D1064131

WITHDRAWN
WILLIAM F. MAAG LIBRARY
YOUNGSTOWN STATE UNIVERSITY

SIR PHILIP SIDNEY:
AN ANNOTATED BIBLIOGRAPHY
OF TEXTS AND CRITICISM
(1554–1984)

A
Reference
Publication
in
Literature

James L. Harner
Editor

SIR PHILIP SIDNEY: AN ANNOTATED BIBLIOGRAPHY OF TEXTS AND CRITICISM (1554–1984)

Donald V. Stump

Project Director

Jerome S. Dees

C. Stuart Hunter

WITHDRAWN

G.K. Hall & Co.
An Imprint of Macmillan Publishing Company
New York

Maxwell Macmillan Canada
Toronto

Maxwell Macmillan International
New York   Oxford   Singapore   Sydney

Copyright © 1994 by Jerome S. Dees, C. Stuart Hunter, Donald Stump

All rights reserved. No part of this book may be reproduced or transmitted in any form or by any means, electronic or mechanical, including photocopying, recording, or by any information storage and retrieval system, without permission in writing from the Publisher.

G.K. Hall & Co.
An Imprint of Macmillan Publishing Company
866 Third Avenue
New York, NY 10022

Maxwell Macmillan Canada, Inc.
1200 Eglinton Avenue East
Suite 200
Don Mills, Ontario M3C 3N1

Macmillan Publishing Company is part of the Maxwell Communication Group of Companies.

Library of Congress Catalog Card Number: 93-12829

Printed in the United States of America

printing number
1 2 3 4 5 6 7 8 9 10

Library of Congress Cataloging-in-Publication Data

Stump, Donald V.
    Sir Philip Sidney : an annotated bibliography of texts and criticism / Donald V. Stump, project director, Jerome S. Dees, C. Stuart Hunter.
        p. cm.—(Reference guide to literature)
    Includes bibliographical references (p.) and index.
    ISBN 0-8161-8238-8 (alk. paper)
    1. Sidney, Philip, Sir, 1554–1586—Bibliography.   I. Dees, Jerome Steele.
    II. Hunter, C. Stuart.   III. Title.   IV. Series.
Z8818.8.S78   1993
[PR2343]
016.821'3—dc20   93-12829
                                                                 CIP

The paper used in this publication meets the minimum requirements of American National Standard for Information Sciences—Permanence of Paper for Printed Library Materials. ANSI Z39.48-1984. ∞™

Z
8818.8
.S18
1993

Contents

WILLIAM F. MAAG LIBRARY
YOUNGSTOWN STATE UNIVERSITY

Contents

Preface

This reference guide is a comprehensive listing of printed material by and about Sir Philip Sidney from 1554 to 1984. It includes not only editions of his works and critical and scholarly commentaries on them, but also biographical and bibliographical studies and literary works written about him, such as funeral elegies and fictional representations of his life. Our aim in compiling the bibliography was twofold: to call attention to a large body of secondary material never before listed, and to provide readers with thorough annotations and detailed subject indexes so that more of their time might be given to Sidney's life and works and less to research.

Although previous bibliographies devoted to Sidney have often accomplished the aims for which they were designed, all have been limited in scope or coverage. Most encompass only a brief period or a single work by Sidney, and nearly all are inconsistent with one another in organization and style. None has an adequate subject index. Taken together, they provide reasonably thorough coverage only for items published since 1940. Moreover, the bibliographies are scattered in numerous sources, and to do a thorough search—even one limited to scholarship of the last fifty years—scholars must consult several sources. Clearly, a single listing will satisfy a pressing need.

The most inclusive of the earlier bibliographies, Samuel A. Tannenbaum's *Sir Philip Sidney (A Concise Bibliography)* (item 268 in our listing) was designed to encompass material published before 1941, but in fact includes only part of the available material. It also adopts an unusual method of organization and citation, and it has no annotations. G.R. Guffey's *Elizabethan Bibliographies Supplements VII: Samuel Daniel 1942–1965, Michael Drayton 1941–1965, Sir Philip Sidney 1941–1965* (item 251), an update of Tannenbaum's work, suffers from similar limitations. Mary A. Washington's helpful book *Sir Philip Sidney: An*

Annotated Bibliography of Modern Criticism, 1941–1970 (item 265), employs a much more useful method of organization and citation and includes annotations, yet it covers only a thirty-year period. Although James L. Harner's *English Renaissance Prose Fiction, 1500–1660: An Annotated Bibliography of Modern Criticism* (252) spans a broader period (beginning in the year 1800), it covers only Sidney's *Arcadia*. Apart from bibliographies in critical books and the annotated listings of major items that appear from time to time in *Sidney Newsletter,* which is published semiannually, the only other guides to the secondary literature are journal articles written in a discursive style. Three useful articles of this sort are W.L. Godshalk's "Recent Studies in Sidney (1965–70)," (item 247); A.J. Colaianne and W.L. Godshalk's "Recent Studies in Sidney (1970–77)" (item 243); and Derek B. Alwes and W.L. Godschalk's "Recent Studies in Sidney (1978–86)," in *Sidney in Retrospect: Selections from "English Literary Renaissance,"* edited by Arthur F. Kinney (University of Massachusetts Press, 1988).

The principal difficulties in using these bibliographies are not only that they are scattered and provide inconsistent information, but also that they do not account for a great deal of material. Together they include only a little more than sixty percent of the scholarship published on Sidney before 1985. None includes the material printed before 1800 on which all modern scholarship is based, such as Renaissance editions of Sidney's works, contemporary commentary on them, and biographical and historical documents. Moreover, none offers an adequate list of literary works written about Sidney.

This reference guide seeks to correct these deficiencies. It includes more than 1,200 items never before listed in the major bibliographies on Sidney, many of them from the twentieth century. It also brings the available materials together in a consistent format, providing extensive annotations, cross-references, and indexes.

In order to ensure that each section of the bibliography was overseen by someone familiar with all the material that it contains, we decided at the outset to divide our labors. Professor Stump had primary responsibility for the sections involving *Arcadia,* the *Defence of Poetry,* the minor prose works and correspondence, the bibliographies, and the literary works pertaining to Sidney. Professor Dees confirmed all the citations in the sections on Sidney's life and poetry, and he and Professor Hunter annotated nearly all the material in those sections. We trust that this procedure has minimized the omissions inevitable in a project that covers more than four centuries and casts its nets wide.

In writing of friendship, the philosopher Francis Bacon once observed, "When all is done, the help of good counsel is that which setteth business straight." We have received much good and friendly counsel—and much material assistance—in preparing this volume. Our greatest debt is to Professors A.J. Colaianne and W.L. Godshalk, who, in 1978, began collecting references, contacting publishers, and laying plans for a comprehensive Sidney bibliography. By 1981, when they turned the project over to us, they had created extensive card files from which we were able to begin the task of locating material and annotating it. Their generosity in providing their preliminary files has allowed us to devote less of our time to searching and more to other tasks, including the creation of a computerized database with powerful retrieval capabilities and automated procedures for compiling indexes. We owe special thanks to Professor Colaianne for early advice and assistance and for initial access to some of the computer software used in the project.

We would also like to offer special thanks to our board of advisors: Walter R. Davis, James L. Harner, Harrison T. Meserole, and Thomas P. Roche, Jr. Without their thoughtful suggestions, the book would be poorer in many ways. We owe a particularly large debt of gratitude to Professor Harner, who, in his double role as a member of the board and as a field editor for G.K. Hall, has devoted hours to our plans and our text, sending us numerous items located in the course of his own research. He has been not just a good editor, but a fellow laborer and a friend as well. Special thanks also go to Carol Kaske and Rita Guerlac for assistance with translations of the French and Latin elegies written after Sidney's death; to Carol Kaske and John Cunnigham for consulting rare items in libraries overseas; and to A.C. Hamilton, Charles Levy, Jean Robertson, and John Shawcross, who studied preliminary samples of the text and made us wiser through their experience.

The computer arrangements and library work required for the project were extensive, and those who assisted us in these tasks deserve special acknowledgment. Heart-felt thanks go to Susan G. Bright, who, with Wanda Baber, Eliza Lau, Peggy Morgan, and many others in the Virginia Tech Department of User Services, worked many hours to make incompatible software compatible, complex coding understandable, and an improbable scheme for a randomly accessible data base workable beyond all our initial hopes. We are also grateful to John B. Smith, designer of the computer programs for the World Shakespeare Bibliography, who generously allowed us to make use of his software and his expertise and who handled more than one phone call at odd hours. Sincere thanks are also due James Stukas of Computing Services at Notre Dame, and Anita Malebranche, Charles Haney, Brenda Evans, and others in the reference and interlibrary loan departments of Newman Library at Virginia Polytechnic Institute and State University, McLaughlin Library at the University of Guelph, Farrell Library at Kansas State, and the Spencer Library at the University of Kansas. We have also received much help from librarians in the research collections that served as our primary resources for rare items: Olin Library at Cornell, the Robarts Library at the University of Toronto, the Library of Congress, the Folger Shakespeare Library, the New York Public Library, the Widener Library at Harvard, the Beinecke Library at Yale, and the Firestone Library at Princeton. Finally, we wish to note a special debt of gratitude to Norman Kretzmann for his friendship and for his assistance in arranging summer working space in the stacks at Cornell.

Financial assistance for the project was generously provided by the Social Sciences and Humanities Research Council of Canada. Supplementary funding for summer travel and research was provided by the Division of Humanities and the College of Arts and Sciences at Virginia Tech. The large burden of computer costs was borne by the English Departments at Virginia Tech and the University of Guelph. To these institutions we offer our sincerest thanks for their generous support.

D.V.S.

Guide for Readers

METHOD OF SELECTION

We have sought to include everything of substance written by or about Sidney from 1554 to 1984, no matter how far afield it may lie. To observe some reasonable limits in an otherwise limitless search, however, we have adopted the following guidelines:

Items Included Comprehensively

1. *Primary editions*. We have cited all printings of Sidney's works that are of historical or scholarly interest. These include virtually all materials from the sixteenth through the nineteenth centuries and all twentieth-century editions and anthologies that contain at least one of Sidney's prose works or poetic collections in its entirety and supply substantive introductions, notes, or other aids. We have not attempted to cite miscellanies that include excerpts from his prose works or scattered selections of his poetry unless these are of historical or textual interest. Nor have we systematically collected school or university textbooks, though we have included all that mention Sidney in their titles.

2. *First printings of Sidney's correspondence*. Since the letters have often been published piecemeal in biographies, calendars of manuscripts, and partial collections, we have attempted to list all the early printings of individual letters that we encountered.

3. *Secondary works of scholarship or criticism*. We have attempted to list all those that mention Sidney or one of his works in their titles. These include books, Ph.D. dissertations, articles in popular and scholarly periodicals, and reprints of such articles.

4. *Literary works written largely or entirely about Sidney.* We have not listed allusions, brief passages in works on other subjects, or imitations of Sidney's works. We have, however, collected elegies, epitaphs, poems of praise, books of historical fiction, and other works that give sustained attention to Sidney or his writings.

Items Included Selectively

1. *Textbook anthologies containing works by Sidney.* We have listed a selection of those that contain substantial prefatory matter and notes.

2. *Literary histories.* Since single-volume surveys of English literature rarely give Sidney detailed or original coverage, we have limited our search to specialized works and to general histories that devote at least a full volume to the English Renaissance.

3. *Scholarly works about Sidney's era or about his social or literary milieu.* We have made an extensive but not exhaustive search of potentially useful works of the following types: books on Elizabethan social, political, and cultural history; biographies of the persons with whom Sidney was most closely associated in private and public life; studies of the principal genres in which he wrote; and books on the authors from whom he drew or on whom he exerted substantial influence.

4. *Reviews.* We have cited only those that make their own contribution to scholarship or concentrate on Sidney in his own right.

5. *Works incorrectly attributed to Sidney.* We have not attempted to list individual lyric poems in this category, since they are well covered in Ringler's edition of *The Poems of Sir Philip Sidney* (see item 92). We have, however, cited longer items published under Sidney's name or sometimes mistaken for his work.

Items Excluded

1. *Manuscripts.* Since those containing works by Sidney have been described elsewhere, we have concentrated entirely on printed material. Full manuscript information is available in Peter Beal's *Index of English Literary Manuscripts* and in the introductions and notes to the Oxford editions of Sidney's works, edited by Katherine Duncan-Jones and Jan van Dorsten, Jean Robertson, and William Ringler (items 22, 55, and 92).

2. *Dictionaries, handbooks, encyclopedias, and other works of general reference.*

3. *Reprints of nineteenth- and twentieth-century books of scholarship and criticism.* Revised editions are listed if the title or the material on Sidney has been substantially altered. Rare books and those published before 1800 are cited in the original edition and also in a more accessible version (if available).

4. *Printed abstracts of unpublished conference papers.*

5. *Masters theses.* A partial listing of these may be found in Patsy C. Howard's *Theses in English Literature, 1894–1970.*

METHOD OF ORGANIZATION

Principles of Division

In organizing a lengthy listing of this kind, there is always some question whether subdividing the table of contents and the indexes is genuinely helpful or not. Keeping the number of divisions small has the advantage of drawing many related items together, so that readers may browse without having to jump from section to section or from one index heading to another. Increasing the number of divisions, however, allows those who know precisely what they are looking for to find it quickly. Our choice was to keep the table of contents headings relatively broad and to provide a very detailed set of indexes.

Principles of Organization

Within the major sections (such as "Texts," "Bibliographical Works," and "General Scholarship and Criticism"), the entries are divided by century. Within each century, they are (with the exception of early editions of Sidney's works) arranged in alphabetical order by the last name of the author or the editor. Anonymous works are listed under the abbreviation "ANON.," and works prepared by an organization such as the Grolier Club are listed under the name of the organization.

Early Editions

In the section entitled "Texts," sixteenth- and seventeenth-century editions and translations of Sidney's works are arranged by date of publication and are generally cited with quasifacsimile title-page transcriptions. The only exceptions are first printings of isolated poems or minor prose works that appeared without title-page acknowledgment in books devoted to other subjects. Such works are listed by date of publication, but without quasifacsimile title-page transcriptions. Within such transcriptions, italic indicates italic in the original and bold indicates either black-letter type or, in a few instances, a display type.

Items First Published in a Century Subsequent to the One in Which They Were Written

All items in the bibliography are listed according to the century in which they were first printed. Consequently, readers interested in early material on Sidney should consult the index as well as the table of contents.

General Works

In the section entitled "General Scholarship and Criticism" and in the first subsection under "Studies of the Poetry," the term "general" means not that the items cited are necessarily broad in their historical or topical coverage, but rather that they cover more than one work by Sidney (or his life and one or more of his works).

Split Entries

In annotating books that include at least two full chapters on Sidney, we have listed each chapter independently in the section that seems most appropriate. In such cases, a brief but complete description of the book appears under "General Scholarship and Criticism," followed by cross-references to more detailed entries listed elsewhere. For example, John Buxton's book *Elizabethan Taste*, which contains a chapter on Sidney's prose fiction and another on his sonnets, appears in three sections: "General Scholarship and Criticism," "*Arcadia*," and the subsection of "Poetry" devoted to *Astrophil and Stella*.

METHODS OF CITATION AND ANNOTATION

Examination Policy

We have sought to see firsthand the title pages and contents of all the works cited in the bibliography. Whenever possible, we have consulted both first editions and later revisions. Those few items that we could not obtain are cited from the best available sources and noted as "not seen" or "not located."

Quasifacsimile Title-Page Information

In citing early editions of Sidney's works, we have included the full text of the title page and a description of the borders and/or ornamentation, with cross-references to Ronald B. McKerrow and F.S. Ferguson's *Title-Page Borders Used in England and Scotland, 1485–1640* (see item 642) and McKerrow's *Printers & Publishers' Devices in England & Scotland 1485-1640* (641). Page numbers include front matter and text as actually counted, not as indicated by printed page numbers. Leading and trailing blank leaves are not included in the count, but blank versos of final pages are included. Since variants of the early printings of Sidney's major works are described in Bent Juel-Jensen's two-part article, "Some Uncollected Authors XXXIV" (256 and 257), we have noted such variants but have not given them separate listings.

Spelling and Orthography

In citing items printed before the nineteenth century, we have preserved the spelling, capitalization, and punctuation of the original title pages, though we have sometimes omitted parts of titles that are unusually expansive, indicating the omissions by elipses. In books where titles or parts of titles appear entirely in capital letters, we have lowered all but the initial letters of main words, according to modern convention. Titles of older works mentioned in the annotations and in the indexes are also cited with modern spellings, unless scholarly convention is strongly in favor of the original—as, for example, in the case of Spenser's *Faerie Queene*.

Cross-References

These are given by author and item number, except when the author is unknown or is the same as for the item in which the cross-reference occurs. In such cases, only item numbers are listed.

Evaluative Judgments

In the annotations, we do not attempt to comment on the merits or faults of the works being described. Such judgments, we think, are best left to our readers.

METHODS OF INDEXING

Index 1

This lists the names of critics, biographers, commentators, and editors of Sidney's works whose publications are cited in the bibliography. Since those who consult this index are most likely to be searching for material by a particular writer, and not for comments on that writer's material offered by other scholars, we list here only items actually written by the person in question. Replies by others may be located through the very extensive set of cross-references provided in the annotations.

Index 2

This lists the names of persons other than Sidney mentioned in the annotations. Titles of works are also provided for the authors listed. Readers interested in the secondary literature on Sidney's connections with the author George Whetstone, for example, will find it by using this index. Those interested in Whetstone's own writings about Sidney, however, will find them listed in Index 1. Literary works of unknown authorship are listed alphabetically by title.

Index 3

This index covers subjects related specifically to Sidney's life and works. In general, we have organized this index to reflect the table of contents, though we have added other headings such as "Poems by Sidney, Misc.," and "Library Collections." We have also subdivided certain broad headings in the table of contents, listing minor works separately by title, for example, and dividing biographical information under two headings: "Biography: General," which is organized by topic, and "Biography: Chronological," which is organized by period and incident in Sidney's life.

Readers interested in Sidney's *Arcadia* should consult both of the primary headings devoted to that work: "*Arcadia*: Original Version" and "*Arcadia*: Revised Versions." To avoid creating yet a third category for studies comparing the two versions, we have cited such studies under both headings when appropriate. Characters such as Pyrocles and Musidorus, who go by various names while in disguise, are always cited by their original names. To eliminate pointless clutter in the subheading "characters," we have listed only items that actually have to do with characterization or character-roles per se. Those that simply allude to characters in passing are ignored.

Wherever possible, we have attempted to keep the subheadings under the titles of each of Sidney's works consistent, so that readers may move rapidly from one section in the index to the next, consulting the same categories. Those interested in Sidney's neo-Platonism, for example, should look under the titles of each of his works for the secondary heading "philosophical background." Whenever further subdivision is warranted, a tertiary heading, "Platonic, neo-Platonic," will also be listed. Discussions of Platonism not tied to particular works are listed under the subheading "views, philosophical" in the section "Biography: General."

To prevent needless duplication of entry numbers in Index 3, we generally cite items only under the lowest appropriate subheading. Thus, if item 48 discussed Sidney's narrative voice in the Old *Arcadia* and item 131 considered narrative technique, but without specific reference to voice, the index for these two items would appear as follows:

Arcadia: **Original Version**
    technique, narrative, 131
      voice, 48

For this reason, it is best to begin a search of Index 3 with the most specific subheadings possible.

Abbreviations

SIDNEY'S POETRY (RINGLER'S CLASSIFICATION)

AS	*Astrophil and Stella*
AT	Poems wrongly attributed to Sidney
CS	*Certain Sonnets*
OA	Old *Arcadia*
OP	Other poems
PS	Psalms
PP	Poems possibly by Sidney

PERIODICALS AND WORKS OF GENERAL BIBLIOGRAHY

ACF	*Annali di Ca' Foscari* (Venice)
AL	*American Literature*
AN&Q	*American Notes and Queries*
Archiv	*Archiv für das Studium der neueren Sprachen und Literaturen*
AUL	*Annali dell' Università di Lecce*
AUMLA	*Journal of the Australasian Universities Language and Literature Association*
BC	*Book Collector*

BHR	*Bibliothèque d'Humanisme et Renaissance*
BJRL	*Bulletin of the John Rylands Library*
BLR	*Bodleian Library Record*
BMC	*British Museum Catalogue*
BNYPL	*Bulletin of the New York Public Library*
CE	*College English*
CentR	*Centennial Review*
CHum	*Computers and the Humanities*
CJ	*Classical Journal*
CL	*Comparative Literature*
CLAJ	*College Language Association Journal*
CLS	*Comparative Literature Studies*
CollG	*Colloquia Germanica, Internationale Zeitschrift für Germanische Sprach- und Literaturwissenschaft*
CritI	*Critical Inquiry*
DA	*Dissertation Abstracts*
DAI	*Dissertation Abstracts International*
DDAAU	*Doctoral Dissertations Accepted by American Universities*
DVLG	*Deutsche Vierteljahrsschrift für Literaturwissenschaft und Geistesgeschichte*
E&S	*Essays and Studies*
EA	*Études anglaises*
EASG	*English and American Studies in German*
EDH	*Essays by Divers Hands*
EIC	*Essays in Criticism* (Oxford)
EIE	*English Institute Essays*
EIRC	*Explorations in Renaissance Culture*
ELH	*English Literary History*
ELN	*English Language Notes* (University of Colorado)
ELR	*English Literary Renaissance*
EM	*English Miscellany*
ES	*English Studies*
ESA	*English Studies in Africa* (Johannesburg)
ESC	*English Studies in Canada*
ESELL	*Essays and Studies in English Language and Literature* (Tohoku Gakuin University, Sendai, Japan)

Expl	*Explicator*
FeL	*Filologia e letteratura*
GHJ	*George Herbert Journal*
GV	*Gesamtverzeichnis des deutschsprachigen Schrifttums 1911–1965*
HLB	*Harvard Library Bulletin*
HLQ	*Huntington Library Quarterly*
HSL	*University of Hartford Studies in Literature*
HudR	*Hudson Review*
ISLL	*Illinois Studies in Language and Literture*
JDJ	*John Donne Journal*
JEGP	*Journal of English and Germanic Philology*
JGE	*Journal of General Education*
JHI	*Journal of the History of Ideas*
JMRS	*Journal of Medieval and Renaissance Studies*
JRMMRA	*Journal of the Rocky Mountain Medieval and Renaissance Association*
JWCI	*Journal of the Warburg and Courtauld Institutes*
KN	*Kwartalnik Neofilologiczny* (Warsaw, Poland)
KR	*Kenyon Review*
KSJ	*Keats-Shelley Journal*
Lang&S	*Language and Style*
LC	*Library Chronicle* (University of Pennsylvania)
LSE	*Lund Studies in English*
LWU	*Literatur in Wissenschaft und Unterricht* (Kiel, Germany)
MLJ	*Modern Language Journal*
MLN	*Modern Language Notes*
MLQ	*Modern Language Quarterly*
MLR	*Modern Language Review*
MP	*Modern Philology*
MSE	*Massachusetts Studies in English*
N&Q	*Notes and Queries*
Neophil	*Neophilologus*
NEQ	*New England Quarterly*
NLH	*New Literary History* (University of Virginia)
NM	*Neuphilologische Mitteilungen*

NOR	*New Orleans Review*
NS	*Die Neueren Sprachen*
NUC	*National Union Catalogue*
PAPS	*Proceedings of the American Philological Society*
PBA	*Proceedings of the British Academy*
PBSA	*Papers of the Bibliographical Society of America*
PCP	*Pacific Coast Philology*
PLL	*Papers in Language and Literature*
PLPLS-LHS	*Proceedings of the Leeds Philosophical and Literary Society, Literary and Historical Section*
PMASAL	*Papers of the Michigan Academy of Science, Arts, and Letters*
PMLA	*Publications of the Modern Language Association of America*
PoetryR	*Poetry Review* (London)
PQ	*Philological Quarterly*
PTRSC	*Proceedings and Transactions of the Royal Society of Canada*
PULC	*Princeton University Library Chronicle*
QJS	*Quarterly Journal of Speech*
QQ	*Queen's Quarterly*
RenB	*Renaissance Bulletin*
RenD	*Renaissance Drama*
RenP	*Renaissance Papers*
RenQ	*Renaissance Quarterly*
RES	*Review of English Studies*
RMS	*Renaissance and Modern Studies*
RomN	*Romance Notes*
SAQ	*South Atlantic Quarterly*
SB	*Studies in Bibliography*
SCN	*Seventeenth-Century News*
SEL	*Studies in English Literature, 1500–1900*
SELit	*Studies in English Literature* (Tokyo)
SELL	*Studies in English Language and Literature* (Kyushu University)
ShJE	*Shakespeare-Jahrbuch* (Weimar)
ShS	*Shakespeare Survey*
SJ	*Shakespeare-Jahrbuch* (pre-1960)

SJH	*Shakespeare-Jahrbuch* (Heidelberg)
SLitI	*Studies in the Literary Imagination* (Georgia State University)
SN	*Studia Neophilologica*
SNew	*Sidney Newsletter*
SP	*Studies in Philology*
SQ	*Shakespeare Quarterly*
SR	*Sewanee Review*
SRen	*Studies in the Renaissance*
SSF	*Studies in Short Fiction*
SSL	*Studies in Scottish Literature* (University of South Carolina)
SSt	*Spenser Studies*
TA	*Theater Annual*
TLS	*Times Literary Supplement* (London)
TQ	*Texas Quarterly* (University of Texas)
TSE	*Tulane Studies in English*
TSL	*Tennessee Studies in Literature*
TSLL	*Texas Studies in Literature and Language*
UMCMP	*University of Michigan Contributions in Modern Philology*
UMSE	*University of Mississippi Studies in English*
UTQ	*University of Toronto Quarterly*
UTS	*University of Texas Studies in English*
VQR	*Virginia Quarterly Review*
WBEP	*Wiener Beiträge zur Englische Philologie*
WHR	*Western Humanities Review*
YES	*Yearbook of English Studies*
YULG	*Yale University Library Gazette*
ZAA	*Zeitschrift für Anglistik und Amerikanistik* (East Berlin)

Introduction

When Sidney died in 1586 while fighting against Catholic forces in the Netherlands, he was mourned in England and on the Continent as few Englishmen below the ranks of royalty had ever been mourned. The Dutch honored him as a national hero, offering to build him a great monument and publishing nearly three dozen elegies in his memory. Many citizens gathered at the docks, along with the 1,200 English soldiers who came to see his coffin off on its journey to England. His own countrymen arranged one of the most elaborate funerals ever given an English subject and published a flood of elegies, including two volumes prepared at Oxford and one at Cambridge that brought together the work of more than 140 contributors. Other memoirs and elegies were published separately by a long and distinguished list of mourners, including Barnabe Barnes, Richard Barnfield, Nicholas Breton, William Byrd, Thomas Campion, Thomas Churchyard, Henry Constable, Samuel Daniel, Michael Drayton, Fulke Greville, George Peele, Sir Walter Ralegh, Edmund Spenser, George and Bernard Whetstone, and Sidney's sister, the Countess of Pembroke.

To understand these extraordinary public expressions of grief and respect, one must not only consider what Sidney accomplished in his brief life but also what others hoped that he would accomplish. In a phrase later remembered by Charles Dickens, he once described himself as a man of "great expectations." It is hard to think of any commoner of his generation who was born with more advantages or more promise. His mother was Lady Mary Sidney, a Dudley, daughter of the Earl of Northumberland and sister-in-law of Lady Jane Grey. His father, Sir Henry Sidney, was a favorite of the young King Edward VI and was—at least at the time of Sidney's birth—extraordinarily wealthy, holding considerable property in his own right and standing as prospective heir to other land-holdings scattered through several counties of England. He

1

later served Queen Elizabeth in several prominent posts, most notably as Lord Deputy of Ireland. Sir Philip's uncles, the earls of Leicester and Warwick, were among the most wealthy and powerful men in the realm, and Sidney was also connected to influential circles at court through his marriage to the daughter of Queen Elizabeth's great secretary, Sir Francis Walsingham.

Throughout his life, Sidney hoped that his expectations would be fulfilled in high office and in great affairs of state. Indeed, from 1575 to 1585 he played limited but visible roles as a courtier, an ambassador, a member of Parliament, and a joint Master of Ordnance. Unfortunately, however, he was too impetuous and too outspoken—particularly in supporting the radical Protestant faction surrounding his uncle, the Earl of Leicester—to gain the confidence of his queen. In consequence, he was never given responsibilities that matched either his abilities or his connections at court. Though many prominent leaders in England and on the Continent regarded him as a promising candidate to lead an international Protestant League against the Catholic forces of France and Spain, his part in that effort was ultimately confined to that of a military governor and field commander fighting limited skirmishes against the Spanish in the Netherlands.

It was not in his public actions, then, but rather in his private character and in his literary works that his "great expectations" were fulfilled. He was the most illustrious English example of what we now call the "Renaissance man," cultivating excellence in a remarkable range of intellectual, artistic, and athletic pursuits. As his friend Fulke Greville remarked in his *Life of Sidney* (item 863), "His end was not writing, even while he wrote; nor his knowledge moulded for tables, or schools; but both his wit, and understanding bent upon his heart, to make himself and others, not in words or opinion, but in life and action, good and great." Though not as learned as Spenser or Jonson or Milton, Sidney was well read in the classics and in contemporary works of literature, philosophy, and history. His languages included Latin and French, Italian and Spanish, a gentleman's Greek and perhaps a smattering of German. He was the most dazzling rhetorician of his generation and a remarkably prolific and innovative writer, both in poetry and in prose. He was also a student of military tactics and a fearless—some say reckless—soldier. He took an active interest in the exploration and colonization of the New World, once attempting to sail with Sir Francis Drake to the West Indies and failing only because the Queen sent messengers to the docks recalling him to court. As a patron, he encouraged artists and musicians, prose stlylists and rhetoricians, philosophers and historians, and—most of all—poets. In return, unprecedented numbers of writers honored him in the prefaces and dedications to their books, and in elegies published after his death.

He was, in short, a man who valued a life of thought and action on a grand scale. Though known for his tendency to seriousness and even melancholy, he was also fond of play, delighting endlessly in the turns and counter-turns of his own wit and taking part in public entertainments at court as well as private amusements at his sister's country estate at Wilton. In both his life and his works, one continually senses a powerful and restless desire to excel, though it is nearly always concealed behind the studied aristocratic ease and self-deprecation that the Italians call "*sprezzatura.*"

Aside from his own self-fashioning, his greatest achievement was the extraordinary body of writings that he left behind unpublished in England when he departed for the Netherlands in 1585. His *Defence of Poetry* was the first major work of literary theory in English and remains one of the most widely read. His sequence of songs and sonnets, *Astrophil and Stella*, began the great English vogue for sonnets in the 1590s and served as a model for the cycles of Spenser, Shakespeare, and many others. For nearly a century, his prose romance *Arcadia* remained the most widely admired and frequently reprinted work of fiction in the language.

In all these literary endeavors, Sidney was important not only as an innovator but also as a transmitter of cultural tradition. He was unusually receptive to literary forms, techniques, and ideas popular on the Continent, and helped to bring many of them across the English Channel for the first time. He was, for example, the first major English author to assimilate the teachings of Aristotle's *Poetics* and the neoclassical criticism of Renaissance Italy. He helped to popularize Hellenistic romance and Italian poetic style, and his treatments of Machiavellian politics and Epicurean philosophy are among the earliest in English literature. Other writers of the age may have written greater works, but none did more to inspire the movement in literature and the arts that we call the "Elizabethan Renaissance."

During the decade following Sidney's death, the dissemination of his works was delayed by his family's slowness in putting them into print. Authorized editions of *Arcadia*, *Astrophil and Stella*, and the *Defence of Poetry* were gradually released, but always under the pressure of unauthorized texts derived from manuscripts that had circulated among his friends and acquaintances. Not until 1598 did his sister finally publish all of his main works in the folio collection that passes under the title of *The Countess of Pembroke's Arcadia*. This compilation became enormously popular, going through ten authorized printings before the end of the seventeenth century and even attracting the attention of literary pirates in Scotland. So popular was the title work in this volume that, although long and complex already, it gradually became encrusted with continuations by other authors. Sir William Alexander began this process in 1616 by supplying material to round out the unfinished Third Book. His continuation appeared in all seventeenth-century English editions of *Arcadia* beginning in 1621. Subsequent printings added Sir Richard Beling's attempt at a Sixth Book and James Johnstoun's supplement to Book III.

Abroad, Sidney's *Arcadia* was also the most popular of his works. In France, parts of it were translated in a manuscript by Jean Loiseau de Tourval between 1607 and 1610. Complete versions were published in the years 1624 and 1625 by two competing translators, Geneviève Chappelain and Jean Boudoin. In Germany, a translation by an unknown author writing under the pen name Valentinus Theocritus von Hirschberg appeared in 1629. With extensive revisions by the well-known author Martin Opitz, five more editions of this version were published between 1638 and 1658. In the Netherlands, a Dutch translation by Felix van Sambix de Jonghe was also successful, going to press three times between 1639 and 1659. In the last year of its run, it was joined by an Italian version by Livio Alessandri.

The list of translations of Sidney's other works reveals a growing interest in them, as well. In the first century and a half, their number included a partial Dutch rendering of the *Defence of Poetry* published in 1619, a complete translation printed in 1712 by Joan de Haes, and a sixteenth-century Spanish manuscript version, most likely by Juan Ruiz de Bustamante. Later publications include another Dutch translation of the *Defence* issued in 1891 by Albert Verwey, a 1946 Italian rendering by Silvio Policardi, extensive selections from *Astrophil and Stella* printed in German by Gräfin Maria Lanckoronska in 1936, and two twentieth-century French versions of the complete sequence by Charles Garnier and Michel Poirier.

The popularity of the early editions and translations of Sidney's works, coupled with his reputation as a national hero, insured the attentions of a long list of imitators, chroniclers, and commentators. In England, a continual stream of literary imitations appeared during the century following his death, mostly in the genres of the sonnet, the chivalric romance, and the pastoral eclogue, but also in tragedy and tragicomedy. *Arcadia* influenced the productions of no fewer than nine playwrights, including Shakespeare, Beaumont and Fletcher, and Shirley. The century also brought forth a good deal of biographical material by John Hooker, John Stow, Fulke Greville, and others, and it produced a scattering of printed comments on Sidney's works. The latter are limited in scope and depth of analysis, but they are not without interest. Early discussions of the poetry, for example, include speculations on the identity of Stella and culturally revealing attempts to minimize the role of Sidney's sister in translating the Psalms. Although early references to the *Defence of Poetry* are surprisingly rare, there are several discussions of the minor prose works and entertainments, including *Four*

Foster Children of Desire, the *Letter to the Queen*, and a translation of du Plessis-Mornay's *Trueness of the Christian Religion* that was begun by Sidney and finished by Arthur Golding.

As one might expect, *Arcadia* received the greatest attention. Soon after its publication, Gervase Markham and Thomas Wilson recognized its debts to earlier literature, notably to Heliodorus's Greek romance *Aethiopica* and to Jorge de Montemayor's Spanish pastoral *Diana* (see 1321, 1827). John Hoskins published numerous excerpts from *Arcadia* as illustrations of the tropes and figures that characterize its widely imitated style (1593). Early commentators also made the first attempts to solve the thorny problem of its genre and intent. Some, such as Fulke Greville, regarded it as an epic poem written to instill serious moral and political principles. Others, including a surprisingly large audience outside the upper classes, read it as a romance of unrequited love and faithful friendship and were drawn by its crowded action and lofty sentiments. Spenser's friend Gabriel Harvey listed five sources of its special appeal: "amorous courting, sage counselling, valorous fighting, . . . delightful pastime by way of pastoral exercises," and "politic secrets of privity" (1319).

Not all readers admired *Arcadia* as much as Greville and Harvey. In *Every Man out of His Humour* and again in published conversations with William Drummond of Hawthornden, Ben Jonson took great pleasure in ridiculing Sidney's style, scoffing at him for "making everyone [from shepherds to kings] speak as well as himself" (365). After the story went around that Charles I had read Pamela's prayer from the Captivity Episode in preparing for his execution, John Milton charged the King with impiety and Sidney with having written "a vain, amatorious poem" (1323). By the end of the seventeenth century, the enormous popularity of *Arcadia* was waning. Commentators tended to repeat the observations of their predecessors without offering much evidence that they had bothered to read the book themselves, and literary authors lost interest in the work. After 1650, only scattered borrowings occurred, and some, such as those in Charles Sorel's *Bergere extravagant*, were parodies.

By 1674, when the last of the seventeenth-century editions of Sidney's works appeared, his literary reputation was in decline. By the second quarter of the eighteenth century, it was in eclipse. To be sure, the Augustan preoccupation with neoclassical criticism preserved some measure of interest in the *Defence of Poetry*, which is reflected in the publication of separate editions in 1752 and 1787. Yet these did not sell well, and the only other reprintings of Sidney's works were the collected editions published in London in 1724 and 1725 and in Dublin in 1739 and Lord Hailes's edition of the correspondence with Languet, which was issued in 1776. Sidney continued to be revered as a half-legendary national hero, but his works were not widely read. Not until Gray's collection of works by Sidney in 1829 would there be another edition of *Astrophil and Stella* or the *Defence*, and *Arcadia* would not appear again until Hain Friswell's condensed version of 1867.

The reasons for the decline are not hard to identify. Sonnets were long out of fashion, as were pastoral romances. The luxuriant Arcadian style, so admired in Sidney's day, did not fare well with readers taught to admire classical simplicity and Royal Society prose. Sidney's *Arcadia* was much too long and involuted to hold the interest of readers who were put off by its style. As William Bond has noted (438), it is no accident that the first simplified paraphrase of the romance, stripped of the eclogues, appears in this period. Horace Walpole seems to have spoken for many when he characterized the book as a "tedious, lamentable, pedantic, pastoral romance, which the patience of a young virgin in love cannot now wade through" (294). Ironically, Walpole's attacks on Sidney's literary reputation may actually have helped to preserve it by rousing a long list of commentators to his defense. For the most part, however, Sidney was allowed to sleep with his fathers, forgotten by nearly everyone except a few learned souls who were still interested in Milton's attacks on Charles I or Shakespeare's borrowings in *King Lear*.

The revival of serious interest in Sidney came with the antiquarian movement of the early nineteenth century. Thomas Zouch's *Memoir of Sir Philip Sidney*, which was the first attempt at a critical biography since the author's death, stirred a good deal of new interest. Bibliographers such as Egerton Brydges and James O. Halliwell-Phillipps stirred more by reexamining the early texts of Sidney's works. Important new editions soon began to appear, including the first printing of the Sidney Psalms in 1823, William Gray's *Miscellaneous Works* in 1829, and Steuart Pears's edition of the correspondence in 1845. William Hazlitt helped keep this newfound interest alive by attacking Sidney even more outrageously and derisively than had Walpole (359), and Isaac Disraeli and Charles Lamb subsequently rose to Sidney's defense (341, 2041). By midcentury, such casual and gentlemanly interest in Sidney began to bear fruit in serious scholarship. In 1862, H. R. Fox Bourne raised the standards for biographical studies by publishing a lengthy memoir on Sidney (318) based on early documents, many of which had sat neglected on the shelves of the State Papers Office for nearly three centuries. In the 1860s and 1870s, periodicals such as *Athenaeum* and *Notes and Queries* began to run frequent articles on Sidney and his place in literary history. In the 1880s and 1890s, there was a flurry of interest in his prose style. At about the same time, scholarly editions began to appear, including well-annotated texts of the *Defence* by Albert Cook and Evelyn Shuckburgh, a new

Astrophil and Stella by Alfred Pollard, a scholarly edition of the same work and the *Defence* by Ewald Flügel, and a facsimile of the 1590 *Arcadia* by Oskar Sommers.

In the first half of the twentieth century, new manuscripts were discovered, and these encouraged even more ambitious scholarly efforts. As early as 1887, Emil Koeppel had noticed that Sidney's contemporaries sometimes quoted a text of *Arcadia* that was different from the published versions, yet twenty years passed before Bertram Dobell finally discovered a manuscript of the Old *Arcadia* (see 1225, 1226). Subsequently, eight other manuscripts came to light, offering scholars a rare opportunity to study a major Renaissance author's methods of composition, revision, and manuscript circulation. Scholars and collectors also discovered a variety of letters and minor poems by Sidney that had never before been edited. With such texts to work with, Albert Feuillerat was able to produce the first nearly complete edition of Sidney's works (23), which appeared between 1912 and 1926. In the same period, Malcolm W. Wallace published his *Life of Sir Philip Sidney* (1171), which long remained the standard biography.

Despite advances in biographical and textual scholarship, however, works such as *Arcadia* and the sonnets were not much better understood in 1926 than they had been a hundred years earlier. Until the middle of the twentieth century, commentators tended to focus on matters external to the works themselves: sources and influences, Sidney's life and Queen Elizabeth's court, and Renaissance styles of prose and metrics. With a few notable exceptions, such as R.W. Zandvoort's comparison of the two versions of *Arcadia* (1316), even the finest studies of the romance tended to isolate one of its elements or to consider the whole only in relation to larger historical developments. Edwin Greenlaw, for example, aroused a good deal of interest in Sidney's use of Epicurean philosophy during Pamela's debate with Cecropia in the Captivity Episode (1565). Kaspar Brunhuber (1443) and Herbert Wynford Hill (1590) began systematic examinations of Sidney's influence on Renaissance drama, which have since been greatly extended by M.C. Andrews (1405–1409) and others. William Dinsmore Briggs (210) sparked interest in Sidney's political philosophy, which subsequently developed into a major topic of scholarly investigation that has been carried on more recently by Martin Bergbusch (1426–1425), Roger Howell (1062), and Martin Raitière (1285). Kenneth O. Myrick (671) and E.M.W. Tillyard (1787) made important contributions by recovering Renaissance theories of genre and exploring Sidney's grounding in literary criticism, particularly that of the Italian neoclassical movement. Not until the advent of New Criticism, however, did substantial numbers of scholars begin systematic internal analyses of *Arcadia*.

 WILLIAM F. MAAG LIBRARY
YOUNGSTOWN STATE UNIVERSITY

Until 1965, the rich inner patterns of Sidney's poetry likewise remained largely unexplored, though an influential section in Hallet Smith's 1952 book *Elizabethan Poetry* (1955) made important strides in that direction. Smith treated *Astrophil and Stella* as a carefully articulated sequence, in which Astrophil is a deliberate persona and the structure of the whole is essentially dramatic. Most scholarship of the period, however, was concerned with individual poems or with external matters such as Sidney's influence on later poets, his experiments with classical prosody and Continental verse forms, or his adaptation of the conventions of earlier sonneteers. The most important debate of the period involved the relation of the sonnets to Sidney's own life. The controversy had its origins in the nineteenth century, when commentators such as Edward Arber and J.A. Symonds read the sequence as a more or less straightforward revelation of Sidney's unrequited love for Lady Penelope Rich (68, 961). Around the turn of the century, however, Sidney Lee and others began to dismiss such heavily autobiographical interpretations as Romantic excesses (620, 2179). In the 1930s, Kenneth Myrick contributed to this change in approach by concentrating on Sidney's self-conscious role as a courtier-poet (671), and in the 1950s, J.W. Lever further undermined the biographical approach by revealing the many ways in which apparently spontaneous and "sincere" sonnets are actually transformations of conventions established by earlier poets on the Continent (1913). In the 1960s, John Buxton took the last step in this process of dismantling the Romantic conception of Astrophil by arguing that Sidney did not write about Lady Rich because he loved her but because, like a painter, he needed a model (2076). Nonetheless, the autobiographical theory never entirely lost its appeal. It continued to appear in the work of scholars such as Mona Wilson (96) and Patrick Cruttwell (2098).

In the same period, the *Defence* enjoyed attention of a more systematic sort than either *Arcadia* or the poetry. Of particular importance were studies of its historical background. Kenneth Myrick, for example, proposed a widely influential analysis of its structure based on the outline of a classical oration (671). He and others, such as Marvin T. Herrick, traced its philosophical roots to the literary criticism of Aristotle and the neo-Aristotelian critics of Renaissance Italy (see 2523–2525, 2527). In 1940, however, this latter view was challenged by Irene Samuel (2627), who argued that the primary influence in Sidney's critical thinking was Plato. During the next two decades, the dispute flared into a major point of controversy, with opinion gradually shifting toward Plato as the major influence. At about the same time, however, a third group of scholars began to argue in favor of yet another major source: Christian arguments against the arts put forward by Cornelius Agrippa and echoed in attacks on the English stage by Stephen Gosson. Proponents of this view included Jacob Bronowski (2420), A.C. Hamilton (2503, 2505), and Harry Berger (2407).

The most notable change in studies of Sidney in the twentieth century took place from the late 1950s to the early 1980s, when the number of publications began to rise exponentially. During that period, scholars recovered more items of Sidney's correspondence and more manuscripts, including the Helmingham Hall text of *The Lady of May* and the Norwich Manuscript of the *Defence of Poetry*. They also undertook new and more carefully researched editions of Sidney's works, including William Ringler's collection of the poetry (92), Jean Robertson's text of the Old *Arcadia* (55), Katherine Duncan-Jones and J.A. van Dorsten's *Miscellaneous Prose* (22), and Geoffrey Shepherd's edition of the *Defence* (141). Scholarly books and dissertations, which once appeared at wide intervals, became an annual harvest, and they tended to concentrate more narrowly on the internal dynamics of Sidney's works than they ever had before. Even historical scholars tended to shift their emphasis, placing research on the political and cultural context of Sidney's works at the service of close analysis. Whatever the ultimate causes of these changes— whether the advent of New Criticism or the proliferation of universities in North America, which increased dramatically the number of publishing scholars and thereby brought about increased specialization and higher rates of publication—the innovations were dramatic.

In studies of the poetry, this change was apparent in the number of books devoted entirely to Sidney, and in the efforts of critics to interrelate various parts of the canon and to explore a wide variety of critical strategies. Robert Montgomery's work in the late 1950s and early 1960s, for example, considered matters of prosody and style, imagery and theme, and set forth a theory that the structure of *Astrophil and Stella* follows shifts in the psychology of Astrophil (1926, 2202–2203). David Kalstone's 1967 book (1907) emphasized the role of sonnet conventions, explicated the poems in more detail than had earlier studies, and also considered elements common to the sonnets and the poems of *Arcadia*. Neil Rudenstine systematically analyzed the entire corpus of Sidney's verse, arguing against the idea that there were major shifts in Sidney's style and emphasizing the recurrent element of dramatic tension and debate (730).

Even more noticeable were changes in the scholarship on *Arcadia*. Older varieties of stylistic analysis, which tended to focus on the standard tropes and figures of classical rhetoric and to set Sidney's prose style against the backdrop of euphuism, gave way to studies of persuasive strategy, narrative tone, and verbal nuance. Beginning with the work of Walter Davis in the 1960s (1498–1499), scholars such as Nancy

Lindheim (1263, 1652), Elizabeth Dipple (1220-1224), and Josephine Roberts (1289, 1739) focused on the interrelations between structure, theme, and generic form. There were also numerous studies of the connections between the major parts of the work: the main plot and the comic subplot, the earlier Asian adventures of the young heroes of the book and their later intrigues in Arcadia, the prose narration and the pastoral eclogues. Such scholarship—represented in the work of Arthur Amos (1399), Jon Lawry (1257, 1639), Franco Marenco (1268–1271), and others—made the coherence of Sidney's complex design more apparent. More detailed studies that later appeared, however, also left the moral and political principles of the work less certain than they had seemed to earlier generations. The work of Richard Lanham (1255), Robert Eril Levine (1260), Dorothy Connell (189), Richard McCoy (638), Alan Sinfield (759, 2636), and others placed new emphasis on such things as the irony and the playful unreliability of Sidney as narrator, the constant cross-currents of dialectically opposed values in the speeches of his characters, and the difficulty of judging the characters' actions. Perhaps because of this new focus, much criticism of the period was based on morally ambiguous scenes: Pyrocles's early debate with Musidorus about love, the lovers' conduct on the night of their elopements (especially in the original version), and the harsh judgments and extraordinary reversals that they undergo at the end of the book.

Examinations of moral and philosophical ambiguity also figured prominently in criticism of the *Defence*. In fact, one of the most frequently debated issues was that of philosophical coherence. Several commentators pressed the case that Sidney had not altogether succeeded in reconciling the Platonic, Aristotelian, and Christian elements of his theory. To this argument were added others: that his mind was deeply divided over the proper relation between sensuous pleasure and moral instruction, between verisimilitude and poetic justice; that he had no settled standard by which to judge poetry and so created conscious "fictions" in defending it; and that his main interest lay in rhetorical maneuvers to win the audience rather than in philosophic coherence. In response to these criticisms, ingenious defenses of the *Defence* were offered. Critics suggested, for example, that Sidney intentionally assumed the mask of an enthusiastic but philosophically naive orator, or that his arguments derived from intellectual traditions now obscure to us, such as humanist forms of neo-Platonism. Prominent in the renewed evaluation of Sidney's philosophical position were Forrest G. Robinson's study of Sidney's visual epistemology (721), S.K. Henninger's studies of his aesthetic and critical assumptions (2516–2521), and Andrew D. Weiner's study of his particular brand of Protestantism (2674).

It may be that, like the moralist Fulke Greville or the romantic Charles Lamb, critics of our own day have refashioned Sidney as a mirror to reflect themselves. Certainly, attempts to portray him as a moral relativist, for example, or as an antiwar satirist or someone torn by existential doubts strike an oddly modern note when applied to the man who defied the Earl of Oxford on the tennis court, opposed the Queen over her plans for a French marriage, and rode half-armed into the caliver fire at Zutphen. Yet it is clear that Sidney was a great deal more complex than earlier generations of scholars recognized. The most comprehensive studies of Sidney's life and works listed in this volume—works such as A. C. Hamilton's *Sir Philip Sidney: A Study of His Life and Works* (550) and Dorothy Connell's *Sir Philip Sidney: The Maker's Mind* (476)—paint an extraordinarily lifelike portrait of this multifaceted man, one that justifies the boundless praise of those who knew the poet personally. As their footnotes attest, however, such books have benefited from the best writings of all the periods represented in this volume. If the scholarship of our own day rises above that of earlier generations— if, using methods such as those of New Historicism, feminism, psychological criticism, and other forms of poststructuralist analysis, we come to understand still better the complexities of Sidney's character and context and the extraordinary richness of his art—it will be, in part, because the insights on which we draw have been accruing and maturing for more than four hundred years.

D.V.S.

Editions and Translations

---

1. COLLECTIONS

Sixteenth Century

1 1598: THE | COVNTESSE | OF PEMBROKES | ARCADIA. | WRITTEN BY SIR | PHILIP SIDNEY | Knight. | NOW THE THIRD TIME | published, with sundry new additions | of the same Author. | London | Imprinted for William Ponsonbie. | *Anno Domini.* 1598, 584 pp. [Title-page border: same as in the 1593 *Arcadia* (item 31).]

Collects for the first time in one folio volume all Sidney's major works: the 1593 composite version of *Arcadia*, *Certain Sonnets*, the *Defence of Poetry*, *Astrophil and Stella*, and *The Lady of May* (here called *The May Day Masque*). Also reprints from the 1593 edition of *Arcadia* Sidney's dedication to his sister and Hugh Sanford's preface. Prepared under the supervision of the Countess of Pembroke.

2 1599: [Ornate rectangular headpiece centered on a rampant lion] | THE | COVNTESSE | OF PEMBROKES | ARCADIA. | *WRITTEN BY SIR* | PHILIP SIDNEY | Knight. | *Now the third time published, with sundry new | additions of the same Author.* | [rectangular ornament] | EDINBVRGH. | *PRINTED BY ROBERT* | *walde-graue, Printer to the* | Kings Majestie. | *Cum priuilegio Regio.* 1599, 556 pp.

Reprints Ponsonby's 1598 edition of *Arcadia* and Sidney's other major works, but derives at least part of *Arcadia* from the 1593 text. See Juel-Jensen (256). Claims to be the third edition *Arcadia* but is, in fact, a pirat-

Sixteenth Century

ed fourth edition published by the Scottish printer Robert Waldgrave. It was seized in a lawsuit by the rightful printer, Ponsonby. See Ferguson (1533), Greg (1568, 1570), Judge (1613), and Plomer (1712).

Seventeenth Century

3 1605: [rule] | THE | [rule] | COVNTESSE | OF PEMBROKES | *ARCADIA.* | [rule] | WRITTEN BY SIR | PHILIP SIDNEY | Knight. | [rule] | NOW THE FOVRTH TIME | PVBLISHED, WITH SVNDRY | NEW ADDITIONS OF THE | *same Author.* | LONDON | Imprinted for SIMON WATERSON | *Anno DOMINI.* | 1605, 584 pp. [Title-page border: at the top left, astrological figures of a king and child with a lion, and at the top right, a woman with a crayfish in front of a bearded man. Between these figures, a personification of Time accompanied by a young man, an old one, and a boy; just below, a globe with the motto "VIRESCIT VVLNERE VERITAS," with Ptolomeus to the left and Marinus to the right. To the right of the title compartment, Strabo and Polibius above personifications labeled "Astronomia" and "Musica." To the left of the title compartment, Aratus and Hipparchus above personifications of "Geometria" and "Arithmetica." Below the imprint compartment, Mercury flanked by two figures embracing (apparently the Gemini) and a seated woman with quill pen (probably Virgo). See McKerrow and Ferguson (642), no. 99.]

Reprints the 1598 edition page for page. A variant was issued with the imprint as follows: LONDON | Imprinted for MATHEW LOWNES | *Anno DOMINI.* | 1605. See Juel-Jensen (256).

4 1613: THE | COVNTESSE | OF PEMBROKES | ARCADIA. | WRITTEN BY SIR | PHILIP SIDNEY | Knight. | NOW THE FOVRTH TIME | published, with some new | Additions. | LONDON | Imprinted by *H.L.* for *Simon* | *Waterson* 1613, 584 pp. [Title-page border: same as in the 1593 *Arcadia* (item 31).]

Reprints page for page the 1605 edition, omitting Sanford's preface. In some issues printed after 1616, includes Sir William Alexander's continuation, which attempts to link the unfinished Book III of the revised *Arcadia* with the ending from the original version. In other issues, inserts at this point an explanation of the lack of completion in Book III. Also inserts one poem not found in the 1605 edition, "A Dialogue betweene two shepherds, utterd in a pastorall shew, at Wilton"

(*PP 1*). Corrects certain textual errors, apparently from a manuscript of the Old *Arcadia*. See Ringler (92). A variant was issued with the imprint as follows: LONDON | Imprinted by *H.L.* for *Mathew* | *Lownes*, 1613. Alexander's continuation exists in three different typesettings, two of which occur in copies of the 1613 edition. See Juel-Jensen (256).

5 1621: *THE* | COVNTESSE | OF PEMBROKES | ARCADIA. | WRITTEN BY SIR | PHILIP SIDNEY | KNIGHT. | [rule] | Now the fift time published, | with some new Additions. | [rule] | *Also a supplement of a defect in* | *the third part of this* | HISTORY. | By Sir W. ALEXANDER. | *DVBLIN*, | Printed by the Societie of | STATIONERS. 1621. | *Cum Privilegio*. 596 pp. [Title-page border: at the top is an arch with the initials "I" at the left and "R" at the right; on either side of the title-compartment are three columns supporting the arch; at the bottom is a pedestal with a compartment for the imprint. See McKerrow and Ferguson (642), no. 274.]

Reprints the 1613 edition, restoring Hugh Sanford's preface. According to Juel-Jensen (256), four variants exist, all showing London as the place of publication and all employing the same title-page border as the 1593 *Arcadia* (31). The first London issue contains the following title page: THE | COVNTESSE | OF | PEMBROKES | ARCADIA. | WRITTEN BY SIR | PHILIP SIDNEY | Knight. | NOW THE SIXT TIME PVB- | LISHED. | LONDON, | Imprinted by *H.L.* for *Simon Waterson*, | and *Mathew Lownes*. 1622. The next issue alters the imprint as follows: LONDON, | Imprinted by *H.L.* for *Simon* | *Waterson*. 1622. Another issue alters the lines after Sidney's name and title: NOW THE SIXT TIME PVB- | LISHED, WITH NEW | ADDITIONS. | LONDON, | Imprinted by *H.L.* for *Mathew* | *Lownes*. 1622. The last issue returns to the pattern of the second London issue but changes the publisher and the date: NOW THE SIXT TIME PVB- | LISHED. | *LONDON* | Imprinted by *H.L.* for *Mathew* | *Lownes*. 1623. Some London copies replace the Dublin printing of Alexander's supplement with one of the two prepared for insertion in the 1613 edition published in London. See also Wiles (1819).

6 1627: THE | COVNTESSE | OF | PEMBROKES | *Arcadia*. | Written by Sir *Philip Sidney* | KNIGHT. | Now the sixt time published, | *with some new Additions*. | [rule] | Also a supplement of a defect in | *the third part of this Historie*, | By Sir W. ALEXANDER. | LONDON, | Printed by *W.S.* for *Simon* |

Seventeenth Century

Waterson. | 1627. 632 pp. [Title-page border: elaborate scrollwork compartment. See McKerrow and Ferguson (642), no. 224.]
Reprints the 1621 edition with an addition by Sir Richard Beling, which narrates the lives of the main characters after the happy conclusion of the 1593 version. This addition had been published separately in Dublin in 1624. Includes a second title page between the end of Sidney's book and Beling's continuation: *A* | SIXTH BOOKE, | TO | THE COVNTESSE | OF PEMBROKES | ARCADIA: | Written by *R.B.* of Lincolnes | Inne Esquire. | [rule] | *Sat, si bene; si male, nimium.* | [rule] | [printer's device] | [rule] | LONDON, | Printed by *H.L.* and *R.Y.* | 1628. Also includes a preface by Beling. A second issue exists with the following title-page: THE | COVNTESSE | OF PEMBROKES | ARCADIA. | Written by Sir PHILIP SIDNEY | KNIGHT. | Now the seuenth time published, | *with some new Additions* | With the supplement of a Defect in the third | *part of this History, by Sir* W. A. *Knight.* | Whereunto is now added a sixth BOOKE, | *By* R.B. *of Lincolnes Inne, Esq.* | [rule] | LONDON printed by H.L. and R.Y. and are | sold by S. WATERSON in S. Pauls Church- | yard, 1629. 632 pp. [Title-page border same as in the 1593 *Arcadia* (item 31).] A variant of the second issue has the following imprint: LONDON printed by H.L. and R.Y. and are | sold by R. MOORE in S. Dunstons Church- | yard, 1629. See Juel-Jensen (256).

7 1633: THE | COUNTESSE | OF PEMBROKES | ARCADIA. | Written by Sir PHILIP SIDNEY | KNIGHT. | Now the eighth time published, | *with some new Additions.* | With the supplement of a Defect in the third | *part of this History, by Sir* W. A. *Knight.* | [rule] | Whereunto is now added a sixth BOOKE, | *By* R.B. *of Lincolnes Inne, Esq.* | [rule] | LONDON, | Printed for SIMON WATERSON and | R. YOUNG, Anno 1633. 632 pp. [Title-page border: same as in 1593 *Arcadia* (item 31).]
Reprints the 1629 edition page for page, with a revised title page preceding Beling's continuation.

8 1638: THE | COUNTESSE | OF PEMBROKES | ARCADIA, | Written by Sir PHILIP SIDNEY | KNIGHT. | Now the ninth time published, with a | twofold supplement of a defect in the third | Book: the one by Sr *W.A.* Knight; the | other, by Mr *Ja. Johnstoun* Scoto-Brit. | dedicated to K. *James*, and now | annexed to this work, for | the Readers be- | nefit. | [rule] | Whereunto is also added a sixth Booke, | By *R.B.* of Lincolnes Inne, Esq. | [rule] |

LONDON, | Printed for *J. Waterson* and *R. Young*, 1638. 652 pp. [Title-page border: same as in 1593 *Arcadia* (item 31).]

Reprints the 1633 edition page for page, with a revised title page for Beling's continuation. Appends James Johnstoun's addition to the unfinished Book III and its dedication to King James. According to Juel-Jensen (256), three early variants exist, all including title page misprints and a turned N in "LONDON" in the imprint and all employing a different layout in Sidney's dedication and Sanford's preface. See "Sir Philip Sidney, 1554–1586: A Check-List of Early Editions of His Works." In *Sir Philip Sidney: An Anthology of Modern Criticism,* edited by Dennis Kay. Oxford: Clarendon Press, 1987, pp. 289–314.

9 1655: THE | COUNTESS | OF | PEMBROKE'S | ARCADIA | WRITTEN BY | Sr PHILIP SIDNEY | *KNIGHT.* | [rule] | *The tenth Edition.* | With his Life and Death; a brief Table of the principal | heads, and som other new Additions. | [rule] | [printer's device] | [rule] | *LONDON,* | Printed by *William Du-Gard*: and are to bee sold by | *George Calvert,* at the half Moon in the new buildings in *Paul's* | Church-yard; and *Thomas Pierrepont,* at the Sun in | *Paul's* Church-yard, M.DC.LV. 686 pp.

Reprints the 1638 edition but adds a biography of Sidney, signed in Greek characters "Philophilipôos"; a passage by Camden (858) describing his death; several elegies and verses written for him; a passage praising *Arcadia* from Peter Heylin's *Cosmography*; the poem "A Remedy for Love"; and a table of the episodes in *Arcadia.* In the biography, discusses Sidney's ancestry, his education at Oxford and on the Continent, his foreign embassies, and his marriage. Discounts the story that he was offered the crown of Poland. Defends *Arcadia* against charges that it is wanton and a waste of the reader's time, treating it as an exposition of moral and political doctrine under the "mystical hieroglyphicks" of a story about lovers. Concludes, however, that the key to the hidden topical allusions in the text is forever lost. Also recounts the story of Sidney's wounding, his request that *Arcadia* be burned, and his death and funeral. Offers possible explanations for the fact that no permanent monument was ever placed over his tomb. According to Woodward (1185), the biography is by Thomas Fuller, but Juel-Jensen (1076) attributes it to the printer, Dugard. The frontispiece is a reversed copy of Elstrack's engraving of Sidney, with his coat of arms printed below. The title page preceding Beling's continuation has been brought up to date. See also Georgas (1029).

10 1662: THE | COUNTESS | OF | PEMBROKE'S | ARCADIA | WRITTEN BY | Sir Philip Sidney | *KNIGHT.* | [rule] | *The*

Seventeenth Century

eleventh Edition. | With his Life and Death; a brief Table of the principal | Heads, and som other new Additions. | [rule] | [printer's device] | [rule] | *LONDON,* | Printed by *Henry Lloyd*, for *William Du-Gard*: and | are to bee sold by *George Calvert*, at the half Moon in the new | buildings; and *Thomas Pierrepont*, at the Sun in St. *Paul's* | Church-yard, MDCLXII. 686 pp.

Reprints the 1655 edition page for page but lacks Sidney's portrait. The title page preceding Beling's continuation has been brought up to date.

11 1674: THE | COUNTESS | OF | PEMBROKE'S | ARCADIA | WRITTEN BY | Sir Philip Sidney | *KNIGHT*. | [rule] | *The Thirteenth Edition*. | [rule] | With his Life and Death; a brief Table of the principal | Heads, and some other new Additions. | [double rule] | *LONDON,* | Printed for *George Calvert*, at the *Golden-Ball* in | *Little-Britain*, MDCLXXIV. 686 pp.

Reprints the 1662 edition page for page, although the portrait in the 1655 has been altered or copied and used again as a frontispiece, without Sidney's coat of arms. According to Juel-Jensen (256), no edition termed the "twelfth" on the title page was ever issued. The title page preceding Beling's continuation has been brought up to date.

Eighteenth Century

12 COLLINS, ARTHUR, ed. *Letters and Memorials of State . . . Faithfully Transcribed from the Originals at Penshurst Place. . . .* Vol. 1. London: T. Osbourne, 1776, pp. 50, 53–54, 61–68, 98–114. Reprint. New York: AMS Press, 1973.

Transcribes for the first time the Penshurst Manuscript of the *Defence of Leicester*, providing introductory comments on its background. Also prints ten letters written by Sidney and seven addressed to him. Among these are included a transcription of the autograph copy of Sir Henry Sidney's letter to his son at Shrewsbury School in 1566 (164) and a transcription of a manuscript of Sidney's *Letter to the Queen*. In the introductory "Memoirs . . . of the Sidneys," traces the family from the thirteenth century through 1743, when the last of the Sidneys died. Recounts Sir Philip's life, citing for the first time many papers at Penshurst, including his license to travel in 1572, the record of his installation as a Gentleman of the Chamber to Charles IX of France, his epitaph, and his will (and related court documents). Also prints Leicester's letter to Sir Thomas Heneage of 23 September 1586, which reports Sidney among the wounded at Zutphen.

Nineteenth Century

13 [HENLEY, JOHN, ed.] *The Works of the Honourable Sir Philip Sidney, Kt. In Prose and Verse.* . . . 14th ed. 3 vols. London: W. Innys, 1724–25.

Reprints the 1674 *Arcadia* (11), but in octavo. Copies issued before William Innys purchased rights to the book show the imprint "London: E. Taylor, A. Bettesworth, E. Curll, W. Mears, and R. Gosling." See Sale (265). Vol. 1, which is dated 1725 (on a second title page after the dedication), includes Henley's dedication to the Earl of Leicester; Sidney's dedication to the Countess of Pembroke; a life of Sidney derived from those in Greville (863), Wood (284), and the 1655 *Arcadia* (9); testimonies by various authors; a brief section entitled "Criticisms on Pastoral Writing"; and Books I and II of *Arcadia*. Vol. 2 (dated 1724) includes Books III–V, paginated as a continuation of the first volume. Vol. 3 (dated 1724) includes a table of characters in *Arcadia*, Richard Beling's continuation of the work, the *Defence of Poetry*, *Astrophil and Stella*, *A Remedy for Love*, *Certain Sonnets*, translations, *The Lady of May*, Psalm 137, a postscript, and a "Table" of titles or first lines of the poems. This is the first illustrated edition in English, containing (in addition to a frontispiece) engravings by G. van der Gucht and I. Pine (after L. Charon), which are placed before each book in *Arcadia*. For further bibliographic information, see Juel-Jensen (256), Sale (265), and Midgley (656).

14 ———. *The Works of the Honourable Sir Philip Sidney, Kt. In Prose and Verse.* . . . 15th ed. 3 vols. Dublin: S. Powell, for T. Moore, 1739.

Reprints item 13, without frontispiece or engravings. For further bibliographic information, see Juel-Jensen (256).

Nineteenth Century

15 FLÜGEL, EWALD. *Sir Philip Sidneys "Astrophel and Stella" und "Defence of Poesie." Nach den ältesten Ausgaben mit einer Einleitung über Sidneys Leben und Werke.* Halle, Germany: Max Niemeyer, 1889, 214 pp.

In the introduction, reprints Flügel's published dissertation (345), with an added appendix containing previously unpublished poems from the Bright Manuscript, the comments on Sidney in Hooker's supplement to Holinshed (272), and Thomas Nashe's preface to the first quarto of *Astrophil and Stella*. Bases the text of *Astrophil and Stella* on the first quarto of 1591, with corrections from other sixteenth-century editions and with variant readings from

Nineteenth Century

the Bright Manuscript and the seventeenth-century folios of *Arcadia*. Adopts the text of the *Defence* in Ponsonby's edition (97), noting variants in Olney's version (98). In a headnote, explains the relation of the two texts. In an appendix, supplies Olney's prefatory matter. Provides no explanatory notes. See also Holthausen (2036) and Koeppel (2038).

16 GRAY, WILLIAM, ed. *The Miscellaneous Works of Sir Philip Sidney, Knt. with a Life of the Author and Illustrative Notes*. Oxford: D.A. Talboys, 1829, 340 pp.

Includes modern-spelling versions of the following: the *Defence*; *Astrophil and Stella*; minor poems, including six "for the first time collected"; *The Lady of May*; the essay *Valour Anatomized in a Fancy*, falsely attributed to Sidney when it was first published in 1651; the *Letter to the Queen*; and the *Defence of Leicester*. Also reprints twenty letters by Sidney, including sixteen from previously unedited manuscripts in the British Library, which are transcribed in the original spelling. In the headnotes to each section, gives publication information but not the copy-texts for the current edition. Includes scattered notes on sources, literary references, and linguistic usage. In the preface, berates the "blunders" in Warton's edition of the *Defence* (103). In the introductory life of Sidney, provides especially detailed accounts of his quarrel with Oxford, his part in defending Leicester from attack, his service in the Netherlands, his death, and the subsequent elegies and tributes. Provides basic information on each of Sidney's major works.

17 MacDONALD, GEORGE, ed. *A Cabinet of Gems, Cut and Polished by Sir Philip Sidney; now, for the more radiance, presented without their setting by George MacDonald*. The Elizabethan Library, 1. London: Elliot Stock, 1892; Chicago: A.C. McClurg, n.d., 210 pp.

Arranges extracts from Sidney's works under the following rubrics: "Men," "Women," "Love and Marriage," "Religion," "Philosophy," "Moral Sayings and Aphorisms," "Human Nature," "Politics and Policy," "Nature and Art," "Horses, Armour, Attire, and Combat," "On Poetry," "Phrases, Similes, Epithets," "From Letters," and "Spoken on His Death-Bed." In the appendices, prints four of the Psalms by Sidney's sister and excerpts from Roydon's elegy for Sidney (2770) and from Greville's *Life* (863). Contains neither indication of sources nor index.

18 PORTER, [JANE]. *Aphorisms of Sir Philip Sidney; with Remarks*. 2 vols. in 1. London: Longman, Hurst, Rees & Orme, 1807, 462 pp.

A collection of passages of various kinds and lengths from a broad range of Sidney's works, grouped according to dominant themes, such as "Love," "Reason and Wisdom," and "Curiosity." Includes "remarks."

Twentieth Century

19 ANON., ed. *"The Defence of Pöesie" and* "Certain Sonnets." *London: Cardoc Press, 1906, 116 pp.*
Prints the works without indicating the copy texts. Includes a preface on the background and nature of the *Defence* but no other aids.

20 COLAIANNE, A[NTHONY] J., ed. *Arcadia (1598): A Photoreproduction.* Scholars' Facsimiles and Reprints, 382. 2 vols. Delmar, N.Y.: Scholars' Facsimiles and Reprints, 1983.
Prints a photographic facsimile of the 1598 edition (1). In the introduction, reviews the composition and publishing history of *Arcadia*, the relation between the major versions of the text, and the influence of the 1593 edition on later English authors. Does not include notes or other aids.

21 CRAIK, T.W. *Sir Philip Sidney: Selected Poetry and Prose* London: Methuen & Co., 1965, 261 pp. Reprint. *Sir Philip Sidney: Selections from "Arcadia" and Other Poetry and Prose.* New York: Capricorn Books, 1966.
Provides substantial modernized extracts from the revised *Arcadia* (Books I-III), from *Astrophil and Stella*, and from the *Defence*, along with miscellaneous poems. In the introduction, examines Sidney's character and provides background and a critical assessment of each of his major works. In the footnotes, glosses difficult phrases, and in the endnotes, explains allusions and provides critical commentary, with cross-references to Sidney's other works. Provides a chronology of Sidney's life and a selective bibliography.

22 DUNCAN-JONES, KATHERINE, and van DORSTEN, JAN A[DRIANUS], eds. *Miscellaneous Prose of Sir Philip Sidney.* Oxford: Clarendon Press, 1973, 248 pp.
Provides a critical, modern-spelling edition of the "Discourse on Irish Affairs," *The Lady of May*, the *Letter to the Queen*, the *Defence of Poetry*, the *Defence of Leicester*, and Sidney's will. Also reprints Gifford (930). In the introduction to each work, discusses dating; literary, intellectual, and historical background; and authoritative manuscripts and editions. Includes full commentary, textual apparatus, and a general index. In the introduction to the "Discourse on Irish Affairs," discusses the occasion, purpose, and style of the document, which supports Sir Henry Sidney's imposition of a land tax on lords in Ireland. Also comments on Sidney's low opinion of the Irish and his allusion to the tax in *Astrophil and Stella* 30. In the introduction to *The Lady of May*, finds both 1578 and 1579 possible as dates of performance and compares the work with other

Twentieth Century

court entertainments, noting its philosophical and political themes. Discounts the theory that the Queen spoiled the ending by choosing the wrong shepherd. Also traces the character Rombus to a comic letter in Thomas Wilson's *Art of Rhetoric*, and compares the country folk with those in *Arcadia*. Hypothesizes that the Helmingham Hall Manuscript is a conflation of Sidney's own record of the performance with last-minute changes made before the performance, the latter not included in the first edition (printed with the 1598 *Arcadia*). In the introduction to the *Letter to the Queen*, argues that it was mild in comparison with other responses to the French marriage and had nothing to do with Sidney's retirement from court. Constructs a stemma of the authoritative texts, concluding that the Penshurst Manuscript is the best. In the introduction to *The Defence of Poetry* discusses dating, sources, rhetorical devices, structure, manuscripts, and early editions. For a detailed annotation, see item 125. In considering Sidney's will, describes the disastrous effects that his debts had on his father-in-law and the financial reasons for Sidney's delayed funeral. See responses by DeNeef (2453) and Heninger (2516).

23 FEUILLERAT, ALBERT, ed. *The Complete Works of Sir Philip Sidney*. 4 vols. Cambridge: Cambridge University Press, 1912–26. Supplies a comprehensive edition with original spelling. Includes a textual apparatus covering editions to 1674 and (with the exception of the Old *Arcadia*) the manuscripts known at the time of publication. In Volume 1, prints the 1590 *Arcadia*. In a prefatory note, discusses the composition of the work and reasons for preferring the 1590 to the 1593 edition. In an appendix, supplies a list of eclogues in the 1593 order and a list of characters in the prose sections of the romance (with chapter references). Includes an index of first lines for the poems. In Volume 2, prints the conclusion of *Arcadia* as it appeared in 1593; miscellaneous poems not printed in the sixteenth century; the 1598 text of *The Lady of May* and *Certain Sonnets*; and Newman's 1591 text of *Astrophil and Stella*. Numbers the sonnets in the last work according to the 1593 edition, though the "Rich Sonnet" (*AS 37*) must be added unnumbered. In an appendix, includes poems of doubtful authenticity. Also provides an index of first lines. In Volume 3, prints without commentary Ponsonby's text of the *Defence*; the Penshurst Manuscript of the *Defence of Leicester*; the autograph manuscript of the "Discourse on Irish Affairs" now in the British Library; the copy of the *Letter to the Queen* in the Bibliothèque Nationale in Paris; transcriptions of 114 letters by Sidney, with notes listing extant manuscripts and their locations; the Woodford Manuscript of Psalms 1–43, which are generally attributed to Sidney; the preface and

Chapters 1–6 of *The Trueness of the Christian Religion*, which Feullierat suggests are the only portions by Sidney; Sidney's will; and the falsely attributed work *Valour Anatomized in a Fancy*. In Volume 4, prints the Clifford Manuscript of the Old *Arcadia*, with emendations from the 1590 and 1593 texts. In a prefatory note, lists the four other manuscripts then known but does not include them in the apparatus. Also adds a table of chapter and page references showing the relation of the Old *Arcadia* to the New, and an index of first lines in the poems. In an appendix, prints the poem "O my thoughts' sweet food, my, my only owner" (*CS 5*) and a letter from Sidney to Joachim [and Philippus] Camerarius of 1 May 1578. See also item 24 and Zandvoort (1316), McClure (637), Gilbert (1893), Robinson (2718), and Tenison (2719).

24 ———. *The Prose Works of Sir Philip Sidney*. 4 vols. Cambridge: Cambridge University Press, 1962.
Reprints item 23, omitting from volumes 2 and 4 the texts of *Astrophil and Stella*, *Certain Sonnets*, and the other poetry. Makes "minor corrections" in the prose works and drops parts of the prefatory notes involving the deleted poetry.

25 KALSTONE, DAVID, ed. *Sir Philip Sidney: Selected Poetry and Prose*. Signet Classic Poetry Series. New York: Signet, 1970, 301 pp.
Following the 1598 *Arcadia*, provides complete texts of *The Lady of May* and *Astrophil and Stella*, along with selections from *Arcadia*, *Certain Sonnets*, and "Other Poems." Also includes six Psalms (based on Bodleian MS. Rawlinson poet. 25) and the complete text of the *Defence* (based on Olney's 1595 edition, with readings from Ponsonby's edition). Relies on Ringler (92) "for many readings, textual references, and notes." In the introduction, emphasizes the "*discovery* of conflict" in Sidney's poems, his "grasp of our resources for self bafflement," and his "animation and play of wit." Contrasts the static, choric, essentially toneless function of the *Arcadia* poems with the "probing and puzzlement" evident in *Astrophil and Stella*, whose "true departure" from earlier verse is its "more intense verbal activity: a liberation of sound, rhythm, and syntax" that participates in, rather than masters, experience. Claims that Sidney's "acuteness as a literary critic is never far from the surface of his verse." See also item 589.

26 KIMBROUGH, ROBERT, ed. *Sir Philip Sidney: Selected Prose and Poetry*. New York: Holt, Rinehart, & Winton, 1969, 571 pp.
Prints the *Defence* and *Astrophil and Stella* in their entirety, along with Book I of the New *Arcadia* and selections from Books II and III. Also prints selections from *The Lady of May*; Book I in its entirety and a selec-

Twentieth Century

tion of poems from the Old *Arcadia*; Psalm 23; six of the *Certain Sonnets*; and one of Sidney's letters to his brother Robert. In the introduction, places Sidney in the humanistic context of the period, provides a biographical sketch, and discusses his works in the context of his life. Suggests that, in both, Sidney saw the practice of art, imitation, and exercise as "an ethic and an esthetic consideration" as well as "an academic program." Also includes separate introductions to the early prose, poetry, and criticism and to each of the major works of Sidney's maturity, providing a context for the selections, identifying the copy text, and, for the major works, discussing the dating. Calls the early work a "pastime," written with a "true, not a studied, casualness." Seeks to show that the conception of art in the *Defence* "concurs completely with that of his age" and that *Astrophil and Stella* was the work that "released [Sidney's] artistic energy totally." Reviews evidence that the New *Arcadia* was meant to be "an epic poem in prose." See also item 27.

27 ——. *Sir Philip Sidney: Selected Prose and Poetry*. 2d ed. Madison: University of Wisconsin Press, 1983, 574 pp.
Without comment, corrects more than 100 printing errors in the first edition (item 26) and expands the bibliography.

28 ROLLINS, HYDER E[DWARD], and BAKER, HERSCHEL, eds. *The Renaissance in England: Non-dramatic Prose and Verse of the Sixteenth Century*. Boston: D.C. Heath & Co., 1954, pp. 323–30, 238–41, 605–24, 737–751.
Prints, without notes, the full text of the *Defence* and excerpts from *Arcadia* and from Sidney's verse.

29 WOODBERRY, G[EORGE] E[DWARD], ed. *"The Defence of Poesie," "A Letter to Q. Elizabeth," "A Defence of Leicester."* The Humanists' Library, 4. Boston: Merrymount Press, 1908, 148 pp.
Prints old-spelling versions of the three works. Follows Flügel's edition of the *Defence of Poetry* (15) and unidentified texts of the others. In the introduction, praises Sidney's broad humanistic education and regards the *Defence of Poetry* as a reflection of his "vital experience" in the world and his religious convictions.

2. *ARCADIA*

Sixteenth Century

30 1590: THE | COVNTESSE | OF PEMBROKES | ARCADIA, | WRITTEN BY SIR PHILIPPE | SIDNEI. | [Sidney coat of arms: a shield encircled with the phrase "HONI SOIT QVI MAL E PENSEE," flanked by a lion and a bear rampant; above the shield a boar, and below it the motto "QVO FATA VOCANT"] | LONDON | Printed for William Ponsonbie. | *Anno Domini*, 1590. 728 pp.

Constitutes the first edition of *Arcadia*, prepared for the press by Fulke Greville and Matthew Gwynne and printed in quarto. Contains Sidney's extensive revisions of Books I-III of the Old *Arcadia*, but not the corrections or the ending of the original version supplied by the Countess of Pembroke and Hugh Sanford in the edition of 1593. Ends in mid-sentence in the episode of Amphialus's rebellion. Includes two poems written specifically for the New *Arcadia*, "Me thought some staves he missed" (*OP 1*) and "Miso, mine own pigsny" (*OP 2*). Also contains Sidney's dedication to his sister, the Countess of Pembroke, and an apology by the "overseer of the print," which notes that the chapter headings and the order of the eclogues were not Sidney's doing. A variant title page shows the imprint as follows: LONDON | Printed by Iohn Windet for william Ponsonbie. | *Anno Domini*, 1590. See Juel-Jensen (256). See also Godshalk (1239).

31 1593: THE | COVNTESSE | OF PEMBROKES | ARCADIA. | WRITTEN BY SIR | Philip Sidney Knight. | NOW SINCE THE FIRST EDI- | tion augmented and ended. | LONDON. | Printed for William Ponsonbie. | *Anno Domini*. 1593. 496 pp. [Title-page border: at the top, the crest of the Sidneys, i.e. a boar on a shield flanked by a bear and a lion; at the sides of the title compartment, scrollwork and two pedestals bearing (at the left) a shepherd and (at the right) an Amazon; at the bottom, a pig with sweet marjoram and the motto "NON TIBI SPIRO" standing before a background of hills and a castle or church. See McKerrow and Ferguson (642), no. 212. See also Eagle (1520 and 1521).]

Reprints the 1590 edition, with corrections and a conclusion drawn from the final three books of the unrevised or Old *Arcadia*. The preparation of this composite folio edition was supervised by the Countess of Pembroke. Includes three poems written for the New *Arcadia* and print-

Sixteenth Century

ed here for the first time: "His being was in her alone" (*OP 3*), "A shepherd's tale no height of style desires" (*OP 4*), and "The lad Philisides"
(*OP 5*). Also contains a preface "To the Reader" by H[ugh] S[anford]
explaining the defects of the 1590 text and the need for the corrections
and additions. See also Godshalk (1239) and Rowe (1293).

Seventeenth Century

32 1625a: L'ARCADIE | DE LA | COMTESSE | DE PEMBROK. |
PREMIERE PARTIE. | *Composee par Messire* PHILIPPES SIDNEY
| *Cheualier Anglois*. | TRADVICTE EN NOSTRE LANGVE | par
vn Gentil-homme François. | *Avec enrichissement de Figures.* |
[ornament depicting a winged satyr bearing a scythe near an
hourglass, with a banderolle before him bearing the inscription
"HANC ASIEM SOL RETUNDIT VIRTVS"] | A PARIS, | Chez
ROBERT FOÜET, ruë sainct | Iacques, à l'Occasion, deuant | les
Mathurins. | M. D. C. XXV | *Avec Priuilege du Roy*. 1:566 + 246
pp.; 2:782 pp.; 3:988 pp.

The first (?) complete French translation of *Arcadia*. On the title pages to
volumes 2 and 3, the printer has supplied the name of the translator,
"D. GENEVIEFVE CHAPPELAIN," in place of the phrase "vn Gentil-
homme François." Each volume includes the following front matter: a
dedication to Madame Diane de Chasteau-Morand signed by the publisher, a preface "Au Lecteur," and an "Extraict du Privilege du Roy."
Following these items, Volume 2 includes a "Table des Vers" and
Volume 3 includes a "Fautes Suruenues à l'impression." Includes
engraved half-title pages and illustrations in each volume. On the dispute between Chappelain and Jean Baudoin for the honor of being the
first French translator of *Arcadia*, see Jusserand (1369). See also Wurmb
(1836) and Hüsgen (1604).

33 1625b: L'ARCADIE | DE LA COMTESSE | DE | PEMBROK, |
Composee par MESSIRE PHILIPPE | SIDNEY, *Cheualier Anglois,* |
ET | Mise en nostre langue, Par I. BAVDOIN. | [device of a hand
reaching out of a cloud with a sheaf of grain above a rural
landscape. Interwoven is the motto "Fertilior Cultu."] | A PARIS,
| Chez TOVSSAINT DV BRAY, ruë sainct | Iacques aux
Espismeurs. | [rule] | M. DC. XXIV. | AVEC PRIVILEGE DV
ROY. | 1:1088 pp.; 2:878 pp.; 3:1064 pp.

The second (?) complete French translation of *Arcadia*, by Jean Baudoin.
On the rivalry between Baudoin and the other major French translator,
Geneviève Chappelain, see Baudoin's prefatory matter and Jusserand

(1369). Each volume begins with an elaborately engraved half-title page by L. Gaultier, includes in the prefatory matter the same full-page portrait of Sidney engraved by I. de Courbes, and ends with a statement of "privilege du Roi." Volume 1 includes a dedicatory epistle from Baudoin to the Queen of France, followed by the de Courbes portrait and a brief life, which praises Sidney's valor and his literary talents. Then follows a longer "Advertissement" praising Sidney as a literary artist and recommending *Arcadia* as a romance and as an exemplary tale; another full-page engraving by de Courbes, which depicts Mary, Countess of Pembroke; and the text of *Arcadia*, Book I and part of Book II. Volume 2 is dated 1625 and includes another dedication to the Queen, followed by another "Advertissment" to the reader discussing changes to English idioms and metaphors needed to make the work comprehensible to a French audience and mentioning contemporary French imitations of Sidney's work. The de Courbes portrait of Sidney follows, then the remainder of Book II and part of Book III. Volume 3, also dated 1625, contains another epistle to the Queen praising her, like Sidney's heroines, for her exemplary conduct. In an "Advertissement pour Response aux Plagiares," discusses problems of translation and the relationship between Sidney's original *Arcadia* and the modifications made after his death. Briefly compares the book with other pastoral romances. Then follows the de Courbes portrait and the remainder of *Arcadia*. See also Wurmb (1836) and Pellison-Fontanier (1325).

34 1629: ARCADIA | **Der Gräffin von Pembrock. | Das ist; | Ein sehr anmüthige | Historische Beschreibung | Arcadischer Gedicht vnd Geschichten / | mit eingemängten Schäffereyen vnd | Poesien. | Warinn nicht allein von den wahren Eygen- | schafften keuscher vnnd beständiger Liebe gehandelt / sondern | auch ein lebendig Bildt deß gantzen menschlichen Wesens vnd | Wandels / auffs zierlichst für Augen ge- | stellet wird: | Allen Hoff- Raths- Kriegs- vnd Weltleuten / Edel vnd Vn- | edel / Hohes vnd Niderstands Personen / die hin vnd wider / sonder- | lich aber an Herrn Höfen / handeln vnd wandeln / | lieblich / nützlich vnd nöthig zulesen: | Angangs in Englischer Sprach beschrieben / durch den weyland Wolge- | bornen / Trefflich-beredten vnd Berümbten Englischen | Graffen vnd Ritter | H. PHILIPPS SIDNEY: | Nachmalen von vnterschiedlichen vornehmen Personen ins Frantzösi- | sche; Nun aber auß beyden in vnser Hochteutsche Sprach / | fleissig vnd trewlich übersetzt | Durch | VALENTINVM THEOCRITVM von Hirschberg. | Mit schönen newen Kupfferstücken gezieret. | Gedruckt zu Franckfurt am Mayn / bey Caspar Rötell / | In**

Seventeenth Century

Verlegung Matthäi Merian. | [rule] | Anno M.DC.XXIX. | **Mit Röm. Kays. Mayt. Freyheit auff 6. Jahr.** | [ornament]. 782 pp.
The first German version of *Arcadia*, translated by an unidentified person using the pseudonym "Valentinus Theocritus von Hirschberg" and printed in quarto. Includes illustrations based upon those in the French translation of Chappelain (32). The translator is frequently, but mistakenly, said to have been Martin Opitz. For the origin of this error, see Lindern (1334) and Wurmb (1836). The front matter of the volume includes a dedication by the publisher, Matthaeus Merian, to Princess Sophien Leonora and a preface by Theocritus justifying his method of translation. According to Wurmb, the translator worked from the French version by Chappelain. See also Geulen (1547), Hüsgen (1604), and Price (1719).

35 1636: "De deughdelycke Parthenia." In *De volstandige Evdoxe*.
   Amsterdam: Gerrit Iansz., 1636. 2d ed., Amsterdam: Gerrit
   Iansz., 1640.
Not seen. According to Schoneveld (267), this is a Dutch translation by J. van Heemskerck of the story of Argalus and Parthenia in Book I of the revised *Arcadia*. It may derive from one of the French translations.

36 1638a: [On a banner held by cherubs, with a chameleon between
   them and a shepherdess with bill on the left and a shepherd with
   bill on the right:] **Den ongestadigen** | HYLAS. | **De
   veranderlijcke** | STELLA. | **De lichtveerdige** | PAMPHILUS. |
   verduijtst | uijt de Fransche | ASTREA. | **en d'Engelsche** |
   ARCADIA. | **den derden druck** | [in an inset, ornamented box
   below:] t'Amsterdam. | voor Gerrit Iansz. opt | hoeckje vande
   Doelestraet. [1638], pp. 251–70. Orig. ed. not located. 2d (?) ed.,
   Amsterdam: Gerrit Iansz., 1636 (not seen).
Includes the stories of Pamphilus and Dido, and Pamphilus and Leucippe, translated into Dutch by J. van Heemskerck. On p. 251 is a separate title page: DE | LICHTVEERDIGE | PAMPHILVS: | *Overgeset uyt d'Engelsche* | *ARCADIA* | vanden Ridder | PHILIPS SIDNEY. | [ornament] | *T'AMSTERDAM* | [rule] | Voor *Gerrit Iansz* Boeck-verkooper | woonende op den hoeck vande | Doel-straet. | 1638. See also item 46 and Schoneveld (267), who suggests that the translator may have worked from one of the French translations of *Arcadia*.

37 1638b: ARCADIA | **Der Gräffin von Pembrock: | Vom Herrn
   Graffen vnd Rittern | Herrn Philippsen | von Sidney | In
   Englischer Sprach geschrieben/ auß dersel- | bigen Frantzösisch/**

28

vnd auß beyden erstlich | Teutsch gegeben | Durch |
VALENTINVM THEOCRITVM | **von Hirschberg: | Jetzo**
allenthalben vffs new vbersehen vnd gebessert: | die Gedichte aber
vnd Reymen gantz anderst gemacht | vnd ubersetzt | Von dem
Edlen vnd Vesten | M. O. V. B. | Auch mit schönen Kupfferstücken
gezieret vnd ver- | legt von | MATTHAEO MERIAN. | [square
ornament: a bridge with "CIRCVMSPECTE" printed over it and a
river flowing in a gorge below; crossing the bridge is a snail
carrying a winged heart] | **Getruckt zu Franckfurt am Mayn/in**
Wolffgang Hoff- | mans Buchtruckerey/im Jahr nach Christi
Geburt | [rule] | M. DC. XXXVIII, 1015 pp. [Some copies contain
a sixth book of 81 pp.]

A revision of the 1629 German translation of *Arcadia* (34) undertaken by
Martin Opitz and printed in octavo. For the nature of Opitz's revisions
and the relation of the text to earlier French translations, see Wurmb
(1836). See also Geulen (1547), Holzinger (1592), Hüsgen (1604), Price
(1719), Szyrocki (1779), and Waterhouse (1800).

38 1639: *D' Engelsche | ARCADIA.* | van de Gravinne | VAN |
PEMBROCK. | Ghestelt door den | Heer PHILIPS SIDNEY, |
Engels Ridder. | *Inde Nederduytsche tale overgheset | door F. V. S. de
Ionghe.* | Het Eerste Deel. | [ornament] | Tot DELF, | [rule] | *By
Felix van Sambix de Ionge, inde Peper-steegh | in't vergulde Schrijf-
boeck Anno 1639.* 1:416 pp.; 2:416 pp.; 3:528 pp.

The Dutch version of *Arcadia*, translated by Felix van Sambix de Jonghe
and published in three volumes duodecimo. The imprint varies. On the
frontispiece of Volume 1, for example, it is "voor Felix van sambix de
Jonghe ende A. Gerritsen," but on that of Volume 2, it is "Bij Adriaen
Gerritsen en Felix Van Sambix de Jonghe." The title page of Volume 2
(dated 1639) shows only the name of Gerritsen, as does that of Volume 3
(dated 1640). Volume 1 contains a preface, "Aen de Nederlantsche
Jonck-vrouwen," dedicating the translation to the widow of Honoré
d'Urfé. Includes frontispieces and illustrations in each volume after
plates in Chappelain's French translation (32), or copies of them in the
German translation (34 or 37).

39 1641: *D' Engelsche | ARCADIA* | Van de Gravinne | VAN |
PEMBROCK. | Ghestelt door den | Heer PHILIPS SIDNEY, |
Engels Ridder. | *Inde Nederduytsche tale overgeset | door F. V. S. de
Jonghe.* | Het Eerste Deel. | *Den tweeden Druck.* | [ornament] | Tot

Seventeenth Century

DELF, | [rule] | *Voor Adriaen Gerritsz en Felix Van Sambix,* | *inde Peper-steegh, Anno 1642.* 1:416 pp; 2:404 pp.; 3:528 pp.
This is the second edition of Felix van Sambix de Jonghe's Dutch translation of *Arcadia*, reprinted from item 38. At the end of Volume 1 is the notation "t'Amsterdam, Ghedruckt by Nicolaes van Ravesteyn, Anno 1642." The imprint on the title pages varies. Volumes 2 and 3 are dated 1641.

40 1642: ARCADIA | **Der Gräffin von Pembrock: Vom** | **Herrn Graffen und Rittern** | **Herrn Philippsen von Sidney** | **In Englischer Sprach geschrieben/ auß dersel-** | **bigen Frantzösisch/ und auß beyden** | **erstlich Teutsch gegeben** | **Durch** | VALENTINUM THEOCRITUM | **von Hirschberg:** | **Hernach allenthalben auffs new vber-** | **sehen vnd gebessert: die Gedichte aber vnd** | **Reymen gantz anderst gemacht** | **vnd vbersetzt** | **Von dem Edlen vnd Vesten** | **Martin Opitz/ V.B.** | **Jetzo auch mit schönen Kupfferstücken** | **gezieret vnd in gewisse Capitel getheilet/ wie denn** | **auch ein Register der Capitel vnd ver-** | **zeichnüß der fürnehmsten Nahmen** | **deren in diesem werck gedacht.** | [ornament of a tree encircled by a vine] | **Gedruckt zu Leyden/** | **Bey Frantz Hegern/** 1642, 1354 pp.
Reprints Opitz's revision of the German translation of *Arcadia* (37), but in duodecimo format and with some of the etchings reversed. Seems to have been planned for two volumes, with the first ending on p. 550. Copies of this issue and its 1646 paginal reprint (42) may be found in which the first volume was bound separately and the second was lost. Other copies were bound as a single volume, with no second title page after p. 550. Contains an engraved frontispiece showing Urania leaving a boy and horse to board a ship, with the shepherds Strephon and Klaius in the background. In the front matter, reprints Merian's dedication and adds an alphabetical table of characters and their roles. Also adds descriptive chapter headings, a brief comment on Sidney's life (pp. 549–50), and a chapter-by-chapter summary of the plot (following p. 1319). See also Wurmb (1836).

41 1643: ARCADIA | **Der Gräffin von Pembrock:** | **Vom Herrn Graffen und Rittern** | **Herrn Philippsen** | **von Sydney** | **In Englischer Sprach geschrieben / auß dersel-** | **bigen Frantzösisch / vnd auß beyden erstlich** | **Teutsch gegeben** | **Durch** | VALENTINVM THEOCRITVM | **von Hirschberg:** | **Jetzo allenthalben auffs new vbersehen vnd gebessert:** | **die Gedichte aber vnd Reymen gantz anderst gemacht** | **vnd übersetzt** | **Von dem Edlen vnd Vesten** | **Martin Opitz von Boberfeldt.** | **Die vierte Edition: mit schönen Kupfferstücken gezieret** | **vnd verlegt durch** | MATHEVM

MERIANVM. | [printer's device] | **Getruckt zu Franckfurt bey Anthoni | Hummen.** | [rule] | M. DC. XLIII. 1092 pp.
Reprints Opitz's revision of the German translation of *Arcadia* (37). On the verso of the final page, provides a brief life of Sidney. For a modern facsimile reproduction, see item 58. See also Wurmb (1836).

42 1646: ARCADIA | **Der Gräffin von Pembrock: Vom | Herrn Graffen vnd Rittern | Herrn Philippsen von Sidney | In Englischer Sprach geschrieben/auß dersel- | bigen Frantzösisch/ vnd auß beyden | erstlich Teutsch gegeben | Durch | VALENTINUM THEOCRITUM | von Hirschberg: | Hernach allenthalben auffs new vber- | sehen vnd gebessert: die Gedichte aber vnd | Reymen gantz anders gemacht | vnd ubersetzt | Von dem Edlen vnd Vesten | Martin Opitz / V.B. | Jetzo auch mit schönen Kupfferstücken | gezieret vnd in gewisse Capitel geth- | eilet / wie denn | auch ein Register der Capitel vnd ver- | zeichnüß der fürnehmsten Nahmen/ | deren in diesem werck gedacht.** | [ornament of a tree encircled by a vine] | **Gedruckt zu Leyden / | Bey Frantz Hegern** / 1646. 1354 pp.
A paginal reprint of the 1642 edition of the German *Arcadia* (40). Retains its frontispiece, which still bears the date 1642. See Wurmb (1836).

43 1658: ARCADIA **Der Gräffin von Pembrock: Vom Herrn Graffen vnd Rittern Herrn Philippsen von Sidney In Englischer Sprach geschrieben, auß derselbigen Frantzösisch, vnd auß beyden erstlich Teutsch gegeben Durch** VALENTINUM THEOCRITUM **von Hirschberg: Hernach allenthalben auffs new vbersehen vnd gebessert, die Gedichte aber vnd Reymen gantz anders gemacht vnd vbersetzt Von dem Edlen vnd Vesten Martin Opitz, V. B. . . . Gedruckt zu Amsterdam, Bey Johan Jansson, Anno** 1658. 1354 pp.
Not seen. Cited in Wendelin von Maltzahn, *Deutscher Bücherschatz des sechszehnten, siebenzehnten, und achtzehnten bis um die Mitte des neunzehnten Jahrhunderts* (Jena: Freidrich Mauke, 1875), p. 357. This is a paginal reprint of the 1642 edition (40). See Wurmb (1836).

44 1659a: *D' Engelsche* | ARCADIA | Van de Gravinne | VAN | *PEMBROCK.* | Ghestelt door den | Heer PHILIPS SIDNEY, | Engels Ridder. | *In de Nederduytsche Tale over-gheset* | *door F. V. S. de Jonghe.* | Het Derde Deel. | [ornament] | t'AMSTERDAM, | [rule] | Voor *Gerrit Willemsz Doornick*, Boeck- | verkooper op de

Seventeenth Century

> Cingel, by Jan-Roon-poorts- | Toorn. *Anno* 1659. 1:430 pp.;
> 2:412 pp.; 3:528 pp.

The third edition of Felix van Sambix de Jonghe's Dutch translation of
Arcadia, reprinted from item 39.

45 1659b: DELL' | ARCADIA | DELLA | CONTESSA | DI
PEMBROCH, | Portata dal Francese | *Dal Signor* | *LIVIO*
ALESSANDRI | PARTE PRIMA. | *Con licenza, & Priuilegio.* |
[Device of armed Minerva seated at the base of a tree, with a
lance in her hand and an owl at her feet] | IN VENETIA,
M.DC.LIX. | [rule] | Presso Combi, & La Noù. 1:758 pp.; 2:518
pp.; 3:776 pp.

Provides the first Italian rendering of *Arcadia*, translated by Alessandri
from an unspecified French version. Includes a dedicatory epistle by
Giovanni la Noù followed by a brief "Vita dell'Avtore," which emphasizes
Sidney's military and diplomatic accomplishments but also touches on his
literary works. Each volume includes its own title page, preceded by a half-
title page engraved by Jac. Picini. The half titles depict the following scenes
from the book: in Volume 1, the initial shipwreck; in Volume 2, Basilius
wooing Pyrocles (disguised as Zelmane); and in Volume 3, the head of
Philoclea, as if severed, in a basin on a table in a gallery, with Pamela in the
background being led blindfolded toward the table. After the life of Sidney
in Volume 1, there is an engraving of the Countess of Pembroke.

46 1670: Den | **Ongestadigen** | HYLAS. | **De Veranderlijcke** |
STELLA. | **De Lichtveerdige** | PAMPHILUS. | **Uyt het Frans en**
Engels vertaelt | **door** J.H. | t'Amsterdam, | voor Jacob Vinckel,
Boeck- | verkooper in de Beurs-Straet, in de | History-Schrijver,
1670, pp. 251–70.

Reprints item 36.

Eighteenth Century

47 [N., J.] *The Famous History of Heroick Acts; or, The Honour of*
Chivalry, Being an Abstract of Pembroke's Arcadia. . . . London: for
William Spiller, 1701, 158 pp.

From an unspecified seventeenth-century edition of *Arcadia*, excerpts the
main plot involving the cross-wooing of the royal lovers, following the
wording of the original text only intermittently. Begins *ab ovo* with the
birth and education of the heroes and ends with parts of Beling's continuation. Also includes condensed accounts of the fall of the King of
Phrygia and Amphialus's rebellion, altering the manner of Amphialus's

apparent death. Omits Cecropia's torment of the Princesses but recounts at length the battle of Clinias and Dametas. Does not mention Sidney on the title page or in the prefatory matter.

48 STANLEY, Mrs., ed. *Sir Philip Sidney's "Arcadia," Moderniz'd.* London: n.p., 1725, 523 pp.

Provides a paraphrase of the 1593 *Arcadia*, following the action and thought of the work but omitting the eclogues.

Nineteenth Century

49 FRISWELL, HAIN, ed. *The Countess of Pembroke's Arcadia.* London: Sampson, Low, Son & Marston, 1867, 510 pp.

Bases the text on an unspecified edition derived from that of 1593. Omits the eclogues, abridges the long episodes, and modernizes spelling. In the notes, supplies numerous philological parallels (cited in a glossarial index at the end of the introduction) and discusses Sidney's influence, particularly on Renaissance dramatists. In an "Introductory and Biographical Essay," provides a concise life of Sidney and examines *Arcadia*. Points out confusions caused by the complex plot, the disguises, and the lack of a consistent time frame. Finds fault with the characters for a lack of human interest, but praises the style. Also comments briefly on sources and influences.

50 SIMROCK, KARL [JOSEPH]. "Zu *König Lear*: 2. Der Bastard nach Sidney's *Arcadia.*" In *Quellen des Shakspeare in Novellen, Märchen und Sagen.* Bibliothek der Novellen, Märchen und Sagen, edited by Theodor Echtermeyer, Ludwig Henschel, and Karl Simrock. Vol. 3. Berlin: Finkeschen Buchhandlung, 1831, pp. 8–16.

Provides a German translation of the story of the Paphlagonian King.

51 SOMMER, H. OSKAR, ed. *The Countess of Pembroke's Arcadia.* London: Kegan Paul, Trench, Trübner & Co., 1891, 415 pp.

Provides a photographic facsimile of the 1590 edition. In the preface, describes the composition of *Arcadia*, Sidney's attitudes toward it, and the reasons that the 1590 text is to be preferred over the folio of 1593. In a "Bibliographical Introduction," gives a thorough history of the text of the revised *Arcadia* from early references to it in a letter from Fulke Greville to Sir Francis Walsingham in 1586 to Friswell's edition (49). Supplies bibliographic descriptions of the various editions, including transcriptions of the title pages, full descriptions of the contents and pagination, reprintings of prefatory matter, and comments on the rela-

Nineteenth Century

tion of each edition to preceding ones. Describes the differences between the 1590 and the 1593 editions, including a table of variants that also shows the position of the eclogues. Also lists supplements to the romance and translations into French and German. See also Wiles (1819).

Twentieth Century

52 BAKER, ERNEST A[LBERT], ed. *The Countess of Pembroke's Arcadia*. Routledge's Library of Early Novelists. London: George Routledge & Sons; New York: E.P. Dutton & Co., [1907], 718 pp.
Prints the 1593 composite version of *Arcadia*, but without indicating the copy text. Also supplies the continuations by Sir William Alexander and Richard Beling. Modernizes spelling and punctuation and includes scattered linguistic and explanatory notes. Reprints a life of Sidney from the 1739 Dublin edition (14). In the introduction, treats *Arcadia* as part of a trend in Renaissance prose fiction away from the traditional embellishment of old legends and toward poetic invention. Links this trend with classical attempts to mingle the imagination of poetry with the reason of prose. In *Arcadia*, however, sees advances in structure, characterization, emotion, and realism that foreshadow the modern novel. Rejects the concept of poetry in the *Defence* as "too broad for poetry, and too narrow for imaginative literature in general," examining the "cloying" style that this definition produced in *Arcadia*. Notes ridicule of this style after Sidney's death, particularly in John Davies of Kidwelly's translation of Sorel's *Berger extravagant*. Provides a full publication history of *Arcadia*, describing its influence on later English drama and fiction.

53 de TOURVAL, JEAN LOISEAU, trans. *Fragment de L' "Arcadie."* Edited by Albert W. Osbsorn. In *Sir Philip Sidney en France*, by Albert W. Osbsorn. Paris: Honoré Champion, 1932, pp. i–xlii.
The first published edition, based on Bodleian Library MS. Rawlinson D920, fols. 365ff., of what Osborn (1103) and Legouis (1642) claim is the first translation of a portion of *Arcadia* into French. Comprises roughly the first six chapters of Book II. Omits the poems, but leaves spaces for them. Osborn reproduces the manuscript text "with its numerous errors of grammar, orthography and punctuation." He suggests that the translation was probably begun in 1607 and completed by 1610, that de Tourval may have failed to find a patron because of the interference of Robert Sidney, and that the manuscript found no publisher because of its author's difficulties with the church. The text is preceded by a dedicatory letter, apparently addressed to the spirit of Sidney himself, since it

begins "here is your *Arcadia*" and later refers to the "bad treatment that I received from *votre brave frère*." This is followed by a more general advertisement.

54 EVANS, MAURICE, ed. *The Countess of Pembroke's Arcadia*. Harmondsworth, England: Penguin Books, 1977, 870 pp.

Provides a modernized text of the 1593 version based on Baker's edition (52), corrected and emended from sixteenth- and twentieth-century editions. In the notes, elucidates mythological references and difficult language and records differences between the Old and the New *Arcadia*. In the introduction, covers dating, composition, publishing history, and the relation between the various versions. Seeks to recapture the Renaissance admiration for the romance. Discusses its brilliant rhetoric, its range of styles and their relation to character and emotional effect. Examines the genre of the work and analyzes it as a "poem" in the sense defined in Sidney's *Defence of Poetry*: a creation of the "erected wit" that offers an image of unfallen goodness and so moves the "infected will" of the reader to action. Analyzes various "speaking pictures" in the book as ways to teach the nature of virtue and vice. Discusses the course of divine providence in the book and the conflict between right reason and passion, identifying these as Sidney's main themes. Notes the central importance of Pamela's debate with Cecropia in the Captivity Episode. Also considers Sidney's ambivalence about the proper role of private codes of chivalric honor and of Machiavellian realpolitik in society. Stresses the continual contrast between the idyllic Arcadia of pastoral tradition and the fallen kingdom portrayed in the romance. Also details the careful articulation of the many strands in the narration, the artful mingling of retrospective and prospective narration, the origins of the action in the natures of the characters, and the narrator's sense of humor.

55 ROBERTSON, JEAN, ed. *The Countess of Pembroke's Arcadia (The Old Arcadia)*. Oxford: Clarendon Press, 1973, 588 pp.

Provides a critical edition with modern spelling. In the commentary, considers textual variants, difficult words and phrases, sources for particular passages, rhetorical figures, and proverbs. In the general introduction, argues that the book was begun in 1577, completed in the spring of 1581, and "tinkered with" in 1581–82, before Sidney began the revised version. Regards the work as "a tragicomedy, with a serious double-plot and a comic underplot, based on a Terentian structure. . . ." Details its debts to Sannazaro's *Arcadia*, Montemayor's *Diana* and its continuations, *Amadis de Gaule*, Ariosto's *Orlando furioso*, Heliodorus's *Aethiopica*, Apuleius's *Golden Ass*, Xenophon's *Cyropaedia*, and works by Aristotle, Plato, and various moral and religious writers. Analyzes the Ciceronian

Twentieth Century

character of Sidney's style and the Aristotelian basis of his rhetoric, discounting the impact of Ramism or euphuism. Minimizes differences
between the styles of the original and the revised versions. In discussing
the genre of the Old *Arcadia*, rejects the possibility that it is a pastoral
romance in which heroes retire from a chivalric world to a pastoral one
for healing. Concludes that the work mingles several genres but fulfills
the essential function of heroic poetry. Notes early allusions to it and
imitations by Robert Greene and Thomas Lodge. In the textual introduction, provides descriptions of eight full scribal manuscripts and one
partial one; eight other manuscripts containing Arcadian poems; and
eight significant printed texts. Constructs a stemma showing the relationships among these texts and discusses Sidney's tendency to continual
revision. Lays out the principles followed in editing the text and providing the apparatus. Also includes maps, a glossary, and indexes of characters, names, places, first lines of poems, and authors and titles mentioned in the general introduction and commentary. The index of
characters provides etymologies of their names.

56 SKRETKOWICZ, VICTOR, Jr. "A Full Critical Edition of Book I
of Sir Philip Sidney's *The Countess of Pembroke's Arcadia* (1590)."
Ph.D. diss., University of Southampton, 1974.
Bases the text of Book I on the 1590 edition, collated against the
Cambridge University Library Manuscript of the New *Arcadia* and
against printed editions through 1613. Normalizes spelling and modernizes punctuation and paragraphing. In the introduction, discusses
the following: date of composition; Sidney's sources in literature and in
personal experience; the heroic form that he followed, particularly as it
derives from Heliodorus's *Aethiopica*; the style of the work; and its influence on later authors. Provides a commentary that clarifies difficult passages, catalogs proverbs, and records rhetorical figures noted in John
Hoskins's *Directions for Speech and Style* (see 1593). Also supplies a glossary; an index of characters, names, and places; an index of general topics; and genealogical tables.

57 SYFRET, ROSEMARY, ed. *Selections from Sidney's "Arcadia."*
Hutchinson English Texts. London: Hutchinson Educational,
1966, 264 pp.
From Feuillerat's edition (23) prints about one-third of Books I-III of
the revised *Arcadia*. Omits the eclogues and all prose material not essential to the main plot (except the story of Argalus and Parthenia).
Summarizes parts of the main action that were omitted, and provides a
glossary and full notes covering linguistic difficulties and matters of cul-

tural and literary background. In the introduction, treats Sidney as an ideal Renaissance gentleman, drawing upon Castiglione and Spenser to characterize his combination of classical and Christian virtues. Reviews his life and works, the composition and publishing history of *Arcadia*, and the development of romance in the sixteenth century. Summarizes the Old *Arcadia*, describing its dramatic structure, methods of characterization, and ethical stance. Reviews changes in the New *Arcadia* and the unsuitability of the conclusion supplied in the 1593 edition. Treats the revision as a prose epic, reviewing the *Defence* to establish Sidney's aims in the genre. Concludes with an examination of Sidney's prose style in relation to euphuism. In a set of "General Introductory Notes," reviews Elizabethan concepts of rhetoric and style and of ethical and political philosophy.

58 THEOCRITUS von HIRSCHBERG, VALENTINUS [pseud.], and OPITZ, MARTIN, trans. *Arcadia der Gräffin von Pembrock.* Darmstadt, Germany: Wissenschaftliche Buchgesellschaft, 1971, 1092 pp.

Reprints in facsimile the German translation of *Arcadia*, working from the 1643 edition (41).

3. POETRY

Sixteenth Century

59 1588: *Svperivs. Psalmes, Sonets, & songs of sadnes and piety, made into Musicke of fiue parts,* by William Byrd. [London]: Printed by Thomas East, the assigne of W. Byrd, 1588, song no. XVI. Reprint. *The English Madrigal School.* Transcribed, scored, and edited by Edmund Horace Fellowes. Vol. 14, *Psalms, Sonnets, and Songs of Sadness and Piety To Five Parts.* London: Stainer & Bell, 1920, pp. 78–83.

Contains the first of Sidney's poems ever to be printed, "O you that hear this voice" (*AS vi*), as set to music by Byrd. The text is corrupt.

60 1591a: Syr P.S. | *His Astrophel and Stella.* | Wherein the excellence of sweete | Poesie is concluded | [ornament] | *To the end of which are added, sundry | other rare Sonnets of diuers Noble | men and*

Sixteenth Century

> *Gentlemen.* | (*) | [ornament] | At London, | Printed for Thomas
> Newman. | *Anno. Domini. 1591.* 88 pp.

The unauthorized first quarto of *Astrophil and Stella*, which was printed
from a faulty manuscript and contains a substantial number of typograph-
ical errors. Includes a dedication by Thomas Newman "To the worshipfull
and his very good Freende, Ma. Frauncis Flower Esquire"; a preface by
Thomas Nashe entitled "Somewhat to reade for them that list"; and 107
unnumbered sonnets from *Astrophil and Stella*. Omits "My mouth doth
water" (*AS 37*); reverses the order of Sonnets 55 and 56; omits lines from
Sonnets 19, 30, 44, 63, and 85; and reverses the opening quatrains of
Sonnet 5. Includes ten songs from the sequence (termed "Other Sonnets
of variable verse"), omitting Song xi altogether and dropping many lines
from viii and x. Adds "Poems and Sonets of sundrie other Noble men and
Gentlemen," which include corrupt versions of twenty-eight sonnets by
Samuel Daniel (twenty-four of which later appeared in *Delia*), five songs
identified by Smith (1155) as the work of Thomas Campion, one sonnet
signed "E.O." but actually by Fulke Greville (Sonnent 28 of *Caelica*), and
an anonymous poem, "If floods be teares." The quarto was not entered in
the Stationers' Register and was recalled in September 1591, apparently at
the order of Lord Burghley. In the dedication, Newman remarks on the
"generall commendation" that has been accorded Sidney's sonnets, con-
ceding, however, that to some the "Argument" may seem "too light." In
the preface, Nashe introduces "Astrophel in pompe," contrasting him with
figures in pastorals and other poetic creations of the day. Calls such works
mere "puppetplay" in comparison with Sidney's "Theater of pleasure,"
where "the tragicommody of loue is performed by starlight." Identifies the
chief actor as Melpomene; "the argument cruell chastitie; the Prologue
hope; the Epilogue dispaire." Comments on his own presumption in
printing the work, which has been hidden "in a cloud." Compares Sidney
with Mercury, to whom "Apollo hath resigned his Iuory Harp" and who
"liuest againe like the Phoenix." Mourns Sidney's death, praising his sister
as "a second Minerua" and satirizing lesser writers. Reprinted in facsimile,
item 88. See also pp. 542–44 in Ringler (92) and see Juel-Jensen (257)
and Case (242).

61 1591b: [ornament] SIR P.S. HIS | ASTROPHEL AND | *STELLA*.
| Wherein the excellence of sweete | Poesie is concluded. |
[ornament] | At London, | Printed for Thomas Newman. | *Anno
Domini.* 1591. 64 pp.

The second quarto of *Astrophil and Stella*, which, according to Ringler
(92), is a "haphazard and slipshod" correction of the first quarto (60)

with reference to a good manuscript. Omits Newman's dedication, Nashe's preface, and the "Poems and Sonets of sundrie other Noble men and Gentlemen." Prints the same poems by Sidney as in the first quarto, and in the same order. Supplies missing lines and corrects some of the errors in Sonnets 1-95, restoring the proper order of the quatrains in Sonnet 5. Does not, however, restore the missing lines of Songs viii and x. See also Juel-Jensen (257) and Case (242).

62 1598?: Syr P.S. | *His Astrophel and Stella.* | Wherein the excellence of sweete | Poesie is concluded. | [ornament] | *To the end of which are added, sundry* | *other rare Sonnets of diuers Noble* | *men and Gentlemen.* | [ornament] | [publisher's device] | *At London* | Printed for *Matthew Lownes.* [80] pp.

The third quarto of *Astrophil and Stella*, which omits Newman's dedication and Nashe's preface, but otherwise reprints the first quarto (60) with few changes. On the likely date of publication and the printer that Lownes may have employed, see Buxton (2077) and Juel-Jensen (257).

Seventeenth Century

63 [DAVISON, FRANCIS, comp.] *A Poetical Rapsody Containing, Diuerse Sonnets, Odes, Elegies, Madrigalls and other Poesies, both in Rime and Measured Verse. Neuer yet Published.* London: V. S[immes] for John Baily, 1602, sigs. A3^r–A3^v, B1^r–B3^v.

Prints "Join mates in mirth to me" (*OP 6*) under the title "Vpon his meeting with his two worthy Friends and fellow-Poets, Sir Edward Dier and Maister Fulke Greuill," and "Walking in bright Phoebus' blaze" (*OP 7*), under the title "Disprayse of a Courtly life." In "To the Reader," claims that Sidney's two pastorals were included by the printer "either to grace the forefront with Sir Ph. Sidneys, and other names, or to make the booke grow to a competent volume." See Ringler (92), pp. 260–64 and 498–99. See also Rollins (724).

Eighteenth Century

64 HARINGTON, Sir JOHN. *Nugae Antiquae: Being a Miscellaneous Collection of Original Papers in Prose and Verse. Written in the Reigns of Henry VIII, Queen Mary, Elizabeth, King James, &c.* Edited by Hen[ry] Harington. Vol. 2. London: Printed for W. Frederick, and Sold by Geo. Robinson and J. Dodsley, 1775, pp. 57–69.

Eighteenth Century

In "Psalmes, Translated by the Countess of Pembroke," provides the texts of Psalms 51, 69, 104, and 137, all thought to be the work of Sidney's sister Mary. These, along with Psalm 137 as published by Steele (66) and Henley (13, 14), are the first selections from the Sidney Psalter to appear in print. See also item 65.

65 ———. *Nugae Antiquae: Being a Miscellaneous Collection of Original Papers in Prose and Verse: Written in the Reigns of Henry VIII, Queen Mary, Elizabeth, King James &c.* 3d ed. Edited by Hen[ry] Harington. Vol. 1. London: Printed for J. Dodsley and T. Shrimpton, 1779, pp. 277–96.

Reprints item 64, adding Psalms 112, 117, and 120, all thought to have been translated by Mary Sidney.

66 [STEELE, Sir RICHARD.] Essay no. 18. In *The Guardian*. Vol. 1. London: J. Tonson, 1714, pp. 73–77.

In an essay on the "Prospect of Death," prints Psalm 137 in the Sidneys' translation, explaining that "a friend" who possessed a complete manuscript provided the transcription. States (incorrectly) that Sir Philip translated all the Psalms. See also Tuckerman (1391).

Nineteenth Century

67 ANON., ed. *Certain Sonnets From the Countess of Pembroke's "Arcadia," Written by Sir Philip Sidney, Kt.* Illustrated by George Wharton Edwards. Cleveland: Barrows Brothers Co., 1890, 36 pp.

An illustrated edition of four poems from *Arcadia* and eight from *Certain Sonnets*. Includes no critical apparatus and no indication of the copy text.

68 ARBER, EDWARD, ed. *Astrophel and Stella*. In *An English Garner: Ingatherings from Our History and Literature*. Vol. 1. London: E. Arber, 1877, pp. 467–579.

Provides a text of *Astrophil and Stella* based on the 1598 edition, but with the songs collected separately at the end. In a lengthy introduction, quotes from Sidney's correspondence and from contemporary documents to establish his reputation and to argue for a biographical (though not a chronological) reading of the sequence. From contemporary evidence, especially that related to her marriages, identifies Lady Rich as Stella. Also relates Godwel's *Brief Declaration* (147) to *Astrophil and Stella* 41, dating the sonnet between 1581 and 1584. Provides transcriptions of the title pages of the two 1591 Newman quartos, accompanied by a brief argument as to which is the unauthorized text.

69 GROSART, ALEXANDER B., ed. *The Complete Poems of Sir Philip Sidney*. Early English Poets. 3 vols. London: Chatto & Windus, 1877. Orig. pub. as part of the Fuller Worthies' Library. 2 vols. London: privately printed, 1873 (not seen).

In Volume 1, prints *Astrophil and Stella*, with *Certain Sonnets* 31 and 32 as Sonnets 109 and 110, gathering the eleven songs at the end. Volume 2 contains "Sidera," consisting of eleven of the *Certain Sonnets*; "Pansies from Penshurst and Wilton," comprised of the remainder of the *Certain Sonnets* and nine additional miscellaneous poems; and fifty of a total of seventy-nine "Poems from . . . Arcadia" (selected from the 1613 edition). Volume 3 prints the remaining poems from *Arcadia* and "The Psalms of David" (*PS 1–43*.) Includes a lengthy introductory essay, prefaces to each section of the edition, and textual notes. At the end of Volume 3, adds "Longer Notes and Illustrations" on textual and linguistic difficulties, an index of first lines, and a "Glossarial Index" of words used in the poems. In the introductory matter, discusses the publishing history of all Sidney's major works, commenting on poems by Sidney published in Renaissance miscellanies. Considers early printings of *Astrophil and Stella*, arguing that the sequence of the sonnets has been intentionally altered to obscure the biographical facts and that Sidney largely confined his wooing of Penelope Devereux to the period before her marriage. In characterizing Sidney's poetry, focuses on the "passion," "thought," and "fineness of art" in the works, quoting at length from Lamb (2041).

70 HANSEN, ADOLF. "Engelske sonetter indtil Milton [English Sonnets to Milton]." *Tilskueren* 9 (February 1892):196–222.

In the introduction to an anthology of English Renaissance sonnets, provides what may be the first Danish translation of *Astrophil and Stella* 31, 39, 41, 64, and 84. Comments on Sidney's contributions to the conventions associated with the form.

71 POLLARD, ALFRED [WILLIAM], ed. *Sir Philip Sidney's Astrophel and Stella. Wherein the Excellence of Sweet Poesy is Concluded. Edited from the Folio of MDXCVIII*. Chicago: McClurg & Co.; London: David Stott, 1888, 273 pp.

Reprints the sequence from the 1598 *Arcadia*, with modernized punctuation and orthography. Adds fourteen poems from *Certain Sonnets*. In the introduction, takes Sidney's death as an "epitome" of his life, discussing what it reveals about his character. Outlines his life, focusing on his relations with Penelope Devereux. Dates *Astrophil and Stella* 1–23, 25–30, and seven poems from *Certain Sonnets* from the period before her mar-

Nineteenth Century

riage to Lord Rich, assuming that Sidney was already in love with her then and that he courted her passionately thereafter. Defends Sidney's pursuit of a married woman on the grounds that an "enforced marriage" is "no marriage." Also discusses early editions of *Astrophil and Stella*, suggesting that poems first printed in 1598 were earlier suppressed out of regard for Lady Rich's reputation. Includes notes on textual, linguistic, and biographical matters. See also Helm (2034).

72 RHYS, ERNEST, ed. *The Lyric Poems of Sir Philip Sidney*. The Lyric Poets. London: J.M. Dent, 1895, 201 pp.

Reprints ninety-six sonnets from *Astrophil and Stella*, thirteen from *Certain Sonnets*, twenty-three poems from *Arcadia*, and other poems, including two wrongly attributed to Sidney. Gives no indication of copy text. In the introduction, provides a brief life of Sidney, critical comments on the poems from *Arcadia*, and biographical comments on *Astrophil and Stella*.

73 RUSKIN, JOHN, ed. *Bibliotheca Pastorum*. Vol. 2, *Rock Honeycomb. Broken Pieces of Sir Philip Sidney's Psalter Laid Up in Store for English Homes*. Part 1. London: Ellis & White; Kent, England: George Allen, 1877, 250 pp.

From the 1823 edition (74), prints modernized and emended selections from Psalms 1–72. In the preface, notes faults in the 1823 edition and finds it impossible to distinguish Psalms traditionally ascribed to Sidney from those attributed to his sister. Feels that the former group includes "many of the feeblest in the volume." Applauds the translators for sacrificing elegance of language in favor of familiarity and accuracy. Examines Greek and Latin theological terms on which the "ethics of the Sidney text" are based. In an introductory essay "Of the Sidney Metres," attempts to justify the use of formal meters and careful symmetries in conveying the powerful emotions of the Psalms. Provides a technical analysis of the meters, inventing a method for diagramming rhyme schemes and scansions. Includes a commentary covering metrical, linguistic, and interpretive matters. Part 2, which was supposed to contain selections from Psalms 73–150 and metrical diagrams of all the Psalms printed, was apparently never published. See also Rathmell (2356).

74 [SINGER, SAMUEL WELLER, ed.] *The Psalmes of David Translated into Divers and Sundry Kindes of Verse, More Rare and Excellent for the Method and Varietie Than Ever Yet Hath Been Done in English. Begun by the Noble and Learned Gent. Sir Philip Sidney, Knt. and Finished by the Right Honorable the Countess of Pembroke, His Sister. Now First Printed from a Copy of the Original Manuscript, Transcribed by John*

Davies, of Hereford, in the Reign of James the First. Early English
Poets. [London:] Chiswick Press, by C. Whittingham, for Robert
Triphook, 1823, 297 pp.

Supplies the first complete edition of the Sidney Psalter, though selections from the portion thought to be by Mary Sidney had appeared in
Harington (64, 65), in the 1724–25 and 1739 editions of Sidney's works
(13, 14), and in Steele (66). Bases the text on the Penshurst Manuscript,
"amended" by comparison with another in the collection of "the Rev.
Dr. Cotton, of Christ Church, Oxford." Does not include notes or commentary. In the "Advertisement," explains that the edition was suggested by James Boswell, who died before he could carry out his intention to
write an introduction. Describes the Penshurst Manuscript, suggesting
that it may have been prepared for Prince Henry. Notes the existence of
yet another manuscript in the library of Richard Heber (British Museum
MS. Additional 12048) and suggests that the earliest manuscript may
still be at Wilton. Accepts a suggestion by a Rev. Bulkeley Bandinel that
"the first portion was written by Sir Philip, and the latter by the
Countess." Quotes Bandinel's description of the Woodford Manuscript
(Bodleian MS. Rawlinson poet. 25) and remarks that Bandinel saw vast
differences between the Woodford MS. and the "first MS. in the
Bodleian." Also records several contemporary and later references to the
existence of the Psalter. For further bibliographic information, see Juel-
Jensen (257).

Twentieth Century

75 BANTOCK, GRANVILLE, and ANDERTON, H. ORSMOND,
eds. *The Melvill Book of Roundels.* London: Roxburghe Club, 1916,
pp. xiv, 27, 139–41.

Prints a manuscript assembled in 1612 by David Melvill, a friend of
George Buchanan, which contains a musical setting of the first six lines
of "Now thanked be the great god Pan" (*OA 5*).

76 BENDER, ROBERT M., ed. *Five Courtier Poets of the English
Renaissance.* New York: Washington Square Press, 1967, pp. xiii,
285–474.

From Ringler's text (92), presents a modernized version of *Astrophil and
Stella*, *Certain Sonnets*, the first 43 Psalms of the Sidney Psalter, and
selected poems from *Arcadia* and Sidney's miscellaneous poetry.
Provides a brief biographical and critical introduction and a short bibliography.

Twentieth Century

77 BULLETT, GERALD [WILLIAM], ed. *Silver Poets of the Sixteenth Century: Sir Thomas Wyatt, Henry Howard, Earl of Surrey, Sir Philip Sidney, Sir Walter Raleigh, Sir John Davies.* Everyman's Library, 985. London: Dent, 1947, pp. xiii–xiv, 171–278, 417–418.

Following Grosart's edition (69), prints all of *Astrophil and Stella* except Songs v and vii; twenty-eight selections from *Arcadia*; and eleven from *Certain Sonnets.* Includes a brief introduction and explanatory notes.

78 DRINKWATER, JOHN, ed. *The Poems of Sir Philip Sidney.* The Muses' Library. London: George Routledge & Sons; New York: E.P. Dutton & Co., 1910, 336 pp.

The text, based on the first two quartos of *Astrophil and Stella* and the 1598 and 1613 editions of *Arcadia*, contains "the whole of his work in verse" with the exception of the Psalms, the poems in *The Lady of May*, a manuscript poem on Elizabeth, and several poems from *Arcadia*. In the biographical introduction, relies on Bourne (319) and Symonds (961). Suggests the Queens's displeasure over Leicester's secret marriage as a probable cause for Sidney's retirement from court late in 1579. In the critical introduction, places Sidney's poetry in its historical context. Dismisses experiments in classical verse but applauds the sincerity and "passion" of *Astrophil and Stella*. Rejects a strictly biographical reading of the sequence, arguing that Sidney was in love with an ideal and chose Lady Rich as a "framework" on which to "build" it. Also comments on Sidney's development of the sonnet form, his diction, and his "vice of conceit-making." Includes scattered linguistic notes and an index of first lines.

79 DUNCAN-JONES, KATHERINE, ed. *Sir Philip Sidney: Selected Poems.* Oxford Paperback English Texts. Oxford: Clarendon Press, 1973, 250 pp.

Drawing on Ringler's edition (92), prints thirty-seven poems from *Arcadia*, twenty-two from *Certain Sonnets*, all of *Astrophil and Stella*, "The Lad Philisides" (*OP 4*), and four of the Psalms. Includes a chronological table, a note on the text, a "Reading List" of primary and secondary sources, a thorough set of notes for the selections, and an index of first lines. In the introduction, provides a biography of Sidney, stressing his career as a courtier and man of action. Taking Philisides's account of himself in *Arcadia* as a glimpse of the early years, suggests that Sidney may first have fallen in love in 1575 when he returned from his tour of the Continent. Notes that, although the *Defence* views literature as a guide to heroic action, Sidney's own poetry concerns itself "with moral and emotional dilemmas of a personal kind." Sketches background information for *The Lady of May*, then turns to the major works. Feels that no other Elizabethan poet "approached either the depth of thought or the astonishing metrical virtuosity" displayed in the poetry of *Arcadia*. Dating *Astrophil and Stella* in 1581–82, discusses the Continental models for the sequence and its biographical content, stressing the importance of Sidney's concept of *energeia* and commenting on the variety of his metrical schemes. Remarks on the shift toward religious subjects that marks the final stages of Sidney's literary career.

80 GARNIER, CHARLES M[ARIE GEORGES], trans. and ed. *Astrophel et Stella*. Collection bilingue des classiques étrangers. Paris: Aubier, 1943, 205 pp.

Using Feuillerat's edition (23) as copy text, provides parallel French and English versions of all of the sonnets from *Astrophil and Stella*, but not the songs, adding the final two sonnets of *Certain Sonnets* as numbers 109 and 110 of the sequence. The first six chapters of the introduction provide a biography, interspersed with brief comments on the works written until Sidney's retirement from court. Discusses his support for Elizabethan voyagers and his contact with Harvey, Ramism, and the Areopagus. Also praise the *Defence*. In Chapter 7, provides a plot summary of *Arcadia*, discusses sources, calls Sidney a "true creator of the English novel," and examines the metrical variety and the classical experimentation in his poems. The discussion of *Astrophil and Stella* in Chapter 8 reviews recent critical commentary, examines Sidney's connections with the Devereux family, reads the sequence biographically (concluding that it "leaves no doubt" as to his love for Lady Rich), analyzes the structure of the sequence, comments on the artistry of both sonnets and songs, and notes that although the two *Certain Sonnets* are customarily included, they "vibrate to a shudder of their own."

81 GENTILI, VANNA, ed. *Astrophel and Stella*. Biblioteca italiana de testi inglesi, 10. Bari, Italy: Adriatica Editrice, 1965, 509 pp.

In the introduction, reviews Sidney's life and discusses nearly all of his literary and political writings. Comments on the relationship between the "Discourse on Irish Affairs" and *Arcadia*; on the Areopagus and Sidney's experiments with quantitative verse; and, in more detail, on *Astrophil and Stella*. In discussing Petrarchan conventions and Sidney's innovations, demonstrates the way in which he altered the Italian material so as to make the sequence more dramatically effective. Follows the text printed with the 1598 *Arcadia*. In extensive footnotes (in Italian), provides detailed commentary on the poems, especially on the biographical context of the sequence.

Twentieth Century

82 HART, KINGSLEY, ed. *Astrophel and Stella*. London: Folio
Society, 1959, 168 pp.
Provides a text based on that in the 1598 folio of *Arcadia*, with some
readings from the quartos. In the introduction, presents a brief biography, stresses the role of the Countess of Pembroke as a literary compan-
ion, sees Stella as Penelope Devereux, dates the sequence between 1578
and 1583, and sees a bipartite organization in which 1–32 deal with
Stella's physical beauty and 33–108 deal with Astrophil as lover.

83 HOBSBAUM, PHILIP, ed. *Ten Elizabethan Poets: Wyatt, Chapman,
Marston, Stanyhurst, Golding, Harington, Raleigh, Greville, Sidney,
Spenser*. Longmans English Series. London: Longmans, 1969, pp.
16–17, 130–38, 190–92.
Contains a sampling of poems from *Astrophil and Stella*, *Arcadia*, and
Certain Sonnets, with brief biographical and explanatory notes.

84 HOWE, ANN ROMAYNE, ed. "A Critical Edition of Sir Philip
Sidney's *Astrophel and Stella* with an Introduction." Ph.D. diss.,
Boston University, 1962, 422 pp.
Offers an edition based upon a collation of "virtually all extant copies of
the three quartos and of the first folio." Records all variants, both sub-
stantive and accidental, and presents a new ordering of the songs "based
on a theory of composition set forth in the Introduction." See *DA* 23
(November 1962):1686.

85 LANCKOROŃSKA, Gräfin MARIA, trans. and ed. *Astrophel und
Stella*. Potsdam, Germany: Privatdruck bei E[duard] Stichnote,
1936, 81 pp.
Includes German translations of sixty-three sonnets from *Astrophel and
Stella* and two of the *Certain Sonnets*, followed by a brief commentary on
the author and his works. Dates the sonnets in 1580 or 1581, identifying
Stella as Penelope Devereux and arguing for a biographical reading
involving an actual affair. Includes in the commentary translations of
four of the Songs.

86 MORREAU, PIERRE. "Un Poème de Sir Philip Sidney traduit
par Paul Claudel." *Bulletin de la Société Paul Claudel* 8 (October
1961):4–5.
Prints the text of "My true love hath my heart" (*OA 45*), with Claudel's
translation into two five-line strophes. Provides a brief appraisal.

87 MOSHER, THOMAS B., ed. *Astrophel and Stella*. Portland, Me.:
Thomas B. Mosher, 1905, 148 pp.
Prints the entire sequence from an unspecified source. Includes a brief
preface, but no notes or other aids.

Twentieth Century

88 NEWMAN, THOMAS, pub. *Astrophel and Stella, 1591*. Menston, England: Scolar Press, 1970, 90 pp.
A facsimile reprint of item 60, the first quarto of *Astrophil and Stella*.

89 POIRIER, MICHEL, ed. and trans. *Astrophel et Stella*. Collection bilingue des classiques étrangers. Paris: Aubier, Éditions Montaigne, 1957, 221 pp.
On facing pages, provides a French translation of the sequence and an edition of the English text (based on the Bright Manuscript, both quartos of 1591, and the 1598 folio of *Arcadia*). Includes an extensive introduction, a selective bibliography, and full notes covering textual variants, linguistic difficulties, literary borrowings and allusions, and scholarship on important cruxes. In the introduction, provides a sketch of Sidney's life, followed by a brief synthesis of his "personality and work," governed by the view that his Protestantism became "more and more the rule of his private life." Prefaces an examination of the biographical elements in *Astrophil and Stella* with the claim that the three best sonnet sequences of the age "were inspired . . . by a real passion." Citing external as well as internal evidence, offers reasons to believe that Sidney "felt a passion for Penelope" both before and after her marriage. In examining Sidney's indebtedness to Petrarchan convention, cites parallels to show that, besides Petrarch himself, his other main sources were French authors. Argues that, in the handling of love themes and motifs, the differences between Sidney and his models are more important than the resemblances. Discusses Sidney's conceits as both characteristically Elizabethan ("the acme of imaginative ornamentation") and protometaphysical, in that they show an intellectuality that is rare in the lyric poetry of this period. Analyzes his versification ("extremely regular"), his rhymes ("as correct as one could demand"), and the structural variety in both the sonnets and the songs. Sees Sidney's chief importance as a domesticator of Italian and French forms and ideas. Summarizes the textual history of the sequence and describes his own principles of translation.

90 PUTZEL, MAX, ed. *Astrophil and Stella*. New York: Doubleday & Co., 1967, 240 pp.
Bases the text on that in the 1598 *Arcadia*, retaining the stanzaic arrangement but modernizing spelling and punctuation and following Ringler (92) in most emendations. In the introduction, argues that the poems "express unmistakably authentic feeling." Views Stella as "a pattern of perfection existing only in the poet's mind" and Astrophil as "a naïve young man filled with grandiose ideas and unassimilated learning, clumsy as a lover and repeatedly caught in absurd predicaments."

Twentieth Century

Defines the nature of Petrarch's poetic, arguing that, whereas Petrarch is "filled with wonder," Sidney is "obsessed with conflict." Contrasts Petrarch's "richly embellished, smooth, and flowing" poetry with Sidney's, which has "a hardness, almost a rasping quality." In considering the "dynamics of Sidney's sonnet form," argues that "in his most characteristic sonnets Sidney begins with a statement uttered in what is technically known as the high style, his public manner. He follows this with the conditions that spring from his statement, and, after achieving complication . . . he resolves it in a swift line or couplet at the end." Argues, in turn, that the complete sequence, like each of the poems, has a "baroque, asymmetrical structure." Suggests that the sequence is unfinished and that Sidney abandoned it in order to work on the revised version of *Arcadia*. Views the cycle as tripartite, suggesting that there is a shift when Astrophil addresses Stella directly (in *AS 30*) and that the dénouement begins with Song viii. Argues that the relationship between the poems and the events and people in Sidney's own life is ambiguous, suggesting that, although there are reasons for assuming that Sidney may have fallen in love with Penelope Rich after her marriage, there are equally good reasons for believing that "the meaning of the poems is ironical." In the "Commentary and Notes," lists variants and provides a discussion of literary and bibliographic matters. An abridgement of Nashe's original preface is included as an appendix.

91 RATHMELL, J[OHN] C.A., ed. *The Psalms of Sir Philip Sidney and the Countess of Pembroke*. The Stuart Editions. Garden City, N.Y.: Doubleday & Co.; New York: New York University Press, 1963, 400 pp.

Prints the entire Psalter, using the manuscript once owned by John Davies of Hereford (British Museum MS. Add. 46372) as the copy-text and including the Countess of Pembroke's revisions of Sidney's work. Provides minimal textual apparatus. Also prints Donne's "Upon the translation of the Psalmes" (2790) and "To the Angell spirit of the most excellent Sir Phillip Sidney" (2799), attributing the latter to the Countess of Pembroke. See also Waller (2360). In the Introduction, differentiates the Sidney Psalter from earlier English translations on the basis of its greater energy, complexity, and variety of emotional effects. Finds the Sidneys' main literary models in the work of Wyatt and Marot. Argues that, more than simply an attempt to create a new school of English poetry, the Psalter represents a genuine effort to duplicate "the sense of intimate, personal urgency" characteristic of the Hebrew originals. Questions Ringler's dating of Sidney's portion of the Psalter (in

92), contending that, since Sidney's work is "decidedly inferior" to that of his sister, his share must have been composed before the completion of *Astrophil and Stella*. Tracing the history of the Psalter, concludes that the only "significant references" to it during the two centuries following the Countess's death are by Steele (66) and Ballard (2334). See, however, Harington (64, 65, 2333), Henley (13, 14), and Wood (284). See also Mesterton (2353).

92 RINGLER, WILLIAM A., Jr., ed. *The Poems of Sir Philip Sidney*. Oxford: Clarendon Press, 1962, 650 pp.

Provides the authoritative edition of Sidney's poetry, supported by a full critical apparatus. For Sir Philip's share of the Psalms (1–43), takes as a copy text the 1695 transcription by Samuel Woodford, attempting to eliminate revisions made by Mary Sidney. For most of the poems in Sidney's other major works, follows the texts published in the 1590 or 1598 *Arcadia*. Under the heading "Other Poems," includes seven judged to be authentic, five from early editions of *Arcadia* and two from Davison's *Poetical Rhapsody*. Under "Poems Possibly by Sidney," prints one from the 1613 *Arcadia*, one from Bodleian MS. Rawl. poet. 85, one transcribed by William Drummond from a portrait of Sidney and preserved in National Library of Scotland MS. 2060, and two from *Four Foster Children of Desire*. Also discusses Sidney's lost translation of du Bartas's *Semaine* and thirty-five poems wrongly attributed to Sidney. In the introduction, provides basic information on Sidney's life and works. Sorts through "influences and sources" important to his development as a poet, discussing his contact with Drant, Rogers, Greville, Dyer, and Spenser at the end of the 1570s. Emphasizes the importance of his quantitative experiments and his contact with Italian vernacular literature, but plays down the influence of contemporary French poetry. Argues that the major sources are "the Latin poets Ovid, Virgil, and Horace, the Italians Petrarch and Sannazaro, and the Spanish poet Montemayor and his continuators." Dating the composition of the Old *Arcadia* in 1577–80 and the beginning of revisions for the New *Arcadia* in 1584, comments on Sidney's experiments with genre and poetic technique. After remarking briefly on the nature, dating, and sources of *Certain Sonnets*, argues that *Astrophil and Stella* was composed on the borders of Wales in the summer of 1582, at about the same time that Sidney wrote the *Defence*. Regards the sequence as "a succession of scenes that illustrate emotional attitudes": Sonnets 1–52 present the young Astrophil in love; Sonnet 53 through Song viii depict his pursuit of physical satisfaction; and Song ix through Sonnet 108 show his rejec-

Twentieth Century

tion. Dates Sidney's share of the Psalms to 1585, commenting on their sources and their metrical dexterity. In considering Sidney's innovations in verse, highlights his "new techniques of rhythm and rhyme, new stanzaic patterns, and new examples of poetic kinds." Also considers the transcription and publication of his poems, commenting on their circulation in manuscript and noting that none of them survives in Sidney's own hand. Discusses his handwriting and habits of spelling, concluding that few traces of the latter survive in the poetry. In the commentary following the poems, discusses matters of composition and dating and constructs stemmata showing the relations among extant manuscripts and printed texts. Also provides detailed glosses on each poem, treating such things as context in the work as a whole, literary allusions, linguistic difficulties, poetic form, and (in the case of the Psalms) wording in other English and Continental translations. Notes that *The Lady of May* did not circulate in manuscript and that it is the earliest English example of "conventionalized pastoral drama." Dates the presentation as either 6–16 May 1578 or 1–2 May 1579 and ponders the political implications of the Queen's final choice. Distinguishes four stages in the composition of the Old *Arcadia*, noting that only three new poems appeared in the New. Argues that the 1590 edition was printed from a manuscript that Sidney left with Greville in 1585 and was edited by Greville and Matthew Gwynne. Comments on the rearrangement of the poetry in the 1593 edition and on revisions and editorial changes made by Sidney's sister. Examining the maps of Greece and Asia Minor that Sidney followed in the revisions, argues that he, not his sister, made (or authorized) the changes in Pyrocles's visit to Philoclea's bedchamber and in Musidorus's intended assault on Pamela. Includes an index of the poems by their "Reciters or Composers." In the commentary on *Astrophil and Stella*, examines the relationship between Sidney and Penelope Devereux, arguing that the sequence was put in its current order and mostly composed after her marriage. Infers that "Astrophil" is the proper spelling of the lover's name. Dates the poems in *Certain Sonnets* over the period 1577–81, denying any connection between them and the poems to Stella. Noting that thirteen of the poems are quatorzains and that several were composed for existing melodies or were set to music, takes the term "Sonnets" in the title to mean "songs." Suggests that the final version of the Psalms, including Mary Sidney's revisions of her brother's work, was completed in time for the Queen's visit to Wilton in 1599. Details the steps followed in attempting to restore Sidney's original wording, arguing that Sidney's chief models were the French metrical translation by

Twentieth Century

Marot and Beza and the prose Psalter in the *Book of Common Prayer*. Includes a bibliography, with detailed descriptions of authoritative manuscripts and printed texts of the poems and of their musical settings. Also includes a "Table of Verse Forms" and an index of first lines. See also Rathmell (91), Lamb (608), Kimbrough (1911), Chalifour (1207), Croft (1211), Lindenbaum (1651), Beal (1864), Brodwin (2068), Gentili (2131), Stillinger (2270), Rudentsine (2326), and Warkentin (2331).

93 [ROGERS, BRUCE, ed.] *Certaine Sonets Written By Sir Philip Sidney*. [Boston and New York]: Riverside Press, [Houghton Mifflin & Co., 1904], 61 pp.
Following the text in the 1613 *Arcadia*, prints thirty-one of the poems, excluding *CS 5*. In the introduction, discusses publishing history and surveys critical opinion on the poems, noting that they owe a debt to Petrarch and Desportes. Casts doubt on attempts to interpret them biographically.

94 SIDNEY, PHILIP (1872–1908), ed. *Sonnets and Songs of Sir Philip Sidney*. London: Thomas Burleigh, 1900, 175 pp.
Prints *Astrophil and Stella*, using the 1598 folio of *Arcadia* as a copy text. Omits all the songs except ii, iv, and xi, which are printed separately. Makes silent emendations from the 1591 quartos. Adds "Thou blind man's mark" and "Leave me, O love" (*CS 31* and *32*) as sonnets 109 and 110 of the sequence. Also prints *Certain Sonnets* 4 and 30 and Old *Arcadia* 45 and 77. In the introduction, provides biographical information on Sidney, his sister, and Penelope Devereux. Includes notes on material that Coleridge took from *Arcadia*, and comments on Sidney's appearance and on the elegy for him entitled "The Doleful Lay of Clorinda" (2741). Also includes sparse notes on the poems.

95 WHITE, H. KELSEY, ed. *Sir Philip Sidney: Sonnets and Miscellaneous Verse. Mary Sidney, Countess of Pembroke: "Hymn to Astraea", etc. Matthew Roydon: "Friend's Passion for His Astrophel."* Pembroke Booklets, 1. Hull, Ontario: J.R. Tutin, 1905, pp. 7–53.
Prints thirty-nine poems from *Astrophil and Stella*, thirteen from *Arcadia*, and eleven from *Certain Sonnets*, without attribution of sources, introduction, or commentary.

96 WILSON, MONA, ed. *Astrophel and Stella*. London: Nonesuch Press, 1931, 231 pp.
Provides a text based on that in the 1598 folio of *Arcadia*, supplemented with selections from *Certain Sonnets* and accompanied by an introduc-

Twentieth Century

tion, textual notes, explanatory notes on the individual poems, and a brief "Index of Usages." In the introduction, presents a summary biography and critical comments on Sidney's place in Elizabethan literature. Views the *Defence* as the means whereby "Philisides, the verse-maker of *Arcadia*, passes into Astrophel of the sonnet sequence." Argues that the order of the sonnets may not be that of composition, but was determined by Sidney himself. Dates composition between 1578 and the autumn of 1580, suggesting that the ending is abrupt and that "Sidney may not have made his final selection." Argues that nothing can be known about the relationship between Sidney and Lady Rich apart from inferences drawn from the poetry itself, but states "I have written of *Astrophil and Stella* as the expression of genuine passion because there is no other way I can hear the later sonnets and songs."

4. *DEFENCE OF POETRY*

Sixteenth Century

97 1595a: THE | DEFENCE OF | Poesie. | By Sir Phillip Sidney, | Knight. | [Printer's device: McKerrow, no. 299] | LONDON | Printed for *William Ponsonby*. | 1595. [72] pp.

The first(?) edition of the *Defence*, printed without prefatory matter and with more errors than in Olney's 1595 edition. Reprinted by the Countess of Pembroke in the 1598 edition of *Arcadia* and also taken as the basis of certain modern editions, notably those of Feuillerat (23) and of Duncan-Jones and van Dorsten (22). Reprinted in facsimile in items 124 and 137. For evidence that this edition preceded that of Olney in 1595, see Juel-Jensen (257). For counterclaims, see Duncan-Jones and van Dorsten, (22, p. 67) and Bond (236).

98 1595b: *AN* | APOLOGIE | For Poetrie. | Written by the right noble, vertu- | *ous, and learned, Sir Philip* | Sidney, *Knight*. | *Odi profanum vulgus, et arceo*. | [rule] | [ornament] | [rule] | AT LONDON, | Printed for *Henry Olney*, and are to be sold at | his shop in Paules Church-yard, at the signe | of the George, neere to Cheap-gate. | *Anno. 1595*. [88] pp.

The second(?) edition of the *Defence*, printed despite a previous "blocking entry" in the Stationers' Register by the Sidney family's preferred printer, William Ponsonby. When this entry was discovered, Olney turned over unsold copies to Ponsonby, who issued a number of them with his own title page. Contains four sonnets by Henry Constable "To Sir Philip Sidney's soul" (2753), a letter by Olney "To the Reader," and a list of errata. Unlike Ponsonby, provides a careful and accurate text, which survives in many copies and is commonly used as the basis of later editions such as those of Arber (104), Smith (142), and Shepherd (141). Omits, however, two important passages in Ponsonby, about which see p. 108, line 4, and p. 118, lines 4–13, in Duncan-Jones and van Dorsten (22). In the letter "To the Reader," calls Sidney "Poesies Messias," who has cleared away the winter that held back the sun of divine poetry. Refers to the edition as a "daring adventure," because the publisher must now be defended against "those great ones, who in themselves have interred this blessed innocent." Whether this edition was printed and offered for sale before that of Ponsonby is difficult to determine. For arguments on both sides of the issue, see item 97.

Seventeenth Century

99 1619: EGLENTIERS | POËTENS | *Borst-weringh.* | DOOR | THEODORE RODENBVRGH, | **Ridder van de Ordre van den Huyze | van Borgongien.** | [Figure of a seated woman in a flowing gown wearing a diadem; in her right hand is a wreath and in her left a staff, and behind her head is the sun. In the rectangular border around her is inscribed "NOBILITAS SOLA EST ATQVE VNICA VIRTVS."] | *T'AMSTERDAM,* | *Ghedruckt by Paulus van Ravesteyn,* | [rule] | Voor Ian Evertsz. Cloppenburgh, 1619. 114 pp.
After an introductory passage, incorporates a partial Dutch translation of the *Defence* into the author's own defence of poetry. Abbreviates certain passages and adds new thought and examples to Sidney's material on the dramatic unities and the abuses of the genre of comedy. Omits altogether his discussions of English poets, of proper poetic style, and of the suitability of English as a poetic language. See Jonckbloet (2369). In the front matter, includes a dedication and a poem to the Prince of Orange, an engraving of him, and several dedicatory poems addressed to Rodenburgh. The title means "Breastplate of a Love [literally 'wild-rose'] Poet." See also Francken (2489).

Eighteenth Century

Eighteenth Century

100 de HAES, J[OAN], trans. *Gedichten van Joan de Haes. Hier by komt F. Sidneis Verdediging der Poëzy uit het Engelsch Vertaelt.* Rotterdam: by Maarten van Loon, 1720, pp. 541–646. Reprint. Delf, Netherlands: Reiner Boitet, 1724.
Reprints item 101, reducing the prefatory matter to Haes's prefatory letter and a letter to Haes by F. van Bochoven.

101 ———. *Verdediging der Poëzy uit het Engelsch van den Ridder Filips Sidnei vertaelt door J. de Haes.* Rotterdam: by Johannes Hofhout, 1712, 152 pp.
The first complete Dutch translation of the *Defence*. In the prefatory matter, includes a dedicatory poem to Joan de Witt; a preface to the reader discussing the need for a Dutch translation and quoting praises of Sidney by other authors; a letter to Haes by David van Hoogstraten; excerpts of commentary on Sidney by earlier writers; and dedicatory poems by Hadrianus Relandus, Hoogstraten, Cornelius van Arckel, and Johann Obreen. Includes occasional glosses.

102 URIE, R., pub. *The Defense of Poesy.* Glasgow: R. Urie, 1752, 108 pp.
Provides the third separate English edition of the *Defence*, with eighteenth-century spelling. Gives no indication of the copy text used and does not include an introduction, notes, or other aids. Reprints a tribute to Sidney by William Temple. See also Baine (2391).

103 [WARTON, JOSEPH, ed.] *The Defence of Poetry.* In *Sir Philip Sydney's Defence of Poetry. And, Observations on Poetry and Eloquence, from the Discoveries of Ben Jonson.* London: for G.G.J. and J. Robinson and J. Walter, 1787, pp. 1–81.
From an unspecified source, prints the text with eighteenth-century spelling. Contains an advertisement, but no introduction or other aids. See also Baine (2391).

Nineteenth Century

104 ARBER, EDWARD, ed. *An Apologie for Poetrie, 1595.* English Reprints, 4. London: Alex. Murray & Son, 1868, 72 pp.
Reprints Olney's text (98) with the original spelling. In the introduction, reviews evidence on the date of the text, the main points in Sidney's rebuttal to Gosson's *School of Abuse*, and the changes in the theory and practice of poetry since the Renaissance. Supplies a bibliography of

other editions and a chronological chart of Sidney's life, with contemporary accounts of his character. Does not include notes.

105 COOK, ALBERT S., ed. *The Defense of Poesy, Otherwise Known as An Apology for Poetry.* Boston: Ginn & Co. 1890, 188 pp.
Provides a modern-spelling text based on Arber's reprint of Olney (in 104) and Flügel's reprint of Ponsonby (in 15). Includes a subject outline of the treatise and very full textual and explanatory notes, with detailed philological data, lengthy quotations from sources and analogues, and cross-references to recurring phrases and images. Also includes references to scholarship on the *Defence*, relevant quotations from Sidney's other works, and comparisons with subsequent works of English criticism. Supplies an index of proper names in the *Defence*, running heads, and line numbers. In the introduction, sketches Sidney's life, dates the *Defence* around 1583, and emphasizes Sidney's reliance on Plutarch, Cicero, and the Bible. Differentiates the style of *Arcadia* from that of the *Defence* or of Lyly's *Euphues*, relating Sidney's prose to that of the early Greeks. Compares Sidney's theory of poetry to that of Shelley, emphasizing Sidney's adaptation of Aristotle's view that poetry is philosophical. Also discusses the influence of Plato and Scaliger on the *Defence* and the greater influence of Aristotle and of Dante, who may have been "Sidney's guide in the conception and arrangement of some of the minor topics of the *Defence*." Sketches the influence of Sidney's book upon George Puttenham, Sir John Harington, and Francis Meres.

106 [MORLEY, HENRY, ed.] *A Defence of Poesie and Poems.* Cassell's National Library, 194. London: Cassell & Co., 1889, 192 pp.
Prints the *Defence* and a selection of poems and songs, mostly from *Certain Sonnets.* Does not identify the copy text. In the notes, supplies organizational headings (e.g., "The Poet's Works and Parts"). In the introduction, dates the *Defence* in 1581 and places it in the context of Sidney's public life.

107 MORLEY, HENRY, ed. *The Defence of Poesie.* In *Shorter Works in English Prose.* Cassell's Library of English Literature. London: Cassell & Co., 1880, pp. 69–86.
Presents the text with brief explanatory and illustrative notes, but without identifying the copy text.

108 QUINN, M.T., ed. *The Defence of Poesie.* Madras, India: Srinivasa, Varadachari & Co., 1890, 132 pp.
Includes an introduction, notes, and index. Not seen. Listed in *BMC* (1964), vol. 222, col. 18, shelf number 011840. f. 78.

Nineteenth Century

109 RHYS, ERNEST, ed. *An Apologie for Poetrie.* In *Literary Pamphlets Chiefly Relating to Poetry from Sidney to Byron.* Vol. 1. London: Kegan Paul, Trench, Trübner & Co., 1897, pp. 13–15, 55–149.
Reprints Olney's text (98) with the original spelling. Supplies notes, mostly on names and allusions in the text. Does not contain an index or other aids, but discusses Sidney briefly in the introduction.

110 SHUCKBURGH, EVELYN S., ed. *An Apologie for Poetrie.* Pitt Press Series. Cambridge: Cambridge University Press, 1891, 228 pp.
Provides an old-spelling version based on Olney's text (98), but one that is collated with the text in the 1598 folio of *Arcadia.* In the preface, explains various states of the text and points out errors in Arber's edition (104). In the introduction, draws upon a manuscript Psalter at Trinity College to correct the date of Sidney's birth from 29 to 30 November 1554. Discusses his character and reputation, his life and works. Remarks on his independence of thought and his reliance upon personal experience in shaping the *Defence.* Dates the work in the fall or winter of 1580–81, noting similar ideas in Sidney's letter to his brother Robert of 18 October 1580. Also analyzes the main divisions of the argument. Supplies few textual notes but provides extensive glosses on philological, stylistic, and literary matters. Identifies borrowings and allusions and cites numerous parallels with other works of Elizabethan literature. Also provides line numbers and a "Glossarial Index."

111 [THURLOW, EDWARD, Lord, ed.] *The Defence of Poesy.* London: W. Bulmer & Co. for White & Cochrane, 1810, 111 pp.
Prints a modern-spelling text of unspecified origin. Also includes two prefatory poems, one on Sidney's portrait at Penshurst (see item 2821). Does not include an introduction or other aids. See also Baine (2391).

112 THURLOW, EDWARD, Lord, ed. *The Defence of Poesy.* London: W. Bulmer & Co., 1811, 112 pp.
Reprints item 111 with three additional prefatory poems, two of which are on Sidney (see item 2821).

113 VAUGHAN, C[HARLES] E[DWYN], ed. *An Apologie for Poetrie.* In *English Literary Criticism.* London: Blackie & Son; New York: Charles Scribner's Sons, 1896, pp. xvi–xxvii, 1–58.
Prints the text from an unspecified source, supplying scattered notes on linguistic problems and literary references. In the introduction, discusses Sidney's immediate English opponents, reviews his arguments, and contrasts his criticism with that of Dryden.

114 VERWEY, ALBERT, trans. *Dichters Verdediging: Shelley's "A Defence of Poetry" en Sidney's "An Apologie for Poetrie."* Amsterdam: S.L. van Looy, 1891, pp. 53–132.

Includes a Dutch translation of the *Defence*, without notes or other aids.

115 YOUNG, ALEXANDER, ed. *"The Defence of Poesie." By Sir Philip Sidney. "Table Talk." By John Selden. With Some Account of the Authors.* Library of the Old English Prose Writers, 2. Cambridge: Hilliard & Brown, 1831, pp. xv–xlvii, 1–88.

Prints a modern-spelling version, without specifying a copy text. In scattered notes, identifies allusions and notes Sidney's influence on later writers. In an introduction, which is "chiefly abstracted from the Life prefixed to Gray's edition" (item 16), reviews Sidney's life and evaluates his works. Stresses the spontaneous and pure style of the *Defence* and its influence.

Twentieth Century

116 ANON., ed. *The Defence of Poesie.* London: Cambridge University Press, 1904, 96 pp.

Prints a text derived from Ponsonby's version (97). Includes a list of emendations but does not provide an introduction or other aids.

117 BATE, WALTER JACKSON, ed. *An Apology for Poetry.* In *Criticism: The Major Texts.* New York: Harcourt, Brace & World, 1952, pp. 77–106.

Reprints Olney's text (98) using modern spelling, with brief notes on literary allusions and difficult phrasing. Includes the *Defence* in the general index to the volume. In the introduction, treats the work as the greatest of all Renaissance critical writings, both because it avoids excessively technical matters and because it unites Christian tradition with the major theories of classical antiquity. Notes Sidney's almost anthropological interest in poetry among primitive peoples, and lists ways in which the book points the way to neoclassical criticism of the seventeenth and eighteenth centuries. The introduction is reprinted in item 2400.

118 BRANCAFORTE, BENITO, ed. *Deffensa de la Poesia: A Seventeenth Century Anonymous Spanish Translation of Philip Sidney's "Defence of Poesie."* North Carolina Studies in the Romance Languages and Literatures, 186. Chapel Hill: University of North Carolina Department of Romance Languages, 1977, 92 pp.

In the introduction, determines that the manuscript composed in 1616(?) was based on Ponsonby's 1595 edition of the *Defence* and may

Twentieth Century

have been the work of Juan Ruiz de Bustamante. Lists departures from Sidney's English version, including some based on religion. Annotates the translation, largely by supplying Sidney's original English to clarify passages in the translation. See also Chambers (121).

119 BUONPANE, ELENA, ed. *Apologia della poesia*. Florence: n.p., 1954.
Not located. Cited as item 237 in Washington (269).

120 CHAMBERS, DWIGHT [O.], ed. *"Deffensa de Poesia*: A Spanish Version of Sir Philip Sidney's *Defence of Poesie*." Ph.D. diss., University of Kansas, 1956, 333 pp.
Provides a diplomatic edition of an anonymous manuscript containing a Spanish translation of the *Defence*. Discusses handwriting, dating, and authorship and concludes that the *Deffensa* was not based on any of the printed texts in English and could, in fact, have been written by Sidney himself. Sets Douglas's reprint of the *Defence* (124) beside the Spanish text and compares them for phonemics, morphology, and syntax. See *DA* 16 (November 1956):2158. See also item 121, Brancaforte (118), and Newels (2585).

121 ———. *Sir Philip Sidney, Deffensa de poesia: A Spanish Version*. N.p. 1968, 44 pp.
Provides a diplomatic text of this anonymous Spanish translation. In the foreword, describes the manuscript, which is at the Biblioteca Nacional in Madrid. Also discusses references to it in earlier bibliographies, evidence of prior ownership by "Juan de Bastamante," and the scribal hand. Concludes that the translation is "somewhat free" but corresponds more closely to Ponsonby's text than to Olney's. Includes a bibliography but no notes. See also item 120, Brancaforte (118), and Newels (2585).

122 CLEMEN, WOLFGANG, ed. *The Defence of Poesie*. Heidelberg: Carl Winter Universitätsverlag, 1950, 57 pp.
Follows Ponsonby's 1595 edition as edited by Feuillerat (23). In the critical apparatus compares the text of Olney (98), the Penshurst Manuscript, and the folio editions of 1598–1674. Retains old spelling and provides brief explanatory notes explaining allusions to other authors.

123 COLLINS, J[OHN] CHURTON, ed. *Sidney's Apologie for Poetrie*. Oxford: Clarendon Press, 1907, 139 pp.
Reprints G. Gregory Smith's old-spelling text (142), which derives from Ponsonby's edition of 1595. Alters slightly Smith's paragraphing and punctuation. Includes full explanatory notes covering obscure phrases,

sources, and allusions. Lacks textual notes, but supplies line numbers and a full index of names and subjects mentioned in the treatise, the introduction, and the notes. Provides a "Memoir of Sidney," which discusses in some detail his life, works, and reputation. Also includes a chart of his ancestors. In a separate "Introduction to the *Apologie*," touches on the controversy with Gosson and the problem of dating. Notes that Sidney's prose here is the first in English to blend so happily "colloquial ease and grace with rhetorical stateliness." Lays out Sidney's chief sources, sketches the main divisions of the treatise, and reviews its publishing history to 1600.

124 DOUGLAS, NOEL, ed. *The Defence of Poesie*. The Noel Douglas Replicas. Bradford and London: Percy Lund, Hamphries & Co., 1928, [72] pp.

Provides a facsimile of the British Museum copy of Ponsonby's 1595 edition (97). Does not contain an introduction, notes, or other aids.

125 DUNCAN-JONES, KATHERINE, and van DORSTEN, JAN [ADRIANUS], eds. *A Defence of Poetry*. In *Miscellaneous Prose of Sir Philip Sidney*. Oxford: Clarendon Press, 1973, pp. 59–121, 185–209.

Provides a modernized critical edition based on the Penshurst Manuscript and Ponsonby's printed text of 1595, with full textual apparatus from the Norwich Manuscript and Olney's first edition. In the introduction, van Dorsten details internal and external evidence for the date of composition, discussing Sidney's experiments with literature, his association with the Areopagus, and his silence about Gosson's *School of Abuse*. Concludes that the winter of 1579–80 is most likely the period of composition. Briefly lists sources, examining the possibility that French theorists, particularly the humanist Henri Estienne, may have played a more direct role than Italian critics. Examines the rhetorical qualities of the *Defence*, supplying an outline based on the parts of a classical oration. Lists translations into foreign languages. Also provides complete descriptions of the two surviving manuscripts and of the first two printed editions, supplying quasifacsimile title-page transcriptions, collations, descriptions of contents, variants, and lists of extant copies. Also touches on William Temple's manuscript analyzing Sidney's book, and discusses the dispute between Olney and Ponsonby over the right to print the work. Explains the difficulty of constructing a stemma, concluding that no two of the four authoritative texts derives from the same original but that Robert Sidney's manuscript and Ponsonby's text are closer to Sidney's fair copy than the others. Urges that "*A Defence of Poetry*" is the

Twentieth Century

most suitable title. Also considers William Temple's treatise on the work, *Analysis Tractationis de Poesie*. Includes full notes on biographical and linguistic matters; information on sources, allusions, and analogues; and references to modern scholarship. Provides a general index to the entire volume, including the introductions and the commentary.

126 ELWOOD, WILLIAM A., ed. "A Critical Old-Spelling Edition of Sir Philip Sidney's *The Defence of Poesie*." Ph.D. diss., University of Chicago, 1967.

Not seen. Cited in *DDAAU*, 1966–67, p. 165. According to Washington (269), bases the text on the Penshurst Manuscript and includes an introduction, annotations, and William Temple's *Analysis Tractationis de Poesi*.

127 ENRIGHT, D[ENNIS] J[OSEPH], and de CHICKERA, ERNST, eds. *An Apology for Poetry*. In *English Critical Texts, Sixteenth Century to Twentieth Century*. London: Oxford University Press, 1962, pp. 3–49, 339–50.

Reprints Olney's edition (98), with a few emendations from Ponsonby's (97). Modernizes spelling and provides concise notes on difficult phrases and allusions. Does not include textual notes or other aids.

128 GILBERT, ALLAN H., ed. *Defence of Poesie*. In *Literary Criticism: Plato to Dryden*. New York: American Book Company, 1940, pp. 404–61.

Reprints Olney's text (98), with corrections from Ponsonby's (97) and with modernized spelling. Supplies section headings from Myrick's outline of the work as a classical oration (in item 671). Also includes full notes on sources, analogues, and allusions, derived mainly from the editions of Cook (105) and Smith (142). Praises Sidney for creating a new form for the *Defence* and for producing an epitome of Renaissance criticism. Provides a brief bibliography and a general index to all the texts in the volume.

129 HARDISON, O.B., Jr., ed. *An Apologie for Poetrie*. In *English Literary Criticism: The Renaissance*. New York: Appleton-Century-Crofts, 1963, pp. 98–146.

Prints an old-spelling version of Olney's text (98), with a brief introduction and a selective bibliography. Supplies occasional notes on allusions and linguistic difficulties.

130 HEBEL, J. WILLIAM; HUDSON, HOYT H[OPEWELL]; JOHNSON, FRANCIS R.; and GREEN, A. WIGFALL, eds. *The Defence of Poesy*. In *Prose of The English Renaissance, Selected from Early*

Editions and Manuscripts. New York: Appleton-Century-Crofts, 1952, pp. 267–304, 882–26.

Prints a modern-spelling edition of Ponsonby's 1595 text (97), emended according to Olney's (98). In a headnote preceding the notes, reviews Sidney's life and works, and provides a bibliography of editions and criticism. In the notes, translates foreign words and explains names, allusions, sources, and difficult phrases. Does not contain an index.

131 LEBEL, MAURICE, ed. and trans. *Un Plaidoyer pour la poésie.* Quebec: Presses de l'Université Laval, 1965, 181 pp.

Provides an English version of the text followed by a complete French translation. In the introduction, provides a biography of Sidney, a discussion of the classical and Renaissance sources for the *Defence* (which follows his arguments in item 2553), and an outline of the argument.

132 MACARDLE, DOROTHY M., ed. *Sir Philip Sidney's "Defence of Poesy."* London: Macmillan & Co., 1919, 89 pp.

Follows Arber's edition (104), with emendations from Ponsonby's text as noted by Cook (105). In the introduction, discusses Sidney's accomplishments, the state of literature in his day, his classicism, and the style of the *Defence.* Includes a chronology of his life, notes on linguistic problems and literary references, questions and exercises for class use, and an index.

133 MAGNUS, LAURIE, ed. *Documents Illustrating Elizabethan Poetry, by Sir Philip Sidney, George Puttenham, and William Webbe.* London: Routledge & Sons; New York: E.P. Dutton & Co., 1906, pp. 22–25, 28–29, 33–107.

Prints the *Defence* in a modernized text, with interpretive notes. Includes a brief, largely biographical introduction and Olney's preface. Views the work, like the criticism of Puttenham and Webbe, as a reply to Gosson.

134 MAHL, MARY R[OBERTA], ed. *The Norwich Sidney Manuscript: The Apology for Poetry.* Northridge, Calif.: San Fernando Valley State College, 1969, 77 pp.

Prints a transcription of the Norwich Manuscript. In the introduction, describes the discovery of the sixteenth-century document in Francis Blomefield's commonplace book (bound in the year 1726) and recounts the research required to identify it. Also traces a possible route by which it may have passed from the Sidney family to Blomefield and gives its history from 1726 to the twentieth century. Concludes that it is probably the earlier of the two known manuscripts of the *Defence*, perhaps dating from before Sidney's death. Fails to identify the scribe, but from spelling

Twentieth Century

and puncutation concludes that the document is no more than one step removed from Sidney's holograph. Notes many variants from other texts, finding the greatest similarities with that printed by Olney (98). Does not include notes or other aids. The introduction is reprinted, with revisions, in item 2564.

135 NEEDHAM, H.A., ed. *Sidney: "An Apology for Poetry." Shelley: "A Defence of Poetry."* Selected English Classics, edited by A.H.R. Ball. London: Ginn & Co., [1931], pp. ix–xv, xxi–xxviii, xxxviii–xlii, 1–63, 111–45, 167–68, 171.

Follows Olney's edition (98), with occasional readings from Ponsonby's (97). In the introduction, supplies a brief life of Sidney and basic information on the *Defence*, including its composition and early editions, its antecedents and contribution to English criticism, its tone and style. Includes a detailed outline of the work, a select bibliography, and an index of proper names. Also supplies notes on verbal difficulties, sources and allusions, and Sidney's positions as a critic.

136 POLICARDI, SILVIO, trans. *La Difesa della poesia*. Padua, Italy: CEDAM, 1946, 129 pp.

Provides an Italian translation, without indicating the text on which it is based. In the introduction, discusses the social context in which the *Defence* was written, considering the question of the moral value of poetry and its relation to the social upheavals of the Renaissance. Sketches the rise of neo-Aristotelian criticism in Italy, its relation to Platonic and Christian thought, and its influence on Sidney. Also considers the largely rhetorical and metrical preoccupations of English critics before Sidney and the controversy over Puritan attacks on the theaters. In this context examines Sidney's concept of poetry, relating it to similar views in the works of Antonio Minturno, J.C. Scaliger, Sir John Harington, Sir Francis Bacon, and Ben Jonson. Reviews Sidney's views on the drama, particularly on comedy and tragedy, the dramatic unities, and decorum, noting the possiblilty that they had an influence on Shakespeare. Does not include notes or other aids.

137 PONSONBY, WILLIAM, pub. *The Defence of Poesie, 1595*. Menston, England: Scolar Press, 1968, [72] pp.

Reprints in facsimile the British Museum copy of Ponsonby's 1595 edition of the *Defence* (97). Does not include an introduction, notes, or other aids.

138 RAJAN, B[ALACHANDRA], and GEORGE, A.G., eds. *Defence of Poetry*. In *Makers of Literary Criticism*. Vol. 1. Bombay: Asia Publishing House, 1965, pp. 105–39.

Provides a modern-spelling edition without specifying the copy text. Contains occasional glosses, but does not provide an introduction, textual notes, or other aids.

139 RHYS, ERNEST, ed. *An Apologie for Poetrie*. In *The Prelude to Poetry: The English Poets in Defence and Praise of Their Own Art*. Everyman's Library: Essays and Belles Lettres. London and Toronto: J.M. Dent & Sons; New York: E.P. Dutton & Co., 1927, pp. 9–60.

Reprints (from item 104) Arber's modern-spelling version of Olney's text. Does not provide an introduction, notes, or other aids.

140 ROBINSON, FORREST G[LEN], ed. *An Apology for Poetry*. Indianapolis, Ind.: Bobbs-Merrill Co., 1970, 123 pp.

Prints a modern-spelling text based on Olney's version (98), with additions and "interesting alternatives" from the Norwich Manuscript and Ponsonby's edition either included or listed in the notes. In the introduction, reviews Sidney's life and works and considers the intellectual and literary context in which the *Defence* was written. Claiming that it "marks the advent of neo-classicism in England," traces its roots to the philosophy, literature, and rhetoric of antiquity and to the writings of English humanists and Italian critics of the sixteenth century. Minimizes the importance of Stephen Gosson in provoking Sidney to write. Outlines the logic of Sidney's argument, focussing on the claim that the poet is a better moral teacher than the historian or the philosopher. Defines what Sidney means by a "speaking picture," by the "Idea or fore-conceit" of a work, and by "an imaginative ground-plot of a profitable invention." Suggests *Arcadia* as the best example of Sidney's literary theory put into practice. Includes extensive notes on linguistic difficulties, on literary references, and on the cultural and intellectual background of particular passages. Also includes an index of subjects and names, which covers both the text and the introduction.

141 SHEPHERD, GEOFFREY, ed. *An Apology for Poetry or The Defence of Poesy*. Nelson's Medieval and Renaissance Library. London: Thomas Nelson & Sons, 1965, 262 pp.

Prints a modern-spelling version based on Olney's text (98), with additions and variants from Ponsonby (97) and the Penshurst Manuscript. Provides extensive notes dealing with textual variants, linguistic difficul-

Twentieth Century

ties, allusions and references to other authors and historical figures, parallels in Sidney's other works and in the writings of classical and Renaissance critics, and the broad intellectual background of the work. In the introduction, notes the English tendency to find "moral springs of political action in poetry," and sees the *Defence* as their best justification. Notes uncertainty about the date and occasion of its composition, dismissing the view that it was written in reply to Stephen Gosson. Sketches Sidney's life, discussing his knowledge of foreign languages, his attainments in various arts and sciences, and his wide reading. Notes his ties to the intellectual circle around the Earl of Leicester and to the scientists who founded Gresham College. Citing Myrick (671), outlines the *Defence* as a classical oration, seeking to clarify its main line of argument. Discusses its background in medieval thought as it was transformed by Renaissance humanism. Argues that Sidney's entire argument rests on the humanist assumption that "Eloquence and Wisdom are indivisible," stressing his elevation of poetry above the other arts and his redefinition of "wisdom" as active piety rather than contemplative devotion. Relates his position to the humanists' tendency to value Plato over Aristotle and Augustine over the scholastic theologians; to their interest in the processes of thinking; and to the Calvinist tendency to see life as a constant struggle between human depravity and divine grace. Considers his political and religious sensibility, commenting on his translations of religious works and his attitude toward sacred poetry in the *Defence*. Examines his rejection of the medieval view of poetry as allegory and his arguments that poetry is superior to law, history, and moral philosophy, relating his position to the Continental debate on the relative value of the arts. In defining what Sidney meant by the term "philosophy," ponders his interest in Ramism, his tendency to merge what the medievals regarded as philosophy with rhetoric, and his caricature of philosophers in the *Defence*. Explains his tendency to take the historian as a more imposing rival for the poet, comparing the *Defence* with defenses of history by Lorenzo Valla, Jacques Amyot, Jean Bodin, and Sir Thomas Elyot. In considering "forces" that helped to shape Sidney's critical views, gives the primacy to Horace, Cicero, and "Renaissance Platonisers," regarding Aristotle's influence as "mainly indirect" and listing possible English influences. Examines key terms in Sidney's discussion of poetry: "imitation," "speaking picture," and "nature" (as related to "art"). Also examines two views of the relation between symbols and reality in his works: the "vaguely Aristotelian and rhetorical" view that the poet "clothes" thought with "fine tropes," and the Augustinian view that he "works by 'pronouncing grace', by transforming the meaning directly into word and voice and gesture." Compares John Hoskins's position on the same issue, noting Sidney's preference for the Augustinian position. Considers his concept of the "other nature" created by the poet and its relation to the first nature created by God. Explains his rejection of the Platonic notion of "divine fury" and his stress on the poet's "Idea, or fore-conceit," relating it to the thought of Federico Zuccaro and Giovanno Paolo Lomazzo. Discusses the intellectual background of Sidney's discussion of "teaching," "delighting," and "moving," noting his respect for pleasure as a legitimate end and his emphasis on poetry as a ground for future action. In balancing his remark that the poet "nothing affirmeth" with his claim that poetry makes truth shine through the fog of sense, stresses his belief in the uncertainty of knowledge and his interest in Ramist dialectic as a means to arrive at "conjectured likelihood." Treats poetry, in his sense, as an embodiment of such likelihood in a particular example that is based on universals. Noting that Sidney sees the poet as a public figure, "beautifying his mother-tongue" and writing as "an instrument of national power and glory," compares him with Castiglione's ideal courtier. Sees connections between this political view of poetry and his strictures against bad poets, his refusal to treat poetry as a "divine" art, and his balancing of the inborn ability of the poet with the need for art, imitation, and exercise. Also examines his position on verse, decorum, traditional genres, the dramatic unities, and the current state of poetry in England, noting that, throughout the work, heroic poetry seems to provide his underlying paradigm. Sketches the influence of the *Defence* on later English poets. Also discusses Sidney's statements on prosody, denying that he ever attempted to recreate Latin meters as an end in itself. Argues that his primary concern was with teaching English poets "to exploit to the full the persuasive and expressive potentialities of the language." Sees his position on diction and style as a shift from older concerns with the sources of vernacular vocabulary and the definition of various figures of speech to a new interest in ways to use such figures well, transforming them into "transparent" figures of thought rather than distracting ornaments, as they had been in euphuism. Includes an index of names in the *Defence* and a selective bibliography. See a response by Craig (2448).

142 SMITH, G[EORGE] GREGORY, ed. *An Apology for Poetry.* In *Elizabethan Critical Essays.* Vol. 1. Oxford: Oxford University Press, 1904, pp. xi–xcii passim, 61–63, 148–207, 382–403.
Follows Olney's edition (98) with the original spelling, adding textual notes from Ponsonby's version (97). In the introduction, discusses

Twentieth Century

Sidney's response to the Puritans, relating it to lines of argument that
became commonplace in Elizabethan criticism: 1) the historical argument that poetry is ancient, universal, and approved by the greatest
authorities, and 2) the moral and artistic argument that it is divine in
origin, imitates nature, presents allegorical truths, and combines teaching with delight. Notes the views of other critics available in the
Renaissance, especially on the following topics: the superiority of poetry
to history and philosophy; the charge that poets are liars and wasters of
time; the various genres of poetry; its current low estate; and its need for
classical reform in matters of decorum, prosody, and diction. Also discusses Sidney's part in the revival of romantic taste and the establishment of criticism as a discipline separate from rhetoric. Traces the origins of his ideas to sources in the classical and patristic periods and to
Renaissance thought in Italy, France, and Spain. Provides a chronological table of publications in the debate over the Puritan attacks on the
stage. Discusses Elizabethan and modern editions of the *Defence* and the
evidence in favor of its other title, *An Apology for Poetry*. In the notes, clarifies phrases, sources, names, and allusions. Also cities numerous analogues, discusses theoretical questions, and cites previous Sidney scholarship. Includes a comprehensive index.

143 SMITH, JAMES HARRY, and PARKS, EDD WINFIELD, eds. *An
Apologie for Poetrie*. In *The Great Critics: An Anthology of Literary
Criticism*. New York: W.W. Norton, 1932, pp. 143–87.
Reprints Arber's text (104), with notes on literary allusions and linguistic
difficulties. In the introduction, sketches Sidney's life, the date and occasion of the *Defence*, and its place in the history of criticism. Includes an
index to the entire volume.

144 SOENS, LEWIS, ed. *Sir Philip Sidney's Defense of Poesy*. Lincoln:
University of Nebraska Press, 1970, 137 pp.
Supplies a modern-spelling version of Ponsonby's text (97), corrected
from Olney's (98) and from the 1598 folio of *Arcadia*. In the introduction, examines Sidney's synthesis of French and Italian criticism and his
influence on later English critics. Notes the mixture of neo-Platonic idealism, Protestant morality, and secular activism that underlie the argument. Compares the views of other authors in Leicester's circle, noting
Sidney's particular emphasis on the need to move readers toward virtue.
Also compares Sidney with Huguenots such as du Bartas and du Plessis-
Mornay and with the poets of the French *Pléiade*, noting Sidney's reluctance to accept their ideas of prophetic inspiration or divine frenzy in
poetry. Relates Sidney's concept of the "fore-conceit" to Ficino's concept

of metaphysical Ideas and their function in shaping the "clay" of post-lapsarian nature. Also remarks on Sidney's dependence on classical rhetoric, both in his notion of the function of poetry and in the form of his defense. Considers the purpose of his digression on English poetry, and examines his prose style. In the footnotes, glosses allusions and difficult phrases, saving commentary on sources, analogues, and modern scholarship for notes at the end of the book. Provides a bibliography and a general index covering the introduction and the notes, as well as the text.

145 SWIEROWICZ, J[AN], trans. *Obrona Poezji.* Lwów: n.p., 1933, 108 pp.

A Polish translation of the *Defence.* Not located. Cited as item 155 in Tannenbaum (268).

146 van DORSTEN, J[AN] A[DRIANUS], ed. *A Defence of Poetry.* London: Oxford University Press, 1966, 112 pp.

Provides a critical edition based on the manuscript at Penshurst and the two editions of 1595, with modern spelling and punctuation. In the introduction, discusses Sidney's character and that of the *Defence*, analyzing it as an *ex tempore* oration embodying common views of his age. Summarizes the central doctrines of the work. Also supplies the following aids: a chronological outline of Sidney's life and works in the context of major cultural and historical events of the age; a select bibliography; an outline of the *Defence* as a classical oration; and an index of names. In the notes, provides full coverage of difficult phrases and Sidney's literary, personal, and cultural references.

5. MINOR WORKS

Sixteenth Century

147 1581: A briefe decla- | *ration of the shews,* | deuices, speeches, and in- | *uentions, done & performed* | before the Queenes Maiestie, & | the French Ambassadours, at the | most valiaunt and worthye Tri- | umph, attempted and executed | on the Munday and Tues- | day in Whitson weeke | last, Anno | 1581 | Collected, gathered, penned & pub- | lshed, by Henry Goldwel, Gen. | *Imprinted at London, by Ro-* | bert Waldegraue, dwelling | without

Sixteenth Century

> Temple-barre, | neere vnto Sommer- | set-House. [40] pp.
> Reprinted in Holinshed (148).

Reports on the background and the performance of *Four Foster Children of Desire*, listing Sidney among the participants. Describes the action and states what "in effect" each participant said, detailing Sidney's armor and trappings and those of his attendants. Includes the first printing of two poems that, according to Ringler (92), are "possibly by Sidney": "Yield yield, O yield, you that this fort do hold" (*PP 4*) and "Alarm, alarm, here will no yielding be" (*PP 5*).

148 1586: *The Third Volume of Chronicles, beginning at duke William the Norman, commonlie called the Conqueror; and descending by degrees of Yeeres to all the kings and queenes of England in their orderlie successions*, by Raphael Holinshed. [London]: n.p., 1586, pp. 1315-21. Reprint. *Holinshed's Chronicles of England, Scotland, and Ireland.* Vol. 4. London: J. Johnson; F.C. & J. Rivington; T. Payne; Wilkie and Robinson; Longman, Hurst, Rees, & Orme; Cadell and Davies; and J. Mawman, 1808, pp. 435–45.

In the supplement from 1578 to 1586 written by John Hooker, the editor of Holinshed's work, reprints Goldwell's *Brief Declaration* (147), a description of the original presentation of *Four Foster Children of Desire*.

149 1587: A | Woorke | concerning the trew- | *nesse of the Christian* | Religion, written | *in French:* | Against Atheists, Epicures, Paynims, Iewes, | Mahumetists, and other Infidels. | *By Philip of Mornay Lord of* | *Plessie Marlie.* | Begunne to be translated into English by Sir | *Philip Sidney* Knight, and at his request | finished by *Arthur Golding.* | ¶ Imprinted at London for *Thomas* | *Cadman.* 1587. 660 pp. [Title-page border: at the top, a winged boy grasping curving trumpets in each hand; in the left margin, a robed figure bearing a lyre; in the right margin, a man in a cape reading a tablet; at the bottom, satyrs seated at left and right, pointing to the winged face of a boy above an oval compartment. See McKerrow and Ferguson (642), no. 117.]

The first of Sidney's writings to appear in print. In a dedicatory epistle to Robert Dudley, Earl of Leicester, Golding includes Sidney among many who have "purposed and attempted" to translate the treatise. States that Sidney "began to put the same into our language, . . . and had proceeded certain chapters therein." Mentions that Sidney then committed "the performance of this piece" to Golding, who offers it to Leicester "as his [Sidney's] and not mine." After Golding's dedication, includes English translations of du Plessis-Mornay's original dedication to Henry of Navarre and of the original preface, followed by a table of contents entitled "The Summes of the Chapters." For a facsimile reprint, see item 163.

150 1592: A | WORKE CON- | cerning the Trewnesse of Christian | *Religion, written in French*: | *Against Atheists, Epicures, Paynims, Iewes, Mahumetists,* | *and other Infidels. By Philip of Mornay* | Lord of Plessie Marlie. | Begunne to be translated into English by Sir *Philip Sidney* | Knight, and at his request finished by | *Arthur Golding.* | [ornament: an oval compartment, surrounded by leaves and branches and inscribed with the words "PERIIT ET INVEN- TA EST." In the compartment is a shepherd bearing a sheep on his shoulders and standing on the near shore of a body of water; on the far shore is a town and, behind it, hills and the sun on the horizon. See McKerrow (641), no. 153ß.] | AT LONDON | Printed by Robert Robinson for *I.B.* dwelling | at the great North doore of *S. Pauls* Church at the | signe of the Bible. *1592.* 576 pp.
Reprints item 149.

Seventeenth Century

151 1604: A | WORKE CON- | cerning the Trunesse of Chri- | stian Religion, written in French: | *Against Atheists, Epicures, Paynims, Iewes, Mahumetists,* | *and other Infidels. By* Philip *of* Mornay | Lord of *Plessie Marlie.* | Begunne to be translated into English by that honourable and wor- | thy Gentleman, Syr *Philip Sidney* Knight, and at his request | finished by *Arthur Golding.* | *Since which time, it hath bene reviewed, and is now the third time publi-* | *shed, and purged from sundrie faultes escaped heretofore, tho-* | *row ignorance, carelesnes, or other corruption.* | [ornament: an oval compartment surrounded by flowers and scrollwork and bearing the inscription "VIRESSIT VVLNERE VERITAS." In the compartment, a naked woman with crown representing Truth, who is holding a book(?) and looking over her shoulder. Behind her, a cloud from which a hand is extended, striking her with a scourge. Between her feet, the initials "TC". See McKerrow (641), no. 299.] | AT LONDON | Printed for George Potter, dwelling at the great | North doore of S. Pauls Church, at the | Signe of the Bible. 1604. 614 pp.
Claims to be a new edition "with corrections." Replaces Golding's dedi- cation to Leicester with a new one by Thomas Wilcocks addressed to Henry Frederick, Prince of Wales, which says of the book that Sidney

Seventeenth Century

"first began to turn it into our tongue." In this printing, the table of contents appears on the last page of the volume. According to Juel-Jensen, the edition was pirated; see "Sir Philip Sidney, 1554–1586: A Check-List of Early Editions of His Works," in *Sir Philip Sidney: An Anthology of Modern Criticism,* edited by Dennis Kay (Clarendon Press, 1987), pp. 289–314.

152 1617: A | WORKE | Concerning the trunesse | of Christian RELIGION: | AGAINST, | *Atheists, Epicures, Paynims, Iewes,* | *Mahumetists,* and other *Infidels.* | Written in French, by PHILIP *of* MORNAY | *Lord of* Plessie *and* Marly. | Begunne to be translated into English, by that honourable and | worthy Gentleman, Sir PHILIP SIDNEY Knight, and at his | request finished by ARTHVR GOLDING. | *Since which time, it hath been reuiewed, and is the fourth time pub-* | lished, and purged from sundry faults escaped heretofore, | thorow ignorance, carelesnesse, or other | corruption. | [ornament: an oval compartment surrounded by scrollwork and bearing the inscription "AVT NUNC, AVT NUNQUAM." In the compartment, a naked female figure representing Opportunity, with exaggerated forelock. In one hand, she holds a knife, and in the other, a circular strip of cloth billowing in the wind. Beneath her feet is a wheel floating on the sea, and behind her are two ships, one afloat and the other sinking before rocks. See McKerrow (641), no. 281.] | LONDON, | Printed by *George Purslowe.* 1617. 624 pp.
Reprints item 151.

153 1646: THE | SOULES | Own evidence, for its own | IMMORTALITY. | In a very pleasant and learned discourse, | Selected out of that excellent Treatise entituled, | *The trunesse of Christian Religion, against* | *Atheists, Epicures, &c.* | *First compiled in French by Famous* | Philip Mornay, Lord of Plessie Marlie, *afterward* | *turned into English by Eloquent Sir* Phillip | Sidney, *and his assistant,* Master | Arthur Golden, *Anno Domini* | *M D LXXX VII.* | And now re-published. | By *John Bachiler* Master of Arts, sometimes of *Emanuell* | Colledge in *Cambridge.* | [ornamental rule] | *Published according to Order.* | [ornamental rule] | *London,* | Printed by *M.S.* for *Henry Overton* in Popes- | head Ally, 1646, 69 pp.
From an unspecified edition, reprints Chapters 14 and 15 of *The Trueness of the Christian Religion.* In the introduction, the editor, John Bachiler, praises the use of pagan and Christian authorities in the work.

Nineteenth Century

154 1663: *A Letter written by Sir Philip Sidney, unto Q. Elizabeth, touching her Marriage with Monsieur.* In *Scrinia Ceciliana: Mysteries of State & Government: In Letters of the late Famous Lord Burghley, And other Grand Ministers of State: In the Reigns of Queen Elizabeth, and King James. Being a further Additional Supplement of the Cabala. . . .* London: for G. Bedel & T. Collins, 1663, pp. 201–9.

Prints an old-spelling version of Sidney's *Letter to the Queen*. Does not identify the copy text. See also item 156.

Eighteenth Century

155 NICHOLS, JOHN [GOUGH], ed. *The Progresses and Public Processions of Queen Elizabeth. Among which are Interspersed Other Solemnities, Public Expenditures, and Remarkable Events, during the Reign of that Illustrious Princess.* 2d ed. Vol. 2. London: Printed by and for John Nichols & Son, 1823, pp. 94–103, 312–29. Orig. pub. as *The Progresses, and Processions, of Queen Elizabeth.* 2 vols. London: Printed by and for the editor, printer to the Society of antiquaries of London, 1788 (not seen).

In "The Queen at Wanstead, 1578," reprints *The Lady of May* from an unspecified folio edition of Sidney's works. In "A Declaration of the Triumph shewed before the Queene's Majestie, and the French Ambassadours, on Whitson Munday and Tuesday," reprints Goldwel's description of the original presentation of *Four Foster Children of Desire* (147), basing the text on that in Holinshed's *Chronicles* (148).

156 STRYPE, JOHN, ed. Appendix to *Annals of the Reformation and Establishment of Religion and Other Various Occurrences in the Church of England, during Queen Elizabeth's Happy Reign Together with an Appendix of Original Papers of State, Records, and Letters.* 4th ed. Vol. 2.2. Oxford: Clarendon Press, 1824, pp. 641–52. 2d ed. (the first containing material on Sidney). London: by and for T. Edlin, 1725–1731 (not seen).

Reprints the *Letter to the Queen*, using item 154 as the source. For Strype's comments on the letter, see item 879.

Nineteenth Century

157 ADLARD, GEORGE. *Amye Robsart and the Earl of Leycester. A Critical Inquiry into the Authenticity of the Various Statements in Relation to the Death of Amye Robsart, and of the Libels on the Earl of*

Nineteenth Century

> *Leycester, with a Vindication of the Earl by His Nephew Sir Philip Sydney*. London: John Russell Smith, 1870, pp. 65-77.

Includes a modernized text of Sidney's *Defence of Leicester* based on Collins's edition (12). Employs it, along with other documents, to vindicate Leicester from charges of murder.

158 KERVYN de LETTENHOVE, Baron HENRY MARIE, ed. *Certaine notes concerninge the state of the Prince of Orange and the Provinces of Hollande and Zeland, as they weare in the monthe of May 1577.* In *Relations politiques des Pays-Bas et de l'Angleterre, sous le règne de Philippe II*, by Baron Henry Marie Bruno Joseph Leon Kervyn de Lettenhove. Vol. 9. Brussels: F. Hayez, 1890, pp. 310-14. Reprinted (from a different manuscript) by Osborn (1108).

A diplomatic communique on the situation in the Netherlands in 1577. According to Osborn (1108) and Howell (1061), the work is most likely by Sidney, but the attribution still remains in question. Describes the attempts by Don John of Austria to entice William of Orange into an alliance against Spain. Observes that, although the Prince is skeptical of Don John's motives, he nevertheless has offered him seven conditions for such an alliance, while at the same time proceeding to fortify his territories. Via this communique, the Prince entreats Elizabeth to join an alliance with him. Offers her trade concessions and naval support, both for commerce and defense, in exchange for her denying harbor to Spanish ships, protecting shipping lanes between England and the Prince's provinces, and guaranteeing, in case of war, loans of 50,000 pounds per year. Suggests that Elizabeth owes Don John a favor for his having thwarted a Spanish plot against England "six yeares past."

Twentieth Century

159 BURGOYNE, FRANK J[AMES], ed. *Letter to Queen Elizabeth, Dissuading Her from Marrying the Duke of Anjou.* In *Northumberland Manuscripts: Collotype Facsimile and Type Transcript of an Elizabethan Manuscript Preserved at Alnwick Castle, Northumberland*. London: Longmans, Green, & Co., 1904, pp. 66-74 and ms. folio 55-61.

Transcribes the letter, supplying missing portions of the manuscript and marginal glosses from Gray's edition (16). In an introductory note, discusses the political context of the letter and Sidney's exclusion from court for writing it.

160 CHAMBERLIN, FREDERICK CARLETON. *Elizabeth and Leycester.* New York: Dodd, Mead, & Co., 1939, pp. 435–37.
Prints Sidney's *Defence of Leicester* from the manuscript in Sidney's own hand.

161 KIMBROUGH, ROBERT, and MURPHY, PHILIP [MICHAEL], eds. "The Helmingham Hall Manuscript of Sidney's *The Lady of May*: A Commentary and Transcription." *RenD*, n.s. 1 (1968):103–19.
Describes the manuscript discovered by Jean Robertson in 1961. Discusses the occasion of the work and its connection with George Gascoigne's "farewell" to the Queen and with the Italian works known as *commedia rusticale.* Points out the aim of the entertainment, which was to gain a gesture of favor for the Earl of Leicester as represented by the shepherd Therion. Notes that the manuscript is important, not only because it is sometimes superior to the 1598 printed text, but also because it includes a private "epilogue" promoting Leicester that was deleted from the 1598 version. Prints a virtually *literatim* transcription.

162 MURPHY, PHILIP MICHAEL, ed. "A Critical Edition of Sir Philip Sidney's *The Lady of May.*" Ph.D. diss., University of Wisconsin, 1969, 156 pp.
Provides a modernized text based on the 1598 edition of Sidney's works and the Helmingham Hall Manuscript, which contains a previously undiscovered epilogue. Also includes a photographic reproduction and a facsimile transcription of the manuscript. In the introductory matter, covers textual problems and provides a history of the genre of the masque and a critical study of *The Lady of May.* See *DA* 30 (June 1970):5432A.

163 SYPHER, F.J., ed. *A Woorke Concerning the Trewnesse of the Christian Religion*, by Philippe de Mornay. Translated by Sir Philip Sidney and Arthur Golding. Delmar, N.Y.: Scholars' Facsimiles & Reprints, 1976, 689 pp.
Provides a facsimile of the 1587 edition (149), with a table of contents and brief summaries of each chapter. In the introduction, sketches the life of du Plessis-Mornay, the value of his book, and his acquaintance with Sidney, noting that it may have begun in Paris in 1572 and included regular correspondence in 1583. Thinks it possible that Sidney saw *De la verité de la religion chrestienne* in manuscript before its publication in 1581. On the question of Sidney's share in the translation, examines Golding's dedication and contemporary references by Fulke Greville,

Twentieth Century

John Florio, and George Whetstone. Dismisses stylistic evidence as inconclusive. Concludes that Golding overstated his role in the project and that Sidney deserves major credit. Sketches the publishing history of the translation, including a detailed bibliographic description and collation of the 1587 edition.

6. CORRESPONDENCE

Sixteenth Century

164 SIDNEY, SIR HENRY. *A Very Godly Letter Made . . . Now XXV. yeeres Past unto Phillip Sidney His Sonne Then of Tender Yeeres, at Schoole in the Towne of Shrowsbury with One M. Astone. . . .* London: T. Dawson for William Gruffith, 1591, [8] pp. Also printed from the autograph manuscript in Collins (12). Reprint. Oxford: Oxford University Press, 1929.

Prints the letter (written in 1566?), with a postscript by Sidney's mother. Survives in the first edition only in the Shrewsbury School library.

Seventeenth Century

165 HARTSOEKER, CHRISTIAN, and van LIMBORCH, PHILLI-PUS, eds. *Praestantium ac Eruditorum Virorum Epistolae Ecclesiasticae et Theologicae. . . .* Amstelaedami: Henricum Wetstenium, 1684, sigs. B1^v–B2^r. Orig. pub. Amsterdam: Henricum Dendrinum, 1660 (not seen).

Prints Justus Lipsius's letter to Sidney of 30 August 1586.

166 LANGUET, HUBERT. *Huberti Langueti, Viri Clarissimi Epistolae Politicae et Historicae. Scriptae quondam Ad Illustrem, & Generosum Dominum Philippum Sydnaeum, Equitem Anglum. . . .* Francofurti: Gulielmi Fitzeri, 1633, 376 pp.

Prints ninety-six Latin letters from Languet to Sidney and one from Languet to a friend concerning Sidney. Does not identify or discuss the manuscript sources, which have never been located. In the prefatory matter, includes a catalog showing where and on what date each of the letters was written. On printing errors in this edition, see John (2733).

167 ————. *Hvberti Langveti Epistolae Politicae et Historicae ad Philippvm Sidnaevm Equitem Anglum, Illustrissimi Pro-Regis Hybernia: filium, Vlissingensem Gubernatorem.* Lvgd. Batavorum [i.e., Leiden]: Elzeviriorum, 1646, 485 pp.
Reprints the letters in the Frankfurt edition of 1633. Combines two of the letters for a total of ninety-six, as against the ninety-seven of 1633. Revises the sequence but continues most of the errors in numbering and text. See John (2733).

168 1633: [Within double rules] PROFITABLE | *Instructions;* | Describing what speciall | Obseruations are to be taken by | *Trauellers in all Nations,* | States and Countries; | Pleasant and Pro- | fitable. | *By the three much admired,* | ROBERT, late Earle of *Essex.* | Sir PHILIP SIDNEY. | *And,* | Secretary DAVISON. | [rule] | LONDON; | Printed for *Beniamin Fisher*, at the | Signe of the *Talbot*, without | Aldersgate. 1633, pp. 74–103.
Prints an undated letter from Sidney to his brother Robert on foreign travel. On p. 25, includes a second title page: [within double rules] TWO | EXCELLENT | LETTERS CON- | cerning Travell: | One written by the | late Earle of ESSEX, | the other by Sir *Philip* | SIDNEY. | [ornament] | LONDON; | Printed for *Beniamin Fisher*, at the | Signe of the *Talbot*, without | Aldersgate. 1633.

Eighteenth Century

169 LANGUET, HUBERT. *Epistolae Ad Philippum Sydneium, Equitem Anglum.* Edited by [Sir] D[avid] Dalrymple, [Lord] Hailes. Edinburgh: A. Murray & J. Cochran; London: J. Murray, 1776, 338 pp.
Reprints Languet's Latin letters to Sidney. Includes an index of names with brief biographical sketches of persons mentioned in the correspondence. Follows the Leiden edition of 1646, with numerous corrections, especially in sequence and numbering. See John (2733).

170 NICHOLS, JOHN [GOUGH], ed. *Progresses and Public Processions of Queen Elizabeth.* 2d ed. Vol. 2. London: John Nichols, 1823, p. 250. Orig. pub. as *The Progresses, and Processions, of Queen Elizabeth.* 2 vols. London: Printed by and for the editor, printer to the Society of Antiquaries of London, 1788 (not seen).
Prints the letter to Lady Kitson of 28 March 1581 in which Sidney mentions his intercession at court on behalf of Sir Thomas Cornwallis.

Eighteenth Century

171 [OLDYS, WILLIAM, ed.]. *The Harleian Miscellany: or, A Collection of Scarce, Curious, and Entertaining Pamphlets and Tracts, As Well in Manuscript as in Print, Found in the Late Earl of Oxford's Library*. Vol. 7. London: for T. Osborne, 1746, pp. 565–66.

From an unspecified manuscript, prints a modern-spelling version of Sir Henry Sidney's letter (164) to Philip at Shrewsbury (without the postscript by Sidney's mother). See item 182.

172 SEWARD, WILLIAM. *Biographiana*. Vol. 2. London: for J. Johnson, 1799, pp. 370–81.

Prints letters from Sidney to his brother Robert (168), advising him on travel, and from Sir Henry to Philip at Shrewsbury (164).

Nineteenth Century

173 BRITISH MUSEUM. DEPARTMENT OF MANUSCRIPTS. *Facsimiles of Royal, Historical, Literary and Other Autographs in the Department of Manuscripts, British Museum*. Edited by George F. Warner. 4th ser. London: Printed by Order of the Trustees, 1899, pp. 3–3a, plate 3.

Transcribes and prints in facsimile Sidney's letter to Leicester dated from Berghen 2 February 1586. (The general table of contents for all five series implies, misleadingly, that the facsimile is on plate 19.)

174 [BUTLER], S[AMUEL, Bishop of] LICHFIELD, ed. *Sidneiana, Being a Collection of Fragments Relative to Sir Philip Sidney Knt. and His Immediate Connections*. London: Roxburghe Club, 1837, pp. 3–5 and plates following title page.

Prints the only extant letter addressed to Sidney from his parents while he was at Shrewsbury School (164). Also includes a facsimile of a letter from Sidney to Jean Hotman.

175 COLLIER, J[OHN] PAYNE. "Sir Philip Sidney, His Life and Death." *Gentleman's Magazine*, n.s. 33 (March 1850):264–69.

Transcribes the following letters: Sidney to Sir Francis Walsingham of 17 December 1581 and 6 March 1583; Sidney to Sir William Cecil of 15 May 1585; and Ralph Lane to Sidney of 12 August 1585.

176 du PLESSIS-MORNAY, [PHILIPPE de, SEIGNEUR du PLESSIS-MARLY]. *Mémoires et correspondance de Duplessis-Mornay, pour servir l'histoire de la Réformation et des guerres civiles et religieuses en France, sous les règnes de Charles IX, de Henri III, de Henri IV et de Louis*

XIII, depuis l'an 1571 jusqu'en 1623. 12 vols. Paris: Chez Treuttel et Würtz; Strasbourg and London: même Maison de Commerce, 1824–25, 2:304–5; 3:158, 488–89.

Transcribes letters from Mornay to Sidney of [20?] July 1583 and 8 July 1585. Also includes Mornay's letter to Walsingham of January 1587 lamenting Sidney's death.

177 GREAT BRITAIN. HISTORICAL MANUSCRIPTS COMMIS-SION. Appendix, Part 4. In *Twelfth Report of the Royal Commission on Historical Manuscripts. The Manuscripts of His Grace The Duke of Rutland, Preserved at Belvoir Castle.* Vol. 1. London: Her Majesty's Stationery Office, 1888, pp. 149, 150, 154, 156, 160, 177, 178, 180–82.

Contains one letter from Sidney to Edward Manners, Earl of Rutland. Other letters to the Earl allude to Sidney's marriage, to his jealousy over a horse, to his commission in the Lowlands, and to the Queen's intervention in his plans to sail with Drake.

178 ———. *Calendar of the Manuscripts of the Most Hon. the Marquis of Salisbury . . . Preserved at Hatfield House, Hertfordshire.* Part 3. London: Eyre & Spottiswoode, for Her Majesty's Stationery Office, 1889, p. 70.

Transcribes a letter from Lady Katherine Paget to Sidney of 13 October [1585].

179 GREAT BRITAIN. PUBLIC RECORD OFFICE. *Calendar of State Papers, Foreign Series, of the Reign of Elizabeth, 1572–74. Preserved in the Public Record Office.* Vol. 10. Edited by Allan James Crosby. London: Her Majesty's Stationery Office, 1876, p. 580.

Prints a letter from Sidney to Burghley commenting on governmental affairs in Poland, Turkey, Constantinople, Egypt, Portugal, Bohemia, and Lithuania.

180 NICHOLS, JOHN GOUGH, ed. *Autographs of Royal, Noble, Learned, and Remarkable Personnages Conspicuous in English History, from the Reign of Richard the Second to That of Charles the Second.* London: J.B. Nichols & Son, 1829, plate 27.

Provides a biographical note and a facsimile of the "commencement" of a 16 December 1572 letter to Leicester requesting leave to be absent from court at Christmas.

181 NICOLAS, Sir [NICHOLAS] HARRIS. *Memoirs of the Life and Times of Sir Christopher Hatton, K.G., Vice-Chamberlain and Lord*

Nineteenth Century

> *Chancellor to Queen Elizabeth*. London: Richard Bentley, 1847, pp.
> 68–69, 127–29, 203, 206, 210–11, 214–15, 327–28, 417–18, 420.

Quotes five letters from Sidney to Hatton from 1579 and 1581 on various political and financial matters; three letters from Walsingham to Hatton regarding suits to the Queen in which Sidney is a party; and one letter from Leicester to the Queen in which he wishes that Sidney "might go to Casimir."

182 OLDYS, WILLIAM, and PARK, THOMAS, eds. *The Harleian Miscellany: A Collection of Scarce, Curious, and Entertaining Pamphlets and Tracts . . . Selected from the Library of Edward Harley, Second Earl of Oxford*. 10 vols. London: White & Cochrane, John Murray, and John Harding, 1808–13, 7:603–4; 10:447–48.

Reprints from Zouch (974) the old-spelling text of the letter from Sir Henry Sidney to Philip at Shrewsbury (164). In Volume 10, reprints the postscript by Lady Mary Sidney and gives the publishing history of the letter, pointing out that the first edition of the *Harleian Miscellany* (171) contained a faulty version "from some unauthorized Ms. copy."

183 PEARS, STEUART A., ed. *The Correspondence of Sir Philip Sidney and Hubert Languet, Now First Collected and Translated from the Latin with Notes and a Memoir*. London: William Pickering, 1845, 322 pp.

Translates into English parts of fifty-eight Latin letters by Languet and the complete texts of seventeen by Sidney. Arranges the entire correspondence chronologically. Also includes an English letter from Sidney to Leicester dated 27 November 1574. In an appendix prints two of Sidney's English letters to his brother Robert: one (undated) from the 1633 volume *Instructions for Travelers* (168) and the other dated 18 October 1580. The remainder of the appendix contains Latin transcriptions of the letters by Sidney translated in the main body of the book. Supplies occasional notes explaining allusions and a full index to the correspondence. In the preface explains the origin of the letters, those from Languet from the 1646 Leiden edition as reprinted by Lord Hailes (169) and those of Sidney from Robinson's edition of *The Zurich Letters* (184) and from the manuscript collection of Wolff (see 2720). In the introduction, provides a life of Sidney, beginning with his Continental tour of 1572–75, his friendship with Languet and with prominent figures in Europe, and his studies. Supplies historical background needed to understand allusions in the letters, concentrating on the Turkish threat to Europe, the protestant rebellions in the Netherlands and France, and the political and religious situation in Germany and Poland. Also discusses Sidney's later life in England, his foreign embassy to Germany in 1577, and his views on the threat from Rome and Spain. Touches on his literary accomplishments and the parody of his Arcadian style in Sir Walter Scott's character, Sir Piercie Shafton. See also John (2733) and Kuersteiner (2734).

184 ROBINSON, HASTINGS, ed. and trans. *The Zurich Letters, (Second Series) Comprising the Correspondence of Several English Bishops and Others with Some of the Helvetian Reformers, during the Reign of Queen Elizabeth.* Cambridge: Parker Society, Cambridge University Press, 1845, pp. 289–94, 296–98, 300; Appendix (paginated separately), pp. 178–84.

Prints English translations and the Latin originals of three letters from Sidney to Languet dated 1 October 1577, 1 March 1578, and 10 March 1578, which were discovered in the city library of Zurich. Provides notes explaining the context and identifying persons mentioned in each letter. In the preface to Pears's edition (183) the editor of this volume is incorrectly identified as Rev. John Hunter.

185 ROZE, ERNEST. *Charles de l'Écluse d'Arras le propagateur de la pomme de terre au XVIe siècle: Sa biographie et sa correspondance.* Paris: J. Rothschild & J. Lechevalier, 1899, pp. 102–3.

Transcribes the letter from l'Écluse to Sidney of 19 March 1576.

186 SCOTT, WALTER, ed. *A Collection of Scarce and Valuable Tracts, on the Most Interesting and Entertaining Subjects: But Chiefly Such as Relate to the History and Constitution of These Kingdoms.* Vol. 1. London: for T. Cadell & W. Davies; W. Miller; R.H. Evans; J. White & J. Murray; and J. Harding, 1809, pp. 492–98.

Prints a modern-spelling version of the letter to Sidney from his father in 1566 (164), without the postscript. Also reprints old-spelling versions of Sidney's letter threatening Edward Molyneux, dated 31 May 1578; Molyneux's reply, dated 1 July 1578; Sidney's letter to his brother Robert on travel, dated 18 October 1580; and the essay *Valour Anatomized in a Fancy*, which is falsely attributed to Sidney. Does not specify sources.

187 ZOUCH, THOMAS. *Memoirs of the Life and Writings of Sir Philip Sidney.* York, England: by Thomas Wilson & Son, for T. Payne & J. Mawman, and for Wilson & Son, 1808, pp. 376–77.

Prints a letter from Robert Dorset to Sidney of 17 May 1576.

Twentieth Century

Twentieth Century

188 BLOK, P[ETRUS] J[OHANES], ed. "Correspondance inédite de Robert Dudley, comte de Leycester, et de François et Jean Hotman." In *Archives du musée Teyler*, 2d ser. Vol. 12, part 2. Haarlem, Netherlands: Héritiers Loosjes; Paris: Gauthier-Villars; Leipzig, Germany: G.E. Schulze, 1911, p. 152.

Transcribes a letter to Sidney from Ruy Lopez dated 2 October 1586, which requests royal protection for Don Antonio, Pretender of Portugal.

189 BOND, WILLIAM H[ENRY]. "A Letter from Sir Philip Sidney to Christopher Plantin." *HLB* 8 (Spring 1954):233–35.

Describes and prints a previously uncollected letter at Harvard, which is apparently to Plantin and is dated from Utrecht on 7 April 1586. Discusses Sidney's relationship with Sir Thomas Heneage, who is mentioned in the letter, and notes that another letter to Plantin may, on the evidence of this one, be redated in March or April of 1586.

190 BRADLEY, WILLIAM ASPENWALL, ed. *The Correspondence of Philip Sidney and Hubert Languet*. The Humanist's Library, 5. Boston: Merrymount Press, 1912, 264 pp.

From Pears's edition (183), reprints the English translations of seventy-six Latin letters in Sidney's correspondence with Languet. In an appendix, adds two English letters on travel from Sidney to his brother Robert. In the introduction, reviews the course of Sidney's friendship with Languet, stressing the humor in their letters, the influence of Melanchthon on their brand of Protestantism, and the humanism that led them to promote a common European culture. Regards Sidney's letters as the first in England with a "modern" view of the world and its history. Sketches his views on the Turks, the Italians, the Spanish, and the war in the Netherlands. Also discusses Languet's aims in guiding his friend's education, his urgings that Sidney marry, and the style of the letters. Does not include notes or an index.

191 BRUGMANS, H[AJO], ed. *Correspondentie van Robert Dudley Graaf van Leycester en andere documenten betreffende zijn gouvernement-generaal in de Nederlanden 1585–1588*. Vol. 1. Werken uitgegeven door het Historisch genootschap (gevestigd te Utrecht), 3d ser., no. 56. Utrecht, Netherlands: Kemink en Zoon N.V., 1931, pp. 85–88, 93–94, 115, 140–41, 160–61.

Prints letters written in 1586 from the Council of Zeeland to Sidney dating from 18/28 February; 19 February/March 1; 7/17 March; 11/21 May;

and 31 May/10 June. Also prints Sidney's letter to the city fathers of
Veere, 7/17 April 1586.

192 BUXTON, JOHN, ed. "An Elizabethan Reading-List: An
Unpublished Letter from Sir Philip Sidney." *TLS*, 24 March 1972,
pp. 343–44.

Prints a letter from Sidney to Edward Denny that was written on 22 May
1580 but preserved in a transcript by John Mansell during the late
1590s, which is now in the Bodleian Library. See also item 2727 and
Buxton's photographic reproduction of the letter (2728).

193 CAMERON, ANNIE I., ed. *The Warrender Papers*. Vol 1.
Publications of the Scottish Historical Society, 3d ser. 18.
Edinburgh: Edinburgh University Press, 1931, p. 146.

From a collection of documents thought to have been compiled in the
seventeenth century by Archbishop Spottiswoode, transcribes Sidney's
letter to George Buchanan dated October 1579.

194 GREAT BRITAIN. HISTORICAL MANUSCRIPTS COMMIS-
SION. *Report on the Manuscripts of the Earl of Ancaster, Preserved at
Grimsthorpe*. Dublin: John Falconer, for His Majesty's Stationery
Office, 1907, p. 34.

Transcribes Sidney's letter to Peregrine Bertie, Lord Willoughby de
Eresby, 4/14 July 1586.

195 GREAT BRITAIN. PUBLIC RECORD OFFICE. *Calendar of State
Papers, Foreign Series, of the Reign of Elizabeth, Preserved in the Public
Record Office*. Vol. 20, *September 1585–May 1586*. Edited by Sophie
Crawford Lomas. London: Published by His Majesty's Stationery
Office, 1921, pp. 50, 92, 131, 167, 176, 180, 198, 214, 216, 407,
409, 415, 458, 462, 553, 565, 607, 628, 670, 673, 694.

Prints and/or summarizes sixteen letters from Sidney to Walsingham,
Burghley, and Thomas Miller; four letters to him from Roger Williams,
William Davison, and the Lords of the Council; and a "minute of her
Majesty's Letters Patent to be made for appointing Sir Philip Sidney to
be governor of Flushing." See the index for more than a hundred additional references to Sidney concerning mainly the governorship but also
the Drake expedition.

196 ———. *Calendar of State Papers, Foreign Series, of the Reign of
Elizabeth, Preserved in the Public Record Office*. Vol. 21, part 2, *June
1586-March 1587*. Edited by Sophie Crawford Lomas and Allen B.
Hinds. London: Published by His Majesty's Stationery Office,

Twentieth Century

> 1927, pp. 68, 102, 129–30, 154, 162, 201, 214–16; 208, 213, 216, 217–18, 219, 235, 243, 251, 360.

The first seven references are to six letters, quoted or summarized, from Sidney to Walsingham, the Lords of the Council, and Jan Wyer, and one letter quoted in full to Sidney from Sir Stephen le Sieur. The remaining pages contain letters referring to his death, eulogies, and epitaphs. See the index for approximately sixty additional references to or comments about him, the majority relating to aspects of his governorship of Flushing, to various military and financial exigencies, and to efforts at governmental continuity after his death.

197 GREG, W[ALTER] W[ILSON]; GILSON, J[ULIUS] P[ARNELL]; JENKINSON, HILARY; McKERROW, R[ONALD] B[RUNLEES]; and POLLARD, A[LFRED] W[ILLIAM], eds. *English Literary Autographs, 1550–1650.* Part 2, *Poets.* Oxford: Oxford University Press, 1928, plate 41.

Reproduces and annotates three samples of Sidney's handwriting (letters to Cecil, 26 February 1570; to Leicester, 6 December 1577; and to Walsingham, 16 December 1585), preceded by a brief standard biography. See also Petti (1111).

198 LEIGH, OLIVER H[ERBRAND] G[ORDON], ed. *Universal Classic Manuscripts.* Washington, D.C., and London: M. Walter Dunne, [1901], unpaginated.

Includes a facsimile reproduction and a transcript of Sidney's letter to Leicester dated 2 February 1586.

199 LEVY, CHARLES SAMUEL, ed. "The Correspondence of Sir Philip Sidney and Hubert Languet, 1573–1576." Ph.D. diss., Cornell University, 1962, 421 pp.

Translates and edits the sixty-six extant letters from 1573 to 1576, reexamining problems of dating and providing annotations on "the persons, the events, and the other circumstances referred to." In the introduction, considers the personal characteristics revealed in the letters and analyzes the Latin styles of their authors. See *DA* 23 (March 1963): 3379–80.

200 LEVY, CHARLES S[AMUEL]. "The Sidney-Hanau Correspondence." *ELR* 2 (Winter 1972):19–28.

Prints two newly discovered manuscripts of letters by Sidney along with the rest of the correspondence that he carried on with Philip Louis, Count of Hanau. Details Sidney's movements at the end of his Continental journey in 1575 and during his embassy to Germany in

1577, arguing that Sidney met Philipp Camerarius in Nuremburg, not in Prague.

201 ———. "An Unpublished Letter of Sir Philip Sidney." *N&Q*, n.s. 13 (July 1966):248–51.
Publishes Sidney's letter of 24 April 1585 to Peter Beutterlich, chief councilor to John Casimir, Count Palatine, and discusses its political context. Focuses on Sidney's view that the English should intervene in the Netherlands and his comments on the religious position of James VI of Scotland, tying these to the Catholic threat posed by the Constitution at Joinville, in which Philip of Spain had made league with the Guises of France.

202 McMAHON, A. PHILIP. "Sir Philip Sidney's Letter to the Camerarii." *PMLA* 62 (March 1947):83–95.
Publishes the letter with "improved readings" and a commentary on its background. Gives a brief account of Sidney's travels on the Continent in 1572–75 and 1577, summarizing his contacts with several printers and humanists, particularly Joachim II and Philipp Camerarius, sons of Joachim Camararius. Suggests that Sidney's promise in the letter to aid in the publication of their father's works was carried out in two volumes printed by Andreas Wechel.

203 MORTON, ANN. *Men of Letters*. Public Record Office Museum Pamphlets, 6. London: Her Majesty's Stationery Office, 1974, p. 3, plate 1.
Contains a facsimile of Sidney's letter to Jan Wyer, 16–26 October 1586, accompanied by a brief account of its content and a translation.

204 MUMBY, FRANK ARTHUR, ed. *Letters of Literary Men*. Vol. 1. New York: E.P. Dutton; London: George Routledge, [1906], pp. 25–31.
After a brief biographical note, prints Sidney's 18 October 1580 letter to his brother Robert, and his 24 March 1586 letter to Walsingham, dealing with difficulties in the Netherlands.

205 OSBORN, JAMES M[ARSHALL]. *Young Philip Sidney: 1572–1577*. New Haven, Conn., and London: Yale University Press, 1972, pp. xx, 308–9, 419–21, 461, 462, 535–40.
Prints for the first time, in modernized English translation, five letters from Sidney: 1) to the Count of Hanau, from Antwerp, 3 May 1575, in Latin, begging pardon for not having seen the Count in Frankfurt in April of that year and alluding to "an illness with which I was severely

Twentieth Century

afflicted" as partial cause; 2) to Languet, 21 April 1576, defending himself warmly against the charge that his friendship has diminished, complaining that "you also imply . . . that you suspect me of deceit and
ingratitude"; 3) to Hanau, from Nuremberg, 30 March 1577, in French,
promising to visit and begging the Count to keep him in favor; 4) to
Charles de l'Éscluse, from Prague, 8 April 1577, in French and Latin,
requesting that its bearer, an unidentified "near relative," be shown "the
memorable parts" of Vienna; and 5) to Edward Denny, from Wilton, 22
May 1580, in English, providing Denny with a reading program and
revealing that Sidney was chafing under his lack of employment in
affairs of state and that he had written songs that he assumed Denney
would know. The letter may contain a reference to Spenser. The program of study advises Denny to read the Scriptures and recommends
special attention to geography, military art, style in writing, draftsman-
ship, and mathematics. It suggests that he follow a methodical plan of
study and outline the books he reads. Provides information on the
sources of the letters and, in Appendix 5, adds contextual background
for the letter to Denny.

206 TAYLOR, HEDLEY V., ed. *Letters of Great Writers from the Time of
Spenser to the Time of Wordsworth.* London: Blackie & Son, 1912,
pp. 9–15.
Reprints a modern-spelling version of Sidney's letter to his brother
Robert dated 18 October 1580.

207 TENISON, E[VA] M[ABEL]. *Elizabethan England: Being the History
of This Country "In Relation to All Foreign Princes."* 12 vols. Royal
Leamington Spa, Warwick, England: n.p., 1933–60, 2:plate 29
following p. 279; 6:34–37.
Prints a photographic facsimile of Sidney's letter to Leicester dated 23
March 1572 and transcribes his letters to Leicester and Queen Elizabeth
of November 1585. Notes that his Italian hand changed as he grew
older. See also item 780.

208 WALLACE, MALCOLM WILLIAM. *The Life of Sir Philip Sidney.*
Cambridge: Cambridge University Press, 1915, pp. 68–70, 142,
280–81, 304–5, 319, 339–40.
Prints in their entirety the following letters to Sidney: from Sir Henry
(and Lady Mary) Sidney (164); from Philip Louis, Count of Hanau, 30
January 1575 (in translation); from Sir Henry Sidney, 27 April 1582;
from Sir Ralph Lane, 12 August 1585; from Lady Katherine Paget, 13
October [1585]; and from [William Davison], 16 November 1585.

Bibliographical Studies

Seventeenth Century

209 DRUMMOND, WILLIAM, [of Hawthornden]. *Auctarium bibliothecae Edinburgenae*. Edinburgh: Haeredes Andreae Hart, 1627. Reprint. Subtitled *sive Catalogus librorum quos Guilielmus Drummondus ab Hawthornden Bibliothecae*. Edinburgh: J. Ballantyne & Co., 1815, 48 pp.

Contains a list of Sidney's works in Drummond's library.

Eighteenth Century

210 AYSCOUGH, SAMUEL. *A Catalogue of the Manuscripts Preserved in the British Museum Hitherto Undescribed*. Vol. 2. London: John Rivington, 1782, p. 738.

Lists a manuscript from the collection of Thomas Birch entitled "Sir Philip Sidney: Short account of his life."

211 [NICERON, JEAN PIERRE.] "Phillipe Sidney." In *Memoirs pour servir a l'histoire des hommes illustres dans la république des lettres: Avec un catalogue raisonné de leurs ouvrages*. Vol. 15. Paris: Chez Briasson, 1731, pp. 217–26.

Provides a brief account of Sidney's life and a list of his works, including several misattributions: *Sir Philip Sidney's Ourania* (2843), which, according to Hunter (363) and others (315), was written by Nathaniel Baxter; *Essay on Bravery*, elsewhere called *Valour Anatomized in a Fancy* (2845), which Beal (230) demonstrates is actually Donne's *Essay of Valour*; *England's Helicon*; and *Almanzor and Almanzaida* (2844). Rightly questions Sidney's authorship of the last item, but wrongly discounts his hand in *Profitable Instructions . . . to Be Taken by Travelers* (168).

Eighteenth Century

212 TANNER, Bishop THOMAS. *Bibliotheca Britannico-Hibernica: Sive, de scriptoribus, qui in Anglia, Scotia, et Hibernia ad Saeculi XVII initium floruerunt, literarum ordine juxta familiarum nomina dispositis commentarius.* London: G. Bowyer, 1748, pp. 670–71.
Lists editions of works by and about Sidney, including elegies, imitations, and spurious works.

Nineteenth Century

213 ARBER, EDWARD, ed. *A Transcript of the Registers of the Company of Stationers of London; 1554–1640 A.D.* 5 vols. London and Birmingham: privately printed, 1875–94, 1:555; 2:295, 458, 460, 463–64, 472, 474, 496, 571, 666; 3:82, 128, 191, 269, 274, 586, 594, 598, 643; 4:66, 176, 180, 195, 205, 224, 245, 346, 513.
Prints entries in the Stationers' Register on the *Defence, Arcadia,* Sidney's translation of du Plessis-Mornay, his lost translation of du Bartas, and *Astrophil and Stella.* Also includes entries on elegies and epitaphs published in Sidney's honor, a portrait of him (one of "9. moderne worthies of the world"), continuations of *Arcadia* by Sir William Alexander and Sir Richard Beling, and Sir Henry Sidney's letter to Philip at Shrewsbury School (164).

214 [BLISS, PHILIP, ed.] *Bibliographical Miscellanies, Being a Selection of Curious Pieces, in Verse and Prose.* Oxford: n.p., 1813, pp. vi, 62–65.
Describes the Rawlinson Manuscript in the Bodleian Library and suggests that five sonnets in it ought to be added to the list of Sidney's works: "A satyr once did run away for dread" (*CS 16*), "The dart, the beams, the sting so strong I prove" (*PP 2*), "Like those sick folks, in whom strange humours flow" (*OA 41*), "Thou pain, the only guest of loathed constraint"(*CS 10*), and "And have I heard her say, 'O cruel pain!'" (*CS 11*).

215 COLLIER, J[OHN] PAYNE. *A Bibliographical and Critical Account of the Rarest Books in the English Language.* Vol. 4. New York: David G. Francis, Charles Scribner, 1866, pp. 50–57.
Provides bibliographical descriptions and a publishing history of *Arcadia* though 1599. Identifies the printer of the 1590 edition as Richard Field and suggests that he may have supplied George Puttenham with the manuscript of *Arcadia* that Puttenham mentions in his *Art of English Poesie.* Also considers the arrangement of the poems in the 1590, 1593,

and 1598 editions of *Arcadia* and discusses Olney's 1595 edition of the *Defence*.

216 ———. "Sir Philip Sidney and His Works." *Gentleman's Magazine* 33 (April 1850):370–77. Reprint. In *The Gentleman's Magazine Library*. Vol. 9, *Bibliographical Notes: A Classified Collection of the Chief Contents of "The Gentleman's Magazine" from 1731–1868*, edited by George Laurence Gomme. London: Elliot Stock, 1889, pp. 192–98.

Discusses the publishing history, contents, variants, and surviving copies of Sidney's major works. Concentrates on the two 1591 quartos of *Astrophil and Stella* and on the 1590 *Arcadia*. Incorrectly attributes the poem by "E.O." at the end of the first quarto of *Astrophil and Stella* to the Earl of Oxford.

217 GRAESSE, JEAN GEORGE THÉODORE. *Trésor de livres rare et précieux: ou nouveau dictionnaire bibliographique. Contenant plus de cent milles articles de livres rares, curieux et recherchés, d'ouvrages de luxe, etc.* Vol. 6. Dresden: R. Kuntze, 1857, pp. 399–400.

Cites eleven editions of Sidney's major works. Mistakenly includes *Almanzor and Almanzaida* (2844).

218 G[RIFFITHS], A[CTON] F[REDERICK]. *Bibliotheca Anglo-Poetica: A Descriptive Catalogue of a Rare and Rich Collection of Early English Poetry in the Possession of Longman, Hurst, Rees, Orme and Brown.* London: Longman, Hurst, Rees, Orme & Brown, 1815, pp. 335–36.

Includes reference to a copy of Dawson's extremely rare 1591 printing of Sir Henry Sidney's letter to Philip at Shrewsbury (164).

219 GROLIER CLUB, NEW YORK. *Catalogue of Original and Early Editions of Some of the Poetical and Prose Works of English Writers from Langland to Wither.* New York: Grolier Club, 1893, pp. 187–92.

Provides full bibliographical descriptions of the 1590, 1598, and 1605 editions of *Arcadia* and the two 1595 editions of the *Defence*. Discusses the dispute between Olney and Ponsonby over the publishing rights to the *Defence*.

220 HALLIWELL[-PHILLIPPS], JAMES O[RCHARD]. *A Brief Account of an Unique Edition of Sir Philip Sydney's "Arcadia."* Brixton Hill, England: n.p., 1854, 7 pp.

Reports that the 1613 edition of *Arcadia* is merely a reprint of the 1605. Considers reasons that the 1605 is rare and provides semifacsimile title-page information, collations, and descriptions.

Nineteenth Century

221 ———. *Descriptive Notices of Works in a Small Collection of Sydneian Literature in the Library of James O. Halliwell.* Brixton Hill, England: n.p., 1854, 8 pp.
Describes copies of the 1591 quartos of *Astrophil and Stella*; the Oxford elegies for Sidney, *Exequiae illustrissimi Philippi Sidnaei* (2760); the 1590, 1593, and Edinburgh 1599 editions of *Arcadia*; and various other works that allude to Sidney or print his poems. Suggests that Francis Davison's *Poetical Rhapsody* affords evidence that the "pleasant Willy" in Spenser's *Tears of the Muses* is Sidney. See also Koeppel (366), Minto (373), and Rollins (724).

222 HAZLITT, W[ILLIAM] CAREW. *Collections and Notes, 1867–1876.* London: Reeves & Turner, 1876, pp. 387–88, 496.
Describes various editions of *Arcadia* through the 1725 edition of the collected works as well as a manuscript of the Psalms (ca. 1610), which varies from that used in the 1823 edition by Singer (74).

223 ———. *Hand-Book to the Popular, Poetical, and Dramatic Literature of Great Britain, from the Invention of Printing to the Restoration.* London: John Russell Smith, 1867, pp. 557–59.
Describes sixteenth- through eighteenth-century editions of *Arcadia*, sixteenth-century editions of *Astrophil and Stella*, and Olney's 1595 edition of the *Defence*. Also lists volumes of elegies on Sidney and continuations of *Arcadia*.

224 [HAZLITT, WILLIAM CAREW, and ELLIS, F.S.] *The Huth Library: A Catalogue of Printed Books, Manuscripts, Autograph Letters, and Engravings, Collected by Henry Huth, with Collations and Bibliographical Descriptions.* Vol. 4. London: Ellis & White, 1880, pp. 1355–57.
Describes Huth Library copies of the 1605 and 1613 *Arcadia*, the 1591 first quarto of *Astrophil and Stella*, Olney's 1595 *Defence*, and the 1725 *Works*. In the annotations, provides information on collations, publishing history, previous ownership, and extant copies.

225 LOCKER-LAMPSON, FREDERICK. *The Rowfant Library. A Catalogue of the Printed Books, Manuscripts, Autograph Letters, Drawings and Pictures.* London: Bernard Quaritch, 1886, p. 116.
Describes copies of early editions in the collection, including a 1590 *Arcadia* and both Ponsonby's and Olney's printings of the *Defence*. Discusses the dispute between the publishers over the latter two.

226 LOWNDES, WILLIAM THOMAS. *The Bibliographer's Manual of English Literature.* Revised by Henry G. Bohn. Vol. 3. London:

Henry G. Bohn, 1864, pp. 2395–97. Orig. pub. London: W. Pickering, 1834 (not seen).

Lists editions of Sidney's works from the sixteenth through the nineteenth centuries, along with various continuations and imitations of *Arcadia* and books about Sidney. Provides descriptions, collations, current owners, and some discussion of contents.

227 [RITSON, JOSEPH.] *Bibliographia Poetica: A Catalogue of English Poets of the Twelfth, Thirteenth, Fourteenth, Fifteenth, and Sixteenth Centuries, with a Short Account of Their Works*. London: C. Roworth for G. & W. Nicol, 1802, pp. 331–33.

Lists several early editions of works by Sidney and two known manuscripts of the Sidney Psalms.

Twentieth Century

228 ANON. "Sir Philip Sidney's Anniversary." *TLS*, 10 December 1954, p. 812.

Describes the Sidney exhibition at the Bodleian Library in 1954. See also Buxton (240).

229 ATKINSON, DOROTHY F. *Edmund Spenser: A Bibliographical Supplement*. Baltimore: Johns Hopkins Press, 1937, pp. 39–42 and passim.

In the section "Spenser and Sidney" and elsewhere, cites scholarship from 1923 to 1937. Provides brief annotations and an index of authors, periodicals, and selected topics.

230 BEAL, PETER. *Index of English Literary Manuscripts*. Vol. 1, *1450–1625*. Part 2, *Douglas–Wyatt*. London: Mansell; New York: R.R. Bowker Co., 1980, pp. 465–88, 633–34.

Lists extant manuscripts of Sidney's works, excluding the correspondence. In the annotations provides (as appropriate) the location of each manuscript; its title, original ownership, scribal hand, contents, and date; printed collations, editions, and textual criticism; and current location and cataloging information. In the introduction, observes that only three of Sidney's literary works survive in his own hand: *Certain Sonnets*, the *Defence of Leicester*, and the "Discourse on Irish Affairs." Discusses Sidney's letters, noting extant manuscripts and their locations, printed facsimiles, and the topics discussed. Also lists books and miscellaneous documents bearing Sidney's signature or handwriting. Notes manuscripts of four poems misattributed to Sidney and one entitled "Blush, Phoebus, blush thy glorie is forlorn" that Robertson argues (2241) may

Twentieth Century

have belonged to *Astrophil and Stella*. Lists several seventeenth-century extracts and translations from *Arcadia* and discusses copies of *Arcadia* associated with the Countess of Pembroke, Gabriel Harvey, and Queen Elizabeth. Points out that the essay *Valour Anatomized in a Fancy* (2845), which bore Sidney's name on the title page, is actually John Donne's *Essay of Valour* and was probably misattributed for satiric reasons.

231 BIES, WERNER. "Recent German Studies of Sidney, 1970–1979." *SNew* 1, no. 2 (1980):47–52.

Provides a review essay of recent German studies.

232 BIES, WERNER; HUNTER, C. S[TUART]; LAMB, M[ARY] E[LLEN]; MONTROSE, LOUIS A[DRIAN]; ROBERTS, JOSEPHINE A[NASTASIA]; RUBIO, GERALD J.; SINFIELD, ALAN; and WALLER, GARY F. "Annotated Bibliography." *SNew* 3, no. 1 (1982):27–37.

Annotates selected articles and notes on Sidney appearing in the years 1979–82.

233 BIES, WERNER; HUNTER, C. S[TUART]; LAMB, M[ARY] E[LLEN]; MOORE, MICHAEL D.; ROBERTS, JOSEPHINE A[NASTASIA]; SALOMON, BROWNELL; and WALLER, GARY F. "Annotated Bibliography." *SNew* 2, no. 2 (1981):20–26.

Annotates a number of books and articles on Sidney from the years 1979–80.

234 BIES, WERNER; HUNTER, C. S[TUART]; LAMB, M[ARY] E[LLEN]; ROBERTS, JOSEPHINE A[NASTASIA]; RUBIO, GERALD J.; and WALLER, GARY F. "Annotated Bibliography." *SNew* 2, no. 1 (1981):8–20.

Annotates a selection of articles, essays, and notes on Sidney from the years 1978–80.

235 BIES, WERNER; LAMB, M[ARY] E[LLEN]; MacLACHLAN, HUGH; MOORE, MICHAEL D.; ROBERTS, JOSEPHINE A[NASTASIA]; and WALLER, GARY F. "Recent Studies of Sidney and His Circle: An Annotated Bibliography." *SNew* 1, no. 2 (1980):61–69.

Covers scholarship and criticism from 1977 to 1980.

236 BOND, WILLIAM HENRY. "The Bibliographical Jungle." *TLS*, 23 September 1949, p. 624.

Reviews circumstantial evidence suggesting that Olney's 1595 edition of the *Defence* preceded that of Ponsonby.

237 BONHEIM, HELMUT. *The English Novel before Richardson: A Checklist of Texts and Criticism to 1970.* Metuchen, N.J.: Scarecrow Press, 1971, pp. 77–83.
Devotes a section to selected twentieth-century studies of *Arcadia*.

238 BRENNAN, MICHAEL [G]. "William Ponsonby: Elizabethan Stationer." *Analytical and Enumerative Bibliography* 7, no. 3 (1983):91–110.
Details Ponsonby's career, discussing his Protestant leanings, his ties to the Leicester/Sidney and the Essex factions at court, and his publication of early editions of works by Sidney, Spenser, and others. In Sidney's case, stresses the unusual nature of the arrangement by which Fulke Greville, and later the Countess of Pembroke, acted as "overseers of the print," since the publisher usually edited the copy-text and supervised the reading and correcting of proofs. Discusses the background and timing of the 1598 *Arcadia* (1) and examines Henry Olney's suppressed edition of the *Defence* (98), the elegies for Sidney published after Spenser's *Colin Clout's Come Home Again* (2740, 2741, 2749, 2768, 2770, 2771), and Thomas Newman's printings of *Astrophil and Stella* (60, 61). Concludes that Newman "was not associated with" Sidney's family and friends and that, to appease them for the unauthorized first quarto, he had to withdraw it from circulation and print a second quarto with corrections, "probably at his own expense." Notes the insertion of a poem by William Percy entitled "Sir Philip Sydneis Song" into of a manuscript of Percy's comedies and pastorals now at the Huntington Library. Also notes Ponsonby's connections with John Windet, the printer of the 1590 *Arcadia*, and his ties (by marriage) to Simon Waterson, who took over the license to print Sidney's works after Ponsonby's death. Includes a chronological list of books published by Ponsonby.

239 BROWN, JAMES; HUNTER, C. S[TUART]; ROBERTS, JOSEPHINE A[NASTASIA]; and WALLER, GARY F. "Annotated Bibliography: Recent Articles and Books on Sidney and Circle." *SNew* 4, no. 1 (1983):20–29.
Annotates selected items on Sidney from 1980 to 1983.

240 BUXTON, JOHN. "The Sidney Exhibition." *BLR* 5 (July 1955):125–30.
Describes the exhibition that opened at the Bodleian Library in November 1954. See also item 228.

Twentieth Century

241 CARPENTER, FREDERIC IVES. *A Reference Guide to Edmund Spenser*. Chicago: University of Chicago Press, 1923, pp. 95–96 and passim.

In the section "Spenser and Sidney," lists selected scholarship to 1923. Includes brief annotations and an index of authors, periodicals, and subjects.

242 CASE, ARTHUR E[LLICOTT]. *A Bibliography of English Poetical Miscellanies, 1521–1750*. Oxford: Oxford Bibliographical Society, Oxford University Press, 1935, pp. 19–21, 302–3.

Contains quasifacsimile title page information, collations, descriptions, variants, and locations for the three volumes of elegies on Sidney published in England in 1587 (2760, 2763, 2765) and for the two 1591 quartos of *Astrophil and Stella* (60, 61).

243 COLAIANNE, A[NTHONY] J., and GODSHALK, W[ILLIAM] L[EIGH]. "Recent Studies in Sidney (1970–77)." *ELR* 8 (Spring 1978):212–33.

Seeks to provide a "reasonably complete" review essay and bibliography organized into three sections: "General," "Studies of Individual Works," and "Canon and Texts."

244 ———. "A Reference Guide to Sir Philip Sidney." *SNew* 1, no. 1 (1980):5–8.

Provides a critique of previous bibliographies and describes plans for a comprehensive Sidney bibliography. (The present volume evolved from those preliminary plans.)

245 ESDAILE, ARUNDELL. *A List of English Tales and Prose Romances Printed before 1740*. London: Blades, East, & Blades, 1912, pp. 126–29.

Lists early editions, translations, imitations, and continuations of *Arcadia*.

246 [EYRE, GEORGE EDWARD BRISCOE.] *A Transcript of the Registers of the Worshipful Company of Stationers; from 1640–1708 A.D.* 3 vols. London: privately printed, 1913–14, 1:18, 298, 300, 328; 2:502.

Includes entries on seventeenth-century editions of *Arcadia*.

247 GODSCHALK [i.e., GODSHALK], WILLIAM L[EIGH] "Bibliography of Sidney Studies since 1935." In *Sir Philip Sidney as a Literary Craftsman*, by Kenneth [Orne] Myrick. 2d ed. Lincoln: University of Nebraska Press, 1965, pp. 352–58.

Provides an annotated listing sorted by author.

Twentieth Century

248 GODSHALK, WILLIAM [LEIGH] "Recent Studies in Sidney." *ELR* 2 (Winter 1972):148–64.
Provides a review essay and bibliography of major scholarship from 1945 to 1969.

249 GREG, W[ALTER] W[ILSON]. *A Bibliography of the English Printed Drama to the Restoration*. Vol. 1, *Stationers' Records, Plays to 1616*. Illustrated Monographs, 24. London: Bibliographical Society, Oxford University Press, 1939, pp. 152–53.
Provides a descriptive bibliography of *The Lady of May* and the editions of *Arcadia* from 1598 to 1674.

250 GROLIER CLUB, NEW YORK. *A Catalogue of Books in First Editions Selected to Illustrate the History of English Prose Fiction from 1485 to 1870*. New York: Grolier Club, 1917, pp. 24–26 and plate 5.
Provides basic information on *Arcadia*, describing editions and a manuscript exibited by the club in 1917.

251 GUFFEY, GEORGE ROBERT. *Elizabethan Bibliographies Supplements*, edited by Charles A. Pennel. Vol. 7, *Samuel Daniel, 1942–1965; Michael Drayton, 1941–1965; Sir Philip Sidney, 1941–1965*. London: Nether Press, 1967, pp. 31–48.
Lists scholarship on Sidney by year. Lacks annotations but provides an index of authors, editors, and titles.

252 HARNER, JAMES L. *English Renaissance Prose Fiction, 1500–1660: An Annotated Bibliography of Criticism*. Boston: G.K. Hall, 1978, pp. 408–78.
Lists bibliographies, editions, and studies of *Arcadia* from 1800 to 1976. Provides annotations and an index of authors.

253 HAYWARD, JOHN. *English Poetry: A Descriptive Catalogue of First and Early Editions of Works of the English Poets from Chaucer to the Present Day Exhibited by the National Book League at 7 Albemarle Street, London, 1947*. Cambridge: National Book League, Cambridge University Press 1947, p. 21.
Provides title-page information, collation, and a description of the 1598 *Arcadia*. Notes that all but one of six known copies are in public libraries.

254 [JACKSON, WILLIAM A., and UNGER, EMMA VA.] *The Carl H. Pforzheimer Library: English Literature 1475–1700*. Vol. 3. New York: n.p., 1940, pp. 963–66.

Twentieth Century

Gives complete descriptive bibliography (including title-page transcription, collation, contents, physical description, publishing history, variants, manuscript data, and the number and location of other extant copies) for the three Sidney volumes in this library: Olney's 1595 quarto of the *Defence* and the 1590 and 1605 printings of *Arcadia*. Suggests that Olney may have been ignorant of Ponsonby's prior right to publish the *Defence* and that, by the time Ponsonby brought out his own text, the market was played out. Gives information on the way the printing rights to Sidney's works changed hands in 1603–1605, following Ponsonby's death.

255 JUEL-JENSEN, BENT. "Contemporary Collectors XLIII." *BC* 15 (Summer 1966):152–74.
In reviewing his personal collection, describes editions of *Arcadia* to 1674. Notes that some copies of the 1613 edition contain Alexander's supplement, which normally appears in the 1621 edition. Also describes the following: the 1587 edition of *The Trueness of Christian Religion*; a manuscript of the Sidney Psalms with an otherwise unknown dedicatory poem by the Countess of Pembroke to Queen Elizabeth; a copy of the Countess's poem "To the Angel Spirit of the Most Excellent Sir Philip Sidney"; early manuscripts of Greville's *Life of Sidney* and Sidney's *Letter to the Queen*; a contemporary account of Zutphen by "a trumpeter"; various works dedicated to Sidney or related to his writings; and a manuscript account of Sidney's death by his chaplain, George Gifford. Notes that Gifford's account includes Sidney's only reference to Penelope Rich outside the sonnets. See also item 2348.

256 ———. "Some Uncollected Authors XXXIV: Sir Philip Sidney, 1554–1586." *BC* 11 (Winter 1962):468–79.
Lists editions of *Arcadia* and variants through 1725. Supplies quasifacsimile title-page transcriptions, collations, bibliographic descriptions, and lists of known copies.

257 ———. "Some Uncollected Authors XXXIV: Sir Philip Sidney, 1554–1586." *BC* 12 (Summer 1963):196–201.
Supplies quasifacsimile title-page transcriptions, collations, detailed descriptions and lists of known copies for the two 1591 editions and the 1598 edition of *Astrophil and Stella*; the 1823 Psalms; the two 1595 editions and the 1752 edition of the *Defence*; Joseph Warton's 1787 edition of the *Defence* and Jonson's *Discoveries*; the 1633 collection containing Sidney's letter to his brother Robert on foreign travel; the 1587 edition of the Sidney-Golding translation of du Plessis-Mornay's *Trueness of the*

Christian Religion; and two works spuriously attributed to Sidney, *Valour Anatomized in a Fancy* (2845) and *Almanzor and Almanzaida* (2844).

258 LAMB, M[ARY] E[LLEN]; MacLACHLAN, HUGH; MOORE, MICHAEL D.; ROBERTS, JOSEPHINE A[NASTASIA]; RUBIO, GERALD J.; and WALLER, GARY F. "Recent Studies of Sidney and His Circle: An Annotated Bibliography." *SNew* 1, no. 1 (1980):15–24.
Compiles an annotated list of "the most significant" books and articles on Sidney from 1977 to 1979.

259 LAMB, MARY ELLEN; POPHAM, ELIZABETH; and ROBERTS, JOSEPHINE A[NASTASIA]. "Annotated Bibliography: Recent Articles and Books on Sidney and the Circle." *SNew* 4, no. 2 (1983):27–33.
Annotates items from the years 1980 to 1983.

260 LEVY, CHARLES S[AMUEL]. "A Supplementary Inventory of Sir Philip Sidney's Correspondence." *MP* 67 (November 1969): 177–81.
Lists sixteen extant manuscripts of letters by Sidney that were not printed by Feuillerat (23) or that have since passed into other hands. Summarizes those that have never been published. Also lists manuscripts (or, in two cases, printed versions) of all the extant letters written to Sidney, with the exception of sixty-five in the hands of James M. Osborn and eleven in the possession of Christ Church College, Oxford, which are described in Sotheby's catalog (2738) for an auction on 26 June 1967. In the footnotes, provides historical information and bibliographic references.

261 LIEVSAY, JOHN L. *The Sixteenth Century: Skelton Through Hooker*. Goldentree Bibliographies in Language and Literature. New York: Appleton-Century-Crofts, 1968, pp. 83–86.
Provides nonspecialists with a selective list of editions and critical works, mostly from the twentieth century. Excludes unpublished dissertations, literary histories, short notes and explications, and older biographical studies.

262 MARENCO, FRANCO. "Sir Philip Sidney: Studi 1965–66." *FeL* 13, no. 3 (1967):216–24.
Surveys Sidney scholarship in 1965 and 1966.

Twentieth Century

263 MOORE, MICHAEL D.; POPHAM, ELIZABETH; and RUBIO, GERALD J. "Annotated Bibliography: Recent Articles and Books on Sidney & Circle." *SNew* 5, no. 1 (1984):28–37.
Covers selected items published between 1978 and 1984.

264 ROCHE, THOMAS P., Jr. "A Library for a Sixteenth-Century Gentleman." *PULC* 38 (Winter–Spring 1977):120–33.
In describing Sidney materials in the Robert H. Taylor collection at Princeton, notes that they include a 1593 *Arcadia*; a 1605 *Arcadia* bound with a discussion of the edition by James Orchard Halliwell-Phillipps; the Chatsworth copy of Ponsonby's 1595 printing of the *Defence*; a 20 March 1583 letter from Sidney to Sir William Blunt; and an autograph letter from Sir Henry Sidney to John Corksham, dated 14 August 1573.

265 SALE, WILLIAM M., Jr. *Samuel Richardson: Master Printer*. Ithaca, N.Y.: Cornell University Press, 1950, p. 204.
Lists the parts of the 1724–25 edition of Sidney's works (13) that were printed by Samuel Richardson. Explains the two states of the title page.

266 SCANLON, PAUL A. "A Checklist of Prose Romances in English, 1474–1603." *Library*, 5th ser. 33 (June 1978):143–52.
Lists early editions of *Arcadia*.

267 SCHONEVELD, CORNELIS W. *Intertraffic of the Mind: Studies in Seventeenth-Century Anglo-Dutch Translation with a Checklist of Books Translated from English into Dutch, 1600–1700*. Publications of the Sir Thomas Browne Institute, Leiden, n.s. 3. Leiden, Netherlands: E.J. Brill, Leiden University Press for the Sir Thomas Browne Institute, 1983, p. 235.
In the checklist, includes early Dutch translations of the *Defence* (99) and *Arcadia* (38, 39, 44). Identifies Johan van Heemskerck as the translator of certain chapters from the romance published separately (see items 35, 36, 46). Also locates extant copies of these works in the Netherlands.

268 TANNENBAUM, SAMUEL A[ARON]. *Sir Philip Sidney (A Concise Bibliography)*. Elizabethan Bibliographies, 23. New York: Samuel A. Tannenbaum, 1941, 79 pp.
Includes a partial list of works by and about Sidney from his lifetime to 1940. Divides the material into editions and translations, selections from works by Sidney and his imitators, musical settings, poems in praise of Sidney, biography and commentary, and fictional depictions of Sidney. Supplies an index of names and subjects.

269 WASHINGTON, MARY A[LDRIDGE]. *Sir Philip Sidney: An Annotated Bibliography of Modern Criticism, 1941–1970*. Columbia: University of Missouri Press, 1972, 209 pp. Orig. a Ph.D. diss., University of Missouri, 1969.

Compiles an annotated list of works by and about Sidney from 1941 to 1970. Divides the bibliography into sections devoted to general criticism, biographical material, each of Sidney's major works, the minor works, foreign studies, and reprints of older studies. Notes selected book reviews, poems dedicated to Sidney, works based on his life, and occasional works published earlier than 1941 not collected in previous bibliographies. Supplies descriptive rather than evaluative annotations, which cover all studies except foreign dissertations. Includes an index of names, which contains references to each of Sidney's works and to the characters in *Arcadia*.

270 [WRIGHT, JAMES OSBORNE, and SHIPMAN, CAROLYN.] *Catalogue of Books by English Authors Who Lived before the Year 1700 Forming a Part of the Library of Robert Hoe*. Vol. 4. New York: n.p., 1904, pp. 175–83.

Provides collations and descriptions of copies of the 1590, 1593, 1598, 1605, and 1627 editions of *Arcadia*; the Ponsonby 1595 *Defence*; the 1823 Psalms; the 1724 *Works*; and other editions of Sidney's writings.

General Scholarship and Criticism

Sixteenth Century

271 FRAUNCE, ABRAHAM. *The Arcadian Rhetoric: Or the Praecepts of Rhetorike made plaine by examples, Greeke, Latin, English, Italian, French, Spanish*. London: Thomas Orwin, [1588], passim. Reprint. In English Linguistics, 1500–1800: A Collection of Facsimile Reprints, 176. Menston, England: Scolar Press, 1969.

Draws numerous examples from the manuscripts of *Arcadia* and from Sidney's poetry.

272 [HOOKER, JOHN, ed.] Supplement from 1578 to 1586. In *The Third Volume of Chronicles, beginning at duke William the Norman, commonlie called the Conqueror; and descending by degrees of Yeeres to all the kings and queenes of England in their orderlie successions*, by Raphael Holinshed. [London]: n.p., 1586, pp. 1315–21, 1553–56. Reprint. *Holinshed's Chronicles of England, Scotland, and Ireland*. Vol 4. London: J. Johnson; F.C. & J. Rivington; T. Payne; Wilkie and Robinson; Longman, Hurst, Rees, & Orme; Cadell & Davies; and J. Mawman, 1808, pp. 435–45, 879–84. Partial reprint, without Goldwel's *Brief Declaration*, in Flügel (15).

Praises Sidney's virtues, mentioning his marriage and daughter Elizabeth, his embassy to the Emperor and the Queen's favorable reaction to it, and the excellence of *Arcadia* (then circulating in manuscript). Supplies "an additament," giving particulars of Sidney's diplomatic successes as Governor of Flushing and his military actions through the Battle of Zutphen. Quotes his Latin letter to Jan Wyer ("Wierus, a very expert and learned physician"), written the night before Sidney died. Also mentions a long Latin letter to "Belerius, a learned divine" composed several days earlier, which was brought to the Queen. Quotes

Henry Stephans's dedicatory epistle to Sidney in his Greek New Testament. Considers the disposition of Sidney's body, his will, and his last motto: "Vix ea nostra voco." Also reprints Goldwel's *Brief Declaration* (147), a description of the original presentation of *Four Foster Children of Desire*. See item 148.

273 MERES, FRANCIS. "A comparatiue discourse of our English Poets, with the Greeke, Latine, and Italian Poets." In *Palladis Tamia. Wits Treasvry, Being the Second Part of Wits Common Wealth*. London: P. Short, for Cuthbert Burbie, 1598, fols. 279^r–87^r.

Praises Sidney's eloquence and compares *Arcadia* with Xenophon's *Cyropaidia* and Heliodorus' *Aethiopica* as "absolute heroicall poems." Calls Sidney "our rarest poet," naming him "one of the most passionate among us to bewaile and bemoane the perplexities of Loue."

274 [SPENSER, EDMUND, and HARVEY, GABRIEL.] *Three Proper, and wittie, familiar Letters: lately passed betweene two Vniuersitie men: touching the Earth-quake in Aprill last, and our English refourmed Versifying*; and *Two other very commendable Letters of the same mens writing: both touching the foresaid Artificiall Versifying, and certain other Particulars*. London: H. Bynneman, 1580, [36] pp. Reprint. *Letters on Reformed Versifying, etc*. In *Elizabethan Critical Essays*, edited by G. Gregory Smith. Vol. 1. Oxford: Oxford University Press, 1904, pp. 87–126.

Provides information on Spenser's early contact with Sidney and with the Areopagus. Discusses their experiments with William Drant's rules of quantitative verse and Sidney's interest in similar rules by Gabriel Harvey. Also notes Stephen Gosson's folly in dedicating *The School of Abuse* to Sidney.

Seventeenth Century

275 DRYDEN, JOHN. "The Authors Apology for Heroique Poetry; and Politique Licence." In *The State of Innocence and Fall of Man: An Opera*, by John Dryden. London: T.N. for Henry Herringman, 1677, sig. C2^r. Reprint. In *Essays of John Dryden*, edited by W.P. Ker. Vol. 1. Oxford: Clarendon Press, 1900, p. 189.

States that Sidney's "connection of epithets, or the conjunction of two words in one" is something "unluckily attempted in English."

276 ———. "A Discourse concerning the Original and Progress of Satire." In *The Satires of Decimus Junius Juvenalis . . . Together with*

Seventeenth Century

the Satires of Aulus Persius Flaccus, translated by John Dryden and others. London: Jacob Tonson, 1693, p. viii. Reprint. In *Essays of John Dryden*, edited by W.P. Ker. Vol. 2. Oxford: Clarendon Press, 1900, p. 28.

Feels that Spenser's Prince Arthur represents Sidney. Explains the unfinished state of *The Faerie Queene* by suggesting that, when Sidney died, Spenser was deprived "both of means and spirit to accomplish his design."

277 [FLORIO, JOHN.] Dedication to *The Essayes or Morall, Politike and Millitarie Discourses of Lo: Michaell de Montaigne. . . .* Book 2. London: Val. Sims for Edward Blount, 1603, sig. R3ʳ. Reprint. In *The Essayes of Michael Lord of Montaigne*, edited by Ernest Rhys. Everyman's Library. London and Toronto: J.M. Dent & Sons; New York: E.P. Dutton & Co., 1910, pp. 5–6.

Finds fault with the 1593 edition of *Arcadia* and praises Sidney's renderings of du Plessis-Mornay's *Trueness of the Christian Religion* and the first part of du Bartas's *Semaine ou la création du monde*. Asks Lady Rich and Sidney's daughter Elizabeth to publish the translation of du Bartas. Also includes two poems praising Sidney (2796).

278 MATHEWS, Sir TOBIE. Preface to *A Collection of Letters, Made by Sr Tobie Mathews Kt. With a Character of the most Excellent Lady, Lucy, Countesse of Carleile*. London: Henry Herringman, 1660, sigs. B5ᵛ–B6ᵛ.

Lists Sidney among a small group of Englishmen with "rare compositions of minds." Reviews his varied attainments, calling *Arcadia* "a Miracle for that time" and praising it for its characters, for its "Deliberations of Counsell," for its "Understandings of naturall Inclination" and "waies of prevailing upon Passion," and for its "Descriptions of Actions, with all the Circumstances thereof." Repeats as a "generall Report" that Sidney was offered the crown of Poland.

279 MILTON, JOHN. *Artis Logicae Plenior Institutio, ad Petri Rami Methodum concinnata, Adjecta est Praxis Annalytica & Petri Rami vita. Libros duobus*. London: Impensis Spencer Hickman, 1672, sig. A4ʳ. Reprint. Edited and translated by Allan H. Gilbert. In *The Works of John Milton*, edited by Frank Allen Patterson, et al. The Columbia Edition. Vol. 11. New York: Columbia University Press, 1935, p. 3.

Agrees "with our countryman Sidney, Peter Ramus is believed the best writer on the art [of logic]."

Seventeenth Century

280 PEACHAM, HENRY, [the Younger]. *The Compleat Gentleman. Fashioning him absolute in the most necessary & comendable Qualities concerning Minde or Bodie that may be required in a Noble Gentleman.* London: for Francis Constable, 1622, pp. 53, 199. Reprint. Edited by Virgil B[arney] Heltzel. Ithaca, N.Y.: Cornell University Press for the Folger Shakespeare Library, 1962.

Names Sidney among "those authors in prose, who speake the best and purest English." Calls his "devises of Tiltings" among "the best" he has seen, and claims to have "once collected" some "with intent to publish them."

281 PHILLIPS, EDWARD. *Theatrum Poetarum, or a Compleat Collection of the Poets, Especially The most Eminent, of all Ages. The Ancients distinguish't from the Moderns in their several Alphabets. With some Observations and Reflections upon many of them, particularly those of our Nation.* London: for Charles Smith, 1675, p. 152.

Remarks that *Arcadia* is "a poem in design" and praises Sidney as being equally "addicted both to Arts and Arms."

282 TEMPLE, Sir WILLIAM. *Miscellanea. The Second Part. In Four Essays.* London: Printed by J.R. for Ri. and Ra. Simpson, 1690, sigs. Aaa1ʳ–Ddd8ʳ. Reprint. In *Five Miscellaneous Essays by Sir William Temple*, edited by Samuel Holt Monk. Ann Arbor: University of Michigan Press, 1963, pp. 173–203.

In "Essay IV. Of Poetry," discusses works including *Arcadia* that mingle poetry and prose. Singles out classical romances such as Heliodorus's *Aethiopica*, remarking that "the true spirit or vein of ancient poetry in this kind seems to shine most in Sir Philip Sidney, whom I esteem both the greatest poet and the noblest genius of any that have left writings [in a modern language] behind them. . . ." Regards him as capable of "the greatest ideas" and "the noblest examples." Includes Spenser, but not Sidney, among authors of "Heroic poetry."

283 WINSTANLEY, WILLIAM. "The Life of Sir Philip Sidney." In *England's Worthies. Select Lives of the Most Eminent Persons of the English Nation from Constantine the Great down to these Times.* London: Printed by J.C. & F.C. for Obadiah Belgrave, 1684, pp. 217–23. Reprint (with minor alterations). In *The Lives of the Most Famous English Poets, or The Honour of Parnassus.* London: H. Clark for Samuel Manship, 1687.

Contains a brief biography and accounts of Sidney's works, with emphasis on *Arcadia* and the translation of du Plessis-Mornay. Also supplies

Seventeenth Century

synopses of sixteenth- and seventeenth-century tributes and an account of Sidney's death.

284 [WOOD, ANTHONY à.] *Athenae Oxonienses: An Exact History of all the Writers and Bishops Who have had their Education in the most ancient and famous University of Oxford, from . . . 1500 to the End of the Year 1690.* Vol 1. London: Tho. Bennet, 1691, cols. 182–85. Reprint. Edited by Philip Bliss. Vol. 1. London: F.C. & J. Rivington et al., 1813, cols. 517–25.

Remarks on Sidney's reputation as a poet and patron, calling him "almost the only person in any age . . . that could teach the best rules of poetry." Discusses his ancestry and character and summarizes his life, providing details of his days at Oxford and his European tour. Corrects Greville (863) on the extent to which Languet traveled with Sidney during the tour and on the circumstances of Languet's visit to England in 1579. Gives information on Sidney's embassy to Germany in 1577, on his contacts with Don John of Austria and William of Orange, and on his *Letter to the Queen*, connecting that document to his quarrel with the Earl of Oxford and his retirement from court in 1580. Sketches his service to the government in the 1580s, noting his interest in America and suggesting that the Queen did not advance him because she feared he would be made King of Poland. Lists works attributed to him (some wrongly). Noting that he wanted *Arcadia* suppressed, discusses its many editions, translations, and continuations. Identifies the character Philoclea and the Stella of the sonnets with Lady Rich. Attributes to Sidney *An Essay upon Valor*, elsewhere called *Valour Anatomized in a Fancy* (2845), citing evidence in the manuscript *Cottoni Posthuma*. Also describes a manuscript of the Psalms at Wilton. Concludes with a detailed description of Sidney's death and funeral, mentioning many of the elegies written in his memory. See also Bliss (317) and Midgley (656).

285 WOOD, ANTHONY à. *Historia et Antiquitates Universitatis Oxoniensis.* Vol. 2. Oxford: e Theatro Sheldoniano, 1674, pp. 264–66.

Provides a brief Latin life of Sidney, stressing his European travels and his public career. Lists his major works in early editions and prints Rainolds's epitaph (2806). See also item 284.

Eighteenth Century

286 BERKENHOUT, JOHN. *Biographia Literaria; or, A Biographical History of Literature: Containing the Lives of English, Scotish, and Irish Authors, from the Dawn of Letters . . . to the Present time.* . . . London: J. Dodsley, 1777, pp. 381–84.

Reviews Sidney's life, attributing his retirement from court to his quarrel with the Earl of Oxford and repeating the myth that he was offered the crown of Poland. Asserts that he obtained for Spenser "the place of poet laureat." Defends Sidney from Walpole (294).

287 BIRCH, THOMAS, ed. Introduction to *The Faerie Queene*, by Edmund Spenser. Vol. 1. London: J. Brindley and S. Wright, 1751, pp. i–xxxvii passim.

Refutes the apocryphal story that Spenser first introduced himself to Sidney at Leicester House by sending in the Despair episode from *The Faerie Queene*. See, for example, Yart (882). Suggests that Spenser turned from pastoral to heroic poetry at Sidney's urging, but dismisses Dryden's surmise (276) that Sidney's death deprived Spenser of "means and spirit" to finish his epic. Regards Spenser's character Prince Arthur as a representation of Sidney.

288 CIBBER, THEOPHILUS. *The Lives of the Poets of Great Britain and Ireland, to the time of Dean Swift.* Vol. 1. London: for R. Griffiths, 1753, pp. 76–84. Reprint. Hildesheim: Georg Olms, 1968.

In "Sir Philip Sidney" lauds the author's achievements as a courtier and statesman, noting the admiration for him expressed by such contemporaries as Don John of Austria. Praises his works, suggesting that *Arcadia* was designed to inculcate virtue and that the *Letter to the Queen* was written at Leicester's request. Discusses the tennis-court quarrel with the Earl of Oxford and contends that the Queen did not allow Sidney to go on Drake's expedition because she needed him elsewhere. Recounts Sidney's exploits in the Low Countries and the circumstances of his death, stressing the widespread mourning that followed. Suggests (mistakenly) that Sidney was the author of *Ourania, Valour Anatomized in a Fancy, Almanzor and Almanzaida,* and "The True Picture of Love."

289 COOPER, E[LIZABETH]. *The Muses Library; Or a Series of English Poetry, from the Saxons, to the Reign of King Charles II.* Vol. 1. London: J. Wilcox, T. Green, J. Brindley, and T. Osborn, 1737, pp. 203–15. Reprint. In *The Historical and Poetical Medley: or Muses Library; Being A Choice and Faithful Collection of the Best Antient*

Eighteenth Century

> *English Poetry, from the Times of Edward the Confessor, to the Reign of King James the First,* by Elizabeth Cooper and William Oldys. London: for T. Davies, 1738, pp. 203–15.

In "Sir Philip Sidney," sketches the author's life and character, misattributing to him the poem "The True Picture of Love." Repeats the myth that he was offered the crown of Poland.

290 GRANGER, JAMES. *A Biographical History of England, from Egbert the Great to the Revolution.* Vol. 1. London: T. Davies, 1769, p. 187.

Praises the variety of Sidney's talents, preferring the style of *Arcadia* to that of *Euphues.*

291 [HURD, RICHARD]. *Moral and Political Dialogues: Being the Substance of several Conversations between Divers Eminent Persons of the Past and Present Age; Digested by the Parties themselves and Now First published from the Original MSS with Critical and Explanatory notes By the Editor.* London: for A. Millar; Cambridge: for W. Thurlborne & J. Woodyer, 1759, pp. 113–14.

In "Dialogue III. On the Golden Age of Queen Elizabeth: between The Hon. Robert Digby, Dr. Arbuthnot, and Mr. Addison. Occasioned by A View of Kenelworth Castle, in the Year 1716," Arbuthnot defends tilting by suggesting that it prepared Sidney for his brave showing at Axel and Zutphen. Addison replies, granting that Sidney was "the very flower of knighthood." A footnote describes the action of *Four Foster Children of Desire,* noting Sidney's part and the occasion on which it was presented. Concludes that "nothing in the Arcadia itself" better shows "the spirit and language of knight errantry."

292 JACOB, GILES. *An Historical Account of the Lives and Writings of Our Most Considerable English Poets, whether Epick, Lyrick, Elegiack, Epigramatists, &c.* London: E. Curll, 1720, pp. 186–89.

Sketches Sidney's life and works, retelling the myth that he was a contender for the crown of Poland and identifying Stella with his wife Frances.

293 UPTON, JOHN. *Critical Observations on Shakespeare.* London: G. Hawkins, 1746, pp. 39, 75–76, 343–44.

Cites Sidney as an example of English chivalry and suggests that Spenser modeled his Prince Arthur on him. Faults his experiments with classical meters.

294 [WALPOLE, HORACE, Earl of Orford.] *A Catalogue of the Royal and Noble Authors of England, With Lists of their Works.* Vol. 1. Strawberry Hill, England: n.p., 1758, pp. 163–68.

In an article on Fulke Greville, notes the "temporary admiration" for Sidney in his own age, but finds his reputation overblown. Admitting that he was the subject of many dedications and elegies, and accepting the myth that he was even nominated for the crown of Poland, finds little to admire in him besides valor. Calls *Arcadia* "a tedious, lamentable, pedantic, pastoral romance, which the patience of a young virgin in love cannot now wade through." Condemns Sidney's attempts at classical meters, suggesting that he "understood little of the genius of his own language." Regards his letter threatening Molyneux as "an instance of unwarrantable violence," and praises the *Defence of Leicester* as the "best presumption of his abilities." Concludes that "he died with the rashness of a volunteer, after having lived to write with the *sang froid* and prolixity of Mademoiselle Scuderi." Subsequent editions add a long note justifying the attacks on Sidney but admitting that they did not take into account the *Defence*, which Walpole had forgotten. See anonymous reactions (303, 309, 1329, 1397) and signed replies by Berkenhout (286), Adams (1338), Brydges (323), Disraeli (341), Hallam (1361), Park (381), Reeve (1336), Zouch (974), and Crossley (1351). See also Walpole's defense of his position in item 398.

295 WARTON, THOMAS. *Observations on the "Fairy Queen" of Spenser.* 2d ed. Vol. 1. London: Printed for R. and J. Dodsley, 1762, p. 88.

Suggests that Sidney's Platonism "contributed not a little" to Spenser's choice of subject for the *Four Hymns.* (This point is not made in the first edition of 1754.)

Nineteenth Century

296 A. "Sir Philip Sidney and Southey." *N&Q,* 2d ser. 11 (1 June 1861):428.

Inquires about Robert Southey's unfinished edition of Sidney's works and receives the reply that the manuscript is in the possession of C.C. Southey. The work was, in fact, a life of Sidney (390), which was published posthumously. See also Southey (391).

297 ADAMS, W[ILLIAM] H[ENRY] DAVENPORT. "Sir Philip Sidney: The Elizabethan Gentleman." In *Records of Noble Lives: A*

Nineteenth Century

> *Book of Notable English Biographies: Sir Philip Sidney, Francis Bacon,*
> *Robert Blake, etc.* London: T. Nelson & Sons, 1868, pp. 11–49.

Uses Greville as a basis for a sketch of Sidney's life and defends the
moral and descriptive passages of *Arcadia*.

298 ADAMS, W[ILLIAM] H[ENRY] D[AVENPORT] [Walter Clinton,
pseud.] *Sword and Pen: or, English Worthies in the Reign of Elizabeth.*
New York: Virtue & Yorston, [1869], pp. 371–445.

In Chapter 1 of "Sir Philip Sidney," quotes various English writers in
praise of Sidney. Describes Penshurst and considers the character and
lineage of his parents, his education and his European tour. In Chapter
2, treats the period from 1575 to 1582, reviewing his trip to Ireland and
his embassy to Germany and regarding Sidney as a "foremost figure" in
Elizabeth's court until his quarrel with Oxford and his retirement to
Wilton. Treats him as the ideal of a gentleman and compares his character with that of Tennyson's King Arthur. Touches on his patronage, listing books dedicated to him and terming him a "warm friend" of
Spenser. Claims that *The Faerie Queene* was written at his instigation and
that *The Shepherd's Calendar* was completed in his company at Penshurst.
Considers the merits and faults of *Arcadia*. In Chapter 3, treats Sidney's
return to court, his interest in America, and his marriage. Praises the
Defence of Leicester for its "literary powers." Recounts the circumstances of
Sidney's appointment as Governor of Flushing, his concerns in that
office, and his actions at Axel and Zutphen. Includes an engraving of
Sidney, borne on a litter, offering his cup to a wounded soldier.

299 AIKIN, LUCY. *Memoirs of the Court of Queen Elizabeth.* Vol. 2.
London: Longman, Hurst, Rees, Orme, Brown, & Green, 1818,
pp. 74–77, 95, 139, 152–62.

Considers the hazards that Sidney braved in writing against the French
marriage in his *Letter to the Queen* and considers his participation in *Four
Foster Children of Desire*, which was performed for the French commissioners. Also notes the weakness of the *Defence of Leicester* and reviews
Sidney's career.

300 ANON. *The Cabinet Portrait Gallery of British Worthies.* Vol. 4.
London: Charles Knight & Co., 1845, pp. 54–74.

Reviews Sidney's life and achievements. Sees in Kalander's house in
Arcadia a description of Penshurst, and compares Sidney's depiction of it
to Jonson's poem "To Penshurst." Attributes Sidney's retirement from
court to his quarrel with Oxford, not to the *Letter to the Queen*. Evaluates
Arcadia, stressing its moral and political astuteness and treating Philoclea

as a portrait of Penelope Rich. Interprets *Astrophil and Stella* biographically.

301 ———. "English Poets and Oxford Critics." *Quarterly Review* 153 (January–April 1882):225–42.
In reviewing Thomas Humphrey Ward's *The English Poets* (London: Macmillan & Co., 1880), argues that Sidney and Sackville "prepared and polished a poetic language and rhythm" for use by Shakespeare and Spenser.

302 ———. "The Faulty Ethical System of Sir Philip Sidney." *N&Q*, 5th ser. 9 (19 January 1878):48.
Asks why Gifford's edition of Jonson refers to Sidney's "faulty ethical system" as the basis for Jonson's "Come My Celia."

303 ———. Review of *The Correspondence of Sir Philip Sidney and Hubert Languet*, edited by Steuart A. Pears. *British Quarterly Review* 5 (1 February 1847):119–48.
Focuses on the character and writings of Languet, providing a history of manuscripts and editions of his correspondence with Sidney and of the relationship between the two men. Also reviews scholarship on Sidney and summarizes his career, rejecting the myth that he was a candidate for the crown of Poland. Defends *Arcadia* from the attacks of Walpole (294) and examines the merits of *Astrophil and Stella* and its biographical background.

304 ———. Review of *The Miscellaneous Works of Sir Philip Sidney*, edited by William Gray. *Southern Review* 5 (May 1830):295–318.
Appraises Sidney's life and works, faulting *Astrophil and Stella* for sensuality and for imitating Petrarch's faults rather than his virtues.

305 ———. Review of *Sir Philip Sidney and the "Arcadia"*, by James Crossley. *Athenaeum*, no. 1367, 5 January 1854, pp. 7–8.
Compares Sidney with the French soldier Bayard and with Sir Walter Ralegh. Seeks to explain the decline in the popularity of Sidney's works during the seventeenth century.

306 ———. "Sir Philip Sidney." *Edinburgh Review* 144 (October 1876):370–406. Reprint. In *Living Age*, 5th ser. 16 (18 November 1876):387–406.
Surveys Sidney's life and works. Evaluates stylistic features of *The Lady of May*, *Arcadia*, and *Astrophil and Stella*, commenting on the metrical experiments of the Areopagus. Also suggests that apostrophes to sleep in Shakespeare's *II Henry IV* and *Macbeth* and in Edward Young's *Night*

Nineteenth Century

Thoughts owe something to the sonnet "Come sleep, O sleep" (*AS 39*). Defends Sidney from charges of immorality over his love of Penelope Rich, identifying her with Philoclea in *Arcadia*.

307 ———. "Sir Philip Sidney." *Hogg's Instructor* 7 (1851):213–15.
Summarizes Sidney's life and works.

308 ———. "Sir Philip Sidney." *[Knight's] Penny Magazine* 8 (30 September 1839):380–82.
Reviews Sidney's life and works, praising his prose style and attributing his failure to win advancement after 1577 to Burghley's "expressed policy of 'suppressing able men.'"

309 ———. "Sir Philip Sidney." *National Quarterly Review* [New York] 5 (June 1862):118–34.
Reviews Sidney's life and political troubles. Evaluates his works, defending *Arcadia* from Walpole (294) and Hazlitt (359) and arguing that his love for Lady Rich was not improper.

310 ———. "Sir Philip Sidney." *North American Review* 88 (April 1859):312–40.
In reviewing the 1622 *Arcadia*, Gray's *Miscellaneous Works* (16), Greville's *Life* (863), and Davis's *Life* (920), discounts *The Lady of May*, praises the *Letter to the Queen*, sees the tennis-court quarrel with Oxford as the reason for Sidney's retirement to Wilton, condemns *Arcadia* and *Astrophil and Stella* on moral and literary grounds (identifying Stella and Philoclea with Penelope Rich), and praises the *Defence*. Concludes with condemnation of Sidney for his affair with Penelope Rich.

311 ———. "Sir Philip Sidney." *The Speaker* 8 (18 November 1893):555–56.
Praises Sidney as "the best educated poet who ever drew breath in England." Counters Hazlitt's condemnation of *Arcadia* (in 359) with Lamb's defense (2041) and praises *Astrophil and Stella*.

312 ———. "Sir Philip Sidney." *Spectator* 60 (15 January 1887):83–84.
Reviews Sidney's life and works.

313 ———. "Sir Philip Sidney." *University of Virginia Magazine* 3 (March 1859):307–16.
Admires Sidney's life and works.

314 ———. "Sir Philip Sidney." *University of Virginia Magazine* 19 (January 1880):205–7.
Praises Sidney as an ideal, but remarks that, despite some fine passages, *Arcadia* "has long since ceased to be read" and the love poems have "sunk into the oblivion they merited."

315 ———. "Sir Philip Sidneys Ourania." *The Philobiblion* 2 (December 1863):270–73.
Supports the view that Nathaniel Baxter, Sidney's one-time tutor, was the author of *Ourania* and not Nicholas Breton.

316 ———. Untitled article. *National Quarterly Review* 5 (June 1862):118–34.
Beginning with a review of Davis's *Life* (920) and the 1724 *Works* (13), condemns *Arcadia* roundly, views the *Defence* as Sidney's best work, and dismisses *Astrophil and Stella*.

317 BLISS, PHILIP, ed. *Antenae Oxonienses: An Exact History of All the Writers and Bishops Who Have Had Their Education in the University of Oxford. To Which Are Added the Fasti, or Annals of the Said University*, by Anthony à Wood. Vol 1. London: F.C. & J. Rivington et al., 1813, cols. 517–25.
Adds various manuscripts to the list of Sidney's works in Wood (284). Also considers acquaintances of the poet, such as William Temple, Thomas Thornton, Richard Carew, and James Perrot. Mentions works dedicated to Sidney and extant portraits of him, and attributes to him a poem, "Ah, poor love! Why dost thou live" (*AT* 5), which Ringler (92) ascribes to Nicholas Breton.

318 BOURNE, H[ENRY] R[ICHARD] FOX. *A Memoir of Sir Philip Sidney*. London: Chapman & Hall, 1862, 573 pp.
Examines Sidney's life and works, consulting many previously unexamined documents, particularly those in the State Papers Office, and quoting extensively from Sidney's correspondence. In Chapters 1–2, considers Penshurst, Sidney's ancestors and parents, and his rearing through the period at Shrewsbury School. Proves that Sidney entered Oxford a year earlier than had been previously supposed and fills out the picture of his relations with Sir William Cecil and the projected marriage to Anne Cecil. Also discusses his companions at Oxford, including Greville, Dyer, Carew, Camden, and Hakluyt. In Chapter 3, details his experiences and contacts during the Continental tour of 1572–75, focusing on the St. Bartholomew's Day Massacre, his friendship with Languet, and his literary and political interests. In Chapters 4–9, considers his royal

Nineteenth Century

service from 1575 through 1579, examining his relations with the earls of Essex and Leicester and his proposed marriage to Penelope Devereux. Establishes his presence at the festivities for the Queen at Kenilworth and Chartley in 1575 and proves that he traveled to Ireland in 1576. Recovers his treatise on Ireland and the Queen's instructions for his embassy to Germany in 1577, detailing his movements during that trip and his diplomatic contacts with William of Orange and Don John of Austria. Demonstrates that he attempted to sail to America as a colonist and supplies letters by Cecil and Walsingham about his later career and his parents' relations with the Queen. Reviews his connections with important figures at court in 1578–79, including Hatton, Sackville, Walsingham, and Knollys. Also examines his literary "training," stressing the influence of Roger Ascham, considering his ties to Spenser and Gabriel Harvey, their interest in establishing a new school of English poetry, and Sidney's early experiment, *The Lady of May*. In Chapters 10–11, takes up Sidney's quarrel with the Earl of Oxford and its connections with Elizabeth's negotiations to marry Alençon, citing evidence that Oxford laid secret plans to have Sidney murdered. Examines the *Letter to the Queen* and its political context, Sidney's retirement from court in 1580, his stay at Wilton with his sister, his return to court, his service in Parliament, his role in the presentation of *Four Foster Children of Desire* before the French ambassadors in 1581, and his trip to Antwerp in 1582. Stresses the discontent with life at court evident in his correspondence with Languet, comparing his public service to Elizabeth with his private devotion to Penelope Rich. In considering his literary work in this period, weighs the faults of *Arcadia* and discusses its debt to Montemayor's *Diana*. Compares its style with euphuism, rejecting allegorical interpretations and stressing its moral teachings. Also criticizes the style of *Astrophil and Stella*. In Chapters 12–14, examines the period 1583–85, including the circumstances in which Sidney was knighted, his marriage, his projects involving America and the West Indies, and his involvement with affairs in Ireland and Scotland. Considers his role as a patron, his translation of Mornay's *Trueness of the Christian Religion*, and his composition of the *Defence of Poetry*, suggesting that George Puttenham and William Webbe read the latter in manuscript before writing their own critical treatises. In Chapters 15–16, records Sidney's opposition to Leicester and the Queen during his service as Governor of Flushing. Details his role in the battles of Axel and Zutphen, his death and burial, and the national mourning that accompanied it. Includes a detailed index of names and subjects discussed, including a chronology of Sidney's life. For an extensively revised version, see item 319. See also items 891, 893 and Long (632), Gordon (931), and Lloyd (949).

319 ———. *Sir Philip Sidney: Type of English Chivalry in the Elizabethan Age*. Heroes of the Nations, 5. New York and London: G.P. Putnam's Sons, Knickerbocker Press, 1891, 402 pp.

An extensively revised version of item 318, augmented with new research, frequently altered in emphasis, and rewritten to fit the format of the Heroes of the Nations series. Adds twenty-seven illustrations, including depictions of Sidney, his family and friends; sketches of his homes and surroundings; and samples of his signature. In Chapter 1, traces his ancestry, identifying him with examples of medieval and Renaissance chivalry. In Chapters 2 and 3, provides details of his education, giving information about his parents and their relations with Leicester and Queen Elizabeth and discussing his appointment at age ten to a living as lay rector in the parish church of Whitford in Wales. Touches on his school days at Shrewsbury and provides details of his studies at Oxford, including his companions there, his relations with Leicester and Sir William Cecil, and proposed marriages to Anne Cecil and a daughter of Lord Berkeley. In Chapters 4 and 5, surveys Sidney's European tour of 1572–75, including his participation in the Earl of Lincoln's embassy to France, his experiences after the St. Bartholomew's Day massacre, and his relationship with Languet. In Chapters 6 and 7, considers Sidney's relations with men prominent in the English court, his participation in the Kenilworth entertainment for the Queen, his visit to Ireland, and proposals that he marry Penelope Devereux. Discusses Sidney's 1577 embassy to Germany, his hopes for a Protestant League, and his contacts with figures such as John Casimir and William of Orange. In Chapters 8–10, examines Sidney's "Discourse on Irish Affairs," his friendship with du Plessis-Mornay, his argument with Molyneux, and his attendance on the Queen, including his presentation of the *Lady of May*. Describes Sidney's interest in the Americas, his *Letter to the Queen*, and the quarrel with Oxford and retirement from court. In Chapters 11–12, considers Sidney's early literary interests, including his acquaintance with the actors Robert Langham and Richard Tarleton and his connection with the Areopagus. Examines his retirement to Wilton and the composition of *Arcadia*. In Chapter 13, looks at Sidney's return to regal favor in the period between 1580 and 1582, recounting details of his financial difficulties, his role in *Four Foster Children of Desire* and the return of the French delegation to Antwerp, and his response to the death of Languet. In providing a biographical reading of *Astrophil and Stella*, corrects the date of Penelope Devereux's marriage to Lord Rich, which occurred in 1581. In Chapter 14, which analyzes Sidney's place in the literary history of England, argues that the *Defence*, *Arcadia*, and *Astrophil and Stella* "are chiefly useful in showing him as a courtier and a

Nineteenth Century

politician, a representative of the chivalrous thought" of his day. In Chapters 15–16, deals with the facts of Sidney's marriage, his association with Giordano Bruno, and his continuing interest in American colonization between 1582 and 1585. Discusses his abortive embassy to France in 1584 and other diplomatic affairs involving Scotland, Spain, and the Netherlands. Touches on his appointment as Master of the Ordnance, his involvement with Sir Francis Drake, and his appointment as Governor of Flushing. In Chapters 17–19, examines his role in the Netherlands, his chivalry on the battlefield, and his death. Comments on the widespread mourning for Sidney, relating it to contemporary opinion that he was the supreme embodiment of Elizabethan chivalry. See also Long (632).

320 BRADLEY, JOHN W. "Benefactors: No. XLVII—Sir Philip Sidney." *Social Notes* 3 (16 August 1879):370–72.
Repeats legends about Sidney and evaluates *Arcadia*.

321 BROWN, T.E. "Sir Philip Sidney: A Causerie." *New Review* 12 (April 1895):415–24.
Praises Sidney's life and attainments.

322 BROWNE, C. ELLIOT. "On Shakespeare's Pastoral Name." *N&Q*, 4th ser. 12 (27 December 1873):509–10.
Suggests that, in Henry Chettle's discussion of Queen Elizabeth's anti-Spanish policy in *England's Mourning Garment*, the name "Philisides" refers to Sidney. See also Nicholson (378, 379).

323 [BRYDGES, Sir SAMUEL EGERTON.] "Memoir of Sir Philip Sidney." In *The British Bibliographer*, edited by [Samuel] Egerton Brydges. Vol. 1. London: R. Triphook, 1810, pp. 81–105, 289–95.
Rehearses Sidney's life, comparing his verse with that of Thomas Sackville's "Induction" to *A Mirror for Magistrates*. Provides bibliographic information and defends Sidney from the attacks of Walpole (294). In passing, prints two sonnets on Penshurst by Brydges and Charlotte Smith that allude briefly to Sidney.

324 [BUTLER], S[AMUEL, Bishop of] Lichfield, ed. *Sidneiana, Being a Collection of Fragments Relative to Sir Philip Sidney Knt. and His Immediate Connections*. London: Roxburghe Club, 1837, 125 pp.
Prints the following: two pieces of Sidney's correspondence (see item 174); a register of scholars at Shrewsbury School (164); the epitaph on Fulke Greville's tomb, which ends with mention of his friendship with

Sidney; William Gryffyth's elegy on Sidney's father; John Philip's "Life, Death, and Funerals of Sir Philip Sidney Knight" (2767); Thomas Churchyard's "Epitaph of Sir Philip Sidney" (2751); Nicholas Breton's "Amoris Lachrymae" (2748); five of the Sidney Psalms (from a hitherto unpublished source, now British Museum MS. Add. 12047); excerpts from *Academiae Cantabrigiensis Lachrymae* (2765); excerpts from *Exequiae Illustrissimi Equitis D. Philippi Sidnaei* (2760); Arthur Collins's account of Sidney's funeral (12); a letter by John Payne Collier (913); a letter from Sir Arthur Basset to Sir Edward Stradlinge on a harp player recommended to Sidney; and an unpublished "memorial" from Thomas Nevitt to Sidney's brother, detailing the estate inherited by Robert from Sir Henry and Sir Philip Sidney and ways in which Robert had used his resources.

325 BUTTERWORTH, WALTER. "Sir Philip Sidney and His *Arcadia.*" *Papers of the Manchester Literary Club* 23 (1897):266–88.
Summarizes Sidney's life and discusses the sources and merits of *Arcadia*.

326 C[ARTWRIGHT, ROBERT.] "The *Faerie Queen* Unveiled." *N&Q,* 3d ser. 4 (11 July 1863):21–22; (25 July 1863):65–66; (8 August 1863):101–3.
Sees the career of Red Cross Knight in Book I of Spenser's *Faerie Queene* as a detailed allegory of Sidney's career at court. Feels that Book II contains a satire of *Arcadia* in which Pyrocles is Sidney's Pyrocles (Sidney himself seeking employment at court). Suggests that Sidney appears again in Book VI in the persons of Calidore and his squire.

327 ——. "'Juliet' Unveiled." *N&Q,* 3d ser. 4 (5 September 1863):181–83.
Claims that *Romeo and Juliet* is an allegory in which Juliet is Sidney's muse, Benvolio is Sidney, and Mercutio is Thomas Nashe. Also lists various sonnets of Shakespeare that may have been written under Sidney's influence, and supports the view that Sidney is "our pleasant Willy" in Spenser's *Tears of the Muses*.

328 CARTWRIGHT, ROBERT. *Papers on Shakspere.* London: John Russell Smith, 1877, pp. 18–25.
Suggests that Stella is not Penelope Rich but "the poet's muse of chivalry" and "in some sense" Frances Walsingham. In *Arcadia*, equates Parthenia with Lady Rich, her lover Argalus with Charles Blount, and Philoclea with Frances Walsingham. Without considering the dates of publication, surmises that some of Shakespeare's advice to the young man of the *Sonnets* is based on Languet's letters to Sidney.

Nineteenth Century

329 C[ARTWRIGHT, ROBERT]. "Shakespeare, Sidney, and Essex."
N&Q, 3d ser. 3 (31 January 1863):82–84; (7 February
1863):103–6; (14 February 1863):124–26.
A single essay published in three parts with the general aim of establishing correspondences between characters in Shakespeare's plays and various public figures of the day, including many in the Sidney circle. Parts
1 and 2 concentrate on *Hamlet*, arguing that the title figure represents
Sidney, that Polonius is Lord Burghley, etc. Part 2 also finds that
Valentine in *Two Gentlemen of Verona* "thinly veils" Sidney and that
Pericles expresses Shakespeare's "love and admiration for the gentle and
heroic character of Sidney." Part 3 contends that *Love's Labor's Lost* was
"in some manner founded on *The Lady of May*" and that the Montague-
Capulet feud in *Romeo and Juliet* pictures the same Burghley-Leicester
rivalry portrayed in *Hamlet*, with Sidney cast as Benvolio. See a response
by Dempewolf (501).

330 CARY, HENRY. *Memoir of the Rev. Henry Francis Cary, M.A.,
Translator of Dante. With His Literary Journal and Letters*. Vol. 2.
London: Edward Moxon, 1847, p. 279.
Notes that, just before Charles Lamb died, he turned down a leaf at the
account of Sidney's death in Phillips (281). Quotes the elder Carey's
"Lines to the Memory of Charles Lamb" (2814), which compares Lamb's
generosity with Sidney's giving of his cup to a soldier at Zutphen.

331 C[HAPIN?], E.H. "Sir Philip Sydney." *Universalist Quarterly and
General Review* 2 (1845):291–312.
Summarizes Sidney's life, works, and reputation.

332 CHURCH, R[ICHARD] W[ILLIAM]. *Spenser*. English Men of
Letters. New York: Harper & Brothers, 1879, pp. 23, 24, 47,
104–7, 157–59.
While acknowledging that Sidney gave Spenser assistance at court, suggests that the two men were not close. Feels that Sidney "led Spenser
astray" by inducing him to "waste his time on the artificial versifying
which was the vogue." Comments on references to Sidney in *The Ruins of
Time*, *The Tears of the Muses*, and *The Faerie Queene*, identifying Sidney
with Calidore and Frances Walsingham with Pastorella.

333 COLLIER, J[OHN] PAYNE, ed. "The Life of Spenser." In *The
Works of Edmund Spenser*. Vol. 1. London: Bell & Daldy, 1862, pp.
xxix–xxxii, xxxvii–xxxviii, xlviii, lii–lvi, cx.
Discusses Sidney's acquaintance with Spenser and the quantitative verse
experiments of the Areopagus. Criticizes the remarks on the *Shepherd's*

Calendar in Sidney's *Defence* and discusses George Whetstone's mistake (in 2776) in attributing the *Calendar* to Sidney. Ponders the authorship of the elegies for Sidney printed at the end of Spenser's *Colin Clout's Come Home Again* (items 2740, 2741, 2749, 2768, 2770, 2771), pointing out that, in Harington's translation of *Orlando furioso* (2364), the "Epitaph upon the Right Honourable Sir Philip Sidney Knight" is attributed to Sir Walter Ralegh. Notes Greville's early plans to publish *Arcadia* and transcribes his letter to Walsingham of November 1586. Also argues against Zouch (974) about the date on which Sidney was made Master of the Ordnance. Prints excerpts from the Stationers' Register on *Arcadia* and Sidney's lost translation of du Bartas's *Semaine*.

334 COLLIER, J[OHN] PAYNE. *The Poetical Decameron, or Ten Conversations on English Poets and Poetry, Particularly of the Reigns of Elizabeth and James I.* 2 vols. Edinburgh: Archibald Constable & Co.; London: Hurst, Robinson, & Co., 1820, 1:62–69; 2:50–54, 103–6, 141–44.

Quotes from George Whetstone's poem on Sidney's death (2776), noting Whetstone's mistaken attribution of *The Shepherd's Calendar* to Sidney and claiming that *Arcadia* must have circulated in manuscript before its publication. From Harington's translation of Ariosto, quotes "Who doth desire that chaste his wife should be" (*OA 65*) and questions its omission from the "printed book." Notes allusions to Sidney in Stafford's *Niobe Dissolved* and in Wither's *Satires* II.iii. Also discusses John Philip's 1587 poem on Sidney (2767); notes Thomas Churchyard's use (in his *True Discourse*) of Whetstone's description of Sidney's wounding at Zutphen; and queries the existence of Raleigh's epitaph on Sidney, which is mentioned by Harington in the notes to Book xvi of *Orlando furioso*.

335 ———. "The Registers of the Stationers' Company." *N&Q,* 2d ser. 12 (10 August 1861):101–2.

Reproduces Ponsonby's entries in the Register (on 23 August 1588) for Sidney's *Arcadia* and his lost translation of *La semaine* by du Bartas. Comments on the publication history of *Arcadia* and notes that John Florio mentions the translation of du Bartas in the introduction to his translation of Bacon's *Essays.*

336 ———. "The Registers of the Stationers' Company." *N&Q,* 2d ser. 12 (24 August 1861):142–44.

Acknowledges the association of the pastoral name "Willy" with Sidney but concludes that the funeral ballad "Peggy's Complaint for the Death of Her Willy" is not for him.

Nineteenth Century

337 COOK, ALBERT S. "Sidney and Giordano Bruno." *MLN* 8 (March 1893):186–87.
Rebuts scholars who believe that Bruno exerted no influence on Sidney. For evidence, refers to Cook's own edition of the *Defence* (105).

338 COURTHOPE, WILLIAM J[OHN]. *A History of English Poetry.* Vol. 2, *The Renaissance and the Reformation: Influence of the Court and the Universities.* London: Macmillan & Co., 1897, pp. 203–33, 250–51, 294, 306.
Recounts Sidney's life and regards his works as expressions of the conflict between the medievalism of Elizabeth's court and the renaissance taking place outside. Examines *Arcadia*, considering its genre, its sources, its merits, and its autobiographical content. Notes the influence on later writers and dramatists exerted by Sidney's female characters, his Arcadian setting, and his plots. Uses external and internal evidence to argue that *Astrophil and Stella* is highly conventional and does not prove that Sidney loved Lady Rich. Credits Sidney with introducing iambic tetrameter to England.

339 CRAIK, GEORGE L[ILLIE]. *Sketches of the History of Literature and Learning in England with Specimens of the Principal Writers. Series Second: From the Accession of Elizabeth to the Revolution of 1688.* Vol. 3. London: Charles Knight, 1845, pp. 57–70 passim.
Covers Sidney's life and works and his association with the Areopagus.

340 CUNNINGHAM, GEORGE GODFREY, ed. *Lives of Eminent and Illustrious Englishmen from Alfred the Great to the Latest Times.* Vol. 2. Glasgow: A. Fullarton & Co., 1836, pp. 260–65.
Summarizes Sidney's life and evaluates the merits of *Arcadia*, the *Defence*, and the poetry, finding "least pleasure" in the last.

341 DISRAELI, I[SAAC]. *Amenities of Literature, Consisting of Sketches and Characters of English Literature.* Vol. 2. London: Edward Moxon, 1841, pp. 352–65.
In "Sir Philip Sidney," evaluates his life and major prose works, defending *Arcadia* against Walpole (294) and Hazlitt (359). Points to the influence of the romance on Shakespeare and other Renaissance poets. Also discusses its descriptions and characters (especially the women), its spirit of chivalry, its narrative diversity, and its diction. Faults the comic elements and the poetry. See also item 1346.

Nineteenth Century

342 DRAKE, NATHAN. *Mornings in Spring; or Retrospections, Biographical, Critical, and Historical.* Vol. 1. London: John Murray, 1828, pp. 113–50, 151–210 passim.

Provides a memoir of Sidney and his sister, emphasizing the development of Sidney's mind and character. Cites poetic and artistic renditions of his death. Also considers the merits of *Arcadia*, emphasizing the role of Mary Sidney in revising it and suggesting that her judgment may have influenced his other works. Discusses manuscripts of the Psalms, providing evidence that the first forty-three are by Sidney and noting the attention that they have received from other writers.

343 ELLIS, ALEXANDER J. *On Early English Pronunciation, with Special Reference to Shakspere and Chaucer.* Part 3, *Illustrations of the Pronunciation of the XIVth and XVIth Centuries: Chaucer, Gower, Wycliffe, Spenser, Shakspere, Salisbury, Barcley, Hart, Bullokar, Gill.* The Chaucer Society, 2d ser., no. 5. London and Berlin: Philological Society, Asher & Co.; London: Early English Text Society, Chaucer Society, Trübner & Co., 1871, pp. 872–74.

Provides an alphabetical listing and commentary for the rhymes in Sidney's Psalms, noting the liberties taken by the poet. Also prints three extracts from *Arcadia* marked with Alexander Gill's phonetic symbols (as published in 1621).

344 ELTON, OLIVER. *An Introduction to Michael Drayton.* Manchester: J.E. Cornish, 1895, pp. 12, 54–55, 57.

Sketches Sidney's influence on Drayton, particularly seen in *Idea's Mirror* and the *Legends*. Notes the lament for Sidney in the Fourth Eclogue of *Idea, or The Shepherd's Garland* (2758) and lists allusions to him and to *Arcadia* elsewhere in Drayton's poetry.

345 FLÜGEL, EWALD. *Sir Philip Sidney.* Halle, Germany: Max Niemeyer, 1888, 91 pp.

Provides a detailed biography of Sidney, documented from original sources. Argues against a close friendship between Sidney and Spenser, and weighs the probabilities that Lady Rich loved Sidney. Discusses the composition of *Arcadia* and its faults in style and characterization. Also examines the ideal of the poet in the *Defence*. In a section entitled "Die Überlieferung der Sonette von *Astrophel and Stella*," provides a descriptive bibliography of the Bright Manuscript, the 1591 quartos, the 1598 folio of *Arcadia* and the poetry, and all subsequents editions through 1888. Weighs evidence and possible explanations for the fact that the Bright Manuscript has greater affinities with the 1598 folio than with the

Nineteenth Century

1591 quartos. For the three printed texts, provides quasifacsimile title-page transcriptions, notes on extant copies, and lists of variants.

346 FREEMAN, R[OWLAND]. *Kentish Poets: A Series of Writers in English Poetry, Natives or Residents in the County of Kent, etc.* Vol. 1. Canterbury: G. Wood, 1821, pp. 79–138.

Provides a life of Sidney and selections from Sidney's works. In discussing *Arcadia*, links Philoclea with Penelope Rich. Also notes an allusion to Sidney in a poem by Christopher Smart.

347 GARNETT, JAMES M. "Notes on Elizabethan Prose." *PMLA* 4 (1889):41–61.

Analyzes the merits and faults of Sidney's prose style.

348 GREAT BRITAIN. HISTORICAL MANUSCRIPTS COMMISSION. *First Report of the Royal Commission on Historical Manuscripts.* London: Her Majesty's Stationery Office, 1870, pp. 47–48, 62.

Among manuscripts at Tabley House, Cheshire, notes copies of Sidney's letters to his brother Robert concerning travel and his *Letter to the Queen.* Also notes a copy of Gifford's "Manner of Sir Philip Sidney's Death" (930) among manuscripts belonging to John Harvey.

349 ———. *Third Report of the Royal Commission on Historical Manuscripts.* London: Her Majesty's Stationery Office, 1872, pp. xvi, 119, 200, 204, 227, 230, 291, 297.

Contains reports of the manuscript collections of the Duke of Northumberland, the Marquis of Bute, the Lord de L'Isle and Dudley, R.E. Edgerton-Warburton, and M. Wilson. Included are several letters from Sidney (including the *Letter to the Queen*), a tailor's bill, and a reference to "Sir Philip Sidney's song" prefixed to Act 4, Scene 3 of a play *Chaunge is no Robberye.* Among the de L'Isle documents are "many volumes of letters to the Sidneys . . . not used by Collins" (12), some cancelled bonds for money borrowed at home and abroad, and a manuscript of the *Defence,* "beautifully written."

350 ———. *Fourth Report of the Royal Commission on Historical Manuscripts.* London: Her Majesty's Stationery Office, 1874, pp. xiii, xiv, xv, 210, 220, 221, 223, 224, 252, 253, 303, 352, 361, 595.

Contains descriptions of the manuscript collections of the Marquis of Salisbury, the Marquis of Hertford, the Earl de la Ware, Lord Mostyn, and Trinity College, Dublin. These include "settlements" for the proposed marriage of Sidney and Anne Cecil; letters from Sidney to Cecil and to Patrick, Master of Gray; two copies of *Letter to the Queen*; three poems to Sidney from Daniel Rogers (2828); a petition by "Mons. Journall" claiming to have translated *Arcadia*; and letters from Sidney to his brother Robert.

351 ——. *Sixth Report of the Royal Commission on Historical Manuscripts*. London: Her Majesty's Stationery Office, 1877, pp. 227a, 343a, 350a.

In reporting the manuscripts of the Duke of Northumberland, Sir Reginald Graham, and Sir Alexander Acland-Hood, notes the purchase in February 1587 of *The Life and Death of Sir Philip Sidney* (probably item 2767) and a copy of Sidney's *Letter to the Queen*. Also lists verses "Upon Sir Philip Sidney's *Defence of Poesie*," described as "sixteen lines, beginning 'The authors name doth that rare book commend'" (not located in print).

352 ——. *Eighth Report of the Royal Commission on Historical Manuscripts*. London: Her Majesty's Stationery Office, 1881, Part 1:585a; Part 2:13b, 33a.

Three parts in one volume, separately paginated and indexed. Notes a copy of the *Letter to the Queen*, a holograph letter of 14 August 1586, and a Sidney family genealogy dating from 1714.

353 ——. *Ninth Report of the Royal Commission on Historical Manuscripts*. London: Her Majesty's Stationery Office, 1883, Part 2:362a.

In three parts, separately paginated and indexed. Notes in the collection of the Earl of Leicester at Holkam Hall, Norfolk, a seventeenth-century collection of epigrams, *Thomae Porteri de Hemell ministri Epigrammata*, which contains an epigram on Sidney. No printed collection by this title was located.

354 GREEN, HENRY, ed. *Whitney's "Choice of Emblemes"*, by Geffrey Whitney. London: Lovell Reeve & Co., 1866, pp. 38, 109–10, 311, 323–26.

In reprinting Whitney's emblem "Non locus virum, sed vir locum ornat," which is dedicated to Sidney, suggests that he learned about the Italian *imprese* through Ruscelli, whose *Imprese illustri* is mentioned in one of the letters to Languet. Notes the prominent use of *imprese* in *Arcadia* and on Sidney's own armor. See also Whitney (2777).

355 GROSART, ALEXANDER B., ed. "Life of Spenser" and Appendix 1, "Spenser's Friendship with Sir Philip Sidney." In *The*

Nineteenth Century

> *Complete Works in Verse and Prose of Edmund Spenser*. Vol. 1.
> London and Aylesbury, England: Hazell, Watson, & Viney, 1882,
> pp. 64–68, 99, 130, 443–56.

Speculates that Spenser's lost Psalms were intended for the collection by
Sidney and his sister and that Spenser visited Wilton in late 1579 or
early 1580. From passages in Spenser's works, concludes that he and
Sidney were intimate and passionate friends and that Spenser dominated Sidney. Suggests that the *Defence* was not published for several years
because it incorporated material from Spenser's lost treatise, *The English
Poet*.

356 HANNAY, DAVID. *Periods in European Literature*. Edited by
[George] Saintsbury. Vol. 6, *The Later Renaissance*. New York:
Charles Scribner's Sons, 1898, pp. 37–38, 200–204, 269–72.

Compares Sidney's *Defence* with Juan de la Cueba's *Egemplar poético* and
Joachim du Bellay's *Défense et illustration de la langue française*. Discusses
the merits and faults of Sidney's poetry and prose, likening *Arcadia* to
the Spanish *Libros de caballerías*, which Sidney had read. Suggests that the
style of *Arcadia* resembles that of Feliciano de Silva.

357 HARINGTON, Sir JOHN. *A Tract on the Succession to the Crown
(A.D. 1602)*. Edited by Clements R. Markham. London:
Roxburghe Club, J.B. Nichols & Sons, 1880, pp. 77–78, 89.

Includes a variant of the sonnet "Of all the kings that ever here did
reign" (*AS 75*), claiming that it genuinely praises Edward IV for his
nobility. Also quotes *Arcadia* in pondering the sort of courage needed in
a successor to Queen Elizabeth.

358 HART, JOHN S[EELY]. *An Essay on the Life and Writing of Edmund
Spenser, with a Special Exposition of "The Fairy Queen"*. New York
and London: Wiley & Putnam, 1847, pp. 31–36, 54–56, 66–67,
104–5.

Comments on Harvey's instrumental role in bringing Sidney and
Spenser together. Also considers the quantitative verse experiments of
the Areopagus and Spenser's allusions to Sidney in *The Ruins of Time*,
Mother Hubberd's Tale, and *Astrophel*.

359 HAZLITT, WILLIAM. *Lectures Chiefly on the Dramatic Literature of
the Age of Elizabeth*. London: Stodart & Steuart, 1820, pp. 265–78.
Reprinted in item 558.

Appraises Sidney as "one of the ablest men and worst writers of the age
of Elizabeth." Condemns the plot of *Arcadia* and rejects the style because
it is "not romantic, but scholastic; not poetry, but casuistry; not nature,

but art." Also attacks *Astrophil and Stella* for its "verbal intricacies and 'thorny queaches.'" Admits that the *Defence* provided Sidney a proper occasion for his "scholastic subtlety." See anonymous responses (309, 311) and replies by Adams (1338), Disraeli (341), Nicoll (380), Crossley (1351), and Kingsley (1370). See also item 558.

360 HENLEY, W[ILLIAM] E[RNEST]. "Sidney." In *Views and Reviews: Essays in Appreciation*. London: David Nutt, 1890, pp. 104–5.

Claims that Sidney's "expression of life" as reflected in *Astrophil and Stella* and *Arcadia* is thin and contrived: "his intellectual life, intense though it were, was lived among shadows and abstractions."

361 HIPPISLEY, J.H. *Chapters on Early English Literature*. London: E. Moxon, 1837, pp. 249–50.

Finds little merit in Sidney's works but admires his character.

362 HUNT, LEIGH. "A Jar of Honey from Mount Hybla," no. 7. *Ainsworth's Magazine* 6 (July 1844):79–86.

Equates Sidney with Sir Calidore in Book VI of *The Faerie Queene*. Suggests that, when Spenser's character Colin Clout breaks his bagpipe, the allegorical meaning is that Spenser is giving up pastoral poetry in reaction to the strictures in the *Defence* against the language of *The Shepherd's Calendar*.

363 HUNTER, JOSEPH. *New Illustrations of the Life, Studies, and Writings of Shakespeare*. 2 vols. London: J.B. Nichols & Son, 1845, 1:354; 2:225, 273.

Argues that the "N.B." who wrote *Sir Philip Sidney's Ourania* was not Nicholas Breton, as scholars had supposed, but Sidney's tutor Nathaniel Baxter. In explaining Hamlet's "tables" recalls the story (recounted by John Aubrey) that Sidney gathered ideas for *Arcadia* in a "table-book" while he hunted. Also comments on Shakespeare's borrowing of the cliff scene in *King Lear* from Sidney's romance.

364 JOHNSTONE, PHILIP H. *The Age of Chivalry: Scenes from the Lives of the Chevalier Bayard and Sir Philip Sidney*. London: Marcus Ward & Co., 1890, pp. 115–75.

Not seen. According to a transcript of the table of contents, Chapters 8–12 examine the life of Sidney as a scholar and student, as a courtier and statesman, as a poet and author, and as a governor and soldier in the Netherlands.

365 JONSON, BEN. *Notes of Ben Jonson's Conversations with William Drummond of Hawthornden. January M.DC.XIX.* Edited by David

Nineteenth Century

> Laing. Shakespeare Society of London Publications, vol. 17, no. 8.
> London: Shakespeare Society, 1842, pp. 2, 10, 15–17, 23, 26.
> Reprint. In *Ben Jonson*, edited by C.H. Herford and Percy
> Simpson. Vol. 1, *The Man and his Work*. Oxford: Clarendon Press,
> 1925, pp. 132, 136–39, 142, 149.

Criticizes Sidney because he "did not keep a decorum in making everyone speak as well as himself." Mentions Sidney's unfulfilled intention to
transform *Arcadia* into a heroic work about King Arthur and states the
opinion of King James I that "Sidney was no poet." Among other allusions, records Jonson's comment that "Sidney was no pleasant man in
countenance, his face being spoiled with pimples and of high blood and
long."

366 KOEPPEL, E[MIL]. "Sidneiana." *Anglia* 10 (1887):522–32. [Title
  page of the volume mistakenly gives the date as 1888.]

In the first printed clue that a version of *Arcadia* remained undiscovered
among unpublished manuscripts of Sidney's works, records numerous
discrepancies between the 1598 texts of *Arcadia* and *Astrophil and Stella*
and the excerpts printed in Abraham Fraunce's *Arcadian Rhetoric* (271).
Points out that Fraunce was working from manuscripts. Also argues that
the pastoral name "Willy" in Fraunce's book refers to Sidney, but denies
that Sidney is the "Willy" mentioned in Spenser's *Tears of the Muses*. See,
however, Halliwell-Phillipps (221), Minto (373), and Rollins (724). See
also item 2038.

367 KRAUSS, FRITZ. "Die schwarze Schöne der Shakespeare-
  Sonette." *SJ* 16 (1881):144–212.

Discusses Philoclea's dispute with Cecropia in *Arcadia* Book III and its
influence on Shakespeare's sonnets urging the young gentleman to
marry. Supports the theory that Shakespeare's Dark Lady was Penelope
Rich and that his Young Man was Sidney's nephew, William Herbert.
Reviews the history of Sidney's relationship with Lady Rich, identifying
her both with Stella and with Philoclea. Quotes references to Stella and
to Lady Rich in elegies by Spenser, Bryskett, and others, sketching her
life and explaining her relations with Lord Herbert. Through verbal
parallels, attempts to demonstrate that Shakespeare's *Sonnets* were written with passages of *Astrophil and Stella* and *Arcadia* in mind. In Rosaline
in *Love's Labor's Lost* and in other dark Shakespearean heroines, sees
reflections of Stella. Identifies Song v of *Astrophil and Stella*, which
renounces her as a devil and a witch, as the direct source for several of
Shakespeare's most bitter sonnets.

Nineteenth Century

368 LANDMANN, F[RIEDRICH]. "Shakspere and Euphuism; Euphues an Adaption from Guevara." *New Shakspere Society's Transactions*, ser. 1 (1880–86):241–76.

Contrasts euphuism with the Latinate prose of Sidney's Rombus in *The Lady of May*. Also touches on the sources and characteristics of Sidney's Arcadian style, noting that it detracted from the popularity of euphuism. See also Schwan (1384).

369 LUCE, ALICE, ed. Introduction to *The Countess of Pembroke's "Antonie."* Litterarhistorische Forschungen, 3. Weimar, Germany: Emil Felber, 1897, pp. 6, 16–28.

Dates the beginning of *Arcadia* and the Psalms in 1580. Rejects suggestions that Sidney's sister rewrote passages of the 1593 *Arcadia*. Compares that edition with the 1590, concluding that she rearranged the poems and introduced "some few omissions and variations." Discusses extant manuscripts and editions of the Sidney Psalter, accepting the tradition that Sidney translated Psalms 1–43. Feels that Mary Herbert's translation of du Plessis-Mornay's *Excellent discours de la vie et de la mort* may have been undertaken at Sidney's suggestion. Also argues for her authorship of "The Doleful Lay of Clorinda" (2771).

370 MacDONALD, GEORGE. *England's Antiphon.* The Sunday Library for Household Reading. London: Macmillan & Co., [1868]; [Philadelphia]: Lippincott, [1869?], pp. 76–86.

Praises Sidney as the man of his age "most variously gifted" and "most in favour with queen, court, and people." Lauds the "wisdom and beauty" of *Arcadia* but faults its prose style and dismisses much of its verse because it follows "false notions of poetic composition." Finds in "Now was our heavenly vault deprived of the light" (*OA 73*) the key to all "righteous questions" of religion. Briefly analyzes a selection of the Psalms, treating several by the Countess of Pembroke as if they were by Sidney.

371 MALONE, EDMOND, ed. *The Plays and Poems of William Shakespeare, with the Corrections and Illustrations of Various Commentators: Comprehending a Life of the Poet, and an Enlarged History of the Stage.* Vol. 2. London: for F.C. & J. Rivington, T. Egerton, et al., 1821, pp. 580–82.

Suggests identities for the authors of all the elegies for Sidney printed with Spenser's *Colin Clout's Come Home Again* (2740, 2741, 2749, 2768, 2770, 2771). See also Bullen (454).

Nineteenth Century

372 MASSEY, GERALD. *Shakespeare's Sonnets, Never before Interpreted: His Private Friends Identified: Together with a Recovered Likeness of Himself.* London: Longmans, Green, & Co., 1866, pp. 36–39, 47, 59, 349–56, 359–61, 364, 382–95. Rev. ed. *The Secret Drama of Shakespeare's Sonnets Unfolded, with the Characters Identified.* London: [Longmans, Green, & Co.,] 1888.
Quotes parallel passages to support the claim that the theme of Shakespeare's "procreation sonnets" was suggested by the scene in *Arcadia* in which Cecropia urges Philoclea to marry. Argues that Shakespeare's Dark Lady was Penelope Rich and compares descriptions of her in the *Sonnets* with those in *Astrophil and Stella*. Concludes, however, that time had changed her and that, "if Penelope Rich be the lady of these sonnets, she is not the Lady Rich of Sidney's love." Treats Shakespeare's Sonnet 135 as an "echo" of Sidney's "Rich" sonnet (*AS 37*) and identifies Lady Rich with Philoclea in *Arcadia*. Discusses the relationship between Sidney and Penelope, taking a biographical approach to *Astrophil and Stella*. Also sees Lady Rich as the "Stella" of Spenser's *Astrophel.* See a response by Peterson (2325).

373 MINTO, WILLIAM. *Characteristics of English Poets from Chaucer to Shirley.* Edinburgh and London: W. Blackwood & Sons, 1874, pp. 238, 242–50, 481–83.
Praises Sidney's pastorals and the technical merit of *Astrophil and Stella*, reading the sequence autobiographically. Argues that, in Thalia's complaint in Spenser's *Tears of the Muses*, Sidney is "our pleasant Willy." See also Halliwell-Phillipps (221), Koeppel (366), and Rollins (724).

374 ———. *A Manual of English Prose Literature, Biographical and Critical, Designed Mainly to Show Characteristics of Style.* 3d ed. Edinburgh and London: William Blackwood & Sons, 1886, pp. 200–213. Orig. pub. Edinburgh: n.p., 1872 (not seen).
Sketches Sidney's life, his emotional makeup, and his critical views. Anatomizes the characteristics of his prose style.

375 MITCHELL, DONALD G[RANT]. *English Lands, Letters, and Kings.* Vol. 1, *From Celt to Tudor.* New York: Charles Scribner's Sons, 1889, pp. 230–39.
In "Philip Sidney," records biographical facts and remarks on the major works. Concludes that "it is, after all, more his personality than his books that draw our attention."

376 MORLEY, HENRY. *English Writers: An Attempt towards a History of English Literature*. Vol. 9, *Spenser and His Time*. London: Cassell & Co., 1892, pp. 115–16, 120–21, 123–45.

Notes Sidney's interest in exploration and his father's early connections with Richard Chancellor, who first opened up trade with Russia. Discusses the composition, publication, sources, and influence of *Arcadia*, contrasting its style with euphuism and noting its affinities with Spanish romances. Also provides basic information on the *Defence*, *Astrophil and Stella*, and Sidney's life.

377 NICHOLSON, BRINSLEY. "Jottings in By-Ways. I. Drayton and Sir Philip Sidney." *N&Q*, 4th ser. 12 (6 December 1873):442–43.

Against Collier's supposition (in 215) that an elegy on Sidney written by Drayton has been lost, argues that it is to be found in the Fourth Eclogue of *Idea, or The Shepherd's Garland* (2758). Notes that, although the eclogue was not published until 1593, it may have been composed several years earlier.

378 ———. "On Shakespeare's Pastoral Name." *N&Q*, 5th ser. 1 (7 February 1874):109–11.

Confirms the assumption of Browne (322) that the name "Philisides" in Henry Chettle's *England's Mourning Garment* means Sidney, not Shakespeare. See also item 379.

379 ———. "'Philisides.'" *N&Q*, 5th ser. 8 (13 October 1877):286.

Adds a further proof that Philisides is Sidney. See item 378.

380 NICOLL, HENRY J[AMES]. *Landmarks of English Literature*. New York: D. Appleton, 1883, pp. xiv, 58–62.

Praises *Arcadia*, noting Hazlitt's censure of it (in 359). Reads *Astrophil and Stella* biographically and praises the *Defence*, particularly for its style.

381 PARK, THOMAS, ed. *A Catalogue of the Royal and Noble Authors of England, Scotland, and Ireland; with Lists of their Works*, by Horace Walpole, Earl of Orford. Vol. 2. London: John Scott, 1806, pp. 201–4, 232–36.

In notes to Walpole's article on the Countess of Pembroke, records earlier differences of opinion about the authorship of the Psalms, concluding that the Sidneys shared in the effort. Attributes to the Countess "The Doleful Lay of Clorinda" (item 2741). In notes to the article on Fulke Greville, defends Sidney from the attacks of Walpole (294), quoting the praises of many of his contemporaries. Notes, however, that Queen Elizabeth once expressed her irritation toward "that rash fellow Sidney."

Nineteenth Century

382 PAYNE, FREDERIC TAYLOR. *Essays on Sir Philip Sidney and Alfred Tennyson.* N.p. 1879, pp. 1–31.

In "Sir Philip Sidney," reviews the author's life and works.

383 PEPYS, SAMUEL. *The Diary of Samuel Pepys.* Edited by Robert Latham and William Matthews. 11 vols. London: G. Bell & Sons, 1970–1983, 6:2; 9:1, 6. Orig. pub. (extensively cut and condensed) as *Memoirs of Samuel Pepys, Esq. F.R.S., Secretary to the Admiralty in the Reigns of Charles II. and James II.; Comprising Diary from 1659 to 1669; Deciphered by the Rev. John Smith . . . from the Original Short-Hand Ms. . . .* London: Henry Colburn, 1825 (not seen).

In the entry for 2 January 1664/5, Pepys notes his anger with his wife for pointing out Nico's song about the jealous husband, "A neighbour mine not long ago" (*OA 64*). Entries for 1 and 2 January 1667/8 note his obtaining a copy of Greville's *Life*, which Pepys claims has become increasingly popular since it has been perceived that the work is an almost prophetic description of the state of Anglo-Dutch relations in the 1660s.

384 PORTER, P. BRYNBERG. "Sir Philip Sidney." *Southern Magazine* 17 (October 1875):488–97.

Reviews Sidney's life and works.

385 R., H.T. "Lady Mary Sidney and Her Writings." *Gentleman's Magazine*, n.s. 24 (August 1845):129–36; (September 1845): 254–59; (October 1845):364–70.

Recounts the education of Philip and Mary Sidney, the circumstances in which *Arcadia* and the Psalms were written, her responses to his death, and her role in preparing his works for publication. Atributes "many of the beauties" of the 1593 *Arcadia* to her revisions. Considers evidence on the extent of Sidney's contribution to the translation of the Psalms and their reputation. Also suggests that family ties led to the naming of the dramatist Philip Massinger after Sidney.

386 RUSKIN, JOHN *Fors Clavigera. Letters to the Workmen and Labourers of Great Britain.* 96 pamphlets. London: Printed for the author, by Smith, Elder & Co., Watson & Hazell, [1871–84], letters 23, 35, 53, 55, and 66. Reprint. In *The Works of Ruskin*, edited by E.T. Cook and Alexander Wedderburn. 39 vols. London: George Allen; New York: Longmans, Green & Co., 1903–12, 27:415–16, 648–59; 28:326–27, 373–75, 615–16, 625.

In discussing contemporary Evangelical values, comments on Sidney's life, on *Astrophil and Stella*, and on Psalms 8, 14, and 15. Attributes Psalm 58 to Sidney, not to his sister.

Nineteenth Century

387 SAINTSBURY, GEORGE [EDWARD BATEMAN]. *A History of Elizabethan Literature*. London and New York: Macmillan & Co., 1887, pp. 40–43, 100–105.

Faults the *Defence* for advocating adherence to the classical unities and *Arcadia* for being a poem in prose. Rejects biographical readings of *Astrophil and Stella* and praises Sidney's poetic skills.

388 SIDNEY, PHILIP [1872–1908]. "Sir Philip Sidney." In *Memoirs of the Sidney Family*. London: T. Fisher Unwin, 1899, pp. 42–86, 222–27.

Surveys Sidney's life, commenting on *Arcadia* and *Astrophil and Stella*, discussing his political and religious views, and calling him "one of the founders of our Colonial Empire." Notes important literary acquaintances and recounts anecdotes illustrating his charm and chivalry.

389 SIMPSON, RICHARD. *An Introduction to the Philosophy of Shakespeare's Sonnets*. London: N. Trübner & Co., 1868, pp. 48, 57, 71–74.

Accepting Massey's contention (372) that Cecropia's advice to Philoclea parallels the advice to procreate in Shakespeare's initial sonnets, suggests that Sidney's "notorious intrigues" with Lady Rich may underlie the plot of Sonnets 137–42, in which Shakespeare is trying to summarize the key ideas of *Astrophil and Stella*. Suggests parallels between Sonnet 146 and "Leave me, O love" (*CS 32*).

390 SOUTHEY, ROBERT. "Life of Sir Philip Sidney." *Fraser's Magazine* 77 (May 1868):591–610; (June 1868):717–33; 78 (July 1868):96–110.

A single essay in three parts, unfinished and published posthumously. In Part 1, presents Sidney's family background, with stress on the characters of his maternal grandmother and his father. Discusses his education, the formation of his friendship with Greville, and his Continental travels, stressing the formative influence of Languet. In each case, emphasizes the moral probity of those seen as shaping Sidney's character. In Part 2, concentrates on the 1577 embassy to Germany and the *Letter to the Queen* opposing the French marriage, analyzing and quoting from the letter at length, with particular concern for the disparity between the almost universal approbation of Sidney's abilities and Elizabeth's refusal to use him in public service. Concludes that "she may have been unwilling to deprive her court of its brightest ornament by calling him to her counsels." In Part 3, views Sidney the courtier, describing at length the pageant *Four Foster Children of Desire* as indicative of life at court. Considers the quarrel

Nineteenth Century

with Oxford and Sidney's retirement to Wilton in 1579. Undertakes a lengthy discussion of his importance in the "reformation" of English literature, suggesting that he "contributed more than any other individual." Also discusses *Astrophil and Stella* as a record of "Sidney's moral and intellectual history," contending that Stella is Frances Walsingham. Claims that "no other English poet has ever made so many experiments in versification," but regrets that his "system of metrification was erroneous." See also item 391.

391 ———. *Southey's Common-place Book, Fourth Series.* Edited by John Wood Warter. London: Longman, Brown, Green, & Longmans, 1851, pp. 240, 321–22, 456, 483, 639.

Records Southey's plan, in 1854, to write a life of Sidney, which Warter says "nearly, if not quite, complete, is in the hands of the Rev. C.C. Southey." (The biography was subsequently published as item 390.) Notes numerous references and allusions to Sidney in the works of Drayton, Joseph Spence, Drummond of Hawthornden, Horace Walpole, and Hannah More. Quotes proverbs and remarks by Sidney, with no attribution of sources.

392 [SOUTHEY, ROBERT.] Untitled article. *Annual Review, and History of Literature* 4 (1805):544–55.

In reviewing Todd's edition of Spenser (963), considers Sidney's acquaintance with Spenser. Defends Sidney as a man and as a poet, praising *Arcadia* but condemning its eclogues as exercises in "versifying upon an impracticable system."

393 STIGANT, WILLIAM. "Sir Philip Sidney." In *Cambridge Essays, Contributed by Members of the University*. Vol. 4. London: John W. Parker & Son, 1858, pp. 81–126.

Rehearses Sidney's life, focusing on ancestry, education, travels, retirement to Wilton, and service in the Low Countries. Discusses his friendships with du Plessis-Mornay, Languet, and other Continental Protestants, noting that he may have met Tasso while in Italy and arguing that he had a close friendship with Spenser. Sees *Astrophil and Stella* as "the history of Sidney's love after the marriage of Lady Rich" and notes its Italian elements. Suggests that Mary Sidney "is supposed to have contributed not a little" to *Arcadia* when she "arranged its scattered and unfinished sheets." Discusses its sources, regretting the choice of Arcadian rather than English locales and heroes and concluding that, despite occasional beauties, "it must be confessed that it is tedious." Attributes its decline in popularity to a general advancement out of the "dark ages." Suggests that the *Defence* is more "sportive" than most believe.

394 STOTSENBURG, JOHN H[AWLEY.] "Sidney's Shake-speare Sonnets." *Baconiana*, n.s. 1 (October 1892):53–61.

In support of his opinion that Sidney was the author of Shakespeare's *Sonnets*, notes that the former's pastoral nickname was Will or Willy. See also item 395.

395 ———. "Sidney's Shake-speare Sonnets." *Baconiana*, n.s. 1 (May 1893):38–48.

Continues to urge the claim that Sidney wrote Shakespeare's *Sonnets*. See item 394. Acknowledges "interesting confirmation" in Brown (2030) and provides stylistic comparisons.

396 T., M. "Sir Philip Sidney: A Character Sketch." *University of Virginia Magazine* 54 (November 1893):67–71.

Praises Sidney as a model of honor and virtue, noting his accomplishments as a statesman, soldier, patron, and writer, and commenting on his "remarkably handsome" appearance. Refers to *Arcadia* as a work of genius, discusses the *Defence*, and provides a brief biographical reading of *Astrophil and Stella*.

397 TRISTRAM, W. OUTRAM. "Sir Philip Sidney." *English Illustrated Magazine* 4 (June 1887):636–40. Reprint. In *Living Age* 174 (9 July 1887):123–27, and in *The Bookmart* 5 (July 1887):45–49.

Reviews Sidney's life, works, and accomplishments, imagining a close friendship with Spenser that was carried on for three years at Penshurst while Spenser was beginning *The Faerie Queene*.

398 WALPOLE, HORACE, Earl of Orford. *The Letters of Horace Walpole, Fourth Earl of Orford.* Edited by Peter Cuningham. 9 vols. Edinburgh: John Grant, 1906, 2:23; 3:151–52; 5:309, 346. Orig. pub. London: R. Bentley, 1857–59 (not seen).

Comments on "delightful" things that he is finding "deep into" Collins's edition of the Sidney papers (1430), including the *Defence of Leceister*. Defends himself against the "offence" given by his having taken "freedom" with Sidney in item 294, concluding that "he was not a great man in proportion to his fame." Speculates that Houghton House might have been built by Sidney, though he can "touch upon no scent of his having lived there." Says that though he has been critical of Sidney, "as an antiquary I venerate him." Refers to having purchased a suit of armor that, he has been assured, is the one mentioned in Sidney's will.

Nineteenth Century

399 WARD, ADOLPHUS WILLIAM. *A History of English Dramatic Literature to the Death of Queen Anne.* Vol. 2. London: Macmillan & Co.; New York: Macmillan Co., 1899, pp. 81, 595–96, 752.
Notes the debts of Shakespeare, Day, and Beaumont and Fletcher to *Arcadia*, commenting briefly on *The Lady of May.* This material is not in the first edition, printed in 1875.

400 WINDSCHEID, KATHARINA. *Die englische Hirtendichtung von 1579–1625: Ein Beitrag zur Geschichte der englischen Hirtendichtung.* Halle, Germany: Max Niemeyer, 1895, pp. 12–13, 21–27 passim, 64–65, 86–88. Orig. a Ph.D. diss., Universität Heidelberg.
Notes that Thomas Watson may have known Sidney well and discusses his "Eclogue upon the Death of . . . Sir Francis Walsingham" (2774), which contains stanzas on Sidney's death. Also discusses the portrayal of Sidney as Elphin in Michael Drayton's *Eclogues* 6 and 8 (2792) and the laments for Sidney in Richard Barnfield's *Affectionate Shepherd* and in Barnabe Barnes's *Parthenophil and Parthenophe* (2743). Touches on Sidney's pastoral poem beginning "Join mates in mirth to me" (*OP 6*) and his "Dispraise of a Courtly Life" (*OP 7*).

401 WOODS, S[AMUEL] B. "Sir Philip Sidney." *University of Virginia Magazine* 15 (October 1876):1–13.
Provides a life of Sidney, emphasizing his death and reading *Astrophil and Stella* biographically. Also comments on the *Letter to the Queen*, and sees *Arcadia* as a *roman à clef* in which Pyrocles is Greville, Musidorus is Sidney, Philoclea is the Countess of Pembroke, Pamela is Penelope Rich, Euarchus is Sir Henry Sidney, and Cecropia is Catharine de Medici.

402 WRANGHAM, FRANCIS. "The Life of Sir Philip Sidney." In *Humble Contributions to a British Plutarch.* London: C. Baldwin, 1816, 77 pp. (each life individually paginated).
Relies heavily on Zouch (974) for biographical information. Comments on the *Defence* and on the sources and early publication history of *Arcadia*, printing lengthy excerpts from the two works.

403 WRIGHT, HENRIETTA CHRISTIAN. *Children's Stories in English Literature from Taliesin to Shakespeare.* New York: Charles Scribner's Sons; London: Ward & Downey, 1889, pp. 299–320.
In "Sir Philip Sidney," provides brief biographical notes on the author's life and a plot summary of *Arcadia.*

Twentieth Century

404 ADOLPH, ROBERT. *The Rise of Modern Prose Style.* Cambridge, Mass., and London: M.I.T. Press, 1968, pp. 74–75, 142, 147.
Notes Sidney's place in the Renaissance debate over Ciceronian prose style. Also comments on the use of the senses in *Arcadia* and in Bacon's *New Atlantis*.

405 AHRENS, RÜDIGER. "Grundzüge des Mäzenatentums in der Tudorzeit: Ein Beitrag zum Verhältnis von Literatur und Aristoktratie im England des 16. Jahrhunderts." *Trierer Beiträge* 7 (1980):1–5.
Considers new attitudes toward patronage in the Elizabethan period, commenting on Stephen Gosson's boldness in dedicating books to Sidney. Also discusses Sidney's tone in the dedication to *Arcadia* and in the "indirect dedication" of the *Defence* to Edward Wotton.

406 ALBRIGHT, EVELYN M. "On the Dating of Spenser's 'Mutabilitie' Cantos." *SP* 26 (October 1929):482–98.
Suggests that Sidney's influence on Spenser began in 1579 and was reflected in the Irish episodes of *The Faerie Queene*.

407 ALDEN, RAYMOND MacDONALD, ed. *The Sonnets of Shakespeare.* Boston and New York: Houghton Mifflin Co., 1916, pp. 16–86 passim.
Cites nearly sixty parallels between Shakespeare's *Sonnets* and *Arcadia* or *Astrophil and Stella*. Presents a synthesis of earlier commentary on the connections between the poets, especially that of Massey (372).

408 ALLEN, PERCY. *The Case for Edward de Vere, 17th Earl of Oxford as "Shakespeare."* London: Cecil Palmer, 1930, pp. 14, 278, 330.
Identifies Sidney with Slender in *The Merry Wives of Windsor* and "in part" with Sir Andrew Aguecheek in *Twelfth Night*. Also links the duel in *Hamlet* with Sidney's challenge to the Earl of Oxford.

409 ——. *The Plays of Shakespeare and Chapman in Relation to French History.* London: Denis Archer, 1933, pp. 89, 242–45.
In *Twelfth Night*, identifies Sidney with Sir Andrew Aguecheek. Also discusses Sidney's Continental tour and French acquaintances.

410 ——. *Shakespeare and Chapman as Topical Dramatists.* London: Cecil Palmer, 1929, pp. 38–39.
Suggests that, in Shakespeare's *Twelfth Night*, Sir Andrew Aguecheek may have been modeled on Sidney.

Twentieth Century

411 ALPERS, PAUL J. *The Poetry of "The Faerie Queene."* Princeton, N.J.: Princeton University Press, 1967, pp. 11–12, 20–22, 72–74, 280–97 passim, 318–19, 332.

Uses the *Defence* to elucidate Spenser's aims in *The Faerie Queene*. Discusses Sidney's description of poetry as "a speaking picture" and compares his notion of the poet's "golden" world with similar views in Tasso. Feels that Sidney emphasizes virtuous characters much more than the world of the poem. Also argues that Spenser's method of moral teaching is different from Sidney's in that Spenser does not ask the reader to judge his characters but only to understand them, whereas Sidney undercuts his characters and brings them to judgment. Feels that this procedure "impoverishes" the pastoralism of *Arcadia*. Notes, however, that Sidney is more skillful than Spenser in dramatizing virtuous action.

412 ALTMAN, JOEL B. *The Tudor Play of Mind: Rhetorical Inquiry and the Development of Elizabethan Drama*. Berkeley: University of California Press, 1978, pp. 87–106, 373, 379.

Compares the contempt for "servile and illiberal" sciences expressed by Marlowe's Dr. Faustus with Sidney's discussion of "serving sciences" in the *Defence*. Also compares *Arcadia* with Castiglione's *Courtier* and More's *Utopia*, suggesting that Sidney was writing a philosophical *quaestio* or dialogue in narrative form. Identifies the central topic as the active versus the contemplative lives and compares the episodes with subquestions and the Arcadian retreat with the traditional garden of such debates. Feels that, by the end of the book, the characters have arrived at a *hypothesis* in which the active life is seen as a necessary complement to the contemplative. Details various devices of debate employed in the work and notes that the Trial Scene follows all the rational procedures prescribed in Renaissance handbooks of rhetoric and still fails. Concludes that the scene is "a wry indictment of the inadequacy of precept . . . before the complexity of experience." Relates this outcome to Sidney's arguments in the *Defence* that poetry is superior to philosophy.

413 ANON. "The Gentleman Poet." *TLS*, 25 January 1963, p. 58.

In reviewing Ringler (92), sketches Sidney's life. Explains his casual attitude toward his works. Touches on the autobiographical content of *Astrophil and Stella*, the difficulty of reading *Arcadia*, and Sidney's experiments with classical meters.

414 ———. "Literaria Rediviva: — Sir P. Sidney's Defence of Poesie."
The London Christian Instructor or Congregational Magazine 5
(1822):42–49.
Praises Sidney as a warrior and a writer, but condemns *Arcadia* as excessively stylized and morally questionable. Treats the *Defence* as his greatest work, providing a popularized commentary with numerous excerpts.

415 ———. *A Monument for Sir Philip Sidney.* N.p. 1913, 10 pp.
Requests subscriptions. Not seen. Listed in *BMC* (1964), vol. 222,
col. 25.

416 ———. "The Pléiade and the Elizabethans." *Edinburgh Review* 205
(April 1907):353–79.
Rebuts arguments by scholars such as Lee (2179) that the Elizabethan
sonneteers were dependent upon Petrarch and the French Pléiade and
hence unoriginal. Includes a comparison of Petrarch's Sonnet 201 ("Real
natura, angelico intelletto") with Sidney's imitation, "Having this day my
horse" (*AS 41*), pointing out the distinctive flavor of Sidney's work. Also
discusses the influence of du Bellay's *Défense et illustration de la langue
française* on Sidney and other Elizabethan critics.

417 BABIN, MARÍA TERESA. "Garcilaso de la Vega y Sir Philip
Sidney." *La Nueva Democracia* 33 (1953):63–75.
Discusses parallels between the authors in their lives and in their works.
Considers them as lovers and courtiers, as political figures and commen-
tators on contemporary poetry. Finds Sidney's ideal of love more sensual
than Garcilaso's.

418 BAKER, HERSCHEL. *The Dignity of Man: Studies in the Persistence
of an Idea.* Cambridge, Mass.: Harvard University Press; London:
Oxford University Press, 1947, pp. 252–53, 296–97.
Considers Sidney's Christian humanism, remarking on the Protestant,
Stoic, and Platonic influences in his thought. Notes similarities between
the ethical assumptions of *Arcadia* and typical catalogs of virtues found in
Renaissance courtesy books.

419 BALDWIN, T[HOMAS] W[HITFIELD]. *On the Literary Genetics of
Shakspere's Plays, 1592–1594.* Urbana: University of Illinois Press,
1959, pp. 178–79, 224.
Suggests that Thomas Watson met Sidney through Frances Walsingham.
Also argues that the Countess of Pembroke's circle discouraged drama
that went against Sidney's views in the *Defence*. Notes that the anony-

Twentieth Century

mous play *Selimus* probably takes its eye-gouging scene from the story of
the Paphlagonian King in *Arcadia*.

420 ———. *On the Literary Genetics of Shakspere's Poems and Sonnets*.
　　　Urbana: University of Illinois Press, 1950, pp. 165, 185–209 pas-
　　　sim, 259, 324.
Considers Shakespeare's borrowings from Sidney in the *Sonnets*, including the music metaphor in Sonnet 8 and the black eyes of the "dark
lady." Traces Shakespeare's arguments on procreation as a means to
immortality, finding their ultimate source in Erasmus but their precise
formulation in *Arcadia*, particularly in Cecropia's speeches in Book III
urging Philoclea to marry.

421 ———. *Shakspere's Five-Act Structure: Shakspere's Early Plays on the
　　　Background of Renaissance Theories of Five-Act Structure from 1470*.
　　　Urbana: University of Illinois Press, 1947, pp. 330, 392–93,
　　　556, 563.
Comments on Scaliger's influence on Sidney. Points out that Sidney's list
of Terentian characters and their "signifying badges" in the *Defence* is a
set of stock illustrations and has a close parallel in a common grammar-
school rhetoric, Joannes Susenbrotus's *Epitome Troporum ac Schematum*.
Notes that Hamlet's expression "the table of my memory" has a parallel
in the *Defence*, which in turn echoes Proverbs 3:3 and 7:3. Also notes that
one of Falstaff's lines in *Merry Wives* III.iii is from *Astrophil and Stella*
Song ii.

422 BARRELL, JOHN and BULL, JOHN, eds. *The Penguin Book of
　　　English Pastoral Verse*. London: Allen Lane, 1974, pp. 16–18.
Notes the close parallel between Sidney (as he was viewed by his contemporaries) and Spenser's character Calidore in *The Faerie Queene*.
Discusses the "nostalgia" in Sidney's pastoral laments for an earlier
world, to which there is no way to return, and feels that "the hopeless-
ness, the impossibility of Arcadia becomes clearer with each fresh artifice
and masquerade. . . ."

423 BASKERVILL, CHARLES READ. *The Elizabethan Jig and Related
　　　Song Drama*. Chicago: University of Chicago Press, 1929, pp. 8,
　　　315.
Argues from the eclogues in *Arcadia* that pastoral games were actually
played in the Renaissance. Also points out a parody of Sidney's sonnet
"Come sleep, O sleep" (*AS 39*) in Jan van Arp's "Singhende klucht, van
drounke goosen."

424 ———. *English Elements in Jonson's Early Comedy*. Austin: University of Texas Press, 1911, pp. 6, 25, 57–59, 143, 217–18, 245–46.

Consider's Ben Jonson's interest in the *Defence*, noting his tendency to turn Sidney's guidelines into rules and relating his "humour" characters to Sidney's comments on characterization. Also discusses Sidney's claim to originality in *Astrophil and Stella* and lists analogues to Philisides's echo poem in *Arcadia* (*OA 31*).

425 BAUGHAN, DENVER EWING. "A Compliment to Sidney in *Hamlet*." *N&Q* 177 (19 August 1939):133–36.

Argues that the lines in *Hamlet* IV.iii on the horseman Lamord do not allude to Peter Mount but to Sidney.

426 BAYLEY, PETER [CHARLES]. *Edmund Spenser: Prince of Poets*. London: Hutchinson & Co., 1971, pp. 57–58, 75–78, 110–11.

Discusses emblems in Spenser's *Ruins of Time* that symbolize Sidney's poetic power and his death. Also examines Spenser's elegy *Astrophel* (2771), discussing the delay in its publication and its cool tone, the references to Sidney's sadness, and the appropriateness of the myth of Venus and Adonis. Draws on the *Defence* to explain the moral purpose of *The Faerie Queene*.

427 BAYNE, RONALD. "Masque and Pastoral." In *The Cambridge History of English Literature*. Edited by A[dolphus] W[illiam] Ward and A[lfred] R[ayney] Waller. Vol. 6, *The Drama to 1642, Part 2*. Cambridge: Cambridge University Press, 1910, pp. 370–420.

Notes the influence of *The Lady of May* on Jonson and Shakespeare, and comments on Sidney's contribution to pastoral.

428 BEHLER, MALLY. "Die Beziehungen zwischen Sidney und Spenser." *Archiv*, n.s. 46 (1923):53–59.

Analyzes the Spenser-Harvey correspondence and other evidence to determine the intimacy of Spenser's friendship with Sidney. Notes how few true friendships Sidney formed in his life and concludes that Spenser had a working relationship with him but regarded him a patron of superior social standing. Finds no evidence to determine which man dominated or the direction of influence between the *Defence* and Spenser's lost treatise *The English Poet*. Concludes that the authors' similar moral and aesthetic views simply reflect a common dependence on Plato and Aristotle. Notes only one close verbal parallel between *The Faerie Queene* and *Arcadia*: Spenser's catalog of trees in I.i, which also occurs in a dialogue between Dorus and Zelmane. Lists numerous char-

Twentieth Century

acters and incidents in *The Faerie Queene* similar to those in *Arcadia*. Also discusses the possible influence of *The Shepherd's Calendar* on Sidney's Arcadian eclogues and Spenser's treatment of Sidney in his minor works. See also Purcell (1122).

429 BENNETT, ALVIN L. "The Renaissance Personal Elegy and the Rhetorical Tradition." Ph.D diss., University of Texas at Austin, 1952, 199 pp.

Abstract not available. According to Washington (269), examines elegies for Sidney, tracing periods of his life in Spenser's *Astrophel* and rhetorical figures in Ralegh's epitaph.

430 BENNETT, JOSEPHINE WATERS. *The Evolution of "The Faerie Queene."* Chicago: University of Chicago Press, 1942, pp. 29, 80, 89–92, 105, 207.

Feels that, because Sidney did not reject Powel's dedication of Lhuyd's *History of Cambria*, he may have favored the Arthurian legend. Notes Dryden's identification of Spenser's Arthur with Sidney and discusses Spenser's account of the Sidneys and the Dudleys in *Stemmata Dudleiana*. Notes several similarities between *Arcadia* and *The Faerie Queene*, arguing that Sidney's shift from a third- to a first-person narrator between the two versions of *Arcadia* has parallels in Spenser's poem. Suggests that Book VI of *The Faerie Queene* "displays a consciousness of the new vogue for pastoral romance, inspired by the publication of *Arcadia*," but that, despite some parallel scenes and themes, there are few direct links between the two works. Identifies Sidney with Sir Calidore.

431 BERLI, HANS. *Gabriel Harvey, der Dichterfreund und Kritiker.* Zürich: Leeman & Co., 1913, pp. 109–12. Orig. a Ph.D. diss., Universität Zürich.

Discusses the Areopagus, comparing Sidney's literary aims with those of Harvey and noting the latter's high regard for *Arcadia*. Also considers the friendship between Sidney and Sir Edward Dyer.

432 BERRY, LLOYD E[ASON], ed. *The English Works of Giles Fletcher, the Elder.* Madison: University of Wisconsin Press, 1964, pp. 419–25.

In the notes to *Licia*, follows Scott (1951) in arguing that Fletcher may have been inspired by *Astrophil and Stella*. Suggests that he may also have known the *Defence*.

433 BERTHELOT JOSEPH A. *Michael Drayton.* Twayne's English Authors Series, 52. New York: Twayne Publishers, 1967, pp. 18–19, 21, 24, 49–50, 54, 104, 122, 135–36.

Discusses Sidney's influence on Drayton, particularly in *Idea's Mirror* and in the eclogues, where Sidney appears as Elphin, a representative of true poetry and virtue in contrast to the false values of King James I. Also considers Drayton's debt to *Arcadia* in *Poly-Olbion* and a possible reference to Sidney in *The Owl.*

434 BIAGI, ADELE. *Sir Philip Sidney: l'aeropago e la difesa della poesia.* Naples: Istituto universitario orientale, 1958, 227 pp.

In Part 1, attempts to reconstruct the origins and development of the "myth" of the Areopagus. In Chapters 1 and 2, examines Spenser's correspondence with Harvey and contrasts what little is known about the Areopagus with the fuller, more concrete information available about the Pléiade. In Chapter 3, examines the "oddity" that the writings of Sidney's contemporaries contain "absolutely no reference" to a literary club such as the Areopagus is supposed to have been. In Chapters 4–7, traces the origins and progression of the myth from Bourne (318) through Wallace (1171), calling it a "tree of vanity, with its roots in the sun, dried out, a pleasant story." In Chapter 8, examines the biographies of Poirier (703), Buxton (998), and Boas (436) to show growing twentieth-century skepticism about the myth, but also to indicate ways in which Sidney's reputation as a patron may have contributed to it. In Chapter 9, shows ways in which Castiglione's theories of the literary accomplishments required of an ideal courtier may also have contributed. In the four chapters of Part 2, surveys the publication history of the *Defence*; examines the biographical and literary relations between Sidney, Gosson, and Amyot; analyzes the *Defence* as a classical oration; and examines the sources of Sidney's ideas in Aristotle and the Italian literary theorists of the Cinquecento.

435 BIEDRZYCKA, HALINA. "Elementy Klasyczne w 'Obronie Poezji' Filipa Sidney." *Roczniki Humanistyczne* 6, no. 2 (1957):105–28.

Analyzes the main arguments of the *Defence*, emphasizing the classical background of Sidney's poetic theory. Traces the Aristotelian, Platonic, and Horatian lines of influence on his notion of the "ends" of poetry, on his concept of poetry as imitation, and on his theories of genre.

Twentieth Century

436 BOAS, FREDERICK S[AMUEL]. *Sir Philip Sidney, Representative Elizabethan: His Life and Writings.* London: Staples Press, 1955, 204 pp.

Provides a general introduction to Sidney's life and writings. Devotes at least a chapter to each of the major works, supplying information on background, manuscripts, printed editions, and literary connections. In discussing the "Discourse on Ireland," notes Sidney's tendency to mingle support for his father's repressive policies and sympathy for the Irish. Summarizes the *Letter to the Queen*, *The Lady of May*, and *Four Foster Children of Desire*. Touches on the genesis and style of Sidney's translation of *The Trueness of the Christian Religion* and notes that the *Defence of Leicester* fails to rebut the charges of Sidney's opponents. See detailed annotations in items 990, 1200, 1865, and 2411.

437 BOND, R[ICHARD] WARWICK, ed. *The Complete Works of John Lyly.* 3 vols. Oxford: Clarendon Press, 1902, 1:18, 46, 80, 133, 146–50; 3:9, 95–97.

Suggests that Sidney probably knew Lyly through Gabriel Harvey and that Lyly's *Endymion* is a court allegory in which Eumenides represents Sidney and Semele represents Lady Rich. Discusses Sidney's criticism of euphuism in the sonnet "Let dainty wits cry" (*AS 3*) and in the *Defence*, noting that Sidney's Arcadian style is looser, more prolix, more "unnatural." Points out satires of Sidney's style in Ben Jonson's *Every Man out of His Humour*, in Shakespeare's characters Amado and Osric, and in Sir Walter Scott's character Sir Piercie Shafton.

438 BOND, WILLIAM HENRY. "The Reputation and Influence of Sir Philip Sidney." 2 vols. Ph.D. diss., Harvard University, 1941, 695 pp.

In Volume 1, examines Sidney's life and influence, citing allusions to Sidney from 1586 to the mid-nineteenth century. Concludes that Sidney's reputation was built in several ways: readers were drawn to his works to learn etiquette and morality and tended to project onto him the virtues of his characters; writers poured out elegies for him, partly because he helped to make the profession of letters respectable; and Renaissance rhetoricians made his style and vocabulary a model for the English language. Ponders the decline of his reputation in the eighteenth century and its rise in the nineteenth following the renewed interest of antiquarians and biographers. In Volume 2, prints allusions to Sidney from 1586 to 1700, excluding books of elegies and other lengthy items. See *Harvard University Graduate School of Arts and Sciences: Summaries of Theses*, 1941, pp. 329–32.

Twentieth Century

439 BORINSKI, LUDWIG. *Englischer Geist in der Geschichte seiner Prosa*. Freiburg, Germany: Verlag Herder, 1951, pp. 20–22.
Contrasts Lyly's style with Sidney's in the *Defence* and *Arcadia*, but notes similarities in their use of metaphor and their dependence upon life at court rather than university book-learning for their sense of style.

440 BOTTRALL, MARGARET [SMITH]. *George Herbert*. London: John Murry, 1954, pp. 120–24.
Argues that Herbert was influenced by Sidney's *Defence*. Compares *Astrophil and Stella* 1 with "Jordan II" (which was originally entitled "Invention") and points out other echoes of Sidney in Herbert's works.

441 BRADBROOK, M[URIEL] C[LARA]. *John Webster: Citizen and Dramatist*. New York: Columbia University Press, 1980, pp. 38–39, 47–55, 151.
Points to Sidney's influence on writers associated with the Inns of Court, particularly the Middle Temple. Suggests that Webster borrows from *Arcadia* his mixture of high and low styles and that he employs material from the Captivity Episode in order to heighten contrasts between the black world of the satirist and the golden world of the pastoral poet. Also remarks on connections between Webster and others in Sidney's circle such as Penelope Rich. Notes that, in the Accession Day Tilt of 1590, her lover, Charles Blount, rode as her knight wearing the colors of Sidney's character Pyrocles. Also points out a speech put in the mouth of Sidney in Webster's *Monuments of Honor* (2810).

442 ———. *Shakespeare and Elizabethan Poetry: A Study of His Earlier Work in Relation to the Poetry of the Time*. London: Chatto & Windus; Toronto: Clarke, Irwin & Co., 1951, pp. 17, 22–27, 57–58, 110–11, 143.
Notes that the Platonism of Pico and Ficino first took root in England in the Sidney circle. Compares Sidney with Castiglione's ideal courtier and discusses the conceits in *Astrophil and Stella* as Ramist "arguments," pointing out that they were meant to conceal, not reveal, the extent of Sidney's passion for Penelope Rich. Also relates the battle between Amphialus and Philantus in Book III of the New *Arcadia* to Ovidian conventions and to Sidney's own life. Notes that lines 57–63 of Shakespeare's *Rape of Lucrece* depend on Sidney's sonnet "Phoebus was judge" (*AS 13*), where the lady's face is likened to a heraldic shield, and compares the exchange of hearts in Sidney's song "In a grove most rich of shade" (*AS viii*) with Shakespeare's Sonnet 22.

Twentieth Century

443 BRADFORD, ALAN T. "Drama and Architecture under Elizabeth
   I: The 'Regular' Phase." *ELR* 14 (Winter 1984):3–28.
In discussing parallels between Sackville and Norton's tragedy *Gorboduc*
and Elizabethan architecture, considers Sidney's judgments about the
tragedy, particularly his claim that it is "inartificially imagined."

444 BRADNER, LEICESTER. *Musae Anglicanae: A History of Anglo-
   Latin Poetry 1500–1925*. New York: Modern Language Association, 1940, pp. 26, 66.
Compares the lifelessness of works by Thomas Challoner and Roger
Ascham with the vitality of Sidney's works. Considers William Gager's
role in editing *Exequiae Sidnaei* (2760) and indicates a number of references to *Arcadia* and *Astrophil and Stella* in the collection.

445 BRETT, PHILIP. "The English Consort Song, 1570–1625."
   Proceedings of the Royal Musical Association 88 (1961–62):73–88.
Suggests that the musicians Edward Paston and William Byrd were in the
"fringes" of the Sidney circle, the latter having been introduced by
Thomas Watson. Also attributes to Sir Edward Dyer two "Funeral Songs"
printed by Byrd (2742), noting that the second ends with the following
words to Sidney: "Thou dead dost liue, thy friend here living dieth."

446 BRIE, FRIEDRICH. "Shakespeare und die Impresa-Kunst seiner
   Zeit." *SJ* 50 (1914):9–30.
Discusses Sidney's role in bringing the art of the *impresa* into English lit-
erature, commenting on his personal mottos and heraldic devices, the
precedents in earlier literature, and the popularity of such devices in the
Sidney circle.

447 ———. "Umfang und Ursprung der poetischen Beseelung in der
   englischen Renaissance bis zu Philip Sidney." *Englische Studien* 50
   (March 1917):383–425.
Examines Sidney's personification of nature and ideas as an important
contribution to the literary style of the period. Places his comments on
personification in the *Defence* in the context of Italian and English criticism and the uses of the device in the Psalms. Classifies various kinds of
personification, distinguishing Sidney's practice from the mythological
personification common in neoclassical literature. Notes that, in the
eclogue "Since that to death is gone the shepherd high" (*OA 75*), Sidney
extends the portrayal of grieving nature found in Moschus's elegy on
Bion. Analyzes other instances of personification in *Arcadia*, tracing the
influence of Petrarch, the Pléiade, and others.

448 BRIGGS, WILLIAM DINSMORE. "Sidney's Political Ideas." *SP* 29 (October 1932):534–42.
From Greville's *Life of Sidney* (863), extracts Sidney's beliefs on the nature and constitutional limits of the English monarchy. Notes that the *Letter to the Queen* was composed with the reign of Mary Tudor in mind and that Sidney's view of the French monarchy is essentially that of Francis Hotman's *Francogallia*. Also shows that George Buchanan's *De Jure Regni* was well regarded in Sidney's circle and may, therefore, have influenced his thought. Concludes that Brie is wrong (in 1202) to dissociate Sidney from the views of the anonymous treatise *Vindiciae contra Tyrannos*.

449 BRINKLEY, ROBERTA FLORENCE. *Arthurian Legend in the Seventeenth Century.* Johns Hopkins Monographs in Literary History, 3. Baltimore: Johns Hopkins Press; London: Oxford University Press, 1932, pp. 155–57.
Points out Sidney's influence on the views of reason adopted in the works of Sir Richard Blackmore.

450 BROOKE, [CHARLES FREDERICK] TUCKER. "Sidney and the Sonneteers." In *A Literary History of England*, edited by Albert C. Baugh. New York and London: Appleton-Century-Crofts, 1948, pp. 388, 472–82. Reprint, with a "Supplement" containing updated bibliographic notes. New York: Appleton-Century-Crofts, 1967.
Emphasizes Sidney's role as a patron who encouraged an "academic spirit" in English letters. Regards him as romantic and independent, whereas his sister was neoclassical and rule-bound. Compares the Old *Arcadia* with a tragicomedy by Philip Massinger and a modern mystery story, and regards the revised version as an outgrowth of Sidney's neoclassical studies for the *Defence*. Notes Sidney's role in starting the vogue for sonnet cycles, discussing the extent of the autobiographical elements in *Astrophil and Stella* and comparing the cycle with the work of later sonneteers. Also notes Sidney's influence on Walter and Francis Davidson and on the unknown poet A.W., whose work appears in Francis Davidson's *Poetical Rhapsody*.

451 BRUSER, FREDELLE. "Concepts of Chastity in Literature Chiefly Non-Dramatic of the English Renaissance." Ph.D., diss., Radcliffe College, 1947, pp. 45, 47–50, 79–85.
Sees in *Astrophil and Stella* a shift from the usual idealization of chastity to the sort of cynicism that marks Sidney's revolt against the conventions of

141

Twentieth Century

the sonnet sequence. Considers the philosophical bases of Pamela's defence of chastity in the Captivity Episode of *Arcadia*, relating it to Sidney's translation of the *Trueness of the Christian Religion*. Also compares Pamela's views with Sidney's handling of the matter elsewhere in the two versions of the romance, noting that the Princess's defense is grounded in the belief that the world is morally ordered.

452 BRYAN, J[OHN THOMAS] INGRAM. *The Interpretation of Nature in English Poetry*. Tokyo: Kaitakusha, 1932, pp. 88–92.
Compares Sidney with the Romantics in his love of nature.

453 BUCHAN, A.M. "The Political Allegory of Book IV of *The Faerie Queene*." *ELH* 11 (December 1944):237–48.
Examines Spenser's political allegory in the marriage of the Thames and the Medway. Feels that, since Penshurst is on the Medway, Elizabethan readers would have associated the river with Sidney. Concludes that Spenser is urging England to adopt the policies advocated by Sidney's party.

454 BULLEN, A[RTHUR] H[ENRY], ed. *An English Garner*. Edited by Thomas Seccombe. Introduction to Vol. 5, *Some Longer Elizabethan Poems*, edited by A[rthur] H[enry] Bullen. Westminster: Archibald Constable & Co., 1903, pp. xvii–xix.
Discusses elegies for Sidney appended to Spenser's *Colin Clout's Come Home Again* (items 2740, 2741, 2749, 2768, 2770, 2771). Touches on their dates of composition, literary quality, and probable authorship.

455 BULLOUGH, GEOFFREY, ed. Introductions to *Narrative and Dramatic Sources of Shakespeare*. 8 vols. London: Routledge & Kegan Paul; New York: Columbia University Press, 1957–75, 1:207, 427; 5:459; 6:234–35, 355–56; 7:47–48, 284–86, 305; 8:125, 128, 395–96.
Compares the transsexual disguise and the outlaw band in *Two Gentlemen of Verona* to similar elements in *Arcadia*. Lists pedants in Renaissance literature that resemble Rombus in *The Lady of May*. Considers the relation between Menenius Agrippa's fable of the parts of the body as recounted in the *Defence* and a similar passage in *Coriolanus*. Also discusses the likelihood that *Arcadia* influenced the anonymous Elizabethan play *Timon*, and traces parts of the life of Pyrocles to the story of Apollonius of Tyre, discounting the possibililty that Sidney's portrayal influenced Shakespeare's *Pericles*. Details parallels between Plexirtus's order that a sea captain slay the heroes of *Arcadia* with a similar incident in *Hamlet*. Rehearses ways in which *Arcadia* shaped *King*

Lear, noting that Plexirtus is also "a partial prototype" for Edmund and the King of Iberia for Gloucester. Finally, lists similarities between the main plot of Sidney's romance and *The Winter's Tale*.

456 BUSH, DOUGLAS. *The Oxford History of English Literature*. Vol. 5, *English Literature in the Earlier Seventeenth Century, 1600–1660*. Oxford: Clarendon Press, 1945, pp. 53–54, 84–85, 94–95, 162–63, 216–17. Rev. ed. New York and Oxford: Oxford University Press, 1962, pp. 53–54, 56, 73, 84–85, 97–99, 145–46, 172, 230–31.

Notes the many seventeenth-century imitators of Sidney's *Arcadia* and Psalms and comments on particular debts to Sidney in the works of Drummond of Hawthornden, Fulke Greville, George Herbert, and Andrew Marvell. Discusses Greville's *Life of Sidney* as "the image of England's ancient vigour" set in contrast to the decadence of the seventeenth century. See also item 1450.

457 BUXTON, JOHN. *Elizabethan Taste*. London: Macmillan & Co., 1963; New York: St. Martin's Press, 1964, pp. 7–8, 100, 106–9, 184–86, 238–39.

Points to evidence in the letters and the prose works that Sidney had an active interest in painting and music and may have known the settings of his sonnets by Charles Tessier and William Byrd. Also compares Sidney's concept of the "right poet" to that of Spenser. Includes chapters on *Arcadia* and *Astrophil and Stella*. See detailed annotations in items 1454 and 2076.

458 ———. "*Peplus*: New College Elegies for Sir Philip Sidney." In *The Warden's Meeting: A Tribute to John Sparrow*, [edited by Evan Davies]. Oxford: Oxford University Society of Bibliophiles, 1977, pp. 23–26.

Identifies ten of the twenty-nine contributors to *Peplus* (2763), the elegies for Sidney prepared by members of New College, Oxford. Concludes that the poems provide "scant" evidence about Sidney's life.

459 CAIN, THOMAS H. *Praise in "The Faerie Queene."* Lincoln: University of Nebraska Press, 1978, pp. 9, 14, 162.

Comments on Spenser's allusions to Sidney as Orpheus in *The Ruins of Time* and as Calidore in *The Faerie Queene*.

Twentieth Century

460 CAMPBELL, LILY B[ESS]. "The Christian Muse." *Huntington Library Bulletin*, no. 8, October 1935, pp. 29–70.

Traces the Renaissance movement to write divine rather than secular poetry, especially the elevation of the goddess Urania to be the Christian Muse. Discusses Sidney's relationship to Guillaume du Bartas, one of the originators of the movement. Sidney not only translated part of his *La semaine* (now lost) but used several arguments in the *Defence* similar to those of du Bartas in favor of rendering Christian subjects in poetry.

461 CARTER, WILLIAM HOYT, Jr. "*Ut Pictura Poesis*: A Study of the Parallel between Painting and Poetry from Classical Times through the Seventeenth Century." Ph.D. diss., Harvard University, 1948, pp. 155–56, 161–64.

Citing Sidney's paraphrase of Simonides in the *Defence*, contends that Sidney views painting as didactic. Notes that, in *Arcadia*, he displays the influence of both Greek and Renaissance Italian theories of painting, particularly in his "word painting" of Kalander's garden and his portraits of women.

462 CASPARI, FRITZ. *Humanism and the Social Order in Tudor England*. Chicago: University of Chicago Press, 1954, pp. 142, 176–80.

Explains Sidney's failure to attain a degree at Oxford as part of the aristocratic disdain of professional scholarship. Discusses similarities between *Arcadia* and Spenser's *Faerie Queene* in purpose, form, and ethical and political thought. Notes common elements in the views of Sidney and other humanists such as Castiglione and Elyot.

463 CAWLEY, ROBERT RALSTON. *The Voyagers and Elizabethan Drama*. Boston: D.C. Heath & Co.; London: Oxford University Press, 1938, pp. 78–79, 256, 303, 306, 355, 363, 370.

Notes Sidney's interest in accompanying Drake to the West Indies in 1585 and discusses Sidney's references to elephants, the climate of Russia, and "Indians." Mentions a passage in the Sidney/Golding translation of the *Trueness of the Christian Religion* in which the word "Cannibals" is mistakenly substituted for "Canada." Suggests that the argument in the *Defence* about Indians who "make and sing songs" derives from Richard Eden's translation of Peter Martyr's *Decades*. See also item 2427.

Twentieth Century

464 CAZAMIAN, LOUIS [FRANÇOIS]. *The Development of English Humor.* Durham, N.C.: Duke University Press, 1952, pp. 138–39.
Traces the pattern of humor in *Arcadia* and the *Defence* to the humanists of the early Renaissance. Compares it with that of Erasmus, Congreve, and Shakespeare (in *Love's Labor's Lost*).

465 CERNY, LOTHAR. *"Beautie and the use thereof": Eine Interpretation von Sir Philip Sidneys "Arcadia."* Anglistische Studien, 6. Cologne and Vienna: Böhlau Verlag, 1984, 371 pp.
Examines the extent to which the theory of the *Defence* and the practice of the New *Arcadia* are informed by the same Calvinistic belief. Starting from the antithesis between *finis* and *utilitas* found in the debate between Cecropia and Pamela in *Arcadia* III.x, argues that Sidney is concerned with "finality" as an all-embracing principle closely linked with his Protestantism. Pamela's ability to argue that beauty is an end in itself, "without further consequence," is broadly grounded in Sidney's Calvinistic belief that only when one has faith in God's freely given grace can actions be pure, untainted by any utilitarian motives. When this is the case, one allows events to fulfill their immanent *finis*, without seeking an additional, utilitarian purpose. Argues that this understanding of finality colors Sidney's poetic theory, claiming that "theologically speaking, the aim of the poet implies a foregoing of reward; it is *utilitas* without the notion of justification by works," and "in terms of poetic theory this means that the poet dispenses with the pursuit of direct effects in life." Finds in this theory a "unified perspective" for interpreting the New *Arcadia*, whose protagonists "take up the process of learning how to act justly by learning how to understand the idea of images. The difficulty of understanding the idea of an image is the same as the difficulty of knowing oneself and of acting in accordance with one's nature as well as the nature of all things in general, and not according to utilitarian aims. This program is carried out and exemplified in the whole range of the protagonists' experience, private, political, and religious." Provides an English summary.

466 CHAMBERS, D.D.C. "Sidney's Rhetoric." *Cambridge Review* 89 (29 October 1966):67–69.
In reviewing Kalstone (1907), suggests that reforming Astrophil's rhetoric is a major concern of *Astrophil and Stella*. Also defends "weaknesses" in the rhetoric of *Arcadia* and *The Lady of May* as intentional reflections of the inner state of the characters.

Twentieth Century

467 CHAMBERS, [Sir] E[DMUND] K[ERCHEVER]. *The Elizabethan Stage*. Vol. 1. Oxford: Clarendon Press, 1923, pp. 144–45, 257–58.

Describes *Four Foster Children of Desire* as it was originally presented in 1581. Identifies the "Will" mentioned in Sidney's letter to Walsingham of 24 March 1586 with the clown Will Kempe. Explains the plays and staging practices that Sidney may have had in mind in the passages of the *Defence* on the dramatic unities. Provides publishing histories for the *Defence, The Lady of May, A Dialogue Between Two Shepherds (PP 1)*, and *Four Foster Children of Desire*. Reprints extracts from the dedications to Sidney in Gosson's *School of Abuse* and *Ephemerides of Phialo*. See also Mithal (2735).

468 CHEADLE, B.D. "The 'Speaking Picture' and the Moral End: Sidney's Difficulties with a Moral Defence of Art." In *Generous Converse: English Essays in Memory of Edward Davis*, edited by Brian Green. Cape Town, South Africa: Oxford University Press, 1980, pp. 25–36.

Notes passages in the *Defence* that do not balance teaching and delight as the ends of poetry but rather suggest that delight is given deceitfully simply to convey a moral lesson. Finds in the revised *Arcadia* three different views of the proper relation between beauty and usefulness and argues that the Old *Arcadia* betrays Sidney's indecisiveness on the issue. Analyzes this ambivalence in the episode of the lion and the bear. Also explicates the opening description of the shipwreck in the New *Arcadia*, suggesting that "it expresses a yearning that runs clearly counter to the work's heroic and moral intentions."

469 CHECKSFIELD, M[URIEL] M[AY]. *Portraits of Renaissance Life and Thought*. London: Longmans, Green & Co., 1964, pp. 191–214.

In "Sir Philip Sidney," treats the writer as an embodiment of Castiglione's ideal gentleman. Reviews his life and works, emphasizing his education and his role at court. Also discusses his reputation in his own age, listing elegies, testimonials, and books dedicated to him. Seeks to explain his fame by a detailed delineation his character.

470 CHILD, HAROLD H. "The Song-books and Miscellanies." In *The Cambridge History of English Literature*, edited by A[dolphus]

Twentieth Century

W[illiam] Ward and A[lfred] Rayney] Waller. Vol. 4, *Prose and Poetry, Sir Thomas North to Michael Drayton*. Cambridge: Cambridge University Press, 1910, pp. 127–46.
Notes works by and/or about Sidney in *The Phoenix Nest, England's Helicon*, and *A Poetical Rhapsody*.

471 CLARK, EVA LEE TURNER. *Hidden Allusions in Shakespeare's Plays: A Study of the Early Court Revels and Personalities of the Times.* 3d ed. Edited by Ruth Loyd Miller. Port Washington, N.Y.: Kennikat Press; London: Minos Publishing Co., 1974, pp. 20, 196–98, 200, 535–45, 678–79, 739–46, 768, 791–93, 897–98.
Expands the material in item 472. Suggests that Shakespeare's *Love's Labor's Lost* IV.i is partly intended to burlesque *The Lady of May*, and identifies Rombus with the Duke of Alençon or Gabriel Harvey. Also suggests that the list of genres in *Hamlet* II.ii is a parody of a similar list in the *Defence*. Identifies Sidney with Perigot in the August eclogue of Spenser's *Shepherd's Calendar*.

472 ———. *Shakespeare's Plays in the Order of Their Writing: A Study Based on the Records of the Court Revels and Historic Allusions.* London: Cecil Palmer, 1930, pp. 24, 60, 372–83 passim, 531–39, 560, 567–69. Reprint. *Hidden Allusions in Shakespeare's Plays: A Study of the Oxford Theory Based on the Records of Early Court Revels and Personalities of the Times.* New York: William Farquhar Payson, 1931.
Considers Sidney's relationship with the Earl of Oxford and possible allusions to it in Shakespeare's plays and in the August eclogue of Spenser's *Shepherd's Calendar*. Asserts that Shakespeare was, in fact, Oxford and that Sidney helped him to have some of his plays produced. Links Sidney with Claudio in *Much Ado about Nothing* and with Ned Poins in *II Henry IV*. Surmises that the shepherd's speech on "two of my best sheep" in *The Winter's Tale* III.iii alludes to Sidney and Fulke Greville and supposes that the funeral speeches in *I Henry VI* were intended for Sidney. See also item 471.

473 CLARK, J. SCOTT, and ODELL, JOHN PRICE. *A Study of English and American Writers: A Laboratory Method.* Chicago: Row, Peterson & Co., 1916, pp. 19–27.
Seeks to list the "distinctive features" of Sidney's poetry and prose, providing comments by noted critics.

Twentieth Century

474 COHEN, EILEEN ZELDA. "Gentle Knight and Pious Servant: A Study of Sidney's Protestantism." Ph.D. diss., University of Maryland, 1965, 208 pp.

Argues against the myth that Sidney was a Puritan, concluding that he was simply a moderate Anglican who advocated a militantly Protestant foreign policy. Considers the religious milieu, Sidney's family and education, his friendship with Languet, his limited acceptance of the teachings of du Plessis-Mornay, and his role in the Leicester camp at court. Also argues that Sidney's views in *Arcadia* and the *Defence* run against the Puritans. See *DA* 26 (June 1966):7312.

475 COLE, HOWARD C. *A Quest of Inquirie: Some Contexts of Tudor Literature.* Pegasus Backgrounds in English Literature. Indianapolis, Ind., and New York: Bobbs-Merrill Co., 1973, pp. 65–66, 108–10, 126–29, 134–36, 162–64, 175–76, 179, 222, 230–31, 264–312 passim, 469–71, 482–84.

Consider's the impact of classical, Italian, and Puritan works on the *Defence*, discussing Sidney's comments on the dramatic unities, poetic inspiration, the term "imitation," mingled genres, and the role of nature versus nurture in creating poets. Questions Sidney's understanding of Aristotle's *Poetics* and of Italian concepts of tragedy and rejects analyses of Shakespeare that rely on the *Defence*. Feels that Sidney preferred Seneca to the Greek tragedians. Also ponders Sidney's comparison of the poet to God, noting that it blurs the distinction between art and nature. Examines his definition of the three kinds of poets, his ambivalent stance toward Plato, and the relation of his definitions of various genres to those of Puttenham and other Elizabethan critics. Considers the autobiographical content of *Astrophil and Stella* and Sidney's strictures against poets who sound insincere. Also cites sixteenth-century appraisals of *Arcadia* and relates the tournament of Phalantus in Book II of the revised version to the Accession Day Tilts of 1581.

476 CONNELL, DOROTHY. *Sir Philip Sidney: The Maker's Mind.* Oxford: Clarendon Press, 1977, 170 pp. Orig. a Ph.D. diss., Harvard University, 1974.

In the introduction, relates Sidney's concept of the poet as "maker" to the humanist view of man as self-maker as enunciated by Pico della Mirandola. Suggests that the key to Sidney's quality of mind is "an ability to encompass and balance contradictions," notably that between his "erected wit" and "infected will." Compares the *Defence* with Erasmus's *Praise of Folly* and with Castiglione's *Courtier*, noting the paradoxes involved in their comparisons of human makers with the divine Maker. In Chapter 1, examines Sidney's views on love, human fallibility, and earthly beauty in contrast to those of Fulke Greville. Traces traditional concepts of earthly love, rejecting the view that the two Princes in *Arcadia* are to be contrasted with Astrophil or that Sidney subordinated earthly to heavenly love. Compares the theme of reason and passion with that in Chaucer's *Troilus*, urging that, in the Trial Scene of *Arcadia*, Sidney adapted the ending of Heliodorus's *Aethiopica* to affirm the law of love over that of society and reason. In Chapter 2, compares Gynecia's love potion with the "medicine of cherries" in the *Defence*, considering Sidney's views on the effects of poetic images of earthly love. Finds the *Defence* intentionally paradoxical and unreliable on this issue. Feels that Sidney's didacticism gives way to human sympathy in passages such as Basilius's poetic dialogue with Boulon (*OA 30*) and that Sidney denied that poets are divinely inspired because his poetic vision is essentially earthly. In Chapter 3, discusses the Renaissance interest in mingling play with serious matters. Compares the allusion to Queen Elizabeth as the Virgin Mary in *The Lady of May* with an incident on one of the Queen's progresses. Also considers Sidney's "play" in tournaments and in his heraldic devices. Following George Puttenham, regards Sidney as a "courtly maker," that is, one who writes lyrics as part of the game of courtly love. Relates this role to the mixture of public and private in *Astrophil and Stella*, to Sidney's playful rivalry with Greville, and to the connections between the French marriage negotiations and *The Lady of May*. Also notes the influence of George Gascoigne's Kenilworth pageant on the latter work and urges that Castiglione influenced the passage in the *Defence* beginning "Now therin of all sciences . . . is our poet the monarch." In Chapter 4, considers Sidney's ambitions as revealed in his correspondence with Languet. Finds more interest in being a statesman and soldier than in writing, though in 1580 he seems to have chosen a quiet life at Wilton over fighting in the Netherlands. Cites his "Discourse on Irish Affairs," his motto "Vix ea nostra voco," and his *Letter to the Queen* as evidence of a shift toward literary aims, noting parallels between the *Letter* and the Old *Arcadia*, especially in Philanax's advice to Basilius and incidents such as the revolt of the commoners and the quarreling of the aristocrats after Basilius's supposed death. In Chapter 5, discusses Sidney's aims in revising the Old *Arcadia* (for a detailed annotation, see item 1210). In the conclusion, discusses the internal "contradictions" characteristic of Sidney's works, relating his faith that they can ultimately be "reconciled" to his religious convictions. In remarking on the deepening interest in religion in his last years, stresses the expanded

Twentieth Century

role of passages on divine providence and religious issues in the revised *Arcadia*. Includes a bibliography and an index.

477 COPE, JACKSON I. "Jonson's Reading of Spenser: The Genesis of a Poem." *EM* 10 (1959):61–66.
Argues that, when Jonson addressed Sidney's daughter in the "Epistle to Elizabeth, Countess of Rutland," he imitated Spenser's *Complaints*, particularly the elegy for Sidney in *The Ruins of Time*.

478 CORY, HERBERT ELLSWORTH. *Edmund Spenser: A Critical Study*. University of California Publications in Modern Philology, 5. Berkeley: University of California Press, 1917, pp. 174–75, 179, 210–16.
Considers Spenser's lost Latin poem *Stemmata Dudleiana* and the English version, *The Ruins of Time*, which celebrate Sidney's family. Suggests that Spenser's grief at the loss of Sidney contributed to the discouragement in the later books of *The Faerie Queene*. From the *Defence* surmises the outlines of Spenser's lost work, *The English Poet*, and compares his *Mother Hubberd's Tale* with Sidney's *Letter to the Queen*. Also discusses the oddly delayed tribute that Spenser paid to Sidney in *Astrophel*.

479 COURTHOPE, W[ILLIAM] J[OHN]. "The Poetry of Spenser." In *The Cambridge History of English Literature*. Vol. 3, *Renascence and Reformation*, edited by A[dolphus] W[illiam] Ward and A[lfred] R[ayney] Waller. Cambridge: Cambridge University Press, 1909, pp. 219–20, 242.
Suggests that the comments in the *Defence* about Spenser's *Shepherd's Calendar* helped to start the vogue for pastoral but prevented others from imitating Spenser's archaic diction. Also identifies Sidney with the "brave courtier" of Spenser's *Mother Hubberd's Tale*.

480 CRAIG, HARDIN. *The Enchanted Glass: The Elizabethan Mind in Literature*. New York: Oxford University Press, 1936, pp. 33–35, 92–94, 153–56, 164–65, 185–86, 227–28.
Takes Sidney as an example of the Elizabethans' attitude toward astrology, diversified education, and formal ethics. In discussing *Arcadia*, analyzes Musidorus's disputation with Pyrocles on the degrading effects of love as a sample of Ramist logic. Also points out the formal oratorical pattern of the *Letter to the Queen*.

481 ———. *A History of English Literature*. Edited by Hardin Craig. Vol. 2, *The Literature of the English Renaissance, 1485–1660*. New

York: Oxford University Press, 1950, pp. 48, 54–59, 111–13, 138, 185–86.

Remarks on the sources and influence of *Arcadia*, the critical background of the *Defence*, and the importance of *Astrophil and Stella* in the history of the sonnet.

482 ———. "Motivation in Shakespeare's Choice of Materials." *ShS* 4 (1951):26–34.

Details ways in which Sidney's stories of the Paphlagonian King and of Plangus guided Shakespeare in transforming the chronicle accounts of King Leir into a tragic play.

483 CRANZ, CORNELIA. "Sir Philip Sidney and His *Arcadia*." *College Folio* 13 (December 1904):79–89.

Gives a popularized account of Sidney's life and assesses the merits of *Arcadia*.

484 CRAWFORD, CHARLES, ed. Introduction and notes to *Englands Parnassus*. Oxford: Clarendon Press, 1913, pp. xiv–xvi, xxiii–xxiv, xxvii, and passim.

Notes that excerpts from *Arcadia* were included in John Bodenham's Elizabethan miscellanies, *Wit's Commonwealth* and *Belvedere*. Also discusses various misattributions involving Sidney that were introduced when Robert Allot compiled *England's Parnassus*. In the notes, suggests that Allot had access to a manuscript of *Astrophil and Stella*. Also traces allusions to *Arcadia* and to *Astrophil and Stella* in the works of John Weever, Alexander Niccholes, Philip Massinger, George Chapman, Robert Burton, John Marston, Sir John Harington, and the unknown author of the *Alcilia* sonnets.

485 CRAWFORD, CHARLES. "John Webster and Sir Philip Sidney." *N&Q*, 10th ser. 2 (17 September 1904):221–23; (1 October 1904):261–63; (15 October 1904):303–4; (29 October 1904):342–43; (12 November 1904):381–82. Reprint. In *Collectanea, First Series*, by Charles Crawford. Stratford-on-Avon: Shakespeare Head Press, 1906, pp. 20–46.

Argues that, in *The Duchess of Malfi* and *A Monumental Column*, Webster constantly imitates Sidney, whereas, in *The Devil's Law-Case*, he merely borrows from him. Notes parallel passages drawn from *Arcadia* (and one from *Astrophil and Stella*) and comments on similarities in plot. Also touches on Sidney's influence on Philip Massinger and on Beaumont and Fletcher.

Twentieth Century

486 CROWDER, RICHARD. "'Phoenix Spencer': A Note on Anne Bradstreet." *NEQ* 17 (June 1944):310.

From a couplet on "Phoenix Spencer" in Anne Bradstreet's "Elegy upon . . . Sir Philip Sidney," concludes that she knew the three elegies in *The Phoenix Nest* but mistakenly assumed that they were by Spenser.

487 CUMMINGS, L. "Spenser's *Amoretti*, VIII: New Manuscript Versions." *SEL* 4 (Winter 1964):125–35.

Argues for a close connection between Sidney, Dyer, Greville, and Spenser, citing evidence of mutual imitation among them found in new manuscripts of *Amoretti* 8.

488 CUMMINGS, R[OBERT] M., ed. *Spenser: The Critical Heritage.* London: Routledge & Kegan Paul; New York: Barnes & Noble, 1971, pp. 40–89 passim.

Records more than fifty references to and comments on Sidney appearing in allusions to Spenser prior to 1715, including the anonymous life attached to the 1679 edition of Spenser's works, which claims that Spenser showed Sidney canto I.ix of *The Faerie Queene*.

489 CUNNINGHAM, J[AMES] V[INCENT]. Introduction to *The Renaissance in England.* New York: Harcourt, Brace & World, 1966. Reprint. In *The Collected Essays of J.V. Cunningham.* Chicago: Swallow Press, 1976, pp. 288–309 passim.

Discusses Sidney's views of Elizabethan social classes and of the proper relation between titled lords and gentlemen, as he presented his position to Queen Elizabeth after the quarrel with Oxford in 1579. Comments again on the similarity between lines in *OA 67* and Donne's epigram on Hero and Leander. From evidence in the *Defence* and *Arcadia*, argues that *Astrophil and Stella* is not "fiction" in Sidney's sense but a "memoir." Compares Sidney's wooing of Penelope Rich with Musidorus's poetic courtship of Pamela in *Arcadia*. Also treats Sidney as the innovator in establishing the "plain style" in English.

490 ———. "Tragic Effect and Tragic Process in Some Plays of Shakespeare and Their Background in the Literary and Ethical Theory of Classical Antiquity and the Middle Ages." Ph.D. diss., Stanford University, 1945.

Examines Sidney's view of the emotional effects of tragedy, namely "admiration and commiseration." See also item 491. Discusses *Astrophil and Stella*, finding in it a scholastic view of moral error in which "reason is not dethroned or suspended, but having committed an error in logic is actively enlisted on the side of wrong desire." See Stanford University,

Twentieth Century

Abstracts of Dissertations for the Degrees of Doctor of Philosophy and Doctor of Education 20 (1944–45):29–34. See also 491.

491 ———. *Woe or Wonder: The Emotional Effect of Shakespearean Tragedy.* [Denver]: University of Denver Press, 1951, pp. 23, 62.
Finds the closest English parallel to Shakespeare's notion of tragic "wonder" in Sidney's views on tragic "admiration" in the *Defence*. Traces the role of wonder in literary theory from classical to Renaissance times. See also Cunningham's Ph.D. dissertation (490), which includes material on *Astrophil and Stella* not printed here.

492 DANBY, J[OHN] F. "The Poets on Fortune's Hill: Literature and Society, 1580–1610." *Cambridge Journal* 2 (January 1949): 195–211.
Traces the shift from the static social hierarchy of the Middle Ages to the dynamic order under Elizabeth, in which success depended on action as much as on birth or title. Notes that Sidney exemplifies one position that poets could hold in this new order: that of the wealthy and well-placed nonprofessional. Contrasts him with four other types of poets who are lower on "Fortune's hill." Relates the kind of literature that each produces to social rank. See also item 1495.

493 DAVENPORT, A[RNOLD], ed. Introduction to *The Collected Poems of Joseph Hall.* Liverpool: University of Liverpool Press, 1949, pp. xli–lx.
Discusses Hall's praise for *Arcadia* and the *Defence* in *Virgidemiae* VI.i.255–60 and its "postscript." Notes similarities between Hall's critical views and those of Sidney.

494 DAVIS, B[ERNARD] E[USTACE] C[UTHBERT]. *Edmund Spenser: A Critical Study.* London: Cambridge University Press, 1933, pp. 12–14, 20, 31, 44, 52, 61, 89, 92.
Plays down the friendship between Spenser and Sidney, but sees many similarities between their views of poetry and between *Arcadia* and Book VI of *The Faerie Queene.*

495 DAVIS, WALTER R. *Idea and Act in Elizabethan Fiction.* Princeton, N.J.: Princeton University Press, 1969, pp. 28-45, 56–72, 80, 82–83.
In Chapter 2, examines the *Defence*, arguing that Sidney regarded fiction as a way of experimenting with possible worlds in order to instill wisdom and so repair the effects of the Fall of Adam. In Chapter 3, considers the

Twentieth Century

carrying out of this theory in the revised *Arcadia*. For detailed annotations, see items 1498 and 2452.

496 DAY, MARTIN S. *History of English Literature*. Vol. 1. Garden City, N.Y.: Doubleday & Co., 1963, pp. 212–13, 215–20.
Sketches connections between Sidney's life and Calidore's encounter with Pastorella in Book VI of *The Faerie Queene*. Reviews Sidney's major works, touching on their background and their influence.

497 DELATTRE, FLORIS, and CHEMIN, CAMILLE. *Les Chansons élizabéthaines*. Bibliothèque des langues modernes, 11. Paris: Librairie Marcel Didier, 1948, pp. 20, 88, 136, 141–45, 324–29.
Comments on Sidney's contribution to the sonnet vogue. Notes his praise for the popular ballad in the *Defence* and discusses his experiments with classical meter, paying special attention to the musicality of poems in *Arcadia, Certain Sonnets*, and *Astrophil and Stella*. Prints parallel French and English texts of "My true love hath my heart" (*OA 45*), "O words, which fall like summer dew on me" (*OA 46*), "The nightengale, as soon as April bringeth" (*CS 4*), and "Ring out your bells" (*CS 30*).

498 del RE, ARUNDELL. *The Secret of the Renaissance and Other Essays and Studies*. Tokyo: Kaitakusha, 1930, pp. 167–76.
In Appendix 3, "Bruno, Florio and the Sidney Circle," suggests that the dispute between Sidney's Areopagus and the court euphuists was "not unconnected" with the War of the Theaters and the Marprelate and the Harvey-Nashe controversies. Links all these rivalries to court politics. Also connects the Areopagus with Ralegh's "School of Night." Asserts that *Astrophil and Stella* has greater affinities with the school of Dante than with that of Petrarch. Finds similarities in outlook between Bruno and Sidney, and concludes that Bruno was intimate with the Sidney circle during his visit to London in 1583–85.

499 de MADARIAGA, SALVADOR. *Shelley and Calderon and Other Essays on English and Spanish Poetry*. London: Constable & Co., 1920; New York: E.P. Dutton & Co., [1921], pp. 72–73.
Points out parallels between the lives and works of Sidney and Garcilaso de la Vega.

500 DEMING, ROBERT H. "Love and Knowledge in the Renaissance Lyric." *TSLL* 16 (Fall 1974):389–410.
Discusses the principles in the *Defence* as the underlying didactic aesthetic of the Renaissance lyric. Views Astrophil as "the complete foolish-wise lover," treating *Astrophil and Stella* 1 as a study in the knowledge of love

and of the self. Uses Sidney to prove that the Renaissance lyric employs a rhetorical strategy displaying "the movement of the conscious radical self in its desire to discover and to understand the totality of its being at the same time that the self is immersed in fragmentary experience."

501 DEMPEWOLF, WALTER. *Shakespeares angebliche Modelle.* Jena, Germany: G. Neuenhahn, 1914, pp. 29, 60, 74–75. Orig. a Ph.D. diss., Grossherzoglich und herzoglich Sächsischen Gesamt-Universität Jena.

Refutes critics like Cartwright (327, 329) who identify Sidney with Shakespearean characters such as Hamlet, Benvolio, and Pericles.

502 DISHER, M. WILSON. "The Trend of Shakespeare's Thought." *TLS*, 20 October 1950, p. 668; 27 October 1950, p. 684; 3 November 1950, p. 700.

Takes the view that Shakespeare's "discipleship to Sidney was fanatical." Considers the power at court of the "Sidney faction" and notes Shakespeare's connections with this group. As evidence, cites Shakespeare's adaptation of the doctrines of love and friendship in *Arcadia*, his verbal borrowings from *Astrophil and Stella* in the *Sonnets*, and the Arcadian material in *King Lear* and *Pericles*. See a reply by Murray (2211).

503 DOHERTY, MARY JANE MARGARET. "The Mistress-Knowledge: Literary Architectonics in the English Renaissance." Ph.D. diss., University of Wisconsin at Madison, 1977.

Considers the definition of an "architectonic science" in Plato, Aristotle, and Augustine and the ways in which this architectural metaphor passed into the Middle Ages and the Renaissance. Discusses poetic theorists from Sidney to Milton who regarded poetry as such a science. Also analyzes *Astrophil and Stella*, considering what it reveals about the private education of a poet and his work in a public medium. See *DAI* 38 (February 1978):4840A.

504 DORAN, MADELEINE. *Endeavors of Art: A Study of Form in Elizabethan Drama.* Madison: University of Wisconsin Press, 1954, pp. 31, 65–66, 80, 86–90, 93, 193–97.

Discusses passages in the *Defence* related to the development of the drama. Also notes the influence of *Arcadia* as a source for plots and as a stage in the development of characterization.

505 DUNCAN-JONES, KATHERINE. "Sidney and Titian." In *English Renaissance Studies Presented to Dame Helen Gardner in Honour of*

Twentieth Century

> *Her Seventieth Birthday*, edited by John Carey. Oxford: Clarendon
> Press, 1980, pp. 1–11.

Examines Sidney's ambivalence toward Italian culture and the lack of
attention to painting in his correspondence. Offers circumstantial evidence that he was familiar with the work of Titian, noting in Book II of
Arcadia a specific allusion to the artist's second rendering of Danae in
the shower of gold. Suggests other allusions to the work of Titian and
Bartholomeus Spranger in *Arcadia* and the *Defence*. Notes that both
Sidney and Titian allude to Sannazaro's *Arcadia* and work in "the larger
tradition of Platonic debate about beauty and love."

506 DUNN, ESTHER CLOUDMAN. *The Literature of Shakespeare's
England*. New York: Charles Scribner's Sons, 1936, pp. 29–30,
70–76, 174, 186–89.

Argues that the "conceited style" of *Arcadia* was intended as poetry and
anticipates the union of rhetoric and feeling in later Elizabethan verse.
Also suggests that the *Defence* reflects the conversational style of the period and that the sonnets reflect the language of high society. Contrasts
Sidney's view of love with those of Shakespeare and of Michael Drayton.

507 EDMUNDS, E.W. "Sir Philip Sidney (1554–86)." In *The Story of
English Literature*, by E.W. Edmunds and Frank Spooner. Vol. 1,
The Elizabethan Period, 1558–1625. London: John Murray, 1907,
pp. 58–87.

Summarizes Sidney's life, listing merits and faults in the *Defence* and
Arcadia and discussing the autobiographical details in *Astrophil and Stella*.
Suggests that Thomas Watson's *Hecatompathia* was inspired by a reading
of *Astrophil and Stella* in manuscript.

508 EINSTEIN, LEWIS. *The Italian Renaissance in England*. New York:
Columbia University Press, 1902, pp. 336–37, 357–58.

Lists Sidney's debts to Petrarch in *Astrophil and Stella* and to the Italian
critics in the *Defence*. Suggests that the Areopagus was an imitation of the
Florentine Academy or that of Baïf in Paris. Traces the dream of an
English Academy from William Thomas to Milton.

509 ELIOT, T[HOMAS] S[TEARNS]. *Use of Poetry and the Use of
Criticism: Studies in the Relation of Criticism to Poetry in England*.
London: Faber & Faber, 1933, pp. 37–52. See also pp. 24–25, 53.

In "Apology for the Countess of Pembroke," defends Sidney's views on
the dramatic unities, treating them as natural laws. Notes the tendency
of modern critics to dismiss Sidney's position on the grounds that
Elizabethan and Jacobean drama continually violates the unities.

Suggests, however, that, where the material allowed, the unities would have made the plays better. Regards *Arcadia* as a "monument of dulness," the *Defence* as an argument with "men of straw," and only a few of Sidney's works as offering "perpetual refreshment." See replies by Rathmell (711) and Mason (2569).

510 ELLRODT, ROBERT. *L'inspiration personnelle et l'ésprit du temps chez les poètes métaphysiques anglais. Seconde partie: Les origines sociales, psychologiques et littéraires de la poésie métaphysique au tournant du siècle.* Paris: Librairie José Corti, 1960, pp. 15–18, 94–179 passim, 208–45 passim, 279, 314–79 passim.

Uses Sidney frequently as a touchstone for generalizations about literary and intellectual developments in the last decade of the sixteenth century, chiefly in discussing 1) shifts in poetic style, including the emergence of the concepts of originality and obscurity; 2) the emergence of new preferences in genres; 3) Continental and Latin influences; and 4) the effects of Ramism. Notes that Sidney seems to have been alone among sonneteers in registering the influence of Catullus, and that he contributes more than any other to the "triomphe de la subtilité d'ésprit" in English poetry.

511 ———. *Neoplatonism in the Poetry of Spenser.* Travaux d'Humanisme et Renaissance, 35. Geneva: Librairie E. Droz, 1960, pp. 23, 97–98.

Suggests that Burghley's displeasure over Spenser's *Astrophel* may have been directed toward "the pastoral travesty of Sidney's heroic death and the emphasis on his love for Stella." Argues that Spenser, long in Ireland, probably felt that the *Astrophil and Stella* poems were intended for Frances and that Spenser meant no disrespect in dedicating the work to her. Claims that Sidney may have read Plato's *Phaedrus* and certainly had studied carefully Cicero's *De officiis*.

512 ELTON, OLIVER. *Michael Drayton: A Critical Study.* London: Archibald Constable & Co., 1905, pp. 35, 53–55, 69.

Notes that Drayton captures Sidney's poetic tone and suggests that Sidney is the model for the character Elphin in Drayton's *Eclogues* (2792), a revised version of his *Idea, or The Shepherd's Garland* (2758).

513 ERNLE, [ROWLAND EDMUND PROTHERO,] Lord. *The Light Reading of Our Ancestors: Chapters on the Growth of the English Novel.* London: Hutchinson & Co., [1927], pp. 89, 120–22, 149–51.

Notes that the *Defence* follows a view, common in the Middle Ages and the Renaissance, that the account of Aeneas by Dares Phrygius was

Twentieth Century

"right" and that of Virgil "feigned." Also evaluates *Arcadia* and comments on its popularity in the seventeenth century.

514 ESPLIN, ROSS STOLWORTHY. "The Emerging Legend of Sir Philip Sidney, 1586–1652." Ph.D. diss., University of Utah, 1970.
Considers those chiefly responsible for spreading Sidney's reputation. Includes balladeers, historians, and biographers; the authors of the several volumes of Sidney elegies; the writers gathered around Mary Sidney; contributors to poetic miscellanies; and pastoral poets such as Spenser, Ralegh, and Greville. See *DA* 31 (November 1970):2341A.

515 EVANS, MAURICE. "Sir Philip Sidney: The Maker." *New Lugano Review* 1 (1979):36–44.
Reviews Sidney scholarship since 1962, adducing further evidence for Connell's thesis (476) that, in much of his writing, Sidney regarded himself as a royal advisor and public mentor. But rejects her view that he thought the heart wiser than the head. Notes his suspicion of love and his idealization of friendship, comparing him in these matters with Shakespeare rather than with Donne or Spenser. Suggests that Sidney may not have finished the New *Arcadia* because, in writing the *Defence*, he had set his sights on more serious genres than romance.

516 EVANS, ROBERT O. "Spenser's Role in the Controversy Over Quantitative Verse." *NM* 57, no. 5–6 (1956):246–56.
Asserts that Sidney's experiments are "highly chaotic" and suggests that, since "in all likelihood" those in *Arcadia* were written after Spenser's *Iambic Trimetrum*, Spenser may have introduced the subject of quantitative verse to Sidney's circle.

517 FARMER, NORMAN K., Jr. "Fulke Greville and Sir John Coke: An Exchange of Letters on a History Lecture and Certain Latin Verses on Sir Philip Sidney." *HLQ* 33 (May 1970):217–36.
Notes that, although the complete text of Greville's memorial poem on Sidney is lost, Coke translated and discussed some lines in a letter of practical criticism to Greville. Touches on Sidney's possible influence on Greville's theory of history.

518 FARNHAM, WILLARD. *The Medieval Heritage of Elizabethan Tragedy*. Berkeley: University of California Press, 1936, pp. 59, 341.
Points out the medieval tradition of *contemptus mundi* behind du Plessis-Mornay's *Trueness of the Christian Religion* and notes that Sidney's sister linked dramatic tragedy with such teachings. Also notes that the description of tragedy in the *Defence* uses the language of medieval *de casibus* tales.

519 FELPERIN, HOWARD. *Shakespearean Romance.* Princeton, N.J.: Princeton University Press, 1972, pp. 30–35, 37–38, 46–47.
Places Sidney among other Protestant authors of romance, including Spenser and Milton, who emphasize inward trials as the means of moral purification. Relates the extremes of virtue and vice in their fictional worlds to this emphasis on testing. Cites the passage on the "golden" world in the *Defence* as the chief justification for creating such imaginary worlds, but notes that Sidney also insists on verisimilitude in such things as the dramatic unities.

520 FOGEL, EPHIM GREGORY. "The Personal References in the Fiction and Poetry of Sir Philip Sidney." Ph.D. diss., Ohio State University, 1958, 495 pp.
Identifies the most probable personal references in *Arcadia* and *Astrophil and Stella* and discusses their place in literary traditions such as Petrarchan and pastoral poetry. Includes an appendix on the chronology and the biographical significance of *Certain Sonnets.* See *DA* 19 (1958):809.

521 FOGLE, FRENCH ROWE. *A Critical Study of William Drummond of Hawthornden.* New York: King's Crown Press, 1952, pp. xvi, 11–18, 39, 177.
Considers Sidney's influence on Drummond's sonnets. Notes that Sidney preferred to imitate nature and ideas, whereas Drummond more often imitated other writers.

522 FRENCH, PETER J. *John Dee: The World of an Elizabethan Magus.* London: Routledge & Kegan Paul, 1972, pp. 126–59.
In "John Dee and the Sidney Circle," notes that Sidney and Dyer studied chemistry with Dee and seeks to connect Sidney's experiments with classical meters to Dee's mystical philosophy. Sees Ramist elements in both Sidney and Dee, placing them in a broader Hermetic and magical tradition. Claims that, for Sidney in the *Defence*, the poet is like an Hermetic magus. Also notes Sidney's connections with Alexander Dickson and Giordano Bruno.

523 FREY, CHARLES. *Shakespeare's Vast Romance: A Study of "The Winter's Tale."* Columbia: University of Missouri Press, 1980, pp. 93–94, 104–7.
Contrasts Sidney's idealization of the poet's "golden" world in the *Defence* with Shakespeare's imitation of nature and his concern about the destructive power of imagination. Notes passages in *Arcadia* in which poetry and its subject seem to merge. Feels that the reader is not asked

Twentieth Century

to form an image of reality but to enjoy "an admitted artifice whose content lies close to or within the form of the reader's temporal encounter with it." Compares similar effects in *The Winter's Tale*.

524 FRIEDERICH, WERNER P[AUL]. *Dante's Fame Abroad, 1350–1850: The Influence of Dante Alighieri on the Poets and Scholars of Spain, France, England, Germany, Switzerland, and the United States. A Survey of the Present State of Scholarship.* Chapel Hill: University of North Carolina Press, 1950, p. 196.

Disputes claims that Sidney's use of *terza rima* in *Arcadia* shows the influence of Dante. Notes that the reference to Dante's Beatrice in the *Defence* is the earliest in English, but concludes that Sidney had no "solid knowledge" of Dante's works.

525 FRIEDRICH, WALTER GEORGE. "The Astrophel Elegies, a Collection of Poems on the Death of Sir Philip Sidney (1595)." Ph.D. diss., Johns Hopkins University, 1936. Printed in part as *The Stella of Astrophel: A Portion of the Astrophel Elegies, a Collection of Poems on the Death of Sir Philip Sidney (1595). A Critical Edition.* Baltimore: Johns Hopkins Univsersity Press, 1936, 30 pp.

Provides a critical edition of the poems on Sidney included in the 1595 quarto of Spenser's *Colin Clout's Come Home Again*. Concludes that Spenser was the editor of the volume and the author of the first poem, *Astrophel* (2771); that "The Doleful Lay of Clorinda" (2741) is probably by the Countess of Pembroke; that "The Mourning Muse of Thestylis" and "A Pastoral Aeglogue" (2749) are by Bryskett; that most of the poems date from 1587, though Spenser's is between 1589 and 1591; and that Spenser's friendship with Sidney was very close and was halted only by Sidney's death. Dissertation not seen. The printed excerpt contains the title page, a summary of contents, and Chapter 4.

526 FUJII, HARUHIKO. *Time, Landscape, and the Ideal Life: Studies in the Pastoral Poetry of Spenser and Milton.* Kyoto, Japan: Apollon-sha, 1974, pp. 134–45.

Examines the role of action, contemplation, and love in Spenser's idealized portrait of Sidney in *Astrophel* (2771). Suggests that, following Sir Thomas Elyot's description of the ideal gentleman, Spenser established Sidney as a model of the Renaissance courtier. Argues that the "Stella" of *Astrophel* is neither Lady Rich nor Sidney's wife but rather an "ideal lady."

527 GARNETT, RICHARD, and GOSSE, EDMUND. *English Literature: An Illustrated Record.* Vol. 2. New York: Macmillan Co., 1904, pp. 35–46.
Ranks Sidney's prose below that of Hooker or Donne. Also lists faults in *Arcadia* and remarks on the literary and biographical background of *Astrophil and Stella.*

528 GASQUET, ÉMILE. *Le courant machiavelien dans la pensée et la littérature anglaises du XVIe siècle.* Études Anglaises, 51. Paris: Didier, [1974], pp. 18–20, 355–69.
In reevaluating the conclusions of Ribner (717, 1731, 1734, 2711), notes the lack of direct evidence that Sidney was seriously influenced by the writings of Machiavelli. Goes on to consider possible parallels between those writings and Sidney's *Letter to the Queen,* "Discourse on Irish Affairs," and *Arcadia.* In discussing *Arcadia,* focuses on the revolt of the Helots, Euarchus's reform of the government of Macedonia, and the views of Basilius and Philanax.

529 GEBERT, CLARA. *An Anthology of Elizabethan Dedications and Prefaces.* Philadelphia: University of Pennsylvania Press, 1933, pp. 45–47, 65–66, 71–76, 112.
Prints Gosson's dedication of *School of Abuse* to Sidney, Sidney's dedication of *Arcadia* to his sister, Nashe's preface to *Astrophil and Stella,* and Olney's preface to the *Defence.*

530 GENOUY, HECTOR. *L'Élément pastoral dans la poésie narrative et le drame en Angleterre, de 1579 à 1640.* Paris: Henri Didier, 1928, pp. 68–79, 117–18, 139–40, 179, 204–6, 237–38, 345–46.
Discusses Spenser's *Astrophel* and other pastoral elegies for Sidney. Also examines the pastoral poems of Sidney that appeared in Elizabethan miscellanies and the pastoral background of *The Lady of May.*

531 GEORGAS, MARILYN DAVIS. "Sir Philip Sidney and the Victorians." Ph.D. diss., University of Texas at Austin, 1969, 434 pp.
Examines Sidney's reputation in the nineteenth century. Notes the desultory interest in the sonnets until late in the period, when they began to eclipse Sidney's other works. Also records a preoccupation with the morality of Sidney's relationship with Penelope Rich, the unfavorable response to *Arcadia,* and the tendency to examine the style but not the substance of the *Defence.* See *DAI* 30 (January 1970):2966A–67A.

Twentieth Century

532 GOLDMAN, MARCUS SELDEN. Review of *Sir Philip Sidney en France*, by Albert W. Osborn. *JEGP* 33 (1934):295–300.
Finds Osborn's discussion (1103) of Sidney's indebtedness to France complicated by the question of Sidney's attitude toward French Roman Catholics. Claims that, since his Protestantism was political rather than religious, he was not actively hostile to Catholics. Stresses the importance of Sidney's friendships with l'Éscluse and Louise de Coligny, and notes that Osborn does not discuss Estienne and overvalues the influence of du Bellay and Scève.

533 ———. "Sidney and Harington as Opponents of Superstition." *JEGP* 54 (October 1955):526–48.
Argues that Sidney had nothing but contempt for the occult arts and for those who desire to avoid danger by consulting astronomers and soothsayers. Discusses his two visits to John Dee, Queen Elizabeth's astrologer; the statements in *Nobilis*, a work by Sidney's physician Thomas Moffet; the remarks in the sonnet "Though dusty wits dare scorn astrology" (*AS* 26); and the oracles in *Arcadia*. Concludes that characters such as Philanax and Musidorus mirror Sidney's own beliefs. Also discusses the relation between Sidney's position and that of Sir John Harington.

534 ———. *Sir Philip Sidney and the "Arcadia."* Illinois Studies in Language and Literature, vol. 17, nos. 1–2. Urbana: University of Illinois Press, 1934, 236 pp. Orig. a Ph.D. diss., University of Illinois at Urbana-Champaign, 1931.
Seeks to understand Sidney's development "as a thinker." After reviewing previous biographies, reexamines his background, education, personal associations, and career. Also evaluates criticism on *Arcadia* since Sidney's lifetime and discusses matters of genre, political content, and sources. In an appendix, reprints Henri Estienne's dedication of his edition of Herodian and Zosimus to Sidney. Includes a full bibliography. For detailed annotations, see items 1032 and 1240.

535 GREAT BRITAIN. HISTORICAL MANUSCRIPTS COMMISSION. *Report on the Manuscripts of Lord de L'Isle & Dudley Preserved at Penshurst Place.* Edited by C.L. Kingsford. 6 vols. London: for His Majesty's Stationery Office, 1925–1966, 1:271–73, 304; 2:2, 24, 32, 48, 51, 53, 68–70, 80, 83, 84, 86, 94–97, 104–5, 170, 192, 201, 218, 367, 575, 580; 3:xxix, xxxii, xxxv, 310, 373–74.
In Volume 1, lists manuscripts related to Sidney, identified by date (7 May 1564 to 1586–87). Briefly describes them and sometimes summarizes or quotes from them at length, especially when they have not previ-

ously been published. In a separate section on "miscellaneous books and manuscripts," notes a copy of the *Defence* bearing Robert Sidney's autograph and a copy of *Defence of Leicester*. In Volume 2, covers papers and correspondence of Sir Henry Sidney and correspondence of Robert Sidney. The former contains letters to and from Sidney, as well as comments about him. The introduction to Volume 3 recounts events in Sidney's governorship of Flushing. The actual manuscripts cited, dating from 1606 and 1607, refer to the enterprise against Axel and to Puritanism in the Flushing garrison under Sidney's command.

536 GREAVES, MARGARET. *The Blazon of Honour: A Study in Renaissance Magnanimity.* London: Methuen & Co.; New York: Barnes & Noble, 1964, pp. 15, 23, 63–76, 78, 113.
Treats Sidney as an example of magnanimity, examining the attitude toward public service and social rank revealed in his life, in his letters, and in *Arcadia*. Notes his conflation of Aristotelian and medieval concepts of nobility with Renaissance interests in art and learning and with Christian faith. Also relates Sidney's concept of delightful teaching in the *Defence* to Spenser's *Faerie Queene* and contrasts Sidney's concept of magnanimity with Milton's.

537 GREENBLATT, STEPHEN [JAY]. *Renaissance Self-Fashioning: From More to Shakespeare.* Chicago: University of Chicago Press, 1980, p. 238.
Connects Astrophil's statement "I am not I, pity the tale me" (*AS* 45) with Shakespeare's *Othello*, noting Iago's words "I am not what I am" and Othello's attempt to win pity by enacting a tale of himself.

538 GREENLAW, EDWIN [A]. *Studies in Spenser's Historical Allegory.* Johns Hopkins Monographs in Literary History, 2. Baltimore: Johns Hopkins Press; London: Humphrey Milford, Oxford University Press, 1932, pp. 104–28 passim, 161–62.
Discusses Spenser's association with Sidney and the Areopagus and the political and literary context of Sidney's *Letter to the Queen*, comparing it with Spenser's *Mother Hubberd's Tale*. Explains Oxford's insult to Sidney on the tennis court as a side effect of Sidney's opposition to the French marriage. From Greville's *Life* extracts Sidney's views on Spain and the proper course of English foreign policy, suggesting that these views had a deep influence on Spenser.

539 GREENLAW, EDWIN [A.]; OSGOOD, CHARLES GROSVENOR; PADELFORD, FREDERICK MORGAN; and HEFFNER, RAY, eds. *The Works of Edmund Spenser: A Variorum Edition.* 10 vols.

Twentieth Century

bound as 11. Baltimore: Johns Hopkins University Press, 1932–57, passim.
Includes a large number of notes on Sidney, all carefully indexed by subject under his name. Identifies him with numerous characters in Spenser's works, particularly *The Faerie Queene*. Relates his life to that of Spenser and considers their personal relations, their political and aesthetic views, and their influence on one another's works. Also discusses the elegies for Sidney published with Spenser's *Colin Clout's Come Home Again* and the connections between *The Faerie Queene* and *Arcadia* and between Spenser's lost work *The English Poet* and the *Defence*.

540 GREGORY, ELMER RICHARD, Jr. "Du Bartas and the Modes of Christian Poetry in England." Ph.D. diss., University of Oregon, 1965, 275 pp.
Explores the "character of English humanism and critical theory to which [du Bartas's] work was assimilable" and the "affinities of thought and technique" of writers, including Sidney, who admired him. See *DA* 26 (March 1966):5434–35.

541 GRIGSON, GEOFFREY. *Poets in Their Pride*. London: Phoenix House, 1962, pp. 15–29.
In "Sir Philip Sidney," provides a popularized sketch of Sidney's life and works.

542 GRUNDY, JOAN, ed. Introduction and notes to *The Poems of Henry Constable*. Liverpool: Liverpool University Press, 1960, pp. 74–75, 218–43 passim.
Considers Constable the first Elizabethan sonneteer to become a "disciple" of Sidney's witty, Continental style. Notes borrowings from Sidney and suggests that one of Constable's sonnets "To Sir Philip Sidney's Soul" (2753) was probably originally entitled "To the Marquis of Piscat's Soul." Also discusses Constable's acquaintance with Sidney.

543 GRUNDY, JOAN. *The Spenserian Poets: A Study in Elizabethan and Jacobean Poetry*. London: Edward Arnold; New York: St. Martin's Press, 1969, pp. 23–24, 46, 56, 58–59, 78, 216–17.
Notes Sidney's influence on Spenserian imitators such as George Wither and Giles Fletcher the Younger, classifying Wither's *Fair-Virtue* as a lengthy paraphrase of lyrics from *Arcadia*. Points out that, according to the definition in the *Defence*, John Donne is not a "right poet," though Spenser is. Also comments on Michael Drayton's *Idea, or The Shepherd's Garland* (2758), in which Elphin represents Sidney. Notes that, in the

revised version published among the *Pastorals* (2792), Sidney comes to represent the old Elizabethan order.

544 HAGER, ALAN. "The Exemplary Mirage: Fabrication of Sir Philip Sidney's Biographical Image and the Sidney Reader." *ELH* 48 (Spring 1981):1–16.

Feels that "Sidney's exemplary image is the product of Elizabethan propagandistic design" and that the key to reading his works is to recover his true character. Applies Sidney's own warnings about history in the *Defence*, suggesting that Leicester and Greville distorted his image to advance their own foreign policy. Attributes to Queen Elizabeth and her "chief propagandist," Sir Henry Lee, the creation of a Sidney cult, which they used to keep other aristocrats in line. Notes that Sidney's lavish funeral served to distract attention from the execution of Mary, Queen of Scots. Examines Sidney's irony and self-deprecation, emphasizing the fault in his character revealed by his improper courtship of Lady Rich. Also argues that the device of a sheep "spotted to be known," borne both by Sidney and by his character Philisides, was a symbol of love melancholy.

545 ———. "'Sweet Smoke of Rhetoric': The *Eiron* and His Irony in the *Defence of Poesie* and Book I of the *1590 Arcadia*." Ph.D. diss., University of California at Berkeley, 1978.

Argues that Sidney adopted an ironic posture, both in his life and in his works. Suggests that the *Defence* often juxtaposes seeming contradictions in a form of internal debate derived from Erasmus's *Praise of Folly*, More's *Utopia*, and Agrippa's *De Vanitate Scientiarum et Artium*. Feels that *Arcadia* sets traps for the readers, persuading them to accept rhetorical appeals and conventions of behavior that are then undercut. Concludes that the lesson of the work is that "we must live by the conventions of rank and role and language, but the conventions themselves are inadequate and arbitrary." See *DAI* 39 (February 1979):4957A–58A.

546 HAGSTRUM, JEAN H. *The Sister Arts: The Tradition of Literary Pictorialism and English Poetry from Dryden to Gray*. Chicago: University of Chicago Press, 1958, pp. 64, 78–79.

Considers the analogy between poetry and painting that figures prominently in the *Defence*. Also examines parts of *Arcadia* in which Sidney describes Kalander's paintings or likens the characters to portraits. Traces the history of such pictorial imagery to the Greeks and Romans and sees Sidney as an influence on similar devices in the Restoration and the eighteenth century.

Twentieth Century

547 HALLIDAY, F[RANK] E[RNEST], ed. Introduction to *The Survey of Cornwall &c*, by Richard Carew of Antony. London: Andrew Melrose, 1953, pp. 26, 42, 62.
Notes that Carew was deeply moved at Sidney's death and that he modeled the poetic style of *Geoffrey of Bulloigne* on the eclogues of *Arcadia*. Also discusses the influence of the *Defence* on Carew's *Excellency of the English Tongue*.

548 HALLIDAY, F[RANK] E[RNEST]. *Shakespeare in His Age.* London: Gerald Duckworth & Co., 1956, pp. 40, 88–90, 112, 201.
Reviews Sidney's career and his influence on Shakespeare, blasting him for defending the classical unities. Notes echoes of the *Defence* in the preface to Ben Jonson's *Every Man in His Humour*.

549 HAMILTON, A.C. "The Modern Study of Renaissance English Literature: A Critical Survey." *MLQ* 26 (1965):150–83.
Recalls Jonson's advice to read Sidney before Donne. Contrasts the temporal effects, the wit, and the colloquial style of Donne with the spatial effects, the relaxed play of imagination, and the formalized style of Spenser and Sidney. Also traces four meanings of "decorum" in classical and Renaissance sources and applies them to speeches by Pamela and Philoclea, suggesting that the sisters represent the neo-Platonic ideas of Beauty and Virtue. Notes Sidney's skill in both the plain and the high styles, and emphasizes his pivotal role in Elizabethan letters. Also surveys recent theories of the relation between autobiography and poetic convention in *Astrophil and Stella*, arguing that the autobiographical element is treated "so obliquely as to be almost meaningless." Traces modern misreadings of the sequence to an inability to understand fully the Renaissance concept of decorum.

550 ———. *Sir Philip Sidney: A Study of His Life and Works.* Cambridge: Cambridge University Press, 1977, 224 pp.
Relates Sidney's literary works to his life and to his age. In Chapter 1, sketches his lineage, expectations, and accomplishments, noting that early creators of the "Sidney legend" largely ignored his literary works. Considers his broad reading and influence, crediting him with creating a renaissance in English literature. Lays out the personal, literary, and social implications of two of his favorite motifs: life as a prison and the gulf between the "erected wit" and the "infected will." In Chapter 2, relates the character Philisides to Sidney in his early, hopeful years at court. Examines *The Lady of May*, considering dating, structure, style, and argument. Relates its central debate over the active and the con-

templative lives to Tasso's *Aminta*. Notes the half-veiled criticism of the court in the masque, relating it to the Queen's refusal to support the Protestant League. Suggests that Elizabeth's judgment at the end of the masque was a response to this criticism. Notes further conflict with the Queen over Sidney's "Discourse on Irish Affairs," his quarrel with Oxford, and his position on the French marriage. Regards his decision to set aside Languet's wishes and become a writer as a way to gain self-knowledge before returning to the active life, noting a parallel in the retirement of Pyrocles and Musidorus to the pastoral world of Arcadia. Examines the autobiographical elements in the Old *Arcadia*, considering Sidney's presence both as the narrator and as Philisides. Ponders the jarring discrepancy between the narrator's sympathy for the lovers and Euarchus's condemnation. Speculates that Sidney may have been "exorcising his private nightmare," the disapproval of his father following his retirement from court. Also discusses Sidney's use of sources in the romance. Points out that the "golden" world of Sannazaro's *Arcadia* provides an Edenic backdrop to the action, which may be compared with the Fall in Genesis. Notes that the chivalric virtues of *Amadis de Gaule* have been inverted to emphasize the degradation of Sidney's heroes and suggests that the vindication of the lovers in the trial scene of Heliodorus's *Aethiopica* has been inverted to stress the shame of Sidney's lovers and their eventual return to virtue. Regards the ambiguity of the trial scene as essential to the "argument" of the Old *Arcadia* as a whole, which may be analyzed as "an anatomy of love: its nature, its working within man, its power both to debase and ennoble, and its conflict with moral and public order." Offers evidence that Euarchus judges from "a pit of darkness" and that the happy outcome is appropriate. Also includes chapters on Sidney's poetry, the *Defence*, and the New *Arcadia*. For detailed annotations, see items 1575, 1897, and 2505.

551 HARKNESS, STANLEY. "The Prose Style of Sir Philip Sidney." In *Studies by Members of the Department of English*. University of Wisconsin Studies in Language and Literature, 2. [Madison]: University of Wisconsin, 1918, pp. 57–76.

Compares the syntax of *Arcadia* and the *Defence*, providing statistics on their differences. Ascribes the stylistic and grammatical faults of *Arcadia* to the author's desire to match his style to the extravagance of the action. Concludes that Sidney was less concerned with sentence architecture or punctuation than with rhythms, which he sometimes took from the Latin *cursus*.

Twentieth Century

552 HARMAN, EDWARD GEORGE. *Edmund Spenser and the Impersonations of Francis Bacon.* London: Constable & Co., 1914, pp. 3, 4, 147–51, 185–92.

Contends that Sir Francis Bacon wrote all of Sidney's major works, that Spenser's *English Poet* is really the work known as Sidney's *Defence*, and that the correspondence between Spenser and Harvey is fictitious.

553 ———. *Gabriel Harvey and Thomas Nashe.* London: J.M. Ouseley & Son, 1923, pp. 74–75, 91, 103, 134–35, 165–67, 190–94.

Claims that the *Defence, Astrophil and Stella,* and the *Letter to the Queen* were actually written by Bacon. Finds parallels between the works of Thomas Nashe and Sidney, especially between the *Anatomy of Absurdity* and the *Defence*. Speculates on possible allusions to Sidney in other works by Nashe and in the Northumberland Manuscript, discovered in 1867 by John Bruce.

554 HARRISON, G[EORGE] B. "Books and Readers, 1591–94." *Library*, 4th ser. 8 (December 1927):273–302.

Discusses the dispute between the printers Olney and Ponsonby over the publication of the *Defence*. Also considers the role of *Astrophil and Stella* in beginning the vogue for sonnets in England.

555 HARRISON, JOHN SMITH. *Platonism in English Poetry of the Sixteenth and Seventeenth Centuries.* Columbia University Studies in Comparative Literature. New York: Columbia University Press, 1903, pp. 84, 127, 137.

Claims that ideas from Plato's *Phaedrus* pervade *Arcadia* and *Astrophil and Stella*. Reads "Leave me, O Love" (*CS 32*) as a Platonic expression of the soul's change from earthly to divine love. Sees the identification of Stella with wisdom in *Astrophil and Stella* 25 as reflecting Plato's description of wisdom as a beautiful woman.

556 HARRISON, T.P., Jr. "The Relations of Spenser and Sidney." *PMLA* 45 (September 1930):712–31.

Seeks to clarify the extent of the friendship between the Sidney and Spenser by comparing their literary works and political views. Discusses their association with the Areopagus, their views of the divine gift required for poetry, their debts to Sannazaro, their concept of epic poetry, and their contempt for court life. Reviews evidence on their views of cosmology, considering the influence of Lucretius, Cicero, and du Plessis-Mornay. Concludes that they neglected Lucretian atomism in favor of an Empedoclean concept of the elements. Points to similarities in Spenser's

Hymn in Honor of Love and Pamela's refutation of Cecropia in the Captivity Episode, and notes that *The Faerie Queene* and *Arcadia* both contain allegories of Elizabeth's French marriage plans. Also finds that the two authors held similar views of political order, the authority of the monarch, and the untrustworthiness of the masses. See also Purcell (1122).

557 HAYDN, HIRAM. *The Counter Renaissance*. New York: Charles Scribner's Sons, 1950, pp. 7–9, 41–42, 331–32, 362, 392–93, 406, 437, 586–87.

Sees a division in Sidney's loyalties between Christian humanism and the anti-intellectual reaction to it. Comments on Platonism in the *Defence*, on Sidney's notions of honor and of atheism, and on his death-bed interest in classical as well as Christian views of immortality.

558 HAZLITT, WILLIAM. *The Collected Works of William Hazlitt*. Edited by A.R. Waller and Arnold Glover. 12 vols. London: J.M. Dent & Co.; New York: McClure, Phillips & Co., 1902–6, 5:303, 318–26; 6:175; 9:9–10; 10:14–15.

In "Table Talk," finds Sidney's sonnets "like riddles." In "Mr. Angerstein's Collection," compares Annibal Caracci's painting "Silenus teaching a young Apollo to play on the pipe" with the passage in *Arcadia* in which a young shepherd pipes "as though he should never be old." Elsewhere attacks Sidney as a "poser," whose *Arcadia* describes a society that never existed and so cannot teach "national manners." Also reprints 359.

559 HEFFNER, RAY. "Essex the Ideal Courtier." *ELH* 1 (April 1934):7–36.

Amasses evidence to demonstrate that Essex was regarded as the "successor of Sidney," and that in 1596 he would have been recognized as the obvious prototype of Spenser's knight of courtesy in Book VI of *The Faerie Queene*. Surveys previous arguments in favor of Sidney and considers "several points in Calidore's character which point more directly to Essex than to Sidney" (i.e., his habit of withdrawing into the country). Also reviews incidents that fit Essex's history but not Sidney's.

560 HEFFNER, RAY; MASON, DOROTHY E.; and PADELFORD, FREDERICK M[ORGAN], eds. *Spenser Allusions in the Sixteenth and Seventeenth Centuries*. "Part I: 1580–1625." *SP* 68 (December 1971):1–172; "Part II: 1626–1700." *SP* 69 (December 1972):175–351. Reprint. Chapel Hill: University of North Carolina Press, 1972, 363 pp. passim.

Lists many allusions to Sidney.

Twentieth Century

561 HELGERSON, RICHARD. *The Elizabethan Prodigals.* Berkeley: University of California Press, 1976, pp. 124–55, 169–71. Orig. a Ph.D. diss., Johns Hopkins University, 1970.

Sees in Sidney and his major works embodiments of the parable of the Prodigal Son, in which good counsel leads to rebellion against reason and eventually to repentance. Stresses the importance of Greville's report that, as Sidney lay dying, he repented for writing *Arcadia*, judging it "apt to allure men to evil." Also finds significant his inability to defend love poetry in the *Defence*, suggesting that *Arcadia* and *Astrophil and Stella* must, even on his own principles, have seemed to him suspect. Argues that Astrophil, Pyrocles and Musidorus, and Philisides are all, in key respects, masks for Sidney himself and that they all behave as prodigals. Points out a trap for the reader in the Old *Arcadia*: "We begin on the side of civic humanism, pass through a stage of detached tolerance, and end excited by vicarious lust." Regards the outcome as a defiant departure from the traditional tale of the Prodigal Son, since the heroes fail to repent and also call into question the very justice of the older generation, which is represented in Euarchus. Stresses the radical nature of Sidney's claims that human reason is darkened and cannot judge such matters rightly. Treats *Astrophil and Stella* as an even bolder rebellion, in which both the technique of the sequence and its subject are the "casting off" of the "conventional self." Traces the process from the explicit strategy of seduction laid out in "Loving in truth" (*AS 1*) to the eventual standoff between Astrophil's passion and Stella's virtue, concluding that the sequence does not meet the moral requirements for poetry set out in the *Defence*. Regards the revisions in *Arcadia*—particularly the more chaste and heroic conduct of Pyrocles and Musidorus—as Sidney's attempt to fulfill the responsibility to teach moral and civic virtue placed on him by such mentors as his father and Languet. Notes, however, that Book III introduces in Amphialus a new prodigal very much like the ones in previous works. Suggests that Sidney simply could not abandon the divided heroes that most intrigued him in favor of more responsible ones. Feels that he may have left the revision unfinished because it would have led back to another immoral subject: the fall of the lovers recounted in Books III–V of the original version. Concludes that he then renounced the works of his youth and turned to religious subjects, concentrating on translations of du Bartas, du Plessis-Mornay, and the Psalms. Considering Sidney's ambivalence about the worth of his own poetry, suggests that the *Defence* be shelved with Erasmus's *Praise of Folly* and other paradoxical *encomia*.

562 HICKSON, S.A.E. *The Prince of Poets and Most Illustrious of Philosophers*. London: Gay & Hancock, 1926, pp. 113–14, 151–278 passim.

On the supposition that Shakespeare was really Sir Francis Bacon, imagines that he enjoyed intimate personal and literary relations with Sidney and his circle.

563 HOFFMAN, NANCY JO. *Spenser's Pastorals: The "Shepheardes Calender" and "Colin Clout"*. Baltimore and London: Johns Hopkins University Press, 1977, pp. 48–49, 84–85.

Contrasts Virgil and Sidney in their attitudes toward nature. Suggests that, in *The Lady of May*, Sidney is far removed from "real nature," working in the "frozen" literary world of conventional pastoral. Explicates Sidney's sestina "Ye goatherd gods" (*OA 71*), urging that he tends to treat nature as ornament or as an allegory of the poet's inner world, whereas Spenser treats it as a real landscape that reflects the inner world of the mind.

564 HOGAN, PATRICK G[ALVIN], Jr. "Sidney and Titian: Painting in the *Arcadia* and the *Defence*." *South Central Bulletin* 27, no. 4 (Winter 1967):9–15.

Provides background for Sidney's description of poetry as a "speaking picture" and seeks to discover his theories of visual art. Analyzes passages in his works that deal with paintings, comparing treatments of the same subjects in the works of Titian, Veronese, Tintoretto, and others. Concentrates on the following subjects: Diana and Actaeon in the New *Arcadia*; Danae and Leda in the same work and in the sonnet "Some lovers speak when they their muses entertain" (*AS 6*); and Lucretia and Tarquin in the *Defence*. Lists paintings and tapestries that Sidney might have seen in England, claiming that Titian is the most likely candidate for seven of Sidney's allusions.

565 ———. "Sidney/Spenser: A Courtesy-Friendship-Love Formulation *Forum* (Houston, Tex.) 9, no. 1 (1971):65–69.

Analyzes the relationship between Sidney and Spenser according to neo-Platonic philosophy, and notes the influence of *Arcadia* on *The Faerie Queene*, especially on Book VI.

566 ———. "Sir Philip Sidney's *Arcadia* and Edmund Spenser's *Faerie Queene*: An Analysis of the Personal, Philosophic, and Iconographic Relationships." Ph.D. diss., Vanderbilt University, 1965, 534 pp.

Twentieth Century

Traces the tradition that Sidney and Spenser were friends and discusses their roles in the Areopagus. Also compares their philosophical interest in Renaissance Christian neo-Platonism, their reliance on graphic arts as the basis for literary imagery, and their uses of iconography. See *DA* 26 (August 1965):1021–22.

567 HÖHNA, HEINRICH. *Der Physiologus in der elisabethanischen Literatur.* Erlangen, Germany: Höfer & Limmert, 1930, pp. 17–19.

Catalogs references to the phoenix, the turtledove, and the viper in the *Defence* and *Arcadia*. Traces such nature lore to the second-century treatise *Physiologus*.

568 HOLLAND, HUBERT H. *Shakespeare Through Oxford Glasses.* London: Cecil Palmer, 1923, pp. 42, 47–48, 56, 76.

In analyzing *Twelfth Night*, identifies Olivia as the Countess of Pembroke and her dead brother as Sidney. Also suggests other Shakespearean characters who resemble Sidney.

569 HOLMES, ELIZABETH. *Aspects of Elizabethan Imagery.* Oxford: Basil Blackwell, 1929, pp. 11–14.

Contrasts the prose styles of Sidney and John Lyly and suggests qualities of metaphysical poetry in the verse of *Astrophil and Stella* and *Arcadia*.

570 HÖLTGEN, KARL JOSEF. "Richard Latewar, Elizabethan Poet and Divine." *Anglia* 89 (1971):417–38.

Lists Latewar's twenty-one contributions to the Oxford elegies, *Exequiae Illustrissimi Philippi Sidnaei* (2760), noting that the main piece alludes to unpublished copies of *Arcadia* and *Astrophil and Stella*. Records Latewar's "intimate" knowledge of Sidney's family and his intention to write three tragedies under Sidney's patronage, though only *Philotas* was completed.

571 HOOG, W. de. *Studiën over de Nederlandsche en Engelsche Taal en Letterkunde.* Vol. 2. Dordrecht, Netherlands: J.P. Revers, 1903, pp. 71–74, 78–81.

In considering Rodenburgh's paraphrase of the *Defence* (99), sketches Sidney's life and works, mentioning Dutch translations and reviewing Sidney's concept of poetry. Notes that Johan van Heemskerk translated passages from *Arcadia* as an opening for his own work *Batavische Arcadia*.

572 HORNE, DAVID H. "The Life." In *The Life and Works of George Peele*, edited by Charles Tyler Prouty. Vol. 1, *The Life and Minor Works of George Peele*, edited by David H. Horne. New Haven, Conn.: Yale University Press, 1952, p. 95.

Notes that, in the prologue to *The Honor of the Garter*, Peele lists Sidney among his favorite authors.

573 HOWELL, WILBUR SAMUEL. *Logic and Rhetoric in England, 1500–1700*. Princeton, N.J.: Princeton University Press, 1956, pp. 204–5, 222–23, 258, 276–77.

Considers Sidney's role in encouraging studies of logic by William Temple and Abraham Fraunce. Notes that illustrations of rhetorical figures in Sidney's writings from John Hoskins's *Directions for Speech and Style* were reused in Thomas Blount's *Academy of Eloquence* and in John Smith's *Mystery of Rhetoric Unveiled*.

574 HUDSON, HOYT HOPEWELL. *The Epigram in the English Renaissance*. Princeton, N.J.: Princeton University Press, 1947, pp. 137, 163.

Mentions poems by Daniel Rogers written to and about Sidney that "might well be consulted by biographers." Also discusses the arrangement of words in Sidney's poem "Virtue, beauty, and speech" (*OA 60*).

575 ———. "Penelope Devereux as Sidney's Stella." *Huntington Library Bulletin* 7 (April 1935):89–129.

Against Purcell (2232) and Brownbill (2072), offers evidence that "intelligent readers" and Sidney's own family and friends thought Stella to be Lady Rich. Cites early references to the proposed match between Sidney and Penelope, the several Sidney poems playing on "rich," and similar puns on and allusions to the names "Rich" and "Stella" by Sidney's contemporaries. Stresses Matthew Gwynne's sonnet to Lady Rich, which was prefixed to Florio's translation of Montaigne (2796), and John Ford's tribute to Charles Blount in *Fame's Memorial*. Sees Anne Bradstreet's treatment of Stella as a "comet" (2785) as a typical response of "moralists in his family." Surveys the treatment of Sidney's reputation by Puritan and theological writers, who "felt that something worldly and faintly scandalous adhered" to it, stressing the life published with the 1655 edition of *Arcadia*. Examines the tradition of those who consider Stella to be Frances Walsingham, claiming that elegies by Spenser (2771) and Bryskett (2749) that imply this identification were written and recognized as "fictions." Rebuts Purcell's analysis of Tyndale's letter to Aubrey (902), claiming that the letter "plumbs the period before the 'whitewashing' began." See a reply by Morris (1125).

173

Twentieth Century

576 HUGHES, MERRITT Y., ed. *John Milton: Complete Poems and Major Prose*. New York: Odyssey Press, 1957, pp. 76, 452, 523.
Suggests that Milton's defence of himself in Sonnet VII is paralleled by Sidney's defence of himself in *Astrophil and Stella* 23. Points out a similarity between *Paradise Regained* IV.346–50 and Sidney's statement in the *Defence* that the best poets were the biblical writers who "did imitate the unconceivable excellencies of GOD."

577 HUNGER, F[RIEDRICH] W[ILHELM] T[OBIAS]. *Charles de l'Éscluse (Carolus Clusius) nederlandsch Kruidkundige, 1526-1609*. 2 vols. The Hague: Martinus Nijhof, 1927–1943, 1:147, 154, 288; 2:69, 71, 340–41, 344.
Notes that l'Éscluse's *Simplicium Medicamentorum* is dedicated to Sidney and Edward Dyer. Summarizes and transcribes a 12 April 1577 Latin letter referring to Greville and Sidney, and an 8 July 1577 letter to Languet discussing Sidney's visit to the Prince of Orange.

578 HUNT, JOHN SCOTT. "Sir Philip Sidney and the Psychology of Imagination." Ph.D. diss., Stanford University, 1984, 331 pp.
Studies the "philosphical considerations" that led Sidney "to regard the writing and reading of poetry from the perspective of human psychology." Juxtaposing passages from the *Defence* with others in *Arcadia*, argues that for Sidney "ethically, epistemologically, [and] aesthetically," human life is "governed by the need to bring speculative insight and practical experience into harmonious conjunction." Examines Sidney's "conception of introspective knowledge" and his "conception of imagination or memory as faculties which order a [divided] soul." See *DAI* 45 (December 1984):1759A.

579 HUNTER, G.K. *John Lyly: The Humanist as Courtier*. London: Routledge & Kegan Paul; Cambridge, Mass.: Harvard University Press, 1962, pp. 190–91, 251–53, 286–90, 298–99.
Rejects the interpretation of Lyly's *Endymion* that equates the character Eumenides with Sidney. Cites evidence that Lyly's comedies were written with the conscious aim of satisfying Sidney's prescriptions in the *Defence*. Details differences between the euphuistic and Arcadian styles in order to explain why Sidney's influence eclipsed that of Lyly among seventeenth-century stylists and authors of romance. Also contrasts Sidney's ideal of noble love with Lyly's more comic view.

580 INGLEBY, CLEMENT MANSFIELD; SMITH, L. TOULMIN; and FURNIVALL, FREDERICK JAMES, eds. *The Shakespeare Allusion Book: A Collection of Allusions To Shakespeare from*

1591–1700. Reedited, revised, and rearranged by John Munro. 2 vols. New York: Duffield & Co; London: Chatto & Windus, 1909, 1:27, 47, 127, 243, 251, 278, 472, 473, 496; 2:7, 66, 137 161, 202, 264.

Records more than a dozen allusions in the sixteenth and seventeenth centuries to Sidney's position as a prominent writer.

581 INGLIS, FRED. *The Elizabethan Poets: The Making of English Poetry from Wyatt to Ben Jonson.* Literature in Perspective Series. London: Evans Brothers, 1969, pp. 71–80.

Sketches Sidney's life and character, stressing his importance as a patron, an importer of Continental culture, and an innovator. Explicates two sonnets: "With how sad steps, O moon" (*AS 31*) and "Leave me, O love" (*CS 32*). Evaluates the strengths and weaknesses of *Astrophil and Stella* and the Psalms.

582 IZARD, THOMAS C. *George Whetstone, Mid-Elizabethan Gentleman of Letters.* Columbia University Studies in English and Comparative Literature, 158. New York: Columbia University Press, 1942, pp. 2, 28, 78, 126, 203, 251–55, 287.

Finds no evidence to prove that Whetstone was in Sidney's circle or that he cast the characters Phyloxenus and Aurelia in his *Heptameron of Civil Discourses* in the likeness of Sidney and his sister. Concludes, however, that Whetstone knew *Arcadia* in manuscript and may have read Sidney's translation of du Plessis-Mornay. Also discusses Sidney's use of Whetstone's preface to *Promos and Cassandra* in writing the *Defence.* Considers the metrical life of Sidney written by Whetstone and his brother Bernard (2776), noting that Bernard was with Sidney when he died and that the poem contains valuable, firsthand information.

583 JAVITCH, DANIEL. *Poetry and Courtliness in Renaissance England.* Princeton, N.J.: Princeton University Press, 1978, pp. 80–81, 93–104, 138, 151–52.

Considers Sidney's "aristocratic bias" in *Arcadia,* particularly his assumption that the royal lovers can catch word play that is beyond the intelligence of the rustic characters. Compares the concept of poetry in the *Defence* with the portrayal of serious aristocratic play in Castiglione's *Courtier.* Notes that both require a withdrawal from the "brazen" world to feign a "golden" one and, by this means, to provide self-knowledge and models for living. Stresses the appeal of "systematic indirection" to the Elizabethan aristocracy and relates this preference to Sidney's view that instruction needs to be combined with delight, that poetry is superi-

Twentieth Century

or to history and philosphy, and that morality is best taught by example. Notes that, in Sidney's day, poetry had begun to supplant oratory as a means of persuasion. Also compares Sidney's views of poetry with those implicit in Spenser's vision of Mount Acidale in Book VI of *The Faerie Queene*. See also item 2159.

> **584** JONAS, LEAH. *The Divine Science: The Aesthetic of Some Representative Seventeenth-Century English Poets.* New York: Columbia University Press, 1940, pp. 8, 85, 88–89, 114.

Draws on the *Defence* to show the Italianate tradition of poetic criticism inherited by the seventeenth century. Notes the influence of *Arcadia* on William Browne of Tavistock, especially in *Britannia's Pastorals*. Also points out that Giles Fletcher's *Christ's Victory and Triumph* is "strongly reminiscent" of the *Defence*.

> **585** JONES, H[ARRY] S[TUART] V[EDDER]. *A Spenser Handbook.* New York: F.S. Crofts & Co., 1930, pp. 23, 26, 79–85 passim, 89–91, 114–15, 201–2, 294–95, 325–32, 391–93.

Examines Spenser's elegy for Sidney in *The Ruins of Time*. Compares Sidney's concept of poetry with Spenser's and reviews speculation that *Muiopotmos* is an allegory of Sidney's quarrel with the Earl of Oxford in 1579. Suggests that Timias's service to Arthur in *The Faerie Queene* II.xi may represent Sidney's aid to his uncle in the *Defence of Leicester* and examines the view that Calidore in Book VI is also modeled on Sidney. Notes that the character Astrophel in *Colin Clout's Come Home Again* also represents Sidney and considers the effects of the *Defence* upon the style of the poem. Examines *Astrophel* (and also John Ford's play *The Broken Heart*) for references to Sidney's life, especially his love of Penelope Rich. Touches on other references to Sidney in Spenser's *Shepherd's Calendar, Mother Hubberd's Tale*, and correspondence.

> **586** JONES, WILLIAM BUFORD. "Nathaniel Hawthorne and English Renaissance Allegory." Ph.D. diss., Harvard University, 1962, pp. 25–44.

Compares Hawthorne's *Blithedale Romance* with *Arcadia*, discussing landscape, characters, clothing, views of poetry, and the generic characteristics of pastoral.

> **587** JUSSERAND, J[EAN] J[ULES]. *Histoire littéraire du peuple anglais.* Vol. 2, *De la Renaissance à la guerre civile.* Paris: Didot, 1904, pp. 262, 264–65, 326–31, 344–49, 462–69, 605, 779, 846.

See item 588.

588 ———. *A Literary History of the English People from the Renaissance to the Civil War*. 2 vols. London: T. Fisher Unwin, 1906–9, 1:287–91, 364–68, 393–97, 531–38; 2:180, 388, 467–68. [The title page labels these as Vols. 1 and 2, but the index treats them as Vols. 2 and 3.]

An English version of item 587. Sketches Sidney's life, discussing the aims and success of his Continental tour. Remarks on the eclectic tastes revealed in the *Defence* and rebuts the view that *Astrophil and Stella* addresses an idealized mistress rather than a real woman. Counters Greville's claim that *Arcadia* is a philosophic poem. Examines the English landscapes and gardens that Sidney had transplanted to Greece, the elements of the Arcadian style, and the influence of the romance on later writers. Discusses its popularity in France, recounting the bitter quarrel between its first French translators, Jean Baudoin and Geneviève Chappelain. Quotes the humorous comparison of Shakespeare and Sidney in *Daiphantus* and notes the influence of *Arcadia* in the speeches of Lady Saviolina in Jonson's *Every Man out of His Humour*. Also discusses Sidney's influence on William Drummond of Hawthornden and on Abraham Cowley's poem "Bathing in the River" in *The Mistress*.

589 KALSTONE, DAVID. "Sir Philip Sidney." In *History of Literature in the English Language*. Vol. 2, *English Poetry and Prose, 1540–1674*, edited by Christopher Ricks. London: Barrie & Jenkins, 1970, pp. 41–59.

Argues that Sidney's works all embody the "critic's prescriptive intelligence," as reflected particularly in the demands of the *Defence* that poetry "move" the reader. Claims that Sidney's career may be viewed "in terms of the growing difficulty his protagonists have envisioning and attaining the perfection of the exemplary heroes mentioned in the *Defence*." Compares the self-mastery and control in *Arcadia*, where "the retrospective narratives of the princes and the highly directive prose of the third-person narrator are constantly demonstrating analytic powers, rich in images which 'enable the judgment,'" to the conflict between fixed ideals and experience in *Astrophil and Stella*, whose protagonist is "engaged in a series of rich encounters with authority, testing the formulas with which others characterize experience." Contrasts the "more intense verbal activity" of the sequence with the "essentially static" poetry of *Arcadia*.

Twentieth Century

590 KASTNER, LEON ÉMILE. "Drummond's Indebtedness to Sidney." *MLR* 6 (April 1911):157–64.
Demonstrates that Drummond made heavy verbatim and paraphrastic borrowings from *Astrophil and Stella* and *Arcadia*, both in his sonnets and in his longer poems.

591 KASTNER, L[EON] É[MILE], ed. Introduction and notes to *The Poetical Works of William Drummond of Hawthornden with "A Cypresse Grove.".* Publications of the University of Manchester, English Series, 5–6. 2 vols. Manchester: Manchester University Press, 1913, 1:xxix–xxx, 164–242 passim; 2:332–410 passim.
Notes Drummond's heavy borrowing from *Arcadia* and *Astrophil and Stella*.

592 KEYNES, Sir GEOFFREY [LANDGON]. "Donne's Books." *TLS*, 13 January 1966, p. 25.
Notes that Donne owned a copy of *Peplus Illustrissimi Viri D. Philippi Sidnaei* (2763), the volume of elegies for Sidney published by scholars at New College, Oxford.

593 KIMBROUGH, ROBERT. *Sir Philip Sidney.* Twayne's English Authors Series, 114. New York: Twayne Publishers, 1971, 162 pp.
Insists that "the life of Sidney and the nature of his art must be studied together." In Chapters 1 and 2, surveys the life and examines the rhetorical strategies of the *Defence*. In Chapter 3, examines *The Lady of May* and discusses the relation between the Old *Arcadia* and its original audience. In Chapter 4, discusses the metrical experiments and poems written in imitation of other authors. In Chapter 5, stresses Sidney's accomplishment in creating the lover's voice in *Astrophil and Stella*, and in the final chapter, suggests that the change in "mode" in the New *Arcadia* reveals a major shift in the author's purpose. Contains a chronology and a selected bibliography. For detailed annotations, see items 1082, 1253, 1911, 2168, 2539, and 2695.

594 KINNEY, ARTHUR F. "Rhetoric and Fiction in Elizabethan England." In *Renaissance Eloquence: Studies in the Theory and Practice of Renaissance Rhetoric*, edited by James J. Murphy. Berkeley: University of California Press, 1983, pp. 385–93.
Argues that, in the *Defence*, Sidney adapts methods of rhetorical disputation to the purposes of poetic fiction. Suggests that "the inherent conflict between icastic and fantastic representation demands a third response. . . : an act of triangulation through which the reader gives the final significance. . . ." Illustrates this view by suggesting that, in Book III of the

New *Arcadia*, Pamela's arguments defeat those of Cecropia and yet are themselves called into question by the surrounding action of the book. Relates this dialectical indeterminacy to other features of the work: the rhetorical excesses of the characters, the problems in judgment raised by the trial at the end, and the lack of a true ending to the action in either version.

> **595** KLEIN, HOLGER MICHAEL. "Das weibliche Portrait in der Versdichtung der englischen Renaissance. Analyse einer literarischen Konvention und Beiträge zum Wandel von Stil und Darstellungstechnik in der englischen Dichtung zwischen 1500 und 1660." Ph.D. diss., Universität München, 1969, 866 pp.

Examines nearly a thousand portraits of women in Renaissance English literature, discussing Sidney's innovations in the idealization of feminine beauty. See *EASG*, 1969, pp. 33–35.

> **596** KLIEM, HANS. *Sentimentale Freundschaft in der Shakespeare-Epoche*. Jena, Germany: Bernhard Vopelius, 1915, pp. 8–15, 34–35. Orig. a Ph.D. diss., University of Jena, 1914.

Considers the Areopagus and Sidney's friendships with Fulke Greville, Sir Edward Dyer, Hubert Languet, and Edmund Spenser. Compares the psychological development of the friendships in *Arcadia* with that in Robert Greene's *Tully's Love*.

> **597** KNIGHT, G[EORGE] WILSON. *The Mutual Flame: On Shakespeare's Sonnets and "The Phoenix and the Turtle."* London: Methuen & Co.; New York: Macmillan Co., 1955, pp. 150, 152, 155.

Citing the elegies for Sidney in *The Phoenix Nest* (2740, 2768, 2770), considers Sidney's association with the symbol of the phoenix.

> **598** KOK, A[BRAHAM] S[EYNE]. *Gedenteeken voor Sir Philip Sidney*. Haarlem, Netherlands: n.p., 1910, 16 pp.

Not seen. Appears to be the same as the partial reprint of item 599, with a Dutch title. Cited in the catalogs of the New York Public Library and Yale University.

> **599** ———. "Sir Philip Sidney." *Onze Eeuw* 10 (May 1910):223–60. Partial reprint. *Sir Philip Sidney*. Pamphlet. Haarlem, Netherlands: n.p., 1910, 16 pp.

Provides, in Dutch, a general introduction to Sidney's life and works. Remarks on the sources of *Arcadia*, its form, and its style. Weighs the importance of the *Defence* in the development of literary theory, compar-

Twentieth Century

ing it to Shelley's *Defence*. Treats *Astrophil and Stella* as autobiographical, and closes with testimonials to Sidney by authors of various nationalities.

600 KOLLER, KATHERINE. "Abraham Fraunce and Edmund Spenser." *ELH* 7 (June 1940):108–20.
Includes a discussion of Fraunce's long connection with Sidney and his circle.

601 ———. "Identifications in *Colin Clout's Come Home Againe*." *MLN* 50 (March 1935):155–58.
Describes annotations, in an early- to mid-seventeenth-century hand, comprising the "earliest record of identifications of people mentioned" in *Colin Clout*. Amyntas is mistakenly identified as Sidney.

602 KRAPP, GEORGE PHILIP. *The Rise of English Literary Prose*. New York: Oxford University Press; London: Humphrey Milford, 1915, pp. 303, 362–82, 482.
Places Sidney's Latin pedant Rombus in a lengthy list of similar carica-tures in Renaissance English literature. Analyzes the style of *Arcadia*, attributing the decline of euphuism to Sidney's influence but suggesting that the heavy ornamentation of the romance does not accord with the ideal of prose poetry advocated in the *Defence*. Also reviews the publish-ing history of *Arcadia* and comments on its reputation among Sidney's contemporaries. Lists "antecedents" of the work, including du Bellay's *Défense et illustration de la langue française*.

603 KUIN, R[OGER] J.P. "Scholars, Critics, and Sir Philip Sidney, 1945–1970." *British Studies Monitor* 2 (Spring 1972):3–22.
Describes major contributions to Sidney scholarship during the period, especially advances in historical and editorial research. Notes the lack of cohesive general works of criticism and fresh approaches to *Arcadia*.

604 LaGUARDIA, ERIC. *Nature Redeemed: The Imitation of Order in Three Renaissance Poems*. Studies in English Literature, 31. The Hague: Mouton, 1966, pp. 36–45, 169.
Comparing Marlowe's treatment of the conflict between passion and purity in *Hero and Leander* with Sidney's in *Arcadia*, points out that Sidney's "shows more rhetoric than drama." Argues that "order" is redeemed in *Arcadia* through the ideals of beauty and chastity: "their mutual sovereignty is a poetic image for the synthesis of nature and spirit." Discusses Sidney's use of the term "imitation" in its historical context.

605 LAIDLER, JOSEPHINE. "A History of Pastoral Drama in England until 1700." *Englische Studien* 35 (1905):193–259.
Notes that *The Lady of May* is the first English play to draw upon the true tradition of the pastoral. Concludes that the main contribution of *Arcadia* to Elizabethan drama was in general atmosphere, not in specific dramatic material. Discusses three plays that did draw specific incidents and characters from the romance: John Day's *Isle of Gulls*, Henry Glapthorne's *Argalus and Parthenia*, and James Shirley's *Arcadia*. Also notes the imitation of Sidney's style in Walter Montague's *Shepherd's Paradise*.

606 LAMB, M[ARY] E[LLEN]. "The Houghton Sale: Items of Interest to Sidney Scholars." *SNew* 2, no. 2 (1981):7–9.
Reports the sale of the Helmington Hall manuscript of the Old *Arcadia* and *The Lady of May*, a manuscript of 100 poems from *Astrophil and Stella* compiled by William Briton of Kelston, early editions of *Astrophil and Stella* and *Arcadia*, and a letter of credit to Sidney for 400 ducats from Tommaso Galbani dated 26 July 1574.

607 ———. "The Myth of the Countess of Pembroke: The Dramatic Circle." *YES* 11 (1981):194–202.
Sets out to demonstrate the unlikelihood that Sidney's sister was at the center of a circle of playwrights influenced or motivated by the views laid out in the *Defence* or that she had any intention of attempting to reform the popular stage according to those views. Discusses tensions between the Countess and Fulke Greville over the publication of the 1590 *Arcadia*.

608 ———. "Three Unpublished Holograph Poems in the Bright Manuscript: A New Poet in the Sidney Circle?" *RES*, n.s. 35 (August 1984):301–15.
Adds new information to the description of the Bright Manuscript provided by Ringler (92). Remarks on the presence of two hitherto unnoted names, both with Sidney family associations, and on the fact that the manuscript has been rearranged since Ringler's description. Considers three poems in the manuscript that are not by Sidney, surveying a complex body of evidence implying that their author was a woman. Transcribes, edits, and comments critically on the three poems, regarding one as imitative of Sidney's themes and techniques.

181

Twentieth Century

609 LAMBIN, G. "De Peele à Sidney, à propos d'une coquille." *Revue anglo-américaine* 2 (1924–25):242–43.
Speculates that Sidney's lost translation of du Bartas was a source used by George Peele.

610 LANGDALE, ABRAM BARNETT. *Phineas Fletcher: Man of Letters, Science and Divinity.* Columbia University Studies in English and Comparative Literature, 125. New York: Columbia University Press, 1937, pp. 122–24, 135.
Points out Fletcher's debt to *Astrophil and Stella* and *Arcadia* in *Sicelides* and his use of the couplet of "Because I breathe not love" (*AS 54*) in his *"Non invisa Cano."*

611 LANHAM, RICHARD A[LAN]. *The Motives of Eloquence: Literary Rhetoric in the Renaissance.* New Haven, Conn., and London: Yale University Press, 1976, pp. 9, 12, 49, 104, 215.
Contrasting a "serious reality" with a "rhetorical reality," argues that the dichotomy underlies Sidney's *Defence*. Feels that Sidney stopped revising *Arcadia* because he could not work out an operant distinction between the "rhetorical reality" of the original version and the "serious reality" toward which the revisions were tending.

612 LANIER, SIDNEY. *Shakespeare and His Forerunners: Studies in Elizabethan Poetry and its Development from Early English.* Vol. 1. New York: Doubleday, Page & Co., 1902, pp. 245–54.
Regards *Astrophil and Stella* as a record of Sidney's passion for Lady Rich, going so far as to term the sonnets "letters from her lover." Analyzes their narrative progression as a five-act tragedy epitomized by sonnets 12, 23, 40, and 64 and *Certain Sonnets* 32 (which he treats as *Astrophil and Stella* 110). Suggests that *Arcadia* is not read now because of its "mazy complications" and its "endless interrelations of antique with medieval characters."

613 LARSON, CHARLES [HOWARD]. *Fulke Greville.* Twayne's English Authors Series, 302. Boston: Twayne Publishers, 1980, pp. 13, 15–16, 25, 27, 30, 35, 41, 84, 94–108, 110, 123–24.
Compares Sidney and Greville in their attitudes toward literature and public service and in their careers at court. Points out contrasts between Greville's *Caelica* and *Astrophil and Stella* and between Greville's *Treaty of Humane Learning* and the *Defence*. Examines the friendship between the two men and Greville's role in publishing the 1590 *Arcadia*. Dates the composition of his *Life of Sidney* (863) between 1610 and 1614, suggesting that a planned life of Queen Elizabeth that Robert Cecil prevented

Greville from writing may have supplied some of the lengthy digressions on politics in the book. Ponders its aims and its loose organization, stressing its mixed function as a biography, as a political tract meant to cast unfavorable light on James I in contrast to Elizabeth, and as a moral tract centered on the example of Sidney as a Protestant martyr and saint. Distinguishes Greville's pessimism about human nature, his belief in progressive social decline, and his limited faith in the value of literature from the views of his friend. Feels that, in the *Life*, Greville tends to distort Sidney's positions about literature to draw them toward his own. Contrasts the poetic styles adopted by the two writers, tracing the differences to larger contrasts in outlook.

614 LASCELLES, MARY. "The Rider on the Winged Horse." In
Elizabethan and Jacobean Studies Presented to Frank Percy Wilson,
[edited by Herbert Davis and Helen Gardner]. Oxford:
Clarendon Press, 1959, pp. 173–98.
Argues that "I never drank of Aganippe well" (*AS 74*) may "have been formerly designed to stand first in the sequence." Following Renwick's commentary in his edition of Spenser's *Complaints*, contends that lines 645–58 of *The Ruins of Time* are an emblem of Sidney.

615 LATHAM, AGNES [MARY CHRISTABEL], ed. *The Poems of Sir
Walter Raleigh*. London: Routledge & Kegan Paul; Cambridge,
Mass.: Harvard University Press, 1951, p. 172.
Notes that the Pierpont Morgan Library sheet containing Raleigh's "The State of France as Now It Stands" also attributes Marlowe's "Passionate Shepherd" to Sidney. See also Bühler (1869).

616 LAWRY, JON S. *Sidney's Two "Arcadias": Pattern and Proceeding*.
Ithaca, N.Y.: Cornell University Press, 1972, 320 pp.
Examines the *Defence* as an exposition of the idea of a heroic poem and, on this basis, undertakes close readings of the Old and New *Arcadia*. See detailed annotations in items 1257, 1639, and 2552.

617 LEA, K[ATHLEEN] M[ARGUERITE]. *Italian Popular Comedy: A
Study of the "Commedia dell'Arte," 1560–1620, with special reference to
the English Stage*. Vol. 1. Oxford: Clarendon Press, 1934, pp. 262,
348, 393.
Notes that Italian comedy was popular in Paris when Sidney was there in 1572 and that Sidney may well have seen troupes of Italian actors in Venice in 1574. Suggests that Rombus in *The Lady of May* may have been the model for Holofernes in Shakespeare's *Love's Labor's Lost*.

Twentieth Century

618 LEE, Sir SIDNEY. *The French Renaissance in England: An Account of the Literary Relations of England and France in the Sixteenth Century.* New York: Charles Scribner's Sons, 1910, pp. 38, 256–67, 293, 327, 342, 442–43.

Notes several close connections with French literature in Sidney's works, including experiments in classical meters that parallel the work of Baïf, and comments in the *Defence* on the dramatic unities that parallel statements by French authors. Discusses Sidney's friendship with such leading French Protestants as du Plessis-Mornay, Ramus, and du Bartas. Also isolates French echoes in *Astrophil and Stella*, concluding that the sequence "gives the first sign of the English sonnet's poetic capacity." Regards the work as the most Continental of all the English sequences.

619 ———. *Great Englishmen of the Sixteenth Century.* New York: Charles Scribner's Sons, 1904, pp. 63–115.

In "Sir Philip Sidney," surveys Sidney's life and works, noting that he "seemed destined to distribute his activities over too wide a field for any of them to bear the richest fruit." Emphasizes Platonic and Petrarchan elements in *Astrophil and Stella*, commenting favorably on its metrical experiments and noting its influence on Spenser and Shakespeare. Also remarks on Sidney's contact with Spenser, Dyer, and Greville and their shared interest in classical versification. Faults the *Defence* because of its low opinion of English drama and because it "underrated the value of poetic expression and poetic form." Comments at length on the sources and style of *Arcadia*, concluding that, despite its "jumble of discordant elements," it shows that Sidney had caught "a distant glimpse of the true art of fiction."

620 ———. "Sidney, Sir Philip (1554–1586)." In *Dictionary of National Biography*, edited by Leslie Stephen and Sidney Lee. Vol. 18. London: Smith, Elder; New York: Macmillan Co., 1909, pp. 219–34.

Includes a survey of Sidney's life and a judgment of his character, along with accounts of his major works. In the former, stresses Sidney's "love of learning," the independence of character that "unfitted him for the permanent role of courtier," his perennial financial difficulties, his long-standing interest in colonization in the New World, and the events surrounding his appointment as governor of Flushing, the battle of Zutphen, and the national adulation succeeding his death and funeral. Considers *Astrophil and Stella* a literal reflection of his relations with Penelope Devereux. Claims that Sidney's "force of patriotism and religious fervor," matched by "much political sagacity and oratorical gifts, and by unusual skill in manly sports," were allied to "a naturally chivalric, if somewhat impetuous temperament." Details locations of "very numerous" portraits. For each of the major works, recounts the publication history and provides a brief analysis and judgment. For *Arcadia*, in addition, discusses sources, style ("diffuse and artificial," abounding in "tricks"), and influence on later English and Continental literature, including translations.

621 LEGOUIS, ÉMILE [HYACINTHE]. *Spenser*. London and Toronto: J.M. Dent & Sons; New York: E.P. Dutton & Co., 1926, pp. 67–68, 75–78.

Praises the "bold metaphoric style" of *Arcadia*, discussing the influence of its visual elements on Spenser. Contrasts the narrative pattern of the *Amoretti* with that of *Astrophil and Stella*, stressing Sidney's failure to resolve the conflict between passion and reason.

622 LEHMANN, GARY PAUL. "A Critical Analysis of the Works of John Day (ca. 1574–ca. 1640)." Ph.D. diss., Duke University, 1980, 307 pp.

Argues that Day "drew his language from the elaborate prose style of Sidney." See *DAI* 41 (October 1980):1612–13A.

623 LEIMBERG, INGE. "Shakespeares Komödien und Sidneys 'Goldene Welt.'" *SJH*, 1969, pp. 174–97.

Finds in Shakespeare's comedies a fulfillment of Sidney's ideal that poetry should represent forms in the imagination rather than objects in the real world. Notes that the catharsis at the end of the play typically results from a recognition of cosmic harmony, whereas in Latin New Comedy it had come from a discovery of inner character. Also points out that Shakespearean comedy resembles *Arcadia* in portraying an inner "golden world" threatened by an outer "iron world."

624 LELAND, JOHN G. "Sidney and Osiris." *SNew* 3, no. 1 (1982):10–12.

Noting that Renaissance mythographers sometimes equated Adonis with Osiris, draws connections between these myths and the circumstances of Sidney's death. Argues that Spenser exploited the parallels in *Astrophel* and *The Doleful Lay of Clorinda* (2741).

625 LEMMI, C[HARLES] W[ILLIAM]. "The Allegorical Meaning of Spenser's *Muiopotmos*." *PMLA* 45 (September 1930):732–48.

Argues that, much like Spenser's *Astrophel*, *Muiopotmos* allegorizes the life and death of Sidney. Claims that the two poems "tell fundamentally the

185

Twentieth Century

same tale," suggesting that the butterfly symbol is "peculiarly suited to Sidney." Also feels that the Astery episode alludes to Lady Rich in her role as Sidney's Stella and that departures from classical sources in the Arachne episode "combine to allegorize" Alençon's courtship of Queen Elizabeth. See also Stein (771), Strathmann (775), Denkinger (1009) and Purcell (1120).

626 ――――. "Italian Borrowings in Sidney." *MLN* 42 (February 1927):77–79.
Points out debts to Dante, Boccaccio, Tasso, Giovanni della Casa, and Francesco Berni in Sidney's works.

627 LEVAO, RONALD LEE. "The Renaissance Mind and Its Fictions: A Comparative Study of Nicholas of Cusa, Sir Philip Sidney, and Shakespeare." Ph.D. diss., University of California at Berkeley, 1978, 426 pp.
Argues that Sidney's works "show the making of fictions to be the mind's characteristic activity, even as they undo the traditional defenses of this activity." Sidney's works show his "inability to free himself from an endless proliferation of poetic images." See *DAI* 39 (February 1979):4960A.

628 LEVIN, HARRY. *The Myth of the Golden Age in the Renaissance.* Bloomington: Indiana University Press, 1969, pp. 93–99, 107–10, 120.
Examines Sidney's adaptation of traditional material about Arcadia, considering the changes he made part of an attempt to transform his romance into a "serious, didactic, and even political [epic], as contrasted with the single-minded amorousness of the Spanish pastoral romances." Contrasts Sidney's *icastic* view of poetry in the *Defence* with the *phantastic*, balancing Bacon's condemnation of the fancy against Sidney's praise of the poet's ideal world.

629 LEVY, F[RED] J[ACOB]. *Tudor Historical Thought.* San Marino, Calif.: Huntington Library, 1967, pp. 243–45, 251, 253, 290.
Considers Sidney's appraisal of history in the *Defence* and in the correspondence. Traces to Machiavelli Sidney's claim that historians must become poets to give a full account of causes, noting this license in the practice of later Renaissance historians and historical poets. Also notes historians whom Sidney knew personally and considers his Continental tour in light of Elizabethan treatises on travel.

630 LEWIS, C[LIVE] S[TAPLES]. *The Oxford History of English Literature*. Vol. 3, *English Literature in the Sixteenth Century Excluding Drama*. Oxford: Clarendon Press, 1954, pp. 324–47.
Sees Sidney as an "aristocrat in whom the aristocratic ideal is really embodied" and as one of the first poets in the sixteenth century to write "Golden poetry," or "poetry in its innocent . . . condition." Considers his pioneering efforts in the poems of *Arcadia*, noting "a much wider range of metrical experiment" than in Spenser and possible influences on Milton, especially in his hymn "On the Morning of Christ's Nativity." Regards *Astrophil and Stella* as "an anatomy of love," a form that "exists for the sake of prolonged lyrical meditation, chiefly on love" and sometimes includes "islands" of narrative and "excursions into public affairs, literary criticism, compliment." Suggests that Sidney works symphonically, with the first thirty-two sonnets introducing "most of the themes on which the sequence is built," especially the conflict between Love and Virtue, Passion and Reason. Argues that, for the literary historian, the composite *Arcadia* of 1593 is the most important version because it has been the most influential. Considers two major sources: Sannazaro's *Arcadia* and Heliodorus's *Aethiopica*, noting the subordination of the pastoral elements to the heroic and amatory. Thinks the female characters better developed than the males, but regards "nobility of sentiment," not characterization, as Sidney's chief interest. Sees *Arcadia* as a representation of nature idealized and a touchstone that tests the depth of our "sympathy with the sixteenth century." Remarking that the *Defence* "springs organically" from Sidney's "whole attitude to life," discusses its sources, its "Golden" poetics, and its style. See also Winters (1971).

631 LOFTIE, Rev. W[ILLIAM] [JOHN]. "Edmund Spenser at Penshurst." In *Poets' Country*, edited by Andrew Lang. Philadelphia: J.B. Lippincott Co.; London and Edinburgh: T.C. & E.C. Jack, 1907, pp. 313–24.
Regards Sidney as the chief influence on Spenser's career. Surmises that Spenser visited Sidney at Penshurst before 1579, the scenery being reflected in *The Shepherd's Calendar*.

632 LONG, PERCY W. "Spenser and Sidney." *Anglia* 38 (1914):173–93.
At odds with Bourne (318, 319) and Higginson (1056), argues that Spenser's connection with Sidney never went beyond casual acquaintance. Feels that Sidney's influence on Spenser's poetry was negligible, and that the term "Areopagus," far from designating a formal group, was "a mere figure of speech for the nonce."

Twentieth Century

633 ———. "Spenser's Sir Calidore." *Englische Studien* 42 (1910):53–60.
Reviews scholarship from the eighteenth century to the present linking Sidney with the knight Calidore in Book VI of Spenser's *Faerie Queene*. Finds most telling the identification of the character Meliboe with Sidney's father-in-law, Sir Francis Walshingham. Argues, however, that Calidore better represents Robert Devereux, Earl of Essex, who married Walshingham's daughter Frances in 1590, four years after Sidney left her a widow. See a reply by Rowe (728).

634 LYON, JOHN HENRY HOBART. *A Study of "The Newe Metamorphosis". Written by J.M., Gent. 1600.* New York: Columbia University Press, 1919, pp. 62–63, 155.
Notes allusions and compliments to Sidney in the works of Gervase Markham.

635 McALEER, JOHN J. "Thomas Lodge's Verse Interludes." *CLAJ* 6 (December 1962):83–89.
Discusses Sidney's influence on Lodge's *Forbonius and Prisceria* and *Rosalynde*.

636 MacCAFFREY, ISABEL G. *Spenser's Allegory: The Anatomy of Imagination.* Princeton, N.J.: Princeton University Press, 1976, pp. 20–21, 120–21, 358.
In the context of Renaissance views of the imagination, discusses Sidney's view of the poet's power to invent, noting its relevance to Spenser's *Faerie Queene* V.vii.2. Compares Spenser's Book VI with Sidney's *Arcadia*.

637 McCLURE, NORMAN EGBERT, ed. *The Letters and Epigrams of Sir John Harington, together with "The Prayse of Private Life."* Philadelphia: University of Pennsylvania Press; London: Oxford University Press, 1930, pp. 11, 15, 229, 235, 390.
Argues that Harington transcribed the copy of Sidney's *Letter to the Queen* preserved by John E.M. Harington, which Feuillerat (23) failed to consult. Suggests that the preface to Sir John Harington's translation of *Orlando furioso* owes much to Sidney's *Defence* and that Harington had read it in manuscript. Notes that, in 1609, Harington owned two copies of the Sidney Psalter.

638 McCOY, RICHARD C[HARLES]. *Sir Philip Sidney: Rebellion in Arcadia.* New Brunswick, N.J.: Rutgers University Press, 1979,

244 pp. Orig. a Ph.D. diss., University of California at Berkeley, 1975.
Examines Sidney's major works in relation to Elizabethan politics. Sees in Sidney's mind continual "conflicts between obedient submission to authority and the recalcitrant urges of desire. . . ." In Chapter 1, describes the "code of obedience" that Queen Elizabeth required of her courtiers and the daring independence that Sidney displayed, particularly in his *Letter to the Queen*. Considers his death at Zutphen, noting the changes in the ethic of heroism brought about by sixteenth-century advances in methods of warfare. Glances at each of Sidney's works, noting their biographical context and finding in all of them "inconclusive development, thematic contradictions, and problems of closure." Compares political constraints with the "sexual politics" of unrequited love that is the subject of *Astrophil and Stella*. Rejects the "rationalistic bias" of Sidney criticism that assumes deliberate planning behind the apparent contradictions and irresolutions in Sidney's works. Also rejects Lanham's assertions (1088, 2174) that Sidney's works are shallow and irrelevant to the true political problems of the age. In subsequent chapters, concentrates on the two versions of *Arcadia* and on *Astrophil and Stella*. For detailed annotations, see items 1266, 1663, and 2191.

639 McGRAIL, THOMAS H[ENRY]. *Sir William Alexander, First Earl of Stirling: A Biographical Study.* London: Oliver & Boyd, 1940, pp. 26, 44–45, 53. Orig. a Ph.D. diss., Cornell University, 1936.
Mentions Sidney as a source for several of Alexander's metrical forms and for his echo poem. Also considers the style of Alexander's continuation of *Arcadia*, comparing it with that of the original. Notes affinities between his *Anacrisis* and the *Defence*.

640 McINTYRE, JOHN PATRICK. "Poetry as Gnosis: The Literary Theory of Sir Philip Sidney." Ph.D. diss., University of Toronto, 1969.
Reads the *Defence* "in the light of the Northern humanist tradition . . . brought to England by Erasmus and Vives." Discusses Sidney's schooling in the tradition, his aristocratic views, and his definition of poetry and the "serving sciences" of philosophy and history. Also considers Sidney's Puritanism and the light that his translation of du Plessis-Mornay sheds on the *Defence*. Relates his religious views in the *Defence* to the political philosophy of *Arcadia*. See *DAI* 31 (August 1970):733A.

Twentieth Century

641 McKERROW, RONALD B[RUNLEES]. *Printers' and Publishers' Devices in England & Scotland 1485–1640*. London: Bibliographical Society, Chiswick Press, 1913, items 153ß, 281, 299.
Describes and reproduces devices used on the title pages of *The Trueness of the Christian Religion* (150, 151, and 152).

642 McKERROW, R[ONALD] B[RUNLEES] and FERGUSON, F[REDERICK] S[UTHERLAND]. *Title-page Borders used in England and Scotland 1485–1640*. London: Bibliographical Society, 1932, pp. 92–93, 102–3, 170–71, 176–77, 204.
Describes and reproduces title-page borders in early editions of *Arcadia* (3, 5, 6, and 31) and of *The Trueness of the Christian Religion* (149).

643 McLANE, PAUL E. "The Death of a Queen: Spenser's Dido as Elizabeth." *HLQ* 18 (November 1954):1–11.
Identifies the Kentish shepherds of line 63 in the November eclogue of Spenser's *Shepherd's Calendar* with Sidney and his family. Relates the poem to Elizabeth's marriage negotiations with the French.

644 ———. *Spenser's "Shepheardes Calender": A Study in Elizabethan Allegory*. Notre Dame, Ind.: University of Notre Dame Press, 1961, pp. 18–26, 48, 56, 67–71, 74–75, 81, 88, 220, 223, 234, 262–63, 266, 271–73, 286–91, 294, 342.
Relates Sidney's *Letter to the Queen* to Stubbs's *Gaping Gulf* and Spenser's *Shepherd's Calendar*, concluding that Sidney's letter "represents . . . probably the reasoned view of the majority of the Privy Council." Suggests that Spenser's shepherd Perigot may represent Sidney, but denies that Dido is Ambrosia Sidney. Also notes Mohl's identification of Sidney with Diggon Davie (662), but argues instead for Bishop Richard Davies. Discusses Sidney's quarrel with Oxford in the context of the February eclogue and treats George Buchanan as a "member *in absentia*" of the Sidney-Leicester circle. Also remarks on Sidney's literary friendships with Dyer, Greville, and Spenser.

645 MACLEAN, HUGH N. "Greville's 'Poetic.'" *SP* 61 (April 1964):170–91.
Argues that "Greville's is a highly individualistic poetic . . . [which] contrasts quite sharply with the theory of poetry enunciated by Sidney in the *Defence*." Shows ways in which the style and content of *Astrophil and Stella* differ from those of *Caelica*. Contrasts the theoretical statements in the *Defence* with Greville's scattered comments on poetry in works including the *Life of Sidney*, *Caelica* 80, and his *Treatie of Humane Learning*.

190

Concludes that Greville was "content with an aggregate of observations reflecting his primary concern with the practical utility of poetry, and only slightly with the image-making function of the poet."

646 McNEIL, DAVID PETER. "The Comic Grotesque and War in Selected Renaissance and Eighteenth-Century Prose." Ph.D. diss., McMaster University, 1983.

Defining "comic grotesque" to mean "examples which emphasize the ludicrous," examines the slaughter of the rebels in *Arcadia*, which "parodies epic-battle motifs." See *DAI* 44 (April 1984):3073A.

647 MAGNUS, LAURIE. *English Literature in Its Foreign Relations, 1300–1800*. London: Kegan Paul, Trench, Trübner & Co.; New York: E.P. Dutton & Co., 1927, pp. 31–36.

Argues that Sannazaro and Sidney provided major links between classical pastoral and its modern derivatives. Feels that "Sidney sought to confine the reform of English metre and diction within [the] strict limits of classico-Italian examples." Compares Sidney with Castiglione's ideal courtier.

648 MAHL, MARY R[OBERTA]. "Sir Philip Sidney's Scribe: The New *Arcadia* and the *Apology for Poetry*." *ELN* 10 (December 1972): 90–91.

Reports that the Norwich Manuscript of the *Defence* and Cambridge University Library MS. KK 1.5 of the revised *Arcadia* are in the same hand. Since both may have been prepared during Sidney's stay at Wilton in 1584, suggests that they may represent his final revisions.

649 MASON, PHILIP. *The English Gentleman: The Rise and Fall of an Ideal*. New York: William Morrow & Co., 1982, pp. 57–59, 144–45.

Considers Sidney's reputation in the sixteenth century, focusing on Spenser's tributes to him. Regards him as a combination of the Renaissance courtier and the English Christian gentleman. Contrasts him with the idealized gentleman of the Victorian period.

650 MATHEW, FRANK. *An Image of Shakespeare*. London: Jonathan Cape, 1922, pp. 14, 62, 83, 135, 178–79, 250–51, 288, 297, 327.

Frequently discusses, in a general way, the influence of the *Defence* and *Arcadia* on Shakespeare's plays.

Twentieth Century

651 MAXWELL, MARJORIE E. "The Renowned Sir Philip Sidney: An Anniversary Tribute." *Time and Tide* 35 (11 December 1954): 1680–81.
Salutes the 400th anniversary of Sidney's birth.

652 MAYR, ROSWITHA. "The Concept of Love in Sidney and Spenser." In *The Concept of Love in Sidney and Spenser*, by Roswitha Mayr, and *John Leanerd's "The Rambling Justice, or the Jealous Husbands": A Restoration Plagiarism of Thomas Middleton's "More Dissemblers Besides Women,"* by James Hogg. Elizabethan and Renaissance Studies, 70. Salzburg: Institut für Englische Sprache und Literatur, Universität Salzburg, 1978, pp. 1–110.
In Chapter 1, reviews conventional concepts of love in the courtly, Petrarchan, and neo-Platonic traditions. In Chapter 2, considers the extent to which Sidney and Spenser followed these conventions. Finds in *Astrophil and Stella* remnants of Courtly Love in the exalted lady who is already married and in the suffering lover dedicated to chivalry and the religion of love. Finds Petrarchan influences in the lady's hardness of heart, in her physical traits, and in the metaphors used to describe her. Notes that Sidney is not so subservient as Spenser, that he makes no claims to immortalize Stella, and that he accepts the final separation philosophically. Discusses the neo-Platonic elements in *Astrophil and Stella*, Sonnets 5, 25, and 71 and Song iii, and in certain poems from *Arcadia*, remarking on ways in which the speakers fail to live up to the demands of the tradition. In Chapter 3, considers other deviations from tradition in the love poetry of Sidney and Spenser. Ponders their stress on physical love, Sidney's inability to reconcile reason with desire, his emphasis on the unconventional conduct of the poet-lover, and his inability to reconcile love with duties at court and in society. Considers the role of irony, wit, and sophistic logic in making the unresolved conflicts within Astrophil bearable, and notes attempts to resolve such conflicts in the endings of *Certain Sonnets* and *Arcadia*. Concludes that Sidney was more critical of convention than Spenser and more successful in expressing "something new, something personal." Sidney included more autobiographical references because he is "concerned with an empirical approach to love" and sets out to test neo-Platonic teachings against reality. Includes a bibliography.

653 MAZZARO, JEROME. *Transformations in the Renaissance English Lyric*. Ithaca, N.Y.: Cornell University Press, 1970, pp. 44, 73–74, 101–7, 111–13, 121, 125, 137–38, 140–43.
Sees Sidney's use of specific detail in *Astrophil and Stella* as a major shift from the technique of Wyatt. Contrasts Astrophil's acceptance of respon-

sibility for loving Stella with Petrarch's claims that he was forced "by the god of love," finding greater individuality in Sidney's position. Sees in *Astrophil and Stella* and the *Defence* a shift in the intended effect of poetry, from instructing readers to moving them. Concludes that Sidney saw the lyric as a rhetorical mode. Citing passages on *energeia* and "speaking pictures" in the *Defence*, illustrates the growing importance of the lyric persona and its usefulness as a mnemonic aid. Claims that the primacy of this mnemonic function is made clear by Sidney's references to the art of memory.

654 MEENAN, DANIEL C. "Sir Philip Sidney." *Holy Cross Purple* 46 (April 1934):460–67.
Reviews Sidney's life and works, tracing to his friendship with Spenser "all the seriousness" in his work.

655 MELCHIORI, GIORGIO. *Shakespeare's Dramatic Meditations: An Experiment in Criticism.* Oxford: Clarendon Press, 1976, pp. 8, 14, 46–48, 56, 122, 197–99.
Using Donow's concordance (2109) as a statistical base, finds that Sidney pays "greater attention to lexical variety" than Daniel or Drayton. Provides statistical tables comparing the style of *Astrophil and Stella* with that of other sonnet sequences. Notes the influence of *Arcadia* on Shakespeare's *Sonnets*, commenting on Lever's claim (1913) that Sonnets 129 and 146 are connected with *Certain Sonnets* 31 and 32.

656 MIDGLEY, GRAHAM. *The Life of Orator Henley.* Oxford: Clarendon Press, 1973, pp. 47–48.
Identifies John Henley as the editor of the 1724–25 printing of Sidney's works (13), noting that Henley claims such an edition in a book listing his publications. Notes that Henley's prefatory "Life" is a pastiche of Greville (863), Wood (284), and the pseudonymous biography in the 1655 *Arcadia* (9).

657 MILLER, DAVID L. "The Pleasure of the Text: Two Renaissance Versions." *NOR* 9 (Fall 1982): 50–55.
Ponders the psychological transaction implied in Sidney's statement in the *Defence* that those who seek only delight in poetry come gradually "to see the form of goodness" and to love it. Traces this progression to Plato's *Symposium* but notes a different view in the *Phaedrus*, namely that love of beauty enslaves the philosopher and must be subdued by reason. Notes in Sidney and Spenser passages in which *eros* leads to *logos*, but not before the poet flirts a good deal with the erotic. Notes the struggle against the erotic in Sidney's sonnet "Who will in the fairest book of nature know" (*AS 71*) and the glimpses of sexually implicit imagery lurk-

ing in the ambiguous phrasing of the sonnet "She comes, and straight therewith her shining twins do move" (*AS 76*). Relates the latter effect to Roland Barthes's concepts of "intermittence" and "text of pleasure."

658 MILLER, EDWIN HAVILAND. *The Professional Writer in Elizabethan England: A Study of Nondramatic Literature.* Cambridge, Mass.: Harvard University Press, 1959, pp. 106, 141–42.

Concludes that "of all the Elizabethan patrons, the Sidneys and the Herberts were by far the most hospitable to literature," but that Sidney himself "probably encouraged artists more through example than through munificence."

659 MILLER, JACQUELINE T. "'What words may say': The Limits of Language in *Astrophil and Stella.*" In *Sir Philip Sidney and the Interpretation of Renaissance Culture: The Poet in His Time and in Ours: A Collection of Critical and Scholarly Essays,* edited by Gary F. Waller and Michael D. Moore. London: Croom Helm; Totowa, N.J.: Barnes & Noble, 1984, pp. 95–109.

Taking issue with Krieger (2172) and Waller (2288), suggests that, in *Astrophil and Stella,* "emphasis on the indeterminancy of words, their lack of fixed points of reference, is often portrayed through the speaker's inability to enforce any single meaning on his language." Shows that, in the *Defence,* Sidney is ambivalent about the reader's ability to misread what the poet intends; likewise, in *Astrophil and Stella,* he "manages to figure forth his own unresolved uneasiness about the complicated relations between readers and writers—the way they can use and abuse each other, and the challenge to the efficacy of words this demonstrates—as Astrophil and Stella alternate roles as writers and readers of their own and each other's texts." Feels that, in both the *Defence* and *Astrophil and Stella,* the emblem of "Hercules as orator" embodies this ambivalence.

660 MILLICAN, CHARLES BOWIE. *Spenser and the Table Round: A Study in the Contemporaneous Background for Spenser's Use of the Arthurian Legend.* Harvard Studies in Comparative Literature, 8. Cambridge, Mass.: Harvard University Press, 1932, pp. 74–75, 78, 94, 171.

Notes the mention of Humphrey Lhuyd's *Commentarioli Britannicae Descriptionis Fragmentum* in Languet's letter to Sidney of 28 January 1574, and Sidney's jocular reply of 11 February. Observes that David Powel's edition of Lhuyd's English translation of Layamon's *Brut* was commissioned by Sir Henry Sidney and dedicated to his son. Repeats Jonson's comment that Sidney intended to rewrite *Arcadia* as an

Arthuriad. Also notes that Richard Robinson dedicated to Sidney his book *The Reverend D. Philip Melanchthon His Prayers.*

661 MILLS, LAURENS J[OSEPH]. *One Soul in Bodies Twain: Friendship in Tudor Literature and Stuart Drama.* Bloomington, Ind.: Principia Press, 1937, pp. 130–31, 214–20.
Discusses Sidney's treatment of friendship in "Dispraise of a Courtly Life" (*OP 7*), "Two Pastorals" (*OP 6*), and *Arcadia.*

662 MOHL, RUTH. *Studies in Spenser, Milton and the Theory of Monarchy.* New York: King's Crown Press, Columbia University Press, 1949, pp. 3–4, 16, 23–30.
Argues that there was a close relationship between Spenser and Sidney dating, perhaps, from contact at Cambridge in 1571–72. Feels that Mary Sidney is the Rosalind of the January and April eclogues in *The Shepherd's Calendar,* and that Philip is Diggon Davie in the September eclogue. See a response by McLane (644).

663 MOLLENKOTT, VIRGINIA R. "George Herbert's Epithet-Sonnets." *Genre* 5 (June 1972):131–37.
Cites *Astrophil and Stella* 39 and 47 as instances of the "epithet-sonnet," a form defined by the way it clarifies its subject by a series of brief descriptive phrases. Without claiming direct influence, suggests that Herbert's sonnets of this type are "sacred parodies of their Elizabethan counterparts."

664 MORLEY, EDITH J[ULIA]. *The Works of Sir Philip Sidney.* The Quain Essay, 1901. London: Hugh Rees, 1901, 60 pp.
Discusses Sidney as an "amateur" writer, viewing the *Letter to the Queen* as a "fitting precursor of his later prose style." Discusses the style and technique of *Arcadia,* noting its place in the development of the English novel, the importance of its verse, and its blending of pastoral and romance elements. Examines *Astrophil and Stella* in terms of sources and traditions, underlying Platonism, and contemporary influences. Calls the *Defence* "a philosophical treatise," tracing its background and commenting on its argument.

665 MORRIS, HARRY. "Richard Barnfield: *The Affectionate Shepherd.*" *TSE* 10 (1960):13–38.
Discusses the "weakness" of Hudson's suggestion (575) that a passage in *The Affectionate Shepherd* allegorizes the Sidney-Rich affair.

666 MORRIS, HELEN [SOUTAR]. *Elizabethan Literature.* Home University Library of Modern Knowledge, 233. London, New

Twentieth Century

York, and Toronto: Oxford University Press, 1958, pp. 30–33, 48, 60–66, 128.

Notes the importance of the *Defence*, praises *Arcadia* as a source of moral instruction, and points out the poetic control in *Astrophil and Stella*, but dismisses the rest of Sidney's works as weak. Noting his acquaintance with Spenser, sees possible images of Sidney in *The Faerie Queene* in the persons of Artegall and Arthur.

667 MORRISSEY, THOMAS J. "1. The Self versus the Meditative Tradition in Donne's *Devotions*. 2. 'Intimate and Unidentifiable': The Voice of Fragmented Reality in the Poetry of T.S. Eliot. 3. Sir Philip Sidney's Poetic Theory and Practice." Ph.D. diss., Rutgers, The State University of New Jersey, 1977, 121 pp.

Discusses ways in which the aims of moving, delighting, and teaching (as defined in the *Defence*), are manifested in all Sidney's major works. See *DAI* 38 (November 1977):2754A–55A.

668 MOULTON, C[HARLES] W[ELLS]. *The Library of Literary Criticism of English and American Authors.* Vol. 1. Buffalo, N.Y.: Moulton Publishing Co., 1901, pp. 320–32.

In "Sir Philip Sidney," presents a summary bio-bibliography, followed by excerpts from previously published comments on Sidney and his works.

669 MUIR, KENNETH. *Introduction to Elizabethan Literature.* New York: Random House, 1967, pp. 34–63.

In "Sir Philip Sidney and the Sonneteers," views the *Defence* as a manifesto for the literary circle involving Sidney, Greville, Dyer, and Spenser. Claims that Sidney's real impact, however, came through the experimental poetry and innovative prose of *Arcadia*. Remarks on the unusual coherence of the story line in *Astrophil and Stella* as compared with that of most other Elizabethan sonnet sequences.

670 ———. *Sir Philip Sidney.* Writers and Their Work, 120. London: Longmans Green & Co., for the British Council and the National Book League, 1960, 40 pp.

After sketching Sidney's life, dismisses the Sidney Psalter as "a work of piety rather than of poetry" and *The Lady of May* as a "courtly trifle." Views the *Defence* as a Renaissance critical milestone. Surveys critical and popular views of *Arcadia*, noting the importance of rhetoric in the work and concluding that it is "incomparably the greatest Elizabethan prose work, the greatest precisely because it was conceived as a poem." Minimizes the biographical element in *Astrophil and Stella* and comments on the way in which the sequence ranges "from conventional compliments and light-hearted conceits to the overflow of powerful feelings and bitter self-questionings." Sees the sequence keyed around "three linked conflicts": between virtue and an adulterous love in Astrophil's mind; between sympathetic love and chastity in Stella's mind; and between Astrophil and Stella, ending with his defeat.

671 MYRICK, KENNETH ORNE. *Sir Philip Sidney as a Literary Craftsman.* Harvard Studies in English, 14. Cambridge, Mass.: Harvard University Press; London: Oxford University Press, 1935, 330 pp.

Attempts a "new synthesis" of well-known facts about *Arcadia* and the *Defence*, with the aim of exposing Sidney's habits of mind and the "sense of values which prompted his instinctive actions." In Chapter 1, discusses Sidney as "Humanist, Courtier, and Poet," stressing his cultural context. Compares his brand of humanism with that of men like Roger Ascham, finding the grounds for both in the Greek ideal of the harmonious life. In actions such as the attempt to sail with Sir Francis Drake, finds the essential traits of Sidney's mind: "energy and gravity . . . exuberance and a finely tempered vitality." Locates the source of this combination in Castiglione's notion of *sprezzatura*, that is, "the quality of urbane poise by which a man is enabled to see himself and his best-loved works as they really are, without self-flattery." In Chapter 2, analyzes the *Defence* as a classical oration, and in Chapter 3, traces the views about heroic poetry expressed there to Italian critics of the sixteenth century, particularly Antonio Minturno. In Chapter 4, treats *Arcadia* as a heroic poem designed according to Minturno's rules, analyzing it against the background of the *Defence*. In Chapter 5, examines Sidney's use of "ornament" in the revised *Arcadia*, taking up the elaborate style of the work and the relation between episodes and the main plot. In Chapters 6 and 7, examines the "purpose" of *Arcadia*, relating it to views set forth in the *Defence* on the function of poetry, particularly the relation between "teaching," "delighting," and "moving." In the final chapter, "*Sprezzatura*," restates the thesis that "fundamental in Sidney's work is a restless creative energy." In the course of asking whether his "courtly temper" is more classical or romantic, points to the "striking sophistication" that underlies his earnestness and vitality, concluding that "chiefly in the passages of comic irony does Sidney show the light touch of the skilled artist and the perfect courtier." For detailed annotations, see items 1691 and 2580. See also item 672 and replies by Stump (776), Ford (1237), Goldman (1555), Bryant (2421), Coogan (2442), and Hardison (2510).

Twentieth Century

672 ⸺. *Sir Philip Sidney as a Literary Craftsman.* 2d ed. Lincoln: University of Nebraska Press, 1965, 362 pp.
Reprints item 671, with minor revisions, two pages of additional notes, an appendix containing a plot summary of the *Arcadia* and a list of its characters, and a bibliography by Godshalk (see item 247).

673 NAKADA, OSAMU. "Sir Philip Sidney no Kutoho." *Kenkyu* (Shizuoka Women's College) 14 (1980):331–45.
Studies Sidney's punctuation, concluding that it "functions partly as punctuation in [the] modern sense and partly as [a] breathing mark."

674 NELSON, T[IMOTHY] G.A. "Sir John Harington as a Critic of Sir Philip Sidney." *SP* 67 (January 1970):41–56.
Reviews Harington's references to Sidney, noting that his highest praise was reserved for *Astrophil and Stella.* Suggests that, in the preface to *Orlando furioso,* he parodied Sidney's defence of love poetry and his high claims for the poet as a "maker" and a moral teacher. Also finds a note of satire and jealousy in Harington's remarks on *Arcadia,* noting his preference for the original over the revised version.

675 NELSON, WILLIAM. *Fact or Fiction: The Dilemma of the Renaissance Storyteller.* Cambridge, Mass.: Harvard University Press, 1973, pp. 1–2, 51-52, 57, 63–64, 70–72, 97, 102.
Relates Sidney's rebuttal of the charge that poets are liars to a widespread defensiveness among literary men of the Renaissance. Compares Sidney's comments on poetry and history with the preface to Jacques Amyot's French translation of Plutarch, noting that Sidney's assertion that poetry is a superior teacher was not widely held. Discusses Sidney's comment in the dedication to *Arcadia* that his romance is a "trifle," comparing a passage in *Don Quixote.*

676 ⸺. *The Poetry of Edmund Spenser: A Study.* New York and London: Columbia University Press, 1963, pp. 56–57, 70, 276–77.
Sees Spenser's Astrophel as "a figure for Sidney's character," and Stella as "a symbol for Sidney's truth in love." Sees Sidney as Spenser's patron, but not as his friend. Plays down Sidney's role as a literary influence on Spenser, and notes that both *Arcadia* and Book VI of *The Faerie Queene* make use of the "hidden identity" motif.

677 NEWDIGATE, BERNARD H[ENRY]. *Michael Drayton and His Circle.* Oxford: Shakespeare Head Press, Basil Blackwell, 1941, pp. 30–31, 132–33.
Argues for a link between Sidney and Drayton on both personal and literary grounds.

Twentieth Century

678 NIXON, LOIS G. "Spenser's 'Incomperable Lanterne': The Dedication Poem of *The Shepheardes Calender.*" Ph.D. diss., University of South Florida, 1980, 121 pp.
Considers reasons that Spenser may have dedicated *The Shepherd's Calendar* to Sidney, stressing their "shared interests and assumptions." See *DAI* 41 (October 1980):1615A–16A.

679 NOHRNBERG, JAMES [CARSON]. *The Analogy of "The Faerie Queene."* Princeton, N.J.: Princeton University Press, 1976, pp. xxii, 27–29, 672, 676–77.
Notes the connection between Sidney and Spenser's character Calidore. Suggests stylistic links between *The Faerie Queene* and *Arcadia* and draws parallels between Spenser's poetic and that of the *Defence.*

680 NUMERATZKY, WILLY. *Michael Draytons Belesenheit und literarische Kritik.* Berlin: Mayer & Müller, 1915, pp. 39–40, 45.
Lists Drayton's allusions to Sidney.

681 OAKESHOTT, WALTER [FRASER]. *The Queen and the Poet.* London: Faber & Faber, 1960, pp. 133, 153.
Argues that Ralegh's epitaph on Sidney (2768) was written at the time of Sidney's death, and that the first two lines of Ralegh's poem "Our passions are most like" derive from *Arcadia.*

682 O'BRIEN, PAULINE W. "The 'Speaking Picture' in the Works of Sidney." Ph.D. diss., Duke University, 1954, 185 pp.
Abstract not available. Cited as item 393 in Washington (269).

683 O'CONNELL, MICHAEL. "*Astrophel*: Spenser's Double Elegy." *SEL* 11 (Winter 1971):27–35.
Argues that *Astrophel* (2771) creates a pastoral fantasy to celebrate the poet of the *Arcadia*, claiming that Spenser's Stella is "representative of the inspiration behind Sidney's poetry." The flower into which the lovers are transformed is symbolic of Sidney's poetry; it consoles the shepherd poet who sings the first part, but does not console Astrophel's sister, who finds Christian consolation in the second part.

684 OGBURN, DOROTHY, and OGBURN, CHARLES. *This Star of England: "William Shake-speare," Man of the Renaissance.* Toronto: Longmans, Green & Co.; New York: Coward-McCann, 1952, pp. 13, 28, 31, 60, 88, 104, 107, 144, 183–90, 199–200, 210, 213–14, 228, 271, 273–80, 294, 303, 317, 445, 466, 487–88, 493, 523, 615, 643, 658, 704, 706, 708, 712, 724–26, 745, 765–66, 1122.
Attempts to demonstrate that Edward de Vere, seventeenth Earl of Oxford, wrote all of Shakespeare's plays. Identifies Sidney with Laertes

Twentieth Century

in *Hamlet*, with Poins in *II Henry IV*, with Boyet in *Love's Labor's Lost*, with Slender in *Merry Wives of Windsor*, with Ajax in *Troilus and Cressida*, with the "dead shepherd" of *As You Like It*, with Sir Andrew Aguecheek in *Twelfth Night*, and with Claudio in *Much Ado about Nothing*. Suggests that the antipathy between Sidney and the Earl of Oxford sprang from Sidney's connection with Leicester, or from Oxford's marriage to Anne Cecil. Argues that the tennis-court quarrel has been "absurdly exaggerated," that Greville's account of it (863) is biased, and that Sidney was the interloper. Finds numerous allusions to it in Shakespeare's plays, especially in the duel scene of *Twelfth Night*, and feels that these show how ridiculous it was. Characterizes Sidney as "emotionally immature, if not insipid," and as a "merely facile" poet, concluding that the Sidney legend is a piece of political propaganda.

685 OLIVEIRA e SILVA, J[OHN] de. "Sir Philip Sidney and the Castilian Tongue." *CL* 34 (Spring 1982):130–45.
Contends that Sidney read both Montemayor's *Diana* and Gil Polo's *Diana enamorada* in their original form. Beginning with Languet's letter to Sidney of 22 Janauary 1574, surveys evidence that Spanish may have been one of the "four languages" that Sidney was "acquainted with." Analyzes Sidney's two translations from Montemayor's *Diana*, "What changes here, O hair" and "Of this high grace with bliss conjoined" (*CS 28, 29*), comparing them with the translations of Bartholomew Yonge and Thomas Wilson. Suggests that, since Sidney's versions are both "better poems" and more faithful to the nuances and complexities of the originals, he did not rely on Yonge or Wilson.

686 OLIVER, H[AROLD] J[AMES]. *The Problem of John Ford*. Melbourne: Melbourne University Press, 1955, pp. 59–60, 79.
Accepts Sherman's thesis (753) that Ford's play *The Broken Heart* reflects the relationship between Sidney and Lady Rich, but notes major differences between Astrophil and Orgilus.

687 ORSINI, [GIAN] NEOPOLEONE [GIORDANO]. *Fulke Greville tra il mondo e Dio*. R. Università di Milano Facoltà di Lettere e Filosofia. 2d. ser., Letteratura Italiana e Filologia Moderna, no. 12. Milan and Messina, Italy: Casa Editrice Giuseppe Principato, 1941, pp. 22, 33–35, 43–50, 89–92.
In "Greville e Sidney" and elsewhere, discusses their friendship, their association with the Areopagus and with Giordano Bruno, their part in performing *Four Foster Children of Desire*, the influence of Sidney's *Defence* on Greville's play *Mustapha*, and Greville's account of his friend's political views in the *Life of Sidney*.

688 OSBORN, LOUISE BROWN. *The Life, Letters, and Writings of John Hoskyns, 1566–1638.* Yale Studies in English, 87. New Haven, Conn.: Yale University Press; London: Oxford University Press, 1937, pp. 4–5, 106–7, 11, 129, 172–84, 277–79.

Notes that, even though Hoskins's *Directions for Speech and Style* extolls the Arcadian style, its author preferred prose that is more direct. Brings up Sidney's lost translations from Aristotle's *Rhetoric*, which Hoskins saw in the possession of Sir Henry Wotton. Also reprints Hoskins's eight elegies on Sidney, first published by Lloyd (2763): "Tandem orata, diu exorata Thalia" (124 lines); "Celebrate funeratum (148 lines); "Mors grauis nimis, ah, nimis grauis mors" (14 lines); Vt inexorabile texi" (57 lines); Collis ô Heliconij" (40 lines); Qvi iam fato meliore viges" (29 lines); "Reddita cognato proles Sidneïa coelo (20 lines); and "Thalia debet omne, quod potest, bonum" (4 lines). Lists passages in Hoskins's *Directions* that are quoted from the revised *Arcadia* and from a manuscript of the original version.

689 OSGOOD, CHARLES G[ROSVENOR]. "The 'Doleful Lay of Clorinda.'" *MLN* 35 (February 1920):90–96.

Cites evidence that Spenser, not the Countess of Pembroke, wrote "The Doleful Lay" (2741). But see item 2826 and Waller (2360).

690 PARADISE, N[ATHANIEL] BURTON. *Thomas Lodge: The History of an Elizabethan.* New Haven, Conn.: Yale University Press, 1931, pp. 66–67, 75, 121.

Discusses Lodge's attack on Gosson and his dedication of the *Alarum against Userers* to Sidney.

691 PARKER, M. PAULINE. *The Allegory of "The Faerie Queene."* Oxford: Clarendon Press, 1960, pp. 246–49.

Argues that, in Book VI of *The Faerie Queene*, Calidore is modeled on Sidney.

692 PARTRIDGE, A[STLEY] C[OOPER]. *The Language of Renaissance Poetry: Spenser, Shakespeare, Donne, Milton.* London: Andre Deutsch, 1971, pp. 52–55.

Summarizes Sidney's contributions to Renaissance literature, with particular emphasis on critical thought.

693 PATTERSON, ANNABEL. *Censorship and Interpretation: The Conditions of Writing and Reading in Early Modern England.*

Twentieth Century

Madison: University of Wisconsin Press, 1984, pp. 24–43, 194–202, 234–35, and passim.

Although Sidney is referred to often, major discussions occur in Chapter 1, which prints an enlarged version of item 1278, and Chapter 4, which considers his influence on the "royal romances" of the later seventeenth century. Shows that the anonymous *Cloria and Narcissus* and Richard Brathwaite's *Panthalia, or The Royal Romance* are to be read in the context of *Arcadia*, and that the *Defence* provided a theoretical rationale for their authors' assumption that "the romancer has as much authority as the historian proper." Suggests that Sidney's awareness of the "cultural significance" of the familiar letter anticipates its importance in the seventeenth century.

694 PATTISON, BRUCE. *Music and Poetry of the English Renaissance*. London: Methuen, 1948, pp. 20, 37, 62–64, 71, 73, 97, 174–75, 179–80.

Comments on the connection between primitive poetry and music that is established in the *Defence*. Identifies similarities between Sidney's views on music and those of Ronsard, arguing that the two knew each other through Leicester and may have met him in Paris in 1572. Notes Sidney's patronage of musicians, suggesting links between the Sidney circle and composers such as Tessier and Dowland. Feels that the musical instruments mentioned in connection with certain lyrics in *Arcadia* "are carefully chosen to underline the moods of the different songs." In discussing quantitative meter in the Queens College manuscript of *Arcadia*, sees a parallel with the techniques of the Pléiade. Comments on Sidney's quantitative experiments and their influence on Campion. Arguing for a close connection between Petrarchan convention and the madrigal, concludes that "Sidney and Spenser had to show that English could adapt itself to the New Poetry before composers could think of following the lead Italy had given." See also item 695 and a reply by Doughtie (1014).

695 ———. "Sir Philip Sidney and Music." *Music and Letters* 15 (January 1934):75–81.

Calls attention to Sidney's "bitter regret" that he was deficient in musical training, but argues that his "very desire for a professional knowledge of the art is evidence of the esteem it held" for him and his class. Discusses his patronage of performers and composers, suggesting that such settings of his lyrics as survive "may have been composed for his special satisfaction." Notes various ways in which his knowledge affects the structure of his poetry and prose. Claims that "in musical details," particularly in *Arcadia*, he is "remarkably concrete," and suggests that "in a primitive way" he "anticipates Bach's obligatos." Sees a strong influence of Italian music on Sidney's "metrical and rhythmical variety," speculating that he "learned Italian measures not as metrical schemes but as tunes to which he fitted English texts."

696 PELLEGRINI, ANGELO MARIO. "Bruno and the Elizabethans." Ph.D. diss., University of Washington, 1941, 224 pp.
Quarrels with Yates's assertion (in 839) that the dedication of Bruno's *Eroici furori* is a reproach to Sidney. Argues that there is no trace of Bruno's influence in Sidney's work. See *Abstracts of Theses, Faculty Bibliography, and Research in Progress*, Publications of the University of Washington, Theses Series 7 (March 1943):211–16.

697 ———. "Bruno, Sidney, and Spenser." *SP* 40 (April 1943): 128–44.
Denies Yates's contentions (2313) that Sidney and Bruno were close friends and that Bruno influenced Sidney's poetry and criticism.

698 PETER, JOHN D[ESMOND]. *Complaint and Satire in Early English Literature*. Oxford: Clarendon Press, 1956, pp. 117, 297, 304–8.
Notes that Sidney's—and Horace's—view of the need for humor in satire is not shared by most satirists of the English Renaissance. Praises Sidney and Shakespeare for avoiding the "cloying sweet" style of most Elizabethan sonneteers. In an appendix, reprints "The Identity of Mavortio" (item 699).

699 ———. "The Identity of Mavortio in Tourner's *Transformed Metamorphoses*." *N&Q* 193 (18 September 1948):408–12. Reprinted in item 698.
Argues that Mavortio represents Henry VIII, not Sidney.

700 PHILLIPS, JAMES E[MERSON]. "Poetry and Music in the Seventeenth Century." In *Stuart and Georgian Moments: Clark Library Seminar Papers on Seventeenth and Eighteenth Century English Literature*, edited by Earl Miner. Berkeley, Los Angeles, and London: University of California Press, 1972, pp. 1–21.
Speculates that Sidney and other members of the Areopagus took from the Pléiade their views on the relationship between music and poetry, which were in line with those of Jean Antoine de Baïf.

Twentieth Century

701 PINTO, V[IVIAN] de SOLA. *The English Renaissance: 1510–1688.*
Introductions to English Literature, 2. New York: Dover
Publications, [1938], pp. 71, 205, 234, 249.
Compares *Arcadia* and *The Faerie Queene*, providing a brief bio-bibliography of Sidney and comments on *Arcadia* and the *Defence*.

702 PLOMER, HENRY R[OBERT] and CROSS, TOM PEETE. *The
Life and Correspondence of Lodowick Bryskett.* Modern Philology
Monographs. Chicago: University of Chicago Press; New York:
Baker & Taylor; Toronto: Macmillan Co. of Canada; London:
Cambridge University Press; Tokyo: Maruzen-Kabushiki-Kaisha;
Shanghai: Commercial Press, 1927, pp. 15, 78, 83.
Records Bryskett's appointment to the Sidney household (ca. 1565) and
his journey to Paris with Sidney in 1572. Suggests that "most, if not all"
of the *Shepherd's Calendar* was written at Penshurst. Equates Sidney with
the "honorable personage" of "To the Reader" in Bryskett's *Discourse*
and notes the entry in the Stationers' Register of 22 August 1587 for
Bryskett's two elegies on Sidney (2749).

703 POIRIER, MICHEL. *Sir Philip Sidney: Le chevalier poète élizabéthain.*
Travaux et mémoires de l'Université de Lille, nouvelle série—
droit et lettres, 26. Lyon: Bibliothèque Universitaire de Lille,
1948, 322 pp.
Examines Sidney's life and works in three books, entitled "Le
Chevalier," "L'Oeuvre," and "Le Poète et Son Temps." In the introduction, surveys the "present state of Sidney studies." In Book 1, devotes
chapters to Sidney's family, his upbringing, his character, his relations
with women, his moral ideas, his political positions, his career at court,
and his religious beliefs. In Book 2, devotes four chapters to Sidney's literary works—his apprentice work, including the poems of *Arcadia*; his
"chef d'oeuvre," *Astrophil and Stella*; his two romances; and the *Defence*.
Frames these chapters with two others devoted to his "culture" (that is,
his intellectual background and aesthetic tastes) and his "language" in
the poetry and the prose works (including such stylistic matters as vocabulary, imagery, figures of speech, and syntax). In Book 3, discusses
Sidney as patron and ponders the development of the "Sidney legend,"
stressing the the Countess of Pembroke's "piété" towards her brother
and the image that emerges from his own literary works. In the final
chapter, examines Sidney's literary reputation in the decades following
his death. Concludes that *Arcadia* enjoyed "une fortune beaucoup plus
durable que ses vers" and that the *Defence* exercised "une influence fort
restreinte" on creative literature. Provides a classified bibliography

(arranged chronologically) and an index. May incorporate "Sir Philip Sidney and Quantitave Verse," the author's Thèse de lettres complementaires, Paris, 1944, which we have been unable to verify. See also detailed annotations in items 1117, 1281, 2008, 2226, and 2602.

704 POPE-HENNESSY, JOHN. "Nicholas Hilliard and Mannerist Art Theory." *JWCI* 6 (1943):89–100.

Cites Sidney's interest in painting and his conversation with Hilliard about perspective. Refers to the distinction in the *Defence* between two kinds of painters in order to demonstrate that Hilliard is an exponent of "anti-realistic representational technique."

705 PRAZ, MARIO. *The Flaming Heart: Essays on Crashaw, Machiavelli, and other Studies in the Relations between Italian and English Literature from Chaucer to T.S. Eliot.* Garden City, N.Y.: Doubleday; Toronto: George J. McLeod, 1958, pp. 6–8, 11, 97–98, 198, 272–76.

Argues that the sources for Sidney's sonnets are French and Italian rather than English and that his Petrarchan and anti-Petrarchan statements are French-based. Noting Sidney's various Italian connections, comments on the Italian sources of the *Defence* and suggests that Sidney was sympathetic to Machiavelli. Concludes that Sidney, "notwithstanding his protests of independent inspiration, was rehearsing most of the hackneyed tropes of the Continental sonneteers, nay, at the very moment he claimed to be no pickpurse of another's brain, was deriving from du Bellay's ode "Contre les Pétrarquistes." Acknowledges, however, that Sidney was "no servile imitator."

706 PRESCOTT, ANNE LAKE. *French Poets and the English Renaissance: Studies in Fame and Transformation.* New Haven, Conn., and London: Yale University Press, 1978, pp. 17, 60–61, 93, 109–10, 178–79, 181, 184, 189–90, 215–16.

Noting parallels between Marot's psalms and the Sidney Psalter, finds similarities in their religious and literary aims. Notes that Daniel Rogers was friends with both Sidney and Ronsard, but argues that Sidney's use of Ronsard was minimal. Cites du Bellay's epitaph for Guillaume Gouffier, Seigneur de Bonnivet, as a source—possibly via its reproduction in Fraunce's *Arcadian Rhetoric*—for some of the Sidney epitaphs, including the anonymous one found in St. Paul's. Comments on Sidney's "lost" translation of du Bartas, arguing that, because the translation was known so widely in manuscript, du Bartas remained unpublished in English long after Sidney's death.

Twentieth Century

707 ———. "The Reception of du Bartas in England." *SRen* 15 (1968):144–73.
Notes that du Bartas praised Sidney as one of the pillars of English poetry and that Sidney was well aware of du Bartas. Comments on Moffet's praise (2827) of Sidney's lost translation of *La Semaine*.

708 PRICE, LAWRENCE MARSDEN. *Die Aufnahme englischer Literatur in Deutschland, 1500–1960*. Translated by Maxwell E. Knight. Bern and Munich: Francke Verlag, 1961, pp. 16, 143.
A German translation of item 709.

709 ———. *The Reception of English Literature in Germany*. Berkeley: University of California Press, 1932, pp. 4, 175–76.
Notes that Sidney was the Elizabethan poet best known in Germany during the seventeenth century. Remarks on his admiration for folk poetry, which appears in the *Defence*.

710 PURDY, MARY MARTHA. "Elizabethan Literary Treatments of the Proposed Marriages of Queen Elizabeth." Ph.D. diss., University of Pittsburgh, 1928.
Relates *The Lady of May* to the *Defence of Leicester* and the *Letter to the Queen* to other literary treatments of the French marriage negotiations. See *Abstracts of Dissertations for the Degree of Doctor of Philosophy, University of Pittsburgh Bulletin* 25, (25 October 1928):147–53.

711 RATHMELL, J[OHN] C.A. "Sidney's *Arcadia* and *Astrophel and Stella*." In *The New Pelican Guide to English Literature*. Vol. 2, *The Age of Shakespeare*, edited by Boris Ford. Harmondsworth, England: Penguin, 1982, pp. 137–48.
Reacting in part against T.S. Eliot's claim that *Arcadia* is a "monument to dullness" (509), reads both works as "characterized by the frequent appearance of a sly and subtle wit" that is always "threatening to call in question" their heroic and romantic values. Reads the sonnet sequence especially in light of Sidney's problems with his own public "great expectations," finding in it "a rueful consciousness of his own inadequacies and self deceptions." In *Arcadia*, which "embodies a genuine effort to grapple imaginatively . . . with problems that were close to the author's heart and conscience," feels that Sidney is neither a "doctrinaire" Calvinist nor a "glib" humanist, but, like Erasmus, "adheres to a sane middle course: men have to live with their imperfections, recognizing their own weaknesses and forgiving them in others."

712 RÉBORA, PIERO. *L'Italia nel dramma inglese (1558–1642)*. Humana biblioteca di cultura, 5. Milan: Casa Editrice 'Modernissima,' 1925, pp. 20, 35, 53, 72, 114.

Notes Italian influences on the *Defence*, *Arcadia* and *The Lady of May*.

713 REDWINE, JAMES D., ed. Introduction to *Ben Jonson's Literary Criticism*, by Ben Jonson. Regents Critics Series. Lincoln: University of Nebraska Press, 1970, pp. xix, l.

Explains the background of Jonson's complaint that, in *Arcadia*, "Sidney did not keep a decorum in making everyone speak as well as himself." Also notes that, in the criticism of Jonson, Sidney, and Dryden, the tragic emotions described by Aristotle are always associated with Fortune's wheel.

714 REES, JOAN. *Samuel Daniel: A Critical and Biographical Study*. Liverpool: Liverpool University Press, 1964, pp. 13, 31–32, 44–46.

Argues that Daniel was drawn to the Sidney circle through his association with the first quarto of *Astrophil and Stella*, though Greville's patronage of Daniel may also have enhanced Sidney's influence. Contrasts *Delia* with *Astrophil and Stella*, noting that Sidney uses myth to make "little dramatised fabliaux," whereas Daniel uses it to supply metaphors. Sees Daniel's *Cleopatra* as directed by the principles laid down in the *Defence*.

715 RELLE, ELEANOR. "Some New Marginalia and Poems of Gabriel Harvey." *RES*, n.s. 23 (November 1972):401–16.

Among Harvey's unpublished marginalia in a volume at Magdalene College, Cambridge, notes a Latin poem of eighty-three hexameters entitled "De tribus viuidis scriptoribus Epigramma. Ad Astrophilum viuidiora delineantum," which begins "Siccinè ais generose? stilo efferuescis Olympi?" Concludes that it was "intended for presentation to Sidney, but the fair copy possibly never found his hands, since he died soon after its composition." The poem suggests that, especially in his pastoral works, Sidney surpassed his predecessors in his ability to produce lively poetic pictures. It appears to have been written late in 1585 or early in 1586.

716 RENWICK, W[ILLIAM] L[INDSAY]. *Edmund Spenser: An Essay on Renaissance Poetry*. London: Edward Arnold & Co., 1925, pp. 25, 79, 87–88, 104, 140, 186–87.

Argues that Sidney must have familiarized Spenser with the ideas of Ronsard and du Bellay, and that he might have introduced Spenser to

Twentieth Century

Italian poetics as well. Views *Arcadia* as, in part, a *roman à clef*. Suggests that Sidney's system for quantitative verse derives from Baïf.

717 RIBNER, IRVING. "Machiavelli and Sir Philip Sidney." Ph.D. diss., University of North Carolina, 1949.
Examines the political ideas, the methods of inquiry, and the philosophical assumptions in Machiavelli's *Prince* and *Discourses*, comparing similar material in both versions of *Arcadia* and in Sidney's political tracts and correspondence. Concludes that, although Sidney's villains sometimes reflect a "warped" opinion of *The Prince* common in Elizabethan literature, Sidney shared many of Machiavelli's views on political theory and practical statecraft. Finds disagreement on only one major issue: the extent to which the personal morality of the ruler is essential to his success in affairs of state. Also suggests that Machivelli's thought was more acceptable in England generally than previous scholars had supposed. See *University of North Carolina Record*, no. 478, *Research in Progress* (January 1949–December 1949), Graduate School Series, no. 58, pp. 113–15.

718 RINGLER, WILLIAM A., Jr. "Spenser, Shakespeare, Honor, and Worship." *Renaissance News* 14 (Spring 1961):159–61.
Supplies evidence that Spenser had originally intended to dedicate *The Shepherd's Calendar* to Leicester, not to Sidney.

719 ROBERTSON, JOHN MacKINNON. *Elizabethan Literature*. London: Williams & Norgate; New York: Henry Holt & Co., 1914, pp. 96–97, 118–22, 143, 208–11.
Reviews the sources of *Arcadia*, regarding it as valuable only for its historical interest. Faults the prose style of *The Trueness of the Christian Religion*, praises the *Defence*, and notes Sidney's impact on the Elizabethan sonnet.

720 ROBIN, P[ERCY] ANSELL. *Animal Lore in English Literature*. London: John Murray, 1932, pp. 83, 112, 131.
Explicates several uses of animal mythology and Renaissance pseudo-science in Sidney's works.

721 ROBINSON, FORREST G[LEN]. *The Shape of Things Known: Sidney's "Apology" in Its Philosophical Tradition*. Cambridge, Mass.: Harvard University Press, 1972, 244 pp. Orig. a Ph.D. diss., Harvard University, 1968.
Considers Sidney's place in a tradition that treats thought as "a form of internal vision." Includes two chapters on the history of this tradition

from the pre-Socratic Greek philosophers through the classical period and the middle ages to the Renaissance, including material on the influence of printing and various arts and sciences. Then considers the influence of the tradition on Sidney's theory of poetry in the *Defence* and the realization of that theory in *Arcadia* and in *Astrophil and Stella*. Concludes with a discussion of the impact of Sidney's theory on selected English literary works of the seventeenth century. Includes an index. For detailed annotations, see items 1742, 1943, and 2618.

722 ROLLINS, HYDER EDWARD, ed. Introduction and notes to *Brittons Bowre of Delights, 1591*. Cambridge, Mass.: Harvard University Press, 1933, pp. xviii-xx, 65, 71–72, 76, 82–84, 88–89.

Discusses the six poems in memory of Sidney included in the miscellany. See Breton (2748). Also points out that the fifth poem is an acrostic based on the name "Penelope Rich" and suggests that, when it was first published, it might have left the impression that Sidney was its author.

723 ———. Introduction and notes to *The Phoenix Nest, 1593*. Cambridge, Mass.: Harvard University Press, 1931, pp. x, xvi, xix, xxxvi, xxxviii–xxxix, 115–32, 157, 160.

Finds connections between the *Phoenix Nest* and Sidney in the variety of lyric forms used in the work and in heraldic associations with the phoenix. Annotates the first three poems in the anthology, which are elegies for Sidney. Notes that one is by Ralegh (2768) and another by Roydon (2770), and attributes a third (2740) to either Greville or Dyer.

724 ———. Notes to *A Poetical Rhapsody, 1602–1621*, compiled by Francis Davison. Vol. 2. Cambridge, Mass.: Harvard University Press, 1932, pp. 49, 72–73, 94, 96, 101, 109–11.

Notes that Davison was a distant relative of Sidney and discusses the two poems by Sidney first published in *A Poetical Rhapsody*: "Join mates in mirth to me" (*OP 6*) and "Walking in bright Phoebus' blaze" (*OP 7*). Notes that, though they were in Davison's possession, they were actually added to the volume by his publisher. Also notes references to Sidney as "Willy" elsewhere in the book and suggests that these lend support to the view that the "Willy" in Spenser's *Tears of the Muses* is Sidney. See also Halliwell-Phillipps (221), Koeppel (366), and Minto (373). Notes that Walter Davison's "Roun-de-lay in Inverted Rhymes" takes its pastoral names from *Arcadia*.

725 ———. *The Sonnets*, by William Shakespeare. 2 vols. A New Variorum Edition of Shakespeare. Philadelphia: J.B. Lippincott,

Twentieth Century

1944, 1:6–7, 18, 39, 47, 64, 78, 90, 121, 136, 298, 323, 329–30, 338, 356, 363, 375, 377; 2:118–21, 275.
Notes Shakespeare's possible debts to Sidney and numerous parallels between the *Sonnets* and *Astrophil and Stella* and *Arcadia*. Considers the surmise that Sidney might even have been the author of the *Sonnets*.

726 ROSE, MARK [ALLEN]. *Heroic Love: Studies in Sidney and Spenser.* Cambridge, Mass.: Harvard University Press, 1968, pp. 1–3, 8–9, 11, 23, 37–41, 53, 77, 78, 113, 127, 138–40.
Notes the moral purpose behind *Arcadia* and sees melancholy behind the moralism of *Astrophil and Stella*. Reads "Leave me O Love" (*CS 32*) as an example of Christian *contemptus mundi* rather than neo-Platonism. Argues that, in *Arcadia*, the treatment of love as a heroic activity is a way of finishing the education of the Princes and preparing them to rule by arming them against the forces of desire. Claims that the neo-Platonism of the Italian epics is tempered in England by Protestantism, so that "to be struck by Cupid's arrow is still to fall from the virtuous state of temperance, but it is also, in the Protestant view, to receive a divine calling to marriage." See a reply by Amos (1399).

727 ROSTON, MURRAY. *Sixteenth-Century English Literature.* Macmillan History of Literature Series. London: Macmillan; New York: Schocken Books, 1982, pp. 139–55.
Presents the traditional view of Sidney as poet, courtier, and soldier. Views *Arcadia* and the *Defence* as landmarks in the development of English literature and *Astrophil and Stella* as an examination of amatory frustration, based in part on Sidney's own experience.

728 ROWE, KENNETH THORPE. "Sir Calidore: Essex or Sidney?" *SP* 27 (April 1930):125–41.
Refutes Long's arguments (633) for Essex as Spenser's model for Calidore in Book VI of *The Faerie Queene*. Supports his own identification of the character with Sidney by noting parallels between Sidney's defence of others, such as Leicester, against slander and the knight's pursuit of the Blatant Beast.

729 ROWSE, A[LFRED] L[ESLIE]. *The Elizabethans and America.* New York: Harper & Brothers, 1959, pp. 189–90.
Comments on Sidney's interest in America and his support of Frobisher's voyages, Gilbert's attempts at settlement, and Ralegh's adventures. Sees in the shipwreck at the beginning of *Arcadia* "the atmosphere of the voyages" to the New World.

730 RUDENSTINE, NEIL L. *Sidney's Poetic Development*. Cambridge, Mass.: Harvard University Press, 1967, 325 pp. Orig. a Ph.D. diss., Harvard University, 1964.

Argues that "Sidney was a sophisticated stylist from the beginning of his career, and that he developed several different manners for specific purposes long before he came to write *Astrophil and Stella*." In Chapter 1, studies Sidney's correspondence in the years 1578–80, highlighting the conflict between Languet's demand for an active life and Sidney's desire for a contemplative one. In Chapter 2, argues for close parallels between the letters and *Arcadia*, with Musidorus representing the demands of the active life and Pyrocles the desire for contemplation. In Chapters 3–7, analyzes the poetry of the *Arcadia*, relating it to the correspondence, analyzing its prosody and style, and noting ways in which it prepared Sidney to write *Astrophil and Stella*. In Chapter 8, discusses *Certain Sonnets*, and in Chapter 9, examines comments on style in the *Defence*, stressing Sidney's anti-Ciceronianism and the importance of his views on decorum and imitation. In Chapter 10, ponders the contrast between the ornamented and patterned poetry of *Arcadia* and the "plainer, more dramatic" verse of *Astrophil and Stella*. Denies that Sidney underwent a clear course of poetic development, however, arguing instead that he varied his style all along, seeking, for example, to preserve decorum in characters of different stations. Feels that the remarks in the *Defence* on artificiality in style are directed against lack of originality and decorum, not against ornament. Sees only one development in Sidney's own poetic style: toward greater *energeia*. Considers passages relevant to this concept in the Old *Arcadia* and the *Defence*, tracing the idea to Aristotle and J.C. Scaliger. Locates the *energeia* of the *Defence* and *Arcadia* in the voices of the speakers and their dramatic contexts. Concludes that Sidney invented the English dramatic lyric and that Astrophil is "the first fully realized, poetically conceived character in modern English literature." In Chapter 11, argues that the form whereby conflicts in the *Arcadia* are resolved by debate is internalized in the debates and dramatic monologues of *Astrophil and Stella*. In Chapter 12, contrasts the poetry of *Arcadia* with the sonnet "Not at first sight, nor with a dribbed shot" (*AS* 2) to show that the latter is freer and more dynamic, courtly, and musical. In Chapter 13, examines the demand for decorum in the style of *Astrophil and Stella*, and in Chapters 14–17, examines the sequence in detail. In the concluding chapter, looks broadly at Sidney's verse, concentrating on matters of style. In Appendix 1, argues for the unity of *Certain Sonnets*, and in Appendix 2, argues that Sidney's portion of the Sidney Psalter was completed in 1580–1581. For detailed annotations,

Twentieth Century

see items 2015, 2245, and 2326. Reprinted in part in item 2622. For a response on the concept of *energeia*, see Robinson (1742). See also Brown (2069).

731 SACCIO, PETER. *The Court Comedies of John Lyly: A Study in Allegorical Dramaturgy*. Princeton, N.J.: Princeton University Press, 1969, pp. 75–76, 130–31, 218–23.

Provides parallels and background for Sidney's reference in the *Defence* to Daedalus as a guide for "the highest flying wit." Details ways in which Lyly's court comedies fulfill prescriptions in the *Defence*, particularly in producing "delight" rather than laughter and in working from a "fore-conceit" to lead the audience to a "profitable invention." Also applies to Lyly Sidney's comments on the "golden world" of poetry and his preference for "icastic" rather than "phantastic" fictions. Compares the feminine disguise worn by Cupid in *Gallathea* with that of Pyrocles in *Arcadia*, considering their traditional associations.

732 SALINGAR, L.G. "The Elizabethan Literary Renaissance." In *The Pelican Guide to English Literature*, edited by Boris Ford. Vol. 2, *The Age of Shakespeare*. Baltimore: Penguin Books, 1955, pp. 51–116. Reprint. *A Guide to English Literature*. The Belle Sauvage Library. Vol. 2, *The Age of Shakespeare*. London: Cassell & Co., Penguin Books, 1961, pp. 43–108. Reprint (without major revisions in the material on Sidney). In *The New Pelican Guide to English Literature*, edited by Boris Ford. Vol. 2, *The Age of Shakespeare*. Harmondsworth, England: Penguin Books, 1982, pp. 51–116.

Discusses the secondary role of literature in Sidney's life. Traces to the humanists his tendency to synthesize sources and his views in the *Defence* on decorum and the popular drama. Also considers *Astrophil and Stella*, noting the Petrachan conflict of earthly and religious love, the combination of Platonic idealism with rhetoric, and the balance of passion with civility and wit. Briefly explicates the sonnets "No more my dear, no more these counsels try" (*AS 64*) and "The nightingale, as soon as April bringeth" (*CS 4*).

733 SANDERSON, JAMES L. *Sir John Davies*. Twayne's English Authors Series, 175. Boston: Twayne Publishers, 1975, pp. 51, 98–99, 120–21, 136–37.

Finds in Davies's "Epithalamion" the influence of the marriage song for Kala and Lalus (*OA 63*). Also places Sidney among other English authors who have translated Psalms and notes the influence of Sidney and Golding's translation of *The Trueness of the Christian Religion* upon Elegy 2 of Davies's *Nosce Teipsum*.

734 SAUNDERS, J[OHN] W[HITESIDE]. *The Profession of English Letters.* London: Routledge & Kegan Paul; Toronto: University of Toronto Press, 1964, pp. 43–53.
Suggests that Sidney's poetry reflected the attitude to literature of a coterie and that the Areopagus acted as a kind of "literary finishing school."

735 ———. "The Stigma of Print: A Note on the Social Bases of Tudor Poetry." *EIC* 1 (January 1951):139–64.
Draws a distinction between the court poet and the "professional" writer. Stresses the coterie atmosphere in which Sidney wrote, citing the condemnation of the "professors of learning" (in the section of the *Defence* on euphuistic "similitudes") as a condemnation of professional writers.

736 SCHANZER, ALICE. "Influssi italiana nella letteratura inglese: Sir Philip Sidney." *Rivista d'Italia* 8 (July 1901):459–81.
Provides general biographical information, representing Sidney's literary career as a response to the climate of thought represented by Stephen Gosson. Noting that, in his need to "defend" literature, Sidney was analogous to Bruno, discusses the *Defence* as a "profession of Sidney's faith." Finds in *Arcadia* the ideals of the Areopagus, excusing its "artificiality" as a convention of the time. In discussing *Astrophil and Stella*, focuses on the biographical context.

737 SCHELLING, FELIX E[MMANUEL]. *Elizabethan Drama 1558–1642: A History of the Drama in England from the Accession of Queen Elizabeth to the Closing of the Theaters, to Which Is Prefixed a Résumé of the Earlier Drama from Its Beginnings.* 2 vols. Boston: Houghton, Mifflin & Co., 1908, 1:130–31, 591–92; 2:4, 59, 98, 145, 152, 176, 178, 194, 365.
Notes a possible allegory of Sidney's love for Lady Rich in the characters of Eumenides and Semele in John Lyly's *Endymion*. Also considers the impact of *Arcadia* on John Webster's *Duchess of Malfi* and on other plays of the period. Notes Sidney's presence at a performance of William Gager's *Meleager* in 1581, and places *The Lady of May* and *Four Foster Children of Desire* in the development of Elizabethan court entertainments.

738 ———. *English Literature During the Lifetime of Shakespeare.* New York: Henry Holt & Co., 1910, pp. 23–33, 41–44, 128, 141, 304, 374–76, 385, 388.
Discusses the nature of the Areopagus, Sidney's experiments in quantitative verse, the historical significance of the *Defence*, the French influence

Twentieth Century

on *Astrophil and Stella*, the technical merit of the poems of the Old *Arcadia*, and Sidney's impact on his contemporaries. Differentiates the *Arcadia* from Lyly's *Euphues* on the basis of prose style and comments on Sidney's expertise with the conceit. Views *Astrophil and Stella* as partly autobiographical and Greville's *Life* as "a species of autobiographical preface to Greville's collected works." Notes Drummond's debt to Sidney; discusses *The Lady of May* as an example of pastoral drama; and notes that *Arcadia* was a source for Day's *Isle of Gulls*.

739 ———. "'Sidney's Sister, Pembroke's Mother': A Consideration of the Elizabethan Woman in Her Sphere as a Patron of Learning." *The Johns Hopkins Alumni Magazine* 12 (November 1923):3–23. Reprint. In *Shakespeare and "Demi-Science": Papers on Elizabethan Topics*. Philadelphia: University of Pennsylvania Press; London: Oxford University Press, 1927.

In seeking to show "how assiduously Lady Pembroke trod in the footsteps of her brother," notes that she "corrected" the *Arcadia* manuscript, that her *Tragedy of Antony* attempted to "sustain the avowed ideals of her brother," and that her entertainment of the Queen in 1599 "followed once more" the tradition exemplified in *Lady of May*.

740 SCHINDL, ERIKA. "Studien zum Wortschatz Sir Philip Sidney: Neubildungen und Entlehnungen." Ph.D. diss., Universität Wien, 1955, 141 pp.

Abstract not available. Cited in *GV*, vol. 114, p. 136.

741 SCHIRMER, WALTER FRANZ. *Antike, Renaissance und Puritanismus: Eine Studie zur englischen Literaturgeschichte des 16. und 17. Jahrhunderts*. Munich: Max Hueber, 1924, pp. 44, 65, 107–8, and passim.

Cites Sidney in discussing the Renaissance revival of classical culture and the development of Puritanism. Compares his comments in the *Defence* on the place of poetry in the church with the attitudes of other Elizabethan critics. Examines the mingling of classical mythology and Christian philosophy in *Arcadia*. Also considers Sidney's Huguenot friends and their role in pushing Protestant English humanism closer to Puritanism.

742 SCHRICKX, W[ILLEM]. *Shakespeare's Early Contemporaries: The Background of the Harvey-Nashe Polemic and "Love's Labour's Lost."* Antwerp, Belgium: De Nederlandsche Boekhandel, 1956, pp. 7, 29–30, 87, 96, 98, 107, 112, 146, 157–59.

Notes Sidney's interest in the art of heraldry, his possible connection with the "School of Night," his relationship with Gabriel Harvey, his

214

contact with Giordano Bruno, and his place in the literary world of his time. Suggests that John Florio helped Greville with the 1590 edition of *Arcadia*. In discussing the dedication to Thomas Nashe's *Lenten Stuff*, considers the attack there on Hugh Sanford for his part in editing the 1593 printing of *Arcadia*.

743 SCHRINNER, WALTER [FRANZ]. *Castiglione und die englische Renaissance*. Berlin: Junker und Dünnhaupt Verlag, 1939, pp. 26, 60, 65–66, 103–13.

Comments on similiarities between Sidney and Castiglione in their moral purposes and in their views on classical and vernacular literature and presents Sidney as the embodiment of Castiglione's ideal courtier. Considers Sidney's acquaintance with Italian arts and literature, including *The Courtier*, and notes the *sprezzatura* in his attitude toward his own literary works. Also notes that fame, social ambition, and Platonism play more of a role in Castiglione's book than in *Arcadia*. Traces to Castiglione Sidney's treatment of music as a cure for tarantula bites. Also discusses suggestions of Sir Thomas Elyot's brand of English humanism in Sidney's concern for the practical and the earthly. Considers such things as his portrayal of the naked human body and his interest in details of horsemanship.

744 SCHÜCKING, LEVIN LUDWIG. *Shakespeare im literarischen Urteil seiner Zeit*. Heidelberg: Carl Winters Universitätsbuchhandlung, 1908, pp. 55–56, 60, 107, 129–41 passim.

Notes Sidney's resistence to native English literary practices and considers his views on the dramatic unities. Notes numerous Elizabethan allusions to Sidney.

745 SCHULZE, IVAN L. "Notes on Elizabethan Chivalry and *The Faerie Queene*." *SP* 30 (April 1933):148–59.

Discusses Sidney's high regard for chivalric training as revealed in his letter to his brother of 1580, in *Arcadia*, and in his own practice, especially at the battle of Zutphen.

746 SCOTT, MARY AUGUSTA. *Elizabethan Translations from the Italian*. Vassar Semi-Centennial Series. Boston: Houghton Mifflin, 1916, pp. lx, lxiii, lxviii, lxix, 74–75, 124, 132, 134, 137, 159, 166, 182, 216, 323, 328, 377, 470, 476, 478–79, 490, 491, 494, 508-10.

Views Sidney as a major figure in the "Italian Renaissance in England," both as a poetic theorist and as a traveller familiar with Italy and its artists. Comments on his contacts with Giordano Bruno and on his imitations of Petrarchan poetry and of Italian madrigals and romances. In providing bibliographical accounts of English works wholly or partially

Twentieth Century

translated from the Italian, notes those who have connections with Sidney.

747 SEATON, ETHEL, ed. Introduction to *The Arcadian Rhetorike*, by Abraham Fraunce. Luttrell Society Reprints, 9. Oxford: Luttrell Society, Basil Blackwell, 1950, pp. viii, xix, xxvi, xxxv–xxxix.
Gives the bare facts of Fraunce's connection with Sidney and his family. Discusses Fraunce's aims, which included building the European reputation of English poets such as Sidney. Argues that the praise for "Rinaldo" in the *Defence* cannot apply to Ariosto's character of that name and must therefore refer to Tasso's. Classifies the quotations that Fraunce selected from *Arcadia* and considers which manuscripts they may have come from. Concludes that the sources cannot be indentified except that they included the Old *Arcadia* and at least some of the revisions. Also discusses variants between Fraunce's versions, the printed texts, and the extant manuscripts.

748 SEATON, ETHEL. *Literary Relations of England and Scandinavia in the Seventeenth Century*. Oxford Studies in Modern Languages and Literature. Oxford: Clarendon Press, 1935, pp. 7–8, 62, 168–69.
Notes Sidney's interest in voyaging to the north and his correspondence with Languet about gold in the Arctic. Suggests Arthur Gorges's castle at Longford as a model for Amphialus's castle in *Arcadia*. Remarks on Ludwig Borrichius's mention of Sidney as a major English poet in his lectures in Copenhagen during the 1670s.

749 SECCOMBE, THOMAS, and ALLEN, J.W. *The Age of Shakespeare.* Vol. 1. London: George Bell & Sons, 1903, pp. 9–16, 103–5, 123–27.
Reviews Sidney's life and comments on his experiments with classical meters. Condemns the poetry of *Arcadia* but praises *Astrophil and Stella*, casting doubts on its autobiographical accuracy and noting the influence of Petrarch and Ronsard. Comments on the thought and style of the *Defence* and notes the influence of *Arcadia*, praising its combination of the chivalric and the pastoral and urging that it be judged "by detached passages."

750 SELLS, A[RTHUR] LYTTON. *The Italian Influence in English Poetry from Chaucer to Southwell*. Bloomington: Indiana State University Press; London: George Allen & Unwin, 1955, pp. 129–49.
In "Sidney; or, The Triumph of Petrarch" considers Sidney's Italian journey and his contact with Veronese and Tintoretto. Argues for strong

216

Italian influences in the style of *Arcadia*. Sees Stella as a "divine pattern," arguing that, in *Astrophil and Stella*, Sidney brings us closer to Petrarch than any other English writer. Also comments on Sidney's contact with Bruno.

751 SEYMOUR-SMITH, MARTIN. *Poets through Their Letters.* Vol. 1. New York: Holt, Rinehart & Winston, 1969, pp. 51–63.

Argues that William Camden, Sidney's fellow student at Cambridge, was responsible for interesting Ben Jonson in Sidney's works. From Sidney's letters, confirms the standard opinion that he was a gentleman *par excellence*. Notes that, though his letters say little about poetry, they do reveal his interest in music.

752 SHEAVYN, PHEOBE [ANNE BEALE]. *The Literary Profession in the Elizabethan Age.* University of Manchester Publications, English Series, 1. Manchester, England: University of Manchester Press, 1909, pp. 13, 34, 37, 67, 131, 179, 184. Reprint, with revisions by J.W. Saunders. Manchester: Manchester University Press; New York: Barnes & Noble, 1967, pp. 13, 34, 37, 67, 85, 138, 150–51, 182–83.

Stresses the fact that Sidney and other court poets of the period avoided print. Notes his activities as a patron, citing Nashe's comments in *Pierce Penniless*. Also discusses Gosson's "impudent" dedication in the *School of Abuse*. Saunders's revisions bring the footnotes up to date and add material on the "battle" between "Courtly poets" such as Sidney and religious and political authorities concerned with the effects of literature on public morality.

753 SHERMAN, STUART P[RATT]. "Stella and *The Broken Heart.*" *PMLA* 24 (June 1909):274–85.

Sees John Ford's play *The Broken Heart* as an allusion to the supposed affair between Sidney and Lady Rich, citing Ford's remarks in the prologue, the parallels between the Sparta of the play and the Sparta of *Arcadia*, and several biographical parallels involving Ford's characters Orgilus and Penthea. Suggests connections between scenes in Ford's play and Sidney's poem "In a grove most rich of shade" (*AS viii*) and notes that Spenser's *Astrophel* depicts the lovers as transformed into an herb with three names: Starlight, Penthia, and Astrophel. See also Oliver (686), Bentley (1423), and Sargeaunt (1751).

754 SHIMAMURA, KAORU. "Sir Philip Sidney: An Introduction." *ESELL* 51–52 (1967):145–72.

Not seen. Cited in "The 1967 Bibliography," by [Kazuyoshi Enozawa and Sister Miyo Takano]. *RenB* 3 (1976):67, item 267.

Twentieth Century

755 SHUSTER, GEORGE N[AUMAN]. *The English Ode from Milton to Keats*. New York: Columbia University Press, 1940, pp. 23–25, 39, 50.

Sees in the *Defence* a desire to blend the Puritan spirit of moral responsibility and the humanist "aesthetic" of reverence for culture. Comments on Sidney's experiments with quantitative verse and on his appreciation of Pindar. Sees a close parallel between the Renaissance ode and the Sidney Psalms, noting praise of the Psalmist in the *Defence*.

756 SIDNEY, PHILIP (1872–1908). *The Sidneys of Penshurst*. London: S.H. Bousfield & Co., 1901, pp. v, 57–108.

In "Sir Philip Sidney," reprints item 388 with minor revisions.

757 SIEBECK, BERTA. *Das Bild Sir Philip Sidneys in der englischen Renaissance*. Schriften der deutschen Shakespeare-Gesellschaft, n.s. 3. Weimar, Germany: Verlag Hermann Böhlaus, 1939, 214 pp. Orig. a Ph.D. diss., Universität Freiburg/Breisgau, 1939.

Consider's Sidney's image in the Renaissance. In Section 1, examines his life as a fulfillment of humanist, Protestant, and courtly ideals. Traces his exalted reputation to the reflection of these ideals in his works and to the manner of his death. Considers the moral teaching and the Platonic background of the *Defence* and the portrait of love and Sidney's personal experience in *Astrophil and Stella*. Examines *Arcadia* for its themes, its genre, and its concepts of friendship, love, heroism, proper government, and the value of poetry. Also considers the revival of poetry and classical concepts of heroism in Sidney's age. In Section 2, reviews the descriptions of Sidney and his character in works by his contemporaries, such as Greville's *Life of Sidney*, the elegies and letters written on the occasion of his death, and early literary and biographical works. In Section 3, considers the Renaissance ideal of manhood that Sidney fulfilled, comparing his reputation with those of Henry V, Sir Thomas More, Queen Elizabeth and her chief courtiers, and Shakespeare. In an appendix, provides a comprehensive catalog of the portraits of Sidney, distinguishing the authentic from the doubtful and spurious. Describes each and discusses past and present ownership, copies and imitations, and scholarly commentary. Also provides an introduction to English portrait art ca. 1600. Includes bibliographies and three chronological lists: works dedicated to Sidney, elegies and epitaphs on him, and printed opinion on his life and character from his death to 1630. See also Judson (1075).

758 ———. "Laudatory Verses on Sir Philip Sidney." *TLS*, 26 February 1938, p. 140.

Queries the whereabouts of the manuscript of poems by Daniel Rogers noted in item 350.

759 SINFIELD, ALAN. *Literature in Protestant England 1560–1660.* London and Canberra, Australia: Croom Helm; Totowa, N.J.: Barnes & Noble Books, 1983, pp. 23–39, 55–63, and passim.

Although brief references to Sidney's theory and practice appear throughout, major discussions are concentrated in Chapter 3, which defines a Puritan form of humanism in terms of a "persistent tension between literature and religion," and Chapter 4, which examines the ambivalence generated by Protestants through their radical alterations of European traditions of love. Argues that Sidney's theory in the *Defence* is "designed to justify literature to the ardent protestant." Draws upon his works to illustrate three "areas of strain and danger" encountered by Puritan humanists: they are "bound to accord preeminence to divine poetry"; they are tempted to "imply a religious validity to pagan imagery"; and they are "inclined to hold the poet in a lofty esteem which is difficult to reconcile with the fall." Examines ways in which Sidney's concern to meet Puritan as well as humanistic criteria creates tensions and ambiguities in the Old *Arcadia*, which he then seeks to "negotiate" in the New. In the revision, he proposes to "supersede the heroic ethos" of his inherited pagan genre by developing a "distinctive protestant heroism which is active as well as humble," and by stressing the role of divine providence in guiding worldly affairs. Reads *Astrophil and Stella* in the context of the thesis that, "in matters of love, literature of the period manifests a dislocation deriving from the co-presence of three discourses: the romantic, Ovidian and Christian." Suggesting that Sidney thought fallen humanity incapable of the sort of chastity demanded by romantic love, argues that the sequence is "contrived as a warning against the dire effects of improper love" and that Astrophil's main characteristic is self-deception. In the New *Arcadia*, sees a further critique of romantic and Ovidian love, in which Sidney emphasizes the value of marriage.

760 ———. "Sidney and Du Bartas." *CL* 27 (Winter 1975):8–20.

Through an examination of the *Defence*, *Arcadia*, and *Astrophil and Stella* in relation to du Bartas's *Semaine*, argues that the religious element in Sidney's major work deserves greater emphasis.

Twentieth Century

761 ———. "Sidney, du Plessis-Mornay, and the Pagans." *PQ* 58 (Winter 1979):26–39.
Summarizes du Plessis-Mornay's religious position in order to clarify Sidney's attitudes to pagans, arguing that Sidney does not follow the *prisca theologia* but instead distinguishes clearly between pagan and Christian thought. Emphasizes Sidney's Calvinism in the *Defence* and studies the implications of du Plessis-Mornay's thought for the characterization of Pamela in *Arcadia*.

762 SINGER, DOROTHEA WALEY. *Giordano Bruno: His Life and Thought*. New York: Henry Schuman, 1950, pp. 116–18, 125–26.
Discusses Bruno's dedication to Sidney of *Lo spaccio de la bestia trionfante* and *Eroici furori*.

763 SLATER, GILBERT. *Seven Shakespeares: A Discussion of the Evidence for Various Theories with Regard to Shakespeare's Identity*. London: Cecil Palmer, 1931, pp. 289–90, 298–300, 305–16.
In Shakespeare's *Much Ado about Nothing*, identifies Claudio with Sidney and Benedick with the Earl of Oxford. Feels that Sidney and Oxford were friends before the latter began to support Elizabeth's plans for a French marriage. After the tennis-court quarrel, he and Sidney were again "very warm." In discussing A.W.'s "Eclogue Made Long Since upon the Death of Sir Philip Sidney" (2809), identifies Collin with Spenser, Thenot with Sir Edward Dyer, and Cuddy with Oxford.

764 SMITH, ERIC. *By Mourning Tongues: Studies in English Elegy*. Totowa, N.J.: Boydell Press, Rowman & Littlefield, 1977, pp. 74, 139, 140.
Notes the possible influence of Sidney on Shelley's *Adonais*.

765 SPRIET, PIERRE. *Samuel Daniel (1563–1619): Sa vie—son oeuvre*. Études anglaises, 29. Paris: Dider, 1968, pp. 28, 38, 63–71, 237–40, 246–47.
Notes the close connection between the Sidney circle and Daniel, contending that many of his works, and particularly the *Defence of Rhyme* and *Musophilus*, cannot be adequately comprehended apart from Sidney's influence. Argues that *Delia* is much closer in spirit to the poems of *Arcadia* and to *Certain Sonnets* than to *Astrophil and Stella*.

766 STANFORD, ANN. "Anne Bradstreet's Portrait of Sir Philip Sidney." *EAL* 1 (Winter 1966):11–13.
Noting Bradstreet's family connections with the Sidneys, discusses her elegy for him (2785) and allusions to him in her poem "The Four Ages

of Man." Sees her identification of "Stella" with Sidney's wife (in the second edition of the elegy) as a way of making *Astrophil and Stella* "more acceptable to the morals of the community."

767 STANFORD, CHARLES LEONARD. "Sir Philip Sidney: Contrasting Views on the Value and Morality of Rhetoric and Poetry." Ph.D. diss., University of Missouri at Columbia, 1978, 170 pp.

Argues that Sidney's attitude toward rhetoric passes through three stages: early positive enthusiasm, middle ambiguity, late distrust that it can be used for moral purposes, an attitude which is strongest in *Defense of Leicester*. See *DAI* 39 (April 1979):6150A.

768 STARRETT, VINCENT. *Books Alive*. New York: Random House, 1940, pp. 109–12.

Comments on *Astrophil and Stella*, dismissing *Arcadia* and the *Defence* as "not of any importance in our day." Recounts the skirmish at Zutphen.

769 STATON, WALTER F., Jr. "Characters of Style in Elizabethan Prose." *JEGP* 57 (April 1958):197–207.

Sees Sidney using the "middle style" in the *Defence*, the "lofty style" at times in *Arcadia*, and the "low style" in his letters.

770 STEBBING, WILLIAM. *Five Centuries of English Verse*. Vol. 1. London and New York: Oxford University Press, [1913], pp. 22–31.

In "Sir Philip Sidney," sees Sidney as a poet unjustly ignored and considers possible causes. Views *Arcadia* as "a mass of preposterous affectation" that "often breaks into loveliness." Praises *Astrophil and Stella*, arguing that Sidney had no immoral designs on Lady Rich but wrote the poems to show her "resisting triumphantly."

771 STEIN, HAROLD. *Studies in Spenser's "Complaints."* New York: Oxford University Press, 1934, pp. 38–40, 48–51, 61, 103–5.

Argues that lines 344–434 of *The Ruins of Time* "grow with perfect ease out of the reflections on Sidney" and that *The Tears of the Muses* reflects the views of the Sidney circle. Identifies Sidney as Astrophel in *Colin Clout's Come Home Again*. Suggests that the claim that Sidney was the model for the "ideal courtier" in *Mother Hubberd's Tale* needs to be balanced with the realization that the passage is largely "Castiglione versified." Comments that some readings of *Muiopotmos* see the poem as a discussion of Sidney's life and death. See Hulbert (1066) and Lemmi

Twentieth Century

(625) as well as refutations by Denkinger (1009), Purcell (1120), and Strathmann (775).

772 STERNBERG, JOACHIM. *Untersuchungen zur Verwendung des antiken Mythus in der Dichtung Sir Philip Sidneys als ein Beitrag zur Interpretation.* Bonn: Rheinischen Friedrich-Wilhelms-Universität, 1969, 382 pp.
Undertakes a comprehensive examination of Sidney's use of the Greek and Roman myth in both the poetry and the prose. Considers the influence of the ancients and of Renaissance poets and mythographers. Uses the "phenomenological method," seeking to interpret, not just to find sources for, Sidney's mythological references. Finds the bulk of them in passages on erotic love but also notes their importance in Sidney's rhetoric and in his theory of poetry. Identifies three principal functions for Sidney's mythological references: to move the reader toward neo-Platonic ideals of beauty and virtue; to heighten satiric or ironic contrasts; and to heighten dramatic or elegaic effects. Gives special attention to the role of Cupid in *Astrophil and Stella*.

773 STEVENSON, DAVID LLOYD. *The Love-Game Comedy.* New York: Columbia University Press, 1946, pp. 94–96, 106, 130–32.
Contrasts the balance of sensual realism and Platonic idealism found in Sidney's works with the less sensual portrayals of love in Spenser and Dante. Also sets Sidney's Stella off against the medieval ideal of femininity and notes the medieval attitude toward worldly passion in the sonnet "Leave me O Love" (*CS 32*).

774 STOTSENBURG, JOHN H[AWLEY]. *An Impartial Study of the Shakespeare Title.* Louisville, Ky.: John P. Morton, 1904, pp. 105, 213, 232–51.
After identifying Sidney as Shakespeare's "pleasant Willy," suggests that Sidney was the true author of Shakespeare's *Sonnets*. Argues that *The Lady of May* was a product of Sidney's association with the Areopagus. See also item 394.

775 STRATHMANN, ERNEST A. "The Allegorical Meaning of Spenser's *Muiopotmos*." *PMLA* 46 (September 1931):940–45.
Criticizes Lemmi's argument (625) that Spenser's *Muiopotmos* is an allegorical presentation of Sidney's life and death, arguing that the parallels drawn do not necessarily accord with the facts. See also Stein (771).

776 STUMP, DONALD V[an GUILDER]. "Sidney's Concept of Tragedy in the *Apology* and in the *Arcadia*." *SP* 79 (Winter 1982):41–61.

Responds to Spingarn (2376) and Myrick (671), who suggest that Sidney's concept of tragedy was based on the plays of Seneca, and to Atkins (2389), who treats it as reminiscent of medieval narrative tragedies. Argues, instead, that Sidney's view is essentially Greek. Examines evidence of his exposure to ancient plays by Sophocles and Euripides and to Renaissance plays by George Buchanan and George Whetstone, who followed important Greek principles of tragic design. Also notes nondramatic sources, such as Heliodorus's *Aethiopica*, that embody many of the same formal principles. Finds few if any distinctively Senecan elements in Sidney's view. Noting that a stronger case can be made for the influence of works in the tradition of Boccaccio's *De Casibus Virorum Illustrium* or the moralized stories of *A Mirror for Magistrates*, suggests that Sidney may have blurred distinctions between his own concept of the genre and that held by his English readers. From parallels that Sidney draws between comedy and tragedy and from his remarks on particular plays, argues that the tragic protagonists he is most interested in are like those recommended in Aristotle's *Poetics*: admirable figures who fall because of a tragic error. To support this conclusion, examines six lines of plot in the 1593 *Arcadia* that Sidney explicitly calls tragic and likens to stage plays: the two strands of the main plot, the account of Amphialus's rebellion, and the episodes of Parthenia and Demagoras, of Helen and Philoxenus, and of the Paphlagonian King. Considers the role of tyrants, the causes of the protagonists' misfortunes, the emotional effects described in the onlookers (often a variant of Aristotle's formula "pity and fear"); and the moral lessons that the stories are best suited to teach. Noting respects in which Sidney did not follow the Greek tradition, concludes nonetheless that he "was the first great English poet to understand and practice Aristotelian principles of tragic design."

777 SUMMERS, JOSEPH H[OLMES]. *George Herbert: His Religion and Art*. Cambridge, Mass.: Harvard University Press, 1954, pp. 31, 146, 147, 148, 163, 179, 205, 228, 229.

Notes the hereditary connection between Sidney and Herbert and identifies a number of Herbert's debts to Sidney, particularly to the metrical experiments in the Psalms.

Twentieth Century

778 SWIFT, CAROLYN RUTH. "Feminine Identity in Lady Mary Wroth's Romance *Urania.*" *ELR* 14 (Autumn 1984):328–46.
Occasionally contrasts *Urania* with *Arcadia* to show ways in which Wroth's views of women's abilities differ from the views of Renaissance men.

779 TAYLOR, HENRY OSBORN. *Thought and Expression in the Sixteenth Century.* Vol. 2. New York: Macmillan Co., 1920, pp. 216–30.
Provides general commentary on *Arcadia* and *Astrophil and Stella* and attempts to date the *Defence.*

780 TENISON, E[VA] M[ABEL]. *Elizabethan England: Being the History of This Country "In Relation to All Foreign Princes."* 12 vols. Royal Leamington Spa, Warwick, England: n.p., 1933–60, 3:62–81 passim, 181–86; 4:120; 5:49–61, 65–95, 266, 273–79, plate 13 after p. 164; 6:34–37, 183–253 passim, 437–59; 9:389–93.
Reproduces the portrait of Sidney ca. 1577 now at the National Portrait Gallery in London, noting that it resembles others at Woburn Abbey and Penshurst and suggesting that all are based on the lost portrait by Paolo Veronese. Examines the political background of his embassy to Germany in 1577, describing it and later reactions at court. Considers Sidney's threat against the life of Edmund Molyneux, his attempt to sail to America with Sir Francis Drake, and his quarrel with the Earl of Oxford, explaining dueling practices of the day. Discusses Sidney's works as the product of experience rather than of literary imitation, considering the relation of the *Defence* to Stephen Gosson's *School of Abuse.* Examines the biographical, financial, and political circumstances of his relationship with Penelope Devereux and his marriage to Frances Walsingham, arguing against Wallace (1171) that the latter was born in 1566 not 1550. Demonstrates that documents purportedly linking her with John Wickerson in an illicit affair refer to another woman. Examines maps and previously unpublished documents on the Battle of Zutphen and discusses Sidney's death, printing Thomas Lant's engraving of the return of his body and the funeral. Also examines the financial difficulties occasioned by Sidney's will and discusses the elegies published in his honor and his later reputation. Includes numerous plates of documents related to Sidney and his works. See item 207. Also considers the Sidney-Golding translation of *The Trueness of the Christian Religion.* See item 2719.

781 THOMAS, DYLAN. *Quite Early One Morning.* New York: New
Directions, 1954, pp. 134–45.
In "Sir Philip Sidney," characterizes the *Defence* as "a defence of the
imaginative life, of the duty, and the delight, of the individual poet living among men in the middle of the turning world that has, in his time,
so little time for him." Sketches Sidney's life, describing Wilton as an
ideal setting for the composition of *Arcadia*. Praises *Astrophil and Stella* as
the work of a major poet.

782 [THOMPSON, FRANCIS.] "The Prose of Poets: Sir Philip
Sidney." *Academy*, no. 1546, 21 December 1901, pp. 615–16.
Briefly analyzes the prose styles of *Arcadia* and the *Defence*, contrasting
their youthful fertility with the decaying languor of late nineteenth-century writing.

783 ———. "Sidney's Prose." In *The Works of Francis Thompson*, edited
by [Wilfred Meynell]. Vol. 3. London: Burns, Oates &
Wishbourne; New York: Charles Scribner's Sons, 1913, pp.
147–52.
Regards Sidney as the first writer of modern English literary prose,
praising his periodic style. Prefers the *Defence* to *Arcadia*.

784 THOMPSON, WALTER, ed. *The Sonnets of William Shakespeare
and Henry Wriothesley, Third Earl of Southampton, Together with "A
Lover's Complaint" and "The Phoenix and Turtle."* Oxford: Basil
Blackwell; Liverpool: Henry Young & Sons, 1938, p. 17.
Suggests that Matthew Roydon's elegy on Sidney (2770) might have
been a source for Shakespeare's poem *The Phoenix and the Turtle*.

785 THORNDIKE, ASHLEY H[ORACE]. *English Comedy.* New York:
Macmillan Co., 1929, pp. 4–6, 64–65.
Discusses Sidney's distinctions between tragedy and comedy and the
relation of *The Lady of May* to other English pastoral plays.

786 TILLEY, MORRIS PALMER. *A Dictionary of the Proverbs in
England in the Sixteenth and Seventeenth Centuries.* Ann Arbor:
University of Michigan Press, 1950, 867 pp. passim.
Cites Sidney's *Arcadia*, *Defence*, *Certain Sonnets*, *Astrophil and Stella*, and
Trueness of the Christian Religion as sources for numerous proverbs in the
period.

787 TILLYARD, E[USTACE] M[ANDEVILLE] W[ETENHALL]. *The
English Renaissance: Fact or Fiction?* Baltimore: Johns Hopkins

Twentieth Century

University Press, 1952, pp. 32–33, 65–68, 79, 86–90, 108–10, 111–14.

Stressing humanistic elements in Sidney's work, analyzes "Go my flock" (*AS ix*) to illustrate the "songlike" and "dramatic" qualities that Sidney inherits from Wyatt. Notes the combination of "radical novelty" and "pious veneration" in the *Defence* and emphasizes the classicism of the revised *Arcadia*, viewing its medievalism as "entirely episodic."

788 ———. *Shakespeare's Last Plays*. London: Chatto & Windus, 1938, pp. 10–14, 32–35, 70–72.

Focuses on similarities between *Arcadia* and Shakespeare's late romances. Sees the lofty reputation of the former as evidence that seventeenth-century audiences would not have regarded Shakespeare's last plays as less "serious" than his previous works. Regards Sidney's book as the primary model for *Cymbeline*, noting similarities in the general course of the action and in specific details of setting, political situation, and characterization. Also praises Sidney's skill in portraying Pamela and Philoclea, first as "symbols" for certain sorts of womanhood and later as fully formed characters.

789 TONKIN, HUMPHREY. *Spenser's Courteous Pastoral: Book Six of the "Faerie Queene."* Oxford: Clarendon Press, 1972, pp. 141, 158, 162, 197, 207–11, 296, 303–4.

Considers neo-Platonic elements in the *Defence*, particularly the view that the artist is a mediator between the iron and golden worlds. In Sidney's view, "Wisdom, the highest entity man's intellect can attain to, is not contained in a book of knowledge, *scientia*, but involves some higher, God-given virtue, *sapientia*. This distinction between utility and virtue . . . implies that Art is a part of, a mark of, a man's humanity." Considers possible connections between *Arcadia* and Book VI of *The Faerie Queene*, treating Calidore and Musidorus as parallel creations.

790 TOURNEY, LEONARD D. *Joseph Hall*. Twayne's English Authors Series, 250. Boston: Twayne Publishers, 1979, pp. 28, 78–79.

Compares Hall's views on the English theatre to those in the *Defence*. Contrasts the "plainness" of Hall's psalmody with Sidney's "more expansive and more rhetorical" style.

791 UHLIG, CLAUS. "Der weinende Hirsch: *As You Like It*, II, i, 21–66, und der historische Kontext." *SJH*, 1968, pp. 141–68.

In seeking the direct source of Jaques's sentiments against deer hunting, notes Sir John Harington's comment in the *Metamorphosis of Ajax* that Sidney disliked hunting and hawking. Considers the humanist tradition behind Sidney's view, contrasting it with the usual position of the aristocracy. Examines Philisides's beast fable in *Arcadia* (*OA 66*), suggesting that it influenced the characterization of Jaques and his views on hunting and on tyranny.

792 UPHAM, ALFRED HORATIO. *The French Influence in English Literature from the Accession of Elizabeth to the Restoration.* New York: Columbia University Press, 1908, pp. 4, 23–50, 67, 71, 75, 109–11, 154, 317, 449–50.

Notes Sidney's many French connections in the 1570s, observing that his Protestantism linked him with many Huguenot writers of the time but concluding that evidence of French influence on Sidney's creative work "is not very positive." Remarks on the French influence on the Areopagus, especially in the production of sonnets and long religious poems. Admits that the narrow purpose of the Areopagus was to experiment with classical meters, but suggests that a wider purpose was to formulate a new English idea of poetry. Argues that *Arcadia* is considerably indebted to Book 11 of Herberay des Essarts's French version of *Amadis de Gaule* and sees Sidney's use of the compound epithet as a French influence, possibly through du Bartas. Contends that Sidney's classical verse experiments and his neoclassical view of drama were also inspired by the French. Draws comparisons between Ronsard's poems and *Astrophil and Stella*, but emphasizes Sidney's adaptation and invention. Discusses several reasons that Sidney should have undertaken a translation of du Bartas's *Semaine*. Also comments on the seventeenth-century continuations and adaptations of *Arcadia*.

793 URE, PETER. "The Poetry of Sir Walter Ralegh." *REL* 1 (July 1960):19–29.

Compares Ralegh's "The Lie" and Sidney's "Walking in bright Phoebus' blaze" (*OP 7*), setting them in a tradition of poems rejecting life at court. Compares Spenser's *Astrophel* (2771) with Ralegh's elegy on Sidney (2768).

794 ———. "Two Elizabethan Poets: Daniel and Ralegh." In *The Pelican Guide to English Literature*, edited by Boris Ford. Vol. 2, *The Age of Shakespeare*. Baltimore: Penguin Books, 1955, pp. 131–46. Reprint. "Two Elizabethan Poets: Samuel Daniel and Sir Walter Ralegh." In *A Guide to English Literature*. The Belle Sauvage Library. Vol. 2, *The Age of Shakespeare*. London: Cassell & Co., Penguin Books, 1961, pp. 123–38. Reprint. In *The New Pelican Guide to English Literature*, edited by Boris Ford. Vol. 2, *The Age of*

Twentieth Century

Shakespeare. Harmondsworth, England: Penguin Books, 1982, pp. 149–64.
Treats works by Daniel and Ralegh as examples of the poetic of Sidney's *Defence*. Notes that Sidney is almost exclusively interested in the "infallible grounds of wisdom" rather than in self-expression or emotional release. Finds a precedent for the metaphysical poets in the sophistry and philosphic speculation of his verse.

795 UTZ, HANS WERNER. *Die Anschauungen über Wissenschaft und Religion im Werke Fulke Grevilles*. Swiss Studies in English, 19. Bern: Verlag A. Francke, 1948, pp. 2–6, 32–34, 38–40, 76–77, 90, 110–12.
Reviews the course of Sidney's friendship with Greville and the literary influence of each one on the other. Also discusses Greville's view that Sidney's *Arcadia* did not entirely accord with his theory in the *Defence*. Considers Sidney's relations with Giordano Bruno, his translation of du Plessis-Mornay, and his tendencies toward Calvinism.

796 van DORSTEN, J[AN] A[DRIANUS]. "Arts of Memory and Poetry." *ES* 48 (October 1967):419–25.
In reviewing Yates's *Art of Memory* (834), notes that the elaborate description of Pyrocles's Amazon disguise in *Arcadia* serves as a mnemonic image to assist Musidorus and the reader in remembering arguments between the characters on the nature of love. Also notes Sidney's comments in the *Defence* on mnemonic as well as poetic uses of imagery.

797 ———. "Gruterus and Sidney's *Arcadia*." *RES*, n.s. 16 (May 1965):174–77.
Announces newly discovered neo-Latin poetic tributes to Sidney. Three of these were published in Janus Gruterus's anthologies of neo-Latin poetry *Delitiae Poetarum Germanorum* and *Delitiae C. Poetarum Belgicorum*. See Melissus (2802) and Gruterus (2795). A fourth is a corrupt manuscript version of Baudius (2784), and a fifth is a manuscript poem in three parts by Gruterus entitled "Gerarti vini.threnvs," which begins "Appulit occiduus vada dum Maurusia Titan, Hesperus et coeli limite pendet eques. . . ." This runs to 232 lines and was enclosed in a letter written on the day that Gruterus heard the news of Sidney's death. Provides summaries of the poems, along with bibliographic information and historical material about their authors.

798 VICKERS, BRIAN. "Epideictic and Epic in the Renaissance." *NLH* 14 (Spring 1983):497–537.

Considers the Renaissance epic, setting aside modern assumptions and concentrating on the expectations of Renaissance readers. Notes a long tradition of epideictic rhetorical theory behind passages in the *Defence* and considers the relation between praise and Sidney's aim of moving the reader to virtuous action. Criticizes his views of poetic justice and the value of history. Feels that *Arcadia* violates Renaissance theories of heroic poetry by portraying royal characters who are "largely corrupt." Connects the revised version with other epics of the period written to present "schematic analyses, by parallels and contrasts, of various types of virtue and vice."

799 ———. "Schriftsteller und Diplomat: Philip Sidneys dichterisches Schaffen." *Neue Zürcher Zeitung*, no. 469, 19–20 October 1974, p. 68.

Provides a general account of Sidney's public life and major works, stressing his importance as a poetic innovator and calling him the greatest "occasional writer" in English.

800 VIGLIONE, FRANCESCO. *La poesia lirica di Edmondo Spenser.* Genoa: Emiliano degli Orfini, 1937, pp. 22, 29, 157–59, 205–6, 210–13.

Comments on Sidney's influence on Spenser, listing allusions and direct references to him in Spenser's works and giving special attention to *Astrophel*.

801 VINES, SHERARD. *The Course of English Classicism from the Tudor to the Victorian Age.* Hogarth Lectures on Literature Series, 12. London: Hogarth Press, 1930, pp. 12, 23–24, 32–34.

Traces classical elements in Sidney's theory and practice, noting the strong impact of Horace and other classical theorists on the *Defence* and the influence of Greek romance and pastoral on *Arcadia*.

802 von STACKELBERG, JÜRGEN, ed. *Humanistische Geisteswelt von Karl dem Grossen bis Philip Sidney.* Baden-Baden, Germany: Holle Verlag, 1956, pp. 295–308.

Summarizes Sidney's career, focusing on his education and his ethical ideals. Considers the occasion that prompted him to write the *Defence*, the circumstances of its publication, and the range of its literary allusions.

Twentieth Century

803 WAIT, R.J.C. *The Background to Shakespeare's Sonnets.* London: Chatto & Windus; New York: Schocken Books, 1972, pp. 22, 82–83.

Sees allusions to *Arcadia* in "the distilled essence imprisoned in glass" of Shakespeare's Sonnet 5 and to "What may words say" (*AS 35*) in his Sonnet 84.

804 WAITH, EUGENE M. *The Pattern of Tragicomedy in Beaumont and Fletcher.* Yale Studies in English, 120. New Haven, Conn.: Yale University Press, 1952, pp. 11–13, 15, 29, 70, 73, 74–77, 79, 80, 86, 171–72.

Argues that Sidney influenced Beaumont and Fletcher, both through *Arcadia* and through statements in the *Defence* implying the rhetorical nature of poetry. Focuses on Fletcher's debt to Sidney for critical positions taken in the preface to *The Faithful Shepherdess.* Notes that *Arcadia* was the source for *Cupid's Revenge* and sees material from both being reworked to shape *Philaster.* Traces the development of the shepherd into the shepherd knight, commenting on the use of disguise and on the development of Arcadian rhetoric.

805 WALLACE, MALCOLM W[ILLIAM]. "The Reputation of Sir Philip Sidney." *The Johns Hopkins Alumni Magazine* 17 (November 1928):1–21.

Discusses Sidney's life, influence, and reputation from the sixteenth to the twentieth century, characterizing him as the incarnation of the spirit of the English Renaissance. See a reply by Georgas (1029).

806 WALLER, GARY F. "British Short Fiction in the Sixteenth and Seventeenth Centuries." In *Critical Survey of Short Fiction,* edited by Frank N. Magill. Vol. 2. Englewood Cliffs, N.J.: Salem Press, 1981, pp. 483–504.

Sees in *Arcadia* the dominance of the Elizabethan court and the strains that would trouble it during the next fifty years. Feels that the book could not be finished and that Sidney's "archaic and regressive" solutions to social problems left him uneasy.

807 ———. "Deconstruction and Renaissance Literature." *Assays: Critical Approaches to Medieval and Renaissance Texts* 2 (1982): 69–93.

Claims to find in the *Defence* an "apparent" hesitation between two conflicting views of language—as transparent instrument of truth ("foreconceit") and as "*jouissance*" (the poet "nothing affirms"). Feels that this hesitation "brings us within sight of Derrida's warning about the elementary confusion between the literary sign and the object it portrays."

Suggests that, in *Astrophil and Stella*, rhetorical strategies of reader-engagement are congenial to deconstructive assumptions about reading.

808 ———. "Mary Sidney's '. . . Two Shepherds.'" *AN&Q* 9 (March 1971):100–102.

Argues that Mary Sidney's "Dialogue Between Two Shepherds" points to a "potential split" between Platonism and Calvinism in the works of Sidney, Greville, and possibly Spenser.

809 ———. "A Review of Recent Reviews." *SNew* 1 (Spring 1980):25–29.

Comments on reviews of books about Sidney published between 1977 and 1980, pointing out trends in scholarship on his life and works.

810 ———. "Sir William Alexander and Renaissance Court Culture." *Aevum: Rassegna di scienze storiche, linguistiche e filologiche* 51 (1977):505–15.

Discusses Alexander's "cult of nostalgia" for Sidney and his association with the old Sidney circle. Also considers the Countess of Pembroke's decision to allow Alexander to publish his continuation of *Arcadia* as part of the 1613 edition.

811 ———. "'This matching of contraries': Bruno, Calvin and the Sidney Circle." *Neophil* 56 (July 1972):331–43.

Notes that, in the *Defence*, Sidney's Calvinist views on "our degenerate soules" are matched with contrary views from the magical tradition represented by Giordano Bruno. These Hermetic views appear in Sidney's statement that the poet is godlike in creating a "golden world" and in "ranging freely in the Zodiac of his own wit." Discusses the tension between these contraries in *Astrophil and Stella*, *Arcadia*, and the Psalms. See also Sinfield (2636).

812 WARD, ADOLPHUS WILLIAM. *Collected Papers Historical, Literary, Travel and Miscellaneous.* Vol. 3. Cambridge: Cambridge University Press, 1921, pp. 187–97.

In "Sir Philip Sidney," locates the author in the literary context of his age, commenting on euphuism in *Arcadia* and on the place of the *Defence* in the history of criticism.

813 WARD, A[LFRED] C[HARLES]. *Illustrated History of English Literature.* Vol. 1, *Chaucer to Shakespeare.* London: Longmans, Green, 1953, pp. 118–19, 137, 158, 165–67.

Praises *Astrophil and Stella* as the epitome of "a cultured Elizabethan gentleman's poetry" but claims that the "true Elizabethan poet's poetry has some driving force that is missing from Sidney's." Argues that Sidney's

Twentieth Century

reputation as a man has given *Arcadia* an unjustifiably high evaluation. Summarizes and comments on the *Defence*, noting how fortunate it was that Shakespeare and his contemporaries ignored its remarks on the unities and on tragicomedy.

814 WARNLOF, JESSICA JEAN. "The Influence of Giordano Bruno on the Writings of Sir Philip Sidney." Ph.D. diss., Texas A & M University, 1973, 212 pp.

Examines biographical evidence on the relationship between Sidney and Bruno. Finds verbal parallels between Bruno's *Lo spaccio* and *Eroici furori* and Sidney's *Arcadia* and *Defence*. Suggests that Bruno aroused Sidney's interest in "the principles of poetry, visual epistemology, the literary emblematic technique, neo-Platonic love, the concept of the heroic, cosmology, and the Hermetic tradition." See *DAI* 34 (January 1974):4222A.

815 WASSERMAN, EARL R. *Elizabethan Poetry in the Eighteenth Century.* Illinois Studies in Language and Literature, vol. 32, nos. 2–3. Urbana: University of Illinois Press, 1949, pp. 36, 141, 164, 170, 213, 218, 257–59.

Noting that Sidney's fame in the eighteenth century rested mainly on the *Arcadia*, lists works of his that were reprinted, modernized, or set to music during the period. Comments on scholarly awareness of him, and analyzes alterations to his language, grammar, and style in Mrs. Stanley's 1725 version of *Arcadia* (48).

816 WATKINS, W[ALTER] B[ARKER] C[RITZ]. *Johnson and English Poetry before 1660.* Princeton Studies in English, 13. Princeton, N.J.: Princeton University Press, 1936, pp. 6–7, 17, 39, 41, 58–59, 67, 69, 73.

Discusses Johnson's comments on and allusions to Sidney in the plan for the *Dictionary* and elsewhere.

817 WATSON, SARA RUTH. "Chivalry in Elizabethan Literature." Ph.D. diss., Western Reserve University, 1932.

Includes a chapter examining *Arcadia* in light of the widespread Elizabethan interest in chivalry. Considers Sidney's descriptions of chivalric life, tournaments, armor and heraldic devices, horsemanship, and methods of combat.

818 WAYNE, DON E. "Mediation and Contestation: English Classicism from Sidney to Jonson." *Criticism* 25 (Summer 1983):211–37.

Discusses Sidney's classicism, comparing it with that of Spenser and Jonson. Argues that, although classicism is traditionally viewed as repressive, it also confirms the authority of reason. Views *Astrophil and Stella* as "mediating" between repression and autonomy, both in the author's manipulation of the established genre and in the character's inability to reconcile desire with virtue.

819 ————. *Penshurst: The Semiotics of Place and the Poetics of History.* Madison: University of Wisconsin Press, 1984, pp. 92–94, 96, 106–7, 112, 127, 140–43, 156, 163, 172.

In a book focusing both on the house and on Ben Jonson's poem, examines the estate in detail in terms of its social, moral, intellectual, and psychological contexts, referring often to Sidney in contrast to Jonson. Contends that the descriptions of Kalander's house and garden in *Arcadia* are modelled on Penshurst, suggesting that Sidney's valuing of the house's "utility" and "lastingness" are symptomatic of an emerging Protestant, bourgeois ethic and are an attempt to legitimize the newness of the Sidney family's titles and power. Contends that Sir Henry's rebuilding of Penshurst and Sidney's *Defence* both reflect the beginnings of a "modern, naturalistic conception of history." Reads Sidney's ironic treatment of love in *Astrophil and Stella* as "a symptom of the anxiety that was widespread among the Elizabethan aristocracy concerning their ancestry." Concludes that Jonson's poem "tries to resolve the contradictions between traditional doctrines according to which house and family are indications of a superior status in society, and an emerging notion of home and family as a natural, universal condition of sociality."

820 WEDGWOOD, C[ICELY] V[ERONICA]. *Seventeenth-Century English Literature.* The Home University Library of Modern Knowledge, 218. London, New York, and Toronto: Oxford University Press, 1950, pp. 46, 49–50, 57.

Discusses James Shirley's dramatic version of *Arcadia* and Sidney's influence on the works of William Drummond.

821 WEINER, ANDREW D[AVID]. "Expelling the Beast: Bruno's Adventures in England." *MP* 78 (August 1980):1–13.

Argues, contra Yates (836), that Sidney was not of the same mind as Bruno and that Bruno recognized this in the dedication of *Lo spaccio de la bestia trionfante* (842). See also Imerti (1068). Views Bruno's dedication of the *De gli eroici furori* to Sidney, not as a proof of Sidney's acceptance of Bruno's views, but rather as an attempt to find a patron for the work.

822 WEISS, WOLFGANG. "Die Fictionalisierung der höfischen Lyrik im England des 16. Jahrhunderts." In *Europäische Hofkultur im 16. und 17. Jahrhundert.* Vol. 2, edited by August Buck, Georg

Twentieth Century

Kauffmann, Blake Lee Spahr, and Conrad Wiedemann. Wolfenbüttler Arbeiten zu Barokforschung, 9. Hamburg: Dr. Ernst Hauswedell & Co., 1981, pp. 89–95.
Stresses Sidney's importance in the gradual "fictionalizing" of the courtly lyric as the sonnet sequence replaced the individual lyric as the norm.

823 WELLEK, RENÉ. *A History of Modern Criticism: 1750–1950*. Vol. 2, *The Romantic Age*. New Haven, Conn.: Yale University Press, 1955, pp. 193–94, 196, 204–5, 209.
Discusses the criticism of Sidney's works by Charles Lamb and William Hazlitt.

824 WENDELL, BARRETT. *The Temper of the Seventeenth Century in English Literature*. The Clark Lectures Given at Trinity College, Cambridge, in the Year 1902–1903. New York: Charles Scribner's Sons, 1904, pp. 20–26.
Stresses the experimental nature of *Astrophil and Stella* and *Arcadia*, treating Pamela's prayer as a "rhetorical experiment." Praises the prose style of *Arcadia* and some of the poems.

825 WHITMAN, CHARLES HUNTINGTON. *A Subject-Index to the Poems of Edmund Spenser*. New Haven, Conn.: Yale University Press; London: Oxford University Press, 1919, pp. 218–19.
Notes numerous references and allusions to Sidney in Spenser's works.

826 WILSON, EDWARD M. "Spanish and English Poetry of the Seventeenth Century." *Journal of Ecclesiastical History* 9 (April 1958):38–53.
Comments on Charles I's borrowing of Pamela's prayer from Book III of the revised *Arcadia* and on Herbert's use of Sidney's poetry.

827 WILSON, ELKIN CALHOUN. *England's Eliza*. Harvard Studies in English, 20. Cambridge, Mass.: Harvard University Press, 1939, pp. 128–30, 170–72, 212–13, 244, 270.
Notes the myths that Elizabeth prevented Sidney's acceptance of the Polish crown and that he exchanged verses for a lock of her hair. Regards *The Lady of May* as the first pastoral masque and *Arcadia* as an expression of chivalric ideals.

828 WILSON, F[RANK] P[ERCY]. *Elizabethan and Jacobean.* Oxford: Clarendon Press, 1945, pp. 17–18, 51–52, 67, 75, 77, 79–80, 100, 136.

Sees *Arcadia* not merely as "amatorious," but as a great humanist work dealing with courage and love. Discusses Sidney's character and his influence on Michael Drayton.

829 WILSON, KATHARINE M[ARGARET]. *Shakespeare's Sugared Sonnets.* London: George Allen & Unwin, 1974, pp. 22–23, 147–48, and passim.

Notes the influence of Geron's songs (*OA 9, 10,* and *67*) on Shakespeare's *Sonnets.* Also considers echoes of *Astrophil and Stella.*

830 WILSON, MONA. *Sir Philip Sidney.* London: Duckworth, 1931; New York: Oxford University Press, 1932, 328 pp.

In a study of Sidney's life and works written for a general audience, seeks to deal "more particularly" than Bourne (318) or Wallace (1171) with Sidney and the "dawn" of Elizabethan literature. Provides the basic facts of Sidney's lineage, life, and death, commenting on the Sidney Psalter, *The Lady of May,* the Areopagus and its experiments with classical meters, and the poetry of *Arcadia.* Summarizes *Arcadia,* discussing the early editions and offering a brief analysis of its style. In discussing the *Defence,* relies heavily on paraphrase. Quotes amply from *Astrophil and Stella* to prove that the sequence goes beyond "love poetry" and the "Stella story" to explore the problems of writing love poetry and the conflict between public and private life. Sees the relationship between Astrophil and Stella as biographical and argues that portions of the sequence were circulated in manuscript. Supplies ample quotations from letters, works, and contemporary documents and includes a bibliography.

831 WOODBERRY, GEORGE EDWARD. *Studies of a Litterateur.* New York: Harcourt, Brace & Co., 1921, pp. 297–304.

Discusses Sidney's character and the nature and background of the *Defence.*

832 WRAIGHT, A[NNIE] D[ORIS], and STERN, VIRGINIA F. *In Search of Christopher Marlowe: A Pictorial Biography.* New York: Vanguard Press, 1965, pp. 82, 83, 110, 125, 147, 155, 166.

Suggests that Marlowe may have written one of the anonymous elegies for Sidney. Attempts to connect the two authors through Sir Francis Walsingham.

Twentieth Century

833 YABU, MORIMINE. "The Theme of Eden in Sidney's Works: A Vision of the Fall." *Kokubungaku Ronshuy* (Ryukyu Daigaku Hobungakubu Kiyo) [Collected Papers (Literature Department), Ryukyu University], no. 16, February 1972, pp. 125–43.
Not seen.

834 YATES, FRANCES A[MELIA]. *The Art of Memory.* London: Routledge & Kegan Paul; Chicago: University of Chicago Press, 1966, pp. 260, 263–64, 283–84, 310, 312–13.
Connects Sidney with the study of memory in the period by noting that the third edition of William Fulwood's *Castle of Memory* was dedicated to Leicester. Links Sidney with John Dee, Alexander Dickson, and Giordano Bruno, speculating that the *Defence* may have been written while Bruno was in England. Argues that Sidney's attitudes to the art of memory are anti-Ramist and that "no pure Ramist could have written the *Defence*." See also van Dorsten (796).

835 ———. "Elizabethan Chivalry: The Romance of the Accession Day Tilts." *JWCI* 20 (1957):4–25. Reprint. In *Astraea: The Imperial Theme in the Sixteenth Century*, by Frances A[melia] Yates. London and Boston: Routledge & Kegan Paul, 1975, pp. 88–111.
In describing the origins and development of the Accession Day Tilts, notes the close association between Sidney and Sir Henry Lee, founder of the tilts. Comments on parallels between *Four Foster Children of Desire* and the tilts of the early 1580s. Mentions the mourning for Sidney after the tilts of 1586 and draws attention to Lee's gift of a copy of the verses from *Arcadia* to his successor, Lord Cumberland.

836 ———. *Giordano Bruno and the Hermetic Tradition.* London: Routledge & Kegan Paul; Chicago: University of Chicago Press, 1964, pp. 176–79, 187–88, 206, 219–21, 228–30, 275, 278, 285, 289, 293, 320, 331, 358, 394.
Argues that Sidney was familiar with and possibly sympathetic to the Hermeticism and neo-Platonism of Bruno, claiming that Sidney was familiar with the *The Divine Pymander of Hermes Trismegistus* and Hermeticism through his translation of du Plessis-Mornay's *De la verité de la religion chrestienne*. Notes that Sidney's contact with John Dee would have given him another viewpoint on the centrality of Hermetic thought. Cites John Dee's diary (922) as evidence that Sidney brought the Polish prince Albert Alasco to visit Dee at Mortlake in June 1583. Discusses Bruno's dedication of *Lo spaccio della bestia trionfante* (842) to

Sidney, particularly its astrological speculations and its offer of friend-ship with Henri III of France. In discussing Bruno's dedication of *De gli eroici furori* to Sidney, suggests that Bruno's attempt to blend Hermeticism and Petrarchanism influenced Sidney and Elizabethan love poetry generally. See a reply by Weiner (821).

837 ——. *John Florio: The Life of an Italian in Shakespeare's England.* Cambridge: Cambridge University Press, 1934, pp. 42–45, 95–96, 104–7, 199, 201, 206.

Notes Florio's apparent success in gaining Sidney's patronage. From quotations in his *Second Fruits*, argues that he had read the *Defence* in manuscript. Also remarks on Sidney's friendship with Bruno and an allu-sion to Penelope Devereux in Bruno's dedication of *De gli eroici furori*. Notes Florio's allusion to Sidney's relationship with her in the dedication to the 1603 edition of his translation of Montaigne. Argues that Florio's condemnation of Hugh Sanford's work on the 1593 *Arcadia* may stem from jealousy, since Florio may have edited the 1590 *Arcadia*.

838 ——. "The Religious Policy of Giordano Bruno." *Journal of the Warburg Institute* 3 (1939):181–207.

Argues that Bruno and Sidney were friends and suggests that Bruno's works "properly understood, might provide an invaluable key to the motive springs of our greatest literature."

839 ——. *A Study of "Love's Labour's Lost."* Cambridge: Cambridge University Press, 1936, pp. 17, 24–25, 104–36, 142–43, 145, 149–51, 171.

Notes parallels between Rombus in *The Lady of May* and Holofernes in *Love's Labor's Lost*, pointing out Shakespeare's allusions to *Arcadia* and *Astrophil and Stella*. Remembering Berowne's anti-Petrarchan sentiments, argues that he was modeled on Giordano Bruno, who, both in Sidney's presence and in the dedication to *De gli eroici furori*, had attacked love sonnets of the sort found in *Astrophil and Stella*. Links Shakespeare's play with Sidney's sequence via John Florio's *Second Fruits*. Examines in detail contemporary evidence linking Stella with Lady Rich. Relates Sidney's sonnets to *Eroici furori*, noting the "vague, Platonic . . . aspiration toward the divine" in "Leave me, O love" (*CS 32*). Also discusses allusions to Sidney in John Eliot's *Ortho-epia Gallica* and to *Arcadia* in an unpublished essay by the Henry Percy, ninth Earl of Northumberland.

Twentieth Century

840 ———. *The Valois Tapestries*. Studies of the Warburg Institute, 23. London: Warburg Institute, 1959, pp. 30, 75, 92, 100.
Notes Sidney's connection with events pictured in or important to the development of the tapestries. Draws parallels between the creation of the tapestries and the creation of *Arcadia*.

841 ZSCHECH, FRITZ. *Die Kritik des Reims in England*. Berliner Beiträge zur germanischen und romanischen Philologie, 50. Berlin: Verlag von Emil Ebering, 1917, pp. 14–21 passim, 32–37.
Considers Sidney's apparent hostility to rhyme at the time of the Areopagus and his later, more sympathetic views in the *Defence*. Notes a similar ambivalence in critics under Sidney's influence, such as Sir John Harington and Frances Meres.

Biographical Studies

Sixteenth Century

842 BRUNO, GIORDANO. "Epistola esplicatoria scritta al molto illustre, et excellente caualliero Signor Philippo Sidneo, dal Nolano." In *Lo Spaccio de la bestia trionfante, proposto da Giove, Effetuato dal conseglo, Reuelato da Mercurio, Recitato da Sophia, Vdito da Saulino, Regostrato dal Nolano. Diviso in tre Dialogi, subdivisi in tre parti.* Parigi: n.p., 1584, sigs. ¶2ʳ–*8ᵛ. Reprint. In *The Expulsion of the Triumphant Beast,* edited and translated by Arthur D. Imerti. New Brunswick, N.J.: Rutgers University Press, 1964, pp. 69–88.

In dedicating the book to Sidney, pays respect to his intellect, customs, and merits, calling his inclinations "truly heroic." Acknowledges, regretfully, some ill will between himself and Greville. Claims that he and Sidney wear the "masks of the mimical and comical and histrionic Sileni," and are thus "far removed" from both the multitude who "laugh at, jest at, mock at and entertain [themselves]," and the "many" who "under their profuse beards and magisterial and grave togas . . . contain ignorance no less vile than haughty." Although the title page gives Paris as the place of publication, the book was actually brought out in London by J[ohn] Charlewood. See also item 980 and Weiner (821)

843 [DIGGES, THOMAS.] *A Briefe Report of the Militarie Seruices done in the Low Countries, by the Erle of Leicester: written by one that serued in good place there in a letter to a friend of his.* London: Arnold Hatfield for Gregory Seton, 1587, sigs. C1ᵛ, C2ᵛ, D1ʳ.

Mentions Sidney in connection with the assault on Elten and Duisburg. In recounting the battle of Zutphen, notes that "not any of name" were lost except Sidney, who was "shot with a musket in the left thigh, but came home on his horse, and died the 25. day after." Essentially the same text as Grimestone (864).

239

Sixteenth Century

844 ESTIENNE, HENRI. "Nobiliss. et modus omnibvs Generosissimo Viro, Philippo Sidneo." In *HERODIANOU HISTORION BIBLIA H. Herodiani Histor. Lib. VIII. Cum Angeli Politiani interpretatione & huius partem supplemento, partim examine Henrici Stephani: utroque margini adscripto.* [Geneva:] Excudebat Henricus Stephanus, 1581, sigs. ¶ii^r–¶ii^v.

In dedicating the volume to Sidney, compares him to Horace and voices the fear that courtly allurements will divert "mi Sidnee" from serious study of works like the one presented.

845 FRAUNCE, ABRAHAM. Prefatory letter "To the Learned Lawyers of England, especially the Gentlemen of Grays Inne." In *The Lawiers Logike, exemplifying the praecepts of Logike by the practise of the common Lawe.* London: William How, 1588, sig. ¶1^r. Reprint. In English Linguistics, 1500–1800: A Collection of Facsimile Reprints, 174, edited by R.C. Alston. Menston, England: Scolar Press, 1969.

States that Sidney first encouraged Fraunce's study of Ramist logic and his treatise on Ramus and Aristotle.

846 GENTILI, ALBERICO. *De Legationibus libri tres. Omnibus omnium ordinum studiosis, praecipue vero. Iuris ciuilis lectu vtiles, ac maxime necessarii.* Hanoviae: Apud Guilielmum Antonium, 1594, sigs. A2^r–A4^v. Reprint in facsimile. Edited by James Brown Scott and translated by Gordon J. Laing. Classics of International Law, 12. 2 vols. New York: Oxford University Press, 1924.

In the dedicatory epistle to Sidney, alludes to their correspondence and "frequent personal interviews" and to Sidney's standing within his own family and at court. Reviews Sidney's role in inspiring and guiding the composition of the treatise.

847 HAKLUYT, RICHARD. "To the right worshipfull and most vertuous Gentleman master Philip Sydney, Esquire." In *Divers voyages touching the discouerie of America and the Ilands adiacent vnto the same, made first of all by our Englishmen and afterwards by the Frenchmen and Britons.* London: for Thomas Woodcock, 1582. Reprint. Edited by J.W. Jones. Hakluyt Society Publications, 1st ser., vol. 7. London: for the Hakluyt Society, 1850, pp. 8–18.

Assuming Sidney's "acustomed fauour" toward voyagers, argues that England should pursue colonization in the Americas more vigorously, sets forth reasons why a northwest passage is likely to be discovered, and pleads for twenty pounds to be applied toward the creation of a lectureship in "the arte of navigation."

848 [HARINGTON, Sir JOHN.] *A New Discovrse of a Stale Svbject, Called The Metamorphosis of Aiax. Writen by Misacmos, to his friend and cosin Philostilpnos.* London: Richard Field, 1596, sig. E1ʳ. Reprint. Edited by Elizabeth Story Donno. New York: Columbia University Press; London: Routledge & Kegan Paul, 1962, p. 108.
Records Sidney's dislike of hunting and hawking.

849 LANT, THOMAS. *Seqvitvr celebritas & pompa funeris quemadmodum a Clarencio Armorum et Jnsignium rege instituta est.* . . . London: Derick Theodor De Brij, 1587, 30 plates. Reprint in facsimile. Edited by Colaianne and Godshalk (2823).
Includes thirty engravings designed by Lant and executed by de Brij, which depict Sidney's massive funeral procession. Includes a title-page description of the funeral, a commentary identifying many of the mourners and giving their functions in the government and/or the ceremony, and a final page of text listing Sidney's attainments, sketching his character and reputation in England and on the Continent, recording Walsingham's role in paying for the funeral, and providing details about the procession and interment. Much of the printed text is in both Latin and English. The plates include depictions of Sidney; the "Black Pynnes" that carried his coffin back from the Netherlands; his tomb in in the old St. Paul's Cathedral; the standard, pennons (bearing Sidney's coat of arms), and banner carried in the procession; articles of his armaments that were carried before the body; the draped coffin; and the most prominent of the seven hundred officials, relatives, foreign dignitaries, and other mourners who took part in the ceremony, many of whom are identified by name. See also Benham (984), Dodds (1012), Doughtie (1014), Hind (1059), and Newdigate (1100).

850 [SEGAR, Sir WILLIAM.] *The Booke of Honor and Armes.* London: Printed by Richard Ihones, 1590, pp. 95, 101. Reprint. Delmar, N.Y.: Scholars' Facsimiles & Reprints, 1975.
Names Sidney as a "defender" in "an Honourable challenge" brought by the Earl of Arundel in 1580 and in one or more Accession Day "exercises in Arms."

851 SMYTHE, Sir JOHN. *Certain Discourses, written by Sir John Smythe, Knight: Concerning the formes and effects of diuers sorts of weapons, and other verie important matters Militarie, greatlie mistaken by divers of our men of warre in these daies.* London: Richard Johnes, 1590, sig. B3ʳ.
Presents Sidney's death from failure to wear his cuisses at Zutphen as a result of misguided modern-day arming practices ("unsoldierlike and fond").

Sixteenth Century

852 STOW, JOHN. *The Annales of England, faithfully collected out of the most authenticall Authors, Records, and other Monuments of Antiquitie, from the first inhabitation untill this present yeere 1592.* London: Ralfe Newbury, 1592, pp. 1180, 1204, 1243–45, 1252–53, 1256, 1257.
Notes Sidney's Whitsunday joust in 1581; his entertainment of the Earl of Leicester while acting as Governor of Flushing; and his exhortation to the troops before the battle of Axel. Describes the taking of Axel, the battle of Zutphen, Sidney's wound, his death, and his funeral procession. Dates the death on 17 October, the landing of the body in London on 5 November, and the burial on 15 February.

853 van METEREN, EMMANUEL. *L'histoire des Pays-bas d'Emmanuel de Meteren. Ou recueil des guerres et choses memorables advenues tant és dits Pays, qu'és Pays voisins, depuis l'an 1313. jusques à l'an 1612. Corrigé et augmenté par l'autheur mesme, et enrichi outre la carte du Pays-bas, de pres de cent pourtraits des principaulx seigneurs desquels it est fait mention en ceste histoire.* Traduite de Flamand en Francoys par I.D.L. The Hague: Chez Hilebrant, Jacob[ssen], & Wou, Imprimeur Ordinaire des Illus. Seig. Estats Generaux, 1618, fols. 263^r–264^r. Orig. pub. in unauthorized translations, in both German (Hamburg: François von Dortt, 1596) and Latin (Cologne: n.p., 1598), before the first Dutch edition appeared (Delft, 1599; not seen).
Refers several times to Sidney's role in Leicester's military preparations between June and October for the siege of Zutphen and briefly describes his death. See also item 872.

Seventeenth Century

854 ANON., ed. *The Works of that Famous English Poet Mr. Edmond Spenser. Whereunto is added An Account of his Life; with other new Additions never before in Print.* London: Henry Hills for Jonathan Edwin, 1679, sig. A1^r.
Records the story that Sidney reacted with munificence to a reading of the manuscript version of the Cave of Despair episode in Spenser's *Faerie Queene* I.ix.

855 [BAUDARTIUS, WILHELMUS.] *Afbeeldinghe, ende beschrijvinghe van alle de Veld-slagen belegeringen en and're notable geschiedenissen ghevallen in de Nederlanden geduerende d'oorloghe teghens den Coningh*

van Spaengien. . . . t'Amsterdam: By Michiel Colijn, 1616, fol. 535ʳ.
Not seen. Cited in *NUC* (pre-1956), Vol. 39, 358. Includes an engraving of Sidney and Prince Maurice at the taking of Axel in 1586, from which van Dorsten reproduces part of the image of Sidney (item 1166, plate 8 following p. 164).

856 ———. *Polemographia Avraico-Belgica. Viva delineatio, ac Descriptio omnium proeliorum, obsidionum, aliarumque rerum memoratu dignarum, qua, durante bello adversus Hispaniarum Regem in Belgij Provincijs, sub ductu ac moderamine Guilelmi & Mauritij Ill. Auraicorum, etc. Principum auspicijs Potentissimorum Ordinum Generalsum, gestae sunt.* Vol. 2. Amstelodami: Apud Michaelem Colinium bibliopolam, 1622, pp. 85–86.
Describes the battle of Zutphen and Sidney's wounding, death, and funeral.

857 BLOUNT, Sir THOMAS POPE. *De Re Poetica: Or, Remarks upon Poetry. With Characters and Censures of the Most Considerable Poets, Whether Ancient or Modern.* London: Richard Everingham for R. Bentley, 1694, pp. 206–9. Reprint in facsimile. New York: Garland Publishing, 1974.
Sketches Sidney's life and character.

858 CAMDEN, WILLIAM. *Remains of a Greater Worke Concerning Britain.* London: G.E. for Simon Waterson, 1605, sigs. Y3ʳ, Z3ᵛ, g3ʳ–g3ᵛ. Reprint. London: John Russell Smith, 1870, pp. 374, 384, 419.
Explains three of Sidney's *imprese*: the Caspian Sea with the motto "Sine refluxu"; the word "Speravi" dashed through; and the sun shining on a withered tree, new blooming, with the motto "His radiis rediviva viresco." Also comments on Sidney's epitaph, noting that it was "imitated out of French of Mons. Bonivet, made by Joach[im] du Bellay, as it was noted by Sir George Buc, in his 'Poetica.'"

859 CAMERARIUS, P[HILIPP]. *The Walking Librarie, or Meditations and Observations Historical, Natural, Moral, Political, and Poetical.* Translated by John Molle. London: Adam Islip, 1621, pp. 98–100. [Variant issue: the same except that the title begins *The Living Library.* . . .] Reprint. In *Bibliographical Memoranda; In Illustration of Early English Literature,* edited by [John Fry]. Bristol, England: n.p., 1816, pp. 167–71.

Seventeenth Century

Records a conversation that the author had with Sidney, Languet, and others during Sidney's embassy to Germany in 1577. Sidney explained that wolves were absent from England because an ancient king of England allowed criminals to bring in their tongues and heads in lieu of punishment. Confirms Sidney's view from contemporary histories.

860 CAREW, RICHARD, of ANTONY. *The Survey of Cornwall.* London: by S.S. for John Iaggard, 1602, p. 102. Reprint in facsimile. Amsterdam: Theatrum Orbis Terrarum; New York: Da Capo Press, 1969.

Relates an incident in his term at Oxford when he was "called to dispute *ex tempore* . . . with the matchless Sir Ph. Sidney."

861 CLARKE, SAMUEL. "The Life and Death of Sir Philip Sidney, who died An. Ch. 1586." In *Lives of Sundry Eminent Persons in this Later Age. In Two Parts, I. Of Divines. II. Of Nobility and Gentry of both Sexes.* Part 2. London: for Thomas Simmons, 1683, pp. 89–97.

Provides an account of Sidney's public life; his parentage; his travels and reputation among important Continental figures; his learning and political "prudence" (here summarizing at length the *Letter to the Queen*); his governorship of Flushing, wounding, and death. Contains an engraved portrait by "F.H. Van Houe, sculp."

862 FULLER, THOMAS. *Anglorum Speculum, or The Worthies of England, in Church and State.* London: Thomas Passinger, William Thackary, and John Wright, 1684, p. 407.

Rehearses basic facts and myths about Sidney's life.

863 GREVILLE, FULKE. *The Life of the Renowned Philip Sidney. With the true Interest of England as it then stood in relation to all Forrain Princes: And particularly for suppressing the power of Spain Stated by Him. His principall Actions, Counsels, Designs and Death. Together with a short Account of the Maxims and Policies used by Queen Elizabeth in her Government.* London: Printed for Henry Seile, 1652, 255 pp. Reprint. Edited by Brydges (908) and Wooden (1184). Reprint. Edited by Nowell Smith. Oxford: Clarendon Press, 1907.

Originally conceived as a "Dedication" to an edition of Greville's early works, the biography of Sidney, occupying the first thirteen of a total of eighteen chapters, presents him as an exemplary pattern of moral and civic virtue and, explicitly and implicitly, as a rebuke to a society that had abandoned his values. The remaining chapters are given to an account of Elizabeth's policies and to Greville's own life and art. In presenting Sidney as "this one man's example," which "did not only encourage Learning and Honour . . . but brought . . . the true use thereof both into the Courte and the Camps," eschews enlivening personal details (omitting, for example, all reference to Penelope Rich or to Sidney's wife and child) but grounds the whole, nevertheless, in Greville's memory of particular times, places, and individuals (e.g., Sidney's refusal to allow Greville to convey William of Orange's praise to the Queen). In presenting Sidney as political exemplar, narrates the tennis-court episode as an incident in a larger discussion of the political situation of the time involving rival factions concerning the French marriage, with Sidney and Oxford standing for contrasting types of courtiers and with the presence of the French ambassadors a reminder of the threat to national honor. In Chapters 5, 8, and 9, turns to larger moral and political issues, particularly Sidney's ideas regarding the danger of Spain and the necessity of strengthening the Protestant alliance. In Chapter 5, offers reasons for Sidney's opposition to the French marriage that differ from those in Sidney's own *Letter to the Queen*. In Chapter 8, details, country by country, the Spanish menace to Europe, and in Chapter 9, sets forth, in an exploratory way, Sidney's arguments for breaking the power of Spain. See also Wooden (1184), Ewing (1017), Zandvoort (1316), and Rees (1726).

864 GRIMESTON, ED[WARD]. *A Generall Historie of the Netherlands: With the genealogie and memorable acts of the Earls of Holland, Zeeland, and west-Friseland, from Thierry of Aquitaine . . . unto Philip the third King of Spaine.* London: A. Islip and G. Eld, 1609, sigs. 4I5^v–4I6^r, 4K2^r–4K3^r.
In phrasing almost identical with that of Digges (843), describes the failed plot by Nicholas Marchant to ambush Sidney in Graveling and recounts the battles of Duisburg ("Doesborch") and Zutphen.

865 H[OLLAND], H[ENRY]. *Herwologia anglica hoc est clarissimorum et doctissimorum.* Arnheim, Netherlands: J. Jansson, 1620, pp. 71–74.
Provides a portrait and a brief biography, including two epigrams (one on *Arcadia*), followed by three short epitaphs. See item 2800.

866 HOOFT, P[IETER] C[ORNIELSZ]. *Nederlandsche Historien, Seedert Ooverdraght der Heerschappye van Kaizar Kaarel den Vyften op Koonig Philips zynen Zoon, tot de doodt des Prinse van Oranje. Met het Vervolgh tot het einde der Landtvoogh dye des Graaven van Leicester.* 3d ed. Amsterdam: by Johan van Someren, Abraham Wolfgangk, Henrik en Dirk Boom, Boekverkoopers, 1677, pp. 1039, 1041, 1065,

Seventeenth Century

1089–90, 1094–95. Orig. pub. 1642 (not seen). Quoted in part by van Dorsten (1166).
Commenting on Sidney's activities in the Netherlands and the possible effects that his life might have had on Dutch history had he survived, views Sidney as possibly capable of reversing the unpopular course of action being taken by Leicester at the time of Sidney's death.

867 [LIQUES, DAVID de]. *Histoire de la Vie de Messire Philippes de Mornay Siegneur du Plessis Marly, &c. Contenant outre la Relation de plusieurs evenemens notables en l'Estat, en l'Eglise, és Covrs, & és Armees, divers advis politiqs, Ecclesiastiqs & Militaires sur beaucoup de mouvemens importans de l'Europe; sovbs Henry III. Henry IV. & Louys XIII.* Leyden, Netherlands: Chez Bonaventure & Abraham Elsevier, 1647, pp. 43, 60.
Comments on du Plessis-Mornay's friendship with Sidney, the latter's support for the Huguenot cause, and his interest in a Protestant League. Praises Sidney's virtues and mentions his translation of the *Trueness of the Christian Religion.*

868 LLOYD, DAVID. "Observations on the Life of Sir Philip Sidney." In *The States-men and Favourites of England since the Reformation. During the Reigns of King Henry VIII. King Edward VI. Queen Mary. Queen Elizabeth. King James. King Charles.* London: Printed by J.C. for Samuel Speed, 1665, pp. 313–22. Partial reprint. "Something of the Character of Sir Philip Sidney." In *The Agreeable Variety. In Two Parts. Containing First, Discourses, Characters, and Poems, Relating to the Most Useful Subjects; and Extracted from Many Worthy Authors.* London: for G. Strahan, A. Boteswsorth, J. Holand, H. Clements, J. Waltho, C. King, and B. Barker, 1717, p. 66.
Surveys Sidney's character, accomplishments, and political views, drawing heavily on Greville (863). Cites "ten ways he laid down [that] a foreign prince might endanger our religion" and nine "motives" that he gave for undertaking an expedition to the Indies. Says of *Arcadia:* "his book is below his spirit: a spirit to be confined with kingdoms, rather than studies, to do what was to be written, than only to write what was to be done." But also says: "Where his great soul could not *improve Europe* he *considered* it; and made that the field of his meditation, that could not be the stage of his actions. England he saw so humoursome and populous, that it was to be refined with war, and corrupted with peace."

869 NAUNTON, ROBERT. *Fragmenta Regalia*. [London]: n.p., 1641, pp. 21–22. Reprint. Edited by John S. Cervoski. Washington, D.C.: The Folger Shakespeare Library; London and Toronto: Associated University Presses, 1985.

Notes briefly the parentage, education, courtiership and two "fictions" about Sidney—that Mars and Mercury argued whose servant he should be and that Art and Nature turned him over to Fortune. Judges that "he seemed to be born to that onely which he went about."

870 [OSBORNE, FRANCIS.] *Historical Memoires on the Reigns of Queen Elizabeth and King James*. London: by F. Grismond, and are to be sold by T. Robinson, 1658, p. 66. Reprint. In *Secret History of the Court of James the First: Containing I. Osborne's Traditional Memoirs. II. Sir Anthony Weldon's Court and Character of King James. III. Aulicus Coquinariae. IV. Sir Edward Peyton's Divine Catastrophe of the House of Stuarts*. Vol. 1. Edinburgh: Printed by James Ballantyne for John Ballantyne & Co.; and Longman, Hurst, Rees, Orme, & Brown, 1811, pp. 81–82.

Suggests that Elizabeth's concern about her subjects wearing the "titles of a forraigne prince" led her to "denie Sir Phillip Sidney the Crowne of Poland."

871 SPEED, JOHN. *The History of Great Britaine under the Conquests of ye Romans, Saxons, Danis, and Normans*. London: for John Sudbury & George Humble, 1611, p. 856.

Refers to Sidney's death at Zutphen.

872 van METEREN, EMMANUEL. *A Trve Discovrse Historicall, of the Svcceeding Governovrs in the Netherlands, and the Ciuill warres there begun in the yeere 1565. with the memorable seruices of our Honourable English Generals, Captaines, and Souldiers, especially vnder Sir Iohn Norice Knight, there performed from the yeere 1577. vntill the yeere 1589*. . . . Translated and collected by T[homas] C[hurchyard] and Ric[hard] Ro[binson]. London: Matthew Lownes, 1602, sigs. L3ᵛ–L4ʳ, O1ʳ–O2ᵛ.

Recounts Sidney's appointment as Governor of Flushing, his death, and funeral, concluding with brief epitaphs, the first "Here under lyes Phillip Sydney Knight" by Bernard Whetstone (2776), the second "usuallie pendant at the said pillar" in St. Paul's Cathedral where Sidney was buried (see item 2782). See also item 853 and Churchyard (2815).

Eighteenth Century

Eighteenth Century

873 BIRCH, THOMAS. *Memoirs of the Reign of Queen Elizabeth, from the Year 1581 till Her Death.* Vol. 1. London: for A. Millar, 1754, p. 35. Reprint. New York: AMS Press, 1970.

Includes a notice of Sidney's marriage to Frances Walsingham, as recorded in the private papers of Anthony Bacon.

874 ———. "Sir Philip Sidney, Knight." In *The Heads of Illustrious Persons of Great Britain, Engraven by Mr. Houbraken, and Mr. Vertue. With their Lives and Characters.* Vol. 2. London: for John and Paul Knapton, 1747–52, pp. 15–16.

In considering the Houbraken engraving of Sidney, provides a brief biographical sketch. On the derivation of this engraving from an Isaac Oliver original, see Judson (1075).

875 CHURCH, RALPH, ed. *"The Faerie Queene," by Edmund Spenser. A New Edition, with Notes Critical and Explanatory.* Vol. 1. London: Printed by William Faden, 1758, pp. xxiii–xxiv.

Quotes "Verses to Spenser" by one W.L. to support the contention that it is "very probable" that Sidney "put him upon" writing the *Faerie Queene.*

876 HOTMAN, FRANCIS. *Francisci et Joannis Hotmanorum patris ac filii, et clarorum virorum ad eos; Epistolae. Quibus accedit, epistolarum miscellanearum Virorum Doctorum, qui hoc & superiore saeculo claruere Appendix.* Ex Bibliotheca Jani Gulielmi Meelii. Amsterdam: apud Georgium Gallet, 1700, p. 341.

Contains a 1586 letter from Francis Hotman to Justus Lipsius noting Sidney's death.

877 LYTTELTON, GEORGE LORD, [1st Baron]. *The History of the Life of King Henry the Second, and of the Age in Which He Lived.* Vol. 3. London: Printed for J. Dodsley, 1769, pp. 178, 359–62.

Compares Sidney with Bayard, concluding that Sidney's attainments were greater. Also compares him with Lord Herbert of Cherbury.

878 [OLDYS, WILLIAM.] "A Collection, Historical and Political, of Letters, Discourses, Memorials, &c. . . . Gather'd, Chiefly, from the Papers of Henry Earl of Derby . . . MS. Fol. 1589, about 280 Pages." *British Librarian*, no. 5, May 1737, pp. 270–86.

Transcribes large parts of Leicester's letter to Sir Thomas Heneage of 23 September 1586, which describes Sidney's actions and his injury at Zutphen.

879 STRYPE, JOHN. *Annals of the Reformation and Establishment of Religion and Other Various Occurrences in the Church of England, during Queen Elizabeth's Happy Reign Together with an Appendix of Original Papers of State, Records, and Letters.* A New Edition. 4 vols. (bound in 7 vols.). Oxford: Clarendon Press, 1824, 2.1:215, 218–23, 226; 2.2:240–41, 641–52; 3.1:85–86, 403–4, 656. 2d. ed. (the first that contained material on Sidney). London: by and for T. Edlin, 1725–31 (not seen).

Records Sidney's arrival in France in 1572 and his presence there during the St. Bartholomew's Day Massacre, arguing that the *Letter to the Queen* took the tone it did because of Sidney's reaction to the massacre. Notes the proposed marriage between Anne Cecil and Sidney and quotes the section of Sidney's will authorizing Walsingham to sell lands to pay the debts of Sidney and his father. In an appendix to Volume 2.2, reprints the *Letter to the Queen*. See item 156.

880 THORPE, J[OHN]. Quoted in "Death and Funeral Procession of Sir Philip Sidney, 1586." In *The Progresses and Public Processions of Queen Elizabeth*, edited by John Nichols. 2d ed. Vol. 2. London: John Nichols & Son, 1823, pp. 483–94. Orig. pub. as *The Progresses, and Processions, of Queen Elizabeth*. 2 vols. London: Printed by and for the editor, printer to the Society of Antequaries of London, 1788 (not seen).

Provides a detailed description of Sidney's funeral procession as it is depicted in Lant's engraving.

881 WALPOLE, HORACE, Earl of Orford. *Anecdotes of Painting in England; With Some Account of the Principal Artists; And Incidental on Other Arts: Collected by the Late Mr. George Vertue; Now digested and published from his original MSS.* 3d ed. "with Additions." Vol. 1. London: Printed for J. Dodsley, 1782, p. 261.

Notes Isaac Oliver's painting of "the whole length of Sir Philip Sidney sitting under a tree."

882 YART, Abbé ANTOINE. *Idée de la Poësie Angloise, ou Traduction des Meilleurs pöetes anglois qui n'ont point encore paru dans notre Langue.* Vol. 4. Paris: Chez Briasson, 1753, p. 108.

Records the myth that Spenser showed Sidney canto ix of Book I of *The Faerie Queene*. See also Birch (287).

Nineteenth Century

883 A., E.H. "Sir Philip Sidney." *N&Q*, 2d ser. 7 (9 April 1859):306–7. Responds to the second query by J.K. (946), claiming to own the portrait by Oliver.

884 ADAMS, WILLIAM HENRY DAVENPORT. *The Sunshine of Domestic Life: or Sketches of Womanly Virtue in the Stories of the Lives of Noble Women*. London: T. Nelson & Sons, 1869, pp. 215–28.
In "A Noble English Mother: The Story of Mary, Countess of Pembroke," discusses Sidney's close relationship with his sister.

885 ANON. "Curious Coats of Arms, Crests, Mottos, and Coronet Devices." *Gentleman's Magazine*, n.s. 12 (July 1819):30–32.
Notes Sidney's device of the Caspian sea with the motto "Sine reflexu."

886 ———. "Extracts from the Parish Registers of St. Olave, Hart-Street, London." Edited by H.H.G. *Collectanea Topographica et Genealogica* 2 (1835):311–17.
Records the baptism of Sidney's daughter Elizabeth on 20 November 1585.

887 ———. "Homes of English Worthies: Penshurst and Sir Philip Sidney." *London Journal* 27 (1858):333–34.
Describes Penshurst for a popular audience, covering the grounds, the house, main rooms, and important portraits. Includes a brief account of the Sidney family.

888 ———. "Junior Branches of the Sidney Family." *Gentleman's Magazine*, n.s. 25 (March 1832):213–16.
Reacting to Collins (12), corrects previous genealogies of the Sidney family, particularly in the collateral lines. Notes descendents in these lines in Thomas Lant's engravings of Sidney's funeral and provides documents on the life of Sidney's brother Thomas. See also J.H. (942).

889 ———. "Leicester in Holland, 1584–1586." *The Monthly Packet*, 3d ser. 2 (September 1881):224–31.
Narrates the events in the Low Countries precipitating Leicester's appointment as Governor General and describes the battle at Zutphen, with attention to the main details of Sidney's wounding and death.

890 ———. "Queen Elizabeth and Sir Philip Sidney." *N&Q* 10 (23 September 1854):241.
Reports the exhibit of a lock of Elizabeth's hair discovered in a copy of *Arcadia*, accompanied by a note "in an early hand," affirming that the

Queen presented the lock to Sidney with "her owne faire hands" and that he responded in 1573 by presenting her with verses "on his bended knee." Quotes six lines of verse in a hand said to be Sidney's own: "Her inward worth all outward worth transcends." See p. 347 in Ringler (92).

891 ———. Review of *A Memoir of Sir Philip Sidney*, by H.R. Fox Bourne. *British Quarterly Review* 37 (1 January 1863):53–83. Reprint. "Life and Times of Sir Philip Sidney." *Eclectic Magazine* 58 (March 1863):269–84. Reprint. "Sir Philip Sidney." *Living Age* 77 (2 May 1863):214–31.

Recounts Sidney's life, seeking to explain why his courtship of Lady Rich did not cause a scandal. Hypothesizes that Sidney had a prior contract with her, interpreting "Ring Out Your Bells" (*CS 30*) in this light. Argues that Bourne misdated Sidney's marriage (in item 318).

892 ———. Review of *Memoirs of the Life and Writings of Sir Philip Sidney*, by Thomas Zouch. *Quarterly Review* 1 (February 1809):77–92.

Sketches Sidney's life, refuting Zouch's view (974) that he met Torquato Tasso in 1574. Suggests that Queen Elizabeth's pet phrase "my Philip" was to distinguish him from her sister's Philip, that is, Philip of Spain. Also rebuts Walpole's attacks on Sidney (294).

893 ———. Review of *Sir Philip Sidney*, by J.A. Symonds. *Athenaeum*, no. 3089, 8 January 1887, pp. 55–56.

Points out important biographical sources not consulted by Symonds (961) or Bourne (318). Notes that Ben Jonson's poem "To Penshurst" is not reliable for data on the house in Sidney's boyhood, since it was rebuilt in 1579. Also touches on the publication history of Matthew Roydon's elegy on Sidney (2770) and the change in the sequence of poems in *Astrophil and Stella* from the editions of 1591 to that of 1598.

894 ———. "Shrewsbury School, Past and Present." *Blackwood's Edinburgh Magazine* 99 (April 1886):422–47.

Discusses Sidney's matriculation at Shrewsbury School, the other prominent figures who enrolled with him, and the circumstances of his father's famous letter to him there.

895 ———. "Sir Philip Sidney." *London Review and Weekly Journal of Politics, Literature, Art, and Society* 4 (19 April 1862):374–75.

Recounts Sidney's life, as set forth in Bourne (318).

896 ———. "Sir Philip Sidney." *University of Virginia Magazine* 4 (February 1860):239–41.

Celebrates Sidney's noble character.

Nineteenth Century

897 ———. "Sir Philip Sidney: Part I. The Prelude." *Oxford and Cambridge Magazine* 1 (January 1856):1–7.
Discusses Sidney's ancestry.

898 ———. "Sir Philip Sidney: Part II. The Learner." *Oxford and Cambridge Magazine* 1 (February 1856):129–36.
Sketches Sidney's youth through 1572, commenting on his intellectual and physical education.

899 ———. "Sir Philip Sidney's Widow and Daughter." *Hogg's Instructor*, n.s. 8 (1852):15–16.
Notes Lady Frances Sidney's subsequent marriages and her conversion to Catholicism. Also discusses the marriage of Sidney's daughter Elizabeth and Ben Jonson's "admiration" of her.

900 ———. "Spenser." *Blackwood's Edinburgh Magazine* 34 (November 1833):824–56.
Claims that Spenser "probably" spent some time at Penshurst "employed in some literary service" and that Sidney was "rather cold" to *The Shepherd's Calendar*. Notes that the intervention of Sidney and Leicester helped Spenser to attain a grant of 3025 acres in County Cork.

901 ———. "The Story of an Old English Mansion: Penshurst—the Home of the Sidneys." *London Society* 1 (1862):42–48.
Sketches Sidney's life and describes the family estate.

902 AUBREY, JOHN. *Lives of Eminent Men.* In *Letters Written by Eminent Persons in the Seventeenth and Eighteenth Centuries: To Which Are Added . . . Lives of Eminent Men by John Aubrey, Esq. The Whole Now First Printed from the Originals in the Bodleian Library and Ashmolean Museum, with Biographical and Literary Illustrations*, edited by [John Walker]. Vol. 2, Part 2. London: Longman, Hurst, Rees, Orme, & Brown; Oxford: Munday & Slatter, 1813, pp. 551–55. Reprint. In *Aubrey's Brief Lives*, edited by Oliver Lawson Dick. London: Secker & Warburg, 1950, pp. 138–40, 278–80.
In "Mary Herbert, Countess of Pembroke," notes that her library at Wilton contains a copy of the Sidney Psalms, "curiously bound in crimson velvet." Attributes the entire translation to Sidney. Noting that he was "much there" at his sister's estate, remarks that "I have heard old Gentlemen say that they lay together, and it was thought the first Philip Earle of Pembroke was begot by him." (Some editions suppress this sentence.) In "Sir Philip Sydney, Knight," calls him a "reviver of poetry in those darke times." Records several anecdotes, including the claims that

Sidney recorded "notions" for *Arcadia* while out hunting; that he ignored Spenser's presentation of *The Faerie Queene*, later read it "delightedly," sent a servant with an unspecified amount of gold, and "ordered an addition"; and that he had "carnall knowledge" with his wife following his wounding at Zutphen, about which was written "some roguish verses." Devotes a paragraph to describing Sidney's "contriving" of tournament *imprese*. Clark's edition adds a letter to Aubrey from D. Tyndale, which provides a "Key of Pembroke's Arcadia" identifying a number of characters. Philoclea, for example, is equated with Lady Rich and Miso with Lady Cox. See also Hudson (575), Fogel (2126).

903 ———. *The Natural History of Wiltshire*. Edited by John Britton. London: J.B. Nichols & Son, 1847, pp. 84, 85, 88, 108, 109.
In discussing the "pictures" at Wilton, notes a portrait of Sidney with verses attached and paintings of scenes from *Arcadia*. Describes several "shields of pasteboard," claiming that their "devices" were "most of them contrived" by Sidney. Claims that the surroundings at Wilton influenced *Arcadia*.

904 B., T. "Sir Philip Sidney." *N&Q*, 3d ser. 2 (13 December 1862):472.
Queries the whereabouts of the Veronese portrait of Sidney. See also item 946.

905 BELTZ, G.F. "Memorials of the Last Achievements, Illness, and Death of Sir Philip Sidney." *Archaeologia* 28 (1840):27–37.
Contends that the skirmish in which Sidney was wounded has been erroneously reported by Zouch (974) and Collins (12), giving in evidence a "hitherto unpublished Postscript" to a letter from Leicester to Burghley. Provides a transcript, with translation, of the letter from Gisbert Enerwitz to Jan Wyer (Johannnes Wierus) to which Sidney's last autograph note is appended, noting that the letter "does not furnish material addition" to the public record.

906 BOURNE, H[ENRY] R[ICHARD] FOX. "Sidney." *Athenaeum*, no. 3663, 8 January 1898, p. 51.
Commenting on the significance of Walsingham's 17 October 1572 letter to Leicester, claims that Walsingham's concern over the "evil practices" of Sidney's servants probably refers only to recklessness with money. Sidney also showed this fault and was impetuous during his European travels.

Nineteenth Century

907 ———. "Sir Philip Sidney." *Athenaeum*, no. 2547, 19 August 1876, pp. 244–45.
Replies to Gordon (931) on documents about Sidney's lands in Sussex. Cites letters of Henry Sidney and Walsingham in arguing that, although Sidney inherited substantial estates shortly before his death, these were encumbered with debts. Sidney died "embarrassed, though hardly poor." See also Gordon's reply (932).

908 BRYDGES, Sir [SAMUEL] EGERTON, ed. *Lord Brooke's Life of Sir Philip Sidney. With a Preface, &c.* 2 vols. Kent, England: Printed at the Private Press of Lee Priory by Johnson & Warwick, 1816.
Includes several genealogical charts, a preface that makes much of Sidney's paternal lineage, eight previously published poems or portions of poems related to Sidney and/or Penshurst (e.g., Jonson's "To Penshurst" and Waller's *Sacharissa*), an appendix containing several tributes to Sidney, and a concluding note that assesses existing memoirs. See also Greville (863).

909 CALVERT, E. *Shrewsbury School: Regestum Scholarium, 1562–1635.* Shrewsbury, England: Adnitt & Naunton, 1892, p. 15.
Lists Sidney and Greville among students entering Shrewbury in 1564.

910 COLBY, FRED. MYRON. "The Last of the Knights." *Potter's American Monthly* 11 (August 1878):113–21.
Reviews Sidney's life and ancestry.

911 COLIGNY, LOUISE DE. *Correspondance de Louise de Coligny Princesse d'Orange (1555–1620).* Edited by Paul Marchegay and Léon Marlet. Paris: Octave Doin & Alphonse Picard, 1887, pp. 25, 28, 31, 36–37.
Includes three letters by the Princess of Orange discussing Sidney's activities in the Netherlands in 1586 and one lamenting his death.

912 COLLIER, J[OHN] PAYNE, ed. *The Egerton Papers. A Collection of Private and Public Documents. Chiefly Illustrative of the Times of Elizabeth and James I.* Camden Society [Publications], 12. London: Camden Society, 1840, p. 92.
In "Sir P. Sidney and the Ordnance," prints Sir Francis Walsingham's letter to Lord Ellesmere of 14 February 1582/3, requesting that Sidney be made joint Master of Ordnance with his uncle, the Earl of Warwick. Suggests that Walsingham intervened because of Sidney's pending marriage with his daughter. Suggests also that Zouch (974) is wrong in

assuming that Sidney's 27 January 1582/83 letter to Cecil, which makes the same request, met with failure.

913 COLLIER, J[OHN] PAYNE. Letter. In *Sidneiana, Being a Collection of Fragments Relative to Sir Philip Sidney Knt. and His Immediate Connections*, edited by S[amuel Butler, Bishop of] Lichfield. London: Roxburghe Club, 1837, pp. 77–80.

Following a clue provided by Harington in the notes to Book XVI of his translation of *Orlando furioso* (2364), ascribes to Sir Walter Ralegh an unsigned epitaph for Sidney (2768) that was printed with Spenser's *Colin Clout's Come Home Again*. Also prints three poems for Sidney: the epitaph that was painted on a tablet and hung near his tomb in St. Paul's Cathedral; an epitaph beginning "Here vnder lies Philip Sydney Knight" (2776), which is here attributed to George Whetstone but is actually by his brother Bernard; and a previously unpublished elegy by Churchyard (2815). Takes the first two from van Meteren (872).

914 ———. "Sir Philip Sidney and American Discoveries." *Gentleman's Magazine*, n.s. 33 (February 1850):116–21.

Cites Sidney's agreement with Humphrey Gilbert (Close Roll 24th Elizabeth, Part 7), giving Sidney the right to colonize Gilbert's grant of land. Sidney sold these rights to George Peckham in 1583, possibly because of his marriage. Notes that Sidney's name is linked with Peckham's in a draft of a letter by Francis Walsingham.

915 ———. "Sir Philip Sidney, His Life and Death." *Gentleman's Magazine*, n.s. 33 (March 1850):264–69.

From Sidney's correspondence, seeks to ascertain the dates on which he began courting and eventually married Frances Walsingham. Transcribes new documents relating to Sidney's office as joint Master of Ordnance and discusses Sir Ralph Lane's suggestion that Sidney embark on an expedition against the Spanish in America. Also considers evidence on Sidney's wound at Zutphen, notably Burghley's letter to Walsingham of 2 November 1586. See also item 175.

916 COOKE [elsewhere COOK], ROBERT. *The Pedigree of Sir Philip Sidney*. Edited by Thomas William King. London: privately printed, 1869, 7 pp.

The document, said to be copied "from the original Roll, in the possession of Alexander Nesbitt, Esq., F.S.A., of Hatchford," records Sidney's ancestry in detail, with drawings of eleven coats of arms. Cooke was Clarenceux King of Arms under Elizabeth. For evidence of its fraudulence, see Kingsford (1083).

Nineteenth Century

917 COOPER, C.H. "Portraits of Sir Philip Sidney." *Gentleman's Magazine*, n.s. 42 (August 1854):152–53.

From the Sidney-Languet correspondence, infers the existence of two portraits of Sidney as of 1574: one in the possession of Languet's friend Antonio Abondio, and the other by Paolo Veronese. Rejects Zouch's view (974) that the portrait from which C. Warren's engraving of Sidney was taken is by Diego Velasquez de Silva. Also presents evidence that a picture at Woburn that had been regarded as Sidney's can hardly be by Antonio More, as some scholars suggest. See also item 918.

918 ———. "Portraits of Sir Philip Sidney." *N&Q*, 2d ser. 7 (26 March 1859):266.

Corrects an error in item 917 and replies to a query by J.K. (946).

919 CURTIS, GEORGE WILLIAM. *Literary and Social Essays*. New York and London: Harper & Brothers, 1894, pp. 149–80.

Gives a popularized account of Sidney's life and character.

920 [DAVIS, SARAH MATILDA HENRY]. *The Life and Times of Sir Philip Sidney*. 3d ed. Boston: Ticknor & Fields, 1859, 287 pp. Orig. pub. Boston: Ticknor & Fields, 1850 (not seen).

A popular, sometimes fictionalized, biography containing lengthy quotations from Sidney's correspondence with Languet and from *Arcadia* and the *Defence*. The following, from an account of the first meeting of Sidney and Henry of Navarre, is typical: "The Magnetism which attracts two kindred natures, revealing to each the mental harmony unobserved by others, drew silently its mysterious cords around the youthful Sidney and the gallant prince." See also 921.

921 ———. *The Life and Times of Sir Philip Sidney*. 4th ed. New York: Fords, Howard, & Hulbert, 1874, 286 pp.

Reprints item 920 with minor revisions, most notably the addition of an index.

922 DEE, JOHN. *The Private Diary of Dr. John Dee and the Catalogue of His Library of Manuscripts, from the Original Manuscripts in the Ashmolean Museum at Oxford, and Trinity College Library, Cambridge*. Edited by James Orchard Halliwell[-Phillipps]. Camden Society Publications, ser. 1, vol. 19. London: Camden Society, 1842, pp. 2, 20.

Mentions two occasions on which Sidney visited Dr. Dee.

923 de L'ISLE and DUDLEY, FRANCES. "Penshurst and Its Memories." *Pall Mall Magazine* 8 (February 1896):202–16.
Describes Penshurst and its grounds, tracing its history from its founding in 1341 until the death of Jocelin, the last of the Sidneys, in 1742. Mentions portraits of Philip still at Penshurst and outlines his life.

924 DIMOCK, JAMES F[RANCIS], ed. *Giraldi Cambrensis Opera.* Rerum Britannicarum Medii Aevi Scriptores, or Chronicles and Memorials of Great Britain and Ireland, 21. Vol. 6. London: Longmans, Green, Reader, & Dyer, 1868, p. liii.
Notes Powel's dedication of his edition of Giraldus's *Itinerary of Cambria* to Sidney and Powel's connection with Sidney's father, to whom he was chaplain.

925 DUDLEY, ROBERT, EARL OF LEICESTER. *Correspondence of Robert Dudley, Earl of Leycester, during his Government of the Low Countries, in the Years 1585 and 1586.* Edited by John Bruce. Camden Society [Publications], 27. London: Camden Society, 1844, pp. 8, 11, 33, 70, 116, 142, 168, 177, 192, 201, 275, 337, 355, 391, 414, 416, 422, 429, 438, 445, 451, 453, 456, 457, 481.
Includes references to such issues as Sidney's finances and the Queen's attitude toward him, both at the time of the Oxford quarrel and at his death.

926 DUGDALE, [Sir WILLIAM]. "Dugale's Mss. Additions to his Baronage." *Collectanea Topographica et Genealogica* 2 (1835): 179–224.
Includes notes on Sidney as a student at Christ Church, Oxford. Also remarks on his travels in the 1570s, his embassy to Emperor Rudolph, and his attempt to sail with Drake.

927 EDGAR, JOHN G. *The Heroes of England.* London: Bickers & Son, 1884, pp. 96–105.
Sketches Sidney's life and exemplary character.

928 FISHER, GEORGE WILLIAM. *Annals of Shrewsbury School.* Revised by J[ohn] Spencer Hill. London: Methuen & Co., 1899, pp. 8–11.
Notes the admission of Sidney and Fulke Greville to Shrewsbury on 17 October 1564. Considers the influence of Thomas Ashton and Sidney's father on his "high qualities of moral and principle."

Nineteenth Century

929 FROUDE, JAMES ANTHONY. *History of England from the Fall of Wolsey to the Defeat of the Spanish Armada.* Vol. 12. New York: Charles Scribner & Co., 1870, pp. 160, 211–13.

Discusses Sidney's position as Governor of Flushing and describes the battle at Zutphen and his death.

930 [GIFFORD, GEORGE?] "The Manner of Sir Philip Sidneyes Death." In *Memoirs of the Life and Writings of Sir Philip Sidney*, by Thomas Zouch. York: by Thomas Wilson & Son, for T. Payne & J. Mawman, and for Wilson & Son, 1808, pp. 267–75. Reprint. *The Manner of Sir Philip Sidneyes Death, Written by his Chaplain M.G. Gifford.* Oxford: New Bodleian Library, 1959, 20 pp. (unpaginated). Reprint. Edited by Duncan-Jones and van Dorsten (22), pp. 161–72.

An eyewitness account of Sidney's death printed here for the first time. Concentrates on Sidney's confrontation with "the guilt of sin, the present beholding of death [and] the terror of God's judgment." Comments on Sidney's acknowledgment that he had "walked in a vain course" during his life and his resolution to reform, should God grant him recovery from his wounds. Claims that, on the morning of his death, Sidney recalled a "vanity wherein I had taken delight, whereof I had not rid myself. It was my Lady Rich. But I rid myself of it, and presently my joy and comfort returned." Provides a detailed account of Sidney's last words and final acts, but makes no mention of the presence of Sidney's wife. Zouch's version is a partly paraphrased, partly reconstructed version of British Museum MS. Cotton Vitellius C.17, fols. 382–87, which is fire-damaged. The 1959 printing is from the Ickwell Bury MS. in the possession of Bent Juel-Jensen, which Duncan-Jones and van Dorsten take as a copy text but correct from the British Museum Manuscript. The Ickwell Bury MS. attributes the work to Fulke Greville, an error perpetuated by Grosart (941).

931 GORDON, H[ENRY] D[ODDRIDGE]. "Sir Philip Sidney." *Athenaeum*, no. 2543, 22 July 1876, pp. 113–14.

On the basis of documents relating to Sidney's lands in Sussex, takes exception to Bourne's assertion (318) that Sidney died "poor and embarrassed." See also Bourne's reply (907) and Gordon's rejoinder (932).

932 ———. "Sir Philip Sidney's Lands in Sussex." *Athenaeum*, no. 2554, 7 October 1876, pp. 464–65.

Replies to Bourne (907) by arguing that Sidney's Sussex estates were much more valuable than the Inquisition Rolls reveal.

Nineteenth Century

933 GOSSE, EDMUND. "Sir Philip Sidney." *Contemporary Review* 50 (November 1886):632–46.
Seeks to strip Sidney's reputation of myths, such as the "Byzantine" falsifications in Spenser's *Astrophel* and Shelley's phrase "sublimely mild, a spirit without spot." Concentrates on Sidney's career as a diplomat, his love of Lady Rich, his relationships with male friends, and his "foolhardy" conduct at Zutphen. Also discusses the Areopagus and its role in introducing new poetic styles.

934 GREAT BRITAIN. HISTORICAL MANUSCRIPTS COMMISSION. *Calendar of the Manuscripts of the Most Hon. the Marquis of Salisbury, K.G., Preserved at Hatfield House, Hertfordshire.* 11 parts. London: Her Majesty's Stationery Office, 1889–1906, 1:146, 415; 2:186, 432, 531; 3:70, 77, 99, 107, 110, 114, 116, 126, 128, 130, 137, 138, 141, 147, 185, 189, 190, 302; 5:409, 410.
Notes letters from Sidney, including two to Cecil, one to the Queen written in 1585, one to Patrick, Master of Gray, and one letter to Sidney from Lady Katherine Paget. Other letters and documents name or refer to him in various social or diplomatic capacities. Includes a 1569 list of "settlements" for Sidney's proposed marriage to Anne Cecil.

935 GREAT BRITAIN. PUBLIC RECORD OFFICE. *Calendar of Letters and State Papers Relating to English Affairs, Preserved Principally in the Archives of Simancas.* Vol. 3, *Elizabeth. 1580–1586,* edited by Martin A[ndrew] S[harp] Hume. London, Her Majesty's Stationery Office, 1896, pp. 172, 178, 384, 547–50, 582, 585, 650.
Prints documents related to Sidney's role in Queen Elizabeth's dealings with Don Antonio, the Portuguese Pretender, and also to Sidney's attempt to sail with Drake. Contains allusions to his activities in the Netherlands and his death.

936 ———. *Calendar of State Papers and Manuscripts, Relating to English Affairs, Existing in the Archives and Collections of Venice, and in Other Libraries of Northern Italy.* Edited by Horatio F. Brown. Vol. 8, *1581–1591.* London: Longman, Green, Longman, Roberts, & Green, 1894, p. 126.
An entry for 6 December 1585 indicates that Leicester had sent Sidney to Flushing "where are Three Thousand English infantry."

Nineteenth Century

937 ———. *Calendar of State Papers, Colonial Series, Preserved in the Public Record Office*. Vol. 1, edited by W. Noel Sainsbury. London: Longman, Green, Longman, & Roberts, 1860, p. 3.
Contains a 1585 letter to Sidney from Ralph Lane, in Virginia, recommending that Sidney "attempt" an expedition against some islands in the West Indies.

938 ———. *Calendar of State Papers, Domestic Series, of the Reign of Elizabeth, 1581-1590, Preserved in Her Majesty's Public Record Office*. Vol. 2, edited by Robert Lemon. London: Her Majesty's Stationery Office, 1865, pp. 23, 33, 38, 40, 98–99, 147, 164, 240, 241, 263, 362, 365, 366, 369.
Provides very brief summaries of letters and other public documents discussing the Earl of Oxford's plot to murder Sidney, Sidney's proposed marriage to Frances Walsingham, his wounding and death, the settlement of his estate, and "information by one Ponsonby . . . that some person was in hands to print Sir Philip Sidney's 'Old Arcadia'" [sic]. See index for other letters and documents that merely refer to Sidney in various legal, personal, and financial capacities or are signed by him.

939 ———. *Calendar of State Papers, Domestic Series, of the Reigns of Edward VI., Mary, Elizabeth, 1547–1580, Preserved in the State Paper Department of Her Majesty's Public Record Office*. Vol. 1, edited by Robert Lemon. London: Longman, Brown, Green, Longmans, & Roberts, 1856, pp. 331, 648, 651, 678.
Contains brief summaries of letters from Sidney (one to Burghley reporting progress on his studies at Oxford) and of a letter referring to him.

940 ———. *Calendar of State Papers, Foreign Series, of the Reign of Elizabeth, 1575–77. Preserved in the State Paper Department of Her Majesty's Public Record Office*. Vol. 11, edited by Allan James Crosby. London: Her Majesty's Stationery Office, 1880, pp. 15–17, 94, 535, 541, 543, 551, 565, 573, 575, 580, 581, 587, 598, 599–600, 603.
Contains summaries of letters from Sidney to Burghley and from Casimir to Sidney and "Instructions for Thomas Wilkes sent to the Count Palatine." Other letters refer to Sidney's movements, audiences, and contacts on the Continent in 1577, including one from Elizabeth expressing to Casimer her "great contentment . . . by the good entertainment accorded him."

941 GROSART, ALEXANDER B., ed. Prefatory note and introduction to *The Works in Verse and Prose Complete of the Right Honourable*

Fulke Greville, Lord Brooke. 4 vols. N.p., 1870, 1:xi–xii, xxiii–xxvii, xxxii, xlix.

Discusses corrections to Greville's *Life of Sidney* made possible by the collation of a manuscript with the 1652 edition. Also touches on major events in Greville's friendship with Sidney and the purpose of the *Life*. On Grosart's misattribution of *The Manner of Sir Philip Sidney's Death* to Greville, see Gifford (930).

942 H., J. "The Sidney Family." *Gentleman's Magazine* 102 (May 1832):400.

Responds to item 888, correcting information about Thomas Sidney's wife.

943 HERMIT OF HOLYPORT [pseud.]. "Dousa's Poem on Sidney." *N&Q* 3 (11 January 1851):22–23.

Inquires about the ode to Sidney by Janus Dousa, describing the volume in which it first appeared (Leiden, 1586). See Dousa the Elder (2755) and Dousa the Younger (2756).

944 HUME, MARTIN [ANDREW SHARP]. *The Courtships of Queen Elizabeth: A History of the Various Negotiations for Her Marriage*. Rev. ed. New York: Brentano's, n.d., pp. 218–19. Orig. pub. London: T.F. Unwin, 1896 (not seen).

Claims that the "disinterested patriotism" that inspired Sidney's *Letter to the Queen* opposing the French marriage "secured" him against the anger that Elizabeth poured on other Protestant objectors.

945 J., W. "Sir Philip Sidney." *N&Q*, 4th ser. 5 (21 May 1870):491.

Requests words and tune to Sidney's "La cuisse rompue," reported by Leicester to be Sidney's "death song." The editors respond that, according to Bourne (318) and Lloyd (949), no copy remains.

946 K., J. "Portraits of Sir Philip Sidney." *N&Q*, 2d ser. 7 (12 March 1859):213.

Comments on an engraving prefixed to Zouch (974) that is supposed to be of a portrait of Sidney by Diego Velasquez de Silva. Remarks that this is impossible, since Velasquez was not born until 1599. By way of inquiring whom the portrait might represent, cites several other portraits, known or alluded to in print, by Veronese and Isaac Oliver. Inquires about a second portrait by Oliver prefixed to Collins (12). See replies by E.H.A. (883) and Cooper (918).

Nineteenth Century

947 KING, ALICE. "Sir Philip Sidney." *Argosy* 21 (May 1876):370–77.
Sketches Sidney's life, with passing reference to his works.

948 KINGSLEY, HENRY. "Sir Philip Sidney." *New Quarterly Magazine*
3 (October 1874–January 1875):416–42. Reprinted in item 1370.
Describes Penshurst, recounting the ancestry of the Sidneys. Considers
Sidney's early marriage prospects with Anne Cecil and regards his rela-
tionship with Lady Rich as the "only dark spot" in his life. Faults the
Queen for her ungrateful and callous treatment of the Sidneys.

949 LLOYD, JULIUS. *The Life of Sir Philip Sidney*. London: Longman,
Green, Longman, Roberts, & Green, 1862, 260 pp.
Aims to supply a "fuller account" of Sidney's life than the numerous
"short memoirs" that were then available. Organizes the material into
chapters corresponding to the major phases of Sidney's life: family and
childhood, foreign travel, service at court and retirement, return to public life, war in the Netherlands, and death, with a central chapter devoted
to the *Defence*, the Psalms, and *Arcadia*. Says of the last that it "reflects
[Sidney's] own mind so vividly, that the examination of its chief characteristics is essential to a compete view of his life." In the preface, notes the
appearance of Bourne's *Memoir* (318) "during the progress of this volume
through the press," and offers several corrections of Bourne based on an
independent examination of manuscript correspondence and documents
in the State Paper Office: Sidney went to Oxford at age 15, his mission to
Paris in 1584 was "revoked," Penelope Rich was married on 10 March.
Accuses Bourne of using Greville's account of Sidney's death "capricious-
ly." Rejects biographical interpretations of *Astrophil and Stella*, remarking
that his own conclusions about the poems "are submitted with diffidence
and . . . sustained by direct proofs." Concludes by reviewing elegies written in Sidney's memory and assessing his character, which was "distinguished by large and refined sympathy" and "near to the ideal of an
Englishman"). In an appendix, prints Pamela's prayer from Book III of
Arcadia and Bernard Whetstone's "Commemoration" (2776). Attempts
throughout a style that "imitates" that of Sidney's period.

950 LODGE, EDMUND. *Portraits of Illustrious Personnages of Great
Britain. Engraved from Authentic Pictures in the Galleries of the Nobility
and the Public Collections of the Country. With Biographical and
Historical Memoirs of their Lives and Actions*. Vol. 3. London: Printed
for Harding, Triphook & Lepard, 1825, item 9. Reprint. In
Museum of Foreign Literature 21 (1837):273–78.
Reproduces the portrait of Sidney ascribed to Antonio More, accompa-
nied by a brief biography that illustrates the variety and power of his

mind and stresses the "playfulness of wit" and the "speculative and practical wisdom" of his writings.

951 MOTLEY, JOHN LOTHROP. *History of the United Netherlands from the Death of William the Silent to the Twelve Years' Truce—1609.* 4 vols. New York: Harper & Brothers, 1880, 1:279, 342, 343, 357, 358–64, 423, 446; 2: 34–40, 50–57. Orig. pub. New York: Harper & Brothers, 1860–67 (not seen).

Rehearses the "well-known" incidents of Sidney's life before he assumed the governorship of Flushing. Remarks on his displeasure at the mismanagement of the campaign in the Netherlands, describing "the awful drunken row" among the English troops and Sidney's exemplary behavior under conditions that embittered most of the English commanders. Reviews the conquest of Axel and the skirmish at Zutphen, basing the account of Sidney's wounding and death on Greville (863).

952 NICHOLSON, B[RINSLEY]. "'A Pastorall Aeglogue upon the Death of Sir Philip Sidney': Its Author." *N&Q*, 5th ser. 6 (14 October 1876):301–2.

Argues that this 1597 poem by "L.B." (2749) cannot be by Lord Brooke, since Greville attained that rank only in 1620, but is rather by Lodowick Bryskett. Cites several references in the correspondence to show that Bryskett accompanied Sidney in Italy in 1572–74.

953 NICOLAS, [Sir] NICHOLAS HARRIS, ed. *The Poetical Rhapsody: To Which Are Added, Several Other Pieces,* by Francis Davison. Vol. 1. London: William Pickering, 1826, pp. lxiii–lxv and table following.

Prints a chronology of Sidney's life and a genealogy showing his blood relation to the Davisons and others associated with *A Poetical Rhapsody.*

954 PEARS, STEUART A. "Portrait of Sir Philip Sidney by Paul Veronese." *N&Q* 2 (5 October 1850):296.

Inquires about the location of the portrait by Veronese, noting that Languet had it in Prague in 1575 and that it passed to du Plessis-Mornay.

955 PETLEY, J[AMES] L[EDGER] W[ARD]. *Penshurst, the House of the Sidneys.* Tunbridge Wells, England: Goulden & Nye, 1890, 101 pp.

Includes material on Penshurst, Sidney, and his family, with notes containing extracts from contemporary documents. In a chapter devoted specifically to Sidney, sketches his life and character, noting that he avoided "contamination" by the "depraved" continent and discussing his

Nineteenth Century

opposition to the French marriage. Praises the intellectual content of his works.

956 [PROCTER, BRYAN WALLER.] *Effigies Poeticae: or, The Portraits of the British Poets, Illustrated by Notes Biographical, Critical, and Poetical.* Vol. 1. London: James Carpenter & Son, 1824, pp. 27–28 and preceding plate.

Eulogizes Sidney, printing an engraving of him by C. Warren from an original in the collection of Charles Cholmondeley Dering.

957 RICHARDSON, [JERUSHA DAVIDSON HUNTING]. *Famous Ladies of the English Court.* London: Hutchinson; Chicago: Stone & Co., 1899, pp. 35–117.

Considers Sidney in consecutive chapters on his mother, on his sister, and on Penelope Rich.

958 SERRELL, GEORGE. "Sir Philip Sidney and His Friend Languet." *Temple Bar* 110 (January 1897):47–65. Reprint. In *Eclectic Magazine*, n.s. 65 (February 1897):248–59.

From the correspondence with Languet, reconstructs the portrait of Sidney as a man of charm, amiability, modesty, and civic responsibility. Stresses his commitment to the Protestant cause and Languet's growing "uneasiness" that Sidney's love of retirement would impede his public mission.

959 SIMPSON, RICHARD. *Edmund Campion, a Biography.* The Catholic Standard Library. London: John Hodges, 1896, pp. 41, 54, 114–17, 123.

Discusses Campion's account, in his letter to John Bovand, of his 1577 meeting with Sidney in Prague, which suggested to Campion that Sidney was ready to convert to Roman Catholicism. Also notes Sir Henry Sidney's protection of Campion in Ireland.

960 STODDART, ANNA M. *Sir Philip Sidney, Servant of God.* Edinburgh and London: William Blackwood & Sons, 1894, 119 pp.

Drawing on Bourne (318) and Symonds (961), supplies a life of Sidney "rather for the general reader than for the student." Begins with an extended description of Penshurst, providing a briefer account of Sidney's childhood ("we can find him pushing through the thickets to gather primroses and ladysmocks"). Describes his schooling at Shrewsbury and Oxford and his travels on the Continent, stressing his social life and studies there. Spends several pages on his entry into court life in 1576–77 and its cost. Describes his return to the "half-attractive and half-wearisome routine of court appearance" following his 1577 embassy to Germany, tracing the events that led to the tennis-court quarrel with the Earl of Oxford and the *Letter to the Queen*. In recounting his retirement from court, concentrates on imagined details of life at Wilton, with only brief notice of his literary activity. Accepts *Astrophil and Stella* as autobiographical. Treats Sidney's governorship of Flushing and his death at Zutphen as exemplifying a religious and chivalric ideal.

961 SYMONDS, J[OHN] A[DDINGTON]. *Sir Philip Sidney*. English Men of Letters. London: Macmillan & Co., 1886; New York: Harper & Brothers, 1887, 213 pp.

Traces Sidney's ancestry, his schooling, his aborted match with Anne Cecil, and his Continental travels, with attention to his meeting with Languet and his sojourn in Italy. Comments on his friendship with the first Earl of Essex and on the failure of his match with Penelope Rich. Also discusses the context of the *Letter to the Queen*. Argues that the Sidney Psalter was begun in the spring of 1580, the same year as *Arcadia*. Presents a critical commentary on the latter, with a plot summary and analysis of the verse. Dates Penelope's marriage to Lord Rich in the spring or summer of 1581. Quotes from and comments on Sidney's letters to his brother and on Sir Henry Sidney's letter to Walshingham of March 1583. Views *Astrophil and Stella* as autobiographical, seeing Stella's rejection of Astrophil as a married woman's virtuous rejection of an ardent suitor. Argues that Newman's edition (60) presents the poems in the proper order, the songs bearing on the surrounding sonnets. Dates the sequence after 1581, arguing that its emotions are "poetically exaggerated." Comments on the Italian and French influences on the sonnet types used. Rejects the argument that "Thou blind man's mark" (*CS 31*) and "Leave me, O love" (*CS 32*) are part of the sequence. Dates the *Defence* in 1581 and provides a critical commentary. Also remarks on Sidney's role as a patron. See also item 893 and replies by Vyvyan (966) and Radford (2045).

962 THOMSON, [KATHERINE BYERLEY]. "Sir Philip Sidney and Sir Fulke Greville." In *Celebrated Friendships*. Vol. 2. London: James Hogg, 1861, pp. 1–50.

A popular biographical sketch, derived largely from Zouch (974) and Collins (12), which gives primary attention to Sidney, but shifts "meantime" to Greville, stressing throughout their proficiency at martial sports and their public responsibilities. Touches on the main events in Sidney's life, with liberal quotations from letters, devoting the greatest detail to his wounding and death.

Nineteenth Century

963 TODD, HENRY JOHN. "Some Account of the Life of Spenser."
In *The Works of Edmund Spenser*, edited by Henry John Todd.
London: Edward Moxon, 1845, pp. ix–lx.
Considers relations between Spenser and Sidney, claiming that Spenser
was "employed in some literary service at Penshurst" and that the dedi-
cation of the *Shepherd's Calendar* to Sidney is a "proof of gratitude."
Points out that *The Ruins of Time* deeply laments Sidney's death, that
Sidney is alluded to in *Mother Hubbard's Tale*, and that *Astrophel* makes
"an elegant use" of Sidney's love for Stella.

964 TURNER, SHARON. *The History of the Reigns of Edward the Sixth,
Mary, and Elizabeth*. Vols. 3 and 4 of *The Modern History of England.
Part the Second: Reigns of Edward VI, Mary, and Elizabeth*. London:
Longman, Rees, Orme, Brown, & Green, 1835, 4:414–15,
420–30.
Quotes Sidney's views of his uncle Leicester, recounts Sidney's death,
and prints extracts from the funeral elegies.

965 TYTLER, PATRICK FRASER. *Life of Sir Walter Raleigh: Founded
on Authentic and Original Documents, Some of Them Never before
Published*. 4th ed. Edinburgh: Oliver & Boyd and Simpkin,
Marshall, & Co., 1844, pp. 36–37, 107–11. Orig. pub. 1833 (not
seen).
Provides a characterization of Sidney drawn partly from Naunton (869),
claiming that his abilities as a writer "cannot be ranked so high" as those
"in war and wisdom." Argues that Sidney, as a member of the
Areopagus, "employed every effort" to dissuade Spenser from writing
rhyme.

966 VYVYAN, EDWARD R. "Sir Philip Sidney." *N&Q*, 7th ser. 3 (15
January 1887):46.
Notes that Symonds (961) incorrectly dates Sidney's admission to
Shrewsbury School and that Sidney went to Christ Church, Oxford, in
1568.

967 WADDINGTON, ALBERTUS. *De Huberti Langueti Vita (1518–81)*.
Paris: apud Ernestum Leroux, 1888, pp. 116–20. Orig. a Ph.D.
diss., University of Paris.
Discusses Sidney's friendship with Languet.

968 WALSINGHAM, Sir FRANCIS. *Journal of Sir Francis Walsingham
from Dec. 1570 to April 1583*. Edited by Charles Trice Martin. The

Camden Miscellaney 6, no. 3. Westminster: The Camden Society, 1870, pp. 30, 31.
In entries for February 1576 and June 1577, notes that Sidney was "dispatched to Themperor" and "came to the Courte."

969 WHIPPLE, E[DWIN] P. "Sidney and Raleigh." *Atlantic Monthly* 22 (September 1868):304–13. Reprint. In *The Literature of the Age of Elizabeth*. Boston: Fields, Osgood, & Co., 1869, pp. 250–57.
Surveys the lives of Sidney and Ralegh.

970 WORDSWORTH, WILLIAM. "The Country Church-yard, and Critical Examination of Ancient Epitaphs." In *The Prose Works of William Wordsworth*, edited by Alexander B. Grosart. Vol. 2, *Aesthetical and Literary*. London: Edward Moxon, Son, & Co., 1876, pp. 41–59. Reprint. "[Essay upon Epitaphs, II]." In *Prose Works of William Wordsworth*, edited by W[arwick] J[ack] B[urgoyne] Owen and Jane Worthington Smyser. Vol. 2. Oxford: Clarendon Press, 1974, pp. 63–79.
Compares Sidney with Charles I, suggesting that his early death led many to question "the dispensations of Providence." Condemns the eight-line anonymous epitaph (2782) originally placed over Sidney's tomb in St. Paul's as a "laboured" adaptation of a French epitaph.

971 WOTTON, MABEL E., ed. *Word Portraits of Famous Writers*. London: Richard Bentley & Son, 1887, pp. 284–86.
In "Sir Philip Sidney, 1554–1587–8 [sic]," collects from several early sources comments on Sidney's appearance.

972 WRIGHT, GEORGE R[OBERT]. "On Sir Philip Sidney and His Father, Sir Henry Sidney, in Connexion with Ludlow Castle." *Journal of the British Archaeological Association* 24 (December 1868):313–27. Reprint. In *Archaeological and Historical Fragments*. London: Whiting & Co., 1887.
Begs leave to "draw a little upon imagination" in fixing Sidney's connections to Ludlow.

973 Z. "Penshurst Castle, and Sir Philip Sidney." *New Monthly Magazine* 8 (December 1823):546–52.
Gives a descriptive tour of the castle and its environs and sketches Sidney's life.

Nineteenth Century

974 ZOUCH, THOMAS. *Memoirs of the Life and Writings of Sir Philip Sidney*. York: by Thomas Wilson & Son, for T. Payne & J. Mawman, and for Wilson & Son, 1808, 389 pp.

Against Walpole's "severe animadversions" (294), sets out to elevate Sidney as a man and a writer, making extensive use of his correspondence and Greville's *Life*. Traces Sidney's ancestry back to Sir William de Sidenie in the time of Henry II, noting that Sidney's paternal grandfather, Sir William Sidney, fought at Flodden. Comments extensively on his parents, quoting their letter to him at Shrewsbury in 1566. Notes the influence of Shrewsbury School and of Thomas Thornton and Robert Dorset on Sidney's early education. Enumerates the places, people, and dates of Sidney's European tour, presenting a graphic account of the St. Bartholomew's Day massacre and placing special emphasis on his associations with Andreas Wechel and Hubert Languet. Speculates that Sidney may have met Tasso while in Padua and Paulo Sarpi, the historian of the Council of Trent, while in Venice. Emphasizes the importance of the dream of a Protestant League in the visit to Germany in 1577, commenting on the efforts of William of Orange in its behalf. Quotes Walsingham's 10 June 1577 letter to Henry Sidney as proof of his son's success as an ambassador. Describes Sidney's defence of his father's Irish policies and quotes at length from the *Letter to the Queen*, claiming, however, that Sidney's quarrel with Oxford occasioned his retirement from the court. Arguing that Heliodorus as well as Sannazaro influenced the composition of *Arcadia*, classifies it as a romance and praises its moral tone, its attempts at classical meters, its classical learning, its characterization, and its enrichment of the language through the use of compound epithets. Defends Charles I's use of Pamela's prayer. From Nichols (155), quotes in full the description of *Four Foster Children of Desire*. Characterizes the *Defence* by quoting extensively from it. Argues that Sir Henry Sidney requested in 1582 that Sidney accompany him to Ireland. Discusses the proposed marriage to Penelope Devereux and the actual marriage to Frances Walsingham; Sidney's appointment to console the King of France on the death of the Duke of Anjou (adding that Sidney does not appear to have carried out the embassy); the murder of Leicester's first wife (arguing that the *Defence of Leicester* ought not to have been written); and Sidney's interest in Drake's voyages. Quotes remarks by Naunton (869) and Fuller (862) regarding the myth that Sidney was nominated for the crown of Poland. Notes two letters from du Plessis-Mornay (July 1583 and July 1585) urging Sidney to support the cause of the Protestant League, and provides much detail (some of it anecdotal) about Sidney's campaign in the Netherlands, including notes on his appointment as Governor of Flushing on 7 November 1585 and his appointment of William Temple as his secretary. Provides information on the battle at Graveling and on the skirmish at Zutphen. Claims that Sidney composed an ode, now lost, on the nature of his wound, and that Sidney's wife was present when he died. In a lengthy account of Sidney's death and burial, draws on Greville (863), Gifford (930, here printed for the first time), Thomas Buckhurst's letter to Robert Dudley, and Thomas Lant's depiction of the funeral procession (849). Concludes with comments on Sidney by contemporaries and later writers and with discussions of his patronage of Spenser, of his association with Bruno, and of his wife and daughter. Includes a bibliography of works attributed to Sidney. See also item 892 and replies by Beltz (905), Collier (912), and Cooper (917).

Twentieth Century

975 ADDEY, JOHN M. *"Mica Mica Parva Stella."* *TLS*, 15 January 1951, p. 69.
Takes issue with Osborn's remarks (1104) on Sidney's horoscope, arguing that it is accurate for the time stated.

976 ALSOP, J.D. "Notes on the Career of Sir Philip Sidney." *N&Q*, n.s. 29 (October 1982):405–6.
Provides four pieces of biographical information relating to Sidney's activities and finances in 1576 and 1577: a bequest by his grandmother, a reference by Griffin Madix to his 1576 Irish visit, a notice of tax assessment, and a notice of attendance before the Council.

977 ANDREWS, MICHAEL CAMERON. "Constable's 'To Sir Philip Sydneyes Soule.'" *Expl* 36 (Spring 1978):34–35.
Interprets the second stanza of the elegy to mean, not that Constable was abroad when news of Sidney's death reached England, but that he was too stunned to take it in.

978 ANGLO, SYDNEY. "Archives of the English Tournament: Score Cheques and Lists." *Journal of the Society of Archivists* 2 (1960–1964):153–62.
Notes two collections in the College of Arms that mention Sidney in connection with at least five tilts between 1574 and 1584.

979 ANON. "An Earthly Paragon." *The Nation* 102 (6 April 1916):388–89.
In reviewing Wallace (1171), suggests faults in Sidney, including "mad extravagance," and intellectual liabilities, such as remaining untouched by philosophical and scientific "stirrings" of the day. Notes with

Twentieth Century

approval several "additions" to the biographical record, especially the identification of Hugh Sanford as author of the prefatory address to the 1593 *Arcadia* and recognition of the major sources of *Arcadia*.

980 ———. "Sidney and Bruno." *TLS*, 16 October 1937, p. 759.
Responds to Henderson (1054), claiming that the only direct evidence concerning Bruno's relations with Sidney are the dedications in two of Bruno's books, neither of which implies "intimacy." See Bruno (842).

981 BAKHUIZEN van den BRINK, J.N. "Het Convent te Frankfort 27–28 September 1577 en de harmonia confessionum." *Nederlandsch Archief voor Kerkgeschiedenis* 32 (1941):235–80.
Discusses Sidney's Continental tour and his embassy to Germany in the 1570s, particularly his Protestant contacts and the mysterious proposal made to him by John Casimir while he was in Frankfurt am Main in September 1577.

982 BAUGHAN, DENVER EWING. "The Question of Sidney's Love for his Wife." *N&Q* 177 (25 November 1939):383–85.
Feels that documentary evidence of the time indicates, contrary to several recent arguments, that the marriage was "plausibly" a loveless one. See also item 983 and Wallace (1171), Purcell (2232), and Friedrich (2128).

983 ———. "Sir Philip Sidney and the Matchmakers." *MLR* 33 (October 1938):506–19.
To settle the dispute over whether *Astrophil and Stella* "literally" records a love affair between Sidney and the woman presumed to be Stella (whether Penelope Devereux or Frances Walsingham), surveys all of the contemporary evidence relating to the four "matches" proposed for Sidney: Anne Cecil, Penelope Devereux, the sister of William of Orange, and Frances Walsingham. Omits consideration of the daughter of Lord Berkeley and Ursula, sister of Prince Casimir, as "lacking corroborative evidence." In none of the four cases is there any evidence of a "love match," and in all, "interests of many relatives and friends," especially Leicester and Languet, were paramount. "On the question of love, the records reveal that [Sidney's] ambitions did not that way tend."

984 BENHAM, W. GURNEY. "Mourners at Sir Philip Sidney's Funeral." *N&Q* 180 (21 June 1941):444–45.
In reply to Newdigate (1100), provides details on Sir Edward Jobsone, one of the mourners mentioned in Lant's engraving of Sidney's funeral procession (849).

985 BEVAN, BRYAN. "Sir Philip Sidney." *Contemporary Review* 186 (1954):346–49.
Sketches Sidney's life and character.

986 BIENFAIT, ANNA. "Penshurst, Geboorteplaats van Philip Sidney." *Eigen Haard*, no. 28, 9 July 1910, pp. 436–41.
Sketches the main events of Sidney's life as part of a tour-guide description and history of Penhurst.

987 BILL, ALFRED H[OYT]. *Astrophel, or the Life and Death of the Renowned Sir Philip Sidney*. New York and Toronto: Farrar & Rinehart, 1937; London: Cassell & Co., 1938, 372 pp.
Provides a biography of Sidney for the general reader, stressing his friendship with Languet, his learning, and his high moral character. In Chapter 1, looks back on Sidney's life from the point of view of Philip II of Spain. In Chapters 2 and 3, surveys the Sidney and Dudley family backgrounds, and in 4 and 5, examines his education at Shrewsbury and Oxford. In Chapter 6, concentrates on the 1573 events in Paris and the acquaintances made there, and in Chapters 7 and 8, recounts the remainder of his European travels and the period from his embassy to Germany in 1577 to the tennis-court quarrel with the Earl of Oxford in 1579. In Chapter 9, examines circumstances surrounding the *Letter to the Queen* and briefly characterizes the *Defence* and the Old *Arcadia*. In Chapter 10, identifies Stella with Penelope Devereux and supports the view that Sidney's love for her was quite real. Also emphasizes Sidney's role as a courtier. In Chapters 11 and 12, attends to his political and scholarly activities in the roughly two years between his marriage to Frances Walsingham and his leaving to become Governor of Flushing, and in the final three chapters, provides a detailed account of his activities in the Low Countries. In the section on his his death and funeral, treats Greville's account of his last words as literally true.

988 BLOK, P[ETRUS] J[OHANES], ed. "Correspondance inédite de Robert Dudley, comte de Leycester, et de François et Jean Hotman." In *Archives du musée Teyler*. Ser. 2, vol. 12, part 2. Haarlem, Netherlands: Héritiers Loosjes; Paris: Gauthier-Villars; Leipzig: G.E. Schulze, 1911, p. 152.
Includes three letters to Leicester relevant to Sidney: one from Henry III of France (dated July 1586) concerning a merchant of Calais accused of plundering; one from Patrick, Master of Gray, naming Sidney as "procurator" for three Scottish gentlemen on diplomatic business; and one from Louise de Coligny offering condolences after Sidney's death.

Twentieth Century

989 BOAS, FREDERICK S[AMUEL]. *Christopher Marlowe: A Biographical and Critical Study.* Oxford: Clarendon Press, 1940, p. 122.

Notes that, although Robert Poley, who played a key role in Marlowe's downfall, was employed by Sidney, the latter "can have had little personal intercourse with him" because of Sidney's departure for Flushing in 1585.

990 ———. *Sir Philip Sidney, Representative Elizabethan: His Life and Writings.* London: Staples Press, 1955, pp. 9–37, 161–200, and passim.

In Chapters 1–6, reviews Sidney's life through his withdrawal from court in 1580, and in Chapters 24–29, covers his remaining years. Considers the "enigmatic or paradoxical elements" in his character: his failure to give credit to his headmaster at Shrewsbury, Thomas Ashton; his scant notice of English plays and poems; his near silence about his time at Oxford; his impulsiveness, especially in threatening Edmund Molyneux; his tendency to leave literary projects incomplete; his financial inprovidence; and his general silence about his wife. Against these oddities sets Sidney's personal magnetism and accomplishments. See also item 436.

991 BOND, WILLIAM H[ENRY]. "The Epitaph of Sir Philip Sidney." *MLN* 58 (April 1943):253–57.

Cites evidence that Sidney's epitaph (2782), which was inscribed on a wooden tablet and fixed on a pillar near his grave in St. Paul's Cathedral, was "one of the sights of the town for at least a generation following his death." Notes the "ironic paradox" that it was not original, but a "clever adaptation" of du Bellay's epitaph for Guillaume Gouffier, Seigneur de Bonnivet.

992 ———. "A Letter of Languet about Sidney." *HLB* 9 (Winter 1955):105–9.

Prints for the first time, with translation, a letter from Languet to Johannes Glauburg dated from Prague on 8 March 1575, which served as an introduction for Sidney in his Continental travels. Discusses Sidney's relations with Languet and with the persons and diplomatic affairs mentioned in the letter.

993 ———. "Two Ghosts: Herbert's *Baripenthes* and the Vaughan-Holland Portrait of Sidney." *Library*, 4th ser. 24 (March 1944):175–81.

"Lays to rest" the two ghosts named, first by demonstrating that the number of references to Sir William Herbert's memorial poem, both contemporary and later, show "definitely" that it existed; and second by showing that an engraved portrait in the 1621 Dublin edition of *Arcadia* "preserves proof" that it was originally prepared for Henry Holland's *Nine Modern Worthies of the World*, which appeared in 1622.

994 BUCK, P[HILO] M., Jr. "Notes on the *Shepherd's Calendar*, and Other Matters Concerning the Life of Edmund Spenser." *MLN* 21 (March 1906):80–84.

By interpreting several details of the poem as "covert" or "clear" allusions to Sidney, comes to the conclusion that Spenser knew Sidney much earlier than 1576 and that most of *The Shepherd's Calendar* was composed in Kent, "probably at Penshurst." See a reply by Higginson (1056).

995 BULLEN, A[RTHUR] H[ENRY]. *Elizabethans*. London: Chapman & Hall, 1924, pp. 28–29, 195–96, 198, 201.

Weighs the possibility that Sidney had met Samuel Daniel. Also discusses the way in which friendship with Sidney shaped the early love poetry of Fulke Greville.

996 BULLOUGH, G[EOFFREY]. "Fulk Greville, First Lord Brooke." *MLR* 28 (January 1933):1–20.

Discusses Greville's mourning at Sidney's death, his plans for a proper tomb (which were never carried out), his role in publishing *Arcadia*, and the part played by the Sidneys in launching Greville's long career at court.

997 BULLOUGH, GEOFFREY, ed. *Poems and Dramas of Fulke Greville, First Lord Brooke*. Vol. 1. London and New York: Oxford University Press, 1945, pp. 2–9.

Recounts Greville's friendship with Sidney. Argues that, although there is little evidence to suggest that the Areopagus was a formal club involving Dyer, Greville, and Sidney, Greville does appear to have written some poetry "in rivalry with his friend."

998 BUXTON, JOHN. *Sir Philip Sidney and the English Renaissance*. London: Macmillan & Co.; New York: St. Martin's Press, 1954, 295 pp.

Pursues the thesis that Sidney and his sister shaped and guided the poetry of the Elizabethan age "toward a fullness of achievement that, in the 1570's, only they foresaw." In Chapter 1, seeks to describe a tradition based on the definition of a patron as not merely one who can afford fine art, but one who has the taste and wit to demand it. Surveys the general state of poetry in England between Chaucer and Spenser, emphasiz-

Twentieth Century

ing the contrast between Elizabethan and postromantic aesthetics. In Chapters 2 and 3, describes "The Education of a Patron," examining in detail Sidney's education and travels, first in France and Germany, with stress on the tutelage of Languet, and then in Italy and at the Imperial Court, emphasizing his "wide knowledge" of Italian poetry and criticism. Focuses mainly on artists and scholars whom he likely met, with liberal quotations from letters and dedications to him. Gives attention to his portraits and to books dedicated to him, such as Estienne's Greek New Testament and Lambert Daneau's *Geographica Poetica*. In Chapter 4, argues that Sidney, Greville, and Dyer (with help from Spenser and Harvey) initiated a "campaign" to create a new poetry that would make England the equal of Italy. Discusses at length their metrical experiments, including those in quantitative verse, contending that the "flowering" of English poetry in the 1590s was not "haphazard accident" but was "brought about by these men's skill and insight." Affirms that Sidney encouraged Spenser's writing of *The Faerie Queene*. In Chapter 5, presents Sidney as a "Generall Maecenas of Learning," concentrating on his influence on "the literary and intellectual life of his time." Also discusses Sidney's involvement with Ramism, with *imprese* and devices, with painting, and with translations of the Psalms, along with his connections with Bruno and other Continental scholars who visited England in the 1580s. In Chapters 6 and 7, considers the Countess of Pembroke and the many gentlemen and ladies "excellently learned" who followed Sidney's example as patron, including Essex, Greville, Mountjoy, Ralegh, Sir Henry Goodere, Sir William Herbert, and Lucy, Countess of Bedford. In an epilogue, reiterates the thesis that "inspiration from Sidney set the English Renaissance on its course." See replies by Doughtie (1014) and Robertson (1130).

999 BUXTON, JOHN, and JUEL-JENSEN, BENT. "Sir Philip Sidney's First Passport Rediscovered." *Library*, 5th ser. 25 (March 1970):42–46.
Describes the discovery at New College Oxford of Sidney's license from Queen Elizabeth to travel on the Continent in 1572. Provides a full description, transcription, and facsimile of the document, comparing it with others of the period and tracing its history.

1000 CAMPBELL, LILY B[ESS]. "Sidney as 'The Learned Soldier.'" *HLQ* 7 (February 1944):175–78.
Reprints the opening paragraph of a 1604 paradox by Dudley Digges as "making some slight contribution to the discussion of Sidney as soldier

vs. Sidney the poet and patron." Citing classical precedent for writing an "Apologie for Souldiers," Digges wishes Sidney had done likewise.

1001 CHAMBERLIN, FREDERICK CARLETON. *Elizabeth and Leycester*. New York: Dodd, Mead, & Co., 1939, pp. 305–7, 309, 319–22.

Relying on contemporary letters, describes the difficulties that Sidney faced in the Netherlands, his valor in battle, and his death.

1002 CHAMBERS, Sir E[DMUND] K[ERCHEVER]. *Sir Henry Lee: An Elizabethan Portrait*. Oxford: Clarendon Press, 1936, pp. 119, 121, 135, 155, 272.

Records Sidney's associations with Lee, including their joust in the 1581 Accession Day Tilts. In Appendix D, notes that the "Ditchley" Manuscript (British Library MS. Add. 41499 A) includes "A remembrance of Sir Ph: Sidnie Knight the 17th Nou' 1586."

1003 CHUBB, EDWIN WATTS. *Stories of Authors: British and American*. New York: Sturgis & Walton Co., 1910, pp. 4–8.

In "Sir Philip Sidney at Zutphen," gives a brief account of Sidney's death.

1004 CHUTE, MARCHETTE. "Getting at the Truth." *Saturday Review*, 19 September 1953, pp. 11–12, 43–44.

Searches out the facts about Sidney's death by examining the testimony of contemporary figures, including Fulke Greville (863), Sir John Smythe (851), and Thomas Moffet (2827). Believes Moffet is the most accurate.

1005 CLIFFORD, JAMES L. *From Puzzles to Portraits: Problems of a Literary Biographer*. Chapel Hill: University of North Carolina Press, 1970, pp. 74–75.

Cites Chute's investigation (1004) of the various accounts of Sidney's death as an example of the problems of "testing authority."

1006 COHEN, EILEEN Z[ELDA]. "Poet in the Service of Protestantism: Sir Philip Sidney as Ambassador." *Historical Magazine of the Protestant Episcopal Church* 38 (June 1969):167–75.

Presents the case for Sidney's failure as ambassador to Germany in 1577: "while Sidney was by nature conciliatory and himself not divided from his Protestant brethren by doctrinal differences, he was [so] single minded in his plan for the League . . . that he was misled by the German princes." Argues that his "credulity" regarding Duke Casimir's inten-

Twentieth Century

tions and abilities made him a "dangerous ambassador," on whose services Elizabeth "would not readily be convinced to chance again."

1007 COLLINS, JOSEPH BURNS. *Christian Mysticism in the Elizabethan
Age, with Its Background in Mystical Methodology.* Baltimore: Johns
Hopkins Press; London: Humphrey Milford, Oxford University
Press, 1940, pp. 95, 233.
Suggests that Sidney's vein of thoughtful melancholy goes back to *A
Mirror for Magistrates* and to the *contemptus mundi* tradition among
English mystics.

1008 DENKINGER, EMMA MARSHALL. "The *Impresa* Portrait of Sir
Philip Sidney in the National Portrait Gallery." *PMLA* 47 (March
1932):17–45.
Identifies the primary source of the *impresa* as a 1562 French *jeton*, with
subsidiary influence from a fifteenth-century Italian device. Interprets
details of the Apollo shield to show that it embodies a particularly
Renaissance concept, at variance with classical notions and deriving
from the Pseudo-Lucian *De Dea Syria*. Contends that the portrait dates
from "1584 at the earliest, surely no later than 1585," that the *impresa*
was especially designed for the 17 November 1584 tilt, and that its
motto, *Inveniam Viam aut Faciam*, alludes to Sidney's plans for New-
World "colonization and plunder." Offers evidence, finally, that the portrait, sometimes challenged, is genuinely of Sidney.

1009 ———. "Spenser's *Muiopotmos* Again." *PMLA* 46 (March 1931):272–76.
Rebuts Lemmi's assertions (625) that Penelope Devereux's marriage was
arranged during Sidney's absence from court; that Sidney would have
objected; that the Queen was jealous when Sidney himself married; and
that Spenser knew of Sidney's love for Penelope. Suggests that Spenser
may have believed that Stella was Frances Walsingham, as allusions in
Colin Clout and *Astrophel* (2771) suggest. See also Purcell (1120).

1010 de SÉLINCOURT, E[RNEST], ed. Introduction to *The Poetical
Works of Edmund Spenser*, edited by E[rnest] de Sélincourt and J.C.
Smith. Oxford Standard Authors Series. Oxford: Clarendon
Press, 1911, pp. xii-xiv.
Argues that Sidney was a major formative influence for Spenser, but that
the relationship was not one of personal intimacy. Attributes the elegy
"To the Angel Spirit of . . . Sir Philip Sidney" (2741) to Spenser. But see
a reply by Waller (2360).

1011 de VRIES, T[IEMAN]. *Holland's Influence on English Language and Literature*. Chicago: C. Grentzebach, 1916, pp. 278–81.
Lauds Sidney's activities as a Protestant activist and a defender of Dutch religious liberty.

1012 DODDS, M. HOPE. "Mourners at Sir Philip Sidney's Funeral." *N&Q* 180 (28 June 1941):463–64.
In response to Newdigate (1100), notes that a portrait of Thomas Lant, not Sidney, appears at the beginning of Pollard's edition of *Astrophil and Stella* (71). Supplies information about one of the mourners at Sidney's funeral, Sir Thomas Perrot.

1013 DOP, JAN ALPERT. *Eliza's Knights: Soldiers, Poets, and Puritans in the Netherlands 1572–1586*. Alblasserdam, Netherlands: Remak, [1981], pp. 2–6, 16–22, 77–85, 98, 153–55, 164–76.
Views Sidney's death at Zutphen as the end of an "epoch" in English military history, one in which the complex politics of the Netherlands and the realities of war were in conflict with England's self-conscious creation of a "national mythology." Regards the development of Elizabethan chivalry as a impediment to English attempts to wage war effectively. In the New *Arcadia* sees a "change in Sidney's perception of England and England's situation in the world." Reads Argalus as a Sidney persona: both are "constant to an ideal from which [their] thinking had moved away, but which publicly [they] must continue to support." Finds Sidney's success at Axel, like his death, ultimately a futile gesture. In the bogs and marshes of Holland, the aristocratic vision was not viable.

1014 DOUGHTIE, EDWARD. "Sidney, Tessier, Batchelar and *A Musical Banquet*: Two Notes." *RN* 18 (1965):123–26.
Argues that Daniell Batchelar, one of the composers represented in *A Musical Banquet*, is noted among the mourners in Lant's engraving of Sidney's funeral (849). Suggests that Batchelar was Sidney's page and that he may have been the one "who provided music for Sidney on his deathbed at Arnheim." Notes also that song VII in *A Musical Banquet* is a setting of the lyric "In a grove most rich of shade" (*AS viii*) and that it was composed by Guillaume Tessier, not Charles Tessier. Argues that the speculation by Pattison (694) and Buxton (998) that Charles Tessier was a member of the Sidney circle is mistaken.

Twentieth Century

1015 EINSTEIN, LEWIS. *Tudor Ideals*. New York: Harcourt Brace, 1921, pp. 43–45, 54, 62, 97, 120, 145–48, 154–56, 255–59, 326–28, 335–38.
Discusses Sidney as the embodiment of the ideal courtier through a comparison of Sir Henry Sidney's letter to him and Philip's letter to his brother Robert. Notes that, while the former deals with decorum and moderation, the latter addresses a more highly developed ideal involving learning and talent. Remarks that, although Sidney had many books dedicated to him, he does not seem to have actively supported writers with financial patronage. Observes that courtiers like Sidney and Ralegh valued their deeds more highly than their literary works.

1016 ELTON, OLIVER. *Modern Studies*. London: Edward Arnold, 1907, pp. 7, 16, 20–21, 24.
Discusses Giordano Bruno's *Cena de le cenari*, an account of a dinner party for Bruno in 1584 that Sidney may have attended. Finds nothing in Sidney's writings to prove that he knew the Italian philosopher or his heretical views. Traces the idea that they met in a secret philosophical "club" to Joseph Warton in the eighteenth century.

1017 EWING, S. BLAINE, [Jr.]. "A New Manuscript of Greville's *Life of Sidney*." *MLR* 49 (October 1954):424–27.
Examines various texts of Greville's *Life of Sidney* (863), giving a bibliographical description of MS. 295 in the Shrewsbury Public Library (S) and summarizing the differences between it and both the printed version of 1652 (P) and the manuscript at Trinity College, Cambridge (M). Notes that, since Chapters 9, 15, 16, and 17 are shorter in S than in P or M, S more nearly accords with Greville's intention that the work be a dedicatory introduction to an edition. Quotes two "unique transition passages" in Chapters 11 and 12 of S that have never been published. Also discusses the implications of different chapter arrangements in S and P.

1018 FALLS, CYRIL [BENTHAM]. "A Window on the World: Sir Philip Sidney and His Age." *Illustrated London News* 10 (July 1954):54.
Reviews Sidney's career, highlighting his literary achievements. Comments on the effect that Victorian studies have had on twentieth-century attitudes toward him.

1019 FAVERTY, FREDERIC E. "A Note on the Areopagus." *PQ* 5 (July 1926):278–80.
Shows that, in the late sixteenth century, *areopagus* meant "any group of persons which arrogated to itself the province of a judiciary body," and argues that any discussion of whether Sidney belonged to an organiza-

tion should consider Thomas Newton's use of the term in this sense in his dedicatory epistle to Thomas Heneage's edition of *Seneca His Ten Tragedies*.

1020 FEINBERG, NONA PAULA. "Elizabeth, Her Poets, and the Creation of the Courtly Manner: A Study of Sir John Harington, Sir Philip Sidney, and John Lyly." Ph.D. diss., University of California at Berkeley, 1978, 231 pp.

Investigates ways in which Sidney fulfilled the humanist ideal of the learned courtier. Concentrates on his use of poetical and political eloquence to win advancement, even though he was striving to portray the image of an amateur. Contrasts his career with the literary career of Ben Jonson. See *DAI* 39 (February 1979):4955A–56A.

1021 FLASDIECK, HERMANN M. *Der Gedanke einer englischen Sprachakademie in Vergangenheit und Gegenwart*. Jenaer Germanistische Forchungen. Jena, Germany: Verlag der Frommannschen Buchhandlung, Walter Biedermann, 1928, pp. 6–9.

Suggests that Sidney may have been a member of the Society of Aniquaries, founded by Archbishop Parker in 1572. Discusses the relation of the Areopagus to literary academies in France and Italy and concludes that it probably was not formally organized and was given its name in jest.

1022 FLENLEY, RALPH, ed. *A Calendar of the Register of the Queen's Majesty's Council in the Dominion and Principality of Wales and the Marches of the Same [1535] 1569–1591 (From the Bodley MS. No. 904)*. Cymmrodorion Record Series, 8. London: Issued by the Honourable Society of Cymmrodorion, 1916, pp. 23, 210–11.

Records the role of Sidney and Sir Thomas Leighton in arbitrating a dispute between Fulke Greville and Charles Foxe.

1023 FREEMAN, ROSEMARY. *English Emblem Books*. London: Chatto & Windus, 1948, pp. 19–20, 35–36, 72.

Brings Sidney into a discussion of the decline of chivalry and the harmonious, allegorical world view of the Middle Ages. Notes a collection of *imprese* once owned by Henry Peacham, which depict Sidney and others at the tilts.

1024 FUJII, HARUHIKO. "Spenser's *Astrophel* and Renaissance Ways of Idealization." *SELit*, English no., 1968, pp. 1–15.

Argues that the lack of private mourning in *Astrophel* is intentional. Notes that Spenser was writing a public eulogy and that his depiction of Sidney as a "Renaissance man" is highly idealized and conventional.

Twentieth Century

Suggests that Spenser's reference to Stella is not an allusion to Lady Rich or to Sidney's wife but to an ideal of love and devotion.

1025 FULTON, EDWARD. "Spenser, Sidney, and the Areopagus." *MLN* 31 (June 1916):372–74.

Adduces evidence from the Spenser-Harvey correspondence and *Ruins of Time* to support the belief that Sidney and Spenser "were on fairly intimate terms . . . before Spenser went to Ireland."

1026 GÁL, ISTVÁN. "Sir Philip Sidney kalauza a korabeli magyar történelemben." [Sir Philip Sidney and the History of Contemporary Hungary.] *Filológiai Közlöny* 17 (January–June 1971):16–25.

Discusses Sidney's European tour of 1572–75, particularly his trip to Hungary, his contacts with Languet and Charles de l'Escluse, and his knowledge of Pietro Bizarri's *Pannonicum Bellum*.

1027 ———. "Sir Philip Sidney's Guidebook to Hungary." *Hungarian Studies in English* 4 (1969):53–64.

Describes the purpose and contents of Pietro Bizari's *Pannonicum Bellum*. Argues that Sidney's acquaintance with members of Johannes Sambucus's circle, coupled with the reading of this book, gave him intimate knowledge of the Hungarian resistance movement, a knowledge that, embedded in his official reports to Burghley in 1574 and Walsingham 1577, hastened the establishment of diplomatic connections between England and Turkey. See a response by Osborn (1107).

1028 GALIMBERTI, ALICE. *Edmondo Spenser "l'Ariosto inglese."* Turin: Casa Editrice Giuseppe Gambino, 1938, pp. 183–91.

In Appendix 1, discusses the extent of Spenser's acquaintance with Sidney.

1029 GEORGAS, MARILYN [DAVIS]. "Mythmaking and Sidney: The Legendary French Geneaology." *Lamar Journal of the Humanities* (Houston, Tex.) 2 (Spring 1976):15–26.

Finds the origins of the myth of Sidney's French ancestry in the pseudonymous "Life" accompanying the 1655 edition of *Arcadia* (9). Traces its "stubborn survival" in the work of subsequent biographers, chastising Wallace (805) for deliberately suppressing Kingsford's revelation (1083) that the pedigree was forged.

1030 GILLIAT, EDWARD. "Sir Philip Sidney, the Peerless Knight." In *Heroes of the Elizabethan Age: Stirring Records of the Intrepid Bravery and Boundless Resource of the Men of Queen Elizabeth's Reign.*

Philadelphia: J.B. Lippincott Co.; London: Seeley & Co., 1911, pp. 234–54.

A popular, and at times misleading, survey that presents, for example, the "effects" of Penelope Rich's marriage on Sidney as though they occurred before the 1577 embassy to Germany or the 1579 tennis-court quarrel with the Earl of Oxford. Focuses on Sidney's wounding at Zutphen and his death.

1031 GODSHALK, WILLIAM L[EIGH]. "A Sidney Autograph." *Book Collector* 13 (Spring 1964):65.

Points out that a manuscript note consisting of Sidney's name, city, and date on the title page of Francesco Guicciardini's *La historia d'Italia*, which appeared in 1569, confirms that he was in Padua on 20 June 1574 and adds to the present knowledge of Sidney's reading while on the Continent.

1032 GOLDMAN, MARCUS SELDEN. *Sir Philip Sidney and the "Arcadia."* Illinois Studies in Language and Literature, vol. 17, nos. 1–2. Urbana: University of Illinois Press, 1934, pp. 17–121. Orig. a Ph.D. diss., University of Illinois at Urbana-Champaign, 1931.

In Chapter 1, discusses the merits and faults of the major biographies of Sidney from 1632 to 1932. Also compares Sidney with the Spanish courtier Bayard. In Chapter 2, relates Sidney's character to that of other Dudleys and Sidneys, noting their tendency to link religion and politics. Considers Sidney's early reading, his training in Greek, his studies at Oxford, and the influence of his father's experiences in Ireland. Suggests that the *Defence* may have been influenced by Henri Estienne's *Poesis philosophia*. In Chapter 3, sorts out Sidney's connections with various French poets, with Languet, and with the Protestant League. Argues that Languet was neither Calvinist nor especially anti-Catholic. In Chapter 4, treats Sidney's political and military affairs from 1575 to 1586, considering the circumstances of the *Letter to the Queen*, its stylistic similarities with *Arcadia*, and the political figures of speech that color even *Astrophil and Stella*. See also item 534.

1033 GOUWS, J.S. "An Edition of Fulke Greville's *A Dedication to Sir Philip Sidney*." D.Phil. thesis, Oxford University, 1976.

Abstract not available. Cited in *Index to Theses Accepted for Higher Degrees in the Universities of Great Britain and Ireland* 26, part 2 (1978):item 6041.

Twentieth Century

1034 GRATTAN FLOOD, W[ILLIAM] H[ENRY]. "Sir Philip Sidney in Ireland." *The Month* 148 (October 1926):358–59.
Provides information from Sir Henry Sidney's "Irish Accounts," contained in the de L'Isle manuscripts (535), allowing the reader "to visualize the surroundings of the young Philip."

1035 GREAT BRITAIN. PUBLIC RECORD OFFICE. *Calendar of State Papers, Foreign Series, of the Reign of Elizabeth, 1577–78. Preserved in the Public Record Office*. Vol. 12, edited by Arthur John Butler. London: Published by His Majesty's Stationery Office, 1901, pp. 22–24, 95, 98, 107, 180, 186, 223, 235, 638, 731.
Summarizes two letters from Casimir requesting that Sidney accompany him on a "march into Flanders," a letter noting the Prince of Orange's "great opinion" of Sidney, minutes of the 24 August 1577 negotiations in Neuestadt concerning Elizabeth's offer of money to aid "the Church of France," and other letters that mention Sidney in various capacities.

1036 ———. *Calendar of State Papers, Foreign Series, of the Reign of Elizabeth, 1578–79. Preserved in the Public Record Office*. Vol. 13, edited by Arthur John Butler. London: Published by His Majesty's Stationery Office, 1903, pp. 122, 391, 395, 421, 477–78.
Summarizes a 1579 letter from William Davison to Sidney asking pardon and a 1578 letter from Leicester to Walsingham discussing the Queen's commissioning Sidney to express her offense at Casimir. Other letters allude to Sidney or convey salutations.

1037 ———. *Calendar of State Papers, Foreign Series, of the Reign of Elizabeth, 1579–1580. Preserved in the Public Record Office*. Vol. 14, edited by Arthur John Butler. London: Published by His Majesty's Stationery Office, 1904, pp. 19, 130, 144.
Summarizes three letters conveying commendations to Sidney.

1038 ———. *Calendar of State Papers, Foreign Series, of the Reign of Elizabeth, January 1581–April 1582. Preserved in the Public Record Office*. Vol. 15, edited by Arthur John Butler. London: Published by His Majesty's Stationery Office, 1907, pp. 71, 625, 634.
Summarizes a 1581 letter to Sidney from Sebastian Pardini expressing sorrow at "your illness and melancholy" and other letters observing Sidney's "suitability" to lead "a certain number of cavalry" and expressing admiration.

1039 ———. *Calendar of State Papers, Foreign Series, of the Reign of Elizabeth, January–June, 1583 and Addenda. Preserved in the Public*

Twentieth Century

Record Office. Vol. 17, edited by Arthur John Butler and Sophie Crawford Lomas. London: Published by His Majesty's Stationery Office, 1913, pp. 177, 249, 355, 370.
Summarizes letters to Walsingham alluding to Sidney in various capacities, one referring to his upcoming marriage.

1040 ———. *Calendar of State Papers, Foreign Series, of the Reign of Elizabeth, Preserved in the Public Record Office*. Vol. 18, *July 1583–July 1584*, edited by Sophie Crawford Lomas. London: Printed under the authority of His Majesty's Stationery Office by The Hereford Times Limited, 1914, pp. 11, 52, 173, 260, 314, 406, 412, 501, 519, 530, 549, 563, 564, 567, 579, 594, 601–2, 603, 605, 611–14, 618, 622, 634, 640, 644–46.
Contains letters to Sidney from Antonio D'Avigne, dated 6 December 1583, and from Nicolo Carenzone, dated 21 June 1584, and a lengthy set of instructions from the Queen concerning envoys to France and the Low Countries. Other letters, largely to and from Walsingham, contain varied allusions to, comments on, commendations, or praises for Sidney. For example, a series of letters from 1584 contains references to Sidney's embassy to convey "condolences" for Orange's death (several containing extended commentary); other allusions are to his having dined in the presence of the Spanish ambassador; to his being put in charge of some "horsemen" in Germany; to his marriage; to payment of "100 livres" to him; and to his having hindered Carenzone's "business."

1041 ———. *Calendar of State Papers, Foreign Series, of the Reign of Elizabeth, Preserved in the Public Record Office*. Vol. 19, *August 1584–August 1585*, edited by Sophie Crawford Lomas. London: Printed under the Authority of His Majesty's Stationery Office by The Hereford Times Limited, 1916, pp. 12, 16–20, 24, 39, 53, 54, 103, 146, 214, 220, 247, 299, 335, 427, 511, 524, 595, 626, 631, 633, 650, 679, 682, 687.
Includes primarily letters to Walsingham from various English agents on the Continent, to Burghley, or to William Davison; also includes two letters from the Queen. References to Sidney include expressions of love for him, allusions to intercessions in legal affairs, "notes" regarding the Queen's instructions upon sending him to France, a comment on his friendship with Andreas Pauli, allusions to his stay at Antwerp, and requests that he be "placed" in Flushing. Contains only one letter to Sidney (from Sir Stephen le Sieur), although a second, to Walsingham, allows Sidney to receive it in the former's absence.

Twentieth Century

1042 ———. *Calendar of State Papers, Foreign Series, of the Reign of Elizabeth, Preserved in the Public Record Office.* Vol. 21, part 1, *June 1586–June 1588,* edited by Sophie Crawford Lomas. London: Published by His Majesty's Stationery Office, 1927, pp. 150, 153, 160, 166, 169, 175, 176, 657.
Summarizes letters expressing grief over and condolences for Sidney's death.

1043 ———. *Calendar of State Papers, Foreign Series, of the Reign of Elizabeth, Preserved in the Public Record Office.* Vol. 21, part 3, *April–December 1587,* edited by Sophie Crawford Lomas and Allen B. Hinds. London: Published by His Majesty's Stationery Office, 1929, pp. 3, 13, 120, 130, 205, 269, 313, 323, 325–26, 340, 348, 368, 369.
Summarizes a series of letters from Edward Burnham to Walsingham concerning attempts to collect pay due to Sidney's estate, and an account of "money paid out . . . for services in the Low Countries." Other letters refer to Sidney's governorship of Flushing and express sorrow at his death. A letter from Edward Norris to the Privy Council refers to Sidney's involvement in his quarrel with Count Hohenlohe.

1044 ———. *Calendar of State Papers, Foreign Series, of the Reign of Elizabeth, Preserved in the Public Record Office.* Vol. 21, part 4, *January–June 1588,* edited by Sophie Crawford Lomas and Allen B. Hinds. London: Published by His Majesty's Stationery Office, 1931, pp. 11, 51, 148, 389, 485.
Contains a letter from the Count Hohenlohe lamenting Sidney's death "daily," and other letters and documents specifying debts and other matters relating to Sidney's governorship of Flushing.

1045 ———. *Calendar of State Papers, Foreign Series, of the Reign of Elizabeth, Preserved in the Public Record Office.* Vol. 22, *July–December 1588,* edited by Richard Bruce Wernham. London: Published by His Majesty's Stationery Office, 1936, pp. 213, 255, 260, 344, 362, 410.
Contains references to or comments on Sidney as "Late Governor of Flushing." One letter alludes to money paid to him.

1046 GREENBERG, STEPHEN JOEL. "Cavalier: Propaganda Stereotypes in Seventeenth-Century England." Ph.D. diss., Fordham University, 1983, 313 pp.
Includes Sidney in a small group of courtiers who provided the great models for the "prototypical Cavalier." See *DAI* 44 (December 1983):1885A.

Twentieth Century

1047 GREENLAW, EDWIN A. "Spenser and British Imperialism." *MP* 9 (January 1912):347–70.

From Greville's *Life*, draws Sidney's opinions on the need for sea power and colonies to oppose Spain, noting that Spenser held the same views.

1048 GROCE, ABEL. *Giordano Bruno, der Ketzer von Nola: Versuch einer Deutung.* Part 1, *Werdegang und Untergang.* Vienna: Europäischer Verlag, 1970, pp. 71–72, 76, 82–83, 120.

Considers Bruno's relationship with Sidney and his circle and suggests that Bruno's dialogue, *La cena de le ceneri* was not set at the house of Fulke Greville, as some scholars assume, but at the house of the French ambassador.

1049 HAND, JEROME MILTON. "Fashioners of Reality: The Courtier in Sixteenth-Century English Literature." Ph.D. diss., Indiana University of Pennsylvania, 1980, 147 pp.

Distinguishes the Renaissance from the "Renaissance Myth," which was supported by the rising middle class and celebrated the material world and the self rather than the spiritual world and God. In the theory of Florentine neo-Platonists such as Marsilio Ficino and Giovanni Pico della Mirandola, the world and the self were seen as avenues to God, but in practice, they often became ends in themselves. Compares the responses of More, Wyatt, Surrey, and Sidney to this "myth," focusing on Sidney's Protestant morality and the extent to which it was "based on what should be rather than on what was." Concludes that, to some extent, all four men became "victims" of the myth, though all were "motivated by a real desire to improve the lot of mankind." See *DAI* 41 (November 1980):2120A–21A.

1050 HARDWICK, [JOHN] MICHAEL, and HARDWICK, MOLLIE. "Penshurst Place, Kent: Philip Sidney 1554–1586." In *Writers' Houses: A Literary Journey in England.* London: Phoenix House, 1968, pp. 33–36.

Provides a brief history and description of "this immaculate example of the less grandiose type of stately home."

1051 HAY, MILLICENT V. *The Life of Robert Sidney, Earl of Leicester (1563–1626).* Washington, D.C.: Folger Shakespeare Library; London and Toronto: Associated University Presses, 1984, pp. 32–34, 36–38, 40, 43–46, 50, and passim.

In discussing Sidney's suggestions for his brother Robert's education, posits that they may have been influenced by a reading of Roger Ascham. Surveys the main events of Sidney's public career to support the claim that "Philip's friends became Robert's allies; his enemies, Robert's

Twentieth Century

opponents; his interests, Robert's avocations." Analyzes the 1580 letter of advice to Robert in order to gauge the latter's interests. Also recounts actions of the two brothers in the Netherlands in 1585–86.

1052 HEINEMANN, MARGOT. *Puritanism and Theatre: Thomas Middleton and Opposition Drama under the Early Stuarts.* Cambridge: Cambridge University Press, 1980, pp. 30, 265, 267.
Suggests that Sidney's patronage favored "Puritan writers and preachers, in accordance with the anti-Spanish and anti-Catholic policies they favored." Lists Sidney's most militant Protestant friends, both in England and on the Continent.

1053 HELTZEL, VIRGIL B[ARNEY], and HUDSON, HOYT H[OPEWELL], eds. and trans. Introduction to *"Nobilis, or a View of the Life and Death of A Sidney" and "Lessus Lugubris"*, by Thomas Moffet. San Marino, Calif.: Huntington Library, 1940, pp. xi–xxiv.
Describes the manuscript of the two poems (Sloan MS. 4014) that was used in the edition (2827), dating *Nobilis* in 1594, providing a life of Moffet and listing his published works. Briefly compares *Nobilis* to nine other contemporary accounts of Sidney's life and death. Claims that all these works share the conviction that Sidney's death was as "great and full of significance as his life—that, indeed, the end crowned the work," and notes that an occasional small detail "brings us close to the man."

1054 HENDERSON, PHILIP. "Sidney and Bruno." *TLS*, 9 October 1937, p. 735.
In response to a reviewer's objections (980), asserts that, in 1584, Bruno was "enthusiastically received" by the Sidney-Greville "academy." Evidence of intimacy between Sidney and Bruno points to a "community of interest" between Sidney and Ralegh.

1055 HERRICK, MARVIN T[HEODORE]. "The Early History of Aristotle's *Rhetoric* in England." *PQ* 5 (July 1926):242–57.
Cites evidence that Sidney knew various works by Aristotle. Notes that he translated the first two books of the *Rhetoric*.

1056 HIGGINSON, JAMES JACKSON. *Spenser's "Shepherd's Calender" in Relation to Contemporary Affairs.* New York: Columbia University Press, 1912, pp. 243–89, 299–310.
From a close examination of Spenser's works, concludes that he had no deep intimacy with Sidney. Traces the notion of a warm, personal friendship to nineteenth-century biographers. Refutes Fletcher's argu-

ments (2368) that the *Shepherd's Calendar* embodies the conscious program of a literary club formed by Sidney. Demonstrates that the view of the Areopagus as an organized society arose no earlier than 1870. Also rejects Buck's early date for the first meeting between Spenser and Sidney (see 994). Concludes that they were first introduced when Leicester presented Gabriel Harvey to the Queen in July of 1578. See also Long (632).

1057 HILL, CHRISTOPHER. *Intellectual Origins of the English Revolution*. Oxford: Clarendon Press, 1965, pp. 132–37, 185, 291–92.

Enumerates Sidney's connections with explorers, scientists, and logicians such as John Dee, Richard Hakluyt the Younger, Michael Lok, Timothy Bright, Giordano Bruno, and Peter Ramus. Points out the personal and intellectual ties between Sidney and Sir Walter Ralegh, and finds political views similar to theirs in a variety of English authors of the Renaissance.

1058 HILLIARD, NICHOLAS. *Treatise Concerning "The Arte of Limning."* In *The First Annual Volume of the Walpole Society, 1911–1912*. Oxford: Walpole Society, Oxford University Press, 1912, p. 12.

Records a conversation between Hilliard and Sidney on the technique of painting short and tall people so that the different proportions of their bodies would be apparent, even if they were drawn the same size.

1059 HIND, A[RTHUR] M. *Engravings in England in the Sixteenth and Seventeenth Centuries: A Descriptive Catalogue with Introductions*. Part 1, *The Tudor Period*. Vol. 1. Cambridge: Cambridge University Press, 1952, pp. 124–26, 132–37.

Provides an account of the Dutch engraver Theodor de Brij's connections with England and a detailed description of his execution of Thomas Lant's designs for thirty engravings depicting Sidney's funeral procession (849). Discusses the figures represented and provides titles, most in English but a few in Latin "where necessary for explanation." Includes collations of the five known sets.

1060 HÖLTGEN, KARL JOSEF. "Why Are There No Wolves in England? Philip Camerarius and a German Version of Sidney's Table Talk." *Anglia* 99, nos. 1–2 (1981):60–82.

Notes that, on his embassy to Nuremberg, Sidney was accompanied by George More. Provides another version of Sidney's remark on the absence of wolves in England.

Twentieth Century

1061 HOWELL, ROGER, Jr. "The Sidney Circle and the Protestant Cause in Elizabethan Foreign Policy." *RMS* 19 (1975):31–46.
Argues that "Sidney had come to think of the Protestant cause in ways that diverged from many of the Protestant activists" with whom he was associated. Suggests that contact with Bruno had made Sidney a Hermeticist and that the Areopagus discussed political policy as well as poetics. Follows Greville (863) in suggesting that Sidney saw Spain as the principal enemy in Europe and that the best way to combat that country was to seize its American possessions. Agrees with Osborn (1105, 1108) that Sidney wrote *Certain Notes Concerning the State of the Prince of Orange* (158).

1062 ———. *Sir Philip Sidney: The Shepherd Knight.* London: Hutchinson & Co.; Boston: Little, Brown & Co., 1968, 317 pp.
Writing "consciously" as a "historian, rather than a specialist in English literature," seeks to "place [Sidney] in his political context." Divides the book into three main parts: "The Courtier-Diplomat," "The Man of Letters," and "The Man of Action." In the introduction, outlines the political fortunes of the Dudley and Sidney families up to Sidney's birth. In Part 1 (Chapters 1–4), deals respectively with the diplomatic mission of 1575–77, with Sidney's involvement in his father's government in Ireland, with his interest in overseas exploration, and with his opposition to the proposed French marriage, all in the context of his connections to the Leicester and Walsingham factions and his "Protestant activism." Also discusses Sidney's "domestic" service to the state in the years 1581–85 and his involvment, during the same period, in foreign affairs, both political (such as the Don Antonio escapade and affairs in Scotland) and intellectual (such as the patronage of Bruno and Sidney's interest in Ramism). In Part 2 (Chapters 5–8), examines Sidney's education, focusing chiefly on his Continental tour of 1572–75. For information on this period, relies heavily on Buxton (998). In Chapter 5, "The Education of an Aristocrat," stresses the influence of Languet. In Chapter 6, discusses *Arcadia*, *The Lady of May*, and the *Defence*, and in Chapter 7, considers *Astrophil and Stella*. In Chapter 8, utilizes *Arcadia* and Greville's *Life* "to form some impression of Sidney's approach to foreign policy, social and political relations, science and superstition." Discusses his "acceptance of the 'mixed state,'" but without reference to the poem "As I my little flock on Ister bank" (*OA 66*), and accepts as authentic sentiments placed in Sidney's mouth by Greville. In Part 3, details Sidney's career in the Netherlands, his death, and the personal response of his friends—thus balancing the account of public mourning

with which the book began. Provides no bibliographical apparatus, but endnotes show frequent recourse to manuscripts and to twentieth-century scholarship.

1063 HUDSON, WINTHROP S. *John Ponet (1516?–1556): Advocate of Limited Monarchy*. Chicago: University of Chicago Press, 1942, pp. 199–200, 202.

Suggests that Sidney may have known Ponet's ideas and communicated them to the two most likely authors of the treatise *Vindiciae contra Tyrannos*, Languet and du Plessis-Mornay. Finds Sidney's opposition to absolute power in the monarchy similar to the position taken by his uncle, Peter Wentworth, and perhaps by his father-in-law, Francis Walsingham.

1064 HUIZINGA, JOHAN. *Address Delivered by J. Huizinga Professor of History in the University of Groningen on the Occasion of Uncovering a Memorial to Sir Philip Sidney at Zutphen on July 2nd 1913*. N.p. 1913, 17 pp.

Apparently an English translation of *Rede bij de Onthulling van een Gedenkteeken for P.S. te Zutphen op 2 Juli 1913*, cited as item 839 in Tannenbaum (268) (not located). The English version places Sidney in the second rank of Renaissance English poets but praises *Astrophil and Stella* and the *Defence*, calling Sidney "almost a Grecian embodiment of the beautiful man." Stresses his service in the Netherlands. See also item 1065.

1065 ———. *Sir Philip Sidney, MDLIIII-MDLXXXVI: An Address*. Oxford: Printed in the Netherlands by Joh. Enschede en Zonen, 1957, 23 pp.

Translates a Dutch address originally delivered at Zutphen on 2 July 1913 at the unveiling of a memorial to Sidney (see item 1064). Explains that the idealized engraving of Sidney was done by S.L. Hartz from Federico Zuccaro's 1577 painting, which is now in the National Portrait Gallery in London. Deals with Sidney's life and historical position in the Netherlands, citing him as a model of the ideal gentleman and noting his contact with "all the grand things of those troublesome times." Feels that Sidney's best poem is the *Defence* and that only a few of his lyrics are still read.

1066 HULBERT, VIOLA BLACKBURN. "A New Interpretation of Spenser's *Muiopotmos*." *SP* 25 (April 1928):128–48.

Interprets Spenser's poem as an allegory of the quarrel between Sidney and the Earl of Oxford, identifying Sidney as the fly, Oxford's ally Lord

Twentieth Century

Burghley as the spider, and the source of conflict as the French marriage. See also Stein (771).

1067 HULTZÉN, LEE SISSON. "Aristotle's *Rhetoric* in England to 1600." Ph.D. diss., Cornell University, 1932, p. 139. Published abstract. Ithaca, N.Y.: n.p., 1932, 5 pp.
Notes evidence that Sidney translated the *Rhetoric*.

1068 IMERTI, ARTHUR D., ed. and trans. *The Expulsion of the Triumphant Beast*, by Girodano Bruno. New Brunswick, N.J.: Rutgers University Press, 1964, pp. 10–11, 21–22, 29–30.
Discusses both possible and documented contacts between Sidney and Bruno, commenting on the strain placed on their friendship by Bruno's argument with Greville. Argues that Sidney was a strong promoter of Bruno's ideas and that the "Explanatory Epistle" to the present work expresses Bruno's indebtedness. See also Bruno (842).

1069 JAMES, J.B. "The Other Sidney." *History Today* 15 (March 1965): 183–90.
Suggests that, after Sidney's death, Queen Elizabeth transferred her dislike of him to his brother, thereby impeding Robert's advancement at court.

1070 JENKINS, ELIZABETH. *Elizabeth and Leicester*. London: V. Gollancz; New York: Coward-McCann, 1962, pp. 220–21, 226, 254–56, 294–96, 322–23, 330–31.
Discusses the importance of Wilton House for Sidney; the "treasury of contemporary detail" woven into his *Arcadia*; the "impression of Elizabeth" given by *The Lady of May*; and Sidney's relations with Spenser. Also considers the close ties within the Sidney family revealed by the *Defence of Leicester*.

1071 JOHN, LISLE C[ECIL]. "Elizabethan Letter-Writer." *PQ* 24 (April 1945):106–13.
Notes Richard Brackenbury's role in arranging the christening of Sidney's daughter, to whom Queen Elizabeth was godmother. From one of Brackenbury's letters dates Penelope Devereux's marriage to Lord Rich "about Allhallow tide" 1581. Concludes that the sonnets of *Astrophil and Stella* that treat her as married must be dated very late in 1581 or in 1582.

1072 ——. "Sir Stephen Le Sieur and Sir Philip Sidney." *MLQ* 17 (December 1956):340–51.
From letters and state papers, quotes passages bearing on le Sieur's services to Sidney and his family, including one 1580 letter that "opens

conjectures" as to whether le Sieur "was employed in making transcripts of the *Arcadia*, or whether any manuscripts of Sidney's works in his hand survive."

1073 JOHNSON, STANLEY D. "The Literary Patronage of Sir Philip Sidney and His Family." Ph.D. diss., Yale University, 1943, pp. 12–47, 109–14.

Noting the financial and intellectual advantages that made Sidney an important patron, comments at length on his contact with English and Continental writers. Points out that Sidney's relationship with Paulus Melissus (Schedius) not only links him with the Pléiade but also with Continental attempts to produce Psalters in the vernacular. Provides a comprehensive list of books dedicated to the Sidneys, quoting from many.

1074 JONES, H[ARRY] S[TUART] V[EDDER]. *Spenser's Defense of Lord Grey*. University of Illinois Studies in Language and Literature, vol. 5, no. 3. Urbana: University of Illinois Press, 1919, pp. 18, 31, 48–50, 64–65.

Sees Sidney as "intermediary" between Spenser's "international" Protestantism and that of the Continent. Notes evidence in the Sidney correspondence that he may have known François de la Noue and Michel de l'Hôspital and would have been therefore an avenue for Spenser's knowledge of their political writings.

1075 JUDSON, ALEXANDER C. *Sidney's Appearance: A Study in Elizabethan Portraiture*. Indiana University Publications, Humanities Series, 41. Bloomington: Indiana University Press, 1958, 105 pp.

Extending and reassessing the earlier studies of Williamson (1180) and Siebeck (757), examines thirty-five representations of Sidney in detail, concluding that "two types" are of "highest authority": the so-called Zuccaro portrait and the van de Passe and Elstracke engravings. Four additional portraits "tempt one to believe that they were intended to represent Sidney"; three others, all miniatures, are more problematical; and twenty-two are "unacceptable on grounds either of provenance or of similarity to the authoritative portraits." Also lists thirteen alleged portraits that are lost or defy identification. Thirty-two plates reproduce the likenesses considered and appendices tabulate opinions regarding the extant potraits and outline relations among the portrait groups. Contains a full bibliography. Preliminary chapters provide accounts of Holbein, Nicholas Hilliard, Isaac Oliver, and other Elizabethan portraitists so as to sugggest "the extraordinary difficulty involved in any

Twentieth Century

study of Tudor portraiture." Also examines all known contemporary written accounts of Sidney's appearance, surveys his comments on painting, and considers the correspondence dealing with the lost Veronese portrait. See also Strong (1160).

1076 JUEL-JENSEN, BENT. Letter. *PBSA* 63 (Second Quarter 1969):121.
Refutes Woodward's theory (1185) that Thomas Fuller wrote the anonymous biography of Sidney in the 1655 *Arcadia* (9), suggesting instead that it was by William Dugard, the printer.

1077 KELLOGG, ELIZABETH R[OCKEY]. *Sir Philip Sidney: Impressions of a Remarkable Character*. Cincinnati, Ohio: C.J. Krehbiel Co., 1960, 124 pp.
Provides a popularized and sometimes fictionalized glimpse at selected moments in Sidney's life. Attempts to link passages in *Arcadia* with facets of Sidney's life at Wilton. See also item 1078.

1078 ———. *Study for a Portrait of Sir Philip Sidney*. Cincinnati, Ohio: printed privately by McDonald Printing Co., 1959, 112 pp.
Presents a fictionalized vignette of Sidney at Shrewsbury, followed by a popularized biography that includes brief comments on Sidney's major works. The following is representative: "He visited Genoa briefly and made a longer stay in Florence to bask in its beauties and meditate on all that Lorenzo the Magnificent had done there to promote the New Learning. Early in January 1574 he took a house in Padua for the quiet study of astronomy, geometry and music. He added German to please Languet although he would have preferred Greek. To this heavy diet he added pageantry and heraldry, to leaven the lump." See also item 1077.

1079 KELSO, RUTH. *The Doctrine of the English Gentleman in the Sixteenth Century*. University of Illinois Studies in Language and Literature, vol. 14, nos. 1–2. Urbana: University of Illinois Press, 1929, pp. 47, 52, 93, 102, 107, 135, 142, 151, 154, 156, 161.
In surveying characteristics of the Elizabethan gentleman, compares Sidney with Castiglione's ideal courtier. Discusses seafaring, dueling, literary composition, travel, swordsmanship, horsemanship, music, holy living, and holy dying.

1080 KEYNES, Sir GEOFFREY [LANGDON]. *Dr. Timothie Bright 1550–1615: A Survey of His Life with a Bibliography of His Writings.* London: Wellcome Historical Medical Library, 1962, pp. 3, 5, 30.
Notes that, in dedicating to Sidney the third book of his *In Physicam Gulielmi Adolphi Scribonii*, Bright recalls taking shelter with Sidney at Walsingham's residence during the St. Bartholomew's Day Massacre.

1081 KHANDALAWA, PHIROZ P. "A Literary Causerie: An Elizabethan Courtier." *The Hindustan Review* 37 (February 1918):152–54.
Provides a brief biography of Sidney.

1082 KIMBROUGH, ROBERT. *Sir Philip Sidney.* Twayne's English Authors Series, 114. New York: Twayne Publishers, 1971, pp. 19–37.
In Chapter 1, surveys Sidney's life, relying heavily on Wallace (1171). Divides the life into five periods: "1554–72: Art"; "1572–75: Exercise:"; "1575–80: 'The expectancy and rose of the fair state'"; "1580–85: Imitation"; and "1585–86: 'We shall have a sore war upon us this summer.'" Discusses the famous stories that Sidney removed his thigh armor before the Battle of Zutphen and that, after being mortally wounded, he offered a wounded soldier his own drink. Concludes that these acts "suggest a man to whom life was a mere gesture and for whom each occasion should be a staged one, whereas the sense of *camaraderie* shown by the first act and the *noblesse* of the second reach deep into the man." See also item 593.

1083 KINGSFORD, C.L. "On Some Ancient Deeds and Seals Belonging to Lord De L'Isle and Dudley." *Archaeologia* 65 (1914):250–59.
Before describing early deeds and seals relating to the Sidney family, traces its descent from John de Sydnei, a yoeman in the reign of Edward I, down to Sir Philip. Shows that the pedigree produced in 1580 by Cooke (916), which traces the family back to William de Sidenie, Chamberlain to Henry II, was a forgery. Finds "no authentic evidence" for his existence. Corrects a number of errors made by Cooke in denominating known husbands and wives. In describing the deeds related to Penshurst, singles out four forgeries, presumably by Cooke, before proceeding to accounts of genuine deeds, the earliest by William de Pulteney in November 1356, showing acquisition of the estate by his father John in September 1339. See also Georgas (1029).

Twentieth Century

1084 KNOLL, ROBERT E. "Spenser and the Voyage of the Imagination." *WHR* 13 (Summer 1959):249–55.

Argues that the painting of Diana and Actaeon described in *Arcadia* and an analogous passage in Spenser's *Muiopotmos* derive from actual paintings by Titian. Suggests that Spenser and Sidney were familiar with them because Sidney brought back to Penshurst from his Venetian visit in 1573–74 several copies of Titian's works.

1085 KOSZUL, A[NDRÉ]. "Argentoratensia Britannica. Les Sidney et Strasbourg (I): I Philip Sidney." *Bulletin de la Faculté des Lettres de Strasbourg* 17 (December 1938):37–44.

Retraces the steps of Sidney's first Continental journey, noting that he met Philippe du Plessis-Mornay, Théophile de Banos, Andreas Wechel, Hubert Languet, Johann Sturm, Henri Estienne, and possibly Peter Ramus.

1086 KUHN, JOAQUIN CHARLES, ed. "An Edition of Fulke Greville's Life of Sir Philip Sidney." Ph.D. diss., Yale University, 1973, 495 pp.

In the Introduction, discusses the *Life* in the context of the friendship between Sidney and Greville and in terms of Greville's biographical technique. In the text, provides a more accurate collation and reproduction of the Trinity College Manuscript of the *Life* than was presented in Alexander B. Grosart's edition of Greville's works (Blackburn: privately printed, 1870). Argues that this manuscript is a more suitable copy text for an edition than the much-revised printed version of 1652 followed by Nowell-Smith (863). In an appendix, examines the various early accounts of Sidney's last battle, his illness, and his death. See *DAI* 34 (May 1974):7236A.

1087 LAMB, MARY ELLEN. "News from Sotheby's: Sidney Letters and a Portrait of Philip Sidney." *SNew* 4, no. 2 (1983):15–16.

Among items related to Robert and Mary Sidney, announces a "splendid portrait of Sir Philip Sidney, c. 1577."

1088 LANHAM, RICHARD A[LAN]. "Sidney: The Ornament of His Age." *Southern Review: An Australian Journal of Literary Studies* 2, no. 4 (1967):319–40.

Probes Sidney's biography to separate fact from legend, arguing that "the nonliterary component of Sidney's reputation stems from exaggerated report and needs revision." Insists that Sidney did not see himself as a scholar or poet, but as a patron. "His role was that of chivalric ornament, and to play it he had to be made over into a work of art, a legend."

1089 LANSDALE, NELSON. "Penshurst Place." *Saturday Review*, 18 February 1956, p. 46.

A brief "tour guide" history, noting that no marker identifies the room where Sidney was born.

1090 LEE, Sir SIDNEY. "Rich, Penelope, Lady Rich (1562?–1607)." In *Dictionary of National Biography*, edited by Leslie Stephen and Sidney Lee. Vol. 16. London: Smith, Elder; New York: Macmillan, 1909, pp. 1006–9.

Claims that the engagement between Sidney and Penelope Devereux "appears to have remained in suspense" nearly four years, during which time Sidney "sent her sonnets declaring his love."

1091 LEVY, F[RED] J[ACOB]. "Philip Sidney Reconsidered." *ELR* 2 (Winter 1972):5–18.

Reviews Sidney's career, arguing that it reveals conflicting desires for both the active and the contemplative lives. Notes the difficulty that the author and others of his circle had in trying to function as statesmen under Elizabeth. Concludes that though "Sidney would . . . have considered his career a failure . . . so were the careers of his associates."

1092 MABIE, HAMILTON WRIGHT. "William Shakespeare: Poet, Dramatist, and Man." *The Outlook* 65 (2 June 1900):283–94.

Reproduces an engraving of a portrait of Sidney ascribed to Antonio More.

1093 MacCAFFREY, WALLACE T. "Place and Patronage in Elizabethan Politics." In *Elizabethan Government and Society: Essays Presented to Sir John Neale*, edited by S[tanley] T[homas] Bindoff, J[oel] Hurstfield, and C[harles] H[arold] Williams. London: Athlone Press, 1961, pp. 95–126.

Claims that Sidney refused to accept royal "cash gifts" derived from such "irregular sources" as recusant fines. See also Wallace (1171). Discusses the Sidney interest in the "Queen's park of Otford" as an example of the significance of "local appointments" within the patronage system.

1094 McKISACK, MAY. *Medieval History in the Tudor Age*. Oxford: Clarendon Press, 1971, pp. 58–59.

Notes that Sidney's father collected medieval books and Welsh antiquities, and discusses the circumstances behind David Powel's dedication of *The History of Cambria* to Sidney in 1584.

Twentieth Century

1095 MALLET, CHARLES EDWARD. *A History of the University of Oxford*. Vol. 2. London: Methuen & Co.; New York: Longman's Green & Co., 1924, pp. 49, 149, 271.
Mentions Sidney as a "famous son" of Christ Church. Asserts that a 1585 production of *Meleager* contained a reference to him and alludes to his dispensation to eat meat during Lent.

1096 MAYNADIER, HOWARD. "The Areopagus of Sidney and Spenser." *MLR* 4 (April 1909):289–301.
Questioning whether the Areopagus "had any reality," examines closely the Spenser-Harvey correspondence as the only "reliable" source of information extant. Concludes that "the Areopagus as a literary society never existed." Contends that, although "the high-sounding name" was only Spenser's joke, there might have been "earnest literary discussion" among Sidney, Spenser, and "other young men who might have been members of an Areopagus."

1097 MORRIS, HARRY. *Richard Barnfield, Colin's Child*. Florida State University Studies, 38. Tallahassee: Florida State University, 1963, pp. 8–11, 25, 26, 51, 58, 63, 71, 74, 128, 131.
Surveys Abraham Fraunce's connections with the Sidney family and briefly discusses Sidney's impact on Barnfield's *Affectionate Shepherd*, *Cynthia*, and *Lady Pecunia*.

1098 MYRES, J[OHN] N[OWELL] L[INTON]. "The Painted Frieze in the Picture Gallery." *BLR* 3 (October 1950):82–91.
In describing the arrangement of figures on the north side of the frieze in the Bodleian Picture Gallery, notes that Sidney was one of "only three Englishmen."

1099 NEALE, J[OHN] E[RNEST]. *Elizabeth I and Her Parliaments, 1559–1581*. London: Jonathan Cape, 1953, pp. 374, 385.
Notes that Sidney was a "newcomer" in Parliament in January 1581, "an ornament rather than a power," and that he was a member of a "grand committee" appointed to draft an "anti-Catholic bill" in February of that year.

1100 NEWDIGATE, B[ERNARD] H[ENRY]. "Mourners at Sir Philip Sidney's Funeral." *N&Q* 180 (7 June 1941):398–401.
Comments on Lant's copperplate engravings of Sidney's funeral (849), now preserved in a "very rare oblong-shaped folio at the British Library." Transcribes in full the corroborating detail found in Bodleian MS. Ashm. 818.9, "perhaps" the source of Lant's designs. Supplies

genealogical information for some of those named. See also Benham (984), Dodds (1012).

1101 O'DONOGHUE, FREEMAN [M]. *Catalogue of Engraved British Portraits Preserved in the Department of Prints and Drawings in the British Museum.* 6 vols. London: Longmans & Co., 1908–1925, 4:106–7, 5:79.

Lists twenty-five engravings of Sidney, as painted by Antonio More, Isaac Oliver, and others, used mainly as title-page or other illustrations in books published from the sixteenth century onwards. Notes that an engraving of Sidney in full armor was made originally for Henry Holland's *The Portraitures at Large of Nine Modern Worthies of the World* and engraved by Robert Vaughan. Also identifies Sidney's head among several on the title page of Edward Phillips's 1678 edition of *The New World of Words*.

1102 ONG, WALTER J. *Ramus, Method, and the Decay of Dialogue.* Cambridge, Mass.: Harvard University Press, 1958, pp. 5, 13, 29, 38, 206, 302.

Suggests that Sidney's interest in Ramism may have come through his contact with Andreas Wechel (Ramus's printer), Théophile de Banos, Hubert Languet, and others in the Huguenot colony at Frankfurt am Main.

1103 OSBORN, ALBERT W. *Sir Philip Sidney en France.* Bibliothèque de la revue de littérature comparée, Vol. 84. Paris: Honoré Champion, 1932, 219 pp.

Explores the nature and extent of French influences on Sidney and his own influence on French literature, chiefly through translations of *Arcadia*. Devotes the first three of eight chapters to the French background of Sidney's works, examining his visits to France, the friendships formed there, and evidence for the writers and works he is likely to have known. Although finding "no marked sign of French genius" in Sidney, contends that the French influence was nevertheless "preponderant" in shaping his spirit. In the next two chapters, presents accounts of Sidney's translators and looks at the quality of the translations themselves. In the final three chapters, surveys his impact on the French during three periods: from his lifetime to 1623, from 1624 (when the first translations of *Arcadia* began to appear) to 1699, and from 1700 to the present. Argues that Jean Loisseau de Tourval's translation of a portion of Book II of *Arcadia* preceded and influenced the work of Baudoin (33) and Chappelain (32), and that de Tourval is the best translator of the

Twentieth Century

three. See also Legouis (1642). In an appendix, prints for the first time de Tourval's translation (53). Rejects Lancaster's thesis (1633, 1635) that Galaut knew the *Arcadia* before Baudoin's translation, arguing instead that the lost *Philoxène* of Antoine du Verdier was one of Sidney's sources. In discussing *Arcadia*, emphasizes its satire of romantic chivalry. Evaluates the evidence for Sidney's knowledge of Joachim du Bellay, Maurice Scève, Pierre de Ronsard, Charles de l'Éscluse, Henri Estienne, Louise de Coligny, and John and Francis Hotman. See responses by Goldman (532) and Lancaster (1634).

1104 OSBORN, JAMES M[ARHSALL]. *"Mica mica parva stella*: Sidney's Horoscope." *TLS*, 1 January 1971, pp. 17–18.
Notes that Sidney's horoscope was cast, not at his birth, but at age sixteen, which explains the disparity between its account of the date and time of his birth and that given by Sir Henry Sidney. The significance of the horoscope is in the sequence of "remarkable incidents" that Sidney reported to the astrologer as the basis for determining "scientifically" the moment of birth. These incidents, four hitherto unknown, include three illnesses and two instances of recognition by the Queen. The second illness corresponds to the 1562 small-pox epidemic and lends evidence to the claim that Sidney's face was scarred. The third illness of 1569–70 seems to have been conjunctivitis. The first appearance before the Queen came during her her 1566 visit to Oxford. The second came when Sidney delivered an oration in 1568, which revealed his assiduous scholarship and, in particular, his interest in astrology. Since the testimony of Moffet (2827) and evidence in *Astrophil and Stella* both suggest a distaste for astrology, conjectures that Sidney "matured" into a loathing for the subject. Suggests that the horoscope was cast by Thomas Allen (1542–1632). See a reply by Addey (975).

1105 ———. "New Light on Sir Philip Sidney." *TLS*, 30 April 1970, pp. 487–88.
Recapitulates the importance of the seventy-six pieces of Sidney correspondence sold at Sotheby's in June of 1967. See items 2738 and 2739. Presents evidence from the letters to suggest that Sidney was the author of *Certain Notes Concerning the State of the Prince of Orange and the Provinces of Holland and Zealand, as They Were in the Month of May 1577.* See also item 1108 and Howell (1061).

1106 ———. "The Osborn Collection, 1934–1974." *YULG* 49 (October 1974):154–70.
The published version of an address at the opening of the Osborn Exhibition in the Beinecke Library of Yale University, 11 October 1974.

Describes the purchase in 1967 of sixty-five letters to Sidney and the research that led to the writing of Osborn's biography (1108).

1107 ———. "Sidney and Pietro Bizari." *RenQ* 24 (Autumn 1971):344–54.

Prints the Italian text of a letter from Bizari to Languet, using it to argue against Gál's belief (1027) that Bizari and Sidney were friends. Notes, however, that they may have met in August of 1572 and/or in May 1577.

1108 ———. *Young Philip Sidney, 1572–1577*. Elizabethan Club, ser. 5. New Haven, Conn., and London: Yale University Press, 1972, 589 pp.

Based on the 1967 discovery of seventy-six hitherto unknown letters to Sidney (2738), closely traces, in twenty-four chapters and six appendices, his activities on the Continent during the period 1572–77. Details his reception at the French court, his contacts there, and his witnessing of the St. Bartholomew's Day Massacre. Traces his journey from Paris to Strasbourg and on to Heidelberg and Frankfurt am Main, describing his contacts with Andreas Wechel, Henri Estienne, Paulus Melissus Schedius, Jean Lobbetius, and Johannes Sturmius. Comments on Sidney's visit to Vienna in the summer of 1573 and his acquaintance with Jean de Vulcob, Jacques Bochetel, and Antonio Abondio. Follows Sidney to Bratislava in August 1573, back to Vienna, and then to Venice in November, remarking on his Venetian friendships with François Perrot de Mésières and Olbracht Laski. Traces Sidney's return to Venice from Padua in February 1574 to have his portrait painted by Veronese. Provides a record of Languet's advice to Sidney on politics and languages and assesses Sidney's abilities in foreign tongues. Also refers to Sidney's training in horsemanship with John Pietro Pugliano. Remarks on Sidney's illness in late September and his brief, and apparently disappointing, journey into Poland. Argues that Languet's introductory letter, with its praise of Sidney as an actor on the political stage of Europe, may have been a source of Naunton's remark (869) on Sidney and the Polish crown. Records Sidney's departure with Languet for Prague, where they arrived in late February 1575, stayed nine days, and then returned to Frankfurt via Dresden. Noting that Sidney was summoned back to England by Thomas Wilkes, acting for Leicester, traces his return, via Antwerp, in the latter part of May. Comments on the death of Ambrosia Sidney, on Sidney's involvement in the education of his brother Robert, and on his involvement with the preparations for Elizabeth's summer progress of 1575, providing an account of Elizabeth's visit to Kenilworth. Deals at length with Sidney's 1576 visit to Ireland and his contact with

Twentieth Century

the Earl of Essex, and records Sidney's visit to Dr. John Dee in January of 1577. Provides details of Sidney's embassy to Germany, including his trip to Prague, his audience with Emperor Rudolph II, and his conversation with Edmund Campion. Concludes with an analysis of Sidney's report of his embassy and with commentary on various marriage proposals, including one for a match between Sidney and Marie of Nassau. Records events following Sidney's return, mentioning the "Discourse on Irish Affairs," Sidney's visits to Wilton, and the demise of the dream of a Protestant League. In six appendices, examines Sidney's horoscope, his patent to bear arms in Italy, instructions for his embassy to Germany, the case for his authorship of *Certain Notes Concerning the State of the Prince of Orange*, his letter to Edward Denny, and Lobbetius's letter to him of 1 October 1581. See also Howell (1061) and Kervyn de Lettenhove (158).

1109 PATERSON, ANTOINETTE MANN. *The Infinite Worlds of Giordano Bruno*. American Lecture Series, 20. Springfield, Ill.: Charles C. Thomas, 1970, pp. 64, 100, 167, 193, 195.

Suggests that Sidney may have introduced Bruno to William Gilbert. Notes that Algernon Swinburne's "For the Feast of Giordano Bruno, Philosopher and Martyr" and "The Monument of Giordano Bruno" both contain allusions to Sidney as a friend of Bruno.

1110 PECK, D.C. "Raleigh, Sidney, Oxford, and the Catholics, 1579." *N&Q*, n.s. 25 (October 1978):427–31.

Quotes hitherto unpublished accounts of the August 1579 tennis-court quarrel, which accuse Oxford of plotting Sidney's murder. These documents, written by Lord Henry Howard and the Earl of Arundel, confirm Greville's account of the sequence of events.

1111 PETTI, ANTHONY G. *English Literary Hands from Chaucer to Dryden*. Cambridge, Mass.: Harvard University Press, 1977, pp. 1, 19, 32, 77; plate 27.

Notes that only one holograph of a Sidney poem exists, that Sidney's general correspondence is in "an extremely cramped sprawling hand," and that his handwriting goes through three "distinct and datable phases." Reproduces Sidney's 27 November 1585 letter to Walsingham, noting the locations of Sidney's holograph material and describing the general characteristics of his hand. See also Greg (197).

1112 PHILLIPS, JAMES E[MERSON]. "Daniel Rogers: A Neo-Latin Link Between the Pléiade and Sidney's 'Areopagus.'" In *Neo-Latin Poetry of the Sixteenth and Seventeenth Centuries*. Papers by James E. Phillips and Don Cameron Allen Presented at a Seminar Held on

October 17, 1964 at the Clark Library. Los Angeles: William Andrews Clark Memorial Library, 1965, pp. 5–28.

Documents Rogers's connections with the group of French intellectuals and artists who, in the 1560s, worked after the flourishing of the Pléiade in the 1550s and before that of Jean Antoine de Baïf's Academy in the 1570s. Argues that the concerns of this group—with finding a means to unify poetry and music, with neo-Platonism and "the Hellenistic spirit," with "divine" literature, and with religious "eirenicism," or "ecumenism"—were also the larger concerns of the Areopagus.

1113 ———. "George Buchanan and the Sidney Circle." *HLQ* 12 (November 1948):23–55.

Presents evidence for close connections between Buchanan and four members of the Sidney circle and for "closeness of thought and feeling" between Buchanan and Sidney regarding the French marriage. Marshals evidence for the high admiration that Sidney and his friends had for Buchanan as educator, political theorist, poet, and historian. Notes similarities between his *De Jure Regni* and *Arcadia*. Argues that the Sidney circle was not interested in Buchanan as a Latinist, but rather as a "divine" poet. Calls Buchanan a "member in absentia" of the circle.

1114 ———. Review of *Poets Patrons and Professors: Sir Philip Sidney, Daniel Rogers and the Leiden Humanists*, by J[an] A[drianus] van Dorsten. *JEGP* 63 (April 1964):341–43.

Notes the existence of a previously unrecorded Latin funeral elegy for Sidney composed by Daniel Rogers (2769).

1115 ———. "Spenser's Syncretistic Religious Imagery." *ELH* 36 (March 1969):110–30.

Cites Sidney's translation of *De la verité de la religion chrestienne* as evidence of his knowledge of sixteenth-century French religious syncretism. Argues that Sidney provided a link between Spenser and such syncretists through his personal contacts with du Plessis-Mornay, Daniel Rogers, and Giordano Bruno. Views the Areopagus as similar to the French Academies in its syncretic leanings.

1116 PIPER, DAVID. "The Chesterfield House Library Portraits." In *Evidence in Literary Scholarship: Essays in Memory of James Marshall Osborn*, edited by René Wellek and Alvaro Ribiero. New York: Oxford University Press; Oxford: Clarendon Press, 1979, pp. 179–95.

Notes that the collection at Chesterfield House includes "a contemporary version of a portrait of Sidney originated by John de Critz, c. 1585, and either by de Critz or from his workshop."

Twentieth Century

1117 POIRIER, MICHEL. *Sir Philip Sidney: Le chevalier poète élizabéthain.* Travaux et mémoires de l'Université de Lille, nouvelle série— Droit et lettres, 26. Lyon, France: Bibliothèque Universitaire de Lille, 1948, pp. 17–145, 253–283.
In Chapter 1 of Book 1, examines the background and "situation sociale" of Sidney's family, his schooling (inferring that he studied law after leaving Shrewsbury), his Continental travels, and his friendship with Languet in the formative years of 1573–74. In Chapter 2, assembles contemporary evidence, both visual and written, to provide a "portrait psychologique," concluding that, although not perfect, Sidney was morally superior to most of those surrounding him and was incompatible with his social milieu. In Chapter 3, argues that Sidney found love less in books than in his own heart, suggesting that the Old *Arcadia* shows evidence of a rivalry with his friend Dyer over "une jeune fille non identifiée" in Elizabeth's court and that the authenticity of Sidney's love for Lady Rich, as recorded in *Astrophil and Stella*, is confirmed by the revised *Arcadia*. In Chapter 4, locates the sources of Sidney's "moral ideas" primarily in Aristotle, Seneca, Castiglione, Elyot, and medieval notions of chivalry. Feels that a preference for the contemplative life, as expressed in *The Lady of May* and other early works, is "adolescent" and is later discarded in favor of a life of action. In Chapter 5, examines Sidney's political beliefs, assuming that he was passionately in love with order and hostile to all violent change. Claims that he was "original" only in supposing that the monarch's authority rests in a contract with the people, an idea that he may have derived from Continental thinkers or from Sir Francis Walsingham. Examines his pronouncements on the Irish question, on the proposed French match for Queen Elizabeth, on foreign relations with several European governments, and on Mary Stuart. In Chapter 6, surveys Sidney's frustrated attempts at political action, suggesting that his disfavor with the Queen may have arisen from his view of her monarchy as a human, not a divine, institution. In Chapter 7, investigates Sidney's religious beliefs, tracing in his writings an evolution from the secular to the religious and finding in his literary works an equilibrium between the Puritan and the humanistic tendencies of his age. In Chapter 1 of Book 3, looks at Sidney as patron, surveying the many works dedicated to him, noting that he was the only English writer with a European reputation, and discussing at length his relations with Spenser. See also item 703.

1118 PRICE, DAVID C. *Patrons and Musicians of the English Renaissance.* Cambridge: Cambridge University Press, 1981, pp. 97, 169–72.
Notes that musicians such as Thomas Paston, William Byrd, and the Kytson family of Hengrave all knew Sidney and had connections with his

circle. Drawing on account-books and letters, discusses the unusual interest in music in Henry Sidney and his offspring. Infers that Philip did not play an instrument but was interested in musical settings of poetry and private musical performances. Notes that William Byrd and Charles Tessier set some of Sidney's poetry, and that Sir Arthur Basset once recommended to Sidney the instrumentalist Thomas Richards.

1119 PROUTY, C[HARLES] T[YLER]. *George Gascoigne: Elizabethan Courtier, Soldier, and Poet*. New York: Columbia University Press, 1942, p. 172.
Noting Gascoigne's connection with Mary Sidney, suggests his possible friendship with Sidney himself.

1120 PURCELL, J[AMES] M[ARK]. "The Allegorical Meaning of Spenser's *Muiopotmos*." *PMLA* 46 (September 1931):945–46.
In replying to Lemmi (625) and Denkinger (1009), argues that there was no affair between Sidney and Penelope Rich and that her marriage to Lord Rich could have taken place at any time after 10 March 1581, though it most likely occurred in October. See also Stein (771).

1121 ———. "The Lost Veronese Portrait of Sir Philip Sidney." *TLS*, 31 October 1929, p. 873.
Points out that Wallace (1171) overlooked an 18 October 1595 letter "proving" that the portrait was in England in the late sixteenth century. Then cites a second letter in Collins (12), dated 1661, "suggesting" that the portrait was in Frankfurt, and explains why it might well have moved from Europe to England and back to the Continent. See replies by Smith (1156) and Wilson (1182).

1122 ———. "The Relations of Spenser and Sidney." *PMLA* 46 (September 1931):940.
In considering the depth of Sidney's relationship with Spenser, compares Harrison (556) with Behler (428), noting that the latter uses "the same and somewhat better material" to come to "conclusions somewhat opposed to those of Harrison."

1123 RAWSON, MAUD STEPNEY. *Penelope Rich and Her Circle*. London: Hutchinson, 1911, pp. 15–95.
Devotes four chapters to accounts of "The House of Sidney": "The Splendid Philip," focusing mainly on comments about marriage in the Languet correspondence; "The Fateful Marriage" between Penelope Devereux and Lord Rich, which was "done before anyone could prevent it"; and "The Starry Way," which reads *Astrophil and Stella* as evidence that "his heart was certainly laid bare by his pen."

Twentieth Century

1124 READ, CONYERS. *Lord Burghley and Queen Elizabeth*. London: Jonathan Cape; New York: Alfred A. Knopf, 1960, pp. 17, 125, 217, 324, 333.
Claims that Sidney spent "considerable time" in the Burghley household. Discusses Sidney's *Letter to the Queen* and quotes letters between Burghley and Leicester in which the latter insists that Sidney, not Burghley's son, should be governor of Flushing.

1125 ———. *Mr. Secretary Walsingham and the Policy of Queen Elizabeth*. 3 vols. Cambridge, Mass.: Harvard University Press; Oxford: Clarendon Press, 1925, 1:220, 299, 347; 2:20, 203; 3:75, 112, 116, 157, 167–68, 402, 423–24.
Discusses major events in Sidney's public career, such as his 1577 embassy to Rudolph II, his *Letter to the Queen* opposing the French marriage, his role in the Netherlands, and the debts left to Walsingham at Sidney's death. Suggests that, in 1583, Sidney was considered as a possible ambassador to the Scottish court and inquires whether Sidney's transmission to George Peckham of three million acres in the New World was to enable his own marriage to Frances Walsingham.

1126 REBHOLZ, RONALD A. *The Life of Fulke Greville, First Lord Brooke*. Oxford: Clarendon Press, 1971, pp. 50–52, 56–61, 75–77, 211–15, 326–28, and passim. Orig. a D.Phil. thesis, Worcester College, Oxford, 1964–1965.
Traces Greville's personal and literary relationship with Sidney, commenting on the almost legendary nature of the friendship. Suggests that Greville valued it more highly than did Sidney. Believes, *pace* Rees (1726), that Greville did the chapter summaries for the 1590 edition of *Arcadia*.

1127 REES, JOAN. "Fulke Greville's Epitaph on Sidney." *RES*, n.s. 19 (February 1968):47–51.
Summarizes a sixteenth-century letter in which Greville proposes a monument to Sidney, including inscriptions that have been lost. Reprints a critical commentary by John Coke on the proposed verses, which describes them as "sombre Grevillean poetry in the process of being hewn out."

1128 REES, JOAN, ed. *Selected Writings of Fulke Greville*. Athlone Renaissance Library. London: University of London, Athlone Press, 1973, pp. 1–7, 139–52, 174–76.
Comments on Greville's relationship with Sidney, printing selections from the *Life of Sidney* and providing a commentary. Contrasts the poetic style of the two authors.

1129 RENWICK, W[ILLIAM] L[INDSAY], ed. *Daphnaïda and Other Poems*, by Edmund Spenser. An Elizabethan Gallery, 4. London: Scholartis Press, 1929, pp. 190–92.

Sees Spenser's dedication of *Astrophel* to Sidney's widow as a clear indication that the relationship between Sidney and Lady Rich was understood by Sidney's contemporaries as "a purely literary *amour courtois* in which there was neither sin nor embarrassment for anyone."

1130 R[OBERTSON], J[EAN]. Review of *Sir Philip Sidney and the English Renaissance*, by John Buxton. *RES*, n.s. 7 (January 1956):69–73.

Reviews evidence on the relations between Sidney and Spenser, arguing that the men were not so close, personally or literarily, as Buxton asserts (998).

1131 ———. "Sidney and Bandello." *Library*, 5th ser. 21 (December 1966):326–28.

Describes a copy of the Boaistuau-Belleforest French translation of Bandello that contains inscriptions attributed to Sidney and Greville. Supplies further external evidence that the book belonged to Sidney at Shrewsbury School.

1132 ———. "Sir Philip Sidney and Lady Penelope Rich." *RES*, n.s. 15 (August 1964):296–97.

Collates two manuscripts of George Gifford's account of Sidney's death and suggests that a reference to "my Ladie Rich" in MS. Juel-Jensen, which is probably the earlier of the two, was excised from the later MS. Vitellius C 17.

1133 RÓNA, E[VA]. "Sir Philip Sidney and Hungary." *Annales Universitatis Scientiarum Budapestiensis de Rolando Eötvös Nominatae: Sectio Philologica* 2 (Spring 1960):46–50.

Argues that Sidney may have accompanied Charles de l'Éscluse to Hungary sometime in mid-1573.

1134 ROSCOE, THEODORA. "An Elizabethan Friendship." *Contemporary Review* 188 (December 1955):394–99.

Interweaves extracts from the Sidney-Languet correspondence with a derivative account of major events in Sidney's life, to compose a narrative of the progress of the two men's friendship from 1572 to Languet's death. Appealing to the poetry as reliable evidence of Sidney's feelings, claims that *Astrophil and Stella* tells us that, "when letters continued to arrive from Languet with news of European affairs, Sidney was in no

Twentieth Century

mood for politics," and that "Leave me O love" (*CS 32*) was prompted by Languet's death.

1135 ROSENBERG, ELEANOR. *Leicester, Patron of Letters*. New York: Columbia University Press, 1955, pp. 174, 175, 289, 319–21, 329–43, 349–50.
Discusses Sidney as a patron, claiming that dedications to him indicate that Leicester was grooming Sidney as his successor in political leadership and literary patronage. Comments on the collections of elegies for Sidney, on his acquaintance with Harvey, and on Nashe's disparagement of it.

1136 ROWE, KENNETH THORPE. "The Love of Sir Philip Sidney for the Countess of Pembroke." *Papers of the Michigan Academy of Science, Arts, and Letters* 25 (1940):579–95.
Responds to Sargent (1142), who claims that Sidney and Dyer were in competition for the love of Mary Sidney. Presents his own contention that both Mira in *Arcadia* and Amarillis in Dyer's poem of that name represent Queen Elizabeth, not Mary. Subjects Aubrey's innuendo (in 902) that Sidney "lay with his sister" to critical scrutiny in the context of Aubrey's general unreliability.

1137 ROWSE, A[LFRED] L[ESLIE]. *The Expansion of Elizabethan England*. New York: St. Martin's Press, 1955, pp. 66, 137, 193, 210, 236, 385, 386–88.
Comments on the prominence of the Sidneys in Elizabethan England, on Sir Henry's role in Ireland, and on Philip Sidney's interest in and support of voyages to America. Recounts Sidney's actions in the battles of Axel and Zutphen, commenting on the reaction to his death, both in England and on the Continent.

1138 ———. *Ralegh and the Throckmortons*. London: Macmillan & Co., 1962, pp. 70, 78, 124–25.
Discusses Sidney's connections at court, remarking on his joust with Sir Christopher Hatton on 2 February 1579.

1139 ROWSE, ALFRED L[ESLIE], and HARRISON, GEORGE B. "Sir Philip Sidney." In *Queen Elizabeth and Her Subjects*. London: G. Allen & Unwin, 1935, pp. 45–55.
Provides a succinct introduction to Sidney, arguing that "the man was greater than the achievement," with commentary on *Astrophil and Stella* ("unsurpassed" in its kind) and the *Defence* ("not particularly original").

Twentieth Century

1140 RUKEYSER, MURIEL. *The Traces of Thomas Hariot.* New York: Random House, 1971, pp. 72–74, 114.
Notes numerous connections between Sidney and Hariot. Also comments on the Ash Wednesday meeting between Sidney and Giordano Bruno in 1584 and on Bruno's apparently mocking attitude toward *Astrophil and Stella.*

1141 SALMON, J[OHN] H[EARSEY] M[cMILLAN]. *The French Religious Wars in English Political Thought.* Oxford: Clarendon Press, 1959, pp. 184–85.
In describing "personal links" between English statesmen and French political theorists such as Languet, du Plessis-Mornay, and the Hotmans, stresses that Sidney's was "the most obvious name in all this network of relationships."

1142 SARGENT, RALPH M[ILLAND]. *At the Court of Queen Elizabeth: The Life and Lyrics of Sir Edward Dyer.* London and New York: Oxford University Press, 1935, pp. 38–39, 40, 42–43, 47–48, 56–71.
Suggests that the friendship between Sidney and Dyer probably began in the winter of 1575–76, after Sidney's return from Italy. Believes that, in his "Mira" poems, Sidney was competing with Dyer for the love of Mary Sidney. Comments on visits that the two men made to John Dee and to the Low Countries in 1578 and on Sidney's interest in Frobisher's voyages. Views the Areopagus as an informal gathering of poets interested in exploring the possibilities of vernacular verse, drawing particular attention to the value of the group's consciously analytical approach to writing. See a response by Rowe (1136).

1143 SCHELLING, FELIX E[MMANUEL]. *The Queen's Progress and Other Elizabethan Sketches.* Boston and New York: Houghton Mifflin & Co., 1904, pp. 75–101.
In "An Old Time Friendship," discusses Greville's relationship with Sidney. Examines the *Life of Sidney*, describes the Whitsuntide tilts of 1581, notes Sidney's attempt to sail with Drake, and comments on the place of Sidney and Greville in the literary world of the times.

1144 SEAVER, PAUL S. *The Puritan Lectureships: The Politics of Religious Dissent, 1560–1662.* Stanford, Calif.: Stanford University Press, 1970, pp. 150, 211.
Notes that the Puritan James Stile, who held two London lectureships, had resigned them by 1582, "apparently to become chaplain to Sir Philip Sidney."

Twentieth Century

1145 SEDGWICK, HENRY DWIGHT. *In Praise of Gentlemen*. Boston: Little Brown & Co., 1935, pp. 100–105.
Praises Sidney as the model gentleman of the age, supporting the view with comments from Sidney's family and friends.

1146 SHELLEY, H[ENRY] C. "The Home of Sir Philip Sidney." *New England Magazine*, n.s. 23 (November 1900):275–83. Reprint. In *Critic* 43 (September 1903):221–31. Reprint. In *Literary Bypaths in Old England*. London: Grant Richards; Boston: Little, Brown & Co., 1909, pp. 57–81. Reprint, in shortened form. In *Book News Monthly* 32 (November 1914):473–75.
With the aim of conveying a sense of "an age of men long passed away," concentrates on the historical relics to be found at Penshurst, including Sidney's helmet and the "card table for which Elizabeth worked the embroidered top." Prints eight photographs, showing both the interior and the exterior.

1147 SHOOSMITH, EDWARD. "Sir Philip Sidney: A 'South Saxon.'" *Sussex County Magazine* 3 (December 1929):864–69.
Suggests that Sidney's name may be Sanskrit, meaning "perfection." Recounts his opposition to the Queen's French marriage plans and his death in battle, adducing evidence to demonstrate that "a good deal of medieval Sussex blood" ran in his veins.

1148 SIDNEY, MARY (d. 1904). *Historical Guide to Penshurst Place*. Tunbridge Wells, England: Goulden & Curry; London: Simpkin, Marshall, Hamilton, Kent & Co., 1903, pp. 15–47.
Discusses Sidney in the context of his family and its connection with Penshurst Place.

1149 SIMONINI, R[INALDO] C., Jr. *Italian Scholarship in Renaissance England*. University of North Carolina Studies in Comparative Literature, 3. Chapel Hill: University of North Carolina Press, 1952, pp. 20, 67, 95.
Comments on Sidney's knowledge of Italian, his disputation with Bruno on Ash Wednesday, 1584, and the "anti-Petrarchist tirade against sonnets to women" in Bruno's dedication to Sidney of his *Eroici furori*.

1150 SKRETKOWICZ, VICTOR, Jr. "Greville and Sidney: Biographical Addenda." *N&Q*, n.s. 21 (November 1974):408–10.
Discusses Sidney's relationship with Christopher Clifford. Suggests that Bryskett remained within the Sidney circle after 1580 and may have provided a link between Sidney and Spenser in the 1580s. Cites additional

evidence to show that Matthew Gwynne (reputed to be the editor of the 1590 *Arcadia*) was Fulke Greville's assistant in the late 1580s.

1151 SMIEJA, FLORIAN. "Poeta amgielski sięga po koronę polską." *Życie*, no. 50, 1950, p. 5.
Discusses the myth that Sidney was offered the Polish crown.

1152 SMITH, D[AVID] NICHOL. "Authors and Patrons." In *Shakespeare's England: An Account of the Life and Manners of His Age.* Vol. 2. Oxford: Clarendon Press, 1916, pp. 182–211.
Details Sidney's influence as a patron, listing books dedicated to him and noting contemporary statements which suggest that, after his death, writers had a harder lot.

1153 SMITH, G[EORGE] C[HARLES] MOORE. "Elizabeth, Daughter of Sir Philip Sidney." *N&Q*, 12th ser. 1 (5 February 1916):108.
Shows that Elizabeth was born 19 October 1585, explaining the cause of earlier errors.

1154 SMITH, G[EORGE] C[HARLES] MOORE, ed. Introduction to *Gabriel Harvey's Marginalia*. Stratford-upon-Avon: Shakespeare Head Press, 1913, pp. 18–20, 23, 27–31.
Recounts Harvey's first meeting with Sidney and his role in introducing Sidney to Spenser. Examines Harvey's correspondence with Spenser about the Areopagus, concluding that Harvey was not part of the circle. See also Harvey (1582).

1155 ———. Introduction to *Victoria, a Latin Comedy*, by Abraham Fraunce. Materialien zur Kunde des älteren englischen Dramas. Louvain, Belgium: A. Uystpruyst; Leipzig: O. Harrassowitz; London: David Nutt, 1906, pp. ix–xxxviii passim.
Discusses Fraunce's relationship with Sidney. Considers their days at Shrewsbury School, Sidney's financial support for Fraunce at Cambridge, the beginning of their personal friendship in 1581 or 1582, and Sidney's patronage of Fraunce's logical treatises. Discusses the dating of the verses on Sidney at the end of Fraunce's *Insignium* and the authorship of the five songs at the end of the first quarto of *Astrophil and Stella* (60).

1156 SMITH, G[EORGE] C[HARLES] MOORE. "The Lost Veronese Portrait of Sir Philip Sidney." *TLS*, 7 November 1929, p. 898.
Challenges Purcell (1121), claiming that the reference to Veronese in a 1595 letter by Rowland Whyte involved a portrait of Languet, not of Sidney. See also Wilson (1182).

Twentieth Century

1157 STAFFORD, JOHN. "The Social Status of Renaissance Literary Critics." *University of Texas Studies in English* 25 (1945–46):72–97.
Discusses shifts in the makeup of the ruling class from the Middle Ages to the Renaissance. Notes that Sidney combines the old ideal with the new.

1158 STEVENSON, GEORGE, ed. Introduction to *Poems of Alexander Montgomerie*. Supplementary Volume. Scottish Text Society, 59. Edinburgh and London: William Blackwood & Sons, 1910, pp. lix–lxii.
Cites documentary evidence on Sidney's connections with the Scottish court, noting James VI's admiration for him and his poetry and Sidney's personal acquaintance with the Master of Gray.

1159 STONE, LAWRENCE. *The Crisis of the Aristocracy, 1558–1641*. Oxford: Clarendon Press, 1965, pp. 224, 477, 643, 693–95, 704, 747.
Uses Sidney as an example of how the lure of the court turned nobles into "shameless mendicants." Mentions the Sidney-Walsingham marriage contract as containing a typical "saving clause," and discusses Sidney's importance as a patron. Also discusses Elizabeth's reproof of him for insulting the Earl of Oxford during a tennis-court incident in 1579.

1160 STRONG, ROY [C.]. *National Portrait Gallery Tudor & Jacobean Portraits*. 2 vols. London: Her Majesty's Stationery Office, 1969, 1:197, 290–93; 2:plates 567–74.
Prints a brief life of Sidney and identifies two kinds of portraits of him: Type A, which shows him at three-quarters length with his right hand on his hip and his left on the hilt of his sword (examples at Warwick Castle, Woburn Abbey, Longleat, and Penshurst); and Type B, which shows his head and shoulders after an original by John de Critz (examples at Knebworth, Penshurst, Hall i' th' Wood Museum, and Blickling Hall). Notes that engravings by Crispin van de Passe and Renold Elstrack are of Type B. Provides a thorough description of three works in the National Portrait Gallery sometimes said to represent Sidney: one actually of his brother Robert, one of an unknown gentleman, and an eighteenth-century copy of an authentic Type A portrait of Sidney. Also lists lost and spurious portraits of him. Among the plates, reproduces four works of Type A, three of Type B, and the two misidentified paintings in the National Portrait Gallery. See also Judson (1075).

1161 STRONG, R[OY] C., and van DORSTEN, J[AN] A[DRIANUS]. *Leicester's Triumph*. Publications of the Sir Thomas Browne Institute, Special Series, 2. London: Oxford University Press; Leiden, Netherlands: Leiden University Press, 1964, pp. 8–11, 14, 15, 18, 27, 35, 42, 56, 58, 62.

In detailing the failure of Leicester's Governor Generalship in the Netherlands in 1585–86, touches on Sidney's role, chiefly as a "mediator" whose close friendship with William of Orange was instrumental in "welding the Orange-Leicester circles into ever closer alignment" in the late 1570s and in softening the impact of Leicester's extravagances in 1585–86.

1162 THOMAS, EDWARD. *Feminine Influence on the Poets*. London: Martin Secker, 1910, pp. 137–40, 235–37.

Notes Mary Sidney's collaboration with her brother on the *Psalms* and her role in revising *Arcadia*. Suggests that Sidney's wife Frances "added to the cause of the sonnets" by "doubling the barrier . . . between [Sidney] and Stella" and that Penelope Devereux's marriage provided the impetus for him to begin *Astrophil and Stella*.

1163 TOOLEY, C.W. "Sidney's Chair." *N&Q*, 9th ser. 5 (12 May 1900):377.

Notes that Sidney's chair is mentioned in Hone's *Table Book* as having been at Penshurst. Inquires about its current location.

1164 TUVE, ROSEMOND. "'Spenserus.'" In *Essays in English Literature from the Renaissance to the Victorian Age Presented to A.S.P. Woodhouse, 1964*, edited by Millar Maclure and F.W. Watt. Toronto: University of Toronto Press, 1964, pp. 3–25.

Discusses Spenser's connection with the Bedford and Russell families, noting in turn their connection with the Sidney/Dudley group. Also discusses Spenser's attitude toward the death of Sidney in *The Ruins of Time*.

1165 van DORSTEN, JAN [ADRIANUS]. "Literary Patronage in Elizabethan England: The Early Phase." In *Patronage in the Renaissance*, edited by Guy Fitch Lytle and Stephen Orgel. Princeton, N.J.: Princeton University Press, 1981, pp. 191–206.

Claims that "no matter how hard one tries to look for alternatives, the new poetry had only one patron: Sidney." Surveys the "inconclusive" evidence for his activities in the "puzzling" years before 1579, contending that his greatest importance is "in terms of international hopes and expectations." Reexamines evidence of Sidney's connection with Spenser, noting that the two "shared a literary ideology" that each seems to have acquired independently from abroad, and concluding that either may have influenced the other. Also reviews evidence about the Areopagus, suggesting that Spenser's *Ruins of Time* contains a "veiled and intimate record of the first Areopagitican experiments."

1166 ———. *Poets, Patrons, and Professors: Sir Philip Sidney, Daniel Rogers, and the Leiden Humanists*. Publications of the Sir Thomas Browne Institute, Leiden. General Series, 2. Leiden, Netherlands: Leiden University Press; London: Oxford University Press, 1962, pp. 23, 29–33, 36–41, 47–58, 60–67, 69–70, 77–169 passim.

Sees the University of Leiden and the Sidney circle as central to the literary, scholarly, and political connnections between England and the Netherlands during the 1570s and 1580s. In Part 1, focuses on Daniel Rogers as an emissary between the two cultures. Includes Rogers with Sidney in the group of Englishmen interested in Ireland, noting that the first English work dedicated to Sidney was John Derricke's poem *The Image of Ireland*. Lists Continental humanists whom Sidney is known to have met in France, Germany, and Austria during his travels of 1572–75, comparing Jan van Hout's defence of Dutch poetry with Sidney's *Defence*. Arguing that Rogers's connection with Sidney may well antedate his 1575 poem "Ad Philippum Sydnaeum Illustrissimae Spei et Indoli Iuvenem" (item 2828), traces evidence of their early friendship and their common interest in religious poetry, particularly that of George Buchanan. In discussing Sidney's embassy to Germany in 1577, details his contacts with humanists such as Languet, Paulus Melissus, and Lambertus Danaeus (who dedicated his *Geographiae Poeticae* to Sidney). Argues that Rogers's poem "In effigiem . . . Sydnaei" (2828) was written about a lost portrait by Veronese. In pondering the Protestant politics of the humanists, notes that George Gilpin's *Beehive of the Romish Church* was dedicated to Sidney. Discusses the biographical details revealed by Rogers's long poem "Ad Philippum Sidnaeum Illustrissimae Indolis ac Virtutis Iuvenem" (2828), which suggests that, in early 1579, Dyer, Greville, and Sidney were discussing "law, God, or moral good," not poetry. In Part 2, documents Sidney's contact with Dominicus Baudius, Georgius Benedicti, Hieronymus Groslotius, Scipio Gentili, Paulus Melissus, Janus Dousa and his son, and perhaps Arnoldus Eickius during a 1585 visit of the Leiden humanists to England, noting that the younger Dousa made "his literary contact with Sidney's milieu through Jean Hotman." Points out that, in the late 1570s, before any of his major English works had been written, Sidney was already known on the

Continent as a poet. From evidence that he wrote early works in Latin, Greek, French, and Italian, concludes that lost juvenilia in these tongues was the basis of his initial literary reputation. Discusses his correspondence with Justus Lipsius, noting that Sidney was his patron and arguing that they first met in 1577, well before Lipsius dedicated to him *De Recta Pronunciatione Latinae Linguae Dialogus*. Discusses the context in which the flood of elegies for Sidney was produced after his death and the need for a Protestant hero in England. Focuses on memorial poetry and letters by the Leiden humanists, noting that Baudius was with Sidney when he died, that he called other Dutch friends to write elegies, and that he offered to write a life of Sidney, which never appeared. Translates and discusses elegies by Baudius, Groslotius, Rogers, Melissus, Benedicti, and Dousa and his son. Distinguishes the volume *Epitaphia in Mortem Sidneij* (2747) from the university collections published in England, noting that it was not prepared by a university printer and was entirely the work of one author, Benedicti. Points out that, except for Groslotius, no Continental writers outside the immediate Leiden circle wrote commemorative verses. Sees the period between the founding of the University of Leiden in 1575 and Sidney's death as one of "experiments towards a 'national' poetry in an international system of service to the state and literary performance." In Appendix 1 and 2, prints the Latin originals of poems and letters discussed in the book, some of which had not been previously recorded.

1167 ———. "Sidney and Languet." *HLQ* 29 (May 1966):215–22.
Offers "preliminary conclusions," principally regarding Sidney's 1574 journey to Poland and his 1577 German embassy, based on eight unpublished letters in the Languet collection in the Bibliothèque Nationale, stressing the formative influence of Languet on Sidney's "political aspirations."

1168 WAINEWRIGHT, JOHN B. "Hangleton." *N&Q*, 11th ser. 11 (24 April 1915):318.
Queries when and how "the isolated church of Hangleton," near Brighton, came into Sidney's possession.

1169 ———. "Sir Philip Sidney's Personal Appearance." *N&Q*, 12th ser. 7 (23 October 1920):329.
Cites several passages from Robert Southey's commonplace book that comment on Ben Jonson's claim that Sidney "was no pleasant man in countenance."

Twentieth Century

1170 WALLACE, ARCHER. "One Crowded Hour of Glorious Life." In *Men Who Played the Game*. New York: Richard R. Smith, 1931, pp. 1–8.

Sketches Sidney's life, with special praise for *Arcadia*.

1171 WALLACE, MALCOLM WILLIAM. *The Life of Sir Philip Sidney*. Cambridge: Cambridge University Press, 1915, 434 pp.

Aims to place Sidney's life more firmly in its historical context than had Bourne (318). In Chapter 1, examines Sidney's family background, tracing his love of learning to his mother. In Chapter 2, details legal impediments to his attainment, as a child, of the incumbancy of Whitford and the office of prebend in Llangulo. In Chapters 3 and 4, follows Thomas Marshall's manuscript record of Sidney's expenses from December 1565 to Michaelmas 1566 (see 1172) to describe life at Shrewsbury School and to speculate about Sidney's participation in the Queen's August 1566 visit to Kenilworth and Oxford. In Chapters 5–6, recounts Sir Henry's tribulations in Ireland from 1566 to 1571 and the failed negotiations for Sidney's marriage to Anne Cecil. Describes the curriculum at Oxford in the 1570s, and sketches several of Sidney's contemporaries there, offering evidence that Sidney also studied at Cambridge, where he may have met Spenser. In Chapter 7, details the experiences of May–September 1572, when Sidney was in Paris to attend the marriage of Charles IX's sister. Records his friendly reception by the French King, noting the famous men whom he met and commenting on the St. Bartholomew's Day Massacre. In Chapter 8, accounts for Sidney's Continental tour of 1572–75 and his contacts with leading intellectuals of the day. Stresses the influence of Languet on Sidney's moral, intellectual, and political development. In Chapter 9, covers Sidney's tenure at court from 1575 to 1577, seeking to locate his first meeting with Penelope Devereux. Recounts the "project of marriage" with Lord Berkeley's daughter; lays to rest the myth that Sidney was offered the Polish crown; and traces his movements in Ireland in the autumn of 1576. In Chapter 10, discusses Sidney's 1577 embassy to Germany, assessing his anti-Catholic feelings, particularly in light of his meeting with Edmund Campion. Recounts his warm reception by William of Orange and the proposed marriage with his sister. Also analyzes Sidney's "Discourse on Irish Affairs." In Chapter 11, concentrates on "thwarted plans and disappointed hopes" in the period between Sidney's return from Ireland and the Oxford quarrel, commenting on the *Letter to the Queen*. Describes the visit by Casimir and Languet to raise support for the Protestant League, analyzing Elizabeth's attitude toward the project. In Chapters 12–13, focuses on the literary activities that enlivened the "inaction and gloom" of the year 1580. Calls *The Lady of May* "slight." Examines the Areopagus, seeing Sidney's relations with Spenser and others at Cambridge as "much more intimate . . . than has ordinarily been supposed," but regarding accounts of his later connections with Spenser as "exaggerated." Dates *Arcadia* in 1580, discussing its influence, its topical references, and its style. Suggests that the *Defence* was composed over a period of three years and that Gosson was not "in any sense responsible" for Sidney's decision to write it. Provides a biographical reading of *Astrophil and Stella*, based on the known relations between Sidney and Penelope Devereux between 1577 and 1581. Makes much of material omitted from the earliest editions but restored in 1598, including Sonnet 24 on the name "Rich." Treats "Leave me, O Love" (*CS 32*) as a fitting conclusion, since Sidney's aim in the sequence was "self mastery." In Chapter 14, considers Sidney's election to Parliament in 1581 and his service on the committee that stiffened laws against recusants; his participation in *The Four Foster Children of Desire*; his attendance on Don Antonio of Portugal; and his attempts to profit from the forfeiture of recusants' estates. In Chapter 15, traces a shift in Sidney's interests from the affairs of the Netherlands to those of Ireland and Wales, noting his desire to participate in the seafaring and colonizing projects of Drake and Gilbert and his efforts to become Master of Ordnance. In Chapter 16, considers the circumstances surrounding Sidney's marriage to Frances Walsingham and signs of his increasing prominence as a public figure, notably his continuing activities on behalf of the Protestants in the Netherlands, his interest in Scottish affairs, and his "intimate contact" with Bruno. In Chapter 17, examines Sidney's aborted embassy to France in 1584 and his service in the Parliament called after the Throckmorton plot. Devotes Chapter 18 to events preceding Sidney's departure for the Netherlands in November 1585, including accounts of his translations of the Psalms and du Plessis-Mornay's *Trueness of the Christian Religion*, his lost translations of du Bartas and Aristotle, and his *Defence of Leicester*. In the final three chapters, covers his govenorship of Flushing; his military actions in the Netherlands; and his wounding, death, and funeral. In a "Postscript," concludes that there is "a large measure of truth in" the popular conception of his character and that "his greatness is not in his works but in his life." In two appendices, prints Thomas Marshall's book of accounts and provides notes on fourteen extant portraits of Sidney. Includes an incomplete and sometimes erroneous index of proper names. See replies by Tenison (780) and Purcell (1121).

Twentieth Century

1172 ———. "Philip Sidney at Shrewsbury School." *University Magazine*
10 (February 1911):110–31.
Provides a brief history of Shrewsbury, describing routine life there in
the 1560s based on the ordinances of Thomas Ashton. Describes the
"ruinous timber houses," the daily regimen, the sports, and the course of
instruction, which was "almost entirely confined to Latin." Examines the
account book of Sidney's servant Thomas Marshall, which gives "many
of the details of Philip's life" from December 1565 to Michaelmas 1566.
Included are costs for clothing, personal care, books, and illnesses.
Considers the influence exerted on Sidney by the characters of his father
and mother. See also item 1171.

1173 WARD, B[ERNARD] M[ORDAUNT]. *The Seventeenth Earl of
Oxford, 1550–1604, from Contemporary Documents*. London: John
Murray, 1928, pp. 165–74, 359–67, and passim.
Discusses at length the tennis-court quarrel, noting that the "only two"
sources of information are biased toward Sidney and claiming to publish
"for the first time *in full*" an English translation of Languet's comments,
which make it "impossible to clear Sidney of all blame." In Appendix D,
presents evidence that the figure named Willy in Spenser's *Tears of the
Muses* represents Sidney.

1174 WARNER, OLIVER. *English Literature: A Portrait Gallery*. London:
Chatto & Windus, 1964, pp. 16–17.
Along with a portrait of Sidney painted in 1577 by an unknown artist,
includes a brief life of Sidney and succinct critical comments on his
works.

1175 WARREN, C[LARENCE] HENRY. *Sir Philip Sidney: A Study in
Conflict*. London: Thomas Nelson, 1936, 250 pp.
A popularized life of Sidney, without documentation of any sort.
Includes chapters focusing on his childhood and schooling; his
European tour; his embassy to Germany and activity at court in the late
1570s; his *Letter to the Queen* and role in the French marriage negotiations; *Astrophil and Stella* and his early relationships with women; his
period of literary work and of relative political inactivity in the early
1580s; his roles in Parliament and the Ordnance Office and his renewed
diplomatic activity in the mid 1580s, along with his interest in Drake's
voyages; and his service and death in the Netherlands. In an epilogue,
describes his funeral and the financial difficulties attendant upon it. Sees
Sidney's life as a constant conflict between the demands of "art" and of
"action," between the life of a poet and that of a soldier. On the basis of
Sidney's letters to Languet between 1575 and 1578, argues that he was

in love in this period. Views the verse of *Arcadia* largely as a poetic exercise with little merit, and sees the *Defence* as defending the imaginative life. Reads *Astrophil and Stella* biographically, suggesting that "Stella" is a composite of Penelope Rich and the unknown woman with whom Sidney was in love in the 1570s and concluding that *Certain Sonnets* 31 and 32 provide a proper ending for the sequence.

1176 ———. "Sir Philip Sidney." In *The Great Tudors*, edited by Katharine Garvin. New York: E.P. Dutton & Co., 1935, pp. 361–75.

Sees Sidney as torn between the life of a courtier and the profession of writer. Reads *Astrophil and Stella* biographically.

1177 WESTCOTT, ALLAN FERGUSON, ed. *New Poems by James I of England, from a Hitherto Unpublished Manuscript (Add. 24195) in the British Museum.* Columbia University Studies in English. New York: Columbia University Press, 1911, pp. lxxix–lxxx, 29, 88, 89, 92, 98.

Notes that Sidney was "the one English poet of the preceding generation to whom the King felt free to pay tribute." Offers evidence that James and Sidney "were on friendly terms and that communication had passed between them."

1178 WHIGHAM, FRANK. *Ambition and Privilege: The Social Tropes of Elizabethan Courtesy Theory.* Berkeley, Los Angeles, and London: University of California Press, 1984, pp. 21, 30, 75, 87, 100, 213.

In discussing the social environment of the Elizabethan court, notes that Sidney's failure to receive extensive royal patronage was not unusual. Comments on the social and courtly implication of Sidney's view of his travels as a means of military reconnaissance.

1179 WILES, A[MERICUS] G[EORGE] D[AVID]. "Sir Philip Sidney: The English Huguenot." *Transactions of the Huguenot Society of South Carolina*, no. 45, 1940, pp. 24–41.

Argues that the "two prominent factors" in Sidney's "deep and lasting" Protestantism are his schooling at Shrewsbury and his witnessing of the St. Bartholomew's Day Massacre. Collects from the correspondence evidence of his "abiding interest in the cause of the Huguenots in France."

1180 WILLIAMSON, G[EORGE] C[HARLES]. "Some Notes on the Portraits of Sir Philip Sidney." *The Connoisseur: An Illustrated Magazine for Collectors* 59 (January–April 1921):217–25.

Considers twenty-two portraits, drawings, and engravings said to be of Sidney. Using as a "touchstone" three portraits by Isaac Oliver, accepts as

Twentieth Century

genuine or probably genuine more than one-half of them, although without any detailed analysis. Offers some evidence for changing the attribution of certain paintings. See also Judson (1075) and Siebeck (757).

1181 WILSON, CHARLES [HENRY]. *Queen Elizabeth and the Revolt of the Netherlands.* London: Macmillan & Co.; Berkeley: University of California Press, 1970, pp. 32, 53, 55, 57, 88–89, 95, 98.
Touches on Sidney's ties to the Leiden humanists, his discussions with William of Orange in 1577, and his service in the Netherlands in 1585–86.

1182 WILSON, MONA. "The Lost Veronese Portrait of Sir Philip Sidney." *TLS*, 7 November 1929, p. 898.
Takes issue with Purcell (1121), claiming that Rowland Whyte's 1595 letter refers to a portrait of Languet. Also draws attention to Languet's letters to Sidney of 11 June 1574 and 6 June 1575, which might indicate that the portrait that Algernon Sidney sought from Frankfurt in 1661 was a copy and not the original. See also Smith (1156).

1183 WILSON, VIOLET A. *Queen Elizabeth's Maids of Honour and Ladies of the Privy Chamber.* London: John Land, 1922, pp. 103–6, 124–27, 136, 145–47, 211, 217, 232, 266.
Alludes to Sidney's role at court, quoting *Astrophil and Stella* as evidence, in the context of characterizing the life there of several of Elizabeth's maids—e.g., "the Maids of Honour were somewhat aggrieved that three such popular young men as Philip Sidney, Fulke Greville and Edward Dyer should be so indifferent to their charms."

1184 WOODEN, WARREN W. Introduction to *The Life of the Renowned Sir Philip Sidney (1652).* Delmar, N.Y.: Scholars' Facsimiles & Reprints, 1984, pp. i–xix.
In reprinting Greville's *Life* (863), discusses matters of dating, text, themes, and "Design and Artistry," guided throughout by the premise that "the moral intent and exemplary function . . . are paramount and consistent." Argues that the "underlying form and traditional structure" of the *Life* derive from the classical demonstrative oration.

1185 WOODWARD, DANIEL H. "Thomas Fuller, William Dugard, and the Pseudonymous Life of Sidney (1655)." *PBSA* 62 (Fourth Quarter 1968):501–10.
Argues that Fuller wrote the life of Sidney prefixed to the 1655 *Arcadia* (9) and that the biography was commissioned by Dugard, the printer. See a rebuttal by Juel-Jensen (1076).

1186 ZANDVOORT, R[EINARD] W[ILLEM]. Review of *Sir Philip Sidney*, by Mona Wilson, and of *Astrophil and Stella*, edited by Mona Wilson. *ES* 13 (October 1931):194–99.
In judging Wilson's portrait of Sidney too "idealistic," argues that Sidney did, in fact, accept money from recusant forfeitures and notes that he profited from several benefices.

1187 ———. "Sidney in Austria." *WBEP* 66 (1958):227–45.
Largely from Languet's correspondence, culls evidence regarding the period from June 1573 to February 1575, when Sidney used Vienna as a "base and starting point" for studying the affairs of central Europe. Surveys the friendships made, the contemporary events mentioned in the letters, and Sidney's probable activities in Vienna when not travelling. Citing several passages omitted from Pears's translation (183), finds that while the exchange is "in part at least, a rhetorical exercise, in which each correspondent casts himself for a set role," Sidney's letters show "a sincere and loving regard for his master."

1188 [ZANDVOORT, REINARD WILLEM.] "Sir Philip Sidney: 1554—November 30—1954." *ES* 35 (1954):262–63.
Pays quatercentenary tribute to Sidney.

1189 ZINS, HENRYK. "Philip Sidney a Polska" [Philip Sidney and Poland]. *KN* 21, no. 2 (1974):147–57.
Argues that Sidney was impressed by the Polish form of government and that this interest led him to Cracow in 1574. Suggests that Sidney considered an invitation to take part in the next Polish election and that Elizabeth knew of his interest.

1190 ———. "Poeta Philip Sidney: Angielski Pretendent do Tronu Polskiego?" *Przeglad Humanistyczny* 18, no. 8 (1974):83–95.
Considers the myth that Sidney was once offered the crown of Poland. Includes a discussion of political elements in *Arcadia*, examining Sidney's political theory in the context of Huguenot and radical Protestant works on theories of monarchy, including *Vindiciae contra Tyrannos* and Buchanan's *De Jure Regni*.

Studies of Arcadia

---

1. ORIGINAL *ARCADIA* AND COMPARISONS WITH THE REVISED EDITIONS

Twentieth Century

1191 AKISHINO, KENICHI. "Sir Philip Sidney no *The Old Arcadia* niokeru 'Dokutsu' no Imi" [Significance of the Cave in Sidney's *The Old Arcadia*]. *Eigo Eibungaku Kenkyu*, no. 25, 1980, pp. 1–19.
Not seen. Cited as item 111 in "The 1980 Bibliography," *Renaissance Bulletin*, no. 10, 1983, p. 33

1192 ASTELL, ANN W. "Sidney's Didactic Method in the *Old Arcadia*." *SEL* 24 (Winter 1984):39–51.
Notes a divided response to the ending of the Old *Arcadia*, with one group of readers assuming that Sidney's didactic meaning is clear and another assuming there is no single lesson. On the basis of theories in the *Defence*, argues that Sidney teaches by "enabling his audience to discover the truth about themselves through their imaginative engagement" in the work. Follows Robinson (1742) in stressing the importance of plot as "the poet's way of letting us see what he means." By retelling the story from different perspectives at the trial, Sidney forces readers to confront their "own blindness" and their "willingness to collaborate," and thus creates a "split reader" who is moved in two directions simultaneously. This bifurcation is "externalized in the two trial judges." Through Euarchus, the readers judge themselves, and only at the end of the trial do they earn the right to pardon themselves.

1193 BARKER, WILLIAM. "Three Essays on the Rhetorical Tradition." Ph.D. diss., Brandeis University, 1968, 151 pp.
Examines the traditional ambivalence about the value of rhetoric, considering the ways in which characters in the Old *Arcadia* move one another with amorous and political speeches. Points out that they are ignorant of something the narrator and the readers understand: "that a *logos* beyond words is ordering . . . their world." Draws parallels with the Mutability Cantos in Spenser's *Faerie Queene*. See *DA* 29 (February 1969):2700A.

1194 BAUGHAN, DENVER EWING. "Sidney's *Defence of the Earl of Leicester* and the Revised *Arcadia*." *JEGP* 51 (January 1952):35–41.
Points out that, in revising the Old *Arcadia*, Sidney added a great deal of genealogical information, which links characters in several of the new episodes. Finds among the Sidneys a strong interest in matchmaking and noble ancestry, which is reflected in Sidney's *Defence of Leicester*. Suggests that this work gave Sidney the idea for the genealogical additions to *Arcadia* and that the revised version must therefore be dated after it.

1195 ———. "Sir Philip Sidney and the Two Versions of the *Arcadia*." Ph.D. diss., Yale University, 1934, 160 pp.
Compares the two drafts of *Arcadia*, arguing that revisions in the original version were dictated by Sidney's interest in noble birth and powerful family connections, in Machiavellian politics and war, and in courtly graces and conventions.

1196 BEATY, FREDERICK L. "Lodge's *Forbonius and Prisceria* and Sidney's *Arcadia*." *ES* 49 (February 1968):39–45.
Considers the circulation of the Old *Arcadia* during Sidney's lifetime, arguing that Lodge had seen one of the manuscripts before writing his own romance, which was published with a dedication to Sidney in 1584. Enumerates parallels between the works in plot, poetic form, phrasing, and prose style. Notes that Lodge and Sidney both attended Oxford and wrote replies to Gosson's *School of Abuse*, and offers evidence that Lodge may have known Sidney personally.

1197 BECKETT, ROBERT DUDLEY. "The Narrative Structure of the Old *Arcadia* and the New *Arcadia* of Sir Philip Sidney: An Analytic Comparison." Ph.D. diss., University of Colorado, 1967, 200 pp.
Compares the two versions, considering narrative technique, the arrangement of episodes, generic classifications, and characterization. Observes that the Old *Arcadia* follows the pattern of comedy, has an

Twentieth Century

obtrusive narrator, and is unified as to kinds of events, moods, themes, and characters. Notes that the New *Arcadia* is not so consistent or unified, has an unobtrusive narrator, and is a mingling of comic and tragic romance. Dates the New *Arcadia* after the *Defence* and the Old *Arcadia* before it, suggesting that Sidney may have left the New *Arcadia* unfinished because he was dissatisfied with its flawed structure. See *DA* 28 (March 1968):3630A–31A.

1198 BEESE, MARGARET. "Manuscripts of Sidney's *Arcadia*." *TLS*, 4 May 1940, p. 224.
Announces the discovery of two manuscripts of the Old *Arcadia*: 1) British Museum MS. Add. 41,498, which originally belonged to Sir Henry Lee and contains "the bulk of the poetry . . . and a long passage of prose"; and 2) Bodleian MS. Jesus C.L., which contains an imperfect copy of the entire text and probably belonged to Lord Herbert of Cherbury.

1199 BERREY, CARYL KADELL. "The Inward Turn of Character: From Rhetorical to Psychological Characterization in Sidney's *Old and New Arcadia*." Ph.D. diss., St. Louis University, 1980, 320 pp.
Drawing on Kellogg and Scholes's distinction between "a more outward, rhetorically conceived kind of narration peopled by orators" and "a more interiorized, psychological projection of human beings in a fictional world," traces Sidney's interest in the "interiority" of his characters. In the Old *Arcadia*, finds that "psychological characterization vies unsuccessfully with rhetorical characterization," winning out only in the depiction of Gynecia. Relates the narrator's own rhetorical stance to Sidney's interest in "character as speechmaker." In the New *Arcadia*, finds a shift in emphasis "from ethos to pathos," evident in the addition of a number of "pathetic histories," which allow the psychological method of characterization to dominate. In the Captivity Episode, "the imprisoned characters defeat the less interiorized, polemic-bound Cecropia because of their moral and psychological integrity, while the military combatants intertwine psyches on the field of blood. . . ." Feels that Sidney's tendency to juxtapose "unequal styles of characterization" may have provided one impediment to his completion of the revised version. See *DAI* 42 (October 1981):1642A–43A.

1200 BOAS, FREDERICK S[AMUEL]. *Sir Philip Sidney, Representative Elizabethan: His Life and Writings.* London: Staples Press, 1955, pp. 57–120.
Provides plot summaries of both versions of *Arcadia* and standard information on manuscripts, printed editions (through the year 1926),

sources, and influence. Evaluates the merits of the two versions, noting the increased range of observation apparent in the similes of the revision. See also item 436.

1201 BORINSKI, LUDWIG. "Die englische Prosaliteratur des 16. Jahrhunderts." In *Literatur der Renaissance*, by Ludwig Borinski and Claus Uhlig. Studienreihe Englisch, 23. Düsseldorf, Germany: August Bagel Verlag; Bern, Switzerland: Francke Verlag, 1975, pp. 56–62.

Reviews sources of *Arcadia* and the ways in which it mingles literary traditions and acts as a model for later hybrids of the same sort, such as d'Urfé's *Astrée*. Considers Sidney's modernization of conventions such as courtly love, chivalric combat, and the heroic journey of adventure. Also considers the topical allegory and Sidney's preoccupation with politics, noting ways in which his views of statecraft are modern rather than medieval. Regards the original version as the first psychologically acute comic novel in English. Discusses prose works by other authors that show the influence of *Arcadia*, even before its first publication in 1590.

1202 BRIE, FRIEDRICH. *Sidneys "Arcadia," eine Studie zur englischen Renaissance.* Quellen und Forschungen zur Sprach- und Kulturgeschichte der germanischen Völker, 124. Strassburg: Karl J. Trübner, 1918, 346 pp.

In Chapters 1 and 2, compares the Old *Arcadia* with the New and discusses the 1590 and 1593 editions. Attempts to date the original version. In Chapters 3 and 4, examines Sidney's aims in *Arcadia*, noting his deathbed wish that it be burned. From the *Defence* infers that he intended to teach through characters who allegorize various virtues and vices. Compares similar aims in Spenser and other Elizabethan writers, tracing such allegories back through the humanists to antiquity. Considers Sidney's political aims and interests, relating Euarchus's attempts to protect Greece from foreign invasion to the Spanish threat in Sidney's day and to the Roman threat to Greece in the third century B.C. (as described by Polybius). Ponders the impact of Renaissance political writers and of ancient historians and philosophers on *Arcadia*, stressing Aristotle's *Politics* and Xenophon's *Cyropaedia*. Notes the importance of subordinate episodes in raising political issues that interested Sidney. In Chapters 5 and 6, discusses moral teaching in *Arcadia*. Sees Pyrocles and Musidorus as embodiments of absolute virtue comparable to Virgil's Aeneas. Analyzes Platonic and Aristotelian influences, concluding that Sidney was creating a new sort of hero, not seen in earlier romances or epics. Discusses the virtues of magnanimity and friendship in Pyrocles

Twentieth Century

and Musidorus, the public virtues of Euarchus, and two kinds of bravery in Pyrocles and Philoclea. Analyzes Sidney's theory of the virtues, the vices, and the passions, noting his use of allegorical names and his borrowings from Roman comedy. Finds in Platonism a resolution of the central conflict between love and virtue, treating Urania as an embodiment of this resolution. Sees Argalus and Parthenia as ideals of married love and Phalantus and Artesia as examples of fashionable amorous display. In the debate between Pamela and Cecropia, examines the relation between chance and divine providence, noting Stoic and Epicurean elements in the passage. In the exchange between Pyrocles and Musidorus about awareness after death, sees Platonic and Christian influences. Also considers the relation of equity to law, the proper education of a prince, the arts of war, and the "laws" of architecture. In Chapter 7, defines *Arcadia* as a chivalric-heroic romance written in the style of a prose poem. Notes elements derived from Greek romance and pastoral poetry, but denies the influence of medieval literature or of euphuism. In Chapters 8–11, examines Sidney's literary sources. Among classical authors, focuses on Heliodorus, Achilles Tatius, Longus, Virgil, Homer, Ovid, Polybius, Pausanias, Justinius, and Strabo. Gives special treatment to the eclogues, considering dating, placement in the work, and the possibility that some were not written for *Arcadia*. Links them with pastoral works by Spenser, Sannazaro, Virgil, and Theocritus and discusses matters of meter and form. Also compares *Arcadia* with Montemayor's *Diana*, Italian *novelle*, and Ariosto's *Orlando furioso*. In Chapter 12, teases out autobiographical references linking Philisides with Sidney, Mira and Philoclea with Penelope Rich, Urania with the Countess of Pembroke, Coridon with Dyer, and Helen with Queen Elizabeth. In Chapter 13, focuses on chivalry. Considers its place in Sidney's life at court, its relation to honor, and its trappings, especially the use of symbolic colors and heraldic devices. Points out passages in which Sidney seems to laugh at medieval combat, discussing the influence of *Amadis de Gaule*. In Chapter 14, relates *Arcadia* to Sidney's cultural context. Notes the aristocratic nature of the book and its reliance on contemporary fashions in painting, architecture, music, dress, and manners. Ends with a discussion of the religious background of the work. See replies by Briggs (448), Zandvoort (1316), and Rowe (1747). See also Lindenbaum (1651).

1203 BROWN, JAMES NEIL. "Elizabethan Pastoralism and Renaissance Platonism." *AUMLA*, no. 44, November 1975, pp. 247–67. Comparing Spenser's view of poetry with that of the *Defence*, contrasts the role of Urania in the Old *Arcadia* as an image of worldly harmony with her function in the New *Arcadia* as "the Muse who presides over planetary motions . . . and as the Celestial Venus." Discusses the romance as a contemplative retreat that educates the Princes for their later reentry into the active life, relating it to pastorals by Shakespeare, Drayton, Marlowe, and others.

1204 BURCHMORE, SUSAN CARTER. "*Imitatio Morum*: Example and Metaphor in Renaissance Characterization." Ph.D. diss., University of Virginia, 1981, 330 pp.

Argues that, in the Renaissance, characterization was regarded as "one aspect of . . . the imitation of mores," which were defined as "attitudes or bents of mind which translated virtue or vice into action." Finds two common "modes" of characterization: one offering examples of mores in action, and another offering "metaphorical" figures, that is, characters created by "transporting attributes of one persona, usually from pagan myth, Classical literature, history or contemporary poetry or politics, into the new context of the poet's own work." In the Old *Arcadia*, finds "almost exclusively" exemplary characters, who illustrate "faulty mores inspired by excessive passion." In the New *Arcadia*, finds a shift toward admirable examples of virtuous love, which show that "the nature of love depends upon its results." See *DAI* 43 (November 1982):1551A.

1205 BUSH, DOUGLAS. *Mythology and the Renaissance Tradition in English Poetry*. Minneapolis: University of Minnesota Press; London: Oxford University Press, 1932, pp. 69–70, 118–19, 161, 169, 194–95.

Touches on Sidney's attitude toward allegory and compares Pamela's refutation of atheism in Book III of the revised *Arcadia* with similar material in Spenser's Mutability Cantos. Supplies a catalog of Renaissance tree-lists that follow the same convention as that in the Old *Arcadia*. Notes similarities between Pyrocles's catalog of Philoclea's beauties and a passage in Phineas Fletcher's *Venus and Anchises*. Also points out the influence of *Arcadia* on William Bosworth's seventeenth-century poem *Arcadius and Sepha*.

1206 CAREY, JOHN. "Structure and Rhetoric in Sidney's *Arcadia*." *Poetica* (Tokyo, Japan) 18 (1984):68–81.

Argues that the elaborate stylistic figuring and the complexities of plotting in *Arcadia* are not ornamental but functional in that they help to set forth a tragic view of the world. Noting that, in *Directions for Speech and Style*, John Hoskins stresses Sidney's use of *antimetabole* and *synoeciosis*, argues that the constant impulse of the Arcadian style is to follow "the principle of binary opposition—the world splitting incessantly into paired qualities; and the principle of frustrated motion—advance is fol-

Twentieth Century

lowed by withdrawal, to by fro." Finds two related principles in the action of the work: "the blindness of humankind, which makes human actions and endeavors produce the opposite of what was intended," and "the principle of conflict, of divided loyalties, of tension and struggle within the soul." Regards Greek tragedy, with its ironies and reversals, as Sidney's model, noting that the Calvinist belief in the "irretrievable wrongness of human reason" provided a "favorable climate for pagan modes of feeling." In discussing the Old *Arcadia*, focuses on Basilius's attempt to avoid the Delphic Oracle and on the inner division between reason and passion suffered by Gynecia and the other royal lovers, noting that the blindness that brings about their reversals originates in this division. Finds two major changes in the New *Arcadia*: the "vast extension and diversification of the narrative" that elaborates the workings of fate and the struggles of reason against passion "as far as the eye can see," and the addition of Amphialus as a personification of the reversals and inner conflicts that dominate the work. Analyzes the ambivalence inherent in Sidney's indirect method of narration and in such things as the descriptions of the landscape, the reflections of the characters, their political debates and class strife during the rebellion, and even their emblematic jewelry. Relates the inner vacillations of the characters to their frequent outward trembling and panting, to their tendency to "fractured speech," and to the rhetorical vacillations of Sidney's style, which draws the reader into "a lived experience of tentativeness, delicacy, and poise." Along the way, identifies a source for Shakespeare's *Two Gentlemen of Verona* I.ii in the New *Arcadia* III.i.

1207 CHALIFOUR, CLARK L. "Sir Philip Sidney's *Old Arcadia* as Terentian Comedy." *SEL* 16 (Winter 1976):51–63.

Against Ringler's classification of the work as a pastoral tragicomedy (92), argues that it is, by sixteenth-century standards, a Terentian comedy. From the *Defence* infers Sidney's concepts of comedy and tragedy, noting three Renaissance criteria for distinguishing them: the final catastrophe, the use of humor, and the rank of the characters. Admits that Sidney's main characters are noble and their actions "nearly tragic," but feels that the rustic setting and the common errors in the action shift the balance toward comedy. Relates Sidney's rhetoric and use of a five-act structure to the study of Terence in the schools. Analyzes the plot, characters, and principles of decorum in *Arcadia* according to Terentian conventions, admitting that Sidney's royal characters, rustics, and women have no precedent in the plays of the Roman dramatist. Relates Gynecia to "the ranting Senecan heroine."

1208 CHAUDHURI, SUKANTA. "The Eclogues in Sidney's *New Arcadia.*" *RES*, n.s. 35 (May 1984):185–202.

Examines closely the placement and prose connections in the 1590 and 1593 editions of *Arcadia*, suggesting "the very strong possibility that 1590 is following a new, authoritative manuscript source for the Eclogues generally." A side-by-side comparison of the 1590 with the Old *Arcadia* shows "an intricate, carefully thought-out dovetailing of clauses selected up and down the whole length of OA," thus providing circumstantial evidence that "the framework of the 1590 Eclogues is authentically Sidneian." A similar side-by-side comparison of the 1593 edition with the Old *Arcadia* shows "less authority." Stops short of claiming "final authorial arrangement" in 1590, but believes it to have "much more authorial sanction" than hitherto claimed.

1209 COHEN, EILEEN Z[ELDA]. "The *Old Arcadia*: A Treatise on Moderation." *Revue belge de philologie et d'histoire* 46 (1968): 749–70.

Examines the Old *Arcadia* for Sidney's position in the dispute between radical Puritans such as Thomas Cartwright and moderate Anglicans such as John Whitgift and Richard Hooker. From the narrator's disapproval of Basilius and the Princes for discarding the garb and responsibilities of royalty, concludes that Sidney could not have accepted the Puritans' desire to eliminate bishops and priestly vestments. Regards Mopsa as a parody of the noble characters and links her with the Puritans through her namesake, the ancient seer Mopsus. Examines the rebellion of the commoners, the intervention of Euarchus, and the beast fable of Philisides (*OA 66*), arguing that Sidney did not share the attitude toward royal authority in the treatise *Vindiciae contra Tyrannos*. Also urges that Sidney shows too much pity for lovers to accept the Puritans' strict moral laws. Concludes that the romance demonstrates his "adherence to kingly authority, ceremony, tradition, law, and the rule of reason."

1210 CONNELL, DOROTHY. *Sir Philip Sidney: The Maker's Mind.* Oxford: Clarendon Press, 1977, pp. 114–42. Orig. a Ph.D. diss., Harvard University, 1974.

In Chapter 5, suggests that Sidney rewrote *Arcadia*, not because he had new models or formal or stylistic revisions in mind, but because he had "more to say on his original themes." Compares Strephon and Claius's opening laments over Urania with the fragment "A shepherd's tale no height of style requires" (*OP 4*) and with Sidney's source in Montemayor's *Diana*. Concludes that, in the revised *Arcadia*, Sidney stresses the benefit of continuing to love, in spite of the pain of such

Twentieth Century

endurance, and gives more attention to tales of love and former adventures. Rejects interpretations of Strephon and Claius that make them models of neo-Platonic love, preferring to compare them with other unrequited lovers such as Astrophil, Pyrocles, and Musidorus. Notes the effect of place-names from Ortelius's maps and from classical literature, suggesting that revision attempts a new sort of verisimilitude. Connects Sidney's remarks on the folly of love with comments on the folly of writing poetry. Also points out the darker evils, the greater tragedies, and the more senseless violence depicted in the revised version. Believes, however, that Sidney intended to end the book more or less as he had the Old *Arcadia*, affirming the comic and heroic possibilities of human nature.

1211 CROFT, P[ETER] J[OHN]. "Sir John Harington's Manuscript of Sir Philip Sidney's *Arcadia*." In *Literary Autographs: Papers Read at a Clark Library Seminar, 26 April 1980*, by P[eter] J[ohn] Croft and Stephen Parks. Los Angeles: William Andrews Clark Memorial Library, University of California at Los Angeles, 1983, pp. 37–75.
Argues that the manuscript, long presumed lost, is in fact the Phillipps Manuscript now at the British Library. Suggests that Harington's quotations from the eclogues of the Old *Arcadia* in his translation of *Orlando furioso* and in the Arundell Harington Manuscript are from a different and superior manuscript. Finds the hands of Harington and two other scribes in the Phillipps Manuscript and dates it between Sidney's death and the 1590 edition of *Arcadia*. Disputes the conclusions of Ringler (92) that other manuscripts of the original version must be dated in the period 1580–82. Posits more intermediate texts than Ringler suggests between Sidney's autograph copy and the extant manuscripts. Argues that Harington's copy text was lent to him by the Sidney family and attributes intentional alterations in the text to his "mischievous wit." Also notes that corrections at the end of the Penshurst Manuscript of the *Defence* are in the hand of Sidney's brother Robert.

1212 CUTTS, JOHN P. "Dametas' Song in Sidney's *Arcadia*." *Renaissance News* 11 (Autumn 1958):183–88.
Prints transcripts of a musical setting of Dametas's song after the death of the bear in the Old *Arcadia*. It survives in Thomas Ravenscroft's *Pammelia* and in manuscript in "Melvill's Book of Roundels." Suggests the possibility that Sidney wrote a masque about Arcadia before he composed his romance, or that portions of the book were presented semi-dramatically. Also lists extant settings of poems from *Arcadia*.

1213 DANA, MARGARET E[LIZABETH]. "The Providential Plot of the *Old Arcadia.*" *SEL* 17 (Winter 1977):39–57.

Examines the apparent contradictions between the final trial and Basilius's pardon of the defendants, and between those judgments and the attitude of the narrator. Argues against Lanham (1255) and Dipple (1224), contending that the narrator only seems to vacillate out of sympathy with the lovers, whereas in fact he handles his role ironically. Stresses the importance of the oracle, relating the narrator's disapproval of Basilius's retirement to Calvin's censures against superstition and Elizabethan views of natural order. Traces the stages by which Basilius's mistake inverts the natural order and leads all the other characters to their unnatural disguises and shifts. Notes the many errors in the final trial that arise from attempts to second-guess divine providence or (in the case of Euarchus) from human ignorance and strict impassivity. Concludes that only providence could fulfill the oracle and correct the errors of the trial, and that the narrator himself, not Euarchus, is the paradigm of justice in the book.

1214 ———. "Sidney's Two *Arcadias*: From Romance Towards Epic." Ph.D. diss., University of California at Riverside, 1971, 257 pp.

Examines the genres of epic and romance as they were regarded in the sixteenth century, especially in the Italian debate over *Orlando furioso* and in Sidney's own *Defence*. Compares the Old *Arcadia* with *Orlando* and the New *Arcadia* with the *Aeneid*, positing a shift in Sidney's conception from romance toward epic. Also argues that recent critics have unnecessarily sacrificed a sense of the noble in Sidney's characters in an attempt to point out ambiguities and complexities, particularly in the trial scene. See *DAI* 32 (November 1971):2636A.

1215 DANCHIN, F.C. "Les deux *Arcadies* de Sir Philip Sidney." *Revue anglo-américaine* 5 (October 1927):39–52.

Seeks to provide some "preliminary reasons" for preferring the Old *Arcadia* to the New. Feels that the revised version splits into "two parts quite unequal in originality and value": Books I and II, which never recapture Sidney's original inspiration, and the finished part of Book III, in which he soars to heights "unimagined" in his original conception. Despite fine descriptions added to Books I and II, the revised version is marred by meandering elaborations of the plot.

1216 DAVIDSON, CLIFFORD. "Nature and Judgement in the *Old Arcadia.*" *PLL* 6 (Fall 1970):348–65.

Argues that the Old *Arcadia* dramatizes the Renaissance dispute over human nature: whether it is a set of inborn inclinations and desires or a

Twentieth Century

rational ideal that must be imposed to redeem such urges. In the New *Arcadia*, the dispute between Pamela and Cecropia makes Sidney's position clear: nature is a rational principle. In the *Defence*, however, both views appear, and in Books IV–V of the Old *Arcadia*, Sidney explores them dialectically without resolving the issue. Suggests that the characters' retreat to pastoral Nature is not an idealized interlude leading to moral improvement but an experience in the "theater of the world," a temptation of the senses that enslaves the characters to a form of love quite contrary to the ideals of neo-Platonism. After the final judgment, however, Sidney reverses himself, suggesting that nature, as a rational principle, can indeed overcome passion and that the two natures of man can be reconciled by divine providence. Also notes that, contrary to Calvin's teaching, Sidney arranges for his virtuous pagans to be redeemed.

1217 DAVIS, WALTER R. "Narrative Methods in Sidney's Old *Arcadia*." *SEL* 18 (Winter 1978):13–33.

Argues that each of the books in the five-act structure of the Old *Arcadia* has a different method of narration. Book I sets up ironic parallels in the actions and debates of Pyrocles and Musidorus and between these and similar scenes involving Basilius and Philanax. The segments of the narrative are nicely closed. Book II also involves closed episodes, but these are branching and involve contrasts rather than parallels. Pyrocles is tragic and acts directly, whereas Musidorus is comic and acts indirectly by creating fictions for Pamela. Book III intensifies the contrasts but brings the two main strands of plot into juxtaposition by interlacing a series of open-ended episodes. Book IV links the two main plot lines even more closely, with Musidorus's failure causing that of Pyrocles. As the comic action of the night gives way to the tragic action of the morning, Sidney emphasizes divine justice. Book V completes the blending of the plot lines and proceeds by three summary narrations that seek to interpret what has happened. Concludes that this method brings out the providential design of the action yet shows the inability of human beings to understand such providence.

1218 de MATTEIS, DANIEL LOUIS. "The Unity and Development of Sidney's *Arcadia*." Ph.D. diss., University of Toronto, 1975.

Examines the shift in narrative techniques between the two versions. Discusses two voices in the original: a "permissive one" in Books I–III and an "evaluative" one in Books IV–V. Compares the first voice with that of Ariosto. Also finds analogous distinctions in the *Defence*, where neo-Platonic psychology alternates with Calvinist psychology, and in the revised *Arcadia*, where the unsuccessful chivalric virtues of the Princes are contrasted with the successful Christian virtues of the Princesses. As an indicator of Sidney's changing attitudes, considers the role of Philisides in the two versions of the romance. See *DAI* 38 (April 1978):6139A–40A.

1219 DENKINGER, EMMA MARSHALL. "Some Renaissance References to '*Sic Vos non Vobis*.'" *PQ* 10 (April 1931):151–62.

Traces Musidorus's *impresa* in Book II of the Old *Arcadia* back to a phrase in an anecdote about Virgil recorded by Asconius Pedianus. Attributes the popularity of the phrase in the sixteenth century to its use as the *impresa* of Antonio da Levya. Seeks to explain Sidney's substitution of the device of a crab when he revised the passage for the New *Arcadia*. Finds that he had used the Virgilian phrase in *Four Foster Children of Desire*, probably as a diplomatic signal preplanned by Elizabeth to reveal that the French marriage plan was off, and that he subsequently avoided the motto.

1220 DIPPLE, ELIZABETH [DOROTHEA]. "The Captivity Episode and the *New Arcadia*." *JEGP* 70 (July 1971):418–31.

Argues that the unfinished 1590 text prepared by Fulke Greville is preferable to the composite 1593 text, discussing Mary Sidney's revisions of the latter. Admits that the oracle in the New *Arcadia* suggests an ending similar to that of the Old, but feels that the late appearance of the prophecy minimizes its importance. Suggests that the Captivity Episode turns the romance in directions incompatible with the original ending. Discusses Sidney's transformation of Arcadia from a *locus amoenus* to a place of both love and war; his refocusing of the love-tragedy on Amphialus; and Sidney's new, more philosophical portrayal of evil and neo-Platonic love in the Captivity Episode. Concludes that Sidney may have left the revised version incomplete because he could not, after such changes, return to the ending of the original.

1221 ———. "Harmony and Pastoral in the Old *Arcadia*." *ELH* 35 (September 1968):309–28.

Ponders the genre of the work, contrasting the idealized pastoral of Sannazaro and Montemayor with Sidney's details of historical and geographical realism, which were drawn from Polybius's *History*. Argues that Sidney continually plays the pastoral setting and the eclogues off against the political and dramatic narrative in order to reveal the impossibility of harmonious paradises in a post-lapsarian world. Discusses the three harmonies of Boethius: *musica mundana*, *musica humana*, and *musica*

Twentieth Century

instrumentalis, finding these in Sidney's opening description of Arcadia. Traces the subsequent loss of harmony, analyzing the Princes as idealized heroes gradually overthrown by "the onslaught of psychological realism." Discusses the role of Dametas as a mirror for the fall of Basilius and notes that a similar fall occurs at the climax of each of the first four books. Regards the excessive punishments meted out in the Trial Scene as a continuation of Sidney's antipastoral realism.

1222 ———. "Metamorphosis in Sidney's *Arcadias.*" *PQ* 50 (January 1971):47–62.
Contrasts the two versions of *Arcadia,* concentrating on metamorphoses in the main characters: "from prince to Amazon or shepherd, from princess to nymph, from sufficient king to dotard." Analyzes the characters' attitudes toward these changes, observing that, in the Old *Arcadia,* the Princes' initial justifications of their actions on the basis of Platonic love are set in ironic contrast to their later actions. These follow Gynecia's more realistic and tragic comments on sexual desire. Calls the work "a study in frustration," in which "virtue, beauty, and canniness" are all insufficient to prevent degradation. Argues that, in the New *Arcadia,* the quasi-Ovidian transformations become more complex. Pyrocles is given the new name Zelmane and is martial and masculine rather than comically feminine. He and Musidorus have a proven heroism that does not decline when they take on disguises. Emphasizes the tale of the original Zelmane as an influence on the entire book. Concludes that the metamorphoses serve "the ideas of love, faithfulness, and unity of being" and that Sidney could not have ended the revised version as he did the original. Includes consideration of Argalus and Parthenia and of the myth of Hercules.

1223 ———. "Sidney's Changing Concept of Arcadia: The Redemption of a Landscape." Ph.D. diss., Johns Hopkins University, 1963.
Abstract not available.

1224 ———. "'Unjust Justice' in the *Old Arcadia.*" *SEL* 10 (Winter 1970):83–101.
Ponders the injustices in Books IV–V, arguing that Sidney leads the reader "away from reductive certainties towards an understanding of the realistic uncertainties that occur when flawed characters confront absolute moral abstractions." Notes diverse narrative voices, from humorous and cynical to sententious, urging that these force the reader to make the final judgment on the action. Notes problems with

Philanax's prosecution and Euarchus's judgments in the Trial Scene. Also considers discrepancies between the laments for the "dead" Basilius and his actual merits, comparing John Case's portrayal of the virtues of Queen Elizabeth in *Sphaera Civitatis*. Admits the Princes' fall from Petrarchan ideals but points to their rise in neo-Platonic and Christian virtues, concluding that Basilius's pardons are a necessary, though imperfect, correction for the excesses of Euarchus's judgments. See a reply by Dana (1213).

1225 DOBELL, BERTRAM. "New Light upon Sir Philip Sidney's *Arcadia.*" *Quarterly Review* 211 (1909):74–100.
Describes the discovery of the first manuscripts of the Old *Arcadia* and compares them to the revised version, considering contents, artistic merit, dating, and the nature of the 1593 edition. Discusses material suppressed by Sidney's sister, and prints poems not previously published.

1226 ———. "Sidney's *Arcadia.*" *Athenaeum*, no. 4167, 7 September 1907, p. 272.
Announces the discovery of the Ashburnham Manuscript of the Old *Arcadia*, listing ways in which it differs from the 1593 version and suggesting that the additions and changes in the later text may not be by Sidney. See also a reply by Greg (1243).

1227 ———. "Sidney's *Arcadia.*" *Athenaeum*, no. 4169, 21 September 1907, p. 336.
Answers Greg (1243), suggesting that the Old *Arcadia* is not "an uncorrected draft" but a finished work more coherent than the versions published in the 1590s.

1228 DORANGEON, SIMONE. "Tensions et ambiguités dans l'*Arcadie* de Sidney en rapport avec l'idée de nature." In *Rhetoric et communication*. Actes du Congres de Rouen (1976). Edited by Hubert Greven. Études Anglaises, 75. Paris: Didier, [1979], pp. 11–24.
Contrasts the concept of "nature" in the Old *Arcadia* with that common in more orthodox pastorals. Finds that Sidney allows two senses of the term, namely "ethical norm" and "physical setting," to remain in unresolved conflict. On the basis of this observation, concludes that he regarded the natural world as ultimately deceptive and did not believe in the value of the "pastoral experience." For him, the natural world was "a neutral environment," intrinsically neither good nor bad, neither better nor worse than city or court. Like Milton, he considered the trials of internal experience more valuable than simple contact with nature.

Twentieth Century

Concludes that, whereas Sidney's attitude toward nature as the "principle of moral judgment" remains constant, his attitude to nature as the physical world varies greatly. This changeability suggests not so much "lack of maturity" as an "absence of authentic pastoral vocation."

1229 DUNCAN-JONES, KATHERINE. "Sidney in Samothea: A Forgotten National Myth." *RES*, n.s. 25 (May 1974):174–77.
In considering Philisides's birthplace in the Old *Arcadia*, cites Elizabethan accounts of the founding of England after Noah's flood under the name "Samothea." Notes its reputation for "stable government, development of the arts, and high and devout philosophical speculation." Traces the myth to a late fifteenth-century fabrication by Annius of Viterbo, who wrote under the pseudonym "Berosus." See also Godshalk (1238).

1230 ———. "Sidney's Personal *Imprese*." *JWCI* 33 (1970):321–24.
Notes that the seven or eight *imprese* recorded as Sidney's and his three mottoes show "skill and fertility in the invention," and "in turn may suggest that the *imprese* in the two *Arcadia*s may be largely his own invention, not borrowed from Italian devices, as has been suggested."

1231 ———. "Sidney's Urania." *RES*, n.s. 17 (May 1966):123–32.
Traces the development of the character Urania. In the Fourth Eclogues of the Old *Arcadia*, she is a country maid of high birth who may allegorize one of Sidney's contemporaries or moral purity. In a poem about the game of barley-break added to the New *Arcadia* (*OP 4*), she again suggests allegorical meanings that are hard to penetrate. In the opening of the revised *Arcadia*, she seems to be Venus Urania, the Muse of Christian poetry, or Platonic virtue itself. Contrasts her lovers, Strephon and Claius, with Pyrocles and Musidorus, who serve Venus Pandemos, or earthly love. The departure of Urania suggests that the rest of the poem will be secular. Also suggests that Strephon and Claius are the two unknown knights who rescue Musidorus from Amphialus in Book III, interpreting their *imprese* as allusions to Urania.

1232 DUNN, UNDINE. "The Arcadian Ethic." Ph.D. diss., Indiana University, 1968, 423 pp.
Examines the private and public ethical values implied in the Old *Arcadia* and compares them with views revealed in Sidney's later life and writings and in the comments of those who knew him. Finds discrepancies between the Arcadian ethic and Sidney's personal beliefs, particularly in his attitude toward the influence of the stars. Also compares Sidney's values with those typical of his social class and suggests that

Twentieth Century

Philoclea represents Mary Agarde, daughter of the Seneschal of Wicklow in Ireland. See *DA* 29 (August 1968):565A.

1233 DURHAM, CHARLES W., III. "Character and Characterization in Elizabethan Prose Fiction." Ph.D. diss., University of Ohio, 1969, 147 pp.

Argues that "there is no progression from a romantic to a realistic delineation of character during the period 1578–1600" but rather a change in the social classes that were romanticized. Finds that John Lyly did not influence Sidney, but that Sidney influenced Robert Greene and Thomas Deloney. In Chapter 3, "Sir Philip Sidney: The Romantic Ideal," suggests that the characters of *Arcadia* are either too idealized or too base. Discusses the function of the contrasts between Basilius and Euarchus and between Basilius and Dametas. Rejects Lanham's thesis (1255) that Pyrocles and Musidorus have faults of character, seeing them as "idealized to a point that is beyond the real." See *DAI* 31 (September 1970):1224A.

1234 EATON, SHARON DIANE. "The Rhetoric of the New *Arcadia*." Ph.D. diss., University of British Columbia, 1979.

Examines Sidney's means of moral persuasion in the work. Traces the change from the ethical ambiguities in the Old *Arcadia* and *Astrophil and Stella* to the affirmation of "a comprehensive system of ethics" in the *Defence*. Explains Sidney's revisions in the New *Arcadia* as attempts to teach this system by providing "a complete spectrum of moral images" and by engaging the readers more actively in discovering the moral design. Discusses the instruction in private love and public duty implicit in the main plot. See *DAI* 40 (October 1979):2070A.

1235 ESTRIN, BARBARA. "The Lost Child in Spenser's *The Faerie Queene*, Sidney's *Old Arcadia*, and Shakespeare's *The Winter's Tale*." Ph.D. diss., Brown University, 1972, 271 pp.

Explores the lost-child motif in the Bible, Greek literature, and works of the English Renaissance. Points out that, in comedy, the rediscovery of the child is contrived by the characters, but in romance it is arranged by the gods. Concludes that *Arcadia* equivocates between these two resolutions. Also examines the narrator's attitude toward the traditional features of such stories. See *DAI* 33 (February 1973):4340A.

1236 FEUILLERAT, ALBERT. Review of *Sidney's "Arcadia": A Comparison between the Two Versions*, by R[einard] W[ilhelm] Zandvoort. *MLN* 46 (March 1931):189–91.

In reviewing Zandvoort (1316), suggests that the Old *Arcadia* was a "trifling" work meant to amuse ladies, but that the New *Arcadia* was intend-

Twentieth Century

ed to exemplify rules of conduct necessary for anyone who would govern. Rejects the notion that Sidney wrote political allegory.

1237 FORD, P[HILIP] JEFFREY. "Philosophy, History, and Sidney's *Old Arcadia*." *CL* 26 (Winter 1974):32–50.
Against Myrick (671), argues that the Old *Arcadia* is as much an epic as the New, even by sixteenth-century Italian standards. Analyzes the original version according to the suggestions in the *Defence* that poetry should combine the best elements in philosophy and history. Examines Italian criteria of verisimilitude, arguing that the Old *Arcadia* fulfills those established for histories. Finds the main philosophical teachings of the work in Basilius's abdication of responsibility and in Sidney's exploration of the limits of royal authority. Pays special attention to the role of the narrator and to the opposition between the "intrigue plot" involving the young lovers and the "political plot." Also considers symmetrical patterns in the act divisions, the conduct of Pyrocles and Musidorus, and the eclogues.

1238 GODSHALK, W[ILLIAM] L[EIGH]. Letter. *RES*, n.s. 29 (August 1978):325–26.
In support of Duncan-Jones's identification of Philisides's birthplace (1229), lists other works that connect Samothea with England. Corrects a detail about the priest "Berosus" (a pseudonym for Annius of Viterbo). Suggests that Sidney may have encountered the myth in William Lambard's *Perambulation of Kent* and notes that it is also appears in the works of Shakespeare and those of the minor Jacobean poet William Slatyer. But see item 1551.

1239 ———. "Sidney's Revision of the *Arcadia*, Books III–V." *PQ* 43 (April 1964):171–84.
Reviews the scholarly debate over revisions in Books III–V of the New *Arcadia* and argues that most were by Sidney, not his sister or Hugh Sanford. Examines the following: Fulke Greville's letter to Sir Francis Walsingham of November 1586; the publication history of the 1590 and 1593 editions (30, 31); Hugh Sanford's preface to the 1593; and John Florio's *World of Words* and preface to Montaigne's *Essays*. Concludes that part of Greville's fair copy of the revised version was lost between 1586 and 1590. Also examines Hugh Sanford's life and his character as an editor, and details the revisions in the 1593 text.

1240 GOLDMAN, MARCUS SELDEN. *Sir Philip Sidney and the "Arcadia."* Illinois Studies in Language and Literature, vol. 17, nos. 1–2. Urbana: University of Illinois Press, 1934, pp. 122–210.

Orig. a Ph.D. diss., University of Illinois at Urbana- Champaign, 1931.

In Chapter 5, surveys trends in Sidney criticism since his death, focusing on *Arcadia*. In Chapter 6, argues against defining *Arcadia* as a pastoral, suggesting that both versions had a similar purpose: to outdo poetic philosophers such as Plato and Sir Thomas More by creating an imaginary world in which theories and passions clash, instructing the reader by the course of the action rather than by preaching. In Chapter 7, rejects "allegory hunting" but connects Philanax's younger brother with Henry II of France, the Helot and Arcadian rebels with the Irish insurgents, Parthenia with Sidney's mother, Philisides and Phalantus with Sidney himself, and the final trial with proceedings against Mary, Queen of Scots. In Chapter 8, examines Sidney's interest in King Arthur and lists similarities between *Arcadia* and the *Morte d'Arthur*, concluding that Malory was a major source. See also item 534.

1241 GÖLLER, KARL HEINZ; MARKUS, MANFRED; and SCHÖWERLING, RAINER. *Romance und Novel. Die Anfänge des englischen Romans.* Sprache und Literatur: Regensburger Arbeiten zur Anglistik und Amerikanistik. Regensburg, Germany: Verlag Hans Carl, 1972, pp. 196–98.

Considers elements of Greek romance in the two versions of *Arcadia*, finding the revised version closer to the ancient form.

1242 GREENLAW, EDWIN A. "Sidney's *Arcadia* as an Example of Elizabethan Allegory." In *Anniversary Papers by Colleagues and Pupils of George Lyman Kittredge*. Boston: Ginn & Co., 1913, pp. 327–37.

Argues that, by Elizabethan standards, *Arcadia* is a heroic poem and that Sidney set out to provide the sort of allegory that contemporary critics expected in the genre. Compares the Old *Arcadia* with the New, urging that the revisions bring the romance more in line with Aristotle's "rules" of epic poetry. Analyzes the Princes' heroic adventures in Book II as an exposition of private ethics that is divided into two groups of episodes: one on education and the other on public and private abuses of love. Argues that the first is modeled on Xenophon's *Cyropaedia* and relates both to the main action of *Arcadia*. Considers Sidney's portrait of the ideal prince, contrasting three allegorical portrayals of Machiavellian statecraft: Plexirtus, Clinias, and Amphialus. Also lists episodes that explore various forms of government and discusses the contrasts between the wise ruler Euarchus and the foolish Basilius. Concludes that Sidney wrote with contemporary crises in England in mind, aiming to

Twentieth Century

educate gentlemen in ethics and politics, much as Spenser did in *The Faerie Queene*. See also replies by Lindheim (1652) and Zandvoort (1316).

1243 GREG, W[ALTER] W[ILSON]. "Sidney's *Arcadia*." *Athenaeum*, no. 4168, 14 September 1907, p. 303; no. 4170, 28 September 1907, p. 368.

Refutes Dobell's suggestion (1226) that many revisions in the New *Arcadia* may not be by Sidney. Discusses the newly discovered manuscripts of the Old *Arcadia*. See also Dobell (1227).

1244 HAGAN, ENID MARGARET. "Pastoral and Romance in Sidney's Two *Arcadia*s." Ph.D. diss., University of Washington, 1971, 171 pp.

Discusses Sidney's mingling of pastoral and romance and concludes that the revised *Arcadia* shifts toward romance and toward a more favorable view of love. Also comments on differences in function between the pastoral elements in the prose narrative and those in the eclogues and discusses "the parallel political and love plots." See *DA* 32 (November 1971):2687A–88A.

1245 HAMILTON, A.C. "Et in Arcadia Ego." *MLQ* 27 (September 1966):332–50.

Reviews Davis (1499), Lanham (1255), and Kalstone (1907). Rejects Davis's choice of texts, his "deliberate forcing" of *Arcadia* to fit a general model of romance structure, and his view that Sidney's heroes proceed from a turbulent outer world to a "pure center." Sees no moral education in their progress to the final trial and no easy Christian moral in Philoclea's speeches to prevent Pyrocles from committing suicide. Qualifies Davis's Platonic reading of the eclogues and refutes his view that the order is significant, noting that it was not set by Sidney. Also considers the relation of the eclogues and the chivalric episodes to the main action. Criticises Lanham for treating passages of high style in the Old *Arcadia* as ironic attempts by the narrator to show the insincerity or the humorous excesses of the characters. Also questions Lanham's classification of the original version as a comic novel and the revision as a comic epic. Against Kalstone, urges that, when *Astrophil and Stella* is set against Petrarchan conventions, "differences far outweigh parallels." Also feels that the sequence should not be read as an exploration of the conflict between heroic virtue and love.

Twentieth Century

1246 ———. "Sidney's *Arcadia* as Prose Fiction: Its Relation to Its Sources." *ELR* 2 (Winter 1972):29–60.
Regards *Arcadia* as a compendium of the best in European fiction and "the first extended work of original prose fiction" in English. Examines the *Defence* for Sidney's theory of the way a poet should learn his art and for comments on the works imitated in *Arcadia*. Beginning with the Old *Arcadia*, considers these sources. Regards Sannazaro's main contribution as an Arcadian state of mind, a "fore-conceit" of an unattainable Eden and a love of beauty mingled with a recognition of its tragic peril. Notes Milton's warnings about the perils of reading *Arcadia* and Sidney's own deathbed wish that it be burned. Reviews parts of the main plot derived from *Amadis de Gaule*, pointing out that Sidney's lovers invert the chivalric ideal by pursuing shameful love in retirement. Notes a similar inversion of a source when Sidney exchanges the purity of the lovers in Heliodorus's *Aethiopica* for the sexual excesses of Pyrocles and Musidorus. Suggests that the final trial was designed to show their true worth again and that it may have moved the book so far from pastoral romance toward heroic poetry that Sidney went back to revise the rest of the book to match. Turns next to the revised *Arcadia*, contrasting its opening with those of Montemayor's *Diana* and Sannazaro's *Arcadia*. Finds that in the sources, sad lovers provide a pattern for succeeding episodes, whereas, in Sidney's work, they offer an ironic contrast. Also traces the influence of Heliodorus on the opening shipwreck and considers the extent of Sidney's originality, particularly in the story of Argalus and Parthenia. Concludes that Sidney succeeded in combining the "soft" delights of pastoral romance with the "hard" virtues and moving action of heroic romance.

1247 HAMM, DIETER. "Sir Philip Sidneys *Old Arcadia*: Selbstthematisierung der Literatur." Ph.D. diss., University of Konstanz, 1972, 184 pp.
Treats the original *Arcadia* as an apology for poetry, comparing it with the *Defence*. Suggests that both works treat poetic imagery as a neo-Platonic *eros* mediating between reality and the realm of Ideas. Sees the kingdom of Arcadia as an idealized Platonic state in a Virgilian landscape. Describes its fall as follows: Basilius's tragic *hubris* leads to the neo-Platonic state of *chorismos*, in which court is separated from country, Princes from Princesses, King from Queen, royalty from aristocracy. At the end, a *catharsis* reunites the kingdom through *eros* and marriage. Considers the King's *hubris* as an attempt to be like God in reshaping Dametas, and defines the Princes' crossing of sexual and class lines as a "masque." Notes Sidney's opposition to tragicomedy and the mingling

Twentieth Century

of classes but concludes that such mixtures allow him to "experiment" with "the whole tragic and comic scale of reality."

1248 HARRISON, T.P., Jr. "A Source of Sidney's *Arcadia*." *University of Texas Bulletin: Studies in English*, no. 6, 22 December 1926, pp. 53–71.
Seeks to define the influence of Montemayor's *Diana* (and its continuations by Gil Polo and Alonso Pérez) upon *Arcadia*. Argues that *Diana* exerted more influence on the pastoral elements of the Old *Arcadia* than did Sannazaro's *Arcadia*. Also argues that, although the New *Arcadia* was more heavily influenced by Greek romance, a number of devices of description, plotting, and narration still hearken back to *Diana*.

1249 ISLER, ALAN D[AVID]. "The Allegory of the Hero and Sidney's Two *Arcadias*." *SP* 65 (April 1968):171–91.
Reviews the history of the classical ideal that an epic hero should embody *sapientia* and *fortitudo*, listing Renaissance works in this tradition and detailing various polarized associations that the two terms carried. Argues that *Arcadia* is built around this polarity, embodied most clearly in Pyrocles (courage) and Musidorus (wisdom), "one soul in bodies twain." Considers etymologies of the Princes' various names, their disguises and conduct, their animal counterparts (the lion and the bear), their role in the wider theme of reason versus passion, and their rhetoric in the Trial Scene. Finds a similar contrast in Philoclea and Pamela and in the characters associated with the two royal lodges.

1250 ———. "Heroic Poetry and Sidney's Two *Arcadias*." *PMLA* 83 (May 1968):368–79.
Discusses the confusion in modern attempts to define the genres of the two versions of *Arcadia* and argues that, in sixteenth-century England, both would simply have been regarded as "heroic poems." Contrasts Renaissance Italian definitions of epic, which emphasize structure and epic machinery, with Elizabethan definitions, which stress serious moral and political teaching in a lengthy, fictional narration. By Italian standards, the two versions of *Arcadia* are not truly epic. Also considers the sense in which both versions are pastoral, noting that they resemble Shakespeare's *As You Like It* and Spenser's *Faerie Queene* in transplanting the court to the country in order to juxtapose art and nature. See a reply by Roberts (1289).

1251 ———. "The Moral Philosophy of Sidney's Two *Arcadia*s: A Study of Some Principal Themes." Ph.D. diss., Columbia University, 1966, 205 pp.

Suggests that modern views of genre and those of Renaissance Italy have obscured the English definition of heroic poetry. Argues that the two versions of the *Arcadia* both satisfy this definition and have the same purpose: to instruct rulers in private and public virtue. Also studies the relationship of the individual to the family and the state and considers the disasters that threaten all three levels if right reason is not obeyed on any one of them. Gives special attention to the role of the family. See *DA* 30 (October 1969):1567A.

1252 KENNEDY, JUDITH M., ed. Introduction to *A Critical Edition of Yong's Translation of George of Montemayor's "Diana" and Gil Polo's "Enamoured Diana."* Oxford: Clarendon Press, 1968, pp. xxxiii–xxxix.

Considers the influence of Montemayor's *Diana* on *Arcadia*, noting early commentary on Sidney's borrowings and concluding that he knew the work in the Spanish. Discusses similarities between the two authors in matters of narrative technique such as irony and humor, in neo-Platonic philosophy, and in versification. Also examines Gil Polo's continuation of *Diana* and its impact on the Old *Arcadia*.

1253 KIMBROUGH, ROBERT. *Sir Philip Sidney*. Twayne's English Authors Series, 114. New York: Twayne Publishers, 1971, pp. 68–88, 125–43.

In Chapter 3, follows previous critics in suggesting that, in the Old *Arcadia*, Sidney brought together the traditional materials of a pastoral courtly romance with those of an academic five-act comedy, but argues that his addition of the four interludes composed of eclogues made the work "his own." Feels that what is "distinctive" about it is that each book "has its own describable tone, each marked by a slight shift from light to serious." Though the work is "complexly experimental," Sidney is in firm control of the narration, which gains much of its power to entertain through his "maintenance of narrative detachment from the action, and through an exploitation of rhetoric in such a way that word rarely answers deed." Claims that the attitudes and tones of the eclogues contrast with those of the prose material and that, although "serious moralizing" enters the work because the eclogues are pastoral, their conventionality "allows them to please more than to instruct." Analyzes this pervasive "spirit of detached delight," showing ways in which it acts as a counterpoint to "slight shifts" in tone from book to book. In Chapter 6,

Twentieth Century

demonstrates that, in recasting the Old, comic *Arcadia* into the New, heroic one, Sidney's attitude and purpose changed drastically. Finds clear signals of the transformation in the new opening and in the variety of styles and voices characteristic of the revised version. Discusses the addition of two new types of characters in Books I and II, some who "take on individuality" and others who "serve to reveal the personalities of those who tell their stories." Agrees with Ringler (92) that the eclogues are out of place in the revised version. Argues finally that, in Book III, an "evolution of seriousness" has occurred in which descriptions of chivalric action no longer serve the aim of projecting courtly and "sacramental" ideals but become "forthrightly realistic." In breaking off in midsentence, "Sidney seems to have quit writing in disgust." See also item 593.

1254 LANGENFELT, GÖSTA. "The Attitude to Villeins and Labourers in English Literature until c. 1600." *ZAA* 8 (1960):337–80.
Condemns Sidney's treatment of commoners and even the lower orders of the aristocracy as scornful, cruel, and Machiavellian. Focuses on the revolt against Basilius in the Old *Arcadia*, noting that the revised version is even more objectionable. Suggests that Sidney's attitude was widely influential.

1255 LANHAM, RICHARD A[LAN]. "The Old *Arcadia*." In *Sidney's Arcadia*. Yale Studies in English, 158. New Haven, Conn.: Yale University Press, 1965, pp. 181–405. Orig. a Ph.D. diss., Yale University, 1963.
In Chapter 1, reviews evidence on composition, dating, manuscripts, and revisions of *Arcadia*. Reviews scholarship on the genre and purpose of the Old *Arcadia* and seeks to examine it without preconceptions fostered by the revised text, the "Sidney legend," or modern preferences in prose style. In Chapter 2, examines the five-act structure of the work and its principal themes. Notes the initial emphasis on the active life and the dangers of retirement, the value of friendship, and the struggle between reason and passion. Argues that all parts of the book are integrated to further these themes and to show the wisdom of Philanax's original warnings to Basilius. Discusses the importance of the first sentence of each book and the role of Euarchus in restoring reason and order at the end. In Chapter 3, defends Sidney's rhetoric. Argues that the set speeches of the characters are frequently calculated for humorous or ironic effect and do not necessarily reflect the views of the narrator. Contrasts the lofty rhetoric of the lovers with the folly of their conduct, noting similarities in the speeches of the base characters. Defends the

rhetoric of Philanax in the Trial Scene and treats Euarchus as the "ethical touchstone of the romance," noting his direct style. In Chapter 4,
discusses Sidney as narrator, distinguishing several voices under two
main heads: Sidney the ignorant and powerless reporter at a play, and
Sidney the "maker," director, and knowing commentator. Argues that
the traditional wisdom voiced by the former is undercut by the irony of
the latter. Feels that the work is dialectical, pitting reason against passion to reveal the limitations of simple moralizing. Also discusses reasons
that Sidney may have reassigned certain speeches from the narrator to
the characters in the New *Arcadia*. In Chapter 5, defends Sidney's
Arcadian style. Reviews rhetorical treatises that he may have known and
discusses his deprecating comments on his own style in the *Defence*.
Details his characteristic tropes and figures, noting his tendency to asso-
ciate love with unpleasant or violent imagery. In Chapter 6, ponders the
genre of the Old *Arcadia*. Notes Sidney's interest in stage analogies and
the affinities between the book and traditional forms of comedy and
tragedy. Feels that the political turmoil of the work moves it in the direction of antipastoral. Rejects tragicomedy and epic as possible genres for
the work and settles on "comic novel." Feels that, in undercutting his
heroes, Sidney is questioning codes of chivalry and courtly love and
advocating Christian marriage and an overriding concern for the welfare
of the state. Finds in the book the "bud" of Shakespeare's romantic
comedies. In Chapter 7, takes up the relation of the Old *Arcadia* to its
sources and to the New *Arcadia*. Finds that genres rather than individual
works were the formative influences, and notes departures from Sidney's
generic models. Constrasts his "architectonic" sense of structure, morality, and rhetoric with the lesser art of the Greek romances. Also finds in
Sidney's work an element of "realism" and a careful regard for causal
connections absent in medieval romance. Notes affinities with George
Gascoigne's *Adventures of Master F.J.* and, to a lesser extent, with the fiction of John Lyly, Robert Greene, and Thomas Lodge. Argues that the
New *Arcadia* is not markedly superior to the Old and that its main new
element is heroic action. Treats it as a "comic epic" and suggests internal
difficulties that may have led Sidney to abandon the revision. Includes a
bibliography. See also replies by Dana (1213), Durham (1233), Hamilton
(1245), Roberts (1289), and Vickers (1307).

1256 ———. "Opaque Style in Elizabethan Fiction." *PCP* 1 (1966):
25–31.

Suggests that Sidney uses rhetoric as a means of characterizing Pyrocles
and Musidorus. Notes ironic contrasts between their words and their

Twentieth Century

deeds, suggesting that they consciously employ devices of rhetoric to seduce the ladies but that readers miss these devices because the book lacks a normative style for comparison. Feels that Euarchus provides such a style, but only at the conclusion.

1257 LAWRY, JON S. *Sidney's Two "Arcadias": Pattern and Proceeding.* Ithaca, N.Y.: Cornell University Press, 1972, pp. 14–153.
In Chapter 1, treats the Old *Arcadia* as a heroic poem, suggesting that its purpose is to provide a "speaking picture" of "essential man." Analyzes the book according to Platonic triads: governors, guardians, and crafts-men in the state; intelligence, will, and appetite in the soul; and so on. Feels that, once the royal lovers abandon their roles as governors, they fall to the middle position in a triad, with wise shepherds and divine providence above and the anarchic mob and changeable fortune below. Considers the theatrical elements of the work and its debates, pointing out the influence of Ramist logic on the latter. Discusses the interrela-tions between two themes: passion versus reason, and providence versus fortune, examining ways in which the subplot involving Dametas and his family is a parody of the main action. In Book I, traces the fall from rea-son suffered by Basilius, Pyrocles, and finally Musidorus, noting the importance of the poem "Transformed in show" (*OA 2*) in laying out the central themes of the work. Also considers the appropriateness of the Princes' disguises, the relation of the lion and the bear to the themes of Book I, and the "choric" function of the eclogues in celebrating order in Arcadia and in warning of unlawful desires. In Book II, traces the decline of Gynecia and the Princesses, suggesting that Gynecia repre-sents uncontrolled desire, Pamela represents intellect, and Philoclea represents will. Treats the rebellion of the commoners as an emblem of the disorder among the principal characters, and notes that the opening poem of the Second Eclogues (*OA 27*) is the key to the entire set. In Book III, sees a redirection of the lovers away from private passion toward public accountability and treats the cave as an emblem for their state. Contrasts the predatory desires of the Princes with the course of divine providence. Sees in the Third Eclogues a foreshadowing of the marriages in Book V and also a reflection of the general structure of the entire work. Suggests that Philisides has little to do with Sidney himself and is included as a spokesman for Platonic views of "divinity and man." Treats his song on the fall of man (*OA 66*) as "the literary and ideologi-cal center of the *Old Arcadia*." In Book IV, sees Dametas as an instrument of divine providence and Basilius's trance as an image of death in love that threatens all the lovers. Examines the debates in the last part of the

work as pitting "providence against despair, and 'higher' laws against retribution." Discusses the "almost Christian" wisdom of the Princesses and the good effects of tribulation on the characters of the lovers. Sees in the Fourth Eclogues a lament for the fallen state of Arcadia and mankind. In Book V, defends the "resurrection" of Basilius as a fitting end to a Terentian and Dantean comedy. Analyzes the character of Euarchus and remarks on the return of the Princes to Stoic patience after their schooling by the Princesses. Urges that Philanax's suppression of letters from the Princesses renders the outcome of the trial suspect, as does the unbending severity of the judge. Contrasts the judgment of the higher powers, approving the final marriages as types of the restored harmony of the state. See also item 616.

1258 LERNER, LAURENCE. "Arkadien und das Goldene Zeitalter." In *Alternative Welten*, edited by Manfred Pfister. Münchner Universitätsschriften, philosophische Facultät, Texte und Untersuchungen zur englischen Philologie, 12. Munich: Wilhelm Fink, 1982, pp. 113–34.
Cites Sidney's "O sweet words, the delight of solitariness!" (*OA 34*) to illustrate the claim that pastoral belongs to a class of literature whose subject matter is "provincial," not courtly, and whose manner of viewing the world is indirect and dreamlike, not direct and objective.

1259 ———. *The Uses of Nostalgia: Studies in Pastoral Poetry*. London: Chatto & Windus, 1972, pp. 16–17, 105–8.
Comments on the simple approval of country over court in the poem "O sweet woods, the delight of solitariness" (*OA 34*). Characterizes *Arcadia* as a whole, however, as antipastoral. Notes that Arcadia is a kingdom and not a retreat; that the disguised Musidorus learns nothing by playing shepherd; that the rustics are ridiculed; and that all the main characters hold conservative, aristocratic views of monarchy and rebellion.

1260 LEVINE, ROBERT ERIL. *A Comparison of Sidney's "Old" and "New Arcadia."* Salzburg Studies in English Literature, Elizabethan & Renaissance Studies, 13. Salzburg: Institut für englische Sprache und Literatur, Universität Salzburg, 1974, 126 pp.
In Chapters 1 and 2, reviews scholarship on the genre of the Old and New *Arcadia*, suggesting a close examination of mood and tone as a way to resolve the disputes. Reviews the composition and publishing history of the various texts. In Chapter 3, argues that the pastoral setting, the rhetoric, and the narrative technique of the revised version are as they had been in the original version: ironic and humorous. They are

Twentieth Century

"beclouding" and lead the characters to speak in one way and to act "in accordance with a plot that moves quite contrary." Notes that the main characters do not belong in a pastoral region, that the more appropriate shepherds are mostly confined to the eclogues, and that the action is too full of realism and the unexpected to suit an idyll. Finds the narrator of the Old *Arcadia* inconsistent and untrustworthy, praising the revision for greater consistency and for delegating most of the retrospective story-telling to the characters themselves. Denies that the opening *in medias res* is an important change related to epic intentions as Myrick had argued (in 1691), noting that Book I might as well begin *ab ovo* because it covers the same essential developments as it had in the original version. Finds Pyrocles's way of falling in love through a picture "sheer ridiculousness" and suggests that virtually all of the material added to Book I in the revision is ironic because it only "frustrates the heroic ambitions of the princes." In Chapter 4, rejects the view that the Princes' Asian adventures in the revised Book II are offered as serious examples for moral and political instruction, seeing them instead as comic because of their aim, which is to advance Pyrocles and Musidorus in the eyes of the Princesses. In Philoclea's bedtime conference with Pamela, finds ironies to undercut her protestations of horror at her apparently lesbian attractions to the disguised Pyrocles, regarding her naked embracement of her sister as hardly "chaste" and Pamela's responses to her sister and to Musidorus as anything but cautious and reasonable, as befits a princess. Notes Philoclea's relish in telling the tale of Cupid's revenge on an unloving Erona just at the time when Philoclea herself has decided to stop resisting love. Also remarks on the humor of having the Princes labor so hard to win by their storytelling ladies who are already won and who are obviously enjoying all the attention. Constrasts Musidorus's honorable attempt to give Pyrocles half his narrative attention, whereas his friend focuses shamelessly on himself. Regards both Princes as inept heroes, finding that few lasting goods are achieved in Asia. Lists bungled actions, particularly those leading to the deaths of Dido, Zelmane, and Daiphantus. Regards Pyrocles as adolescent and naive to tell a lady such stories to impress her, but suggests that she enjoys them "as mindlessly as he does." In Chapter 5, notes ironies in his quelling of the rebellion in Arcadia. Finds it comic that a hero should do battle with millers and tailors, then win them by false rhetoric, and finally be taken in himself by the rhetoric of a man like Clinias. In Chapter 6, returns to the initial question of genre, classifying the New *Arcadia* as a humorous romance and arguing that it is not significantly different in structure or manner from the original version. Believes that the revisions are generally calculated to make the comedy more urbane, refined, and effective. In Book III, however, allows that the humor is overbalanced with sadness, as Sidney makes a gruesome mockery of chivalry itself and shows his aristocrats to be little more honorable in battle than Clinias and Dametas. Attributes the unifinished state of the revision to the fact that Sidney had "found himself writing a different kind of work in Book III" and "had tired of it." Includes a selective bibliography.

1261 LINDENBAUM, PETER ALAN. "The Anti-Pastoral Pastoral: The Education of Fallen Man in the Renaissance." Ph.D. diss., University of California at Berkeley, 1970, 354 pp.
Finds that English pastorals often oppose earlier foreign models by attacking "that habit of mind which seeks to find an Edenic, easy, carefree existence anywhere in man's present world." Considers the similarities between the two versions of *Arcadia* and argues that both treat the pastoral sojourn as a means to educate Pyrocles and Musidorus about their limitations as fallen human beings. See *DAI* 32 (August 1971):973A–74A.

1262 ———. "Sidney's *Arcadia*: The Endings of the Three Versions." *HLQ* 34 (May 1971):205–18.
Defends the ending of the Old *Arcadia* against critics who feel that it goes against justice or is merely a convention of romance. Suggests that Euarchus represents the best use of reason available to man, but points out many passages on human fallibility and divine providence that prepare the reader for the overturning of Euarchus's decision and make it appropriate. Believes that the true flaw in the ending is that the Princes have behaved too reprehensibly to deserve the happy outcome. Argues that Sidney made (or authorized) revisions in Pyrocles's behavior to Philoclea in her bedchamber and in Musidorus's attempt to rape Pamela because the Princes had to be made more honorable to deserve the ending. Also argues that Sidney had singled out several badly edited pages in the 1593 version for the same sort of revision, particularly those reporting the behavior of the Princes during the trial.

1263 LINDHEIM, NANCY [ROTHWAX]. *The Structures of Sidney's "Arcadia."* Toronto: University of Toronto Press, 1982, 234 pp. Orig. a Ph.D. diss., University of California at Berkeley, 1966.
Defines three unifying patterns in *Arcadia*: 1) rhetorical structure, or "local organization of language and ideas"; 2) tonal structure, or "local textural devices" and arrangements of events to convey attitudes and judgments; and 3) narrative structure, or the arrangement of plot and

Twentieth Century

episode "without emphasizing linear or causal movement." In Chapter 1, considers the essentially rhetorical nature of *Arcadia* in its style, its frequent set speeches, and its underlying aim to move the will. Defines similarities between Sidney's outlook and that of the ancient Sophists and notes the limited impact of neo-Platonism and Christianity upon the work. In Chapter 2, considers Sidney's habit of thinking in antitheses, suggesting that *Arcadia* emphasizes two: matter versus spirit and doing versus suffering. Also analyzes *topoi* of praise and blame, noting fine distinctions of character between Argalus and Amphialus, Pyrocles and Musidorus, Pamela and Philoclea. Finds the females better differentiated than the males. Notes Sidney's "peculiar habit of constructing and superseding antithetical relationships," tracing it to his view of order among warring elements in the cosmos. Examines images of perfection in the landscape, the state, and the union of lovers, stressing the continual tension between the ideal and the actual. In Chapter 3, examines the antithesis between reason and passion. Explores Pyrocles's association with the myth of Hercules and Omphale, noting that, in Sidney's revision of the myth, love becomes a servant of heroic action. Also explores classical and Christian formulations of the relation between knowledge and virtue. Notes that Sidney vacillates, making Gynecia act according to the Christian view, Pyrocles according to the classical view, and Philoclea according to neither. In Chapter 4, argues that Sidney often orders events in a three-part "tonal structure." First a positive instance is given, then a negative one, then a comic parody. Finds this sequence in the single combats undertaken by Amphialus and his servant Clinias in Book III; in the Princesses sufferings at the hands of Cecropia; and in the three sections of Book I, which center on the accounts of Parthenia, Helen, and the tournament of Phalantus. Relates the three-part structure to stylistic and thematic antitheses and to the tragicomic form of the work. Also examines Sidney's narrative stance, concluding that he moved away from the intrusive narrator of the Old *Arcadia* toward a "transparent" one without independent personality. With reference to Freudian psychology, discusses figures such as Amphialus as "surrogate" heroes who suffer what the central heroes cannot be allowed to suffer. In Chapter 5, examines the relation of the main plot to the Asian adventures of Book II. Notes that Musidorus deals with public concerns that he and Pyrocles were educated to handle, and that his narration proceeds from education, to simple problems, to complex ones ending in a shipwreck. Pyrocles deals with matters of private integrity for which they had no preparation, and his stories proceed in similar stages to a shipwreck. Discusses the different narrative techniques employed by the two

Princes and treats the story of Erona as an epitome of their Asian experiences. In Chapter 6, argues that Sidney's political and social concerns do not derive from his sources. Examines his departures from chivalric romance, pastoral, and particular models such as Xenophon's *Cyropaedia* and Heliodorus's *Aethiopica*. Finds that Sidney was chiefly moved by his own temperament and his didactic theory of poetry, by Renaissance concepts of the epic, and by the ideals of Tudor humanism. Feels that the New *Arcadia* was written in imitation of Virgil's *Aeneid*. In Chapter 7, considers the relation of the main plot to the episodes. Evaluates the ending supplied in the 1593 *Arcadia*, accepting it in certain respects. Argues that Pyrocles does not undergo a process of moral education, noting little change in him after his attempts at suicide or his prison meditations. Despite the destructive effects of passion, sees Pyrocles and Musidorus as essentially heroic. Notes that, in revising the Old *Arcadia*, Sidney made them more noble, their story more consonant with the eclogues, and the work as a whole more clearly heroic. Analyzes the personal relationships in the book according to Aristotle's *Nicomachean Ethics* and notes the many conflicts between public and private responsibily. Evaluates Euarchus's judgments in the trial, admitting the importance of rigor in maintaining public order but noting the lack of legal equity or Christian mercy in his decisions. Finds the providential overturning of his judgments "a fitting culmination" of the work. Includes an appendix discussing the epic practice of beginning *in medias res* and another diagramming the personal relationships in *Arcadia*.

1264 ———. "Vision, Revision, and the 1593 Text of the *Arcadia*." *ELR* 2 (Winter 1972):136–47.
Using Aristotle's distinction between plot and episode, discusses the new episodes in Books I and II of the New *Arcadia* and the revised plot of Book III. Lists ways in which the revisions are not compatible with the completion that Sidney's sister supplied in 1593 and argues that "Sidney had changed his basic conception of [his] characters." Rejects recent scholarship that treats material in the Old *Arcadia* on Pyrocles's attempted suicide and the two Princes' discussion of death before the trial as if these were the outgrowth of material in the Captivity Episode in the New *Arcadia*. Argues that Sidney's characters do not undergo education or change but rather realize traits that were present in them from the outset. Regards the prison dialogue between Pyrocles and Musidorus, therefore, not as evidence of altered views but as a justification of the active life of heroism that they were already leading in Books I and II. Relates their discussion of memory after death to Socrates's justification

of himself in the *Phaedo* and to Renaissance debates on immortality. Focuses on the teachings of Aristotle, Averroes, and Pietro Pomponazzi.

1265 McCANLES, MICHAEL. "Oracular Prediction and the Fore-Conceit of Sidney's *Arcadia.*" *ELH* 50 (Summer 1983):233–44.
Explores the paradoxes generated by the Delphic Oracle in the two versions of *Arcadia*: an external and prior "blueprint" of the plot becomes its "fore-conceit," generating the plot despite attempts by the characters to avoid it. Ponders the dialectical interplay between free will and determinism that arises from their attempts. Compares Basilius with Oedipus, suggesting that Sidney's king flees, not just the events prophesied, but also the irrationality of the apparent contradictions in the oracle. Notes questions of interpretation that arise from the placement of the prophecy later in the revised version, where it is juxtaposed with Basilius's false but plausible view that it has already been fulfilled. Concludes that Sidney catches the reader in one of the mysteries of life: "that determinism generates freedom while denying it; freedom chooses restraint while seeking to escape it."

1266 McCOY, RICHARD C[HARLES]. *Sir Philip Sidney: Rebellion in Arcadia*. New Brunswick, N.J.: Rutgers University Press, 1979, pp. 36–68, 110–37. Orig. a Ph.D. diss., University of Calfornia at Berkeley, 1975.
In Chapter 2, discusses both versions of *Arcadia*, noting parallels with political events in England. Examines the conduct of Pyrocles, Musidorus, and Amphialus, finding in them an inability to establish a proper balance between political authority and individual autonomy. Focuses on the Huguenot doctrine of legitimate rebellion by subaltern magistrates. Also notes the inconclusiveness of the many debates in *Arcadia*, treating that between Reason and Passion in the Second Eclogues as a mirror for the main plot. Notes that both involve conflict with authority and lead to "grimly punitive" judgments, but that they ultimately allow the judgment to be evaded and end in moral confusion. Finds parallels between speeches in *Arcadia* and Sidney's letters to Languet. Sees in Sidney a conflict between desires for sympathy and indulgence and a need for punishment and forgiveness. Also lists characters in *Arcadia* who act as Oedipal father and mother figures. In Chapter 4, discusses the narrative sequence of the Old *Arcadia*. Notes a recurrent pattern of successful intrigue by the Princes, followed by reversals. Analyzes Pyrocles's debate with Philoclea after his attempted suicide and the Princes' discussion of immortality before the Trial Scene, pondering issues of divine authority and human autonomy. Interprets the

final trial as a test of paternal authority. Rejects Euarchus's "ruthlessly impersonal" legalism, relating it to Sidney's fear of his own father's judgment. Also rejects Basilius's claim that divine providence has governed the outcome, since the harmonious ending is based on "falsehood and evasion." Accuses Sidney of "blatant favoritism" toward the Princes, urging that "filial claims are satisfied without being fully vindicated, and paternal authority is thwarted without being denied." See also item 638.

1267 MAGISTER, KARL-HEINZ. "Philip Sidneys *Arcadia*: Ein höfisch-humanistischer Renaissance-Roman." *ShJE* 117 (1981):109–26.
Traces the social forces leading to the union of the medieval chivalric ideal of faith and fortitude with the Renaissance humanist ideal of polite learning and service to the state. Comments on the dilemma posed by Sidney's role as a courtier to an absolutist monarch and his background as a member of an independent aristocracy that opposed such absolutism. Sees the modern preference for the Old *Arcadia* as a failure to recognize Sidney's chosen role as a proponent of humanist political ideals and points to the importance of these ideals in the New *Arcadia*. Suggests that the work presents a utopian vision in which the authority of the state and the self-determination of the people are balanced, much as they are in Hooker's *Laws of Ecclesiastical Polity*. Contrasts the chivalric ideal of Malory, and comments on the way in which Sidney's new ideal affects style, point of view, structure, and characterization. Also discusses Sidney's adaptation of the pastoral tradition.

1268 MARENCO, FRANCO. *Arcadia Puritana: L'uso della tradizione nella prima "Arcadia" di Sir Philip Sidney.* Biblioteca di Studi Inglesi, 9. Bari, Italy: Adriatica Editrice, 1968, 240 pp.
Argues that the Old *Arcadia* is "one of the most important works in all of Elizabethan literature, and, moreover, that it possesses a very solid structure which espouses very clear ideas, and that under a frivolous and amusing appearance, it contains a profound allegory of human life, compared to which the much celebrated allegory of *The Faerie Queene* is an obscure labyrinth." Examines the Old *Arcadia* in the context of its literary tradition and concludes that, contrary to much critical commentary, it is not dominated by pastoral and epic conventions, but rather by "a vision antithetical to these conventions." It is a tentative effort at renewal, inspired by noteworthy cultural ambitions that appeared in the last quarter of the sixteenth century. Believes that it "resists interpretation based on preconceived external norms," but is "validated from within" (*valida per se stessa*) for its intelligence and its singular literary talent. In Chapter 1, describes a passage in Book III, finding in it themes and

Twentieth Century

structures characteristic of the whole work. Through five succeeding chapters, which form a "vast commentary" on this episode, proceeds to a "global interpretation" that seeks to situate the work within its cultural milieu. Each of the five chapters is divided into four sections, the first of which develops a particular aspect of the episode on which the rest of the chapter will focus. In Chapter 2, the focus is on the nature of kingship; in Chapter 3, on the concept of the hero; in Chapter 4, on the contradictory and illusory nature of social constructs; and in Chapter 5, on the problematic structure of the Old *Arcadia*. The second and third sections of each chapter examine themes relevant to the subject, and the fourth examines the literary traditions from which these themes emerge. In Chapter 6, maintains the four-part structure, focusing however, on Sidney's place in the culture of his century. Argues that the Old *Arcadia* is a "manifesto of a literary avant-garde" whose purposes are controlled by the ideas of Calvin and his adherents, and that recognition of this fact demands a reassessment of Sidney's character and place in his culture. Rather than the aristocratic courtier holding humanistic hands with Castiglione and Petrarch, we must see the dedicated scholar who uses literature as a powerful weapon to defend his political ideas and his religion: he is, in effect, the originator of a new school of thought. Claims that "we should not be surprised to find this 'paragon of his time' in the company of Puritan theologians: Puritanism and civil conventions coexisted at Elizabeth's court before parting company in the turbulent century of Charles I and Milton." Incorporates, in revised form, the substance of four articles: items 262, 1269, 1270, and 1271. See a reply by Roberts (1289).

1269 ———. "Double Plot in Sidney's Old *Arcadia*." *MLR* 64 (April 1969):248–63.

Laments the modern emphasis on generic and political studies of *Arcadia*, arguing that these have led critics to undervalue the Old *Arcadia* because it is not epic and lacks clear heroes. Regards it as "an allegory of the soul's pilgrimage" comparable to *The Faerie Queen* and as "a gloomy, almost desperate book" that mocks the wordly hero. Examines the interruptions in each of the first four acts by the lion and bear, the drunken Paphlagonians, the band of rebels, and Dametas, noting that each evil involves a greater participation of reason than the last. Points out that these invasions all mark crucial stages in the love intrigues of the royal characters and penetrate ever deeper into their seclusion. Regards the intruders as mirrors of Pyrocles and Musidorus, who are the main causes of disorder and death in Arcadia. Analyzes linguistic devices linking the intrusions with the main plot and traces the gradual degradation of the two Princes. See a reply by Roberts (1289).

1270 ———. "Per una nuova interpretazione dell'*Arcadia* di Sidney." *EM* 17 (1966):9–48.

Proposes that *Arcadia* be read as "an allegory of human life inspired by Calvinist thought." Analyzes "three crucial moments" in acts 1, 3, and 5 of the Old *Arcadia*, where Pyrocles and Musidorus discuss their fortunes and state, claiming that the recasting of these passages in the New *Arcadia* does not affect Sidney's intentions. Reads the Princes' initial debate concerning the active and contemplative lives as setting the moral and intellectual framework for the entire work: the Princes' capitulation to love "fragments" their internal equilibrium and leads to moral confusion. It is the complexity and thoroughness with which Sidney investigates the internal experience of his protagonists that marks his originality. Finds the second debate, turning on a conflict between love and friendship, "perfectly parallel" to the first. Whereas the first outcome was the Princes' isolation from the external world, the second is their isolation from each other. Events between the second and third debates drive the Princes to the brink of a "tragic human situation" from which there seems no escape. The ambiguity of the third debate is typical of Sidney's technique generally, in that it shows equally the Princes' infected wills and their erected wits. Noting that the passage has caused critical disagreement about Sidney's religious beliefs, argues that his view is the same as that in Davies's *Nosce teipsum* and Greville's *Treaty of Humane Learning*, i.e., that man's aim is to know inwardly both the fullness of his glory and the depth of his degradation. Traces the background of this idea to a form of Christian neo-Platonism that conflates the thoughts of St. Augustine, Ficino, and Calvin, contending that its proximate source for the three Englishmen was the Ramist reformation at Cambridge. Concludes that *Arcadia* enacts dramatically the principle, at once Protestant and humanist, epitomized by Calvin's injunction that "it is necessary for our conscience to inform us particularly of our misfortune [*mal-heureté*] before we can draw near to any knowledge of God."

1271 ———. "Sidney e l'*Arcadia* nella critica letteraria." *FeL* 12 (1966):337–76.

Governed by the premise that it is necessary to keep Sidney the author separate from Sidney the cultural "myth," surveys in detail the changing critical evaluations of *Arcadia* from the late eighteenth century to the present. Finds in the nineteenth and early twentieth centuries two major critical strains. The first, exemplified by Hazlitt (359, 558) and Symonds

Twentieth Century

(961), saw Sidney the author in conflict with Sidney the hero and preferred the latter. The second, exemplified by scholars such as Jusserand
(587, 1369) and Raleigh (1381), was bothered by the mingled genres of
Arcadia and became preoccupied with attempts to define the nature of
the work. Divides modern criticism into five main classes: one that is
allegorical, another that is formal, a third that is thematic (including
commentaries that regard *Arcadia* as a treatise on the education of the
prince), a fourth that seeks to reconcile the split between the man and
the writer, such as Goldman (534) and Lewis (630), and a fifth that
ignores or disparages the Old *Arcadia*. In a concluding section, sets forth
formal, allegorical, and thematic grounds for a critical resuscitation of
the original version.

1272 MOORE, DENNIS MICHAEL. "Elizabethan Poets and Politics:
Spenser's *Complaints* and Sidney's *Arcadia*." Ph.D. diss., Princeton
University, 1978, 239 pp.
Examines the form, imagery, and historical context of the Philisides
poems in the Old *Arcadia* (*OA* 9, 24, 31, 62, 66, 73, 74). Notes the corre-
spondences between Mira and Queen Elizabeth, suggesting that Sidney
was mingling allegories of love and politics in just the way that he did in
Four Foster Children of Desire. See *DAI* 39 (March 1979):5529A.

1273 ———. "Philisides and Mira: Autobiographical Allegory in the
Old *Arcadia*." *SSt* 3 (1982):125–37. Reprint in revised, expanded
form. In *The Politics of Spenser's "Complaints" and Sidney's Philisides
Poems*. Salzburg Studies in English. Elizabethan and Renaissance
Studies, 101. Salzburg: Institut für Anglistik und Amerikanistik,
Universität Salzburg, 1982.
Argues that in the Old *Arcadia* Sidney figures himself in the character of
Philisides and suggests that Mira may figure as Queen Elizabeth.
Analyzes the imagery of the mythological dream in "Now was our heav-
enly vault" (*OA* 73), drawing connections between the poem's situation
and Sidney's political problems. Contends that the proper analogy with
Philisides's choice and its effects is not the judgment of Paris but
Tiresias's judgment in favor of Zeus. Philisides, like Tiresias, suffers for
interfering in matters "too high."

1274 NORBROOK, DAVID. *Poetry and Politics in the English Renaissance*.
London, Boston, and Melbourne: Routledge & Kegan Paul, 1984,
pp. 1, 12, 15, 91–108, 117, 158, 171, 184, 196, 198, 203, 243,
274.
Sees in the Old *Arcadia* a society in which love and contemplation are
valued but are also subjected to criticism. Suggests that Sidney "politi-

cised Italian courtly romance, enclosing it within a carefully organized humanist framework" and sounding in it a note of republicanism that can be traced from him to the radicals of the 1650s. It is this tendency in his political thought that may account for some of Elizabeth's reluctance to entrust to him sensitive political offices. Notes, however, that Sidney's Protestant republicanism is tempered by an awareness of the need for ceremony and structure in society, both of which are weakened if there is no monarch. In the revisions of *Arcadia*, finds an attempt to "synthesize the aristocratic cult of honour with humanist and Protestant didacticism, to produce a work that men like Languet or Buchanan could respect on political as well as literary grounds." Feels that, in his later years, Sidney turned to "more explicitly Protestant literary forms," such as his translations of du Plessis-Mornay and du Bartas. Concludes that his politics became more Protestant and radical as he matured. Considers the impact of Sidney and his *Arcadia* on the views of Fulke Greville, Ben Jonson, and others in the Jacobean and Caroline periods.

1275 OLIVEIRA e SILVA, JOHN de. "The *Arcadias* of Sir Philip Sidney in the Context of the *Dianas* of Jorge de Montemayor and Gaspar Gil Polo: Religious Themes and the Language of Love." Ph.D. diss., City University of New York, 1977, 183 pp.

Examines philosophical themes in the Spanish *Dianas*, particularly the divergence between Montemayor's view that the human will cannot govern love with reason and Gil Polo's view that it can. Suggests that Sidney reconciles his Spanish sources by glorifying love and yet emphasizing the importance of the lover's will. Contrasts Sidney's heroes with those of Montemayor, noting that Sidney's do not require a magical intercessor like Felicia. Such a figure is unnecessary because divine providence is constantly working in harmony with the heroes' own virtuous wills. Concludes that, "in affirming . . . the integrity of the human intellect without denying the efficiency of providence, Sidney has followed the . . . moderate Reformers of his time." See *DAI* 38 (September 1977):1418A.

1276 PARKER, ROBERT WESLEY. "Narrative Structure and Thematic Development in Sidney's Original *Arcadia*." Ph.D. diss., Columbia University, 1965, 291 pp.

Attempts "to set forth the total structure, narrative and thematic," of the Old *Arcadia* in order to find a solution to problems of justice in the outcome. Contrasts Sidney's tightly knit sequence of cause and effect with the loose, episodic structure of his major sources, *Amadis de Gaule* and Heliodorus's *Aethiopica*, and concludes that Sidney modeled his plot on Terentian comedy. Suggests that Sidney supported Euarchus's judg-

Twentieth Century

ments and that the ending is problematic largely because his moral lessons clash with expectations aroused by the comic structure. See *DA* 28 (October 1967):1406A.

1277 ———. "Terentian Structure and Sidney's Original *Arcadia*." *ELR* 2 (Winter 1972):61–78.
Details sixteenth-century criteria for judging a work as "heroic" and concludes that the Old *Arcadia* is "the one significant heroic poem completed in English prior to *Paradise Lost*." Notes, however, the vagueness of the Elizabethan concept of the genre and the Continental view that epic was the origin of all the other genres and includes them. Argues that Sidney therefore sought a more precisely defined form in Terentian comedy. Discusses the wide dissemination of theories of Terentian comedy, analyzing Sidney's work according to Gregorius Wagnerus's description of the five-act structure of Terence's *Andria*. Compares the relative unity of Sidney's plot, defined in Aristotelian terms, with the disunity of his source *Amadis de Gaule*, noting that Sidney's characters are more like those of comedy than like traditional heroes of romance. Also reveals Sidney's sense of probability and causality by comparing his handling of the oracle and the climactic trial with that of a second source, Heliodorus's *Aethiopica*. In comparison with most other Renaissance works of prose fiction and drama, finds Sidney's "taut syllogistic structure" revolutionary. Discusses the importance of this structure for the world portrayed in the work, where clear laws of cause and effect prevail and moral choices are crucial. Locates the main dramatic conflict in the unresolved clash between the laws of the love-chase and the laws of public order.

1278 PATTERSON, ANNABEL. "'Under . . . Pretty Tales': Intention in Sidney's *Arcadia*." *SLitI* 15 (Spring 1982):5–21. Reprint, with additions, in item 693.
Viewing *Arcadia* as "an elegant test case for theories of interpretation," examines the extent to which "its fictionality, its generic affiliations, its plot and other textual procedures" relate to the "problem of restricted or proscribed communication." Sees in Sidney's revisions in the New *Arcadia* evidence for his "loss of confidence in indirect or covert discourse, or in messages accomodated to the forms of Elizabethan courtship." Whereas the Old *Arcadia* offers rather openly "an analysis of Elizabethan culture, finding it wanting," the New *Arcadia* creates a "medium of expression that may, with luck, break through the political restraints and cultural assumptions" and so allows Sidney "to keep faith with himself."

1279 PENN, SUSAN FAULKNER. "The Treatment of Love in Spenser and Sidney: A Comparison of Books III–V of the *Faerie Queene* and Sidney's (Old) *Arcadia*." Ph.D. diss., University of Kansas, 1983, 272 pp.

Finds similarities in theme and organization between the Old *Arcadia* and Books III–V of Spenser's *Faerie Queene*, arguing that both "seek to counter the influence of the courtly love tradition and to reconcile romantic love and Protestant marriage." Sees the works as "explorations of the nature of good love, one consonant with friendship and justice," in which the lovers are equals and friends and their love leads to "bounteous deeds" rather than obsessive desire. See *DAI* 44 (October 1983):1094A.

1280 PERKINSON, RICHARD H. "The Epic in Five Acts." *SP* 43 (July 1946):465–81.

Traces the origin of the five-act structure in classical drama and criticism and its adaptation for use in epic poetry. Notes Aristotle's comparisons of epic and tragedy and the medieval blurring of distinctions between narration and drama. Analyzes parallels between the five "books or acts" of the Old *Arcadia* and the structure of Senecan tragedy, suggesting that Sidney abandoned the structure in the New *Arcadia* because it restricted the variety and scope of the action.

1281 POIRIER, MICHEL. *Sir Philip Sidney: Le chevalier poète élizabéthain.* Travaux et mémoires de l'Université de Lille, nouvelle série— Droit et lettres, 26. Lyon, France: Bibliothèque Universitaire de Lille, 1948, pp. 198–218.

In Chapter 4 of Book II, discusses Sidney's revisions of *Arcadia*, stressing the expanded chivalric element, the nonchronological arrangement, the rapid narrative rhythms, the "flagrant anachronisms," and the attempts at psychological verisimiltude. Concludes that the New *Arcadia* is neither a point of departure nor a useful link in the evolution of a literary form, but rather a grand finale for genres whose brilliance had already faded. See also item 703.

1282 POPHAM, ELIZABETH [ANNE]. "Poetic Courtship, Policy, and the Remaking of Sidney's *Arcadia*." *SNew* 4, no. 2 (1983):3–12.

Argues that the "same idiom" ("the serious concerns of a would-be counsellor") is continually transformed in Sidney's major works from *The Lady of May* through the New *Arcadia*. Claims that *Four Foster Children of Desire* provides the crucial bridge from the Old *Arcadia* to the New. Extending Hamilton's observation (550) that Sidney employs the "indi-

Twentieth Century

rect" strategy of the narrator in More's *Utopia*, argues that the world of *Arcadia* is "sufficiently parallel" to the Elizabethan socio-political world to "offer alternative readings of contemporary issues, but flexible enough to permit the general application and explication of humanist counsel or rule." Notes the "unusually high" number of queens "brought by right of birth" to their thrones, as well as their "propensity to choose their suitors unwisely."

1283 PRAZ, MARIO. "Sidney's Original *Arcadia*." *London Mercury* 15 (March 1927):507–14. Reprint, with minor revisions. In *Ricerche anglo-italiane*, by Mario Praz. Rome: Instituto Grafico Tiberino, 1944, pp. 63–78.

Criticizes the Old *Arcadia* for its slow pace, medieval crudity, and "immature" methods of characterization. Compares it with d'Urfé's *Astrée* and with the New *Arcadia*. Argues that the revised version is worse than the original, commenting on the Countess of Pembroke's alteration of the final books for the edition of 1593. Notes precedents for the gruesome humor of Sidney's mob scenes in classical epigrams and in Marino's *Strage degl'innocenti*.

1284 PRINCE, RONALD FRANK. "'The Knowledge of a Mans Selfe': A Reading of Sidney's *Old Arcadia*." Ph.D diss., University of Pittsburgh, 1972, 221 pp.

Proposes that, in the Old *Arcadia*, Sidney tests the humanist doctrine of self-knowledge and finds that it fails to deal adequately with sexual passion. Considers the dialectic of reason and passion in the narrator as well as the major characters and finds a harmonious synthesis only at the end. Also proposes two ways to analyze the structure of the romance: 1) by relating the first two books to the private sphere, the last two books to the public sphere, and the middle book to both, as an allegory of the mind of a hero; or 2) by setting in parallel the main plot involving Pyrocles and those who love him, the comic plot involving Musidorus and those who love him, and the eclogues, which form a pastoral subplot.

1285 RAITIÈRE, MARTIN N[ORMAN]. *"Faire bitts": Sir Philip Sidney and Renaissance Political Theory*. Duquesne Studies in Language & Literature, ser. 4. Pittsburgh: Duquesne University Press, 1984, 166 pp.

Seeks to define the political views expressed in Sidney's writings and the nature of his affinities with contemporary Protestant political theory, especially that of Languet. Two chapters study the themes of rebellion and civil war in *Arcadia* as preliminary to two others devoted specifically to the Ister bank poem in the Third Eclogues (*OA 66*), seen as a "specific comment on that most notorious of Protestant works, *Vindiciae contra tyrannos*." Two appendices set forth the reasons for believing that Hubert Languet authored the anonymous 1579 treatise and examine Greville's several connections with the Ister bank poem. Assuming that "Sidney's politics have been misconstrued because we have put undue emphasis on some obvious biographical facts," Raitière acknowledges Sidney's "solid" connections to "the conventional architects of modern constitutional- ism," but argues that he commented on the Protestant League in order to reject it. Claims that, even as a young man, Sidney had doubts about the "rhetoric of kingfighters." Rejects claims by previous critics that the Ister bank poem contains "topical historical allegory," reading the fable instead as more generally devoted to "Nature and Art, beast and man."

1286 READ, PATRICIA ELINOR. "The Disfigured Mind: A Study of Art and Moral Vision in Sir Philip Sidney's Old and New *Arcadias*." Ph.D. diss., Rice University, 1971, 257 pp.

Analyzes ways in which Sidney's "treatment of moral vision and of the visual arts . . . reflects tension between Renaissance optimism about the capacity of man to see clearly and to create reasonable order and Puritan pessimism about it." Argues that Sidney's "increased use of arti- facts and the complex structure of the revision show his increased con- cern with exercising the mind of the reader so that he may become aware of the difficulties of seeing clearly." Suggests that he is "painfully aware" of the "limitations of human vision." See *DAI* 32 (October 1971):2068A.

1287 REES, JOAN. *Exploring "Arcadia."* Birmingham, England: University of Birmingham, 1981, 15 pp.

An "apology" for the study of *Arcadia*, warning against merely consider- ing it "characteristic of its age" and providing a brief outline of its con- tents. Contends that, in rewriting the original version, Sidney sought "an outlet for energies and skills which he was prevented from applying in the world of action." Finds the "distinction" of *Arcadia* in its blend of "political analysis and psychological penetration" and its generic com- plexity. Seeks to show that the Paphlagonian king episode is "deeply embedded in the soil of *Arcadia*," arguing that the story raises questions about the individual's duty to society and to other individuals that ramify throughout the entire narrative structure. Claims "firm evidence" that changes in the New *Arcadia* would not have affected the general outline of events as given in the Old. Emphasizes Sidney's authorial control over his materials: "the structure of *Arcadia* may be described in terms of co-

Twentieth Century

existing confusion and control, anarchy and order." Finds Sidney almost the equal of Shakespeare in his capacity "to enlarge our imaginative sympathies and our moral understanding," and to "disturb our prepared expectations and to invigorate our responses."

1288 ———. "Fulke Greville and the Revisions of *Arcadia*." *RES*, n.s. 17 (February 1966):54–57.
Reexamines statements by Greville and by John Florio on the state of the manuscripts of *Arcadia* and the ending envisioned for the revised version. Concludes that Sidney's "direction" to revise the romance may have referred, not to the New *Arcadia*, but to the Old. Thus, by 1593 there may have been three versions: the original; a "corrupt" copy of it revised by the Countess of Pembroke at Sidney's direction; and the extensively revised version written by Sidney himself and entrusted to Greville. If so, the ending supplied by the Countess may follow Sidney's directions and yet still not contain the ending that he envisioned for the New *Arcadia*.

1289 ROBERTS, JOSEPHINE A[NASTASIA]. *Architectonic Knowledge in the "New Arcadia" (1590): Sidney's Use of the Heroic Journey.* Salzburg Studies in English Literature: Elizabethan and Renaissance Studies, 69. Salzburg: Institut für englische Sprache und Literatur, Universität Salzburg, 1978, pp. 18–59. Orig. a Ph.D. diss., University of Pennsylvania, 1975.
In Chapter 1, examines the five-act structure of the Old *Arcadia* and Sidney's comparisons of the action with that of a play. Treating the two disguised Princes as comic actors, suggests that, in their encounter with the lion and the bear, they abandon heroism for self-interest. Notes imagery of disease and poison applied to their desires and relates their inner state to the rebellion of the Arcadian commoners. Sees Pyrocles's attempted suicide and their conduct at the trial as evidence of their decline, noting similar changes in Philisides, Erona, and Plangus. Considers the genres represented in the book, refuting suggestions by Davis (1499) and Isler (1250) and noting problems with those of Lanham (1255) and Marenco (1269, 1268). Argues that the work is a Roman comedy, involving traditional conflicts between young lovers and an old father, complications brought about by low characters, and musical interludes. Suggests that, in writing the New *Arcadia*, Sidney largely obliterated this comic pattern. For a detailed summary of chapters on the revised version, see item 1739.

1290 ———. "Herculean Love in Sir Philip Sidney's Two Versions of *Arcadia*." *EIRC* 4 (Spring 1978):43–54.

Discusses the Pyrocles of the Old *Arcadia*, noting allusions linking him with the myth of Hercules and Omphale. Finds in each book of Sidney's romance a parallel to one of the twelve labors of Hercules. Suggests, however, that Sidney undermines the heroic comparison by adding touches of irony and frequent reminders of Pyrocles's youthfulness and passion. Notes that Spenser makes similar ironic uses of the myth in *The Faerie Queene* and that, in the *Defence*, the story is treated as comic. Contrasts the allusions to the myth in the New *Arcadia*, where Pyrocles is portrayed more seriously as a heroic figure. Regards Amphialus as his foil, brought in to demonstrate the dangers of an unresolved conflict between erotic passion and heroic virtue. Sees in Pyrocles a gradual process of development into heroic maturity.

1291 ROBERTSON, JEAN. "Euarchus/Evarchus in Sidney's *Arcadia*." *RenQ* 28 (Summer 1975):298–99.

Notes that early manuscripts and editions offer no sure guidance, but argues for the pronunciation "Euarchus."

1292 ROCKWELL, PAUL EDMUND. "Comic Elements in Sidney's *Old Arcadia*." Ph.D. diss., University of Maryland, 1980, 185 pp.

Emphasizes "Sidney's intention to entertain," studying comic techniques in the narration, the characterization, and the use of language. Examines Renaissance lore about Amazons, finding positive as well as negative associations. Also examines Sidney's frequent allusions to Ovid and his use of a comic style of erotic narration derived from the *Metamorphoses*. Suggests that Sidney's damping of comic effects in Book IV is necessary to build suspense for the climax. See *DAI* 41 (December 1980):2619A.

1293 ROWE, KENNETH THORPE. "The Countess of Pembroke's Editorship of the *Arcadia*." *PMLA* 54 (March 1939):122–38.

Examines Hugh Sanford's preface to the 1593 *Arcadia* (item 31), particularly its comments on the editing done by Sidney's sister. Against scholars who have accused her of rearranging, revising, and bowdlerizing the last three books, infers from Sanford's preface that she merely corrected printing errors in the 1590 edition (item 30) and supplied the conclusion of the Old *Arcadia*, adding nothing that Sidney had not himself written or determined. Suggests that Sidney made revisions in Book III–V of *Arcadia* in just one manuscript, his sister's, and that she followed these revisions in the 1593 edition. In support of this hypothesis, under-

Twentieth Century

takes a comparative analysis of all the important discrepancies between the Old *Arcadia* and the last books of the 1593 edition, as well as the rearrangement of the eclogues.

1294 ———. "Elizabethan Morality and the Folio Revisions of Sidney's *Arcadia*." *MP* 37 (November 1939):151–72.
Examines two major revisions of the last books of the Old *Arcadia* as they appeared in the 1593 edition: Pyrocles's consummation of his love of Philoclea and Musidorus's contemplated rape of Pamela. Draws upon social history and each of the major literary sources of *Arcadia* to demonstrate that it was common and accepted for betrothed couples to consummate their marriages before the formal ceremony. Suggests, therefore, that Sidney's sister would probably not have revised the text because she found the sexual nature of either scene shocking. Discusses her role in publishing material no less shocking in *Astrophil and Stella*. Drawing on principles stated in the *Defence*, argues that Sidney meant his heroes to be complete models of virtue throughout *Arcadia* and that he himself made the revisions, not because their sexual conduct was wrong, but because it was "frivolous," "lacking in magnitude and vigor of purpose."

1295 SCANLON, PAUL A. "Sidney's *Old Arcadia*: A Renaissance Pastoral Romance." *Ariel* 10 (October 1979):69–76.
Against critics who minimize the pastoral elements in the Old *Arcadia*, points out the importance of the enchanted rural setting. Identifies the cave with the "feminine principle" and suggests that the book is in the tradition of pastoral celebrations of love exemplified by Montemayor's *Diana*. Allows that Sidney poses problems about love not easily solved, but suggests that Euarchus provides an ideal standard at the end.

1296 SCHLEINER, WINFRIED. "Differences of Theme and Structure of the Erona Episode in the *Old* and *New Arcadia*." *SP* 70 (October 1973):377–91.
Analyzes the original version of the Erona story as an object lesson in the vengefulness of Cupid, and relates it to the character of Histor, who narrates it. Points out that, in the revised version, many of the references to Cupid are dropped or weakened, and the central issue becomes the discrepancy in rank between Erona and her husband Antiphilus. Concludes that Sidney's main aim in revising the episode was to show that the lower classes are uncontrolled and cannot properly separate private desires from public responsibilities. Also examines the stories told by Miso and

Mopsa and the accounts of Plangus and Andromana, Pamphilus and Dido, the Paphlagonian King, and the mutinous commoners.

1297 SKRETKOWICZ, VICTOR, [Jr.]. "Hercules in Sidney and Spenser." *N&Q,* n.s. 27 (August 1980):306–10.
Traces the origins of the error that Hercules traded clothes with Iole rather than with Omphale. Concludes that Sidney followed this late medieval tradition in both versions of *Arcadia,* but also drew upon the story of Omphale. Discusses ironies in his comparisons between Amphialus and Hercules.

1298 ———. "Sidney and Amyot: Heliodorus in the Structure and Ethos of the *New Arcadia.*" *RES,* n.s. 27 (May 1976):170–74.
Examines the influence of Heliodorus upon Sidney's revisions of the original *Arcadia.* Concentrates on the analysis of the *Aethiopica* in the proem to Amyot's translation, noting the correspondences between Amyot's theory and Sidney's practice, particularly in the method of narration and in the moral and martial conduct of the heroes.

1299 SMART, MARGARET JANE McCALLUM. "Sir Philip Sidney as Ironist: An Examination of Some Rhetorical Structures in the *Old Arcadia.*" Ph.D. diss., University of Toronto, 1976.
Considers "epistemological contradictions" arising from Sidney's divided view of the human mind. Concentrates on "the ironic structures of the *Old Arcadia* in relation to the rhetorical tradition and to sixteenth-century theories of cognition and communication," particularly those of Plato, Aristotle, Peter Ramus, and the Christian neo-Platonists. Considers the apparent division between thought and style in the poetic theory of the *Defence* and the role that this division plays in the Old *Arcadia.* Suggests that the romance begins with Plato's ideal of rational harmony in the soul and moves toward a Christian emphasis on the need for divine grace and the limits of human understanding. See *DAI* 39 (October 1978):2265A.

1300 STILLMAN, ROBERT E. "The Perils of Fancy: Poetry and Self-Love in *The Old Arcadia.*" *TSLL* 26 (Spring 1984):1–17.
Argues that, unlike the *Defence,* which is "agressively optimistic" about the effects of poetry on the audience, the Old *Arcadia* provides a "critique of the dangers of the imagination." In that work, "the psychological distortions of the impassioned mind are linked to the poetic logic of romanticizing fiction to provide what is simultaneously a lesson in reading and a lesson in evaluating modes of thought." Shows that Sidney is "ambivalent" about the "imaginative tools" that Pyrocles and Musidorus

Twentieth Century

use to persuade their mistresses; their songs "indicate potential perils of the fancy in alienating mankind from . . . the virtue and contentment which a life led in harmony with nature supplies." Examines in two parts the consequences when a poet-lover uses imagination to impose desire on nature and on an audience.

1301 ———. "Sidney's Arcadian Eclogues and Renaissance Pastoral Traditions." Ph.D. diss., University of Pennsylvania, 1979, 532 pp. In Part 1, argues that the Old *Arcadia* asks us to evaluate several competing versions of the idle life as "a way of determining how to make a just response to fortune"; the Old *Arcadia* is Sidney's "*gesture* to obtain for himself and for England the relief from misfortune that justice alone can supply." In Part 2, claims that the Old *Arcadia* is a Stoic version of pastoral, which achieves a synthesis between Italianate aestheticism and the "moral authority of the Christian bucolic." It defends pastoral by redefining its traditional values. In Part 3, studies the relationship between the eclogues and the books adjacent to them, and in Part 4 examines Sidney's attitude toward "the capacity of poetry to reconcile man to his world, while showing his awareness of poetry's limitations and the dangers of 'fancy.'" See *DAI* 40 (April 1980):5457A.

1302 TILLYARD, E[USTACE] M[ANDEVILLE] W[ETENHALL]. *The English Epic and Its Background.* New York: Oxford University Press, 1954, pp. 230, 254–61, 291, 294–319, 373–74.
Cites evidence that the Elizabethans regarded *Arcadia* and *The Faerie Queene* as epics and as the greatest works in the English language. Compares them with Shakespeare's histories, emphasizing their philosophical and political character. In Chapter 10, "Sidney," discusses the reputation of *Arcadia* and classes the original version as a romantic novel and the revision as more nearly an epic. Emphasizes the range of styles Sidney had mastered. Examines Continental theories of the epic and Sidney's application of them, touching on his adaptation of Virgilian battle scenes and Aristotelian methods of characterization. Counters critics who regard the New *Arcadia* as more political than the Old, contending that the Christian doctrine of the Captivity Episode is the main distinguising feature. Lists three main conflicts in the work: the active versus the contemplative, the Aristotelian versus the Christian, and the misgoverned versus the well-governed. Ponders the problems caused by Sidney's tendency to mix literary convention with direct, personal observation. Also seeks to differentiate Sidney's "plastic and pictorial" writing from the more "literary and progressive" method of other great authors.

Points out the influence of *Arcadia* on William Chamberlayne's *Pharonnida* and compares *Arcadia* with Honoré d'Urfé's *Astrée* and John Barclay's *Argenis*.

1303 TOLIVER, HAROLD E. *Pastoral Forms and Attitudes*. Berkeley: University of California Press, 1971, pp. 15–16, 38–39, 45–62, 113–14, 211.

Suggests that Sidney's Christianity made his pastoral world likely to be ransacked and his heroes and shepherds resistant to moral change. Contrasts Shakespeare's "green worlds," in which large groups of characters are transformed by experience. Also compares the radical naturalism of Montaigne's and Milton's view that there are no "green worlds" left outside the imagination. In Chapter 3, "Sidney's Knights and Shepherds," examines the opening of the revised version in order to demonstrate its complex balance of romantic and pastoral elements. Contrasts the original version, finding that it interweaves romance and pastoral more closely. Notes the mutual dependence of the noblemen and the rustics, but also their separation, one embodying the active life, discipline, and the Aristotelian mean between luxury and poverty, and the other embodying the contemplative life, hopeless longing for perfection, and greater poverty. Contrasts this social order in Arcadia with the chaos among the Helot rebels. Regards much of the book as an exploration of "the imperfections of nobility and rusticity and their relations." Suggests that those who cross the class lines learn something but are not transformed by their experiences.

1304 TOWNSEND, FREDA L. "Sidney and Ariosto." *PMLA* 61 (March 1946):97–108.

Suggests that Ariosto's *Orlando furioso* provided the method of plotting for both versions of *Arcadia*. Against Myrick (1691), argues that Sidney did not follow Aristotelian principles of epic design, even as these were adapted by Antonio Minturno. Notes that Minturno distinguished carefully between epic and romance and disapproved of the many persons and incidents in romances like *Orlando*. Contrasts the approval of Ariosto by Renaissance critics in Italy and England, including Sidney himself (in the *Defence*). Discusses Sidney's tendency to break off episodes, his addition of tangential adventures and episodes utterly unconnected with the main action, and his combination of medieval and modern warfare.

Twentieth Century

1305 TURNER, MYRON [MARTIN]. "'Disguised Passion' and the Psychology of Suicide in Sidney's Old *Arcadia.*" *PLL* 15 (Winter 1979):17–37.

Suggests that the romance "teaches that virtue is . . . passion in disguise" and so reveals what Pamela calls "the darkest of all natural secrets, which is the heart of man." Considers the discrepancy in the main characters between outward virtues and inward sins, suggesting that Sidney was following the radical psychology of the Calvinists, which made the cognitive faculty subject to the affective faculty and virtually denied free will. Discusses the conflict between Stoic and Christian elements in the passage on Pyrocles's attemped suicide. Examines his underlying motives in the light of Reformed doctrine.

1306 ———. "Distance and Astonishment in the Old *Arcadia*: A Study of Sidney's Psychology." *TSLL* 20 (Fall 1978):303–29.

Undertakes to explain "the structures and dynamics of consciousness" in Sidney's characters, considering the origins and effects of their mental states. Contrasts the rational, temperate mind of Euarchus, which exemplifies Stoic humanism, with the blinded, intemperate minds of the royal lovers, in which reason is overpowered by continual experiences of wonder or astonishment. Notes that the Stoic Pamela of the New *Arcadia* is not present in the original version and treats Philanax's excesses in Book V as failed Stoicism. Traces the origin of irrationality in Arcadia to Basilius's "prelapsarian" curiosity about the oracle and his subsequent astonishment and fall. Considers Renaissance philosophical debates over the role of reason and imagination in cognition, noting that Sidney's characters rely on imagination, which originates in the senses and is thus uncertain. Considers the classical, medieval, and Protestant elements in Sidney's concept of constancy, defining it as the "compulsion to recover the lost sense of wholeness that antedated astonishment." Contrasts imagery of stone and intricate webs in the romance, considering the role of providence in controlling time and chance and the failure of the characters to be provident. Regards Euarchus's judgment in the trial as a final indication of the limitations of Stoic rationalism and the need for faith in divine grace.

1307 VICKERS, BRIAN. "In Search of *Arcadia.*" *Cambridge Review* 89 (29 October 1966):62–64.

Argues that Sidney's style is not uniformly "luscious, over-elaborated" but varies according to scene and matter. Praises the plotting and the revealing juxtaposition of characters, noting the major changes introduced in the revision. Also reviews Davis (1499) and Lanham (1255).

Against Davis, argues that the book is not a pastoral and does not include a circular journey of neo-Platonic enlightenment. Against Lanham, contends that the narrator is not untrustworthy.

1308 WEINER, ANDREW DAVID. "'Erected Wit' and 'Infected Will': A Study of Sir Philip Sidney's *Old Arcadia*." Ph.D. diss., Princeton University, 1969, 249 pp.

Following the clue in the *Defence* that poetry must be read "allegorically and figuratively," sets the Old *Arcadia* in the context of Elizabethan attitudes toward allegory and Protestant Biblical exegesis. Examines the morality of the main characters, concluding that all are negative *exempla* and hence that the work is not a heroic romance but "a pastoral which uses romance materials in a comic mode." Notes that the eclogues and the Terentian five-act structure of the work clarify the moral evil of the main characters and set them in contrast to such ideal figures as Lalus, Kala, and Euarchus. See *DA* 31 (August 1970):736A.

1309 WHITE, R.S. "'Comedy' in Elizabethan Prose Romances." *YES* 5 (1975):46–51.

In seeking antecedents for Elizabethan romantic comedy, examines the Old *Arcadia*, pointing out the romantic elements of the plot and suggesting that Sidney took the sense of wonder and supernatural mystery from Greek romance and "provided a rational explanation . . . in the interests of verisimilitude." Notes the same tendency in Shakespeare. Points out that, whereas the classical view of comedy emphasizes the correction of vices, Sidney's *Defence* also gives the genre a role in teaching virtue, as did many Elizabethan plays.

1310 ———. *Shakespeare and the Romance Ending*. Newcastle upon Tyne, England: R.S. White, 1981, 147 pp. passim. Orig. a D.Phil. thesis, Oxford University, 1974.

Regards the New *Arcadia* as, by its very nature, "endless," in that the reader's expectation of an ending is gradually subordinated to a "self-generating" multiplicity of complications and digressions. Contrasts the clear sense of an ending in the Old *Arcadia*. Feels that, in the original version, Sidney was crossing Greek romance with Italian *novelle*, whereas, in the revised version, he was following medieval romance. Relates the New *Arcadia* to the romances of Shakespeare, particularly *Cymbeline*, in which the Queen resembles Sidney's character Cecropia and Cloten resembles Clinias.

Twentieth Century

1311 WILES, AMERICUS GEORGE DAVID. "Continuations of Sir
Philip Sidney's *Arcadia*." Ph.D. diss., Princeton University, 1934.
As background for discussing the continuations, provides parallel analyses of the Old *Arcadia* and the New, discussing epic sequence and
defending Sidney's style. Finds little merit in the continuations, especially those by Anne Weamys and Gervase Markham. Rates most highly the
continuations of the New *Arcadia* by Sir William Alexander and by James
Johnstoun and the supplemental episodes by Richard Beling.

1312 ———. "Parallel Analyses of the Two Versions of Sidney's
Arcadia." *SP* 39 (April 1942):167–206.
Prints in parallel columns synopses of the Old *Arcadia* and those portions of the New *Arcadia* that were revised or relocated. Discusses major
improvements: a new epic structure, added variety and unity in the
episodes, and closer ties between the main plot and the subplots.
Concludes that the revisions heighten suspense, verisimilitude, and dramatic effectiveness.

1313 WILLIAMS, KENT F. "Theme and Structure in the Third
Eclogues of Sidney's *Old Arcadia*." *Selected Papers from the West
Virginia Shakespeare and Renaissance Association* 4 (Spring
1979):1–9.
Rejects Kalstone's view (1907) that Sidney regarded his rustics with
"comic irony," finding them "incapable of the higher ranges of feeling
that characterize his heroes." Identifies the views of the shepherds in the
Third Eclogues with those of Sidney. Explicates each poem in the group
(*OA 64–67*), noting that they begin with a celebration of marital harmony, turn to examine disharmony extending from the family to the state,
and finally return to the possibility of happiness in marriage.

1314 WILSON, MONA. Review of *Sidney's Arcadia: A Comparison between
the Two Versions*, by R[einard] W. Zandvoort. *RES* 6 (October
1930):466–67.
In responding to Zandvoort (1316), urges that Sidney's own instructions,
not his sister's "Puritanism," were responsible for the Princes' improved
sexual conduct in the 1593 version. Also argues that Cecropia's atheism
owes nothing to Lucretius's *De Rerum Natura*.

1315 YOUNG, FRANCES CAMPBELL BERKELEY. *Mary Sidney,
Countess of Pembroke*. London: David Nutt, 1912, pp. 24–26,
40–41, 46–49, 57, 119, 123–32, 134–40. Orig. a Ph.D. diss.,
University of Wisconsin, 1911.
Relates Sidney's life to that of his sister. Discusses recently discovered
manuscripts of the Old *Arcadia* and the Countess's revisions of the 1593

edition, concluding that she "added no more than she could help; left out only those things that she deemed too personal to be printed; and employed the only possible means of completing the story." Also discusses "The Doleful Lay of Clorinda" (2741) and the Sidney Psalms, considering extant manuscripts and evidence of authorship.

1316 ZANDVOORT, R[EINARD] W[ILLEM]. *Sidney's Arcadia: A Comparison between the Two Versions.* Amsterdam: N.V. Swets & Zeitlinger, 1929, 228 pp.

In Chapter 1, covers sixteenth-century allusions to *Arcadia* and the publication history and date of the romance. Provides a detailed description and a partial collation of six manuscripts and the 1590 and 1593 editions, examining Mary Sidney's corrections in the 1593, noting her errors, and giving her credit for radical changes, particularly in the morality of the young couples. Also notes faults in Feuillerat's edition (23). In Chapter 2, examines Sidney's progress as a storyteller, reviewing opinions on *Arcadia* of Sidney's contemporaries and modern critics. Compares extracts from the two versions, arguing that the revised version is superior in characterization, verisimilitude, and narrative technique. Gives special attention to new complexity in the characters of Pamela, Philoclea, and Gynecia and to new powers of construction in the episodes of Amphialus's rebellion and the story of Erona and Plangus. In Chapter 3, takes up Sidney's progress as a thinker. Rejects the view of Greville (863) and Greenlaw (1242) that Sidney's main intent was moral and political instruction. Also quarrels with Brie (1202) on the influence of Aristotle and Plato and on the prevalence of allegory in *Arcadia*. Probes Sidney's views on pictorial art; on friendship and love; and on the ideal ruler. Finds in Euarchus affinities with Queen Elizabeth and with Sidney himself. Also discusses Sidney's brutal tone with the lower classes and reviews the philosophical and political debates in the book, particlularly the one between Cecropia and Pamela on atheism. In Chapter 4, examines style in the two versions, arguing that it is diverse rather than homogeneous. Analyzes Sidney's most common schemes and tropes and concludes that the revised version is superior in most respects. In Chapter 5, reviews previous scholarship on Sidney's sources, summarizing William Vaughan Moody's unpublished 1894 Harvard University M.A. thesis, "An Inquiry into the Sources of Sir Philip Sidney's *Arcadia*." See also Feuillerat (1236) and Wilson (1314).

1317 ———. "The Two versions of Sidney's *Arcadia*." *Archiv* 157 (1930):261.

Provides basic information on the manuscripts and the early printed versions of *Arcadia*.

Twentieth Century

1318 ZEEVELD, W. GORDON. "The Uprising of the Commons in Sidney's *Arcadia*." *MLN* 48 (April 1933):209–17.
Argues that the uprising in Book II of the Old *Arcadia* was written as an allegory protesting the proposed marriage between Elizabeth and Alençon. Contrasts the revised version, in which Sidney has removed all dangerous allegorical parallels. In explaining these deletions, notes that, by 1580, the Queen had shown her inclination to punish vocal critics of the match, and Sidney's party at court had ceased its opposition.

2. REVISED EDITIONS OF 1590 AND 1593

Sixteenth Century

1319 HARVEY, GABRIEL. *Pierces Supererogation or A New Prayse of the Old Asse*. London: John Wolfe, 1593, sigs. G3^r–G4^r. Reprint. In *The Works of Gabriel Harvey*, edited by Alexander B. Grosart. The Huth Library, Vol. 2. London and Aylesbury: Hazell, Watson, & Viney, 1884, pp. 99–102. Reprint in facsimile. Menston, England: Scolar Press, 1970.
Recommends *Arcadia* for four things: amorous courting, sage counselling, valorous fighting, and "delightful pastime by way of pastorall exercises." Compares Sidney with "the most sententious historians" and praises the romance for containing "some politic secrets of privity" and good counsel on the use of weapons. Compares the romance with the epics of Homer.

Seventeenth Century

1320 LANGBAINE, GERARD. *An Account of the English Dramatick Poets*. Oxford: L.L., for George West and Henry Clements, 1691, pp. 232, 476. Reprint. Oxford and New York: Burt Franklin, 1964. Reprint in facsimile. Menston, England: Scolar Press, 1971.
Notes that several plays published before 1691 adapt plots from *Arcadia*, including Glapthorne's *Argalus and Parthenia* and Shirley's *Arcadia*.

1321 MARKHAM, JARVIS [elsewhere GERVASE]. Preface to *The English Arcadia, Alluding his beginning from Sir Philip Sidneys ending*. London: Edward Allde, for Henrie Rocket, 1607, sigs. A2^r–A2^v.
Defends his own imitation of *Arcadia* by pointing out Sidney's debt to Montemayor and Heliodorus. See also item 1322.

1322 M[ARKHAM], G[ERVASE] [elsewhere JARVIS]. Preface to *The Second and Last Part of the First Booke of the English Arcadia.* London: Nicholas Okes, for Thomas Sanders, 1613, sigs. A4ʳ–A4ᵛ.
Reacts to those who criticized his view (1321) that *Arcadia* was influenced by Montemayor and Heliodorus.

1323 M[ILTON], I[OHN]. ΕΙΚΟΝΟΚΛΑΣΤΗΣ *in Answer to a Book Intitl'd* ΕΙΚΩΝ ΒΑΣΙΛΙΚΗ., *The Portrature of his Sacred Majesty in his Solitudes and Sufferings.* London: Matthew Simmons, 1649, pp. 11–13. Reprint. In *The Works of John Milton*, edited by Frank Allen Patterson, et al. The Columbia Edition. Vol. 5, *Eikonoklastes*, edited by William Haller. New York: Columbia University Press, 1932, pp. 85–86.
Attacks Charles I for attempting "to attribute to his own making other mens whole Prayers," namely Pamela's prayer from Book III of "the vain amatorious Poem of Sr *Philip Sidneys Arcadia*; a Book in that kind full of worth and witt, but among religious thoughts, and duties not worthy to be nam'd." See reactions by Wagstaff (1326), Johnson (1331), Lauder (1332), Nichols (1335), Almack (1339), Masson (1376), Symmons (1388), Alexander (1396), Empson (1525), Hughes (1599), Liljegren (1650), Madan (1670), and Smart (1768).

1324 PELLIS[S]ON[-FONTANIER], PAUL. *The History of the French Academy, Erected at Paris by the late Famous Cardinal de Richelieu, and consisting of the most refined Wits of the Nation. Wherein is set down its Original and Establishment, its Statutes, Daies, Places, and manner of Assemblies, etc. With the Names of its Members, and Character of their Persons, and a Catalogue of their Works.* London: by J. Streater for Thomas Johnson, 1657, p. 218.
Provides an English translation of item 1325.

1325 ———. *Relation Contenant L'Histoire de L'Académie François.* Paris: Chez Augustin Covrbé, 1653, p. 504.
Claims that Baudoin was commissioned by Queen Marie de Médicis to produce his French version of *Arcadia* (33) and that he travelled to England for the purpose, meeting there a "French gentlewoman" who helped with the translation and later married him. See also item 1324.

1326 [WAGSTAFF, THOMAS.] *A Vindication of K. Charles the Martyr: Proving That His Majesty was the Author of "EIKON BASILIKE."* London: H. Hindmarsh, 1697, 54 pp.
Includes the first attempt to prove that Milton himself arranged to insert Pamela's prayer into Charles I's prayer book. Supplies the testimony of

Seventeenth Century

the printer to this effect, listing early editions that did not include the prayer. Urges that Charles was not especially fond of *Arcadia* but that Milton took it "as a pattern, to mend his style and invention." See also Milton (1323) and Liljegren (1650).

Eighteenth Century

1327 ALEXANDER, Sir WILLIAM, Earl of Stirling. *Anacrisis; or, A Censure of some Poets Ancient and Modern.* In *The Works of William Drummond of Hawthornden.* Edinburgh: James Watson, 1711, pp. 159–62. Reprint. In *Critical Essays of the Seventeenth Century*, edited by J[oel] E[lias] Spingarn. Vol. 1. Oxford: Clarendon Press, 1908, pp. 180–89.
Calls *Arcadia* "the most excellent work . . . written in any language." Regards each of the characters as an example of a particular virtue and notes the union of epic and pastoral in the book, comparing it with Honoré d'Urfé's *Astrée.* Explains his own intentions in completing the unfinished third book.

1328 ANON. Letter. *Gentleman's Magazine* 35 (May 1765):229.
Explains the conventions of chivalric battle behind the phrase in *Arcadia* "defying him in a mortal affray from the bodkin to the pike upward."

1329 ———. Letter. *Gentleman's Magazine* 37 (February 1767):57–60.
Notes Shakespeare's borrowings from *Arcadia*, especially in *King Lear*, and rebuts Walpole's attacks on the romance (294).

1330 CRITO [pseud.]. "Sequel to the Poetical Balance, Being Miscellaneous Thoughts on English Poets." *Scots Magazine; or, Edinburgh Magazine and Literary Miscellany* 20 (March 1758):138–40.
Contrasts Spenser's "natural" style with the "tortured" prose of *Arcadia.* Sees Sidney's work as a disguised attempt "to justify putting Mary Queen of Scots to death."

1331 JOHNSON, SAMUEL. *Milton.* In *The Lives of the English Poets; and a Criticism on Their Works.* Dublin: Whitestone, Williams, Colles, et al., 1779, pp. 156–57.
Inclines to the view that Milton or his party interpolated Pamela's prayer into Charles I's prayer book, *Eikon Basilike.* See Milton (1323).

1332 LAUDER, WILLIAM. *King Charles I. Vindicated From the Charge of Plagiarism, Brought against him by Milton, and Milton himself convicted* *of Forgery, and a gross Imposition on the Public. To the Whole is sub-joined the Judgment of several Learned and Impartial Authors concerning Milton's Political Writings.* London: Printed for W. Owen, 1754, pp. 21–34.

Not seen. Argues that Milton himself was responsible for inserting Pamela's prayer into the published version of Charles I's prayer book, *Eikon Basilike*. See Milton (1323).

1333 [LENNOX, CHARLOTTE RAMSEY.] *Shakespear Illustrated; or, The Novels and Histories on which the Plays of Shakespear Are Founded.* Vol. 3. London: A. Millar, 1754, pp. 291–301.

Reprints the story of the Paphlagonian King, noting similarities with the subplot of *King Lear*.

1334 LINDERN [elsewhere LINDNER], KASPAR GOTTLIEB. *Umständliche Nachricht von des weltberümten Schlesiers, Martin Opitz von Boberfeld, Leben, Tode, und Schriften.* Vol. 2. Hirschberg, Germany: Immanuel Krahn, 1741, pp. 25–26.

Originates the disputed theory that the name "Valentinus Theocritus von Hirschberg" given the translator of the first German version of *Arcadia* (34) was a pseudonym for Martin Opitz. See counterarguments by Wurmb (1836), but see also Dünnhaupt (1519).

1335 NICHOLS, JOHN [GOUGH]. *Biographical and Literary Anecdotes of William Bowyer, Printer . . . Containing an Incidental View of the Progress and Advancement of Literature in This Kingdom from the Beginning of the Present Century to the End of the Year MDCCLXXVII.* London: John Nichols, 1782, pp. 633–34. Reprint. In *Literary Anecdotes of the Eighteenth Century; Comprizing Biographical Memoirs of William Bowyer, Printer.* Vol. 1. London: John Nichols, 1812, pp. 525–26.

Quotes Bowyer's evidence that Milton interpolated Pamela's prayer in Charles I's prayer book, *Eikon Basilike*. See Milton (1323).

1336 R[EEVE], C[LARA]. *The Progress of Romance, Through Times, Centuries, and Manners; with Remarks on the Good and Bad Effects of It, on Them Respectively; in a Course of Evening Conversations.* Vol. 1. Colchester, England: W. Keymer, 1785, pp. 75–79.

Defends *Arcadia* against Walpole (294), rating its prose above its poetry.

Eighteenth Century

1337 STEEVENS, G[EORGE]. Commentary on *King Lear* IV.iii. In *The Plays of William Shakespeare*, edited by S[amuel] Johnson and G[eorge] Steevens. Vol. 9. London: C. Bathhurst, 1773, p. 440. Reprint. In *King Lear*, edited by Horace Howard Furness. A New Variorum Edition of Shakespeare, 5. Philadelphia: J.B. Lippincott Co., 1880, p. 252.
Suggests that, in the passage describing Cordelia's reaction to letters from England, the phrase "sunshine and rain" derives from a description of Philoclea in *Arcadia*.

Nineteenth Century

1338 ADAMS, W[ILLIAM HENRY] DAVENPORT. *Famous Books*. New York: R. Worthington, [1879], pp. 114–44.
In "Sidney's *Arcadia*," attacks Walpole (294) and Hazlitt (359) for their low opinion of Sidney's works, reviewing the praises of other commentators. Considers the style and the sources of *Arcadia*.

1339 ALMACK, EDWARD. *A Bibliography of the King's Book or "Eikon Basilike."* London: Blades, East, & Blades, 1896, pp. 47–48.
Notes the origins of the charge that Milton inserted Pamela's prayer into Charles I's prayer book. Lists editions of *Eikon Basilike* that contain the prayer. See Milton (1323).

1340 ANON. "The Literary World: Its Sayings and Doings." *The Critic: London Literary Journal* 13 (1 February 1854):64.
Explains an attempt to pirate an article on *Arcadia* by Crossley (1351), which led to its printing as a book (1352).

1341 ———. "Sidney, Spenser, and Elizabethan Romance." *Tait's Edinburgh Magazine* 22 (October 1855):577–82.
Considers the social conditions that led to the English Renaissance, focusing on the life of Sidney and *Arcadia*.

1342 ———. "Sir Philip Sidney's *Arcadia*." *Bookworm* 1 (1888):145–49.
Gives basic information on the composition and publication of the work.

1343 BASSE, MAURITS. *Stijlaffectatie bij Shakespeare vooral uit het Oogpunt van het Euphuisme*. Université de Gand. Recueil de travaux publiés par la Faculté de Philosophie et Lettres, 14. Gand, Belgium: Librairie H. Engelcke; The Hague: Martinus Nijhoff, 1895, pp. 30–37.
In the section on "Arcadianisme," argues that Sidney's prose style was shaped by Italian and Spanish influences, especially that of Don Luis de

Nineteenth Century

Gongora y Argote. Considers such characteristic devices as hyperbole, antimetabole, repetition, and personification. Also notes Sidney's influence on the style of John Dickenson's *Arisbas* and Gervase Markham's *English Arcadia*.

1344 BOLTE, JOHANNES, ed. Introduction to *Mucedorus, ein englisches Drama aus Shaksperes Zeit*, translated by Ludwig Tieck. Berlin: Wilhelm Gronau, 1893, pp. v–vi.

Suggests that *Arcadia* influenced the anonymous Elizabethan play *Mucedorus*.

1345 BRYDGES, [Sir] SAMUEL EGERTON. *Censura Literaria, Containing Titles, Abstracts, and Opinions of Old English Books*. Vol. 3. London: T. Bensley for Longman, Hurst, Rees, & Orme and J. White, 1807, pp. 389–94.

Weighs the merits of *Arcadia*.

1346 C., W.A. "Sir Philip Sidney's *Arcadia*." *N&Q*, 5th ser. 1 (4 April 1874):269.

Inquires whether anyone has carried out Disraeli's suggestion (341) that a copy of *Arcadia* with marginalia by Gabriel Harvey be published. The replies (on pp. 353, 396, and 498) give no answer. See also Godshalk (1550) and Harvey (1582).

1347 C[ARTWRIGHT, ROBERT]. "The *Arcadia* Unveiled." *N&Q*, 3d ser. 3 (6 June 1863):441–43; (29 June 1863):481–83; (27 June 1863):501–3; 4 (19 September 1863):237.

Suggests that Spenser's Red Cross Knight is an allegorical portrait of Sidney and that Sidney's works also require allegorical interpretation. Cites biographical data to show that Stella represents Sidney's muse, the goddess of chivalry, and that nearly all the persons and places in the *Arcadia* have historical counterparts. For example, Arcadia is England and Laconia is France; Basilius is Burghley; Gynecia is Elizabeth; Pyrocles is Sidney himself; Musidorus is Fulke Greville; Pamela is Mary Sidney (or Christian Philosophy); Philoclea is Frances Walsingham; Cecropia is Mary Stuart; and Amphialus is her son, James VI of Scotland. See a rebuttal by Howard (1367).

1348 CHILD, CLARENCE GRIFFIN. *John Lyly and Euphuism*. Münchener Beiträge zur romanischen und englischen Philologie, 7. Erlangen and Leipzig: A. Deichert'sche Verlagsbuch-handlung, Georg Böhme, 1894, pp. 49–50, 54–55, 101, 107–12.

Finds the clearest distinction between Sidney's Arcadian style and euphuism in the use of metaphor: Lyly's are few and unnatural, whereas

375

Nineteenth Century

Sidney's are frequent and have "a natural relation to their objects." Rejects Landmann's conclusion (1373) that euphuism was extinct after 1590, when Arcadianism came into vogue. Also feels that Landmann was wrong (1374) to attribute Sidney's style to the influence of Montemayor, contending instead for Schwan's view (1384) that Sidney was following the Italianate style of Wyatt and Surrey.

1349 CROFTS, ELLEN. *Chapters in the History of English Literature from 1509 to the Close of the Elizabethan Period.* London: Rivingtons, 1884, pp. 66–68, 71–75, 81–85.
Considers the artificiality of the poetic experiments of the Areopagus and characterizes *Arcadia* as euphuism popularized. Also traces the background of the *Defence* in the Puritan attacks on the stage and blames Sidney for prescribing the dramatic unities.

1350 CROSS, WILBUR L. *The Development of the English Novel.* New York: Macmillan Co.; London: Macmillan & Co., 1899, pp. 11, 25–26.
Compares the episodic structure of *Arcadia* with that of the picaresque novel and subsequent, more linear forms of prose fiction.

1351 [CROSSLEY, JAMES.] "*The Countess of Pembroke's Arcadia* . . . 1633 . . . ." *Retrospective Review* 2, part 2 (1820):1–44. Reprint. As "Sir Philip Sidney's *Arcadia*." *Museum of Foreign Literature, Science, and Art* 37 (November 1839):369–86.
Examines Sidney's greatness as a man and as a literary craftsman, defending *Arcadia* against the detractions of Hazlitt (359), Walpole (294), and others. Praises its prose style and its portrayals of nature, heroism, love, and friendship, but censures the comic passages and the poetry. Also comments on the continuation by Sir William Alexander. See also items 1340 and 1352.

1352 ———. *Sir Philip Sidney and the "Arcadia."* London: Chapman & Hall, 1853, 94 pp.
Reprints item 1351, with minor revisions and a brief life of Sidney. See item 1340.

1353 DODGE, R.E. NIEL. "An Allusion in Coleridge's 'First Advent of Love.'" *Anglia* 18 (1896):132.
Notes that Coleridge alludes to Sidney's description of Urania.

Nineteenth Century

1354 DRAKE, NATHAN. *Shakespeare and His Times*. 2 vols. London: T. Cadell & W. Davies, 1817, 1:444–45, 467–68, 548–52, 573, 652–53; 2:54–55, 283.
Comments on Sidney's life, character, and major works, discussing the sources of *Arcadia* and its mixture of artificiality with verisimilitude. Suggests that, in addition to the subplot in *King Lear*, Shakespeare's borrowings from *Arcadia* include parts of *Two Gentlemen of Verona* IV.i and the epithet "little hangman" applied to Cupid in *Much Ado About Nothing* III.ii. Surmises that the name "Pericles" in the play of that name is a corruption of "Pyrocles."

1355 DUNLOP, JOHN [COLIN]. *Geschichte der Prosadichtung, order Geschichte der Romane, Novellen, Märchen u.s.w.* Translated by Felix Liebrecht. Berlin: Verlag von G.W.F. Müller, 1851, pp. 364–68.
A German translation of item 1356.

1356 ———. *The History of Fiction: Being a Critical Account of the Most Celebrated Prose Works of Fiction, from the Earliest Greek Romances to the Novels of the Present Age*. Vol. 3. Edinburgh: Longman, Hurst, Rees, Orme, & Browne, 1814, pp. 164–78. Rev. ed. *The History of Prose Fiction*. Revised by Henry Wilson. Vol. 2. London: George Bell & Sons, 1888, pp. 394–402.
Examines *Arcadia* on the topics of genre, prose style, poetic merit, and influence.

1357 FIELDS, JAMES T[HOMAS]. *Yesterdays with Authors*. Boston: James R. Osgood & Co., 1872, p. 62.
Originates the story that Nathaniel Hawthorne had an early copy of *Arcadia*, which "he had read so industriously for forty years that it was nearly worn out of its thick leathern cover." But see Charney (1466) and Julian Hawthorne (1583).

1358 [GENEST, JOHN.] *Some Account of the English Stage, from the Restoration in 1660 to 1830*. Vol. 4. Bath, England: H.E. Carrington, 1832, pp. 395–96.
Summarizes the plot and reports the first performance of McNamara Morgan's *Philoclea*, an eighteenth-century play based on the main plot of *Arcadia*.

Nineteenth Century

1359 GIRARDIN, SAINT-MARC. *Cours de littérature dramatique ou de l'usage des passions dans le drame.* Vol. 3. Paris: G. Carpentier, 1886, pp. 273–302. Orig. pub. Paris: Carpentier, 1843 (not seen).
In Chapter 46, "L'Arcadie de Sydney.—La pastorale dans Shakspeare," compares Sidney's work with other pastorals of the Renaissance, stressing the contrast between his aristocratic and rustic characters and the prominence of love and politics as central concerns. Regards the work as a mixture of comedy and idyll, noting that Sidney rejects the giants and satyrs common in the pastoral romances of Spain and Italy in favor of greater verisimilitude. (This essay is not in the English translation of the work published by Robert Gibbes Barnwell in 1849.)

1360 GRAVES, ISABEL. "Sir Philip Sidney's Use of Arcadianism and Its Source." Ph.D. diss., University of Pennsylvania, 1899.
Abstract not available.

1361 HALLAM, HENRY. *Introduction to the Literature of Europe, in the Fifteenth, Sixteenth, and Seventeenth Centuries.* Vol. 2. London: John Murray, 1839, pp. 312, 411–12, 431, 438–41.
Defends *Arcadia* against Walpole (294) and suggests that it influenced Edmund Waller's poem "Fair! that you may truly know."

1362 [HAZLITT, WILLIAM CAREW, ed.] Introduction to "The Sources of *King Lear*." In *Shakespeare's Library: A Collection of the Plays, Romances, Novels, Poems, and Histories Employed by Shakespeare in the Composition of His Works,* edited by J[ohn] Payne Collier. 2d ed. Revised [by William Carew Hazlitt]. Vol. 2. London: Reeves and Turner, 1875, pp. 312–13.
Notes that Sidney's story of the Paphlagonian King was a source for *King Lear.* (Collier's original edition of 1843 does not contain this introduction.)

1363 HAZLITT, W[ILLIAM] CAREW. *A Manual for the Collector and Amateur of Old English Plays.* London: Pickering & Chatto, 1882, p. 62.
Asserts that the plot of Thomas Jevon's late eighteenth-century play *The Devil of a Wife* is based on Sidney's account of Mopsa in *Arcadia.* See also Brunhuber (1443).

1364 HEATH, H. F[RANK]. "*Arcadia* and Its Sources." Ph.D. diss., University of Strassburg, 1890.
Not located. Cited as item 813 in Tannenbaum (268).

Nineteenth Century

1365 HILLS, ERATO. "Passage in the *Arcadia*." *N&Q*, 4th ser. 1 (11 April 1868):342.
Requests a source for Sidney's phrase "making a perpetual mansion of this poor baiting place of man's life." For replies, see Rumage (1382), Shaw (1385), and Tennent (1389).

1366 HOLLINGSHEAD, JOHN. *Gaiety Chronicles*. Westminster: Archibald Constable & Co., 1898, pp. 193–94.
Mentions that the "germ" of the story for W.M. Balfe's opera *Letty the Basket-Maker* came from *Arcadia*.

1367 HOWARD, FRANK. "The *Arcadia* Unveiled." *N&Q*, 3d ser. 4 (22 August 1863):150–51.
Rejects Cartwright's allegorical interpretations (1347).

1368 IGNOTO [pseud.]. "Sir Philip Sidney's *Arcadia*: 'Wrong-Caused Sorrow.'" *N&Q*, 4th ser. 11 (18 January 1873):56.
Notes the passage in Book I in which nightingales "recount their wrong-caused sorrow" and queries the expression. Receives the reply that the passage refers to Ovid's story of Philomela, who was changed into a nightingale.

1369 JUSSERAND, J[EAN] J[ULES]. *The English Novel in the Time of Shakespeare*. Translated by Elizabeth Lee. London: T. Fisher Unwin, 1890, pp. 217–83, 287–90.
In "Sir Philip Sidney and Pastoral Romance," regards the pastoral as an ideal form for experimenting and for requesting patronage. After rehearsing Sidney's life, treats *Arcadia* as a light romance for ladies, commenting on its disguises, its tournaments, and its settings. Notes Italian sources and praises Sidney for his depiction of love, particularly in Gynecia. Blames him for his handling of comic scenes, comparing Rombus in *The Lady of May* with a similar character of Rabelais. Also considers Sidney's influence on popular romance, particularly Francis Quarles's *Argalus and Parthenia* and Lady Mary Wroth's *Urania*. Notes the attention given *Arcadia* in seventeenth-century France, beginning with the feud over precedence between the first two French translators, Jean Baudoin and Geneviève Chappelain. Touches on Charles Sorel's satire of Sidney in *Berger Extravagant*, noting that it was translated into English by John Davies of Kidwelly, who also ridiculed Sidney in his preface. In addition, considers Antoine Mareschal's tragicomedy *Cour Bergère*, which was based on *Arcadia*.

Nineteenth Century

1370 KINGSLEY, HENRY. *Fireside Studies*. Vol. 2. London: Chatto & Windus, 1876, pp. 171–254.
Reprints item 948, adding a rebuttal of Hazlitt's attacks on *Arcadia* (359). Includes a brief discussion of Sidney's characters, an evaluation of his eclogues, and a comparison of *Arcadia* to Scott's *Guy Mannering*.

1371 KOEPPEL, EMIL. *Quellen-Studien zu den Dramen Ben Jonson's, John Marston's und Beaumont's und Fletcher's*. Münchener Beiträge zur romanischen und englischen Philologie, 11. Erlangen and Leipzig: A. Deichert'sche Verlagsbuchhandlung, George Böhme, 1895, pp. 46–48.
Discusses Beaumont and Fletcher's use of *Arcadia* as a source for *Cupid's Revenge*.

1372 KRAUSS, FRITZ. "Shakespeare und seine *Sonette*." *Nord und Sud* 8 (1879):226–43.
Argues that Cecropia's speeches aimed at convincing Philoclea to marry Amphialus were the source of similar arguments to the young man in Shakespeare's *Sonnets*. Also cites Languet's friendship with Sidney as a parallel for Shakespeare's friendship with the young man.

1373 LANDMANN, FRIEDRICH. *Der Euphuismus, sein Wesen, siene Quelle, seine Geschichte*. Giessen, Germany: Wilhelm Keller, 1881, pp. 92–94, 102. Orig. a Ph.D. diss., Universität Giessen.
Contrasts Sidney's style with that of Lyly, crediting *Arcadia* with helping to supplant euphuism but noting excesses in Sidney's own imitators. See a reply by Child (1348).

1374 LANDMANN, FRIEDRICH, ed. Introduction to *"Evphves: The Anatomy of Wit." To Which Is Added the First Chapter of Sir Philip Sidney's "Arcadia."* Englischen Sprach- und Literaturdenkmale, 4. Heilbronn, Germany: Verlag von Gebr. Henninger, 1887, pp. xxvii–xxxii.
Distinguishes the Arcadian style from euphuism, noting the influence of the former on John Dickenson's *Arisbas*. Suggests that, in Shakespeare's *Love's Labour's Lost*, it is Sidney's style rather than John Lyly's that is being parodied. Also touches on the sources of *Arcadia* and its place in the history of pastoral romance. See a reply by Child (1348).

1375 MASSON, DAVID. *British Novelists and Their Styles, Being a Critical Sketch of the History of British Prose Fiction*. Cambridge: Macmillan & Co.; Boston: Gould & Lincoln, 1859, pp. 61–69.
Evaluates *Arcadia*, defending it against charges of vagueness and lack of realism.

1376 ———. *The Life of John Milton: Narrated in Connexion with Political, Ecclesiastical, and Literary History of His Time.* Vol. 4. London: Macmillan & Co., 1877, pp. 138–40, 248–50.

Discusses Milton's attack (1323) on Charles I for using Pamela's prayer from Book III of the revised *Arcadia*. Reprints the original text and the version in *Eikon Basilike*. Also discusses Milton's amplification of his charge in the second edition of *Eikonoklastes* and traces the history of the accusation that Milton himself had the prayer added to *Eikon Basilike*.

1377 MILTON, JOHN. *A Common-Place Book of John Milton, and a Latin Essay and Latin Verses Presumed to Be by Milton.* Edited from the Original MSS. in the Possession of Sir Frederick U. Graham, Bart., by Alfred J. Horwood. Camden Society Publications, n.s. 16. London: For the Camden Society, 1876, pp. 4, 34, 35. Reprint. Edited by James Holly Hanford. In *The Works of John Milton*, edited by Frank Allen Patterson, et al. The Columbia Edition. Vol. 18. New York: Columbia University Press, 1938, pp. 133, 187, 189.

Quotes or refers to *Arcadia* under the headings "*Ebrietas,*" "*Aulici,*" and "*Astutia Politica.*"

1378 MOORMAN, FREDERIC W[ILLIAM]. *William Browne: His "Britannia's Pastorals" and the Pastoral Poetry of the Elizabethan Age.* Quellen und Forschungen zur Sprach- und Kulturgeschichte der Germanischen Völker, 81. Strassburg: Karl J. Trübner, 1897, pp. 8, 28, 83–84.

Compares sections of *Britannia's Pastorals* with passages in *Arcadia*. Despite Browne's own claim, concludes that Sidney's influence was minimal.

1379 MOUNT, C.B. "Sir Philip Sidney and Shakspeare." *N&Q,* 8th ser. 3 (22 April 1893):305.

Notes a verbal parallel between a passage in *Arcadia* Book III and *The Winter's Tale* IV.iii, urging that Shakespeare's Mopsa derives from Sidney's.

1380 PRIDEAUX, HUMPHREY. *Letters of Humphrey Prideaux Sometime Dean of Norwich to John Ellis Sometime Under-Secretary of State 1674–1722.* Edited by Edward Maunde Thompson. Westminster: Camden Society, 1875, pp. 20–21.

Regards *Arcadia* as "a bare translation of Sannazaro" held in "high esteem among women and fools."

Nineteenth Century

1381 RALEIGH, WALTER. *The English Novel, Being a Short Sketch of Its History from the Earliest Times to the Appearance of "Waverley."* New York: Charles Scribner's Sons, 1894, pp. 51–64, 100–101.
Sketches Sidney's life and works and reviews the sources and faults of *Arcadia*. Attributes its success to sentiment and to its portrayals of love. Discusses its influence on Samuel Richardson and on John Crowne's *Pandion and Amphigenia*.

1382 RUMAGE, CRAUFURD TAIT. "Sir Philip Sidney's *Arcadia.*" *N&Q*, 4th ser. 1 (30 May 1868):516.
Replies to Hills (1365) on the origins of the phrase "making a perpetual mansion of this poor baiting place of man's life." Suggests that Sidney adapted an idea found in Cicero's *De Senectute* and Seneca's Epistle 120. See also Shaw (1385) and Tennent (1389).

1383 SCHLOSSER, J.F.H. "Über Opitz und Philip Sidney." In *Aus der Nachlass von J.F.H. Schlosser*, edited by S. Schlosser. Vol. 4. Mainz, Germany: n.p., 1859, pp. 94–108.
Not located. Cited as item 1117 in Tannenbaum (268).

1384 SCHWAN, EDUARD. Review of "Shakspere and Euphuism," by Friedrich Landmann. *Englische Studien* 6 (1883):94–111.
Criticizes Landmann's attribution (368) of the artificial style of several of Shakespeare's courtly characters to the influence of euphuism. Notes Sidney's connection of Lyly's style with a wider pattern of Italianate affectation. From evidence such as Jonson's allusions to the Arcadian style in *Every Man out of His Humour*, argues that Sidney's own style was more fashionable at court and was more likely to have influenced Shakespeare. See also Child (1348).

1385 SHAW, J.B. "Passage in the *Arcadia.*" *N&Q*, 4th ser. 2 (5 December 1868):541.
In reply to Hills (1365) notes parallels to Sidney's phrase "making a perpetual mansion of this poor baiting place of man's life" in Cicero's *De Senectute* and *Consolatio*. See also Ramage (1382) and Tennent (1389).

1386 SOUTHEY, ROBERT, ed. *Palmerin of England*. Vol. 1. London: Hurst, Rees, & Orme, 1807, p. xliv.
Notes that the Spanish romance *Amadis of Greece* provides the source for the character of Zelmane, daughter of Plexirtus, in *Arcadia*.

1387 SOUTHEY, ROBERT. *Selections from the Letters of Robert Southey*. Edited by John Wood Warter. 4 vols. London: Longman, Brown,

Nineteenth Century

Green, & Longmans, 1856, 1:222–24, 287, 315; 2:4, 15, 97, 104, 123.
Comments on *Arcadia*, praising it as "the one book in our language which has most of Shakespeare in its manner." Defends it against the censures of Zouch (974). Suggests that the Spanish romance *Amadis of Greece* was Sidney's source for the character Zelmane, daughter of Plexirtus.

1388 SYMMONS, CHARLES. *The Prose Works of John Milton; with a Life of the Author, Interspersed with Translations and Critical Remarks.* Vol. 7. London: T. Bensley for J. Johnson, et al., 1806, pp. 278–82.
In the biography later published separately as Symmons's *Life of John Milton*, argues that Milton's condemnation (1323) of Charles I for having used Pamela's prayer was too severe. Documents the course of the controversy that followed.

1389 TENNENT, J. EMERSON. "Sir Philip Sidney's *Arcadia*." *N&Q*, 4th ser. 1 (25 April 1868):397.
In reply to Hills (1365), notes that Sidney's phrase "making a perpetual mansion of this poor baiting place of man's life" has analogues in Moore's *Irish Melodies* and Washington Irving's *Bracebridge Hall*. See also Ramage (1382) and Shaw (1385).

1390 TORRACA, FRANCESCO. *Gl'imitatori stranieri di Jacopo Sannazaro.* Rome: Ermanno Loescher, 1882, pp. 77–78.
Discusses references to Sannazaro in the *Defence* and his negligible influence on *Arcadia*.

1391 TUCKERMAN, BAYARD. *A History of English Prose Fiction from Sir Thomas Malory to George Eliot.* New York: G.P. Putnam's Sons, 1882, pp. 90–101.
Characterizes Sidney and evaluates *Arcadia*, suggesting that a passage in the romance prompted Sir Richard Steele to write item 66.

1392 UNDERHILL, JOHN GARRETT. *Spanish Literature in the England of the Tudors.* New York: Columbia University Press, Macmillan Co.; London: Macmillan & Co., 1899, pp. 170–71, 177, 247, 260-316 passim, 324.
In "Sidney and Oxford: Patrons of Learning," details the many connections between the Sidney and Pembroke circles and the politicians and writers of Spain. Notes that Sidney's translations of lyrics by Montemayor were the first in English. Also reviews the influence of

Nineteenth Century

Montemayor's *Diana* upon *Arcadia*, denying that it was especially important in shaping Sidney's style.

1393 WARD, A[DOLPHUS] W[ILLIAM], ed. "Sir Philip Sidney." In
English Prose: Selections, edited by Henry Craik. Vol. 1, *Fourteenth
to Sixteenth Century*. New York: Macmillan Co.; London:
Macmillan & Co., 1893, pp. 401–22.
Places *Arcadia* in the development of Renaissance pastoral, emphasizing
its artificiality and adherence to convention. Evaluates the style, condemning euphuistic influences and contrasting it to the "Attic lightness
and gracefulness" of the *Defence*.

1394 WARREN, F[REDERICK] M[ORRIS]. *A History of the Novel
Previous to the Seventeenth Century*. New York: Henry Holt & Co.,
1895, pp. 336–38.
Faults *Arcadia* for its mixture of genres and its misleading pastoral title.

1395 WEST, ELIZA M. *Shakesperian Parallelisms, Chiefly Illustrative of the
"Tempest" and "A Midsummer Night's Dream," Collected from Sir Philip
Sidney's "Arcadia."* London: Printed for the editor by Wittingham
& Wilkins, 1865, 29 pp.
Prints in parallel brief excerpts from *Arcadia* and from Shakespeare,
making no attempt at critical evaluation.

Twentieth Century

1396 ALEXANDER, PETER. *"Milton's God."* *TLS*, 16 February 1962,
p. 105.
Faults Empson (1525) for accepting the allegation that Milton inserted
Pamela's prayer into Charles I's prayer book, *Eikon Basilike*. See Milton
(1323). For further exchanges printed in *TLS*, see Empson, 2 March, p.
137; P.L. Heyworth, 9 March, p. 161; Alexander, 16 March, p. 185;
Empson, 23 March, p. 201; B.A. Wright, 30 March, p. 217; Alexander, 6
April, p. 240; Empson, 27 April, p. 281; Alexander, 11 May, p. 339;
Empson, 25 May, p. 380; and Merritt Y. Hughes, 27 July, p. 541.

1397 ALMON, LISELOTTE. "Die Staatsidee in Sidneys *Arcadia*,
Barclays *Argenis* und Anton Ulrichs *Aramena*." Phil.F. diss.,
University of Marburg, 1944, 187 pp.
Abstract not available. Cited in *GV* 3:23.

1398 ALPERS, PAUL [J.]. "What Is Pastoral?" *CritI* 8 (Spring 1982): 437–60.

Argues that, since "shepherds" are seen as "representatives of men," pastoral is fundamentally realistic. Sees Sidney's reshaping of the genre in *Arcadia* as in keeping with its dynamic, realistic nature.

1399 AMOS, ARTHUR K[IRKHAM], Jr. *Time, Space, and Value: The Narrative Structure of the "New Arcadia."* Lewisburg, Pa.: Bucknell University Press; London: Associated University Presses, 1977, 203 pp. Orig. a Ph.D. diss., University of Oregon, 1970, 238 pp.

In Chapter 1, sets forth two structural principles to guide analysis of the New *Arcadia*. First is the use of parallel episodes to bring out "permutations" in various virtues and vices. Second is the use of different ordering principles in each of the work's three books: in Book I, pictorial and spatial relations; in Book II, causal and temporal relations; and in Book III, moral and political values. Compares the original and the revised versions, stressing differences in the narrator's attitudes toward his heroes and in the means employed for moral instruction. In Chapter 2, considers the opening of the New *Arcadia*, suggesting that, by beginning *in medias res*, Sidney diminishes the role of the omniscient narrator and makes spatial rather than temporal relations dominant. Rejects interpretations of Urania by Davis (1499) and Rose (726), seeing her only as a shepherdess who symbolizes the force of love and its effects on lovers' perceptions. Notes the oddly pictorial quality of several passages, relating them to Sidney's descriptions of paintings in the book and arguing that perception is analogous to artistic or poetic creation, in which a "fore-conceit" shapes the world being created. Stresses two themes in *Arcadia*: the erotic and the political, and feels that, in both, perceptions are creative. In the episodes of Helen and Amphialus, Phalantus and Artesia, sees excesses of this creative process leading to solipsism. In the landscapes of Laconia and Arcadia, sees the effects of the differing perceptions of their peoples. Notes the intertwining of the erotic and the political in the Helot rebellion and in the episode of Argalus and Parthenia, seeing the latter as an "emblem" of true love, which validates Pyrocles's succeeding love of Philoclea. The story of Helen and Amphialus, by contrast, lends support to Musidorus's rejection of love. Defends Pyrocles's transvestism and his position in the debate with Musidorus, and treats the tournament of Phalantus as a comic comment on the lust of Basilius and Gynecia. Also considers the erotic and political themes in the eclogues, relating the beast fable (*OA 66*) to Basilius's

Twentieth Century

retirement after consulting the Delphic Oracle. In Chapter 3, argues that Book II is primarily about temporal relations. Finds a change in style from the static, pictorial descriptions of Book I to dynamic narratives of "process," such as Philoclea's complex change in feelings toward the disguised Pyrocles. Relates Musidorus's retrospective narrations to his desire to convince Pamela of his nobility, and Pyrocles's narrations to his need to convince Philoclea of his ethical judgment and integrity. Traces chains of causality from the prophecies before the birth of Musidorus through his encounters with the Kings of Phrygia and Pontus, contrasting these rulers with Euarchus. Sees the episode of the King of Paphlagonia as a shift to more complex ethical issues and a start of causal chains important later in the book. Compares the king with Basilius. Sees Pyrocles's reactions to Amphialus and to the naked Princesses in the bathing incident as evidence of his superiority to other lovers in the book. Relates the stories of Erona and of Plangus to one another and to the main plot, considering the function of intervening passages by Miso and Mopsa. Explores the complex relations among Anaxius's deferred joust with Pyrocles, the episode of Dido and Pamphilus, Andromana's treatment of Pyrocles and Musidorus, their release by Palladius and Zelmane, their involvement in the Bithynian civil war, and their last encounters with Plexirtus. Feels that these problems reveal the inadequacy of absolute ethical codes, "the inconclusive nature of moral action," and the inextricable relation between erotic and political affairs. Also discusses the rebellion of the Arcadian commoners and the balance between the serious and the comical throughout Book II and its eclogues. In Chapter 4, urges that, since the characters in Books I and II are hard to judge morally, "*Arcadia* goes on to create a structure of value and to test one value system against another." Analyzes the assumptions underlying the arguments of Cecropia and the Princesses during their debates in Book III, seeing in Cecropia's "egotistical" position a radical form of relativism in which "the only constraints on the individual come from within the self because there is no order intrinsic in the world." Feels that Pamela's position is superior because it it "maximizes rewards and minimizes punishments." In the increasingly brutal private combats fought against Amphialus, sees the failure of the chivalric ideal and a rejection of idealizations of war. Analyzes the characters of Anaxius and Amphialus, noting in the latter an inability to accept moral responsibility, even at the end of his rebellion. Relates Pyrocles's reaction to the mock execution of Philoclea to Argalus's reaction to the disfigurement of Parthenia. Concludes that, although the fortunes of the characters are in the hands of the gods (as revealed in the oracles), the ethical norms by which the gods operate is, in part, a mystery. In the conclusion, rejects the view that Sidney left the New *Arcadia* unfinished because revision had made the original ending unworkable or incongruous in tone. Finds the revision "architectonically sound." Includes a selective bibliography.

1400 ANDERS, H[ENRY] R.D. *Shakespeare's Books: A Dissertation on Shakespeare's Reading and the Immediate Sources of His Works.* Berlin: Georg Reimer, 1904, pp. 96, 102–3, 276, 280, 282, 283.
Lists Shakespeare's borrowings from the *Arcadia*, denying that Sidney influenced *Two Gentlemen of Verona* or the procreation arguments in the *Sonnets*.

1401 ANDERSON, D.M. "The Dido Incident in Sidney's *Arcadia*." *N&Q*, n.s. 3 (October 1956):417–19.
Remarks on the violence of the Dido episode, noting its slim connection with the context. Suggests that Sidney was drawing on an unidentified Italian story and that he incorporated the incidents to show Pyrocles's willingness to set aside reputation to aid the distressed.

1402 ———. "The Trial of the Princes in the *Arcadia*, Book V." *RES*, n.s. 8 (November 1957):409–12.
Argues against Rowe's view (1747) that the trial scene is meant to exemplify the conflict between romantic love and parental authority. Denies Rowe's assumption that the ending of the Old *Arcadia* can be used in interpretations of the New *Arcadia* and argues that the true conflict in the scene is between justice to the two young princes and the need to maintain the state by administering its rather severe laws. Cites the *Trueness of the Christian Religion* to suggest that Sidney minimized the importance of injustices to individuals when the state is in danger.

1403 ANDREWS, MICHAEL CAMERON. "*Arcadia* and *King Lear*." *N&Q*, n.s. 31 (June 1984):205.
Cites a "further instance" of Sidney's influence on the description of Cordelia's tears in *King Lear* IV.iii.

1404 ———. "*Jack Drum's Entertainment* as Burlesque." *RenQ* 24 (Summer 1971):226–31.
Examines the influence of Sidney's tales of Argalus and Parthenia and of Helen and Amphialus on two Elizabethan plays: the anonymous *Trial of Chivalry* and John Marston's *Jack Drum's Entertainment*.

Twentieth Century

1405 ———. "Sidney's *Arcadia* and *Soliman and Perseda*." *AN&Q* 11
(January 1973):68–69.
Suggests that Parthenia's death in Book III of the revised *Arcadia* was
Kyd's source for the death of Perseda. Accordingly, proposes that
Soliman and Perseda be dated no earlier than 1590.

1406 ———. "Sidney's *Arcadia* and *The Winter's Tale*." *SQ* 23 (Spring
1972):200–202.
Suggests that Polixene's exchange with Camillo concerning Prince
Florizel in *The Winter's Tale* IV.ii is based on the story of Plangus in the
New *Arcadia*.

1407 ———. "Sidney's *Arcadia* on the English Stage: A Study of the
Dramatic Adaptations of *The Countess of Pembroke's Arcadia*." Ph.D.
diss., Duke University, 1966, 206 pp.
Examines the nine English plays that have the *Arcadia* as their principal
source. Concludes that John Marston's play *Jack Drum's Entertainment*
and the anonymous *Trial of Chivalry* and *Mucedorus* make no effort to
emulate Sidney but merely exploit his characters and incidents to entertain. Believes that two Jacobean works, John Day's parody *The Isle of
Gulls* and Beaumont and Fletcher's *Cupid's Revenge*, imitate Sidney more
consistently. Asserts that two later seventeenth-century plays, the anonymous *Andromana* and Henry Glapthorne's *Argalus and Parthenia*, show
the influence of *Cupid's Revenge*, but that James Shirley's *Arcadia* and
McNamara Morgan's *Philoclea* show no influence of earlier adaptions. In
an appendix, briefly summarizes two manuscript plays: the anonymous
Love's Changelings' Change and Thomas Moore's *Arcadian Lovers*. See *DA*
27 (May 1967):3860A–61A.

1408 ———. "The Sources of *Andromana*." *RES*, n.s. 19 (August 1968):
295–300.
Argues that the anonymous seventeenth-century play *Andromana* is more
heavily dependent on Beaumont and Fletcher's play *Cupid's Revenge*
than on Sidney's *Arcadia*.

1409 ———. "*The Virgin Martyr* and Sidney's *Arcadia*." *AN&Q* 14
(March 1976):107–8.
Notes that Dorothea's exchange with Angelo in IV.iii of Thomas Dekker
and Philip Massinger's play *The Virgin Martyr* echoes Pyrocles's words to
Philoclea in Book III when he discovers that her apparent execution was
only a trick.

Twentieth Century

1410 APTEKAR, JANE. *Icons of Justice: Iconography & Thematic Imagery in Book V of "The Faerie Queene."* New York and London: Columbia University Press, 1969, p. 36.
Compares Artegal's use of eloquence against his giant opponent in *Faerie Queene* V.ii with Pyrocles's eloquent calming of the the rebels in *Arcadia* II.26.

1411 ARCULUS, MARGARET JOAN. "The Ending of Romance: Sidney, Spenser, and the Unresolved Narrative." Ph.D. diss., Yale University, 1984, 390 pp.
Analyzes earlier romances in order to establish their common "poetics." Drawing on the work of Jacques Lacan for theories of the self, argues that romance genres arise in periods when the concept of identity is changing from one defined by relation to a community to one defined by "solitary quest." Notes, however, that identity in romance is usually "bestowed" by others, particularly by a lover or a family, and that the reunions common at the end "image the impossibility of independently achieving unified identity." Noting the typical family reunion at the end of the Old *Arcadia*, suggests that the revised version fails to reach a conclusion because of Sidney's "inability to achieve a unified authorial identity." See *DAI* 46 (November 1985):1283A.

1412 ARMSTRONG, WILLIAM A. "*King Lear* and Sidney's *Arcadia*." *TLS*, 14 October 1949, p. 665.
Suggests that Shakespeare borrowed Edmund's opportunistic philosophy and Gloucester's famous simile "as flies to wanton boys, are we to the gods" from Cecropia's debate with Pamela in Book III of *Arcadia*. Also finds the various conceptions of nature in the play clearly set forth in one of Pamela's replies to Cecropia. See also a reply by Pyle (1723).

1413 ASCOLI, GEORGES. *La Grande-Bretagne devant l'opinion Française au XVIIe siècle.* Vol. 2. Paris: Librarie Universitaire J. Gambier, 1930, pp. 132–37.
In "L'*Arcadie* de Sidney," discusses the influence of the romance on Jean Galaut's tragedy *Phalante*, noting that Galaut changes the name of Amphialus to Phalante. Also notes Jean Baudoin's use of verse instead of prose in his translation of *Arcadia*, praising the quality of the undertaking. Comments on Chappelain's translation, comparing it somewhat unfavorably with that of Baudoin. Remarks on the impact of *Arcadia* on numerous minor writers.

1414 ATKINS, J[OHN] W[ILLIAM] H[EY]. "Elizabethan Prose Fiction." In *The Cambridge History of English Literature*. Vol. 3,

Twentieth Century

> *Renascence and Reformation*, edited by A[dolphus] W[illiam] Ward
> and A[lfred] R[ayney] Waller. Cambridge: Cambridge University
> Press, 1909, pp. 351–55.

Reviews the sources of *Arcadia* and discusses its "shadowy" characters
and "rich confusion" of form and setting. Notes its chivalric elements,
but sees it as a departure into sheer fancy from the "specious" realism of
medieval romance. Lists faults in its style and enumerates works in fiction and drama written under its influence.

1415 ATKINSON, DOROTHY F. "The Pastorella Episode in *The Faerie
Queene*." *PMLA* 59 (June 1944):361–72.

Rejects the view that Spenser's episode involving Pastorella was based
primarily on *Arcadia*, citing closer parallels in the anonymous work *The
Mirror of Knighthood*.

1416 BABB, LAWRENCE. *The Elizabethan Malady: A Study of
Melancholia in English Literature from 1580 to 1642*. East Lansing:
Michigan State College Press, 1951, pp. 89, 143–44, 155, 158–60,
173, 181.

Cites the King of Phrygia in *Arcadia* as one of only two melancholic villains in Elizabethan prose fiction. Notes the tension between two traditional views of love in *Arcadia*: the classical position that it is a dangerous
sickness and the courtly love doctrine that it is ennobling. Lists traditional symptoms of melancholic lovesickness illustrated in *Arcadia*, noting
that Amphialus's symptoms go beyond the usual love-languor in that
they are complicated by physical wounds and melancholy, associated in
Renaissance medical texts with grief rather than love. Includes Sidney
himself in a list of notable Elizabethan melancholics.

1417 BAKER, ERNEST A[LBERT]. *The History of the English Novel*. Vol.
2, *The Elizabethan Age and After*. London: H.F. & G. Witherby,
1929, pp. 13, 15, 54–55, 67–89, 104–5, 119–20.

Dismisses *Arcadia* as a book in which "there is nothing of any importance
going on." Characterizes its style in contrast to euphuism, relating both
to the prose of Heliodorus's *Aethiopica* and Apuleius's *Golden Ass*. Covers
the sources of *Arcadia*, reviewing the history of Renaissance pastoral and
its confluence with chivalric romance. Surveys the influence of *Arcadia* on
later literature, particularly on Robert Greene's *Pandosto* and Thomas
Lodge's *A Margarite of America*. Remarks on Sidney's characters, treating
all but Gynecia as types. Also touches on the role of fortune and divine
providence. See a response by Pruvost (1721).

1418 BASKERVILL, C[HARLES] R[EAD]. "Sidney's *Arcadia* and *The Tryall of Chevalry.*" *MP* 10 (October 1912):197–201.
Points out that the story of Philip and Bellamira in the anonymous Elizabethan play *The Trial of Chivalry* is drawn from Sidney's story of Argalus and Parthenia. Believes that the action involving Ferdinand and Katharine is based on Sidney's account of Helen and Amphialus. Also notes that John Marston's play *Jack Drum's Entertainment* draws on the same two passages, and George Chapman's play *The Gentleman Usher* draws on the Parthenia episode. Suggests that *The Trial of Chivalry* came first and attracted Marston and Chapman to the story.

1419 BEACH, DONALD MARCUS. "Studies in the Art of Elizabethan Prose Narrative." Ph.D. diss., Cornell University, 1959, 237 pp.
Describes English fiction from 1575 to 1600, distinguishing three main subjects: sentiment, separation, and adventure. Points out that *Arcadia* combines all three. See *DA* 20 (1959):2274–75.

1420 BEER, GILLIAN. *The Romance.* The Critical Idiom, 10. London: Methuen & Co., 1970, pp. 33–37.
Suggests that Sidney's "playfulness in the midst of splendour" may owe something to chivalric entertainments at Elizabeth's court. Considers the changes in the Arcadian landscape as signs of the political lessons of the romance. Also contrasts Sidney's attitude toward language with that of John Lyly.

1421 BEILIN BROWN, ELAINE V. "The Uses of Mythology in Elizabethan Romance." Ph.D. diss., Princeton University, 1973, 336 pp.
Examines "mythographic manuals, encyclopediae, dictionaries, emblem books, the Greek and Roman classics and their commentaries" in order to elucidate mythology in romances such as *Arcadia*. Discusses Sidney's allegorical meanings and "non-novelistic" methods of composition. See *DAI* 34 (May 1974):7180A–81A.

1422 BENJAMIN, EDWIN B. "Fame, Poetry, and the Order of History in the Literature of the English Renaissance." *Studies in the Renaissance* 6 (1959):64–84.
Briefly compares Sidney's attitude toward fame in the *Arcadia* with the views of other Renaissance authors.

Twentieth Century

1423 BENTLEY, GERALD EADES. *The Jacobean and Caroline Stage.* 7
vols. Oxford: Clarendon Press, 1941–68, 3:440; 4:480, 933;
5:1035, 1074–75, 1139, 1367; 7:16–128 passim.

Discounts Sherman's suggestion (753) that Sidney's love of Lady Rich
was the basis for Ford's play *The Broken Heart*, allowing, however, that
"*Arcadia* was often on the author's mind." Also considers the influence of
Arcadia on Henry Glapthorne's *Argalus and Parthenia*, Thomas Nabbes's
Covent Garden, J.S.'s *Andromana; or, The Merchant's Wife*, James Shirley's
Arcadia and *Politician*, and the anonymous *Love's Changelings' Change*.
Places these works in a chronological list of publications, performances,
and other events relevant to the Jacobean and Caroline stage.

1424 BERGBUSCH, MARTIN LUTHER THEODORE. "Political
Thought and Conduct in Sidney's *Arcadia*." Ph.D. diss., Cornell
University, 1971, 277 pp.

Seeks to determine whether *Arcadia* embodies a coherent political theory. Compares the two versions, Sidney's other writings, the works of history and political theory that Sidney knew, and certain of his literary
sources. Concludes that his views on royal authority and its relation to
the law are conventional and resemble those of Sir Thomas Smith and
Richard Hooker. Yet on the topics of sovereignty, rebellion, and foreign
intervention, sees Sidney as less orthodox. Believes that Sidney follows
radical Protestant theorists such as Bishop Ponet, George Buchanan,
and the French Huguenots. Finds the speeches of Philanax especially
indebted to Huguenot thought. See *DAI* 31 (June 1971):6590A.

1425 ———. "Rebellion in the *New Arcadia*." *PQ* 53 (January 1974):
29–41.

Against Ribner's contention (1734) that Sidney regarded rebellion as
unjustifiable no matter what the circumstances, supports Briggs's argument (1438) that he sanctioned rebellion so long as the monarch "egre-
giously and repeatedly oversteps his constitutional limitations." Traces
this position to Sidney's Huguenot connections and his knowledge of
tracts such as the anonymous *Vindiciae contra Tyrannos*. Analyzes the five
rebellions in *Arcadia* and the comments of the narrator, concluding that
Sidney "approves of the rebellions in Laconia, Pontus, and Phrygia, but
disapproves of those in Arcadia."

1426 ———. "The 'Subaltern Magistrate' in Sir Philip Sidney's *Arcadia*:
A Study of the Character of Philanax." *English Studies in Canada* 7
(Spring 1981):27–37.

Argues that Philanax's behavior after Basilius's supposed death is a "logical extension" of his earlier actions. Shows that the narrator's attitude,

though complex, is consistent: his comments are unfavorable when Philanax acts out of personal loyalty or a desire for revenge; they are favorable when Philanax's actions accord with duty to Arcadia. Shows that, in revising the character of Philanax, Sidney heightens the possibilities for conflict between love for Basilius the man and love for Basilius the ruler. Suggests that, in bringing this issue to the fore in the revised *Arcadia*, Sidney may have been influenced by Huguenot political thought, particularly that of the anonymous treatise *Vindiciae contra Tyrannos*.

1427 BISWAS, D[INESH] C[HANDRA]. *Shakespeare in His Own Time.* Delhi: Macmillan Co. of India, 1979, pp. 21, 23–28, 30, 48.
Compares *Arcadia* with Lyly's *Euphues*, noting conventions from Greek romance and the use of parallelism and antithesis as techniques of style and structure.

1428 BLISS, LEE. "Defending Fletcher's Shepherds." *SEL* 23 (Spring 1983):295–310.
Asserts that *Arcadia* had a "pervasive" influence on the general tone of John Fletcher's play *The Faithful Shepherdess*.

1429 BLOOR, R[OBERT] H[ENRY] U[NDERWOOD]. *The English Novel from Chaucer to Galsworthy.* London: Ivor Nicholson & Watson, 1935, pp. 73–82.
Sketches Sidney's life and the development of pastoral romance. Evaluates *Arcadia*, rejecting its mixture of classical, medieval, and modern elements but praising its depictions of love.

1430 BLUESTONE, MAX. *From Story to Stage: The Dramatic Adaptation of Prose Fiction in the Period of Shakespeare and His Contemporaries.* Studies in English Literature, 70. The Hague and Paris: Mouton, 1974, pp. 35–41, 67–68, 110, 114, 143–44, 157–62, 212, 272–85 passim, 316.
Links Sidney with Jonson, Chapman, and others who distrust sensuous spectacle, noting that *Arcadia* rarely particularizes about material things or physical action. Examines the debasement of Arcadian characters in Beaumont and Fletcher's *Cupid's Revenge* and in Shakespeare's *King Lear*. Examines Sidney's dislike of mixed forms and changing times or locales, attributing it to his desire for a perfect order in which social groups do not mingle haphazardly and the world is not "chancy."

Twentieth Century

1431 BOKLUND, GUNNAR. *"The Duchess of Malfi": Sources, Themes, Characters.* Cambridge, Mass.: Harvard University Press, 1962, pp. 25–28, 37–41, 44–46, 50–55, 60–63, 66–67, 73.
Discusses Webster's possible borrowings from *Arcadia*. Suggests that Sidney's Erona is the most likely source for Webster's portrayal of the Duchess in prison. Notes similarities between Cecropia's mock executions in the Captivity Episode and Ferdinand's use of similar devices in the play. Also notes the use of echo poems in both works and compares Webster and Sidney in their attitudes toward revenge, suicide, and marriage across class lines.

1432 BORINSKI, LUDWIG. "Mittelalter und Neuzeit in der Stilgeschichte des 16. Jahrhunderts." *SJ* 97 (1961):109–33.
Treats *Arcadia* as transitional because it combines medieval elements with neoclassical structures and psychological realism.

1433 BOYCE, BENJAMIN. *The Theophrastan Character in England to 1642.* Cambridge, Mass.: Harvard University Press, 1947, pp. 50–51, 89–91.
Drawing upon John Hoskins's comments on *Arcadia* in *Directions for Speech and Style* (1593), discusses Sidney's adherence to Aristotelian notions of decorum and to Theophrastan methods of character analysis. Also ponders the influence of medieval models.

1434 BRADNER, LEICESTER. "From Petrarch to Shakespeare." In *The Renaissance: A Symposium. February 8–10, 1952.* New York: Metropolitan Museum of Art, 1953, pp. 63–76.
Relates *Arcadia* to the work of Sannazaro and Montemayor.

1435 BRIE, FRIEDRICH. "Deismus und Atheismus in der englischen Renaissance." *Anglia* 48 (1924):54–98, 105–68.
In surveying the influence of atheist and deist thought in the English Renaissance, cites Cecropia's speeches in Book III of *Arcadia*. Suggests that Pamela's arguments against Cecropia may have been inspired by Sidney's quarrel with the reputed atheist Edward de Vere, Earl of Oxford. Also relates Sidney's interest to du Plessis-Mornay's *De la verité de la religion chrestienne*. Traces Cecropia's arguments to the ancient Epicureans and Sophists as represented in Cicero's *De Natura Deorum*. Links her comments on the value of religion in subduing the masses, not with Machiavelli, but with the Greek tyrant Critias. Also considers the influence of Lucretius, Sidney's acquaintance with Giordano Bruno, and his references to Machiavelli's *Prince*.

1436 ———. "Das Volksbuch vom 'gehörnten Siegfried' und Sidneys *Arcadia*." *Archiv*, n.s. 21 (1908):287–90.

Discusses Sidney's description of the battle of Dametas and Clinias in Book III of *Arcadia* and its influence on a similar comic battle in the folk tale of "gehörnten Siegfried." See also Brockstedt (1439).

1437 BRIGGS, JULIA. *This Stage-Play World: English Literature and Its Background, 1580–1625*. Oxford and New York: Oxford University Press, 1983, pp. 1–2, 34–35, 127–33, 148–49, 189–90, 197, 200–201.

Contrasts the ideal of Arcadia presented early in the romance with the baser reality that emerges later, suggesting that Sidney's view of conventional pastoral is ironic. Discusses his neo-Platonism, his *sprezzatura*, and his humanist interest in moral teaching. Lists ways in which the New *Arcadia* is like a heroic poem and considers reasons that the classical meters in the eclogues are hardly audible.

1438 BRIGGS, WILLIAM DINSMORE. "Political Ideas in Sidney's *Arcadia*." *SP* 28 (April 1931):137–61.

Regards *Arcadia*, not as an allegory of England's recent past, but as an illustration of her possible future. Examines Sidney's position on the right of rebellion, finding it in accord with the Huguenot tract *Vindiciae contra Tyrannos* and similar works. Considers his stand on the insurrections in France and the Netherlands and his portrayals of rebels and monarchs in *Arcadia* and the *Defence*. Concludes that Sidney believed in a divinely ordained monarchy, administered through a trained aristocracy and limited by the law of nations. Also notes that the King of Phrygia resembles Filippo Maria Visconti and that Sidney's views on limited monarchy bore upon the case of Mary, Queen of Scots. See also Bergbusch (1425).

1439 BROCKSTEDT, GUSTAV. "Zu der Abhandlung Friedrich Bries: Das Volksbuch vom 'gehörnten Siegfried' und Sidneys *Arcadia*." *Archiv*, n.s. 23 (1909):155–59.

Accepts Brie's argument (1436) that the combat of Clinias and Dametas in *Arcadia* was a source for the Volksbuch but defends the unknown author's originality.

1440 BROOKE, RUPERT. *John Webster and the Elizabethan Drama*. New York: John Lane Co., 1916, pp. 145–60 passim.

Examines Webster's borrowings from *Arcadia*, suggesting that the dramatist worked from a commonplace book.

Twentieth Century

1441 ———. "A Note on John Webster." *Poetry and Drama* 1 (1913):27–32.
Argues that Webster's borrowings from *Arcadia* must have been collected in a notebook. Defends Webster, showing that he improved on his sources.

1442 BRÜCKL, O. "Sir Philip Sidney's *Arcadia* as a Source for John Webster's *The Duchess of Malfi*." *ESA* 8 (March 1965):31–55.
Discusses in detail Webster's borrowings, weighing the likelihood that he worked from a notebook of phrases and passages or that he intentionally played his language off against the audience's memories of *Arcadia*.

1443 BRUNHUBER, K[ASPAR]. *Sir Philip Sidneys "Arcadia" und ihre Nachläufer: Literarhistorische Studie.* Nuremberg, Germany: M. Edelmann, 1903, 63 pp.
In Part 1, lists ways in which Sidney drew upon his sources: Sannazaro's *Arcadia*, Montemayor's *Diana*, the anonymous *Amadis de Gaule*, Heliodorus's *Aethiopica*, Achilles Tatius's *Clitophon and Leucippe*, and Chariton's *Chaereas and Callirrhoe*. Argues that Sidney borrowed less from Montemayor and more from *Amadis* than previous scholars had supposed. Also notes Sidney's adaptation of the Greek romance motif of the revenge of Cupid in his story of Erona and lists his various borrowings from Virgil and Terence. In Part 2, examines the influence of Sidney's romance on plays of the seventeenth century: John Day's *Isle of Gulls*, Beaumont and Fletcher's *Cupid's Revenge*, Henry Glapthorne's *Argalus and Parthenia*, James Shirley's *Arcadia*, the anonymous *Andromana*, Antoine Mareschal's *La cour bergère*, and the Italian opera by Flaminio Parisetti and Giovanni Battista Alveri entitled *Il rè pastore, overo: Il Basilio in Arcadia*. This last work was translated into German by F.C. Bressand, set to a new score by Reinhard Keiser, and published and performed in Hamburg as *Der königliche Schäfer, oder Basilius in Arcadien*. Rejects W. Carew Hazlitt's view (1363) that Thomas Jevon's farce *The Devil of a Wife* is based on the account of Mopsa in *Arcadia*.

1444 BRYAN, J[OHN THOMAS] INGRAM. *The Feeling for Nature in English Pastoral Poetry.* Tokyo: Kyo-Bun-Kwan, 1908, pp. 45–52. Orig. a Ph.D. diss., University of Pennsylvania, 1907.
In "The Pastoral School of Sidney," discusses Sidney as the chief English proponent of the strain of pastoral derived from Sannazaro and Montemayor, asserting that it leads to the conventional insipidity of Pope. Contrasts the strain begun by Spenser, noting that Sidney stripped pastoral of the magical and supernatural and emphasized

action more than natural beauty. Comments on Sidney's influence on Robert Greene and Thomas Lodge.

1445 BUCHIN, ERNA. "Sidney's *Arcadia* als Quelle für *Cymbeline*." *Archiv* 143 (1922):250–52.
Identifies the story of Plangus and Andromana in Book II as a likely source for the Queen's machinations to put Cloten on the throne in Shakespeare's play. Also links Cloten with Sidney's Dametas and the apparent poisoning of Imogen in the cave with the "death" of Basilius.

1446 BUCK, EVONNE PATRICIA. "The Renaissance Pastoral Romance: A Study of Genre and Theme in Sannazaro, Montemayor, Sidney and D'Urfé." Ph.D. diss., University of Michigan, 1975, 276 pp.
Examines the Renaissance genres of pastoral, romance, and antipastoral for their underlying class affiliations and attitudes toward life. Suggests that, in *Arcadia*, Sidney resolved the tension between the three genres "in favor of the pastoral tradition and the contemplative life of the mind." See *DAI* 36 (April 1976):6663A.

1447 BUCKLEY, GEORGE T. *Atheism in the English Renaissance.* Chicago: University of Chicago Press, 1932, pp. 16, 75–77. Reprint. *Rationalism in Sixteenth Century English Literature.* Chicago: University of Chicago Libraries, University of Chicago Press, 1933. Orig. a Ph.D diss., University of Chicago, 1931.
Notes that Pamela's refutation of Cecropia in the New *Arcadia* is the first known English response to the mechanistic philosophy of Lucretius. Agrees with Greenlaw (1565) that Cecropia may represent Catharine de Medici and Pamela may represent Queen Elizabeth. Concludes that Sidney's contact with Epicureanism probably came through his French connections. Also identifies a comment in the *Defence* on "philosophers who, shaking off superstition, brought in atheism" as an allusion to Plutarch's treatise in the *Moralia* "On Superstition."

1448 BUGGE HANSEN, NIELS. *That Pleasant Place: The Representation of Ideal Landscape in English Literature from the 14th to the 17th Century.* Copenhagen, Denmark: Akademisk Forlag, 1973, pp. 84–87, 122–23, 132, 154.
Notes that, after Book I, the New *Arcadia* rarely describes the landscape and makes little of the pastoral setting. The descriptions are unusually panoramic and laden with conceits, but otherwise conventional. Finds that Sidney's panoramic view becomes common in seventeenth-century pastorals by William Browne, John Denham, and Milton.

Twentieth Century

1449 BURNS, RAYMOND S[TEPHEN], ed. Introduction to *The Isle of
Guls*, by John Day. Renaissance Drama: A Collection of Critical
Editions. New York and London: Garland Publishing, 1980, pp.
16, 23, 27, 37–39. Orig. a Ph.D. diss., University of Pennsylvania,
1963, 305 pp.
Points out that Day's play owes its main plot, its chief characters, and
much of its phrasing to *Arcadia* but that Sidney's moral sentiments have
been debased. Suggests that Sidney's character Basilius has been transformed into a satire of James I.

1450 BUSH, DOUGLAS. "Marvell and Sidney." *RES*, n.s. 3 (October
1952):375.
Notes that his own discussion (456) of Marvell's debt to *Arcadia* in the
poem "The Definition of Love" antedates that of Martin (1675).

1451 BUSHMAN, MARY ANN. "The Case Against Rhetoric: Problems
of Judgment in Jacobean Tragedy." Ph.D. diss., University of
California at Berkeley, 1982, 208 pp.
Claims that Sidney exhibits a "deeply critical, questioning attitude
toward rhetoric's claims to knowledge." Sidney's subject in *Arcadia* is the
conflict between a "human institution of judgment" and a "truly over-
powering opponent—the world of Arcadia itself," and in the trial he
"reveals the potential tragedy of relying on rhetorical methods to
explain and judge a very complex and human actuality." See *DAI* 44
(July 1983):173A.

1452 BUTRICK, LYLE HOWARD. "*The Queenes Arcadia* by Samuel
Daniel, Edited, with Introduction and Notes." Ph.D diss., State
University of New York at Buffalo, 1968, 355 pp.
Notes Sidney's influence on the title of the play. See *DAI* 29 (December
1968):1863A

1453 BUXTON, JOHN. *A Draught of Sir Philip Sidney's Arcadia.* In
Historical Essays, 1600–1750: Presented to David Ogg, edited by
H[enry] E[smond] Bell and R.L. Ollard. London: A. & C. Black;
New York: Barnes & Noble, 1963, pp. 60–77. Orig. pub. Oxford:
printed at the New Bodleian Library, 1961 (not seen).
Publishes for the first time an anonymous, mid-seventeenth-century
poem that adapts Sidney's *Arcadia* to the circumstances that led to the
outbreak of the civil war. Discusses the possible political allegory in the
work and the attitude toward *Arcadia* adopted by the author and the
Puritans and courtiers of the period. Also reports the existence of an
elaborate subject and character index of *Arcadia* in the same manuscript.

Twentieth Century

1454 ———. *Elizabethan Taste*. London: Macmillan & Co., 1963; New York: St. Martin's Press, 1964, pp. 246–68.
Provides publishing history for the 1590 and 1593 editions of *Arcadia* and examines the reputation of the book. Divides readers into two classes: those like Mary Sidney who treat it as a light romance, and those like Fulke Greville who regard it as a serious heroic poem. Notes that Abraham Fraunce thought it worthy of comparison with the epics of Homer and Virgil. Drawing upon Hoskins (1593), lists elements of the romance that Sidney's contemporaries most admired. Also records contemporary opinion on the contrasts between the Arcadian style and euphuism.

1455 ———. "Sidney and Theophrastus." *ELR* 2 (Winter 1972):79–82.
Examines evidence that Sidney's method of describing comic character was influenced by Theophrastus. Cites comments by Renaissance rhetoricians, the *Characters* of Sidney's friend Henri Estienne, and the manuscript of a seventeenth-century index to *Arcadia*.

1456 CAREY, JOHN. "Sixteenth and Seventeenth Century Prose." In *History of Literature in the English Language*, edited by Christopher Ricks. Vol. 2, *English Poetry and Prose, 1540–1674*. London: Sphere Books, Barrie & Jenkins, 1970, pp. 339–431.
Regards the political sections of *Arcadia* as "a stage for the posturing aristocrats" rather than as explorations of practical principles of government. Attacks the passage on the rebellion of the commoners as "elegant barbarity" and "class warfare," and dismisses the book as "fake civilization." Also condemns as "sterile" the ornamentation of Sidney's style, treating echoes of it in Nashe's *Unfortunate Traveller* as ambivalent attempts at satiric parody.

1457 CARNEY, JO ELDRIDGE. "Female Friendship in Elizabethan Literature." Ph.D. diss., University of Iowa, 1983, 222 pp.
Includes a discussion of Sidney's representations of female friendships in *Arcadia*. See *DAI* 44 (January 1984):2151A.

1458 CARNICELLI, D.D., ed. Introduction to *Lord Morley's "Tryumphes of Fraunces Petrarcke": The First English Translation of the "Trionfi."* Cambridge, Mass.: Harvard University Press, 1971, pp. 54, 56–57, 63.
Points out similarities between the triumphal pageant of Artesia in Book I of *Arcadia* and Petrarch's "Trionfo d'amore." Concludes that Sidney was parodying conventions drawn from the illustrations of the *Trionfi* or from Elizabethan pageants created under its influence.

Twentieth Century

1459 CARRARA, ENRICO. *Storia dei generi letterari italiani: La poesia pastorale*. Milan: Dottor Francesco Vallardi, [1909], p. 439.
Notes the influence of *Arcadia* on Renaissance pastoral and compares Sidney with Garcilaso de la Vega.

1460 CARROLL, WILLIAM MEREDITH. *Animal Conventions in English Renaissance Non-Religious Prose (1550–1600)*. New York: Bookman Associates, 1954, pp. 46, 80–82.
Explains the philosophy behind Sidney's statement in *Arcadia* that beasts cannot perceive beauty. Compares the episode of the lion and the bear with similar encounters in other Elizabethan romances, concluding that such scenes reveal the "vertue" of the Renaissance man in overcoming evil. Traces to medieval romances the animal imagery used in the heraldic devices of Sidney's knights.

1461 CARSANIGA, GIOVANNI M. "'The Truth' in John Ford's *The Broken Heart*." *CL* 10 (Fall 1958):344–48.
Discusses parallels between the play and *Arcadia*, noting that both involve oracles and include characters with Greek names signifying moral qualities. Adds that the love affair in the main plot of the play resembles Sidney's frustrated relationship with Penelope Rich.

1462 CHALLIS, LORNA. "The Use of Oratory in Sidney's *Arcadia*." *SP* 62 (July 1965):561–76.
Examines the set speeches in *Arcadia*, contrasting Sidney's use of all three classical forms—the deliberative, the forensic, and the epideictic—with the tendency of other Elizabethans to emphasize the third. Notes that Sidney excels over early Elizabethan playwrights in the variety and dramatic force of his style. Traces to Cicero his sense of rhythm and to Aristotle his ability in argument, particularly his adaptation of speeches to the speaker, the audience, and the occasion. Concludes that Sidney anticipated seventeenth-century reactions against excessive ornament.

1463 CHAMBERS, R[AYMOND] W[ILSON]. *"King Lear": The First W.P. Ker Memorial Lecture Delivered in the University of Glasgow 27th November, 1939*. Glasgow: Jackson, Son & Co., 1940, p. 45.
Discusses the influence of the story of the Paphlagonian King on the deaths of Shakespeare's King Lear and Gloucester.

1464 ———. "Poets and Their Critics: Langland and Milton." Warton Lecture on English Poetry. *PBA* 27 (1941):109–54.
Discusses Milton's comments on Pamela's prayer in the Captivity Episode and argues against the charge that Milton himself interpolated the passage in the prayer book of Charles I.

1465 CHANG, H[SIN] C[HANG]. *Allegory and Courtesy in Spenser: A Chinese View.* Edinburgh University Publications: Language and Literature, 8. Edinburgh: Edinburgh University Press, 1955, pp. 114–51 passim.

In "*The Faerie Queene,* Sidney's *Arcadia* and the Romances," concludes that Sidney sought to teach an inconsistent and limited code of chivalry but that Spenser sought to translate the code into more universal principles. Notes Sidney's transformation of traditional loci of Greek romance: the stronghold of the bandits becomes the Renaissance castle of Amphialus; the haunt of shepherds becomes the royal retreat; the cave of defeated rebels becomes the trysting place of princes. Argues that the half-savage insurgents described by Sidney and Spenser derive from their personal knowledge of Irish rebels. Also suggests parallels between Sidney's tale of Amphialus and Helen and Spenser's account of Timias and Belphoebe, and between Sidney's story of Erona and Spenser's account of Mirabella.

1466 CHARNEY, MAURICE. "Hawthorne and Sidney's *Arcadia.*" *N&Q,* n.s. 7 (July 1960):264–65.

Dispels the myth, apparently begun by Fields (1357), that Hawthorne read an old copy of *Arcadia* regularly. Notes that *Mosses from an Old Manse* alludes to the story of Sidney's generosity in giving his cup to a soldier at Zutphen, but concludes that Hawthorne hardly regarded Sidney as a favorite author. See also Julian Hawthorne (1583).

1467 CLEMEN, WOLFGANG. *Shakespeares Bilder: Ihre Entwicklung und ihre Funktionen im dramatischen Werk.* Bonner Studien zur englischen Philologie, 27. Bonn: Peter Hanstein, 1936, pp. 317–22. [The English translation, *Shakespeare's Imagery,* omits this section on Sidney.]

Compares the similes and metaphors of *Arcadia* with those of Lyly's *Euphues,* suggesting that Sidney's imagery is superior in that it is functional, organic, and harmoniously connected with the subject at hand. Discusses Sidney's tendency to personify Nature and his use of dynamic rather than static images. Relates his idealization of a humanized, "golden" world in the *Defence* to the fantastic quality of imagery in *Arcadia.*

1468 CLUETT, ROBERT. "Arcadia Wired: Preliminaries to an Electronic Investigation of the Prose Style of Philip Sidney." *Lang&S* 7 (Spring 1974):119–37.

Provides "a partial quantitative account of Sidney's style in prose fiction measured against those of Lodge, Lyly, and Nashe." Describes computer techniques and the classifications employed and supplies numerous

Twentieth Century

graphs. Concludes that "it is not that Sidney was hypotactic, Lyly paratactic; it is rather that Sidney was hypotactic in an irregular way and that Lyly was symmetrical, anaphoric, seriated." Also suggests that Sidney's style is more adverbial than scholars have recognized.

1469 COFFEE, JESSIE A. "Arcadia to America: Sir Philip Sidney and John Saffin." *AL* 45 (March 1973):100–104.
Discusses the many excerpts from *Arcadia* in the commonplace book of a seventeenth-century American judge. See Saffin (1748).

1470 COMITO, TERRY [ALLEN]. "Beauty Bare: Speaking Waters and Fountains in Renaissance Literature." In *Fons Sapientiae: Renaissance Garden Fountains*, edited by Elisabeth B. MacDougall. Dumbarton Oaks Colloquium on the History of Landscape Architecture, 5. Washington, D.C.: Dumbarton Oaks, 1978, pp. 15–58.
Traces traditions behind references in *Arcadia* to reflecting water and fountains. Concentrates on the neo-Platonic philosophy implicit in the description of Philoclea bathing in the river Ladon.

1471 ———. "The Lady in a Landscape and the Poetics of Elizabethan Pastoral." *UTQ* 41 (Spring 1972):200–218.
Examines "Come Dorus, come, let songs thy sorrows signify" (*OA* 7) and *Colin Clout's Come Home Again* in terms of the story of the lady who mysteriously both "inhabits and transcends" the landscape. Considers the description of Urania in *Arcadia*, where the poet seeks out the natural objects haunted by his memory of her. Notes that lovers in *Arcadia* continually attempt to discover in the pastoral world some testimony of the lady's presence. While Lalus thinks in terms of concrete images, Musidorus complains because he can only celebrate the elusiveness of the lady. Believes that Sidney uses the dual awareness of rustic and prince to embody conflict between the lady's presence and her elusiveness. "The whole romance adheres to a difficult faith in the potentialities of experience, and works toward the reconciliation of a whole set of polarities revolving about the mind's relation to the world."

1472 ———. "Renaissance Gardens and Elizabethan Romance." Ph.D. diss., Harvard University, 1968, pp. 539–52.
Views *Arcadia* as "an intellectual anatomy of pastoral." Discusses ways in which the characters are continually acting in response to their surroundings, attempting "to press the data of the physical world into service of aspiring thought."

Twentieth Century

1473 CONSTABLE, KATHLEEN M[ARY]. "The Rival Poet and the Youth of the Sonnets." *TLS*, 9 November 1933, p. 774.
Links Dorus and Pamela with characters of the same name in Drayton's sonnet sequence *Idea's Mirror*.

1474 COOK, ALBERT S. "'Never less alone than when alone.'" *MLN* 24 (February 1909):54–55.
Notes many instances of this paradox from Cicero to Edward Gibbon, including two in *Arcadia*.

1475 COOKE, PAUL J. "The Spanish Romances in Sir Philip Sidney's *Arcadia*." Ph.D. diss., University of Illinois at Urbana-Champaign, 1939.
Abstract not available. Cited in *Comprehensive Dissertation Index 1861–1972*, vol. 33, p. 920.

1476 CORBETT, MARGERY, and LIGHTBOWN, RONALD. *The Comely Frontispiece: The Emblematic Title-Page in England, 1550–1660*. London: Routledge & Kegan Paul, 1979, pp. 58–65.
In Chapter 2, "Sir Philip Sidney," examines the title page of the 1593 *Arcadia*, discussing similar engravings of the period, the characters and incidents of the book represented on the title page, and the emblems. Traces the pig and marjorum bush from its origin in Lurcretius to its treatment in Renaissance emblem books by Pierio Valeriano and Joachim Camerarius. Links statements in Hugh Sanford's preface to this emblem and discusses later printed attacks on Sanford by John Florio and Thomas Nashe that also employ the emblem.

1477 COTTON, SEABORN. "The Reverend Seaborn Cotton's Commonplace Book." Transcribed by Samuel Eliot Morison. *Publications of the Colonial Society of Massachusetts* 32 (April 1935):320–52.
Includes several extracts from *Arcadia* in a partial transcription of a seventeenth-century manuscript by Seaborn Cotton.

1478 COULMAN, D. "Spotted to be Known." *JWCI* 20 (January–June 1957):179–80.
Notes that there is a manuscript at Penshurst containing a major part of Abraham Fraunce's *Insignium, Armorum, Emblematum . . . Explicatio*, in which two of Sidney's devices not mentioned in the published version are described. One, a sheep marked with pitch over the motto "Spotted to be known," is Philisides's device in *Arcadia*.

403

Twentieth Century

1479 COUTON, M[ARIE]. "Didactisme et romanesque dans le roman élisabéthain." Ph.D. diss., University of Lyon, 1982, 864 pp.
Draws on contemporary theories of narratology to analyze the blend of romantic and didactic elements in Elizabethan prose fiction. Examines the discursive, narrative, and rhetorical techniques of *Arcadia*, contrasting the work of other authors of Arcadian prose fiction such as Thomas Lodge and Robert Greene. Points out that, although *Arcadia* is an important influence on later fiction, Elizabethan writers "utterly misunderstood" Sidney's poetics. See *DAI* 47 (Summer 1986):284C–85C.

1480 COUTON, MARIE. "Variations arcadiennes dans le roman pastoral élisabéthain." In *Le Genre pastoral en Europe du XVe au XVIIe siècle*. Actes du Colloque International tenu à Saint-Étienne du 28 septembre au 1er octobre 1978: Centre d'Études de la Renaissance et de l'Age Classique. Edited by Claude Longeon. Saint-Étienne, France: Publications de l'Université de Saint-Étienne, 1980, pp. 151–59.
Contrasts Sidney's handling of pastoral characters and activities in *Arcadia* with that of Lodge in *Rosalynde*. Seeks to show that, although the two works seem similar, their respective "interpretations" of pastoral (revealed in the way elements are "organized" and "commented on" at the level of *récit*) "diverge profoundly." Whereas for Sidney the pastoral realm is a place where his heroes' illusions of harmony and serenity are "picked to pieces" (*déchirer*), for Lodge it is the scene of an "expérience privilégiée insoupçonée." Whereas for Lodge love is reconciliatory, for Sidney it provides irreconcilable tensions. Whereas Lodge's characters pass clearly through a purgatory of exile and trial to a "new life," Sidney's heroes discover that love in the pastoral world is "indissolubly purgatory and paradise." Concludes that Lodge's world permits escape from time but Sidney's does not, and that Sidney has a better command of the complexities of human experience.

1481 COYLE, MARTIN [J]. *"Arcadia* and *King Lear." N&Q*, n.s. 27 (April 1980):140.
Considers the influence of *Arcadia* on *Lear* IV.iii.

1482 ———. "The Composition of *King Lear* and Its Sources." Ph.D. diss., University of Nottingham, 1972–73.
Abstract not available. Cited in *Index to Theses Accepted for Higher Degrees in the Universities of Great Britain and Ireland* 23 (1972–73): Item 327.

1483 CRAFT, WILLIAM JEFFREY. "Love in *Arcadia*: A Study of Sidney's Heroic Romance." Ph.D. diss., University of North Carolina at Chapel Hill, 1980, 238 pp.

Notes that, although the 1593 *Arcadia* seems to have been designed as a heroic work of the highest sort and thus as an image of virtues, it nonetheless presents heroes who suffer an ethical fall because of love. Investigates Sidney's conception of love and its relation to heroism, offering two resolutions for the tensions between them. First, suggests that "love and valor can strengthen one another in an even higher heroism than the principals—for all their splendor—display," as we can see from the stories of Helen, Plangus, and Argalus and Parthenia. These characters are set in contrast to others, such as Andromana, Amphialus, Basilius, and Gynecia, who move toward destruction because of "relentless, possessive desire." Second, feels that the inner division between heroic aspiration and passionate desire seen in Pyrocles and Musidorus leads readers to praise the one and reject the other, recognizing "the difficulty and desirability" of the sort of right loving that is "the essence of heroic man and womanhood." Considers the fictional world of Arcadia, arguing that it is suited to portray conflicts between love and heroism in ways that the modern novel cannot. Also considers the importance of the idealized education of Pyrocles and Musidorus in the larger pattern of the work. See *DAI* 42 (August 1981):712A.

1484 ———. "The Shaping Picture of Love in Sidney's *New Arcadia*." *SP* 81 (Fall 1984):395–418.

From the premise that long narrative passages in *Arcadia* "are meant to be viewed as shaping pictures of what love should or should not be," extends the arguments of Lawry (1639) by suggesting that the work is "an ongoing pageant of the possibilities to which love can lead: to the denial of self in the heroic pursuit of the beloved's good; to the destruction of self in the abandoned pursuit of one's desire." First examines the "pictorial traditions" that Sidney inherited and the "views of love" available in three literary traditions. Then examines two contrasting groups of pictures—heroic, self-denying, and devoted versus ignoble, self-seeking, and inconstant—that enforce on us "the necessity of making a choice in love."

1485 CRAIG, HARDIN. "The Composition of *King Lear*." *RenP*, 1961, pp. 57–61.

Suggests that Sidney's story of the Paphlagonian King moved Shakespeare to turn the history of King Lear, which was not tragic in

Twentieth Century

Geoffrey of Monmouth, into a tragedy. Lists details in Shakespeare's main plot that derive from Sidney's story.

1486 CRANE, WILLIAM G. *Wit and Rhetoric in the Renaissance: The Formal Basis of Elizabethan Prose Style.* New York: Columbia University Press, 1937, pp. 41, 43, 56, 79, 91–92, 107, 175–78, 194.

Notes the material by Sidney collected in the anonymous Elizabethan commonplace book *Politeuphuia: Wit's Commonwealth* and in Luis de Granada's *Collectanea Moralis Philosophiae.* Also links the rhetoric of Sidney and Abraham Fraunce with Audomarus Talaeus's *Institutiones Oratoriae.* Contrasts Sidney's favorite rhetorical tropes and figures with those of John Lyly, providing a technical analysis of Sidney's devices and their sources in earlier romances and sentimental novels. Suggests that Lyly's derogatory remarks in *Euphues* directed against those who use "superfluous eloquence" may well refer to *Arcadia*, since it was circulating in manuscript. Also notes that John Dickenson's *Arisbas* imitates *Arcadia*.

1487 CREHEN, BARBARA. "The Sense of Experience in Sidney's *New Arcadia*." Ph.D. diss., Columbia University, 1980, 499 pp.

Contends that the central concern of the New *Arcadia*, conceived "altogether afresh," is no longer the "moral and political consequences of a pursuit of a mere personal gratification," but rather an "urgent interest in the conditioned nature of human experience in general." Men are not "utterly free," but are determied by particular circumstances, which include intentions and actions of others as well as the consequences of their own past actions. This "vision of experience" is related to "new categories" that Machiavelli and Guicciardini were applying to the understanding of history. See *DAI* 42 (June 1982):5127A.

1488 CROLL, MORRIS W[ILLIAM]. "*Arcadia*." *MLN* 16 (February 1901):124–25. [Page numbers cited are for the volume, as printed at the top of the pages, not those for the issue, which appear at the bottom.]

Suggests that Penshurst was the prototype of Kalander's house in *Arcadia*. Notes parallel descriptions in Ben Jonson's poem "To Penshurst."

1489 CROMPTON, N.J.R. "Sidney and Symbolic Heraldry." *Coat of Arms* (London) 8 (April 1965):244–48.

Traces the shift from purely genealogical heraldry, with its symbolic "badges," to the use of *imprese*, that is, symbolic emblems with mottos that indicate the bearer's present psychological state. Discusses the symbolism behind *imprese* in *Arcadia*. (Apparently, a promised continuation was not published.)

1490 CURTIUS, ERNST ROBERT. *European Literature and the Latin Middle Ages*. Translated by Willard R. Trask. Bollingen Series, 36. Princeton, N.J.: Bollingen Foundation, Princeton University Press, 1953, p. 237.

Rejects the view of Pollert and Kindervater (1715) that Shakespeare's line "Find tongues in trees, and books in running brooks" in *As You Like It* II.i echoes a passage in *Arcadia*. Cites other analogues to show that the metaphors are commonplace.

1491 CUTTS, JOHN P. "More Manuscript Versions of Poems by Sidney." *ELN* 9 (September 1971):3–12. Reprint. Introduction to *"Loves Changelinges Change": An Anonymous Play Based on Sidney's "Arcadia."* North American Mentor Texts and Studies Series, 2. Fennimore, Wis.: James Westburg & Associates, 1974, pp. vii–xix.

Reports on the manuscript of *Love's Changlings' Change*, which is a paraphrase (and often an almost word-for-word adaptation) of portions of *Arcadia*. The play includes three previously unpublished variants of poems by Sidney: "Transformed in show, but more transformed in mind" (*OA 2*); "Come shepherd's weeds, become your master's mind" (*OA 4*); and "We love, and have our loves rewarded" (*OA 6*).

1492 ———. "Pericles in Rusty Armour, and the Matachine Dance of the Competitive Knights at the Court of Simonides." *YES* 4 (1974):49–51.

Puts forward the possibility that the tournament of Phalantus in Book I of the revised *Arcadia* and Pamela's description of Musidorus's matachine dance in Book II may have influenced Shakespeare's presentation of the tournament and dance in *Pericles*.

1493 CUVELIER, ÉLIANE. "Les Dialogues d'amour dans le roman élisabéthain." In *Le Dialogue au temps de la Renaissance*, edited by M[arie-] T[hérèse] Jones-Davies. Université de Paris-Sorbonne, Institut de recherches sur les civilisations de l'Occident moderne, Centre de recherches sur la Renaissance, 9. Paris: Jean Touzot, 1984, pp. 75–97.

In comparing dialogues between lovers as they appear in Elizabethan fiction between 1578 and 1600, cites the 1593 *Arcadia* to illustrate several main "structural" features: the division of dialogues into three "phases";

Twentieth Century

the presence of a "véritable stratégie féminine," which consists in pretending to repulse the wooer while all along encouraging him a bit, so as finally to accept him; and "alternative strategies" of dialogue, including epistolary exchanges. Claiming concision and directness for Sidney's dialogues, suggests that their style reflects an increasing concern for rapid plot development in Elizabethan fiction. Presents Sidney's account of Argalus and Parthenia in Book III as a "sublime exception" to the rule that love dialogues are designed to lead to marriage rather than to represent conjugal life. Notes Sidney's tendency to locate his dialogues in moments of crisis and remarks on his inventiveness in handling indirect dialogues, such as Musidorus's professions of love to Pamela via Mopsa. Calls Pyrocles's debate with Philoclea about suicide "the most brilliant example" of a love dialogue that incorporates social and philosophical ideas.

1494 DANA, MARGARET E[LIZABETH]. "Heroic and Pastoral: Sidney's *Arcadia* as Masquerade." *CL* 25 (Fall 1973):308–20.
In seeking the reason that Sidney gave his epic the title of a lowly pastoral, suggests an analogy with Musidorus's diguise as a shepherd. Brings up traditions of pastoral, courtly love, and Christian humility that advocate "being low in order to be high," finding examples in Urania and in the shepherds Strephon and Claius. Discusses the importance of disguise in Elizabethan royal entertainments, noting Italian uses of masques to free nobleman from the decorum of rank. Points to entertainments with similar purposes in *The Faerie Queene*. Also discusses the disguises as tests of integrity and as metaphors for the transforming power of love and "the ambiguous surfaces life can present." Argues against critics who feel that the Princes fail the test. Also relates diguise to Castiglione's concept of *sprezzatura* and to C.L. Barber's analysis of festival elements in Shakespearean comedy.

1495 DANBY, JOHN F. *Poets on Fortune's Hill: Studies in Sidney, Shakespeare, Beaumont and Fletcher*. London: Faber & Faber, 1952, pp. 17–19, 31–32, 35–36, 46–107 passim, 155–56. Reprint. *Elizabethan and Jacobean Poets: Studies in Sidney, Shakespeare, Beaumont and Fletcher*. London: Faber & Faber, 1954.
Places Sidney at the top of "Fortune's hill," relating his high social position to the sort of books that he wrote. Defines his typical stance as *ironia*. Contrasts his career with that of Spenser. In Chapter 2, "Sidney's *Arcadia*: The Great House Romance," urges that the book was written to instruct "princes and gentlemen, in prosperity and adversity, limning out exact pictures of every posture in the mind." Regards elements of

romance and pastoral, including the eclogues, as only "vaguely perti-nent" to the main purposes of the book. Examines the initial shipwreck, noting the the implicit comparison between the macrocosm and the microcosm of the soul. Notes Sidney's interest in balancing pairs of con-trasting characters, incidents, or ideas. Defines his moral ideal as a wed-ding of "feminine" Christian patience with "masculine" classical magna-nimity. Analyzes the main characters as combinations of these elements and offers reasons that the four young lovers are paired as they are. Treats the Captivity Episode as the supreme test of patience and magna-nimity, pondering Sidney's concept of evil as revealed in Cecropia and Amphialus. Considers the trial and condemnation of the royal lovers as Sidney's way of exploring the relation of human virtue and divine provi-dence. Notes parallels between *Arcadia* and *King Lear* and contrasts Sidney with Shakespeare, regarding one as the product of a great house and the other as the product of rural nature and the playhouses. In Chapter 3, "Sidney and the Late-Shakesperian Romance," seeks to define the moral and political "mechanisms" governing both *Arcadia* and the plays of Shakespeare. Concentrates on the relations among rulers, aristocrats, and commoners; the nature of villainy; and the requirement that public order be founded on private virtue. Analyzes Sidney's world-view as a series of concentric spheres: virtue perfected, surrounded by human imperfection, surrounded by fortune, surrounded by the divine. Finds this scheme in the second description of the initial shipwreck and relates it to Boethius's *Consolation of Philosophy* and to Shakespeare's *Pericles*. Compares incidents and characters in *Arcadia* with analogues in Shakespeare's other late romances. Also compares the work of Beaumont and Fletcher. For a reply, see Rose (726). See also item 492.

1496 D[AVENPORT], A[RNOLD]. "Possible Echoes from Sidney's *Arcadia* in Shakespeare, Milton, and Others." *N&Q* 194 (24 December 1949):554–55.

Finds echoes of *Arcadia* in Shakespeare's *Antony and Cleopatra*, *King Lear*, *Midsummer Night's Dream*, and *Julius Caesar*; in Milton's *Paradise Lost*, *Samson Agonistes*, and "Lycidas"; in Drummond of Hawthornden's com-ments on Donne; and in Fuller's description of wit-combats between Shakespeare and Jonson.

1497 DAVIS, WALTER R. "Actaeon in Arcadia." *SEL* 2 (Winter 1962):95–110.

Analyzes the cave scene between Gynecia and Pyrocles, arguing that it is "the central episode of the plot." Links the cave with the grotto in Ovid's *Metamorphoses* where Actaeon saw Diana naked, noting verbal echoes and

Twentieth Century

tracing the tradition of similar caves in pastoral literature, art, and emblem books. Finds traditional interpretations of the myth relevant to Sidney's cave scene: reason brought down by passion; love destroyed by curiosity; the mind illuminated by self-knowledge. Suggests that Pyrocles sees his own lust mirrored in the cave and in Gynecia, and that this self-knowledge prepares him for a process of Christian regeneration, which he begins after his attempt to commit suicide.

1498 ———. *Idea and Act in Elizabethan Fiction*. Princeton, N.J.: Princeton University Press, 1969, pp. 56–72, 80, 82–83.
In Chapter 3, "Pastoral Romance: Sidney and Lodge," considers Sidney's way of presenting and testing ideas in *Arcadia*, arguing that he aims to exalt "ordinary man by mimesis into the realm of the mythical." Suggests that Asia Minor represents heroic action and the actual world of human experience and that Arcadia (especially in the central cave) represents contemplation, love, and a meeting of ideal with real. Places the romance among other Renaissance fictions in which the hero leaves the real world, dons a disguise reflecting a change of values, gains new self-knowledge in an idealized world, and returns to the world he first left. Treats *Arcadia* as an exploration of the diverse fortunes possible under the rule of the goddess of love and, more particularly, of Plato's conception of love and the just order of the soul and the state. Considers the Princes' disguises, the ambivalent effects of their love, the lessons of passages such as the final prison scene and the trial, and the constant failure of precept in the face of experience. Traces Sidney's influence on later English pastoral romances such as Gervase Markham's *English Arcadia*, John Dickenson's *Arisbas*, and works by Robert Greene. Also compares *Arcadia* with Thomas Lodge's *Euphues's Shadow*.

1499 ———. "A Map of *Arcadia*: Sidney's Romance in Its Tradition." In *Sidney's "Arcadia*," by Walter R. Davis and Richard A. Lanham. Yale Studies in English, 158. New Haven, Conn.: Yale University Press, 1965, pp. 1–179. Orig. a Ph.D. diss., Yale University.
In the introduction, discusses various states of the text and explains the reasons for selecting the 1593 version for study. Rejects attempts to classify it as an epic in prose, treating it instead as a pastoral romance. In Chapter 1, traces the development of pastoral poetry and romance from antiquity through the Renaissance. Finds two main precedents for the structure of Sidney's work: Sannazaro's *Arcadia*, in which the protagonist progresses from pain to education and regeneration, and Montemayor's *Diana* (with its continuation by Gil Polo), in which subplots reflect the

main plot, eclogues mingle with a prose narrative, and the main action follows a five-act comic structure. Emphasizes the pastoral setting of such works, noting that it often involves concentric circles: a central cave or place of revelation, surrounded by a harmonious pastoral world, set off from a wider world of politics, commerce, and war. Points out that the heroes tend to travel from the outer circle to the center and back, undergoing education and regeneration in the process. In Chapter 2, considers the immediate sources of *Arcadia*, relating its structure to the conventions of Renaissance pastoral romance. Explains the vastness and complexity of Sidney's design as an attempt to introduce a full range of moral and political *exempla* and to provide occasions for argumentation. Maintains that Pyrocles and Musidorus undergo a carefully planned process of moral education, passing from a public sphere (active, political, chivalric) to a private sphere (contemplative, amorous, pastoral) and back again. In Chapter 3, regards the debates between Pyrocles and Musidorus as indicators of their progress toward perfection. Notes that, in Book I, they abandon the active life for the contemplative, setting out on a neo-Platonic ladder of love (as defined by Plotinus and Macrobius). Suggests that, until Book III, the Princes are governed by Aristotelian views of ethics and make little progress because their minds are divided between reason and passion. In the Captivity Episode of Book III, the Princesses teach the men to control passion through Christian patience and faith in divine providence, virtues that they master in prison before the Trial Scene. In Chapter 4, examines Strephon and Claius as examples of the effects of the neo-Platonic ladder of love and their mistress Urania as a representation of Heavenly Love derived from Platonic conceptions of the goddess Aphrodite Ourania. Also considers the influence of the openings of Heliodorus's *Aethiopica* and Montemayor's *Diana*. Discusses the function of the eclogues in dividing the main action into sections with universal themes: love, suffering and division of mind, marriage, and death. In Chapter 5, supplies a revised version of item 1501, which considers the function of the episodes and their relation to the main plot. In Chapter 6, traces interrelations between microcosm and macrocosm in *Arcadia* using as guides Renaissance interpretations of Plato's *Republic* and the Christian story of the Fall. Finds that Basilius recapitulates the sin of Adam by doubting, then fleeing from, divine providence. The disorder in the King's soul then leads to disorder in his family and the state. Sees emblems of this progression in the scenes that close each of the first four books, and regards the King's reawakening at the end of Book V as an appropriate means to restore faith in providence and natural order. Feels that Pyrocles and Musidorus progress

411

Twentieth Century

from mere seekers of glory to potential philosopher kings, who combine active virtues with contemplative wisdom and have been broken so that they submit to divine providence. Regards Euarchus as such a philosopher king and as a picture of the "natural justice" lost by Adam, which the Princes attain in prison before their trial. Analyzes the various versions of recent events given by the characters at the trial and concludes that Euarchus's judgment is deliberately "by law and not by philosophy or reason." In Chapter 7, concludes that *Arcadia* is not an epic but a pastoral romance pushed to the limits of the form. It records changes in the soul, not merely changes in fortune, and it has the fullness and detail of a moral treatise. Discusses the balance in Sidney's mind between appreciation for active and contemplative virtues and for the good and bad effects of love. Regards the final trial as an exercise in antithesis leading dialectically to a new synthesis. See replies by Hamilton (1245), Amos (1399), Roberts (1289), Vickers (1307), and Rose (726).

1500 ———. "Masking in Arden: The Histronics [sic] of Lodge's Rosalynde." *SEL* 5 (Winter 1965):151–63.
Contrasts Sidney's inner pastoral realm of love and contemplation with the surrounding world of violent heroic action. Lists other works designed on the same pattern, in which characters pass from the outer to the inner and back to the outer again, gaining harmony of soul in the process. Finds more intellectualizing and moralizing in *Arcadia* than in Continental pastoral.

1501 ———. "Thematic Unity in the New *Arcadia*." *SP* 57 (April 1960):123–43.
Argues that, in the greater complication of the revised *Arcadia*, "the matter of the original main plot is diffused, reflected, moralized, and generally clarified." Compares the episodes in Book I involving Argalus and Parthenia, Amphialus and Helen, Phalantus and Artesia, arguing that they shed important light on the main plot. They "define the nature of the Arcadian retreat" and foreshadow the changes in Pyrocles and Musidorus as they penetrate the retreat and fall in love. Observes that all the episodes of Book II concern private passion and public disorder, two themes united in the complex episode of Plangus and Erona, which in turn foreshadows the course of the main plot in Book II. From the disordered minds of the Princes in Book I comes disorder in the royal family and the kingdom in Book II. Finally, in Book III, Sidney presents two possible outcomes of such disorder: for Amphialus, who lacks Christian patience, there is outward and inward war leading to tragedy; for the Princesses, who move toward patience, there is an inward harmony of

reason and passion leading to victory. Also relates the eclogues to these developments. See a reply by Lindheim (1652).

1502 DAVISON, MARY CAROL. "The Metamorphoses of Odysseus: A Study of Romance Iconography from the *Odyssey* to *The Tempest*." Ph.D. diss., Stanford University, 1971, 474 pp.
Examines the genre of romance as it emerged in classical antiquity, noting that it encompassed much that genres like pastoral excluded. Examines *Arcadia* in light of this tradition, concentrating on the elaborate system of symbolic iconography common in ancient romances. See *DAI* 32 (September 1971):1467A.

1503 DELASANTA, RODNEY. *The Epic Voice*. De Proprietatibus Litterarum, Series Maior, 2. The Hague: Mouton, 1967, pp. 60–81. Orig. a Ph.D. diss., Brown University, 1962, 242 pp.
Defends the complicated plot of the New *Arcadia* by comparison with Homer's *Odyssey*, pointing out that both employ an omniscient narrator and several characters who act as "delegated" narrators. Evaluates Sidney's success in making the alternation of these "voices" an integral part of the epic design, noting that it allows the author to begin *in medias res*. Also discusses ways in which Sidney's episodes are romantic rather than epic. Concludes that they contain parallels and contrasts that help to reinforce the ideals of love and political action embodied in the main plot.

1504 DENKINGER, EMMA MARSHALL. "The *Arcadia* and 'The Fish Torpedo Faire.'" *SP* 28 (April 1931):162–83.
Examines ancient and Renaissance sources in order to explain allusions to the fish in the Second Eclogues and in Amphialus's *impresa* at the tournament of Phalantus. Concludes that Sidney's immediate source was Bernardo Tasso, who used the fish as his personal *impresa*.

1505 DENT, R[OBERT] W. *John Webster's Borrowing*. Berkeley: University of California Press, 1960, 331 pp. passim.
Details Webster's many borrowings from *Arcadia*. Concludes that they tend to stitch together widely scattered bits of Sidney's prose in order to add to the plays' imagery, *sententiae*, and argumentative wit.

1506 DESVIGNES, LUCETTE, ed. *La cour bergère ou l'Arcadie de Messire Philippes Sidney*, by André Mareschal. 2 vols. [Saint-Étienne]: Publications de l'Université de Saint-Étienne, 1981.
Volume 2 contains a photoreproduction of the 1640 Paris edition of Mareschal's "tragi-comédie," based on Sidney's *Arcadia*. In Volume 1, a

Twentieth Century

general introduction includes a sketch of Sidney's life and a brief discussion of *Arcadia* and its reception in France, insisting that Mareschal based his play on Baudoin's translation (33). Also provides two "guides," one to the general idea of "Arcadia," the other to Sidney's "superiority" to other pastoral writers. In both, draws on de Tourval's dedicatory epistle (53) on the assumption that seventeenth-century readers understood the complexities of *Arcadia* better than twentieth-century French critics. Seeks to show that Mareschal's "judicious" selection and adaption of details from the *Arcadia* remain "attentive" to the psychology of Sidney's characters. See also item 1507.

1507 DESVIGNES, LUCETTE. "De l'*Arcadie* de Sidney à *La cour bergère*, ou du roman pastoral à la tragi-comédie." In *Le Genre pastoral en Europe du XVe au XVIIe siècle*. Actes du Colloque International tenu à Saint-Étienne du 28 septembre au 1er octobre 1978: Centre d'Études de la Renaissance et de l'Age Classique. Edited by Claude Longeon. Saint-Étienne: Publications de l'Université de Saint-Étienne, 1980, pp. 311–18.
Provides a shorter version of material presented in the introduction to her edition of *La cour bergère* (1506).

1508 DOBYNS, ANN. "Character Definition Through Dialogue in Three Romances: A Rhetorical Analysis." Ph.D. diss., University of Oregon, 1983, 152 pp.
Considering "linguistic characteristics within selected units of discourse," compares the speech patterns of "parallel characters" in similar and different narrative contexts in *Morte d'Arthur*, New *Arcadia*, and *Wuthering Heights*. Concludes that, in *Arcadia*, Sidney's characters "use similar speech conventions when representing their similar social types," but "markedly different manners of speaking" when representing "contrasting philosophical types." See *DAI* 44 (January 1984):2152A.

1509 DONALD, ROSLYN L. "Another Source for Three of John Donne's Elegies." *ELN* 14 (June 1977):264–68.
Cites Sidney's blazon on Philoclea, "What tongue can her perfections tell" (*OA 62*), as a likely source for Donne's elegies "The Anagram," "The Comparison," and "Love's Progress."

1510 DONOVAN, LAURENCE. "How John Leyden Died." *The Carrell: Journal of the Friends of the University of Miami [Florida] Library* 20 (1979):9–24.
Compares the style of Sidney's revised *Arcadia*, Thomas Nashe's *Unfortunate Traveller*, and John Donne's sermon "Death's Duel." Feels

that Sidney's "hyper-poetic" and artificial style diverts attention from his subject and prevents realistic characterization, yet also allows refined analysis. Concludes that Sidney points the way to Henry James, whereas Nashe anticipates more realistic authors such as Hemingway and Faulkner, and Donne exploits both styles.

1511 DORAN, MADELEINE. "Elements in the Composition of *King Lear*." *SP* 30 (January 1933):34–58.
Examines the influence of *Arcadia* on the original version of *King Lear* and on Shakespeare's revision, observing that the changes reflect Sidney's views on political authority and its abuse.

1512 DORANGEON, SIMONE. *L'églogue anglaise de Spenser à Milton*. Études anglaises, 49. Paris: Didier, 1974, pp. 31–45 passim, 80, 133, 151–52, 168, 171–77, 192–95, 226–27, 276, 287–88, 302, 466–67.
Emphasizes Sidney's contribution to the development of the genres of pastoral and romance and the Platonism apparent throughout his works. Sees in the eclogues of *Arcadia* the influence of Spenser's *Shepherd's Calendar*. Notes a contrast between the verse forms assigned to rustics and to noblemen, but dismisses the poems as mediocre when taken out of context.

1513 DOWDEN, EDWARD. *Essays Modern and Elizabethan*. London: J.M. Dent & Sons; New York: E.P. Dutton, 1910, pp. 375–79.
In "Elizabethan Romance," considers the sources, the appeal, and the faults of *Arcadia*.

1514 DUHAMEL, P[IERRE] ALBERT. "Sidney's *Arcadia* and Elizabethan Rhetoric." *SP* 45 (April 1948):134–50.
Distinguishes between the styles of Lyly's *Euphues* and Sidney's *Arcadia*, analyzing Pyrocles's debate with Musidorus in Book I according to the method of the Renaissance rhetorician John Brinsley. Concludes that Lyly followed Erasmus and the Ciceronian stylists in focusing on tropes and figures, whereas Sidney resembles Thomas Wilson and Francis Bacon in focusing on a worthy choice of subject, clear organization, and sound argument. Contrasts Sidney and Lyly in their use of ornament and in their understanding of the "topics of invention."

1515 ———. "Sir Philip Sidney and the Traditions of Rhetoric." Ph.D. diss., University of Wisconsin, 1945, 166 pp.
Places Sidney in the development of rhetoric from the Greek Sophists through Francis Bacon. In analyzing *Arcadia*, discusses passages of

Twentieth Century

description and narration as well as oratory, applying the method of the
Renaissance rhetorician John Brinsley. By comparing matters of invention and argument with those of elocution, establishes Sidney's reliance
on Ramistic and Aristotelian theories of rhetoric. See *University of
Wisconsin Summaries of Doctoral Dissertations* 9 (1949):483–84.

1516 DUNCAN-JONES, E.E. "Henry Oxinden and Sidney's *Arcadia*."
N&Q 198 (August 1953):322–23.
Notes that one of Oxinden's letters is "a mosaic of unacknowledged quo-
tations from Sidney's *Arcadia*."

1517 DUNCAN-JONES, KATHERINE. "Nashe and Sidney: The
Tournament in *The Unfortunate Traveller*." *MLR* 63 (January
1968):3–6.
Details points in which Thomas Nashe's description of the tournament
at Florence in *The Unfortunate Traveller* is a parody of passages in the
1593 *Arcadia*, particularly Phalantus's tournament in Book I and other
descriptions of armor and *imprese*.

1518 ———. "Philip Sidney's Toys." *PBA* 66 (1980):161–78.
Calls into question the prevailing view of Sidney as simultaneously a
man of action and a heroic poet, claiming that "obviously all his poetry
is *early* poetry," and concluding that "what he had finished by the time of
his death were, for the most part, poetic toys, to be enjoyed as such."
Finds in *The Lady of May*, in the eclogues of the Old *Arcadia*, and in
Astrophil and Stella a poetry that "takes us deep into a world of internalized brooding." Argues that all of the longest poems in *Arcadia*, including "As I my little flock on Ister bank" (*OA 66*) and "A shepherd's tale no
height of style desires" (*OP 4*), are "in different ways disappointing as
the work of a man who set a high value on action." Although believes
them to be technically outstanding, feels that all are by Sidney's "own
most exacting standards, *empty*." Finds in *Astrophil and Stella* "few links
with the ideas on which the *Defence* is based," viewing its two main characters as "social cowards." Sees Sidney's famed *sprezzatura* as perhaps "a
fitting framework for what was in the last analysis only splendid trifles."

1519 DÜNNHAUPT, GERHARD. "Altes und Neues zur
Opitzbibliographie." In *Martin Opitz: Studien zu Werk und Person*,
edited by Barbara Becker-Cantarino. Amsterdam: Rodopi, 1982,
pp. 247–52. Also pub. in *Daphnis* 3, no. 2 (1982):683–88.
Cites new discoveries about Martin Opitz's early career as an author and
a translator that make more plausible the largely discredited view that
he wrote the 1629 German translation of *Arcadia* (34), which appeared

under the pseudonym Valentinius Theocritus von Hirschberg. See also Lindern (1334) and Wurmb (1836).

1520 EAGLE, R[ODERICK] L. "The *Arcadia* (1593)—Spenser (1611) Title-Page." *Baconiana* 29 (July 1945):97–100.

Notes that the same block was used to print the emblems on both title pages and corrects a misinterpretation of the figures in *Baconiana* 28 (April 1944):76. Identifies the human forms with Pyrocles and Musidorus and the boar at the top with Francis Bacon or "the Arcadian boar." Provides the meaning and the history of the bottom emblem, that of a pig drawing back from sweet marjoram. See also Walters (1799).

1521 ———. "The *Arcadia* (1593) Title-Page Border." *Library*, 5th ser. 4 (June 1949):68–71.

A revised version of item 1520. Adds a list of books by other authors that used the same title-page border and notes that the 1638 edition of *Arcadia* was the last to use it.

1522 ECCLES, MARK. "A Survey of Elizabethan Reading." *HLQ* 5 (January 1942):180–82.

Lists *Arcadia* among the books most widely read in England prior to 1642.

1523 EISINGER, FRITZ. *Das Problem des Selbstmordes in der Literatur der englischen Renaissance*. Überlingen, Germany: Seebote, [1926], pp. 64–69. Orig. a Ph.D. diss., Universität Freiburg.

Discusses attempted and successful suicides in *Arcadia*, in particular those involving Andromana, Amphialus, and Pyrocles. Suggests that, though Sidney may have sympathized with Amphialus, he held firmly to Aristotle's arguments against suicide in the *Ethics*.

1524 ELTON, WILLIAM R. *"King Lear" and the Gods*. San Marino, Calif.: Huntington Library, 1966, pp. 34–63, 84, 105, 128, 164–65, 183–84, 192, 211, 275. Orig. a Ph.D. diss., Ohio State University, 1957, 302 pp.

In Chapter 3, "Sidney's *Arcadia*: Four Attitudes to Providence," treats the romance as a link between Calvin's theology and Shakespeare's *Lear*. Lists Sidney's Calvinist teachers at Shrewsbury School and Oxford and his later Puritan and Huguenot associations. Finds in *Arcadia* the following Calvinist views: "the *Deus absconditus*; the gods as somehow not consonant with human happiness; human reason as corrupted and dark; man's position in relation to cosmic forces as one of helpless despair; and mankind as a 'worm.'" Argues that Sidney departed from most

Twentieth Century

Protestants in taking the view that pagans such as Pamela could anticipate Christian virtues and be saved. Compares Cecropia's atheistic arguments, focusing on Epicurean philosophy and scepticism in the
Renaissance. Also examines Basilius's ambiguous attitude toward the
oracle and Pyrocles's belief in a deity who is mysterious and possibly
cruel. Finds in theological discussions in *Arcadia* and *Lear* similar
metaphors of ripeness, thunder, and lower forms of life.

1525 EMPSON, WILLIAM. *Milton's God.* Norfolk, Conn.: New
      Directions Books, 1961, pp. 121–22.
Considers the accusation that Milton himself had Pamela's prayer added
to Charles I's prayer book, and concludes that the trick would have been
justified. See Milton (1323). For a lengthy series of replies, see
Alexander (1396).

1526 ERNLE, [ROWLAND EDMUND PROTHERO, Lord.] "Tudor
      Novels and Romances II." *Nineteenth Century* 92 (November
      1922):748–59.
Evaluates the faults of *Arcadia*, attributing its success to its portrayals of
love and to Sidney's own personality.

1527 EVANS, MAURICE. "Divided Aims in the *Revised Arcadia.*" In *Sir*
      Philip Sidney and the Interpretation of Renaissance Culture: The Poet in
      His Time and in Ours: A Collection of Critical And Scholarly Essays,
      edited by Gary F. Waller and Michael D. Moore. London: Croom
      Helm; Totowa, N.J.: Barnes & Noble, 1984, pp. 34–43.
Working from the premise that Sidney's genius was mimetic, explores
the "problems to which his peculiar eclecticism gave rise." Instead of the
"rapprochement" between Platonism and Aristotelianism posited by
Heninger (2520), sees in the *Defence* a "confusion of philosophies,"
resulting in a "very uncertain control of the 'speaking pictures' which
form the basis of [Sidney's] 'delightful teaching.'" Although Sidney
agrees with Aristotle that "mimesis by its very nature gives pleasure," he
"seems never to quite trust this," and tends instead to "embellish" dramatic moments with a "display of fine and witty rhetoric," as if "he cared
more for his picture than for what it was saying."

1528 EWING, S. B[LAINE], Jr. "Burton, Ford, and *Andromana.*" *PMLA*
      54 (December 1939):1007–17.
Examines the alterations of Sidney's story in this anonymous Caroline
play.

1529 FADER, DANIEL NELSON. "Aphthonius and Elizabethan Prose
Romance." Ph.D. diss., Stanford University, 1963, 265 pp.
Seeks "to account for certain common structural elements in Elizabethan
prose romance . . . by examining the grammar-school precepts of Latin
composition taught to Lyly, Sidney, and Lodge." Concentrates on
Aphthonius's *Progymnasmata*, noting its influence on passages of *Arcadia*.
Blames Aphthonius for retarding the "vital movement" of the romances,
but credits him for helping to develop Sidney's rhetoric. See *DA* 24
(February 1964):3335.

1530 FALKE, ANNE. "'The Work Well Done that Pleaseth All':
Emanuel Forde and the Seventeenth-Century Popular Chivalric
Romance." *SP* 78 (Summer 1981):241–54.
Places *Arcadia* in the traditions of interlaced romance and of aristocratic
fiction read largely by women. Suggests that Forde adapted Sidney's
techniques for the middle class.

1531 FARMER, NORMAN K., Jr. *Poets and the Visual Arts in Renaissance
England*. Austin: University of Texas Press, 1984, pp. 1–18,
108–110.
In Chapter 1, "Visual Art in the *New Arcadia*," observes that, in revising
the original version, "Sidney recast much of his narrative and a great
deal of his description in an apparent effort to appeal more vividly to his
reader's sense of specific pictorial genres: landscape, paintings on
mythological themes, portraits, statuary, jewelry, emblems, impresas."
Noting Greville's remark that Sidney was "an excellent image maker,"
discusses Sidney's knowledge of the visual arts, stressing his interest in
the "expressiveness" of images that invite readers "to imagine a concrete
visual experience as though it were already shaped by the hand of the
artist." Considers Sidney's choice of Veronese to paint his portrait, his
questions about painting as recorded by Hilliard (1058), and other evidence, citing theories about and responses to art by contemporaries
including Daniel Rogers, Giovanni Paolo Lomazzo, and Francesco
Bocchi. Analyzes the sense of visual space created by the opening of the
New *Arcadia* and in the description of Kalander's garden and "house of
pleasures," tracing the way in which Sidney guides the inner eye of the
reader's imagination to the use of framing and perspective by contemporary painters. Relates the descriptions of works of art belonging to
Kalander to larger themes in the romance: nature versus art and passion
versus reason. Suggests that Musidorus makes the mistake of identifying
uncritically with the subjects of the paintings he sees, whereas the reader

Twentieth Century

is encouraged to keep at a critical distance from the passionate scenes represented. Relates the expressive visual techniques of *Arcadia* to Sidney's discussion in the *Defence* of the "second nature" and the "speaking pictures" created by poets. Relates Kalander's statue of Venus and his paintings of Hercules and Omphale, Diana and Actaeon, Hippomenes and Atalanta to later events in *Arcadia* and analyzes the expressive technique employed in Sidney's description of other portraits, including those at the tournament of Phalantus and several of Philoclea. Analyzes emblems and impresas in Books II and III, seeing Miso's description of the "fiend" Cupid, with its accompanying poem (*OA 8*) and Mopsa's story of Cupid and Psyche as emblems of the incompleteness of love in "the fictive Arcadia." Identifies paintings that may have served as sources for three of Sidney's allusions to Ovidian myths. Concludes that "there is a conscious order in the progression from landscape to portraiture to emblem and impresa in the three existing books of the *New Arcadia*." The forms "become increasingly abstract, openly symbolic, and intellectual" and gradually increase the "psychological depth" of the narrative.

1532 FEHRENBACH, ROBERT J., ed. Introduction to *A Critical Edition of "The Politician" by James Shirley*. Renaissance Drama: A Collection of Critical Editions. New York and London: Garland Publishing Co., 1980, pp. xlii–xlvii.
Argues against Huberman's view (1595) that Sidney's story of Plangus was the direct source for Shirley's play, suggesting instead that Lady Mary Wroth's *Urania* acted as an intermediary.

1533 FERGUSON, F[REDERICK] S[UTHERLAND]. "Relations between London and Edinburgh Printers and Stationers (–1640)." *Library*, 4th ser. 8 (September 1927):145–98.
Summarizes the career of the printer Robert Waldgrave, commenting on his pirated edition of *Arcadia* (2) and on the lawsuit that followed.

1534 FIELD, B[RADFORD] S., Jr. "Sidney's Influence: The Evidence of the Publication of the History of Argalus and Parthenia." *ELN* 17 (December 1979):98–102.
Traces Sidney's influence in the following seventeenth-century works: Francis Quarles's poem *Argalus and Parthenia*, John Quarles's continuation, Henry Glapthorne's play of the same name, and two anonymous prose works, *The Most Pleasant and Delightful History of Argalus and Parthenia* and *The Unfortunate Lovers: The History of Argalus and Parthenia*.

1535 FIRESTONE, CLARK B. *The Coasts of Illusion: A Study of Travel Tales*. New York: Harper, 1924, pp. 246–48.
Discusses Sidney's land of Arcadia as a country and as a "province of the imagination."

1536 FOGEL, EPHIM G[REGORY]. "Milton and Sir Philip Sidney's *Arcadia*." *N&Q* 196 (17 March 1951):115–17.
Discusses Milton's attitude toward *Arcadia*, noting evidence in his commonplace book that he admired the work. Also considers Milton's reasons for opening *Samson Agonistes* with lines derived from Sidney's story of the Paphlagonian King.

1537 FORD, PHILIP JEFFREY. "*Paradise Lost* and the Five-Act Epic." Ph.D. diss., Columbia University, 1967, 289 pp.
Relates Sidney's use of a five-act structure in the Old *Arcadia* to sixteenth-century Italian criticism. Both Sidney and the Italians emphasized teaching; verisimilitude; chronological order; the unities of time, place, and action; multiple episodes; and symmetrical design. See *DA* 28 (December 1967):2207A.

1538 FORKER, CHARLES R. "Robert Baron's Use of Webster, Shakespeare, and Other Elizabethans." *Anglia* 83 (1965):176–98.
Mentions that Baron's *Cyprian Academy* is in the fashion of *Arcadia* and that two of his other works, *Pocula Castalia* and *Mirza*, also draw upon Sidney.

1539 FORSYTHE, ROBERT STANLEY. *The Relations of Shirley's Plays to the Elizabethan Drama*. Columbia University Studies in English and Comparative Literature. New York: Columbia University Press, 1914, pp. 38, 268–79, 345, 428.
Details the relation of James Shirley's play *Arcadia* to Sidney's work, pointing out that the main plot and nearly all the characters are borrowed. Also lists allusions to Sidney's romance in Shirley's other plays and in Thomas Nabbes's *Covent Garden*. Notes a further dramatization of *Arcadia* in McNamara Morgan's eighteenth-century play *Philoclea*.

1540 FOX, ALICE. "'What right have I, a woman?': Virginia Woolf's Reading Notes on Sidney and Spenser." In *Virginia Woolf: Centennial Essays*, edited by Elaine K. Ginsberg and Laura Moss Gottlieb. Troy, N.Y.: Whitston, 1983, pp. 249–56.
Argues that Woolf's holograph notes show that, even though it is not apparent in the printed version of her essay, she read *Arcadia* "from a feminist perspective." Contends that Sidney's treatment of women frus-

Twentieth Century

trated Woolf's hopes for an enlightened view of them, expressed in an early note.

1541 FROST, DAVID L. *The School of Shakespeare: The Influence of Shakespeare on English Drama 1600–42.* Cambridge: Cambridge University Press, 1968, pp. 79, 214–17, 219–20, 274.

Notes in the works of Shakespeare and Philip Massinger parallels for the figure in Book I of the New *Arcadia* in which Sidney contrasts a "hillock" with "lofty Olympus." Also compares Sidney's romance with similar minglings of pastoral and epic material in Spenser's *Faerie Queene* and in Shakespeare's late romances. Notes that Shakespeare, like Sidney, used the form for instructive reflections and debates and for offering models of conduct under adversity. Compares Sidney's attitude toward the allegorical interpretation of fiction with that of Edwin Sandys, and notes verbal parallels in Shakespeare's *Troilus and Cressida* I.ii, Webster's *Duchess of Malfi* V.ii, and Sidney's passage beginning "Eagles we see fly alone . . ." in *Arcadia* I.ix.

1542 F[ULLER], H. de W. "Sidney's *Arcadia.*" *Nation* 96 (20 February 1913):174–77.

Faults *Arcadia* for lacking unity, but praises the comic scenes, the characters (especially the women), and the language.

1543 GAYLEY, CHARLES MILLS. *Beaumont, the Dramatist: A Portrait.* New York: Century Co., 1914, pp. 106, 111, 150–74.

Notes the influence of *Arcadia* on Beaumont and Fletcher's plays, including *The Maid's Tragedy* and perhaps *Philaster.* Suggests that *Cupid's Revenge* derives from two of Sidney's plots: Cupid's punishment of Erona and the career of Plangus. Also discusses the close ties of John and Francis Beaumont with the Sidney family.

1544 GENOUY, H[ECTOR]. *L'"Arcadia" de Sidney dans ses rapports avec l'"Arcadie" de Sannazaro et la "Diana" de Montmayor.* Paris: Henri Didier, 1928, 211 pp.

In Chapter 1, sets forth the circumstances under which *Arcadia* was composed and summarizes its publication history (claiming, however, that the 1593 edition is "non révisée"). Provides accounts of the Greek pastoral romances and of the Italian *novelle*. In Chapters 2 and 3, summarizes and compares Sannazaro's *Arcadia* with Montemayor's *Diana.* In Chapter 4, concentrates on Sidney's conception of the pastoral romance, on his theory of imitation, and on his borrowings from the works of Sannazaro and Montemayor. In Chapter 5, pursues a comparative analysis of the three authors, seeking to define Sidney's originality under four headings: differences in basic conception; theme, plot, and characters;

"constitutive elements"; and "moral and political considerations." Among the constitutive elements, compares each author's blending of the following: pastoralism, romance, and love theory; principles of chivalry and the picaresque; and the use of magic and disguise. In Chapter 6, examines the prose style and versification of each writer, stressing the "note gaie" that modifies Sidney's moral and political seriousness and sets his work apart from that of his predecessors. Finds Sidney's originality mainly in 1) the greater prominence he gives to the chivalric element (claiming without discussion that this prominence derives from *Amadis de Gaule*), and 2) "les qualités de forme," especially in a prose style which, despite certain *longeurs* and preciosity, "attains a remarkable ease and clarity in many passages, notably in descriptions and portraits," and which exercised great influence on Shakespeare. Includes an annotated bibliography.

1545 GEROULD, GORDON HALL. *The Patterns of English and American Fiction: A History*. Boston: Little, Brown, & Co., 1942, pp. 22–28.

Discusses Sidney's reputation and the composition of *Arcadia*, defending its style and structure, reviewing its sources, and comparing it with Spenser's *Faerie Queene*.

1546 GESNER, CAROL. *Shakespeare and the Greek Romance: A Study of Origins*. Lexington: University Press of Kentucky, 1970, pp. 48–49, 75, 98, 117.

Rehearses scholarly opinion on Sidney's debt to Greek romance, particularly Heliodorus's *Aethiopica*, and notes ways in which *Arcadia* helped to transmit the tradition to Shakespeare.

1547 GEULEN, HANS. "'Arcadische' Simpliciana: Zu einer Quelle Grimmelshausens und ihrer strukturellen Bedeutung für seinen Roman." *Euphorion* 63 (1969):426–37.

Discusses Theocritus von Hirschberg's translation of *Arcadia* (34) and its revision by Martin Opitz (37), weighing their influence on Hans Jakob Christoffel von Grimmelshausen's *Simplicissimus*. Also ponders Grimmelshausen's allusion to Sidney later in the book and his adoption of the pseudonym Samuel Greifnson vom Hirschfeld.

1548 ———. *Erzählkunst der frühen Neuzeit: Zur Geschichte epischer Darbietungsweisen und Formen im Roman der Renaissance und des Barock*. Tübingen, Germany: Verlag Lothar Rotsch, 1975, pp. 140–47, 301–2.

Discusses Sidney's adaptation of the narrative techniques of Heliodorus. Considers Sidney's rhetoric and his narrative voice, noting its ironic

Twentieth Century

ambivalence and arguing that it introduces a note of relativism in Sidney's moral teaching. Explicates the opening involving Strephon, Claius, and Urania. Because of his ironic play upon the conventions of chivalric and pastoral romance, links Sidney with Ariosto and Cervantes and with the German authors Heinrich Anselm von Zigler und Kliphausen and Hans Jakob Christoffel von Grimmelshausen.

1549 GILBERT, ALLAN H. *Machiavelli's "Prince" and Its Forerunners: "The Prince" as a Typical Book "De Regimine Principum."* Durham, N.C.: Duke University Press, 1938, pp. 44–45, 99–100, 200–201.
In the context of Renaissance theories of monarchy, examines passages in *Arcadia* and the correspondence on the prince's duty to correct his subjects and to obey the laws. Notes Sidney's approval of Machiavelli's view that the monarch must sometimes be severe.

1550 GODSHALK, W[ILLIAM] L[EIGH]. "Gabriel Harvey and Sidney's *Arcadia*." *MLR* 59 (October 1964):497–99.
From analysis of the handwriting, concludes that marginalia in a copy of the 1613 *Arcadia* previously attributed to Gabriel Harvey are not, in fact, his. Also considers dating and traces the ownership of the book. See also item 1346.

1551 ———. "Samothea Again." *RES*, n.s. 31 (May 1980):192.
From correspondence with Jean Robertson and William Ringler, corrects item 1238. Acknowledges that Arthur Kelton was the first to place imaginary descendents of Annius of Viterbo (or "Berosus") in the British Isles.

1552 ———. "Sidney and Shakespeare: Some Central Concepts." Ph.D. diss., Harvard University, 1964, 288 pp.
Compares *Arcadia* with plays by Shakespeare, focusing on the use of heroic and pastoral conventions and on attitudes toward monarchy. Finds the major difference between the two authors in Shakespeare's more conservative view of kingship. Analyzes elements in the story of the Paphlagonian King that Shakespeare did not adopt in writing *King Lear*.

1553 GOHLKE, MADELON SPRENGNETHER. "Narrative Structure in the New *Arcadia*, *The Faerie Queene* I, and *The Unfortunate Traveller*." Ph.D. diss., Yale University, 1972, 356 pp.
Answers critics who find the three works formless. Suggests that each is designed to throw the reader into a world where purpose and design are useless, and then to dispel the confusion as the moral issues of the work become clear. The structure of the works thus reflects the author's view

that the cosmos itself is not "luminous, stable and harmonious" but dark and difficult to understand. See *DAI* 33 (August 1972):723A.

1554 GOHN, ERNEST S. "Primitivistic Motifs in Sidney's *Arcadia*." *PMASAL* 45 (1960):363–71.
Argues in general against twentieth-century interpretations of *Arcadia* that overemphasize Sidney's commitment to the active world of the state, and in particular against Whitney's view (1816) that Sidney was not a primitivist. Points out a "minor theme" of primitivism in the romance, but concludes that Sidney did not develop it consistently.

1555 GOLDMAN, MARCUS SELDEN. Review of *Sir Philip Sidney as a Literary Craftsman*, by Kenneth O. Myrick. *JEGP* 38 (1939):136–41.
Offers evidence that Sidney's Greek was better than Myrick suggests (in 671); that heroic literature (especially Malory) helped to shape *Arcadia*; and that Castiglione's letter to Vittoria Colonna in *The Courtier* resembles Sidney's dedicatory epistle to his sister in *Arcadia*. Also suggests that *Arcadia* contains a good deal of contemporary political allusion.

1556 GÖLLER, KARL HEINZ. "Die Bedeutung der Vulgaria-Sammlung von Samuel Pepys." *Archiv* 216, no. 1 (1979):109–16.
Discusses a 1672 chapbook version of Sidney's story of Argalus and Parthenia found in the Pepys collection.

1557 GORDON, IAN A. *The Movement of English Prose*. English Language Series. Longmans, Green & Co., 1966, pp. 20, 78–81, 94, 146.
Compares Sidney's definition of "caesura" with that of George Puttenham. Traces from Quintilian to the English humanists the sort of syntax displayed in *Arcadia*, noting its influence in later centuries.

1558 GREEN, GLADYS. "Trollope on Sidney's *Arcadia* and Lytton's *The Wanderer*." *Trollopian*, no. 3, September 1946, pp. 45–54.
Transcribes the handwritten comments in Trollope's copy of *Arcadia*, which note the improvements in fiction since the Renaissance and the felicities and faults of Sidney's style.

1559 GREEN, PAUL D[AVID]. "Doors to the House of Death: The Treatment of Suicide in Sidney's *Arcadia*." *Sixteenth Century Journal* 10 (Fall 1979):17–27.
Examines the background of the suicidal incidents in *Arcadia*, considering such works as Plato's *Phaedo*, Virgil's *Aeneid*, and the Greek romances. Defines Sidney's position according to the Stoic and Christian doctrine that one must submit to adversity without despair. Concludes

Twentieth Century

that the author condones Parthenia's suicide and has mixed feelings about other attempts in which altruistic motives play a part, such as those of Amphialus, the Paphlagonian King, and Pyrocles.

1560 ———. "'Long Lent Loathed Light': A Study of Suicide in Three English Nondramatic Writers of the Sixteenth Century." Ph.D. diss., Harvard University, 1971, pp. 97–185.
Argues that Sidney's attitude to suicide in *Arcadia* varies from character to character and circumstance to circumstance, contending that, for Sidney, some forms of suicide are less culpable or cowardly than others.

1561 GREEN, ROSEMARY M. "The Treasure Chest of the Mind: Uses of Memory in Sidney, Shakespeare, and Renaissance Lyric Poetry." Ph.D. diss., Boston University, 1976, 315 pp.
Argues that Renaissance poets recognized three uses for images in the memory: 1) to provide ideal forms for experience, 2) to aid in moralizing or teaching, and 3) to "eternize" themselves and those they loved. Suggests that the pastoral sections of *Arcadia* represent the first use: an escape into poetry and romance. The heroic sections represent the second and third: a search for virtue and lasting fame. See *DAI* 37 (September 1976):1563A.

1562 GREENBLATT, STEPHEN [JAY]. "Murdering Peasants: Status, Genre, and the Representation of Rebellion." *Representations* 1 (February 1983):1–29.
Compares Sidney's account of Pyrocles and Musidorus doing battle with the mob in the New *Arcadia* with other Renaissance representations of class conflict. Emphasizes Sidney's concern that the mob not gain honor by an encounter with their betters. Traces to this concern the fact that the Princes are disguised, that the rebels are dehumanized, and that Sidney indulges in morbid comedy at their expense. Treats the painter who loses his hand as a momentary representation of Sidney himself, left idle by his queen, and notes that he "mutilates" this image. Also discusses the role of rhetoric in calming the Arcadian mob.

1563 ———. "Sidney's *Arcadia* and the Mixed Mode." *SP* 70 (July 1973):269–78.
Discusses the critical background for the mingling of genres in the revised *Arcadia*. Argues that, "by shifting generic perspectives, Sidney exposes the limitations of modes of conduct and versions of reality." Contrasts the simple moralism of the *Defence* with the effect of *Arcadia*, suggesting that the romance reveals the uncertainty of human judgment and the view that "values are not *given* but generated from within the

individual." Comments on the way one genre undercuts another in the main plot.

1564 GREENFIELD, THELMA N. *The Eye of Judgment: Reading the "New Arcadia."* Lewisburg, Pa.: Bucknell University Press; London and Toronto: Associated University Presses, 1982, 229 pp.

Introduces nonspecialists to the "basic narrative and poetic methods" of *Arcadia*. In the introduction, sees Sidney's purpose as epistemological in that he brings readers, not just to learn, but to observe the process of learning. Focuses on the immediate and visible, suggesting that Sidney's most memorable insights involve "knowing through seeing." Considers matters of genre, composition, and early publishing history. In Chapter 1, infers the poetic theory or "myth of creation" that guided Sidney, seeing in the opening shipwreck echoes of Platonic creation myths. Examines Strephon and Klaius's recollection of Urania, stressing the role of memory in Renaissance faculty psychology, in the theory of poetic creation described in the *Defence*, in the debate between Pyrocles and Musidorus on the night before their trial, and in the trial itself. Urges that Sidney's aim was to enrich the "transtemporal" memories of his readers. Considers views of creation in Pamela's debate with Cecropia, tracing comments there on the one and the many to Plato's *Philebus* and relating these comments to the *discordia concors* formed by the many parts of *Arcadia*. Also examines Sidney's use of metaphors of clothing. In Chapters 2 and 3, analyzes Sidney's characters: his method of defining them in relation to one another and his use of visual detail and symbolism to link them with universal ideas. Notes the importance of the process of penetrating disguises and so of moving from visual detail to an understanding of internal and external nature. Considers Pyrocles's disguise in light of classical and Renaissance glorifications of transvestism and hermaphrodism, bringing in the views of Carl Jung. Sees Pyrocles as (in Sidney's words) the "uttermost in mankind that might be seen." Relates Musidorus's mean apparel to qualities of noble humility and patient service. Links Sidney's pictorial descriptions to paintings by Protestant artists in Germany. In Chapter 4, considers the narrator, discussing his handling of romance conventions, problems in public affairs, sequences of cause and effect, and details of human psychology, manners, and morals. Sees in the episodes of Book II a "dialectic of language, narrative, and images" that provides lessons in the difficulty of moral choice, the uncertainty of earthly rewards, and the power of love. Relates various storytellers to their tales, showing that narrative style reveals their characters and the limits of their knowledge. Pyrocles is

Twentieth Century

elegant, Musidorus is discursive and didactic, and Basilius is blunt and earthy. Sees the use of multiple narrators as a means of providing variety while maintaining unity and of portraying transcendent beauty while revealing the limitations of the senses. Compares the more conventional narration of Book III. In Chapter 5, argues that the work is a "poem," not just in its fictional matter and moral intent, but also in its "rhetorical intensities and organizations." Samples Sidney's rhetoric, from long set speeches to single sentences, tropes, and words. In Chapter 6, considers the three "thematic structures" that unify the work: love, fortune, and the Delphic Oracle. Suggests that, together, these define "the limits of human knowledge and freedom." Feels that the book is intended to fix Philoclea in the memory of the reader. As the focus of the love theme, she is "the sun and center of the *New Arcadia*" and is connected with Penelope Rich. Also considers references to fortune, treating Musidorus as "the living emblem of Fortune's tyranny." Discusses Philoclea's lessons to Pyrocles in Book III on the proper response to misfortune, and notes the many characters who suffer "fortune's worst" and survive. Rejects the view that Sidney abandoned the revision because he had no good way to end it in accordance with the oracle. In Chapter 7, discusses the main sources of his narrative technique: Xenophon's *Cyropaedia*, Heliodorus's *Aethiopica*, *Amadis de Gaule*, and Montemayor's *Diana*. Also compares the Old *Arcadia* with the New, focusing on the role of the narrator, the placement of the poems, and the philosophical themes. In Chapter 8, traces Sidney's interest in "psychological verisimilitude within decidedly unrealistic fictions" to the techniques of Elizabethan court entertainments. Relates *Arcadia* to *Four Foster Children of Desire*, the *Letter to the Queen*, and *The Lady of May*. In Chapter 9, considers *Arcadia* as an attempt to match in fiction the variety of God's creation, comparing similar attempts at plenitude in the Psalms and the *Defence*. Suggests that, in the latter, "fore-conceit" does not mean "preconceived abstract principle" but "overmastering thought" about a character, which the author develops as he writes. Applies to *Arcadia* the concept of the "golden" world of poetry, rejecting recent criticism that treats the heroes as bad moral examples. In Chapter 10, discusses the epistemological processes involved in reading *Arcadia*, which involves "exercising imaginatively in the ring of experience" and seeing in visible things "the constancy of Idea." Feels that the book cannot be limited to a single genre, moral structure, or meaning. In Appendix A, argues against narrow conceptions of Sidney's moral and religious views, and in Appendix B, reviews judgments of *Arcadia* by Sidney's contemporaries. Includes a bibliography.

Twentieth Century

1565 GREENLAW, EDWIN [A]. "The Captivity Episode in Sidney's *Arcadia*." In *The Manly Anniversary Studies in Language and Literature*. Chicago: University of Chicago Press, 1923, pp. 54–63.
Connects the captivity of the Princesses in Book III with the danger that Queen Elizabeth would marry Alençon in 1580. Suggests that Cecropia represents Catharine de Medici and Clinias her ambassador Simier. Suggests that Spenser echoed the passage in the episodes of *The Faerie Queene* involving Braggadoccio and Tromparte. Argues that Sidney's episode also draws upon attacks against Epicurean mechanistic philosophy in the writings of du Plessis-Mornay and du Bartas. Details Sidney's allusions to Lucretius's *De Rerum Natura*, concluding that they reveal a thorough knowledge of the philosophical issues involved. See also Buckley (1447) and a reply by Levinson (1645).

1566 ———. "Shakespeare's Pastorals." *SP* 13 (April 1916):122–54. Reprint. In *Pastoral and Romance: Modern Essays in Criticism*, edited by Eleanor T[erry] Lincoln. Englewood Cliffs, N.J.: Prentice-Hall, 1969, pp. 83–107.
Interprets *As You Like It*, *Cymbeline*, and *The Winter's Tale* in relation to "a well-defined type of plot-structure which, originating in *Daphnis and Chloe* and modified by certain Italian and Spanish elements, found its first complete English expression in Sidney's *Arcadia*." Argues that *Arcadia* provided Spenser with the outlines of the episode involving Pastorella in *The Faerie Queene* and that both works influenced Shakespeare. Also makes a case that Spenser's character Colin Clout and Shakespeare's Jaques derive from Sidney's Philisides and that Shakespeare's character may be a good-humored satire of Sidney himself.

1567 GREER, RICHARD ALLEN. "Adaptations of the Greek Romances in the English Renaissance as Reflections of the Debate between Fortune and Virtue." Ph.D. diss., Harvard University, 1972, pp. 80–85, 165–68.
Summarizes the Greek sources of *Arcadia*, considering their influence on Sidney's presentation of divine providence. Compares two sorts of love in the book, one leading to the overthrow of reason and one leading to virtue, relating these to the contrast in Greek romance between apparently ruinous fortune and providence.

Twentieth Century

1568 GREG, W[ALTER] W[ILSON]. "The Decrees and Ordinances of the Stationers' Company, 1576–1602." *Library*, 4th ser. 8 (March 1928):395–425.

Discusses the outcome of the lawsuit occasioned by Robert Waldgrave's 1599 pirating of *Arcadia* (2). William Ponsonby had instituted proceedings in Star Chamber against John Legatt and a number of London booksellers for contracting with Waldgrave to print the edition. The suit was finally referred to the Court of the Stationers' Company, where Legatt and John Harrison were fined. See also item 1570.

1569 ———. *Pastoral Poetry and Pastoral Drama: A Literary Inquiry, with Special Reference to the Pre-Restoration Stage in England*. London: A.H. Bullen, 1906, pp. 121–22, 147–54, 318–34, 362, 368, 371, 418–20.

Discusses the popularity of pastoral in the Sidney circle, attributing the rare "bantering eclogue" of Nico and Pas (*OA 29*) to the influence of Theocritus's Idyll 5. Details the circumstances in which early editions of *Arcadia* were published, and summarizes its sources and its influence, particularly on Shakespeare and Thomas Lodge. Characterizes and condemns the Arcadian style. Finds no true pastoral characters or action in the book. Examines its influence on Renaissance drama, including James Shirley's *Arcadia*, John Day's *Isle of Gulls*, the anonymous *Mucedorus* and *Andromana*, Beaumont and Fletcher's *Cupid's Revenge*, Henry Glapthorne's *Argalus and Parthenia*, and two manuscript plays. Provides plot summaries and comparisons with *Arcadia*. Also notes Sidneian influence in Abraham Cowley's play *Love's Riddle* but not in the Latin play *Parthenia*. Finds "barely an excuse" for calling Sidney's *Lady of May* a pastoral.

1570 GREG, W[ALTER] W[ILSON], and BOSWELL, E., eds. *Records of the Court of the Stationers' Company 1576 to 1602—from Register B*. London: Bibliographical Society, 1930, pp. lix–lxx, 80–82, 87–88.

In a section of the *Records* not published by Arber (213), prints Star Chamber minutes recording the progress and outcome of litigation brought by Ponsonby against John Legatt and others over Waldgrave's Edinburgh 1599 pirating of *Arcadia* (2). See also item 1568.

1571 GRUND, GARY R. *John Hoskyns, Elizabethan Rhetoric and the Development of English Prose*. Harvard Dissertations in American and English Literature. New York: Garland, 1987, pp. 128–37, 147–74. Orig. a Ph.D. diss., Harvard University, 1972.

In "The Sources of *The Directions*," seeks to demonstrate that Hoskins's work is a "new form of criticism" that "reveals the conscious art of Sidney:

his use of figures as a constituent oratorical element, his function in the general rhetorical tradition, and his awareness of the necessity of an expressive prose style." Cites figures (e.g., *antimetabole*) by which Sidney attains stylistic diversity, "functionality," and amplification. In "The Legacy of Arcadianism," claims that it was through a "nexus of associations" running from Hoskins to Charles Hoole's *A New Discovery of the Old Art of Teaching School* that Sidney's style was "made an example to the generation that grew up after the last sequel was written." Compares Hoskins work with Thomas Blount's *Academy of Eloquence* and John Smith's *Mystery of Rhetoric Unveiled* in order to show how "Arcadianism" is gradually "absorbed into the general rhetorical tradition."

1572 HAINSWORTH, G[EORGE]. "L'*Arcadia* en France: trois Nouveaux témoignages de son succès." *Revue de littérature comparée* 10 (July 1930):470–71.

Cites three pieces of evidence to show Sidney's early influence on French literature: a 1625 abridgement of Nicolas de Montreux's *Bergeries de Juliette*; an allusion in the Bishop of Belley's *Cléoreste*, which appeared in 1626; and François Boisrobert's *La folle gageure*, which was published in 1653. Each work contains in its title either a direct reference to Sidney or the names "*Arcadia*" or "Countess of Pembroke."

1573 HALLAM, GEORGE WALTER, Jr. "Functional Paradox in Sidney's Revised *Arcadia*." Ph.D. diss., University of Florida, 1959, 266 pp.

Argues that, if the plot of the revised *Arcadia* is disentangled and considered chronologically, it amounts to a unified use of Ramist logic to prove the paradox that "adversity best discovers virtue." Sees the true foundation of the work in a series of "paradoxes of situation" that reveal the discrepancy between things as they seem and things as they really are. Suggests that the unity of the work is not apparent to modern readers because Sidney took Ramus's advice and concealed the logical structure by beginning *in medias res*. Distinguishes four levels of meaning in the romance: practical, historical, literary, and ontological. See *DA* 20 (September 1959):1014.

1574 HAMILTON, A.C. "Elizabethan Prose Fiction and Some Trends in Recent Criticism." *RenQ* 37 (Spring 1984):21–33.

Considers problems with modern criticism of romance, tracing the principal difficulty to the fact that the genre is highly conventional and popularized rather than complex and "literary." Notes that, although *Arcadia* requires more analysis than most romances, it suffers from the same difficulty. Considers recent critical trends that may prove more

Twentieth Century

fruitful than historical criticism or New Criticism, among them archetypal criticism, reader-response criticism, structuralism, and deconstruction.

1575 ———. *Sir Philip Sidney: A Study of His Life and Works*. Cambridge: Cambridge University Press, 1977, pp. 123–74.

In Chapter 5, treats the revised *Arcadia* as Sidney's attempt to write the sort of heroic poem described in the *Defence* and to prove to his father that he had not wasted his talents. Contrasts the openings of Sannazaro's *Arcadia* and Montemayor's *Diana* with Sidney's initial account of Strephon and Claius, noting that the beneficial effects of their love are not repeated in the experience of the other lovers in the work. Considers the shipwreck scene, which derives from Heliodorus, and suggests that, in the story of Argalus and Parthenia, Sidney attempts to overgo Heliodorus by portraying "the form of goodness" itself. Sees the constancy of their love as a pattern for the rest of the book and contrasts it with the constant but mismatched love between Helen, Amphialus, and Philoxenus. Treats the tournament of Phalantus as an instructive parody of true love and virtue and the parade of portraits as an examination of the kinds of feminine beauty. Also considers the debates in Book I, Sidney's deathbed views on the moral dangers of his romance, its early reputation, and the effect of Sidney's revisions in raising the moral level of the work. Treats the Princes' Asian adventures in Book II as delineations of heroic virtue and its vulnerability to treachery. Ponders ways in which Book III would have made it difficult for Sidney to return to the original plot of the Old *Arcadia* following Amphialus's rebellion. Sees the besieged castle as the central image of Book III, combining as it does active, masculine virtue with passive, feminine endurance. Discusses Sidney's emphasis on the latter, distinguishing the characters of Pamela and Philoclea and treating them as images of the harmony between beauty and virtue. From contemporary evidence, argues that the 1593 edition of *Arcadia* is an "unnatural hybrid" and that the 1590 edition is as well finished as it needed to be. Considers Sidney's great aim to move a nation to virtuous action through works of literature, concluding that it sustained the English Renaissance through the time of Milton. See also item 550.

1576 HAMPSTEN, ELIZABETH MORRIS. "A Study of Romance." Ph.D. diss., University of Washington, 1965, 296 pp.

Regards *Arcadia* as an "anti-war" book, which reveals the consequences when a ruler fails to fulfill his obligation to wield power effectively. See *DA* 26 (August 1965):1021.

Twentieth Century

1577 HANFORD, JAMES HOLLY and WATSON, SARA RUTH. "Personal Allegory in the *Arcadia*: Philisides and Lelius." *MP* 32 (August 1934):1–10.
Reviews attempts from the seventeenth through the nineteenth centuries to link characters in *Arcadia* with Elizabethan political figures. Identifies Helen of Corinth with Queen Elizabeth and Helen's knight Lelius with Sir Henry Lee. Notes Lee's connections with Sidney and suggests that Andromana's tournament represents the Accession Day Tilts established by Lee. Discusses the trappings of the Frozen Knight and of Philisides, noting that Sidney actually jousted with Lee on Accession Day, 1581. Also treats Andromana as a parody of Elizabeth.

1578 HANKINS, JOHN ERSKINE. *Shakespeare's Derived Imagery*. Lawrence: University of Kansas Press, 1953, pp. 244–45.
Regards Cecropia's advice to Philoclea about marriage and motherhood in *Arcadia* III.v as a probable source for *Romeo and Juliet* I.i, parts of *Venus and Adonis*, and passages in Shakespeare's *Sonnets*.

1579 HANNAY, MARGARET P. "'Faining Notable Images of Vertue': Sidney's *New Arcadia* as *Legenda Sanctorum*." *HSL* 15–16 (1983–1984):80–92.
Argues that the revised *Arcadia* in some degree seeks to replace the saints' lives that had gradually in the sixteenth century been discouraged by Protestantism. Offering a "model for living," it "filled a popular need for heroes." Shows that the male protagonists conform in four respects to a "mythic paradigm" for "confessor saints." Examines the Cecropia episode at length in terms of its parallelisms to "the usual paradigm for a female saint," who, like Saint Agnes, is a virgin and martyr.

1580 HARMAN, EDWARD GEORGE. *"The Countesse of Pembrokes Arcadia" Examined and Discussed (With a Chapter on Thomas Lodge)*. London: Cecil Palmer, 1924, 243 pp.
Supposes that *Arcadia* and *Astrophil and Stella* were both composed by Francis Bacon. Finds hidden topical allegories in *Arcadia*, identifying most of the young male characters with Bacon and most of the young females with the Countess of Pembroke or with Queen Elizabeth. Relates the mutiny of the Arcadian mob to the anonymous play *Sir Thomas More*. Also relates the "naked paganism" of *Arcadia* to the lack of Christian emphasis in the works of Spenser and Shakespeare.

Twentieth Century

1581 HARRISON, T.P., Jr. *"The Faerie Queene* and the *Diana." PQ* 9
(January 1930):51–56.
Discusses similarities between the main plot of *Arcadia* and Spenser's
Pastorella episode. Compares both with a similar story in the continua-
tion of *Diana* by Alonzo Perez, and concludes that Spenser's main source
was Sidney.

1582 HARVEY, GABRIEL. *Gabriel Harvey's Marginalia.* Edited by G.C.
Moore Smith. Stratford-upon-Avon: Shakespeare Head Press,
1913, pp. 86, 168–70.
Mentions Harvey's 1613 folio of *Arcadia,* which he had divided into
chapters and summarized. Also evaluates the style of the romance.

1583 HAWTHORNE, JULIAN. *Hawthorne Reading: An Essay.* Cleveland, Ohio: Rowfant Club, 1902, pp. 35, 46–61.
Mentions that a folio edition of *Arcadia* was in the Hawthorne family
library but that Nathaniel made no use of it after he first left for college.
See also Charney (1466) and Fields (1357). Recounts a séance with
Robert and Elizabeth Barrett Browning in which a woman whose name
was inscribed in this volume materialized.

1584 HAZARD, MARY ELIZABETH. "'Pregnant Images of Life':
Sidney's Use of Visual Imagery in *The New Arcadia."* Ph.D. diss.,
Bryn Mawr College, 1970, 310 pp.
Examines "the Renaissance theory of ornament" and the historical context of Sidney's iconographic portraits, pageants, processions, tilts,
masques, and dreams. Also examines Sidney's sometimes unconventional use of emblems and his method of defining the place that his characters hold in a moral hierarchy by revealing their attitude toward certain
images. See *DAI* 32 (September 1971):1474A.

1585 HELGERSON, RICHARD. "Lyly, Greene, Sidney, and Barnaby
Rich's *Brusanus." HLQ* 36 (February 1973):105–18.
Discusses Rich's occasional borrowings from *Arcadia,* noting that they are
from a manuscript of the original version, though Rich was probably
writing after the publication of the revised text in 1590.

1586 HELTZEL, VIRGIL B[ARNEY]. "The Arcadian Hero." *PQ* 41
(January 1962):173–80.
From contemporary evidence on Sidney's bearing and character, and
from the conduct of Pyrocles and Musidorus, infers Sidney's "ideal of
gentility." Considers birth and bodily form; virtues such as courtesy,

valor, and friendship; ability in philosophy and the arts; and skill in arms and recreations.

1587 HERBST, CARL. *"Cupid's Revenge" by Beaumont and Fletcher und "Andromana, or the Merchant's Wife" in ihrer Beziehung zu einander und zu ihrer Quelle.* Königsberg: Hartungsche Buchdruckerei, 1906, 76 pp. passim. Orig. a Ph.D. diss., Albertus-Universität zu Königsberg, 1906.

Examines the influence of *Arcadia* on Beaumont and Fletcher's play *Cupid's Revenge* and on the anonymous *Andromana*. Finds various borrowings from the stories of Plangus and Andromana and of Erona and Antiphilus. Also discusses two common motifs in these stories: Cupid's punishment of those who resist him and lovers wooing in disguise.

1588 HERPICH, CHA[RLE]S A. "Shakespeare's 'Virtue of necessity.'" *N&Q*, 10th ser. 1 (6 February 1904):110–11.

Suggests that Shakespeare derived the phrase "virtue of necessity" from *Arcadia*.

1589 ———. "Sonnet III. and Sidney's *Arcadia.*" *N&Q*, 10th ser. 8 (31 August 1907):164.

Points out several lines in Shakespeare's Sonnet 3 that apparently derive from Book III of the 1590 *Arcadia*. Similar language occurs in Daniel's *Delia* 32 and in *The Rape of Lucrece*, lines 1758–59.

1590 HILL, HERBERT WYNFORD. "Sidney's *Arcadia* and the Elizabethan Drama." *University of Nevada Studies* 1 (1 January 1908):1–59.

In "Part I: The Arcadia," analyzes Sidney's sources, with parallel passages ·and commentary. Concludes that both Sannazaro and Montemayor have been overrated; that Greek romances are more important; and that *Amadis de Gaule* is the primary source. Analyzes Sidney's style and considers the influence of *Arcadia*, citing allusions well into the seventeenth century. In "Part II: The Influence of the *Arcadia* on the Elizabethan Drama," lists incidents, characters, and stylistic elements derived from Sidney in the following pastoral plays: the anonymous *Mucedorus*, John Day's *Isle of Gulls*, James Shirley's *Arcadia*, Henry Glapthorne's *Argalus and Parthenia*, and Beaumont and Fletcher's *Cupid's Revenge*. Mentions Sidney's slight influence on the plays of Robert Greene and Ben Jonson and more important borrowings in Beaumont and Fletcher's *Maid's Tragedy* and *Philaster*. Concludes that Shakespeare's direct debt to *Arcadia* in *The Winter's Tale* and *As You Like It* was slight,

Twentieth Century

though Sidney exerted an indirect influence through Robert Greene's *Pandosto* and Thomas Lodge's *Rosalynde*. Also notes the ties between *King Lear* and Sidney's story of the Paphlagonian King.

1591 HOLLIDAY, CARL. *English Fiction from the Fifth to the Twentieth Century*. New York: Century Co., 1912, pp. 164–73.
Gives basic information on Sidney's life and on *Arcadia*.

1592 HOLZINGER, WALTER. "*Der Abentheurliche Simplicissimus* and Sir Philip Sidney's *Arcadia*." *CollG* 2 (1969):184–98.
Details Hans Jakob Christoffel von Grimmelshausen's allusions to *Arcadia*, which suggest his intent to translate Sidney's high romance into the "low, bawdy, cynical" style of a picaresque novel. Prints parallel passages from Grimmelshausen's book, Martin Opitz's revision of the German translation of *Arcadia* (37), and Sidney's original English text. Notes that Grimmelshausen is more sympathetic to commoners than is Sidney.

1593 HOSKINS, JOHN. *Directions for Speech and Style*. Edited by Hoyt H[opewell] Hudson. Princeton Studies in English, 12. Princeton, N.J.: Princeton University Press, 1935, 162 pp. passim.
Written ca. 1599 but not published, except in pirated extracts, until this edition. Includes more that 180 passages from *Arcadia* analyzed as illustrations of good writing. Concentrates on epistolary style and some forty figures of speech. For discussion, see Boyce (1433), Buxton (1454), Robinson (1742), and Hudson (1596).

1594 HOY, CYRUS. "Shakespeare, Sidney, and Marlowe: The Metamorphoses of Love." *VQR* 51 (Summer 1975):448–58.
Notes the emphasis in *Arcadia* on the transforming power of love, discussing Pyrocles's debate with Musidorus in Book I. Relates plot lines in the book to Shakespeare's plays, comparing the episode of Helen in Book I with *Twelfth Night*. Contrasts the willingness of Sidney's characters to accept the risks of love with the resistance to change and affection in Marlowe's protagonists.

1595 HUBERMAN, EDWARD. "James Shirley's *The Politician*." Ph.D diss., Duke University, 1934, pp. 16, 19–20.
Suggests that Sidney's story of Plangus was a direct source for Shirley's play and notes the influence of the story on other seventeenth-century playwrights. Not seen; cited in a reply by Fehrenbach (1532).

1596 HUDSON, HOYT H[OPEWELL], ed. Introduction to *Directions for Speech and Style*, by John Hoskins. Princeton Studies in English,

12. Princeton, N.J.: Princeton University Press, 1935, pp. xii–xl, 53–101 passim.

Examines Hoskin's relations with Sidney and his use of *Arcadia* for illustrations in teaching rhetoric. Suggests the pervasive influence of the Arcadian style in the seventeenth century, noting critical praise for it and wholesale borrowings from Hoskins's *Directions* (1593) in two popular rhetorics: Thomas Blount's *Academy of Eloquence* and John Smith's *Mystery of Rhetoric Unveiled*.

1597 HUDSON, HOYT H[OPEWELL]. "An Oxford Epigram-Book of 1589." *HLQ* 2 (January 1939):213–217.

Attributes an anonymous epigram book to Matthew Gwynne and John Lloyd. Notes that the dedication contains direct evidence for the common assumption that Fulke Greville was responsible for printing the 1590 *Arcadia*.

1598 HUEBNER, ALFRED. "Das erste deutsche Schäferidyll und seine Quellen." Ph.D. diss., Universität Königsberg, 1910, 119 pp.

Treats the name given by the first German translator of *Arcadia*, Valentinus Theocritus von Hirschberg, as a psedonym for Martin Opitz. Examines the influence of *Arcadia* on Opitz's *Hercinie*.

1599 HUGHES, MERRITT Y., ed. *The Complete Prose Works of John Milton*. Edited by Don M. Wolfe. Vol. 3, *1648–1649*, edited by Merritt Y. Hughes. New Haven, Conn.: Yale University Press, 1962, pp. 152–60.

Reviews evidence indicating that Milton did not arrange to have Pamela's prayer added to Charles I's prayer book, *Eikon Basilike*. Also examines reasons that Milton took offence at the King's use of the prayer. See Milton (1323).

1600 HUGHES, MERRITT Y. "New Evidence on the Charge that Milton Forged the Pamela Prayer in the *Eikon Basilike*." *RES*, n.s. 3 (April 1952):130–40.

Clarifies the significance of Madan's disproof (in 1670) of the charge that Milton inserted Pamela's prayer. Covers evidence from early editions of *Eikon Basilike*, concluding that "if Milton had ignored Pamela's prayer in *Eikonoklastes* no one would ever have questioned its use by the King." Also seeks to explain Milton's strong reaction against Charles's use of the prayer. See also item 1599 and Milton (1323).

Twentieth Century

1601 ————. "Spenser's Debt to the Greek Romances." *MP* 23 (August 1925):67–76.

Regards *Arcadia* as the chief influence on Books III–VI of *The Faerie Queene*, especially in the Greek elements and the descriptions of works of art.

1602 HUNTER, G.K. "The Marking of *Sententiae* in Elizabethan Printed Plays, Poems, and Romances." *Library*, 5th ser. 6 (December 1951):171–88.

Discusses the use of punctuation and italics to mark *sententiae* in early editions of *Arcadia*.

1603 HURRELL, J[OHN] D[ENNIS]. "Themes and Conventions of Elizabethan Prose Fiction (1558–1603)." Ph.D. diss., University of Birmingham, 1955.

Abstract not available. Cited as item 139 in *Index to Theses Accepted for Higher Degrees in the Universities of Great Britain and Ireland* 5 (1954–55).

1604 HÜSGEN, HILDEGARDIS. *Das Intellektualfeld in der deutschen "Arcadia" und in ihrem englischen Vorbild.* Emmerich am Rhein, Germany: Franz Massing, [1935], 95 pp. Orig. a Ph.D. diss., Westfälischen Wilhelms-Universität zu Münster, 1935.

Studies in detail the terms that Sidney uses for the human mind and their German equivalents in Martin Opitz's revision (37) of Valentinus Theocritus von Hirschberg's translation (34). Considers both positive words such as "reason," "wit," "sense," and "wisdom," and negative ones, including "unreasonableness," "beastliness," "folly," and "simplicity." Notes the influence of Chappelain's French translation (32) on the German version. Also traces the philosophical roots of Sidney's terminology, noting particularly the impact of Aristotle and Plato and the lack of Roman influence.

1605 ISLER, ALAN D[AVID]. "Moral Philosophy and the Family in Sidney's *Arcadia*." *HLQ* 31 (August 1968):359–71.

Lays out Sidney's views on the moral and political ends of poetry and explores the place of the family in Elizabethan discussions of order or "degree." Discusses the sequence of events by which Basilius's failure of right reason and consequent retirement to the lodges early in *Arcadia* leads to the later disorder in his family and the state. Finds a similar pattern of spreading disorder in the story of the Paphlagonian King and in Shakespeare's *King Lear*.

Twentieth Century

1606 ———. "Sidney, Shakespeare, and the 'Slain-Notslain.'" *UTQ* 37 (January 1968):175–85.
In seeking to explain Sidney's apparent cruelty toward the mob of commoners in Book II of the New *Arcadia*, compares similar scenes in Spenser's *Faerie Queene* and in Shakespeare's *II Henry VI* and *Julius Caesar*. Following Samuel Barber, suggests connections between such mob scenes and Saturnalia that turn the world upside down. Concludes that the note of harsh comedy allows Sidney to keep decorum in mixing aristocrats with commoners and also allows the audience to assess the action with the detachment needed to judge it properly.

1607 JEHENSON, MYRIAM YVONNE. *The Golden World of the Pastoral: A Comparative Study of Sidney's "New Arcadia" and d'Urfé's "L'Astrée."* Speculum Atrium, 8. Ravenna, Italy: Longo, 1981, 163 pp. Orig. a Ph.D. diss., Columbia University, 1974.
Seeks to demonstrate "how radically different Sidney and d'Urfé are in the manner in which they present the themes, values, and ideas . . . associated with the pastoral genre." Connects Sidney with the Christian humanists, who idealized an unchanging natural order in which mankind is free to become godlike or bestial. Links d'Urfé, however, with the Mannerists, who accepted Montaigne's view of human limitations, Machiavelli's belief in the political efficacy of fraud and cunning, and the belief that the order of the world is "constantly shifting and elusive." In Chapter 1, examines the myth of the Golden Age in classical and Renaissance pastoral literature. Focuses on three "dialectical oppositions" between idealized and everyday views of reality: nature versus civilization, *otium* versus *negotium*, and innocence versus passion. Also traces the development of these oppositions in Renaissance pastoral romance. In Chapter 2, argues against the view that the Old *Arcadia* is a tragicomedy with a serious double plot, stressing its "Ovidian playfulness." Feels that Sidney's portrayal of the Golden Age is often parodic and lacks the melancholy, the nostalgia, and the spiritual or religious ends of other Renaissance pastorals. Finds in Sidney much tolerance of error in his characters and a "positive view" of their love, suggesting that the apparent injustices of the final trial are not meant to be taken seriously. In Chapter 3, considers the more serious moral issues in the 1590 *Arcadia*, concentrating on Petrarchan and neo-Platonic influences. Considers conflicts between spiritual and sensual forms of love and the difficulty in distinguising irony from sympathy in the narrator's attitude toward his characters. Also discusses the relation between ideas, natural objects, and works of art, turning to the *Defence* for Sidney's views on

Twentieth Century

the "second nature" created by the poet, the role of ideas in the creative process, and the moral ends of poetry. Sees the changes from one version of *Arcadia* to the other as an "evolution from pastoral as a criticism of poetic idyllism, to a more heroic exploration of idealized forms, to an ultimate critique of both earlier phases." Discusses idealization in the account of Strephon, Claius, and Urania; the relation of ideal to actual in the main characters; and the effect of the pathetic fallacy on the characters' own descriptions of the world. In Chapter 4, suggests that, in Book III, idealization gives way to verisimilar depictions of post-lapsarian nature, to more restrained sensuality, and to virtual parodies of idealized fiction. Stresses the pitiable humanity of Cecropia and other treacherous characters and the pathos of the battle scenes. Suggests that Sidney left the revision unfinished because he could no longer reconcile the realism he sought with the unrealistic form of the pastoral romance. In Chapters 5–7, contrasts *Astrée* with *Arcadia*, noting that Sidney lacks d'Urfé's interest in the dialectical oppositions in classical romance, that he offers truer examples of virtue, and that he is less intrusive as a narrator (at least in the revised version). Also notices differences in Sidney's way of handling mythological allusions, disguises and changes of name, love letters, suspended narrations, and allusions to divine providence.

1608 JEWKES, W[ILFRED] T. "The Literature of Travel and the Mode of Romance in the Renaissance." *BNYPL* 67 (April 1963):219–36. Reprint. In *Literature as a Mode of Travel: Five Essays and a Postscript*, edited by Warner G. Rice. New York: New York Public Library, 1963, pp. 13–30.

Discusses similarities between Elizabethan voyage literature and romance. Cites *Arcadia* to show that both kinds of writing are imaginative and idealized and both focus on the heroic virtues of *sapientia et fortitudo* directed to the service of the state. Suggests that the literary criticism of the period—particularly Sidney's *Defence*—provided the theoretical basis for the combination of imagination and pragmatism found in the travel literature.

1609 JOHNSON, PAULA [COPELAND]. *Form and Transformation in Music and Poetry of the English Renaissance.* Yale Studies in English, 179. New Haven, Conn.: Yale University Press, 1972, pp. 82–90. Orig. a Ph.D. diss., Yale University, 1969.

Analyzes the opening and Book II of the New *Arcadia*, comparing Sidney's method of multilineal plot construction with the composition of a motet. Ponders Sidney's "passion for linear continuity" as revealed in his constant use of grammatical and logical connectives. Notes that these work against the division of the work into books and Chapters. Also considers the author's frequent alternations between past and present; his dislike of firm conclusions or hierarchical arrangements in the episodes; and his tendency to make the sequence of the main action clear only in retrospect. Compares these structural characteristics of *Arcadia* with similar ones in Montemayor's *Diana* and in motets by William Byrd.

1610 JOHNSON, R[EGINALD] BRIMLEY, ed. *The Birth of Romance from "Euphues": Sidney's "Arcadia": Romantics and Pastorals*. London: John Lane, Bodley Head Press, 1928, pp. 85–98.
Provides an introduction and excerpts from *Arcadia*.

1611 JONES, FREDERIC L. "Another Source for *The Trial of Chivalry*." *PMLA* 47 (September 1932):668–70.
Attributes incidents in the play involving Ferdinand and Pembroke to the influence of Book I of *Arcadia*, in which Pyrocles and Musidorus are similarly separated and fight in single combat before recognizing one another.

1612 JORDAIN, V.L. "Webster's Change of Sidney's 'Wormish' to 'Womanish.'" *N&Q*, n.s. 24 (April 1977):135.
Suggests that, when (in *The Duchess of Malfi* V.v) Webster altered Sidney's phrase "in such a shadowe, or rather pit of darkness, the wormish mankinde lives," he had in mind the proverb "Revenge is womanish."

1613 JUDGE, CYRIL BATHURST. *Elizabethan Book-Pirates*. Harvard Studies in English, 8. Cambridge, Mass.: Harvard University Press, 1934, pp. 90, 100–111, 156–59.
Examines the circumstances in which Robert Waldgrave pirated the 1598 *Arcadia* and printed it in Edinburgh in 1599 (see item 2). Reprints legal documents in the case and discusses its final disposition.

1614 JUEL-JENSEN, BENT. "Sidney's *Arcadia*, 'London, 1599': A Distinguished Ghost." *BC* 16 (Spring 1967):80.
Explains that the mysterious edition was, in fact, printed in 1613 but had found its way into the library of Alexander Pope without a title page. Asserts that Pope invented a fictitious title page.

1615 ———. "Sidney's *Arcadia*, 1638." *Library*, 5th ser. 22 (December 1967):355.
Acknowledges that the book reported in item 1616 came to him from another collector, who had first recognized its importance.

Twentieth Century

1616 ———. "Sir Philip Sidney's *Arcadia*, 1638: An Unrecorded Issue." *Library*, 5th ser. 22 (March 1967):67–69.
Reports a version in which the initial four pages contain errors and differ in type and ornament from previously recorded copies. See also item 1615.

1617 JUNKE, GISELA. "Die Formen des Dialogs im frühen englischen Roman." Ph.D. diss., Universität Köln, 1975, 152 pp.
Contrasts passages of dialogue in *Arcadia* with samples by other authors of Elizabethan prose fiction. Finds that Sidney's speeches are unusually long and often involve prolonged examination of a single moral theme. The dialogue is "not used to its potential as a means of interaction between persons." See *EASG*, 1975, pp. 70–72. See also *DAI* 37 (Autumn 1976):136C.

1618 KEACH, WILLIAM. *Elizabethan Erotic Narratives: Irony and Pathos in the Ovidian Poetry of Shakespeare, Marlowe, and Their Contemporaries*. New Brunswick, N.J.: Rutgers University Press, 1977, pp. 43–44, 152–53, 167–72, 215.
From evidence in *Glaucus and Scilla*, suggests that Thomas Lodge had read in manuscript the bathing scene in *Arcadia*. Links the same scene to lines in John Marston's *Metamorphosis of Pygmalion's Image* and in Francis Beaumont's *Salmacis and Hermaphroditus*. Examines the influence of *Arcadia* on John Weever's *Faunus and Melliflora*.

1619 KELLEHER, HARRY G. "Sidney's Argumentative Prose and the New *Arcadia*: Classical Rhetorical Structures." Ph.D. diss., University of Denver, 1977, 324 pp.
Discusses Sidney's training in rhetorical treatises by Aristotle, Cicero, Quintilian, and the author of *Rhetorica ad Herennium*. Argues that the *Letter to the Queen* takes the form of an accusatory forensic oration and that the *Defence of Leicester* and the *Defence of Poetry* follow that of a defensive forensic oration. Feels that the New *Arcadia* also adopts such methods of organization. Concludes that, for Sidney, "the ends of rhetoric and literature are the same." See *DAI* 38 (November 1977):2809A–10A.

1620 KERLIN, ROBERT T[HOMAS]. "Scott's *Ivanhoe* and Sidney's *Arcadia*." *MLN* 22 (May 1907):144–46.
Details numerous correspondences between the two works, especially in their "three chief moments": the tournaments, the capture and imprisonment of the hero and heroines, and the siege. Also finds the works similar in their mingling of pastoral and chivalric romance, in their

treatment of outlawry, in their reliance on disguises, and in their retelling of Asiatic adventures outside the main action.

1621 KERMODE, [JOHN] FRANK. *Shakespeare, Spenser, Donne: Renaissance Essays.* London: Routledge & Kegan Paul; New York: Viking Press, 1971, pp. 222, 229, 249.

Analyzes the combination of improbable romantic plots and serious ethical and political thought that characterizes Shakespeare's last plays, attributing it in part to the influence of *Arcadia.*

1622 KÉRY, LÁSZLÓ. "Romance and Renaissance." In *Actes du VIIIe Congrès de l'Association Internationale de Littérature Comparée/ Proceedings of the 8th Congress of the International Comparative Literature Association.* Vol. 1, *Trois grandes mutations littéraires: Renaissance—Lumières—Début du vingtième siècle/Three Epoch-Making Literary Changes: Renaissance, Enlightenment, Early Twentieth Century,* edited by Béla Köpeczi and György M. Vajda. Stuttgart, Germany: Erich Bieber, Kunst und Wissen, 1980, pp. 101–3.

Presents Sidney as among the first to "preserve and revitalize" the legacy of medieval romance while "keeping with the secular spirit of the Renaissance." His open-minded, synthesizing spirit provided a "bridge" to Shakespeare's "universality."

1623 KINNEY, ARTHUR F. "Humanist Poetics and Elizabethan Fiction." *RenP*, 1978, pp. 31–45.

Examines the relation between Sidney's "poetics," as theorized in the *Defence* and practiced in *Arcadia,* and "humanist poetics," grounded in the practice of disputation. Claims that Sidney "displays an acute and penetrating conception of humanist poetics." For Sidney, as for More and Erasmus, truth rests not only, or finally, in the "fore-conceit" of the poet but in the judgment of the reader. Examines the debate between Pamela and Cecropia as representative of Sidney's strategy of "simultaneously referring to icastic and fantastic art so as to force upon the reader an act of triangulation." Argues that Sidney shares his humanist poetics with Robert Greene and that *Pandosto* and *Arcadia* should be read in the same way.

1624 KIRK, DAVID MORRISON. "The Digression: Its Use in Prose Fiction from the Greek Romance through the Eighteenth Century." Ph.D diss., Stanford University, 1960, 268 pp.

Includes *Arcadia* and its chief sources in an examination of digressive episodes. See *DA* 21 (October 1960):874–75.

Twentieth Century

1625 KITE, EDWARD. "Wilton House, and Its Literary Associations." *Wiltshire Notes and Queries* 5 (June 1907):433–42.
Refers briefly to *Arcadia*, quoting Aubrey (902) in support of the claim that many of its "pastoral descriptions of scenery were probably taken from Wilton Park."

1626 KIYOHARA, YOSHIMASA. "Gloucester higeki no gengo-Paphlagonia-O gojitsu monogatari" [The Sequel of the Paphlagonian Story: Prototype of the Gloucester Tragedy]. *Ronshu* (Bungaku-kai, Konan Daigaku), no. 36, March 1968, pp. 101–24.
Discusses the influence of the story of the Paphlagonian King on Shakespeare's *King Lear*.

1627 ———. "Sir Philip Sidney no *Arcadia* ni tsuite" [On Sir Philip Sidney's *Arcadia*]. *Albion* (Kyoto-daigaku), n.s., no. 8, November 1961, pp. 11–27.
Not seen. Listed in "English Renaissance Studies in Japan, 1961–63," by Kazuyoshi Enozawa and Sister Miyo Takano, *RenS* 1 (1974):31.

1628 KOEPPEL, E[MIL]. *Ben Jonson's Wirkung auf zeitgenössische Dramatiker und andere Studien zur inneren Geschichte des englischen Dramas.* Anglistische Forschungen, 20. Heidelberg: Carl Winter, 1906, pp. 69, 94–99.
Discusses parodies and references to Sidney's *Arcadia* in Jonson's *Every Man out of His Humour* and *Bartholomew Fair*, in Shackerley Marmion's *Antiquary*, and in other plays by Jonson, Shakespeare, Thomas Nashe, James Shirley, Thomas Nabbes, and Thomas Heywood.

1629 KOPPENFELS, WERNER VON. "Two Notes on *Imprese* in Elizabethan Literature: Daniel's Additions to *The Worthy Tract of Paulus Iovius*; Sidney's *Arcadia* and the Tournament Scene in *The Unfortunate Traveler*." *RenQ* 24 (Spring 1971):13–25.
Details the ways in which Nashe's tournament at Florence parodies scenes in *Arcadia*, particularly the tournament in which Amphialus kills Argalus and Parthenia.

1630 KRIEGER, GOTTFRIED. "Gedichteinlagen im englischen Roman." Ph.D. diss., Universität Köln, 1969, 274 pp.
Considers the connection between the verse interludes in *Arcadia* and the "larger issues" of the romance. See *EASG*, 1969, pp. 52–55.

Twentieth Century

1631 KUDCHEDKAR, S.L. "Castiglione's *Courtier* and Elizabethan Literature." *Indian Journal of English Studies* 3, no. 1 (1962):12–24.
Notes similarites between Castiglione's ideal courtier and Sidney's heroes, particularly Argalus.

1632 LaGUARDIA, ERIC. "Figural Imitation in English Renaissance Poetry." In *Actes du IVe Congrés de l'Association Internationale de Littérature Comparée/Proceedings of the 4th Conference of the Institute of Comparative Literature Association, Fribourg, 1964*, edited by François Jost. The Hague and Paris: Mouton, 1966, pp. 844–54.
Sees Amphialus's dream as a "minor paradigm for the figural character of poetic mimesis in English Renaissance poetry, for it combines in a single image the quality of both the concrete world of sensual experience and the absolute world of the mind of God in which the idea of virtue is contained." Distinguishes medieval from Renaissance figural imitation, focusing on Renaissance metaphors of love, nature, and art.

1633 LANCASTER, HENRY C[ARRINGTON]. *A History of French Dramatic Literature in the 17th Century.* 5 parts in 9 vols. Baltimore: Johns Hopkins Press; Paris: Les Belles Lettres; London: Oxford University Press, 1929–40, 2.1:250–52, 366–67; 2.2:575, 766; 3.1:63.
Notes examples of the influence of *Arcadia* on French drama, largely in pastoral tragicomedies. Discusses plays by Jean Galaut, Gauthier de Costes La Calprenède, Antoine Mareschal, and (possibly) François le Metel de Boisrobert. See also item 1635 and Osborn (1103).

1634 ———. Review of *Sir Philip Sidney en France*, by Albert W. Osborn. *MLN* 48 (April 1933):269–73.
Rebuts two arguments about which Osborn (1103) had taken Lancaster to task: whether Alexandre Hardy's *Partenie* is derived from a French translation of *Arcadia*, and whether Galaut's *Phalante* was influenced by *Arcadia*, thus making it the first example of the influence of English literature upon French.

1635 ———. "Sidney, Galaut, La Calprenède: An Early Instance of the Influence of English Literature upon French." *MLN* 42 (February 1927):71–77.
Argues that Jean Galaut's borrowings from *Arcadia* in his play *Phalante*, which was written ca. 1605, are the earliest instances of English literary influence in France. For a reply, see Osborn (1103). Suggests that apparent echoes of *Arcadia* in Gauthier de Costes La Calprenède's *Phalante* derive from Galaut. See also Magendie (1671).

Twentieth Century

1636 LANGFORD, GERALD. "John Barclay and His *Argenis.*" Ph.D. diss., University of Virginia, 1940, 460 pp.
Details similarities between *Arcadia* and *Argenis.* Argues that Barclay "was merely writing the sort of book Sidney had done, adding, however, an historical allegory to it."

1637 La RAGIONE, COLOMBA. "Sir Ph. Sidney: Un cortigiano polemico alla corte di Elisabetta." *Annali della Facoltà di Lettere e Filosofia dell'Università di Napoli* 19 (1976–1977):163–97.
Argues that Sidney created Musidorus as a model of the Elizabethan courtier. Contends that the model is not convincing because it is based on a nostalgic ideal of feudalistic culture that attempts to resist economic, political, and religious evolution.

1638 LAWRENCE, JUDIANA. "'Postures against brief nature': Irony and Romance in *Cymbeline.*" Ph.D. diss., University of Rochester, 1983, 285 pp.
Places *Cymbeline* in a tradition of romance extending from Heliodorus's *Aethiopica* to Sidney's *Arcadia* and Spenser's *Faerie Queene.* See *DAI* 44 (December 1983):1800A.

1639 LAWRY, JON S. *Sidney's Two "Arcadias": Pattern and Proceeding.* Ithaca, N.Y.: Cornell University Press, 1972, pp. 154–289.
In Chapter 2, examines the New *Arcadia* as a heroic poem. Analyzes the major changes introduced when Sidney revised the original version: exemplary stories replacing dramatic dialogue; tournaments near the end of each book overshadowing the eclogues; heroism and multiplicity of action replacing comic error and simple plot; appeals to the eye supplanting those to the ear; and a new heroism of patience replacing the old heroism of chivalric combat. Notes that the emblems of disorder that ended the early books of the Old *Arcadia* have, in the New, been linked to one malevolent source: Cecropia. Also points out that the eclogues "serve less as reflectors of the developing action . . . than as thematic lines back to the lamenting adoration of Urania." Throughout the book, notes parallels with Homer's *Odyssey.* Treats marriage as "both the fore-conceit and emblem" of the New *Arcadia.* In Book I, stresses the three episodes narrated by the main characters, noting that they provide emblems of three kinds of love: the ideal, represented by Argalus and Parthenia; "love *a là mode*," portrayed in Amphialus and Helen; and self-ish, deluded love, revealed in Phalantus and Artesia. Relates such "speaking pictures" to Platonic Ideas, to the "places" used in the art of memory, to the portrait galleries common in Elizabethan buidings, and to the successive "stages" of late medieval drama. Emphasizes the role of

the episodes as moral examples to guide the main characters, listing numerous parallels in their own situations. In discussing the main action, notes that it begins with disorder in the shipwreck and in Basilius's response to the oracle and ends with disorder in the attack of the lion and the bear. Contrasts the house of Kalander as an emblem of harmony and compares Strephon and Claius with Pyrocles and Musidorus. In Book II, sees the "tyrannous lusts" of Basilius and Gynecia against a background of Asian episodes about masculine tyranny and feminine lust. Treats the episodes as lessons for the young lovers of the main plot and as analogues for the rebellion of the commoners at the end of the book. Stresses revisions in the Old *Arcadia* that change the lovers from comic to heroic figures. Notes their frequent imitation of one another and their common struggle to mediate between ideal love and natural desire. Compares the Princes' shipwreck in Asia with that of Book I. Analyzes the episodes as mirrors to the main plot: those of the kings of Phrygia, Pontus, and Paphlagonia portray misrule, and the rest explore "love's errors" in the public and the private spheres. Stresses those of Erona and Antiphilus; Plangus and Andromana; Dido and Pamphilus; and Andromana, Zelmane, and Palladius. Links Gynecia's jealous fury near the end of Book II with the rebellion of the commoners that follows it. Also considers good and bad uses of rhetoric in the addresses to the mob delivered by Pyrocles and Clinias and notes the changes in effect produced by the rearrangement of the eclogues in the New *Arcadia*. In Book III, sees the two sides in the civil war as images of virtue and vice and the external attacks on Amphialus's castle as parallels for the internal attacks on the virtue of the Princesses. Points out that the characters' earlier concern with love gives way to issues of death, faith, and patience and that the lovers in the three episodes of Book I are all parted from each other or killed in Book III. Sees their calamities as warnings against excessive love of honor and unrestrained grief. Also regards Book III as "a nostalgic farewell to heroic chivalry," which is satirized in the comic battle between Dametas and Clinias and criticized in Amphialus's killing of Parthenia and Anaxius's brutality toward the Princesses. Notes ways in which the final oracle changes the direction of the revised version and speculates on Sidney's intentions for the ending. See also item 616.

1640 LEE, ERNEST DARE. *The Papers of an Oxford Man: Essays and Criticisms*. London: Ingpen & Grant, 1928, pp. 58–61.
In "Sidney's *Arcadia*," sketches the merits and faults of the work, praising its depictions of love.

Twentieth Century

1641 LEED, JACOB. "Richardson's Pamela and Sidney's." *AUMLA* 40 (November 1973):240–45.
Suggests that Richardson's Pamela resembles Sidney's in character as well as in name. Also notes that both ladies endure captivity and are involved in a courtship that crosses class lines.

1642 LEGOUIS, ÉMILE [HYACINTHE]. "Le Premier traducteur français de l'anglais littéraire." *Revue anglo-américaine* 10 (June 1933):418–21.
Confirming Osborn's discovery (1103) that Jean Loiseau de Tourval was the first French translator of *Arcadia*, shows that, unlike Baudoin or Chappelain, he was a *"traducteur scrupulous."*

1643 LEIGHTON, JOSEPH. "On the Reception of Sir Philip Sidney's *Arcadia* in Germany from Opitz to Anton Ulrich." In *From Wolfram and Petrarch to Goethe and Grass: Studies in Literature in Honour of Leonard Forster*, edited by Dennis Howard Green, L.P. Johnson, and Dieter Wuttke. Saecvla Spiritualia, 5. Baden-Baden, Germany: Verlag Valentin Koerner, 1982, pp. 473–88.
Argues that, because of poor translations, *Arcadia* made a "relatively small impact" in Germany but that, at the same time, its reception conforms to a "pattern which applies to the reception of other novels." Shows that translations of both the poetry and the prose of *Arcadia* suffered because of dependence on intermediary French versions. In seeking to ascertain the extent to which *Arcadia* was actually read, shows that its "most ardent champions" were associated with Wolfenbüttel and that, like other novels in seventeenth-century Germany, it supplied material for the operas that became increasingly the preferred "aristocratic" art form. Discusses the use of *Arcadia* in a 1679 masque and in operas performed in 1690 and 1691.

1644 LEVINE, NORMAN. "Aspects of Moral and Political Thought in Sidney's *Arcadia*." Ph.D. diss., Columbia University, 1972, 216 pp.
Seeks to relate Sidney's moral teachings to his political views. Discusses the relations between reason and passion in the soul and between political authority and the common good in the state. Details Sidney's views on the limitations of human reason and will, and argues that the author "qualifies the rational Aristotlian ethic in terms of an ethic of 'kindnesse.'" Also discusses Sidney's views on "the preferred form of government, the functions of magistrates, and the limits of political obedience." See *DAI* 35 (April 1975):6670A.

1645 LEVINSON, RONALD B. "The 'godlesse minde' in Sidney's *Arcadia*." *MP* 29 (August 1931):21–26.
Argues that Pamela's rebuttal of Cecropia's attack on religion in Book III of *Arcadia* is based on Cicero's *De Natura Deorum*, not on a careful study of Lucretian philosophy, as Greenlaw had argued (1565).

1646 LEWIS, C[LIVE] S[TAPLES]. *Spenser's Images of Life*. Edited by Alastair [D.S.] Fowler. Cambridge: Cambridge University Press, 1967, pp. 25–26, 33.
Notes that, in *Arcadia*, Sidney distinguishes between a true and a false Cupid, much as Spenser does in *The Faerie Queene*.

1647 LEWIS, JOSEPH WOOLF. "Unfinished Works of the Sixteenth Century: *The Faerie Queene*, *The New Arcadia*, and *The Ocean to Scinthia*." Ph.D. diss., Temple University, 1982, 231 pp.
Evaluates "the (rather slim) possibility that an aesthetic of incompletion . . . flourished in the latter part of the sixteenth century." Considers earlier explanations of the unfinished state of Sidney's *Arcadia*, which are mostly biographical. Then undertakes a close reading of the work to establish that "an incomplete structure may be appropriate, though certainly not mandatory." See *DAI* 43 (September 1982):809A.

1648 LEWIS, PIERS INGERSOLL. "Literary and Political Attitudes in Sidney's *Arcadia*." Ph.D. diss., Harvard University, 1964, 149 pp.
Examines the relations between social and political issues and such things as "style, form, [and] genre, as they are used for describing people, actions and feelings." Noting that Sidney continually connects his own literary works with his life, draws attention to ways in which the literary devices of *Arcadia* bring out social and political implications of the action.

1649 LILJEGREN, S[TEN] B[ODVAR]. "Milton and the King's Prayer." *Beiblatt zur Anglia* 37 (March 1926):91–94.
Responds to Smart (1768) on Milton's possible role in inserting Pamela's prayer in Charles I's prayer book.

1650 ———. *Studies in Milton*. Lund, Sweden: C.W.K. Gleerup, 1918, pp. 37–152.
Examines Milton's possible role in inserting the prayer of Pamela into *Eikon Basilike*. Considers the prayers at the time of Charles I's execution, Milton's words on them in *Eikonoklastes*, the printing history of *Eikon Basilike*, Wagstaff's charges against Milton (in 1326), and the various

Twentieth Century

scholarly exchanges over the case since the seventeenth century. Concludes that Milton inserted the prayer. See Milton (1323).

1651 LINDENBAUM, PETER [ALAN]. "The Geography of Sidney's *Arcadia*." *PQ* 63 (Fall 1984):524–31.
Combining the observations of Ringler (92) and Brie (1202), shows that Sidney used both Strabo's and modern maps in taking "considerable pains to get his geographical details correct" in the New *Arcadia*. Argues that this care results from Sidney's "redefinition" of Arcadia as "an actual historical place."

1652 LINDHEIM, NANCY ROTHWAX. "Sidney's *Arcadia*, Book II: Retrospective Narrative." *SP* 64 (January 1967):159–86.
Faults Greenlaw (1242) and Davis (1501) for oversimplifying the role of the heroic tales told retrospectively in Book II of the New *Arcadia*. Considers the moral problems for the Princes posed in these tales as well as their importance as moral *exempla*, contrasting those told by Musidorus with those narrated by Pyrocles. Believes that Musidorus's adventures exemplify the principles of ethics and politics that the Princes learned in growing up, whereas Pyrocles's adventures involve more complex problems and demand "relativistic" solutions for which neither prince was prepared. Examines the two shipwrecks that begin and end their travels, contrasting the sort of heroism required in each. Notes parallels between the three phases of each Prince's adventures and sees the Erona episodes as a "bridge" between the simple problems of Musidorus's narrative and the moral confusions in Pyrocles's. Concludes that, though the Princes' characters are static, their moral responsibility increases in complexity throughout the book.

1653 LINDSAY, JEAN STIRLING. "A Survey of the Town-Country and Court-Country Themes in Non-Dramatic Elizabethan Literature." Ph.D. diss., Cornell University, 1943, 214 pp.
Suggests that the "fundamental conception" of *Arcadia* is a contrast between the delights of country life and the evil of the court. Also mentions similar sentiments in Sidney's poem "Dispraise of a Courtly Life" (*OP* 7).

1654 LORING, KATHERINE M. "Sidney's *Arcadia*." *Expl* 39 (Fall 1980):28.
Discusses the balance in *Arcadia* between solitude and social life.

Twentieth Century

1655 LOVETT, ROBERT MORSS, and HUGHES, HELEN SARD. *The History of the Novel in England*. Boston: Houghton Mifflin Co.; Cambridge, Mass.: Riverside Press, 1932, pp. 7–10, 15–16.

Characterizes the revised *Arcadia*, focusing on its mingling of sources. Classifies Books I and II as a union of Renaissance pastoral and Greek romance. Regards Book III as chivalric romance and Book IV as an Italian *novella*.

1656 LOWERS, JAMES K. *Mirrors for Rebels: A Study of Polemical Literature Relating to the Northern Rebellion, 1569*. University of California Publications: English Studies, 6. Berkeley: University of California Press, 1953, pp. 108–10.

Notes parallels between the polemical pamphlets issued in support of the Queen at the time of the Northern Rebellion of 1569 and Sidney's arguments against rebellion in *Arcadia*. Suggests that readers would have connected the rebellion with Amphialus's revolt in Book III.

1657 LUCAS, F[RANK] L[AURENCE], ed. *The Complete Works of John Webster*. 4 vols. London: Chatto & Windus, 1927, 1:252; 2:140, 162–63, 167–68, 174–80, 190–94, 197–99, 323–25, 328–29, 334, 343, 358; 3:287, 289; 4:133, 136.

Cites numerous passages in which Webster was influenced by Sidney. Notes especially the impact of *Arcadia* on *The White Devil*, *The Duchess of Malfi*, *The Devil's Law Case*, *A Monumental Column*, and *Anything for a Quiet Life*.

1658 LUCE, MORTON. *Rich's "Apolonius and Silla," an Original of Shakespeare's "Twelfth Night."* London: Chatto & Windus, 1912, pp. 86–87.

Notes "traces" of *Arcadia* in *Twelfth Night*, especially the resemblance between Viola and Sidney's disguised female page Zelmane.

1659 MACAULAY, ROSE. "John Lyly and Sir Philip Sidney." In *The English Novelists: A Survey of the Novel by Twenty Contemporary Novelists*, edited by Derek Verschoyle. London: Chatto & Windus; New York: Harcourt, Brace, & Co., 1936, pp. 29–47.

Lambasts Sidney as "a dull, even a disastrous novelist," who did "long damage to literature and to literary taste." Prefers Lyly's *Euphues*, contending that *Arcadia* lacks distinct characters and suffers from "stilted and rambling formlessness and drowsy periods."

Twentieth Century

1660 McCANLES, MICHAEL. "Reading Description in Sidney's New
Arcadia: A Differential Analysis." *UTQ* 53 (Fall 1983):36–52.
Considers the complaint that Sidney's descriptions are unrealistic
because they are encrusted with rhetorical ornament. Points out that this
view assumes that the author intended his words as a "transparent medium through which the reader passes easily into contact with a nonverbal,
physical reality. . . ." To disprove this assumption, explicates several
descriptions, including the initial shipwreck, Kalander's garden and
house, and Pamela's description of Musidorus's equestrian skill. Argues
that such passages do not follow the Ramist epistemology described by
Robinson (1742), but agrees that "Sidney dealt with highly articulated
structures of information that were intended to be reconstructed in the
reader's mind with equal articulation." Concludes that Sidney envisions
"structures articulated and filled out by a dialectical interplay of verbal
segments bound together by . . . logical differentials" involving mutual
implication and mutual exclusion. Suggests, then, that Arcadian descriptions are the most realistic possible because they are not transparent:
"Whatever reality such figuration mediates lies nowhere else save in this
figuration."

1661 ———. "The Rhetoric of Character Portrayal in Sidney's New
Arcadia." *Criticism* 25 (Spring 1983):123–39.
Feels that "Sidney's character portraits can in no way be separated from
his recuperating and understanding the rhetorical figuration and dialectical logic that textualizes these portraits." Asserts that Sidney follows
Aristotle in defining a spectrum of potentialities in which "a person's
ethical make-up . . . is constituted out of not only the moral qualities that
positively define it, but also those that do not but might have." Works
out six permutations in which virtues imply or exclude other virtues or
vices. Relates these "ethical dialectics" to the rhetorical figures of *synoeciosis*, *antithesis*, *syncrisis*, and *anatanogoge*. Explicates minutely the process
by which readers move from rhetorical figure to logical pattern to an
understanding of Sidney's characters. Focuses on the portraits of
Philoclea and Pamela, Helen, the King of Phrygia, Tydeus and Telenor,
and Anaxius. Also touches on the mixed genres of *Arcadia*.

1662 McCLUNG, WILLIAM A. *The Country House in English Renaissance
Poetry*. Berkeley, Los Angeles, and London: University of California Press, 1977, pp. 35–37, 48, 50, 53.
Contrasts Kalander's house with Basilius's star-shaped lodge: the former
suggests the "charitable virtues" of its owner, the latter "Basilius' conspicuous failure to fulfil his role." Includes three plates of Penshurst.

1663 McCOY, RICHARD C[HARLES]. *Sir Philip Sidney: Rebellion in Arcadia.* New Brunswick, N.J.: Rutgers University Press, 1979, pp. 138–217. Orig. a Ph.D. diss., University of Calfornia at Berkeley, 1975.

In Chapter 5, examines the Asian adventures of Book II. Argues that, as soon as Pyrocles and Musidorus leave the authority of Euarchus and begin to choose for themselves, they lose control of events. Following Freud, relates the authority of parents to that of God and asserts that Sidney leaves questions about both unresolved. Finds that, as the Asian journey progresses, ethical conflicts become harder to resolve and the entire "evaluative framework" of the romance is called into question. In Chapter 6, examines Amphialus's rebellion. Feels that the initial concern with politics and warfare gives way to "dreamy" chivalric tournaments, which allow Sidney to escape the serious implications of the rebellion. Argues that the early descriptions of the battles are realistic and even satiric, whereas later ones show a wonder at carnage that makes it almost beautiful. Traces Sidney's ambivalence about war to the Elizabethan cult of chivalry. Notes a similar ambivalence in Amphialus's attitude toward the doctrine of rebellion by subaltern magistrates. Notes that Sidney's male characters often find ways to evade punishment, whereas the females and commoners do not and become "scapegoats." Traces to Epicurean and Machiavellian teachings the position that Cecropia takes on religion, suggesting that the heroes of the romance tend to waffle between her view and that of Pamela and Euarchus. Finds in Pamela's arguments against Cecropia, and also in the opening description of Arcadia in Book I, a Calvinist tendency to regard God as a despot. Sees as the corollary of this view a tendency to portray the heroes of the book as men without true moral responsibility. Concludes that Sidney could not accept the "painful clarity" of Pamela's theology and that he left the revised *Arcadia* unfinished because he preferred not to risk a clear resolution of the issues he had raised. Finds in his death a similar escape from the need to reconcile obedience with autonomy. See also item 638.

1664 MacCRACKEN, H.N. "The Sources of *Ivanhoe*." *Nation* 92 (19 January 1911):60.

Comments on Sir Walter Scott's use of the *Arcadia* as a source for the Torquilstone Castle episode in *Ivanhoe*. For a reply, see Wolff (1829).

1665 McKEITHAN, D.M. "*King Lear* and Sidney's *Arcadia*." *University of Texas Studies in English*, no. 14, 8 July 1934, pp. 45–49.

Points out similarities between Edmund's plotting against Edgar in *Lear* and Andromana's machinations against Plangus in *Arcadia*.

Twentieth Century

1666 McKILLOP, ALAN DUGALD. *Samuel Richardson: Printer and Novelist.* Chapel Hill: University of North Carolina Press, 1936, p. 34.
Minimizes the link between Richardson's *Pamela* and Sidney's *Arcadia*, suggesting that Richardson may have taken the name "Pamela" from Steele's *Tender Husband*.

1667 McNEIR, WALDO [F]. "The Behaviour of Brigadore: *The Faerie Queene* V.3.33–34." *N&Q* n.s. 1 (March 1954):103–4.
Cites Musidorus's horsemanship in *Arcadia* as a possible source for Brigadore's behavior.

1668 ———. "Trial by Combat in Elizabethan Literature." *NS* 15 (March 1966):101–12.
Argues that, in *Arcadia*, Sidney uses the medieval tradition of trial by combat with a blend of "chivalry and psychology," ultimately subjecting the romantic notion to the rule of law in the "thoroughly modern court trial" of Book V. Concludes that, for Sidney, "common law had superceded the old-fashioned chivalry that he loved and laughed at and lived by."

1669 McPHERSON, DAVID C. "A Possible Origin for Mopsa in Sidney's *Arcadia*." *RenQ* 21 (Winter 1968):420–28.
Suggests that the name "Mopsa" is a bilingual pun, combining the name of one of Virgil's shepherds with the Dutch word "*mops*," meaning "pug dog" and, by extension, "country lout." Contrasts Virgil's Mopsus with Sidney's cruder Mopsa, suggesting that the latter was designed as a comic contrast for Pamela and for the high sentiments of the noble characters. Notes a similar mock-pastoral yoking of Virgil's Mopsus and a Dutch *mops* in a 1570 Dutch engraving based on a drawing by Peter Bruegel the Elder. From evidence of Sidney's connections with various Dutchmen, suggests that he may have encountered the engraving.

1670 MADAN, FRANCIS F. *A New Bibliography of the "Eikon Basilike."* Oxford Bibliographical Society Publications, n.s. 3. Oxford: Oxford Bibliographical Society, Oxford University Press, 1950, pp. 120–24, 140, 144, 146–47, 156, 170.
Supplies a bibliography of works on the charge that Milton himself inserted Pamela's prayer into Charles I's prayer book. From the printing history of *Eikon Basilike* and from contemporary testimonies, demonstrates that the charge is false. See also Hughes (1600), Morand (1685), and Milton (1323).

1671 MAGENDIE, MAURICE *Le Roman français au XVIIe siècle: De "L'Astrée" au "Grand Cyrus."* Paris: Librairie E. Droz, 1932, pp. 71–77.
Discusses the impact of *Arcadia* and its French translations on the development of French prose fiction in the first half of the seventeenth century. Suggests that it is indirectly responsible for a "bien mauvaise roman français," the anonymous *Arcadie françoise de la nymphe Amarille*. See also Lancaster (1635).

1672 MARGOLIES, D.N. "Author and Audience in Elizabethan Fiction: The Social Basis of a Changing Relationship." Ph.D. diss., University of Essex, 1973.
Abstract not available. Cited as item 306 in *Index to Theses Accepted for Higher Degrees in the Universities of Great Britain and Ireland* 26, Part 1 (1977).

1673 MARINO, JAMES ARTHUR. "The Cult of Ideal Friendship in Three Elizabethan Novels." Ph.D. diss., Louisiana State University and Agricultural and Mechanical College, 1972, 226 pp.
Concludes that, in *Arcadia*, Sidney treats friendship as "a measure of character, . . . the goad to heroic action and a major factor in achieving social and political stability." Notes that the structure of the romance emphasizes the contrast between the heroism of the Princes as friends and their subsequent decline as lovers. Sees the ending as an opportunity to unite love and friendship. See *DAI* 33 (June 1973):6876A–77A.

1674 MARSH, T.N. "Elizabethan Wit in Metaphor and Conceit: Sidney, Shakespeare, Donne." *EM* 13 (1962):25–29.
Argues that Sidney anticipates Donne's "The Anagram" in his ironic praise of Mopsa in "What length of verse can serve brave Mopsa's good to show" (*OA 3*). Contrasts Shakespeare's use of the mingling of blood and tears in *Titus Andronicus* III.i with the use of the image in *Arcadia* as Strephon, Claius, and Musidorus search the sea for Pyrocles.

1675 MARTIN, L.C. "Marvell, Massinger, and Sidney." *RES*, n.s. 2 (October 1951):374–75.
Points to Philoclea's soliloquy in *Arcadia* II.v as a likely source for Andrew Marvell's poem "The Definition of Love." See also Bush (1450).

Twentieth Century

1676 MATHEWS, ERNST GARLAND. "Studies in Anglo-Spanish Cultural and Literary Relations, 1598–1700." Ph.D. diss., Harvard University, 1938.
Evaluates the influence on *Arcadia* exerted by Montemayor's *Diana* and by the continuations of Gil Polo and Alonzo Pérez. Argues that earlier scholars overestimated the influence, which was mainly in general matters of style, structure, genre, and narrative voice, not in particular episodes or characters. See *Harvard University Graduate School of Arts and Sciences: Summaries of Theses*, 1938, pp. 304–13.

1677 MERMEL, ANN RAUCH. "Mythological Allegory in Sidney's *Arcadia*." Ph.D. diss., University of Houston, 1974, 249 pp.
Seeks to resolve the apparent contradiction between Sidney's suggestion that poets imitate actions in the world of nature and his view that they create "golden worlds" beyond the realm of nature. Suggests that, in *Arcadia*, "Sidney imitated mythological actions which, in turn, imitated divine Ideas." Argues that several major characters in the romance have counterparts in myth. For example, Basilius is a type of Saturn, Pyrocles of Hercules, Musidorus of Apollo, and Plangus of Hippolytus. Examines each mythological association on four neo-Platonic levels of being: the natural, the cosmological, the astrological, and the theological. Concludes that the concealed mythological associations of the romance affirm man's "freedom and the power to ascend to God." See *DAI* 35 (January 1975):4440A–41A.

1678 MERTEN, MARIA. *Michael Draytons "Poly-Olbion" im Rahmen der englischen Renaissance*. Oranienburg, Germany: Immaculatahaus, 1934, pp. 31–36.
In Chapter 5, "Draytons *Poly-Olbion* und Sidneys *Arcadia*," suggests that Kalander's hunt in Book I influenced Song 13 of Drayton's work. Also notes resemblances between the falconry that Basilius displays for the disguised Pyrocles and Drayton's Song 20.

1679 MILLARD, BARBARA C. "Thomas Nashe and the Functional Grotesque in Elizabethan Prose Fiction." *SSF* 15 (Winter 1978):39–48.
In considering the background of Nashe's *Unfortunate Traveller*, notes that Sidney, too, is interested in abnormal relationships, such as those involving Pyrocles's disguise as an Amazon, and in comic inversions of chivalric conventions.

1680 MILLER, ANTHONY PHILIP. "Structure, Style, and Thought in Sidney's New *Arcadia*." Ph.D. diss., Harvard University, 1977, 221 pp.

Seeks "to show how the form and disposition of the New *Arcadia*, and pervasive features of its verbal texture, derive from the identifiable materials of Sidney's religious and philosophic thought." Classifies the work as a romance, noting, however, Sidney's modifications of the genre. Stresses his Christian presuppositions and his concern, not only with moral virtues, but also with God's way of governing a fallen world.

1681 MILLER, PETER MacNAUGHTON, Jr. "The Rhetoric of Sidney's *Arcadia*." Ph.D. diss., Princeton University, 1939, 262 pp. Abstract not available.

1682 MILWARD, PETER. "Jojishi" [epic poetry]. In *Eikoku Runessansuki no Bungei Yoshiki*, edited by Peter Milward and Ishi Shonosuke. Tokyo: Aaratake, 1982, pp. 3–14.

Not seen. Cited as item 676 in the *MLA International Bibliography*, 1982, vol. 1. See also item 3973 in the Modern Humanities Research Association's *Annual Bibliography of English Language and Literature* 58 (1983).

1683 MITCHELL, ALISON, and FOSTER, KATHARINE. "Sir William Alexander's *Supplement* to Book III of Sidney's *Arcadia*." *Library*, 5th ser. 24 (September 1969):234–41.

Seeks to establish the printer and the period of publication for early issues of Alexander's continuation. On the basis of variants, argues that the author may have made changes before the second printing.

1684 MONTGOMERY, R[OBERT] L[ANGFORD, Jr.] "Sidney's *Arcadia*: The Critics' Book." *MLQ* 44 (June 1983):198–206.

In reviewing Greenfield (1564) and Lindheim (1263), notes the tendency of modern scholars to focus on the genre and the themes of *Arcadia* or on its biographical and intellectual backgrounds. Points out the limitations of thematic and ideological analyses, arguing that Sidney's complex style and wit forestall simple statements of his meaning.

1685 MORAND, PAUL PHELPS. *The Effects of His Political Life upon John Milton*. Paris: Henri Didier, 1939, pp. 23–51, 93.

Examines evidence that Milton inserted Pamela's prayer into Charles I's prayer book, reviewing twentieth-century scholarship on the issue. Concludes that Milton is guilty. See also Madan (1670) and Milton (1323).

Twentieth Century

1686 MORRIS, JOSEPH E. "Shakespeare's Use of the *Arcadia.*" *N&Q*
175 (3 December 1938):409.
In reply to Watson (1802), suggests that Shakespeare's description of the
Dauphin's horse in *Henry V* III.vii was based on the work of Thomas
Blundeville and not on *Arcadia*.

1687 MUIR, KENNETH. "*King Lear*, IV,i,10." *TLS*, 3 June 1949, p.
365.
Citing Sidney's phrase "poorely arayed" in the story of the Paphlagonian
King, emends the crux in *Lear* to read "But who comes heere? My father
poorely 'rayd?"

1688 ———. *Shakespeare's Sources. I: Comedies and Tragedies.* London:
Methuen & Co., 1957, pp. 13, 29, 74, 145–47, 223.
Cites scholarship demonstrating that Shakespeare knew *Astrophil and
Stella*, the *Defence*, and *Arcadia*. Notes that Romeo's speech to the "dead"
Juliet just before his suicide contains several echoes of the sonnet "I see
the house, my heart thy self contain" (*AS 85*). Dismisses claims by Pyle
(1724) that Viola's male disguise and Maria's letter trick in *Twelfth Night*
are borrowed from *Arcadia*, since both are commonplace. Notes the
influence of *Arcadia* on *King Lear*, particularly Sidney's account of the
death of the Paphlagonian King, his story of Plangus, and the eclogue of
Plangus and Basilius (*OA 30*). Also notes that *Coriolanus* echoes the version of Menenius's fable of the belly found in the *Defence*. See also item
1689.

1689 ———. *The Sources of Shakespeare's Plays.* New Haven, Conn.: Yale
University Press, 1978, pp. 9–10, 45, 138, 196, 201–2, 238.
Supplies a revised version of item 1688.

1690 MUIR, KENNETH, and DANBY, JOHN F. "*Arcadia* and *King
Lear.*" *N&Q* 195 (4 February 1950):49–51.
Notes several passages of *Arcadia* that are echoed in *King Lear*: the story
of the Paphlagonian King, the poetic debate between Plangus and
Basilius (*OA 30*), Miso's poem on blind Cupid (*OA 8*), the weeping of
Philoclea in Cecropia's prison, and Basilius's foolish admiration for
Dametas.

1691 MYRICK, KENNETH ORNE. *Sir Philip Sidney as a Literary
Craftsman.* Harvard Studies in English, 14. Cambridge, Mass.:
Harvard University Press; London: Oxford University Press,
1935, pp. 110–297.
In Chapter 4, "*Arcadia* as an Heroic Poem," argues that, both in subject
and in structure, the New *Arcadia* follows Minturno's rules for an epic.

Suggests that such departures from Minturno as we see simply show Sidney's recognition that "to regard the end, not to follow a mechanical rule, is for any classicist the first rule of art." In the opening exchange between Strephon and Claius, sees a "conscious adaptation" of the epic invocation. Compares Sidney's theory in the *Defence* with his practice in *Arcadia*, focusing on issues such as the proper role of the supernatural, the suitability of prose as a medium for epic, and the propriety of mingling pastoral and historical matters. Feels that Sidney's "rational temper" and "religious reverence" led him to reject supernatural machinery. Finds that, in subject and narrative method, the New *Arcadia* conforms better to Minturno's idea of the "fundamental principles of heroic poetry" than does the Old *Arcadia*. In Chapter 5, "Ornament in the *New Arcadia*," argues that its "elaborate style, varied episode, and large design all reflect the love of magnificence" that distinguishes the art of both Sidney and Minturno from that of the ancients. Examines Minturno's distinctive theory of the relation between episodes and the main action, pointing to passages in *De Poeta* that "justify" the "grandiose plan" of the New *Arcadia*. Shows ways in which Sidney conforms to "four elastic principles" governing the length of the fable. Feels that, in its confusing multiplicity of episodes, the New *Arcadia* "fails by the standards of true art," but praises it as an "experiment." In considering the style of *Arcadia*, suggests that Sidney thinks of it as a "garment that may be changed at will." Sees the rhetorical variety within the work as an attempt to find forms of refined speech suitable for "artistic expression." In Chapter 6, "Sidney's Theory of Poetic Truth," discusses the "purpose" of *Arcadia*, examining the *Defence* for Sidney's theory of the function of poetry. Seeks to ajudicate prior critical disagreements, first whether poetry teaches by allegory or by "ideal imitation," then whether its chief aim is to teach or to delight. Insists that, in Sidney's view, teaching cannot be separated from delight. Argues that Sidney's view of imitation differs from Aristotle's in "the importance he assigns to character as compared with action and to the possible as compared with the probable." In Chapter 7, "Poetic Truth in the *New Arcadia*," seeks to reveal ways in which the work applies the aesthetic principles of the *Defence*. After arguing that *Arcadia* is not primarily an allegory, considers whether it is a philosophical treatise, examining the "range of problems treated by Sidney"—those related to social conditions, to political, philosophical, or ethical beliefs, and so on. Contends that, although Sidney's teaching is deliberate, it is always subordinate to the imaginative appeal of the work, to its attempt to "show noble conduct as beautiful" and thus to "inflame 'the minde with the desire to be woorthie.'" See also item 671 and replies by Levine (1260), Townsend (1304), and Rowe (1747).

459

Twentieth Century

1692 NASON, ARTHUR HUNTINGTON. *James Shirley, Dramatist: A Biographical and Critical Study*. New York: Arthur H. Nason, 1915, pp. 243–45.
Treats Shirley's dramatic adaptation of *Arcadia* as the beginning of a major shift toward romance in the dramatist's career.

1693 NEELY, CAROL THOMAS. "Speaking True: Shakespeare's Use of the Elements of Pastoral Romance." Ph.D. diss., Yale University, 1969, 226 pp.
Exploring "the achievement of an adequate style" as an important theme in Renaissance romance, argues that *Arcadia* exhibits a tension between "the capriciousness suggested by the multiple threads of the story, the security created by the circular romance plot and controlling narrator, and the cyclical pattern implied by the analogies and contrasts." Claims that neither its characters nor the work itself fully achieves integration. See *DA* 30 (February 1970):3433A–34A.

1694 NEWDIGATE, B[ERNARD] H[ENRY]. "The Rival Poet and the Youth of the Sonnets." *TLS*, 9 November 1933, p. 774.
Identifies the Dorus and Pamela of Drayton's *Idea's Mirror* with characters of the same names in *Arcadia*.

1695 O'CONNOR, JOHN J[OSEPH]. *"Amadis de Gaule" and Its Influence on Elizabethan Literature*. New Brunswick, N.J.: Rutgers University Press, 1970, pp. 151–52, 183–201.
In *"Amadis* and Sidney's *Arcadia,"* discusses the influence of the French romance on the names, incidents, and characters of *Arcadia* and also on its view of sexual love, its use of transvestism, its humor, and its prose style. Also suggests that the *chanson* of Arlanges in Book XI of *Amadis* supplied Sidney with the pattern for "In a grove most rich of shade" (*AS viii*).

1696 ———. "Studies in the Theory and Practice of Prose Fiction 1600–1640." Ph.D. diss., Harvard University, 1951, pp. 4, 49–75.
Calling *Arcadia* the "most influential single piece of fiction to appear in England before *Pamela*," notes that it was most popular between 1620 and 1629. Discusses the major formative role that it played in the fiction of the period, particularly as a model for the heroic poem in prose.

1697 OEFTERING, MICHAEL. *Heliodor und seine Bedeutung für die Litteratur*. Litterarhistorische Forschungen, 18. Berlin: Verlag von Emil Felber, 1901, pp. 93–96.
Lays out similarities between *Arcadia* and the *Aethiopica* of Heliodorus, concentrating on the opening *in medias res* and the episode of Plangus and Andromana.

1698 OGILVY, J.D.A. "Arcadianism in *1 Henry IV.*" *ELN* 10 (March 1973):185–88.

Notes in the opening of *Arcadia* parallels to Hal's tavern speech imitating his father. Suggests that Shakespeare was parodying the Arcadian style.

1699 O'HARA, JAMES EUGENE, Jr. *The Rhetoric of Love in Lyly's "Euphues and His England" and Sidney's "Arcadia" (1590)*. Salzburg Studies in English Literature: Elizabethan and Renaissance Studies, 76. Salzburg: Institut für Englische Sprache und Literatur, Universität Salzburg, 1978, 175 pp. Orig. a Ph.D diss., University of Michigan, 1974, 210 pp.

Examines passages of "love rhetoric" by each author, conducting tests and statistical comparisons in matters of rhetorical organization, balance and length of the periods, and figures of thought and speech. Finds that earlier scholarly opinion on the distinctions between the Arcadian and the euphuistic styles is unreliable. Concludes that antithesis combined with *isocolon-parison* is the most distinctively euphuistic characteristic and that *polyptoton* is more common in Arcadian prose. Contrasts Sidney's flexible, sometimes euphuistic prose, with Lyly's more consistent style.

1700 OKUDA, HIROYUKI. "Sidney no Pastoralism" [Sir Philip Sidney's Pastoralism]. *Kenkyu Sburoku. [Gaikokugo/Gaikokubungaku.]* (Kyoyobu, Osaka Daigaku), no. 6, March 1970, pp. 19–35.

Not seen. Cited as item 208 in "The 1970 Bibliography," by [Kazuyoshi Enozawa and Sister Miyo Takano], *RenB* 5 (1978):38.

1701 OLIVEIRA e SILVA, J[OHN] de. "Naming and Literary Context: Backgrounds to Sir Philip Sidney's Philisides." *Literary Onomastics Studies* 7 (1980):139–48.

Traces the literary history of the name "Filli" or "Phyllis" from antiquity through the Renaissance, noting associations with discontented love and pastoral settings. Also examines analogous names in Montemayor's *Diana* based on Latin roots suggesting catlike guile and bitterness as well as felicity. Argues that Sidney would have rhymed the name with "felicities" as an ironic comment on his own unhappy love.

1702 ———. "Recurrent Onomastic Textures in the *Diana* of Jorge de Montemayor and the *Arcadia* of Sir Philip Sidney." *SP* 79 (Winter 1982):30–40.

Observes that, just as Montemayor derives three of his main characters' names from *felix*, so Sidney uses character names from the root *philo*, though in a different way. For Sidney, love and happiness are less dependent on external influences; they "thrive or wither" as a result of the lovers' inner resources. Asks why Cecropia has a name and a function so different from that of Montemayor's Felicia, who is in many ways her counterpart. On the evidence of a lost 1585 play based on the *Diana*, entitled *Felix and Philomena*, suggests that Cecropia (whose name has associations with Philomena, daughter of Cecrops) is a veiled allusion to Felismena. If so, the captivity is an "extended episode of self-scrutiny and self-conquest on the part of the sisters, not merely an experience in temptation from without." Concludes that Sidney "borrows a precedent" from Montemayor's poem, but "far exceeds it" in complexity and scope.

1703 OTTEN, KURT. *Der englische Roman vom 16. zum 19. Jahrhundert.* Grundlagen der Anglistik und Amerikanistik, 4. Berlin: Erich Schmidt Verlag, 1971, pp. 26–30, 39, 79.

Relates Sidney's dedication of *Arcadia* to his sister to the courtly tradition in which women inspire masculine achievement. Discusses the mixture of genres in the work and the history of the myth of Arcadia from classical to modern times. Relates the plot to the "myth of redemption" found in Greek romance and tragedy, emphasizing the importance of divine providence and the oracle. Regards the preservation of chastity as the main thematic thread of the work, relating it to order in the individual and in the state and contrasting it with the concerns of classical epic. Also discusses the style and narrative technique of the work and its importance as a model for later fiction.

1704 PARROTT, THOMAS MARC, ed. *The Plays and Poems of George Chapman.* Vol. 2, *The Comedies.* London: George Routledge & Sons; New York: E.P. Dutton & Co., 1914, pp. 754–55.

Considers the mutilation of the heroine's face in three early seventeenth-century plays: the anonymous *Trial of Chivalry*, John Marston's *Jack Drum's Entertainment*, and George Chapman's *Gentleman Usher*. Suggests that all rely on Sidney's story of Parthenia in Book I of the revised *Arcadia*.

1705 PARRY, GRAHAM. "Lady Mary Wroth's *Urania*." *PLPLS-LHS* 16 (July 1975):51–60.

Notes the origin of the name "Urania" in *Arcadia* and discusses the character's associations with Aphrodite Urania in Plato's *Symposium*, with the muse of astronomy, with the Christian muse of du Bartas, and perhaps with the Countess of Pembroke. Compares Mary Wroth's literary skills with those of Sidney, noting ways in which her *Urania* imitates *Arcadia*.

1706 PASICKI, ADAM. "A Rhetorical Figure in Lyly and Sidney." In *Between Language and Literature: Papers by Members of the English Institute Delivered at the Session Held 22–24 October 1971.* Zeszyty Naukowe Uniwersytetu Jagiellońskiego, 293: Prace Historyczno-literackie, 24. Cracow, Poland: Jagellonian University of Cracow, 1973, pp. 23–34.

Offers a syntactic and morphological analysis of *antimetabole* (a figure of repetition) in order to establish a quantitative basis for affirming G.K. Hunter's judgments (579) that "Lyly's style was basically argumentative; Sidney's was basically descriptive," and that "the most obvious figure of Arcadianism is periphrasis, not balance, which allows Sidney greater scope in varying the appearance of his figures."

1707 PATCHELL, MARY. *The Palmerin Romances in Elizabethan Prose Fiction.* Columbia University Studies in English and Comparative Literature, 166. New York: Columbia University Press, 1947, pp. 71, 73, 99, 115–127.

Suggests that Emanuel Forde's *Ornatus and Artesia* may owe its episode of a prince wooing in feminine attire either to *Arcadia* or to *Amadis de Gaule*. Also details the many parallels between *Arcadia* and the Spanish Palmerin romances, both in episode and theme and in attitude toward such things as divinely ordained fortune and marital chastity. Contends that Moody was wrong (in his unpublished M.A. thesis, Harvard University, 1894) to single out *Amadis* as "the source" for the main plot and various episodes of the revised *Arcadia*.

1708 PAULIN, BERNARD. *Du couteau à la plume: Le suicide dans la littérature anglaise de la renaissance (1580–1625).* Lyon, France: L'Université de St. Étienne, 1977, pp. 189–95.

From passages in *Arcadia*, infers that, for Sidney, suicide is a deserved end for an evil character, whereas the rejection of suicide enobles a good one.

1709 PETTET, E.C. *Shakespeare and the Romance Tradition.* London: Staples Press, 1949, pp. 23–37, 75–100 passim, 162.

Characterizes *Arcadia* as a traditional romance of love and friendship, pointing to surprise and suspense as its main appeals. Notes its fairy-tale coincidences and improbabilities; its typical catalogue of marvels from older romances; its use of disguises, mistaken identities, and recognitions; its adherence to poetic justice; and its strained psychology and artificial sentiments. Comments on its mixture of aristocratic and rustic characters and its mingling of Greek and medieval, pastoral and chivalric settings. Compares similar mixtures in Elizabethan drama, particularly in Shakespeare's romances. Discusses reasons that Sidney was drawn to romance, noting that it produces delight and laughter, a combination discussed in the sections of the *Defence* devoted to comedy. Also notes that Lyly must have known Sidney's position on comic delight and the dramatic unities.

1710 PHILLIPS, HELEN M. "Human Nature and Art in Sidney's *Arcadia*." Ph.D. diss., Cornell University, 1933, 426 pp. Published abstract: n.p., 1933, 3 pp.

Considers the view of human nature revealed in the characters of *Arcadia*, comparing it with Sidney's own character. Discusses his adaptation of material from Erasmus's *Praise of Folly*, the Greek romances, and works by Aristotle, Xenophon, and Plutarch. Also analyzes pictorial descriptions in *Arcadia*, suggesting that Sidney knew the work of Venetian artists and the comparisons of painting and poetry common in the works of the Italian critics. Also touches on the influence of Theocritus's *Idylls* and Francesco Colonna's *Hypnerotomachia*. Includes a list of references to all the characters in *Arcadia*.

1711 PHILLIPS, JAMES E[MERSON]. "Arcadia on the Range." In *Themes and Directions in American Literature: Essays in Honor of Leon Howard*, edited by Ray B. Browne and Donald Pizer. Lafayette, Ind.: Purdue University Studies, 1969, pp. 108–29.

Suggests that American literature about the western cowboy took up the dying pastoral tradition of Europe. Compares Sidney's lyric "Go my flock" (*AS ix*) with the anonymous cowboy song "Ten Thousand Cattle." Also details the parallels in setting, characters, action, poetic interludes, episodes, and moral teaching between *Arcadia* and Owen Wister's novel *The Virginian*.

1712 PLOMER, HENRY R[OBERT]. "The Edinburgh Edition of Sidney's *Arcadia*." *Library*, n.s. 1 (March 1900):195–205.

Discusses the pirated edition of 1599 (2) and William Ponsonby's legal battle to protect his copyright. From ornaments on the title page identifies the printer of the 1598 edition as Richard Field. Adduces evidence that Robert Waldgrave, not printers in Cambridge, was responsible for the pirating.

1713 POGGIOLI, RENATO. "The Oaten Flute." *HLB* 11 (Spring 1957):147–84. Reprint. In *The Oaten Flute: Essays on Pastoral Poetry and the Pastoral Ideal*, edited by A. Bartlett Giamatti. Cambridge, Mass.: Harvard University Press, 1975, pp. 1–41.

Sees Sidney's as "the aristocratic view of pastoral justice, which, like all aristocratic views, is a retrospective utopia, a backward-looking dream."

1714 POIRIER, MICHEL. "Sidney's Influence upon *A Midsummer Night's Dream*." *SP* 44 (July 1947):483–89.
Lists borrowings from the *Arcadia* in *King Lear*, *Twelfth Night*, *As You Like It*, *The Taming of the Shrew*, and *Macbeth*. Concentrates on the parallels between the hunt in Book I of the revised *Arcadia* and Theseus's exchange with Hippolyta on the baying of the hounds in *A Midsummer Night's Dream* IV.i. Traces subsequent borrowings from the same passage of *Arcadia* in Gervase Markham's *Country Contentments* and in other works. Also suggests that, in *A Midsummer Night's Dream* V.i, Theseus's comments on "the lunatic, the lover, and the poet" derive from remarks in the *Defence* on the "divine fury" of the poet.

1715 POLLERT, HUBERT, and KINDERVATER, JOS[EF] WILH[ELM]. "Zeitschriftenschau." *SJ* 69 (1933):189.
Suggests that Shakespeare's line "Finds tongues in trees, and books in running brooks" in *As You Like It* II.i may be borrowed from *Arcadia* II.i: "Thus both trees and each thing else be the books of fancy." But see Curtius (1490).

1716 POPHAM, ELIZABETH ANNE. "The Concept of Arcadia in the English Literary Renaissance: Pastoral Societies in the Works of Sidney, Spenser, Shakespeare, and Milton." Ph.D. diss., Queen's University at Kingston, Ontario, 1982.
Examines "the critical understanding of pastoral in the English Renaissance; the 'genealogy' of the fictional country of Arcadia; and the exploitation of the pastoral image . . . as an emblem of the well-ordered state." Describes the development of literary Arcadias from Sidney and Spenser to Shakespeare. Considers the mingling of classical and medieval elements in Renaissance pastoral and suggests that Sidney's work is utopian and undertakes "an anatomy of social and ethical behaviour in the world encompassing the shepherd society." See *DAI* 43 (April 1983):3326A.

1717 POTEZ, HENRI. "Le premier roman anglais traduit en Français." *Revue d'histoire littéraire de la France* 11 (1904):42–55.
Argues that Baudoin's translation of *Arcadia* (33) is not the earliest rendering of an English novel into French. Regnault's translation of Robert Greene's *Pandosto* preceded it by nine years.

1718 PRAZ, MARIO. "*The Duchess of Malfi*." *TLS*, 18 June 1954, p. 393.
Discusses the parallel between John Webster's scene with wax corpses and the mock executions in Book III of *Arcadia*.

465

Twentieth Century

1719 PRICE, LAWRENCE MARSDEN. *English-German Literary Influences: Part I. Bibliography.* University of California Publications in Modern Philology, 9. Berkeley: University of California Press, 1919, pp. 130–31, 133.

Considers the influence of *Arcadia* in Germany, noting that it is first mentioned in 1624 in Martin Opitz's *Aristarchus.* Also discusses the relation of Valentinus Theocritus's German translation (34) to earlier French versions and to Opitz's revision of 1638 (37).

1720 PRUVOST, RENÉ. *Matteo Bandello and Elizabethan Fiction.* Paris: Librarie Ancienne Honoré Champion, 1937, pp. 205–6, 217, 325.

Notes that *Arcadia* owes nothing to the English novels written in imitation of Bandello. Suggests that the popularity of Sidney's romance hastened the end of the vogue for such novels.

1721 ———. "Réflexions sur l'euphuisme à propos de deux romans élisabéthains." *Revue anglo-américaine* 8 (October 1930):1–18.

Contending in part with Baker (1417), argues that Greene's *Menaphon* is thoroughly indebted to *Arcadia.* Notes that the "extravagant romance," the "lyricism," and the "idealism" of both works are "at the antipodes" from Lyly's *Euphues.*

1722 PSILOS, PAUL DENNIS. "Sidney's *Arcadia*: A Critical Study." Ph.D. diss., Northwestern University, 1970, 222 pp.

Seeks to demonstrate the "narrative and logical consistency" of the New *Arcadia* by examining its apparently disjointed structure in the light of the *Defence.* Relates the pastoral elements in *Arcadia* to Sidney's thematic concerns and to his use of metaphor. See *DAI* 31 (April 1971):5373A.

1723 PYLE, FITZROY. "*King Lear* and Sidney's *Arcadia*." *TLS*, 11 November 1949, p. 733.

Replies to Armstrong (1412), suggesting that Shakespeare does not directly echo Sidney's phrasing in the play and that similarities arise "from the common stock of medieval and Elizabethan thought."

1724 ———. "*Twelfth Night, King Lear* and *Arcadia*." *MLR* 43 (October 1948):449–55.

Argues that *Arcadia* influenced Shakespeare's *Twelfth Night*, not just in the comic duel of cowards but also in much of the subplot and tone of the play. Notes parallels between the works in the initial shipwrecks that separate two kinsmen and in the sex changes, and argues that Malvolio is derived from Sidney's Dametas. Also considers the parallels between *King Lear* and *Arcadia*, emphasizing Shakespeare's debt in the main plot as well as the subplot. Concludes that *Lear* may have been conceived while Shakespeare was consulting *Arcadia* for *Twelfth Night*. See a reply by Muir (1688).

1725 RAITIÈRE, MARTIN N[ORMAN]. "Amphialus' Rebellion: Sidney's Use of History in *New Arcadia*." *JMRS* 12 (Spring 1982):113–31.

Examines Sidney's attitude toward the doctrine of rebellion by subaltern magistrates, as it was set forth by Huguenots such as Hubert Languet and Francis Hotman. Adduces evidence that, although Amphialus uses the doctrine to justify his revolt in Book III of *Arcadia*, Sidney opposed such arguments. Finds the inspiration for Amphialus's rebellion in one of the favorite illustrations used by the Huguenots: the Duke of Alençon's revolt against Henry III of France in 1575. Lists similarities between Alençon's published justification and that issued by Amphialus, but notes evidence in the *Letter to the Queen* and elsewhere that Sidney condemned Alençon's attempt. Suggests that Sidney allowed Amphialus a certain nobility out of respect for the theory but ultimately undercut him by making Amphialus appear feudal and selfish. Concludes that McCoy is wrong (in 1663) to equate Amphialus's ambivalence toward authority with that of Sidney himself.

1726 REES, JOAN. *Fulke Greville, Lord Brooke, 1554–1628: A Critical Biography.* Berkeley: University of California Press, 1971, pp. 1–3, 22–25, 43–70, 74–77, 87–103, 141, 171–72, 199–201.

Characterizes Sidney and the nature of his friendship with Greville, discussing the latter's unfinished elegy for him, plans that they should share a tomb in St. Paul's Cathedral, and their acquaintance with Giordano Bruno. Reviews Greville's role in publishing the New *Arcadia*, his reasons for preferring it over the Old, and his limited view of the book as an exercise in political reasoning. Attributes the chapter headings added in 1590 to Matthew Gwynne. Ponders the editor's arrangement of the eclogues and his elimination of Philisides from them, urging that the 1590 edition is probably closer to Sidney's wishes than that published in 1593. Also discusses Greville's *Life of Sidney* (863), noting that its original title (*A Dedication*) is more accurate than the one now in use. Suggests that the book aims to portray Sidney as a public figure, not as a private man. Notes contrasts between Sidney and the courtiers of James I and sees the comparisons between Sidney and Essex as an emblem of the contemplative and the active lives. Suggests that Greville's discussion of the French marriage represents Sidney's private views, whereas the *Letter to the Queen* represents the public views of his faction at court. Also

Twentieth Century

takes Greville's suggestions on England's policy toward Spain as the results of Sidney's own thinking. Notes parallels between numerous poems by Greville and those in *Astrophil and Stella* and *Arcadia,* suggesting that Sidney was engaged in "singing matches" with Greville and Dyer and that Greville's later poetry contains ironic commentaries on Sidney's excessive love of Stella. Identifies Greville with the disapproving friend in *Astrophil and Stella* 21, 69, and perhaps 14, and takes Greville's reproof of "witty fictions" (in the *Life of Sidney*) as a comment on *Arcadia.* Contrasts his poetic style with that of Sidney. See a reply by Rebholz (1126).

1727 ———. "Juliet's Nurse: Some Branches of a Family Tree." *RES,* n.s. 34 (February 1983):43–47.
Suggests that the manners and speech of the nurse in Shakespeare's *Romeo and Juliet* may have been modeled on Miso's discourse on Cupid in Book II of *Arcadia.*

1728 REEVES, ROBERT NICHOLAS, III. *The Ridiculous to the Delightful: Comic Characters in Sidney's "New Arcadia."* LeBaron Russell Briggs Prize: Honors Essays in English, 1973. Cambridge, Mass.: Harvard University Press, 1974, 61 pp.
Examines the comic subplot, considering irony, satire, and the narrator's use of multiple voices. Finds precedents for the subplot only in Roman comedy and notes that the theory of comic delight in the *Defence* is more advanced than that in Aristotle or Trissino. Argues that the comic characters in the *Arcadia* exist to expose the flaws as well as to exalt the virtues of Sidney's heroes and heroines. Suggests that Sidney's purpose is to portray the education of the young lovers, and all the other characters may be diagrammed as the spokes of a wheel with these four at the hub. Distinguishes low comic scenes, which arouse scornful laughter, from high comic passages, which arouse delight and set up parallels between the mean and the noble characters. Also points out, in an appendix, that Dametas's antics in the bear episode resemble Falstaff's actions at the battle of Shrewsbury in *I Henry IV* V.iv.

1729 RIBNER, IRVING. *The English History Play in the Age of Shakespeare.* Princeton, N.J.: Princeton University Press, 1957, pp. 106, 245, 250–51.
Suggests that *Arcadia* may well have influenced *As You Like It, Midsummer Night's Dream,* and *Twelfth Night,* as well as *King Lear.*

1730 ———. *Jacobean Tragedy: The Quest for Moral Order.* London: Methuen & Co., 1962, p. 156.
Notes parallels in the setting and in the names of characters between Ford's play *The Broken Heart* and *Arcadia*.

1731 ———. "Machiavelli and Sidney: The *Arcadia* of 1590." *SP* 47 (April 1950):152–72.
While admitting that Sidney sought to discredit Machiavellian tactics in the actions of Plexirtus, Clinias, and Amphialus, argues that the political philosophy of *Arcadia* agrees with that of Machiavelli. Examines the character of Basilius, noting qualities condemned by Machiavelli and treating Philanax as a more suitable ruler. Relates the latter's letter to Basilius in Book I to Sidney's *Letter to the Queen*. Analyzes the rebellion of the Helots for Sidney's views on insurrection and the best way to govern a conquered people. Finally, examines Euarchus's reformation of his realm, comparing Machiavelli's remedies for governmental corruption.

1732 ———. "A Note on Sidney's *Arcadia* and *A Midsummer Night's Dream*." *Shakespeare Association Bulletin* 23 (October 1948):207–8.
Suggests that the entanglement of the four lovers in Shakespeare's play is based on the cross-wooing of Philoclea, Zelmane, Basilius, and Gynecia.

1733 ———. "Shakespeare and Legendary History: *Lear* and *Cymbeline*." *SQ* 7 (Winter 1956):47–52.
Cites Shakespeare's borrowings from *Arcadia* as evidence that *King Lear* is concerned with contemporary political problems.

1734 ———. "Sidney's *Arcadia* and the Machiavelli Legend." *Italica* 27 (September 1950):225–35.
Examines the "Machiavels" in *Arcadia*, including Plexirtus, Clinias, Amphialus, and the kings of Phrygia and Pontus. Argues "1) that the characteristics with which Sidney endows these villains have little relation to Machiavelli's actual writings, but are instead reflections of the prevalent popular misinterpretation, 2) that these villains all fail in their purposes not because they follow Machiavelli, but precisely because they fail to follow certain of Machiavelli's basic precepts . . . , and 3) that the 'Machiavels' of the *Arcadia*, rather than offer evidence that Sidney was opposed to Machiavelli's ideas, serve instead to reinforce the conclusion . . . that Sidney and Machiavelli were in essential agreement." See a reply by Bergbusch (1425).

Twentieth Century

1735 ———. "Sidney's *Arcadia* and the Structure of *King Lear*." *SN* 24, no. 1–2 (1952):63–68.

Points to similarities in the ways in which the subplots of *Arcadia* and *King Lear* serve to emphasize and universalize the same central theme: the danger of turning away from public responsibilities to lead a private life. Compares Sidney's position in the *Letter to the Queen*, which also stresses the need to exercise power rather than to relinquish it to another.

1736 ———. "Sir Philip Sidney on Civil Insurrection." *JHI* 13 (April 1952):257–65.

Traces two views of civil obedience: that of the Tudors that even tyrants must be obeyed, and that of extreme English Puritans that subjects may depose a tyrant. Argues from evidence in *Arcadia* that Sidney followed Tudor orthodoxy and that he also rejected the Huguenot doctrine that the monarch is bound by contract to his people and is subject to law.

1737 RICHMOND, VELMA E. BOURGEOIS. "The Development of the Rhetorical Death Lament from the Late Middle Ages to Marlowe." Ph.D. diss., University of North Carolina, 1959, 367 pp.

Includes a discussion of death laments in *Arcadia*, noting that they are part of a trend toward more dramatic laments. See *DA* 20 (January 1960):2807.

1738 RIVERS, ISABEL. *The Poetry of Conservatism, 1600–1745: A Study of Poets and Public Affairs from Jonson to Pope*. Cambridge: Rivers Press, 1973, pp. 40–45.

Argues that Jonson uses Sidney and his family as examples of the proper relationship between nobles and their monarch, noting that Jonson's view of Penshurst parallels Sidney's depiction of Kalander's house. Argues that the political ideas of *Arcadia* are reflected throughout Jonson's works.

1739 ROBERTS, JOSEPHINE A[NASTASIA]. *Architectonic Knowledge in the "New Arcadia" (1590): Sidney's Use of the Heroic Journey*. Salzburg Studies in English Literature: Elizabethan and Renaissance Studies, 69. Salzburg: Institut für englische Sprache und Literatur, Universität Salzburg, 1978, 335 pp. Orig. a Ph.D. diss., University of Pennsylvania, 1975.

In the introduction, rehearses the Renaissance debate over the genre of Ariosto's *Orlando furioso*, considering Italian definitions of romance, epic, and the "mixed mode." Regards the New *Arcadia* as "mixed," comparing it with the story of Hercules and Omphale. In Chapter 1, analyzes the Old *Arcadia* as a Roman comedy. For a full annotation, see item 1289. In

Chapter 2, reviews criticism of Book II of the New *Arcadia*, tying its stories to the concerns of the characters who narrate and listen to them.
Notes that, in portraying the male narrators, Sidney stresses a single flaw
that endangers each of them: pride in Musidorus, lack of self-control in
Pyrocles, and lack of judgment in Basilius. Sees Musidorus as an embodiment of *sapientia* and Pyrocles of *fortitudo*, Pamela of all that is
admirable and Philoclea of all that stirs affection. In their stories, finds
that they deal with problems very like the ones that they currently face.
Sees a progression from clear moral choices to murky ones. In Chapter
3, discusses sources for the narrations of Book II. In Homer's *Odyssey*,
finds analogues for the setting, the heroic journey framed by shipwrecks,
the heroes' discovery of their own weaknesses, and their acquisition of
"architectonic" knowledge. Comments on Sidney's lack of interest in
monsters or supernatural "machinery." Sees in his heroes similarities
with Aeneas in that they encounter various kinds of monarchs and
become entangled in love affairs, but differences in that they face
tougher moral choices and receive less help from the higher powers.
Notes that, like Heliodorus, Sidney replaces epic monsters with evil people, makes romantic love the central subject, and sets up a subplot to
illuminate the main action. Lists numerous parallels between Musidorus
and Odysseus, Pyrocles and Hercules. In Chapter 4, considers the range
of fictional forms in Book II. Treats the accounts of the Kings of
Phrygia, Pontus, and Paphlagonia as tragedies, comparing the first two
with stories in *A Mirror for Magistrates* and the last with Sackville and
Norton's *Gorboduc*. Contrasts Musidorus's involvement in political
tragedies with Pyrocles's entanglement in domestic tragedies, such as
those of Dido and Zelmane. Analyzes the story of Erona as a romance
modeled on the account of Olympia in *Orlando furioso*; Mopsa's story as
similar to Chaucer's "Tale of Sir Thopas"; and the tragedy of Plangus as
a modification of a story in Heliodorus. In Pyrocles's Asian adventures,
finds characters out of Terence, and in the story of Zelmane, finds
romance material like that in Montemayor's *Diana*. Stresses the impact
of love on politics throughout Book II. Analyzes the tournaments of
Phalanatus, Andromana, and Amphialus as "arenas for the clash of
opposed ideals." In Chapter 5, examines Sidney's departures from traditional pastoral, particularly his strong interest in political problems, his
wide range of characters, and his incorporation of heroic material. Notes
ways in which the opening shipwreck reveals limitations in high and low
characters alike. Treats Arcadia as an "ideal haven of contemplation" but
also as a place of ignorance confused with wisdom. In Book III, considers the intrusion of Asian violence into the pastoral world. Contrasts

Twentieth Century

Musidorus with Amphialus, analyzing their heraldic devices and stressing their departure from the ideals represented by Strephon and Claius.
Discusses reminders of an unspoiled pastoral world in the elegy for
Amphialus (*OA 75*) and in Pamela's embroidery. In Chapter 6, treats
Amphialus as a portrait of medieval heroism, which seeks "glory in a single-minded quest." Traces his division of mind to his mixed lineage,
linking his mother with the half-serpent Cecrops. Also compares him
with Malory's Tristram, remarking that his courtesy is not grounded in
virtue. Sees criticism of chivalry throughout the romance, defining
Sidney's ideal as responsible public service, not private glory. Contrasts
the medieval heroism of Amphialus with the classical heroism of
Argalus. Drawing on the the notion of "architectonic" knowledge in the
Defence, sees the Asian journey and the Arcadian interlude as crucial in
developing such knowledge in Pyrocles and Musidorus, who excel
Amphialus in their grasp of "the actual nature of the passions, the difficulty of making ethical choices, and the problem of conflicting values."
Sees Euarchus as the ideal of heroism toward which they are moving. In
an appendix, discusses the Cambridge Manuscript of the New *Arcadia*,
pointing out that its altered character names reflect the process by which
Sidney revised the original version. Includes a lengthy bibliography. See
also item 1289.

1740 ———. "*Daiphantus* (1604): A Jacobean Perspective on Hamlet's
    Madness." *LC* 42 (Winter 1978):128–37.
Notes allusions to *Arcadia* in this anonymous poem.

1741 ———. "Extracts from *Arcadia* in the Manuscript Notebook of
    Lady Katherine Manners." *N&Q*, n.s. 28 (February 1981):35–36.
Lists excerpts of six poems and three prose passages from the 1593
Arcadia. Notes that Lady Katherine was the niece of Sidney's daughter
Elizabeth.

1742 ROBINSON, FORREST G[LEN]. *The Shape of Things Known:
    Sidney's "Apology" in Its Philosophical Tradition*. Cambridge, Mass.:
    Harvard University Press, 1972, pp. 137–73. Orig. a Ph.D. diss.,
    Harvard University, 1968.
In the first section of Chapter 4, traces ways in which Sidney's concern
with visual epistemology in the *Defence* is put into practice in the New
Arcadia. Noting Greville's view that Sidney's aim in the work was "to turn
the barren Philosophy precepts into pregnant Images of life," treats the
work as a "full gallery of moral images," with "exemplary instruction in
how those images are to be viewed." Argues that Sidney intended the

reader to "disregard words" in favor of the universal images of moral and political virtue embodied in the characters. Noting Hoskins's analysis of Sidney's method in *Directions for Speech and Style* (item 1593), discusses the characterization of the King of Pontus, Euarchus, and Pamela. Also discusses the balance between the almost photographic and the abstract in moralized descriptions such as that of the initial shipwreck. Stresses the importance of heraldic *imprese* and of emblems, such as that involved in "Poor painters oft with silly poets join" (*OA 8*), in bringing ideas together with images. Regards the addition of nearly eighty such verbal pictures to the revised *Arcadia* as evidence of Sidney's desire to bring the romance into line with the critical "manifesto" worked out in the *Defence*. Relates such changes to his prose style, in which language is seen as the "apparel" of thought, pointing out the anti-Ciceronian and pro-Ramist implications of this view. Emphasizes the conceptual basis of Sidney's style by examining passages on tyranny and war, noting ways in which passion and disordered thought are depicted in disordered language. Contrasts these with other passages, such as that on the happy beginning of the sea voyage of Pyrocles and Musidorus in Book I, in which concord is reflected in harmonious language. Considers, finally, ways in which dialogue acts as a "verbal emblem" for states of mind in the characters, contrasting the logic of Pamela's speech in Book I with the illogic of Pyrocles's outbursts in Book III, and the righteous anger of the captive Pamela with the artful guile of her captor Cecropia. Suggests that Sidney shifted from a dominant narrator in the Old *Arcadia* to a less intrusive narrator and greater reliance on dialogue in the New because he wanted to combine thought and expression in the characters' own voices, as he had in *Astrophil and Stella*. Notes the tendency of love to magnify things seen by lovers, relating such effects to the *energeia* characteristic of their speech. Disagreeing with Rudenstine (730), traces this *energeia* to the clarity of the concepts behind language, not to the language per se. As an illustration, analyzes the concepts and the dramatic context of Pyrocles's confession of love to Musidorus in Book I, noting Sidney's ability to make the reader see the lover's own "fore-conceit," rather than the author's, as the controlling Idea behind the words. See also item 721, Astell (1192), and McCanles (1660).

1743 ROLFE, FRANKLIN PRESCOT. "The Use of Verse in Elizabethan Prose Fiction and the Traditions Which Precede It." Ph.D. diss., Harvard University, 1931.

Traces from antiquity through the Renaissance literature that mingles poetry with prose. Suggests that, by the time Sidney wrote *Arcadia*, the

Twentieth Century

tradition was "running to seed."See *Harvard University Graduate School of Arts and Sciences: Summaries of Theses*, 1931, pp. 239–42.

1744 ROSE, MARK [ALLEN]. *Heroic Love: Studies in Sidney and Spenser.* Cambridge, Mass.: Harvard University Press, 1968, pp. 1–3, 35–73, 138–40. Orig. a Ph.D. disertation, Harvard University, 1967.

Considers the genre of the classical epic and the innovation of Sidney and Spenser in adding love as a principal theme. Contrasts the follies and excesses of the heroes in the Old *Arcadia* with the more "sophisticated" view of love in the revised version of 1593. Focuses on the latter text, discussing the departure of Urania and the subsequent spread of disorder once Venus and Cupid rule in her place. Considers the debate between Pyrocles and Musidorus in Book I as a clash between humanist rationality and romantic passion. Traces the process by which the action tests both ideals and proves them naive. Contrasts the comic view of love in Book I with the tragic view in Book II, concluding that Sidney regarded the Princes' love as heroic because it entails a battle within the soul. Argues that the main characters are not Christian but Stoic, analyzing the debate between Pamela and Cecropia in Book III as the traditional one between Stoicism and Epicureanism. Suggests that all the main characters move back and forth between these two poles. Disagrees with the arguments of Danby (1495) and Davis (1499) that the scene in which Philoclea persuades Pyrocles not to commit suicide is a lesson in Christian patience. Sees it instead as an example of Pyrocles's Stoic magnanimity. Interprets the prison scene before the final trial as a further illustration of Stoic nobility. Evaluates Euarchus's final judgment as an application of legal justice without equity or mercy and therefore welcomes Basilius's subsequent pardoning of the royal lovers. Concludes that, although Sidney initially pits love against heroism, he ultimately portrays love as a higher stage in the education of his heroes. See a reply by Amos (1399).

1745 ———. "Sidney's Womanish Man." *RES*, n.s. 15 (November 1964):353–63.

Rejects the view of several modern critics that the transvestism of Pyrocles's disguise would have been accepted by Renaissance readers as a literary convention. Reviews Renaissance views of Amazons, transvestism, the proper relation between reason and passion, the contrast between true love and "bastard love," and the relation between effeminacy and the Christian doctrine of the Fall. Discusses the heraldic devices given Pyrocles: the eagle with feathers of a dove and Hercules governed by Omphale. Concludes that Musidorus's initial arguments against Pyrocles's conduct reflect Sidney's own views.

1746 ROTA, FELICINA. *L'"Arcadia" di Sidney e il teatro: Con un testo inedito.* Biblioteca di studi inglesi, 6. Bari, Italy: Adriatica Editrice, 1966, 391 pp.

Examines the use of *Arcadia* as a source for plays of the seventeenth century. In Chapter 1, describes the various versions of *Arcadia* and the literary and social contexts in which they were written. In Chapter 2, examines four plays based loosely on the general structure of *Arcadia*: the anonymous *Love's Changelings' Change* and *The Arcadian Lovers*, James Shirley's *Arcadia*, and John Day's *Isle of Gulls*. Concentrating primarily on ways in which the language of narrative is transposed into the language of the stage, finds that the first two plays best succeed in making this transition. Both deal with the love theme in *Arcadia*, the first concentrating on Sidney's satirical treatment of this theme, the second more on its "poetic quality." Shirley's play differs from the preceeding two in that he "lowers" Sidney's themes into a "more familiar, well-designed framework," which condenses various scenes into one and eliminates details. He restores to the plot some of the formal unity possessed by the Old *Arcadia*, emphasizing the love theme and the "nota sentimentale" that are characteristic of his other plays. In *The Isle of Gulls*, Day adjusts Sidney's principal intrigues to plot devices of equivocation and disguise inherited from Roman comedy, diminishing the love element and eliminating the pastoral altogether. In Chapter 3, considers plays based on particular "tales" in *Arcadia*, chiefly Beaumont and Fletcher's *Cupid's Revenge*, Henry Glapthorne's *Argalus and Parthenia*, and J.S.'s *Andromana*. Notes that Beaumont and Fletcher find in the tales of Andromana and of Erona "possibilities for analyzing guilty love affairs and intrigues," which enable them to contrast sentimental love with melodramatic death. Feels that Glapthorne and J.S. "push certain elements of the *Arcadia* to their extreme limits," creating plays without "equilibrium" and with an atmosphere that is "artificial and forced." Comparing these plays with Sidney's work, shows that he achieved a "harmony" and a "poetic tone" despite flaws in narrative design. Concludes that, although Sidney's own genius was narrative and not dramatic, his work was effectively brought to the stage by others "with a praxis to which Elizabethans were accustomed."

1747 ROWE, KENNETH THORPE. *Romantic Love and Parental Authority in Sidney's "Arcadia."* University of Michigan Contributions in

475

Twentieth Century

Modern Philology, 4. Ann Arbor: University of Michigan Press, 1947, 58 pp.

Examines Sidney's response to the Elizabethan controversy over the proper way to contract marriages. Sees in *Arcadia* a conscious balance between the claims of young lovers to choose for themselves and the authority of the parents to arrange matches. In the first section, examines treatments of the issue in sources and analogues including *Amadis de Gaule*, Heliodorus's *Aethiopica*, Achilles Tatius's *Clitophon and Leucippe*, Montemayor's *Diana*, Malory's *Morte d'Arthur*, Ariosto's *Orlando furioso*, Lyly's *Euphues*, and Castiglione's *Courtier*. Finds Sidney's sexual ethics purer than that of most of these works and his justification of parental authority unprecedented, since they all champion the free choice of lovers. In the second section, analyzes the trial scene in *Arcadia*. Reviews devices by which the author wins the reader's sympathies for the lovers and, at the same time, establishes Euarchus as an ideal governor and judge. Points out improbabilities in Philanax's sudden vengefulness but notes that Elizabethan prosecutors were similarly extreme in their rhetoric. Justifies the harshness of speech displayed by Pyrocles and Musidorus as expected rhetorical strategies in a life-and-death verbal combat. Points out contrasts between the view of marriage revealed by the lovers, who see it as a culmination of romantic love in virtuous union, and that of Euarchus, who sees it as a beginning of childbearing and social responsibility from which love may grow. Takes Brie (1202) and Myrick (1691) to task for "rationalizing" Sidney's ethics by supporting Euarchus against the Princes. Argues that Sidney presents them all as ideals of virtue and does nothing to resolve the ethical confusion bred by their opposition. Concedes, however, that divine providence seems to favor the position of the lovers. Concludes that Sidney intended to create, not a coherent philosophical system, but an accurate reflection of the confused social situation of his age. In the third and fourth sections, finds precedents for the character and position of Euarchus in Xenophon's *Cyropaedia*, Cicero's *De Officiis*, Aristotle's *Nicomachean Ethics*, Elyot's *Governor*, Ascham's *Schoolmaster*, and Vives's *Instruction of a Christian Woman*. Finds the view of Sidney's lovers expressed in Lyly's *Euphues* and the plays of Shakespeare. Also examines actual marriage practices in the Elizabethan aristocracy and in Sidney's own experience. Concludes that Sidney saw the "virtue and beauty" possible in both forms of marriage. See a reply by Anderson (1402).

1748 SAFFIN, JOHN. *John Saffin His Book (1665–1708): A Collection of Various Matters of Divinity, Law & State Affairs Epitomiz'd Both in*

Verse and Prose. Edited by Caroline Hazard. New York: Harbor Press, 1928, pp. 148–50, 155–58.

Includes seventy-one quotations from *Arcadia* in Saffin's private miscellany. See Coffee (1469).

1749 SAMMUT, ALFONSO. *La Fortuna dell'Ariosto nell'Inghilterra elisabettiana*. Milan: Vita e Pensiero, 1971, pp. 17, 21, 23, 132–34.

Citing Townsend (1304), notes Sidney's debt to Ariosto for matters of narrative technique, phraseology, insertion of apparently irrelevant episodes, parallel characters, and other devices in *Arcadia*.

1750 SANDYS, JOHN EDWIN. *Harvard Lectures on the Revival of Learning*. Cambridge: Cambridge University Press, 1905, p. 107.

Discusses the background of the bear that attacks the royal party in Book II, pointing out that "Arcadia" means "land of the bears." Cites sources to show that the beasts actually inhabited the region.

1751 SARGEAUNT, M[ARGARET] JOAN. *John Ford*. Oxford: Basil Blackwell, 1935, pp. 111–12.

Argues, *pace* Sherman (753), that there are no parallels between the plot line of Ford's play *The Broken Heart* and Sidney's connection with Lady Rich. Notes parallels in setting between that play and *Arcadia* and between the subplot of Ford's *Love's Sacrifice* and the actions of Pamphilus in Sidney's romance.

1752 SATIN, JOSEPH, ed. Headnote. In *Shakespeare and His Sources*. Boston: Houghton Mifflin Co., 1966, pp. 446–47.

Discusses the influence of the story of the Paphlagonian King on *King Lear*, focusing on the storm, the characters, and the final scene of death.

1753 SAVAGE, JAMES E. "Beaumont and Fletcher's *Philaster* and Sidney's *Arcadia*." *ELH* 14 (September 1947):194–206.

Argues that materials in *Philaster* first attributed to the influence of Montemayor's *Diana* actually derive from *Arcadia*, with Beaumont and Fletcher's earlier play *Cupid's Revenge* as an intermediary. Discusses stock characters present in both plays and the influence on these of Sidney's stories of Erona and Antiphilus, Plangus and Andromana.

1754 ———. "Notes on *A Midsummer Night's Dream*." *UMSE* 2 (1961):65–78.

Discusses Sidney's description of Kalander's hunt in Book I, arguing that it influenced Shakespeare's *A Midsummer Night's Dream* IV.i. Suggests that the bear in the latter passage may derive from Sidney's episode of the lion and the bear.

Twentieth Century

1755 SCANLON, PATRICK McRAE. "Sir Philip Sidney's *Arcadia* (1590): Emblematic Narrative and the Evolution of Sidney's Style." Ph.D. diss., University of Rochester, 1984, 158 pp.
Argues that Sidney employs several emblematic devices—*imprese*, "symbolic livery," emblems, and emblematic scenes and tales—to "externalize character and emotion" and to "lend an objective reality to conflicts and themes." As *Arcadia* progresses, Sidney uses "more elaborately emblematic subplots to represent the effects of passion to family, community and state." In Book III, he "seems to be moving beyond his emblematic narrative method to a style closer to that of the novel." See *DAI* 45 (December 1984):1761A–62A.

1756 SCANLON, P[AUL] A. "Elizabethan Prose Romance." Ph.D. diss., Trinity College, Dublin, 1966.
Abstract not available. Cited as item 365 in *Index to Theses Accepted for Higher Degrees in the Universities of Great Britain and Ireland* 17 (1966–67).

1757 SCHIPPER, J[AKOB]. *James Shirley: Sein Leben und seine Werke, nebst einer Übersetzung seines Dramas "The Royal Master."* Vienna and Leipzig: Wilhelm Braumüller, 1911, pp. 67–75.
Discusses Shirley's close adherence to the main plot of Sidney's romance in the play *Arcadia*.

1758 SCHLAUCH, MARGARET. *Antecedents of the English Novel, 1400–1600 (from Chaucer to Deloney)*. Warsaw: Polish Scientific Publishers; London: Oxford University Press, 1963, pp. 176–85.
Discusses the mingled generic tradition behind the New *Arcadia* and the influence of Heliodorus's *Aethiopica* and Montemayor's *Diana*. Points out faults in structure, probability, and style but notes Sidney's facility with colloquial speech and folktale motifs as well as with the mannered style and concerns of the aristocracy. Comments on the mingling of medieval codes of conduct and "type" characters with Renaissance Platonism, and finds the key to the structure of the book in themes of private passion and public responsibility.

1759 SCHNEIDER, PAUL STEPHEN. "The Labyrinth of Love: A Reading of Sir Philip Sidney's *New Arcadia*." Ph.D. diss., University of Wisconsin at Madison, 1973, 292 pp.
Examines the psychological realism and the complex structure of the work. Takes the opening chapter as a model of behavior for the rest of the romance, discussing the backgrounds of Sidney's neo-Platonism and his views on the role of selfless love in reordering the fallen world. Takes the story of Argalus and Parthenia in Book I as a paradigm of selfless

love and examines the role of such love in reordering personal and political relationships in Book II. Points out the destructive selfishness of various characters in Book III. Concludes that the young couples of the main plot learn "to distinguish between true love and self-love, and this will allow them to restore order." See *DAI* 35 (July 1974):416A.

1760 SCOULAR, KITTY W. *Natural Magic: Studies in the Presentation of Nature in English Poetry from Spenser to Marvell.* Oxford: Clarendon Press, 1965, pp. 24, 32, 97, 189.

Touches on Sidney's descriptions of nature, particularly in *Arcadia*. Considers his use of clothing to express the character or function of the wearer, his interest in oxymoron and paradox, and his use of "as if" and "it seems" in describing natural settings.

1761 SCRIBNER, SIMON. *Figures of Word-Repetition in the First Book of Sir Philip Sidney's "Arcadia."* Washington, D.C.: Catholic University of America Press, 1948, 141 pp.

Sets out "to make a systematic and complete survey of the figures of word-repetition" employed by Sidney. Draws on the *Defence* to define the purpose and nature of *Arcadia* and then on sixteenth-century rhetorical treatises to understand the general function of word-repetitions. Analyzes the nature and extent of various "forms of composition" in *Arcadia*, such as narration, description, and exposition, and considers different "voices," including those of the narrator and of his characters. Classifies the figures of word-repetition and discusses their use in all the various "forms of composition" and "voices" in the book. Concludes that the more complex and impressive word-repetitions commonly associated with the Arcadian style actually comprise only twenty percent of the total. Finds that the figures are usually functional rather than merely ornamental and that they are used according to "definite theoretical convictions and critical principles."

1762 SHAPAZIAN, ROBERT MICHAEL. "Sidney's *Arcadia*: The Metaphorics of Artificiality." Ph.D. diss., Harvard University, 1970, 245 pp.

Examines the conscious artificiality of *Arcadia*, considering its background in Renaissance rhetorical theory and in Sidney's own critical views, as expressed in the *Defence*. Suggests that "artifice is associated with the Ideal and man's quest for it" and that "in its imitative 'falseness,' artifice also reflects the limited nature of the human condition."

Twentieth Century

1763 SHERIDAN, RICHARD BRINSLEY. *The Letters of Richard Brinsley Sheridan*. Edited by Cecil Price. Vol. 1. Oxford: Clarendon Press, 1966, pp. 59–63.
In a letter to Thomas Grenville dated 30 October 1772, recommends *Arcadia* for its ideal portrayals of love and friendship.

1764 SHURGOT, MICHAEL WILLIAM. "Characterization in Elizabethan Comedy: Theory and Practice." Ph.D. diss., University of Wisconsin at Madison, 1977, 213 pp.
Considers Sidney among the novelists who anticipated the romantic comedies of John Lyly, Robert Greene, and Shakespeare. Argues that, whereas classical comedy is based on distinctions of age and class, the comedy of *Arcadia* is based on Renaissance theories of love and the passions. See *DAI* 38 (June 1978):7350A.

1765 SICHEL, WALTER [SYDNEY]. *Sheridan*. Vol. 1. New York: Houghton Mifflin; London: Constable & Co., 1909, pp. 95, 403.
Comments on the influence of *Arcadia* on Sheridan.

1766 SINNING, HEINRICH. *"Cupid's Revenge" von Beaumont und Fletcher und Sidney's "Arcadia."* Halle, Germany: n.p., 1905, 74 pp. Orig. a Ph.D. diss., Friedrichs-Universität zu Halle-Wittenberg.
Details borrowings from Sidney's stories of Erona and Antiphilus, Plangus and Andromana, as they inform *Cupid's Revenge*. Compares the play with its source, scene by scene.

1767 SKRETKOWICZ, VICTOR, [Jr.]. "Symbolic Architecture in Sidney's New *Arcadia*." *RES*, n.s. 33 (May 1982):175–80.
Suggests that Sidney's description of Basilius's star-shaped retreat in the revised *Arcadia* is based on a hunting lodge and garden designed and built by Archduke Ferdinand of Tirol, which is described by Fynes Moryson in *An Itinerary*. During one of Sidney's two diplomatic missions to Prague, he may actually have seen the complex, which was "built with six corners in the form of a star" and called "Stella."

1768 SMART, JOHN S. "Milton and the King's Prayer." *RES* 1 (October 1925):385–91.
Exonerates Milton from the charge that he inserted Pamela's prayer in captivity into Charles I's prayer book, *Eikon Basilike*. Also refutes Milton's view that the prayer is heathen, pointing out that variants in Charles I's text give it "a definitely Christian character." See also Milton (1323) and Liljegren (1649).

1769 SMITH, HALLETT [DARIUS]. "Shakespeare's Romances." *HLQ* 27 (May 1964):279–87.

Suggests that Shakespeare first turned to the techniques of his late romances while adapting material from *Arcadia* for *King Lear*.

1770 SMITH, RICHARD HORTON. "Paměa, Pamēla." *N&Q*, 9th ser. 12 (22 August 1903):141.

Thinks Sidney the first to have used the name in literature. Notes metrical evidence that Alexander Pope pronounced it with a stressed, long *e*, whereas Samuel Richardson pronounced it with a short *e* and stressed the first syllable. Argues that Richardson's pronunciation then became the accepted norm. The article brought a lengthy series of responses, which offer further evidence of the common pronunciation of the name in English, Latin, and French, particularly in the eighteenth century. See the following replies: W.F Prideaux (9th ser. 12 [24 October 1903]:330); Richard Horton Smith, Samuel Gregory Ould, and John Pickford (10th ser. 1 [16 January 1904]:52); Robert Pierpoint (10th ser. 1 [13 February 1904]:135–36); G. Krueger (10th ser. 1 [28 May 1904]:433–34); L.L.K (10th ser. 1 [18 June 1904]:495–96); Richard Horton Smith (10th ser. 2 [16 July 1904]:50–52); and Austin Dobson (10th ser. 2 [30 July 1904]:89–90).

1771 STADLER, ULRICH. *Der einsame Ort: Studien zur Weltabkehr im heroischen Roman*. Basler Studien zur deutschen Sprache und Literatur, 43. Bern, Switzerland: Francke Verlag, 1971, pp. 89–105.

In an appendix, "Grimmelshausen und die *Arcadia* Philip Sidneys," notes borrowings from the romance in the works of Hans Jakob Christoffel von Grimmelshausen. Focuses on the Battle of Wittstock in *Simplicissimus*, printing it beside the appropriate passage in the German translation of *Arcadia* (37). Compares Sidney's realistic descriptions with those in other romances of the period.

1772 STEVENSON, LIONEL. *The English Novel: A Panorama*. Boston: Houghton Mifflin Co.; Cambridge, Mass.: Riverside Press, 1960, pp. 17–21, 32, 91, 493.

Provides basic information on *Arcadia*, summarizing its influence on Robert Greene, Thomas Lodge, and John Barclay. Relates Sidney's views on poems in prose to Henry Fielding's classification of *Joseph Andrews* as a comic epic.

Twentieth Century

1773 STILLINGER, JACK, ed. *Anthony Munday's "Zelauto: The Fountaine of Fame," 1580.* Carbondale: Southern Illinois University Press, 1963, pp. xvi, xvii.
Notes that Munday is the first Elizabethan novelist to use romance themes and incidents that later become prominent in Sidney's *Arcadia*. Draws several comparisons between *Arcadia* and *Zelauto*, including their use of pastoral motifs and of chapter divisions.

1774 STUMP, DONALD V[an GUILDER]. "Greek and Shakespearean Tragedy: Four Indirect Routes from Athens to London." In *"Hamartia": The Concept of Error in the Western Tradition: Essays in Honor of John M. Crossett*, edited by Donald V. Stump, J.A. Arieti, Lloyd Gerson, and Eleonore Stump. Texts and Studies in Religion, 16. New York: Edwin Mellen Press, 1983, pp. 211–46.
Identifies *Arcadia* as one of several sources used by Shakespeare that might have taught him the form of Greek tragic plot recommended in Aristotle's *Poetics*. Discusses Sidney's knowledge of the treatise and of literary works written in imitation of Greek tragedy. Explicates the story of Helen, examining Sidney's use of stage metaphors, the nature of his characters, the role of the gods, and the design of the plot. Concludes that Aristotelian critical terms have proved useful in analyzing Shakespearean tragedy because the playwright was influenced by works such as *Arcadia* that owe indirect debts to Greek tragedy.

1775 ———. "Sidney's Concept of Tragedy and the Function of *Hamartia* in the *Arcadia*." Ph.D. diss., Cornell University, 1978, 332 pp.
Examines lines of plot in the 1593 *Arcadia* that were apparently designed to remind the reader of stage tragedies. Reviews evidence that Renaissance authors and critics linked the genres of tragedy and epic and compares the concept of tragedy in the *Defence* with that implicit in *Arcadia*. Argues that, although Sidney's wording in the *Defence* suggests a quasi-medieval definition of tragedy, the plot lines in *Arcadia* are essentially Aristotelian. Examines possible sources of Sidney's concept in critical treatises by Aristotle, Antonio Minturno, Lodovico Castelvetro, and J.C. Scaliger and in literary works by Euripides, Heliodorus, Seneca, George Buchanan, Sackville and Norton, and George Whetstone. Analyzes the main plot of *Arcadia* as a neoclassical tragedy that turns on Basilius's error (or *hamartia*) in seeking to avoid the oracle. Also details ways in which Sidney's tragic plot lines anticipate the form of Shakespearean tragedy. See *DAI* 38 (June 1978):7351A–52A.

Twentieth Century

1776 SYFORD, CONSTANCE MIRIAM. "The Direct Source of the Pamela-Cecropia Episode in the *Arcadia.*" *PMLA* 49 (June 1934):472–89.

Notes the passage in the *Defence* linking Plutarch with the thought that the superstitious poets of antiquity were to be preferred to the philosophers, "who shaking off superstition brought in atheism." Locates similar notions in Plutarch's *Moralia*, particularly in "Of Isis and Osiris" and "On Superstition." Finds throughout the *Moralia* close parallels to the debate in *Arcadia* III.10, particularly to Cecropia's rejection of Pamela's "divinity" as mere superstition, Pamela's arguments on the roles of chance and Nature in the Creation, and her final praise of the Creator.

1777 SYKES, H[ENRY] DUGDALE. *Sidelights on Elizabethan Drama: A Series of Studies Dealing with the Authorship of Sixteenth and Seventeenth Century Plays.* London: Oxford University Press, Humphrey Milford, 1924, pp. 131, 142–43, 146, 154, 165, 168, 217.

Notes frequent borrowing from *Arcadia* in the plays of Webster, particularly *The Duchess of Malfi* and *The Devil's Law Case.* From allusions to *Arcadia* and other evidence, infers that Webster had a hand in anonymous plays such as *Appius and Virginia* and *The Fair Maid of the Inn* and in Thomas Middleton's *Anything for a Quiet Life.*

1778 ———. *Sidelights on Shakespeare.* Stratford-upon-Avon: Shakespeare Head Press, 1919, pp. 98, 174–76, 186, 196–97.

Notes that Pyrocles's speech to Philoclea in Book II of *Arcadia* is used in *A Yorkshire Tragedy.* Indicates major borrowings from *Arcadia* in Shakespeare's *Pericles.*

1779 SZYROCKI, MARIAN. *Martin Opitz.* Neue Beiträge zur Literaturwissenschaft, 4. Berlin: Verlag Rütten & Loening, 1956, p. 92. Rev. ed. Munich: Verlag C.H. Beck, 1974, p. 117.

Discusses Opitz's revisions (37) of the German translation of *Arcadia* published in 1629 by Valentinus Theocritus von Hirschberg (34).

1780 TALBERT, ERNEST WILLIAM. *The Problem of Order: Elizabethan Political Commonplaces and an Example of Shakespeare's Art.* Chapel Hill: University of North Carolina Press, 1962, pp. 89–117.

In "Sir Philip Sidney," discusses *Arcadia* in its political context, noting Sidney's heritage of Christian Aristotelianism, and pointing out his connections with George Buchanan, Hubert Languet, and others with "radical" political and religious views. Notes that, in *Arcadia*, difficulties are resolved by "sound discipline" based on "good parts acquired by gentle

Twentieth Century

blood." Views Sidney's political attitudes as consonant with those of such contemporaries as Richard Hooker.

1781 TAYLOR, A.B. "A Note on Ovid in *Arcadia*." *N&Q*, n.s. 16 (December 1969):455.
Suggests that, when Sidney compares Philoclea with Arethusa at the end of Book I of the New *Arcadia*, he is inadvertently drawing on Ovid's description of Daphne.

1782 TEAHAN, JAMES THOMAS. "The Graeco-Italian Pastoral and Its Imitations in English Renaissance Literature." Ph.D diss., University of Florida, 1977, 252 pp.
Considers the *Arcadia* in a historical survey of pastoral literature. See *DAI* 38 (MAY 1978):6703A–4A.

1783 TEETS, BRUCE E. "Two Faces of Style in Renaissance Prose Fiction." In *Sweet Smoke of Rhetoric: a Collection of Renaissance Essays*, edited by Natalie Grimes Lawrence and J.A. Reynolds. University of Miami Publications in English and American Literature, 7. Coral Gables, Fla.: University of Miami Press, 1964, pp. 69–81.
Differentiates Sidney's style from that of John Lyly, and contrasts both with "more realistic" Elizabethan prose.

1784 THOMPSON, ANN. "Jailers' Daughters in *The Arcadia* and *The Two Noble Kinsmen*." *N&Q*, n.s. 26 (April 1979):140–41.
Suggests that the scene with Mopsa in the tree (*Arcadia* IV.i) was in John Fletcher's mind when he wrote of the jailer's daughter in *Two Noble Kinsmen* V.ii.

1785 THRASHER-SMITH, SHELLEY. *The Luminous Globe: Methods of Characterization in Sidney's "New Arcadia."* Salzburg Studies in English Literature: Elizabethan and Renaissance Studies, 94. Salzburg: Institut für Anglistik und Amerikanistik, Universität Salzburg, 1982, 241 pp. Orig. a Ph.D. diss., University of Houston, 1980.
Defends Sidney's female characters from the charge that they are representatives of ideals and lack depth. In Chapter 1, reviews scholarly commentary on the subject and considers the role of characterization in Sidney's larger aims to teach and delight. Examines three "structural devices" employed in depicting his women: descriptive portraits, which act as "speaking pictures" and advance the action; two-part narrations, which build curiosity about minor characters in the episodes and often

contrast the ideal with the real; and delayed dramatic presentations, which build suspense about the main characters and lend them credibility. In Chapter 2, examines paired characters, noting ways in which their style of speech reveals their inner natures. Sees Helen as a contrast to Cecropia and Miso as a mirror for Gynecia. Also traces the tradition behind Miso's demonic portrait of Cupid, treating it as a comment on the Queen's debased love of Pyrocles. Contrasts Mopsa and Urania with Pamela, then Pamela with Philoclea. In Chapter 3, discusses Sidney's use of dialogue, monologue, and soliloquy, finding them unusual in the period because they are restricted to key points in the action, are integral to the characterization, and follow the structures of formal oratory only as the occasion demands. Analyzes the rhetoric of Cecropia, seeing it as an extension of her Machiavellian politics. Notes that most of the soliloquies occur in Book II and are reserved for the most guilt-ridden of the female characters, Cecropia and Philoclea. In Book III, soliloquy gives way to monologue addressed to another party. Also examines the effect on characterization of poems, songs, and prayers, noting that the first is reserved almost exclusively for men and the last for women. Analyzes Sidney's use of classical tropes and figures, seeing in his style foreshadowings of the achievements of the great Elizabethan dramatists. In Chapter 4, considers Sidney's skill in characterizing his women through the stories that they tell, hear, or have told about them. Details devices by which this is accomplished, such as differences in style and rhetoric and the incorporation of narrative asides, multiple narrators, character sketches, love complaints, letters, and dreams. Gives special attention to the stories told in Book II, noting that Gynecia and Cecropia are too isolated to take part. Concludes that Sidney gave to his characters much of the task of narration so that he could reveal their natures and avoid moralizing in his own voice. In Chapter 5, concentrates on methods of characterization in passages narrated by Sidney himself. Following definitions in the *Defence*, treats such passages in Books I and II as comic and those in Book III as tragic. Notes more dialogue in I and II than in III, where action predominates. Also considers Sidney's use of exposition and description, focusing on the role of metaphors, mythological allusions, and personifications. Finds more nature imagery applied to Philoclea than to Pamela and surmises that the sparsity of classical allusions in their speech is meant to suggest a Christian outlook. In Chapter 6, considers references to contemporary social and intellectual life that lend verisimilitude to the characters. Links Philoclea with Penelope Rich, Parthenia with Sidney's mother, Argalus with his father, Cecropia with Catharine de Medici, and Helen

Twentieth Century

and Andromana with Queen Elizabeth. Also considers references to the common pastimes of Elizabethan women, to the medical practices of the period, and to the Accession Day Tilts. Notes that Sidney differentiates his characters according to the geographical regions from which they come. Also takes up references to faculty psychology, Calvinist theology, neo-Platonic philosophy, literary theory, and Renaissance feminism. In the conclusion, notes ways in which Sidney's techniques of characterization anticipate developments in later works of prose fiction.

1786 TIEJE, ARTHUR JERROLD. *The Theory of Characterization in Prose Fiction Prior to 1740.* University of Minnesota Studies in Language and Literature, 5. Bulletin of the University of Minnesota, December 1916. Minneapolis: [University of Minnesota,] 1916, pp. 6–7, 9, 11, 43–44, 83.
Contrasts the characterization in the anonymous romance *Palmerin of England* with more advanced techniques in *Arcadia*, particularly the individuation of minor characters and the contrasts between paired characters. Notes the subsequent trend in fiction away from Sidney's "ideality."

1787 TILLYARD, E[USTACE] M[ANDEVILLE] W[ETENHALL]. *The English Epic Tradition.* Warton Lecture on English Poetry. *PBA* 22 (1936):35–55. Reprint, as a pamphlet. N.p. 1936, 21 pp.
Argues that, in Renaissance criticism, *Arcadia* would be classed as an epic, and suggests that Sidney's vindication of prose poems in the *Defence* was meant to legitimize his own prose epic. Also compares Sidney's control of plot and character with that of Spenser in *The Faerie Queene*. Notes that Basilius fulfills Aristotle's requirements for a tragic hero.

1788 ———. "Milton and Sidney's *Arcadia*." *TLS*, 6 March 1953, p. 153.
Notes an echo of the opening of *Arcadia* in *Paradise Lost* II.836–39.

1789 TING, NAI TUNG. "Studies in English Prose and Poetic Romances in the First Half of the Seventeenth Century." Ph.D. diss., Harvard University, 1941, 360 pp.
Examines the influence of *Arcadia* on seventeenth-century romances, particularly Thomas Gainsford's *History of Trebizond* and Lady Mary Wroth's *Urania*. See *Harvard University Graduate School of Arts and Sciences: Summaries of Theses*, 1941, 350–53.

1790 TRENEER, ANNE. *The Sea in English Literature from "Beowulf" to Donne*. Liverpool: University Press of Liverpool; London: Hodder & Stoughton, 1926, pp. 145–48.

Notes that *Arcadia* includes "the first picture of a ship destroyed by fire in English imaginative writing." Discusses Sidney's style in the two passages involving shipwrecks.

1791 TRIENENS, ROGER J[OHN]. "The Green-Eyed Monster: A Study of Sexual Jealousy in the Literature of the English Renaissance." Ph.D. diss., Northwestern University, 1951, 312 pp.

Places instances of jealousy in *Arcadia* in the contexts of the medieval fabliau and Renaissance works about amorous rivalry. See *Summaries of Doctoral Dissertations Submitted to the Graduate School of Northwestern University in Partial Fulfillment of the Requirements for the Degree of Doctor of Philosophy* 19 (June–September 1951):45–49.

1792 TURNER, MYRON [MARTIN]. "The Disfigured Face of Nature: Image and Metaphor in the Revised *Arcadia*." *ELR* 2 (Winter 1972):116–35.

Examines the relationship between metaphysical or ontological problems in *Arcadia* and the more commonly discussed ethical ones. Focuses on metaphors relating nature to a disfigured face. Explicates the neo-Platonic, Petrarchan, and Christian humanist associations in the opening description of Urania's face, juxtaposed immediately with an image of death when Musidorus's body washes ashore and then with the sight of the godlike man Pyrocles. Sees in Sidney's treatment of the naked human body the more general belief that "the beauty, order, and functionalism of the universe reflect the divine wisdom." Nonetheless, man, like nature, is disfigured. Traces similar contrasts throughout the romance. Relates them to Sidney's portrayal of faith as a way to discover "a meaningful universe despite the disfigured face of nature." Focuses on the emblem Pamela sews upon her purse in the Captivity Episode.

1793 ———. "The Heroic Ideal in Sidney's Revised *Arcadia*." *SEL* 10 (Winter 1970):63–82.

Links the characterization of Pyrocles and Musidorus with Renaissance notions of godlike heroism and Christian liberty, particularly those exemplified in Sir Thomas Elyot's *Governor*, Aristotle's *Ethics*, Cicero's *De Officiis*, Calvin's *Institutes*, and Castiglione's *Courtier*. Argues that Sidney sought to reconcile "the pride and self-sufficiency of the hero with Christian humility and dependence upon God." Contends that Pamela in captivity in Book III is the most complete example of this reconcilia-

Twentieth Century

tion. Examines her character according to neo-Platonic conceptions of temperance and Petrarchan views of the ideal mistress. Concludes that the two Princes learn to balance their early heroism with Petrarchan love and humility.

1794 ———. "Majesty in Adversity: The Moral Structure of Sidney's
   Arcadia." Ph.D. diss., University of Washington, 1965, 292 pp.
Contrasts the Renaissance critical theory that heroic poems are concerned with heroic deeds with Sidney's apparent view in the New *Arcadia* that a heroic mind is more important. Discusses the passages in which the main characters are helpless against adversity or the power of love, and explores Sidney's attempt to present an ideal of magnanimous contempt for fortune united with humble dependence upon God. Concludes that, for Sidney, the ideal ruler must be majestic, inspiring awe and even terror, and yet he must also be loving and recognize human weakness from the experience of his own fallen nature. See *DA* 26 (September 1965):1636.

1795 Van der GAAF, W. "Gill's Mopsae." *ES* 16 (April 1934):59.
In order to explain Alexander Gill's use of *"Mopsae"* in *Logonomia Anglica*, traces the pastoral name Mopsus back to Virgil and the feminine form to Sidney. Also notes that Gill provides phonetic transcriptions of passages from *Arcadia*. See also Ellis (343).

1796 van GELDER, H[ERMAN] A[REND] ENNO. *The Two*
   Reformations in the Sixteenth Century: A Study of the Religious Aspects
   and Consequences of Renaissance and Humanism. The Hague:
   Martinus Nijhoff, 1961, pp. 336–38.
Discusses Sidney's awareness of atheist teachings in his age, focusing on the reflections of Musidorus and Pyrocles on the eve of their expected execution and on the debates between Cecropia and Pamela.

1797 WALKER, D.P. "Ways of Dealing with Atheists: A Background to
   Pamela's Refutation of Cecropia." *BHR* 17 (May 1955):252–77.
In examining *Arcadia* III.10, ponders Sidney's possible reading of atheism in Cicero, Peter Ramus, John Lyly, and others. Emphasizes the importance of du Plessis-Mornay's *De la verité de la religion chrestienne.* Weighs Elizabethan claims that "atheism" was widespread and enumerates forms that such beliefs could have taken. Also examines the motives behind the many refutations of atheism in the period. Suggests that Pamela is a *prisca theologus*, that is, a pagan who has attained Christian salvation by reading the Book of Nature. Provides background on Pamela's argument for God's existence, noting the "sophistry" of her

remarks on chance and the psychological strategy that she employs against Cecropia. Concludes that Sidney was in the "liberal camp" in his belief that pagans could reach religious truth and in his Platonized theology, which may have contributed to the later flowering of the Cambridge Platonists.

1798 WALLERSTEIN, RUTH. *Studies in Seventeenth-Century Poetic.* Madison: University of Wisconsin Press, 1950, pp. 63, 169–70.

Notes the influence of the lament for the "dead" Basilius on William Drummond of Hawthornden's *Tears on the Death of Moeliades.* Discusses the use of wordplay in otherwise serious scenes of *Arcadia* and compares similar tensions in Shakespeare's *Hamlet.*

1799 WALTERS, PERCY. "The Hidden Meaning of the Title Pages of *Arcadia*, etc." *Baconiana* 29 (October 1945):159–60.

In reply to Eagle (1520), asserts that the title page includes numerous hidden codes and allusions, and concludes from them that Sir Francis Bacon wrote *Arcadia.*

1800 WATERHOUSE, GILBERT. *The Literary Relations of England and Germany in the Seventeenth Century.* Cambridge: Cambridge University Press, 1914, pp. 18–37.

In "Sidney's *Arcadia* in Germany," comments on the popularity of *Arcadia* throughout the seventeenth century, comparing in detail the 1629 translation by "Valentinus Theocritus" (34) and its 1638 revision by Opitz (37).

1801 WATSON, HAROLD FRANCIS. *The Sailor in English Fiction and Drama, 1550–1800.* New York: Columbia University Press, 1931, pp. 51–53, 66.

Points out that the portrait of Pyrocles riding a spar in the opening of the revised *Arcadia* hearkens back to Homer's *Odyssey.* Concludes that most of Sidney's sea material derives from Greek romance and has parallels in Robert Greene's *Alcida.*

1802 WATSON, SARA RUTH. "Shakespeare's Use of the *Arcadia*: An Example in *Henry V.*" *N&Q* 175 (19 November 1938):364–65.

Argues that the description of Argalus's horse in Book III was the source for the description of the Dauphin's mount in *Henry V* I.vii. Also suggests that the passage in *Arcadia* may derive from a treatise on horsemanship by Thomas Blundeville. See a reply by Morris (1686).

Twentieth Century

1803 ———. "Sidney at Bartholomew Fair." *PMLA* 53 (March 1938):125–28.
Cites Reginald Scot's *Discovery of Witchcraft* as a possible source for the beheading tricks in the Captivity Episode. Prefers, however, the explanation that Sidney saw the trick performed "by one Kingsfield of London" at Bartholomew Fair in 1582.

1804 WATT, IAN [P.]. "Elizabethan Light Reading." In *The Pelican Guide to English Literature*, edited by Boris Ford. Vol. 2, *The Age of Shakespeare*. Baltimore: Penguin Books, 1955, pp. 119–30. Reprint. *A Guide to English Literature*. The Belle Sauvage Library. Vol. 2, *The Age of Shakespeare*. London: Cassell & Co., Penguin Books, 1961, pp. 111–22. Reprint. "Elizabethan Fiction." In *The New Pelican Guide to English Literature*, edited by Boris Ford. Vol. 2, *The Age of Shakespeare*. Harmondsworth, England: Penguin Books, 1982, pp. 195–206.
Lists the sources of *Arcadia*, contrasting its Christian Platonism with the naturalism of a modern novel. Objects that the psychological realism of Sidney's characters is lost in artificialities of plot, style, and setting.

1805 ———. "The Naming of Characters in Defoe, Richardson, and Fielding." *RES* 25 (October 1949):322–38.
Offers reasons that Samuel Richardson took from *Arcadia* the name of the heroine in the novel *Pamela*.

1806 WATTERSON, WILLIAM COLLINS. "Elizabethan Pastoral Satire." Ph.D. diss., Brown University, 1976, 163 pp.
Discusses Sidney's satiric depictions of "rustic types" in *Arcadia*, treating them as part of an attempt to "revolutionize the aristocratic form of pastoral romance." Noting Sidney's familiarity with medieval pastoral complaint, argues that, in the eclogues, he "indulges in literary satire on pastoral conventions." See *DAI* 46 (March 1986):2703A–4A.

1807 WEIMANN, ROBERT. "'Appropriation' and Modern History in Renaissance Prose Narrative." *NLH* 14 (Spring 1983):459–95.
Discusses Sidney's differentiation between poetry and history and his innovation in making "the means and meanings of the fictional enterprise his own." Also examines the passage in Book II of the revised *Arcadia* in which the Princes set out on their Asian adventure. Notes that they value personal choice in a way not common in earlier epics and romances but that they fail to control the course of the action as they had intended. Relates this failure to similar ones in works by Cervantes, Shakespeare, and others.

Twentieth Century

1808 ———. "Change and Growth in Renaissance Fiction and Drama." In *Actes du VIIIe Congrès de l'Association internationale de Littérature Comparée/Proceedings of the 8th Congress of the International Comparative Literature Association.* Vol. 1, *Trois grandes mutations littéraires: Renaissance—Lumières—Début du vingtième siècle/Three Epoch-Making Literary Changes: Renaissance—Enlightenment—Early Twentieth Century,* edited by Béla Köpeczi and György M. Vajda. Stuttgart, Germany: Erich Bieber, Kunst und Wissen, 1980, pp. 53–60.

In arguing that Renaissance fiction and drama reveal "a new mode of apprehending the world," claims that *Arcadia* exhibits "new forms of correlation between action and character." A Sidneian hero "has to achieve his distinction, which is his character, deliberately and personally, not in reference to any pre-ordained standards, or to any previously expanded heroical labour, but 'by his owne choice, and working.'" Sidney's characters thus set the pattern of an action that, "since it is no longer given, assumes an unpredictable quality."

1809 ———. *Realismus in der Renaissance: Aneignung der Welt in der erzählenden Prosa.* Berlin and Weimar: Aufbau-Verlag, 1977, pp. 77, 82, 94, 141, 165.

Contrasts *Arcadia* with classical epic and medevial romance, noting that Sidney's heroes seek their adventures out of desire for personal honor and are not compelled by chance or necessity. Also considers Sidney's stance as a member of the landed aristocracy and applies his views in the *Defence* on the relation between history and poetry in order to explain his fiction.

1810 WEIS, RENÉ J.A. "*Antony and Cleopatra*: The Challenge of Fiction." *English* 32 (Spring 1983):1–14.

Examines Cleopatra's defence of her dream of Antony in V.ii of Shakespeare's play, tracing it to Sidney's *Defence*. Notes that both authors turn neo-Platonic arguments against Plato and that both presuppose an Idea or "fore-conceit" that is independent of and superior to the products of nature.

1811 WEISS, ADRIAN. "The Rhetorical Concept of *Narratio* and Narrative Structure in Elizabethan Prose Fiction." Ph.D. diss., University of Ohio, 1969, 222 pp.

Examines traditional teachings about the second part of a classical oration, the *narratio*, arguing that they "determined the very nature" of *Arcadia*. Considers methods of narration, characterization, plot develop-

Twentieth Century

ment, and description in both versions of the romance. See *DAI* 30 (December 1969):2503A–4A.

1812 WHITE, R.S. "Metamorphosis by Love in Elizabethan Romance, Romantic Comedy, and Shakespeare's Early Comedies." *RES*, n.s. 35 (February 1984):14–44.
In exploring the evolution from prose and verse romance to an "entirely new strain" of romantic comedy, examines the "hinge" of both romance and comedy, which is "the transformation of the personality effected by love between the sexes." Although by and large Elizabethan romance writers present the motif of metamorphosis as a conventional assumption about the golden world, sees Sidney as an exception. In *Arcadia*, he explores the emotions attending transformation, which "dislocates" the reason and "provokes dark pain." Although for him the consequences of love are morally questionable, love itself is "psychologically inevitable." Concludes that the energy of *Arcadia* is in "a tension between its explicit moral message and the emotional conviction of its narrative."

1813 ———. "Sidney's *Arcadia* as a Possible Source for *The Eve of St. Agnes*." *KSJ* 28 (1979):11–17.
Argues that Pyrocles's visit to Philoclea's bedroom in Book III of the 1593 *Arcadia* is a close parallel to Keats's poem in "narrative development, themes, imagery, and occasional words."

1814 WHITEFORD, ROBERT NAYLOR. *Motives in English Fiction.* New York: G.P. Putnam's Sons, 1918, pp. 35–41.
Praises *Arcadia* for prose style and plot construction. Lists works of fiction written under its influence.

1815 WHITMAN, ROBERT F. "Webster's *Duchess of Malfi*." *N&Q*, n.s. 6 (May 1959):174–75.
Cites Sidney's story of Tydeus and Telenor as the source of one of Bosola's speeches in *The Duchess of Malfi* IV.ii.

1816 WHITNEY, LOIS. "Concerning Nature in *The Countesse of Pembrokes Arcadia*." *SP* 24 (April 1927):207–22.
Examines the several definitions of the term "nature" in the 1593 *Arcadia*, concentrating on "natural" ethics. Notes Sidney's combination Christian, Stoic, Aristotelian, and neo-Platonic metaphysics, emphasizing his borrowings from Aristotle and Cicero and his weak grasp of Lucretius. Demonstrates that the characters use the term "nature" in many senses but seeks to distinguish Sidney's view from theirs. Suggests that Philoclea and Pyrocles have a beauty of soul largely bestowed by

nature without the need for education, and that Pamela and Musidorus reveal the effects of good nature strengthened by education. Also discusses the antinomianism of Basilius and Cecropia, who support their unlawful desires by appeals to "nature" rather than to reason. See also Gohn (1554).

1817 WHITTEMORE, NENA [LOUISE] THAMES. "The New Palm Tree Impresa in the New *Arcadia*." *AN&Q* 14 (September 1975):3–5.

Cites Pliny's *Natural History* and Samuel Daniel's addendum to Paulus Jovius's *Worthy Tract* to explain Argalus's *impresa* in Book III: to thrive, palm trees must be planted in pairs, male and female. Notes two other passages in *Arcadia* that refer to this point.

1818 ———. "Unity and Variety in Sir Philip Sidney's *New Arcadia* (1590)." Ph.D. diss., City University of New York, 1968, 261 pp.

Discusses the means by which Sidney attained the epic unity required by Italian critics such as Antonio Minturno and also the romantic variety advocated by Giraldi Cinthio. Considers the way in which the adventures and combats that Sidney introduced in the revised version help to bring thematic unity to the book by foreshadowing and commenting on the main plot. Also discusses the new variety of pastoral sports and the role of genealogy in uniting the large cast of characters. Points out that each book has the same structure: "it begins with a love lament, includes idle sports or pastimes, and reaches a high point in a tournament or battle." This structure emphasizes the unifying themes of the work: love and heroic action. See *DA* 29 (November 1968):1521A–22A.

1819 WILES, A[MERICUS] G[EORGE] D[AVID]. "The Date of Publication and Composition of Sir William Alexander's Supplement to Sidney's *Arcadia*." *PBSA* 50 (Fourth Quarter 1956):387–92.

Argues that Alexander's supplement was not included in editions of *Arcadia* prior to 1621. Also discusses its date of composition and casts doubt on Sommer's claim (51) that the supplement was published separately in Dublin in 1621.

1820 ———. "James Johnstoun and the *Arcadian* Style." *RenP*, 1957, pp. 72–81.

Analyzes Johnstoun's continuation of Book III of the New *Arcadia*, identifying qualities of style that it shares with Sidney's original. In the notes, covers the publication history of the continuation and problems in identifying the author.

Twentieth Century

1821 ———. "Sir William Alexander's Continuation of the Revised
Version of Sir Philip Sidney's *Arcadia*." *SSL* 3 (April 1966):
221–29.
Assesses the merit of Alexander's continuation, considering its failures in
style and its successes in plotting and characterization.

1822 WILKINS, ERNEST HATCH. "Arcadia in America." *PAPS* 101
(15 February 1957):4–30.
Sketches the role in history of the region of Greece known as Arcadia.
Discusses the influence of Sidney and Sannazaro in popularizing
"Arcadia" as a place name in the New World.

1823 WILLIAMS, GEORGE WALTON. "The Printer of the First Folio
of Sidney's *Arcadia*." *Library*, 5th ser. 12 (December 1957):274–75.
Rejects the accepted view that Thomas Creede was the printer of
Ponsonby's 1593 *Arcadia*. From ornaments in the book, proves that the
printer was John Windet.

1824 WILLIAMS, GORDON. "Humanist Responses to War: Sidney's
Contribution." *Trivium* 16 (May 1981):45–61.
Examines the growth of antiwar sentiment during the Renaissance,
focusing on *Arcadia*. Discusses the revolt of the commoners, suggesting
that Sidney's brutal humor is satiric and shows genuine concern for the
lower classes. Also discusses the tournament of Amphialus as an
antichivalric satire, in which the absurd pomp of battle contrasts unfavorably with the patience of the captive Princesses. Relates the brutality
of chivalry to the theme of rape in the incident in Book III involving
Anaxius and his brothers. Points to the influence of Machiavelli and
Rabelais on Sidney's descriptions of war and records a Saxon custom in
which a defiled maiden pricked her assailant with bodkins or pins, a
punishment meted out to Sidney's Pamphilus.

1825 ———. "Sidney's Protestant Epic." *Trivium* 14 (May 1979):
135–53.
Considers problems of morality in *Arcadia*, concluding that Sidney recognized that there are no "absolute or theoretical standards" capable of
resolving them. Discusses the complexities in Pyrocles's sexual awaken-
ing, the ambiguous associations of androgyny and disguise in the work,
the subtleties of its rhetorical figures, and the limitations of Euarchus's
final judgments.

1826 WILLIAMS, J.B. "Dr. Johnson's Accusation against Milton." *British Review* 9 (March 1915):431–40.

Examines the evidence that Charles I actually used Pamela's prayer as part of his private devotions. Finds Milton innocent of the charge that he incorporated the prayer in Charles's prayer book.

1827 WILSON, THOMAS. "Diana de Monte Mayor Done Out of Spanish by Thomas Wilson (1596)." Edited by H. Thomas. *Revue Hispanique* 50 (1920):367–418.

In the dedication to Fulke Greville, comments on Sidney's debt to Montemayor in *Arcadia*.

1828 WOLFF, SAMUEL LEE. *The Greek Romances in Elizabethan Prose Fiction*. New York: Columbia University Press, 1912, pp. 239–40, 262–366, 461–64, 470–76.

In Chapter 2, "Sir Philip Sidney," considers the dating and composition of the two versions of *Arcadia* and focuses on the text of 1593. Traces to Greek romance the initial shipwreck and the incidents in which people who scorn love become its slaves. Regards Heliodorus's *Aethiopica* as Sidney's primary source, noting his borrowing of the following major elements: Musidorus's elopement with Pamela; the Trial Scene; Pyrocles's leadership of the Helots; several incidents among the Asian adventures of Book II; the captivity of Pyrocles and Philoclea in Book III; and the episodes of the Paphlagonian King and of Erona. Traces to Achilles Tatius's *Clitophon and Leucippe* the character of Sidney's Gynecia, the aborted rescue of Pyrocles from the initial shipwreck, Plexirtus's scheme to drown the Princes after their Asian journey, the feigned executions in the Captivity Episode, and various details of the Trial Scene. Also notes the influence of *Amadis de Gaule* on the feigned double rendezvous of Pyrocles with Gynecia and Basilius in the cave. Finds much of Greek romance in Sidney's view of chance and divine providence, but little in his methods of characterization. Finds a precedent for his description of Kalander's garden in Achilles Tatius. Feels that, in revising the original *Arcadia*, Sidney heightened suspense and satisfied criteria for the plot of an epic. Finds the best precedent for his narrative method in Helidorus. Also considers Sidney's style, his use of humor, his interest in emblems and *imprese*, and his impact on seventeenth-century drama and the English novel. In Appendix B, describes the Clifford Manuscript of the Old *Arcadia*.

Twentieth Century

1829 ——. "The Sources of *Ivanhoe*." *Nation* 92 (2 February 1911):114.
Replies to MacCracken (1664), discussing Scott's use of *Arcadia* as a source.

1830 WOODBRIDGE, LINDA. *Women and the English Renaissance: Literature and the Nature of Womankind, 1540–1620*. Urbana and Chicago: University of Illinois Press, 1984, pp. 158–59.
Cites Pyrocles's Amazon disguise as an example of ambivalence toward "the softened man and the toughened woman." Concludes that both Sidney and others of his age wavered between thinking of such people as "monsters" and regarding them as "symbols of human wholeness."

1831 WOOLF, VIRGINIA. *The Common Reader, Second Series*. London: Leonard and Virginia Woolf, Hogarth Press; New York: Harcourt, Brace, & Co., 1932, pp. 40–50.
In "*The Countess of Pembroke's Arcadia*," treats the romance as an escape from "the present and its strife." Ponders the dominant impressions of the work: "beauty of scene; stateliness of movement; sweetness of sound." Feels that Sidney "leads us without any end in view but sheer delight in wandering" and pleasure in beautiful words. Notes that he occasionally observes his scenes and characters closely, like a modern novelist, but that his characters do not long behave like ordinary men and women. Complains that the narrator too often provides generalized emotions, landscapes, and long discourses rather than the pointed observations characteristic of Sidney's poems. Praises the book for its blending of "romance and realism, poetry and psychology," concluding that, "in the *Arcadia*, as in some luminous globe, all the seeds of English fiction lie latent."

1832 WRIGHT, CELESTE TURNER. "The Amazons in Elizabethan Literature." *SP* 37 (July 1940):433–56. [Certain page numbers from the April issue were duplicated in the July issue.]
Lists Sidney's references to Amazons and places his portrayal of Pyrocles in the guise of Zelmane in the context of other literary treatments of the tribe.

1833 WRIGHT, LOUIS B. *Middle-Class Culture in Elizabethan England*. Chapel Hill: University of North Carolina Press, 1935, pp. 111, 382–83.
Notes the popularity of *Arcadia*, even among people of the lower social orders.

1834 ———. "The Reading of Renaissance English Women." *SP* 28 (October 1931): (October 1931):671–88.

Demonstrates that *Arcadia* was read by middle-class women in the Renaissance by citing Wye Saltonstall's character of "A Maide" in *Picturae Loquentes*, the condemnation of *Arcadia* in Thomas Powell's *Tom of All Trades*, and its appearance in a list of books in the library of a brothel in John Johnson's *Academy of Love*.

1835 WRIGHT, THOMAS EDWARD. "The English Prose Anatomy." Ph.D. diss., University of Washington, 1963, 238 pp.

Argues that *Arcadia* was revised according to the eight rhetorical forms of the Renaissance prose anatomy: diatribe, paradoxical encomium, essay collection, character collection, debate, dialogue, letter collection, and fantastic journey. See *DA* 24 (April 1964):4181.

1836 WURMB, AGNES. *Die deutsche Uebersetzung von Sidneys Arcadia (1629 und 1638) und Opitz' Verhältnis dazu.* Hanover, Germany: Aug. Eberlein & Co., 1911, 67 pp. Orig. a Ph.D. diss., Ruprecht-Karls-Universität zu Heidelberg, 1911.

In Chapter 1, outlines *Arcadia*, reviewing its publishing history and that of its continuations. Describes the French translations of Baudoin (33) and Chappelain (32), discussing the controversy surrounding their publication and the authorship of the first volume of the one attributed to Chappelain. Finds that the German translation of Theocritus (34) was based on Chappelain, not Baudoin. Describes the revisions and reprintings of the German translations from 1638 to 1658, supplying partial title page information, descriptions of contents, and comments on variants and the location of the poems. In Chapter 2, characterizes the Chappelain translation as loose, detailing its departures from the English text. Demonstrates that the 1629 German version is "slavishly" true to it, even in matters of prosody, where Chappelain took few pains to imitate Sidney. Denies that Opitz's revisions (37) were improvements, noting that obvious errors are retained and that the changes were generally in single words or in minor matters of syntax. Finds a decrease in foreign loanwords and major changes in the style and prosody of the poems. In Chapter 3, disputes Theocritus's claim to have consulted the English text and denies that Opitz consulted either French version. Finds Opitz's translation of Beling's continuation close and accurate. Notes poems in Sidney's part that suggest Opitz's knowledge of the English originals. In Chapter 4, rejects Lindner's claim (1334) that "Valentinus Theocritus" was all along a pseudonym for Opitz. See, how-

Twentieth Century

ever, further evidence by Dünnhaupt (1519). Also argues that a third, anonymous translator rather than Opitz was responsible for the translation of Beling's continuation.

1837 YOUNG, DAVID. *The Heart's Forest: A Study of Shakespeare's Pastoral Plays.* New Haven, Conn., and London: Yale University Press, 1972, pp. 17–22, 75, 77, 80, 115.

Treats *Arcadia* as an illustration of developments in pastoral romance that allowed the genre to be adapted for the stage. Discusses the royal sojourn in the countryside as a way to mingle social classes, to open opportunities for plotting, to establish an urbane point of view, and to bring changes in the characters and their society that prepare for a return to court. Also considers Sidney's use of natural settings and his attitude toward patterns of causation involving human error, fortune, and divine providence. Compares the work with Robert Greene's *Pandosto* and *Menaphon* and Shakespeare's *King Lear*. Regards Sidney's incident of the lion and the bear in Book I as a source for the attack of the bear in *The Winter's Tale*.

1838 ZANDVOORT, R[EINARD] W[ILLEM]. "Brutus's Forum Speech in *Julius Caesar*." *RES* 16 (January 1940):62–66. Reprint. In *Collected Papers: A Selection of Notes and Articles Originally Published in "English Studies" and Other Journals*, by R[einard] W. Zandvoort. Groningen Studies in English, 5. Groningen, Netherlands: J.B. Wolters, 1954, pp. 58–61.

Contrasts the euphuistic style of Brutus's funeral oration with the Arcadian style of Antony's speech. Notes other instances of the Arcadian style in *The Merchant of Venice* and in *Romeo and Juliet*.

1839 ———. "Fair Portia's Counterfeit." *Rivista di letterature moderne*, n.s. 2 (September 1951):351–56. Reprint. In *Collected Papers: A Selection of Notes and Articles Originally Published in "English Studies" and Other Journals*, by R[einard] W. Zandvoort. Groningen Studies in English, 5. Groningen, Netherlands: J.B. Wolters, 1954, pp. 50–57. Reprint. In *Atti del V congresso internazionale di lingue e letterature moderne nei loro rapporti con le belle arti*. Florence, 27–31 March 1951. Florence: Valmartina, 1955.

Compares descriptions of works of art in *Arcadia* and in works by Shakespeare. Rejects scholarly opinion that the authors studied contemporary paintings, noting that all the descriptions follow similar rhetorical patterns and praise "deceptive realism" as the ideal. Discusses the conventions in painting that Sidney was following, tracing them from antiquity through the nineteenth century.

1840 ———. "What Is Euphuism?" In *Mélanges de linguistique et philolo-gie: Fernand Mossé in memoriam*. Paris: Didier, 1959, pp. 508–17. Reprint. In *Collected Papers II: Articles in English Published between 1955 and 1970*, by R[einard] W. Zandvoort. Groningen Studies in English, 10. Groningen, Netherlands: Wolters-Noordhoff, 1970, pp. 12–21.

Details differences between the Arcadian and the euphuistic styles, pointing out that Sidney's prose is hardly uniform and often illustrates the characteristics found in Lyly's more uniform work. Also surveys previous scholarship and popular handbooks of literature for their definitions of the two styles.

1841 ZSCHAU, WALTHER WOLFGANG. *Quellen und Vorbilder in den "Lehrreichen Schiften" Johann Balthasar Schupps*. Halle, Germany: Druck von Ehrhardt Karras, 1906, pp. 92–93. Orig. a Ph.D. diss., Vereinigten Friedrichs-Universität zu Halle-Wittenberg, 1905.

Argues that the sixteenth-century German author Schupps was familiar with Sidney's *Arcadia*.

Studies of the Poetry

1. GENERAL

Seventeenth Century

1842 H[OWELL], J[AMES]. *Cottoni Posthuma: Divers Choice Pieces of that Renowned Antiquary Sir Robert Cotton, Knight and Baronet, Preserved from the Injury of Time, and Exposed to Public Light, for the Benefit of Posterity*. London: by Francis Leach for Henry Seile, 1651, item 13.
Wrongly attributes the poem "Faint Amorist" to Sidney. See p. 350 in Ringler (92).

Nineteenth Century

1843 BOWEN, MARY. "Some New Notes on Sidney's Poems." *MLN* 10 (April 1895):cols. 236–46.
Notes that the earliest printed texts of Sidney's poetry were Byrd's settings of "O you that hear this voice" and "O dear life, when shall it be" (*AS vi* and *x*) in his 1588 *Psalms, Sonnets, and Songs* (59). Discusses Bodleian Rawlinson MS. Poet. 85, which includes twenty-two poems by Sidney, including eight from *Arcadia*, nine from *Certain Sonnets*, three from *Astrophil and Stella*, and two others. Suggests that songs from *Astrophil and Stella* may have circulated alone in manuscript. Attributes to Sidney the poem "At my heart there is a pain," (*AT 5*). Suggests that several poems attributed to Nicholas Breton may indeed belong to Sidney, a viewpoint that is challenged by Ringler (92, 1941).

500

1844 COX, F[REDERICK] A[RTHUR], ed. *English Madrigals in the Time of Shakespeare*. The Lyric Poets. London: J.M. Dent & Co., 1899, pp. 13, 93, 105, 115, 117, 123, 148.
Notes that "In a grove most rich of shade" (*AS viii*), "Go my flocke, go get you hence" (*AS ix*), "Come shepheard's weedes" (*OA 4*), "O sweet woods the delight of solitarines" (*OA 34*), and "My true love hath my hart" (*OA 45*) were all set as madrigals between 1588 and 1624. Includes madrigal settings of Sidney's poems from a number of songbooks printed during this period.

1845 HEWLETT, HENRY G. "Poets of Society: Prior; Praed; Locker." *The Contemporary Review* 20 (July 1872):238–68.
Calls Sidney a poet of "pure emotion and sentiment"; his appeal is "mainly to the immortal elements of human consciousness, which are independent of time and space."

1846 HUNT, LEIGH. "An Essay on the Cultivation, History, and Varieties of the Species of Poem Called the Sonnet." In *The Book of the Sonnet*, edited by Leigh Hunt and Samuel Adams Lee. Vol. 1. London: Samson Low, Son, & Marston, 1867, pp. 40, 69.
Praises the verse in *Arcadia*, but finds fault with the poem "Virtue, beauty, and speech" (*OA 60*). Notes the Italian influence on Sidney's sonnets.

1847 MAIN, DAVID M. *A Treasury of English Sonnets*. New York: Worthington Co., 1889, pp. 14–18, 251–58.
Prints several of Sidney's sonnets. In the notes, defends *Astrophil and Stella* from its nineteenth-century detractors. Suggests that a sonnet by Wordsworth and Shelley's fragment "To the Moon" owe debts to Sidney's "With how sad steps, O moon" (*AS 31*). Also notes borrowings from "Since nature's works be good" (*OA 77*) in William Drummond of Hawthornden's *Cypress Grove*.

1848 MAYER, S.R. TOWNSHEND. "Westminster Abbey." *N&Q*, 5th ser. 7 (20 January 1877):48.
Questions Sidney's authorship of an unfinished forty-stanza poem on Mary Magdalene printed in the February 1869 issue of *Westminster Abbey; or, Reminiscences of Past Literature*. According to p. 352 in Ringler (92), "the only recorded file of that periodical . . . was destroyed in World War II."

Nineteenth Century

1849 NOBLE, J[AMES] ASHCROFT. *The Sonnet in England and other Essays*. London: Elkin Matthews & John Lane, 1893, pp. 3, 18, 19–21.

Compares Sidney with the courtly versifiers of the period, noting that his sonnets are unusually humane, natural, and spontaneous.

1850 SCHIPPER, J[AKOB]. *Englische Metrik in historischer und systematischer Entwickelung dargestellt*. Part 2, *Neuenglische Metrik*. 2 vols. Bonn: Verlag von Emil Strauss, 1888, passim.

Provides extensive technical information on meters and forms used by Sidney, analyzing individual poems and comparing them with examples by other poets.

1851 ———. *Grundriss der englischen Metrik*. Wiener Beiträge zur englischen Philologie, 2. Vienna and Leipzig: Wilhelm Braumüller, 1895, pp. 258, 261–62, 307, 335, 366, 375, 382–85, 387.

Analyzes various meters and forms in Sidney's verse.

1852 STONE, WILLIAM JOHNSON. *On the Use of Classical Metres in English*. London: Henry Frowde, 1899, pp. 11–12.

In surveying "stumbling blocks" that prevented the proper use of classical meters in English, condemns Sidney for his "perversion of natural rules," denying that his principles came from Gabriel Harvey.

1853 SYMONDS, J[OHN] A[DDINGTON]. "The Debt of English to Italian Literature." *Fortnightly Review*, n.s. 17 (March 1875): 371–81.

Argues that Sidney's familarity with Italian literature enabled him to perceive greater possibilities for complexity and interweaving of rhyme than some of his contemporaries.

1854 ———. Review of *The Complete Poems of Sir Philip Sidney*, edited by Alexander Grosart. *Academy* 5 (20 June 1874):681–82.

In reviewing Grosart (69), discusses Sidney's adapatation of metrical schemes from classical and Italian Renaissance poetry, noting examples in *Arcadia* and *Astrophil and Stella*.

1855 WARD, MARY A. "Sir Philip Sidney." In *The English Poets*, edited by Thomas Humphrey Ward. Vol. 1, *Chaucer to Donne*. London and New York: Macmillan Co., 1890, pp. 341–47.

Stresses the impact of Sidney as a poet and critic on the writers of the sixteenth and seventeenth centuries, faulting the eighteenth century for ignoring Sidney's works. Reads *Astrophil and Stella* biographically, distinguishing three stages of development: "impetuous passion," "a period of

. . . joy," and "a period of widening separation." Rejects the practice of printing *Certain Sonnets* 31 and 32 as a conclusion to the sequence. Views Sidney's classical experiments as a blemish and dismisses the poetry of *Arcadia*.

Twentieth Century

1856 ALDEN, RAYMOND MacDONALD, ed. *English Verse: Specimens Illustrating Its Principles and History*. New York: Henry Holt & Co., 1903, pp. 330–33.
Offers representative samples of English prosody from *Astrophil and Stella* and *Arcadia*. Discusses the use of classical measures by Sidney, Harvey, and Spenser.

1857 ALDEN, RAYMOND MacDONALD. *Shakespeare*. Master Spirits of Literature Series. New York: Duffield & Co., 1922, pp. 125–26, 128.
Notes Sidney's influence on Shakespeare, particularly in sonnet imagery and in Italian forms of prosody.

1858 ALONSO, DÁMASO. "Poesia correlativa inglesa en los siglos XVI y XVII." *Filología moderna* 1 (February 1961):1–47.
In providing a theory of "correlative poetry" ("conjuntos semejantes") and in surveying its occurrences among English poets from Wyatt to Milton, illustrates the first of three "kinds" of parallel structure by citing "Vertue, beauty, and speech" (*OA 60*). Lists other examples in *Astrophil and Stella*.

1859 ANON. "Sir Philip Sidney." *TLS*, 16 June 1910, p. 213. Reprint. In *Living Age*, 7th ser. 48 (6 August 1910):374–78.
In reviewing Drinkwater's edition of Sidney's poems (78), discusses the poet's place in the development of English verse, his mingling of fact and ideal in Stella, and his use of English in its modern form.

1860 APPLEGATE, JAMES. "Sidney's Classical Meters." *MLN* 70 (April 1955):254–55.
Lists Sidney's experiments in classical prosody in *Certain Sonnets* and *Arcadia*, naming the meters and pointing out that most are from Horace and Catullus. Corrects the errors of earlier scholars.

Twentieth Century

1861 BAILEY, JOHN CANN. *Poets and Poetry, Being Articles Reprinted from the Literary Supplement of "The Times."* Oxford: Clarendon Press, 1911, pp. 28–36.

Places Sidney in the development of sixteenth-century poetry and modern English idiom. Treats Stella as an ideal rather than as a strict portrait of Penelope Devereux.

1862 BARTENSCHLAGER, KLAUS. "Die Situation des Sprechers im Gedicht. Wyatt, Sidney, Spenser. Ein historisch-typologischer Versuch." Ph.D. diss., Universität München, 1970, 125 pp.

Rejecting the term "dramatic" to describe Sidney's poetry, suggests instead more refined ways to describe the "situation of the speaker." Notes that, whereas ancient and Renaissance authorities generally assume that a lyric poet speaks in his own person, Sidney does not. Infers that he considered the lyric as a "mimetic" genre, that is, one representing a persona "speaking in a significant situation." In this respect, places *Astrophil and Stella* in a tradition derived form Catullus and Ovid. Compares Sidney's verse with that of Wyatt and Spenser.

1863 BEAL, PETER. "The Ottley Manuscript of Poems by Sidney." *Library*, 6th ser. 3 (June 1981):157.

Accepts two of the three corrections offered by Robertson (1942) to his earlier remarks (1864) about the Ottley Manuscript. Argues, however, for his reading of line 22 of "Near Wilton sweet huge heaps of stones are found" (*CS 22*), concluding that the phrase "Thames breeds" is a "genuine alternative reading," and that the Ottley Manuscript has "more serious textual implications" than Robertson allows. See also Warkentin (2331).

1864 ———. "Poems by Sir Philip Sidney: The Ottley Manuscript." *Library*, 5th ser. 33 (December 1978):284–95.

Describes twenty-four poems from *Arcadia* and seventeen poems from *Certain Sonnets* in the Ottley Manuscript in the National Library of Wales. Records variants from the texts printed by Ringler (92) and suggests that the manuscript may represent early, unaltered versions of the poems. See also item 1863 and Robertson (1942).

1865 BOAS, FREDERICK S[AMUEL]. *Sir Philip Sidney, Representative Elizabethan: His Life and Writings.* London: Staples Press, 1955, pp. 121–58.

Discusses the metrical experiments in the eclogues of *Arcadia* and surmises that the Philisides-Mira poems relate to a love affair that preceded Sidney's attraction to Penelope Devereux. Contrasts Philisides with

Astrophil and argues that the earlier sonnets "Thou blind man's mark" (*CS 31*) and "Leave me, O Love" (*CS 32*) cannot properly be added to *Astrophil and Stella* as its conclusion. Praises the metrical virtuosity of Sidney's Psalms. See also item 436.

1866 BRAY, Sir DENYS. "The Art-Form of the Elizabethan Sonnet Sequence and Shakespeare's Sonnets." *SJ* 63 (1927):159–82.

Examines seven methods for linking sonnets within a sequence. Names Sidney among those who practice the "echoing rhyme series." See also Bullitt (2074).

1867 BREWER, WILMON. *Sonnets and Sestinas*. Boston: Cornhill Publishing Co., 1937, pp. 143–44, 146, 197–98, 199.

Praises Sidney for the variety of his sonnet forms and for introducing the French sestet. Discusses his use of the sestina in *Arcadia*.

1868 BROADBENT, J[OHN] B[ARCLAY]. *Poetic Love*. London: Chatto & Windus, 1964, pp. 129–42.

In a chapter on Sidney, claims that working against the pressure of Petrarch and Ronsard led him to begin to write in a fashion of "metaphysical asperity" that prefigures Donne. Claims that both "Leave me, O love" (*CS 32*) and "With how sad steps, O moon" (*AS 31*) are quite conventional. Sees the poems of *Astrophil and Stella* as rhetorical in that, despite their irony and skepticism, "their dialectic is external, not inward." Feels that "Sidney understood the ideal nature of poetic love, but the tendency of his eloquence to hypnotize itself prevented him from realizing it." At times, however, he seems to go beyond the merely conventional and rhetorical to glimpse love realistically and colloquially.

1869 BÜHLER, CURT F. "Four Elizabethan Poems." In *Joseph Quincy Adams Memorial Studies*, edited by James G. McManaway, Giles E. Dawson, and Edwin E. Willoughby. Washington, D.C.: Folger Shakespeare Library, 1948, pp. 695–706.

Prints Marlowe's "Passionate Shepherd" from a seventeenth-century manuscript in which the poem is called "A sonnet Madrigal by Sr Philipp Sydney." See also Latham (615).

1870 BULLOUGH, GEOFFREY. *Mirror of Minds: Changing Psychological Beliefs in English Poetry*. London: Athlone Press; Toronto: University of Toronto Press, 1962, pp. 10, 32–35.

Discusses *Astrophil and Stella* as an example of the Renaissance expression of psychology through rhetoric. Sees in Sidney's poetry "a renewal

Twentieth Century

of the consciousness of mental processes" found in Dante and his contemporaries. Also sees pastoral solitude as an important element in the
sort of meditations found in the eclogues of *Arcadia*.

1871 BUXTON, JOHN. *A Tradition of Poetry*. London, Melbourne,
Toronto: Macmillan; New York: St. Martin's Press, 1967, pp. 19,
52, 61, 63.
Discusses Sidney's influence on and participation in the tradition of aristocratic amateur poetry in sixteenth- and seventeenth-century England.

1872 CELLINI, BENVENUTO. *Vita e arti nei sonetti di Shakespeare col
testo dei sonetti riordinati e commentati*. Rome: S.A. Editrice
Tumminelli "Studium Urbis," 1943, pp. 164–68 passim, 183–85,
188, 204, 206.
Notes parallels between Shakespeare's *Sonnets* and several poems in
Arcadia and *Astrophil and Stella*.

1873 CROSLAND, THOMAS WILLIAM HODGSON. *The English
Sonnet*. London: Martin Secker, 1917, pp. 141–57.
In "Sir Philip Sidney, 1554–1586," faults the rhyme schemes in *Astrophil
and Stella* for "melodic defect" resulting from failure to grasp the full significance of the Petrarchan form. Praises the sequence, but concludes
that the sonnets of *Arcadia* are finer.

1874 CRUSE, AMY. *The Elizabethan Lyrists and Their Poetry*. London:
George G. Harrap & Co., 1919, pp. 34–50.
Provides biographical information on Sidney and brief critical com-
ments, interspersed with excerpts from his poetry.

1875 DENONAIN, JEAN-JACQUES. *Thèmes et formes de la poésie
"Metaphysique": Étude d'un aspect de la littérature anglaise au dix-sep-
tième siècle*. Paris: Presses Universitaires de France, 1956, pp. 89,
119, 408–9, 418, 449.
Notes Sidney's possible influence on George Herbert's two New Year's
sonnets. Considers the date and manuscript circulation of *Astrophil and
Stella* and comments on its place in the sonnet vogue. Points out that,
although Donne and Herbert were aware of Sidney's experiments with
stanzaic form in the Psalms, neither they nor their contemporaries
shared his interest in quantitative verse.

1876 DONOW, HERBERT S. *A Concordance to the Poems of Sir Philip
Sidney*. Cornell Concordances. Programming by Trevor J.
Swanson. Ithaca, N.Y.: Cornell University Press, 1975, 624 pp.
Using Ringler (92) as the base text, lists keywords in context and pro-
vides title as well as page and line references. In the introduction,

explains basic programming parameters. An appendix provides a word-frequency listing.

1877 DONYO, VICTOR A., ed. *Parthenophil and Parthenophe: A Critical Edition*, by Barnabe Barnes. Carbondale and Edwardsville: Southern Illinois University Press; London and Amsterdam: Feffer & Simons, 1971, pp. liv, lxii, 145, 147, 169, 171, 174, 180, 191, and passim.

Notes Sidney's influence on Barnes's metrical experiments and sonnet forms. Points to verbal parallels in poems by Sidney.

1878 DRINKWATER, JOHN. *Prose Papers*. London: Elkin Mathews, 1917, pp. 74–93.

In "Philip Sidney," argues that *Astrophil and Stella* was written when Sidney had "ceased to think of verse-making as a pleasant and polished accomplishment and wrote with fire and passion as all true poets write, to ease his mind." Condemns Sidney's quantitative experiments, arguing that *Astrophil and Stella* is biographical and "sincere" in its expression of love. Claims that Sidney took the sonnet, "which was at the time experimental," and gave it a "sweetness" rarely excelled.

1879 DUNN, CATHERINE MARY. "A Survey of the Experiments in Quantitative Verse in the English Renaissance." Ph.D. diss., University of California at Los Angeles, 1967, 355 pp.

Calls Sidney the "major figure" in the spiral of quantitative experiment in England. His poetry was "never surpassed in quality and metrical variety." See *DA* 28 (July 1967):193A.

1880 EMERSON, OLIVER FARRAR. "Shakespeare's Sonneteering." *SP* 20 (April 1923):111–36.

Briefly discusses Sidney's use of the English form of sonnet in *Arcadia*. Speculates on his reason for choosing the Italian rather than the English form in *Astrophil and Stella*. Notes instances of Sidney's influence on other sonneteers, focusing in particular on the alexandrine sonnet in Shakespeare's *Love's Labor's Lost*.

1881 ERSKINE, JOHN. *The Elizabethan Lyric: A Study*. Columbia University Studies in English, 2. New York: Columbia University Press; London: Macmillan & Co., 1903, pp. 92–94, 122–24, 128–29, 131, 133.

Argues that the sonnets in *Astrophil and Stella* fall into two groups—the autobiographical and the conventional—and that, since Sidney did not intend to publish his sequence, it is more intimate in tone and appears to be more genuine than Petrarch's. Locates the greatness of Sidney's sonnets in his ability to arrange his themes dramatically, giving the impression of sincere self-revelation. Faults the poems in *Arcadia* for lacking lyric emotion.

1882 FABRY, FRANK J. "Sidney's Poetry and Italian Song-Form." *ELR* 3 (Spring 1973):232–48.
Discusses the influence of fixed Italian song forms on Sidney's use of feminine and masculine rhymes and argues that Italian vocal forms appear in the poetry of *Arcadia*. Notes also the influence of French theory, especially that of Ronsard, on *Astrophil and Stella* and the Psalms.

1883 FELLOWES, EDMUND HORACE. *The English Madrigal Composers*. London: Clarendon Press, 1921, pp. 106, 141–43, 162, 257, 279.
Comments on the use made of Sidney's works by the madrigal writers, suggesting that Sidney's connection with the Kytson family may have encouraged such settings.

1884 FELLOWES, E[DMUND] H[ORACE], ed. *English Madrigal Verse, 1588–1632*. Oxford: Clarendon Press, 1920, pp. 11, 38, 57, 163, 180, 199, 202–4, 398, 454, 457, 503, 506, 549.
Prints seventeen poems by Sidney set to music before 1632. Includes settings by Robert Dowland, William Byrd, Thomas Ravenscroft, Henry Youll, Thomas Morley, John Ward, and Francis Pilkington. See also item 1885 and Pilkington (1976).

1885 ———. *English Madrigal Verse, 1588–1632*. Rev. and enl. by F.W. Sternfield and David Greer. Oxford: Clarendon Press, 1967, pp. 218, 265.
Adds two new poems to those collected in the first edition (1884).

1886 FELLOWES, EDMUND H[ORACE]. *William Byrd*. London: Oxford University Press, 1936, pp. 152, 154, 158, 168, 244–45.
Comments on Byrd's settings of Sidney's works.

1887 FERRY, ANNE DAVIDSON. *All in War with Time: Love Poetry of Shakespeare, Donne, Jonson, Marvell*. Cambridge, Mass., and London: Harvard University Press, 1975, pp. 134–35, 139–49, 220–23, 226–27, 231, 263.
Traces Sidney's influence on poetry of the seventeenth century. Discusses Shakespeare's Sonnet 18 in light of statements in the *Defence* on the poet's ability to create a "golden world." Claims that "His mother dear, Cupid offended late" (*AS 17*) mythologizes the poet-lover, comparing the sonnet with Jonson's Epigram 126. Sees the note of praise in

Jonson's "To Mary Lady Wroth" (Epigram 103) as similar to that in Sidney's sonnet "You that with allegory's curious frame" (*AS 28*), and notes a similarity of view in the poet's search for the true source of invention in Sonnet 1 and in Jonson's Epigram 76. Contrasts Marvell's presentation of the lover's relationship to the world of nature in "The Mower's Song" with that displayed in "Over these brookes trusting to ease mine eyes" (*OA 21*).

1888 ———. *The 'Inward' Language: Sonnets of Wyatt, Sidney, Shakespeare, Donne*. Chicago and London: University of Chicago Press, 1983, pp. 119–214, and passim.

Refers to Sidney on nearly every page, devoting Chapters 3, "Sidney," and 4, "Shakespeare and Sidney," to an extended and detailed analysis of *Astrophil and Stella*. Argues that a revolution in the language of poetry moved Sidney and his contemporaries to a new view of the self and a new way of expressing awareness of that self in poetry. Claims that, among the earlier poems, only "Leave me, O love" (*CS 32*) uses language in ways that show "an awareness of the ambiguities and shifting relations between words and what is in the heart," a self-consciousness that defines the essential difference between the love sonnet and other forms of love lyric in the sixteenth century, and which defines also the essential nature of *Astrophil and Stella* as a sonnet sequence. Sees Sidney's poet-lover as different from both Wyatt's and Petrarch's, the only two prior models that Sidney could have had. Reads *Astrophil and Stella* as an elaborate and detailed working out of the first line of its first sonnet, "the earliest poem in English to make its central concern the relation between what may be felt 'in truth' and what may show 'in verse.'" Feels that its first line "changes poetry in our language." Provides extended readings of Sonnets 3, 5, 6, 18, 22, 27, 32, 35, 80, and 86. Argues that Shakespeare was also concerned with the treacherous relation between poetic language and inward experience, concluding that he "understood the issues in Sidney's terms, and learned his means for exploring them."

1889 FORBIS, JOHN F. *The Shakespearean Enigma and an Elizabethan Mania*. New York: American Library Press, 1924, pp. 285–91.

In "The English Petrarchists: Sir Philip Sidney," argues that Sidney's sonnets, like Shakespeare's, are the product of an addiction to wine and that the moral problem confronted in the poems involves overcoming alcoholism. Views Stella not as a person but as a glass of wine. Claims that "Who hath ever felt the change of love" (*CS 24*) records Sidney's "reform."

Twentieth Century

1890 FOWLER, ALASTAIR [D.S.] *Conceitful Thought: The Interpretation of English Renaissance Poems*. Edinburgh: Edinburgh University Press, 1975, pp. 38–58, 98–101.
Discusses the complexity of conceits in *Astrophil and Stella* 1 and 9. Also considers the sestina structure of "Ye goatherd Gods" (*OA 71*), surveying scholarship on the poem, emphasizing its genre as a singing contest, and distinguishing between the characters of Klaius and Strephon. Describes the intricate way in which Lamon's tale and the game of barley-break and its players fit the basic form of the sestina. See also Litt (2002).

1891 FROST, WILLIAM. *Fulke Greville's "Caelica": An Evaluation*. Battleboro, Vt.: n.p., 1942, 62 pp. passim.
Argues that Sidney had neither the emotional depth of Greville nor the sincere commitment to neo-Platonism. Points to Sidney's extensive borrowings from Ronsard and Petrarch and suggests that the new language advocated by the Areopagus was intended "to cloak this borrowed imagery and philosophy." Also discusses a number of Sidney's literary devices that Greville rejected, including classical allusions, pastoral elements, medieval archaisms, and "sugared ornamental imagery." Examines the verbal parallels between the work of the two poets and concludes that, after the early Cupid poems, Greville diverged from Sidney. Contrasts *Astrophil and Stella 8* with *Caelica 11* and discusses the Puritan leanings of the two poets.

1892 FUCILLA, JOSEPH G. "*Parole identiche* in the Sonnet and Other Verse Forms." *PMLA* 50 (June 1935):372–402.
Surveys the *sonnetto equivoco*, in which rhymes are identical in sound but different in meaning, as a "new type of sonnet" in European Renaissance poetry. Cites Sidney's "Now that of absence the most irksome night" (*AS 89*) and "Since that the stormy rage of passions dark" (*OA 39*) as English examples of the form.

1893 GILBERT, ALLAN H. "A Poem Wrongly Attributed to Sidney." *MLN* 57 (May 1942):364.
Shows that a nine-line poem "Such is the cruelty," which is attributed to Sidney in Feuillerat's edition (23), is actually Spenser's *Faerie Queene* V.v.25.

1894 GRIEM, EBERHARD. "Die elisabethanische Epoche." In *Epochen der englischen Lyrik*, edited by Karl Heinz Göller. Düsseldorf, Germany: August Bagel Verlag, 1970, pp. 79–99.
Analyzes the rhythms of "Come let me write" (*AS 34*), noting Sidney's attempt to capture the sound of daily speech. Also considers Sidney's

influence on later Elizabethan lyric poets, particularly those who moved away from Petrarchan conventions.

1895 GRUNDY, PRISCILLA NOBLE "The Nature and Function of Poetics in the Poems of Sir Philip Sidney." Ph.D. diss., Northern Illinois University, 1979, 249 pp.

Argues that Sidney knew Continental prosody better than English, and that each of his poetic works shows a "distinct prosodic personality," determined by such things as stanza patterns, foot reversals, use of pause and enjambment, type of feet, and use of elision. See *DAI* 39 (February 1979):4957A.

1896 HAMER, ENID [HOPE (PORTER)]. *The Metres of English Poetry.* London: Methuen; New York: Macmillan Co., 1930, pp. 191–93, 300–302.

Comments on the sonnet form in *Astrophil and Stella* and on the classical experiments in *Arcadia*, praising Sidney's sapphics.

1897 HAMILTON, A.C. *Sir Philip Sidney: A Study of His Life and Works.* Cambridge: Cambridge University Press, 1977, pp. 58–106.

In Chapter 3, considers Sidney's conscious desire to present the English with models of poetic craftsmanship. Examines the debate of Dicus and Lalus (in a prose section of the First Eclogues of the Old *Arcadia*) over the relation of poetry to music, relating Dicus's position to Sidney's use of quantitative measures in "Fortune, nature, love" (*OA 11*) and "My muse, what ails this ardour" (*OA 32*). Relates such metrical experiments to the claim in the *Defence* that rhyme and verse are not essential to poetry. Examines connections between one eclogue and another, between whole sets of eclogues and the main action, and between imbedded poems and the surrounding prose. Regards the cave near the royal lodges as an image of the darkness of man's fallen state, which is conquered in the sole poem of Book V: "Since nature's works be good" (*OA 77*). Explores Sidney's aims in translating the Psalms, discussing passages in the *Defence* and Donne's "Upon the Translation of the Psalms." Also discusses links between poems that clarify the structure of *Certain Sonnets*. Treats the work as an appendix to the Old *Arcadia*, suggesting that it was written to sing "the poor hopes of poor Philisides." Remarks that, in *Astrophil and Stella*, love seems more overwhelming than in the earlier sonnets, where the lover has the capacity to turn away from irrational passion. Considers the autobiographical elements in the later sequence, concluding that Sidney's aim was to examine various "postures" of a lover's mind and, to this end, transformed the facts of his relationship with Penelope Rich into fiction. Analyzes the work as follows: an introduction in which the "programme" of the sequence is

Twentieth Century

announced (*AS 1–13*); Astrophil's sight of Stella, growing isolation from the world, and realization that words and reason are inadequate and his love cannot be satisfied (*AS 14–35*); his hearing of Stella's song, heightened desire, and demands for greater intimacy (*AS 36–71*); and his kissing of Stella, attempt to satisfy desire, and request that she allow him to return to the active life (*AS 72–108*). Considers the background for this progression in Castiglione's *Courtier* and notes Sidney's various departures from the Petrarchan tradition. See also item 550.

1898 HÄUBLEIN, ERNST. *Strophe und Struktur in der Lyrik Sir Philip Sidneys*. Europäische Hochschulschriften, ser. 14, vol. 2. Bern, Switzerland: Hubert Lang; Frankfurt am Main: Peter Lang, 1971, 238 pp. Orig. a Ph.D. diss., Universität Würtzburg.
Combines a "systematic inqui[r]y into the structural implications of the stanza with a historical survey of the poetic technique of Sidney and his contemporaries." Analyzes in detail poems from *Arcadia*, *Certain Sonnets*, *Astrophil and Stella*, and the Sidney Psalter. In Chapter 1, identifies three kinds of logical relation among stanzas: 1) "light stimulus," in which each stanza comes to a clear end but is part of a logical progression running through the entire poem; 2) "unfixed stanzas," in which each is totally independent of the others and could be moved to another place in the poem; and 3) "strong stimulus," in which stanzas lack clear ends and so tend to run together. Finds that, though Sidney mixes the three kinds, he prefers the first. In Chapter 2, considers links between stanzas formed, not logically, but by correlation of "identical or semantically related words or word groups." See Alonso (1858). In Chapter 3, considers "problems of construction and unity in single stanzas. Noting that Sidney never repeats a stanzaic form in any of his forty-three Psalms, examines ways in which he turned the less formally structured and regular English translations that were his primary sources into stanzaic verse. Considers the function of rhyme and rhetorical figures in achieving stanzaic unity. Also notes the need for additions, paraphrases, and changes in the original syntax in order to make the meter regular. Includes an English summary.

1899 HEDLEY, JANE. "What Price Energeia: Personification in the Poetry of Sidney and Greville." *SLitI* 15 (Spring 1982):49–66.
Argues that, whereas Greville uses personification "to facilitate the apprehension of universal truths in their ideality," Sidney uses it to give abstractions "a vivid human presence and topicality." The contrast may result from the differing values that each places on the roles of the philosopher and poet.

1900 HOLLANDER, JOHN. *Vision and Resonance: Two Senses of Poetic Form.* New York: Oxford University Press, 1975, pp. 61–67, 82, 184.

Notes the claim in the *Defence* that "the glories of Classical scansion utilized certain structural elements of the Greek language, and that English poetry must make full use of the analogous resources of the English language for the same purposes." Concludes that Sidney's "myriad attempts at all sorts of lyric forms were, in the main, experimental: whether in the variety of meters in which he versified the Psalter, or the quantitative poems in the *Arcadia*, sheer compositional exuberance, and the exigencies of a particular moment seem to be at work."

1901 HOLLOWELL, B.M. "The Elizabethan Hexametrists." *PQ* 3 (January 1924):51–57.

Discusses Sidney's role in introducing classical meters into English poetry.

1902 HUGHEY, RUTH, ed. *The Arundel Harington Manuscript of Tudor Poetry.* 2 vols. Columbus: Ohio State University Press, 1960, 1:30, 38, 61, 68; 2:66–68, 74–76, 253–54, 309–12, 317–19, 352–58, 361–64.

In the introduction and notes, provides detailed information on the eight poems by Sidney in the manuscript. Discusses other extant manuscripts of each poem, publication dates and history, textual variants, and scholarly studies. In covering "Ring out your bells" (*CS 30*), notes similar invectives against women in the verses of Sir Thomas Wyatt and the Earl of Surrey. Considers Sir John Harington's access to manuscripts of Sidney's poetry, notably *Astrophil and Stella*, and points out that he is the only contemporary who explicitly links Penelope Rich with Stella. Also discusses the evidence that Ralegh wrote the elegy on Sidney beginning "To praise thy life and wail thy worthy death" (2768), pointing out that, in lines 45–48, it resembles the epitaph that once hung near Sidney's tomb in St. Paul's Cathedral (2782).

1903 HUNTER, G.K. "Drab and Golden Lyrics of the Renaissance." In *Forms of Lyric: Selected Papers from the English Institute*, edited by Reuben A. Brower. New York and London: Columbia University Press, 1970, pp. 1–18.

Distinguishes between poetry "presented as part of a social mode, being manipulated by sophisticated but real people," like the poetry of Gascoigne, and poetry that creates "a world possessed by its symbols, and so cut off from 'real' life," as in *Arcadia* and *Astrophil and Stella*. The difference is between "figures of words" and "figures of thought,"

Twentieth Century

between poetry sparse in imagery and symbol and poetry filled with them. Sees in Sidney's poetry a group of parallel, self-explanatory "emblems rather than a straight-forward narrative."

1904 JAYNE, SEARS. "Ficino and the Platonism of the English Renaissance." *CL* 4 (Summer 1952):214–38.
Argues against the direct influence of Ficino on most English varieties of "Platonism" in the period, suggesting that Sidney is unusual in going beyond the French Petrarchan poets to explore Italian sources directly. Compares the Ficinian views of idealized love and beauty in Sidney's Sonnet "Leave me, O Love" (*CS 32*) with those in Sonnet 207 of Michelangelo's *Rime*.

1905 JEHMLICH, REIMER. "Die Bildlichkeit in der Liebeslyrik Sir Philip Sidneys, Michael Draytons und John Donnes." Ph.D. diss., Universität Kiel, 1970, 202 pp.
Examines the distinction between Elizabethan and metaphysical poetry, challenging "Donne's 'modernism' and his alleged revolt against Elizabethan conventions." Compares the metaphors in Sidney's *Astrophil and Stella*, Drayton's *Idea*, and Donne's *Songs and Sonnets*, examining the background of particular images from antiquity to the Renaissance. Argues that Donne has more in common with Sidney than with Drayton. Notes Sidney's portrayal of "realistic" situations, his interest in challenging conventional views of love through wit and irony, and his tendency to argue or ratiocinate. Distinguises the imagery of all three authors from "modern" associative uses of metaphor. See *EASG*, 1970, pp. 31–33.

1906 JORGENS, ELISE BICKFORD. *The Well-Tun'd Word: Musical Interpretations of English Poetry 1597–1651*. Minneapolis: University of Minnesota Press, 1982, pp. 13, 25, 30, 91–92, 94, 241.
Noting Sidney's concern that the structural details of a poem's first stanza be repeated in succeeding ones, suggests that the "attitude" implied here is similar to "fitting musical notation to poetic meter." Contends that "the controlling effect of metrical pattern" is part of the effect he desired.

1907 KALSTONE, DAVID. *Sidney's Poetry: Contexts and Interpretations*. Cambridge, Mass.: Harvard University Press, 1965, 203 pp. Orig. a Ph.D. diss., Harvard University, 1961.
In the introduction, argues that, while revitalizing the Petrarchan tradition, Sidney also called the values of the tradition into question. Sees the poems of *Arcadia* "as part of an attempt to give dramatic shape to a singular view of pastoral retirement and a world of love." Suggests that the sonnets of *Astrophil and Stella* be read in the context of *Arcadia*, where the

conflict between love and the heroic life is a central concern. In Chapters 1–3, takes up the poetry of *Arcadia*, differentiating the songs of the rustics, which occur in interludes between books, from those of the courtiers, which occur incidentally throughout the text. Examines ways in which Sidney tests the values of classical and Italian pastoral against the demands of the heroic world. After glancing at *The Lady of May*, focuses on the depiction of Philisides in the Third Eclogues of *Arcadia*, regarding him as an instance of the conflict between the active and contemplative lives. Analyzes "Ye goatherd gods" (*OA 71*), distinguishing Sidney's technique from that of Sannazaro and pointing out that Sidney's Arcadian poems criticize "the easy resolution of Sannazaro's *Arcadia*." Concludes that Sidney's interest lies in the conflict between the "heroic world," which offers a model of "reasonable activity," and a "pastoral world," which "presents in the vicissitudes of love a heightened example of the unavoidable obstacles to heroic striving." In Chapters 4–5, deals with the poetry of *Astrophil and Stella* and regards it as dynamic, whereas Petrarch's verse tends to be static. Contrasts Petrarch's preoccupation with Laura with Astrophil's focus on himself, noting that the distant and idealized love of *Rime* 248 is quite different from the open, physical desire of Sidney's "Who will in fairest book of Nature know" (*AS 71*). Argues that Astrophil acts out a dual role, playing both the lover and the critic of love and, in the process, adopting various "poses and attitudes" toward Petrarchan conventions. Suggesting that Sidney's mastery of his persona is what gives the poems force, divides the sequence into three parts, locating the climax in Sonnets 69 through 72 and suggesting that the work "comes to no fitting conclusion." Finds the only possible resolution in the last two poems of *Certain Sonnets*. Concludes that "Sidney's achievement in *Astrophil and Stella* is to fashion the Petrarchan sonnet into a form responsive to the antagonisms he felt so deeply" and that the sequence "raises explicitly the question of the fate of Petrarchism in England and poses more problems about Neoplatonic love in English poetry than it answers." See responses by Hamilton (1245), Williams (1313), Brodwin (2068), Brown (2069), and Kimbrough (2168, 2695).

1908 KALUZA, MAX. *A Short History of English Versification from Earliest Times to the Present Day*. Translated by A.C. Dunstan. London: George Allen & Co.; New York: Macmillan Co., 1911, pp. 348, 374, 375, 377, 383.

Notes Sidney's use of various metrical patterns and comments briefly on the Italianate nature of the octaves in *Astrophil and Stella*.

Twentieth Century

1909 KAUN, ERNST. *Konventionelles in den elisabethanischen Sonnetten mit Berücksichtigung der französischen und italienischen Quellen.* Greifswald, Germany: Buchdruckerei Hans Adler, 1915, pp. 12–13, 16, 22–23, 27–28, 32–33, 35, 39, 41, 47–48, 50, 63, 65–67, 75–76, 90, 92, 97–98, 108, 110–11, 115. Orig. a Ph.D. diss., Königlichen Universität zu Greifswald.

Isolates a variety of conventional motifs, attitudes, metaphors, and expressions in the Italian and French as well as English sonnets of the period. Cites Sidney's use of these conventions.

1910 KERMAN, JOSEPH. *The Elizabethan Madrigal: A Comparative Study.* American Musicological Society Studies and Documents, 4. New York: American Musicological Society, 1962, pp. 10, 11, 15–19, 31, 112, 113, 115.

Describes settings of Sidney's poems and parts of poems, noting that he is "sparsely represented in the madrigal books."

1911 KIMBROUGH, ROBERT. *Sir Philip Sidney.* Twayne's English Authors Series, 114. New York: Twayne Publishers, 1971, pp. 89–106.

In Chapter 4, discusses Sidney's metrical experiments in the Psalms, his efforts to write quantitative verse, and his "Imitations, Foreign and Native." Against Ringler (92), argues that the Psalms are early work and that Sidney did not finish the translation because he felt that "this particular effort to reform vernacular poetry was not worth the effort." Finds that, although Sidney's manner shows him "consciously departing from native practice, he unconsciously is true to it." Claims that the only factor that "saves" any of the quantitative poems is that they were intended as songs and, when performed, their musical settings help to reinforce the sense of meter. Divides the poems of the Old *Arcadia* into two classes: lyrics, such as "My true love hath my heart" (*OA 45*), and formal poems, such as "Ye goatherd gods" (*OA 71*). Finds that none of the first sort is extraordinary, whereas many of the second are, though generally as *tours de force* rather than as good poems. Contrasts the poems of *Certain Sonnets* with those of *Arcadia* and *Astrophil and Stella*, suggesting that, because the former have no larger context, the reader can get closer in them to Sidney the poet and discover "the first signs of a developing voice." Analyzes what is "new" in them, finding "Thou blind man's mark" (*CS 31*) the "most complete" before *Astrophil and Stella*. See also item 593.

1912 KREMER, CHARLES FREDERICK. "Studies in Verse Form in Non-Dramatic English Poetry from Wyatt to Sidney." Ph.D. diss., Northwestern University, 1942.

Discusses Sidney's use of foreign verse forms, providing a summary of his poetic output according to kinds of verse form, variety within the form, repetitions, number of poems in the form, and number of lines. See *Summaries of Doctoral Dissertations Submitted to the Graduate School of Northwestern University in Partial Fulfillment of the Requirements for the Degree of Doctor of Philosophy* 10 (June–August 1942):30–32.

1913 LEVER, J[ULIUS] W[ALTER]. *The Elizabethan Love Sonnet.* London: Methuen & Co., 1956, pp. 51–91.

In a chapter on Sidney, surveys twentieth-century criticism of *Astrophil and Stella*, commenting on its blending of tradition and convention. To demonstrate Sidney's adaptation of conventional themes, forms, and devices, compares Sonnet 71 with Petrarch's *Sonnetto in Vita* 210, Sonnet 17 with Pontano's *De Stella*, and Sonnet 8 with Epigram 268 in the *Greek Anthology*. Discusses Sidney's depiction of emotional states that are also "intellectual and spiritual dilemmas." Suggests that his sonnet form has its source in Wyatt and that the content of the sequence is a blend of conventional Petrarchan and Platonic elements with intense personal emotion. Connects Shakespeare's *Sonnets* 129 and 146 with *Certain Sonnets* 31 and 32. See also Melchiori (655) and Montgomery (2203).

1914 LEVÝ, JIŘÍ. "On the Relations of Language and Stanza Pattern in the English Sonnet." In *Worte und Werte: Bruno Markwardt zum 60. Geburtstag*, edited by Gustav Erdmann and Alfons Eichstaedt. Berlin: Walter de Gruyter & Co., 1961, pp. 214–31.

On the basis of statistical analysis, which shows the importance of binary intonation patterns and of midline and endline pauses, argues that the "prosodic qualities of the language" were responsible for the development of the sonnet in England. Noting that Sidney's fondness for midline pauses allows him to use the Petrarchan form with force, concludes that "the Italian or French forms could reach any standard of perfection only with those English poets who inclined to an obligatory antithetical construction of lines, especially with Sidney and Spenser."

1915 LOONEY, J. THOMAS, ed. *The Poems of Edward de Vere (Seventeenth Earl of Oxford)*. London: Cecil Palmer, 1921, pp. ix, 38, 39.

Compares Oxford's verse with Sidney's, praising the former. Prints Oxford's "Were I a King" and the poem sometimes thought to be

Twentieth Century

Sidney's parody of it, "Wert thou a King" (*AT 29*), noting that these poems identify Oxford as "Willie." Applies this identification to the characters of the same name in the August Eclogue of the *Shepherd's Calendar* and in *The Tears of the Muses*.

1916 McCOY, DOROTHY SCHUCHMAN. *Tradition and Convention: A Study of Periphrasis in English Pastoral Poetry from 1557–1715.* Studies in English Literature, 5. The Hague, London, Paris: Mouton, 1965, pp. 54–61. Orig. a Ph.D. diss., University of Pittsburgh, 1962.

In "Sir Philip Sidney: Periphrase in Arcadia," argues that Sidney's ornamentation is largely rhetorical. Suggests that he controls mythological allusion, *paronomasia*, *antonomasia*, and *periphrasis* through the implementation of three levels of style.

1917 McPEEK, JAMES A[NDREW] S[CARBOROUGH]. *Catullus in Strange and Distant Britain.* Harvard Studies in Comparative Literature, 15. Cambridge, Mass.: Harvard University Press, 1939, pp. 156–59, 240–41. Orig. a Ph.D. diss., Harvard University, 1932.

Calling Sidney the "first poet writing in English who genuinely appreciated Catullus and left definite evidence of his appreciation," suggests that he may have been introduced to Catullus by Henri Estienne. Sees "Let mother earth now deck her self in flowers" (*OA 63*) as "apparently the first epithalamy in English conforming to the tradition set by Catullus," and argues that echoes of Catullus in this poem are independent of references in Gil Polo's *Diana Enamorada*. Suggests that the sparrow mentioned in *Arcadia* and in "Good brother Philip, I have borne you long" (*AS 83*) may be linked with *Carmen* 2. Feels that Sidney's one direct translation, "Unto no body" (*CS 13*), which translates *Carmen* 70, is weak.

1918 MARTZ, LOUIS L[OHR]. *The Poetry of Meditation: A Study in English Religious Literature of the Seventeenth Century.* Yale Studies in English, 125. New Haven, Conn.: Yale University Press, 1954, pp. 261–82.

Notes Sidney's direct and indirect influence on Herbert in terms of verbal patterns, concepts, and poetic technique. Argues that "Herbert as poet developed away from an early enthusiasm for Donne's manner toward a style much closer to Sidney's." Compares the two sonnets of Herbert's *Temple* to "Leave me, O love" (*CS 32*), noting numerous other parallels in themes and style between *Astrophil and Stella* and Herbert's poetry. Claims that Sidney's translation of Psalms 1–43 represents "the closest approximation to the poetry of Herbert's *Temple* that can be found anywhere in preceding English poetry," and that Sidney's "subdued and controlled variety" of stanza form is also found in the work. Comments in detail on the translation of Psalm 6, on its overall theme of simplicity and on its evocation of the "artful verse of Elizabethan song." Concludes that the Sidney Psalter represents "the attempt to bring the art of Elizabethan lyric into the service of psalmody, and to perform this in a way that makes the psalm an intimate, personal cry of the soul to God."

1919 MARX, STEVEN RUDOLPH. "The Pastoral Debate of Youth and Age: Genre and Life Cycle in Renaissance Poetry with Special Reference to Edmund Spenser's *The Shepheardes Calender*." Ph.D. diss., Stanford University, 1981, 347 pp.

Proposes a "new way of reading all pastoral poetry" as "generated by a rejection of adulthood and middle-age." The debate structure of bucolic poems, "submerged" in Sidney and others, "leads the reader . . . through a dualistic world view to a disturbing relativity of perspective." See *DAI* 42 (February 1982):3611A.

1920 MILES, JOSEPHINE. "Ifs, Ands, Buts, for the Reader of Donne." In *Just So Much Honor: Esays Commemorating the Four-Hundredth Anniversay of the Birth of John Donne*, edited by Peter Amadeus Fiore. University Park and London: Pennsylvania State University Press, 1972, pp. 273–91.

Argues that, in his use of conjunctions, Sidney is more like Donne than like other contemporaries and that "it is Sidney in fact whose sonnets move, though with simpler thought, in the way Donne's move."

1921 ———. *Renaissance, Eighteenth Century, and Modern Language in English Poetry: A Tabular View.* Berkeley: University of California Press, 1960, pp. 5, 18, 42, 46, 54, 58, 62, 66, 70.

Provides statistical analyses of word frequency, major words, use of adjectives and adverbs, types of proportions, and types of measures used by 200 poets, including Sidney. Major nouns for Sidney include "beauty," "breast," "day," "desire," "eye," "fool," "fortune," "friend," "hand," "heart," and "love." Major verbs include "make," "see," "love," "think," "show," and "speak." Major adjectives are "fair," "gold," "good," "great," "happy," "high," and "sweet."

Twentieth Century

1922 MILL, ADAIR. *"Tottel's Miscellany* and *England's Helicon." Ingiliz Filolojisi Dergisi: Studies by Members of the English Department, University of Istanbul* 3 (1952):42–60.
Sees Sidney's advances in poetic technique as part of a trend toward greater attention to sound in Tudor poetry and to the relations between verse and music.

1923 MILLER, AUDREY BERRYMAN. "Themes and Techniques in Mid-Tudor Lyric Poetry: An Analytical Study of the Short Poems from Wyatt to Sidney." Ph.D. diss., Northwestern University, 1949.
Classifies the poems of Sidney and his contemporaries according to their themes and their poetic techniques, locating them in larger poetic "trends." See *Summaries of Doctoral Dissertations Submitted to the Graduate School of Northwestern University* 17 (June–September 1949):35–41.

1924 MILLER, JACQUELINE T. "Authority and Authorship: Some Medieval and Renaissance Contexts." Ph.D. diss., Johns Hopkins University, 1980, 263 pp.
Concerned with the "sometimes complementary, sometimes conflicting concepts of 'authority' and 'authorship,' and the motives that work to merge or separate them," investigates several texts by Chaucer, Spenser, Sidney, and Herbert. Examines in the love lyrics "the way problems of creative autonomy and authoritative sanction can be employed as rhetorical techniques that mediate between the speaker and the object of his poetry." See *DAI* 41 (July 1980):264A.

1925 MIROLLO, JAMES V. *Mannerism and Renaissance Poetry: Concept, Mode, Inner Design.* New Haven, Conn.: Yale University Press, 1984, pp. 124, 150–51.
As examples of mannerist description, cites *Astrophil and Stella* 22 and the description of Philoclea's hand in "What tongue can her perfections tell" (*OA 62*). See also item 2005.

1926 MONTGOMERY, ROBERT L[ANGFORD], Jr. *Symmetry and Sense: The Poetry of Sir Philip Sidney.* Austin: University of Texas Press, 1961, 141 pp. Orig. a Ph.D. diss., Harvard University, 1956.
Aims to "locate and describe the ornate and plain styles in Sidney's poems and to suggest where each begins and ends." In Chapter 2, examines "symmetry" in the poetry of *The Lady of May*, the Psalms, and *Arcadia*, working from the premise that they "reflect a strong experimental spirit" not found in *Astrophil and Stella*, one "deriving from a different

creative principle." Finds in them a "geometrical, balanced use of ornament," as well as a tendency to amass it at the expense of other elements
in the poetry. Finds, however, that in some of the songs in both the Old
Arcadia and *Certain Sonnets*, he "reaches a more sophisticated concept of
structure." In Chapters 3 and 4, examines the poetry of *Arcadia*, considering the effects that Sidney achieves by incorporating "figures of amplification" and the style and attitudes of Petrarchism. In Chapter 5, discusses Sidney's "Artless Style," treating the *Defence* as a theoretical bridge
between the earlier lyrics and those of *Astrophil and Stella*. In Chapters 6
and 7, considers "The Structures of Artless Style," providing a sustained
reading of *Astrophil and Stella* with the premise that its mixture of styles
results from a tension between convention and feeling. In three appendices, provides definitions of rhetorical figures, tabulates all appearances
of the "blazon," and lists all poems that include personifications. For
detailed annotations, see items 2006, 2204, and 2574.

1927 NICHOLS, J[OHN] G[ORDON]. *The Poetry of Sir Philip Sidney: An
Interpretation in the Context of His Life and Times*. New York: Harper
& Row; Liverpool, England: Liverpool University Press, 1974,
181 pp. Orig. a Ph.D. diss., University of Liverpool, 1971.

Discusses Sidney's poetry in the light of his ideals and those of his age,
concentrating on *Astrophil and Stella* but also giving considerable attention to the poems in *Arcadia* and *Certain Sonnets*. In Chapter 1, suggests
that Sidney is at his best "when his sense of humour has full play."
Traces his humor, along with his wit and "a certain lordly air," to his
practice of *sprezzatura*, which was made possible, in part, by his being
above the need for patronage. Discusses his quantitative experimentation within the broader context of his views on and his practice of "imitation." Quoting copiously, elucidates his mastery of "complicated and
subtly varied rhetorical effects," and through extended comparisons with
Shakespeare and Spenser, argues that a "sense of continual movement
and development is a more constant feature of Sidney's verse than, say,
the use of complex . . . imagery." Finds his images "not so much striking
in themselves as appropriate as means of conveying the argument of the
poem," but claims at the same time that they derive a "force and subtlety" from their very commonness. Finds tendencies toward allegory in his
poetry, but insists that it is Sidney's "ability to write straight fiction which
should be stressed." Except in the Psalms, which were "written with a
flair for tedium," notes a strong sense of the dramatic. In Chapters 2–4,
argues against treating *Astrophil and Stella* either as biographical or fictional, proposing a way of seeing it as "dramatic" instead. See a detailed
annotation in item 2216.

Twentieth Century

1928 OMOND, T[HOMAS] S[TEWART]. *English Metrists, Being a Sketch of English Prosodical Criticism from Elizabethan Times to the Present Day*. Oxford: Clarendon Press, 1921, pp. 2, 7, 9–10, 20, 25, 45, 277, 283.
Argues that Sidney's attempts at classical meters failed because of the nature of the English language, not his ineptitude.

1929 OTSUKA, SADANORI. "Sidney no Palinode." In *Ogoshi Kazugo: Ryokyoju Taikan Kinnen Ronbunshu*, edited by Suga Yasuo. Kyoto, Japan: Apollonsha, 1980, pp. 43–56.
Not seen. Cited as item 1332 in the *MLA International Bibliography*, 1981, vol. 1.

1930 PARSONS, ROGER LOREN. "Renaissance and Baroque: Multiple Unity and Unified Unity in the Treatment of Verse, Ornament, and Structure." Ph.D. diss., University of Wisconsin, 1959, 516 pp.
Contrasts Sidney's images with Donne's to show that a sixteenth-century image is "developed as an object which though relevant to the whole is in addition of interest in itself, [whereas] in seventeenth-century poetry the image tends to be subordinated to its relevance." See *DA* 19 (May 1959):2958.

1931 PAULUSSEN, HANS. *Rhythmik und Technik des sechsfüssigen Jamus im Deutschen und Englischen*. Bonn: Peter Hanstein, 1913, pp. 63–65.
Provides a technical analysis of the alexandrines in *Arcadia* and in *Astrophil and Stella*.

1932 PEBWORTH, TED-LARRY. "The Net for the Soul: A Renaissance Conceit and the Song of Songs." *RomN* 13 (Autumn 1971):159–64.
Traces the Petrarchan image of the lady's hair as a net for the soul back to the Song of Songs 7:1–5. Discusses Sidney's use of this image in "What tongue can her perfections tell" (*OA 62*) and "All my sense thy sweetness gained" (*CS 27*).

1933 POIRIER, MICHEL. "Quelques sources des poèmes de Sidney." *EA* 11 (April–June 1958):150–54.
Quoting parallel passages, notes "rapprochements" between several of Sidney's poems from *Arcadia* and *Certain Sonnets* and works by Ovid, Petrarch, Gosson, and Spenser. Proposes the "règle" that Sidney borrowed from poems quite unlike the ones he was composing.

1934 POLICARDI, S[ILVIO]. *Lyrical Poetry in Renaissance England.* Biblioteca di saggi e lezioni accademiche, 9. Milan: Montuoro, 1943, pp. 60–64, 74–77, 79–87.

Sees *Arcadia* as the "most finished expression" of Elizabethan pastoral and praises the technique of its lyrics. Divides *Astrophil and Stella* into poems that deal with established Petrarchan themes and others that appear autobiographical, concluding that the sequence is largely conventional. Praises its songs for combining "conscious aesthetic devices" with "spontaneous song." Also discusses the appearance of many of Sidney's lyrics in late sixteenth-century poetic miscellanies.

1935 POMEROY, ELIZABETH W. *The Elizabethan Miscellanies: Their Development and Conventions.* University of California Publications: English Studies, 36. Berkeley, Los Angeles, and London: University of California Press, 1973, pp. 14, 17–18, 74–92, 103, 104, 114.

Views Howell's *Devises* (2762) as the "link between the traditions of Surrey and Sidney." Notes that Sidney's poems appear in *England's Helicon*, Davison's *Poetical Rhapsody* (63), and *Britton's Bower of Delights* (2748). Arguing that *The Phoenix Nest* is an extended elegy for Sidney, documents Sidney's connection with the phoenix. Points out links between Sidney and poems in the collection, concluding that "the first section recalls Sidney and some medieval modes; the second commemorates him practically, in contemporary poetic styles." See item 2740, Ralegh (2768), and Roydon (2770). See also Rollins (723).

1936 POTTER, JAMES LAIN. "The Development of Sonnet-Patterns in the Sixteenth Century." Ph.D. diss., Harvard University, 1954, pp. 85–107.

Dating the sonnets of *Arcadia* between 1577 and 1581 and those of *Astrophil and Stella* between 1581 and 1583, notes that the former are mainly English in form and the latter Italian. Points to the more Shakespearean and experimental nature of those in *Certain Sonnets*.

1937 QUITSLUND, JON A. "Sidney's Presence in Lyric Verse of the Later English Renaissance." In *Sir Philip Sidney and the Interpretation of Renaissance Culture: The Poet in His Time and in Ours: A Collection of Critical and Scholarly Essays,* edited by Gary F. Waller and Michael D. Moore. London: Croom Helm; Totowa, N.J.: Barnes & Noble, 1984, pp. 110–23.

Works from three hypotheses: that Sidney is "mannerist" in his embodiment of "contrary abilities"; that, *pace* Harold Bloom, Sidney more than

Twentieth Century

any other determined the "lack of priority" of lyric poets over the next fifty years; and that his early tragic death "liberated energies and encouraged emulation," rather than producing anxiety of a guilty, post-Romantic sort. Examines Greville's "strengths" by comparing *Astrophil and Stella* 99 with *Caelica* 100; discusses the "strangeness of Sidney's presence" in Shakespeare's Sonnets 24, 84, and 127; notes a number of "allusions to and transformations of Sidney's models" among Donne's poems; and contends that Herbert is "indebted more deeply and broadly than Donne" to Sidney's "colloquialism, playfulness, intertwining narrative and discourse, surpassing twists in . . . thought, and . . . controlled ironies."

1938 REICHERT, JOHN FREDERICK. "Formal Logic and English Renaissance Poetry." Ph.D. diss., Stanford University, 1963, 233 pp.

Finds that the majority of Sidney's sonnets oppose two points of view in the manner of a logical debate. In some, the debate remains unsettled and concludes with a logical paradox. More often, however "the octet presents a proposition which is then refuted by an enthymeme in the sestet," with the last line often being the major premise of the enthymeme. See *DA* 24 (September 1963):1174–75.

1939 RIGIK, ELNORA MARYANNE. "'No Eloquence Like It': Stylistic Rhetoric in the Poetry of Sir Philip Sidney." Ph.D. diss., University of Delaware, 1981, 179 pp.

Examines Sidney's use of rhetorical figures and schemes to "emphasize themes and messages," to "recreate the motions of the mind thinking," and to "arouse emotions in the reader." Sees a "limited use" of rhetorical devices in the Old *Arcadia* poems, with a "sameness of effect." In *Certain Sonnets*, sees a "wider selection of varied figures to capture the lover's emotions and states of mind." In *Astrophil and Stella*, finds figures "so skillfully assimilated into the texture of the poems that they nearly escape notice." See *DAI* 41 (May 1981):4723A–24A.

1940 RINGLER, WILLIAM [A., Jr.]. "Master Drant's Rules." *PQ* 29 (January 1950):70–74.

Beginning with Spenser's reference (274) to the "rules" of William Drant, sets out to clarify Sidney's theories of quantitative verse. Cites statements in the First Eclogues of the Old *Arcadia*, the relevant passage in Ponsonby's 1595 edition of the *Defence*, and the "Nota" written in the margin of the manuscript of the Old *Arcadia* at St. John's College, Cambridge.

1941 ———. "Poems Attributed to Sir Philip Sidney." *SP* 47 (April 1950):126–51.

Surveys the poems attributed to Sidney since his death, arguing that at least 278 are genuine: seventy-six in the Old *Arcadia*, thirty-two in *Certain Sonnets*, 119 in *Astrophil and Stella*, three in *The Lady of May*, five in the New *Arcadia*, and the first forty-three Psalms in the Sidney Psalter. Argues that, since Sidney himself collected his miscellaneous poems and since he seems to have spent the latter part of his literary career working on religious subjects, the "probability of there being any considerable number of miscellaneous poems that he did not include in *Certain Sonnets* is slight." Discusses the case in favor of thirty other poems attributed to Sidney, concluding that two (or possibly three) are authentic and that two more are probably by Sidney. See also Bowen (1843).

1942 ROBERTSON, JEAN. "A Note on 'Poems by Sir Philip Sidney: The Ottley Manuscript.'" *Library*, 6th ser. 2 (June 1980):202–5.

Praises Beal's comments (1864) on the poems from *Arcadia* and *Certain Sonnets* in the Ottley Manuscript, but challenges three of his readings, arguing that Ringler's (92) are better. See also Warkentin (2331).

1943 ROBINSON, FORREST G[LEN]. *The Shape of Things Known: Sidney's "Apology" in Its Philosophical Tradition.* Cambridge, Mass.: Harvard University Press, 1972, pp. 173–204. Orig. a Ph.D. diss., Harvard University, 1968.

In the second section of Chapter 4, considers the effects of Sidney's "visual epistemology" on the poems in *Arcadia* and *Astrophil and Stella*. Defines the role of love as "the refiner of invention," suggesting that "when the compelling clarity—the *energia*—of the lover's amorous Idea is accurately set forth in words, the result is good love poetry." From "In vain, mine eyes, you labour to amend" and "Since so mine eyes are subject to your sight" (*OA 14, 16*), infers the relation between vision and knowledge in Sidney's early poetry, relating it to *trattati d'amore* that Sidney may have read in Italy. Notes that Pyrocles and Musidorus are "almost completely powerless to abandon the image of a body for the image of an Idea." Analyzes the Christian elements in five poems addressed by Basilius to the sun (*OA 26, 38, 52, 55, 69*), tracing the causes of the King's loss of reason and his "apostasy" in preferring Zelmane over Apollo. Argues that Basilius illustrates a principle true of Sidney's lovers in general, that "infected mindes infect each thing they see" (*CS 18*) by projecting amorous "conceits" onto the things seen. Analyzes "My sheep are thoughts" and "Feed on my sheep" (*OA 17, 23*) as speaking pictures of Musidorus's passion, and "Ye living powers" and "My words,

Twentieth Century

in hope to blaze my stedfast mind" (*OA 18, 19*) as emblems for Philoclea's emotions. Compares such poems with Giordano Bruno's *Eroici furori*, which uses a similar emblematic technique, and with the poems of *Astrophil and Stella*, which are not static in the same way but portray "mental movement." Stressing the role of Stella's image made "visible" as a "concrete universal" in the heart of the lover in Sonnet 1, discusses "the way aesthetic and amorous intentions overlap" in the sequence and the relation between Stella's varying responses and Astrophil's "conceits" of her. Ponders his difficulties in climbing the Platonic "ladder of love" in Sonnets 5, 25, 28, 50, 67, 101 and Song v, discussing the lover's departure from "bookish convictions" to embrace "the illogic of love's invention." Concludes that, both in *Arcadia* and in *Astrophil and Stella*, Sidney's "first and most urgent impulse is to make thoughts and ideas visible to the eye of the reader's mind," but that the sonnets "figure forth the complex and irregular rhythms of conscious-ness itself." Treats *Astrophil and Stella* as "an antidote for the clear-eyed optimism of the [*Defence*]" in that it explores the distortions possible in the relation between seeing and thinking. See also item 721 and Weiner (2298).

1944 ROBINSON, PETER. "In Another's Words: Thomas Hardy's Poetry." *English* 31 (Autumn 1982):221–46.
Argues that Hardy's "Lausanne in Gibbon's Old Garden 11–12 p.m." shares several technical devices (e.g., rhetorical question) with Sidney's sonnet "With how sad steps, O moon" (*AS 31*).

1945 RUBEL, VERÉ L[AURA]. *Poetic Diction in the English Renaissance from Skelton through Spenser*. New York: Modern Language Association, 1941, pp. 20, 104, 107, 113–16, 123–26, 133, 145, 152–58, 203–10, 211.
Comments on Sidney's use of polysyllabic rhyme, his "borrowings," and his interest in the question of proper poetic diction, analyzing at length "As I my little flock on Ister bank" (*OA 66*). Contrasts the argument against archaisms in the *Defence* with their use in the poems of *Arcadia*, suggesting that, in Spenser's *Shepherd's Calendar*, Sidney may have disap-proved of the dialect words more than the archaisms. Notes that *Astrophil and Stella* is free of such words. Discusses Sidney's use of figures, listing those used in *Astrophil and Stella* and analyzing Sonnets 33, 36, and 47 to illustrate their use. Argues that the diction of the Psalms is similar to that of *Astrophil and Stella*. Also considers Sidney's experiments in classical versification and the possible influence of the Pléiade on the use of compounding in the Sidney circle.

General

1946 RUHRMANN, FRIEDRICH G. *Studien zur Geschichte und Charakteristik des Refrains in der englischen Literatur.* Anglistische Forschungen, 64. Heidelberg: Carl Winter, 1927, pp. 53–56.
Discusses the use of refrains in Sidney's poetry.

1947 RUTHVEN, K.K. *The Conceit.* The Critical Idiom, 4. London: Methuen & Co., 1969, pp. 23, 27–28, 31–32, 37–38, 59.
Views "What tongue can her perfections tell" (*OA 62*) as the best English example of the blazon on a lady's beauty and "What length of verse can serve brave Mopsa's good to show" (*OA 3*) as a good example of the comic reversal of the same form. Suggests that Sidney's ability to achieve a balance between serious and comic, between literal and figurative, maintains the freshness in his conceits. Discusses the heraldic metaphors in *Astrophil and Stella* 13 and 65, rejecting Yates's view of them (2313). Suggests that a failure to understand the conceit as a poetic device may lie behind biographical readings of Sonnet 59.

1948 SALOMON, LOUIS B[ERNARD]. *The Devil Take Her: A Study of the Rebellious Lover in English Poetry.* Philadelphia: University of Pennsylvania Press, 1931, pp. 21, 66–67, 83, 291–93, 320, 332, 351. Orig. a Ph.D. diss., University of Pennsylvania, 1931.
Regards "Leave me, O Love" (*CS 32*) as an extreme example of the "farewell to love" motif and "Ring out your bells" (*CS 30*) and "What, have I thus betrayed my liberty?" (*AS 47*) as examples of a "pseudo-revolt" against love. Cites other instances of such rebellion in Sidney's works.

1949 SATTERTHWAITE, ALFRED W. *Spenser, Ronsard, and Du Bellay: A Renaissance Comparison.* Princeton, N.J.: Princeton University Press, 1960, pp. 40, 52–53, 56.
Finds Sidney the most likely channel of influence between French and English poetry in the 1570s and 1580s.

1950 SCHIPPER, JAKOB. *A History of English Versification.* Oxford: Clarendon Press, 1910, pp. 205, 262–68, 308–9, 334, 354, 365, 373–74, 380, 382, 383.
To illustrate Sidney's role as an innovator, cites his use of a wide variety of metrical forms and stanza patterns.

1951 SCOTT, JANET G[IRVAN]. *Les sonnets élisabéthains: Les sources et l'apport personnel.* Bibliothèque de la Revue de Littérature

Twentieth Century

Comparée, 60. Paris: Librairie Ancienne Honoré Champion, 1929, pp. 15–53.

Compares the sonnets of *Arcadia* with those in *Astrophil and Stella*, commenting on anti-Petrarchan elements and noting in *Arcadia* more imitation of foreign sources. Considers the relationship between Sidney and Penelope Rich, arguing for a biographical reading of *Astrophil and Stella*. Also touches on matters of poetic technique in *Certain Sonnets*. Notes Sidney's debts to French sonneteers, both in form and in content, but praises his originality in giving a new form to an old subject.

1952 SCOTT, WILLIAM O. "Structure and Repetition in Elizabethan Verse." Ph.D. diss., Princeton University, 1959, 224 pp.

In a study of ways in which techniques of repetition derived from rhetorical handbooks influenced Renaissance poets, argues that Sidney "adjusts repetition and syntax more closely [than Wyatt] to context, so that syntax becomes imitative of the mind's workings in a given situation. Syntax expresses internal colloquy or meditation. Repetition portrays a mental grasping and seizing upon words for the sake of greater self-knowledge." Compares Spenser and Donne to Sidney. See *DA* 20 (March 1960):3752.

1953 SMITH, BARBARA HERRNSTEIN. *Poetic Closure: A Study of How Poems End*. Chicago and London: University of Chicago Press, 1968, pp. 21, 25, 50, 148–50, 213–14.

Analyzes "Ye goatherd gods" (*OA 71*), "Come, let me write" (*AS 34*), "Who will in fairest book of nature know" (*AS 71*), and "Thou blind man's mark" (*CS 31*) as examples of four different techniques of poetic closure.

1954 SMITH, EGERTON. *The Principles of English Metre*. London: Oxford University Press, Humphrey Milford, 1923, pp. 5, 112, 158, 266, 271, 273–74.

Cites examples from Sidney's poetry to illustrate the emotional effect of rhythm, the syllabic theory of versification, the use of classical meters, and the sonnet form. Notes parallels between Sidney's rhymes in the sonnets and those of Ronsard.

1955 SMITH, HALLETT [DARIUS]. *Elizabethan Poetry: A Study in Convention, Meaning, and Expression*. Cambridge, Mass.: Harvard University Press, 1952, pp. 10, 51–54, 58–59, 142–57, 162–66, 271, 280, 325.

Compares the pastoral eclogues in *Arcadia* with those of Spenser in *The Shepherd's Calendar*. Distinguishes comedy from satire in "And are you there old Pas" (*OA 29*) and "What length of verse can serve brave Mopsa's good to show" (*OA 3*). Calling *Astrophil and Stella* arguably the most important Elizabethan sonnet cycle, claims that it establishes the "vitality" of the Petrarchan tradition, as distinct from its "manner." Approaches the sonnets "through the critical comments in the poems themselves," claiming that they "involve" the critical theories of the *Defence* and that, from them, we can infer a "doctrine about love poetry, and perhaps by implication about all poetry." Examines in detail the problem of the two audiences in the sequence, Stella herself and other readers. Also analyzes the style and diction by which an "individual role" is created for Astrophil. Argues that the sonnets are structured according to a "system in which the feelings work two ways and have an object in the reconciliation of opposites," with the "most extended and pervasive conflict" being that between reason and passion. This conflict accounts for roughly one-fifth of the sonnets, "disposed throughout the cycle in such a way that they influence most of the others." Focusing on the eleventh song, discusses the inconclusiveness of the sequence. Suggests Sidney's influence on Spenser's *Amoretti* and on Drayton's 1599 revisions of *Idea's Mirror*. Discusses the failure of the quantitative verse experiments of the Areopagus and their relation to Campion's *Observations on the Art of English Poesy*. Also discusses Sidney's moralized view of Virgil's *Aeneid* and of heroic poetry in general.

1956 SOUTHALL, RAYMOND. "Love Poetry in the Sixteenth Century." *EIC* 22 (October 1972):362–80.

Argues that the shift from Wyatt's plain style to Sidney's more ornate one was the result of a shift in poetic sensibilities, in which economics was a major factor. Finds that metaphors based on wealth became more prominent as money gained importance in daily life.

1957 SPENCER, THEODORE. "The Poetry of Sir Philip Sidney." *ELH* 12 (December 1945):251–78.

Draws attention to the importance of "art, imitation, and exercise" in Sidney's early poetic efforts and to the attempt to break through convention in the later works. Sees the Sidney Psalms, whose "intrinsic merit is small," as important for their experiments in metrics and diction. Noting the "astonishing variety of forms" in the poems of the Old *Arcadia*, argues that the experiments in classical meters taught Sidney how to achieve variety within the individual line, whereas his imitation of Italian models gave him practice in variations from one line to another, training his ear in "more elaborate melody and counterpoint." In *Astrophil and Stella*, sees Sidney trying deliberately "to put convention

Twentieth Century

aside, and to speak for himself," an attempt which was his "legacy, not only to the generation of poets which immediately followed, but to all poets since." Comparing "In a grove most rich of shade" (*AS viii*) with Donne's "Ecstasie," finds Sidney "more elemental, more direct." Concludes that Sidney, not Spenser, is "the most central of English poets in the generation that was soon to know Shakespeare."

1958 SPIEGEL, GLENN S. "Perfecting English Meter: Sixteenth-Century Criticism and Practice." *JEGP* 79 (April 1980):192–209.
Examines a variety of works, including "Transformed in show" (*OA 2*), "Loving in truth" (*AS 1*), and "What ails this heathenish rage?" (*PS 2*), to show Sidney's contribution to the development of a new kind of English meter.

1959 STACK, RICHARD CATESBY. "From Sweetness to Strength: A Study of the Development of Metrical Style in the English Renaissance." Ph.D. diss., Stanford University, 1968, 223 pp.
Seeks to provide a general description of the "style-shift" from the "sweet" line of Sidney and Spenser to the "strong line" of Donne. Remarks on Sidney's "ability to manipulate conventional linguistic and rhythmic counters within a legalistically defined framework." Suggests that variety is achieved, "not by tapping the rhythmic unpredictability of speech, but by virtuosity in this manipulation of counters." Locates the primary unit of composition in the line, not the sentence. See *DA* 29 (August 1968):616A.

1960 STULL, WILLIAM L. "Elizabethan Precursors of Donne's 'Divine Meditations.'" *Comitatus* 6 (1975):29–44.
Notes Sidney's influence on Donne's adaptation of the concept of *energeia* and his use of "moving, dramatic metaphors." Shows that Sidney's influence was also transmitted to Donne through the poetry of Henry Constable, Barnabe Barnes, and Henry Lok.

1961 SWALLOW, ALAN. "Principles of Poetic Composition from Skelton to Sidney." Ph.D. diss., Louisiana State University, 1941.
Compare's Sidney's poetry with that of Wyatt, concluding that the two men had "similar intentions and the same techniques" and that Sidney "provides the link between Wyatt and the later poets who were to use the method for great poetry." See *The Graduate School: Abstracts of Theses, University Bulletin, Lousiana State University*, n.s. 34, (January 1942): 21–23.

1962 TANNENBAUM, SAMUEL A[ARON]. "Unfamiliar Versions of Some Elizabethan Poems." *PMLA* 45 (September 1930):809–21.

Records two poems attributed to Sidney, "How can the feeble forts" (*AT 12*) and "Are women fair?" (*AT 4*), in a mid-seventeenth-century commonplace book in the possession of Dr. Rosenbach of New York City.

1963 THOMPSON, JOHN. "Sir Philip and the Forsaken Iamb." *KR* 20 (Winter 1958):90–115. Reprint, with minor changes. "Sir Philip Sidney." In *The Founding of English Metre*. London: Routledge & Kegan Paul; New York: Columbia University Press, 1961, pp. 139–55. Orig. a Ph.D. diss., Columbia University, 1957.

Asks "What has the meter to do with meaning?" and in "going back to the beginning" for an answer, claims that, in Sidney's poetry, "the metrical system of modern English reaches perfection for the first time." Argues that Sidney extended Gasgoigne's recognition that metrical pattern was something "that could be thought of as a thing apart from the language itself" by "using" meter in two ways. In the poems of *Arcadia*, he "perfects an ability to make features of the language correspond to the same features in the metrical pattern," with psychological insight and with a "thoroughness of organization unknown before." In *Astrophil and Stella*, the language is fitted to metrical pattern "no less exactly" than in the earlier poems, "but the relation of the syllable of language to its similacrum in the meter is more formal, more a matter of technical agreement. The metrical control allows the full sense of the difference between the metrical pattern and the language to become plain. The art of poetry achieves the degree of sophistication that allows it to recognize its own limitations." To illustrate the first of these "two ways," provides detailed metrical analyses of lines from *The Lady of May* and from *Arcadia*, calling the former "pure Gascoigne in meter." By similar analyses of lines from *Astrophil and Stella*, defines a "new kind of poetry," which is "our English meter at last."

1964 TUVE, ROSEMOND. *Elizabethan and Metaphysical Imagery: Renaissance Poetic and Twentieth-Century Critics*. Chicago: University of Chicago Press, 1947, pp. 29–31, 39–42, 85, 90, 111–13, 182–85, 205, 320–22.

Uses Sidney's poetic as a touchstone for Renaissance literary theory. Analyses "Because I oft in dark abstracted guise" (*AS 27*) to show the effects of logical and rhetorical training upon his poetry. Argues that Sidney's emphasis on *energeia* and his concern with universals would have led him to didacticism, even if he had not followed the Horatian dictum that poets should teach and delight.

Twentieth Century

1965 WAGNER, BERNARD MATHIAS. "New Poems by Sir Philip Sidney." *PMLA* 53 (March 1938):118–24.

Argues that thirteen poems in MS. Harley 7392—compiled by St. Loe Kniveton between 1584 and 1600—are by Sidney. The list includes "Ring out your bells" (*CS 30*) and ten poems from *Arcadia*. See also Ringler (92), who rejects the attribution to Sidney of two of the poems: "Philisides, the shepherd good and true" (*AT 19*) and "The gentle season of the year" (*AT 25*).

1966 WARKENTIN, GERMAINE [THERESE]. "The Meeting of the Muses: Sidney and the Mid-Tudor Poets." In *Sir Philip Sidney and the Interpretation of Renaissance Culture: The Poet in His Time and in Ours: A Collection of Critical and Scholarly Essays*, edited by Gary F. Waller and Michael D. Moore. London: Croom Helm; Totowa, N.J.: Barnes & Noble, 1984, pp. 17–33.

Argues that Sidney learned invaluable lessons about "the architecture of whole collections" of poems from carefully reading mid-century "gentleman's miscellanies." Briefly analyzes the collections of Barnaby Googe, George Turberville, and George Gascoigne to show that their informing principles are predominantly those of the Dantean *libello* rather than the Petrarchan *canzonieri*. In particular, finds them strongly schematic and moral in tone. Argues that Sidney found in them "three elements of supreme importance": a public and civic ethical perspective, a "special role played by woman," and a "peculiarly circumstantial texture." Argues that *Certain Sonnets* was composed and, in the Bodleian Manuscript version, consciously revised both "within the parameters established by such collections" and as a critique of them. Calls *Astrophil and Stella* the first true Petrarchan *canzoniere* in English, but one with a difference for which "the mid-Tudor *libello* is accountable." Contends, finally, that "we have always subconsciously heeded" this influence in a repeated feeling that *Certain Sonnets 31* and *32* provide a telling conclusion to *Astrophil and Stella*.

1967 WASWO, RICHARD. *The Fatal Mirror: Themes and Techniques in the Poetry of Fulke Greville*. Charlottesville: University Press of Virginia, 1972, pp. 43–44, 56–57, 97, 103–5.

Discusses the relationship between *Caelica* and the poetry of *Astrophil and Stella* and *Arcadia*, noting Greville's appropriation of Sidney's techniques for embodying abstract concepts. Finds that the two poets differ, not on the moral purpose of poetry, but rather on its moral efficacy and therefore on issues of style. Compares the treatment of the Cupid legend in "His mother dear Cupid offended late" (*AS 17*) and *Caelica* 73. Drawing on Sidney's views of *energeia* in the *Defence*, discusses changes in the rhetoric of *Astrophil and Stella* according to the audience addressed.

1968 WEISS, WOLFGANG. *Der Refrain in der Elisabethanischen Lyrik: Studien zur Entwicklungsgeschichte eines literarischen Formelements.* Munich: n.p., 1964, pp. 41–49. Orig. a Ph.D. diss., Ludwig-Maximilians-Universität zu München, 1964.
Provides a technical analysis of Sidney's innovations in poems structured around a refrain.

1969 WELLS, HENRY W[ILLIS]. *Poetic Imagery Illustrated from Elizabethan Literature.* New York: Columbia University Press, 1924, pp. 42–45.
Faults Sidney's conceits for being overelaborate and his images for being "conspicuous as metaphorical excrescences."

1970 WEST, BILL C. "Anti-Petrarchism: A Study of the Reaction against the Courtly Tradition in English Love-Poetry from Wyatt to Donne." Ph.D. diss., Northwestern University, 1950.
Includes Sidney among Elizabethan poets who "repudiated the Petrarchistic love-conventions in both ideology and style in their most characteristic and successful work." See *Summaries of Doctoral Dissertations Submitted to the Graduate School of Northwestern University* 18 (June–September 1950):35–37.

1971 WINTERS, YVOR. "English Literature in the Sixteenth Century." *HudR* 8 (Summer 1955):281–87. Reprint. In *The Function of Criticism: Problems and Exercises*, by Yvor Winters. Denver: Alan Swallow, 1957, pp. 189–200.
In reviewing Lewis (630), rejects two common views: that Sidney and others in the "Petrarchan movement" displaced Elizabethan poets who preferred the plain style, and that Donne wrote in reaction against Sidney and his imitators.

1972 ———. *Forms of Discovery: Critical and Historical Essays on the Forms of the Short Poem in English.* Denver: Alan Swallow, 1967, pp. 29–34.
Notes Sidney's part in popularizing the Petrarchan style. Analyzes "Highway, since you my chief Parnassus be" (*AS 84*) and "Leave me, O love" (*CS 32*), noting unevenness in their quality.

Twentieth Century

1973 ———. "The Sixteenth Century Lyric in England: A Critical and Historical Reinterpretation." *Poetry* 53 (February 1939):258–72; (March 1939):320–35; 54 (April 1939):35–51.

Presents a case for downplaying the importance of the Petrarchan poetry of the Elizabethan age in favor of poems in a less ornate style. Contends that, because Sidney is caught up in the pleasures of rhetoric for its own sake, he often introduces "a mode of perception too complex for his own poetic powers" and is "forced to seek matter in the precious and the trivial." Notes in particular the faults in "Highway, since you my chief Parnassus be" (*AS 84*). Allows, however, that Sidney's songs are "nearly all perfect in execution; the slighter songs display extraordinary wit and polish, and some of the most ambitious have considerable depth." Suggests that Jonson, Donne, and later writers owe Sidney a considerable debt for his contributions to the development of the English song. See also Paterson (2222).

1974 WOODS, SUSANNE. "Aesthetic and Mimetic Rhythms in the Versification of Gascoigne, Sidney, and Spenser." *SLitI* 11 (Spring 1978):31–44.

Sets out to show how certain "rhythmic varieties" developed within "the new accented-syllabic security of English Renaissance versification" and go beyond such prevailing stylistic categories as "plain" or "eloquent." Distinguishes mimetic rhythms (those that "directly imitate, represent, or promote" either the speaking voice or the poem's statement) from aesthetic ones (those that are pleasurable but not directly imitative of voice or statement). Argues that, unlike either Spenser or Gascoigne, whose variations from the iambic pattern are aesthetic, Sidney's rhythmic tensions are strongly imitative. Examines *Astrophil and Stella* 41 and 31 to suggest that he has "far greater control over the rhythmic movement of his lines than was possible" before the Renaissance.

2. POEMS FROM *ARCADIA*

Seventeenth Century

1975 DOWLAND, JOHN. *The Second Booke of Songs or Ayres, of 2. 4. and 5. partes: With Tableture for the Lute or Orpherian, with the Violl de Gamba.* London: by Thomas Este, 1600, sig. F2ᵛ.

In Song 10, dedicated to Hugh Holland, provides a setting for four voices of "O sweet woods" (*OA 34*). Does not identify the poem as by Sidney. See also Willetts (2028).

Twentieth Century

1976 PILKINGTON, FRANCIS. *The Second Set of Madrigals and Pastorals, of 3. 4. 5. and 6. Parts, Apt for Violls and Voyces*. London: by Thomas Snodham, 1624, no. 14.
Presents a setting for five voices of the text of lines 5–10 of "Come shepherd's weeds" (*OA 4*). See Fellowes (1884).

Nineteenth Century

1977 SMITH, T.C. "Poetical Coincidences: Sheridan." *N&Q* 4 (18 October 1851):291.
Notes that a poem beginning "O yield, fair lids," which occurs in an unfinished, untitled play by Sheridan, is an adaptation of "Lock up, fair lids" (*OA 51*).

Twentieth Century

1978 ADLER, DORIS. "Imaginary Toads in Real Gardens." *ELR* 11 (Autumn 1981):235–60.
Briefly discusses Sidney's references to frogs in poems such as "Ister bank" (*OA 66*), noting that other political writings of the age employ that creature to represent the Duke of Alençon. Considers Sidney a "spokesman" for the Leicester party at court.

1979 ATTRIDGE, DEREK. *Well-Weighed Syllables: English Verse in Classical Metres*. Cambridge: Cambridge University Press, 1974, pp. 173–87. Orig. a Ph.D. diss., Cambridge University, 1972.
In "Scholarship and Sensitivity—Sir Philip Sidney," argues that Sidney was aware of the attempt to reform Latin pronunciation and its implications for metrical quantity, despite the fact that he "probably read Latin verse with an unclassical pronunciation." Compares him with Stanyhurst, concluding that Sidney's quantitative verse neither accurately imitates Latin verse nor ignores natural length and accent in English, but is instead an "attempt to introduce into English poetry those features of classical verse so highly admired by the Elizabethans, without losing too much of the rhythmical quality of traditional English verse." Discusses in detail the use of classical meters in the poems of *Arcadia*.

1980 BLANK, PHILIP E., Jr. "Auden's Poetic Models: 'Paysage moralisé' and Sidney's 'Ye Gote-heard Gods.'" *PLL* 16 (Winter 1980):90–99.
Argues that Auden's uncharacteristically close imitation of "Ye goatherd gods" (*OA 71*) owes a debt to Empson's commentary (1986) and reflects

535

Twentieth Century

the view that "we are bound to revive the past." Argues that Auden follows the verbal and architectonic structure of Sidney's poem in a fashion that "not only links past and present but expands a correlation of times into an evocation of the tide of history."

1981 BOLTE, JOHANNES. "Das Echo in Volksglaube und Dichtung." *Forschungen und Fortschritte* 11 (1 September 1935):320–21.
Discusses the long tradition of echo poems, touching on the eclogue "Fair rocks, goodly rivers" (*OA 31*).

1982 BREWER, WILMON. *Concerning the Art of Poetry*. Francestown, N.H.: Marshall Jones Co., 1979, pp. 129, 155–62 passim.
Places Sidney in the history of the English sonnet, discussing the Italian origin of poems designed around parallel lists of nouns and verbs such as his "Virtue, beauty, and speech" (*OA 60*).

1983 COLBY, ELBRIDGE. *The Echo Device in Literature*. New York: New York Public Library, 1920, pp. 21–23.
Notes that Sidney did not use the echo device in his short lyrics and sonnets, where it would be most common, but in a longer eclogue, "Fair rocks, goodly rivers" (*OA 31*), which invites comparison with a poem in Sir William Alexander's *Aurora*.

1984 CUNNINGHAM, J[AMES] V[INCENT]. "The Problem of Form." *Shenandoah* 14 (Winter 1963):3–6. Reprint. In *The Collected Essays of J.V. Cunningham*. Chicago: Swallow Press, 1976, pp. 247–50.
Compares Donne's epigram on Hero and Leander with two lines in Sidney's eclogue "In faith, good Histor, long in your delay" (*OA 67*).

1985 DIPPLE, ELIZABETH [DOROTHEA]. "The 'Fore Conceit' of Sidney's Eclogues." In *Literary Monographs*, 1, edited by Eric Rothstein and Thomas K. Dunseath. Madison and London: University of Wisconsin Press, 1967, pp. 3–47, 301–3.
Considers Sidney's concepts of the poet's "golden world" and of the "fore-conceit" as central to an understanding of the eclogues of *Arcadia*. Argues that they function in opposition to, as well as in accord with, the general movement of the work. Discusses the contrast between the noble characters and the rustics, suggesting that the speakers in the eclogues advance from a state of ignorance to a vision of harmony.

1986 EMPSON, WILLIAM. *Seven Types of Ambiguity*. London: Chatto & Windus, 1930, pp. 45–50.
Analyzes the poem "Ye goatherd gods" (*OA 71*). Points out the slow accretion of feelings and implications attained by the double sestina

536

form, which repeats line endings from stanza to stanza. See also Blank (1980) and Ransom (2010).

1987 GALM, JOHN A[RNOLD]. *Sidney's Arcadian Poems.* Salzburg Studies in English Literature: Elizabethan and Renaissance Studies, 1. Salzburg: Institut für Englische Sprache und Literatur, Universität Salzburg, 1973, 229 pp. Orig. a Ph.D. diss., Yale University, 1963.

Using the 1593 *Arcadia,* discusses the distribution of poems in the text and draws comparisons with Sannazaro, Montemayor, and Gascoigne. Examines the eclogues in detail, suggesting that the variety of their styles is a reflection of the complex diversity of the work as a whole. Concludes that the "pastoral society is not an ideal one juxtaposed to the princely, but it does more often possess some natural virtues like simplicity and common sense which focus attention on the excesses of the more sophisticated Arcadians." Takes little notice of criticism after the year 1962.

1988 GARKE, ESTHER. *The Use of Songs in Elizabethan Prose Fiction.* Bern, Switzerland: Francke Verlag, 1972, pp. 15–71 passim.

Considers the function of the songs in *Arcadia,* classifying them and considering their function in the plot, the characterization, and the setting. Discusses the precedents for mingling prose and verse in a romance. Points out that the songs sung by Sidney's shepherds evoke the pastoral setting and are simple, whereas those of the royal characters lack pastoral description and are sophisticated. Analyzes Basilius's hymn to Apollo (*OA 38*) as a blasphemous parody of Christian hymnody, regarding his public display of emotion as a breach of aristocratic decorum. Notes that, during performances of the eclogues, time stands still and the seasons reflect the singers' moods rather than the actual time of year. Also discusses the loss of supernatural associations in Sidney's adaptation of the traditional echo song (*OA 31*).

1989 GIBSON, WENDY. "Sidney's Two Riddles." *N&Q,* n.s. 24 (December 1977):520–21.

Offers "a pregnant woman" as the answer to both riddles in the poem "And are you there old Pas?" (*OA 29*).

1990 GRANT, W[ILLIAM] LEONARD. *Neo-Latin Literature and the Pastoral.* Chapel Hill: University of North Carolina Press, 1965, pp. 203–4.

Compares the poem "Virtue, beauty, and speech did strike, wound, charm" (*OA 60*) with other examples of the same rhetorical scheme, called *contraria contrariis.*

Twentieth Century

1991 GREENBLATT, STEPHEN J[AY]. *Sir Walter Raleigh: The Renaissance Man and His Roles.* Yale Studies in English, 183. New Haven and London: Yale University Press, 1973, pp. 88–90.
Notes that, although there are similarities in literary method between Ralegh's *Ocean to Cynthia* and Sidney's "Ye goatherd gods" (*OA 71*), such as ambiguity in the imagery and the breaking down of terminal words in successive stanzas, Sidney's poem is more controlled.

1992 HANSSEN, SELBY. "An Analysis of Sir Philip Sidney's Metrical Experiments in the *Arcadia.*" Ph.D. diss., Yale University, 1942.
Not seen. Cited in *DDAAU* 9 (1942):109.

1993 HENDRICKSON, G.L. "Elizabethan Quantitative Hexameters." *PQ* 28 (April 1949):237–60.
Notes Sidney's prominence among Englishmen interested in classical versification during the last decades of the sixteenth century. Cites poems from *Arcadia* to illustrate his interest in a variety of meters and his care in adapting them from the Latin.

1994 HOLLANDER, JOHN. *The Untuning of the Sky: Ideas of Music in English Poetry, 1500–1700.* Princeton, N.J.: Princeton University Press, 1961, pp. 126–27, 139–43.
Considers the imagery underlying Gynecia's song "My lute, within thyself thy tunes enclose" (*OA 54*), noting Sidney's musical awareness and commenting on his distinction between ancient and modern methods of versification. Finds parallels in the thought of Jean Antoine de Baïf and his circle. Notes Sidney's awareness of the divergence of poetry from music, discussing the eclogue "Come Dorus, come, let songs thy sorrows signify" (*OA 7*) as his most elaborate statement on the relations between the two.

1995 HUGHEY, RUTH. "The Harington Manuscript at Arundel Castle and Related Documents." *Library*, 4th ser. 15 (March 1935): 388–444.
In the course of describing documents "closely related" to the Arundel Harington Manuscript, notes a manuscript of the metrical Psalms of Sidney and the Countess of Pembroke. The Harington Manuscript itself contains eight of Sidney's poems, several in Sir John's hand, and a version of Ralegh's epitaph on Sidney (2768) that validates Ralegh's authorship.

1996 JAKOBSON, ROMAN. "The Grammatical Texture of a Sonnet from Sir Philip Sidney's *Arcadia.*" In *Studies in Language and Literature in Honour of Margaret Schlauch*, edited by Mieczysław

Brahmer, Stanisław Helsztyński, and Julian Krzyżanowski. Warsaw: PWN—Polish Scientific Publishers, 1966, pp. 165–73. Provides a technical analysis of the Arcadian sonnet "Loved I am, and yet complain of love" (*OA 20*). Points out patterns of sound, grammatical form, and rhetoric.

1997 JERNIGAN, JOHN CHARLES. "The Sestina in Provençe, Italy, France, and England (1180–1600)." Ph.D. diss., Indiana University, 1970, 290 pp. Discusses the three sestinas in *Arcadia* (*OA 70, 71, 76*), remarking on the connection of the form with pastoral romance. Notes that Sidney introduced the sestina to England. See *DAI* 31 (June 1971):6554A–55A.

1998 JONES, DOROTHY. "Sidney's Erotic Pen: An Interpretation of One of the *Arcadia* Poems." *JEGP* 73 (January 1974):32–47. Argues that "What tongue can her perfections tell" (*OA 62*) is "dominated by two pairs of contrasting ideas; nature and art on the one hand, passion and chastity on the other." Comments on Sidney's erotic imagery and on his adaptation of the blazon formula.

1999 KABELL, AAGE. *Metrische Studien II: Antiker Form sich Nähernd.* Uppsala Universitets Årsskrift 1960, no. 6. Uppsala, Sweden: A.B. Lundequistska Bokhandeln, 1960, pp. 174–77, 217. Discusses the metrical experiments of the Areopagus as reflected in the eclogues of *Arcadia*. Provides a technical analysis of the influence of Latin and French prosody, noting that Sidney learned the art in France and uses many French loanwords.

2000 KALSTONE, DAVID. "The Transformation of *Arcadia*: Sannazaro and Sir Philip Sidney." *CL* 15 (Summer 1963):234–49. Traces the dramatic qualities of Sidney's eclogues to Petrarch's *Rime* and Sannazaro's *Arcadia*, but finds that the verse forms and topics come almost entirely from the latter. Notes in Sidney's poems a new emphasis on the "foul ways" of love and a tension between the chivalric prose and the pastoral eclogues. Explicates "Ye goatherd gods" (*OA 71*), comparing it with the double sestina by Sannazaro from which it derives. Concludes that, whereas Petrarch balances the joys of pastoral imagination with the pains of exiled love and Sannazaro emphasizes the harmony of love, Sidney brings out the "nightmare quality" of the lover's plight. Sees Sidney's poem as "a criticism of the uncomplicated happiness of Sannazaro's *Arcadia*."

Twentieth Century

2001 KERLIN, ROBERT THOMAS. *Theocritus in English Literature.* Lynchburg, Va.: J.P. Bell Co., 1910, pp. 15, 26–27.
Notes comments on Theocritus in the *Defence* and argues that the singing match "And are you there old Pas" (*OA 29*) is modeled on *Idyl* 5.

2002 LITT, GARY L. "Characterization and Rhetoric in Sidney's 'Ye Goatherd Gods.'" *SLitI* 11 (Spring 1978):115–24.
Shows that the poem (*OA 71*) uses imagery, diction, syntax, grammar, and metaphor to differentiate Strephon as a type of the Renaissance literary shepherd from Klaius as a shepherd-hunter. Differs from Fowler (1890) in stressing the "chaotic disentegration and *reversal* of character" in stanzas 9 and 10, where Sidney "crystalizes the essential styles and characters" and "evaluates the relative merits" of the two shepherds' approaches to experience.

2003 McCOWN, GARY MASON. "The Epithalamium in the English Renaissance." Ph.D. diss., University of North Carolina, 1968, 595 pp.
Includes a discussion of the epithalamium for Lalus and Kala (*OA 63*). See *DAI* 29 (January 1969):2220A–21A.

2004 MILL, ADAIR. "Quantitative Verse and the Development of Sixteenth Century English Prosody." *Ingiliz Filolojisi Dergi[si]: Studies by Members of the English Department, University of Istanbul* 2 (1951):29–54.
Distinguishes the quantitative verse experiments of Sidney and others in the Areopagus from those of earlier humanists. Sees Campion's attempts as superior to those of Sidney because, though both related poetry to music, Campion faced the practical problems of musical setting. Draws connections between the Areopagus and the Accademia della Nuova Poesia in Italy and Jean-Antoine de Baïf's Académie de Musique et de Poésie and the Académie du Palais in France. From the poem "If mine eyes can speak" (*OA 12*), infers Sidney's "rules" of quantitative versification, which seem to depend on Elizabethan spelling rather than on actual pronunciation and hence are "founded on no really valid basis." Finds the same problem in Spenser's attempts. Regards as likely Harvey's claim that Spenser and Sidney distorted English pronunciation to accord with such "rules." Suggests, however, that the experiments contributed to the development of "that subtle and melodious interplay of stress and quantity which distinguishes later Elizabethan verse from Tudor poetry."

2005 MIROLLO, JAMES V. "In Praise of *La bella mano*: Aspects of Late Renaissance Lyricism." *CLS* 9 (March 1972):31–43.

In examining Sidney's description of the hand in "What tongue can her perfections tell" (*OA 62*), concludes that this example presents "a grotesque, microcosmic image signifying . . . all the traditional themes associated with love, beauty, [and] the lady." See also item 1925.

2006 MONTGOMERY, ROBERT L[ANGFORD], Jr. *Symmetry and Sense: The Poetry of Sir Philip Sidney.* Austin: University of Texas Press, 1961, pp. 30–63. Orig. a Ph.D. diss., Harvard University, 1956.

In Chapter 3, examines the poems of *Arcadia* for their use of "figures of amplification," emphasizing their "abundant, forceful, and extended treatment of feeling" but finding that many of them "seem to lack complexity or tension" and are "unequipped to render a particular experience in depth." Contends that Sidney uses imagery for "uniform effects" rather than to imitate states of mind or mental processes. Discusses "lack of conciseness" as a valid means of building emotional energy. In Chapter 4, examines Sidney's adaptation of the style and attitudes of Petrarchism in the *Arcadia* poems, contending that his treatment of love is "more informed by rationalism" than are the poems of his contemporaries, while, at the same time, "he can more feelingly render its religious impulse." Sees Sidney's presentation of "idealistic and idealized love" as "more than connoisseurship; it is a total commitment." See also item 1926.

2007 MOORE, DENNIS [MICHAEL]. *The Politics of Spenser's "Complaints" and Sidney's Philisides Poems.* Salzburg Studies in English: Elizabethan and Renaissance Studies, 101. Salzburg, Austria: Institut für Anglistik und Amerikanistik, Universität Salzburg, 1982, pp. 63–173.

Concerned in general ways with the part played by patronage in sixteenth-century political poems, with the forms that they took, and with the relation between political allegories and other allegorical works, considers in detail the poems in the Fourth Eclogues of the Old *Arcadia*. To the question "Why did Sidney leave court?" answers that his "melancholy temperament, strength of mind, and contempt for much of Elizabeth's careful statecraft" joined with his poverty to drive him away. Identifies Mira with Queen Elizabeth in many of the Philisides poems, especially in "Now was our heavenly vault" (*OA 73*) and "Unto the caitif wretch" (*OA 74*), where "in the symbolic underpinning of Philisides' vision we find

Twentieth Century

the elements into which Sidney has translated his angering of England's goddess." The Philisides poems allow Sidney to "praise [Elizabeth] loyally even while indirectly criticizing her conduct of affairs." Reads "As I my little flock" (*OA 66*) as "an anatomy of tyranny as a national phenomenon," with the two sorts of beasts representing two classes of nations. Suggests that Elizabeth may have "graciously commissioned" *Four Foster Children of Desire*, knowing that Sidney and his friends would "welcome the opportunity" to produce it.

2008 POIRIER, MICHEL. *Sir Philip Sidney: Le chevalier poète élizabéthain*. Travaux et mémoires de l'Université de Lille, nouvelle série—Droit et lettres, 26. Lyon, France: Bibliothèque Universitaire de Lille, 1948, pp. 164–79.

In Chapter 2 of Book 2, focuses on the poems of *Arcadia*, discussing the tradition of pastoral poetry from which they derive, noting the English settings they often suggest, and remarking on their tendency to raise the mind from the creation toward the Creator. In the love lyrics, finds a mediocre form of Petrarchism, and in the quantitative verse experiments, notes a dependence on the French academies. Stresses the influence of Jean Antoine de Baïf and the experiments pursued at Cambridge from the 1540s to the 1580s, which involved or had an influence on writers such as William Drant, Thomas Blennerhasset, James Sandford, Gabriel Harvey, and the authors of the Areopagus. Examines Sidney's principles of versification in relation to those of other English and Continental writers. Also discusses *The Lady of May*, concentrating on its place in the development of the masque and discussing the comic character Rombus. See also item 703.

2009 QUAINTANCE, RICHARD E., Jr. "The French Source of Robert Greene's 'What Thing is Love.'" *N&Q*, n.s. 10 (August 1963):295–96.

Argues that Greene's "Doron's eclogue joined with Carmelas" is not an imitation of Sidney's mock blazon of Mopsa (*OA 3*) but rather a mock pastoral.

2010 RANSOM, JOHN CROWE. *The New Criticism*. Norfolk, Conn.: New Directions, 1941, pp. 103–14.

Discusses Empson's analysis (1986) of "Ye goatherd gods" (*OA 71*).

2011 RICHMOND, H[UGH] M. *Renaissance Landscapes: English Lyrics in a European Tradition.* De Proprietatibus Litterarum, Series Practica, 52. The Hague and Paris: Mouton, 1973, pp. 78–79, 90.

Notes Sidney's literary kinship with Ronsard and quotes from "O sweet woods" (*OA 34*) to show Sidney's interest in landscape and the virtues of solitude.

2012 ROGERS, EVELYN GIBBS. "Sidney the Perfectionist Poet: Changes in Text and Context of the New *Arcadia* Poems." Ph.D. diss., University of Maryland, 1970, 264 pp.

Compares the poems of the 1590 *Arcadia* and their contexts with earlier versions of the poems and their settings in the Old *Arcadia*. Concludes that the revisions are virtually all improvements in imagery, rhetoric, and decorum. Suggests that some of the changes seem to be Sidney's doing and that "others are so logical as to be perhaps according to his intentions." See *DAI* 31 (February 1971):4133A.

2013 ROSENMEYER, THOMAS G. *The Green Cabinet: Theocritus and The European Pastoral Lyric.* Berkeley and Los Angeles: University of California Press, 1969, pp. 73, 165, 226–27, 250.

Relates the infrequent use of metaphor in the poetry of *Arcadia* to the plain style of the pastoral tradition, arguing that Sidney's presentation of *otium* is complex in that it features "both the Epicurean-pastoral delight in its pleasures, and the Stoic doubts concerning its feasibility in a sinful world." Credits Sidney with introducing the particularly melancholy tone of British pastoral in "Ye goatherd gods" (*OA 71*).

2014 RØSTVIG, MAREN-SOFIE. "Elaborate Song: Conceptual Structure in Milton's 'On the Morning of Christ's Nativity.'" In *Fair Forms: Essays in English Literature from Spenser to Jane Austen,* edited by Maren-Sofie Røstvig. Totowa, N.J.: Rowman & Littlefield, 1975, pp. 54–84.

Compares the structure of Milton's poem with that of Sidney's epithalamium "Let mother earth now deck herself" (*OA 63*). Finds that both poems are organized symmetrically around a central stanza, with a positive theme before and a negative theme after. Stanzas equidistant from the center are paired off against each other. Discusses the numerological reasons for Sidney to center the poem in stanza 6, which celebrates virtue as the "knot" of the marriage.

Twentieth Century

2015 RUDENSTINE, NEIL L. *Sidney's Poetic Development*. Cambridge, Mass.: Harvard University Press, 1967, pp. 23–45, 53–114, and passim. Orig. a Ph.D. diss., Harvard University, 1964.

Provides a thorough analysis of the poems of *Arcadia*. In Chapter 3, views Pyrocles as an apologist for Sidney's poetic view of experience, seeing the indecisiveness of *Arcadia* concerning the conflict between love and duty as a reflection of Sidney's own concerns ca. 1580. Argues that eclogues such as those between Geron and Philisides ("Up, up Philisides, let sorrows go," *OA 9*) and between Boulon and Plangus ("As I behind a bush did sit," *OA 30*) reflect the Sidney-Languet correspondence of 1577–1580. In Chapter 4, argues that the *Defence* marks a revision in Sidney's thinking: it suggests "that accommodations between the delights of beauty and the demands of virtue are easier to arrange than either the Old *Arcadia* or the letters would imply. In this it is like the revised *Arcadia*." In Chapter 5, discusses the suitability of the style of the poetry in *Arcadia* to the aims of the work. Argues that the poetry "is much more diverse than has been generally noticed" and that "this diversity in itself forces us to be more attentive to the motives that tend to govern Sidney's changes of style from poem to poem within the work." The poems reveal "a style of life and speech whose manner is indissolubly part of its matter as expressive of a whole range of courtly and romantic values, feelings, and ideals." In Chapter 6, examines the prosody of the poems in *Arcadia*, finding them conventional in that their rhetorical complexity parallels "the stylized movements of classical theatre or ballet, where a cultivated artificiality of gesture and expression is a primary vehicle of meaning." In Chapter 7, argues that one "source of the dramatic style of *Astrophil and Stella* . . . lies in *Arcadia*'s eclogues, and particularly in the speech of Philisides. The eclogues are largely written in a plain and energetic manner, with all the roughness accorded to them by tradition, and in the young courtier-shepherd one can see some of the aggressiveness, satiric spirit, and eroti-cism of Astrophel." Shows that "Philisides is much less sophisticated and assured than Astrophel, but it is he who begins to develop that tone of satiric bravado and strong-minded willfulness which pervades the verse of Sidney's later hero." See also item 730.

2016 S., H.K. St. J. "Plato and Sidney." *N&Q*, 10th ser. 1 (12 March 1904):207.

Asks which work Grosart (69) may have had in mind when he traced to Plato the phrase "all thy starry eyes" in "As I behind a bush did sit" (*OA 30*).

Twentieth Century

2017 SCHÖN, HILDA. "Catulls Epithalamion und seine englischen Nachahmer bis 1660." Ph.D. diss., Universität Wien, 1940, 131 pp. Abstract not available. Cited in *GV*, vol. 116, p. 367.

2018 SCHUMAN, SHARON. "Sixteenth-Century English Quantitative Verse: Its Ends, Means, and Products." *MP* 74 (May 1977): 335–49.
Refers to Sidney's Arcadian poems in a discussion of the principles behind various attempts to adapt quantitative verse to English poetry.

2019 SOUTHALL, RAYMOND. "*Troilus and Cressida* and the Spirit of Capitalism." In *Shakespeare in a Changing World*, edited by Arnold Kettle. New York: International Publishers; London: Lawrence & Wishart, 1964, pp. 217–22.
Notes that the growth of the bourgeois, mercantile ethic in the sixteenth century prompted the use of imagery of trade and commerce even in love poetry. Cites as an example "My true love hath my heart" (*OA 45*).

2020 STILLMAN, ROBERT E. "Poetry and Justice in Sidney's 'Ye goat-herd gods.'" *SEL* 22 (Winter 1982):39–50.
Contending that prior analysis of the poem (*OA 71*) paid inadequate attention to its sources, shows that its purposefulness and power derive from an "elaborate network of syntactic parallels" with Gil Polo's "Pues ya se esconde el sol" from Book 1 of *Diana enamorada*, combined with the "built-in repetitive sestina devices" of the Fourth Eclogue of Sannazaro's *Arcadia*. At one level, this combination "increases our awareness of the painful monotony suffered by the lover in the prison of his desires"; but at a deeper level, Sidney is "able to coalesce into a single image the action of poetry and justice as a kind of harmony." Both operate by means of a *discordia concors*. Concludes that "the balance which makes good poetry can also lead to the contentment of a good life." Sidney's intention is thus to "reconcile the two most important trends in the history of pastoral romance."

2021 STRATTON, CLARENCE. "The Italian Lyrics of Sidney's *Arcadia*." *SR* 25 (July 1917):305–26.
Examines various Italian verse forms, sketching their history and discussing their use in two of Sidney's sources: Sannazaro's *Arcadia* and Montemayor's *Diana*. Using numerous illustrations from *Arcadia*, discusses Sidney's mastery of the madrigal, sesta rima, sestina and double sestina, canzone, strambotto, sonnet, and terza rima.

Twentieth Century

2022 TRUESDALE, CALVIN WILLIAM. "English Pastoral Verse from Spenser to Marvell: A Critical Revaluation." Ph.D. diss., University of Washington, 1956, 342 pp.
In a Chapter dealing with "the sad shepherd," briefly treats Sidney's handling of the theme of rejection in love. See *DA* 17 (May 1957):1087.

2023 TUFTE, VIRGINIA. "England's First Epithalamium and the *'Vesper Adest'* Tradition." *EM* 20 (1969):39–51.
Argues that the "Fifth Day" of Sir Henry Wotton's *A Courtly Controversy of Cupid's Cautels* was modeled on Catullus's *Carmen* 62, the "Vesper Adest," and was written before Sidney's epithalamium in *Arcadia*, "Let mother earth now deck herself" (*OA 63*). See also item 2024 and Wöhrmann (2029).

2024 ——. *The Poetry of Marriage: The Epithalamium in Europe and Its Development in England*. University of Southern California Studies in Comparative Literature, 2. Los Angeles: Tinnon-Brown, 1970, pp. 141, 152–56.
Argues that Sidney's "Let mother earth now deck herself" (*OA 63*) was not the first epithalamium in English. Discusses its sources, its congruity with the principles of the *Defence*, and its meticulous structure, relating it to the tradition of the classical epithalamium. See also item 2023.

2025 TURNER, MYRON [MARTIN]. "'When Rooted Moisture Failes': Sidney's Pastoral Elegy (*OA 75*) and the Radical Humour." *ELN* 15 (September 1977):7–10.
Defines Sidney's "rooted moisture" as "natural humidity," and shows how this concept, derived ultimately from Aristotle, influences the imagery of "Since that to death is gone the shepherd high" (*OA 75*).

2026 UNDERDOWN, MARY EBBA INGHOLT. "Sir Philip Sidney's 'Arcadian' *Ecologues*: A Study of his Quantitative Verse." Ph.D. diss., Yale University, 1964, 304 pp.
Argues that Sidney was "virtually unique" in regarding "rimed" and "measured" verse as alternatives. His quantitative verse is a metrical imitation of Latin verse, based on "quantitative English prosody," one that "adapts Latin rules to the English language, emphasizing 'position' and maintaining the distinction between stress and length." His metrics also replace Latin polysyllables with "English word-groups (sense units)." Suggests that his use of "phrasing" implies a "significant relation between the Latin metrics familar to all educated Elizabethans, comtemporary music and English versification." See *DA* 25 (August 1964):1222.

2027 van DORSTEN, JAN ADRIANUS. *Terug naar de tekomst* [Return to the Future]. Leiden, Netherlands: University Press of Leiden, 1971, 25 pp.

Considers Philisides as he appears in the Third Eclogues of *Arcadia*, drawing parallels with Sidney's own life. Focuses on the comments of Geron and on Philisides's poem "As I my little flock on Ister bank" (*OA 66*), arguing that they bear on a theme of responsibility that runs throughout the book.

2028 WILLETTS, PAMELA J[OAN]. *The Henry Lawes Manuscript*. London: Trustees of the British Museum, 1969, pp. 34–35, 36–37, plates xii, xiii.

Records Lawes's settings for "My Lute, within thy self" (*OA 54*) and for one verse of "O sweet woods" (*OA 34*). Plate xiii, which illustrates this latter setting, faces plate xii, which shows John Dowland's setting for the entire poem (see item 1975).

2029 WÖHRMANN, KURT. *Die englische Epithalamiendichtung der Renaissance und ihre Vorbilder*. Borna-Leipzig, Germany: Universitätsverlag von Robert Noske, 1928, pp. 8–15. Orig. a Ph.D. diss., Albert-Ludwigs-Universität zu Freiburg.

Discusses the eclogue "Let Mother Earth now deck herself in flowers" (*OA 63*), treating it as the first epithalamium in English. But see Tufte (2023, 2024). Details verbal and formal similarities with its apparent source, Bartholomew Young's translation of Arsileo's marriage song for Syreno and Diana in Gil Polo's *Diana enamorada*, suggesting that Sidney must have seen it in manuscript. Notes elements in Sidney's poem that become standard in later English epithalamia: personifications of Nature, the refrain, and the form of the stanza. Traces imagery of the elm and the vine from Horace through Johannes Secundus and Ronsard to Sidney.

3. *ASTROPHIL AND STELLA*

Nineteenth Century

2030 BROWN, HENRY. *The Sonnets of Shakespeare Solved, and the Mystery of His Friendship, Love, and Rivalry Revealed*. London: John Russell Smith, 1870, pp. 212–25.

In "The Love of Sir Philip Sidney for Penelope Devereux, and Lady Rich's Illicit Amours Revealed," sees the Dark Lady sonnets as "covertly

Nineteenth Century

leveled at Lady Rich," whom Shakespeare attacks for her reputation in later life. Argues that Sidney painted her fair to please his sister while Shakespeare painted her foul to warn his patron about women. Identifies Penelope Rich as the model for Philoclea in *Arcadia*.

2031 CRAIK, GEORGE LILLIE. *The Romance of the Peerage or Curiosities of Family History*. Vol. 1. London: Chapman & Hall, 1848, pp. 81–108, 208–9.

After discussing the relationship between Sidney and Penelope Rich, explicates *Astrophil and Stella* as an autobiographical poem. Discusses the contemporary events alluded to in "Whether the Turkish new-moon" (*AS 30*), dating the sonnet and the rest of the sequence in 1585. Finds it impossible to reconcile the contradiction between the celebration of Astrophil's affair with Stella in Spenser's *Astrophel* and the dedication of that work to Sidney's wife.

2032 GROSART, ALEXANDER B. "Barnabe Barnes: Shakspere, Sidney, etc." *Academy* 7 (1 May 1875):455.

Suggests that Barnes's *Parthenophil and Parthenophe* contains "unrecorded celebrations" of Sidney and Stella.

2033 GUGGENHEIM, JOSEF. *Quellenstudien zu Samuel Daniels Sonnettencyklus "Delia."* Berlin: E. Ebering, 1898, pp. 43–44. Orig. a Ph.D. diss., Friedrich-Wilhelms-Universität zu Berlin, 1898.

Finds little evidence that Daniel's sonnet sequence was influenced by *Astrophil and Stella*.

2034 HELM, K. "Zur Entstehung von Ph. Sidney's Sonetten." *Anglia* 19 (1897):549–53.

In examining Pollard's reconstruction (71) of events in Sidney's relations with Lady Rich, accepts his dating of incidents reflected in *Astrophil and Stella* 22, 24, 30, 37, and 41. Also allows that the first thirty-two sonnets can, with the exception of Sonnet 24, be read as if written before Penelope married Lord Rich, and those after Sonnet 32 can be taken as coming after the marriage. Contends, nonetheless, that an "ordering hand" such as that of Mary Sidney was at work in preparing the printed version and that the sequence of the poems cannot be proven to follow the strict chronology of Sidney's life during the period in question.

2035 [HITCHCOCK, ETHAN ALLAN.] *Spenser's Poem, Entitled "Colin Clouts Come Home Againe," Explained; with Remarks upon the "Amoretti" Sonnets, and also upon a Few of the Minor Poems of Other Early English Poets.* New York: James Miller, 1865, pp. 149–54.

Regards Stella as an ideal of beauty and goodness, treating the sonnet "I on my horse, and love on me" (*AS 49*) as an allegory of body, soul, and divine spirit.

2036 HOLTHAUSEN, F. "Zu Sidneys *Astrophel and Stella,* ed. Flügel." *Archiv* 87 (1891):435–37.

Supplies corrections to Flügel's edition (15).

2037 JAMESON, ANNA BROWNELL. *Memoirs of the Loves of the Poets: Biographical Sketches of Women Celebrated in Ancient and Modern Poetry.* Boston: Houghton, Mifflin & Co.; Cambridge: The Riverside Press, [1895], pp. 190–200.

In "Sidney's Stella," quotes from several sonnets in *Astrophil and Stella* to construct a portrait of Stella, claiming that Song viii "describes a secret interview which took place between [Sidney] and Lady Rich shortly after her marriage."

2038 KOEPPEL, E[MIL]. Review of *Sir Philip Sidneys "Astrophel and Stella" und "Defence of Poesie,"* edited by Ewald Flügel. *Englische Studien* 14 (1890):129–37.

In response to Flügel (15), discusses the sonnet "I might, unhappy word" (*AS 33*) and the reasons that Sidney did not marry Penelope Devereux. Reports from correspondence with Flügel that a manuscript of the cycle, found previously in the library of the College of King James, Edinburgh, and mentioned in item 366, has disappeared. Describes the volume and gives cataloging information. Advances reasons for regarding the 1598 edition as more than a reprinting from the second quarto of 1591, contending that it must have been prepared with reference to a reliable manuscript and is the best basis for an edition. Discusses at length textual problems, comparing the Bright Manuscript, the 1591 quartos, and the 1598 folio edition.

2039 ——. "Studien zur Geschichte des englischen Petrarchismus im sechzehnten Jahrhundert." *Romanische Forschungen* 5 (1890): 65–97.

Discusses Sidney's reaction against Petrarchan conventions, tracing the sort of phrasing satirized in the sonnet "Some lovers speak" (*AS 6*) back to Petrarch's own *Rime.* Demonstrates, however, that Sidney borrowed

Nineteenth Century

heavily from the tradition he was attacking. Identifies as his most obvious departure from it his irreverent depictions of Cupid.

2040 ———. "Zu *Astrophel and Stella*." *Anglia* 13 (1891):467–68.
Rejects possible emendations of the phrase "day-nets" in the sonnet "Cupid, because thou shinest in Stella's eyes" (*AS 12*). Notes the same phrase in a similar context in George Pettie's *Petite Palace of Pettie His Pleasure*.

2041 LAMB, CHARLES. "Nugae Criticae. By the Author of Elia. No. 1. Defence of the Sonnets of Sir Philip Sidney." *London Magazine* 8 (September 1823):248–52. Reprint. "Some Sonnets of Sir Philip Sidney." In *The Works of Charles and Mary Lamb*, edited by E.V. Lucas. Vol. 2. London: Methuen, 1903, pp. 213–20.
Defends Sidney from charges levelled by Hazlitt (359), providing a sympathetic reading of *Astrophil and Stella*. Prints selections with some emendations, praising the rhythm, diction, description of time and place, display of "transcendent passion," and evocation of the historical moment. See also Muir (2205), Nichols (2216), and Ogden (2217).

2042 LOWELL, JAMES RUSSELL. *The Old English Dramatists*. London: Macmillan & Co.; Boston and New York: Houghton Mifflin Co., 1892, pp. 29–31.
Quotes *Astrophil and Stella* 30 as an example of the "ease and simplicity" that Elizabethan English had attained as a literary language.

2043 MARQUIS, T.G. "Sidney's *Astrophel & Stella*." *PL* 8, no. 8 (1896):570–77.
Praises the sequence and "the mild unspotted soul of the writer," finding his love "pure and true."

2044 NICHOLSON, BRINSLEY. "'Jubilant Song upon the Stolen Kiss.'" *N&Q*, 7th ser. 3 (12 February 1887):135.
Replies to Watkiss (2047), arguing that, in "Have I caught my heavenly jewel" (*AS ii*), the last line should read, "Foole, and more foole, for no more taking."

2045 RADFORD, ADA. "Astrophel and Stella." *Hobby-Horse* 7 (April 1892):85–98.
Aiming to rebut Symonds's claim (961) that Sidney was "not an eminently engaging or . . . interesting personage," surveys *Astrophil and Stella* as evidence of "the great love of his life." Cites sonnets that "bear the plain stamp of sincerity."

2046 STODDARD, RICHARD HENRY. "The Sonnet in English Poetry." *Scribner's Monthly* 22 (October 1881):905–21.

Reads *Astrophil and Stella* biographically, comparing Sidney's poetic technique with that of Wyatt and Surrey.

2047 WATKISS, LLOYD W. "'Jubilant Song upon the Stolen Kiss.'" *N&Q*, 7th ser. 3 (January 1887):29.

Queries the source of Symonds's use of "mere" and "more" in his emendation (961) of the last line of "Have I caught my heavenly jewel" (*AS ii*): "Fool, more fool, for no mere taking." See the reply by Nicholson (2044).

Twentieth Century

2048 ADAMS, ROBERT M[ARTIN]. *Strains of Discord: Studies in Literary Openness.* Ithaca, N.Y.: Cornell University Press, 1958, pp. 4–6, 121.

Uses *Astrophil and Stella 1* as an example of the contrast between direct and indirect approaches to a subject. Points out stylistic links between the poem and Herbert's "Jordan II": both use artifice to prepare the reader for simple directness. See also Fish (2123).

2049 AHRENDS, GÜNTER. *Liebe, Schönheit und Tugend als Strukturelamente in Sidneys "Astrophel and Stella" und in Spensers "Amoretti".* Bonn, Germany: Rheinische Friedrich-Wilhelms-Universität, 1966, pp. 5–182. Orig. a Ph.D. diss., Universität Bonn, 1965.

Reads *Astrophil and Stella* in the context of neo-Platonic love theory, dividing the sequence into three main parts, each with subgroupings. The first part, Sonnets 1–40, elaborates an "argument" between desire and reason, asking whether following the path of virtue can enable one to subdue physical desire, and concludes that it cannot. Part 2, Sonnets 41–83, develops the theme that the virtuous lover cannot overcome desire by himself, but needs the aid of the beloved. Part 3, Sonnets 84–108, explores the power of the senses to achieve the ends of spiritual love, contending that Astrophil does achieve the capacity to love virtuously.

2050 ALDEN, RAYMOND MacDONALD. "The Lyrical Conceit of the Elizabethans." *SP* 14 (April 1917):129–52.

Divides the conceit into "Verbal," "Imaginative," and "Logical" types and illustrates each with examples from *Astrophil and Stella*.

Twentieth Century

2051 ———. "A Point in Sidney's Versification." *Nation* 88 (18 February 1909):164.
Points out that Saintsbury's comment (2624) on the decasyllabic final line of "Loving in truth" (*AS 1*) is based on a faulty text in Arber's edition (68).

2052 ALLEN, DON CAMERON. *The Star-Crossed Renaissance: The Quarrel about Astrology and Its Influence in England*. Durham, N.C.: Duke University Press, 1941, pp. 158–59.
Sees *Astrophil and Stella* 26, in which Stella's eyes are likened to stars, as the prototype for English astrological sonnets, especially those in Giles Fetcher's *Licia* and Henry Constable's *Diana*.

2053 BANKS, THEODORE HOWARD. "Sidney's *Astrophel and Stella* Reconsidered." *PMLA* 50 (June 1935):403–12.
Argues that the sonnets "do not record a deeply felt love of Sidney for Stella," but were prompted solely by Sidney's desire to write poetry.

2054 BARKAN, LEONARD. *Nature's Work of Art: The Human Body as Image of the World*. New Haven and London: Yale University Press, 1975, pp. 175–200. Orig. a Ph.D. diss., Yale University, 1971.
In "*Astrophil and Stella*: The Human Body as Setting for the Petrarchan Drama," argues that, like other literature that makes use of the body, Sidney's sonnets demonstrate "a tension between fragmentation and union." Although the most basic function of the body is "as a literal locus for action," "in objectifying the complexity of his own feelings and experiences, Sidney often uses the body as the vehicle for multiple metaphors." Claims that "Sidney uses the body metaphor to multiply and diversify his characters, and to establish the three basic forces which animate the sequence: the attraction of Stella, the strength of Love, and the transforming power of Astrophil's spirit."

2055 BAWCUTT, PRISCILLA. "A Crux in *Astrophil and Stella*, Sonnet 21." *N&Q*, n.s. 29 (October 1982):406–8.
Argues that the obsolete word "geres" is more appropriate to the context of the poem than the word "gyres" of line 6. For earlier opinions, see Ringler (92) and Wilson (96).

2056 BERNARD, JOHN DANA. "Studies in the Love Poetry of Wyatt, Sidney, and Shakespeare." Ph.D. diss., University of Minnesota, 1970, 297 pp.
Argues that, in these three poets, "an underlying empiricism subjects Neoplatonic, rational love to the test of experience." In *Astrophil and*

Stella, sees the poet-lover's failure to circumscribe his struggles within the order of art as a judgment on Sidney's part that poetry has its limits as a "'golden' harmonizer of the antinomies of existence." See *DAI* 31 (January 1971):3538A.

2057 BERNT, JOSEPH PHILIP. "Sir Philip Sidney and the Politics of *Astrophil and Stella*." Ph.D. diss., University of Nebraska at Lincoln, 1979, 323 pp.
Argues that the sequence contains a political allegory commenting on the French marriage and praising Elizabeth's rejection of it. Feels that the *Defence* provides a theoretical justification for such an interpretation. The poem's narrative pattern "offers an obvious parallel with the marriage negotiations," and the jealousy sonnets indirectly allude to the controversy. See *DAI* 40 (April 1980):5449A.

2058 BERRY, J. WILKES. "Unnamed Lady in *Astrophil and Stella* 97." *AN&Q* 12 (May/June 1974):135–37.
Identifies "Dian's peere" in Sonnet 97 with Queen Elizabeth.

2059 BLUDAU, DIETHILD. "Sonettstruktur bei Samuel Daniel." *ShJE* 94 (1958):63–89.
Compares *Astrophil and Stella* with Daniel's sonnet sequence *Delia*. Finds that the latter is traditional and concerned with harmony and close observation of life, whereas Sidney's sequence is innovative and preoccupied with logic and inner debate. Sees in Shakespeare's *Sonnets* a union of both sets of characteristics.

2060 BLUM, IRVING D. "The Parodox of Money Imagery in English Renaissance Poetry." *SRen* 8 (1961):144–54.
In arguing generally that Renaissance poets use money imagery to express "even the highest spiritual value," shows that, in *Astrophil and Stella*, economic terms "define Stella's endearing qualities."

2061 BOLIEU, LOUIS SHERMAN, Jr. "Michael Drayton, Transitional Sonneteer: The Place of Drayton in English Renaissance Sonnet Development." Ph.D. diss., Texas A & M University, 1972, 218 pp.
Argues that *Astrophil and Stella* contains a "balance of external and internal drama," both of which Sidney develops by the same techniques that Drayton later uses in *Idea*. Drayton, however, "excels at external drama." See *DAI* 33 (May 1973):6301A–2A.

Twentieth Century

2062 BOND, WILLIAM H[ENRY]. "Sidney and Cupid's Dart." *MLN* 63 (April 1948):258.

Suggests that, in the sonnet "It is most true, that eyes are formed to serve (*AS 5*), the line on Cupid's dart "which for ourselves we carve" refers to "a pheon [or dart head] azure" on Sidney's coat of arms.

2063 BONTOUX, GERMAINE. *La chanson en Angleterre au temps d'Élisabeth*. Oxford: Oxford University Press, 1936, pp. 209–14, 450–54, 544–49.

Discusses the use of songs from *Astrophil and Stella* in songbooks such as Robert Dowland's *Musical Banquet* and William Byrd's *Psalms, Sonnets, and Songs*. Prints and analyzes Charles Tessier's setting of "In a grove most rich of shade" (*AS viii*), Byrd's setting of "O you that hear this voice" (*AS vi*), and a funeral song for Sidney set to music by Byrd (2742).

2064 BOOTH, STEPHEN. *An Essay on Shakespeare's Sonnets*. New Haven, Conn., and London: Yale University Press, 1969, pp. 179–180.

Argues that, in some of Sidney's sonnets, the effect depends on the reader's familiarity with the genre, so that the reader hears only the manner and not the matter of the poem. Remarks on Sidney's use of final couplets, suggesting that the mastery of such endings was "possibly his chief technical accomplishment." Notes that, while Sidney's sonnets were models for many later writers, they were technically complex and difficult to imitate. The skillful superimposition of prose rhythm and syntax on patterns of rhyme and meter in *Astrophil and Stella* 2, for example, is an effect that few sought to reproduce.

2065 BORGHESI, PETER. *Petrarch and His Influence on English Literature*. Bologna: Nicholas Zanichelli, 1906, pp. 93–98.

Provides a general discussion of Petrarch's influence on *Astrophil and Stella*, claiming that Stella "had all the qualities of Petrarch's Laura," that Sidney "obtains a greater degree of perfection" when not writing about Stella, and that his "clear and concise" style "is not to be found in any other Petrarchist."

2066 BRANNIN, JAMES. "Astrophel, the Puritan." *Sewanee Review* 16 (1908):452–57.

Reads *Astrophil and Stella*, emphasizing its moral conflicts. Sees in it the sensibility of "the earlier Puritan, to whom breadth of view was not impossible," and who was "not blinded by that little facet of life which the later Puritan saw fit to emphasize, not too anxious to save his own soul."

2067 BRIE, FRIEDRICH. Review of *Sidney's Stella*, by James M. Purcell. *Englische Studien* 70, no. 2 (1935):289–90.

Supports the dating of some sonnets in *Astrophil and Stella* before the Old *Arcadia*, perhaps as early as 1573–74. Takes Purcell (2232) to task for denying references to Lady Rich in the first sonnet of *Britton's Bower of Delights* and for arguing that Stella represents Frances Walsingham, discussing evidence in Puttenham's *Art of English Poesy* and Spenser's *Astrophel* (2771).

2068 BRODWIN, LEONORA LEET. "The Structure of Sidney's *Astrophel and Stella*." *MP* 67 (August 1969):25–40.

Reviews the structural hypotheses of Ringler (92), Young (2316), and Kalstone (1907). Using "source of action" in the poems as a clue to their arrangement, suggests that Sonnets 1–35 stress Astrophil as the sole motivator for the love action, that 36–87 take Stella as their main focus, and that 88–108 depict Astrophil again with "no moral armour against the unrelieved despair caused by Stella's final rejection of his love." This tripartite structure is complemented by patterns of light and darkness: "the total pattern of imagery in the sequence may be viewed in terms . . . of Stella's eyes," producing a night/day/night pattern that parallels the structural one. Considers chastity and virtue as major thematic concerns throughout the sequence.

2069 BROWN, RUSSELL M[ORTON, Jr.] "Sidney's *Astrophil and Stella*, 1." *Expl* 32 (November 1973):item 21.

Like Kalstone (1907), traces Sidney's use of "sunne-burn'd" to Thomas Wilson's *Art of Rhetoric*, pointing out that "the word would suggest something being invisibly affected by its surroundings, and would have the particular associations of the way a man's habits of speech are inevitably colored by his reading." Thus, because Astrophil searches for inspiration in others' writings, his poems "will inevitably reflect the very love sonnet tradition that he strives to reject." See also Cotter (2090) and Rudenstine (730).

2070 ———. "Sidney's *Astrophil and Stella*, Fourth Song." *Expl* 29 (February 1970):item 48.

Noting the ambiguity of the song's final stanza, suggests that "Stella may actually yield to Astrophil's desires," which would account for the change seen in Sonnet 86, "Alas, whence came this change of looks?"

Twentieth Century

2071 ———. "'Through All Maskes My Wo': Poet and Persona in *Astrophil and Stella*." Ph.D. diss., State University of New York at Binghamton, 1972, 277 pp.

In light of sixteenth-century poetic theory, argues that some of Astrophil's statements about poetry are "ironic and parodic," important for their revelations about the speaker rather than as a theory of poetics. Astrophil is an unreliable narrator, "often a *poseur*, sometimes self-deceiving, and occasionally dishonest." The sequence "satirizes" Petrarchan love as "inevitably productive of intolerable and unresolvable conflicts." See *DAI* 33 (November 1972):2317A.

2072 BROWNBILL, J. "Philip Sidney and Penelope Rich." *TLS*, 20 September 1928, p. 667.

Documents the history of Penelope Devereux's liaison with Charles Blount, pointing out that it preceded her marriage to Lord Rich and arguing that it remained secret until 1606, when he died. Suggests that the story of love between Penelope and Sidney is a nineteenth-century fiction and that few sonnets in *Astrophil and Stella* refer to her specifically.

2073 BUCHLOH, PAUL GERHARD, and JEHMLICH, REIMER. "Sir Philip Sidney." In *Die englische Lyrik. Von der Renaissance bis zur Gegenwart*, edited by Karl Heinz Göller. Vol. 1. Düsseldorf, Germany: August Bagel, 1968, pp. 55–64.

Explicates *Astrophil and Stella* 76 as a representative example of Sidney's poetic genius, analyzing its structure, its imagery (particularly light and dark, and heat and cold), its position in the sequence, and its special relationship to Petrarch's *Rime* 19 and 223.

2074 BULLITT, JOHN M. "The Use of Rhyme Link in the Sonnets of Sidney, Drayton, and Spenser." *JEGP* 49 (January 1950):14–32.

Applying the work of Bray (1866), which suggests that some of Shakespeare's sonnets are deliberately linked by rhyme words, finds similar links in the sonnets of *Astrophil and Stella*. In thirty-five cases, rhyme words are repeated in successive sonnets; in twenty-two cases rhymed sounds recur; and in others, composite rhymes form the link. Concludes that many of the repetitions are deliberate.

2075 BURHANS, CLINTON S., Jr. "Sidney's 'With How Sad Steps, O Moon.'" *Expl* 18 (January 1960):item 26.

Concludes that "although Sidney was forced by metrical requirements to write the [last] line as he did, I think he means it to be read with the words virtue and ungratefulness transposed." See responses by Combellack (2088) and Essig (2116).

2076 BUXTON, JOHN. *Elizabethan Taste*. London: Macmillan & Co., 1963; New York: St. Martin's Press, 1964, pp. 269–94.

From omissions in the pirated edition of 1591, concludes that two versions of *Astrophil and Stella* circulated in manuscript: one complete and one purged of material that might have compromised Lady Rich. Rejects the autobiographical interpretations of the Romantics, arguing that Sidney consciously mingled fact with fiction. Suggests that Penelope was a willing model for Sidney but loved Charles Blount all along. Also rejects the Romantic emphasis on Sidney's spontaneity, arguing that he consciously employed all the rhetorical and metrical devices of the Petrarchan tradition in an attempt to reform English poetry. Notes the importance of Sidney's circle in freeing the generation of Shakespeare from the plain didacticism of earlier English verse.

2077 ———. "On the Date of *Syr P.S. His Astrophel and Stella.* . . . Printed for Matthew Lownes." *Bodleian Library Record* 6 (August 1960):614–16.

Cites evidence to suggest 1597 or 1598 as the year of publication for the undated third quarto of *Astrophil and Stella* (62).

2078 CAMPBELL, MARION. "Unending Desire: Sidney's Reinvention of Petrarchan Form in *Astrophil and Stella*." In *Sir Philip Sidney and the Interpretation of Renaissance Culture: The Poet in His Time and in Ours: A Collection of Critical and Scholarly Essays*, edited by Gary F. Waller and Michael D. Moore. London: Croom Helm; Totowa, N.J.: Barnes & Noble, 1984, pp. 84–94.

Examines *Astrophil and Stella* in light of current readings of Petrarch, especially that of John Frecerro. Concludes that "no consistent psychological or narrative structure can be identified" in the sequence, because it "dramatises the process of creating a self and of narrating a self's history without those processes ever crystallising into the product of a self created or a story told." Claims that any perception of a unified form is a construction by a particular reader.

2079 CARR, JOHN WAYNE. "'That Love and Honor Might Agree': An Ethical Study of *Astrophil and Stella*." Ph.D. diss., Stanford University, 1975, 224 pp.

Examining individual sonnets in terms of "Elizabethan psychology as adapted from classical discussions of ethics," argues that Sidney is "Aristotelian in emphasizing the harmonious relationships between reason and sensation necessary for the moral life," while his treatment of the will's difficulty in obeying reason is Stoic and Christian, and especial-

Twentieth Century

ly Calvinistic. Contends that, in all his major works, Sidney "questions and often ridicules" the way both Petrarchism and neo-Platonism "subordinate" practical virtue to contemplative transcendence. See *DAI* 35 (March 1975):6090A–91A.

2080 CASTLEY, J.P. "*Astrophel and Stella*—High Sidnaean Love, or Courtly Compliment?" *Melbourne Critical Review* 5 (1962):54–65.
Argues that the sequence is not a narration but a "playful but highly intelligent" use of the language and courtly compliment written to figure forth attitudes and poses of the lover. Stresses the "lightness, touching feeling, and sophisticated good humour" of the sonnets.

2081 CAWLEY, ROBERT RALSTON. *Unpathed Waters: Studies in the Influence of the Voyagers on Elizabethan Literature*. Princeton, N.J.: Princeton University Press; London: Oxford University Press, 1940, pp. 30, 130.
Discusses Sidney's interest in America and the phrase "new-found paradise" in the sonnet "O kiss, which dost those ruddy gems impart" (*AS 81*).

2082 CHAN, MARY. "*The Strife of Love in a Dream* and Sidney's Second Song in *Astrophil and Stella*." *SNew* 3, no. 1 (1982):3–9.
Identifies the source of "Have I caught my heavenly jewel" (*AS ii*) in Ovid's myth of Priapus and Lotis. Discusses connections between the song and the motif of the sleeping nymph in Renaissance visual art, observing its appearance in one of the woodcuts in Francesco Colonna's *Hypnerotomachia Poliphili*, an English translation of which, by one R.D., was published in 1592 and dedicated to Sidney's memory. Analyzes the place of the song in the sequence, concluding that it "sums up and re-expresses the inner drama of Sonnets 69–72 rather than being simply a comic relief and the starting point for a new theme." Includes a setting for the Song from British Library MS. Additional 15117, f.19.

2083 CHERUBINI, WILLIAM. "The 'Goldenness' of Sidney's *Astrophel and Stella*: Test of a Quantitative-Stylistics Routine." *Lang&S* 8 (Winter 1974):47–59.
Uses *Astrophil and Stella* as a base text for the development of a computer-assisted program for the analysis of poetic style. A test run of the system defines the "golden" style, best exemplified in *Astrophil and Stella* 6, as "poetry rich in syntactical and tropological complexity."

2084 CLITHEROE, FRED R. *"Astrophil and Stella." Library*, 6th ser. 2 (September 1980):335.

Responds to Wilson (2309), suggesting that Sidney himself wrote lines replying to a poem by the Earl of Oxford that were published in Newman's 1591 edition of *Astrophil and Stella*.

2085 COGHLAN, DAVID T. "Fluid Fashion: The Infrastructures of *Astrophel and Stella* and *Ideas Mirrour* and Sonnet Cycle Popularity in the 1590's." Ph.D. diss., Temple University, 1984, 270 pp.

Employs a structuralist methodology to show that three interrelated motifs, "especially representative of Elizabethan cycles," express "attempts to reestablish individual identity in the face of a collapsing 'medieval' hierarchy." These motifs are the sonnet mistress, who fails as a defining end; the poetic image, which "represents sense divorced from essence"; and the sonnet suitor, who must "employ verbal mastery even as he maintains a posture of solicitous dependency." See *DAI* 45 (December 1984):1758A.

2086 COLIE, ROSALIE L. *Paradoxia Epidemica: The Renaissance Tradition of Paradox*. Princeton, N.J.: Princeton University Press, 1966, pp. 89–95, 195.

Argues that, in *Astrophil and Stella*, the Petrarchan scheme "shows through the surface of Sidney's style, in the punctuation of sonnets with songs, [and] in the kind of imagery and conceit [used,]" but that the sequence is also deliberately anti-Petrarchan. Suggests that Sidney's originality lies "in his brilliant and self-conscious manipulation of language and ideas about language" and points out that Sidney uses his own style as a major theme, calling into question "assertions made in the very language [he] examines." Noting that Sonnets 6, 15, 28, 55, and 74 all deal with issues of literary criticism and the artificiality of various poetic conventions, considers the relation between Astrophil and Sidney, observing that, in the end, Sidney appeared to turn away from the affectations of poetry.

2087 COLLINS, MICHAEL JOHN. "Comedy in the Love Poetry of Sidney, Drayton, Shakespeare and Donne." Ph.D. diss., New York University, 1973, 211 pp.

In considering how and why certain poems are comic, examines Astrophil's last-line reversals and his various comic roles. See *DAI* 34 (June 1974):7743A.

Twentieth Century

2088 COMBELLACK, C.R.B. "Sidney's 'With How Sad Steps, O Moon.'" *Expl* 20 (November 1961):item 25.
Corrects Burhans (2075), suggesting that, in the last line of the sonnet (*AS 31*), Sidney uses "ungratefulness" in the sense of "unpleasantness" rather than "unthankfulness." See also Essig (2116).

2089 COOPER, SHEROD M., Jr. *The Sonnets of Astrophel and Stella: A Stylistic Study*. Studies in English Literature, 41. The Hague and Paris: Mouton, 1968, 183 pp. Orig. a Ph.D. diss., University of Pennsylvania, 1963.
Centrally concerned with Sidney's "craft," devotes Chapter 1 to an examination of Sidney's theories regarding style, emphasizing the *Defence* but also drawing upon *Arcadia*. In Chapter 2, follows Courthope (338) in arguing that *Astrophil and Stella* is an "integral work," not because it is a sequential narration but because it is an "exercise of the imagination on a set theme." Sees the work as "a display of the wit of the poet, partly in placing a single thought in a great number of different lights, partly in decorating it with a vast variety of far-fetched metaphors." In the remaining six chapters, examines versification, rhyme schemes, vocabulary, rhetoric, imagery, and "English and French stylistic influences" in the sequence. Concludes that from the analyses "emerges a poet who knew intimately the mechanics of verse, the resources of his language, and the ways in which it could be manipulated to produce effective and ingenious statements." Argues that Sidney seeks to avoid monotony, not through metrical variation, but through caesura placement and enjambment. Suggests that the sequence is so overwhelmingly iambic that, "where there is a question whether a given foot represents a deviation, the reader must consider it iambic if he wishes to read the line as Sidney probably intended it." Notes that, although there are fifteen different rhyme schemes, a small number accounts for the bulk of the sonnets, one being used sixty times. Applying Josephine Miles's concepts of majority and minority vocabularies (1921), isolates twenty-eight nouns, adjectives, and verbs that are "instrumental in determining the orientation of the sequence." Drawing on Henry Peacham's *Garden of Eloquence*, examines some of the "most interesting and obvious" of Sidney's rhetorical figures, arguing that he used them consciously. Studies the images along the lines provided by Caroline Spurgeon for Shakespeare, classifying them according to the "areas" of experience from which they come. Seeks to determine whether *Astrophil and Stella* is, stylistically, more English or French, finding that Sidney "relied on his knowledge of both traditions," fusing

and remaking them through his genius. In an appendix, supplies a word count of nouns, adjectives, and verbs.

2090 COTTER, JAMES FINN. "The 'Baiser' Group in Sidney's *Astrophil and Stella*." *TSLL* 12 (Fall 1970):381–403.
Attempts to show that a concern with poetry underlies the poems in praise of the kiss (Song ii and Sonnets 73–83). Offers a close analysis of the twelve poems and their influence on the poems that follow, emphasizing Sidney's ironic stance. Argues that "poetry is a fit mirror of life because it is distinct from life; it reflects the real without replacing it."

2091 ———. "A Glasse of Reason: The Art of Poetry in Sidney's *Astrophil and Stella*." Ph.D. diss., Fordham University, 1964, 204 pp.
Argues that Sidney's purpose in his "masterwork" was to "put into practice his theory of poetry, to give it concrete embodiment, to present in poetic form his . . . correctives for contemporary verse." Studies *Astrophil and Stella* in light of the five parts of classical rhetoric, by the use of which Sidney sought to "revitalize" poetry. See *DA* 24 (June 1964):5382.

2092 ———. "The Last Act of *Astrophil and Stella*." *Mid-Hudson Language Studies* 2 (1979):61–76.
Contends that the controversial reference to "this great cause" in line 8 of Sonnet 107 is to "the writing of the sequence itself as an *ars poetica*, seen in the larger context of the enrichment of English letters." Argues that *Astrophil and Stella* puts into practice Sidney's "declaration of meaning" in the *Defence*: to show "spots of the common infection," so that "we may bend to the right use both of matter and manner." Calls the sequence "architectonic," its aim being to "realize art concretely by embodying it within the poem as the matter of knowledge."

2093 ———. "Sidney's *Astrophil and Stella*, Sonnet 40." *Expl* 27 (March 1969):item 51.
Notes that sections of Dante's *Convivio* link love, astrology, and rhetoric in a fashion similar to that in Sidney's sonnet "As good to write" (*AS 40*).

2094 ———. "Sidney's *Astrophil and Stella*, Sonnet 75." *Expl* 27 (May 1969):item 70.
Reads the sonnet ironically, seeing references to venereal disease and linking them with references to the debauchery of Edward IV. See also Nelson (2215).

Twentieth Century

2095 ———. "The Songs in *Astrophil and Stella*." *SP* 67 (April 1970):178–200.
After reviewing comments in the *Defence* on the connection between poetry and reason, examines the songs in *Astrophil and Stella*, accepting their placement in the sequence as indicated in Ringler's edition (92). Provides a close reading of each one, noting Sidney's skill in handling dialogue. Demonstrates an antiphonal relationship between the songs and the sonnets.

2096 COWAN, STANLEY A. "Sidney's *Astrophel and Stella* IX, 12–14." *Expl* 20 (May 1962):item 76.
Argues, *pace* Putzel (2234), that "touch" can refer both to "touchstone" and to "tinder-box," thereby uniting "the mineral metaphor and the imagery of fire." See also Dudley (2111).

2097 CROLL, MORRIS W[ILLIAM]. *The Works of Fulke Greville*. Philadelphia: J.P. Lippincott, 1903, pp. 3–4, 8–15, 19–20, 26–27.
Considers the "obvious and significant" relation between Sidney's *Astrophil and Stella* and Greville's *Caelica* and the two men's shared Platonism. Argues that Greville's natural poetic bent demands that he escape Sidney's influence: "his object is not to gild reality, but to reproduce the very color and touch of its brass."

2098 CRUTTWELL, [MAURICE JAMES] PATRICK. *The English Sonnet*. Writers and Their Work, 191. London: British Council and National Book League, Longmans, Green, & Co., 1966, pp. 13–18.
Argues that, in *Astrophil and Stella*, Sidney is following his own experience, "but the experience itself is varied, changeable, often self-contradictory."

2099 CUTTS, JOHN P. "Falstaff's 'Heauenlie Iewel': Incidental Music for *The Merry Wives of Windsor*." *SQ* 11 (Winter 1960):89–92.
Notes that Falstaff's exclamation to Mistress Ford "Have I caught thee, my heavenly jewel?" in *Merry Wives* III.iii comes from the opening line in Song ii of *Astrophil and Stella*. Discusses the relevance of the song to the play, providing a transcript of the setting found in the British Library MS. Add. 15117.

2100 DAHL, CURTIS. "Sidney's *Astrophel and Stella*, LXXXIV." *Expl* 6 (May 1948):item 46.
Assuming that Stella is Lady Rich, identifies the "highway" in Sonnet 84 as Whitechapel Road, which led to the house of her mother at Wanstead.

Considers possible symbolism in the poem, particularly that connected with highways.

2101 D[AVENPORT] A[RNOLD]. "Shakespeare's Sonnets." *N&Q* 196 (6 January 1951):5–6.

Points out several parallels between Shakespeare's Sonnet 29 and "No more my dear, no more these counsels try" (*AS 64*).

2102 DAVIE, DONALD. *Articulate Energy: An Enquiry into the Syntax of English Poetry*. London: Routledge & Kegan Paul; New York: Harcourt, Brace, 1955, pp. 45, 46, 53.

Uses techniques displayed in Ernest Fenollosa's "The Chinese Written Character as a Medium for Poetry" to explicate "Come sleep, O sleep" (*AS 39*). Argues that Sidney's metaphors are not metaphors but "particulars of the abstraction sleep" and that, "under Fenollosa's scrutiny, [the poem] will come off very badly. It is poetry where the verb is evaded whenever possible." Also criticizes the Ramist logical pattern underlying Sonnet 27.

2103 de GRAZIA, MARGRETA. "Lost Potential in Grammar and Nature: Sidney's *Astrophil and Stella*." *SEL* 21 (Winter 1981):21–35.

Explores the nature of the grammatical conflict between the indicative and the potential mood, citing Sidney's use of the moods as a way of playing out the conflict between sense and reason. In the *Defence* cites the contrasts between history and poetry, sense and wit. In *Astrophil and Stella* suggests that Astrophil's libidinous longings make him unable to escape from the power of sense and lead to his loss of potential.

2104 de MOURGUES, ODETTE. *Metaphysical, Baroque and Précieux Poetry*. Oxford: Clarendon Press, 1953, pp. 12–20, 23, 125, 131, 141.

Compares *Astrophil and Stella* with Maurice Scève's *Délie* as examples of premetaphysical and *précieux* poetry. Notes *précieux* elements in Sidney's sequence, including the rhymes in Sonnet 89, the rhetoric in Sonnet 49, and the "stiff personifications of Virtue, Reason, Love, Beauty" throughout. Argues that Sidney possessed "that faculty of eclectic discrimination and suppleness in adapting foreign themes to English diction which represents almost the highest possible creative power in a *précieux* poet." Concludes that, "if Sidney was in no way a forerunner of the metaphysical poets, it was precisely because he was a typical *précieux* poet and his *préciosité* owed a great deal to his Italian models."

Twentieth Century

2105 DEVEREUX, E.J. "A Possible Source for 'Pindare's Apes' in Sonnet 3 of *Astrophil and Stella*." *N&Q*, n.s. 24 (December 1977):521.
Suggests that the phrase may have its source in Pindar's *Second Pythian Ode*.

2106 DICKSON, ARTHUR. "Sidney's *Astrophel and Stella*, Sonnet 1." *Expl* 3 (October 1944):item 3.
Analyzes the metaphors in the sestet of Sonnet 1.

2107 DINGLEY, R[OBERT] J. "'Sir Foole': *Astrophil and Stella* 53." *Parergon*, n.s. 1 (1983):105–12.
Seeks to redress the "tacit neglect" of the tournament sonnet "In martial sports I had my cunning tried" (*AS 53*). Examines it in the context of Elizabethan pageantry, arguing that it "seeks to disorient its reader in the same way that its protagonist is disoriented by Stella" by a "nimble juxtaposition of disparate levels of reality." Sees in Astrophil a "schizo-phrenic dislocation," which is contrary to the usual harmonious balance implied by the conjunction of Venus and Mars and which has as its ulti-mate source "the ambivalent position of the Elizabethan courtier."

2108 DONOW, HERBERT S. "Concordance and Stylistic Analysis of Six Elizabethan Sonnet Sequences." *CHum* 3 (March 1969):205–8.
Discusses the principles behind the construction of computer-generated concordances and of stylistic tests. Considers specific applications to son-net sequences, including *Astrophil and Stella*.

2109 ———. *A Concordance to the Sonnet Sequences of Daniel, Drayton, Shakespeare, Sidney, and Spenser*. Carbondale and Edwardsville: Southern Illinois University Press; London and Amsterdam: Feffer & Simons, 1969, 781 pp.
Provides a computer-generated concordance of *Astrophil and Stella* as printed in Ringler's edition (92). In the preface, describes the basic parameters of the programs and their capabilities. In an appendix, pro-vides word lists and word-frequency counts.

2110 DUANE, CAROL L. "The English Renaissance Poet in the World: Wyatt, Gascoigne, Sidney, Shakespeare, and Jonson. Ph.D. diss., Michigan State University, 1984, 256 pp.
Places Sidney among other Englishmen of the Renaissance who were concerned with the poet's ability and responsibility to shape the order of society and who sought to put "active humanism" into practice. Takes Astrophil as a "negative example," who turns away from his social and

poetic responsibilities as the sequence progresses. See *DAI* 45 (February 1985):2532A.

2111 DUDLEY, FRED A. "Sidney's *Astrophel and Stella*, IX, 12–14." *Expl* 20 (May 1962):item 76.

Points out, *pace* Putzel (2234), that "touch" can mean "touchstone," "touchwood or tinder," and "touch powder" or blasting powder, and that it "carries a clear hint of carnal meaning." See also Cowan (2096).

2112 DUNCAN-JONES, KATHERINE. "'Rosis and Lysa': Selections from the Poems of Sir Robert Sidney." *ELR* 9 (Spring 1979):240–63.

Notes ways in which *Astrophil and Stella* served as a model for poems by Sidney's brother.

2113 EASTHOPE, ANTHONY. "Poetry and the Politics of Reading." In *Re-Reading English*, edited by Peter Widdowson. London and New York: Methuen, 1982, pp. 136–49.

Drawing on Roman Jakobson's distinction between "enunciation" and "enounced," anaylzes "Having this day my horse" (*AS 41*) as a representative moment in the "founding" of the "English bourgeois tradition." Defines that tradition as a "continuing mode of poetic representation" that seeks to "disavow enunciation in favor of the subject of the enounced," thereby creating the "sense of presence" on which all modern "literary criticism" is grounded.

2114 EICHHOFF, THEODOR. *Unser Shakespeare: Beiträge zu einer wissenschaftlichen Shakespeare-Kritik.* Vol. 2. Halle, Germany: Max Niemeyer, 1903, pp. 131–39.

Regards *Astrophil and Stella* as coterie literature that lacks concern with "the great human problems." From the *Defence*, concludes that Sidney could not have taken the sonnets seriously either, and suggests that they were imitated only because he was a war hero.

2115 ENDICOTT, ANNABEL. "Pip, Philip and Astrophil: Dickens's Debt to Sidney?" *Dickensian* 63 (September 1966):158–62. [In this issue the volume number 62 appears erroneously on the title page.]

Suggests that Sidney inspired Dickens's portrait of the ideal gentleman in *Great Expectations* and also that there may be links between the names "Pip" and "Philip," and "Estella" and "Stella." Finds in the novel verbal echoes of three sonnets: "What, have I thus betrayed my liberty?" (*AS 47*); "Good brother, Philip" (*AS 83*); and especially "Your words, my

Twentieth Century

friend, right healthful caustics" (*AS 21*). The last refers to "that friendly foe,/ Great expectation." Sees in Estella the cold Petrarchan mistress who, like Penelope Rich, has been married off for "riches." Also connects Miss Havisham with Queen Elizabeth.

2116 ESSIG, ERHARDT H. "Sidney's 'With How Sad Steps, O Moon.'"
  Expl 20 (November 1961):item 25.
Points out that Burhans's solution (2075) to the crux in the last line of Sonnet 31 is identical to the solution reached by Charles Lamb (2041). See also Combellack (2088).

2117 EVANS, MAURICE. *English Poetry in the Sixteenth Century.*
  London: Hutchinson & Co., 1955, pp. 87–89, 97–99, 103–6.
Argues that there are clear resemblances between Sidney and Astrophil and between Penelope Rich and Stella, but notes that the relationship could only have lasted between Penelope's marriage and the spring of 1582, the only time that they were together at court. Suggests that "Sidney may have been following humanist literary theory in attributing a fictional but credible love affair to real characters, in order to give to his sonnet cycle the verisimilitude which he felt to be lacking in the love poetry of the time." Claims that Sidney, like Petrarch, uses the sonnet sequence as a meditative, introspective form of verse. Noting that the pastoral setting of Song viii is out of place in the quotidian realism of the rest of the piece, suggests that "Sidney had not finished off this section of the poem, or that the publisher included materials not intended for the purpose."

2118 EWBANK, INGA-STINA. "Sincerity and the Sonnet." *Essays and Studies*, n.s. 34 (1981):19–44.
Offers a "gathering of some thoughts on ways in which the problems of sincerity—of knowing yourself and your 'true' feelings, expressing them 'truly,' and thereby creating 'true' art—are explored and exploited." Reads Sidney, "who dazzles and impresses us by the wholeness and self-containedness of his fiction," in contrast to Shakespeare, who "involves us by the sense that he is going beyond fiction." Notes the "interwoven, interacting, and deeply interdependent" relation between the love story and the poetic self-consciousness, emphasizing the importance of speech in Astrophil's courtship. Finds the songs (particularly Song viii, with its shifting "modes of speech") crucial in allowing the "epigrammatic para-doxes and reversals of the sonnets to be expanded and examined." Contends that *Astrophil and Stella* is "rendered to the reader with such self-consciousness of its own art as to make it, as a tale, more akin to *Lolita* than to *Clarissa*."

2119 FALLS, CYRIL [BENTHAM]. *Mountjoy: Elizabethan General*. London: Odhams Press, 1955, pp. 54–67, 220–32.

Comments on the relationship between Sidney and Penelope Devereux, noting that Sidney's father probably did not draw up a formal marriage contract with Essex. Sees no suggestion that Penelope was ever in love with Sidney, although, for Sidney's part, the sonnets of *Astrophil and Stella*, with their "passion, and in places . . . remorse", seem to "bear the stamp of reality and experience."

2120 ———. "Penelope Rich and the Poets: Philip Sidney to John Ford." *EDH*, n.s. 28 (1956):123–37.

Provides a biography of Penelope Devereux and a review of comments on her, arguing that her identification with Sidney's Stella was common knowledge. Reads *Astrophil and Stella* as autobiographical, arguing that, at the time the sonnets were written, Penelope, far from being in love with Sidney, was already in love with Blount.

2121 FERRUOLO, ARNOLFO. "Sir Philip Sidney e Giordano Bruno." *Convivium*, n.s. 17 (1948):686–99.

Claims that, though Bruno did not directly influence Sidney, the two had a "spiritual affinity." Sees similarities between *Eroici furori* and *Astrophil and Stella*, especially in the renunciation at the end of the respective sequences, in the coincidence of certain images from mythology, and in repeated sonnet motifs. In support, comments on Bruno's dedication of his sequence to Sidney and their shared anti-Petrarchan stance.

2122 FINNEGAN, ROBERT EMMET. "Sidney's *Astrophil and Stella* 14." *Expl* 35 (Winter 1976):22–23.

Examines the numerous suggestions of "rhubarb" in the poem, including "bitter," "barbed," and "rueful."

2123 FISH, STANLEY E[UGENE]. *Self-Consuming Artifacts: The Experience of Seventeenth-Century Literature*. Berkeley, Los Angeles, and London: University of California Press, 1972, pp. 198–99.

Contrasts Herbert's "Jordan II" with *Astrophil and Stella* 1. See also Adams (2048).

2124 FLETCHER, JEFFERSON B[UTLER]. "Did 'Astrophel' Love 'Stella'?" *MP* 5 (October 1907):253–64. Reprint. In *The Religion of Beauty in Woman and other Essays on Platonic Love in Poetry and Society*. New York: Macmillan Co., 1911, pp. 147–65.

Surveys the scholarship on Astrophil's love of Stella, arguing that it is Platonic. Also examines Spenser's *Astrophel*.

Twentieth Century

2125 FLOWER, TIMOTHY FRANK. "1. Forms of Re-creation in
Nabokov's *Pale Fire*. 2. Charles Dickens and Gothic Fiction. 3.
Making It New: Problems of Meaningful Form in the Sonnets of
Sidney and Keats." Ph.D. diss., Rutgers University, 1972, 169 pp.
Argues that Sidney creates a "pointedly non-Petrarchan variant" in his
sestets, which, in "half resembling" those of Petrarch, formally embody
"Astrophil's conflict with Petrarchan love." The sonnets "question"
Petrarchan conventions in an ambivalent way. See *DAI* 32 (June
1972):6927A.

2126 FOGEL, EPHIM G[REGORY]. "The Mythical Sorrows of
Astrophil." In *Studies in Language and Literature in Honour of
Margaret Schlauch*, edited by Mieczysław Brahmer, Stanisław
Helsztyński, and Julian Krzyżanowski. Warsaw: PWN—Polish
Scientific Publishers, 1966, pp. 133–52.
Tries to mediate between "the iconoclastic fallacy" (which denies any significant relationship between Sidney and Astrophil or between Lady
Rich and Stella) and "the biographical fallacy" (which seeks to read the
sequence historically). Focuses on the common assumption that the
sequence involves "the poet's regret and self-reproach for failing to lay
siege to Penelope Devereux's heart before she became Lady Rich." Aside
from Tyndale's unreliable surmises (quoted by Aubrey in item 902),
finds no contemporary testimony to support Sidney's "mythical sorrows." Argues that neither the general themes and structure of the
sequence, nor specific poems within it, require such an interpretation.
Points out that the two sonnets usually cited as evidence (*AS* 2 and *33*)
have precedents in the work of earlier sonneteers, such as Ronsard and
Petrarch, and therefore seem conventional rather than biographical.
Concludes that the sequence follows the "classic five-stage pattern of the
romances of courtly love": Introduction (Sonnets 1–14), Development
(15–65), Culmination (66–85), Reversal (Songs iv–viii), and Denouement
(ix–108).

2127 FOWLER, ALASTAIR [D.S.]. *Triumphal Forms: Structural Patterns
in Elizabethan Poetry*. Cambridge: Cambridge University Press,
1970, pp. 175–80.
Examines *Astrophil and Stella* numerologically as a long poem written in
fourteen-line stanzas, in which the total number of sonnets alludes to the
game played by Penelope's suitors in Homer's *Odyssey*, with the absence
of the 109th indicating Astrophil's failure as a lover. Points out several
other numerological possibilities in the various patterns of the sequence.
See also Roche (2243).

2128 FRIEDRICH, WALTER G[EORGE]. "The Stella of Astrophel." *ELH* 3 (June 1936):114–39.
Argues that: 1) accounts of the Sidney-Rich affair have been based solely on the 1598 *Astrophil and Stella* and the elegies published with Spenser's *Colin Clout's Come Home Again*; 2) since the latter celebrate Frances Sidney as Stella, they cannot serve as evidence for a Sidney-Rich story; 3) there is no evidence that contemporaries regarded Lady Rich as Stella; and 4) seventeenth-century identifications are based solely on the same internal evidence as in number 1. Feels that the poems were written individually or in small groups, and although some "unmistakably" deal with Lady Rich, these do not prove that the sequence is the story of a love affair with her.

2129 FRYE, PROSSER HALL. *Literary Reviews and Criticisms*. New York and London: G.P. Putnam's Sons, 1908, pp. 1–18.
In "The Elizabethan Sonnet," discusses "With how sad steps, O moon" (*AS 31*), noting Sidney's heavy reliance on French sources.

2130 GAYLON, LINDA. "Puttenham's *Enargeia* and *Energia*: New Twists for Old Terms." *PQ* 60 (Winter 1981):29–40.
Defends the sound effects of "I never drank of Aganippe well" (*AS 74*), noting that the Elizabethans were fond of figures of repetition.

2131 GENTILI, VANNA. "La 'tragicomedy' dell' *Astrophil and Stella*." *Annali dell'Università di Lecce* 1 (1963):57–92.
Argues that the Sidney legend has been harmful to scholars because it has encouraged too much emphasis on biography and on Petrarchan convention. Claims that the narrative line of *Astrophil and Stella* should not be read as a conventional framework but rather as "an internal structure with each sonnet having a precise function," which is predominantly dramatic. Proposes a three-part structure (Sonnets 1–43, 44–85, Song iv–end), which differs from those offered by Young (2316) and Ringler (92). Claims that Sidney opposes the Petrarchan conventions that entrap Astrophil. Provides explications of Sonnets 4, 5, 10, 18, and 19 in order to correct the "meditative" emphasis of former critics while stressing the dramatic qualities of the poems. Concludes that *Astrophil and Stella* precludes a happy ending, its irresolution making it a "tragicomedy." See also Hamilton (2142).

Twentieth Century

2132 GILES, MARY DOOLEY. "The Elizabethan Sonnet Sequence: Segmented Form in its Earliest Appearances, *Astrophil and Stella*, *Hecatompathia*, and *Delia*." Ph.D. diss., University of Virginia, 1977, 261 pp.

Following the theory of Paula Johnson in *Form and Transformation in Music and Poetry of the English Renaissance* (Yale University Press, 1972), derives the term *segment* from the musical concept of "periodic analogy." Argues that, unlike the other sonneteers, for whom the "segment" is a theme, for Sidney it consists of the individual sonnet. See *DAI* 39 (August 1978):872A–73A.

2133 GODSHALK, W[ILLIAM] L[EIGH]. "Cicero, Sidney, and the 'Sunne-Burn'd Braine.'" *N&Q*, n.s. 27 (April 1980):139–40.

Cites possible sources for the imagery in the sonnet "Loving in truth" (*AS 1*), including Thomas Wilson's *Art of Rhetoric*, Cicero's *De Oratore*, E.K.'s glosses on *The Shepherd's Calendar*, and Gascoigne's *Adventures of Master F.J.* Suggests that the lines involve a deliberate ambiguity.

2134 ———. "Sidney's Astrophel." *AN&Q* 17 (September 1978):19–20.

Argues for the spelling "Astrophel" rather than "Astrophil," on the grounds of a possible bilingual pun: "fell" in the sense of "vicious" and also of "fallen."

2135 GOLDMAN, LLOYD NATHANIEL. "Attitudes toward the Mistress in Five Elizabethan Sonnet Sequences." Ph.D. diss., University of Illinois, 1964, 297 pp.

Examines each poet's attitude toward his conceits (which determines his attitude toward his mistress) and finds the fundamental organization of each sequence to be based on the poet's "understanding of the Petrarchan tradition." Sidney employs his sonnets as "tools for the logical examination of his persona," and his attitude toward his mistress shows an awareness of classical mythology, which accounts for his feelings of attraction and repulsion. Argues that Sidney was analyzing amorous love in "the light of Christian Agape and pagan Eros." See *DA* 25 (May 1965):6590–91.

2136 GOLDSTEIN, NEAL L. "*Love's Labour's Lost* and the Renaissance Vision of Love." *SQ* 25 (Summer 1974):335–50.

Suggests parallels between the play and Sidney's sonnets, especially in their ambivalent attitudes toward sensuality and Platonic spirituality.

2137 GOTTFRIED, RUDOLF. "Autobiography and Art: An Elizabethan Borderland." In *Literary Criticism and Historical Under-*

standing: Selected Papers from the English Institute, edited by Phillip Damon. New York: Columbia University Press, 1967, pp. 109–34. Discusses the mingling of autobiography and fiction in *Astrophil and Stella*. Notes that Sidney goes beyond Petrarch in realistic details, such as the allusions to the Sidney and Devereux coats of arms in Sonnets 13 and 65, and that other sonneteers followed Sidney's lead.

2138 GOULSTON, WENDY. "The 'Figuring Forth' of Astrophil: Sidney's Use of Language." *Southern Review: Literary and Interdisciplinary Essays* 11 (November 1978):228–46.

Argues that Astrophil's "audaciously witty tongue circumvents the promptings of his reason" and that "he wilfully persists in the self-degrading pursuit of a self-centered love." Examines all facets of his misuse of language and reason, arguing that his speech is a "parody of the Christian lexicon" that insists blasphemously on "vainly personal meanings." Contrasting Astrophil's language with that of the Psalms and distinguishing between his voice and Sidney's, shows that Astrophil's use of animal images "degrades the 'golden world'" by misusing metaphor. Feels that his use of false logic and distortion of grammar are an "obsession with and abuse of the outer forms of language," which in turn parallel his sexual obsession with Stella's body. Also feels that, in avoiding "I" as the grammatical subject of his sentences and relegating that function, instead, to personification of parts of himself or "Cupid," he "misuses language as revelation." Concludes that "throughout *Astrophil and Stella* Sidney uses paradox to draw attention to Astrophil's deceptive manner of expression, to show simultaneously both Astrophil's twisting of meaning and Sidney's teaching of God-given truth."

2139 GRUNDY, JOAN. "Shakespeare's Sonnets and the Elizabethan Sonneteers." *ShS* 15 (1962):41–49.

In discussing the nature of the Elizabethan sonnet sequence, asserts that Sidney's concept of poetry as a "speaking picture" governs the development of the genre. Regards Shakespeare and Sidney as the only poets of the period to question the nature of the conventional sonnet.

2140 GUNN, THOM, ed. Introduction to *Selected Poems of Fulke Greville*. Chicago: University of Chicago Press; London: Faber & Faber, 1968, pp. 9–10, 12, 16–18, 26.

Considers literary influences between Sidney and Greville, noting their friendship and shared Calvinism. Compares the ornate, sophisticated style of *Astrophil and Stella* with the plain style of earlier Elizabethan

Twentieth Century

poets. Explicates *Astrophil and Stella* 31 and 99, and compares Sonnet 33 with Greville's *Caelica* 56.

2141 HAMILTON, A.C. "The 'mine of time': Time and Love in Sidney's *Astrophel and Stella*." *Mosaic* 13, no. 1 (1979):81–91.
Points out that, despite its status as the major English Petrarchan poem, *Astrophil and Stella* does not have "time and love" as a major motif. Argues that Sidney uses time "on the level of structure and form," introducing the metaphor of time as a "Pioneer, Underminer, or Sapper" that will both reveal Stella's true worth and undermine Astrophil "through violence and fraud." Compares Sidney's sequence with Petrarch's to show that Sidney neither moves out of time nor attempts to redeem it. Argues that, in wooing Stella, "Astrophel had acted out the fullness of loving in the unfolding of time," and that "the completeness of that experience sets him apart from it." Concludes that "Astrophel triumphs over time but not by escaping: he redeems time by transforming it."

2142 ———. "Sidney's *Astrophel and Stella* as a Sonnet Sequence." *ELH* 36 (March 1969):59–87.
Seeks to show that *Astrophil and Stella* may be read as a single, long poem on the theme of "loving in truth." Focuses on the "story" of the sequence, considering its biographical foundations and noting that it provides the only "external structure or framework." After reviewing earlier discussions of this framework, suggests three main parts, comprising Sonnets 1–35, 36–72, and 72–108. Notes that the sequence can be divided even more precisely by theme: Sonnets 1–6: introduction; 7–13: object of affection; 14–35: Astrophel loving in truth; 36–72: Astrophel's problems as lover and poet; and 72–108: "all the events of the 'affair' between the lovers." See also Young (2316).

2143 HANSEN, ADOLF. "Stella." *Tilskueren*, 1907, pp. 423–27.
In comparing depictions of "Stella" in the works of Sidney, Swift, and Goethe, paraphrases *Astrophil and Stella* to show its varied emotional states.

2144 HARFST, B.P. "Astrophil and Stella: Precept and Example." *PLL* 5 (Fall 1969):397–414.
Building on Howe's discussions (2151 and 84), argues that the sonnet sequence reflects closely the concerns of the *Defence*. Not only do many of the sonnets repeat points raised about poetry in the *Defence*, but both works also follow a seven-part structural pattern and Astrophil's love for Stella embodies "each of the specific sins that Gosson charged against poetry."

2145 HASSELKUSS, HERMANN KARL. *Der Petrarkismus in der Sprache der englischen Sonettdichter der Renaissance*. Münster, Germany: n.p., 1927, pp. 37–44. Orig. a Ph.D. diss., Westfälischen Wilhelms-Universität zu Münster, 1927.

Considers Sidney's probable exposure to Italian sonnets during his European tour and his dislike of Petrachan imitations. Lists passages in *Astrophil and Stella* with close parallels in Petrarch's *Rime*, but attributes the similarities to Sidney's interest in the common themes and conventions of Continental sonneteers and not to direct influence.

2146 HENDERSON, KATHERINE USHER. "A Study of the Dramatic Mode in the English Renaissance Love Lyric: Sidney's *Astrophil and Stella* and Donne's *Songs and Sonnets*." Ph.D. diss., Columbia University, 1969, 310 pp.

Defining a dramatic lyric as "the poetic representation of verbal action," seeks to establish that the majority of sonnets in *Astrophil and Stella* are dramatic lyrics and that the sequence constitutes a dramatic unit. The sonnets are of three kinds: "dramatic encounters" (in which the speaker directs an action toward his audience), soliloquies (in which he directs an action toward himself), and formal, set pieces, which are "dramatic by virtue of their context." Sidney's departures from Petrarch are related to the dramatic nature of his sequence. See *DAI* 30 (April 1970): 4413A–14A.

2147 HENINGER, S.K., Jr. *A Handbook of Renaissance Meteorology with Particular Reference to Elizabethan and Jacobean Literature*. Durham, N.C.: Duke University Press, 1960, p. 52.

Notes that lines 7–8 of *Astrophil and Stella* 1 echo a commonplace found in Bartholomaeus's *De Proprietatibus Rerum*: rain "is more fresh and sweet then other waters . . . [and it] maketh the lande to beare fruit."

2148 HINELY, JAN LAWSON. "The Sonnet Sequence in Elizabethan Poetry." Ph.D. diss., Ohio State University, 1966, 306 pp.

Argues that Sidney followed Petrarch in creating a sequence "unified by the dominant, individualized speaking voice of the poet lover" and in suggesting that this persona might be a mask for the poet himself. He "stressed the expressive use of poetry by emphasizing the truth and singularity of Astrophil's experience." See *DA* 27 (March 1967):3011A.

2149 HIRAKAWA, TAIJI. "Astrophel no Nigai Humour." In *Ogoshi Kazugo: Ryokyoju Taikan Kinnen Ronbunshu*, edited by Suga Yasuo. Kyoto, Japan: Apollonsha, 1980, pp. 57–70.

Not seen. Cited in the *MLA International Bibliography*, 1981, vol. 1, item 1335.

Twentieth Century

2150 HOUGH, GORDON RICHARD. "A Quiet Image of Disquiet:
The Persona in the Lyrics of Wyatt, Sidney and Donne." Ph.D.
diss., State University of New York at Buffalo, 1975, 191 pp.
Discusses Astrophil on the basis of formulations by the British psychoan-
alyst D.W. Winnicott about "true" and "false" selves. Contends that
Sidney writes "as though he has perfect faith in the expressiveness of his
art, though his persona is only able to control his ambivalence as a lover
with that art and not able to gain active satisfaction of his desire." See
DAI 36 (April 1976):6705A.

2151 HOWE, ANN ROMAYNE *"Astrophel and Stella*: 'Why and How.'"
SP 61 (April 1964):150-69.
Surveys the battle over whether the sequence is to be read as biography
or convention, discussing Sidney's methods of characterization and his
ways of working with and against Petrarchan conventions. In his principle that poetry is "delightful teaching," sees a way of promoting an
active Christian life. Provides a detailed analysis of the various rhetorical
devices used in the sequence, and suggests a reordering of the songs.
Sees ironies in Sonnet 75. See also Harfst (2144) and Nelson (2215).

2152 HUNTER, C. STUART "Erected Wit and Infected Will: Sidney's
Poetic Theory and Poetic Practice." *SNew* 5, no. 2 (1984):3–10.
Argues that, by using Astrophil as a negative example and drawing the
reader into sympathy with him, Sidney "begins to move the reader from
vice to virtue" by making the negative aspects of his character "increasingly evident." The sequence puts into practice principles in the *Defence*
involving *mimesis* and the poet's power to move by way of well-tuned language.

2153 HUNTER, G.K. "The Dramatic Technique of Shakespeare's
Sonnets." *EIC* 3 (April 1953):152–64.
Contrasts Sidney with Shakespeare, noting that Sidney's "intellect is
more analytical" and his use of simile "has the objective quality of a
rational self-criticism which Shakespeare lacks." Argues that the distance
between speaker and reader in *Astrophil and Stella* leads the reader to
take a "less biographical view of the situation."

2154 ———. "Spenser's *Amoretti* and the English Sonnet Tradition." In
A Theatre for Spenserians. Papers of the International Spenser
Colloquium, Fredericton, New Brunswick, October 1969. Edited
by Judith M. Kennedy and James A. Reither. Toronto: University
of Toronto Press, 1973, pp. 124–44.
Argues that, whereas *Astrophil and Stella* concentrates on the speaker,
Amoretti focuses on the relationship with the beloved. By means of come-

dy, irony, personification, and drama, the former stresses the "disproportion between inner and outer." The latter emphasizes the blending of the two.

2155 IMANISHI, MASAKI. "Sir Philip Sidney no *Astrophel & Stella* no Hyogen to Giho *Elizabeth-cho Love-Sonnet* Shiron" [Expression and Technique in *Astrophil and Stella*: An Essay on the Elizabethan Love Sonnet]. In *Gengo to Buntai: Higashida Chiaki Kyoju Kaureki Kuien Roubunshu* [*Language and Style: Collected Essays Commemorating the Sixtieth Birthday of Professor Chiaki Higashida*], edited by Chiaki Higashida. Osaka, Japan: Osaka Kyoiku Tosho, 1975, pp. 30–42.

Discusses the use made of "comic posture" and "colloquialism and plain speech" as elements of style in *Astrophil and Stella*.

2156 INGRAM, W.G. "The Shakespearean Quality." In *New Essays on Shakespeare's Sonnets*, edited by Hilton Landry. New York: AMS Press, 1976, pp. 41–63, 255–57.

Argues that *Astrophil and Stella* differs from Shakespeare's *Sonnets* because of Sidney's decorative and functional use of "the wide gamut of Ramistic rhetoric."

2157 ISOBE, HATSUE. "Astrophel no Settoku." In *Muraoka Isamu Sensei Kiju Kinen Ronbunshu: Eibungaku Shiron*. Tokyo: Kinseido, 1983, pp. 1–15.

Not seen. Cited in the *MLA International Bibliography*, 1984, vol. 1, item 1691.

2158 JACKSON, MacD[ONALD] P. "The Printer of the First Quarto of *Astrophil and Stella* (1591)." *SB* 31 (1978):201–3.

On the basis of close bibliographic analysis and comparison with another book published in the period, argues that the printer of the first quarto was John Charlewood and that he was working from a carelessly copied manuscript.

2159 JAVITCH, DANIEL. "The Impure Motives of Elizabethan Poetry." *Genre* 15 (Spring–Summer 1982):225–38.

Arguing from the premise that much Elizabethan poetry was written to display verbal accomplishments of a sort to commend the writer for preferment to positions at court, and citing the example of George Gascoigne, contends that one of the principle aims of *Astrophil and Stella* "was to rebuke prior Elizabethan writers of amatory verse, not solely for the inferior quality of their verse but for the extra-amatory and extra-literary motives that had prompted it." Finds that Astrophil indirectly

Twentieth Century

mocks these motives whenever he insists that Stella is all that matters to
him. Citing "I never drank of Aganippe well" (*AS 74*), identifies "disin-
terestedness" as the quality that Astrophil "most wants to convey to set
himself apart from contemporary versifiers." See also item 583.

2160 JEHMLICH, REIMER. "Feurige Liebesdämpfe: Zu drei Sonetten
Sir Philip Sidneys." *LWU* 4 (1971):147–57.
Deals with three sonnets: "In nature apt to like" (*AS 16*), "O eyes, which
do the spheres of beauty move" (*AS 42*), and "Farewell, O sun" (*AS 76*).
Considers their importance in the sequence and their imagery of flaming glances and burning hearts, tracing it to Ficino, Dante, Petrarch,
and Ronsard.

2161 JENKINS, ANNIBEL. "A Second Astrophel and Stella Cycle."
RenP, 1970, pp. 73–80.
Suggests that, since they were first printed as "Other Sonnets of Variable
Verse," the songs of *Astrophil and Stella* should be considered as a separate cycle. Argues that they may be divided into two groups, each of
which has a sequential development. The first, including Songs ii, iv, vi,
viii, and x, contains "the episodes of incident"; the second, including
Songs i, iii, v, vii, and ix, contains "the pattern of emotional response" to
the first group. The final song then repeats "both incident and emotion
to complete the whole."

2162 JOHN, LISLE C[ECIL]. "The Date of the Marriage of Penelope
Devereux." *PMLA* 49 (September 1934):961–62.
Quotes a letter "which seems to refer unmistakably to the marriage to
Lord Rich" and that fixes the date after 18 September 1581. This is sig-
nificant since most of the poems in *Astrophil and Stella* were written after
October of that year.

2163 ———. *The Elizabethan Sonnet Sequences: Studies in Conventional
Conceits*. Columbia University Studies in English and Comparative
Literature, 133. New York: Columbia University Press, 1938, pp.
179–94.
In "The English Petrarch," challenges the view that *Astrophil and Stella* is
conventional and imitative, and denies the claim that Stella is Frances
Walsingham. Reviewing internal evidence and contemporary events,
dates Penelope Devereux's marriage to Lord Rich in the autumn of
1581 and suggests that the sonnets were written soon after, most of them
"presumably" in 1582.

2164 JONES, ANN ROSALIND. "The Lyric Sequence: Poetic Performance as Plot (Dante's *Vita nuova*, Scève's *Délie*, Sidney's *Astrophil and Stella*, Drayton's *Idea*, La Ceppède's *Théorèmes*)." Ph.D. diss., Cornell University, 1976, 327 pp.

Seeks to define the "organizational principle and poetic implications" of the five named sequences. Finds that they all record the writer's development as poet as well as lover. Although in individual poems the poet may act dramatically, in the sequence as a whole he stands apart and arranges logically to clarify meaning. Argues that Astrophil's love corrupts his search for direct, sincere language, his final sonnets revealing his "isolation and paralysis." See *DAI* 37 (April 1977):6464A–65A.

2165 JONES, ANN ROSALIND, and STALLYBRASS, PETER. "The Politics of *Astrophil and Stella*." *SEL* 24 (Winter 1984):53–68.

Begins from the premise that "the contradictory tyrannies of court life (the need to succeed at any cost versus the ideal pose of disinterested advisor) find their counterparts in the contradictory tyrannies of love (the amorous passion . . . versus 'Tyran honour')." In *Astrophil and Stella*, identifies "strategies of manipulation which were the techniques of aspiring lover and courtier alike" and suggests that poems in the sequence "function as a complex displacement of the ideological pressures of the court." Argues, for example, that, in sonnets such as 23, 69, and 107, the "logic" of the poet coincides with "political rhetoric" in ways that allow Astrophil to control and dominate everything in the sequence. Identifying a "set of homologies" between lover/beloved and courtier/prince, argues that Petrarchan love is a game in which three powerful discourses meet: love, religion, and politics. Notes, however, that the homology breaks down on the crucial point of the woman's chastity. Since her giving is the opposite of the prince's giving, the three discourses conflict irreconcilably. Concludes that Sidney's sequence "takes the search for transcendence or the hopeful resolution of other sonnet sequences to an absolute dead end."

2166 KALSTONE, DAVID. "Sir Philip Sidney and 'Poore *Petrarchs* Long Deceased Woes.'" *JEGP* 63 (January 1964):21–32.

Argues that Astrophil's contrary attitudes, "his alternate mockery and acceptance of Petrarchan rhetoric," reveal Sidney's distrust of a poetic tradition that was breaking down. Views the uncertainties of the sequence as a prologue to the poetry of Shakespeare and Donne.

Twentieth Century

2167 KENNEDY, WILLIAM J[OHN]. *Rhetorical Norms in Renaissance Literature*. New Haven, Conn., and London: Yale University Press, 1978, pp. 57–78.
In the chapter on *Astrophil and Stella*, notes that, although Sidney's sequence reflects the influence of Petrarch and the French sonneteers, it has three things that they lack: moral satire, humorous self-deprecation, and practical rhetorical persuasion. Noting Sidney's familiarity with Aristotle's *Rhetoric*, shows that his use of rhetorical devices generates irony in the sequence and that Sidney employs playfulness, wit, and experimentation to create a "dramatic impulse, with a covert, though very definite moral purpose."

2168 KIMBROUGH, ROBERT. *Sir Philip Sidney*. Twayne's English Authors Series, 114. New York: Twayne Publishers, 1971, pp. 107–24.
In Chapter 5, argues that, in *Astrophil and Stella*, Sidney achieved a "voice . . . so realized that we take it for his," and in doing so "showed his fellows how to combine meter and rhythm in creating poetry that moves, instructs, and delights," an achievement that makes the sequence "one of the world's great collections of lyric poetry." Shows how, despite the sequence's "highly conventional" Petrarchism, "everything comes alive." Concurs with Kalstone's judgment (1907) that Astrophil's "significant activity is the discovery of conflict, and he delights in it," but maintains that "it is only Astrophil the persona who sees no resolution to the conflict of love." The duality of voice allows Sidney to show Astrophil's "Byronic delight in discovery of life's delusions and, at the same time, show him as blind to the principles of natural law." Analyzes individual sonnets to differentiate between those in which "we do not trouble to distinguish between poet and persona" and those in which we must, as in "It is most true" (*AS* 5). Contends that the story is "the least important aspect of the sequence," and that even if it records a real affair with Penelope Rich, the affair "was not very serious." See also item 593.

2169 KINSMAN, ROBERT S. "Sidney's *Astrophel and Stella*, Sonnet XII, 1–2." *Expl* 8 (June 1950):item 56.
Approves the reading "day-nets" from the second quarto and elucidates the significance of the image for the poem.

2170 KLEMP, P[AUL] J. "Sidney's Astrophil and Homer's Love Triangles." *PLL* 19 (Summer 1983):326–30.
Discusses the significance of the number of sonnets in the sequence, which is 108, a number important in Homer. Views Astrophil as an

intrusive third party, who forms a love triangle between Penelope and Lord Rich, arguing that the verbal allusions in "Rich fools there be" (*AS 24*), "I might, unhappy word" (*AS 33*) and "What may words say" (*AS 35*) "encourage the reader to see Astrophil's relationship as an ironic re-enactment of important love triangles in Homer's epics." Claims that these allusions provide a moral context for the reader in judging Astrophil's actions and that it is one of Sidney's "great achievements" that Astrophil is never aware of the many ironies behind his allusions to Homer.

2171 KRIEGER, MURRAY. "The Continuing Need for Criticism." *Concerning Poetry* 1 (Spring 1968):7–21.
Sees "What may words say" (*AS 35*) as "the Petrarchan sonnet to end all Petrarchan sonnets" in that it reveals the limitations of language by using language itself and shows that language can be transformed by the poet into something more.

2172 ———. "Presentation and Representation in the Renaissance Lyric: The Net of Words and the Escape of the Gods." In *Mimesis: From Mirror to Method, Augustine to Descartes*, edited by John D. Lyons and Stephen G. Nichols, Jr. Hanover, N.H., and London: University Press of New England, 1982, pp. 110–31.
Argues that the language in *Astrophil and Stella* indicates Sidney's awareness both of the poem's need to "invoke and contain its object, its goddess," and of "the illusory nature of his attempt." Views Sidney's sonnets and the work of other Renaissance lyric writers as attempts to come to grips with the ways in which language functions. See also Miller (659).

2173 KUIN, ROGER [J.P.]. "A Little World Made Cunningly: Semiosis in a Sidney Sonnet." *SNew* 4 (Spring 1983):6–11.
Applies the semiotic methods of Michael Riffaterre's *Semiotics of Poetry* (Indiana University Press, 1978) to the sonnet "Like some weak lords" (*AS 29*). In its structure of "literal ungrammaticalities," of "semantic ambiguities," and of "catechretic metaphors" (all three unusual in *Astrophil and Stella*), sees "neurotic" signs of an "invariant matrix" showing Cupid to be a "*false* god." While at a mimetic level the poem depicts Astrophil's helpless devotion to Stella, its "significance" is that it "proclaims a dark malignancy which prefigures the cycle's unhappy ending."

2174 LANHAM, RICHARD A[LAN]. "*Astrophil and Stella*: Pure and Impure Persuasion." *ELR* 2 (Winter 1972):100–115.
Reads *Astrophil and Stella* as caused by sexual frustration, suggesting that Astrophil is forced to assume roles that are not essentially poetic but

Twentieth Century

rhetorical in that they aim to persuade. Questions the need for consistency in a poetic persona. For a counterargument, see Montgomery (2202).

2175 LATHAM, JACQUELINE E.M. "Shakespeare's Sonnet 21." *N&Q,* n.s. 25 (April 1978):110–12.
Argues that Shakespeare's repudiation of convention in Sonnet 21 links him and the poem with Sidney. Works out an elaborate series of connections between the sonnet and *Astrophil and Stella*.

2176 ———. "Sidney's *Astrophil and Stella*, Sonnet 30." *Expl* 33 (February 1975):item 47.
Reviews the political background of the sonnet, drawing attention to the "ingenious play on ideas and words" that accompanies the allusions. Suggests that "weltring" alludes to recurrent border disputes between England and Scotland.

2177 LAVIN, J[OSEPH] A[NTHONY]. "The First Two Printers of Sidney's *Astrophil and Stella*." *Library,* 5th ser. 26 (September 1971):249–55.
Argues that the printers of the first and second quartos were John Charlewood and John Danter, respectively, though evidence for the latter is not conclusive.

2178 LEE, Sir SIDNEY. "The Elizabethan Sonnet." In *The Cambridge History of English Literature,* edited by A[dolphus] W[illiam] Ward and A[lfred] R[aney] Waller. Vol. 3, *Renascence and Reformation.* New York and Cambridge: Cambridge University Press, 1909, pp. 281–310.
Notes Thomas Watson's influence on Sidney's sonnets. Argues that, though probably based on fact, *Astrophil and Stella* is not a poetic autobiography. Mentions Sidney's influence on Henry Constable and Barnabe Barnes.

2179 LEE, Sir SIDNEY, ed. Introduction to *Elizabethan Sonnets, Newly Arranged and Indexed.* In *An English Garner,* edited by Edward Arber. Rev. ed. Vol. 1. Westminster: n.p., 1904, pp. ix–cx.
Dismisses attempts to treat *Astrophil and Stella* as a series of "autobiographic confessions." Emphasizes, instead, Sidney's practice of imitating Petrarch and Ronsard to advantage, comparing "Having this day my horse, my hand, my lance" (*AS 41*) with Petrarch's Sonnet 201, and "Dear, why make you more of a dog than me?" (*AS 59*) with Ronsard's

Amours I.78. Praises Sidney for retaining more or less Italianate schemes of meter and rhyme.

2180 LeGALLIENNE, RICHARD. "Old Love Stories Retold: 1. Sir Philip Sidney and Lady Penelope Devereux." *Cosmopolitan* 33 (June 1902):211–17.

In a biographical reading of *Astrophil and Stella*, argues that Sidney lost Penelope when Leicester's son was born and Sidney could no longer expect to inherit his uncle's estate. Cites internal evidence of her affection for Sidney and sees "Leave me, O love" (*CS 32*) as a fitting conclusion for the sequence.

2181 LEGOUIS, PIERRE. *Donne the Craftsman: An Essay upon the Structure of the "Songs and Sonnets."* Paris: H. Didier, 1928, pp. 55–61.

Compares Donne's use of an interlocutor in "The Canonization" with Sidney's in "Alas have I not pain enough my friend" (*AS 14*) and in "Your words my friend, right healthfull caustics, blame" (*AS 21*).

2182 LEISHMAN, J[AMES] B[LAIR]. *Themes and Variations in Shakespeare's Sonnets.* London: Hutchinson & Co., 1961, pp. 60, 90, 116–17, 182.

Argues that Sidney learned self-dramatization from Ronsard. Claims that the apostrophe to the moon in *Astrophil and Stella* 31 is indebted to a line in the pseudo-Virgilian *Lydia*, and that Sonnets 3, 6, 15, and 74 may have inspired Shakespeare's Sonnet 21.

2183 LeVAY, JOHN P. "Sidney's *Astrophel and Stella*, Sonnet 18." *Expl* 40 (Spring 1982):10–12.

Argues that, in "With what sharp checks" (*AS 18*) as throughout the sequence, Sidney treats reason ambiguously, praising its power in the octave, but deeming it inferior to mystical love in the sestet.

2184 LEVY, CHARLES S[AMUEL]. "Sidneian Indirection: The Ethical Irony of *Astrophil and Stella*." In *Sir Philip Sidney and the Interpretation of Renaissance Culture: The Poet in His Time and in Ours: A Collection of Critical and Scholarly Essays*, edited by Gary F. Waller and Michael D. Moore. London: Croom Helm; Totowa, N.J.: Barnes & Noble, 1984, pp. 55–56.

From "the perspective afforded by feminist criticism," contends that Astrophil "fails systematically to take Stella seriously as a moral and emotional being." Seeks to account for an "ironic structure" in the sequence that highlights "incongruity and partiality by reference to a

Twentieth Century

broad and rich field of human experience," similar to an age's "méntal-ité." Reexamines the series of sonnets studied by Warkentin (2294), showing that Astrophil's "inability to understand the implications and likely consequences of his behavior" derives from his "field of experience."

2185 LONG, PERCY W. "Astrophel." *Nation* 91 (14 July 1910):33.
Finds the origin of the name "Astrophel" in Rabelais, suggesting that it "must have been encountered by members of the Areopagus, and may have been adopted, rather than coined anew, by Sidney."

2186 LOWBURY, EDWARD; SALTER, TIMOTHY; and YOUNG, ALISON. *Thomas Campion: Poet, Composer, Physician*. London: Chatto & Windus; New York: Barnes & Noble, 1970, pp. 56–57.
Compares Campion's ironic last line in "When thou must home to shades of underground" with Sidney's in "With how sad steps, O moon" (*AS 31*).

2187 LOWES, JOHN LIVINGSTON. *Convention and Revolt in Poetry*. Boston and New York: Houghton Mifflin Co., 1919, pp. 15, 104.
In the closing lines of *Astrophil and Stella* 1 and 15, finds "the eternal triangle of the poet's art—what you feel, what you see, what you say." Feels that Sonnet 15 shows the "progressive dessication" of the sonnet form.

2188 LUTHER, SUSAN M. "Sidney's *Astrophil and Stella*, Sonnet 29." *Expl* 33 (January 1975):item 40.
In "Like some weak lords" (*AS 29*), argues that Sidney's "irony and sexual implication" give the touch of anti-Petrarchism that keeps the sonnet "from being only bad verse, without removing it from the love tradition." Asserts that, by subtle changes in diction, Sidney mocks the convention in which he works.

2189 LYLES, ALBERT. "A Note on Sidney's Use of Chaucer." *N&Q* 198 (March 1953):99–100.
Suggests that "Come sleep, O sleep" (*AS 39*) reflects Chaucer's *Book of the Duchess*, lines 242–64.

2190 McCABE, RICHARD A. "Conflicts of Platonic Love and Sensual Desire in *Astrophil and Stella*." In *Literature and Learning in Medieval and Renaissance England: Essays Presented to Fitzroy Pyle*, edited by John Scattergood. Dublin: Irish Academic Press, 1984, pp. 103–26.
Argues that Sidney had Castiglione's *Courtier* in mind while writing *Astrophil and Stella* and that "the movement of the sequence, especially

that of the transition from the kiss to the pains of absence, seems to have been fashioned after the pattern of Cardinal Bembo's discussion." Holds that the reader is to sympathize with Astrophil as one of those "yong men as yelde to sensuall love," whom Bembo says may be excused. Sees, then, no resolution to the conflict in the sequence between the intellectual and the sensual.

2191 McCOY, RICHARD C[HARLES]. *Sir Philip Sidney: Rebellion in Arcadia*. New Brunswick, N.J.: Rutgers University Press, 1979, pp. 69–109. Orig. a Ph.D. diss., University of Calfornia at Berkeley, 1975.

In Chapter 3, examines the theme of rebellion versus submission in *Astrophil and Stella*, relating it to Sir Thomas Wyatt's resistance to the traditional submissiveness of the courtly lover. Sees the sonnet "O joy too high" (*AS 69*) as pivotal, since it portays Astrophil briefly as a "King" over Stella, and regards the song "Only joy, now here you are" (*AS iv*) as an allusion to her sexual capitulation. Concludes, however, that Astrophil's dominance is illusory, for Stella quickly regains control and the sequence ends in frustrated desire. See also item 638.

2192 McGINN, DONALD J. *Thomas Nashe*. Twayne's English Author Series, 317. Boston: Twayne Publishers, 1981, pp. 25, 32–33, 36, 39, 115, 138, 142, 144, 147.

Notes Nashe's allusions to Sidney and comments on his preface to the first quarto of *Astrophil and Stella*.

2193 MAHONEY, JOHN F. "The Philosophical Coherence and Literary Motive of *Astrophel and Stella*." In *Essays and Studies in Language and Literature*, edited by Herbert H. Petit. Duquesne Studies, Philological Series, 5. Pittsburgh: Duquesne University Press, 1964, pp. 24–37.

Argues that the sequence is a "poetic application" of the neo-Platonic theory of love and beauty expressed in Castiglione's *Courtier*, contending that inclusion of "Thou blind man's mark" and "Leave me O love" (*CS 31, 32*) would render the sequence "a true literary version of the *cursus* of an erring courtier's love." Provides parallel passages from *Astrophil and Stella* and Hoby's translation of *The Courtier*, the former "chosen not so much for aptness as for convenience, for in fact it would seem in the end that almost all the sonnets reflect statements of Bembo."

2194 MAIBERGER, MAX. *Studien über den Einfluss Frankreichs auf die elisabethanische Literatur*. Part 1, *Die Lyrik in der zweiten Hälfte des XVI. Jahrhunderts*. Frankfurt am Main: Gebrüder Knauer, 1903,

Twentieth Century

pp. 22–26, 49. Orig. a Ph.D. diss., Ludwig-Maximillians-Universität zu München, 1903.
Discusses Sidney's possible debt to Philippe Desportes. Emphasizes the influence of Sonnet 75 of *Amours d'Hippolyte* and the poem "Priere au Sommeil" in *Diana* on Sidney's sonnet "Come sleep, O sleep" (*AS 39*). Also considers borrowings from Pierre de Ronsard and Jean Antione de Baïf in several sonnets of *Astrophil and Stella*.

2195 MARENCO, FRANCO. "*Astrophil and Stella.*" *FeL* 13 (1967): 72–91, 162–91.
Provides a detailed analysis and evaluation of the sequence in five sections. In the first, draws an analogy between "She comes, and straight therewith" (*AS 76*) and Caravaggio's "Amore Vittorioso" to show that both fall between mannerism and baroque. In Section 2, analyzes the song "If Orpheus' voice had force" (*AS iii*) to establish the underlying neo-Platonism of the sequence. In Section 3, rejects the importance of biographical details in favor of "internal drama," tracing the progress of Astrophil's capitulation to his passionate love for Stella and comparing Sidney's psychological acumen with that of Shakespeare. In Section 4, rereads the sequence in terms of parallels between Sidney/Astrophil's rejection of literary artificialities and his helplessness in his love for Stella, stressing historical and cultural context rather than the psychology of the lover. In the last section, compares several sonnets, particularly "Who will in fairest book of nature know" and "The wisest scholar of the wight most wise" (*AS 25, 71*), to illustrate the nature of the two principal problems of the sequence: "quello sentimentale e quello letterario." Concludes that what was most important for Sidney was "to discuss, to criticize, to transcend love in the name of a severe vision of life. For this reason, that love could not be absolutely, painfully conventional; and that transcendence could not be solely in the direction of moral education."

2196 MAROTTI, ARTHUR F. "'Love is not love': Elizabethan Sonnet Sequences and the Social Order." *ELH* 49 (Summer 1982): 396–428.
Argues that *Astrophil and Stella* addresses concerns about social status characteristic of an "ambitious, educated elite" in Elizabethan England. In metamorphosing these concerns into love poetry, it reenacts, in another mode, the painful frustrations of life at court, presenting political courtship under the guise of amorous courtship. Argues that, through this transformation, Sidney's work established the sonnet sequence of the 1590s.

2197 MATHEWS, G.M. "Sex and the Sonnet." *EIC* 2 (April 1952):119–37.

Notes Petrarchan and anti-Petrarchan elements in *Astrophil and Stella*. Stresses the function of "arranged marriage" in promoting adultery and argues that a moral problem arises in which "the contradiction between Sidney's passion for Penelope Rich and his religious veneration for married chastity is expressed through an interesting dichotomy in his use of the word 'virtue.'" Claims that those "who doubt the reality of the experience behind the sequence—or its physical fulfillment—should note the critical point in the narrative at which the conflict of 'Virtues' suddenly ceases. The word does not occur at all in the last 28 sonnets."

2198 MATTISON, ALICE EISENBERG. "Astrophil and the Wofull Lover: Love Poems by Sidney and His English Predecessors." Ph.D. diss., Harvard University, 1968, 247 pp.

Examines theoretical views of the purpose of *Astrophil and Stella*, arguing that it does not focus on the intellect but rather on the emotions. Investigates the development of sonnet conventions in England, briefly examining poems from *Arcadia* and *Certain Sonnets*. In *Astrophil and Stella*, analyzes Sidney's use of the conventions of the "wofull lover," who suffers sleeplessness and continual indignities, who neglects reason and is dissatisfied with the lady, and who ponders the difficulties in being a poet. Arguing that the methods of the sequence are those of Sidney's English predecessors, contends that it moves from the "recording of public, physical gestures which identify a lover" to the "dramatization of internal states of mind."

2199 MICHELAGNOLI, ALFREDO. *Il Sonetto nella letteratura inglese con cento sonetti dal Wyatt allo Swinburne*. Padua, Italy: Casa Editrice Dott. Antonio Milani, 1938, pp. 1–19.

In tracing the history of the English sonnet from Wyatt to Swinburne, comments on *Astrophil and Stella*, emphasizing Lady Rich's role as an inspiring force.

2200 MILLER, JACQUELINE T. "'Love Doth Hold My Hand': Writing and Wooing in the Sonnets of Sidney and Spenser." *ELH* 46 (Winter 1979):541–58.

Compares "Let dainty wits cry on the sisters nine" (*AS 3*) with Herbert's "Jordan" poems, showing that Sidney's work has more poetic control. In "Stella, the fullness of my thoughts of thee" (*AS 50*), finds Sidney playing with this control by pretending to surrender his art to Stella "in order to

Twentieth Century

create an acceptable, effective, and persuasive artifact." What Sidney only pretends to do, Herbert actually does.

2201 MÖNCH, WALTER. *Das Sonett: Gestalt und Geschichte*. Heidelberg: F.H. Kerle Verlag, 1955, pp. 77, 131, 135–36.

Ponders the oddity that, although Sidney followed Petrarchan conventions in *Astrophil and Stella*, Giordano Bruno felt free to take an anti-Petrarchan line in dedicating *Eroici furori* to him. Relates Sidney's claims that English excels as a poetic language to similar claims made for other languages on the Continent. While noting the French influence on the form of Sidney's sonnets, suggests that *Astrophil and Stella* is, in technique and themes, closer to Petrarch's *Rime*.

2202 MONTGOMERY, ROBERT L[ANGFORD, Jr.]. "Astrophil's Stella and Stella's Astrophil." In *Sir Philip Sidney and the Interpretation of Renaissance Culture: The Poet in His Time and in Ours: A Collection of Critical and Scholarly Essays*, edited by Gary F. Waller and Michael D. Moore. London: Croom Helm; Totowa, N.J.: Barnes & Noble, 1984, pp. 44–55.

Contending against the "biographical" readings of Lanham (2174) and others, argues that, as a persona, Astrophil permits "a kind of indeterminancy, giving the sequence a subtle interplay not only between biography and fiction, but also between Astrophil as a single, coherent fictional character and the consciously shaped and articulated selves deliberately fashioned and offered to the attention of Stella." Examines two sets of unresolved "alternatives" in Astrophil's presentation of himself as lover and poet: in the first instance, between the "fixed ethos of the Petrarchan servant" and the Donne-like, "volatile and agressive" witty seducer (as in Sonnets 76 and 77); in the second, between a "jaunty," assertive poet of simplicity and sincerity, and one whose composition "offers neither relief from suffering nor persuasive results." Cites Sonnet 2, treating it as "introductory to the entire sequence" and arguing that it demonstrates "the paradoxical results of a poetic whose coherence and value are dissolved in the lover's self delusion."

2203 ———. "Reason, Passion, and Introspection in *Astrophil and Stella*." *University of Texas Studies in English* 36 (1957):127–40.

Following the lead of Lever (1913) and Smith (1955), shows that the "dialectics of Astrophil's mental conflict" are "finally responsible for the seriousness with which Sidney, in spite of frequent indulgence in wit and insouciant playfulness, treats the love affair." Contends that Sidney's aim is not to "gauge the intensity of feeling," but to "focus attention analyti-

586

cally on Astrophil's state of mind, searching out the sources and motives for feeling." Suggests that Astrophil himself becomes "skeptical of the wholeness of these motives." Claims that this internal focus helps to explain the "dramatically unsatisfying conclusion" of the sequence.

2204 ———. *Symmetry and Sense: The Poetry of Sir Philip Sidney.* Austin: University of Texas Press, 1961, pp. 77–120. Orig. a Ph.D. diss., Harvard University, 1956.
Devotes Chapters 6 and 7 to discussions of "The Structures of Artless Style" and to a sustained reading of *Astrophil and Stella.* From the premise that its mixture of styles, its "quick, often bewildering shifts," result from a tension between convention and feeling, argues that the unity of the sequence is established, not by the style, but by the continuing narrative thread and by the single, controlling sensibility of Astrophil. Suggests that the conflict between reason and passion in the final sonnets forces Astrophil to "end as the standard Petrarchan lover." Concludes that "*Astrophel and Stella*, as an artistic whole, clearly moves further [than the poems in *Arcadia*], both in concealing the structure which makes it a whole and in establishing, for English poetry at least, a broad, dramatically oriented context in which lyric develops the order and technique of larger forms." See also item 1926.

2205 MUIR, KENNETH. "'Astrophel and Stella', XXXI." *N&Q,* n.s. 7 (February 1960):51–52.
Disagrees with Lamb (2041) about the final line of "With how sad steps, O moon" (*AS 31*). Suggests that, after blaming Stella in the preceding lines, Astrophil suddenly turns his irony on himself.

2206 ———. *Shakespeare's Sonnets.* Unwin Critical Library. London: George Allen & Unwin, 1979, pp. 17, 22–23, 30–33, 35–38, 55–56.
Remarks on the composition and publication history of *Astrophil and Stella,* Sidney's dramatic and colloquial style, and his use of the sonnet form. Argues that, despite conventions, the story of Astrophil's love for Stella "had some basis in fact" and sees "I on my horse" (*AS 49*) as a source for Shakespeare's Sonnets 50 and 51.

2207 MULRYAN, JOHN. "Sidney as Scrivener: Pen-and-Ink Imagery in *Astrophel and Stella.*" *SNew* 1 (Fall 1980):58–59.
Sees the image as an extended pun wittily directed toward Astrophil's amatory and Sidney's financial problems.

Twentieth Century

2208 MURPHY, KARL M. "The 109th and 110th Sonnets of *Astrophel and Stella*." *PQ* 34 (July 1955):349–52.
Surveys past criticism on the issue before asserting that there were only 108 sonnets in the sequence.

2209 ———. "Studies in *Astrophel and Stella*." Ph.D. diss., Harvard University, 1949, 262 pp.
In Chapter 1, discusses both the early printed versions and the three manuscripts of the sequence. In Chapters 2 and 3, examines respectively the development of the sonnet form and Sidney's adaptation and manipulation of the sonnet tradition. In Chapters 4, 5, and 6, considers the biographical context of *Astrophil and Stella*, proposing a four-act narrative sequence of love, courtship, acceptance, and rejection. Summarizes theories regarding the identity of Stella up to 1900 and then to the late 1940s. In Chapter 7, argues that the sonnets were composed in the order that they follow in the initial quartos and that they were written in the spring and summer of 1582. In Chapters 8 and 9, discusses the impact of the circulation of the sequence in manuscript and in print up to the time of Shakespeare, and traces the fortunes of the sequence down to the twentieth century. Three appendices discuss "The Baconians," "Rhyme Schemes," and "Numbering of the Sonnets and Songs" in all editions and known manuscripts.

2210 MURPHY, WILLIAM M. "Thomas Watson's *Hecatompathia* [1582] and the Elizabethan Sonnet Sequence." *JEGP* 56 (July 1957): 418–28.
Argues that Watson's *Tears of Fancy* was inspired by Sidney. Suggests that, whereas Watson's *Hecatompathia* followed a pedestrian path, *Astrophil and Stella* "transcended" Petrarchism. Ponders the reasons that most English imitators followed Watson rather than Sidney.

2211 MURRAY, HOWARD. "The Trend of Shakespeare's Thought." *TLS*, 5 January 1951, p. 7.
Replying to Disher (502), compares "Highway, since you my chief Parnassus be" (*AS 84*) and Shakespeare's Sonnet 50 to argue that Sidney did not influence Shakespeare.

2212 NEELY, CAROL THOMAS. "The Structure of English Renaissance Sonnet Sequences." *ELH* 45 (Fall 1978):359–89.
Argues that, in a typical English sequence, the initial sonnets set out the key components: the lover's passion, the beloved, and the poetry that unites them. Suggests that these components are usually linked by a metaphor of breeding. The sequence then develops in two unequal

parts: an establishment of the static Petrarchan relationship, followed by a resolution in favor of passion. Argues that *Astrophil and Stella* splits around Sonnet 63.

2213 NELSON, LOWRY, Jr. "The Matter of Rime: Sonnets of Sidney, Daniel, and Shakespeare." In *Poetic Traditions of the English Renaissance*, edited by Maynard Mack and George deForest Lord. New Haven and London: Yale University Press, 1982, pp. 123–42.

Studies Sidney's rhymes under nine headings: those between monosyllables, those between the same or different grammatical categories, "slant-rimes," and the like. Finds that one of the poet's virtues is the ability to "convey a sense of the sweep and wholeness of a colloquial utterance." Supports this judgment by comparing *Astrophil and Stella* 55 with 56, regarding the rhymes in the latter as "ill-used." Analyzes examples of "unusual inventiveness" in the rhymes.

2214 NELSON, THOMAS EDWARD. "The Syntax of Sidney's Poetry." Ph.D. diss., Ohio University, 1975, 140 pp.

Comparing the syntax of *Astrophil and Stella* with that of other poetry of the period, argues that Sidney, unlike his contemporaries, "developed the potential of the clause, rather than the line, as the basis of structure in his sonnets," with the result that his poetry emphasizes "features different from those by which the poetry of his era is usually identified." See *DAI* 36 (April 1976):6710A–11A.

2215 NELSON, T[IMOTHY] G.A. "*Astrophel and Stella*: A Note on Sonnet LXXV." *AUMLA* 27 (May 1967):79–80.

Argues, contra Howe (2151) and others, that the sonnet is not ironic. Cites Harington's *Metamorphosis of Ajax* and Thomas More's *Life of Richard III* to demonstrate that not all sixteenth-century writers saw Edward IV as an evil lecher. See also Cotter (2094).

2216 NICHOLS, J[OHN] G[ORDON]. *The Poetry of Sir Philip Sidney: An Interpretation in the Context of his Life and Times*. New York: Harper & Row; Liverpool: Liverpool University Press, 1974, pp. 52–154. Orig. a Ph.D. diss., University of Liverpool, 1971.

In Chapter 2, examines and rejects four inadequate approaches to *Astrophil and Stella*: the purely biographical, which does not allow for conventional elements obviously present; the purely fictional, which ignores the biographical elements; the mostly biographical, which regards the sequence as based on Sidney's personal experience but which, although admitting some dramatic, fictional, and conventional

Twentieth Century

elements, overstresses the "passionate love affair which we can know of
only from the sequence itself"; and the thematic, which necessitates a
"straitjacket of which the poems are always madly and gaily bursting."
Proposes in their stead a "dramatic" approach that is based in part on
Lamb's understanding of the poems as "full, material, circumstantiated"
(see item 2041). In Chapter 3, proposes that *Astrophil and Stella* is "dramatic" without necessarily being a "dramatic *fiction*," and that it was
designed specifically to be read biographically by those in the know, but
as fiction by outsiders. Seeks to bring out the ways in which the persona
who speaks the poems merges "occasionally and in varying degrees"
with the author. Argues that the "biographical intrusions" into the
sequence exist to "make us more aware of the poetry as art, and consequently more aware that art is related to things outside itself," an effect
that was consciously calculated by Sidney. Suggests that the poems
"teased, and to some extent mystified," their first readers just as they do
us. Surveys the large cast of characters in the drama, including the
Muses and Cupid, and examines its varied conflicts, following Gentili
(81) in calling the dominant one a "dialettica dell'ostacolo." Argues that
the sequence is unified, not by a narrative progression, but by the
author's meditation on one main experience, seen "in different lights,"
and by the "recurrence of themes and imagery." Surveys the varied ways
the songs perform their main function of "abstracting emotions . . . and
giving them a more emphatic and extended voice." In Chapter 4, isolates some "comparatively small matters of technique" that allow Sidney
to treat each individual sonnet as a "specific dramatic moment" within
the larger "play." Pays particular attention to Sonnets 39, 69, 75, and
103. See also item 1927.

2217 OGDEN, JAMES. "Hazlitt, Lamb and *Astrophel and Stella*."
Trivium 2 (May 1967):141–42.
Suggests that Lamb (2041) was the first modern critic who "knew exactly" that Sidney's sequence was biographical, and that Lamb's knowledge
may have come from a new edition of Wood (284).

2218 OKUDA, HIROYUKI. *"Astrophel and Stella* o Megutte: Ronsard to
Sidney Ogoegaki." In *Yamakawa Kozo Kyoju Taikan Kinen
Ronbunshu*. Toyonaka, Japan: n.p., 1981, pp. 55–69.
Not seen. Cited in the *MLA International Bibliography*, 1982, vol. 1, item
1294.

2219 OTSUKA, SADANORI. *Ai no Tonkyu: Sidney kara Shakespeare e* [A Quest for Love: from Sidney to Shakespeare]. Kenkuysha Selected Writings, 31. Tokyo: Kenkyusha, 1983, pp. 9–68.

Part 1 of the material on Sidney includes three chapters: "A Sonnet on 'Suffering': Love as a Game," "A Sonnet Calling on the Moon: Buffoonery of Love," and "*Astrophil and Stella*: Love of Palinode and Truth." Part 2 focuses on Shakespeare without mentioning Sidney.

2220 OWEN, DANIEL E[DWARD]. "Relations of the Elizabethan Sonnet Sequences to Earlier English Verse, Especially That of Chaucer." Ph.D. diss., University of Pennsylvania, 1903, p. 34.

Notes the similarity between *Astrophil and Stella 39* and Chaucer's *Book of the Duchess*, lines 231ff., but argues that Chaucer was not Sidney's immediate source.

2221 PEARSON, LU EMILY. *Elizabethan Love Conventions.* Berkeley: University of California Press, 1933, pp. 84–102.

In "Sir Philip Sidney's Analysis of Love," provides a survey of Sidney's intellectual career and a reading of *Astrophil and Stella*, governed by the premise that "underneath the story of a seemingly all-pervading passion for a very human woman is in reality the yearning of the Renaissance—a cry in which lingers the melancholy note of romantic idealism."

2222 PETERSON, DOUGLAS L[EE]. *The English Lyric from Wyatt to Donne: A History of the Plain and Eloquent Styles.* Princeton, N.J.: Princeton University Press, 1967, pp. 186–201. Orig. a Ph.D. diss., Stanford University, 1957.

Following Winters (1973), distinguishes between "plain" and "ornate" styles in the sixteenth-century lyric, placing Sidney "within the framework of the eloquent poetic." Analyzes *Astrophil and Stella* 9, 13, 22, 29, and 32 as "examples of praise in the old eloquent mode" and 89 and 108 as examples of "complaints written in the old manner." Contrasts the latter two with the analytical, anti-Platonic Sonnets 1, 2, 4, 5, 25, 28, and 52, which are complaints "conceived psychologically" rather than in terms of the precepts of courtly love. Concludes with an analysis of *Certain Sonnets* 31 that regards Sidney as moving toward the contemplative tradition of Donne.

2223 PETTET, E.C. "Sidney and the Cult of Romantic Love." *English* 6 (Summer 1947):232–40.

In *Astrophil and Stella*, finds a romantic attitude to love that links Sidney with Chaucer and the medieval romance tradition. Also notes his departures from this tradition.

Twentieth Century

2224 PETTIT, HENRY. "Sidney's *Astrophel and Stella*." *Expl* 1 (February 1943):item 26.
Answers an earlier query by R.U. (2285) by claiming that the sestet of "Loving in Truth" (*AS 1*) contains a single parturition metaphor referring to two kinds of children.

2225 PIRKHOFER, ANTON M. "The Beauty of Truth: The Dramatic Character of Shakespeare's Sonnets." In *New Essays on Shakespeare's Sonnets*, edited by Hilton Landry. New York: AMS Press, 1976, pp. 109–28, 260–64.
Contrasts the "highly tensional beginning" of Shakespeare's first sonnet with Sidney's practice in *Astrophil and Stella*, which is "much less forthright." Concludes that Sidney's sonnets "are almost too 'decorated' to allow of direct utterance of emotion or thought."

2226 POIRIER, MICHEL. *Sir Philip Sidney: Le chevalier poète élizabéthain*. Travaux et mémoires de l'Université de Lille, nouvelle série—Droit et lettres, 26. Lyon, France: Bibliothèque Universitaire de Lille, 1948, pp. 180–97.
In Chapter 3 of Book 2, discusses ways in which *Astrophil and Stella* represents an advance over the poetry of *Arcadia*. Considers Astrophil's moral problem in courting a married Stella, the tone of the work, and the heterogeneity of the sonnets and songs. Examines their troubadour, Petrarchan, and neo-Platonic backgrounds, assessing their "originality" and concluding that Sidney's imitations are never servile. Compares the sonnets with the work of French poets, particularly Ronsard. See also item 703.

2227 PRINCE, F[RANK] T[EMPLETON]. Review of *Elizabethan Sonnet Themes and the Dating of Shakespeare's "Sonnets"*, by Claes Schaar. *SN* 35, no. 2 (1963):307–10.
Suggests that "When Nature made her chief work, Stella's eyes" (*AS 7*) is the source for Shakespeare's Sonnet 132.

2228 ———. "The Sonnet from Wyatt to Shakespeare." In *Elizabethan Poetry*. Stratford-upon-Avon Studies, 2. New York: St. Martin's Press; London: Edward Arnold, 1960, pp. 11–29.
Praises Sidney for his revival of Petrarch, but faults him for abandoning the strict Italian form.

2229 PURCELL, J[AMES] M[ARK]. "A Note on Sonnet II of *Astrophel and Stella*." *PQ* 11 (October 1932):402–3.
In "Not at first sight, nor with a dribbed shot" (*AS 2*), reads "dribbed" as meaning "indirect."

2230 ———. "Sidney a Source for Sir John Davies." *PQ* 12 (January 1933):85–88.
Argues that "Whether the Turkish new-moon minded be" (*AS 30*) was a source for Davies's "Meditations of a Gull" and that other sonnets from the sequence provided sources for "Ten Sonnets to Philomel."

2231 ———. "Sidney's *Astrophel and Stella* and Greville's *Caelica*." *PMLA* 50 (June 1935):413–22.
Analyzes the two works in detail, finding "striking similarities" in thought and phrasing in poems numbered the same in each sequence. On the basis of the many correspondences in the first forty, argues that the two poets were in communication and perhaps even suggested to one another the topics on which they were both to write. Concludes that the parallels suggest "consultation" but not "plagiarism."

2232 ———. *Sidney's Stella*. New York and London: Oxford University Press, 1934, 122 pp.
In response to critics who equate Stella with Lady Rich, asserts that *Astrophil and Stella* reveals "an imaginary relationship between the poet and an ideal lady" and that the sonnets "are merely exercises to show the poet's skill in sonneteering." In Chapter 1, attempts to date the sequence, noting parallels in the thought of Sidney's letters to Languet during the years 1573–74. Dates "The curious wits, seeing dull pensiveness" (*AS 23*) no later than 1574, identifying "the Prince" mentioned there with a ruler encountered on Sidney's Continental tour. Denies that "Having this day my horse, my hand, my lance" (*AS 41*) refers to a tournament in 1581, as is often supposed, and from historical allusions, dates "Whether the Turkish new-moon minded be" (*AS 30*) before 1575, the earliest year in which the poet could have met Penelope Devereux. Concludes that Stella existed in "prototype" before they met. In Chapter 2, argues that a sonnet to Lady Rich printed by Florio (2796) may not refer to Sidney's sonnets but to those of Henry Constable or John Davies of Hereford. Finds no reliable evidence of a connection between Stella and Lady Rich in other contemporary literature or in the work of seventeenth-century biographers. Provides evidence that Sidney loved his wife and that she is the Stella of Spenser's *Astrophel* and Bryskett's *Mourning Muse of Thestylis* (2771, 2749). In discussing Richard Barnfield's *Affectionate Shepherd*, resists attempts to identify the "lusty youth" and Gwendolen with Sidney and Lady Rich. From historical documents, concludes that Sidney never sought a romantic liaison with Penelope. In Chapter 3, dismisses the likelihood that a sonnet sequence of the Elizabethan period would be autobiographical. Considers contemporary

Twentieth Century

notions of literary "imitation" and the conventions of the Petrarchan sonnet, finding little in *Astrophil and Stella* that is new or personal or "sincere." In Chapter 4, treats Stella as little more than an imitation of Petrarch's Laura. From the *Defence*, concludes that Sidney "did not think highly of the poetic emotions." Finds even the name "Stella" conventional, and cites parallels in a lyric by Clément Marot to support the notion that Sidney's puns on the word "rich" are simply references to wealth, not to Lord Rich. Argues that neither Sonnet 37 nor other parts of the sequence were omitted from early editions because they revealed too much. Concludes that *Astrophil and Stella* is a Platonic work and that Stella symbolizes divine beauty. Includes a bibliography. See a response by Brie (2067).

2233 ———. "Sonnet CV of *Astrophel and Stella* and *Love's Labour's Lost*." *PQ* 10 (October 1931):399.
Suggests that, in "Unhappy sight, and hath she vanished by" (*AS 105*), "glass" means "tears," as it does in Shakespeare's play.

2234 PUTZEL, MAX. "Sidney's *Astrophel and Stella*, IX." *Expl* 19 (January 1961):item 25.
In "Queen virtue's court" (*AS 9*), takes "touch" to mean "touchstone" and elucidates the imagery of the poem. See Cowan (2096) and Dudley (2111).

2235 RAY, ROBERT H. "Sidney's *Astrophil and Stella*, Sonnet 5." *Expl* 41 (Spring 1983):7–9.
Finds in Hebrews 12:13–16 the source for the pilgrim reference in "It is most true, that eyes are formed to serve" (*AS 5*). Argues that Astrophil ought to be rejecting the appeal of the physical world, which is personified in Stella.

2236 REED, EDWARD BLISS. *English Lyrical Poetry from Its Origins to the Present Time*. London: Oxford University Press; New Haven, Conn.: Yale University Press, 1912, pp. 147–56, 177–80.
Dates *Astrophil and Stella*, singling out eight of its sonnets as autobiographical. Calls the metrical experiments of the Old *Arcadia* "poor."

2237 REES, D.G. "Italian and Italianate Poetry." In *Elizabethan Poetry*. Stratford-upon-Avon Studies, 2. New York: St. Martin's Press; London: Edward Arnold, 1960, pp. 53–69.
In discussing *Astrophil and Stella*, praises Sidney for capturing much of the Italian lyric impulse, but faults him for "a formidable list of Italianate sillinesses."

2238 REGAN, MARIANN S. "Astrophel: Full of Desire, Emptie of Wit." *ELN* 14 (June 1977):251–56.

Points out that Astrophil sometimes plays the conventional "foolish lover" of earlier lyrics, a role exploited to convince readers that he is a true lover.

2239 RICHMOND, H[UGH] M. *The School of Love: The Evolution of the Stuart Love Lyric.* Princeton, N.J.: Princeton University Press, 1964, pp. 9, 45–46.

Discusses the ways in which Sidney's analytical style in *Astrophil and Stella* influenced the development of the Stuart love lyric. Pays particular attention to the condemnation of "sugaring" in "Because I breathe not love" (*AS 54*) and to the revelation of the processes of Astrophil's thought in "Muses, I oft invoked your holy aid" (*AS 55*).

2240 ROBERTSON, JEAN. "Macbeth on Sleep: 'Sore Labour's Bath' and Sidney's *Astrophel and Stella*, XXXIX." *N&Q*, n.s. 14 (April 1967):139–41.

Notes verbal links between *Macbeth* and "Come sleep, O sleep" (*AS 39*), particulary in the terms "bathing," "bating," and "bat."

2241 ———. Review of *The Arundel Harington Manuscript of Tudor Poetry*, edited by Ruth Hughey. *RES*, n.s. 13 (November 1962):403–6.

Suggests that, in the Arundel Harington Manuscript, a poem of three six-line stanzas in iambic pentameter, which begins "Blush, Phoebus, blush, thy glory is forlorne" and is found with a group of poems by Sidney and his circle, may well be from Sidney's pen and belong before the Fourth Song in *Astrophel and Stella*. Prints the poem with regularized spelling and punctuation.

2242 ———. "Sir Philip Sidney and His Poetry." In *Elizabethan Poetry*. Stratford-upon-Avon Studies, 2. New York: St. Martin's Press; London: Edward Arnold, 1960, pp. 111–29.

Comments that "those who close their eyes to the fact that a story is being told" in *Astrophil and Stella* and who "persist in treating the sonnets as meditations on love or explorations of the lover's emotions not only ignore the nature of the sonnet cycle but also disregard the purpose of the renaissance lyric—to persuade and to praise." Discusses Sidney's relationship with Lady Rich and with his friend Languet, stressing the "semi-auto-biographical, semi-fictional" nature of the story. Minimizes Bruno's influence. Concludes that "Sidney did more than any other writer to make the Continental experience and practice of poetry and

Twentieth Century

criticism accessible to his countrymen while at the same time speaking in his own voice as an English poet."

2243 ROCHE, THOMAS P., Jr. "Astrophil and Stella: A Radical Reading." *SSt* 3 (1982):139–91.

Reads *Astrophil and Stella* as a "negative example of how to go about the business of love." Views Astrophil in his role as unrequited lover, not as a heroic figure but as an example of man's obsessive concerns with his own desires, man creating for himself his own private hell, in which his every hope brings him ever closer to the despair that marks the conclusion of the sequence. In the first section, analyzes the imagery of blackness, "perversely" presented as light, and the equally perverse imagery of the uniqueness of Astrophil's star, which first becomes his sun and then becomes two black stars. Examines the relation of this imagery to "Morpheus, the lively son of deadly sleep" (*AS 32*). In the next two sections, discusses Homeric parallels, bawdy puns, and blasphemous metaphors, first in the sonnets and then in the songs, claiming that the latter have never been treated as an integral part of the sequence. In the last section, attempts to determine the structural principles of the sequence on the basis of numerological analyses of the placement of the sonnets and songs, confirming and extending the earlier analysis of Fowler (2127). Refines Fowler's argument by analyzing the structure of the first sixty-three sonnets and by proposing a rationale for the placement of the hexameter sonnets. Concludes that there is no development in Astrophil: all the sonnets and songs are "recapitulations of the same crisis: human desire and its effects."

2244 ROGERS, DONALD O. "Nature and Art in Sidney's *Astrophel and Stella*." *South Central Bulletin* 31 (Winter 1971):211–14.

Uses the *Defence* to distinguish between "ideal" and "empirical" art and nature, a disjunction caused by the Fall. Argues that "Astrophel is only a particularization of what Sidney would term the common tragedy of mankind." Views Sonnets 69–72 as the climax of the disjunction, concluding that Sidney seems to reject "the exclusive claims of both empirical and ideal Nature."

2245 RUDENSTINE, NEIL L. *Sidney's Poetic Development*. Cambridge, Mass.: Harvard University Press, 1967, pp. 172–269, and passim. Orig. a Ph.D. diss., Harvard University, 1964.

Provides a close reading of *Astrophil and Stella*, comparing techniques and attitudes found there with those in Sidney's earlier verse and in the *Defence*. In Chapter 11, compares the poetry of *Astrophil and Stella* with that of *Arcadia*, analyzing Astrophil's aesthetic. Notes tensions in the poetry, relating them to matters of theme and prosody and remarking on the way in which such tensions form the character of Astrophil early in the sequence. Treats the conflict between love and virtue in these poems as a more sophisticated exploration of a dominant theme in the eclogues of *Arcadia*. In Chapter 12, analyzes Sonnet 2 at length to establish basic conflicts within Astrophil, which are "played out" on "three fronts" in the first twenty-one poems: against other poets, against Stella's coldness, and against Virtue. Devotes Chapter 13 to the poems that criticize other courtly poets and Chapter 14 to the tensions that arise as Astrophil commits himself to love. In Chapter 15, shows how the changing style of Sonnets 22–40 embodies "changes in manner" that "deepen our sympathy" for Astrophil. In Chapter 16, analyzes ways in which the style of Sonnets 41–68 maintains a "double perspective" on Astrophil's gradual yielding to desire. In this group of poems, sees a more aggressive speaker, with heightened *energeia* and a tendency to colloquialism. In Chapter 17, considers Astrophil's degeneration. In discussing Sonnets 69–93 and the intervening songs, singles out Songs iv and viii and Sonnets 71 and 72 as crucial. Concludes that, if sonnets 94 through 102 "in one sense . . . declare the debilitating and destructive power of [Astrophil's] passion, they also give sustained and elevated expression to his sorrow, a fit ceremony for the failure of a love that has been movingly portrayed." See also item 730.

2246 RYKEN, LELAND. "The Drama of Choice in Sidney's *Astrophel and Stella*." *JEGP* 68 (October 1969):648–54.
Argues that the sequence is structured around Astrophil's choice to pursue physical passion, which dooms him to a progressive movement from freedom to bondage and, inevitably, defeat. In its focus on this choice, *Astrophil and Stella* resembles works by Milton and Spenser.

2247 SANDERS, GERALD. "Sidney's *Astrophel and Stella*." *Expl* 1 (February 1943):item 26.
Answers R.U. (2285) by arguing that the sestet of "Loving in truth" (*AS 1*) is "a succession of metaphors, each suggested in turn by the preceding one, and all, of course, based on the 'brain child' motif."

2248 SCANLON, JAMES J. "Sidney's *Astrophil and Stella*: 'See what it is to Love' Sensually!" *SEL* 16 (Winter 1976):65–74.
Discusses the ethical implications of Astrophil's emotional states, arguing that Sidney is interested in demonstrating the lack of validity in Astrophil's unconventional love ethic, in which passion holds sway over

Studies of the Poetry

Twentieth Century

reason. Argues that Astrophil is an Elizabethan paradigm for the folly of emotional love. As the pivot of the argument, cites the final line of "Stella, since thou so right a princess art" (*AS 107*).

2249 SCHAAR, CLAES. *An Elizabethan Sonnet Problem: Shakespeare's Sonnets, Daniel's "Delia" and Their Literary Background*. Lund Studies in English, 28. Lund, Sweden: C.W.K. Gleerup, 1960, pp. 45, 97–102.
Comments on Sidney's use of the sonnet form and claims that his images "largely derive their themes from the military, mythological, and feudal spheres, and a minor number suggest homely and trivial activities."

2250 SCHIRMER, WALTER F[RANZ]. "Das Sonett in der englischen Literatur." *Anglia* 49 (1926):1–31.
Considers adaptations of Italian and French rhyme schemes in *Astrophil and Stella*, remarking that, despite protestations to the contrary, Sidney borrows heavily from other Petrarchan sonneteers. Sees the sequence as a mixture of the "scholastic" and the erotic.

2251 SCHLÜTER, KURT. "The Influence of the Greek Prayer Hymn on the English Renaissance Sonnet: Aspects of Genre in Relation to Form of Verse." *Anglia* 102, no. 3 (1984):323–48.
Analyzes Sidney's "Come sleep, O sleep" (*AS 39*) as a "subtle" example of how the Greek hymnic form of invocation, praise, and petition has influenced the generic form of the sonnet. Finds that the "real status" of Sidney's sleep as a god becomes "continually more definite" as the poem progresses. Situates the poem in relation to similar sonnets by Daniel, Drummond, and particularly Bartholomew Griffin, whose "Care-charmer Sleep" is a "considerably coarsened" imitation.

2252 ———. "Die Lyrik der englischen Renaissance." In *Neues Handbuch der Literaturwissenschaft*, edited by Klaus von See. Vol. 10, *Renaissance und Barock (II. Teil)*, edited by August Buck. Frankfurt am Main: Akademische Verlagsgesellschaft Athenaion, 1972, pp. 216–56.
Sees in *Astrophil and Stella* a conflict between inner drives and the norms of domestic life. Considers the interplay of Sidney's personal experience with the conventions of Petrarchan poetry and Platonic love. Traces the change in Stella from unattainable goddess to nearly attainable woman, discussing the return of Petrarchan distance and frustration late in the sequence. Contrasts the sonnets with Spenser's *Amoretti*.

598

2253 SCOTT, JANET G[IRVAN]. "Minor Elizabethan Sonneteers and their Greater Predecessors." *RES* 2 (October 1926):423–27.
Cites six samples of "plagiarism" by Bartholomew Griffin, William Smith, and Richard Linche, and appends a list of sonnets for further comparison, including eight from *Astrophil and Stella*.

2254 ———. "The Names of the Heroines of Elizabethan Sonnet-Sequences." *RES* 2 (April 1926):159–62.
Points out that the name "Stella" may have been suggested by Sidney's reading of Pontano's *De Stella*, the only prior usage with "literary reminscence."

2255 ———. "Parallels to Three Elizabethan Sonnets." *MLR* 21 (April 1926):190–91.
Notes parallels to *Astrophil and Stella* 17 and 25 by Giovanni Pontano and Marc-Claude de Buttet, respectively.

2256 SELLS, A[RTHUR] LYTTON. *Animal Poetry in French and English Literature and the Greek Tradition.* Indiana University Publications, Humanities Series, 35. Bloomington: Indiana University Press, 1955, pp. 78–79.
Traces the ancestry of Sidney's sonnets on the sparrow and the lapdog (*AS 59, 83*) to poems by Catullus, Marot, Saint-Gelais, du Bellay, and Ronsard.

2257 SERONSY, CECIL [C]. *Samuel Daniel.* Twayne's English Author Series, 49. New York: Twayne Publishers, 1967, pp. 18, 20–21, 25, 34, 43.
Notes Daniel's high opinion of Sidney but suggests that the two authors probably never met. Considers poems by Daniel first published in Newman's unauthorized printing of *Astrophil and Stella*. Contrasts Sidney's sonnets with *Delia*, arguing that Sidney's sequence was written before *Arcadia*.

2258 SHIRREFF, A.G. "A Suggested Emendation of Sidney's Sonnets." *N&Q* 194 (19 March 1949):129.
Against Siegel (2260), argues that the phrase "Pindar's apes" in line 3 of "Let dainty wits cry on the sisters nine" (*AS 3*) alludes to Horace's poem "Pindarum quisquis studet aemulari" (*Odes* IV.2).

2259 SIEGEL, PAUL N. "The Petrarchan Sonneteers and Neo-Platonic Love." *SP* 42 (April 1945):164–82.
Surveys the use of Petrarchan and neo-Platonic conventions in the sonnets of Sidney and his contemporaries.

Twentieth Century

2260 ———. "A Suggested Emendation for One of Sidney's Sonnets."
N&Q 194 (19 February 1949):75–76.
Suggests changing line 3 of "Let dainty wits cry on the sisters nine" (*AS*
3) to read "Petrarch's Apes" on the grounds that the opposition between
neo-Platonic idealism and Petrarchan formalism established by such an
emendation is consonant with a similar opposition in Sonnets 6 and 15.
But see Shirreff (2258).

2261 SINFIELD, ALAN. "Astrophil's Self-Deception." *EIC* 28 (January
1978):1–18.
Argues that Sidney manipulates Astrophil so that the reader will identify
with him and, at the same time, see beyond the lover and thereby perceive
that Astrophil's primary psychological characteristic is self-deception.

2262 ———. "Double Meanings: II: Sexual Puns in *Astrophil and Stella*."
EIC 24 (October 1974):341–55.
Argues that "sexual *double entendre* is an important feature of Sidney's
verbal skill" and that "Astrophil's love for Stella is sexual right from the
beginning of the sequence."

2263 ———. "Sidney and Astrophil." *SEL* 20 (Winter 1980):25–41.
Reviews attempts to deal with the "dilemma" of Sidney-Astrophil's relationship with Stella. Notes that "if Astrophil and Sidney are fairly close
then there is no problem, but if the poem is Sidney's dire warning of the
dangers of the overthrow of reason and all Christian values by sexual
passion . . . then it is very strange that he should wish us to identify himself at all with his protagonist." Argues for a "radical separation between
the moral stance of Astrophil and the poem as a whole." Claims that
Astrophil's fall places the "passionate and adulterous implications of
much traditional writing on love" into a Protestant and critical focus.
Notes that both *Astrophil and Stella* and *Arcadia* provide critiques of marriage. Concludes that the distinction between Astrophil and Sidney provides the reader with a chance to feel "with the speaker but . . . not sus-
pend his human responsibility to assess rationally the speaker's
emotions."

2264 SLOAN, THOMAS O. "The Crossing of Rhetoric and Poetry in
the English Renaissance." In *The Rhetoric of Renaissance Poetry from
Wyatt to Milton*, edited by Thomas O. Sloan and Raymond B.
Waddington. Berkeley, Los Angeles, and London: University of
California Press, 1974, pp. 212–42.
Argues that, whereas *Astrophil and Stella* seems "almost thoroughly
Ramistic," it is "decidedly non-Ramistic" in its "sense of audience or
presence of others."

2265 SMITH, G[EORGE] C[HARLES] MOORE. "Astrophel and Stella." *TLS*, 18 September 1930, p. 735.
In reply to Wilson (2311), provides evidence that the "dead glasse" of line 3 of "Unhappy sight, and hath she vanished by" (*AS 105*) may be the eye.

2266 SNELL, MARY. *Vom Lesen zum Interpretieren am Beispiel englischer Lyrik*. Munich: Max Hueber Verlag, 1972, pp. 31–53.
In "'A Moment's Monument'—Neun Sonette," compares "With how sad steps, O moon" (*AS 31*) with sonnets by authors ranging from Michael Drayton to Gerard Manley Hopkins.

2267 SOKOL, B.J. "Numerology in Fulke Greville's *Caelica*." *N&Q*, n.s. 27 (August 1980):327–29.
Points out that, in the Warwick Manuscript of *Caelica*, Greville included 108 poems. Sees this as a tribute to Sidney, whose *Astrophil and Stella* includes the same number of sonnets—probably, as Fowler suggests (2127), as a witty allusion to the number of suitors that Penelope entertained in Homer's *Odyssey*. Draws connections between Sidney's sonnet "Have I caught my heavenly jewel" (*AS ii*) and the central sonnet of Greville's manuscript sequence.

2268 STEVENSON, RUTH. "The Influence of Astrophil's Star." *TSL* 17 (1972):45–57.
Claims that the structure of the sequence and its general thematic movement are governed by the fluctuating character of Stella. Argues that Sonnets 1–43 treat Stella as an abstract idea; that the material from Sonnet 44 to the end of the songs following sonnet 85 presents a flesh-and-blood person; and that the sonnets following 85 present Astrophil's direct reaction to the first two Stellas and his puzzlement concerning the reality of each.

2269 STILLINGER, JACK. "The Biographical Problem of *Astrophel and Stella*." *JEGP* 59 (October 1960):617–39.
Surveying the autobiographical readings of *Astrophil and Stella* from Arber (68) to Young (2316), stresses five points: that the date of composition for the poems is unknown; that they circulated in manuscript; that none was suppressed or withheld; that the order of the sonnets is fixed; and that the sequence is finished. Examines the documentary evidence for the connection between Sidney and Penelope Rich, concluding that her father, the Earl of Essex, was fond of Sidney, that he once wished Sidney to marry Penelope, and that some sort of marriage treaty existed. Notes the following grounds for identifying her with Stella: the pun on "rich" in "Rich fools there be" (*AS 24*); the claim of "What may words

Twentieth Century

say" (*AS 35*) that Stella's name is "Rich"; and the use of "rich" through-out "My mouth doth water" (*AS 37*). Notes, however, that neither Sonnet 24 nor 37 mentions Stella, and that to recognize the Stella of 35 as Lady Rich requires prior knowledge. Although contemporaries such as Matthew Gwynne, Thomas Campion, and Sir John Harington identified Stella with Lady Rich, Spenser and the other authors of the "Astrophel" elegies connected her with Frances Walsingham. Notes that, despite expressions of Platonic love, Astrophil's feelings for Stella are sexual. Yet, considering relations between the Sidney and the Essex families, sees little possibility of anything more than friendship between Philip and Penelope. Concludes that, although Stella sometimes seems to rep-resent Lady Rich, the sequence as a whole may simply be the exercise of a courtier expected to write love poetry.

2270 ———. Review of *The Poems of Sir Philip Sidney*, edited by William A. Ringler, Jr. *JEGP* 62 (April 1963):372–78.
Argues against Ringler's emendation (92) of "Astrophel" to "Astrophil," and introduces new evidence against his dating of some of the sonnets in *Astrophil and Stella*.

2271 STROUP, THOMAS B. "The 'Speaking Picture' Realized: Sidney's 45th Sonnet." *PQ* 29 (October 1950):440–42.
Sees "Stella oft sees the very face of woe" (*AS 45*) as an embodiment of the mimetic principles at the core of *Defence*.

2272 STULL, WILLIAM L. "Antanaclasis in *Astrophil and Stella* 31." *AN&Q* 20 (September–October 1981):3–4.
Contends that "there" in line 14 of the sonnet homonymically means also "their," thus giving the meaning "Do they call their ungratefulness a virtue?" as well as "Do they term virtue their ungratefulness?"

2273 SUDDARD, S[ARAH] J[ULIE] MARY. *Keats, Shelley and Shakespeare: Studies and Essays in English Literature.* Cambridge: Cambridge University Press, 1912, pp. 162–76.
In "*Astrophel and Stella*," argues that Sidney's sequence is a sincere state-ment of his love.

2274 TAKAMATSU, YUICHI. "Sonnet: Sono Igirisu-teki Tokusei ni tsuite." In *Eikoku Renaissance-ki no Bungei Yoshiki.* Tokyo: Aratake, 1982, pp. 65–87.
Not seen. Cited in *MLA International Bibliography*, 1982, vol. 1, item 712.

2275 TAYLOR, ARVILLA KERNS. "The Manège of Love and Authority: Studies in Sidney and Shakespeare." Ph.D. diss., University of Texas, 1969, 467 pp.

Explores the nature and significance of imagery derived from the art of horsemanship, where, metaphorically, the rider represents the trained statesman or graceful courtier, who attempts to "restore the Great Horse to his prelapsarian harmony with man." In *Astrophil and Stella*, manège imagery allows Astrophil to display "frank, even arrogant prurience." It also is a means of "viewing with a detached and humorous irony the conflicting demands of passion and reason." The "breakdown" of this imagery at the end of the sequence reflects Astrophil's "debilitation," resulting from his "increasingly intense libidinous desires." See *DA* 30 (January 1969):3025A–26A.

2276 THOMAS, EDWARD. *The Tenth Muse*. London: Martin Secker, 1911, pp. 15–19.

In "Sir Philip Sidney," discusses Lady Rich as the inspiring force behind *Astrophil and Stella*.

2277 TOKUMI, MICHIO. "On the Rhyme Scheme in *Astrophel and Stella*." *SELL* 32 (January 1982):1–11.

Following the lead of Williamson (2306), analyzes the rhyme patterns in *Astrophil and Stella* 5, 71, and 72, contrasting that of *Certain Sonnets* 11. Claims that Sidney's CDCDEE rhyme pattern in the sestet, counterpointed with a 3/3 or 3/2/1 pattern of syntax and sense, is a "new creation." In his experiments with the sonnet form, Sidney "enhances its power of expression to investigate a new love."

2278 TRAISTER, DANIEL HARRIS. "'Pity the Tale of Me': A Reading of Sidney's *Astrophil and Stella*." Ph.D. diss., New York University, 1973, 496 pp.

Argues that Sidney uses the persona of Astrophil as a "negative exemplum" of the consequences of lust, which include both worldly and spiritual decline. The sequence concludes with a "'speaking picture' of spiritual sleep, *Acedia*," with Astrophil having "failed as a lover, as a courtier, as a poet, and a human being." Draws support for this reading from Sidney's biography. Sees in Sonnets 9 and 29 "issues of appearance and change which permeate the entire sequence." See *DAI* 34 (June 1974):7724A.

Twentieth Century

2279 ———. "Sidney's *Astrophil and Stella*, Sonnet 89." *Expl* 42 (Winter 1984):2–3.
Argues that, in "Now that of absence the most irksome night" (*AS 89*), the "massive repetition" of the rhythms of the diurnal cycle strips the words "night" and "day" of their meanings. The poem thus functions thematically in the last section of the sequence, where there is "no significance to time at all."

2280 ———. "Sidney's Purposeful Humor: *Astrophil and Stella* 59 and 83." *ELH* 49 (Winter 1982):751–64.
Discusses the use of animal imagery in "Dear, why make you more of a dog than me?" and " Good brother Philip, I have borne you long" (*AS 59, 83*). In light of Sidney's theory in the *Defence* that comedy finally works by providing a negative example, argues that, in laughing at Astrophil's comparison of himself to a lapdog and a sparrow, readers soon realize that they are laughing at Astrophil's "collapse . . . into bestiality." This realization then leads them to reevaluate their initial reaction to the poem.

2281 ———. "'To Portrait That Which in This World Is Best': Stella in Perspective." *SP* 81 (Fall 1984):419–37.
Examines the sonnets "Queen virtue's court" and "Like some weak lords" (*AS 9, 29*), suggesting that they "alter our understanding of the development of Sidney's narrative" and that Astrophil's uncertainties press readers into "sympathetic awareness" by thrusting confusion upon them and forcing them to choose and judge. Argues that Sonnet 29 employs techniques of conflicting perspective from anamorphic painting, as well as aspects of the "ugly mistress poem," in order to prevent readers from adopting one simple and manageable perspective on Stella. Likewise, Sonnet 9, which was designed fundamentally for praise, turns Stella into a "less than human composition of earthen objects." Sees these poems as typical of the sequence as a whole, which leads the reader to question Astrophil's goals and his own participation in those goals.

2282 TUCKER, VIRGINIA ACHESON. "'Directing Threds . . . Through the Labyrinth': The Moral Use of Platonic Conventions and Patterns of Imagery in Sidney's *Astrophil and Stella*." Ph.D. diss., University of North Carolina at Greensboro, 1973, 221 pp.
Argues that the conventions of literature and of love in *Astrophil and Stella* are both "essentially Platonic." Feels that, in Sonnet 52, Astrophil deliberately chooses appetite over reason, thus corrupting his will, and

concludes that the four major image patterns of the sequence (those that idealize Stella's person, those of light and dark, images associated with the Platonic "hierarchy of the senses," and images for Stella's eyes) parallel this "fall into the Brazen world." Suggests further that the songs fall into two groups, depending on whether they are iambic (associated with the ideal) or trochaic ("where the sensual is given rein"). See *DAI* 34 (November 1973):2583A.

2283 TUVE, ROSEMOND. *Essays by Rosemond Tuve: Spenser, Herbert, Milton.* Edited by Thomas P. Roche, Jr. Princeton, N.J.: Princeton University Press, 1970, pp. 115, 147, 150–53, 175, 201.

Comments on Sidney's relations with the Russell family, on Spenser's view of Sidney, and on the relationship between *Astrophil and Stella* 1 and 3 and Herbert's "Jordan II," noting in the last case that, despite the verbal echoes, the poems are "a world apart" in theme: one deals with poetic imitation, the other with *imitatio Christi*.

2284 TWYNE, BRIAN. Commentary on *Astrophil and Stella.* In "Brian Twyne's Commentary on *Astrophel and Stella*," by James J. Yoch. *Allegorica* 2, no. 2 (1977):116.

Provides terse comments on Sonnets 9, 11, 15, 63, 74, 79 and Song v, primarily relating to figures of speech and the appropriateness of images. For example, says of the touchstone image in Sonnet 9 that it "doth not drawe strawe but iron . . . wherefore indeed this touchstone wanteth ye touchstone of truth." See Yoch (2315).

2285 U., R. "Sidney's *Astrophel and Stella* Sonnet 1." *Expl* 1 (October 1942):question 8.

Asks whether the last six lines of the poem are a single metaphor. See replies by Pettit (2225) and Sanders (2247).

2286 VICKERS, BRIAN. *Classical Rhetoric in English Poetry.* London: Macmillan & Co.; New York: St. Martin's Press, 1970, pp. 109–10, 125–50, 155–56.

Illustrates various rhetorical figures with quotations from Sidney. Playing down Sidney's connection with Ramus, notes his clear grasp of the psychological function of rhetoric in the *Defence*. Presents a rhetorical analysis of "My words I know do well set forth my mind" (*AS 44*), arguing that *Astrophil and Stella* "is perhaps the most rhetorically complex series of poems in English."

Twentieth Century

2287 VOSS, ANTHONY EDEN. "The Search for Words: The Theme of Language in Four Renaissance Poems." Ph.D. diss., University of Washington, 1967, 170 pp.
Feels that Sidney had to "dismiss the more pervasive even if less clearly articulated orders of society and civility" if he was to forge his "own rule of words." Concludes that, in *Astrophil and Stella*, he "dismisses grammar, philosophy, and even the Petrarchan idiom." See *DA* 28 (March 1968):3690A–91A.

2288 WALLER, GARY F. "Acts of Reading: The Production of Meaning in *Astrophel and Stella*." *SLitI* 15 (Spring 1982):23–35.
Taking a deconstructionist position that *Astrophil and Stella* is "less a definable literary 'text' than a field of potential meaning," indicates the ways in which its openendedness encourages the reader to create meaning through reading. Notes that whatever meanings the poems disclose for a modern reader, "they show us that they can be treated in a traditional New Critical manner, as 'complete and closed,' only if we ignore that they demand performance, not passivity." See also Miller (659).

2289 ———. "The Rewriting of Petrarch: Sidney and the Languages of Sixteenth-Century Poetry." In *Sir Philip Sidney and the Interpretation of Renaissance Culture: The Poet in His Time and in Ours: A Collection of Critical and Scholarly Essays*, edited by Gary F. Waller and Michael D. Moore. London: Croom Helm; Totowa, N.J.: Barnes & Noble; 1984, pp. 69–83.
Concerned mainly with "testing a methodological question," argues that Sidney's *Astrophil and Stella*—as, indeed, all of Sidney's work—is a battleground in which the two major cultural discourses of the age, Petrarchanism and Protestantism, contest over what has been, "at least since Descartes, at the center of the discursive and social structures of Western civilization," that is, the concept of the individual or unitary self. Finds that both discourses are "primarily part of a struggle to fix or create the self by means of language" and that the two intersect "to create in [Sidney's] work a distinctive set of contradictions." These "two great master codes reinforced each other's peculiar anxieties beneath their obvious intellectual differences." Urges that more work be done on the "discursive *structures*" of Protestantism, as distinct from its theology and practices, and that scholars probe Sidney's works more deeply for contradictions between Protestant piety and courtly ambition.

2290 ———. "Sir Philip Sidney". In *Critical Survey of Poetry: English Language Series*, edited by Frank [Northen] Magill. Vol. 6. Englewood Cliffs, N.J.: Salem Press, 1982, pp. 2569–81.

Examines *Astrophil and Stella* in its "courtly" context, emphasizing ways in which Sidney forces the reader to become actively involved in the "performance" of the poems.

2291 WALTER, J[OHN] H[ENRY]. "*Astrophel and Stella* and *The Romaunt of the Rose*." *RES* 15 (July 1939):265–73.

Argues that Sidney modeled *Astrophil and Stella* on the English *Romaunt of the Rose*, eschewing its allegorical method but incorporating many of its personifications into the character of Stella herself and dividing the arguments of Reason between Astrophil's friends and Stella. As a model, the *Romaunt* "had the advantage of high chivalric morality."

2292 WARKENTIN, GERMAINE THERESE. "*Astrophil and Stella* in the Setting of Its Tradition." Ph.D. diss., University of Toronto, 1972.

Argues that *Astrophil and Stella* most resembles the *canzonieri* of Jacques Peletier du Mans, noting in particular that, like Sidney, du Mans begins with "the fundamental moral crisis of the *giovenile errore*" and depicts "an experience of purification." Stresses the importance of two other traditional characteristics of the Italian *canzonieri* in Sidney's sequence: a concern with *varietas*, which recalls Petrarch and finds expression in Astrophil's "energy and changeability," and a "process of illumination," which hearkens back to Dante and appears most clearly in six songs at the heart of the sequence but also in the final sonnets. See *DAI* 34 (February 1974):5211A.

2293 ———. "'Love's sweetest part, variety': Petrarch and the Curious Frame of the Renaissance Sonnet Sequence." *Renaissance and Reformation* 11, no. 1 (1975):14–23.

Contrasts *Astrophil and Stella* with Watson's *Hecatompathia* in surveying the growth of the Renaissance *canzonieri*, defining that form as a "a work exhibiting the variety of moods of a lover, set forth in *rime sparse* or separate lyrics, and with a formal introductory poem constituting a proem or *excusatio*."

2294 ———. "Sidney and the Supple Muse: Compositional Procedures in Some Sonnets of *Astrophil and Stella*." *SLitI* 15 (Spring 1982):37–48.

Examines sonnets from *Astrophil and Stella* to demonstrate ways in which Sidney uses conventional poetic and rhetorical *topoi* as compositional strategies. Argues, for example, that *contraria* produce the various groupings of the sequence. Examines the distinction between "study" and "invention" in "Loving in truth" (*AS 1*), defining "invention" as the use of commonplaces for exploration and elaboration. Argues that the premium placed on the latter shows Sidney moving toward an Aristotelian emphasis on reason. Views "With How Sad Steps" (*AS 31*) and "O tears, no tears" (*AS 100*) as examples of this trend. Finds similar uses of *topoi* in other Renaissance poems.

2295 WATSON, GEORGE. *The English Petrarchans: A Critical Bibliography of the "Canzoniere."* Warburg Institute Surveys, 3. London: Warburg Institute, University of London, 1967, pp. 1, 3, 17–18, 31.
In the introduction, points out that Sidney wrote no direct imitations of Petrarch's *Rime* and that his critique of the Petrarchans in the *Defence* employs the Petrarchan oxymoron of icy fire. Notes Sidney's verbal borrowings from the *Rime* in *Astrophil and Stella* 1, 48, and 71.

2296 WEBSTER, JOHN. "'The Methode of a Poete': An Inquiry into Tudor Conceptions of Poetic Sequence." *ELR* 11 (Winter 1981):22–43.
Argues that Ramist notions of arrangement underlie differences between the plain (drab) and eloquent (golden) styles of sixteenth-century poetry. Analyzes "Having this day my horse" (*AS 41*), an example of the eloquent style, showing that it is structured according to Ramus's "prudential method," which initially withholds its purpose in favor of "searching out the means and antecedents" that lead to the poem's main point.

2297 WEINER, ANDREW D[AVID]. "'In a grove most rich of shade': A Figurative Reading of the Eighth Song of *Astrophil and Stella*." *TSLL* 18 (Fall 1976):341–61.
Distinguishing between "allegorical reading," in which "we are compelled to discover one particular meaning," and "figurative reading," which offers the "freedom to construct alternate meanings for a given passage," argues that Song viii seeks to remind us that "love need not be limited to passionate desire for physical consummation." Contends that "we are led to sit in judgment upon Astrophil and Stella from the moral perspective the figures invite us to adopt and from which we view them as fugitives from God and the light." Sees the poem as balancing rational and emotional perspectives, but argues that "for Sidney, idolatrous, passionate love is a disaster because it draws us away from God, who should be the true object of our devotion."

2298 ———. "Structure and 'Fore Conceit' in *Astrophil and Stella*." *TSLL* 16 (Spring 1974):1–25.

Using Robinson's concept of "fore-conceit" as the structural framework of the sequence (see item 1943), argues that it is divided into five parts beginning, respectively, at Sonnets 1, 20, 45, and 69 and Song viii. Discusses changes in the character of Astrophil that define each part, concluding that his "final desolation allows no renewal, for he still clings to what destroyed him, his worship of Stella to the exclusion of all else."

2299 WEISER, DAVID K. "Berryman's Sonnets: In and Out of the Tradition." *AL* 55 (October 1983):388–404.

Calls attention to several similarities between Berryman's sonnets and Sidney's, claiming that "O how the pleasant airs of true love be" (*AS 78*) was a source for Berryman's Sonnet 51.

2300 WEISS, WOLFGANG. *Die Elisabethanische Lyrik.* Erträge der Forschung, 55. Darmstadt, Germany: Wissenschaftliche Buchgesellschaft, 1976, pp. 20–22, 42–43, 64–65, 78–81.

Discusses Sidney's remarks in the *Defence* on *energeia* in the love lyric and considers the effects of Ramism on his theory of poetry. Evaluates his experiments with classical meters and their effects on *Astrophil and Stella*, noting particularly the refined interaction of meter with the rhythms of normal, lively speech. Also considers Sidney's use of Italian meters; the role of *energeia* in making conventional sonnet material seem autobiographical; the rich characterization of Astrophil and his social, religions, and political circumstances; and Stella's unconventional responses to him.

2301 WELSH, ANDREW. *Roots of Lyric: Primitive Poetry and Modern Poetics.* Princeton, N.J.: Princeton University Press, 1978, pp. 197–98.

Argues that Sidney's style in *Astrophil and Stella* is based on "consummately skillful and artistic use of metrical tension, the interplay between the abstract metrical pattern and the rhythms of speech." Feels that it established the standard for metrical poetry in English for three hundred years.

2302 WENTWORTH, MICHAEL DOUGLAS. "Studies in Selected Elizabethan Sonnet Sequences: *Astrophel and Stella, Delia, Amoretti, Idea*." Ph.D. diss., Bowling Green State University, 1979, 307 pp.

Seeking to explain the structural design of the four works, claims that the concept of wit accounts for "various conflicts" in *Astrophil and Stella*

Twentieth Century

and for Astrophil's poetic performance, which is "often abrasive." See *DAI* 40 (April 1980):5458A.

2303 WHIGHAM, R.G., and EMERSON, O[LIVER] F[ARRAR]. "Sonnet Structure in Sidney's *Astrophel and Stella*." *SP* 18 (July 1921):347–52.
Discusses the various forms of sonnet used in the sequence, citing three predominant rhyme schemes, which appear in sixty, eighteen, and nine sonnets respectively. Also notes two less important schemes and nine variants. Surveys Sidney's use of the sonnet form in other works besides *Astrophil and Stella*.

2304 WHITAKER, VIRGIL K[EEBLE]. *Shakespeare's Use of Learning: An Inquiry into the Growth of His Mind and Art*. San Marino, Calif.: Huntington Library, 1953, pp. 99, 120.
Discounts the possibility that *Astrophil and Stella* influenced Berowne's thoughts on his lady's "blackness" in *Love's Labor's Lost* IV.iii. Links *Astrophil and Stella* 10 with Thomas Watson's *Hecatompathia* and Shakespeare's *Rape of Lucrece*.

2305 WICKES, GEORGE. "A Portrait of Penelope Rich." *RenP*, 1957, pp. 9–14.
Uses "the many sketches done by the poets," starting with Sidney's, to reconstruct a portrait of Lady Rich, warning that "we shall not find out what the lady looked like." Concludes that Sidney's portrait, "almost completely stylized," was the source of inspiration for all the others.

2306 WILLIAMSON, COLIN. "Structure and Syntax in *Astrophil and Stella*." *RES*, n.s. 31 (August 1980):271–84.
Argues that "the demonstration of the capabilities of a particular form, for whatever purpose, was exactly the kind of contribution to English poetry that exercise, as Sidney understood it, could properly make." Remarks that, in the sestets of many of his sonnets, Sidney was particularly interested in the superimposition of an unusual pattern on a more familiar one. Concludes that tension and conflict in the themes of the sequence are mirrored in the sonnet form. See also Tokumi (2277).

2307 WILLIAMSON, GEORGE. *A Reader's Guide to the Metaphysical Poets: John Donne, George Herbert, Richard Crashaw, Abraham Cowley, Henry Vaughan, Andrew Marvell*. London: Thames & Hudson, 1968, pp. 73, 94, 105, 126.
Links Donne's "Extasie" with *Astrophil and Stella viii* and sees Herbert's "Jordan II" as an attempt to outdo "Loving in truth" (*AS 1*).

2308 ———. *Seventeenth Century Contexts.* Chicago: University of Chicago Press; London: Faber & Faber, 1960, pp. 63–77.
In "The Convention of *The Extasie*," suggests a number of connections between "In a grove most rich of shade" (*AS viii*), Greville's *Caelica* 75, and Donne's "The Extasie."

2309 WILSON, CHRISTOPHER R. "*Astrophil and Stella*: A Tangled Editorial Web." *Library*, 6th ser. 1 (December 1979):336–46.
Suggesting that Daniel may have had a hand in the preparation of Newman's 1591 edition, focuses on the "other rare Sonnets" appended to Sidney's. See also Clitheroe (2084).

2310 WILSON, HAROLD S. "Sidney's *Astrophel and Stella*, Sonnet 78." *Expl* 2 (November 1943):item 17.
Reads the sonnet as "a vituperation upon Lord Rich," viewing him as an evil beast, described only generally in the octave but in terms of specific bodily parts in the sestet.

2311 WILSON, MONA. "*Astrophil and Stella*." *TLS*, 11 September 1930, p. 716.
Considers the possibility that the "Dead glasse" mentioned in "Unhappy sight, and hath she vanished by" (*AS 105*) may be a telescope, pointing out that the telescope was not invented until 1609. See a reply by Smith (2265).

2312 WINN, JAMES ANDERSON. *Unsuspected Eloquence: A History of the Relations between Poetry and Music.* London and New Haven, Conn.: Yale University Press, 1981, pp. 127, 150.
Discusses connections between Sidney and Petrarch, stressing ways in which the form of their sonnets reflects conflicts within the speaker. Sees rhymes such as that on "joy" and "annoy" in "My words I know do well set forth my mind" (*AS 44*) as "the best equivalent poets had for the more obvious harmonic and contrapuntal simultaneity available to composers."

2313 YATES, FRANCES A[MELIA]. "The Emblematic Conceit in Giordano Bruno's *De gli eroici furori* and in the Elizabethan Sonnet Sequences." *JWCI* 6 (1943):101–21.
Argues that, in writing *Astrophil and Stella*, Sidney was influenced by Bruno's style and by his rejection of Petrarchan imitations. See replies by Pellegrini (697) and Ruthven (1947).

Twentieth Century

2314 ———. "Fulke Greville." *TLS*, 7 August 1937, p. 576.
Suggests that Greville chose the name "Caelica" (heavenly) for his sequence of songs and sonnets because Sidney had addressed his sequence to Stella (star). Both titles may reflect "interest in Giordano Bruno's *nuova filosofia* with its imaginative flights into stellar space."

2315 YOCH, JAMES J. "Brian Twyne's Commentary on *Astrophel and Stella.*" *Allegorica* 2, no. 2 (1977):114–16.
Transcribes, with a brief introduction, the whole of the commentary recorded in Corpus Christi College MS. 263, fols. 250–70, observing that although Ringler (92) had distributed much of it in his edition, having it in its entirety will enable readers "to evaluate more readily the limits of a young collegian's reading in the last decade of the sixteenth century." Observes that Twyne is consistently aware of the division between Sidney's perception and Astrophil's. See Twyne (2284).

2316 YOUNG, RICHARD B. "English Petrarke: A Study of Sidney's *Astrophel and Stella.*" In *Three Studies in the Renaissance: Sidney, Jonson, Milton.* Yale Studies in English, 138. New Haven, Conn.: Yale University Press, 1958, pp. 1–88.
Suggests that, in *Astrophil and Stella*, Sidney "has exploited the technical problem, the poetic relation of manner and matter, as the chief means of presenting the dramatic problem, the relation of lady and lover." Feels that the sequence gains its dramatic vitality by engaging lover, writer, and reader in discovering the goal of the sequence. In discussing the biographical elements, distinguishes between "literary" and "literal" sincerity, analyzing the persona of Astrophil in terms of the conventional behavior of the Petrarchan lover and of the the themes of the sequence. Details the didactic and rhetorical functions of Sidney's use of Petrarchan conventions. Claiming that the order of the 1598 folio edition is the right one, views the sequence as tripartite: Sonnets 1–43 define the essential values of the experience; Sonnet 44–Song iii comment on the lady's virtue but also focus on Astrophil's feelings; and Sonnets 84–108 show Astrophil becoming a part of "the very [Petrarchan] convention he had attempted to eliminate." Contends, finally, that the structure of the sequence "is one of analysis and synthesis, with the Petrarchan convention as its subject matter," claiming that, though the final sonnet may not appear "conclusive in the sense of a complete resolution," that very fact "constitutes its dramatic function." See also Brodwin (2068), Gentili (2131), and Hamilton (2142).

2317 YUASA, NOBUYUKI. "Rhetoric in the Sonnets of Sidney, Spenser and Shakespeare: A Morphology of Metaphor, Antanaclasis and Oxymoron." *SELit*, English Number, 1977, pp. 33–52.

Surveys samples of Sidney's use of each of the figures, arguing that, in Sonnets 9, 39, and 49, he seeks to "breathe fresh life into formal rhetoric by giving it greater flexibility than before."

4. CERTAIN SONNETS

Twentieth Century

2318 BROOKS, CLEANTH and WARREN, ROBERT PENN. *Understanding Poetry: An Anthology for College Students*. New York: Henry Holt & Co., 1938, pp. 341–45.

Analyzes "Ring out your bells" (*CS 30*) as an example of a litany. The analysis remains unchanged through the third edition, but is shortened in the fourth.

2319 CROFT, P[ETER] J[OHN], ed. *Autograph Poetry in the English Language: Facsimiles of Original Manuscripts from the Fourteenth to the Twentieth Century*. Vol. 1. London: Cassell; New York: McGraw-Hill, 1973, plate 14.

Reproduces Sidney's autograph of "Sleep baby mine" (*CS 6*), written on the foot of the last page of Jean Bouchet's *Les Annales d'Aquitaine*. Comments on Sidney's distinctive hand and notes that the holograph suggests a "certain nonchalance" in matters of punctuation and capitalization.

2320 DEMPSEY, PAUL K. "Sidney's 'And Have I Heard Her Say? O Cruell Paine!'" *Expl* 25 (February 1967):item 51.

Argues that the theme of *Certain Sonnets* 11 is "the Christian injunction to transform suffering into ethical insight," concluding that "the lady, who should rule pain, is herself abused by 'false', that is physical pain."

2321 FABRY, FRANK J. "Sidney's Verse Adaptations of Two Sixteenth-Century Italian Art Songs." *RenQ* 23 (Autumn 1970):237–55.

Locates the musical models for "The fire to see my woes" (*CS 3*), "The nightingale, as soon as April bringeth" (*CS 4*), and "No, no, no, no, I

Twentieth Century

cannot hate my foe" (*CS 26*) in an unnumbered manuscript of Italian madrigals and *villanelle* in Winchester College library. Praises Sidney's ability to construct verse forms that follow both the melodic line and the harmonic voices of the various pieces.

2322 FUCILLA, JOSEPH G. "A Rhetorical Pattern in Renaissance and Baroque Poetry." *SRen* 3 (1956):23–48.
Cites "In wonted walks, since wonted fancies change" (*CS 18*) as an example of the "disseminative-recapitulative pattern" in lyric poetry.

2323 HOFFMAN, DAN G. "Sidney's 'Thou Blind Man's Mark.'" *Expl* 8 (February 1950):item 29.
Points out that Sidney uses seven metaphors in *Certain Sonnets* 31 to characterize desire and to suggest "a train of implications to man's subjection to desire".

2324 LAMB, MARY ELLEN "'Nett which paultrye prayes disdaines': Sidney's Influence on Two Unattributed Poems in the Bright Manuscript." *SNew* 5 (Spring/Summer 1984):3–14.
Provides readings of two lyrics in British Library MS. Add. 15232, both of which imitate *Certain Sonnets* 27. Drawing on Harold Bloom's theory of the "anxiety of influence," finds both poems to be, in contrasting ways, essentially "about" their own relation to the Sidneian tradition that empowered them. One, "In a greene wood thick of shade," expresses "fear of engulfment" by the tradition; the other, "All my senses weare bereaved," expresses "anxiety about acceptance of the poem, on which the poet's virility as a poet . . . seems to depend."

2325 PETERSON, DOUGLAS L[EE]. "A Probable Source for Shakespeare's *Sonnet CXXIX*." *SQ* 5 (Autumn 1954):381–84.
Rejects Massey's claim (372) that the source of Shakespeare's Sonnet 129 is "Thou blind man's mark" (*CS 31*).

2326 RUDENSTINE, NEIL L. *Sidney's Poetic Development*. Cambridge, Mass.: Harvard University Press, 1967, pp. 115–30, 277–83. Orig. a Ph.D. diss., Harvard University, 1964.
Dates the composition of *Certain Sonnets* between 1577 and 1581 and argues that the poems "suggest a curve from the narrator's reluctant acceptance of love through stages of frustration and bitterness, indecisiveness, re[s]traint and self-sacrifice to final rebellion." Compares *Certain Sonnets* with the *Arcadia* poems, arguing that at every important level of form—phrasing, metrics, the lyric sequence—Sidney is just on the verge of the discoveries that will soon make *Astrophil and Stella* what

it is. Concludes that *Certain Sonnets* "contains all the essential elements for a substantial poetry of serious but sophisticated love. It has the suggestion of a plot, a variety of moods and tones, and strong intimations of an assured, controlling poetic voice." In Appendix 1 argues, contra Ringler (92), in favor of the view that *Certain Sonnets* is a unified whole. See also item 730.

2327 RYKEN, LELAND. "Sidney's 'Leave Me, O Love': An Interpretation." *Christian Scholar's Review* 1 (Fall 1970):19–26.
Explicates the poem (*CS 32*), noting biblical allusions and remarking on the lover's alternation between renunciation and affirmation. Concludes that the poet's craft in the poem complements its Christian content, that it implies a theocentric worldview, and that it embodies principles shared by Platonism and Christianity.

2328 ———. "Sidney's 'Leave Me, O Love Which Reachest But to Dust.'" *Expl* 26 (September 1967):item 9.
Explains Sidney's linking of images of "yoke" and "light" in lines 6–7 of *Certain Sonnets* 32 as a pun deriving from Matthew 11:30.

2329 THOMAS, H., ed. Introduction to "Diana de Monte Mayor Done Out of Spanish by Thomas Wilson (1596)." *Revue Hispanique* 50 (1920):367–418.
Suggests that, when Bartholomew Yonge mentions other translators in the preface to his English version of Montemayor's *Diana*, he may refer to Sidney, who translated the first and third poems as "What changes here, O hair" and "Of this high grace with bliss conjoined" (*CS 28, 29*).

2330 THOMAS, W[ALTER] K[EITH]. "Sidney's 'Leave me, o Love, which reachest but to dust.'" *Expl* 28 (January 1970):item 45.
Argues that the coherence of *Certain Sonnets* 32 is based on biblical allusions.

2331 WARKENTIN, GERMAINE [THERESE]. "Sidney's *Certain Sonnets*: Speculations on the Evolution of the Text." *Library*, 6th ser. 2 (December 1980):430–44.
Analyzes the three manuscripts of *Certain Sonnets*: Clifford (Cl), Bodleian (Bo), and the 1598 folio (98). Focuses on the fact that the arrangement of the poems in Bo differs significantly from that in the other two versions. Presents evidence that Bo represents a "deliberate reorganization" by Sidney "made on principles which were leading him by a process of experimentation towards the variety of organization, fluidity of design, and narrative strength of *Astrophil and Stella*." On the basis of known

practices for compiling manuscript books, argues that Ringler (92) was wrong to conclude that Bo was written from loose sheets. Its prototype (X-Bo) was likely "either an annotated paper quire or vellum-bound notebook, or a bundle of bifolia fairly heavily written and then annotated in the margin." In appendices, discusses the Otley Manuscript and others containing several of the poems in *Certain Sonnets*, relating them to the present argument. See also Robertson (1942) and Beal (1863).

2332 WILSON, HAROLD S. "Sidney's 'Leave Me, O Love, Which Reachest But to Dust.'" *Expl* 2 (April 1944):item 47.
Discusses biblical allusions that form the spine of *Certain Sonnets* 32.

5. PSALMS

Seventeenth Century

2333 HARINGTON, Sir JOHN. *A Briefe View of the State of the Church of England, As it stood in Q. Elizabeths and King James his Reigne, to the Yeere 1608.* . . . London: Printed for Jos. Kirton, 1653, sigs. G5ᵛ–G6ʳ.
Suggests that Gervase Babington, chaplain to the Earl of Pembroke, aided Mary Sidney in her translation of the Psalms: "for it was more then a womans skill to express the sense so right . . . , and more then the English or Latine translation could give her." See also Thomas (2335) and Ballard (2334).

Eighteenth Century

2334 BALLARD, GEORGE. *Memoirs of Several Ladies of Great Britain Who Have Been Celebrated for Their Writings or Skill in the Learned Languages, Arts and Sciences.* Oxford: Printed by W. Jackson, for the author, 1752 (not seen). Reprint. Edited by Ruth Perry. Detroit: Wayne State University Press, 1985, pp. 249–52.
In "Mary, Countess of Pembroke," discusses the Sidney Psalms as if they were translated entirely by the Countess, noting a copy "bound in velvet" in the library at Wilton. Rebuts Harington (2333) and others who suppose that she was aided by Gervase Babington, her chaplain.

2335 THOMAS, WILLIAM. "An Account of the Bishops of Worcester . . ." In *A Survey of the Cathedral-Church of Worcester; With an Account of the Bishops thereof, From the Foundation of the See, to the year 1600.* London: Printed for the author [by] John Clarke, 1737, p. 221 (separately paginated). Orig. pub. London: Printed for the author, 1736 (not seen).
Repeats, without attribution, Harington's inference (2333) that Gervase Babington assisted Mary Sidney in translating the Psalms.

Nineteenth Century

2336 COTTON, H. "On Psalmody." *Christian Remembrancer* 3 (June 1821):327–31.
Evaluates the Sidney Psalms.

2337 HOLLAND, JOHN. *The Psalmists of Britain. Records, Biographical and Literary, of Upwards of One Hundred and Fifty Authors, Who Have Rendered the Whole or Parts of the Book of Psalms, into English Verse.* Vol. 1. London: R. Groombridge, Ridge, & Jackson, 1843, pp. 194–98, 215–18.
Reviews Sidney's life and works, regarding Psalms 1–43 as his and remarking on their stanzaic variety and classical metrical patterns. Prefers those translated by Mary Sidney.

2338 NICHOLSON, BR[INSLEY]. "The Sidneian Psalms." *Athenaeum,* no. 2803, 16 July 1881, p. 79.
Noting four classes of "great and manifest differences" between Psalms 120–27 and all the rest in Singer's edition (74), suggests that they are by Abraham Fraunce. Notes differences between this edition and the two manuscript copies in the British Museum.

Twentieth Century

2339 BAROWAY, ISRAEL. "The Accentual Theory of Hebrew Prosody: A Further Study in Renaissance Interpretation of Biblical Form." *ELH* 17 (June 1950):115–35.
Without "direct documentary evidence," suggests that Sidney's interest in accentual Hebrew versification may have developed from the works of Augustinus Steuchus. Promises to explore (in a second article that apparently never appeared) Sidney's reason for versifying the Psalms:

Twentieth Century

"he may have wished to exemplify . . . the proper moral use of native English versification . . . as the English equivalent of the Hebrew form."

2340 BRENNAN, MICHAEL [G.]. "The Date of the Countess of Pembroke's Translation of the Psalms." *RES*, n.s. 33 (November 1982):434–36.

Argues that a reference in the dedication of Henry Parry's *Victoria Christiana*, published in 1594, is evidence for the existence in manuscript of a completed translation of the entire Sidney Psalter "soon after the publication of the 1593 *Arcadia*."

2341 ———. "Licensing the Sidney Psalmes for the Press in the 1640s." *N&Q*, n.s. 31 (September 1984):304–5.

Shows that, in the mid–seventeenth century, perhaps between 1643 and 1648, a complete text of Psalms was approved for printing by the official licenser, but that "for reasons unknown" it was not delivered to a printer.

2342 CAMPBELL, LILY B[ESS]. *Divine Poetry and Drama in Sixteenth Century England.* Cambridge: Cambridge University Press; Berkeley and Los Angeles: University of California Press, 1959, pp. 50–53, 84–87.

Notes Sidney's attitude to the Psalms in the *Defence* and treats his own translations as valuable experiments in versification. Like Smith (2359), argues that the idea of varying the meters may have come from Marot, though it had English precedents. Also comments on Sidney's interest in du Bartas.

2343 CLEMENTS, A.L. *The Mystical Poetry of Thomas Traherne.* Cambridge, Mass.: Harvard University Press, 1969, p. 195.

Suggests that Traherne's poetry owes a debt to Sidney's Psalms, either directly or through the work of George Herbert.

2344 CROWN, RACHEL MAE. "The Art of Sidney in the Psalms." Ph.D. diss., University of Kansas, 1975, 228 pp.

By comparing Sidney's poems with two primary and two secondary sources, discovers that the basic principle governing his "metaphrase" is "a faithful adherence to the substance and form of the original Psalms," and "confirms the consistency of his translation practice" by examining his treatment of terms for the diety. Argues that, "hewing to the original, he based his linear art upon the diction, the 'thought rhythms,' and the verbal proportion of the given stylistic unit (the biblical verse), and planned his stanza according to a logical and affective grouping of biblical verses." See *DAI* 37 (July 1976):327A–28A.

Twentieth Century

2345 FREER, COBURN. *Music for a King: George Herbert's Style and the Metrical Psalms*. Baltimore and London: Johns Hopkins University Press, 1972, pp. 72–108.

In "Sir Philip Sidney and the Countess of Pembroke," discusses the varied stanza forms of the Sidney Psalter. Lauds Sidney's "skill in suiting form to meaning" and indicates ways in which Herbert's style incorporates elements from the Sidney Psalms. See also item 2346.

2346 ———. "The Style of Sidney's Psalms." *Lang&S* 2 (Winter 1969):63–78.

Argues that, more like Herbert and the devotional poets of the next century than like his contemporaries, Sidney in the Psalms is a "poet who thinks *through* or by means of his forms." Analyzes his use of enjambment, feminine rhyme, rhythm and "motion within groups of lines," syntax, and meter, stressing throughout "the extent to which Sidney's stanza depends on relations between syntax and idea." Pays special attention to Psalms 6, 10, 13, 16, and 38. Calls Psalm 13 "probably the most impressive" among all of Sidney's more successful translations, and shows that its "stanza shape" of question and answer (with affinities to the echo form used in *Arcadia*) "imposes a new pattern on its original." See also item 2345.

2347 GIBBON, JOHN MURRAY. *Melody and the Lyric from Chaucer to the Cavaliers*. London and Toronto: J.M. Dent; New York: E.P. Dutton, 1930, pp. 68–74.

Discusses Sidney's interest in music, expressed both in letters to Languet and Robert Sidney and in the musical references in his works. Argues that the meter of many of Sidney's Psalms derives from the popular airs selected by Marot for his tunes in the Huguenot Psalter, which Sidney encountered through Languet.

2348 JUEL-JENSEN, BENT. "The Tixall Manuscript of Sir Philip Sidney's and the Countess of Pembroke's Paraphrase of the Psalms." *BC* 18 (Summer 1969):222–23.

Discusses the provenance of the manuscript (noted in item 255). Concludes that it may have been a gift from King James to its original owner, Sir Walter Aston.

2349 KINNAMON, NOEL J. "*Melle de petra*: The Sources and the Form of the Sidneian Psalms." Ph.D. diss., University of North Carolina, 1976, 230 pp.

Argues that the two Sidneys use different paraphrase techniques, with Philip preferring "to retain as much of the prose Psalm text as possible."

Twentieth Century

Both treat the Psalms as "chiefly personal and dramatic prayers" rather than as cultural texts. Although they "looked to the French metrical psalter of Marot and Beza as an aesthetic model," they almost never translate it directly. Both are more concerned than the French with the "inner form" of the Psalms. See *DAI* 37 (February 1977):5143A–44A.

2350 LEWALSKI, BARBARA KIEFER. *Protestant Poetics and the Seventeenth-Century Religious Lyric*. Princeton, N.J.: Princeton University Press, 1979, pp. 45, 241–45, 253, 275–76, 301.
Considers the importance of the Sidney Psalter, with its new English voice and its many experiments in rhyme scheme and stanzaic pattern, as a model for religions lyrics of the English Renaissance. Finds in it precedents for Donne's dramatic use of colloquial openings; for George Herbert's voices and rhythms and his interest in acrostics; and for the graphic imagery of metaphysical poetry. Points to Psalm 13 as a "suggestive precedent" for George Herbert's echo poem "Heaven," and to Psalm 23 as a source for the feast metaphor in Herbert's "Love (III)." Also discusses Donne's appraisal of the Psalter in the poem "Upon the Translation of the Psalms" (2790).

2351 LIFSCHUTZ, ELLEN ST. SURE. "David's Lyre and the Renaissance Lyric: A Critical Consideration of the Psalms of Wyatt, Surrey and the Sidneys." Ph.D. diss., University of California at Berkeley, 1980, 350 pp.
Examines the Sidney Psalter in the context of Renaissance lyric imitations of David. Argues that Sidney began the translations as a poetic exercise and stopped when he did because he had derived the benefit he sought. Asserts that Mary continued the work under his guidance. See *DAI* 41 (January 1981):3118A.

2352 LOW, ANTHONY. *Love's Architecture: Devotional Modes in Seventeenth-Century English Poetry*. New York: New York University Press, 1978, pp. 19–21, 28–29, 74–76.
In the context of Donne's poem of praise (2790), discusses the Sidney Psalter in detail, noting that the "varied stanza forms" of Donne, Herbert, and Vaughan owe much to it. Argues that the verse forms of the Sidneys were chosen to fit the Psalms "to the new style of music." Sees Donne's poem on the Psalter as "primarily an act of devotion inspired by the Sidneys' work." Suggests that the Psalms provide a link between Sidney and Herbert.

2353 MESTERTON, ERIK. "Correspondence." *London Magazine* 6 (December 1959):60.

Corrects a fault in Rathmell's list (91, 2356) of printings of the Sidney Psalter.

2354 PRATT, WALDO SELDEN. *The Music of the French Psalter of 1562: A Historical Survey and Analysis. With the Music in Modern Notation.* New York: Columbia University Press, 1939, pp. 30–31, 81, 83, 89–90, 97, 100, 102, 105, 114, 119, 121–22, 129, 133, 149, 154, 157–58, 178, 184, 190, 192–95, 200.

Discusses the possibility that, while he was in France, Sidney may have heard the music for the French Psalter. Notes tunes that appear to have been used for the Sidney Psalter.

2355 PRESCOTT, ANNE LAKE. "The Reputation of Clément Marot in Renaissance England." *SRen* 18 (1971):173–202.

Argues that Sidney's Psalms "show striking similarities" with the translations that Marot made while in exile in Geneva. Also notes that Donne was probably thinking about the Geneva Psalter when he compared Continental translations with those in English.

2356 RATHMELL, J[OHN] C.A. "Exploration and Recoveries—I: Hopkins, Ruskin, and the *Sidney Psalter*." *London Magazine* 6 (September 1959):51–66.

Argues that Hopkins was directly indebted to the Psalter in his "terrible sonnets," and contends that, when the Psalter is properly appreciated, "the history of the metaphysical revival of our own time will have to be rewritten." Noting the "closeness of Sidney's renderings to the movement of the original Hebrew Psalms," compares specific passages by Hopkins (without discriminating Sidney's efforts from his those of his sister). Argues that Hopkins's awareness of the translation came via Ruskin's essay "Of the Sidney Metres" (which introduces item 73) and that Hopkins's fondness for Milton reflects their common interest in the Sidney Psalter. See also Mesterton (2353).

2357 RIESE, TEUT. *Die englische Psalmdichtung im sechzehnten Jahrhundert.* Universitäts-Archiv anglistische Abteilung, 4. Münster, Germany: Heinrich Buschmann, Abteilung Helios-Verlag, 1937, pp. 4–5, 102–17.

Discusses the comments on the Psalms in the *Defence*, noting the Protestant and humanist assumptions that underlie Sidney's poetic. Covers the manuscripts, the reputation, and the composition of the Psalms. Supports the view that Sidney's sister (or someone helping her)

Twentieth Century

consulted the original Hebrew and argues that she and her brother relied more on the Geneva Bible than on the Vulgate or other translations. Compares the styles of the two translators, noting that both depart from the direct diction and syntax of the original for more artful and expressive phrasing. Concludes that Mary's reworkings are more extensive and vivid. Infers the aims of the translators: 1) to clarify the text by making connections more logical and emphatic and dark metaphors more explicit, and 2) to beautify it by adding epithets, by substituting unusual expressions for everyday ones, and by extending metaphors, personifications, and antitheses. Also considers the failings of the metrical experiments in the Sidney Psalter, comparing similar attempts by Richard Stanyhurst and Abraham Fraunce.

2358 SERONSY, CECIL C. "Another Huntington Manuscript of the Sidney Psalms." *HLQ* 29 (February 1966):109–16.
Describes and partially collates Huntington Library Manuscript Ellesmere 11673, designating it O, after the manner of Ringler (92) and Rathmell (91). Concludes that, while belonging to a large, derivative group of manuscripts, it is no more than two removes from the lost original of B and that D, which most clearly resembles it, is derived from it. Indicates ways in which it differs from other manuscripts in text, in psalm titles, and in preliminary and marginal details.

2359 SMITH, HALLET [DARIUS]. "English Metrical Psalms in the Sixteenth Century and Their Literary Significance." *HLQ* 9 (May 1946):249–71.
Examines motives for translating the Psalms into English verse, and surveys the contents of five classes of translations. Treats Sidney's as part of a group influenced by Marot, arguing that his main interest was in verse experimentation, which led him to inaugurate a "School of English Versification." See also Campbell (2342).

2360 WALLER, G[ARY] F., ed. Introduction and appendix to *The Triumph of Death, and other Unpublished and Uncollected Poems by Mary Sidney, Countess of Pembroke (1561–1621)*. Salzburg Studies in English: Elizabethan and Renaissance Studies, 65. Salzburg: Institut für Englische Sprache und Literatur, Universität Salzburg, 1977, pp. 3–5, 9, 18–26, 44–45, 48–59, 211–21.
In the Introduction, comments on Mary Sidney's role in translating the Sidney Psalter, in editing her brother's works, and in carrying on his "revolution" in English literature through her own patronage. Concludes that all her own works "were directly inspired by his example

and dedicated to his memory." Discusses extant manuscripts of the Psalms, including two not known at the time of Ringler's edition (92). Constructs a stemma and discusses variants, accepting the traditional view that Sidney translated the first forty-three Psalms and his sister revised those and translated the rest. Details stages in her revisions. Argues that the poem "To the Angel Spirit of . . . Sir Philip Sidney" (2799), long attributed to Samuel Daniel, is, in fact, by Mary Sidney. Prints a later version (2826) that she included in a presentation volume of the Psalms, detailing her revisions and what they show about her relationship with her brother. Also reprints the "Doleful Lay of Clorinda" (2741), arguing that the traditional attribution of the elegy to the Countess is correct and rebutting de Sélincourt (1010), Osgood (689), and others who first ascribed it to Spenser. In an appendix, discusses in detail the recently discovered manuscript of the Psalms in the Houghton Library of Harvard University (MS. 69M-142).

2361 WALLER, G[ARY] F. "A 'Matching of Contraries': Ideological Ambiguity in the Sidney Psalms." *Wascana Review* 9 (Spring 1974):124–33.
In the Psalms, sees the Sidneys bringing "into play an intellectual tension . . . between the theological drives of Protestant piety and the attitudes derived from courtly neo-Platonic, even Magical, philosophies." Stresses the imaginative autonomy and intellectual independence of the translators.

2362 ———. "The Text and Manuscript Variants of the Countess of Pembroke's Psalms." *RES*, n.s. 26 (February 1975):1–18.
Discusses the changes made by the Countess in her extensive revisions, distinguishing between Sidney's close adherence to his originals and the Countess's experimentation with metrics and figures.

2363 WARDROPPER, BRUCE W. "The Religious Conversion of Profane Poetry." In *Studies in the Continental Background of Renaissance English Literature: Essays Presented to John L. Lievsay*, edited by Dale B.J. Randall and George Walton Williams. Durham, N.C.: Duke University Press, 1977, pp. 203–21.
Notes that Marot "appropriated the tunes of popular airs for his translations of the Psalms, some of which are clearly reflected in Sidney's English versions."

Studies of the Defence of Poetry

Sixteenth Century

2364 HARINGTON, [Sir] JOHN. "A Preface, or Rather a Briefe Apologie of Poetrie, and of the Author and translator of this Poem." In *Orlando Fvrioso in English Heroical Verse*. [London: Richard Field,] 1591, sigs. ¶2ʳ–¶8ᵛ. Reprint. In *Elizabethan Critical Essays*, edited by G[eorge] Gregory Smith. Vol. 2. London: Oxford University Press, 1904, pp. 194–222. Reprint in facsimile. New York: Da Capo Press; Amsterdam: Theatrvm Orbis Terrarvm, 1971.

Cites the *Defence* four years before its publication. Uses Sidney's works to support claims about the poetic "gift," the propriety of breaking off episodes in the middle, and the beauty of feminine rhymes. See also Williams (2379).

Eighteenth Century

2365 GILDON, CHARLES. *The Complete Art of Poetry*. Vol. 1. London: Charles Rivington, 1718, pp. 48–72. Reprint in facsimile. New York: Garland, 1970.

In a lengthy oration in praise of poetry spoken by the character Laudon, plagiarizes extensively from the *Defence*, abridging and paraphrasing most of the work from the end of the exordium through Sidney's discussion of art, imitation, and exercise in the digression on the current state of English poetry. Borrows many phrases and sentences nearly verbatim.

Nineteenth Century

2366 ANON. Review of *An Apologie for Poetry*, edited by Evelyn S. Shuckberg, and *The Defence of Poesy*, edited by Albert S. Cook. *Athenaeum*, no. 3333, 12 September 1891, pp. 348–49.
Discusses sixteenth-century editions of the *Defence*, suggesting that the printer Olney called his pirated edition *An Apology for Poetry* to avoid detection. Argues that the *Defence* was written in London at the time when the Areopagus was gathering there in 1579 and early 1580.

2367 ———. "Sir P. Sidney's Defence of Poesy." *Retrospective Review* 10 (1824):43–59. Reprint. In *The Museum of Foreign Literature, Science, and Art* 32 (March 1838):343–49.
Analyzes the *Defence* as a "logical discourse," stressing its influence on early nineteenth-century "dissertations" on poetry published in magazines and reviews. Compares Sidney's views with those of Byron, and discusses the merits and faults of *Astrophil and Stella*.

2368 FLETCHER, JEFFERSON B[UTLER]. "Areopagus and Pléiade." *JEGP* 2, no. 4 (1898):429–53.
Draws heavily on Sidney's aesthetic views in the *Defence*, asserting their consonance with Spenser's views in *The Shepherd's Calendar*, to argue that the English and French coteries exhibit "apparent identities of purpose and performance." Compares the two "programmes" with respect to three main issues: each adopted a mediating or "trimming" stance toward classical imitation; each defined and defended a new "poetic diction," both in vocabulary and syntax; and each "reformed versification," developing the "national rhyme principle" into "the rich harmonies" of which it was capable. See a reply by Higginson (1056).

2369 JONCKBLOET, W[ILLEM] J[OZEF] A[NDRIES]. *Geschiedenis der Nederlandsche Letterkunde.* 4th ed., revised by C. Honigh. Groningen, Netherlands: J.B. Wolters, 1889, pp. 200–202. Orig. pub. Groningen: J.B. Wolters, 1868 (not seen).
Discusses Theodore Rodenburgh's early Dutch rendering of the *Defence*, remarking that, though rough, it is "crisp" and accurate. Points out, however, that it sometimes abbreviates and that it omits altogether Sidney's discussion of English poetry and drama and his sections on style and the suitability of the English language as a medium for poetry. Prints a substantial excerpt from Rodenburgh on the tendency of modern poets to abuse the classical unities and the genre of comedy, noting

Nineteenth Century

that it is only partly derived from the *Defence*. Notes that less than a quarter of Rodenburgh's work is devoted to translating Sidney.

2370 JONES, W[ILLIAM] ALFRED. *Essays upon Authors and Books*. New York: Stanford & Swords, 1849, pp. 79–87.
In "Sir Philip Sidney's *Defence of Poesy*," summarizes the *Defence*, with asides on nineteenth-century authors.

2371 [LONGFELLOW, HENRY WADSWORTH.] "Defence of Poetry." *North American Review* 34, no. 74 (January 1832):56–78. Reprint. In *Essays from the "North American Review,"* edited by Allen Thorndike Rice. New York: D. Appleton & Co., 1879, pp. 303–33. Partial reprint. In *The Achievement of American Criticism: Representative Selections from Three Hundred Years of American Criticism*, edited by Clarence Arthur Brown. New York: Ronald Press Co., 1954, pp. 219–33.
Briefly considers Sidney's character, the decline in the popularity of *Arcadia*, and the value of the *Defence*. Uses the latter as inspiration for his own defence of poetry.

2372 QUOSSEK, C. "Sidney's *Defence of Poesy* und die Poetik des Aristoteles." In *Jahresbericht über die Städtische Realschule I. Ordnung zu Crefeld*. Crefeld: Gustav Kühler, 1880, pp. 3–38.
Sketches Sidney's life and seeks to explain the flowering in literature that he helped to bring forth, discussing the state of classical studies in the period. Reviews Sidney's arguments in the *Defence* in light of this background, emphasizing the impact of Aristotle, Plato, and other classical authors.

2373 SCHELLING, FELIX E[MMANUEL]. *Poetic Verse Criticism of the Reign of Elizabeth*. Series in Philology, Literature and Archaeology, vol. 1, no. 1. Philadelphia: University of Pennsylvania Press, 1891, pp. 25–29, 33, 60, 69–79 passim, 96–97.
Discusses the controversy behind the *Defence* and its influence on later criticism. Defends Sidney's definition of poetry to include poetic prose and his strictures against the English drama, noting the influence of George Whetstone on his doctrine of the dramatic unities. Also points out Sir John Harington's reliance on the *Defence* in the preface to his translation of *Orlando furioso*.

2374 SCOTT, FRED N. "Boccaccio's *De Genealogia Deorum* and Sidney's *Apologie*." *MLN* 6 (April 1891):97–101.
Speculates that Sidney had read Boccaccio's book. Points out parallels with the *Defence*, particularly on the following points: the need to defend

poetry, the enmity of philosophers, the example of poetry in Scripture, the definition of poetry, and the chief objections against it.

2375 SHERMAN, L[UCIUS] A[DELNO]. *Analytics of Literature: A Manual for the Objective Study of English Prose and Poetry.* Boston: Ginn & Co., 1893, pp. 265, 297.
Provides a technical analysis of the prose style in the *Defence*. Tabulates average numbers of predications per sentence and numbers of simple sentences and clauses saved. Compares the work of other authors from the Middle Ages to the nineteenth century.

2376 SPINGARN, JOEL ELIAS. *A History of Literary Criticism in the Renaissance, with Special Reference to the Influence of Italy in the Formation and Development of Modern Criticism.* New York: Macmillan Co., Columbia University Press; London: Macmillan & Co., 1899, pp. 34, 51, 104, 142, 268–310 passim. Reprint (with revisions) in item 2642.
Regards the *Defence* as an "epitome of the literary criticism of the Italian Renaissance." Traces Sidney's views on the preeminence, antiquity, and universality of poetry to Minturno; his definition of poetry to the Italian neo-Aristotelians; his view of the aims of poetry to Scaliger; and his distinction between poetry and history to Scaliger and Minturno. Considers the background of the *Defence* in attacks on poetry by Stephen Gosson and Cornelius Agrippa, and stresses Sidney's importance as the first Englishman to put forth a coherent theory of the drama. Examines the roots of his concepts of tragedy and comedy, noting that, in considering the distinction between delight and laughter and the importance of the dramatic unities, Sidney takes positions similar to those of Trissino. Also discusses the verse experiments of the Areopagus and remarks on the similarity between certain of Sidney's critical views and those of Sir John Harington, Sir Francis Bacon, and Ben Jonson. See a reply by Stump (776).

2377 STAPFER, PAUL. *La poétique de Philip Sidney.* Grenoble, France: Dauphin et Dupont, 1877, 35 pp.
Presents a brief biography of Sidney and comments on the *Defence*.

2378 ———. *Shakespeare and Classical Antiquity: Greek and Latin Antiquity as Presented in Shakespeare's Plays.* Translated by Emily J. Carey. London: C. Kegan Paul & Co., 1880, pp. 46–50.
In "Classical Precepts Enforced by Sir Philip Sidney," discusses Sidney's comments on the dramatic unities and other classical rules.

Nineteenth Century

2379 WILLIAMS, ADIN. *"The Apologie for Poetry." Athenaeum*, no. 2714, 1 November 1879, p. 563.
Citing comments by Harington (2364), suggests that Sidney may have printed his book for friends prior to 1595.

2380 WOODBRIDGE, ELISABETH. "Boccaccio's Defence of Poetry; As Contained in the Fourteenth Book of the *De Genealogia Deorum." PMLA* 13, no. 3 (1898):333–49.
Discounts Scott's suggestion (2374) that the *Defence* owes a debt to Boccaccio.

2381 WYLIE, LAURA JOHNSON. *Studies in the Evolution of English Criticism.* Boston: Ginn & Co., 1894, pp. 11–13. Orig. a Ph.D. diss., Yale University, 1893.
Touches on Sidney's "Romanticism" and classicism and his interest in quantitative verse.

Twentieth Century

2382 ABRAMS, M[EYER] H[OWARD]. *The Mirror and the Lamp: Romantic Theory and the Critical Tradition.* New York: Oxford University Press, 1953, pp. 14–15, 273–74, 323.
Differentiates Sidney's form of neoclassical criticism from the Aristotelian mimetic tradition and from Romantic expressive criticism. Classes Sidney with "pragmatic" theorists in that he sees literature as an instrument for achieving a moral effect in the audience. Discusses Sidney's comments on "another nature" in poetry and his assertion that the poet "never lieth."

2383 AHRENS, RÜDIGER. "Literaturtheorie und Aristokratie in der Tudorzeit: Ein Beitrag zur Funktion des Mäzens im England des 16. Jahrhunderts." *Anglia* 99, nos. 3/4 (1981):279–311.
Examines the role of the Sidneys as patrons. Considers Stephen Gosson's error in dedicating his *School of Abuse* to Philip, arguing that the work was not based on Puritanism so much as on the "new learning" of the universities. Also discusses Gosson's dedication of subsequent works to Sidney and his father-in-law. Explains the opening of the *Defence* as an attempt to make poetry, like horsemanship, a distinctive ornament of the ideal courtier. Traces the influence of Sidney's exalted conception of the poet upon the activities of English literary patrons such as his sister Mary.

2384 ———. "The Poetics of the Renaissance and the System of Literary Genres." In *Functions of Literature: Essays Presented to Erwin Wolff on His Sixtieth Birthday*, edited by Ulrich Broich, Theo Stemmler, and Gerd Stratmann. Tübingen, Germany: Max Niemeyer Verlag, 1984, pp. 101–17.

Aiming to elucidate connections between "the classifications of the typology of genres and the broader intellectual movements of the time," examines Sidney's view of traditional genres in the *Defence*. Contends that his literary theory was "above all concerned with filling the vacuum created by the retreat of the Church." Argues that, because he placed the genres "at the service of the social, ideological, and religious changes and ambitions of the age," their "cultural functions" mirror accurately "the sociological realities of Elizabethan times."

2385 ALI, S.M. MUHFUZ. "A Note on Aristotle's Theory of Imitation as Reflected in Shakespeare's Use of North's Plutarch." *Venture: A Review of English Language and Literature* (Karachi University) 3 (1963):60–63.

Not seen. According to item 618 in Washington (269), argues that, in adapting matierial from Plutarch, Shakespeare was following precepts in the *Defence*.

2386 ALLEN, DON CAMERON, ed. Introduction to *Francis Meres's Treatise "Poetrie": A Critical Edition*. University of Illinois Studies in Language and Literature, vol. 16, nos. 3–4. Urbana: University of Illinois Press, 1933, pp. 34, 43, 53–60.

Details Meres's almost verbatim borrowings from the *Defence*.

2387 ANDERSON, JUDITH H. *Biographical Truth: The Representation of Historical Persons in Tudor-Stuart Writing*. New Haven, Conn., and London: Yale University Press, 1984, pp. 124–25, 164–68.

Compares Sidney with Bacon on the relations of poetry to history and of each to truth. Suggests that Bacon had Sidney in mind when he "so carefully limited the province and value of poetry."

2388 ARMSTRONG, WILLIAM A. "*Damon and Pythias* and Renaissance Theories of Tragedy." *ES* 39 (October 1958):200–207.

Argues that *Damon and Pythias* follows the theory of tragedy held by Sidney and other contemporary English critics. The play examines the vices of a tyrant and demonstrates that only tragedy, not philosophy or history, can move such rulers to reform.

Twentieth Century

2389 ATKINS, J[OHN] W[ILLIAM] H[EY]. *English Literary Criticism: The Renascence.* London: Methuen & Co., 1947, pp. 113–38, 227–28, 256–58.

Places the *Defence* in the context of other English works defending poetry. Considers its date and the outline of the argument. Offers evidence that Sidney is more inclined to regard verse as necessary to poetry than he avows, and that his comments on divine inspiration may be more consistent than they appear. Notes the interrelation of Sidney's various classical and Renaissance sources, suggesting that he and Aristotle are close in their view of the nature of poetry. Explains the force of attacks on poetry by Cornelius Agrippa and Plato and Sidney's method of reply. Analyzes the rhetorical methods by which Sidney attracts his court audience, noting that his satiric sketches of the philosopher and the historian anticipate the vogue for "characters." Regards his theory of tragedy as a "composite" formed mainly from "medieval tradition, together with fragments drawn from Aristotle as interpreted by Italian critics." Notes that Sidney's demand for verisimilitude in drama is not from Aristotle, but finds Aristotelian elements in his remarks on comedy. Relates Sidney's comments on the lyric to *Astrophil and Stella*, those on diction to *Arcadia*, and those on prosody to the experiments of the Areopagus. Concludes that Sidney judges less by rules and classical authorities than by aesthetic and moral effect. Takes Plato as "perhaps" the predominant influence on the *Defence*. Also argues that Sidney must have known Gosson's *Plays Confuted in Five Acts*, published in 1582, and so must have written the *Defence* in 1582–83. Discusses the extensive influence of Sidney's thought on the criticism of Ben Jonson. See a reply by Stump (776).

2390 AUBERLEN, ECKHARD. *The Commonwealth of Wit: The Writer's Image and His Strategies of Self-Representation in Elizabethan Literature.* Studies and Texts in English. Tübingen, Germany: Gunter Narr, 1984, pp. 74–80, 89–90, 130, 183–84, 205–6.

Contrasts Sidney as a "cultivated amateur" apologist for poetry with Lodge as a "professional" apologist or *literatus*. Claims that their differences are in style and manner rather than in "poetological content" and may be traced to their social positions. Sees Sidney's aims in both the *exordium* and the peroration of the *Defence* as a successful effort to distance himself, through an act of *sprezzatura*, from the "role of apologist," which was "potentially just as one-sided as Pugliano's professionalism."

2391 BAINE, RODNEY M. "The First Anthologies of English Literary Criticism, Warton to Haselwood." *SB* 3 (1950–51):262–65.

Notes that the edition of the *Defence* published in 1752 was the first separate reprint of any work of English criticism and that the 1787 printing with Jonson's *Discoveries* was the first "anthology." Identifies the copy-texts of the 1787 edition by Warton (103) and the 1810 edition by Thurlowe (111), inferring that neither sold well.

2392 BAKER, HERSCHEL. *The Race of Time: Three Lectures on Renaissance Historiography.* Toronto: University of Toronto Press, 1967, pp. 15–16, 83–84.

Places Sidney's derisive comments on historians in the context of Renaissance assumptions about their exalted role. Suggests that Sidney's unorthodox view inaugurated a lengthy reappraisal of this role in the later English Renaissance.

2393 BAKER, HOWARD. *Induction to Tragedy: A Study in a Development of Form in "Gorboduc," "The Spanish Tragedy" and "Titus Andronicus."* University: Louisiana State University Press, 1939, pp. 196–97.

Argues that Seneca was not the primary influence on early English tragedy, pointing out that Sidney bases his points on the structure of drama mainly on Euripides, Plautus, and Terence. Regards Sidney's concept of tragedy as medieval with a single Aristotelian note.

2394 BALDWIN, CHARLES SEARS. *Renaissance Literary Theory and Practice: Classicism in the Rhetoric and Poetic of Italy, France, and England, 1400–1600.* New York: Columbia University Press, 1939, pp. 46, 178–80, 189.

Explains Sidney's reference in the *Defence* to "Nizolian paper books" as a derision of writers who rely on a thesaurus of Cicero's vocabulary. Accuses Sidney of lacking a reasoned theory of poetry. Also discusses his reading as revealed in the *Defence*.

2395 BARKER, ARTHUR E. "An Apology for the Study of Renaissance Poetry." In *Literary Views: Critical and Historical Essays*, edited by Carroll Camden. Chicago: University of Chicago Press, for William Marsh Rice University, 1964, pp. 15–43.

Defends the *Defence* against modern scholars who treat it merely as a self-contradictory fusion of neo-Aristotelian mimetic theory with neo-Platonic idealism, or who simplify it as "stultifying moralism." Notes Sidney's commitment to the religious and secular struggles of his day, suggesting that the *Defence* may not have been published until seven years after the Armada because it goes against the Protestant "rigorism and . . . enthusiasm" of the period. Notes that Sidney valued the poetic experience and did not wish to see poetry "scourged out of the church of God." Examines Sidney's views on the superiority of poetry to history and philosophy, suggesting that his teachings on *mimesis* have been mis-understood because he intentionally assumes the "mask of one who does

Twentieth Century

not know clearly what he is talking about, in order to induce us to figure it out." Concludes that, for Sidney, "good poetry or fiction is not fantastic or transcendental but, through a conscious and disciplined art making good use of the providential gifts of nature . . . , represents this creative process [of divine providence], with its corrective ironies and its sustaining energy. . . ."

2396 BARNES, CATHERINE. "The Hidden Persuader: The Complex Speaking Voice of Sidney's *Defence of Poetry.*" *PMLA* 86 (May 1971):422–27.
Argues that the Defence wins support by "sophisticated exercises in audience psychology rather than by intellectually cogent argumentation." Suggests that Sidney draws the reader into two "dramas": a trial in which Sidney is a public defender of "poor poetry" and the reader is part of the jury, and a self-conscious form of irony in which he subtly ridicules himself. Details the techniques by which Sidney evokes scorn for his enemies and self-interested support from the audience, citing the *exordium* about Pugliano as a paradigm of the author's rhetorical method and tone of voice.

2397 BAROWAY, ISRAEL. "Tremellius, Sidney, and Biblical Verse." *MLN* 49 (March 1934):145–49.
Shows that Sidney's narrowly restricted list of "the poeticall part of scripture" in the *Defence* is based on a discriminating reading of the preface to the third division of the Tremellius-Junius translation of the Bible, where the authors distinguish "lyric" from other kinds of Biblical poetry.

2398 BASKERVILL, C[HARLES] R[EAD]. "The Early Fame of *The Shepheards Calender.*" *PMLA* 28 (1913):291–313.
Argues against Greenlaw's view (2497) that, in the *Defence*, Sidney was cool in praising the *Calendar* because Spenser was in political disfavor. Discusses Sidney's patronage and Spenser's delay in writing an elegy for him, suggesting that the two had fallen out over Spenser's poem *Virgil's Gnat*.

2399 BASU, NITISH K. *Literature and Criticism.* Calcutta: Bookland Private Publishers, 1963, pp. 22–33, 211–12, 259.
Summarizes the *Defence*, discussing Sidney's attacks on Ciceronian style and his role in turning English poets away from accentual verse toward rhyme.

2400 BATE, WALTER JACKSON. *Prefaces to Criticism.* Garden City, N.Y.: Doubleday & Co., 1959, pp. 44–51.
Reprints the introduction to the *Defence* in item 117.

2401 BAUGHAN, DENVER EWING. "Swift's Source of the Houyhnhnms Reconsidered." *ELH* 5 (September 1938):207–10.
Suggests that the passage on the riding master Pugliano at the beginning of the *Defence* inspired Book IV of *Gulliver's Travels*, where horses are treated as superior to men. Notes that Swift alludes to the *Defence* several times in "A Letter of Advice to a Young Poet." See also Frantz (2490).

2402 BAXTER, JOHN. *Shakespeare's Poetic Styles: Verse into Drama.* London: Routledge & Kegan Paul, 1980, pp. 7–45.
In Chapter 2, "Sidney's *Defence* and Greville's *Mustapha*," suggests that the *Defence* first champions the "golden style" of poetry, then the "plain style." Rejects, however, the arguments of Hardison (2510) that the work is composed of two inconsistent parts. Also discusses Sidney's comments on the emotional effects of tragedy, arguing that he accepted all three mentioned by Aristotle: pity, fear, and wonder. Examines Greville's tragedy *Mustapha* as an illustration of the golden and plain styles employed to arouse these emotions. Notes parallels between the play and poems by Sidney.

2403 BEACH, D[ONALD] M[ARCUS]. "The Poetry of Idea: Sir Philip Sidney and the Theory of Allegory." *TSLL* 13 (Fall 1971):365–89.
Argues that, in Sidney's view, "poesy invents for ethics a concrete history of its own and, conversely, encourages man to see through the concrete to certain principles of conduct which lie behind and inform history and fable." Claiming that poems "grow from precepts conceived analogically," analyzes the *Defence* to show how each device mentioned there contributes to a forceful presentation of the "fore-conceit." Contrasts Sidney's views with other conceptions of allegory.

2404 BEAUCHAMP, VIRGINIA WALCOTT. "Sidney's Sister as Translator of Garnier." *Renaissance News* 10 (Spring 1957):8–13.
Argues that, in translating Robert Garnier's *Marc Antoine* in 1590, Mary Sidney was "setting herself the task of . . . justifying [Sidney's] views" of tragedy as set forth in the *Defence*. Because there were no native examples, she was forced to look to France.

2405 BENNETT, A[LVIN] L. "The Moral Tone of Massinger's Dramas." *PLL* 2 (1966):207–16.
Finds reminiscences of the *Defence* in Paris's defence of acting in *The Roman Actor*.

Twentieth Century

2406 BENSON, DONALD R. "'Ideas' and the Problem of Knowledge in Seventeenth-Century English Aesthetics." *EM* 19 (1968): 83–104.
Examines Sidney's epistemology, concluding that his definition of poetry depends on Platonic Ideas. Notes that seventeenth-century aesthetics carries on traditional views of epistemology such as Sidney's rather than turning to the skepticism fashionable in other areas of thought.

2407 BERGER, HARRY, Jr. "The Renaissance Imagination: Second World and Green World." *Centennial Review* 9 (Winter 1965): 36–78.
Discusses the *Defence* as the *locus classicus* of the "true poet's" attitude toward imagination and fiction. Distinguishes poets like Sidney from neo-Platonic idealists in that the poets value the fiction itself, not just the ideals embodied in it. Considers the historical origins of Sidney's view, emphasizing the importance of Christianity in teaching Renaissance poets the value of creating "second worlds" that mirror the "first world" created by God. Traces the changing value placed on each of these two "worlds" by writers and scientists from the fourteenth through the seventeenth centuries. Also examines 1) the relation between this "second world" and the audience, using the example of perspective in painting; and 2) the relation between the "second world" and an ideal or "green world," exemplified in More's *Utopia*. See also Fargnoli (2476).

2408 BLACKBURN, THOMAS H. "Edmund Bolton's *The Cabanet Royal*: A Belated Reply to Sidney's *Apology for Poetry*." *SRen* 14 (1967):159–71.
Argues that, without mentioning the *Defence*, Bolton's unpublished seventeenth-century manuscript seeks to refute Sidney's view that poetry is superior to philosophy. Contrasts the two writers in their attitude toward imagination and imitation in poetry, and notes that they were carrying on the ancient "civil war among the Muses." Also prints a passage in which Bolton asserts that, in *Arcadia*, Sidney was imitating Greek and Latin historians.

2409 BLUNDEN, EDMUND [CHARLES]. *Addresses on General Subjects Connected with English Literature Given at Tokyo University and Elsewhere in 1948.* Tokyo: Kenkyusha, 1949, pp. 183–95.
In "Criticism: Sidney to Arnold," summarizes the *Defence*.

2410 BOAS, FREDERICK S[AMUEL]. *Shakspere and his Predecessors.* London: John Murray, 1902, pp. 29–31.
Characterizes Sidney's comments on tragedy as "rigidly Senecan." Disapproves of his tendency toward rules, such as those on the dramatic unities.

2411 ———. *Sir Philip Sidney, Representative Elizabethan: His Life and Writings.* London: Staples Press, 1955, pp. 45–56.
Finds the originality of the *Defence* in its style rather than its ideas. Concludes that the work is a "classic" because it insists on "the predominance of imaginative over historical truth." Rejects Sidney's views on the English drama, calling them a "perverted standard" instilled by his classical education. Also dislikes his tendency to value moral teaching and to advocate imitation of "perfect" models rather than experimental freedom. See also item 436.

2412 BOGDAN, DEANNE GAIL. "Northrop Frye and the Educational Value of Literature." Ph.D. diss., University of Toronto, 1980.
Sees Frye's literary criticism as a "defence of poetry," comparing it with earlier defenses by Sidney and Shelley. See *DAI* 41 (December 1980):2493A–94A.

2413 BÖHLER, REINHARD. "Die Funktion des Dichtung in der Theorie Sir Philip Sidneys." Ph.D. diss., Universität Erlangen-Nürnberg, 1971, 250 pp.
Argues that the *Defence* is not fundamentally Aristotelian but neo-Platonic. Discusses Sidney's alteration of Aristotle's notion of *mimesis* so that the object of imitation is not nature but Platonic Ideas. Examines Sidney's terms *"vates"* and *"maker"* and the neo-Platonic basis for his assertion that poetry is superior to philosophy and history. Also finds in the *Defence* the neo-Platonic view that poetry emanates a mysterious moral and "erotic" force that draws readers to the good, which is also the beautiful. Concludes that the ends of poetry (teaching, delighting, and moving) are not three for Sidney but one, all accomplished by the "erotic" force. Also touches on Sidney's reasons for listing the various genres of poetry in the order that he does. See *EASG*, 1972, pp. 51–53. See also *DAI* 39 (Summer 1979):4693C.

2414 BOND, WILLIAM H[ENRY]. "Casting Off Copy by Elizabethan Printers: A Theory." *PBSA* 42 (4th Quarter 1948):281–91.
Seeks to explain variations in the spacing of the type in the 1595 Ponsonby edition of the *Defence*.

Twentieth Century

2415 BOYD, JOHN D. *The Function of Mimesis and Its Decline.* Cambridge, Mass.: Harvard University Press, 1968, pp. 138, 165, 178, 197–99, 251.
Notes the "rather low rhetorical conception of poetry" implicit in Sidney's description of it as a sweetener for philosphical medicine. Traces the same view in eighteenth-century criticism. Argues that Sidney's concept of poetry "is theoretically inconsistent in its effort to blend Platonism, Aristotelianism, and the notions of Horace, especially in questions of the didactic function of poetry." Notes an echo of the *Defence* in George Farquhar's *Discourse on Comedy*.

2416 BRADBROOK, M[URIEL] C[LARA]. *The Growth and Structure of Elizabethan Comedy.* London: Chatto & Windus, 1955, pp. 29–31, 39–40, 114.
Notes ways in which Sidney's comments on comedy foreshadow the actual comedies written later in the period. Suggests that the prologue to Lyly's *Sapho and Phao* may echo the *Defence*, specifically Sidney's rejection of laughter as the chief end of comedy. Notes in Ben Jonson's works a parallel for Sidney's phrase "the poet never affirmeth and so never lieth."

2417 BRETT, R.L. "Thomas Hobbs." In *English Literature and British Philosophy: A Collection of Essays*, edited by S.P. Rosenbaum. Chicago: University of Chicago Press, 1971, p. 46.
Feels that when, in his *Brief Art of Rhetoric*, Hobbs takes the position that literature should provide examples to illustrate the truths of philosophy, he is echoing the *Defence*.

2418 BRINCKMANN, CHRISTINE N., and KELLER, ULRICH. "Erzählen und Lügen: Zur Auslegung von Henry James' *The Turn of the Screw*." In *Miscellanea Anglo-Americana: Festschrift für Helmut Viebrock*, edited by Kuno Schuhmann, Wilhelm Hortmann, and Armin Paul Frank. Munich: Pressler, 1974, pp. 26–77.
In the introduction, examines the implications of Sidney's claim that the poet "nothing affirmeth, and therefore never lieth."

2419 BRINK, J.R. "Philosophical Poetry: The Contrasting Poetics of Sidney and Scaliger." *Explorations in Renaissance Culture* 8–9 (1982–83):45–53.
Examines three issues that illustrate the "significant differences" between Scaliger and Sidney, while contending that Scaliger's theory was the more immediately influential. Sidney's Aristotelian insistence on

poetry as "imitation" obligates him, unlike Scaliger, to "exclude" philosophical and historical poets or to "relegate them to second-class status."

2420 BRONOWSKI, J[ACOB]. *The Poet's Defence.* Cambridge: Cambridge University Press, 1939, pp. 19–86. See also pp. 10–11, 89–125 passim, 152, 172–73.

In "Sidney and Shelley," contrasts Sidney's belief in ideal truth with Shelley's reliance on scientific truth, seeking to trace changing attitudes toward poetry from the Renaissance to the nineteenth century. Feels that Sidney avoids the true issues in Stephen Gosson's attack on poetry and so fails to make an adequate defense. Points to similarities in the Protestant views of poetry held by both men: their distrust of the senses and their reliance on ideal truths received from God, not from the world. Feels that Sidney was simply content to accept the use of the senses in poetry in order to convey ideal truths and shape conduct, and Gosson was not. Notes that Sidney introduces an inconsistency when he adopts Aristotle's view of imitation. Traces attitudes toward the moral power of poetry from Sidney to Coleridge, focusing on similarities between Sidney's views and those of Jonson and Dryden. Notes that all three see poetry as a means to create an ideal "second nature," though Jonson shifts the final goal from virtue to knowledge and allows pleasure and the senses a larger role. Sees Wordsworth as the last of the great English poets to accept a concept of poetry like that of Sidney. In analyzing Shelley's *Defence of Poetry,* points out ways in which Shelley rejected Sidney's traditional views of poetic truth. Also touches on *Astrophil and Stella,* treating it as a record of Sidney's discovery of a concept of virtue combining thought and sensuous experience.

2421 BRYANT, DONALD C[ROSS]. "'A Peece of Logician': The Critical Essayist as Rhetorician." In *The Rhetorical Idiom: Essays in Rhetoric, Oratory, Language, and Drama Presented to Herbert August Wichelns,* edited by Donald C[ross] Bryant. Ithaca, N.Y.: Cornell University Press, 1958, pp. 293–314. Reprint. In *Der englische Essay: Analysen,* edited by Horst Weber. Darmstadt, Germany: Wissenschaftliche Buchgesellschaft, 1975, pp. 38–47.

Examines rhetorical strategies in the *Defence,* arguing against Myrick (671) that Sidney's *propositio* is not a definition of poetry but a demonstration of its excellence. Regards the central strategy as argument from authority and from history. Analyzes Sidney's rebuttal of Plato according to the *topoi* in forensic oratory that are used to dispose of a hostile witness.

Twentieth Century

2422 BUCHLOH, PAUL GERHARD. *Michael Drayton: Barde und Historiker, Politiker und Prophet.* Neumünster, Germany: Karl Wachholtz Verlag, 1964, pp. 65–69.
Weighs Sidney's influence on Drayton, employing the comments on divine and historical poetry in the *Defence* to define Drayton's aim in *The Harmony of the Church* and comparing the two authors' interest in Welsh bards.

2423 BUCK, AUGUST. "Dichtungslehren der Renaissance und des Barocks." In *Neues Handbuch der Literaturwissenschaft*, edited by Klaus von See. Vol. 9., *Renaissance und Barock. (I. Teil)*, edited by August Buck. Frankfurt am Main: Akademische Verlagsgesellschaft Athenaion, 1972, pp. 28–60.
Compares the *Defence* with criticism on the Continent. Considers Sidney's preference for vernacular rather than Latin poetry, his definition of poetry (especially epic), and his strictures against English tragicomedy.

2424 BUNDY, MURRAY W[RIGHT]. "Bacon's True Opinion of Poetry." *SP* 27 (April 1930):244–64.
Notes similarities between Bacon and Sidney in their views on the imagination and on the superiority of poetry to history.

2425 ———. "'Invention' and 'Imagination' in the Renaissance." *JEGP* 29 (October 1930):535–45.
Discusses the origins of the Renaissance concept of poetic imagination. Finds that Sidney and other critics of the period borrowed from classical rhetoric the term "invention" and redefined it for poets, using the medieval concept of imagination. Notes that Sidney departs from Aristotle in discussing "fore-conceit" and imitation.

2426 BUNDY, MURRAY W[RIGHT], ed. *Navgerivs, sive De Poetica Dialogvs*, by Girolamo Fracastoro. Translated by Ruth Kelso. University of Illinois Studies in Language and Literature, vol. 9, no. 3. Urbana: University of Illinois Press, 1924, p. 10.
Regards Sidney's theory of poetry as too apologetic and too concerned with ethics to match the practice of Renaissance poets or even their ideals. Finds in Fracastoro a similar mingling of Aristotelian and Platonic theories but a more frankly aesthetic view, which better represents the age.

638

2427 CAWLEY, R[OBERT] R[ALSTON]. "'Areytos' in the *Defence of Poesie.*" *MLN* 39 (February 1924):121–23.
Corrects Cook's note (in 105) on Sidney's observation about "barbarous and simple Indians," showing that it could have come from Richard Eden's *History of the West Indies* or from Fernandez de Oviedo's *Historia general de las Indias.* Finds the most likely source in Eden's English translation of a passage in Peter Martyr's *Decades.* See also item 463.

2428 CHARLTON, H[ENRY] B[UCKLEY]. *Castelvetro's Theory of Poetry.* Manchester, England: Manchester University Press, 1913, pp. 15–16, 62, 152–53.
Traces Sidney's phrase "a speaking picture" to Horace via Minturno. Notes the possibility that Sidney could have seen the 1564 edition of Tasso's *Discorsi dell'arte poetica* and comments on the neo-Platonism implicit in Sidney's association of beauty with virtue.

2429 CHATTERJEE, VISVANATH. "Sidney and the Critical Tradition." *Essays and Studies* (Department of English, Jadavpur University, Calcutta, India) 1 (1968):6–18.
In appraising Sidney's claim to be the father of English criticism, surveys other commentators from Richard de Bury to Dryden. Details ways in which the *Defence* draws upon Plato, Aristotle, Horace, Boccaccio, Minturno, Scaliger, and Castelvetro. Also counters the view that Sidney did not write in response to Stephen Gosson's *School of Abuse.*

2430 CHEADLE, B.D. "The 'Form of Goodness' in English Renaissance Literature." *ESA* 21 (March 1978):1–16.
Consider's Sidney's position that poetry is the highest form of learning, tracing it to the humanists' belief in the civilizing power of literature. Notes, however, that Sidney does not accept the moral pragmatism of humanists such as Sir Thomas Elyot but sees goodness as "comely." Urges that, "For Sidney, active virtue . . . lives in the generous expansiveness of men's responses to what is brave and free in 'the form of goodness.'" Feels that Sidney's is not a morality of the will but of perfected feeling, and concludes that, when Sidney compares poetry with a picture, he has in mind both exemplary images and "the total action rationally set forth." Compares Sidney with William Butler Yeats.

2431 ———. "'The Truest Poetry is the Most Feigning': Sidney on the Poet As Maker." *Theoria* 52 (1979):39–49.
Suggests that there is a "strain" between the moral arguments in the *Defence* and Sidney's aesthetic feelings. Notes an apparent contradiction in his remarks on Plato's notion of a "divine fury" in the poet, compar-

Twentieth Century

ing Sidney's distinction between "right poetry" and divine or philosophical poetry with similar views in the criticism of William Webbe. Also finds a strain between Sidney's emphasis on "feigning" and his lack of interest in sustained, realistic fiction, except as it offers moral *exempla*.

2432 CLARK, A.C. "Ciceronianism." In *English Literature and the Classics*, edited by G.S. Gordon. Oxford: Clarendon Press, 1912, pp. 112, 138–39.
Notes Sidney's unusual ability to reproduce the rhythms of Cicero's prose.

2433 CLARK, DONALD LAMEN. *Rhetoric and Poetry in the Renaissance: A Study of Rhetorical Terms in English Renaissance Literary Criticism*. New York: Columbia University Press, 1922, pp. 83–87, 93–94, 145–49, 156.
Notes the importance of the *Defence* in turning English criticism from medieval to classical models. Lists Sidney's borrowings from Aristotle, J.C. Scaliger, and others, noting the influence of rhetorical theory on Sidney's views of *energeia* and the ends of poetry. Also remarks on Sidney's lack of interest in allegory and his influence on Ben Jonson.

2434 CLARK, EARL JOHN. "Spenser's Theory of the English Poet." Ph.D. diss., Loyola University of Chicago, 1956, 339 pp.
Surmises that Spenser's lost treatise *The English Poet* influenced the *Defence*. Finds Sidney less concerned with the "poetic process" than Spenser but more emphatic about the superiority of poetry to other disciplines.

2435 CLAYTON, THOMAS. "Catharsis in Aristotle, the Renaissance, and Elsewhere." *Journal of the Rocky Mountain Medieval and Renaissance Association* 2 (January 1981):87–95.
In arguing that Milton offered the "most defensible interpretation" of Aristotle's concept of *catharsis*, remarks on the "explicitly moral and didactic emphasis" in Sidney's definition of tragedy and on his view that the genre aims to arouse "admiration and commiseration." Sees Sidney's concept of tragedy as "notably different" from that of Aristotle.

2436 CLEMEN, WOLFGANG. *English Tragedy before Shakespeare: The Development of Dramatic Speech*. Translated by T.S. Dorsch. London: Methuen & Co.; New York: Barnes & Noble, 1961, pp. 39, 73.
Relates Sidney's emphasis on moral teaching in tragedy and his comments on the "stately speeches" in *Gorboduc* to Elizabethan views on the nature and function of set speeches in the drama.

2437 CLEMENTS, ROBERT J. *Picta Poesis: Literary and Humanistic Theory in Renaissance Emblem Books.* Temi e Testi, 6. Rome: Edizioni di Storia e Letteratura, 1960, pp. 97–98, 131.

Notes that, like Sidney, authors of emblem books claimed that poetry was superior to and embodied philosophy. Also points out that Alciati anticipated Sidney in using the analogy of a pill with a sugar coating.

2438 COLLINS, JOHN CHURTON. *Greek Influence on English Poetry.* Edited by Michael MacMillan. London: Sir Isaac Pitman & Sons, 1910, pp. 88–89.

Contrasts Sidney's reliance on Greek sources with the practice of other Elizabethan critics. Lists points in the *Defence* derived from Aristotle, applauding Sidney for recognizing that, in the *Poetics*, poetry has a moral as well as an aesthetic function.

2439 CONDON, HELEN MARGARET. "The Ethical Element in Literary Criticism of the English Renaissance." Ph.D. diss., Stanford University, 1953, 185 pp.

Draws upon Sidney and others in assessing the role of ethics in the criticism of the period. Concludes that the absolutist Christian ethics of the age are "integrally related" to such critical concepts as imitation, allegory, poetic rationality, the function of art, and the nature of the major genres. Also considers the moral views expressed by Renaissance opponents of poetry. See *DA* 14 (February 1954):354–55.

2440 CONGLETON, J[AMES] E[DMUND]. *Theories of Pastoral Poetry in England, 1684–1798.* Gainesville: University of Florida Press, 1952, pp. 9, 42–43.

Notes that the *Defence* contains the first recorded use of the English term "pastoral" to describe a literary genre. Discusses Sidney's comments on the form.

2441 COOGAN, ROBERT [M.]. "More Dais Than Dock: Greek Rhetoric and Sidney's Encomium on Poetry." *SLitI* 15 (Spring 1982):99–113.

Argues that the *Defence* is not a forensic but an epideictic oration, one shaped around an "informing vision" of poetry crowned and triumphant. Analyzes the work according to the schema for an encomium in Aristotle's *Rhetoric* and in Aphthonius's *Progymnasmata*. Notes five divisions: a *prooimion*, arguments praising poetry, a *refutatio* of objections, a *digressio* on English poetry, and an epilogue. Analyzes each of these sections according to Aristotle's topics of invention. Notes that Sidney does not adopt the stance of a public defender and does not include a

Twentieth Century

narratio, a section required in a forensic oration. Analyzes the appropriateness of his diction to each of the topics he employs. Argues that an epideictic reading clarifies the unity of the work and accounts for its particular combination of logical, emotional, and ethical appeals. Notes that, in the first main section, Sidney is not attempting a formal definition of poetry, since he limits his attention largely to its final cause, delightful teaching. Concludes that the *Defence* may have been written to counter the low esteem in which poetry was held at Oxford.

2442 ———. "The Triumph of Reason: Sidney's *Defense* and Aristotle's *Rhetoric.*" *PLL* 17 (Summer 1981):255–70.
Rejects Myrick's widely accepted outline (671) of the *Defence*. Argues that the *confirmatio* in the first part of the work is epideictic rather than forensic, in that it praises poetry and seeks to win for it a laurel crown. Notes the lack of a true *narratio*, which is necessary in a forensic oration. Sees the second part of the work (after the sentence beginning "But because we have ears as well as tongues . . .") as a *refutatio* of objections against poetry, which is followed by a *digressio* on English poetry and a *peroratio*. Finds support for this simplified outline in Aristotle's *Rhetoric*. Rejects the view that the first part of the work is an emotional appeal or that Sidney speaks through a persona. Emphasizes the logic of Sidney's argument, discussing the classical *topoi* that it employs. Also distinguishes his "description" of poetry as a mimetic art from a formal definition and argues that his comments on divine inspiration are not logically inconsistent.

2443 COOK, ALBERT S. "A Plagiarist of Sir Philip Sidney." *JEGP* 5, no. 2 (1903):159–60.
Points out that the anonymous author of the preface to Nahum Tate's 1697 edition of Sir John Davies's *Nosce Teipsum* plagiarized Sidney's *Defence*.

2444 COOPER, LANE. *The Poetics of Aristotle, Its Meaning and Influence.* Ithaca, N.Y.: Cornell University Press, 1956, pp. 131–33.
Notes Aristotelian doctrines in the *Defence* and likely Italian sources for them.

2445 COSTA, RICHARD HAUER. "Intimations of *Don Quixote* in Sidney's *Defense of Poetry.*" *Ball State University Forum* 11, no. 4 (Autumn 1970):60–63.
Notes that Sidney and Cervantes shared views on the dramatic unities, Aristotelian imitation, the relation of poetry to the other arts, the role of

poetry in perfecting nature, and the folly of simply mimicking other poets.

2446 COURTHOPE, WILLIAM JOHN. *Life in Poetry: Law in Taste. Two Series of Lectures Delivered in Oxford, 1895–1900.* London and New York: Macmillan & Co., 1901, pp. 69–71, 280–81.

Attacks Sidney for failing to grasp the aims of writers such as Zenophon and Plato, but praises him for allowing that poetry may be written in prose.

2447 COWL, R[ICHARD] P[APE]. *The Theory of Poetry in England: Its Development in Doctrines and Ideas from the Sixteenth Century to the Nineteenth Century.* London: Macmillan & Co., 1914, pp. 3, 42, 84–85, 156, 187, 224–25, 242, 298–301.

Juxtaposes quotations from the *Defence* and comparable passages from other works of English criticism, organized by topic.

2448 CRAIG, D.H. "A Hybrid Growth: Sidney's Theory of Poetry in *An Apology for Poetry*." *ELR* 10 (Spring 1980):183–201.

Rejects Shepherd's view (141) that Sidney's description of the poet as a God-like creator is related to the Mannerist theory of painting set forth by Federico Zuccaro and others. Discounts MacIntyre's suggestion (2563) that Sidney's theory is neo-Platonic, noting major differences in the views of true neo-Platonists such as Cristoforo Landino. Also rejects Weiner's argument (2672) that Sidney's poetic is Calvinist. Turns instead to the ideal of wisdom presented by the northern humanists, noting Sidney's stress on the power of the poetic image or "speaking picture" to move men to virtue. Analyzes the hybrid of Aristotelian and Platonic elements in Sidney's concept of poetic imitation, noting that Sidney's arguments resemble those in favor of painting put forward by Leonardo da Vinci. Cites passages in *Arcadia* and *Astrophil and Stella* that reflect Sidney's position.

2449 CRAIGIE, JAMES. "Sidney's 'King James of Scotland.'" *TLS,* 20 December 1941, p. 648.

Argues that the "King James" mentioned in the *Defence* is not James I of Scotland but James VI (the future James I of England). Lists diplomatic contacts through which Sidney may have learned of James's interest in literature, and uses the reference to date the *Defence* in 1584–85.

Twentieth Century

2450 DAICHES, DAVID. *Critical Approaches to Literature*. Englewood Cliffs, N.J.: Prentice-Hall, 1956, pp. 50–72, 77–78, 86, 98, 155, 158–59.

In Chapter 3, "The Poet as Moral Teacher," reviews the the major arguments of the *Defence* and discusses their historical significance. Equates Sidney's view that the fables of poetry can teach morality with "the old doctrine of allegory" that goes back to Philo of Alexandria's attempts to reconcile Scripture with Platonism by reading it allegorically. Notes that, early in the *Defence*, poetry seems to have no value apart from the moral, philosophical, and historical knowledge that it communicates. In the later argument that the poet is like the divine Maker, sees a better case for intrinsic value than Aristotle made against the attacks of Plato. Remarks that, although Sidney borrows Plato's concept of Ideas for this argument, he does not seem to recognize the power of his own reasoning to disarm Plato's objections to poetry. Suggests that Sidney transfers the process of imitation from the poet to the reader, who is drawn to imitate in real life what the poet presents in fictions. Supposes that, for Sidney, heroes must always be "perfect" and successful, whereas villains must be "obviously villainous" and doomed. Distinguishes Sidney's argument that poetry is superior to history from a similar line of reasoning in Aristotle's *Poetics*. Stresses Sidney's tendency to divorce form from content, noting that the purely "esthetic" side of poetry comes into his theory only in so far as it helps to move the reader to moral goodness. Nonetheless, sees the discussion of style late in the work as an important forerunner of "purely esthetic points of view." Finds Sidney and Wordsworth in agreement on the need for "passion" and "liveliness" in poetry, but rejects the view that Sidney was a "romantic" or that he valued emotion for its own sake. Examines the basis for Sidney's hierarchy of literary genres. Concludes that Sidney defended poetry at the cost of its independence from moral philosophy.

2451 DAVIES, HUGH SYKES. *Realism in the Drama*. Cambridge: Cambridge University Press, 1934, pp. 29–34.

Criticizes Sidney's rigidity in requiring the dramatic unities and in censuring English tragicomedy.

2452 DAVIS, WALTER R. *Idea and Act in Elizabethan Fiction*. Princeton, N.J.: Princeton University Press, 1969, pp. 28–45.

In Chapter 2, "Acting Out Ideas in Sidney's Theory," distinguishes Sidney's theory of fiction from that of other Elizabethan critics, particularly in his concepts of "making" and "feigning." Examines the Christian Platonism behind his view that poets imitate eternal ideas and, like God, create a "second nature." Considers his reasons for exalting poetry over philosophy and history, urging that he saw poetry as the best means to restore the damage done by the Fall. Traces his view of poetry to Greek, French, and Italian sources. Also explores his use of Plutarch's metaphor of the "speaking picture," relating it to Renaissance theories of sight, knowledge, and prophecy and noting its importance in Sidney's definition of the ends of poetry: teaching, delighting, and moving. Corrects misimpressions about these, arguing that delighting is inseparable from the other two. Links Sidney's concept of poetry to neo-Platonic theories of love as an intermediary between the actual and the Ideal. Also brings in Renaissance science, particularly its use of hypothetical worlds, and concludes that "Sidney points out the exploratory rather than the imitative function of fiction."

2453 DeNEEF, A. LEIGH. "Opening and Closing the Sidneian Text." *SNew* 2, no. 1 (1981):3–6.

Complains that twentieth-century editions, including that of Duncan-Jones and van Dorsten (22), have failed to record crucial variants in the passages of the *Defence* where Sidney defines poetry as a "speaking picture" and comments on its "Idea or fore-conceit." On the basis of these variants, suggests that Sidney may have seen the process of imitation as twofold: "The conceit is an initial conceptual metaphor which imitates the originating Idea; the text is a verbalized metaphor which imitates the conceit." Relates this reading to Sidney's comments on history and philosophy, reader and ethical action, poet and poem, Logos and language, God and nature. See also Heninger (2516) and van Dorsten (2665).

2454 ———. "Rereading Sidney's Apology." *JMRS* 10 (Fall 1980): 155–91.

Reviews recent attempts to deal with apparent inconsistencies in the *Defence*, suggesting that the logic of Sidney's position depends on his definition of poetry as an art of imitation. First, examines the relation between God and the poet and between the poet and nature. Focuses on the epistemological gap between the poet's mental Idea and the verbal imitation of that Idea, suggesting that the main teaching of the work is not the Idea itself but the ability to translate the Idea into ethical action. Stresses the importance of the Fall of Adam in creating the epistemological problems that the poet resolves and examines the relation between the divine Logos and human language. Second, argues that the process of poetic imitation moves from Idea (a universal abstraction) to "fore-conceit" (a generalized, potential action formed in imitation of the Idea)

Twentieth Century

to text (a particularized, fictional action written in imitation of the "fore-conceit"). Hence, the "fore-conceit" is central because it mediates between Idea and act. Traces Sidney's term "Idea" to Plato, regarding it as an innate memory formed without the influence of perceptions gathered through the senses. Notes that, since the process of imitating such Ideas introduces distortions, Sidney is "very close to reaffirming Plato's principal charge" against poetry. Relates Sidney's three-stage process of imitation to Augustine's discussion in *De Trinitate* of the divine Word in relation to mental and spoken words. Notes that, at each stage in the process, the poet can only make metaphors for the Idea and, hence, that Sidney writes advisedly when he terms poetry an art of "figuring forth to speak metaphorically." Stresses the need for the reader to participate in recreating the "fore-conceit" and the Idea, noting that Sidney calls fiction "an imaginitive ground-plot of a profitable invention." Third, inquires how it is that poetry leads to ethical action, exploring the faculty psychology underlying Sidney's theory. Finds the answer in his explanation of the mediating role of poetry between philosophy (which deals with Ideas) and history (which deals with actions). Also considers Sidney's sketchy comments on the power of poetry to delight and move. Relates Sidney's theory of poetry to his Protestant concern with the reformation of society and the restoration of fallen human nature.

2455 ———. *Spenser and the Motives of Metaphor.* Durham, N.C.: Duke University Press, 1982, pp. 5–13, 17–19, 28–34, 38–40, 43–44, 63, 77–79, 110, 120–21, 125, 136, 143, 156, 158–59, 176.

Argues that Sidney is the first theoretician to give Elizabethan poets a definition of why and a model for how poetry speaks metaphorically. Both theory and model are grounded in the relation between the three key terms in the *Defence*: "Idea" (an abstract universal), "fore-conceit" (a latent potential), and "work" (a concrete manifestation of the Idea). This relation is analogous to that between a noun (such as "love"), an infinitive ("to love"), and a verbal (specific acts of "loving"), a paradigm which is implicit in Sidney's complaint against ignorant "faultfinders," who will "correct the verb before they understand the noun." Sidney's theory implies a mutual relationship in which the poet's "transference" of an Idea into a text must be matched by the reader's transference of text into an Idea: one's senses receive the images in the poem, one's imagination perceives its structure, one's intellect meditates on the Idea, and one's will gives rise to imitative action. This view of the reading process is analogous to Ficino's explanation of the way in which an architect's Idea becomes realized in an actual building by means of an intermediary "plan." For Sidney, the "ending end" of this process is the "reformation of man," not just a rehashing of humanist ideals but a "careful and logical extension of those theories." Thus poetry is a means of grace by which man can re-form himself "according to the *imago Dei* by which he was originally formed and which remains implanted but forgotten in the human mind." It is also "an art of imitation which figures forth in order to speak metaphorically," in which capacity it can be abused and misunderstood. This latter danger accounts for much of the defensive tone, not only in Sidney himself, but also in such followers as Spenser, whose desire to be a "right poet" was "dependent upon his ability to marshall an adequate defense against the abuses Sidney identifies"—the poet's own internal errors, errors brought about by his language, or external threats from poor or perverse readers. Argues that, for Sidney, genre is the "formal fore-conceit of literary perception," that "pastoral," for example, embodies the same position between "poetry" and "Ye goatherd gods" (*OA 71*) as does "fore-conceit" between Idea and text. Reads all of Spenser's poems in light of this theory, with particular stress on the way *Ruins of Time* "pays the dead Sidney the highest of literary compliments by demonstrating in practice the principal theorems of the *Apology*." Sees in *The Faerie Queene* Spenser's "growing awareness" that Sidney's ideals for poetry are "too dependent upon a perhaps unwarranted faith in the good will of its readers."

2456 DENNIS, CHRISTOPHER MARKEE. "Literary Conceptions of David in the English Renaissance." Ph.D diss., Princeton University, 1979, 180 pp.
Discusses references to David in the *Defence* and suggests that Sidney regarded the Psalms as ideal models to follow in reforming English poetry.

2457 DEVEREUX, JAMES A. "The Meaning of Delight in Sidney's *Defence of Poesy*." SLitI 15 (Spring 1982):85–97.
Discusses the relation of delight to teaching and moving in Sidney's poetic theory. Notes that delight is subordinated to the other ends, that it leads to them, that it sometimes involves the senses as well as the mind, and that it can be violent. Considers Sidney's sources in classical and Renaissance rhetoric and criticism and in neo-Platonic philosophy. Against Roberts (2616), argues that delight is intrinsic to poetic teaching. Suggests that, for Sidney, the power of the poem lies in its "speaking pictures" and that these delight because of "conveniency, that is, . . . the proper correspondence that exists between the poetic representation and the objects or actions in nature that are represented." Finds the ulti-

Twentieth Century

mate source of Sidney's concept of "conveniency" in Aquinas's adaptation of Aristotle's notion of pleasure. Notes that, because this theory treats delights of the senses as more intense than those of the intellect, Sidney had a sound basis for his claim that poetry is more forceful than philosophy.

2458 DIEDE, OTTO. *Der Streit der Alten und Modernen in der englischen Literaturgeschichte des XVI. und XVII. Jahrhunderts.* Greifswald, Germany: Hans Adler, 1912, pp. 33–36. Orig. a Ph.D. diss., Königlichen Universität Griefswald, 1912.

Considers Sidney's position in the dispute between Renaissance "classicists" and "modernists." Notes that only in discussing lyric poetry does he have much praise for modern authors.

2459 DITLEVSEN, TORBEN. "'Truth's Journey to Word': On the Concept of 'Imitation' in Sidney's *Apology for Poetry.*" *Language and Literature* (University of Copenhagen) 2, no. 1 (1973):54–70.

Considers the way in which Sidney's ideal poet turns his subject into fiction. Suggests that the poet imitates, not Nature itself, but the divine reason in Nature. Lays out reasons that poetry is, in Sidney's view, superior to history and philosophy. Defines three "levels of reality": 1) the Real World of particulars, with which historians are concerned; 2) the Fictive World, which is "false" by the standards of the Real World; and 3) the Truth of universals, which "does not immediately correspond to 'the true' in the Real World or differ from 'the false' on the Fictional level." Defines the true poet, in Sidney's sense, as one who creates a world on the second level that is a perfect image of things on the third. Relates this scheme to Sidney's claim that the poet creates a "second nature," noting Plato's different position in the *Ion.* Undertakes a semiotic analysis of Sidney's view. Truth enters the mind and is perceived as an Idea or "fore-conceit" in the internal language of the mind. This Idea, in turn, conceives a "Fiction" that is then expressed in the external language of the "Word." Sees the process of reading as the reverse of these steps. Examines points at which the process is dependent on the perceiver and hence fallible, and notes steps that need further explanation. Feels that, in Sidney's semiotic system, reading leads only to "Truths" predetermined from the outset and hence that the process is "self-confirming."

2460 DONNO, ELIZABETH S[TORY]. *"Admiration* and *Commiseration* in Marlowe's *Edward II.*" *NM* 79, no. 4 (1978):372–83.

Suggests that Sidney's inclusion of "admiration" as a principle effect of tragedy sets his view of the genre apart from Aristotle's and ties it to a growing Renaissance interest in the wonderful or astonishing, especially among Italian critics. Feels that a number of critical objections to Marlowes's *Edward II* do not take into account this trend, which also helps to explain Shakespeare's evil tragic protagonists in *Richard III* and *Macbeth*.

2461 ———. "Old Mouse-eaten Records: History in Sidney's *Apology*." *SP* 72 (July 1975):275–98.
In reply to Hearsey (2515), considers Sidney's attitude toward history, examining his correspondence and the *Defence* and listing histories that he had read. Records a shift in emphasis from theoretical works of value in public service to more pragmatic works involving private virtues. Focuses on Sidney's letters to his brother Robert and to Edward Denny, listing the things that Sidney expects them to learn from the study of history: systematic analysis of actions, skills in rhetoric and poetic speech, and the ability to discourse in various arts. Argues that he derived his main argument against history from a work praising it, namely Jacques Amyot's preface to his translation of Plutarch's *Lives*. Suggests that the irony of this procedure is part of Sidney's deliberately playful and brilliantly illogical stance in the *Defence* and is not to be taken seriously.

2462 DOWLIN, CORNELL MARCH. "Sidney and Other Men's Thought." *RES* 20 (October 1944):257–71.
Argues against scholars who treat Sidney as a mere conveyer of Italian critical thought. Illustrates his originality by showing that his classification of Heliodorus's *Aethiopica* as an epic does not come from J.C. Scaliger, as some commentators suggest. Notes that no Continental critic had yet recognized the possibility of a prose epic. Also distinguishes Sidney's views on poetic "feigning" from those of Aristotle, Cicero, and various Italian critics.

2463 ———. "Sidney's Two Definitions of Poetry." *MLQ* 3 (December 1942):573–81.
Argues that, in defining poetry as "the feigning of notable images of virtues, vices," Sidney was drawing upon Plato's *Republic* rather than Minturo's *De Poeta*. Suggests that Sidney's true opponent in the *Defence* was not the Puritans but Plato and that he used Plato's own ideas against him.

Twentieth Century

2464 DUDEK, LOUIS. "Art, Entertainment and Religion." *QQ* 70 (Autumn 1963):413–30.
Asserts that Christianity is inherently opposed to secular entertainment and that, after the Middle Ages, works such as Sidney's *Defence* were required "to justify the very existence of art and literature."

2465 DUNCAN-JONES, KATHERINE. "A Note on Irish Poets and the Sidneys." *ES* 49 (October 1968):424–25.
Suggests that one of the curses at the end of the *Defence*, "to be rhymed to death, as is said to be done in Ireland," is a reference to the political power of Irish poets. In 1560, Sir Henry Sidney encouraged his supporters to despoil them, and Thomas Churchyard records their counterthreat: "to rhyme these gentlemen to death."

2466 DURLING, ROBERT M. *The Figure of the Poet in Renaissance Epic.* Cambridge, Mass.: Harvard University Press, 1965, pp. 131, 236–37.
Contrasts Ariosto's practice as a poet with Sidney's ideal in the *Defence*. Finds Sidney's views closer to those of Spenser.

2467 EAGLE, R[ODERICK L.]. "Sir Philip Sidney and *Love's Labour's Lost*." *Baconiana*, 3rd ser. 13 (July 1915):154–57.
Suggests that a manuscript of the *Defence* guided Shakespeare in *Love's Labor's Lost*, giving him the hint for the characters Berowne and Holofernes.

2468 EAGLETON, TERRY. *Criticism and Ideology: A Study in Marxist Literary Theory.* London: NLB; Atlantic Highlands, N.J.: Humanities Press, 1978, pp. 19, 75.
Treats the Sidney of the *Defence* as a spokesman for a "hegemonic class" opposed to "an assertive bourgeois puritanism." Notes certain of his views that are consonant with twentieth-century materialist criticism.

2469 EICHNER, HANS. "In Defence of Literature." In *Humanities in the Present Day*, edited by John Woods and Harold G. Coward. Waterloo, Ontario: Wilfrid Laurier University Press, 1979, pp. 75–89.
Feels that, though literature is currently in need of defenses, those provided by Sidney and Shelly "no longer ring true." Notes that Sidney placed little emphasis on literature as a way to preserve knowledge, and feels that his lofty moral expectations are unrealistic because literature often portrays an unjust world, and if it does not, it misleads the reader. Concludes that the only part of Sidney's defence that is sound is his emphasis on the pleasure of the "second nature" created by the poet.

2470 ELIA, R.L. "Platonic Irony in Sidney's *An Apology for Poetrie*." *Revue des langues vivantes* 36 (1970):401–5.
Argues that Sidney unconsciously confirmed Plato's worst fears about poets by propounding a "second nature" by which the poet draws our minds away from reality toward mere fictions. Compares Oscar Wilde's views in "The Decay of Lying."

2471 ESTALL, H.M. "Philosophy's Dry Light." *QQ* 71 (Summer 1964):226–37.
Notes Sidney's reply to Plato's charges against poetry in the *Republic* and compares Sir Francis Bacon's defence of philosophy in *The Advancement of Learning*.

2472 EVANS, FRANK B. "The Concept of the Fall in Sidney's *Apologie*." *RenP*, 1969, pp. 9–14.
Finds the true "starting point" of Sidney's argument, not in classical philosophy, but in the Christian doctrine of the Fall. Suggests that Sidney exalted poetry because, of all human arts, it best works on the "infected will" and so can repair the effects of original sin. Notes that his view that man's "wit" is "erected" goes against Calvin and hearkens back to Aquinas.

2473 EVANS, MAURICE. "Guyon and the Bower of Sloth." *SP* 61 (April 1964):140–49.
Suggests that the passage in the *Defence* on the second nature created by poets influenced Spenser's Bower of Bliss, both in conception and in language. Concludes that Spenser was suspicious of Sidney's theory of art because it aims to create things "more beautiful than life."

2474 ———. *Spenser's Anatomy of Heroism: A Commentary on "The Faerie Queene."* Cambridge: Cambridge University Press, 1970, pp. 148–50.
Citing the *Defence*, examines Renaissance views on the nature and purpose of the heroic poem. Differentiates between Sidney's faith in the power of "erected wit" to move the "infected will" and Spenser's more skeptical attitude.

2475 FAIRCHILD, HOXIE NEALE. *The Noble Savage: A Study in Romantic Naturalism*. New York: Columbia University Press, 1928, pp. 444–45.
In analyzing Sidney's comments on primitive peoples in the *Defence*, discusses the ancient and widespread tradition that the noble savage is a natural poet.

Twentieth Century

2476 FARGNOLI, JOSEPH. "Patterns of Renaissance Imagination in Sir Philip Sidney's *Defence of Poesie*." *MSE* 8, no. 3 (1982):36–42.
Advances the view that the opening account of John Pietro Pugliano "embodies the form and content of the *Defence* in embryo." Draws upon the theoretical distinction between "first," "second," and "green" worlds as defined by Berger (2407), arguing that the *exordium* "follows the *Defence's* style, epitomized by *energeia* and *sprezzatura*, and includes its categorical shifts from the historical to the subjective to the imaginary and back again."

2477 FARMER, NORMAN [K.], Jr. "Fulke Greville and the Poetic of Plain Style." *TSLL* 11 (Spring 1969):657–70.
Examines Greville's poetic theories as they emerge from his *Life of Sidney* and *A Treaty of Humane Learning*. Finds Greville in frequent agreement with Sidney and notes their common interest in faculty psychology.

2478 FERGUSON, ARTHUR B. *Clio Unbound: Perception of the Social and Cultural Past in Renaissance England*. Duke Monographs in Medieval and Renaissance Studies, 2. Durham, N.C.: Duke University Press, 1979, pp. 29, 33–35, 71, 333.
Treats Sidney's comments on history in the *Defence* as part of a general backlash against Cicero's exaltation of the subject. Feels that Sidney stacks the cards by ignoring the best sort of history being written on the Continent.

2479 FERGUSON, MARGARET W. "Border Territories of Defence: Freud and Defenses of Poetry." In *The Literary Freud: Mechanisms of Defence and the Poetic Will*. Psychiatry and the Humanities, 4. Edited by Joseph H. Smith. New Haven and London: Yale University Press, 1980, pp. 149–80.
Compares Freud on the ego's defences and the interpretation of drama with Sidney on the defence of poetry and the interpretation of literary texts. Notes that defences of poetry such as those by Sidney, Shelley, and Boccaccio break several traditional literary boudaries: they are part of a dialogue beyond their pages; they are often part of another work; and they merge imaginative and critical discourses. Examines Freud's defenses of his own field of psychoanalysis, noting that his strategy, like Sidney's, "involves a complex double movement of attack and courtship, and its aim is not so much to win a verdict of 'innocent' as to lead the prosecution to see that . . . it shares the defendant's position." In Sidney's argument, the philosopher and the historian are shown to share the methods of the poet. Takes Sidney's version of Menenius's "Fable of

the Belly" as an analogue in which Menenius is Sidney and the belly is the poet in conflict with society.

2480 ———. "Sidney's *A Defence of Poetry*: A Retrial." *Boundary 2: A Journal of Postmodern Literature* 7 (Winter 1979):61–95.

Compares Freud's theory of the three main dangers to the ego with Sidney's defense against three sorts of opponents: historians, with their factual truths; immoral poets, with their provocations to the passions; and philosophers or Puritans, with their moralistic aim to banish poets. Regards Menenius Agrippa in the "Fable of the Belly" as an emblem of Sidney's ideal poet and of Sidney himself as a defender of poetry, because Menenius is "at once orator and poet, master and servant" to his audience. Sees the poet as a mediator between reason and the passions and also as a peacemaker in the "civil war among the Muses." Feels that Sidney's claim that the poet is superior to the historian and the philosopher "implies a double standard of value and leads to a questioning as well as an assertion of the poet's claim to superiority." Traces his comments on love poetry to Plato's attacks in the *Republic* and examines Sidney's adaptation of replies in Plutarch's "How the Young Man Should Study Poetry" in the *Moralia*. Sees a major shift in Sidney's argument when he considers love poetry, suggesting that he begins to put limits on the poet's "high-flying wit" and to enlist historians and philosophers as allies. Considers the ironic stance generated by Sidney's comparison of his own defense with Pugliano's defense of horsemanship. Concludes that Sidney's peroration both confirms and denies all that came before it, creating a "circle of irony" from which there is no exit. Suggests that Sidney is ambiguous about self-love, seeing it as both the ground of sin and the ground of education, since the delight that leads to virtue is founded in self-love. Sees the *Defence* as an allegory in which "the reader may find himself in Sidney's images of self-reading," which involve "the Christian's (and, more problematically, the courtier's) paradoxical duty to be master and servant at once." Concludes that Sidney has a Christian and Platonic desire to attack the ego: "By dramatizing the philosopher's and the historian's lack of self-knowledge, by offering examples of an act of critical self-observation, the *Defence* becomes, like the poetry it paradoxically praises, an 'exercise of the mind' aimed at turning the reader 'inward for thorough self-examination.'" Sees the very exercise as egotistical, however, since "the desire to promote virtue in others is also the desire to promote the self in the eyes of others." Discusses his problems in dealing with Queen Elizabeth, comparing his *Letter to the Queen* with the stories of Menenius and of Nathan, the prophet mentioned in the *Defence*.

Twentieth Century

2481 ———. *Trials of Desire: Renaissance Defenses of Poetry*. New Haven, Conn.: Yale University Press, 1983, pp. 137–62, 226–34.
In "Sir Philip Sidney: Pleas for Power," employs Freudian notions of "resistance" and "defence" to explain the ways in which Sidney's "egoistic project" does its work within and upon a "body of culture" that Sidney perceives as a "system of dependent relations." In the first half, considers his defense against philosophy and history as a "revision" of the pastoral convention of the singing match, in which Sidney first "attacks" each of poetry's opponents and then "concedes" to each in such a way as to "imply a double standard of value" that "leads to a questioning as well as an assertion of the poet's claim to superiority." In Sidney's view, the power of poetry is "questionable" because, as an expression of desire, it can be either rightly used or abused. Sidney's defense is thus a "diplomatic" or "mediatory" one, in which the "I" repeatedly stages a "dialogue between a self which speaks and a self which responds critically to that speech." In the second half, examines this "dialogic defense" (in Bakhtin's terms) first as "irony," then as "allegory." Contends that the Pugliano anecdote in the *exordium* is a paradigm of the whole oration: both there and in the *peroratio*, "the text offers the reader a choice not between error and truth but between error and the recognition of the inevitability of error in the self." As one who continually "reflects on his own mode of discourse," Sidney is preoccupied with "the weariness of language," with an "endless turning" that recognizes the likelihood that its designs on the reader may fail. Contending that Sidney's "desire to promote virtue in others is also the desire to promote the self in the eyes of others," discusses Sidney's ambivalent recognition that "neither the courtier nor the author of a written text . . . can make an audience [read "queen"] 'note' his words." This fact makes the *Defence* oscillate between two modes of allegory, an "old" one associated with classical oratory and a "new" one closer to Puttenham's notion of it as the "courtly figure."

2482 FIRESTINE, MARTHA WARN. "The Doctrine of Imitation in the English Renaissance: Roger Ascham, Sir Philip Sidney, and Ben Jonson." Ph.D. Diss., Indiana University, 1974, 295 pp.
Argues that, in the English Renaissance, imitation was not regarded as servile reproduction of a model but as a method of education that required discretion and allowed extensive changes in matter or style. Concludes that, for Sidney, the goal of imitation was general: to emulate the aims and the judgment of the greatest authors. See *DAI* 35 (July 1974):447A.

2483 FLEMING, RUDD. "Plutarch in the English Renaissance." Ph.D. diss., Cornell University, 1935, pp. 216–18. Published abstract. N.p. 1935, 6 pp.

Lists references and allusions to Plutarch in the *Defence* and cites the sources from which they come. Notes that the Renaissance commonplace comparing poetry with a "speaking picture" comes ultimately from Plutarch.

2484 FLOWER, ANNETTE C. "The Critical Context of the Preface to *Samson Agonistes*." *SEL* 10 (Spring 1970):409–23.

Points out similarities between the opening lines of Milton's preface and Sidney's justification of tragedy in the *Defence*.

2485 FOSTER, LESLIE D[ONLEY]. "'I Speak of the Art, and not of the Artificer': The Logical Structure of Sidney's *Defence of Poetry* and the Concessive Arguments." *Hebrew University Studies in Literature* 5 (Autumn 1977):155–81.

Seeks to discover the logical rather than the oratorical structure of the *Defence*. Finds three main arguments: a "Theoretical Defence," in which the value of poetry is demonstrated inductively by a process of definition; a "concessive Practical Defence," which considers the value of poetry in its mode of operation, its genres, and its qualities; and a "concessive Historical Defence," which is concerned with poetry in England and "formulates the poet's power very modestly as reason and good sense." Locates the heart of the book in the first argument, which explores relations between "expressions of the spirit of God and those of the spirit of man." Also suggests that the second argument focuses, not on the poetic artifact, but on spirit as the power (or efficient cause) of poetry.

2486 ———. "Sidney's Praise of Man: A Reassessment of the Nature of the Literary Theory in *The Defence of Poesie*." Ph.D. diss., University of Notre Dame, 1974, 207 pp.

Argues that Sidney sees poetry as a "creative power" which is the "divine essence" and that his fundamental purpose in the *Defence* is to "praise the true nature of man" on the grounds that "to be most fully human is to be most nearly true to the 'divine essence.'" Suggests that he develops his praise of man in contrast to that of Pugliano, in whose view civilization is based on the power of the military or the police rather than on the divine nature. Analyzes three main arguments in the *Defence*: "The first treats poetry as a human *power* or faculty and praises the true spirit of poetry. The second treats poetry as a human *activity* or action (resulting from that power) and praises the morality of that action. The third

Twentieth Century

treats poetry as a human *artifact* (which should be the product of that power) and praises what poetry might be." Concludes that Sidney is a transitional figure between, on the one hand, Christian theologians and classical and medieval theorists of literature and, on the other, critics of the Romantic period. See *DAI* 34 (April 1974):6590A.

2487 FOWLER, A[LASTAIR] D.S., trans. and ed. Introduction to *De Re Poetica*, by Richard Wills. Oxford: Luttrell Society, Basil Blackwell, 1958, pp. 21–38 passim.
Points out many similarities between Wills's Latin treatise and the *Defence*: both are classical orations defending poetry; both employ similar arguments from such sources as J.C. Scaliger, Aristotle, and Plato; and both are Christian as well as classical in their stance. Concludes that Sidney may have used *De Re Poetica* as a formal model and that Wills deserves credit as the first to make Italian criticism available in England.

2488 FOWLER, A[LASTAIR] D.S. "Protestant Attitudes to Poetry, 1560–1590." D.Phil. thesis, Pembroke and Queen's College, Oxford, 1957–58.
Abstract not available. Cited in *Index to Theses Accepted for Higher Degrees in the Universities of Great Britain and Ireland* 8 (1957–58):item 156.

2489 FRANCKEN, EEP. "Rodenburghs bewerking van Sidneys Defence." In *Reisgidsen vol Belluno's en Blauwbaarden: Opstellen over S. Vestdijk en anderen aangeboden aan Dr. H.A. Wage.* Leiden, Netherlands: Publikaties van de Vakgroep Nederlandse Taal- & Letterkunde, 1976, pp. 57–65.
After introductory information on Rodenburgh, discusses his Dutch paraphrase of the *Defence* (99). From details of phrasing suggests that the author followed Ponsonby's version as well as that of Olney, or perhaps a manuscript incorporating features of both. Notes abridgments, errors, and the omission of much of Sidney's digression on English poetry, concluding that the work is of poor quality and obscures the meaning of the original.

2490 FRANTZ, R.W. Letter. *ELH* 6 (March 1939):82.
Responds to an article by Baughan (2401), which suggests that the *Defence* played a part in Swift's creation of the rational horses in Book IV of *Gulliver's Travels*. Points out that Smith first made this connection (in 2638).

2491 FRASER, RUSSELL [A.]. *The Dark Ages and the Age of Gold.* Princeton, N.J.: Princeton University Press, 1973, pp. 3–4, 49, 53,

73–75, 93–94, 127, 140–44, 150–51, 183–84, 262–317 passim, 361–62.

Noting Sidney's tendency to see the Middle Ages as distant and "unciv-il," focuses on the *Defence* as a major contributor to the "great divide" between that period and the "modern" age. Sets out to criticize the modern conception of literature, calling Sidney "the chief of the academy in which the new esthetic [was] fashioned." Sees as crucial his addition of "moving" to "teaching" and "delighting" as one of the ends of poetry, since it makes virtuous action rather than contemplation the aim and implies "a receding of the City of God before the City of Man." Regards Sidney's denigration of his own *Arcadia* and his deathbed wish that the book be burned as signs of guilt that it was not sufficiently useful in the world. Stresses Greville's analysis of the work as a series of "morall Images" and Sidney's characterization of poetry as "medicine" and the beauties of the art as a mere "garment" for truth, noting that these phrases tend to reduce poetry to a form of philosophy tricked out in alluring rhetoric. Pondering Sidney's restless rhetorical inventiveness in *Astrophil and Stella* and his less adorned style in the Psalms, infers that the latter shows the rationalist's faith that "the truth is ascertainable and simple" and needs no metaphors to express it. Contrasts Sidney's claim that poets should use art "to hide Art" with his own practice of showing off his art, as in "Ye goatherd gods" (*OA 71*). Sees him shifting the proper province of poetry from "the business of life" to romance, where he may escape from "his lowly habitation on the bestial floor" to a "golden and more fastidious world." By taking "wit" to mean "imagination" and idealizing the poet who ranges "only within the Zodiac of his own wit," Sidney helped to begin the gradual constriction of the sphere of poetry from the court and the world of affairs to "the nursery or the boudoir." Regards his desire to teach virtue forcefully as the root of the neoclassi-cal tendency to bind art with rules. Since clarity is essential to the pro-ject, the writer must adhere to such conventions as the classical unities and decorum in the drama, simple causal structure in the main plot of the epic, and classical meters in verse. Concludes that, in the modern aesthetic inaugurated by Sidney and others in the Renaissance, "as the motive of art is not to pay homage to the visible world but to recast it, so the motive of life is not simply to live but to query and reconstitute the basis of living."

2492 ———. "Sidney the Humanist." *SAQ* 66 (Winter 1967):87–91. Defines humanism as the "devotion to use, rather than to beauty as an end in itself" and suggests that Sidney is the humanist par excellence.

Twentieth Century

Emphasizes the pragmatism and social expediency of the *Defence*, suggesting that Sidney considered poetry something of only temporary usefulness, which may be discarded as people become better able to handle reality. Discusses Fulke Greville's comments on Sidney's "moral images" and compares the practice of Shakespeare.

2493 FRYE, NORTHROP. "The Critical Path: An Essay on the Social Context of Literary Criticism." In *In Search of Literary Theory*, edited by Morton W. Bloomfield. Studies in the Humanities. Ithaca, N.Y.: Cornell University Press, 1972, pp. 91–193.

Discusses statements in the *Defence* on early oral poets such as Homer. Feels that Sidney shows the bias of his culture in that he treats prose as the "primary verbal expression of reality" and regards poetry simply as a persuasive expression of things more precisely said in prose. Thus, he prizes poetry primarily for its sententious statements and illustrations. Also seeks to explain the loss in later criticism of Sidney's sense of the poet's social relevance, specifically in teaching religion. Contrasts the views in Shelley's *Defence of Poetry*.

2494 GORDON, IAN A. *John Skelton: Poet Laureate*. Melbourne: Melbourne University Press; London: Oxford University Press, 1943, pp. 63–66.

Considers ways in which Skelton's *Replycacion* anticipates Renaissance works such as Sidney's *Defence*.

2495 GRAFF, GERALD. *Poetic Statement and Critical Dogma*. Evanston, Ill.: Northwestern University Press, 1970, pp. 161, 180–83.

Discusses Sidney's concept of decorum. Also argues for a middle ground between critics who assert that Sidney regards poetry as a mere sugarcoating on a philosophical pill and those who feel that he denies the poet's responsibility to convey any truths whatever.

2496 GREENE, THOMAS. *The Descent from Heaven: A Study in Epic Continuity*. New Haven, Conn.: Yale University Press, 1963, pp. 295–98.

Notes Sidney's reluctance to urge poets to imitate the classics, classifying his concept of epic poetry as medieval.

2497 GREENLAW, EDWIN A. "The Shepheards Calender." *PMLA* 26, no. 3 (1911):419–51.

Explains Sidney's "cold praise" for *The Shepherd's Calendar* as a prudent response to Spenser's outspoken opposition to the French marriage. Notes that, at the time Sidney was composing the *Defence*, he was suffering the Queen's displeasure for addressing a letter to her on the same subject. Concludes that it would not have been "politic" to praise "a work under suspicion in itself and written by a man whom it had been found expedient to send out of the country." For a reply, see Baskervill (2398).

2498 GREGORY, E[LMER] R[ICHARD], Jr. "Du Bartas, Sidney, and Spenser." *CLS* 7 (December 1970):437–49.

Rebuts the idea that Sidney and du Bartas were opposed in their poetic theories. Emphasizes their common belief that poetry has a serious religious function and that it leads to evil only if misused.

2499 HALIO, JAY L. "The Metaphor of Conception and Elizabethan Theories of the Imagination." *Neophilologus* 50 (October 1966):454–61.

Points out that the *Defence* is one of the few works of the English Renaissance that suggests that "the imagination was not . . . merely a reproductive faculty of the intellect, but was frequently, and even essentially, creative."

2500 HALL, VERNON. *Renaissance Literary Criticism: A Study of Its Social Content.* New York: Columbia University Press, 1945, p. 212. Orig. a Ph.D. diss., University of Wisconsin at Madison, 1940.

Considers Sidney's views on tragicomedy and on the role of poetry in teaching aristocratic virtues.

2501 HALLAM, GEORGE W[ALTER, Jr.]. "Sidney's Supposed Ramism." *RenP*, 1963, pp. 11–20.

Considers Milton's statement in his *Fuller Institution of the Art of Logic* that Sidney held Ramus as "the best writer on this art." Reviews evidence linking Sidney with Ramus, noting that there is no reference to the logician in Sidney's writings. Analyzes the structure of the *Defence* as an illustration of Ramus's "prudential" and "natural" methods of argument and of his ten "topical places of invention." Discusses William Temple's manuscript treatise *Analysis Tractationis de Poesi*, which also traces Ramist arguments in the *Defence*. Concludes that, as "a piece of a logician," Sidney accepted Ramism, but that, as a poet, he saw its limitations.

2502 HAMILTON, A.C. "Elizabethan Romance: The Example of Prose Fiction." *ELH* 49 (Summer 1982):287–99.

Contends that the "defining characteristic" of Elizabethan prose fiction is "found in the immediate, powerful impact on the reader of the separate episodes, each of which calls for a full response, and [is] complex in being both primitive and sophisticated." Suggests that the poetics for

Twentieth Century

this romance was "first provided" by Sidney's *Defence*, specifically the doctrine that the poet's golden world "enchants, even ravishes the reader with delight."

2503 ———. "Sidney and Agrippa." *RES*, n.s. 7 (April 1956): 151–57. Reprinted with revisions in item 2506.
Details parallels between the *Defence* and Cornelius Agrippa's *De Vanitate Scientiarum et Artium*. Notes that both authors defend poetry by attacking the other arts, arguing that only poetry aims at self-knowledge and is not bound to the senses but to incorruptible ideas. Suggests that Sidney saw in Agrippa's treatise, not a scurrilous attack on learning, but a defense of Christian liberty—a vision of things as they should be rather than a "knowledge" of things as they are.

2504 ———. "Sidney's Idea of the 'Right Poet.'" *CL* 9 (Winter 1957):51–59. Reprinted with revisions in item 2506.
Contends that Sidney's definition of the "right poet" is not simply borrowed from J.C. Scaliger but is an original integration of material from Aristotle, Plato, and Horace. Notes Sidney's brilliance in responding to Plato by creating a kind of poet that the philosopher had not discussed and then by giving this poet the very Platonic function of imitating Ideas. Also notes Sidney's refinements of Scaliger's views on the ends of poetry and its function in creating a second nature. Regarding the neo-Platonic and Christian background of Sidney's position, points out that his poet not only moves but "moves *upwards* and so supplements the power of grace." See a reply by Pontedera (2604).

2505 ———. *Sir Philip Sidney: A Study of His Life and Works*. Cambridge: Cambridge University Press, 1977, pp. 107–22.
In Chapter 4, considers the *Defence*, discussing its date, its personal tone, its logic, and its "revolutionary" originality. Notes Sidney's departures from the criticism of J.C. Scaliger, his ingenuity in eluding the attacks of Plato, and his Christian assumptions in defining his poetics. Considers his emphasis on the doctrine of the Fall and his "Augustinian-Calvinist" conception of the infected will. Examines the way in which his ideal poet surpasses nature and draws souls to virtue, concluding that, in Sidney's view, the poet's aim is to provide a secular analogue to a religious vision, an image of outward beauty that displays inward virtue. Finds an example of the fulfillment of this aim in the New *Arcadia*. See also item 550.

2506 ———. *The Structure of Allegory in "The Faerie Queene."* Oxford: Clarendon Press, 1961, pp. 17–30, 56–57, 60–61, 124–27, 208. Orig. a Ph.D. diss., Jesus College, Cambridge University, 1953.

Presents a revised and expanded version of material in 2503 and 2504. Also rejects the view that Sidney opposed allegory, finding in his statement that poets imitate Ideas rather than nature an implicit theory of allegory. Compares the *Defence* with Spenser's prefatory letter to Ralegh and treats Sidney's views as the critical basis for reading *The Faerie Queene*. Sees Book I as a tragedy of the sort described in the *Defence*. Also argues that Sidney's "real enemy" was not Stephen Gosson but du Bartas and others who sought to write religious poetry.

2507 HAMILTON, K.G. *The Two Harmonies: Poetry and Prose in the Seventeenth Century.* Oxford: Clarendon Press, 1963, pp. 78, 86–89, 121, 123, 131–34, 138, 146–47.

Considers the mixture of Aristotelian, Horatian, and Platonic elements in the *Defence*. Concludes that, in the seventeenth century, the treatise was important because it analyzed poetry philosophically and didactically rather than rhetorically and because it gave the science of poetics a place outside the trivium. Places John Dryden, Sir Francis Bacon, and Ben Jonson in the same tradition of criticism as Sidney. Also discusses the historical context of Sidney's theory of imagination.

2508 HANSEN, DAVID A. "Addison on Ornament and Poetic Style." In *Studies in Criticism and Aesthetics, 1660–1800: Essays in Honor of Samuel Holt Monk.* Minneapolis: University of Minnesota Press, 1967, pp. 94–127.

Offers reasons that Joseph Addison and John Dennis take exception to Sidney's comments on the ballad *Chevy Chase*.

2509 HARDISON, O.B., Jr. *The Enduring Monument: A Study of the Idea of Praise in Renaissance Literary Theory and Practice.* Chapel Hill: University of North Carolina Press, 1962, pp. 7, 43–44, 49, 53–54, 88, 95, 104, 193.

Places the *Defence* in a long tradition of works suggesting "that poetry is (or at times can be) a form of theology." Argues that the book is organized as an answer to Plato's charges against poetry in the *Republic*. Suggests that, when Sidney proposes "to weigh this latter sort of poetry by his works, and then by his parts," the word "works" means "moral effects" and draws upon a long tradition in which poetry is defended on the grounds that it praises virtue and blames vice. Notes the influence of Plato on Sidney's definition of lyric poetry.

Twentieth Century

2510 ———. "The Two Voices of Sidney's *Apology for Poetry.*" *ELR* 2 (Winter 1972):83–99.
Discusses Sidney's adherence to the form of a classical oration, noting its presence in two other poetic treatises: Bernardino Daniello's *Poetics* and John Rainolds's *Oratio in Laudem Artis Poeticae*. Arguing against Myrick's outline of the *Defence* (671), which is based on Cicero and Quintilian, contends that Sidney's interest in Aristotle's *Rhetoric* and in Ramism freed him from such rigidity of outline. Proposes that Sidney originally composed the work in the "voice" of a humanist in the tradition espoused by Boccaccio, Politianus, and Tasso. The work followed a simple outline: introduction, three major proofs, refutation, and peroration. Later, Sidney became interested in neoclassical poetics in the manner of J.C. Scaliger, Lodovico Castelvetro, and Ben Jonson and therefore inserted the long neoclassical critique of English poetry. Explicates key passages in the *Defence* according to this scheme, noting parallels in other treatises from the humanist and neoclassical traditions. See replies by Baxter (2402), Raitière (2607), and Sinfield (2636).

2511 HARRIER, RICHARD. "Invention in Tudor Literature: Historical Perspectives." In *Philosophy and Humanism: Renaissance Essays in Honor of Paul Oskar Kristeller*, edited by Edward P. Mahoney. New York: Columbia University Press, 1976, pp. 370–86.
Argues that Sidney, like other Tudor writers, regarded prose and poetry as rhetorical "instruments" of persuasion or proof. Examines Sidney's attempt in the *Defence* to combine the neo-Platonic view that art imitates Ideas with the Aristotelian position that it imitates nature. Argues that Sidney's central premise is that "poetry, oratory, and reason" all work "through participation in man's divine essence, his erected wit." Contrasts Sidney's definition of the term "style" with our own, emphasizing the greater freedom for invention in Sidney's view. Suggests that he analyzed all uses of language in terms of rhetorical tropes and figures.

2512 HATHAWAY, BAXTER. *The Age of Criticism: The Late Renaissance in Italy*. Ithaca, N.Y.: Cornell University Press, 1962, pp. 132, 326–27.
Considers Sidney's position that poetry lies midway between philosophy and history, noting similar views in the work of Agnolo Segni. Links Sidney's discussion of the "golden" world of poetry with the criticism of Sperone Speroni and Girolamo Fracastoro.

2513 ———. *Marvels and Commonplaces: Renaissance Literary Criticism.* New York: Random House, 1968, pp. 88–109 passim, 116, 159, 165.

Differentiates the *Defence* from genuine works of literary criticism and connects it with antecedents in the first half of the sixteenth century rather than in the second. Discusses the relative influence of Plato, Ficino, and Aristotle, distinguishing Sidney's concept of poetic imitation from Aristotelian *mimesis*. Links Sidney's concept of the "golden world" of poetry with similar notions in the work of Girolamo Fracastoro and Sperone Speroni. In the long controversy over the proper use of poetic imagination, places Sidney with Italian proponents of the marvelous and the feigned. Traces the English tradition derived from Sidney's brand of Platonism to George Puttenham, Sir John Harington, George Chapman, and Sir Francis Bacon. Notes that Thomas Hobbs follows the same line as Sidney in giving poetry a place above philosophy in teaching morality. Contrasts Sidney with Giraldi Cinthio and other Italians who regard the fantastic elements of romance as decorative rather than instructive.

2514 HAYDEN, JOHN O. *Polestar of the Ancients: The Aristotelian Tradition in Classical and English Literary Criticism.* Newark: University of Delaware Press; London: Associated University Presses, 1979, pp. 14, 17–27, 100–117, 176.

Defines the Aristotelian tradition in English criticism on the basis of five characteristic aims: *mimesis*, universality, morality, empiricism, and flexibility. In Chapter 5, "Sir Philip Sidney," lists the principal critics that Sidney drew upon in the *Defence*. Rejects the view that he was writing in response to Stephen Gosson's *School of Abuse*, citing more important opponents such as Savanarola and Cornelius Agrippa. Suggests that Sidney's literary theory shows the first signs of neoclassical dogmatism, noting ways in which it does and does not follow Aristotelian doctrine. Emphasizes his failure to harmonize Platonic idealism with Aristotle's doctrines of *mimesis* and universality. Feels that Sidney's views on the moral effects of literature are more simplistic and "narrow" than Aristotle's. Also notes that Wordsworth's "Reply to 'Mathetes'" echoes Sidney's statement that "the ending end of all earthly learning [is] virtuous action."

2515 HEARSEY, MARGUERITE. "Sidney's *Defence of Poesy* and Amyot's *Preface* in North's *Plutarch*: A Relationship." *SP* 30 (October 1933):535–50.

Discounts the possibility that Sidney wrote the *Defence* in reply to Stephen Gosson's *School of Abuse* or that he borrowed his ideas on the

Twentieth Century

nature of poetry chiefly from the Italians. Suggests a better source for these ideas in Jacques Amyot's preface to Plutarch's *Lives*, which extols the value of history. Finds in Amyot "not only claims for history which needed refutation, but arguments that could be well turned to the defence of poetry, and also a model in manner and style. . . ." Also considers the possibility that both Sidney and Amyot were influenced by Boccaccio's *De Genealogia Deorum*.

2516 HENINGER, S.K., Jr. "'Metaphor' and Sidney's *Defence of Poesie*." *JDJ* 1 (1982):117–49.

Considers the *Defence* as a means to further Sidney's Protestant social agenda. Notes the confluence in his thought of neo-Platonic idealism, Protestant faith in the word, humanist concern with arts of persuasion, and Aristotelian theories of the power of imagery. Examines his terms "imitation" and "metaphor," noting that his definition of poetry depends on a crux. Prefers the punctuation in Ponsonby's edition ("figuring forth to speake Metaphorically. A speaking *Picture* . . .") to that in Olney's ("figuring foorth: to speake metaphorically, a speaking picture . . ."). Examines authoritative texts, arguing against van Dorsten's punctuation (22) and noting that Ponsonby's punctuation neatly separates Aristotle's contribution to the definition from that of Plutarch and Horace. Explicates passages on metaphor in Aristotle's *Poetics* and *Rhetoric*, emphasizing the concept of *energeia*, in which a metaphor becomes a means to produce quasi-visual images to heighten vividness. Traces the Aristotelian concept through Cicero and Quintilian to Erasmus and Elizabethan rhetoricians such as Thomas Wilson. Concludes that Sidney "is thinking of poetry as one of the arts of discourse, an *ars dicendi*, using the technique of energeiac metaphor and having the aim of persuading an audience." See also DeNeef (2453) and van Dorsten (2665).

2517 ——. "Sidney and Boethian Music." *SEL* 23 (Winter 1983): 37–46.

Argues that the *Defence* was written at a cultural turning point, when poetry ceased to be associated most closely with music and came to be associated with painting. Explores the implications of Sidney's final comments on the "planet-like music of poetry," discussing the interrelations between three sorts of music defined in Boethius's *De Musica*: *musica mundana*, *musica humana*, and *musica instrumentalis*. Explains these interrelations on the basis of Platonic epistemology, in which the sensuous experience of reading a poem leads to the intellectual conception of divine Ideas. Suggests that, in Sidney's words, the poem leads to "the knowledge of a man's self" because it reveals that, like the cosmos, the mind is ordered by divine providence, and this harmony of soul leads naturally to virtuous ethical and political action. Also explores Sidney's comments on metrics—the weighing of syllables "by just proportion." Suggests a correlation between Sidney's poet and God, the arch-geometer, who created the cosmos by number, weight, and measure. Considers the influence of the French Pléiade upon the quantitative verse experiments of Sidney and his circle. Notes, however, that Sidney's interest in virtuous action and in Aristotelian imitation led him to a poetic related to painting. Sees *Arcadia* as a poem without meter, based on a poetic aimed at "feigning notable images of virtues, vices, or what else."

2518 ———. "Sidney and Milton: The Poet as Maker." In *Milton and the Line of Vision*, edited by Joseph Anthony Wittreich, Jr. Madison: University of Wisconsin Press, 1975, pp. 57–95.

Lists Milton's references to Sidney's works, finding no direct evidence that he knew the *Defence*. Argues, however, that he was writing in the tradition of Sidney and Spenser and shared their poetic. For all three, the poet imitates God by creating a "second nature" and employs literature to religious and political ends. Discusses Sidney's concept of the poetic "maker" as an image of the divine Maker, tracing it back through du Bartas's *La semaine* to Plato's *Timaeus*. Notes that, in this view, both nature and the "second nature" of the poem derive from the same "archetypal idea" and follow the same creative process: from "fore-conceit" to something made. Relates this view to Raphael's lesson to Adam in *Paradise Lost* VII.176–79 that the acts of God, which are "immediate," must be rendered sequentially by "process of speech." Points out that the reading of such a poem is thus a process of drawing from the sequential narration a single underlying Idea or "form" of the work. Contrasts this process with the reading of allegory. Relates Sidney's poetic to the practice of Spenser in the *Shepherd's Calendar* and of Milton in *Paradise Lost* and the lesser poems.

2519 ———. "Sidney and Serranus' *Plato*." *ELR* 13 (Spring 1983): 146–61.

Describes a Greek edition of Plato by Henri Estienne with a Latin translation by Jean de Serres, noting that Sidney had connections with the compilers and was sent a complimentary copy. Translates the *argumentum* printed before the *Ion*, suggesting that it was an intermediate between J.C. Scaliger's poetics and Sidney's. Lists points that Sidney may have borrowed from de Serres, notably his division of poets into three classes; his definitions of *eikastike* and *phantastike*; and his derivation of

Twentieth Century

the word "poet" from the Greek verb meaning "to make." Concludes that "in no other treatise of even considerably greater length is there a comparable concentration of topics, terms, and phrases that Sidney thought of sufficient importance to dwell upon."

2520 ———. "Speaking Pictures: Sidney's Rapprochement between Poetry and Painting." In *Sir Philip Sidney and the Interpretation of Renaissance Culture: The Poet in His Time and in Ours: A Collection of Critical and Scholarly Essays,* edited by Gary F. Waller and Michael D. Moore. London: Croom Helm; Totowa, N.J.: Barnes & Noble, 1984, pp. 3–16.

Traces the convergence of a number of forces, from classical times to the Renaissance, in a "time-honored tradition for interrelating poetry and painting, and for seeing both as systematic systems that borrowed from one another and that were most expressive when used in conjuction." Appearing at a "node in our cultural history, where the prevalent esthetics was turning from a dependence upon the formal criteria of proportion and verging toward an empirical basis in the accurate observation and description of physical nature," Sidney introduces a "syncretic poetics" in which "images direct their sensuous appeal to the mind's eye." See also Evans (1527).

2521 ———. *Touches of Sweet Harmony: Pythagorean Cosmology and Renaissance Poetics.* San Marino, Calif.: Huntington Library, 1974, pp. 3–7, 287–309, 325, 338–39, 344, 365–66, 382–93 passim.

Places Sidney's statement on the "planet-like music of poetry" in the Pythagorean tradition, which suggests musical correspondences between the cosmic order of nature and the earthly order of art. Also examines Sidney's concept of the poet as "maker," tracing it to Cristoforo Landino and to Plato (in the *Timaeus*). Notes that, like God, the poet begins the act of creation with a Word—an Idea or "fore-conceit"—from which he creates a "second nature." Distinguishes such a poet from a *vates,* who writes by divine revelation, and from a philosophical or didactic poet, who merely produces an Aristotelian imitation of nature. Finds the essence of poetry, in Sidney's view, in the framing of metaphors that link abstract generalities with concrete particulars. Considers the influence of Sidney's concept of the "maker" on other critics such as William Webbe, George Puttenham, and Ben Jonson, and on poets such as Shakespeare and Milton. Notes that an altogether different poetic underlies metaphysical and Augustan poetry. Also notes an implication of Sidney's theory: that the reader must reread in order to perceive the inherent Idea. Since it is embodied in the relationship between all the parts, it cannot be grasped in one sequential reading.

2522 HERFORD, C.H., and SIMPSON, PERCY, eds. *Ben Jonson*. Vol. 1, *The Man and His Work*. Oxford: Clarendon Press, 1925, pp. 10–11, 335–42 passim.

Notes the strong influence of the *Defence* on Jonson's critical writings and on his play *Every Man in His Humour*.

2523 HERRICK, MARVIN T[HEODORE]. *Comic Theory in the Sixteenth Century*. Illinois Studies in Language and Literature, 34. Urbana: University of Illinois Press, 1950, pp. 21–23, 26, 37, 53–55, 75, 87–88, 146.

Discusses the traditions behind Sidney's terms *prosopopoeias* and *mimesis*, his emphasis upon delight as an aim of poetry, his preference for poetry over history, his dislike of popular tragicomedy, and his classical theory of comedy. Traces his warning against provoking vain laughter to Aristotle's *Nicomachean Ethics*.

2524 ———. *The Fusion Of Horatian and Aristotelian Literary Criticism, 1531–1555*. Illinois Studies in Language and Literature, 32. Urbana: University of Illinois Press, 1946, pp. 1, 26, 36–37, 46–47, 56, 65–66, 82.

Points out that Sidney was part of a broad Renaissance trend to mingle the poetic theories of Aristotle and Horace. Discusses Sidney's debts to them on the topics of nature and art, imitation, the aims of poetry, decorum, epic versus tragic poetry, and the dramatic unities.

2525 ———. *The Poetics of Aristotle in England*. Cornell Studies in English, 17. New Haven, Conn.: Yale University Press; London: Oxford University Press, for Cornell University, 1930, pp. 24–29, 38–39.

Lists works of Aristotle that Sidney seems to have known and discusses the influence of the *Poetics* on the *Defence*. Gives Sidney credit for establishing Aristolelian criticism in England. Feels, however, that Sidney did not understand Aristotle's theory of organic unity and that he was closer to Minturno than to Aristotle in his moral interpretation of *catharsis* and in his stress on "admiration" in tragedy. Traces to Sidney several Aristotelian ideas in the criticism of Ben Jonson.

2526 ———. "The Theory of the Laughable in the Sixteenth Century." *QJS* 35 (February 1949):1–16.

Traces the classical and Italian roots of a passage in the *Defence* in which Sidney seems to suggest that the laughter aroused by comedy should be mingled with admiration.

Twentieth Century

2527 ———. "Trissino's *Art of Poetry.*" In *Essays on Shakespeare and Elizabethan Drama in Honor of Hardin Craig*, edited by Richard Hosley. Columbia: University of Missouri Press, 1962, pp. 15–22.

Examines three passages in the *Defence* on which Giangiorgio Trissino's *Poetica* may have exerted a direct influence: the discussion of laughter and delight in comedy; the definition of poetry; and the praise of epic for its portrayal of virtuous heroes. Concludes that the latter two involved nothing but commonplaces of Renaissance criticism and that only the passage on comedy bears the identifiable imprint of Trissino's theories. Also seeks to explain Sidney's moral strictures against excessive laughter, considering Cicero's *De Oratore* and Renaissance mistranslations of the term "*hamartêma*" in Aristotle's *Poetics*.

2528 HERRON, DALE. "The Focus of Allegory in the Renaissance Epic." *Genre* 3 (June 1970):176–86.

Considers the failure of late medieval and Renaissance poets to create an epic like Virgil's that "sums up" contemporary society. Cites the *Defence* in arguing that Sidney and other poets of the period were less concerned with contemporary life than with a timeless, golden, prelapsarian world.

2529 HORTON, RONALD ARTHUR. *The Unity of "The Faerie Queene."* Athens: University of Georgia Press, 1978, pp. 57–58, 81–82, 184.

Notes that Spenser and Sidney held comparable views on the ends of poetry. Also considers Sidney's ambivalence toward lawyers in the *Defence*, suggesting that he found civil justice noble but limited in its power to improve morality.

2530 HYDE, MARY CRAPO. *Playwriting for Elizabethans, 1600–1605.* New York: Columbia University Press, 1949, pp. 10–12.

From the passage on English plays in the *Defence*, concludes that Sidney had "no real understanding" of the theater, made a "faulty interpretation of Aristotle," and focused on trivia.

2531 HYMAN, VIRGINIA RILEY. "Sidney's Definition of Poetry." *SEL* 10 (Winter 1970):49–62.

Examines the survey of other theories of poetry that precedes Sidney's own definition. Argues that his discussion of these other theories is not merely a rhetorical embellishment but an integral part of Sidney's method of definition. He proceeds by selecting views similar to his own but more extravagant in their claims. He then wins the audience by setting more modest and rational boundaries for the term "poetry." By these means, he also arrives at a definition that is "the sum of the other theories reduced to their ethical and rational level."

2532 JENKINS, OWEN. "The Art of History in Renaissance England: A Chapter in the History of Literary Criticism." Ph.D. diss., Cornell University, 1954.

Examines the modern divorce between history and poetry, pointing out that English writers of the early Renaissance do not endorse the separation. Both history and poetry "were thought to provide examples of the precepts of philosophy, and for most purposes . . . it was not necessary to distinguish between them." Suggests that Sidney began the modern trend by emphasizing the differences between the two arts. See *DA* 15, no. 1 (1955):123–24.

2533 JONES, THORA BURNLEY, and NICOL, BERNARD de BEAR. *Neo-Classical Dramatic Criticism 1560–1770.* Cambridge: Cambridge University Press, 1976, pp. 36–43.

Reviews Sidney's critical position and its origins in Italian criticism.

2534 KAHN, VICTORIA ANN. "Authority and Interpretation in the Renaissance: Erasmus, Sidney, and Montaigne." Ph.D. diss., Yale University, 1979, 302 pp.

Concerned with ways in which the authors question medieval notions of authority and show renewed interest in "prudence, or excellence in deliberation about the right cause of action," argues that the *Defence* tries to ensure the persuasiveness of poetry through a neo-Platonic "strategy" of referring ideas in the individual's mind to those in the mind of God. See *DAI* 40 (December 1979):3283A.

2535 KAMHOLTZ, JONATHAN Z. "Ben Jonson's Green World: Structure and Imaginative Unity in *The Forrest.*" *SP* 78 (Spring 1981):170–93.

Feels that, though Jonson "redefines Sidney's goals," the spirit of Sidney hovers over *The Forest*. Claims that, in comparing himself to Sidney, Jonson sees himself as the ideal poet of the *Defence*: a creator imitating God's primary act of creation.

2536 KELTY, JEAN McCLURE. "The Frontispiece of Ben Jonson's 1616 Folio: A Critical Commentary on the Elizabethan Stage." *TA* 17 (1960):22–35.

Suggests that Jonson's frontispiece protests satirically against "a generation that . . . did not fulfill its responsibility to the priest-like purpose of art. . . . It represents pictorially the critical comments of Sir Philip

Twentieth Century

Sidney." Notes that the folio addresses itself to concerns about the English stage expressed in the *Defence*.

2537 KER, W[ILLIAM] P[ATON]. *Form and Style in Poetry: Lectures and Notes.* Edited by R[aymond] W[ilson] Chambers. London: Macmillan & Co., 1928, pp. 196, 337.
Praises the *Defence* as "one of the strangest mixtures in literature—the work of an ironical wit who at the same time respected and reverenced the pedantic authorities, and ideals that are conventionally planned, lacking in true life." Notes that the "great dialogue on romance and the drama at the end of the first part of *Don Quixote*" contains striking parallels with the *Defence*. Also finds a link between Sidney and Cervantes in the latter's use of Heliodorus in *Persiles y Sigismunda*.

2538 KIEFER, FREDERICK. *Fortune and Elizabethan Tragedy.* [San Marino, Calif.: Huntington Library, 1983, pp. 72–73.
Regards Sidney's definition of tragedy in the *Defence* as essentially Senecan, comparing it with similar passages by Alexander Neville and George Puttenham. Sees in all three a tension between pagan notions of fortune and Christian or Stoic concepts of divine justice.

2539 KIMBROUGH, ROBERT. *Sir Philip Sidney.* Twayne's English Authors Series, 114. New York: Twayne Publishers, 1971, pp. 38–62.
In Chapter 2, using Thomas Wilson's *Art of Rhetoric* as a guide, examines the rhetorical structure and strategies of the *Defence*, assuming that Sidney worked on it over a period of four years (1578–82) and that it is "a cumulative expresssion of theories and ideas to which [he] had been exposed from grammar school on." Underlying Sidney's theory is an idea of "imitation" based on "integrity," that is, on writers having made what they learn "wholly theirs." Differs with Myrick (2580) on the divisions within the oration, placing greater stress on the *narratio*, and arguing that *sprezzatura* is only part of the work's ethos. Also contends that the speaker's masks are more varied than Myrick had assumed. Contends that Sidney's definition of imagination "lies behind" that of Wordsworth and Keats. Claims that critical emphasis on the rhetorical organization of the *Defence* tends to obscure its "simple but profound" aesthetic theory, in which the prime attribute of poetry is that it delights: "the manner stimulates; the delight of matter instructs." Finds Sidney's idea that the poem moves to "well doing" grounded in the Aristotelian, Thomistic tradition, which, though nowhere referred to explicitly, is "assumed throughout." Notes that, unlike most Italian critics, Sidney was "interested in a variety of qualities and not rigorously defined categories." Argues that he evalu-

ates and criticizes the current state of English poetry from the premise that the inner experience of the poet is "all important." Concludes that the *Defence* is the "perfect fruition" of Sidney's education, "at the center of which was rhetoric [disposition], framed by grammar [elocution] and logic [invention]." See also item 593.

2540 KINNEY, ARTHUR F. "Parody and Its Implication in Sydney's *Defense of Poesie.*" *SEL* 12 (Winter 1972):1–19.
Argues that the *Defence* "consciously parallels and burlesques Stephen Gosson's *School of Abuse.*" Discusses the form of the classical oration employed by both authors and numerous similarities in the issues examined, the authorities and illustrations cited, and the euphuistic style employed in the two works. Concludes that, since he disliked the crudity of Gosson's work, Sidney "resorted to parody to mask the similarity of his own argument." Dates the *Defence* in the months just after Gosson's book appeared.

2541 KISHLER, THOMAS C. "Aristotle and Sidney on Imitation." *CJ* 59 (November 1963):63–64.
Compares the concept of imitation in Aristotle's *Poetics* with that in the *Defence.* Concludes that, whereas Sidney's ideal poet transcends philosophy by his "glimpses of the ideal world," Aristotle's ideal poet merely approaches philosophy by discovering universal forms in concrete objects.

2542 KLEIN, K.L. "Rhetorik und Dichtungslehre in der elizabethanischen Zeit." In *Festschrift zum 75. Geburtstag von Theodor Spira*, edited by H[elmut] Viebrock and W[ilhelm] Erzgräber. Heidelberg: Carl Winter Universitätsverlag, 1961, pp. 164–83.
Claims that Sidney's theory of poetic style, unlike that of Ascham and Puttenham, maintains a dichotomy between matter and manner. The "dress" of eloquence is not always tailored to the "body" of idea.

2543 KNOWLTON, EDGAR C. "Sir Philip Sidney on Italian Rhymes." *N&Q,* n.s. 16 (December 1969):455–56.
Refutes Sidney's claim in the *Defence* that there are no masculine rhymes in Italian.

2544 KOHL, NORBERT. "Zur Rezeption der Antike in Sir Philip Sidneys *Defence of Poesie.*" *Literaturwissenschaftliches Jahrbuch* (Görres-Gesellschaft) 21 (1980):39–56.
Reviews ways in which ancient criticism, philosophy, rhetoric, and history contributed to the *Defence.* After tracing Sidney's education and his contact with intellectuals during his European tour of 1572–75, discusses

the aims of the *Defence*, its organization as a classical oration, and its rhetorical strategies. Relates Sidney's position on the moral function of poetry to Aristotle's concept of *mimesis*, to Christian notions of virtue, and to contemporary views of the moral value of historical writing. Lists Continental authors who exalt history over poetry, suggesting that Sidney's work may have been directed against them as well as the English Puritans. Because Sidney's letters to his brother Robert and to Edward Denny stress, not poetry, but history, moral philosophy, and the Bible, concludes that the *Defence* may have been written "tongue in cheek" as a rhetorical exercise.

2545 KRIEGER, MURRAY. "The Critic as Person and Persona." In *The Personality of the Critic*, edited by Joesph P. Strelka. Yearbook of Comparative Criticism, 6. University Park and London: Pennsylvania State University Press, 1973, pp. 70–92.

Discusses the ambivalence in Sidney's view that the poet is both a free creator and an imitator of neo-Platonic universals.

2546 ———. *The New Apologists for Poetry*. Minneapolis: University of Minnesota Press, 1956, pp. 171–72, 177.

Discusses Sidney's response to Plato's rejection of poets in the *Republic*. Asserts that, by treating poetry as a conveyor of "propositional truth," Sidney made the art essentially decorative—a sugarcoating on a philosophical pill. Contrasts Sidney's view with that of F.W.J. Schelling.

2547 ———. "Northrop Frye and Contemporary Criticism: Ariel and the Spirit of Gravity." In *Northrop Frye in Modern Criticism: Selected Papers from the English Institute*, edited by Murray Krieger. New York: Columbia University Press, 1966, pp. 1–26.

Compares Frye's critical position with Sidney's, noting in common the distinction between brazen and golden worlds, the comparison of poetic imagination with the zodiac, and the distinction of wit from will. The two differ because, while Frye can "go all the way to the golden world of man's wit and remain in it," Sidney is "pulled back to the dully imitative by the conservative Italian critical tradition that claims him." Notes that, unlike Sidney, "Frye explicitly and continually divorces his humanistic-romantic attitude from all metaphysical claims, so that his golden world is the product only of the human imagination and has no other sanction."

2548 ———. "Poetic Presence and Illusion: Renaissance Theory and the Duplicity of Metaphor." *CritI* 5 (Summer 1979):597–619. Reprint. In *Poetic Presence and Illusion: Essays in Critical History and*

Theory, by Murray Krieger. Baltimore and London: Johns Hopkins University Press, 1979, pp. 3–25.

Finds conflicts between the passages in the *Defence* which suggest that the poet creates "another nature" and those that suggest that he aims at universals and moral teaching. Also claims that Sidney had "a need to summon the sublime presence; and the act of invocation itself—together with the presence with which it unites—dissolves the empty incapacities of the language that normally struggles on its own." Sees *Astrophil and Stella* as "an invocation for [Stella's] presence to invade the present poem and to dissolve its differences into her identity." Feels that her presence "turns words against themselves, using their self-contradictions to reveal the bankruptcy of language." Concludes that poets such as Sidney and Shakespeare "can accept words as insubstantial entities existing on their own, not to be confounded with their signifieds" but that Sidney goes on to "create a willful illusion of verbal substance."

2549 KROUSE, F. MICHAEL. "Plato and Sidney's *Defence of Poesie*." *CL* 6 (Spring 1954):138–47.

Argues that Samuel (2627) overstates Plato's influence on the *Defence*, pointing out that she ignores possible intermediaries between Plato and Sidney and fails to take account of Plato's views on myth. Suggests that the *Defence* "relies principally upon Plato for its fundamental conceptions of the nature of poetry and poetry's ethical effects, but principally upon Aristotle for its treatment of the formal aspects of poetry and . . . the relationship between form and function." Sees a connection between Sidney's comments on the power of poetry to move as well as to teach and Plato's view that myth is needed to arouse the passions in support of the conclusions reached by dialectic.

2550 KUHN, URSULA. "English Literary Terms in Poetological Texts of the Sixteenth Century." Ph.D. diss., Universität Münster, 1972, 1072 pp.

Prints passages by Sidney and fourteen other English critics, arranging them by subject heading and providing extensive cross-references. See *EASG*, 1972, p.48.

2551 LANGDON, IDA. *Materials for a Study of Spenser's Theory of Fine Art*. Ithaca, N.Y.: printed for the author, 1911, pp. i, xxi, xliii–xlv.

Discusses Sidney's concept of the "golden world" of poetry and the superiority of poetry to history, noting parallels in the works of Spenser and J.C. Scaliger.

Twentieth Century

2552 LAWRY, JON S. *Sidney's Two "Arcadias": Pattern and Proceeding.* Ithaca, N.Y.: Cornell University Press, 1972, pp. 1–13.
In the introduction, examines the *Defence* as an exposition of the idea of a heroic poem. Discusses the role of poetry as a mediator between precept and practice, or between a "fore-conceit" and its manifestation. Sees Sidney's principle aim as the restoration of the "erected wit" as the governor of the "infected will." Considers the relation between poetic invention and Platonic or Christian "ideas," comparing the poet with God in three respects: like God the Father, the poet brings about an incarnation of the "word"; like God the Son, he offers a "speaking picture" of the beauty of virtue; and like God the Holy Spirit, he moves men to action. Finds three "partially obscured principles of movement" in Sidney's theory: 1) poetic imitations elevate the reader to enjoy the Platonic Idea of virtue; 2) the characters move through the action of the poem toward greater knowledge; and 3) the education of the characters equips the reader for moral choices and "great-mindedness." See also item 616.

2553 LEBEL, MAURICE. "Sir Philip Sidney (1554–1586) et son *Plaidoyer pour la poésie* (1595)." *PTRSC*, 4th ser. 1 (June 1963): 177–86.
Argues that Sidney's "new poetic" shows clear signs of his familiarity with contemporary critical thought in Italy and France as well as with Aristotle. See also item 131.

2554 LEE, RENSSELAER W. "*Ut pictura poesis*: The Humanistic Theory of Painting." *Art Bulletin* 22 (December 1940):197–269. Reprint, revised as a monograph. New York: W. W. Norton & Co., 1967, 86 pp.
Relates Sidney's statement in the *Defence* that painting is a popular form of philosophy to the views of Horace, Dante, and Girolamo Fracastoro.

2555 LEIDIG, HEINZ-DIETER. *Das Historiengedicht in der englischen Literaturtheorie: Die Rezeption von Lucans "Pharsalia" von der Renaissance bis zum Ausgang des achtzehnten Jahrhunderts.* Bern, Switzerland: Herbert Lang; Frankfurt am Main: Peter Lang, 1975, pp. 30–67 passim, 82–83, 103–4, 143, 167.
Examines Sidney's distinction between "right poets" and historical poets such as Lucan, who deal with "matters philosophical." Compares the views of Sir Francis Bacon, Edmund Spenser, George Puttenham, William Webbe, and other Renaissance and late seventeenth-century authors. Also distinguishes Sidney's concept of *mimesis* from Aristotle's, noting that the difference affects Sidney's discussion of the superiority of poetry to history. Examines each of the grounds that Sidney gives for preferring poetry, comparing his views with those of authors on the Continent.

Twentieth Century

2556 LEIMBERG, INGE. "Die Dichtungstheorie der englischen Renaissance unter dem Gesichtspunkt von Kunst und Natur." In *Englische und amerikanische Literaturtheorie: Studien zu ihrer historischen Entwicklung*, edited by Rüdiger Ahrens and Erwin Wolff. Vol. 1, *Renaissance, Klassizismus und Romantik*. Anglistische Forschungen, 126. Heidelberg: Carl Winter Universitätsverlag, 1978, pp. 95–120.

Working from the hypothesis that Sidney is not typical of his age, and relying heavily on the first sonnet of *Astrophil and Stella* to corroborate theories in the *Defence*, examines the effects that attitudes toward art and nature have on theories of originality, of invention and imitation, of poetic diction, of prosody, and of the idea that *ars est celare artem*. Argues that Sidney has no overriding theory, but multiple theories. Finds that, though he and Edmund Campion differ in their valuation of rhyme, the underlying "structure of their thought" is the same, since meter is for Sidney what rhyme is for Campion: a symbol of cosmic order. Contends that Sidney locates the failure of his contemporaries in their lack of artistry.

2557 ———. "'Kein Wort darf fehlen': Das Thema und seine Variationen in der elisabethanischen Dichtungs-theorie." In *Studien zur englischen und amerikanischen Sprache und Literatur: Festschrift für Helmut Papajewski*, edited by Paul G. Buchloh, Inge Leimberg, and Herbert Rauter. Neumünster, Germany: Karl Wachholtz Verlag, 1974, pp. 267–93. Reprint. In *Englische Literaturtheorie von Sidney bis Johnson*, edited by Bernfried Nugel. Darmstadt, Germany: Wissenschaftliche Buchgesellschaft, 1984, pp. 391–420.

Considers the implications of Sidney's statement in the *Defence* that, in a poem, "one word cannot be lost or the whole work fails," relating it to his phrase "the planet-like music of poetry." Traces the history of this claim in Aristotle's *Poetics*, Cicero's *De Oratore*, Quintilian's *Institutio Oratoria*, Horace's *Ars Poetica*, and Longinus's essay *On the Sublime*, noting the prominence of similar ideas in literature and criticism from the sixteenth through the twentieth centuries. Discusses the meaning of Sidney's claim in three senses. First, considers the metrical precision valued in the Renaissance and the relations between poetry, mathematics, music, and astronomy. Adds to these the demands of Renaissance rhetoric and grammar. Second, relates the claim to Renaissance theories of imitation, in which the poet's words are inextricably bound to the things they imitate and poetic creation is an analogue of divine creation.

Twentieth Century

Third, connects Sidney's claim with Renaissance theories of the psychological effects of music, rhetoric, and poetry, discussing the interrelations of *musica mundana* and *musica instrumentalis* with *musica humana*.

2558 ———. *Shakespeares "Romeo und Julia": Von der Sonnetdichtung zur Liebestragödie*. Beihefte zu Poetica, 4. Munich: Wilhelm Fink, 1968, pp. 45–63.

Within the larger context of Renaissance rhetoric, examines Sidney's concept of *energeia*, suggesting that it provided a theoretical basis for the representation of "love-feeling" in *Romeo and Juliet*. Feels that Sidney's theory of emotional expression in love poetry is a key link between the "tragicomedy of love" in the Petrarchan sonnet and its "proper dramatization" on the stage.

2559 LEVAO, RONALD [LEE]. "Sidney's Feigned *Apology*." *PMLA* 94 (March 1979):223–33.

Argues that, though Sidney calls to mind neo-Platonic or Augustinian doctrines on the divine origin of poetry and its power to reshape the world according to metaphysical ideas, he falls back to a position in which the poet is regarded as an autonomous creator and poetry must be defended on the basis of moral effects rather than metaphysical truths. Points out that, if the poet has no law but wit, there is no way to demonstrate that the product of his wit is good. Suggests that Sidney sees all discourse as fiction and conjecture and consciously creates rhetorical and poetic fictions throughout the *Defence*, advancing different arguments for different readers without a strict regard for consistency. Concludes that Sidney's affinities are not with Ficino and the neo-Platonists but with thinkers like Nicholas of Cusa.

2560 LEVY, F[RED] J[ACOB]. "Sir Philip Sidney and the Idea of History." *BHR* 26 (September 1964):608–17.

Discusses the arguments in the *Defence* that history is inferior to poetry as a moral teacher and the comments on the value of history in a letter from Sidney to his brother Robert suggesting books to be read. Argues that Sidney's statements reveal a widespread change in the status of history in late sixteenth-century England. Whereas history had been regarded as a branch of moral philosophy, it came to be regarded as a division of politics, teaching causes and circumstances and their effects on political choices. Collects evidence that, despite his complaints in the *Defence*, Sidney was deeply interested in history and had an effect on the historical writings of Camden, Heywood, and Bacon.

Twentieth Century

2561 McGRATH, LYNETTE. "John Donne's Apology for Poetry." *SEL* 20 (Winter 1980):73–89.
Draws from Donne's prose works "the kind of apology for poetry that [he] himself might have made," comparing it with Sidney's *Defence* and with the larger humanistic tradition in which both were writing. Concentrates on the section of the *Defence* often designated as the "narration," noting many similarities between the two authors and concluding that Sidney probably helped to shape Donne's views.

2562 MacINTIRE, ELIZABETH JELLIFFE. "French Influences on the Beginning of English Classicism." *PMLA* 26 (September 1911):496–527.
Sees the Areopagus as the "English cognate to the Pléiade" and asserts that Sidney's critical theory is essentially Horatian and derives from William Drant by way of Spenser.

2563 McINTYRE, JOHN P[ATRICK]. "Sidney's 'Golden World.'" *CL* 14 (Fall 1962):356–65.
Examines the *Defence* in order to demonstrate that the neo-Platonism of the Florentine Academy, not the mimetic theory of Aristotle, was Sidney's most immediate source. Traces his distinction between *icastic* and *phantastic* imitation to Plato's *Sophist*, noting later alterations introduced by Plotinus and by Christians such as the poets of the Chartres school. Considers the Platonic assumptions behind Sidney's comments on the following: the parallel between divine and human creation, the divine inspiration of the poet, and the dualism between the "erected wit" and the "infected will." Relates these views to Sidney's emphasis on decorum, *energeia*, and moral didacticism. Also considers the influence of Ramism and of the neo-Platonic doctrine of emanation and return. Concludes that "whatever Sidney has borrowed from Aristotle and Horace he has transposed into the hierarchical universe of the Christian Platonists." See also Craig (2448).

2564 MAHL, MARY R[OBERTA]. "The Norwich Sidney Manuscript: Adventures of a Literary Detective." *Coranto* 8, no. 1 (1972): 18–32.
A revised version of the introduction to item 134.

2565 ———. "A Treatise on Horsman Shipp." *TLS*, 21 December 1967, p. 1245.
Announces the discovery of the Norwich Sidney Manuscript of the *Defence* and promises an edition of it.

Twentieth Century

2566 MAINUSCH, HERBERT. "Die Dichtungstheorie Sir Philip Sidneys." Phil.F. diss., Westfälische Wilhelms-Universität zu Münster, 1956, 159 pp.
Abstract not available. Cited in *GV*, vol. 83, p. 335.

2567 MALLOCH, A.E. "'Architectonic Knowledge' and Sidney's *Apologie.*" *ELH* 20 (September 1953):181–85.
Outlines Sidney's theory of poetry, concentrating on the importance of the concept of "architectonic" knowledge.

2568 MARKS, EMERSON R. *Relativist and Absolutist: The Early Neoclassical Debate in England.* New Brunswick, N.J.: Rutgers University Press, 1955, pp. 9, 22, 38, 136.
Sees the *Defence* as an absolutist document, an example of "Christian didacticism."

2569 MASON, H.A. "An Introduction to Literary Criticism by Way of Sidney's *Apologie for Poetrie.*" *Cambridge Quarterly* 12, nos. 2–3 (1983): 77–173.
Introduces the *Defence* to undergraduates. In Lecture 1, establishes criteria for judging works of criticism. In Lecture 2, discusses the occasion of the *Defence*. Dismisses Gosson's *School of Abuse* in favor of an "internal" occasion, but questions whether Sidney had anything new to add to the critical theories of his day. In Lecture 3, discusses the Roman tendency to mingle theories of poetry and oratory, finding it behind Sidney's metaphors that treat poetry as a set of ideas clothed with words. Discusses the background of the Renaissance charge that poets are liars and the ancient struggle between truth and beauty as proper ends of poetry. Finds Horace's compromise position—that poetry aims to teach *and* delight—logically impossible. Also rejects Renaissance theories that attempt to yoke reason and fancy. Concludes that great poetry does not begin with ideas but with the words themselves. In Lecture 4, considers Plato's reasons for attacking poetry in the *Republic* and Sidney's use of Platonic arguments to defend against Plato's attack. In Lecture 5, notes that Sidney's doctrine of the dramatic unities does not derive from Aristotle but from "Italian pedants." Reproves T.S. Eliot (509) for defending Sidney's position. Also discusses the origins of Sidney's concept of tragedy. In Lecture 6, asks what the *Defence* is defending and concludes that it is not poetry but something that poetry serves as an ornament: the ideal of the courtier. Attacks this ideal as a "noble lie" because it does not admit the inevitable corruption of court life. In Lecture 7, questions whether the *Defence* has any claim to sound judg-

ment, seriousness, or originality. Concludes that Sidney succeeds by style rather than by substantive arguments.

2570 MEAGHER, JOHN C. *Method and Meaning in Jonson's Masques.* Notre Dame, Ind.: University of Notre Dame Press, 1966, p. 178.
Argues that Jonson's poetic in the masques is that of the *Defence* in that they are designed "to show the splendor of a golden world" and to move men to desire virtue.

2571 MINER, EARL [ROY]. "Assaying the Golden World of English Renaissance Poetics." *Centrum* 4 (Spring 1976):5–20.
Cites Sidney in discussing the importance of decorum and its relation to the "unjust social hierarchy" of the Renaissance. Seeks to defend the unchanging usefulness of the main critical ideas of the Renaissance.

2572 ——. *The Restoration Mode from Milton to Dryden.* Princeton, N.J.: Princeton University Press, 1974, pp. 27–28, 29, 42–43, 46, 48, 55, 62, 105, 139, 141, 328, 539.
Indicates ways in which Sidney's critical principles become commonplace in later seventeenth-century literary theory.

2573 MONTGOMERY, ROBERT L[ANGFORD, Jr.]. *The Reader's Eye: Studies in Didactic Literary Theory from Dante to Tasso.* Berkeley: University of California Press, 1979, pp. 6–7, 117–41, 169–85 passim.
In Chapter 4, suggests that the *Defence* goes further than most works of Italian criticism in stressing "the need to manage the affective nature of the audience." Notes that, in Sidney's view, sensory images and the pleasure that they produce are crucial in conveying knowledge, and considers whether pleasure precedes knowledge or vice versa. From the description of Kalander's garden in the revised *Arcadia*, infers that pleasure arises primarily from "the perception of the artist's skill at mimetic illusion." Discusses the relation of the lifelike to the artificial in such passages, arguing that both must be present. Contrasts Sidney's view of poetic universals with that of the neo-Platonists, tracing it instead to Girolamo Fracastoro, who describes universals as ideas embodied in visual images. Notes the importance of the imagination in Sidney's theory, discussing its relation to the emotions and noting that, in defending the various genres of poetry, Sidney associates each with a particular emotion. Contrasts Sidney's position with that of Torquato Tasso.

Twentieth Century

2574 ———. *Symmetry and Sense: The Poetry of Sir Philip Sidney*. Austin: University of Texas Press, 1961, pp. 64–76. Orig. a Ph.D. diss., Harvard University, 1956.
In Chapter 5, discusses Sidney's "Artless Style." Dating the *Defence* after most, if not all, of the *Arcadia* poems were written, treats it as a theoretical bridge between the earlier, more ornamental lyrics and *Astrophil and Stella*. Argues that Sidney's view of the lyric in the *Defence* "rests upon a close analogy to prose oratory" which is "anti-Ciceronian" in its biases in that it invokes "stylistic restraint" so as "to further the vitality of content." Denies, however, that Sidney opposes ornament; rather, he rejects excessive or misplaced uses of it. See also item 1926.

2575 MOORE, JOHN W., Jr. "Sir Philip Sidney: The Role of Prophecy and Delight in Moral Education." *JGE* 23 (January 1972):322–27.
In reviewing Robinson (721), outlines Sidney's theory of moral education by pleasurable examples. Seeks to explain the resurgence of interest in Sidney.

2576 MOORE, MICHAEL D. Review of *William Temple's Analysis of Sir Philip Sidney's "Apology for Poetry": An Edition and Translation*, edited by John Webster. *SNew* 5, no. 2 (1984):27–29.
Claims that Temple's aim is to "classify and redispose the implicit conceptual structure of Sidney's reasoning," making explicit the "propositional technicalities of Sidney's argument qua argument." Indicates that, though not a "crypto-post-structuralist," Temple is "skeptical and relentless" in the manner of many current critics.

2577 MUIR, KENNETH. "Menenius's Fable." *N&Q* 198 (June 1953): 240–42.
Cites nine ancient and Renaissance sources for the fable, arguing that the version in Shakespeare's *Coriolanus* was influenced, in part, by remarks in the *Defence*.

2578 ———. "Shakespeare and Politics." In *Shakespeare in a Changing World*, edited by Arnold Kettle. New York: International Publishers; London: Lawrence & Wishart, 1964, pp. 65–83.
In considering the background of Shakespeare's political views, argues that Sidney accepts "without questioning" the "dubious moral" of Menenius's fable of the belly.

2579 MURRIN, MICHAEL. *The Veil of Allegory: Some Notes Toward a Theory of Allegorical Rhetoric in the English Renaissance*. Chicago and London: University of Chicago Press, 1969, pp. 4, 169–70, 185–88, 191.

Argues that Sidney, like Puttenham and Jonson, "rejected the traditional identification [of poetry] with allegory and tried to bring the poet closer to the orator." Claims that Sidney's emphasis on the poet as maker and his rejection of "divine inspiration" are anti-allegorical, since the poet is given, not truth, but the ability to make. Sees Sidney's objections to Spenser's *Shepherd's Calendar* as oratorically based. Places Sidney's view of poetry between the allegorical and the neoclassical in that, though "he considered the poet's creations to be other worlds . . . which surpassed the creations of nature," he never "claimed that the poet's world actually reflected the objective series of relationships which existed in the cosmos."

2580 MYRICK, KENNETH ORNE. *Sir Philip Sidney as a Literary Craftsman*. Harvard Studies in English, 14. Cambridge, Mass.: Harvard University Press; London: Oxford University Press, 1935, pp. 46–109.

In Chapter 2, "*The Defence of Poesie* as a Classical Oration," argues that Sidney follows Ascham in stressing the importance of rules, imitation, and practice. Details ways in which the *Defence* conforms to the structure of the seven-part classical forensic oration as conceived by Cicero and Quintilian. Sees in Sidney's prose style the classical virtues of lucidity, conciseness, credibility, and magnificence. Also argues that the *confirmatio* adheres to the third and fifth rules of logic in Thomas Wilson's *Rule of Reason*. In Chapter 3, "Sidney's Classical Background," considers the influence of neoclassical criticism on his conception of the language, structure, and characters of a heroic poem. Asking whether Sidney knew Greek, concludes that his "first-hand knowledge" was very limited. Examines possible debts to Italian theorists including Bernardino Daniello, Benedetto Varchi, Giovanni Giorgio Trissino, Julius Caesar Scaliger, Lodovico Castelvetro, and Antonio Minturno. Finding little evidence of influence by the first three, goes on to argue that "it is from Minturno . . . that Sidney is most likely to have learned the theory of the epic," especially his theory of "the moving power of poetry, an idea which . . . is fundamental to [Minturno's] whole argument." See also item 671, Kimbrough (2539), and Poirier (2602).

2581 NAKADA, OSAMU. "Sir Philip Sidney's *A Defence of Poetry*: A Note on the Two Modern Texts." *Shizuoka Joshi Daigaku Kenkyu*

Twentieth Century

Kiyo [Shizuoka Women's University Research Bulletin] 16 (February 1983):1–7 (separate issue).
Compares the editions of Feuillerat (23) and Smith (142) with the two editions of 1595. Finds the modern texts accurate, but notes "silence in the notes where some reference is expected."

2582 NARAYANACHAR, K.S. "The Poet as Critic—Some Comparisons in Indian and English Literary Criticism." In *Literary Criticism: European and Indian Traditions,* edited by C.D. Narasimhaiah. Mysore, India: Department of Postgraduate Studies and Research in English, University of Mysore, n.d., pp. 60–77.
Compares Coleridge and Sidney with various poets and critics in Sanskrit literature. In particular, considers Sidney's division of poetry into three distinct kinds and his statement of the aims of poetry.

2583 NAUMANN, JULIUS. *Die Geschmacksrichtungen im englischen Drama bis zur Schliessung der Theater durch die Puritaner nach Theorie und Praxis der Dichter charakterisiert.* Rostock, Germany: Universitäts-Buchdruckerei von Adlers Erben, 1900, pp. 14–18, 35–37. Orig. a Ph.D. diss., Universität Rostock.
Discusses Sidney's comments in the *Defence* on tragicomedy and the dramatic unities, comparing those in George Whetstone's preface to *Promos and Cassandra* and the views of the Countess of Pembroke and her circle.

2584 NELSON, WILLIAM. "The Boundaries of Fiction in the Rennaissance: A Treaty between Truth and Falsehood." *ELH* 36 (March 1969):30–58.
Undertakes "to describe the way in which fiction comes to be recognized, defined, and distinguished from history in the Renaissance." From the *Defence,* infers that fiction writers still faced accusations of lying and could not tell their stories "for true."

2585 NEWELS, KLEMENS. "Eine spanische Übersetzung der *Defence of Poesie* von Sir Philip Sidney." *Anglia* 72, no. 4 (1955):463–66.
Reports the discovery of a manuscript in the Bibliotéca Nacional in Madrid that contains an anonymous Spanish translation of the *Defence* (118, 121). Provides a full bibliographic description, reprinting the translator's chapter headings. Infers that the translator was Juan Ruiz de Bustamante and dates the handwriting around 1600. See also Chambers (120).

2586 NEWTON, RICHARD C. "Ben. Jonson: The Poet in the Poems." In *Two Renaissance Mythmakers: Christopher Marlowe and Ben Jonson.*

Twentieth Century

Selected Papers from the English Institute, 1975–76, n.s. 1. Edited by Alvin Kernan. Baltimore and London: Johns Hopkins University Press, 1977, pp. 165–95.
Sees Sidney as the "genius" of Jonson's lyric poetry. Jonson's desire to "fulfill the Sidneian vision of the poet" was blocked only by a change in contemporary attitudes toward poetry and poets and by Jonson's own "Baconian predispositions."

2587 NITCHIE, ELIZABETH. *Vergil and the English Poets.* Columbia University Studies in English and Comparative Literature. New York: Columbia University Press, 1919, pp. 66, 93. Orig. a Ph.D. diss., Columbia University.
Discusses references to Virgil in the *Defence*, particularly the remark that his Aeneas is "feigned."

2588 NUGEL, BERNFRIED. *The Just Design. Studien zu architektonischen Vorstellungsweisen in der neoklassischen Literaturtheorie am Beispiel Englands.* Berlin and New York: Walter de Gruyter, 1980, pp. 125–32.
Places the architectural metaphors in the *Defence* in a tradition running through classical criticism into that of the Italian and English Renaissance. Relates these metaphors to others involving music and compares Sidney's usage with that of George Puttenham.

2589 O'BRIEN, GORDON WORTH. *Renaissance Poetics and the Problem of Power.* Institute of Elizabethan Studies Publications, 2. Chicago: Institute of Elizabethan Studies, 1956, pp. xv–xvi, 86–87.
Finds in Sidney's translation of du Plessis-Mornay a possible source for statements in the *Defence* that poetry should teach with delight and also instill virtue. Defines virtue in Sidney's sense and discusses metaphors in *The Trueness of the Christian Religion* that link the order within the soul with that governing the earth and stars.

2590 ONG, WALTER J. "Oral Residue in Tudor Prose Style." *PMLA* 80 (June 1965):145–54.
Cites the oratorical structure of the *Defence* as an example of "organizational formula," one of several classes of "oral residue" that exhibit "the formulary state of mind" in sixteenth-century prose.

2591 ORWEN, WILLIAM R. "Spenser and Gosson." *MLN* 52 (December 1937):574–76.
Questions Spenser's statement in his letters to Gabriel Harvey that Sidney "scorned" Stephen Gossen for writing the dedication in the

Twentieth Century

School of Abuse. Cites as evidence Gosson's dedication of two later works to Sidney and to his father-in-law.

2592 OSGOOD, CHARLES G[ROSVENOR]. Introduction to *Boccaccio on Poetry: Being the Preface and the Fourteenth and Fifteenth Books of Boccaccio's "Genealogia Deorum Gentilium."* Princeton, N.J.: Princeton University Press, 1930, pp. xlv–xlvi.
Lists views of Boccaccio that recur in the *Defence*, allowing that verbal echoes in Sidney's treatise may derive from intermediate sources rather than from Boccaccio directly.

2593 PADELFORD, FREDERICK MORGAN. "Notes on Sidney's *Defense of Poesy*." *MLN* 21 (May 1906):159–60.
Points out several passages in Scaliger's *Poetics* that Sidney drew upon: one arguing that historians imitate poets, another on "filthy" passages in Plato, and a third on epic as the supreme form of poetry.

2594 ———. "Sidney's Indebtedness to Sibilet." *JEGP* 7 (January 1908):81–84.
Regards several comments in the *Defence*, particularly those on religious poetry, as more indebted to Thomas Sibilet's *Art poetique françois* than to Minturno's *De Poeta*.

2595 PAPAJEWSKI, HELMUT. "An Lucanus sit Poeta." *DVLG* 40 (December 1966):485–508.
Examines the distinction between poet and historian held by authors from J.C. Scaliger to Voltaire, using their classification of Lucan as a test case. Contrasts the clear distinction in the *Defence* with the lack of one in Scaliger's *Poetices Libri Septem*. Also discusses the Aristotelian principles behind Sidney's argument, particularly the concept of universals.

2596 PARTEE, MORRISS HENRY. "Anti-Platonism in Sidney's *Defence*." *EM* 22 (1971):7–29.
Points out that Sidney rejected Plato's doctrine that poets are divinely inspired and took the more Christian view that secular poetry cannot rise above human "invention." Suggests that Sidney and other Elizabethans such as Thomas Lodge saw the implications of Plato's *Ion* more clearly than many modern scholars. Discusses Sidney's ingenuity in refuting Plato's attack on poets, noting that Sidney's "right poet" resembles Plato's ideal philosopher.

2597 ———. "Plato and the Elizabethan Defence of Poetry." Ph.D. diss., University of Texas, 1966, 278 pp.
Contrasts Sidney with other Elizabethan critics in that he knew Plato's dialogues thoroughly and directly. Concludes that, in all his major

works, Sidney reveals an attraction to Plato's concepts of love and beauty. He also agrees with Plato on the didactic ends of poetry and on the concept of absolute virtue, but disagrees in his views of poetic inspiration and imitation. See *DA* 27 (August 1966):459A–60A.

2598 ———. "Sir Philip Sidney and the Renaissance Knowledge of Plato." *ES* 51 (October 1970):411–24.
Argues that, unlike other Elizabethan critics, Sidney had "an extensive and generally accurate knowledge of the dialogues." Discusses allusions to Plato and Socrates in the *Defence, Astrophil and Stella,* and the correspondence, noting indirect sources from which these may derive. Suggests that references in the *Defence* to the unworldly astronomer and to *icastic* and *phantastic* imitation have their source in *Theaetetus* and *The Sophist*. Examines Sidney's strategy for rebutting Plato's attack on poets, noting that he "consistently limits Plato's mistrust of poets only to their religious teachings" and so avoids a broader attack on Book X of *The Republic*.

2599 PERKINSON, RICHARD H. "Additional Observations on the Later Editions of *Nosce Teipsum*." *Library*, 5th ser. 2 (June 1947):61–63.
Notes three previously unnoticed "borrowings" from the *Defence* in the preface by a "Learned and Ingenious Divine" to Nahum Tate's 1697 edition of *The Original, Nature, and Immortality of the Soul*.

2600 PLETT, HEINRICH F. *Rhetorik der Affekte. Englische Wirkungsästhetik im Zeitalter der Renaissance.* Studien zur englischen Philologie, n.s. 18. Tübingen, Germany: Max Niemeyer Verlag, 1975, pp. 133–41 and passim. Orig. a Ph.D. diss., Universität Bonn, 1970.
Compares treatises on poetics, rhetoric, music, and prosody that helped to shape Elizabethan thought on the emotional effects aroused by literature. Examines Sidney's comments in the *Defence* on *energeia* and the aims of poetry: to teach, to delight, and to move. Considers his innovation in adapting the last of these from the theory of rhetoric, distinguishing his views from those of Sir Thomas Elyot and J.C. Scaliger. Also examines the metaphoric imagery that Sidney uses in discussing poetry and rhetoric and relates his views on meter and "music" in poetry to the emotional effects that the imagery arouses.

2601 ———. "Typen der Textklassifikation in der englischen Renaissance." *Sprachkunst* 12, no. 1 (1981):212–27.
Presents a systematic and inclusive taxonomy for classifying Renaissance texts as "rhetorical," "poetological," or "rhetorical-poetological."

Twentieth Century

Considers the order in which various English critics list the genres of poetry, noting that Sidney is unusual in exalting lyric to the second position, between heroic poetry and tragedy. Also discusses Sidney's distinction between three kinds of poets, his adaptation of traditional terms for the effects of rhetoric to describe poetry, and his influence on Francis Meres's discussion of poetic genres.

2602 POIRIER, MICHEL. *Sir Philip Sidney: Le chevalier poète élizabéthain.* Travaux et mémoires de l'Université de Lille, Nouvelle série— Droit et lettres, 26. Lyon, France: Bibliothèque Universitaire de Lille, 1948, pp. 219–35.

In Chapter 5 of Book 2, discusses the *Defence*, considering its origins in the critical debate involving Gosson's *School of Abuse*. Stresses Sidney's borrowings from the preface to Amyot's translation of Plutarch's *Lives* and from the work of Italian critics such as Minturno. Also considers the moral emphasis of the *Defence*, its position on the divine inspiration of poets, its denial that verse is an essential characteristic of poetry, its treatment of the classical genres, and its assessment of the vernacular literature of England. Concurs with Myrick (2580) on its logical and rhetorical structure, finding little in its thought that is original. See also item 703.

2603 POND, VIRGINIA THOMAS. "Imagination in the Poetic Theory of Pierre de Ronsard and Sir Philip Sidney." Ph.D. diss., University of North Carolina at Chapel Hill, 1981, 323 pp.

Compares Sidney's views on verse, rhyme, and the unities with those of Ronsard, arguing that the similarities are less important than the differences. Traces the latter to different views of the imagination. Though both men distrust the faculty, Sidney gives it a key place in his theory, focusing on its importance for both poets and their audiences. Ronsard prefers to stress divine inspiration by the Muses or Apollo rather than human mental processes. Discusses the effect of this difference on each author's statements on invention and imitation, concluding that, "while Ronsard is clearly in the Platonic/Neoplatonic tradition, Sidney is more consistently in the Aristotelian tradition than many critics have thought him to be." See *DAI* 42 (June 1982):5113A.

2604 PONTEDERA, CLAUDIO. "Poetica e poesia nell' *Apology for Poetry*." *ACF* 6 (1967):125–47.

Argues that, in his synthesis of Aristotle, Plato, and Horace, Sidney was superior to all other English theorists and to most Italians. Claims that attempts such as Hamilton's (2504) to establish the philosophical basis of the *Defence* fail because they consider only parts of the treatise, not the whole. Arguing that readers should prefer Olney's text to that of Ponsonby, provides a close examination of Sidney's major terms: imitation, fiction, fable, and representation. Discusses their connotations in the work of previous critics, suggesting that they embody both Aristotelian and Platonic concepts in such a way that the sources complement rather than exclude one other. Finds the value of the *Defence* in its *completezza*, a result not of its "analytical and circumscribed attention to particular theoretical or technical problems of literary theory, but rather to its confronting in depth problems of the aesthetic experience and connecting them to a unified vision of life."

2605 POTTS, L[EONARD] J[AMES]. "Ben Jonson and the Seventeenth Century." In *English Studies: 1949*, edited by Philip Magnus. London: John Murray, 1949, pp. 7–24.
Argues that, whereas Sidney expects poetry to represent what "should be," Jonson follows Aristotle and Bacon in expecting it to express "the life of man." Contrasts Jonson's neoclassicism with Sidney's "high moral idealism."

2606 PURSGLOVE, GLYN. "Erected Wit and Infected Will: Some notes Towards a Reading of *Meeting Ends*." In *Francis Warner: Poet and Dramatist*, edited by Tim Prentki. Knotting, Bedfordshire, England: Sceptre Press, 1977, pp. 39–52.
Uses Sidney's phrase as a counterpoint for discussing Warner's display of sexual erection and venereal infection in *Meeting Ends*.

2607 RAITIÈRE, MARTIN N[ORMAN]. "The Unity of Sidney's *Apology for Poetry*." *SEL* 21 (Winter 1981):37–57.
Argues that the apparent inconsistencies in the *Defence* noted by Hardison (2510) are actually part of a larger unity. Focuses on the syntax of Sidney's claim that the "speaking picture" of poesy is superior to the "learned definition" of philosophy. Feels that Sidney pointedly omitted the claim that poetry is a "moderator" between the external, material things treated by the historian and the social and political abstractions of the philosopher. Examines Sidney's illustrations of the value of a "speaking picture," noting than none embodies a clear philosophical precept. Also examines his digression on English poetry, particularly the shift from talk of the poet's liberty to talk of his discipline and the need for neoclassical rules. Explains this shift on the basis of Sidney's image of Icarus and Daedalus, which suggests that neither liberty nor rules are acceptable alone. Finds in them a dilemma that Sidney refused to

Twentieth Century

resolve, noting it in the syntax, structure, and style of the entire work. Also sees this tension in Sidney's other major works.

2608 RAM, TULSI. *The Neo-Classical Epic (1650–1720): An Ethical and Historical Interpretation.* Delhi: National Publishing House, 1971, pp. 31, 41, 240–41.
Relates Sidney's views on the moral function of poetry to those of seventeenth-century authors and critics of the neoclassical epic. Also notes similarities in the definitions of tragedy given by Chaucer, Sidney, and Dryden.

2609 RANSOM, JOHN CROWE. *The World's Body.* New York: Scribner's, 1938, pp. 56–58.
Uses comments in the *Defence* as a basis for defining the poet's traditional function.

2610 REIDEL, WOLFGANG. *Die Arbeit der Dichter: Vergleichende Studien zur dichterischen Subjektivität in der englischen Romantik und Moderne.* Frankfurt am Main; Bern, Switzerland; Las Vegas, Nev.: Peter Lang, 1979, pp. 17–19.
Locates the *Defence* in the development of new views of subjectivity and objectivity in Renaissance philosophy. Considers Sidney's concept of the poet as the creator of a "golden" world, noting ways in which this view departs from Aristotelian and Christian assumptions.

2611 RENWICK, W[ILLIAM] L[INDSAY]. "The Critical Origins of Spenser's Diction." *MLR* 17 (January 1922):1–16.
Places Sidney's rejection of the archaic language in Spenser's *Shepherd's Calendar* in the context of other French and English discussions of diction. Also traces Sidney's admiration of the compound epithet to his contact with the poets of the Pléiade.

2612 RINGLER, WILLIAM A., [Jr.], ed. *Oratio in laudem artis poeticae [circa 1572]*, by John Rainolds. Princeton Studies in English, 20. Princeton, N.J.: Princeton University Press, 1940, pp. 2, 20, 23.
Argues that Rainolds' *Oration* "anticipates many of the fundamental positions and arguments" of Sidney's *Defence*, particularly those having to do with the moral function of poetry. Sees the similarities, not as proof that the *Oration* was a source for the *Defence*, but as evidence of "the pervasive influence of the academic tradition."

2613 RINGLER, WILLIAM [A., Jr.]. *"Poeta Nascitur non Fit:* Some Notes on the History of an Aphorism." *JHI* 2 (October 1941):497–504.

Traces the history of the aphorism from its classical sources through Sidney to the Romantic writers to show the relative emphasis placed on "inspiration" and "natural talent" by the poetic theorists of the various periods.

2614 ———. *Stephen Gosson: A Biographical and Critical Study.* Princeton Studies in English, 25. Princeton, N.J.: Princeton University Press, 1942, pp. 36–37, 117–24. Orig. a Ph.D. diss., Princeton University, 1937.

Discusses Gosson's mistake in dedicating his *School of Abuse* and *Ephemerides of Phialo* to Sidney. In pondering the extent to which the *Defence* may be regarded as a reply to Gosson, notes that the *School of Abuse* is the only sixteenth-century attack on poetry that contains all the major charges that Sidney addresses. Also notes points of agreement between Sidney and Gosson.

2615 RISTINE, FRANK HUMPHREY. *English Tragicomedy: Its Origin and History.* New York: Columbia University Press, 1910, pp. 71–73, 91, 93–94, 146.

Suggests that Sidney's criticism of "tragicomedies" inhibited use of the term in England for twenty-five years.

2616 ROBERTS, MARK. "The Pill and the Cherries: Sidney and the Neo-Classical Tradition." *EIC* 16 (January 1966):22–31.

Sees the *Defence* as dealing with "fundamental issues" but not always showing "a full theoretical grasp" of the principles concerned. Argues that a basic ambiguity in Sidney's answer to Plato and in other aspects of the *Defence* allows him to claim that poetry can both teach and delight. See a response by Devereux (2457).

2617 ROBERTSON, D.W. "Sidney's Metaphor of the Ulcer." *MLN* 56 (January 1941):56–61.

Traces Italian theories that explain, in medical terms, Aristotle's concept of *catharsis*. Finds that none of these corresponds to Sidney's statement that tragedy "showeth forth the ulcers that are covered with tissue." From contemporary English definitions of tragedy and uses of the ulcer metaphor, concludes that it simply means that hidden crimes will be revealed.

Twentieth Century

2618 ROBINSON, FORREST G[LEN]. *The Shape of Things Known: Sidney's "Apology" in Its Philosophical Tradition.* Cambridge, Mass.: Harvard University Press, 1972, 244 pp. Orig. a Ph.D. diss., Harvard University, 1968.

Argues that Sidney's theory of poetry "takes root in the assumption that thought is a form of internal vision" and that poetry is "a verbal rendering of ideas visible in the poet's mind as he composes and in the reader's mind as he reads." In the introduction, traces analogies between thought and vision from Plato through medieval authors to Sidney, citing illustrations in *Arcadia* and *Astrophil and Stella*. In Chapter 1, undertakes a more thorough history of visual epistemology, noting changes from the pre-Socratics to Aristotle and Plato (especially in the *Republic*). Discusses Greek influence on the Epicureans and Stoics and on Plotinus. Also considers visual epistemology in Christian thought from the Bible and the church fathers through medieval and Arab writers to thirteenth-century Dominicans and Franciscans, including Aquinas and Roger Bacon. Finds Renaissance views "less philosophical" and more intensely visual. Focuses on Nicholas of Cusa, Marsilio Ficino, Giovanni Pico della Mirandola, John Colet, Philip Melanchthon, and Pietro Pomponazzi, noting increasing emphasis on nature and the human soul as sources of knowledge about the divine. In Chapter 2, considers increasingly visual conceptions of thought encouraged by the printing press and by Renaissance views of love psychology, mathematics, painting and emblem books, and theories of "method." In all these, finds that "the symbol somehow bridges the chasm that divides . . . the temporal from the eternal." Notes widespread distrust of language as necessarily sequential and imprecise and an increasing tendency to equate words with visual images. In Chapter 3, identifies the "cornerstone" of Sidney's poetic theory as the premise that "moral abstractions have the greatest pedagogical efficacy when they are made visible to the mind's eye." Ponders the phrase "speaking picture," concluding that it means "the poetic fusion of moral abstractions with actual characters." Of Sidney's slight attention to religious poetry, remarks that his theory could not deal with things "invisible to mortal eyes." Notes similarly neo-Platonic elements in the visual epistemology of du Plessis-Mornay's *De la vérité de la religion chrestienne* and Sidney's *Defence*. Also finds similarities with Mannerist theories of painting, conventional views of emblems, and Continental works of rhetoric and criticism by Bruno and Fracastoro. Noting the visual nature of "ideas" and "conceits" in Sidney's theory, remarks on his easy division between form and matter, concluding that, for him, poetry was an art of presentation that borrows its matter from philosophy. Argues that, from the "method" of Peter Ramus, Sidney borrowed "pictorial machinery," a "penchant for defining the arts in terms of their practical ends," and a concept of "inward light" that guides the soul to truth. Links Sidney's position to John Dee and the Renaissance "arts of memory." In Dee, finds a source for the term "ground-plot," suggesting that Sidney saw reading poetry as the reverse of the process of creating it. Rejecting Rudenstine's analysis of Sidney's concept of *energeia* (in item 730), defines the term as "conceptual clarity" that arises "when the writer has his moral abstraction—whether of a virtue, vice, or passion—clearly in view." Concludes that the *Defence* is "not so much a hand-book on poetry as it is a scientific theory of communication." In Chapter 4, discusses the New *Arcadia* and *Astrophil and Stella* as realizations of the theory presented in the *Defence* (for details, see items 1742 and 1943). In Chapter 5, suggests that Sidney's visual epistemology "virtually dominated English critical theory from Jonson to Johnson," but confines discussion of its impact to the work of character writers in the seventeenth century and to the masques of Ben Jonson. Notes the opinions of John Hoskins and Fulke Greville that, in describing characters in *Arcadia*, Sidney imitated the *Characters* of Theophrastus. While acknowledging similarities in matter and method, rejects the view on the grounds that Theophrastus's work was inaccessible to Sidney. Argues that the seventeenth-century English imitators of the *Characters* were often closer to Sidney than to Theophrastus because they began with similar aesthetic assumptions, particularly the Platonic view that virtue need only be made visible to be desired. Compares Sidney's conception of characters as "speaking pictures" with that of Joseph Hall, Wye Saltonstall, and others. In examining the relation between the visual and the conceptual elements of Jonson's masques, finds Jonson's critical statements on topics such as invention, speaking pictures, and the aims of teaching and delight similar to those of Sidney. See also item 721.

2619 ROSSKY, WILLIAM. "Imagination in the English Renaissance: Psychology and Poetic." *SRen* 5 (1958):49–73.

Argues that, whereas most Renaissance theorists condemned the "fancy" for distorting reality, Sidney approves of the poet's ability to create versions of the ideal because the poet's feigning is directed to "rational and moral effects." Such imagination is "a glorious compounding of images beyond life, of distortions which are yet verisimilar imitations, expressing a truth to reality and yet a higher truth also, controlled by the practical purpose, the molding power and, in almost every aspect, by the reason and morality of the poet."

Twentieth Century

2620 ROTHSTEIN, ERIC. "English Tragic Theory in the Late Seventeenth Century." *ELH* 29 (September 1962):306–23.
Discusses Sidney's comments on tragedy in the *Defence* as "inchoate" attempts to define the genre as Aristotle had: on the basis of the emotions that it arouses. Also examines the later, more fully developed "affective" theories.

2621 ROUTH, JAMES. *The Rise of Classical English Criticism: A History of the Canons of English Literary Taste and Rhetorical Doctrines, from the Beginning of English Criticism to the Death of Dryden.* New Orleans, La.: Tulane University Press, 1915, pp. 30–48 passim, 70–78 passim, 91–92, 100.
Compares Sidney with other English critics on points of controversy such as the way in which evil is to be portrayed, the mnemonic value of verse, and the mingling of tragedy and comedy. Notes Sidney's letter to his brother Robert of 18 October 1580 on the proper materials for "a story." Also discusses Sidney's views on style, rhyme, figures of speech, and the classical unities.

2622 RUDENSTINE, NEIL [L.]. "Sidney and Energia." In *Elizabethan Poetry: Modern Essays in Criticism*, edited by Paul J. Alpers. New York: Oxford University Press, 1967, pp. 210–34.
Reprints Chapter 10 from item 730.

2623 SAINTSBURY, GEORGE [EDWARD BATEMAN]. "Elizabethan Criticism." In *The Cambridge History of English Literature.* Vol. 3, *Renascence and Reformation*, edited by A[dolphus], W[illiam] Ward and A[lfred] R[ayney] Waller. Cambridge: Cambridge University Press, 1909, pp. 289–312.
Summarizes the *Defence*, suggesting that Sidney got "the general drift of Italian criticism" but owed no great debt to any particular author.

2624 ———. *A History of Criticism and Literary Taste in Europe.* Vol. 2, *From the Renaissance to the Decline of Eighteenth Century Orthodoxy.* New York: Dodd, Mead, & Co.; Edinburgh and London: William Blackwood & Sons, 1902, pp. 45, 171–76, 226–27, 348.
Regards Girolamo Fracastoro's *Naugerius sive de Poetica* as "the first drawing up of the creed which converted Sidney." Sees Sidney's criticism as a defence "not so much of Poetry as of Romance" and evaluates its faults and its influence. Notes similarities between Sidney's statements on improbabilities in the drama and a passage in Cervantes's *Don Quixote* I.iv. See also item 2625 and Alden (2051).

692

2625 ————. *A History of English Criticism, Being the English Chapters of "A History of Criticism and Literary Taste in Europe."* Edinburgh and London: William Blackwood & Sons, 1911, pp. 54–59, 100–101.
Reprints the parts of item 2624 devoted to English criticism.

2626 SALMAN, PHILLIPS. "Instruction and Delight in Medieval and Renaissance Criticism." *RenQ* 32 (Autumn 1979):303–32.
Includes an examination of the *Defence* in the light of Renaissance faculty psychology. Traces the use of the faculties as the poet composes and as his ends of teaching, delighting, and moving are realized in the minds of the audience. Also examines the concepts of *energeia* and *praxis*, noting that Sidney's faculty psychology differs from that typical of medieval poets in that it leads to action rather than to contemplation.

2627 SAMUEL, IRENE. "The Influence of Plato on Sir Philip Sidney's *Defense of Poesy.*" *MLQ* 1 (September 1940):383–91.
Argues that Plato, not Aristotle, is the main source for the *Defence*, providing both the imputations against which Sidney must defend and the doctrines used in the defense itself. Lists references to Plato in Sidney's works and the dialogues he seems to have known. Notes the Platonic influence in Sidney's discussion of moral teaching, universal patterns or "images," the role of the beautiful in leading men to virtue, and the divine inspiration of the poet. See a reply by Krouse (2549).

2628 SASTRI, P.S. *The History of Literary Criticism.* Agra, India: Lakshmi Narain Agarwal Educational Publishers, 1969, pp. 107–31. See also pp. 102, 104–6.
In a chapter on the *Defence*, draws together information on its sources, organization, and content. Discusses Sidney's Platonism and Puritanism and his views on the superiority of poetry over history and philosophy. Notes affinities between his definitions of poetic genres and those of earlier critics. Also discusses Sidney's views on rhyme and meter and on English poetic style.

2629 SCHABERT, INA. *Die Lyrik der Spenserianer. Ansätze zu einer absoluten Dichtung in England, 1590–1660.* Tübingen, Germany: Max Niemeyer Verlag, 1977, pp. 15–76 passim, 192, 209.
Considers the influence of Sidney's concept of poetry on the Spenserian poets of the seventeenth century. Sees his criticism as more pragmatic than theirs and less concerned with imitations of nature. Also considers his views on divine inspiration and on the abuse of Petrarchan conventions in English love poetry. Notes his impact on the poetry of John Davies.

Twentieth Century

2630 SCHÄFER, JÜRGEN. "'Twins by Birth': Literaturtheoretische Aspekte elisabethanischer Rhetorik." In *Englische und amerikanische Literaturtheorie: Studien zu ihrer historischen Entwicklung*, edited by Rüdiger Ahrens and Erwin Wolff. Vol. 1, *Renaissance, Klassizismus und Romantik.* Anglistische Forschungen, 126. Heidelberg: Carl Winter Universitätsverlag, 1978, pp. 45–72.
Uses Sidney's *Defence* as a touchstone in surveying the relations between poetic and rhetorical theory. Finds that Sidney differs from other theorists of the period in viewing the narrator of the prose romance as a heroic poet rather than an orator.

2631 SCHULZE, KONRAD. *Die Satiren Halls: Ihre Abhängigkeit von den Altrömischen Satirikern und ihre Realbeziehungen auf die Shakespeare-Zeit.* Palaestra: Untersuchungen und Texte aus der deutschen und englishen Philologie, 106. Berlin: Mayer & Müller, 1910, pp. 258, 275–76.
Considers likely allusions to Sidney in Hall's *Satires*, including an echo of Sidney's strictures against mingling clowns and kings in tragedy.

2632 SCOTT-JAMES, R[OLFE] A[RNOLD]. *The Making of Literature: Some Principles of Criticism Examined in the Light of Ancient and Modern Theory.* London: M. Secker, 1928; New York: H. Holt & Co., 1929, pp. 116–19.
Argues that the *Defence* "does not seriously deal with the arguments of Plato."

2633 SESSIONS, WILLIAM A. "Spenser's Georgics." *ELR* 10 (Spring 1980):202–38.
Examines two appraisals of the hero Aeneas: that of Sidney in the *Defence* and that of Cristoforo Landino. Concludes that Sidney followed J.C. Scaliger in treating Aeneas as the highest model of virtue. Contrasts Spenser's view of heroism laboring in history with Sidney's view of it triumphing in an idealized, "golden" world.

2634 SEWELL, ELIZABETH. *The Orphic Voice: Poetry and Natural History.* New Haven, Conn.: Yale University Press, 1960, p. 72.
Notes that Sidney's comments on Orpheus and orphic poetry in the *Defence* match almost exactly those in Thomas Spratt's *History of the Royal Society*, but that Sidney's are "illogical."

2635 SHULTE-MIDDELICH, BERND. *"Apology for Poetry.* Dichtungstheorie im Widerstreit mit den Theorien benachbarter Disziplinen in der elisabethanischen Zeit." Ph.D. diss., Universität Bochum, 1977, 412 pp.

Considers the discrepancy between the rare and limited attacks on literature by the Puritans and the elaborate defences they are often said to have provoked. Finds a more likely provocation in attacks by writers in history, philosophy, mathematics, and medicine. Finds that the *Defence* is part of a tendency to break up the traditional unity of the liberal arts and to promote rival disciplines. See *EASG*, 1983, pp. 38–40.

2636 SINFIELD, ALAN. "The Cultural Politics of the *Defence of Poetry*." In *Sir Philip Sidney and the Interpretation of Renaissance Culture: The Poet in His Time and in Ours: A Collection of Critical and Scholarly Essays,* edited by Gary F. Waller and Michael D. Moore. London: Croom Helm; Totowa, N.J.: Barnes & Noble, 1984, pp. 124–43.

Determined to see the *Defence* as an "intervention at a particular cultural and political conjuncture aimed at appropriating literature to earnest protestant activism," extends observations by Waller (811) and Hardison (2510) that it is "constituted of diverse elements." Examines Sidney's handling of four "main anxieties about pagan writing": the gods, love, heroism, and "human capacity in a fallen world." Although Sidney "handles the issue of the gods rather well," on love poetry he is "less secure," because he deals with "diverse elements within an unsettled cultural apparatus." As for heroism, it is "problematized in a zealously protestant environment." With respect to man's fallenness, Sidney offers two rationales: the first "justifies all poetry, though not at a very exalted pitch," whereas the second "justifies Christian poetry, but not the pagan writing which figured so largely in the Elizabethan cultural apparatus." See also item 759.

2637 SISSON, C[HARLES] H[UBERT]. "Poetry and Myth." In *British Poetry since 1970: A Critical Survey,* edited by Peter Jones and Michael Schmidt. New York: Persea Books; Manchester, England: Carcanet Press, 1980, pp. 172–77.

Against Philip Larkin's pronouncements on the nature of poetic originality, cites Sidney's comments on *mimesis*, arguing that the poet must "invent" rather than "preserve." Views Sidney's notion of "imitation" as a "doctrine of *creation*."

Twentieth Century

2638 SMITH, D[AVID] NICHOL. "Jonathan Swift: Some Observations." *EDH*, n.s. 14 (1935):29–48.
Connects Pugliano's praise of horses at the beginning of the *Defence* with Jonathan Swift's exaltation of the Houyhnhnms in Book IV of *Gulliver's Travels*. See also Baughan (2401).

2639 SMYTH, MARIAM. "The Ethical Conception of Literature in English Literary Theory." Ph.D. Diss., University of Kansas, 1941, 603 pp.
Relates the *Defence* to the age-old debate over the role of the poet as an ethical teacher. See *Microfilm Abstracts* 3, no. 1 (1941):17–18.

2640 SNARE, GERALD [HOWARD]. "Dissociation of Sensibility and the *Apology for Poetry* in the Twentieth Century." *SLitI* 15 (Spring 1982):115–28.
Discusses scholars of the last hundred years who see in the *Defence* an antagonism between classicism and romanticism. Relates this view to T.S. Eliot's thesis that, in the seventeenth century, passion was "dissociated" from intellect and classical rules supplanted imaginative impulse in literature. Notes the tendency of late Romantic critics to prefer Sidney's practical criticism of English authors to his theoretical discussions, or his passages on creative imagination to his advocacy of neoclassical rules. Finds in recent scholarship the same critical terminology and the same assumption of polar opposition between romanticism and classicism.

2641 SPELLMEYER, KURT. "Plotinus and Seventeenth-Century Literature: A Prolegomenon to Further Study." *PCP* 17 (November 1982):50–58.
Briefly identifies the "distinctly Plotinian concepts" informing Sidney's poetics. Underlying his theory of imitation finds a "tenet central to Plotinian aesthetics—that the artist . . . holds the mirror to the Ideal Forms themselves." Also feels that Sidney "endorses a Plotinian conception of the Ideal as literally visible in the images surveyed by the mind's eye."

2642 SPINGARN, J[OEL] E[LIAS], ed. *La critica letteraria nel Rinascimento: Saggio sulle origini dello spirito classico nella letteratura moderna.* Translated by Antonio Fusco. Bari, Italy: Gius. Laterza & Figli, 1905, pp. 249–310 and passim.
Provides a revised version of item 2376, which the author describes in the preface to the 1924 reprinting of the English version as "so much fuller and maturer than the original version that the latter is completely

superseded by it." In passages on the *Defence*, follows the substance of the English text but adds numerous comparisons with the work of various Italian critics.

2643 ———. Introduction to *Critical Essays of the Seventeenth Century.* Vol. 1, *1605–1650.* Oxford: Clarendon Press, 1908, pp. xiii–xviii.
Concludes that the *Defence* shaped Ben Jonson's conceptions of poetry and drama and reinforced his classical bias. Cites parallels between Sidney's book and the prologue to *Every Man out of His Humour.* Also considers reasons that Jonson later drew back from Sidney's position.

2644 STARNES, D[e WITT] T[ALMAGE]. "Purpose in the Writing of History." *MP* 20 (November 1922):281–300.
Considers the traditional role that Sidney assigns to the historian: to teach virtue by providing examples to be imitated or avoided. Examines the development of the convention from classical antiquity through the Renaissance, giving special attention to English chroniclers and historians.

2645 STAUFFER, DONALD ALFRED. *The Nature of Poetry.* New York: W.W. Norton & Co., 1946, pp. 95–98, 127–28.
Calls the statements in the *Defence* on the moral function of poetry "narrow and rigid," suggesting that Sidney himself was "uneasy" about them and about the capacity of poetry to tell the truth. Labels his scant comments on lyric as "puritan" and notes that Sidney's own sonnets are not "moral" in his sense. Also notes the importance of concrete imagery in his theory.

2646 STEADMAN, JOHN M[ARCELLUS]. *The Lamb and the Elephant: Ideal Imitation and the Context of Renaissance Allegory.* San Marino, Calif.: Huntington Library, 1974, pp. xxxix–xli, 96–97, 201.
Places Sidney's views on *mimesis*, allegory, and invention in the historical context of Renaissance allegory.

2647 ———. *Milton and the Renaissance Hero.* Oxford: Clarendon Press, 1967, pp. 3–4, 9, 11.
In discussing Renaissance concepts of the epic, examines Sidney's views on the moral function of poetry and the virtues associated with classical heroes.

2648 STROZIER, ROBERT M. "Poetic Conception in Sir Philip Sidney's *An Apology for Poetry.*" *YES* 2 (1972):49–60.
Approves the trend since the 1940s to treat Plato as the dominant influence on the *Defence* and opposes the view that the treatise lacks a single, coherent theory of poetry. Identifies Sidney's central concern as the

Twentieth Century

means by which poets may teach ideas of virtue and beauty, even though poetry operates by sensory images and cannot present ideas directly. Suggests that Sidney regarded nature as a primary, visible expression of such ideas and that he saw the arts as secondary expressions that imitate nature. Finds the unity of the *Defence* in the view that poetry is the art closest to nature. Traces this view to Democritus, with J.C. Scaliger as a likely intermediary. Defines Sidney's brand of Platonism as an outgrowth of Renaissance humanism, which preferred to move from the ideal to the actual (that is, to virtuous activity in the world) rather than from the actual to the ideal.

2649 ———. "Roger Ascham and Cleanth Brooks: Renaissance and Modern Critical Thought." *EIC* 22 (October 1972):396–407.
Submits that Renaissance works such as the *Defence* are relevant to the underlying concerns of New Criticism.

2650 SYMMES, HAROLD S. *Les Débuts de la critique dramatique en Angleterre jusqu'à la mort de Shakespeare.* Paris: Ernest LeRoux, 1903, pp. 103–15. Orig. a Ph.D. diss., University of Paris.
Examines Sidney's remarks on tragedy and comedy, on the dramatic unities, and on dramatic decorum, noting the major classical and Renaissance sources from which they derive.

2651 SYMONDS, JOHN ADDINGTON. *Shakspere's Predecessors in the English Drama.* London: Smith, Elder, & Co., 1884, pp. 228, 253–58, 593.
Feels that Sidney's remarks on *Gorboduc* reveal the "bondage" of the best minds of his age to a false ideal of drama fostered by Seneca: "solemn diction, sonorous declamation, conformity to the unities." Also discusses Sidney's debt to Aristotle, Horace, and the Italians.

2652 TATLOCK, J[OHN] S[TRONG] P[ERRY]. "Bernardo Tasso and Sidney." *Italica* 12 (August 1935):74–80.
Discusses the possible influence of Bernardo Tasso's *Ragionamento della poesia* on Sidney's *Defence*.

2653 TEMPLE, WILLIAM. *William Temple's "Analysis" of Sir Philip Sidney's "Apology for Poetry."* Edited by John Webster. Medieval and Renaissance Texts and Studies, 32. Binghamton, N.Y.: Medieval & Renaissance Texts & Studies, 1984, 186 pp.
Examines Sidney's arguments in the *Defence* from the position of a moral philosopher responding to a poet, with the overriding aim of insisting that poetry is to be valued, not for its difference from all other arts, but

for what it shares with them. Follows closely the organization of Sidney's work, sometimes paraphrasing, sometimes objecting, in order to make clear the course of the argument. Bases objections on the central premise that Sidney's aesthetic does not sufficiently value conceptual problems of understanding. In contrast to Sidney's view of poetry as an instrument of the will, with its chief power that of moving, Temple consistently sees it as a logical art, a vehicle of reason. For example, in countering Sidney's claim that the truth of a poet's Ideas "is manifest, by delivering them forth in such excellencie as hee hath imagined them," Temple contends that their truth can be assured only if they have been derived dialectically, by the proper precepts of rational thought. In considering Sidney's defense of the poet against lying, Temple notes that his notion of "affirmation" boxes him into a logical dilemma: if the poet does not affirm, he cannot lie; but unless he affirms, neither can poetry have truth value. See also Thorne (2657).

2654 THALER, ALWIN. *Shakespeare and Sir Philip Sidney: The Influence of the "Defense of Poesy."* Cambridge, Mass.: Harvard University Press, 1947, 112 pp.

Argues that "almost every major idea or principle in the *Defense* can be illustrated in some measure in Shakespeare's practice." In Chapter 1, illustrates his borrowing of both the phrasing and the substance of Sidney's book. Also suggests that Shakespeare's early connection with the Earl of Leicester's acting company may have brought Sidney's theories to Shakespeare's attention. Lists allusions to the *Defence* in other literary and critical works of the period, particularly the plays of Ben Jonson. In Chapter 2, concentrates on the third section of the *Defence*, that on the English poets. Notes plays of Shakespeare that adhere to or echo Sidney's descriptions of comedy and tragedy. Also considers Shakespeare's disregard of Sidney's "rules": the classical unities, the definitions of literary genres, and the "three wings" of the poet (art, imitation, and exercise). Notes in both authors a tension between fondness for ornamented language and dislike of rhetorical excesses. In Chapter 3, takes up the first section of the *Defence*, that on the nature of poetry. Considers Sidney's views on the Horatian ends of instruction and delight and the Platonic doctrine that virtue and beauty are one. Notes passages in which Shakespeare endorses Sidney's distinction between "versing" and poetry and his statements on the role of exercise in strengthening natural genius. Also finds Shakespearean analogues for Sidney's conception of "fore-conceit." Suggests that Shakespeare trusted more to his audience's imaginations than Sidney did but had a greater distrust of

Twentieth Century

vain fantasy. Gathers passages in Shakespeare's works revealing his views on the Puritan attacks on the stage, on the nondramatic genres of poetry, and on the value of history and philosophy. In Chapter 4, compares Sidney and Shakespeare in their responses to the opponents of poetry, particularly those who charge that poets are liars and encourage immorality.

2655 THOMPSON, ELBERT N[EVIUS] S[EBRING]. *The Controversy between the Puritans and the Stage.* Yale Studies in English, 20. New York: Henry Holt & Co., 1903, pp. 12, 90–91.
Seconds Sidney's claim that Plato was not consistently opposed to poetry. Regards very few passages in the *Defence* as replies to Stephen Gosson.

2656 THOMPSON, GUY ANDREW. *Elizabethan Criticism of Poetry.* Menasha, Wis.: Collegiate Press, George Banta Publishing Co., 1914, 216 pp. passim.
Relates the criticism of Sidney and his contemporaries to the poetry of the period. Covers such topics as the unsatisfactory state of English poetry, its causes and remedies; the nature and function of poetry; and poetic form. Notes that Sidney's main attack is not against the Puritans but against base "poet-apes" writing for reward. His remedy is to provoke national pride in the "mother tongue" and to link poetry with learning, noble action, and the aristocracy. Also notes that Sidney's view of poetry emphasizes matter over style or form and largely ignores allegory.

2657 THORNE, J.P. "A Ramistical Commentary on Sidney's *An Apologie for Poetrie.*" *MP* 54 (February 1957):158–64.
Details the divergences of opinion between the *Defence* and William Temple's manuscript commentary on it (item 2653). Describes the manuscript, discusses dating, and explains Temple's underlying Ramism. Concludes that the conventional gentleman of Sidney's day, embued with Ramus's view that all knowledge is "dialectical" and that poetry is simply such knowledge versified, would have viewed the *Defence* as "false even to the extent of perversity."

2658 TILLYARD, E[USTACE] M[ANDEVILLE] W[ETENHALL]. *The Elizabethan World Picture.* London: Chatto & Windus, 1967, pp. 22, 45. Orig. pub. London: Chatto & Windus, 1943 (not seen).
From comments in the *Defence* on the "erected wit" and "infected will," infers Sidney's views of order in a world disrupted by sin and his attitude toward human perfectibility.

2659 ———. "Sidney's *Apology*." *TLS*, 14 June 1941, pp. 287, 290.
Comments on the passage of the *Defence* on the "second nature," noting
that the "he" in the phrase "when with the force of a divine breath he
bringeth things forth" refers to man, not God, as one modern edition
suggests. Analyzes the passage in light of Christian Platonism.

2660 TRIMPI, WESLEY. "The Ancient Hypothesis of Fiction: An Essay
on the Origins of Literary Theory." *Traditio* 27 (1971):1–78.
Notes Sidney's view that poetry holds an ideal position between philosophy and history, comparing Sir Francis Bacon's claim that science holds
the middle ground between rationalism and empiricism with similar
views in twentieth-century philosophy and literary criticism. Attributes
much disagreement about Platonic and Aristotelian influences in the
Defence to a misunderstanding of Renaissance ambivalence over the
terms "example" and "image."

2661 TUVE, ROSEMOND. *Allegorical Imagery: Some Medieval Books and
Their Posterity*. Princeton, N.J.: Princeton University Press, 1966,
pp. 122, 127, 142, 171, 175, 184, 247, 335, 359, 368.
Alludes to the *Defence* as a touchstone to support the claim that, "however varied the definitions of allegory, they are at one in raising to an
extreme Sidney's remarks about poetry, that it deals with things 'in
their universal consideration' so that we view abstractions themselves
interacting."

2662 UHLIG, CLAUS. "Sidneys *Defence of Poesie* und die Poetik der
Renaissance. In *Englische und amerikanische Literaturtheorie: Studien
zu ihrer historischen Entwicklung*, edited by Rüdiger Ahrens and
Erwin Wolff. Vol. 1, *Renaissance, Klassizismus und Romantik*.
Anglistische Forschungen, 126. Heidelberg: Carl Winter
Universitätsverlag, 1978, pp. 73–93.
Considers Sidney's theory of poetry in relation to the classical rhetorical
tradition as it influenced the major Italian theorists. Views his poetic as
fundamentally Aristotelian in its notion of the relation between universals, which are the province of the poet, and particulars, which are the
domain of the historian. In this respect, his theory is of a piece with
other Renaissance theory. However, Sidney's "own accent" resides in a
"didacticism" that, though clearly marked, is not "pedantic." Claims that
the *Defence* must be read in terms of its "ethical aims," which are Sidney's
real weapon against the enemies of poetry. These aims are fundamentally rhetorical, grounded in his emphasis on "moving."

Twentieth Century

2663 ULREICH, JOHN C., Jr. "'The Poets Only Deliver': Sidney's Conception of *Mimesis*." *SLitI* 15 (Spring 1982):67–84.
Considers the appearance that the *Defence* mingles two inconsistent concepts of poetic imitation, one Aristotelian and the other Platonic. Lays out Aristotle's views that poets imitate nature and that forms exist only in so far as they are inherent in matter. Contrasts Plato's position that poets "figure forth" Ideas that exist independent of matter. Argues, however, that the two positions are not contradictory but contrary and hence "necessarily interdependent" and that Sidney sought implicitly to reconcile them. Finds the key to this reconciliation in the dynamic process of imitation: Aristotle saw it as "form realizing matter"; Plato considered it "matter expressing form." Cites evidence from the *Defence* to show that Sidney's concept of *mimesis* comprehends both, as did that of Milton. Also considers the apparent contradiction between Sidney's statements that the poet has "the works of Nature for his principal object" and that he disdains "to be tied to any such subjection," imitating instead a "golden" world of the imagination. Argues, however, that these views can be reconciled if one takes a neo-Platonic tack and regards the object of poetic imitation as nature's working (*Natura naturans*), instead of nature's works (*Natura naturata*). Relates Sidney's position here to his concept of *energeia*, to his comparison of the poetic maker to the divine Maker, and to his concepts of decorum and unity of action. Concludes that "what the poet delivers, finally, is not so much a product of his imagination as the imaginative process itself."

2664 VANDERHEYDEN, JAN F. "De vertaling van Sir Philip Sidney's *Defence of Poesie* door Joan de Haes (1712)." *Verslagen en Mededelingen van de Koninklijke Vlaamse Academie vor Tall- en Letterkunde*, September–December 1964, pp. 315–51.
Provides a brief biography of de Haes and discusses the relations between the three editions of 1712, 1720, and 1724 (see items 100 and 101). Is unable to decide which of the English editions most likely served as his translation text, proposing as most likely 1621, 1633, 1638, or 1674. In seeking to answer the question "Why translate?" examines de Haes's intellectual milieu, suggesting a "community of spirit" with Sidney. Analyzes the quality of the translation, its accuracy and fidelity to the nuances of Sidney's ideas and to his "baroque" prose style. Concludes that de Haes's translation is a genuine transformation of Sidney's work into Dutch.

2665 van DORSTEN, JAN [ADRIANUS]. "How Not To Open the Sidneian Text." *SNew* 2, no. 2 (1981):4–7.
Replies to DeNeef (2453), discussing a crux in Sidney's basic proposition describing poetry as a "speaking picture." Defends the punctuation of the passage in the Oxford edition (22). See also Heninger (2516).

2666 ———. "Sidney and Franciscus Junius the Elder." *HLQ* 42 (Winter 1978):1–13.
Argues that comments in the *Defence* on teaching, delighting, moving, and other important topics may have been inspired by Junius's dedicatory epistle to John Casimir in Part 3 of the Tremellius-Junius Bible. Notes that the dedication in Junius's *Grammatica Hebraeae Linguae* is to Sidney and suggests that the two had met, probably in 1577 during Sidney's embassy to Germany. Lists friends that the two men had in common and discusses the possibility that Sidney promised to introduce the Tremellius-Junius Bible to England as a way to further the Protestant League.

2667 VICKERY, JOHN B. "William Faulkner and Sir Philip Sidney?" *MLN* 70 (May 1955):349–50.
Suggests that Faulkner's phrase "Momus Nilebarge clatterfalque," used of a Mardi Gras float in his novel *Pylon*, is a compression of Sidney's mention of the Nile's cataracts and of Momus in the final paragraph of the *Defence*.

2668 VIEBROCK, HELMUT. *Defence of Poetry. Englische Argumente für den Bildungswert von Dichtung.* Sitzungberichte der wissenschaftlichen Gesellschaft an der Johann Wolfgang Goethe-Universität, Frankfurt am Main, vol. 14, no. 2. Wiesbaden, Germany: Franz Steiner Verlag, 1977, 38 pp.
Compares defenses of literature by Sidney, Shelley, and Ezra Pound in order to assess contemporary views on the subject. Considers the implications of Sidney's assertion that the poet "never lieth," connecting it with his comparison of the human "maker" with the divine Creator. Sees in this view a major departure from Aristotelian poetics, which aims only at *mimesis*. Also suggests that Renaissance nationalism changed the interpretation of Horace's dictum that poetry should teach and delight, making the ultimate aim the creation of a common national culture. From Sidney's arguments favoring poetry over history and philosophy, concludes that he valued the "instructive" over the "true." Considers ways in which Sidney's poetic was adapted or overthrown in the Romantic period.

Twentieth Century

2669 WALDEN, MICHAEL SETH. "Word, Image, and Representation in the Poetry of Sidney, Spenser, Jonson, and Donne." Ph.D. diss., University of California at Berkeley, 1981, 217 pp.

Considers "the truth value of representations" in Sidney's theory and practice. Finds in the *Defence* "an Aristotelian confidence that words might fashion true images, and a Platonic reticence to confirm the accuracy of representations." Examines the author's self-representation in *Astrophil and Stella,* noting that he simultaneously elicits sympathy and suspicion for that image. See *DAI* 42 (January 1982):3169A.

2670 WEBSTER, JOHN, ed. Introduction to *William Temple's "Analysis" of Sir Philip Sidney's "Apology for Poetry."* Medieval and Renaissance Texts and Studies, 32. Binghamton, N.Y.: Medieval & Renaissance Texts & Studies, 1984, pp. 11–56.

Clarifies Temple's three aims: to explicate the conceptual structure of *Defence,* to outline its organization, and to comment on its issues. Explains how his Ramist logic worked and "how such a system could come to concern itself" with a text like Sidney's, indicating where the two men disagree on aesthetic positions. Provides accounts of Temple's life, of the text, and of the principles of translation, along with a glossary of logical terms. Analyzes in close detail Temple's objections to three of Sidney's key arguments: that poetry is imitation; that, since it affirms nothing, poetry does not lie; and that poetry has a special capacity to move to virtuous action. In each case, "Temple thinks Sidney slights problems inherent in knowing, and thereby exaggerates poetry's position among the arts." Notes that Temple's remarks—"as close as we will ever come to seeing how educated Tudor readers actually responded to Sidney's work"—remind us that Sidney's aesthetic was but one of several "among which any serious reader had to find a place."

2671 WEBSTER, JOHN. "Oration and Method in Sidney's *Apology*: A Contemporary's Account." *MP* 79 (August 1981):1–15.

On the basis of William Temple's manuscript treatise *Analysis Tractationis de Poesi,* the earliest known commentary on the *Defence,* questions Myrick's outline of the *Defence* as a classical oration (671). Points out that Temple regards Sidney's work as a treatise, not as a forensic oration, and that he divides it into only four parts: a preface, a confirmation of the true nature of poetry, a refutation of possible objections, and an epilogue. Notes that Temple links the work with the humanist theory of discourse known as "method," which focuses on strategies appropriate for exposition rather than for persuasion. Surveys the theory of "method" from Philip Melancthon to Peter Ramus, noting that Elizabethan gentlemen were thoroughly exposed to the theory and that it accounts for Sidney's pattern of organization better than theories of oration. Notes, however, ways in which Temple distorts the *Defence* to fit his theory and concludes that Sidney's book draws strength from both forensic rhetoric and "method."

2672 WEINER, ANDREW D[AVID]. "Moving and Teaching: Sidney's *Defence of Poesie* as a Protestant Poetic." *JMRS* 2 (Fall 1972): 259–78.

Points out that Calvin and the Puritans were not generally opposed to poetry. Suggests, then, that Sidney was defending it against another group, those who accepted a medieval view of poetry. Argues that, before the Reformation, poetry was thought to drive the reader to seek knowledge (often concealed in allegory), and the reader was expected to use that knowledge to act well. But Luther had undercut that view by asserting that fallen man has no capacity to chose the good. Suggests that Sidney solves this problem on the basis of Calvinist theology. First he asserts that the poet is not dependent on the forms of fallen Nature but ranges "within the Zodiack of his owne wit," inspired directly "with the force of a divine breath." Then he solves the problem of the "infected will" by asserting that the poet bypasses the corrupt senses by working directly upon the imagination, which in turn bypasses the corrupt reason by working directly on the will. Points out two other ways in which Sidney's poetic is Protestant: 1) it avoids allegory in favor of figurative language, and 2) it does not affect salvation (which is predestined) but rather moral and political behavior. See a response by Craig (2448).

2673 ———. "'Multiformitie uniforme': *A Midsummer Night's Dream*." *ELH* 38 (September 1971):329–49.

Draws on the *Defence* to elucidate the debate between Hyppolyta and Theseus on the power of the imagination, the comments of the mechanicals about the effect of the Pyramus and Thisbe interlude on its audience, and the contrast Shakespeare establishes between his play and that of the mechanicals. Sees in the play Shakespeare's own *Defence of Poetry*.

2674 ———. *Sir Philip Sidney and the Poetics of Protestantism: A Study of Contexts*. Minneapolis: University of Minnesota Press, 1978, 243 pp.

In Chapter 1, examines Sidney's religious position, classifying him as one of the "godly," that is, a Protestant zealous in applying his faith to daily life. Regards Calvin as the "definitive interpreter" of the faith for

Twentieth Century

Sidney and his circle. Following the *Second Helvetic Confession* and du Plessis-Mornay's *Trueness of the Christian Religion*, attempts to reconstruct Sidney's views on the depravity of man and Christian regeneration. Examines his role in Queen Elizabeth's French marriage negotiations and in plans for a Protestant League, regarding Basilius's retirement in *Arcadia* as a comment on Elizabeth's opposition to the league. Argues that the *Defence* was prompted by a desire for a theory of poetry consonant with Reformed views of human nature. Interprets the work in that light, denying that Sidney confines "right poetry" to natural rather than divine philosophy. Urges that his works aim at the sort of self-knowledge that leads to a desire for salvation, though not to consideration of spiritual matters per se. In Chapter 2, analyzes characters in the Old *Arcadia* as "major classical formulations of the nature of man" and the narrator as a Protestant with a low opinion of human nature. Classifies the book as a comedy that illustrates the "common errors" of mankind rather than heroic virtues. Analyzes Book I in light of the biblical story of Adam, seeing Basilius as an Epicurean and Philanax as a Stoic. Considers the Aristotelian and neo-Platonic positions taken by Pyrocles and Musidorus, noting their later decline from these ideals. Discounts the theory that Philoclea educates Pyrocles after he attempts suicide in Book III or that the Princes are reconciled with God in the later prison scene. Accepts Euarchus's judgment of them as just and argues that their conduct has been no better than that of Gynecia, who acts as a mirror to show the evil of all the royal lovers. Also judges Pamela for her rebelliousness and Philoclea for her immodesty. In Chapter 3, defines the Mantuan tradition of pastoral and distinguishes two sorts of eclogue in *Arcadia*: those by main characters that magnify love into idolatry, and those by shepherds that diminish it to human proportions. Suggests that the eclogues after Books I and II present an ideal vision of love; those after Book III actualize this ideal and consider difficulties in attaining it; and those after Book IV consider the disordered love of the royal characters. Drawing on Sir Thomas Elyot's *Book of the Governor*, examines Renaissance associations between love, music, and cosmic order. Treats the debate of Reason and Passion (*OA 27*) as Sidney's solution to the problem faced by the royal lovers: they are to subordinate both reason and passion to religious faith. Contrasts the religious doubt and blasphemy of noble lovers such as Gynecia and Plangus with the harmonious faith of rustic lovers such as Lalus and Kala, whose marriage offers a contrast to the illicit love being pursued in the main plot. Treats the poem "Let mother earth now deck herself" (*OA 63*) as the completion of the "ideological core" of the eclogues and as a contrast to the conduct of

706

Pyrocles and Gynecia during their meeting in the cave in Book III. Interprets "On Ister bank" (*OA 66*) as a poem on the Fall of Adam and the need for obedience to Christ. In the Fourth Eclogues, allows that the shepherds lack Christian grace, but concludes that the eclogues in general offer hope through faith. In Chapter 4, considers the relation between the Terentian structure of the Old *Arcadia* and the sequence of emotions aroused by the book. Relates the fall suffered by the royal lovers and the attack of the lion and the bear to the fall of Adam and the consequent disruption of nature. In Book II, sees the disruptions spreading to society at large, most obviously in the rebellion of the commoners. Regards Book III as an unmasking of the true evil of the royal lovers. In Book IV, ponders the narrator's unexpected sympathy for the lovers and notes the importance of references to divine providence. In Book V, divides the main characters according to the wrong doctrines that have guided their actions, noting that all have trusted in their own strength rather than in the grace of God. Compares Euarchus with Abraham, obeying "heavenly rules" even at the cost of his son, and offers reasons that his judgments go unfulfilled. Dismisses the narrator's complaints of injustice at the end, concluding that the work as a whole teaches faith in providence.

2675 ———. "Sir Philip Sidney (1554–1586)." In *A Milton Encyclopedia*, edited by William B. Hunter, et al. Vol. 7. Lewisburg, Pa.: Bucknell University Press; London: Associated University Presses, 1979, pp. 195–99.
Claims that Milton assigns to the orator the task of "moving" that Sidney gave the poet. Sees Milton's manipulation of genre foreshadowed in Sidney's analysis of genre in the *Defence*.

2676 WETZEL, GÜNTER. "Die literarische Kritik in England von Sidney bis Dryden." Ph.D. diss., Christian-Albrechts Universität zu Kiel, 1941, 168 pp.
Abstract not available. Cited in *GV*, vol. 144, p. 148.

2677 WHITAKER, VIRGIL K[EEBLE]. *The Mirror up to Nature: The Technique of Shakespeare's Tragedies.* San Marino, Calif.: Huntington Library, 1965, pp. 58, 76–80.
Remarks on the importance of the *Defence* for the development of Renaissance drama, focusing on Sidney's concept of *mimesis*, his concern with universal precepts conveyed in concrete examples, and his view that art should be didactic.

Twentieth Century

2678 WHITE, HAROLD OGDEN. *Plagiarism and Imitation during the English Renaissance: A Study in Critical Distinctions.* Harvard Studies in English, 12. Cambridge, Mass.: Harvard University Press, 1935, pp. 60–64, 73–74, 78–79, 108.
Examines Sidney's doctrine of imitation in the *Defence* and *Astrophil and Stella*, particularly his views on borrowing from other authors, as the Ciceronian and Petrarchan poets do. Acquits John Harington of charges that he plagiarized from the *Defence* in his preface to *Orlando furioso.*

2679 WILLCOCK, GLADYS DOIDGE, and WALKER, ALICE, eds. *The Arte of English Poesie*, by George Puttenham. Cambridge: Cambridge University Press, 1936, pp. c–cii, 327–28.
Compares Sidney and Puttenham, noting that both emphasize the power of poetry to move the reader. Finds, however, that Sidney has more regard for authorities in classical antiquity and the Italian Renaissance and that he is less comfortable with love poetry. Lists poems from *Certain Sonnets* and the Old *Arcadia* that Puttenham had seen in manuscript.

2680 WILSON, HAROLD S. "Some Meanings of 'Nature' in Renaissance Literary Theory." *JHI* 2 (October 1941):430–48.
Classifies the usage of Sidney and others according to thirty-five definitions of the term "nature."

2681 WIMSATT, WILLIAM K[URTZ], Jr., and BROOKS, CLEANTH. *Literary Criticism: A Short History.* New York: Alfred A. Knopf, 1957, pp. 167–74, 422.
Characterizes the attacks on poetry by Elizabethan moralists and the nature of Sidney's response. Finds his definition of poetry as a moral teacher inconsistent with his later admission that some poems are immoral. Relates his theory that poetry imitates ideas to statements by Plotinus, Shakespeare, and Sir Francis Bacon. Also compares Sidney's criticism with that of Jonson and Shelley.

2682 WINTER, HELMUT. *Literaturtheorie und Literaturkritik.* Studienreihe Englisch, 19. Düsseldorf: August Bagel Verlag; Bern, Switzerland, and Munich: Franke Verlag, 1975, pp. 87–91.
Lays out Sidney's theory of poetry and notes its major sources.

2683 WITHERSPOON, ALEXANDER MACLAREN. *The Influence of Robert Garnier on Elizabethan Drama.* Yale Studies in English, 65. New Haven, Conn.: Yale University Press, 1924, pp. 65–85 passim.
Considers the various translations and imitations of the plays of Garnier written by the Countess of Pembroke and by others in the Sidney circle.

Sees these plays as attempts to reform English tragedy along the lines that Sidney had laid out in the *Defence*. Also discusses Sidney's participation in the Areopagus.

2684 WOLFF, ERWIN. "Einleitung: Funktionsgeschichtliche Aspekte der englischen Literaturtheorie." In *Englische und amerikanische Literaturtheorie: Studien zu ihrer historischen Entwicklung*, edited by Rüdiger Ahrens and Erwin Wolff. Vol. 1, *Renaissance, Klassizismus und Romantik*. Anglistische Forschungen, 126. Heidelberg: Carl Winter Universitätsverlag, 1978, pp. 11–44.

Locating the *Defence* within the larger history of "apologetic" literature (religious, scientific, and aesthetic), claims that it raises three major lines of defense. From a "sociological" perspective, Sidney sees poetry as the origin of all culture, suggesting that its value resides in the social utility of its power to move people to virtuous action. From a religious perspective, poetry functions as a substitute for the role of the church. From a philosophical perspective, Sidney's treatise "opens up" a gap between poetry and science that will not be fully felt until the eighteenth century. It does so through its insistence that poetry can reach the ideal realm directly, whereas science must take a detour through reality.

2685 WOLFLEY, LAWRENCE C. "Sidney's Visual-Didactic Poetic: Some Complexities and Limitations." *JMRS* 6 (Fall 1976):217–41.

Criticizes Robinson (2618) for suggesting that Sidney's *Defense* is philosophically perfect. Also rejects Shepherd's view (141) that it is "basically Aristotelian." Notes that Aristotelian *mimesis* is concerned with particular men, but Sidney is concerned with imitations of virtues, vices, and passions. Finds the originality of the *Defence* in its concern with the psychological processes by which images are transferred to the reader's mind. Lays out the Renaissance humanists' distinction between words and the mental entities to which they refer, which were regarded as primarily visual. Also distinguishes the term "fore-conceit" from "Idea." Argues that Sidney followed a Ramist distinction in offering two models for the way a poet affects the mind: the "Idea" or "fore-conceit" teaches dialectically through mental images, and the actual words of the poem move the will rhetorically. Concludes that Sidney was wrong in thinking that poetry necessarily moves men to virtuous action.

2686 WRIGHT, NEIL HUTCHISON. "Shakespeare and Redemptive Illusion." Ph.D. diss., Florida State University, 1982, 187 pp.

Argues that Shakespeare was "deeply indebted to the idea of redemption through poetic illusion" as set forth in the *Defence*. Traces Sidney's concept of the *vates* and his theory of divine truth in poetry to Plato's

Twentieth Century

Ion, suggesting that Shakespeare inherited but altered Sidney's Platonic concepts. Treats Prospero, the magus in *The Tempest,* as "Shakespeare's realization of the Vates or 'right poet'" of the *Defence.* See *DAI* 43 (January 1983):2356A.

2687 ZOLBROD, PAUL GEYER. "The Poet's Golden World: Classical Bases for Philip Sidney's Literary Theory." Ph.D. diss., University of Pittsburg, 1967, 202 pp.
Investigates Sidney's concept of "fore-conceit." Points out that it is a form of universal idea different from that of the philosophers in that it "is invariably expressed in concrete terms" and delights as well as teaches. Traces the concept to Plato's *Phaedrus* and Aristotle's *Poetics,* noting that its origins are probably pre-Socratic. Considers the relevance of the concept to twentieth-century criticism. See *DA* 28 (June 1968):5033A.

Studies of the Minor Works

1. THE LADY OF MAY

Nineteenth Century

2688 HALPIN, N[ICHOLAS] J. *Oberon's Vision in the "Midsummer-Night's Dream," Illustrated by a Comparison with Lylie's "Endymion."* Shakespeare Society of London, Publications, vol. 14, no. 16. London: Shakespeare Society, 1843, pp. 99–100.

Surmises that, in writing *The Lady of May*, Sidney's aim was to gain Queen Elizabeth's permission for some young noblewoman to marry. Equates Rombus with Stephen Gosson and weighs reasons that the Queen's final judgment was not printed.

Twentieth Century

2689 AXTON, MARIE. "The Tudor Mask and Elizabethan Court Drama." In *English Drama: Forms and Development: Essays in Honour of Muriel Clara Bradbrook*, edited by Marie Axton and Raymond Williams. Cambridge: Cambridge University Press, 1977, pp. 24–47.

Discusses the political context of *Four Foster Children of Desire* and *The Lady of May*, relating them to other entertainments for the Earl of Leicester that involve a struggle between masculine desire and feminine beauty. Dates *The Lady of May* in 1578. Suggests that the controversy between the shepherds and the foresters represents Leicester's "anti-selves." Considers elements of the masque in the work and traces the

Twentieth Century

characters Therion and Espilus to entertainments written for Henry VIII. Discusses the meaning of Therion's name, tracing it to Aristotle's *Politics*, and suggests that the entertainment was designed to allow Queen Elizabeth to give Leicester a clear decision on his proposal of marriage.

2690 BROTANEK, RUDOLF. *Die Englischen Maskenspiele.* Wiener Beiträge zur Englischen Philolgie, 15. Vienna and Leipzig: Wilhelm Braumüller, 1902, pp. 47–48, 83, 156.

Touches on Sidney's pastoral style and *The Lady of May*, commenting on ways in which it anticipates the characteristics of later, more fully developed masques. Traces the pedant in John Beaumont's *Masque of the Inner Temple and Gray's Inn* to the influence of Sidney's Rombus.

2691 CRAIGIE, SIR WILLIAM A. *The Critique of Pure English from Caxton to Smollett.* Society for Pure English, tract no. 65. Oxford: Clarendon Press, 1946, pp. 132–34, 154.

Points out that most of Rombus's Latinisms in *The Lady of May* were in actual use.

2692 FLETCHER, JEFFERSON BUTLER. *Literature of the Italian Renaissance.* New York: Macmillan Co., 1934, p. 289.

Points out the similarity between Sidney's *Lady of May* and the pastoral farces of an Italian troup known as *I Rozzi*, which mingled rustic slapstick with mythology. Notes that the question put to Sidney's Lady is also a typical Italian *dubbio*.

2693 HOGAN, PATRICK G[ALVIN], Jr. "Neoplatonic Elements in Sidney's Masque-like *Lady of May*." SNew 1, no. 2 (1980):53–57.

Considers the background of the work and suggests that it foreshadows the ethical concerns of Sidney's major works. Discusses the neo-Platonic implications of Sidney's concept of the "erected wit" in the *Defence* and Rixon's argument for the active life in the *Lady of May*, probing the reasons behind Queen Elizabeth's choice of the contemplative shepherd Espilus.

2694 HOTSON, LESLIE. "Who Wrote *Leicester's Commonwealth?*" *Listener* 43 (16 March 1950):481–83.

Notes that, at the time Sidney was writing the *Defence of Leicester*, his father-in-law, Sir Francis Walsingham, knew that Thomas Morgan was the author of *Leicester's Commonwealth* but concealed the information from Sidney.

2695 KIMBROUGH, ROBERT. *Sir Philip Sidney.* Twayne's English Authors Series, 114. New York: Twayne Publishers, 1971, pp. 63–68.

In Chapter 3, claims that *The Lady of May* has the same spontaneous quality as Gascoigne's 1575 Kenilworth entertainment, but argues that, more importantly, it shows Sidney's "academic" imitation of the Italian *commedia rusticale.* Finds in the work "two aspects of his art which became more apparent as he wrote more: his ability to reveal character through speech and his refusal to see life as a series of simple oppositions." Disagrees with Orgel (2698) and Kalstone (1907), who suggest that Queen Elizabeth was not paying attention to the May Lady's request for judgment. Concludes that, "like Caesar, she knew what kind of men she wanted around her." See also item 593.

2696 MONTROSE, LOUIS ADRIAN. "Celebration and Insinuation: Sir Philip Sidney and the Motives of Elizabethan Courtship." *RenD*, n.s. 8 (1977):3–35.

Concerned with persuasion and manipulation as the means by which courtiers could achieve preferment from Elizabeth, argues that Sidney's *Lady of May* was designed "less to praise than to oppose, instruct, and petition his queen." Sees it as a prime example of the Elizabethan attempt "to obliterate the distinction between life and art." Finds in it a contrast between time-servers and free spirits, which serves to criticize the role of the courtier at Elizabeth's court. Sees the Queen's choice at the end as a conscious rejection of Sidney's aspirations. In the *Defence*, finds a justification for Sidney's pursuit of literature as the only course of action open to him.

2697 ORGEL, STEPHEN K. *The Jonsonian Masque.* Cambridge, Mass.: Harvard University Press, 1965, pp. 22, 44–57, 188.

Reprints, with slight revisions (including a few added examples), the argument of item 2698.

2698 ———. "Sidney's Experiment in Pastoral: *The Lady of May.*" *JWCI* 26 (1963):198–203.

Examines Sidney's adaptation of conventions of the court masque. Argues that *The Lady of May* questions the pastoral tradition, particularly its emphasis on the contemplative life, much as *Arcadia* shows the limitations of pastoral romance and *Astrophil and Stella* offers a critique of the Petrarchan convention of the unattainable mistress. Notes the inadequacy of the contemplative characters Lalus and Rombus. Explicates the debates in the work, noting that the foresters are continually successful

Twentieth Century

in undercutting the arguments of the shepherds. Regards the Queen's choice of the shepherd Espilus as an attempt to follow pastoral tradition and a failure to grasp Sidney's antipastoral intentions. Also suggests that the lack of dance and spectacle in the work anticipates the emphasis on poetry that characterizes later masques by Jonson and Milton. See item 2697 and a response by Kimbrough (2695).

2699 PICKETT, PENNY. "The Secretest Cabinet: The Theory of the Soul in Sir Philip Sidney and Philippe du Plessis de Mornay." Ph.D. diss., Brown University, 1974, 195 pp.
Identifies the edition of Plato that was most important to Sidney and discusses Sidney's knowledge of the dialogues, arguing that it is "direct, thorough, and primary." Also considers links between du Plessis-Mornay and Sidney, both in their lives and in their ideas on the soul. Suggests that Sidney rejected Mornay's theory and that the *Defence* was written against him and others who distrusted the human imagination. Links the *Defence* to passages in Plato favorable to poets. Analyzes *The Lady of May*, asserting that it contains a veiled use of Plato's image of the soul as a chariot. See *DAI* 35 (May 1975):7265A–66A.

2700 ———. "Sidney's Use of *Phaedrus* in *The Lady of May*." *SEL* 16 (Winter 1976):33–50.
Analyzes *The Lady of May* as a poetic analogue to Plato's image of the soul as a charioteer drawn by a mild horse and a wild one. From etymologies of the names "Espilus" and "Therion," and from evidence about the temperaments of these characters, concludes that they correspond with Plato's horses. Identifies the May Lady as reason and the "good," as these are discussed in Plato's *Symposium*. Considers the choice between the two suitors offered to Queen Elizabeth, arguing that Sidney does not mean for either to be eliminated but for the two to be brought into harmony. Discusses problems raised by attempts to identify the characters with Leicester and other contemporary political figures, treating Rombus as a representation of "the failure of rhetoric to join man's soul with that which his soul desires (beauty, the good, the one, God)." Also treats the epilogue in the Helmingham Hall Manuscript as a parallel to Socrates's final prayer in *Phaedrus*, and concludes that the entire entertainment illustrates the concept of poetry in Sidney's *Defence*.

2701 PURCELL, J[AMES] M[ARK]. "A Few Notes on Sidney's *Lady of May*." *MLN* 47 (June 1932):386–87.
Cites words in *The Lady of May* used well before the earliest date recorded in the *Oxford English Dictionary*.

2702 PURDY, MARY MARTHA. "Political Propaganda in Ballad and Masque." In *If by Your Art: Testament to Percival Hunt*, edited by Agnes Lynch Starrett. Pittsburgh: University of Pittsburgh Press, 1948, pp. 264–93.

Discusses the political context of *The Lady of May*, equating the Lady with Queen Elizabeth, Espilus with Leicester, and Therion with the Duke of Alençon. Considers the personal and political aims behind the allegory, surmising that the masque encouraged topical allegories and allusions in Spenser's *Shepherd's Calendar*, Lyly's *Endymion*, and Harvey's *Gratulationes Valdinenses*.

2703 REYHER, PAUL. *Les masques anglais: Étude sur les ballets et la vie de cour en Angleterre (1512–1640)*. Paris: Hachette & Co., 1909, pp. 30–31, 98–99, 178.

Comments on the literary importance of the Kenilworth entertainments of 1575 and on the possible influence of *The Lady of May* on Francis Beaumont's development of the antimasque.

2704 STILLMAN, ROBERT E. "Justice and the 'Good Word' in Sidney's *The Lady of May*." *SEL* 24 (Winter 1984):23–38.

Offers a "new argument" about the entertainment, claiming that "*all* of its diverse concerns" may be thematically unified through a consideration of "the connection which Sidney draws between justice and good works." At the center of the work is Sidney's concern for a just relation between *res* and *verba*. In contrast to post-Saussurean linguistics, Sidney's own concepts "interpret meaning . . . as a function of similarity": language is a "rational totality like that of a philosophical system." *The Lady of May* "is filled with characters unable to match words and things properly." In the debate between Dorcas and Rixus, Sidney is concerned with "the way in which an abuse of language both mirrors and creates an abuse of passion." This is the "moral matter," the *res* at the heart of the entertainment's *verba*. Sidney's purpose in publishing it may have included criticizing Elizabeth's misjudgment, her injustice, in awarding the May Lady to Espilus. *The Lady of May* is important for understanding Sidney's literary career in the degree to which it "anticipates his concerns about language in *Defence*."

Twentieth Century

2. *FOUR FOSTER CHILDREN OF DESIRE*

Twentieth Century

2705 BERGERON, DAVID M. *English Civic Pageantry 1558–1642.* Columbia: University of South Carolina Press, 1971, pp. 36–37, 44–46.
Describes *The Lady of May* and *Four Foster Children of Desire*, relating them to other pageants of the day and to Queen Elizabeth's French marriage negotiations.

2706 COUNCIL, NORMAN. "*O Dea Certe*: The Allegory of *The Fortress of Perfect Beauty*." *HLQ* 39 (August 1976):329–42.
From circumstantial evidence, infers that the court and the French commissioners expected the entertainment (also called *Four Foster Children of Desire*) to deal allegorically with the prospects that Queen Elizabeth would marry the Duke of Alençon. Argues that it did. Discusses the meaning of Sidney's motto and the Queen's shifting role, first as the goddess of natural beauty and later as the goddess of heavenly beauty. Sees in both roles the suggestion that Elizabeth is not a suitable match for the Duke. Notes parallels with neo-Platonic philosophy, Christian allegories of the New Adam and Eve, and contemporary events at court. Also traces the development of the modern dislike of such allegories.

2707 FOGEL, EPHIM G[REGORY]. "A Possible Addition to the Sidney Canon." *MLN* 75 (May 1960):389–94.
Examines two opening sonnets in *Four Foster Children of Desire*, along with the prose delivered by the challengers. Argues that these passages are probably by Sidney and ought to be included among his works.

2708 SCHULZE, IVAN L. "The Final Protest against the Elizabeth-Alençon Marriage Proposal." *MLN* 58 (January 1943):54–57.
Suggests that *Four Foster Children of Desire* was the final symbolic attempt of the antimarriage faction to break off Queen Elizabeth's match with the Duke of Alençon. Points out that the comparison of Elizabeth with the sun echoes secret correspondence from Alençon's emissary, Jehan de Simier, which could only have come to Sidney's knowledge through Sir Francis Walsingham or the Earl of Leicester.

2709 WELSFORD, ENID. *The Court Masque: A Study in the Relationship between Poetry and the Revels.* Cambridge: Cambridge University Press, 1927, pp. 159–60.
Regards the *Four Foster Children of Desire* as crude by the standards of the French ambassadors for whom it was performed.

3. *A LETTER WRITTEN . . . TO QUEEN ELIZABETH*

Twentieth Century

2710 BRENNECKE, ERNEST. "Shakespeare's 'Singing Man of Windsor.'" *PMLA* 66 (December 1951):1188–92.
Argues that "the singing man in Henry the IV's time," who is mentioned as an example of treachery in Sidney's *Letter to the Queen*, is the priest John Maudelen. Notes that he was a conspirator against Richard II and was associated with Windsor. Infers that, in *II Henry IV* II.i, Shakespeare uses the phrase "the singing man of Windsor" to suggest villainy.

2711 RIBNER, IRVING. "Machiavelli and Sidney's *Discourse to the Queenes Majesty*." *Italica* 26 (September 1949):177–87.
Compares ideas in Sidney's *Letter to the Queen* with those in Machiavelli's *Prince* and *Discourses*. Concludes that both men use the same utilitarian and empirical method of argument, based on historical experience of cause and effect rather than on abstract principles of morality. Points out numerous principles in Sidney's letter that have parallels in Machiavelli's works.

2712 WOUDHUYSEN, H.R. "A Crux in the Text of Sidney's *A Letter to Queen Elizabeth*." *N&Q*, n.s. 31 (June 1984):172–73.
Citing eight readings culled from "the more immediately accessible" manuscripts discovered after Duncan-Jones's edition of *Letter to the Queen* (22), suggests a resolution to the crux "such ivy knots" by comparing a passage in Old *Arcadia*, Book V, which reads "such very knots."

4. *DEFENCE OF THE EARL OF LEICESTER*

Twentieth Century

2713 ANON. Notice of sale. *N&Q* 152 (7 May 1927):326.
Describes a manuscript of the *Defence of Leicester* containing letters from Leicester, his wife, and Lord Burghley.

2714 ———. "Sidney's *Defense of Leicester*." *TLS*, 19 May 1927, p. 360.
Notes the sale of an autograph manuscript of the *Defence of Leicester*. Describes the manuscript and its history.

Twentieth Century

5. *THE TRUENESS OF THE CHRISTIAN RELIGION*

Twentieth Century

2715 DANIELSON, DENNIS R. "Sidney, Greville, and the Metaphysics of 'Naughtinesse.'" *ESC* 10 (September 1984):265–77.

Although mainly concerned with two of Greville's poems, shows that Sidney's "brilliant" translation of a passage in du Plessis-Mornay's *Trueness of the Christian Religion*, where he renders the concepts of moral evil and metaphysical nothingness as "naughty" and "naughtinesse," provides Greville with terms whose considerable philosophical freight has been misunderstood.

2716 [MORNAY, CHARLOTTE ARBALESTE de.] *A Huguenot Family of the XVI Century: The Memoirs of Philippe de Mornay, Sieur du Plessis Marly, Written by His Wife.* Translated by Lucy Crump. London: George Routledge & Sons; New York: E.P. Dutton & Co., [1926], pp. 169–70.

Mentions Sidney's intimacy with Mornay, his translation of *The Trueness of the Christian Religion*, and his role as godfather to Mornay's daughter.

2717 MURPHY, CHARLES D. "John Davies's Versification of Sidney's Prose." *PQ* 21 (July 1942):410–14.

Claims that Davies's versification of Sidney's translation of du Plessis-Mornay's *Trueness of the Christian Religion* in his *Mirum ad Modum* "lacks the coherence of the prose original."

2718 ROBINSON, FORREST G[LEN]. "A Note on the Sidney-Golding Translation of Philippe de Mornay's *De la verité de la religion chrestienne*." *HLB* 17 (January 1969):98–102.

Argues against attempts such as that of Feuillerat (23) to assign particular parts of the treatise to Sidney or to Arthur Golding. Concludes that stylistic analysis cannot discriminate in this case.

2719 TENISON, E[VA] M[ABEL]. *Elizabethan England: Being the History of This Country "In Relation to All Foreign Princes."* Vol. 7. Royal Leamington Spa, Warwick, England: n.p., 1940, pp. 145–60 passim.

Notes the popularity of the Sidney-Golding translation, explaining Golding's stated aim "to reforme the malicious and stubborn-hearted" as a reference to the Puritans. Rejects attempts by Feuillerat (23) to determine the parts written by Sidney by analyzing the prose style. Finds that the mediocre sections have stylistic parallels in *Arcadia* and reflect badly written passages in the French original. Quotes the testimony of Fulke Greville, George and Bernard Whetstone, and other contemporaries that Sidney wrote "a great part" of the translation. See also item 780.

Studies of the Correspondence

Eighteenth Century

2720 WOLFIUS, JO[HANN] CHRISTOPHORUS. *Conspectus Supellectilis Epistolicae et Literariae*. Hamburg: Sumtibus Felginerianis, 1736, pp. 59, 98, 128, 238.

Catalogs manuscripts of letters in the Sidney correspondence, including fourteen from Sidney to Languet later printed by Pears (183).

Nineteenth Century

2721 ANON. Review of *The Correspondence of Sir Philip Sidney and Hubert Languet*, edited by Steuart A. Pears. *Athenaeum*, no. 948, 27 December 1845, pp. 1237–39.

Suggests that Sidney's fame greatly exceeds his achievements. Discusses his relationship with Languet, the discovery of the new letters in Pears's edition (183), and the wisdom of Languet in perceiving the faults in Sidney's character.

2722 BRUCE, JOHN. "Who Was 'Will, My Lord of Leycester's Jesting Player'?" *Shakespeare Society's Papers* 1 (1844):88–95.

Quotes at length from Sidney's letter to Sir Francis Walsingham of 24 March 1586, discussing its background and the several actors named "Will" to which it may refer. Argues in favor of Will Kempe and weighs the possibility that Leicester's entire company of players, including Shakespeare, may have been with him in the Netherlands.

2723 GREAT BRITAIN. HISTORICAL MANUSCRIPTS COMMIS-SION. *Second Report of the Royal Commission on Historical Manuscripts*. London: Her Majesty's Stationery Office, 1871, pp. ix, 82, 97.

Nineteenth Century

Notes among manuscripts of C. Cottrell Dormer several letters from Sidney to Leicester. Among the "Charter Chests of the family of Neville of Holt" are Elizabeth's instructions to Sidney "beinge sent to the Emperor the viith of Februarie 1576."

Twentieth Century

2724 BALD, R.C. "'Will, My Lord of Leicester's Jesting Player.'" *N&Q*, n.s. 6 (March 1959):112.
Documents the Continental travels of Will Kempe in order to refute arguments by Mithal (2735) that Kempe could not possibly be the actor mentioned in Sidney's letter to Sir Francis Walsingham of 24 March 1586.

2725 BUFORD, ALBERT H. "History and Biography: The Renaissance Distinction." In *A Tribute to George Coffin Taylor: Studies and Essays, Chiefly Elizabethan, by His Students and Friends*, edited by Arnold Williams. Chapel Hill: University of North Carolina Press, 1952, pp. 100–112.
Examines Sidney's letter to his brother Robert of 18 October 1580, comparing its notions of biography and history with similar concepts in Bacon's *Advancement of Learning* and Plutarch's *Lives*.

2726 BÜHLER, CURT F. "On the Date of the Letter Written by Sir Philip Sidney to Christopher Plantin." *RES* 12 (January 1936):67–71. Reprint. In *Early Books and Manuscripts: Forty Years of Research*, by Curt F. Bühler. [New York]: Grolier Club, Pierpont Morgan Library, 1973, pp. 317–21.
Argues that the letter in vol. 3, p. 134, of Feuillerat (23) was not written in 1580/1, as Feuillerat supposed, but in the summer of 1585. Identifies the three books that Sidney requested as Abraham Ortelius's *Theatrum Orbis Terrarum*, the *Speculum Nauticum*, and most likely Aurelio de Pasino's *Discours sur plusieurs poincts de l'architecture de guerre*. Relates the request to Sidney's hope to sail with Drake against Spain in September 1585. See also Bond (189).

2727 BUXTON, JOHN. "An Elizabethan Reading-List: An Unpublished Letter from Sir Philip Sidney." *TLS*, 24 March 1972, pp. 343–44; 31 March 1972, p. 366.
In the first issue listed, prints a letter from Sidney to Edward Denny dated 22 May 1580 and preserved in a transcript by John Mansell. Supplies a biographical introduction and explanatory notes, suggesting

Humphrey Tyndall as the likely source from whom Mansell received the letter. In the following issue, points out that the portrait chosen by *TLS* to accompany the letter is not, in fact, of Sidney. See also items 192 and 2728 and the original description of the manuscript by Sotheby & Co. (2739). See also a response by Davids (2729).

2728 ———. "A New Letter from Sir Philip Sidney," *ELR* 2 (Winter 1972):four-page insert following p. 28.
Supplies photographs of Mansell's copy of Sidney's letter to Edward Denny, dated from Wilton on Whitsunday (22 May) 1580, which gives advice about a future course of study. Reviews Denny's life and his relations with Sidney, identifying in the letter an allusion to *Certain Sonnets* and noting that the books listed by Sidney reveal his own reading. See also items 192 and 2727.

2729 DAVIDS, ROY L. "Philip Sidney." *TLS*, 7 April 1972, p. 394.
Notes that a letter to Edward Denny printed by Buxton (2727) was first printed in Sotheby's sale catalog for 15 June 1971. Argues that the manuscript of the letter was copied from the holograph, and disputes Buxton's reading of one of the words. Begins a long correspondence. See subsequent issues of *TLS*: Buxton's reply and Ronald Mansbridge's addition, 14 April 1972, p. 421; Davids's reply to Buxton and Bent Juel-Jensen's comment, 28 April 1972, p. 495; Buxton's reply to Davids, 5 May 1972, p. 521; and R.E. Alton's support for Davids, 12 May 1972, p. 548.

2730 DEAN, LEONARD F. "Bodin's *Methodus* in England Before 1625." *SP* 39 (April 1942):160–66.
Notes Sidney's reference to Jean Bodin in a letter to Robert Sidney dated 18 October 1580, and suggests that the *Methodus* increased Sidney's scorn for historians.

2731 DIX, WILLIAM S., ed. "Letters of English Authors: From the Collection of Robert H. Taylor." *PULC* 21 (Summer 1960):200–236.
In a catalog of letters exhibited at Princeton in 1960, includes one from Sidney to his banker dated from Frankfurt on 20 March 1573.

2732 GREENLAW, EDWIN A. "The Influence of Machiavelli on Spenser." *MP* 7 (October 1909):187–202.
Cites Sidney's mention of *Il principe* in correspondence with Languet as evidence that Spenser had encountered Machiavelli's ideas though the Sidney circle.

Twentieth Century

2733 JOHN, LISLE CECIL. "The First Edition of the Letters of Hubert
Languet to Sir Philip Sidney." *JEGP* 48 (July 1949):361–66.
Corrects the assertion of Pears (183) that the 1646 Leiden edition of
Languet's correspondence with Sidney (167) was the first. Points out the
1633 Frankfurt edition (166), listing extant copies and identifying the
printer as William Fitzer. Lists printing errors in the 1633 version, most
of which were carried over to that of 1646. Traces Lord Hailes's edition
(169) to the 1646 edition and Pears's text to Lord Hailes, noting corrections and new errors in the course of transcription. Infers that Sir
Stephen le Sieur, to whom the 1633 version is dedicated, had a hand in
collecting the letters.

2734 KUERSTEINER, AGNES DUNCAN. "A Note on Sir Philip
Sidney." *N&Q* 193 (26 June 1948):268–69.
Argues that Pears (183) mistranslates a passage in Sidney's 19 December
1573 letter to Languet, leading later biographers to view Sidney as "bad-
tempered and unjust."

2735 MITHAL, H.S.D. "'Will, My Lord of Leicester's Jesting Player.'"
N&Q, n.s. 5 (October 1958):427–29.
Seeks to refute the view of Chambers (467) and others that the "Will"
mentioned in Sidney's letter to Sir Francis Walsingham of 24 March
1586 was Will Kempe. Points to records of Kempe's travels and the lack
of evidence that he was in Leicester's acting company. Argues instead in
favor of a known member of the company, Robert Wilson. See a reply by
Bald (2724).

2736 PARKS, STEPHEN. "The Osborn Collection, 1934–1974: A
Catalogue of Manuscripts Exhibited in the Beinecke Rare Book
and Manuscript Library, October 1974–February 1975." *YULG* 49
(October 1974):171–211.
Lists the authors in James M. Osborn's collection of sixty-five letters to
Sidney. See also item 2738.

2737 REICHELT, WALTER ERIC. "Sir Philip Sidney's Reading Lists
and Sixteenth-Century English Education." Ph.D. diss., Columbia
University, 1977, 198 pp.
Examines Sidney's letters recommending programs of study to his
brother Robert and to Edward Denny. Places them in the context of
humanist thought about the proper way to study history, suggesting that
they were intended to provide practical political and military skills not
available in the grammar schools and universities. Citing Jean Bodin's
Methodus ad Facilem Historium Cognitionem as their "probable source,"

notes that they proceed from the whole to the parts and from the general to the particular and are designed to instill knowledge of probable chains of cause and effect in matters affecting the commonwealth. Reflects on the active and virtuous life that Sidney expected of a gentleman, tracing his ideals to Scripture, Aristotle's *Nicomachean Ethics*, Cicero's *De Officiis*, and Plutarch's *Moralia*. See *DAI* 38 (July 1977):287A.

2738 SOTHEBY & CO. "Bibliotheca Phillippica: Catalogue of the Celebrated Collection of Manuscripts Formed by Sir Thomas Phillipps, Bt. (1792–1872)." n.s. 3d part. Sale of 26 June 1967. London: Sotheby & Co., [1967], pp. 88–90.

In Lot 741, describes for sale sixty-five original letters in Latin, French, and Italian addressed to Sidney by scholars and diplomats on the Continent during the period of June 1573–June 1576 (with one letter dated 10 October 1581). Notes that none of Sidney's replies is thought to have survived. Also includes a letter from Pietro Bizari to Jean de Vulcob, Sieur de Sassy, which is "almost certainly" the one that Languet sent to Sidney as a model of eloquence and referred to in a letter of 19 November 1573 (to which Sidney replied on 5 December 1573). Notes that all the letters were, until 1967, "apparently unpublished and unknown to scholars." Lists their authors as follows: Jean Lobbetius, a "learned lawyer" of Strasbourg (nineteen letters); Wolfgang Zindelini, tutor to Christopher, Prince Palatine (twelve letters); Andreas Pauli, counsellor to August I, Elector of Saxony; Jean Vulcob, French diplomat; Matthew Wacker, diplomat and poet; François Perrot; Théophile de Banos, disciple of Peter Ramus; Zacharius Ursinus; Otto, Count Solms; Favian, Burgrave and Baron of Donau; Dr. George Purkircher; Michael Slavata, Baron of Cossumberg; and others. Notes that Sir Thomas purchased them in 1844 from Benjamin Heywood Bright. Sketches broadly the subjects they deal with, the places from which they originated and to which they were addressed, and their styles of address. Concludes that the letters represent "much the largest collection" of letters to Sidney to be found anywhere. In Lot 743, describes eleven Latin letters to Sidney from Robert Dorset, the tutor of Sidney's brother Robert, dating from 3 June 1575 to 23 June 1576. Describes their major topics, which center around Oxford University and the education of Robert Sidney. Only one of the letters was previously known to scholars, that published by Zouch (187).

2739 SOTHEBY & CO. "Bibliotheca Phillippica: Catalogue of the Celebrated Collection of Manuscripts Formed by Sir Thomas

Twentieth Century

Phillipps, Bt. (1792–1872)." n.s. 7th part. Sale of 15 June 1971. London: Sotheby & Co., [1971], pp. 141–43 and preceding plate. In Lot 1660, describes for the first time John Mansel's transcript of Sidney's letter to Edward Denny outlining suggestions for Denny's education. Notes that the letter was previously unknown and that it contains the only reference in Sidney's letters to his own "songs," which the poet asks Denny to sing. Also notes a likely allusion to Spenser, suggesting that Sidney helped the poet obtain his appointment in Ireland by exercising influence through Denny and his family. In considering the authors whom Sidney recommends, claims that the list includes fourteen who have not previously been proved to have had any direct influence on him: Didorus Siculus, Quintus Curtius, Polybius, Valerius, Zonarus, Procopius, Paulus Aemilius, Polydore Vergil, Stephanus (Henri Estienne), Abraham Ortelius, Jean Froissart, Monstrelet, Francesco Guicciardini, and Sacro Bosco. Also notes Sidney's reference to Holinshed's *Chronicles*, which formerly could only be linked with him by inference. Includes a photograph of the letter, biographical information on Denny and Mansell, and speculations on the way in which Mansell may have obtained the letter. See also Buxton (2727, 2728) and Davids (2729).

Literary Works Pertaining to Sidney

1. ELEGIES, EPITAPHS, AND POEMS OF PRAISE

Sixteenth Century

2740 ANON. "Another of the same. Excellently written by a most woorthy Gentleman." In *The Phoenix Nest. Built vp with the most rare and refined workes of Noble men, woorthy Knights, gallant Gentlemen, Masters of Arts, and braue Schollers*. London: Iohn Iackson, 1593, sigs. C1ᵛ–C2ʳ. Reprint in facsimile in Rollins (723), pp. 18–19. Reprint in Spenser (2771), sigs. K3ᵛ–K4ʳ.

An elegy of ten quatrains beginning "Silence augmenteth griefe, writing encreaseth rage." Describes the lament of personified abstractions, such as Knowledge, Time, and Fame. Bids farewell to joy and hope, now that "the wonder of our age" is dead. For speculation on the identity of the author, see Malone (371), Rollins (723), and Pomeroy (1935).

2741 ———. The "dolefull lay" of Clorinda. Appended to *Colin Clovts Come home againe*, by Ed[mund] Spencer [sic]. London: [T.C., for] William Ponsonbie, 1595, sigs. G1ʳ–G3ʳ. Reprint. The English Experience: Its Record in Early Printed Books Published in Facsimile, 187. Amsterdam: Theatrvm Orbis Terrarvm; New York: Da Capo Press, 1969.

A pastoral funeral elegy of 108 lines, beginning "Ay me, to whom shall I my case complaine." Traditionally said to be by the Countess of Pembroke, but often attributed to Spenser. See de Sélincourt (1010), Friedrich (525), Malone (371), Osgood (689), and Waller (2360). Complains against the heavens for allowing Astrophel to die and against

Sixteenth Century

men for killing him, likening him to the flower astrophel, "Vntimely cropt." Calls on shepherd lasses to break their garlands and cease to sing lays of love, since the finest maker of such lays is dead. Asks Death what it has done with him and imagines his soul among the flowers of paradise, beholding "immortall beauties."

2742 ———. "The funerall Songs of that honorable Gent. Syr Phillip Sidney, Knight." In *Svperivs. Psalmes, Sonets, & songs of sadnes and piety, made into Musicke of fiue parts*, by William Byrd. [London]: Printed by Thomas East, the assigne of W. Byrd, 1588, nos. XXXIV, XXXV. Reprint. In *The English Madrigal School*. Transcribed, scored, and edited by Edmund Horace Fellowes. Vol. 14, *Psalms, Sonnets, and Songs of Sadness and Piety To Five Parts*. London: Stainer & Bell, 1920, pp. 190–215.

In no. 34, a twenty-line song in five stanzas (plus one repeated as a refrain) beginning "Come to mee grief for euer," mourns Sidney's death and calls him "hope of land strange" (i.e., the Netherlands) and "floure of England." In no. 35, a fourteen-line song beginning "That most rare brest," the author calls himself a "friend" and praises Sidney's "princely Hart" and "spirit heroic," singling him out as one whom princes mourned and "three cities strange desired." Since this song ends with the words "thy friend here living dieth," Brett (445) suspects a pun and suggests that both poems are by Sidney's friend Sir Edward Dyer. Both songs are set to music in five parts by William Byrd.

2743 [BARNES, BARNABE.] *Parthenophil and Parthenophe. Sonnettes, Madrigals, Elegies, and Odes*. [London: John Wolf, 1593,] sigs. P1ʳ–P2ʳ. Reprint. In *Parthenophil and Parthenophe: A Critical Edition*, edited by Victor A. Doyno. Carbondale: Southern Illinois University Press; London and Amsterdam: Feffer & Simons, 1971, pp. 94–96.

In "Canzon 2," a pastoral echo poem of sixty-five lines that begins "Sing sing (Parthenophil)," celebrates Sidney's birthday. Among the shepherds paying him tribute are Stella, Colin, and Eliza ("Arcadiaes Queene").

2744 [BARNFIELD, RICHARD.] *Poems: In diuers humors*. London: G.S. for Iohn Iaggard, 1598, sig. E4ʳ. Reprint. In *Poems of Richard Barnfield*, edited by Montague Summers. London: Fortune Press, [1936?], p. 134.

In "An Epitaph vpon the Death, of Sir Philip Sidney, Knight: Lord-gouernour of Vlising," reflects on Sidney's learning and valor, his family, and his death. The poem is ten lines long and begins "That England lost, that Learning lov'd."

2745 BAUDIUS, DOMINICUS. *Dominici Bavdij Insvlensis Carmina, quorum seriem Pagina sequens indicabit, Ad D. Petrvm Regemortervm.* Lvgdvni Batavorum [i.e., Leiden]: Ex officina Ioannes Paetsij, 1587, pp. 28–29, 66–68, 70–73, 98. Reprint in van Dorsten (1166), pp. 182–84, 186–88.

Includes four Latin poems written for or about Sidney. In "Ad illustrissimum heroëm Philippum Sidneium" (a poem of forty lines beginning "Non quod vetusta nobilis ab domo"), calls him "the leader of Britain's youth" and praises him for his eloquence and wisdom. Also praises the English for their intervention in the war in the Netherlands, seeing Sidney as an avenger for Belgium. In "Ad illustrissimum dominum meum Philippum Sidneium" (fifty lines beginning "Ecce iterum Iani auspicijs redit annus in orbem"), praises him for his nobility, virtue, and wit, noting his cultivation of Apollo and the Muses. Mentions plans to write a historical book on Leicester and Sidney, asking Sidney to be his Maecenas and alluding to Sidney's part in the war against the Spaniards. In "Ad nobilissimum equitem Robertum Sidneium" (seventy-seven lines beginning "O Sidneianae columen unicum domus"), laments Sidney's death in the voice of his brother Robert, whose life is now like death. Looks to the day when Robert can join his brother as "a new citizen of the heavens." In the poem "In obitum fortissimi herois Philippi Sidneii" (twenty-eight lines beginning "Viderat hostili grassantem caede Philippum"), Mars envies Sidney and takes revenge for his great deeds in battle, seeing in him the form of the goddess Pallas Athena. Recounts his death at the "trembling hand" of a "hiding Spaniard," but takes consolation from the fact that Sidney triumphed "in true virtue."

2746 [BENEDICTI, GEORGIUS.] *De Rebvs Gestis Illustriss Principis Guilielmi, Comitis Nassonij, etc.* Lvgdvni Batavorvm [i.e., Leiden]: Ex officina Ioannis Paetsij, 1586, pp. 47, 54. Reprint in van Dorsten (1166), p. 183.

In "Illustro viro D Philippo Sidneo" (a poem of six lines beginning "Si tibi Sidneae non essent nomina gentis") and "Illustri viro D. Philippo Sidneo" (a poem of two lines beginning "Ingenium, doctrina, genus"), praises Sidney for his noble birth, his learning, and his virtues.

2747 ———. *Epitaphia in Mortem Nobilissimi et Fortissimi Viri D. Philippi Sidneij Equitis ex Illustrissima Waruicensium Familia. Qvi Incomparabili Damno Reip. Belgicae Vulnere in praelio contra Hispanos*

Sixteenth Century

> *fortiter accepto paucis post diebus interijt.* Lvgdvni Batavorvm [i.e.,
> Leiden]: Ex officina Ioannis Paetsij, 1587, 12 pp. Reprint in fac-
> simile in Colaianne and Godshalk (2823). Reprint in van Dorsten
> (1166), pp. 194–98.

Includes twenty Latin funeral elegies for Sidney, which range in length
from two to twelve lines and frequently address a passing wayfarer to tell
the great loss incurred at Sidney's death. Notes his cultivation of Astraea
and the Muses, his knighthood in the Order of the Garter, the circumstances in which the envious god Mars struck him down, and the
moment of his death. Finds comfort in the thought that those who
believe that he is dead are deceived because he lives in heaven, honored
by Mars and the Muses, by Belgium and Britain. In reply to the question
why Sidney sought the heavens, answers that "he could not conquer the
earth."

2748 B[RETON], N[ICHOLAS]. *Brittons Bowre of Delights. Contayning
Many, most delectable and fine deuices, of rare Epitaphes, pleasant
Poems, Pastorals and Sonets.* London: Richard Ihones, 1591, sigs.
A1ʳ–B2ᵛ, C3ʳ–C4ʳ, D3ʳ–D3ᵛ. Reprint in facsimile in Rollins (722).

Includes six poems in memory of Sidney. In "Amoris Lachrimae: A most
singular and sweete Discourse of the life and death of S.P.S Knight,"
mourns Sidney as his dearest friend. Lists his virtues, noting that "in
childish years, he was esteemed a man." Remarks on his devotion in religion, his constancy in love (which was always directed to his "star"), and
his joy in martial deeds. Personifies Nature, Art, Wisdom, Beauty, and
other abstractions as mourners at his tomb, complaining that Death has
taken the only phoenix. Imagines the end of the world, with the Queen,
the shepherds, the classical gods, and a procession of scholars, soldiers,
and peers all grieving for his loss. The poem is 366 lines long and
begins "Among the woes of those unhappie wights." In "An Epitaph on
the death of a noble Gentleman," a poem of eighty-six lines that begins
"Sorrow come sit thee down," calls on the gods, the Muses, the court, the
army, and various allegorical figures to lament Sidney's death. Praises
his education and virtue, likening him to the phoenix and terming him
"the flower of chivalry." Pictures Sidney in "highest Paradise," and the
Queen leading a procession of mourners: courtiers, knights, scholars of
Oxford and Cambridge, and clergymen. In "The summe of the former
in four lines," which begins "Grace, Vertue, Valor, Wit," lists Sidney's
virtues and laments his death. See also three other brief elegies, each
entitled "A Poem": no. 28, which runs to twelve lines and begins "Powre
downe poore eies the teares of true distresse"; no. 29, which runs to six

lines and begins "Peace all the world, your weeping is but vaine"; and no. 30, which is in twelve lines and begins "Perfection peereles, Vertue without pride." These exalt Sidney for his virtues and mourn his death.

2749 [BRYSKETT, LODOWICK.] "The mourning Muse of Thestylis" and "A pastorall Aeglogue vpon the death of Sir Phillip Sidney Knight, etc." Appended to *Colin Clovts Come home againe*, by Edmund Spencer [sic]. London: [T.C., for] William Ponsonbie, 1595, sigs. G3ʳ–H4ᵛ. Reprint. The English Experience: Its Record in Early Printed Books Published in Facsimile, 187. Amsterdam: Theatrvm Orbis Terrarvm; New York: Da Capo Press, 1969. Reprint in facsimile, with a transcript of the Lambeth Palace Manuscript. In *Literary Works of Lodowick Bryskett*, edited by J[ohn] H[enry] P[yle] Pafford. [Farnsborough, England]: Gregg International Publishers, 1972, pp. 281–89, 297–315.

In "The Mourning Muse," a 195-line poem beginning "Come forth ye Nymphes," complains against Mars for taking Sidney, despite the cries that would rise from England and the Netherlands. Pictures the river gods of the Western world, the nymphs, the Muses, and the forest gods appealing to have his fate altered, and Ocean urging them to silence. Imagines Sidney's deathbed prayer, in which he recalls his service to the Lord in seeking justice for the oppressed and asks for longer life or "th'euerlasting blis." Depicts the laments of "his lovely Stella" and his sister and the disturbances in heaven and earth that accompanied his death. Envisions Sidney with the gods and warriors of antiquity, standing before the throne of God. In "A Pastoral Eglogue," a dialogue of 162 lines between Lycon and Colin that begins "Colin, well fits thy sad cheare this sad stownd," offers elegies for the death of Philisides. Imagines Pallas Athena grieving with her nymphs and oreads. Calls Sidney "cureous, valiant, and liberall" and pictures him in life scaling the "craggie rocks of th'Alpes and Appenine." Seeing Neptune and the river gods of England grieving, recalls that his songs could tame beasts and points out "the name of Stella, in yonder bay tree." Pictures Sidney gazing down from heaven and listening to their song. See also Friedrich (525), Hudson (575), Nicholson (952), and Purcell (2232).

2750 CAMPION, THOMAS. *Thomae Campiani Poemata. Ad Themesin. Fragmentum Vmbrae. Liber Elegiarum. Liber Epigrammatum.* Londoni: Richardi Field, 1595, sig. E3ᵛ.

In the eight-line epigram "De interitu Philippi Sydnei," addresses Venus's doves, asking why they seek (and say) "Philip" among the flowers and bidding them tell Venus of his death. Alludes to "Good brother

Sixteenth Century

Philip" (*AS 83*). The poem begins "Passeres Cypriae alites petulci." See also item 2787.

2751 [CHURCHYARD, THOMAS.] *The Epitaph of Sir Phillip Sidney Knight, lately Lord Gouernour of Floshing.* London: George Robinson for Thomas Cadman, [1587], 8 pp.

In the dedication to Sidney's wife, notes the outpouring of elegies after Sidney's death. In the poem (84 lines, beginning "A Greater losse then world well waies"), alludes to Sidney's promise as a statesman, his schooling in Cicero, his intellectual virtues, his embassy to Germany, his skill at the tilts, and his literary accomplishments. Praises his deathbed wish to live longer to serve his country and to amend his life, and joins in the national mourning at his death.

2752 ———. *A Mvsical Consort of Heauenly harmonie (compounded out of manie parts of Musicke) called Chvrchyards Charitie.* London: by Ar. Hatfield, for William Holme, 1595, sigs. E3^r–G4^r. Reprint in facsimile. N.p.: James Sutherland, for Alexander Boswell at the Auchinleck Press, 1817.

In "A Praise of Poetrie, some notes therof drawen out of the Apologie, the noble minded Knight, sir Phillip Sidney wrate," lists poets of many nations and ages who fostered learning and virtue. Includes several stanzas granting Sidney the "garland lawreate." Calls his verse "Nectar" that provides "Christian comfort" and ensures its author immortality, both on earth and in heaven. The poem runs to 336 lines and begins "When world was at the very woorst."

2753 CONSTABLE, HENRY. "Foure Sonnets written by Henrie Constable to Sir Phillip Sidneys soule." In *An Apologie for Poetrie*, by Sir Philip Sidney. London: Henry Olney, 1595, sigs. A4^r–A4^v. Reprint. In *The Poems of Henry Constable*, edited by Joan Grundy. Liverpool: Liverpool University Press, 1960, pp. 166–69.

In the sonnet beginning "Giue pardon (blessed Soule) to my bold cries," asks pardon for interrupting Sidney's singing among the angels and for being slow to lament his death. In "Sweet Soule which now with heau'nly songs doost tel," pictures Sidney in heaven, surpassing other poets in his songs. The poem was originally dedicated "To the Marquesse of Piscats soule," that is, to Vittoria Colonna, and Grundy (542) surmises that Olney made the change. In "Even as when great mens heires cannot agree," Sidney's virtues "sue" for parts of his body: Courage for his heart, Eloquence for his tongue, and so on. Suggests that, in dying, Sidney gained two lives: eternal life in heaven and life though fame on earth. In "Great Alexander then did well declare," compares Sidney with the Greek general, concluding that no man now living encompasses all his virtues.

2754 [DAY, ANGEL.] *Vpon the life and death of the most worthy, and thrise renowmed knight, Sir Phillip Sidney: A Commemoration of his worthines, Contayning a briefe recapitulation, of his valiant vsage and death taken, in her Maiesties seruices of the warres in the Low-countries of Flaunders.* London: Robert Walde-graue, [1586], 12 pp. Reprint in facsimile in Colaianne and Godshalk (2823).

An allegorical elegy in which the Muses (especially Thalia and Calliope) mourn for Sidney, along with the Fates and figures such as Mischance, Bellona, and Fame. Mentions *Arcadia* and Sidney's skill in poetic meters. Catalogs his virtues, noting his Christian care and guidance of his soldiers, and describes his wounding at Zutphen. Describes his last hours, including his final confession, his charge to his brother Robert, and his dying call to God. The poem is in thirty-four stanzas of rhyme royal and begins "What meanes this calme."

2755 DOUSA, JANUS, [the Elder]. "Dousiani voti solutio. Ad illustrem virum Dn. Philippum Sidneium Henrici Pro-Regis Hiberniae f. Cum eidem Petronium arbitrum muneri mitteret." In *Iani Dovsae a Noortvviick Odarvm Britannicarvm liber, ad D. Elisabetham Britanniarum Franciae Hiberniae que Reginam. Item Iani Dovsae filij Britannicorvm carminum silua,* by Janus Dousa [the Elder] and Janus Dousa [the Younger]. Lvdgvni Batavorvm [i.e., Leiden]: Ex Officina Plantiniam, apud Franciscum Raphelengium, 1586, pp. 21–22 (not seen; cited in *National Union Catalog, Pre-1956 Imprints*, vol. 146, p. 44). Reprint in van Dorsten (1166), pp. 179–80.

In a poem of thirty-two lines, beginning "Arbitrum en tandem tibi," offers Sidney a copy of the elder Dousa's edition of Petronius's *Satyricon*. Apologizes for having taken so long to send it.

2756 DOUSA, JANUS, [the Younger]. "Illustrissimo principi Philippo Sidnaeio, Henrici Hiberniae Proregis filio, gubernatori valachriae." In *Iani Dovsae a Noortvviick Odarvm Britannicarvm liber, ad D. Elisabetham Britanniarum Franciae Hiberniae que Reginam. Item Iani Dovsae filij Britannicorvm carminum silua,* by Janus Dousa [the Elder] and Janus Dousa [the Younger]. Lvdgvni Batavorum [i.e., Leiden]: Ex Officina Plantiniam, apud Franciscum Raphelengium, 1586, pp. 54–55 (not seen; cited in *National Union*

Sixteenth Century

> *Catalog, Pre-1956 Imprints*, vol. 146, p. 44). Reprint in van Dorsten
> (1166), pp. 181–82.

Lists gifts that the classical gods have bestowed on Sidney, praising his
ancestral line, his virtue, his wit, and his skill in Greek and Latin.
Alludes to his embassy to Germany and to a visit to the "city of Antenor"
(or Padua). Referring to the epics of Homer and Virgil, compares Sidney
with Nestor, Odysseus, and Aeneas. The poem begins "O Sidnaeie, suas
Pallas cui tradidit artes" and is twenty-eight lines long.

2757 ————. *Rervm Caelestivm Liber Primus. In Lavdem Vmbrae Declamatio
et Carmen, unam cum aliquot Poëmatiis, quorum seriem sequens pagina
indicabit. Quibus additae sunt Orationes Fvnebres in obitus aliquot ani-
malium, interprete Gvlielmo Canter, nunquam antehac editae.* Lvgdvni
Batavorvm [i.e., Leiden]: Ex officiana Plantiniana, apud
Franciscum Raphelengium, 1591, pp. 54–61 (not seen; cited in
National Union Catalog, Pre-1956 Imprints, vol. 146, p. 45). Reprint
in van Dorsten (1166), pp. 189–93; English trans., pp. 158–61.

In "D.M. ilustr. herois Philippi Sidnaei" (an elegy of 125 lines beginning
"Qualiter Arcadio Typhin dum pendet ab astro"), laments the death of
Sidney, calling him "our only hope, the Spaniard's terror" and regretting the audacity that led to his leg-wound. Mentions his visit to Venice
during the European tour of 1572–75 and also his embassy to Germany
in 1577, noting that he was raised in "the two arts of Minerva." Portrays
laments by his wife and words of condolence offered to her by the Earl
of Leicester. In "In eiusdem obitum Daphnis ecloga" (a pastoral elegy of
102 lines, which begins "Forte pedo stabat Lycidas innixus agresti"),
portrays the shepherd Lycidas mourning on the bank of the Thames for
Daphnis (Sidney). Imagines bad omens, seen by his wife Frances at his
departure from England, and laments the decline of all nature since his
death. Portrays him in Elysian fields, speaking words of consolation to
Lycidas.

2758 [DRAYTON, MICHAEL.] *Idea[,] The Shepheards Garland, Fashioned
in nine Eglogs. Rowlands Sacrifice to the nine Muses.* London:
Thomas Woodcocke, 1593, sigs. D2ᵛ–E2ʳ. Reprint. In *The Works of
Michael Drayton*, edited by J. William Hebel. Vol. 1. Oxford:
Shakespeare Head Press, Basil Blackwell, 1961, pp. 60–64.

In the "Fovrth Eglog" (155 lines beginning "Well met good wynken,"),
laments the death of Sidney (under the pastoral name Elphin). Winken
calls the poet "Rare substance . . . / Of Pastorall," "Spell-charming
Prophet, sooth-divining seer," "The essence of all Poets divinitie,/ Spirit
of Orpheus." Winken then sings for his friend Gorbo a funeral elegy that

he attributes to his friend Rowland, which invokes the Muse Melpomene and the wood nymphs to mourn Sidney's death and takes consolation from the idea that the poet has found immortality in verse and in the afterlife. (The "Sixt Eglog" is largely devoted to the praises of Sidney's sister Mary in the figure of Pandora.) See also a thoroughly revised version of these eclogues in item 2792 and see Elton (344, 512), Nicholson (377), and Grundy (543).

2759 EICKIUS, ARNOLDUS. *Elogium Illvstrissimi Principis, Roberti, Comitis Leycestrii, Baronis de Denbigh, etc., Belgiae Gubernatoris Generalis. Recognitum et auctum. . . . Cum Elogio. Clarissimi, D. Philippi Sidnei. Vrbis Flessingae Praefecti. Seu de vera nobilitate.* Trajecti [i.e., Utrecht, Netherlands]: n.p., 1586, sigs. B1ʳ–B4ᵛ.
Includes a lengthy Latin poem in praise of Sidney, written before his death. Text of the poem not seen.

2760 [GAGER, WILLIAM, ed.] *Exeqviae Illvstrissimi Eqvitis, D. Philippi Sidnaei, Gratissimae Memoriae ac Nomini Impensae.* Oxonii [i.e., Oxford]: ex officina Typographica Iosephi Barnesii, 1587, 96 pp. Reprint in facsimile in Colaianne and Godschalk (2823).
A collection of Latin elegies on Sidney published at Oxford. Gager's epistle dedicatory to the Earl of Leicester is followed by more than a hundred poems, including epitaphs, classical elegies, epigrams, pastoral eclogues, and shape poems. The forty-one contributors include William Camden, George Carleton, Thomas Cooper, Richard Eedes, William Gager, Matthew Gwynne, Laurence Humphrey, Richard Lateware, Francis Mason, and Thomas Thornton. According to Wilson (830), pp. 319–21, the elegy "Clarissimi Eqvitis Philippi Sidneii Memoriae Sacrvm" by Robert Dow (sigs. D1ᵛ–D2ᵛ) may be the origin of the myth that Sidney was once offered the crown of Poland. For further bibliographic information, see Case (242).

2761 HARVEY, GABRIEL. *Gratulationum Valdinensium Libri Quatuor. Ad Illustriss. Augustissimamque Principem, Elizabetam. . . .* Londoni: Henrici Binnemani, 1578, sigs. K3ʳ–L3ʳ. Reprint, with an English translation. In *The Works of Gabriel Harvey, D.C.L.*, edited by Alexander B. Grosart. The Huth Library. Vol. 1. London and Aylesbury, England: Hazell, Watson, & Viney, 1884, pp. xxxvii–xxxviii; English trans., pp. xli–xliii.
In Liber IV, "Ad nobilissimvm, humanissimumque Iuuenum, Philippum Sidneivm, mihi multis nominibus longe charissimum" (a poem of seven-

Sixteenth Century

ty-one lines beginning "Tene ego, te solum taceam, praeclare Philippe"), praises Sidney for his liberal education, the honor gained in his Continental travels, and his varied accomplishments in religion and the arts.

2762 H[OWELL, THOMAS]. *H. His Deuises, for his owne exercise, and his Friends pleasure.* London: H. Iackson, 1581, sigs. E4ᵛ–F1ʳ. Reprint. *Howell's Devises, 1581.* Edited by Walter Raleigh. Tudor & Stuart Library, 1. Oxford: Clarendon Press, 1906, pp. 44–45.

In "Written to a most excellent Booke, full of rare inuention," offers the first known comments on *Arcadia*. Suggests that it teaches the vanity of seeking to avoid the will of the "high powers," and laments that the work has not been published. Also praises its conceits and "saws well mixed," which conceal "mysteries deep."

2763 [LLOYD (elsewhere LHUYD), JOHN, ed.] *Peplvs. Illvstrissimi Viri D. Philippi Sidnaei Svpremis Honoribvs Dicatvs.* Oxonii [i.e., Oxford]: Excudebat Iosephus Barnesius, 1587, 54 pp. Reprint in facsimile in Colaianne and Godschalk (2823).

A collection of seventy-two Latin poems in Sidney's memory that were dedicated to Henry Herbert, Count of Pembroke, by the members of New College, Oxford. The twenty-nine contributors include Thomas Bastard, Richard Daniel, Matthew David, John Gifford, John Hunt, John Hoskins, John Lloyd (or Lhuyd), Henry Martin, John Owen, Roger Ravenscroft, and William Watson. See Buxton (458). For further bibliographic information, see Case (242).

2764 MELISSUS SCHEDIUS, [PAULUS]. *Melissi Schediasmata poetica.* 2d ed. Lvtetiae Parisiorum [i.e., Paris]: Apud Arnoldvm Sittarvm, 1586, pp. 161–62, 265–67 (not seen; cited in *National Union Catalog, Pre-1956 Imprints*, vol. 374, p. 498). Reprint in van Dorsten (1166), pp. 173–74, 180–81; English trans., p. 50.

In "Ad Philippum et Robertum Sydneios, viros illustres" (a poem of eight five-line stanzas beginning "Philippe Musarum nitor"), praises Sidney and his brother, asking them to accept the poet's "unornamented verses," since "a simple maid needs no cosmetics." In "Ad Philippum Sidnaeum Elizabethae reginae Angliae ad Rom. Imp. legatum" (which begins "Sydnee Musarum inclite cultibus" and runs to forty lines), pictures Sidney departing down the Rhine after his embassy to Germany in 1577, having held the Emperor's "eyes and speech spellbound" and now returning to his Queen, who is "eager" to hear his report. Suggests that he is protected by the Nereids and calls him "renowned for [his] study of the Muses."

2765 NEVILLE, ALEXANDER, ed. *Academiae Cantabrigiensis Lachrymae Tvmvlo Nobilissimi Equitis, D. Philippi Sidneij Sacratae per Alexandrum Nevillum.* Londini: ex officina Ioannis Windet impensis Thomae Chardi, 1587, 130 pp. Reprint in facsimile in Colaianne and Godschalk (2823).

A volume of 124 funeral elegies for Sidney by sixty-eight contributors, which was issued by Cambridge University and dedicated to Sidney's uncle, the Earl of Leicester. The poems in the volume are mainly in Latin, though a few are in English, Greek, and Hebrew. Contributors include Thomas Bing, Edward Chapman, Giles Fletcher the Elder, Gabriel Harvey, Thomas Holland, James VI of Scotland, Sir Robert Naunton, Alexander Neville, William Temple, and one "R.S.," possibly the unidentified editor of *The Phoenix Nest*. In the prose dedication, which is dated on the day of Sidney's funeral, Neville remembers the widespread mourning at Sidney's death, his virtues and attainments, his reputation in England and on the Continent, and his devotion to the Muses. For further bibliographic information, see Case (242).

2766 PEELE, GEORGE. *An Eglogue Gratulatorie. Entituled: To the right honorable, and renowmed Shepheard of Albions Arcadia: Robert Earle of Essex and Ewe, for his welcome into England from Portugal.* London: Richard Jones, 1589, sig. A3ᵛ. Reprint. In *The Works of George Peele*, edited by A[rthur] H[enry] Bullen. Vol. 2. London: John C. Nimmo, 1888, pp. 267–77.

In lines 60–75 of the poem, which celebrates Essex's triumphal return from Portugal in 1589, alludes to England as "Arcady" and commends Sidney and Essex for keeping "the grim wolf from Eliza's gate." Pictures Essex mourning for Sidney, proclaiming that, in him, Sidney's virtues are "revived."

2767 [PHILIP, JOHN]. *The Life and Death of Sir Philip Sidney, late Lord governour of Flushing: His funerals Solemnized in Paules Churche where he lyeth interred; with the whole order of the mournfull shewe, as they marched thorowe the citie of London, on Thursday the 16 of February, 1587.* London: by Robert Walde-grave, 1587, 16 pp. Reprint in Butler (324). Reprint in facsimile in Colaianne and Godshalk (2823).

Includes fifty-four stanzas in rhyme royal presented as Sidney's own words spoken from beyond the grave. In the first half, which is cast as a

Sixteenth Century

strongly Protestant "plea," Sidney urges readers to "stand at od" against Rome and to be grateful for the peace of Elizabeth's reign. In the second half, which is cast as a description of his funeral, Sidney comforts the mourners, saying, for example, "O Devorax, my deare . . . / Mourne not for me."

2768 RALEGH, Sir WALTER. "An Epitaph vpon the right Honorable sir Philip Sidney knight: Lord gouernor of Flushing." In *The Phoenix Nest. Built vp with the most rare and refined workes of Noble men, woorthy Knights, gallant Gentlemen, Masters of Arts, and braue Schollers.* Compiled by R.S. London: by Iohn Iackson, 1593, sigs. B4ᵛ–C1ᵛ. Reprint in facsimile in Rollins (723), pp. 16–18. Reprint in Spenser (2771), sigs. K2ʳ–K3ʳ.

A poem in fifteen quatrains, beginning "To praise thy life, or waile thy worthie death." Remembers Sidney's royal lineage and name, his rearing in Kent and education at Oxford, his embassy to Emperor Rudolph and his role in the Netherlands. Suggests that God regarded Sidney's mind as too "kingly" to remain in "this base world." Finds even envy, spite, and malice mollified by his death, calling him "Scipio, Cicero, and Petrarch of our time." As Hughey notes (1902), stanzas 12–13 resemble the epitaph (2782) originally hung on a pillar in St. Paul's Cathedral over Sidney's tomb. See also Rollins (723), Pomeroy (1935), and Hughey (1902, 1995).

2769 ROGERS, DANIEL. Latin funeral elegy. In *Chronicon Saxoniae & vicinarum aliquot Gentium: Ab Anno Christi 1500. vsque ad M.D.XCIII*, by David Chytraeus. Lipsiae [i.e., Leipzig]: Impensis Heningi Grosii, [1593], pp. 826–29.

In an untitled poem of ninety-two lines beginning "Caelo receptos, flere licet nefas," lists the gifts given Sidney by gods such as Pallas, Hermes, and Mars. Pictures the moment in which he was shot in the leg at Zutphen and the mourning in Belgium and England that followed his death. Ponders the vanity of life and takes comfort in the belief that he is in heaven. First cited by Phillips (1114).

2770 ROYDON, MATTHEW. "An Elegie, or friends passion, for his Astrophill. Written upon the death of the right Honorable sir Philip Sidney knight, Lord gouenor of Flushing." In *The Phoenix Nest. Built vp with the most rare and refined workes of Noble men, woorthy Knights, gallant Gentlemen, Masters of Arts, and braue Schollers.* Compiled by R.S. London: Iohn Iackson, 1593, sigs. B1ʳ–B4ᵛ.

Reprint in facsimile in Rollins (723), pp. 9–16. Reprint in Spenser (2771), sigs. I1ʳ–K2ʳ.

A poem of 234 lines beginning "As then, no winde at all there blew." Portrays a dream vision of animals and birds (including the phoenix) gathered in the forest around a man in mourning. He delivers a complaint describing Sidney's noble bearing and virtues, his fondness for "woods of Arcadie," the eternal glory that he bestowed on Stella, his death (ascribed to the envy of Mars), and the sorrow of the natural world. On connections between Sidney and the phoenix, see Knight (597), Rollins (723), and Pomeroy (1935).

2771 [SPENSER, EDMUND.] "Astrophel." Appended to *Colin Clovts Come home againe*, by Ed[mund] Spencer [sic]. London: [T.C., for] William Ponsonbie, 1595, sigs. E3ʳ–F4ᵛ. Reprint. The English Experience: Its Record in Early Printed Books Published in Facsimile, 187. Amsterdam: Theatrvm Orbis Terrarvm; New York: Da Capo Press, 1969.

A pastoral elegy of 216 lines, beginning "Shepheards that wont on pipes of oaten reed." Laments the death of Astrophel, recounting his rearing in "Arcady" on the banks of Haemony, where he was the "shepheards praise" and "lasses loue." Finds one failing in him, that he was "not so happie as the rest." Notes his ability to "pipe," dance, carol, and write lays of love, which he addressed to Stella, who was "his lifes desire" and the only one to whom he "vowd the seruice of his daies." Lists his skills in athletics, shooting, and hunting, seeing "proud desire of praise" as the end that led him to seek prey "abroad." Portrays the "toyles and subtil traines" that he laid "the brutish nation to enwrap" and the "ill mynd" that led him to attack at Zutphen, "vnmyndfull" of his own safety. Lamenting the wound in his thigh and the absence of friends to treat it, imagines him carried to his "loued lasse," who cares for him and follows him in death. Pictures the pair transformed to the flower that bears his name, with the shepherds mourning as they never had before. Introduces the succeeding song, the "dolefull lay" of Clorinda, as one sung by "his sister." See Fujii (526). On the disputed identity of "Stella," see especially Purcell (2232), Brie (2067), Hudson (575), Friedrich (2128), John (2163), and Stillinger (2269).

2772 SPENSER, ED[MUND]. *The Faerie Qveene. Disposed into twelue books, Fashioning XII. Morall vertues.* London: Printed for William Ponsonbie, 1590, sig. Qq4ᵛ. Reprint. In *The Poetical Works of Edmund Spenser*, edited by E[rnest] de Sélincourt and J.C. Smith.

Sixteenth Century

Oxford Standard Authors Series. Oxford: Clarendon Press, 1911, p. 413.
In the dedicatory sonnet "To the right honourable and most vertuous Lady, the Countesse of Penbroke," praises Sidney as "the glory of our daies." Picturing him in heaven, "crownd with lasting baies," states that it was he "Who first my Muse did lift out of the flore,/ To sing his sweet delights in lowlie laies." Sees Sidney's likeness in his sister.

2773 [SPENSER, EDMUND] [Immeritô, pseud.]. *The Shepheardes Calender Conteyning twelue AEglogues proportionable to the twelue monethes. Entitled to the Noble and Vertuous Gentleman most worthy of all titles both of learning and cheualrie M. Philip Sidney.* London: Hugh Singleton, 1579, sig. ¶1ᵛ. Reprint in photographic facsimile. Edited by Oskar Sommer. London: John C. Nimmo; Manchester: Spenser Society, 1889. Reprint in facsimile. Menston, England: Scolar Press, 1968.
In "To His Booke," an eighteen-line dedicatory poem that begins "Goe little booke: thy selfe present," suggests that the work was left unsigned for fear of "Envie." Sends the volume to Sidney, calling him "president/ Of noblesse and of cheualree." Expects his protection and promises to send more poetry after the book is "past ieopardee."

2774 WATSON, THOMAS *An Eglogue Vpon the death of the Right Honorable Sir Francis Walsingham, Late principall Secretarie to her Maiestie, and of her most Honourable Priuie Councell. Written first in latine by Thomas Watson Gentleman, and now by himselfe translated into English.* London: by Robert Robinson, 1590, 20 pp.
An English translation of item 2775.

2775 ———. *Meliboevs Thomae Watsoni Siuè, Ecloga in Obitum Honoratissimi viri, Domini Francisci Walsinghami Equitis aurati, Divae Elizabethae secretis, & sanctioribus consilius.* Londini: Excudebat Robertus Robinsonus, 1590, 22 pp.
A Latin eclogue, in which Arcadia stands for England, Diana for Queen Elizabeth, Meliboeus for Sir Francis Walsingham, and Astrophil for Sidney. Includes stanzas portraying Sidney fighting the "lion that devoured Belgium." Mourns his death.

2776 WHETSTONE, GEORGE, and W[HETSTONE], B[ERNARD]. *Sir Philip Sidney, his honorable life, his valiant death, and true vertues. A perfect Myrror for the followers both of Mars and Mercury. . . . Whereunto is Adjoyned, one other briefe Commemoration of the Universall Lamentation, the neverdying praise, and most sollemne funerall of the sayd right hardie and noble Knight. By B.W. Esquire.* London: for Thomas Cadman, [1587], sigs. A1ʳ–C4ʳ. Reprint in Colaianne and Godshalk (2823).

In George Whetstone's "Sir Philip Sidney, his honorable life and valiant death," a fifty-stanza elegy in rhyme royal, compares Sidney to Alexander the Great, surveying his life from "the sweete disposition of his youth" to his death, emphasizing the latter and citing the names of many of his followers. In Bernard Whetstone's "Commemoration," which is in sixty-eight lines of poulter's measure, concentrates on responses to Sidney's death and describes the funeral, closing with a six-line epitaph. Since, according to Izard (582), Bernard Whetstone was with Sidney in the Netherlands, the book probably contains firsthand information about his death.

2777 WHITNEY, GE[O]FFREY. *A Choice of Emblemes, and Other Devises, For the moste parte gathered out of sundrie writers, Englished and Moralized. And Divers Newly Devised.* Leyden: In the house of Christopher Plantyn, by Francis Raphelengius, 1586, sigs. b2ʳ–b3ʳ. Reprint. The English Experience: Its Record in Early Printed Books Published in Facsimile, 161. Amsterdam: Theatrvm Orbis Terrarvm; New York: Da Capo Press, 1969.

A sixty-line poem beginning "When frowning fatall dame," which is printed below the emblem "Pennae gloria perennis" and is dedicated to Sir Edward Dyer. Pictures Apollo, Minerva, and the Muses mourning at the death of Surrey, then recovering their "mirth" at the birth of Sidney. Imagines Jove and the other gods giving him their gifts and Sidney maturing into a poet whose work "matcheth former times." Mentions works circulating among his friends and his fame at home and abroad, recounting Whitney's offer to dedicate the emblem to him rather than to Dyer and Sidney's refusal of it as "not his proper due." Citing Homer as an example, applies to Dyer and Sidney the moral that the pen gives more lasting fame than marble monuments built by princes. See also Green (354).

Seventeenth Century

Seventeenth Century

2778 ANON. "An Epigram to Sir Phillip Sydney in Elegicall Verse, Translated out of Iodelle, the French Poet." In *A Poetical Rapsody Containing, Diuerse Sonnets, Odes, Elegies, Madrigalls, and other Poesies, both in Rime, and Measured Verse,* edited by Francis Davison. London: V.S. for Iohn Baily, 1602, sig. I8ʳ. Reprint in facsimile in Rollins (724), vol. 1, p. 189.
An eight-line poem based on a similar epigram by Étienne Jodelle. Beginning "Cambridge, worthy Philip, by this verse builds thee an Altar," follows the precedent of "Greece and Italy" in seeking to immortalize Sidney. See also Davison (63).

2779 ———. "Hexameters, Vpon the neuer-enough praised Sir Phillip Sidney." In *A Poetical Rapsody Containing, Diuerse Sonnets, Odes, Elegies, Madrigalls, and other Poesies, both in Rime, and Measured Verse,* edited by Francis Davison. London: V.S. for Iohn Baily, 1602, sig. I8ᵛ. Reprint in facsimile in Rollins (724), vol. 1, p. 190.
Takes consolation for Sidney's death from the thought that he lives in eternity and that his fame will preserve his memory on earth. Portrays the grief of three Muses in particular: Melpomene, Calliope, and Thalia. Blames the gods for allowing Sidney to die and seeks to sing so that even the lions, bears, and boars of Arcadia will pause to listen. The poem is nine lines long and begins "What can I now suspect?" See also Davison (63).

2780 ———. "Others vpon the same." In *A Poetical Rapsody Containing, Diuerse Sonnets, Odes, Elegies, Madrigalls, and other Poesies, both in Rime, and Measured Verse,* edited by Francis Davison. London: V.S. for Iohn Baily, 1602, sigs. I9ᵛ–I10ᵛ. Reprint in facsimile in Rollins (724), vol. 1, pp. 192–94.
In an elegy of forty-two lines beginning "Whom can I first accuse?" blames the gods (including Apollo, Mars, Minerva, and the Muses) for not preventing the Fates from ending Sidney's life. Lists reasons that each refused. Seeks grace to sing so that men and beasts from other lands (including "Arcady") will stand "astonished" at his glory. See also Davison (63).

2781 ———. "An other vpon the same." In *A Poetical Rapsody Containing, Diuerse Sonnets, Odes, Elegies, Madrigalls, and other Poesies, both in Rime, and Measured Verse,* edited by Francis

Davison. London: V.S. for Iohn Baily, 1602, sig. I9ʳ. Reprint in facsimile in Rollins (724), vol. 1, p. 191.
A fifteen-line elegy beginning "What strange aduenture?" Pictures the Muses having left the mountains of Boetia for London, where Melpomene, Calliope, and Thalia weep for dead Philip, "the care and praise of Apollo." See also Davison (63).

2782 ———. Sidney's epitaph (which was inscribed on a wooden tablet and hung on a pillar near his tomb in St. Paul's Cathedral in London). In *A Trve Discovrse Historicall, of the Svcceeding Governovrs in the Netherlands, and the Ciuill warres there begun in the yeere 1565. with the memorable seruices of our Honourable English Generals, Captaines, and Souldiers, especially vnder Sir Iohn Norice Knight, there performed from the yeere 1577 vntill the yeere 1589 . . .* , by Emmanuel van Meteren. Translated and Collected by T[homas] C[hurch-yard] and Ric[hard] Ro[binson]. London: Matthew Lownes, 1602, sig. O2ᵛ. Reprint in Weever (2811).
So far as is known, provides the first printed text of Sidney's epitaph in St. Paul's Cathedral. The original tablet on which it was written is now lost. The poem (in eight lines, beginning "England, Netherland, the Heauens and the Arts,") observes that Sidney cannot be enclosed by "a small heape of stones" and that he has been divided into six parts: "His bodie hath England, for she it fed,/ Netherland his blood in her defence shed:/ The Heauens haue his soule, the Arts haue his Fame,/ All Souldiers the griefe, the World his good Name." See also van Meteren (872), Bond (991), and Hughey (1902).

2783 BANCROFT, THOMAS. *Two Bookes of Epigrammes, and Epitaphs.* London: I. Okes, for Matthew Walbancke, 1639, sig. C4ʳ.
In "On Sir Philip Sidney," offers a two-line epigram praising Sidney's wit.

2784 BAUDIUS, DOMINICUS. *Poematvm nova editio, quorum seriem pagina sequens indicabit.* Lvgdvni Batavorvm [i.e., Leiden]: T. Basson, 1607, p. 603 (not seen; cited in *National Union Catalog, Pre-1965 Imprints*, vol. 39, p. 433). Reprint in van Dorsten (1166), p. 188.
A two-line Latin chronogram, beginning "hIC IaCet eXtInCtVs." For a corrupt manuscript version of this poem, see van Dorsten (797).

2785 [BRADSTREET, ANNE.] *The Tenth Muse Lately sprung up in America. Or Severall Poems, compiled with great variety of Wit and Learning*, [by Anne Bradstreet]. London: Stephen Bowtell, 1650,

Seventeenth Century

pp. 191–96. Reprint in facsimile. Edited by Josephine K. Piercy. Gainsville, Fla.: Scholars' Facsimiles & Reprints, 1965.
In "An Elegie upon that Honourable and renowned Knight, Sir Philip Sidney," treats Sidney and his *Arcadia* as perfections of the lore of Apollo and the Muses. Compares his deeds in the Netherlands with the battles of Achilles. Finds dangerous temptations of Cupid in *Arcadia* and compares Sidney's relations with Lady Rich to Hercules's service to Omphale. The poem is eighty-six lines long and begins "When England did enjoy her halcyon days." The six-line poem "His Epitaph" begins "Here lies in fame under this stone." Calls Sidney "Philip and Alexander both in one," the "quintessence" of men.

2786 BROWNE, WILLIAM, [of Tavistock]. *Britannia's Pastorals. The Second Book.* London: Thomas Snodham for George Norton, 1616, p. 36. Reprint. In *The Poems of William Browne of Tavistock*, edited by Gordon Goodwin. Vol. 1. London: Lawrence & Bullen, 1894, pp. 237–39.
In the "Second Song," lines 247–80, praises Sidney as "Astrophel," comparing him with Orpheus and Cicero and acknowledging him as the first to write in the English pastoral tradition that Browne himself is continuing.

2787 CAMPION, THOMAS. *Epigrammatvm libri II. Vmbra. Elegiarum liber unus.* Londoni: Excudebat E. Griffin, 1619, sig. C7ʳ. Reprint. In *The Works of Thomas Campion: Complete Songs, Masques, and Treatises with a Selection of the Latin Verse*, edited by Walter R. Davis. Garden City, N.Y.: Doubleday & Co., 1967, p. 424; English trans., p. 425.
In the nine-line epigram "De obitu Phil: Sydnaei equitis aurati generosissimi," prints an extensively revised version of item 2750. Begins "Matris pennigerum alites Amorum."

2788 CARLETONO, GEORGIO. *Heroici characteres. Ad Illvstrissimvm Eqvitem, Henricum Nevillum.* Oxoniae [i.e., Oxford]: Iosephus Barnesius, 1603, sigs. G1ʳ–G3ᵛ.
In "P. Sidnaei Fvnvs" (a poem of 222 lines beginning "Hectorei cineres, & si quid in orbis Eoi"), compares Sidney's death with that of Hector, lamenting that Sidney did not die at the hand of a hero like Achilles so that he might have greater fame. Defends modern heroes, saying that they deserve the same glory as the ancients for similar deeds. Compares Sidney with his father, tracing their lineage to Mars and noting that, even as a boy, Sidney was moved by love of glory and preeminence.

Mentions his education at Oxford and his abilities in both war and peace, portraying France, Italy, and particularly the Netherlands as eager to claim him as one of their own. Praises him, however, as one of those who are at home everywhere and who "give life to the ages." Laments that, except through poetry, such fame as his would have been lost. Calls on the Arcadians to sing of him as he sang of them, and invokes the Thames to carry tears of mourning for him to the sea. Prophesies lasting fame for him as hero and *vates*, imagining Leicester and Peregrine Bertie, Lord Willoughby, taking vengeance on the Spanish for his death. Depicts the battle of Zutphen in some detail, naming particular combatants and depicting Sidney and his enemies as Homeric heroes. Suggests that Sidney was wounded after charging superior forces to rescue Willoughby and that he kept his wound secret. Pictures soldiers of many nations lamenting at his death, and closes with an image of the Muses releasing a fountain of tears that others may drink from forever.

2789 DAVIES, JOHN, of Kidwelly. *The Extravagant Shepherd: or, The History of the Shepherd Lysis. An Anti-Romance; Written originally in French and Now made English.* London: T. Newcomb, for Thomas Heath, 1654, sigs. Hhh4ʳ, Kkk2ʳ.

In "The Oration of Clerimond against Poetry, Fables, and Romances" and "The Oration of Philiris in vindication of Fables and Romances," Clarimond complains of Sidney's introduction of the minor characters Strephon and Claius before the major persons of *Arcadia* have appeared. Also objects that the two speak obscure verses and never appear again. Philiris replies by praising Sidney's "discourses of love and discourses of state." Neither passage is in the French original, *Le berger extravagant*, by Charles Sorel.

2790 D[ONNE], J[OHN]. *Poems, by J.D. With Elegies on the Authors Death.* London: Printed by M.F. for John Marriot, 1635, sigs. Aa5ᵛ–Aa6ᵛ. Reprint. In *The Poems of John Donne Edited from the Old Editions and Numerous Manuscripts. . . . ,* edited by Herbert J.C. Grierson. Vol. 1. London: Oxford University Press, 1912, pp. 348–50.

In "Vpon the translation of the Psalmes by Sir Philip Sydney, and the Countesse of Pembroke his Sister," blesses God for giving his spirit to the Sidneys. Praises them for having "John Baptist's holy voice" and for teaching Englishmen what and how to sing. Laments the lack of a good translation for use in the churches, suggesting that the version by the Sidneys may "Be as our tuning" to sing in the choirs of heaven. The poem, which runs to fifty-six lines and begins "Eternal God, for whom

Seventeenth Century

who ever dare," was not included in the first edition of Donne's poems, published in 1633. See also Lewalski (2350).

2791 DOUSA, JANUS, [the Younger]. *Poemata: olim a patre collecta, nunc ab amicis edita.* Lugduni Bat. [i.e., Leiden]: apud A. Cloucquium, 1607, p. 100 (not seen). Reprint in van Dorsten (1166), p. 194.
In "D.M. ilustr. herois Philippi Sidnaei" (a poem of fourteen lines beginning "Quod SIDNAEE, tuum decorent tot carmina funus"), portrays Apollo, Minerva, and the Muses lamenting Sidney's death and asks, "What wonder, then, if men also write funeral songs . . . ?" In "Codri Athenarum regis, ed Philippi Sidnaei comparatio" (a six-line poem beginning "Ob Patriam Codrus mentito occisus amictu est"), draws a comparison between Sidney and Codrus, an Athenian king who gave his life for his homeland.

2792 [DRAYTON, MICHAEL.] *Poemes Lyrick and pastorall. Odes, Eglogs, The man in the Moone.* London: R.B. for N.L. and I. Flasket, [1606], sigs. E7^r–F2^r. Reprint, with numerous minor revisions. In *Poems by Michael Drayton Esqvire.* London: W. Stansby for Iohn Swethwicke, 1619. Reprint of the 1619 text. In *The Works of Michael Drayton*, edited by J. William Hebel. Vol. 2. Oxford: Shakespeare Head Press, Basil Blackwell, 1961, pp. 546–51.
In the "Sixth Eglog" (168 lines beginning "Wel met good Winken"), offers an extensively rewritten version of item 2758. Winken rejects his friend Gorbo's urging that he maintain a "mean" in mourning and laments instead the decline of virtue since the days of Elphin (who represents Sidney). Depicts all of nature mourning and the shepherds subjected to "beastly clowns." Suggests that Sidney foresaw that the world would bring forth "strange monsters" and pictures him in a choir of angels, "laughing euen Kings, and their delights to skorn/ and all those sots them idly deify." Omits Rowland's song for Elphin, adding that Rowland, "like a gracelesse and vntutord lad," has departed for "southern fields." Predicts "mickle woe" for him. (The "Eighth Eglog" includes an extensively revised celebration of Mary Sidney, to whom Sidney is said to have "bequeath'd the secrets of his skill." See the original version, item 2758, "Sixth Eglog." See also Grundy (543).

2793 FitzGEFFREY, CHARLES [Caroli FitzGeofridi]. *Affaniae: sive Epigrammatvm Libri tres: Ejusdem Cenotaphia.* Oxoniae [i.e., Oxford]: Excudebat Josephvs Barnesivs, 1601, sigs. D5^r, M4^v.
Contains a two-line epigram "De Philippo Sydnaeo" and a sixteen-line epitaph entitled "Phillipo Sydnaeo. E. Aurato," which begins "Dona

744

Philippe tibi viuo, lachrymasque cadenti." The epitaph lists the blessings given to Sidney by Mars, Venus, Minerva, Pan, and Calliope.

2794 GAMAGE, WILLIAM. *Linsi-Woolsie. Or, Two Centvries of Epigrammes.* Oxford: Joseph Barnes, 1613, sigs. B6ʳ, D1ʳ.
Includes two epigrams on Sidney: First Century, Epigram 49, "To Zutphen, a towne in Gilderland, at the Beleagring of which, the renowned Sir Phillip Sidney was killed," and Second Century, Epigram 11, "On Sir Phill: Sidneys Arcadia."

2795 GRUTERUS, JANUS. Epigram. In *Delitiae C. poetarum belgicorum.* Vol. 2. Frankfort: n.p., 1614, p. 739 (not seen). Reprint. In van Dorsten (797), p. 176.
An eight-line epigram beginning "Quidquid amorum habet ipsus amor, quidquidque leporem," which, according to van Dorsten (797), was probably written before Sidney's death. Mentions Pamela and Philoclea, thus perhaps suggesting that Gruterus had seen *Arcadia* in manuscript.

2796 GWYNNE, MATTHEW. ["Il Candido."] "To the Right Honorable, Elizabeth Countesse of Rutland" and "To the Honorably-vertuous Ladie, La: Penelope Rich." In the dedication to Book 2 of *The Essayes or Morall, Politike and Millitarie Discourses of Lo: Michaell de Montaigne. . . .*, translated by John Florio. London: Val. Sims for Edward Blount, 1603, sigs. R3ᵛ–R4ʳ. Reprint. In *The Essayes of Michael Lord of Montaigne,* edited by Ernest Rhys. Everyman's Library, 440–42. Vol. 2. London and Toronto: J.M. Dent & Sons; New York: E.P. Dutton & Co., 1910, pp. 5–6.
Two dedicatory sonnets that mingle praise for Sidney with compliments to his daughter and Lady Rich. On the sonnet to Lady Rich, see also Hudson (575), Purcell (2232), and Yates (837).

2797 HARINGTON, Sir JOHN. "Of Sir Philip Sidney." In *The Most Elegant and Witty Epigrams of Sir Iohn Harrington, Knight, Digested into Fovre Bookes: Three whereof neuer before published.* London: G.P. for John Budge, 1618, sig. H7ʳ. Reprint. In *The Letters and Epigrams of Sir John Harington together with "The Prayse of Private Life,"* edited by Norman Egbert McClure. Philadelphia: University of Pennsylvania Press; London: Oxford University Press, 1930, p. 235.
A nine-line epigram deprecating his own works in contrast to Sidney's and noting the fame of the latter.

Seventeenth Century

2798 HERBERT, EDWARD, Baron of Cherbury. "Epitaph on Sir Philip Sidney lying in St. Paul's without a Monument, to be fastned upon the church door." In *Occasional Verses of Edward Lord Herbert, Baron of Cherbury and Castle-Island.* London: T.R. for Thomas Dring, 1665, sig. E3ʳ.
In five lines, notes that Sidney lies within and declines to praise him lest "men adore."

2799 [HERBERT, MARY (SIDNEY), Countess of Pembroke.] "To the Angell Spirit of the most excellent, Sr. Phillip Sidney." In *The Whole Workes of Samvel Daniel Esquire in Poetrie.* London: Nicholas Okes, for Simon Waterson, 1623, sigs. M7ᵛ–M8ᵛ. Reprint. In *The Complete Works in Verse and Prose of Samuel Daniel*, edited by Alexander B. Grosart. Vol. 1. [London: Hazell, Watson, & Viney,] 1885, pp. 267–68.
A poem of seventy-five lines, beginning "To the pure Spirit, to thee alone addrest." Praises Sidney's Psalms and laments his early death. Acknowledges an "infinite" literary debt to him and praises his virtues, concluding that he was "too fair for earth." The elegy was first published among the works of Daniel but appears in revised form in a manuscript of the Sidney Psalms, where it is explicitly attributed to Sidney's sister. See item 2826.

2800 H[OLLAND], H[ENRY]. *Herwologia anglica hoc est clarissimorum et doctissimorum.* Arnheim: J. Jansson, 1620, pp. 72–74.
Includes five short poems: "Quod sit ab antiquo tantum cantatus Homero," which praises Sidney for his superiority as a man of action and a man of letters; "Ipse tuam moriens (sed conjuge teste) jubebas," which offers a witty comment on his deathbed request that *Arcadia* be burned; "Sis quoque carminibus nostris celebratior Heros," which depicts Sidney's surviving brothers lamenting that they must live after him; "Cur atra sim quaeris? Sydneii ad sydera rapti," which depicts the ship that returned his body to London; and "Qui dignos ipsi vita scripsere libellos," which takes comfort in the fact that Sidney's short life brought "gloria longa." See also item 1060.

2801 LOVELACE, RICHARD. "Clitophon and Lucippe translated." In *Lucasta: Epodes, Odes, Sonnets, Songs, &c. To which is Added Aramantha, A Pastoral.* London: by Tho. Harper, 1649, pp. 80–82. Reprint. In *The Poems of Richard Lovelace*, edited by C.H. Wilkinson. Oxford: Clarendon Press, 1930, pp. 68–69.
Beginning "Pray Ladies breath, awhile lay by/ Celestial *Sydney's Arcady*," the poem provides a brief meditation on the love ethic of *Arcadia*, claim-

ing at one point that "Gallant *Pamelas* Majesty,/ And her sweet Sisters Modesty/ Are fixt in each of you; you are/ Distinct, what these together were."

2802 MELISSUS [SCHEDIUS], PAULUS. Two epigrams. In *Delitiae poetarum germanorum*. Vol. 4. Frankfort: n.p., 1612, pp. 439, 479.
Not seen. According to van Dorsten (797), one poem is a twelve-line epigram beginning "Principibus mos est infantis ab unius ortu Treis susceptorum conciliasse manus . . . ," which "considers the unhappy plight of nine young girls who, in the event of [Sidney's] death, would be fatherless; and so, suggesting that Queen Elizabeth might spare a place for them, commends the orphaned muses to the protection of 'dux Robertus' and 'comes Philippus.'" The other is a ten-line epigram beginning "Unica si tantas comprendere chartula posset Virtutesque tuas . . . ," which (according to van Dorsten) calls Sidney "the golden sun of the morn" and praises his achievements as "fiery stars."

2803 OWEN, JOHN. *Epigrammatum Ioannis Owen Cambro-Britanni Libri Tres. Ad Illustrissinam D. Mariam Neuille, Comitis Dorcestriae filiam, Patronam suam*. 3d ed. Londoni: ex officinam Humfredi Lownes, sumtibus Simonis Waterson, 1607, sigs. C1ᵛ–C2ʳ, C6ʳ.
Reprints item 2804, renumbering the four epigrams (now II.28, 29, 31, 67). Bound following this work is another, separately collated, which has its own title page: *Epigrammatum Ioannis Owen, Cambro-Britanni, Ad Excellentissimam & doctissimam Heroinam, D. Arbellam Stuart, liber singularis*. Londoni: Ex officinam Humfredi Lownes, sumtibus Simonis Waterson, 1607. This work contains a fifth poem, entitled "Vita Philippi Sidneij. Ad eiusdem fratrem, D. Robertum Sidney, vicecomitem de Lisle" (Liber Vnvs. 142, sig. C7ᵛ), which is an epigram in four lines beginning "Qvi dignos ipsi vitam scripsere libellos."

2804 ———. *Epigrammatvm libri tres*. Londoni: Apud Ioannem Windet, Sumptibus Simonis Watersonii, 1606, sigs. C8ʳ–C8ᵛ, D3ʳ.
Includes four Latin epigrams on Sidney: "Philippus Sidnaeus" (II.27, four lines beginning "Quod sit ab antiquo tantum cantatus Homero"); "Ad eundem" (II.28, four lines beginning "Qui scribenda facit, scribit ue legenda, beatus"); "Ad Elizabetham Comitissam Rutlandiae, Philip. Sidnaei filiam" (II.30, two lines beginning "Quod pater ille tuus fuerit"); and "Ad D. Philippum Sidnaeum de ipsius Arcadia" (II.66, six lines beginning "Ipse tuam moriens (vel coniuge teste) iubebas"), which mentions Sidney's deathbed wish that *Arcadia* be burned. See also items 2803, 2805.

Seventeenth Century

2805 ———. *Epigrams of That most wittie and worthie Epigrammatist Mr. Iohn Owen.* Translated by John Vicars. London: W. S[tansby] for John Smethwicke, 1619, sig. B3ᵛ.

Provides an English translation of Epigram II.28 as printed in item 2804.

2806 RAINOLDS, JOHANNE. Epitaph. In *Historia et Antiquitates Universitatis Oxoniensis*, by Anthony à Wood. Vol. 2. Oxford: e Theatro Sheldoniano, 1674, pp. 265–66.

One of two Latin prose epitaphs written to adorn the adjoining tombs of Sidney and his father-in-law, Sir Francis Walsingham. Recounts Sidney's parentage, titles, and honors, mentioning that he was educated in "good letters," that he served as an ambassador to Emperor Rudolph II, and that he fought "more courageously than cautiously" in the Netherlands. The epitaph begins "Philippus Sidneius, Henrico patre natus, viro nobili" and is preserved in MS. Cotton Vespasian, C, XIV, fol. 206.

2807 SHEPPARD, S[AMUEL]. *Epigrams Six Bookes Also the Socratick Session, or The Araignment of Julius Scaliger, with Some Select Poems.* London: Printed by G.D., for Tho. Bucknell, 1651, sigs. E8ᵛ, F7ᵛ.

In the epigram "On Sir Phillip Sydneys Decease" (six lines, beginning "When Aericina saw brave Sydney die"), Venus laments Sidney's death as a dual loss: of Mars and of Apollo. In "Sir Philip Sydney's *Arcadia*" (six lines, beginning "Sir, you are at the Races end before us"), remarks on Sidney's debt to Heliodorus and suggests that the fame of the book "had been eclips'd, had any other name/ Troubled the Title Page."

2808 STRADLING, JOHN. *Joannis Stradlingi Epigrammatum Libri Quatuor.* London: George Bishop and John Norton, 1607, sigs. B4ᵛ–B5ʳ, C5ᵛ.

Contains an eight-line epitaph on Sidney, "Non tibi detuerant artes, non bellica virtus"; a four-line one, "Túne Philippe iaces saxi sub mole reclusus"; and a two-line epigram, "Qui Marti Musiquem."

2809 W., A. "Eglogve. Made long since vpon the death of Sir Phillip Sidney." In *A Poetical Rapsody Containing, Diuerse Sonnets, Odes, Elegies, Madrigalls, and other Poesies, both in Rime, and Measured Verse*, edited by Francis Davison. London: V.S. for Iohn Baily, 1602, sigs. C3ᵛ–C7ᵛ. Reprint in facsimile in Rollins (724), vol. 1, pp. 36–44.

A pastoral dialogue of 216 lines beginning "Perin, arreed what new mischance betide." Laments the loss of Sidney as a fellow shepherd. Questions why Collin Clout [i.e., Spenser] has not written an elegy and suggests that "want of wealth, and loss of love so dear" has oppressed him.

Substitutes a lament composed by Cuddy, which asks the shepherds to leave the songs of Colin Clout in order to lament for Willy [i.e., Sidney]. Envisions Apollo, the Muses, and other deities mourning for his death, which "turned shepherd's peace to strife." At the end Cuddy breaks his pipe, Colin is said to be "killed with care," and Phillis (i.e., Sidney's wife) is portrayed in her grief. See also Davison (63) and Slater (763).

2810 WEBSTER, JOHN. *Monuments of Honor. Deriued from remarkable Antiquity, and Celebrated in the Honorable City of London.* . . . London: Nicholas Okes, 1624, sigs. B1ᵛ–B2ʳ. Reprint. In *The Complete Works of John Webster*, edited by F[rank] L[aurence] Lucas. New York: Oxford University Press, 1937, p. 320.

In a verse speech of eight lines beginning "To Honor by our Wrightings Worthy men," Sidney treats the praise of worthy men as the duty of a poet and expects virtue and "high deedes" to follow. Sidney appears in the pageant with four other "famous Schollers and Poets of this our Kingdome," namely Geoffrey Chaucer, John Lydgate, John Gower, and Sir Thomas More. Sidney, however, is called the "glory of our clime" and is the only one of the four to speak.

2811 WEEVER, JOHN. *Ancient Funerall Monuments within the United Monarchie of Great Britaine, Ireland, and the Ilands adjacent, with the dissolved Monasteries therein contained.* London: Thomas Harper for Laurence Sadler, 1631, pp. 320–22.

In describing monuments at Penshurst, prints du Bellay's epitaph on Guillaume Gouffier, Seigneur de Bonnivet (in French), along with the English imitation for Sidney's tomb (2782), which was "written upon a Tablet, and fastened to a pillar in S. Pauls Church London." Also prints King James's two elegies on Sidney in Latin and English.

Nineteenth Century

2812 BILDERDIJK, KATHARINA WILHELMINA. "Sir Philip Sidney." In *Nieuwe Gedichten van Vrouwe K.W. Bilderdijk*. Brussels: Brest van Kempen, 1829, pp. 78–79 (not seen.) Reprint. In *Nederlandsche Dicht- en Prozawerken. Bloemlezing uit de Nederlandsche Letteren.* . . . , edited by Georg Penon. Groningen, Netherlands: J.B. Wolters, 1893, pp. 151–52.

A poem of 44 lines composed in 1808, which begins "Gewond, en onder duizend lijken." Imagines the famous incident in which Sidney, wounded on the battlefield at Zutphen, called for water. After it was brought, a

Nineteenth Century

humble soldier came by who was also injured and in need of a drink, and when Sidney saw his need, he offered him the cup instead.

2813 BRETON, NICHOLAS. "Sr Ph. Sydney's Epitaph." In *The Works in Verse and Prose of Nicholas Breton,* edited by Alexander B. Grosart. Chertsey Worthies' Library. Vol. 1. [Edinburgh]: Printed for private circulation, Edinburgh University Press, Thomas and Archibald Constable, 1879, sect. t (*Daffodils and Primroses*), p. 17.
A thirty-line epitaph beginning "Deepe lamenting losse of treasure," printed here for the first time from a manuscript owned by F.W. Cosens. Pictures Wisdom, Honor, Virtue, and Love lamenting for the death of Sidney. Praises his reason and learning, where "muses had their meeting," and despairs at his loss. At the end, takes comfort that his soul is in heaven.

2814 CARY, HENRY FRANCIS. "Lines to the Memory of Charles Lamb." In *Memoir of the Rev. Henry Francis Cary, M.A., Translator of Dante. With His Literary Journal and Letters,* by Henry Cary. Vol. 2. London: Edward Moxon, 1847, p. 279.
Portrays Lamb at the moment of his death lying with an account of Sidney's death before him. Compares Lamb's generosity with Sidney's giving of his cup to a soldier at Zutphen. See also item 330.

2815 CH[URCHYARD], TH[OMAS]. Poem on Sir John Norris and Sir Philip Sidney. In a letter by J[ohn] Payne Collier. In *Sidneiana, Being a Collection of Fragments Relative to Sir Philip Sidney Knt. and His Immediate Connections,* edited by S[amuel Butler, Bishop of] Lichfield. London: Roxburghe Club, 1837, pp. 79–80.
A poem of twenty lines, which Collier found written by hand in a copy of Churchyard and Robinson's translation of van Meteren (872). Sees Sidney triumphant over death, "victorious ouer enemies, victorious ouer time." In thinking of him and of Sir John Norris, asks, "Why could not Churchyarde die with them[?]"

2816 GROSLOT[IUS, HIERONYMUS]. ["Tumulus V.C.M. Philippi Sydnaei equitis illustrissimi, ac doctrina et virtute incomparabilis."] In *Mémoires-Journaux,* by Pierre de L'Estoile. Edited by G. Brunet, A. Champollion, E. Halphen, Paul Lacroix, Charles Read, and Tamizey de Larroque. Vol. 10. Paris: Librairie des Bibliophiles, 1881, pp. 42–43. Reprint from manuscript in van Dorsten (1166), pp. 184–85.
A ten-line Latin epitaph beginning "Ecce arto terrae in tumulo," in which Sidney is pictured as receiving the honor of Mars and the Muses.

Although included in the section of L'Estoile's manuscript dated October 1609, according to van Dorsten (1166), pp. 164–65, the poem was written no later than 12 December 1586.

2817 HOOD, THOMAS. *The Poetical Works of Thomas Hood*. Boston: Crosby, Nichols, Lee & Co., 1860, pp. 181–82.

In "Sonnet to a Sonnet," praises Sidney as courtier, but faults him for referring to France as a "sweet enemie" in the sonnet "Having this day my horse, my hand, my launce" (*AS 41*).

2818 IRELAND, W[ILLIAM] H[ENRY]. *Ballads in Imitation of the Antient*. London: Biggs & Cottle, for T.N. Longman and O. Rees, 1801, pp. 187–92.

In "Ballad of the doleful Death of that Mirrour of true Knighthood, the noble Sir Philip Sydney," laments Sidney's death, focusing on the incident in which he gave his cup to another wounded soldier. The poem is fifty-six lines long and begins "Weep my Country, weep your Glory."

2819 ———. *Rhapsodies*. London: D.N. Shury, for Longman & Rees, 1803, pp. 103–4.

In "On the Oak in Penshurst Park," a poem of twenty-four lines that begins "Still peaceful flow the Medway's stream," meditates on Penshurst, alluding to *Astrophil and Stella* and *Arcadia* and to the oak planted at Sidney's birth.

2820 SWINBURNE, ALGERNON. "Astrophel: After Reading Sir Philip Sidney's *Arcadia* in the Garden of an Old English Manor-House." *Pall Mall Magazine* 1 (May 1893):1–7. Reprint. In *Astrophel and Other Poems*. London: Chatto & Windus, 1894 (not seen). Reprint. In *The Complete Works of Algernon Charles Swinburne*, edited by Sir Edmund Gosse and Thomas James Wise. Vol. 6. London: W. Heinemann, 1925, pp. 62–67.

A poem in three parts, the first in eight-line tetrameter stanzas, the second in octameter tercets, the third a mixture of the two. Contrasts the spirit of Sidney's England with her present state, "enmeshed and benetted/ With spiritless villanies round." Concludes "Hers thou art: and the faithful heart that hopes begets upon darkness dawn."

2821 THURLOW, Lord EDWARD, ed. *The Defence of Poesy*. London: W. Bulmer & Co., 1811, 112 pp.

Includes three prefatory poems on Sidney, apparently by Lord Thurlow. In the sonnet "On Beholding the Portraiture of Sir Philip Sidney in the Gallery at Penshurst" (which begins "The man that looks, sweet Sidney,

Nineteenth Century

in thy face"), lists Sidney's virtues and imagines Spenser looking at the portrait, "Framing thence high wit and pure desire,/ Imagined deeds, that set the world on fire." In the sonnet "On the Divine and Never-Ending Memory of Sir Philip Sidney" (which begins "Yet shall thy name be to all ages dear"), calls him "the tongue of love," imagining the spheres stopping to intone his praises and shepherds singing "the triumph of Arcadia's blissful days." In "A Song to Sir Philip Sidney" (an unfinished poem of sixty-seven lines, which begins "Spirit, whose bliss beyond this cloudy sphere"), depicts Astrophel in heaven, crowned with flowers and surrounded by celestial choirs. Seeks to come to him, praising his "influence" among the shepherds. See also items 111 and 112.

Twentieth Century

2822 ANON. "A rem[em]brance of Sir Ph: Sidnie Knight the 17th Nou' 1586 in the 29 yeare of her ma[jes]ties most gratious raigne." In *Sir Henry Lee: An Elizabethan Portrait*, by [Sir] E[dmund] K[erchever] Chambers. Oxford: Clarendon Press, 1936, p. 272.
Two Latin poems of three lines each, headed in English "the first" and "the second," followed by a third of two lines "Vpon the morning horse." The first speaker announces, "We were three, joined in a faithful covenenant, of whom one fell. . . ." The second says that the funeral of the fallen friend will be a kind of death for them, too, and pledges to render him yearly honors. The third speaker, the mourning horse, contrasts former days, when it wore purple and bore its "glittering lord," with the present occasion, on which it bears his funeral trappings. As Yates suggests (835), these were presented before the Queen at the Accession Day Tilts of 1586, perhaps by Sidney's friends Dyer and Greville, with the riderless horse calling to mind the dead Sidney.

2823 COLAIANNE, A[NTHONY] J., and GODSHALK, W[ILLIAM] L[EIGH], eds. *Elegies for Sir Philip Sidney (1587)*. Delmar, N.Y.: Scholars' Facsimiles & Reprints, 1980, 430 pp.
A facsimile reprint of the engravings of Sidney's funeral procession by Lant (849); the volumes of funeral elegies prepared at Oxford and Cambridge by Neville (2765), Gager (2760), and Lloyd (2763); and other works by individual authors, including George [and Bernard] Whetstone (2776), John Philip (2767), Angel Day (2754), and George Benedicti (2747). In the introduction, examines the reasons for Sidney's "long-lived popularity." Describes his wounding and death, the return of his body to England, his funeral, and the literary activity that followed.

Provides brief discussions of each of the works reprinted, including information on the types of poems and the most prominent contributors involved in the university volumes and biographical data on the authors of the other works. Attributes the Whetstone volume entirely to George. But see Izard (582), who notes that the title page of the book indicates that it includes poems by both George and Bernard and that it was Bernard who was actually with Sidney in the Netherlands at the time of his death.

2824 CONSTABLE, HENRY. *The Poems of Henry Constable*, edited by Joan Grundy. Liverpool: Liverpool University Press, 1960, pp. 154–55.

In the sonnet "To the Countesse of Pembroke," beginning "Ladie whome by reporte, I only knowe," seeks to honor Sidney's sister by praising Sidney. In the sonnet "To the Countesse of Essex vpon occasion of the death of her First husband, Sir Philip Sydney," which begins "Sweetest of Ladies if thy pleasure be," urges his wife to take revenge on Spain for his death. Suggests that she go there and kill his foes by letting them gaze upon her eyes. The poems are printed here for the first time from the Todd Manuscript.

2825 GROSLOTIUS, HIERONYMUS. "Epitaphe d'Illustrissime Messire Philippe de Sydney Chevalier" and "Epitaphium eiusdem." In *Poets, Patrons and Professors: Sir Philip Sidney, Daniel Rogers, and the Leiden Humanists*, by J[an] A[drianus] van Dorsten. Publications of the Sir Thomas Browne Institute. General Series, 2. Leiden, Netherlands: Leiden University Press; London: Oxford University Press, 1962, pp. 165–66, 185–86.

In the French epitaph (a sonnet which begins "Passant arreste icy. Icy dans ce tombeau"), calls Sidney the "soul of England" and imagines his soul in heaven. Laments that, at his death, the Fates cut short the reign of Mars, the Graces, and the Muses. Prophesies that poetry will bring him universal renown. In the Latin epitaph, (which is forty-four lines long and begins "Siste, heus Viator"), speaks in Sidney's voice to such "Travellers" as may stop to listen. Recounts his literary accomplishments, celebrating both his English poetry and a group of works no longer extant, which were evidently composed in Italian, French, Latin, and Greek. Also evokes his military prowess, claiming that Mars slew him out of envy and then rewarded him, afterward, with deathless fame. Both epitaphs are printed here for the first time from British Museum MS. Burney 370.

Twentieth Century

2826 [HERBERT, MARY (SIDNEY), Countess of Pembroke.] ["To the Angell spirit of the most excellent Sir Phillip Sidney."] In *Two Poems by the Countess of Pembroke*, edited by Bent Juel-Jensen. Oxford: Privately printed, 1962 (not seen). Reprint in Waller (2360), pp. 92–95.
A revised version of item 2799 printed here for the first time. Appears as a dedicatory poem in a presentation volume of the Sidney Psalms prepared by Mary Sidney. Drops two of the original stanzas, adds three others, and makes numerous minor revisions that contribute a note of deeper personal grief and devotion. In the manuscript, the poem is said to be "By the Sister of that Incomparable Sidney." For a discussion of the centuries-old misattribution of the poem to Samuel Daniel, see Waller (2360), pp. 44–45.

2827 MOFFET, THOMAS. *"Nobilis, or a View of the Life and Death of a Sidney" and "Lessus Lugubris."*. Edited and translated by Virgil B[arney] Heltzel and Hoyt H[opewell] Hudson. San Marino, Calif.: Huntington Library, 1940, 170 pp.
Two Latin works on Sidney, written ca. 1594 and printed here for the first time, with an introduction (see item 1053), English prose translations, explanatory notes, and an index. In *Nobilis*, a prose biography, follows the form of a Latin oration, seeking to provide the young William Herbert with an example to emulate. Traces Sidney's life from boyhood and adolescence to life at the university and at court, concluding with his martial service in the Netherlands, his wounding at Zutphen, and his death. Places primary stress on his piety and love of learning. Also emphasizes his patriotism and skill in dealing with men, his poetic ability, his martial valor, his friendships and family relations, and his noble descent. In *Lessus Lugubris* (a poem of 368 lines beginning "Talem ego te cerno Sydni? te exangue cadaver?") offers a lengthy apostrophe to Sidney's "pale corpse," addressing respectively his Head ("encircled with fiery beams which pious faith sent forth from the inmost secret places of the mind"), his Breast (site of "that gentle heart, serene, heroic, upright, temperate, heavenly"), his Right Hand (emblematic of civic and martial achievement), his Left Hand, and his Feet. Concludes with a "parenthesis," which records the lament of Peregrine Bertie, Lord Willoughby of Eresby, who is described in *Nobilis* as having been rescued by Sidney just before the latter received his fatal wound.

2828 ROGERS, DANIEL. Three Latin poems on Sidney. In *Poets, Patrons and Professors: Sir Philip Sidney, Daniel Rogers, and the Leiden Humanists*, by J[an] A[drianus] van Dorsten. Publications of the Sir

Thomas Browne Institute. General Series, 2. Leiden: Leiden University Press; London: Oxford University Press, 1962, pp. 173, 174–79; English trans., pp. 39, 55–56, 62–66.

In "Ad Philippum Sydnaeum illustrissimae spei et indoli iuvenem" (written in 1575–76), mentions the countries that Sidney visited on the European tour of 1572–75, assuming that he is now on his way to Ireland, where things learned on the Continent will allow him "to cultivate those barbarians." Sees it as Sidney's destiny to rule Ireland as viceroy, as his father had before him. The poem begins "Ergo pererratis Latii regionibus orbis" and is twenty lines long. In "In effigiem illustrissimi iuvenis D. Philippi Sydnaei" (1577?), wonders at the skill of the artist (Paulo Veronese) who painted Sidney's portrait. In the picture's inability to speak, sees Sidney's own habits: like a "follower of Pythagoras's praised silence, you seem to hear much and to speak little." The poem is twenty lines long and begins "Fare age (sic longum molli lanugine cingat." In "Elegia XIIIa. Ad Philippum Sidnaeum illustrissimae indolis ac virtutis iuvenem," imagines Sidney in attendance on the Queen at Richmond on her birthday. Pictures allegorical figures of Religion, Justice, Prudence, and Constancy as her counselors, the Muses and Graces as her musicians, and "Heroines" such as Sidney's mother and sister as her ladies. Sees Sidney (and Dyer) as poets inspired by Jupiter and worthy to praise such ladies, whether in Latin, French, or Italian. Imagines the "Weird Sister" who spun his fate standing by Sidney's cradle, prophesying that he would learn from wide travels, become a "master of the arts of peace and war," "establish God in his Churches," "protect equality of rights," and "be sacred to Virtue, the Muses, and the gods." Sees the prophecy as fulfilled, noting the gifts each god has bestowed and alluding to incidents on his Continental travels, including his meetings with Languet and Sturmius. Thinks of Sidney as high in Elizabeth's favor and possessed of "the deepest secrets of her mind." Recounts his embassy to the Emperor in 1577, his meeting with Casimir, and his eagerness to fight in the Netherlands. Sees the Earls of Warwick and Leicester as furthering his career and friends such as Dyer and Greville as fellow "favourites almost" at court. The elegy, dated 14 January 1579, begins "Te tenet Attalicis Ricemondia compta tapetis" and runs to 190 lines. All three poems are from the Hertford Manuscript.

2829 STRODE, WILLIAM. *The Poetical Works of William Strode*. Edited by Bertram Dobell. London: Bertram Dobell, 1907, p. 43.

In "A Superscription on Sir Philip Sidney's Arcadia, Sent for a Token," compares the recipient to Pamela and Philoclea as images of virtue. Dobell prints the poem from a manuscript in his possession, undated.

Nineteenth Century

2. WORKS OF FICTION

Nineteenth Century

2830 KNIGHT, CHARLES. *Once Upon a Time*. 2d ed. Vol. 1. London: John Murray, 1859, pp. 162–69.
In "Philip Sidney and Fulke Greville," presents an imaginary conversation between Sidney and his father and a longer dialogue between Sidney and Greville, both set at Shrewsbury School in 1569.

2831 LANDOR, WALTER SAVAGE. *Imaginary Conversations of Literary Men and Statesmen*. Vol. 1. London: Taylor & Hessey, 1824, pp. 13–26.
In "The Lord Brooke and Sir Philip Sidney," has Sidney converse with Greville on the nature of happiness. Sets the conversation at Penshurst, but makes little reference to the actual life or views of either man. Has Sidney concede that he has no rank among the poets, that he was unwise in trying to mingle the ancient with the modern, and that his "expatiating in the regions of romance" was in bad taste. Landor seems to have cut the text for the first edition, for at the end he notes, "This conversation was longer," and quotes part of the remainder. See also 2832 and 2833.

2832 ———. *Imaginary Conversations of Literary Men and Statesmen*. Vol. 1. London: Henry Colburn, 1826, pp. 17–38.
A revised and expanded version of item 2831.

2833 ———. *The Works of Walter Savage Landor*. Vol. 1. London: Edward Moxon, 1853, pp. 4–9.
A still longer version of item 2831.

2834 MARSHAL, EMMA. *Penshurst Castle in the Time of Sir Philip Sidney*. Collection of British Authors, Tauchnitz Edition, 2971. Leipzig: Bernhard Tauchnitz, 1894, 304 pp.
Following Bourne (318), provides a fictional account of Sidney's life from 1581 to 1586, including a description of his funeral.

2835 [YONGE, CHARLOTTE MARY.] *The Chaplet of Pearls; or, The White and Black Ribaumont*. Collection of British Authors, Tauchnitz Edition, 1001–2. Leipzig: Bernard Tauchnitz, 1869, 1:54–161 passim, 328–29; 2:71, 86, 303–4.
In a historical novel about the wars between French Catholics and the Huguenots, portrays Sidney during his stay in Paris in 1572.

Twentieth Century

2836 COMSTOCK, SETH COOK. *The Rebel Prince*. London: John Long, 1905, 535 pp.
Portrays the activities of Dick Harrod, a fictional secret agent of Queen Elizabeth said to be a childhood friend of Sidney. Harrod is preferred and preserved through Sidney's influence at court.

2837 FOOTE, DOROTHY NORRIS. *The Constant Star*. New York: Charles Scribner's Sons, 1959, pp. 1–160.
A historical novel about affairs of the Elizabethan court from 1584 to 1603, largely as seen through the eyes of Sidney's wife Frances. For the first half of the book, focuses on the life of Sidney from his marriage until his death, with special attention to his love of Penelope Rich, his plans to sail with Drake, and his part in opposing Spain in the Netherlands.

2838 POLLARD, ELIZA FRANCES. *A Gentleman of England: A Story of the Time of Sir Philip Sidney*. London: Partridge, [1911], 411 pp.
Not seen. Cited as item 1330 in Tannenbaum (268).

2839 WESTCOTT, JAN. *The Walsingham Woman*. New York: Crown Publishers, 1953, 346 pp.
Sidney plays a secondary role in this novel, which begins in a violent storm on the afternoon of August 10, 1585, when Frances Walsingham's intended elopement with one John Wickerson is foiled by one Rickard [sic] de Burgh and she is returned to her father to await impassioned courtship by and marriage to a romanticized Sidney. Sidney's appointment as Governor of Flushing, his wounding, and death are treated as background for the political intrigues of Sir Francis Walsingham and a developing relationship between Frances and de Burgh.

2840 WHITMAN, G.I. *The Glory of His Day*. N.p., n.d.
Not located. Cited as item 1332 in Tannenbaum (268).

2841 WILLARD, BARBARA. *He Fought for His Queen: The Story of Sir Philip Sidney*. London and New York: Frederick Warne & Co., 1954, 178 pp.
A historical novel, which begins with his mother's illness and return to Penshurst from court when he was eight and ends with his funeral. Includes illustrations.

2842 ———. *Portrait of Philip*. London: Macmillan & Co., 1950, 387 pp.
Provides a fictionalized version of Sidney's life and death.

Seventeenth Century

3. WORKS WRONGLY ATTRIBUTED TO SIDNEY

Seventeenth Century

2843 B[AXTER], N[ATHANIEL]. *Sir Philip Sydneys Ourania, That is, Endimions Song and Tragedie, Containing all Philosophie*. London: Printed by Ed. Allde, for Edward White, 1606, 104 pp.

A long poem containing several allusions to Sidney (more occur in the several dedicatory poems at the front of the volume). The title clearly is meant to imply a poem for Sidney, not by him, but later writers unfamiliar with the work have occasionally attributed it to Sidney himself. See Niceron (211) and Cibber (288). For evidence that the poem is by Sidney's tutor, Nathaniel Baxter, rather than (as some had thought) by Nicholas Breton, see item 315 and Hunter (363).

2844 [de La ROCHE-GUILHELM, Mlle.] *Alamanzor, and Almanzaida. A Novel. Written by Sir Philip Sidney, And found since his Death amongst his Papers*. London: Printed for J. Magnes and R. Bentley, 1678, 120 pp.

This hoax puzzled or fooled unwary bibliographers for nearly two centuries. See, for example, Niceron (211), Graesse (217), and Cibber (288).

2845 H[OWELL], J[AMES], ed. *Valour Anatomized in a Fancie. By Sir Philip Sidney. 1581*. In *Cottoni Posthuma. Divers Choice Pieces of that Renowned Antiquary Sir Robert Cotton, Knight and Baronet, Preserved from the injury of Time, and Expos'd to public light, for the benefit of Posterity, By J[ames] H[owell] Esquire*. London: Printed by Francis Leach, for Henry Seile, 1651, sigs. Y1ʳ–Y4ʳ.

As Beal (230) has pointed out, this is John Donne's *Essay of Valour*, perhaps published under Sidney's name for satiric reasons. The misattribution is perpetuated by writers and editors including Gray (16), Scott (186), Niceron (211), Wood (284), and Cibber (288).

Index 1: Authors Listed in the Bibliography

All index references are by item number rather than by page.

A. [sic], 296
A., E.H., 883
Abrams, Meyer Howard, 2382
Adams, Robert Martin, 2048
Adams, William Henry Davenport, 297, 298, 884, 1338
Addey, John M., 975
Adlard, George, 157
Adler, Doris, 1978
Adolph, Robert, 404
Ahrends, Günter, 2049
Ahrens, Rüdiger, 405, 2383, 2384
Aikin, Lucy, 299
Akishino, Kenichi, 1191
Albright, Evelyn M., 406
Alden, Raymond MacDonald, 407, 1856, 1857, 2050, 2051
Alexander, Peter, 1396
Alexander, Sir William, Earl of Stirling, 1327
Ali, S.M. Muhfuz, 2385
Allen, Don Cameron, 2052, 2386
Allen, J.W., 749
Allen, Percy, 408, 409, 410
Allesandri, Livio, 45
Almack, Edward, 1339
Almon, Liselotte, 1397
Alonso, Dámaso, 1858
Alpers, Paul J., 411, 1398

Alsop, J.D., 976
Altman, Joel B., 412
Alton, R.E., 2729
Amos, Arthur Kirkham, Jr., 1399
Anders, Henry R.D., 1400
Anderson, D.M., 1401, 1402
Anderson, Judith H., 2387
Anderton, H. Orsmond, 75
Andrews, Michael Cameron, 977, 1403, 1404, 1405, 1406, 1407, 1408, 1409
Anglo, Sydney, 978
Applegate, James, 1860
Aptekar, Jane, 1410
Arber, Edward, 68, 104, 213
Arculus, Margaret Joan, 1411
Armstrong, William A., 1412, 1723, 2388
Ascoli, Georges, 1413
Astell, Ann W., 1192
Atkins, John William Hey, 1414, 2389
Atkinson, Dorothy F., 229, 1415
Attridge, Derek, 1979
Auberlen, Eckhard, 2390
Aubrey, John, 902, 903
Axton, Marie, 2689
Ayscough, Samuel, 210

B., T., 904
Babb, Lawrence, 1416

759

Index 2: Names Mentioned in the Annotations

All index references are by item number rather than by page.

Index 3: Subjects Discussed in the Annotations

All index references are by item number rather than by page.